GOVERNMENT ASSISTANCE ALMANAC
★2000-2001★

GOVERNMENT ASSISTANCE ALMANAC
★2000-2001★

The Guide to Federal Domestic Financial and Other Programs

Covering Grants, Loans, Insurance, Personal Payments and Benefits, Subsidies, Fellowships, Scholarships, Traineeships, Technical Information, Advisory Services, Investigation of Complaints, Sales and Donations of Federal Property — with Funding Summaries, over 4,000 Program Headquarters and Field Office Addresses and Phone Numbers, an Agency Index, and a Comprehensive Master Index

★FOURTEENTH EDITION★

by J. Robert Dumouchel

Omnigraphics

615 Griswold Street, Detroit, MI 48226
Phone (800) 234-1340 • Fax (800) 875-1340 • www.omnigraphics.com

GOVERNMENT ASSISTANCE ALMANAC 2000-2001:
The Guide to Federal Domestic Financial and Other Programs
Covering Grants, Loans, Insurance, Personal Payments and
Benefits, Subsidies, Fellowships, Scholarships, Traineeships,
Technical Information, Advisory Services, Investigation of
Complaints, Sales and Donations of Federal Property —
with Funding Summaries, over 4,000 Program Headquarters
and Field Office Addresses and Phone Numbers, an Agency
Index, and a Comprehensive Master Index

by J. Robert Dumouchel

Co-published and distributed by:

Omnigraphics, Inc.
615 Griswold Street
Detroit, Michigan 48226
www.omnigraphics.com

Co-published by:

Foggy Bottom Publications
P.O. Box N-7776
Nassau, Bahamas

Copyright © 2000 by J. Robert Dumouchel
Printed in the United States of America

The Library of Congress has assigned the following International Standard Serial Number:
ISSN 0883-8690

Library of Congress card number: **86-658073**

International Standard Book Number:
ISBN 0-7808-0342-6

CONTENTS

PART II. Program Information
(*Note: the organization and sequence of the described programs are explained on page 12. For an* alphabetical listing *of administrative units and sub-units consult the* **AGENCY INDEX** *beginning on page 747.*)

DISCLAIMER/INVITATION

We have attempted to compile and present the information in this book accurately and in the most helpful form possible. The information is intended to provide basic guidance concerning programs and benefits available from the federal agencies cited.

Federal program policies, regulations, funding levels, addresses, and phone numbers tend to change. There could be unintentional errors in the information, caused by changes in government programs or organization, inaccuracies in the source material, omissions, or typographical or other inadvertent mistakes. A great deal of care was taken to avoid such errors.

The information in this publication was compiled from the sources cited and from other sources considered reliable. While every possible effort has been made to ensure reliability, the publisher and the editor will not assume liability for damages caused by inaccuracies in the data, and make no warranty, express or implied, on the accuracy of the information contained herein.

Users of *GOVERNMENT ASSISTANCE ALMANAC* are invited to send their observations about the book, its form, and their experience in referring to the information, to the editor at the address below. Suggestions for improvements in any aspect of the book will be especially appreciated.

> J. Robert Dumouchel, Editor
> GOVERNMENT ASSISTANCE ALMANAC
> c/o Omnigraphics, Inc.
> 615 Griswold Street
> Detroit, MI 48226

Abbreviations Used in This Book

ACF   Administration for Children and Families
ACP   Agricultural Conservation Program
ADA   Americans with Disabilities Act
AFDC   Aid to Families with Dependent Children
AHEC   Area Health Education Centers
AIBC   American Indian Business Consultant
AIDS   acquired immunodeficiency syndrome
AMS   Agricultural Marketing Service
AOA   Administration on Aging
ARS   Agricultural Research Service
ATF   Bureau of Alcohol, Tobacco and Firearms

BEA   Bureau of Economic Analysis
BHCDA   Bureau of Health Care Delivery and Assistance
BIA   Bureau of Indian Affairs
BLM   Bureau of Land Management
BLS   Bureau of Labor Statistics
BRSG   basic research support grant
BRSG   biomedical research support grant

C of C   chamber of commerce
CCC   Commodity Credit Corporation
CDBG   community development block grant
CDCP   Centers for Disease Control and Prevention
CDCU   Community Development Credit Union
CEIF   Coastal Energy Impact Fund
CEPP   Chemical Emergency Preparedness and Prevention
CERCLA   Comprehensive Environmental Response, Compensation
               and Liability Act ("Superfund")
CERT   Council of Energy Resource Tribes
CFDA   Catalog of Federal Domestic Assistance
CMHS   Center for Mental Health Services
CNCS   Corporation for National and Community Service
CODIS   Combined DNA Index System
CPD   Community Planning and Development
CRIPA   Civil Rights of Institutionalized Persons Act
CRP   Conservation Reserve Program

CRS	Community Relations Service
CSAP	Center for Substance Abuse Prevention
CSAT	Center for Substance Abuse Treatment
CSBG	community services block grant
CSREES	Cooperative State Research, Education and Extension Service
DC	District of Columbia
DEA	Drug Enforcement Administration
DIC	dependency and indemnity compensation
DOD	Department of Defense
DOE	Department of Energy
DOED	Department of Education
DOI	Department of the Interior
DOJ	Department of Justice
DOL	Department of Labor
DOT	Department of Transportation
DVA	Department of Veterans Affairs
EBS	Emergency Broadcast System
ECOA	Equal Credit Opportunity Act
EDA	Economic Development Administration
EEOC	Equal Employment Opportunity Commission
EFN	exceptional financial need
EHS	environmental health center
EIS	environmental impact statement
EMI	Emergency Management Institute
EMS	emergency medical services
EOC	emergency operating center
EPA	Environmental Protection Agency
ERC	educational resource center
ESA	Economics and Statistics Administration
ESEA	Elementary and Secondary Education Act
ESL	English as a second language
EST.	estimate
ETA	Employment and Training Administration
FAA	Federal Aviation Administration
FACE	Freedom of Access to Clinic Entrances Act
FAPRS	Federal Assistance Programs Retrieval System
FAS	Foreign Agricultural Service

FC	foster children
FCC	Federal Communications Commission
FCIC	Federal Crop Insurance Corporation
FCS	Food and Consumer Service
FDA	Food and Drug Administration
FEMA	Federal Emergency Management Agency
FFB	Federal Financing Bank
FFP	federal financial participation
FHA	Federal Housing Administration
FHAP	Fair Housing Assistance Program
FHIP	Fair Housing Initiatives Program
FHWA	Federal Highway Administration
FIP	Forestry Incentives Program
FLAS	foreign language and area studies
FMCS	Federal Mediation and Conciliation Service
FmHA	Farmers Home Administration *(Note: FmHA functions now are within FSA and RHS)*
FNS	Food and Nutrition Service
FRA	Fund for Rural America
FSA	Farm Service Agency
FTA	Federal Transit Administration
FTC	Federal Trade Commission
FTZ	foreign trade zone
FY	Fiscal Year *(Federal fiscal year: October 1 through September 30)*
GAA	Government Assistance Almanac
GPO	U.S. Government Printing Office
GSA	General Services Administration
HBCU	Historically Black College and University
HCFA	Health Care Financing Administration
HEA	Higher Education Act
HEAL	health education assistance loan
HHS	Department of Health and Human Services
HIP	housing improvement program (BIA)
HIV	human immunodeficiency virus
HMO	health maintenance organization
HOPE	Housing Opportunities for People Everywhere
HQ	headquarters
HRSA	Health Resources and Services Administration

HSA	health system agency
HUD	Department of Housing and Urban Development
IBDC	Indian business development center
IDEA	Individuals with Disabilities Education Act
IDG	industrial development grant
IHE	institution of higher education
IHS	Indian Health Service
IMLS	Institute of Museum and Library Services
INS	Immigration and Naturalization Service
IRS	Internal Revenue Service
ISDEAA	Indian Self-Determination and Education Assistance Act
ITA	International Trade Administration
JDRP	Joint Dissemination Review Panel
JJDPA	Juvenile Justice and Delinquency Prevention Act
JTPA	Job Training Partnership Act
LC	Library of Congress
LEA	local education agency
LSCA	Library Services and Construction Act
MARC	minority access to research careers
MB&IA	minority business and industry association
MBDA	Minority Business Development Agency
MBDC	minority business development center
MBE	minority business enterprise
MBRS	minority biomedical research support
MBS	minority biomedical support
MECEA	Mutual Educational and Cultural Exchange Act
MFB	marine and freshwater biology
MHSSRA	minority high school student research apprentice
MI	minority impact
MIA	missing in action
MIP	mortgage insurance premium
MRTP	Minority Research and Teaching Program
MSA	Metropolitan Statistical Area
N.A.	not available, or not applicable
NASA	National Aeronautics and Space Administration
NASS	National Agricultural Statistics Service

NBS	National Bureau of Standards (*Note: as of 1988, NBS became NIST*)
NCIC	National Crime Information Center
NCSCI	National Center for Standards and Certification Information
NCUA	National Credit Union Administration
NEA	National Endowment for the Arts
NEH	National Endowment for the Humanities
NEIC	National Energy Information Center
NET	nutrition education and training
NFIP	National Flood Insurance Program
NHA	National Housing Act
NHSC	National Health Service Corps
NIAAA	National Institute on Alcohol and Abuse and Alcoholism
NICE3	National Industrial Competitiveness through Energy, Environment, and Economics (DOE)
NIDA	National Institute on Drug Abuse
NIEHS	National Institute of Environmental Health Sciences
NIH	National Institutes of Health
NIMH	National Institute of Mental Health
NINDS	National Institute of Neurological Disorders and Stroke
NIOSH	National Institute for Occupational Safety and Health
NIS	New Independent States (of the former Soviet Union)
NIST	National Institute for Standards and Technology
NLRB	National Labor Relations Board
NMFS	National Marine Fisheries Service
NOAA	National Oceanic and Atmospheric Administration
NOS	National Ocean Service
NPS	National Park Service
NRC	Nuclear Regulatory Commission
NRCS	Natural Resources Conservation Service
NRSA	National Research Service Award
NSA	National Security Agency
NSEP	National Security Education Program
NSF	National Science Foundation
NSRDS	National Standard Reference Data System
NTIA	National Telecommunications and Information Administration
NTIS	National Technical Information Service

OAA	Older Americans Act
OBEMLA	Office of Bilingual Education and Minority Languages Affairs
OCCSSA	Omnibus Crime Control and Safe Streets Act
OCSE	Office of Child Support Enforcement
OEA	Office of Export Administration
OERI	Office of Educational Research and Improvement
OESE	Office of Elementary and Secondary Education
OFCCP	Office of Federal Contract Compliance Programs
OJJDP	Office of Juvenile Justice and Delinquency Prevention
OMB	Office of Management and Budget
OMEI	Office of Minority Economic Impact
OPE	Office of Postsecondary Education
OPIC	Overseas Private Investment Corporation
OPM	Office of Personnel Management
OS	Office of the Secretary
OSERS	Office of Special Education and Rehabilitative Services
OSFA	Office of Student Financial Assistance
OSHA	Occupational Safety and Health Administration
OSTI	Office of Scientific and Technical Information
OSWER	Office of Solid Waste and Emergency Response
OTAA	Office of Trade Adjustment Assistance
OVAE	Office of Vocational and Adult Education
PACA	Perishable Agricultural Commodities Act
PHS	Public Health Service
PIK	payment-in-kind
PL	Public Law
PR	Puerto Rico
PRWORA	Personal Responsibility and Work Opportunity Reconciliation Act of 1996
PTFP	Public Telecommunications Facilities Program
PWBA	Pension and Welfare Benefits Administration
RBCS	Rural Business-Cooperative Service
RC&D	resource conservation and development
RCRA	Resource Conservation and Recovery Act
RCWP	Rural Clean Water Program
RDLF	rural development loan fund
REA	Rural Electrification Administration *(Note: REA functions now are within RUS)*

RHS	Rural Housing Service
RMA	Research and Marketing Act of 1946
RMA	Risk Management Agency
RSVP	Retired and Senior Volunteer Program
RUS	Rural Utilities Service
SAMHSA	Substance Abuse and Mental Health Services Administration
SARA	Superfund Amendments and Reauthorization Act
SBA	Small Business Administration
SBIC	Small Business Investment Center
SBIR	small business innovation research
SCOR	specialized center of research
SCORE	Service Corps of Retired Executives
SCS	Soil Conservation Service *(Note: SCS functions now are within NRCS)*
SDWA	Safe Drinking Water Act
SEA	state education agency
SED	serious emotional disturbances
SEOG	supplemental educational opportunity grant
SEPA	Science Education Partnership Award
SERCA	Special Emphasis Research Center Award
SESA	state employment security agency
SIG	shared instrumentation grant
SLIAG	State Legislation Impact Assistance Grants
SMSA	Standard Metropolitan Statistical Area
SPRANS	special projects of regional and national significance
SRM	Standard Reference Materials
SRO	single room occupancy
SSA	Social Security Administration
SSBG	Social Services Block Grant
SSI	Supplemental Security Income
STD	sexually-transmitted disease
STORET	storage and retrieval
STTR	Small Business Technology Transfer
SWDA	Solid Waste Disposal Act
TAAC	Trade Adjustment Assistance Center
TANF	Temporary Assistance to Needy Families
TDD	telecommunications devices for the deaf
TDHE	tribally-designated housing authority

TERO	tribal employment rights office
TRIO	three—i.e., neither an acronym nor an abbreviation *(Per DOED, when the "TRIO" programs began in the Division of Student Services, Office of Postsecondary Education, three programs were established; the original nomenclature has remained.)*
TSCA	Toxic Substances Control Act
TVA	Tennessee Valley Authority
U.S.C.	United States Code
USCG	U.S. Coast Guard
USDA	U.S. Department of Agriculture
USDC	U.S. Department of Commerce
USDOD	U.S. Department of Defense
USGPO	U.S. Government Printing Office
USIA	U.S. Information Agency
USIP	U.S. Institute of Peace
USIS	U.S. Information Service
VA	Veterans Administration *(Note: as of 1989, VA became DVA)*
VCCLEA	Violent Crime Control and Law Enforcement Act
VI	Virgin Islands (U.S.)
VISTA	Volunteers in Service to America
VOCA	Victims of Crime Act
WIC	Women, Infants, and Children
WIN	Work Incentive Program

PART I

Obtaining Federal Assistance

What This Book Gives You

GOVERNMENT ASSISTANCE ALMANAC has two purposes: (1) to provide information enabling users to identify *all domestic programs* available from federal agencies; (2) to help users reach the point of obtaining assistance.

In the December 1999 update of *Catalog of Federal Domestic Assistance*, the General Services Administration reports 1,424 federal domestic programs available in 2000 as the government enters Fiscal Year 2001. The total includes programs offering either financial or nonfinancial assistance.

The *ALMANAC* reduces the information in the federal catalog's more than 2,400 pages, including the "Update," to the essentials needed by most persons seeking federal assistance. Modifications in the presentation of the information, especially the *ALMANAC*'s indexes, enable users to identify available programs and their features more easily and quickly.

PART I provides *basic guidance on using this book* to identify and obtain available assistance. The guidelines are intended for newcomers to federal programs; the more experienced may find some helpful reminders.

PART II outlines *every domestic financial and other assistance program available as of 1 January 2000.* For each program the following is provided:

- the established program number and title, and the popular title when applicable;
- the type or types of assistance included;
- a description of objectives, permitted uses of funds, and project examples when they clarify program purposes; the enacting legislation is noted when it helps to define program purposes;

1

- eligibility factors concerning both applicants and beneficiaries;
- range and average amounts awarded through programs providing financial assistance;
- a summary of recent activity;
- the address and phone number for program headquarters, as well as other referrals when applicable.

PART III provides tables showing *funding levels for all programs* and their *administering agencies* for the last *four fiscal years*. To our knowledge such comprehensive tables showing allocations specifically for federal domestic programs are exclusive to the *ALMANAC*. The tables also serve as a *listing of the programs in the numerical sequence* in which they appear in PART II. The *fifty largest and the fifty smallest programs* are identified.

PART IV provides *addresses and phone numbers for more than 3,000 field offices*, organized to correspond with the program numbers for which these offices have administrative responsibility. This system was established specifically for users of the *ALMANAC*; like the tables, this system exists nowhere else.

The **AGENCY INDEX** provides an *alphabetical listing of federal administrative units and sub-units*—including the program numbers within their respective responsibility. (The *Catalog of Federal Domestic Assistance* does not provide an alphabetical listing.) While administrative units also are incorporated within the MASTER INDEX, the AGENCY INDEX may expedite user searches specifically for these entities.

ALMANAC users will find the **MASTER INDEX** unique and exhaustive, particularly its subject headings, references, and cross-references. This index locates all available federal domestic assistance. It also includes: administrative units and cross-references to sub-units; official and popular program titles; abbreviated program, agency, and other titles and terms; well-known laws and their section and title numbers; and, general program references not found in other indexes of government assistance. The format enables users to distinguish programs providing financial assistance from those that do not, through the use of italicized program numbers. The copyright for *GOVERNMENT ASSISTANCE ALMANAC* makes its index an exclusive feature.

The list of **Abbreviations Used in This Book** preceding this section does not appear in the federal catalog.

By definition, "domestic programs" do not necessarily include assistance available through ongoing government activities—e.g., operation of federal facilities and services, public information activities, enforcement of most federal laws and regulations, or products or services obtained through contractors, etc. The section entitled "Types of Federal Assistance Available," beginning on page 4, explains what assistance is and is not covered in the *ALMANAC*.

Encountering the information in this book for the first time, some will be surprised by the scope of available federal assistance, which may seem very broad or rather meager in many areas. The assistance is available subject to program eligibility criteria, discussed under "Who May Obtain Federal Assistance?" (see page 9).

Timeliness of the Information

The thirteenth edition of the *ALMANAC* (1999-2000), based on the *1998 Catalog of Federal Domestic Assistance,* identified 1,386 federal programs. During the last year 74 programs were added and 36 were deleted, producing the present total of 1,424 as of 1 January 2000; this fourteenth edition incorporates the new programs and all program changes.

Federal programs rarely are terminated unless similar assistance is available through another program; this book helps in identifying those other programs. The accompanying table shows an almost steady increase in the total number of domestic programs since the mid-1980s.

Currently 56 departments, commissions, agencies, bureaus, and other federal entities administer the assistance programs. They manage the programs either through their main offices, through some 166 "administrative sub-units," or through field offices.

Regarding the reliability of addresses and phone numbers, generally, ten to twelve percent of phone numbers and five to seven percent of office addresses change in the course of a year, based on federal directories studied. It can reasonably be expected that few changes in program contact information will be encountered.

Changes are inevitable in program application requirements, governmental organization, and addresses and phone numbers. Keeping abreast of all changes would require a daily compilation, such as is provided in

---

DOMESTIC ASSISTANCE PROGRAM TOTALS
1984 THROUGH 2000

Per *GOVERNMENT ASSISTANCE ALMANAC*, 1st-14th editions.

GAA 1985-86	—	989 programs in 1984
		1,013 programs in 1985
GAA 1988	—	1,025 programs in 1987
		1,052 programs in 1988
GAA 1989-90	—	1,117 programs in 1989
GAA 1990-91	—	1,157 programs in 1990
GAA 1991-92	—	1,183 programs in 1991
GAA 1992-93	—	1,246 programs in 1992
GAA 1993-94	—	1,288 programs in 1993
GAA 1994-95	—	1,335 programs in 1994
GAA 1995-96	—	1,370 programs in 1995
GAA 1996-97	—	1,392 programs in 1996
GAA 1997-98	—	1,327 programs in 1997
GAA 1998-99	—	1,368 programs in 1998
GAA 1999-00	—	1,386 programs in 1999
GAA 2000-01	—	1,424 programs in 2000

---

the *Federal Register*. However, most substantive program changes affect the details of regulations, seldom affecting the factors included in the *ALMANAC*'s program entries; in pursuing programs with federal officials, inquirers will be advised of major changes.

Types of Federal Assistance Available

Fifteen types of federal domestic assistance are available through existing programs—providing financial or nonfinancial resources.

Programs that provide *financial assistance* are classified as:

Direct loans: programs offering the loan of federal funds for a specific term, with or without interest, with repayment expected. Example: FSA's "Emergency Loans" program provides USDA loans directly to farmers and others (see **10.404**).

Direct payments/specified use: programs providing funds for a specified purpose, with no repayment expected. Example: "Payments for Essential Air Services" to air carriers by DOT (see **20.901**).

Direct payments/unrestricted use: programs providing federal funds for use at will by the recipient, with no repayment expected. Example: "Social Security—Retirement Insurance," administered by SSA (see **96.002**). Programs in this classification may be known as "entitlements."

Formula grants: programs through which federal funds are distributed to states or other recipients according to a formula (often based on population), for continuing activities not confined to a specific project. No repayment is expected. Example: DOED's "Adult Education—State Grant Program" (see **84.002**). Programs in this classification also may be known as "entitlements."

Guaranteed/insured loans: programs offering private or public lending institutions a guarantee or insurance against loan defaults, covering all or a portion of the amount borrowed. Example: HUD's "Mortgage Insurance—Homes" program (see **14.117**).

Insurance: programs assuring reimbursement for losses under specified conditions. Insurance coverage may be provided directly by a federal agency or through a private company, depending on specific program provisions. Example: "Foreign Investment Insurance," administered by OPIC (see **70.003**). Some programs also provide for federal payment of a portion of insurance premiums. Example: USDA's "Crop Insurance" program (see **10.450**).

Project grants: programs granting federal funds for specific projects, services, products, or other activities—such as scholarships, construction, research, planning, technical assistance. Some project grants cover cooperative agreement arrangements with state governments or other organizations to assist the federal granting agency in the performance of a certain function. No repayment is expected. Project grants do not necessarily cover 100 percent of project costs. Example: NSF's "Geosciences" program (see **47.050**).

The classifications of programs providing *nonfinancial assistance* are:

Advisory services/counseling: programs through which federal specialists provide consultation, advice, or other assistance—delivered through conferences, workshops, personal contacts, or published information. Example: NRCS-USDA's "Soil and Water Conservation" program (see **10.902**).

Federal employment: programs offering jobs with the federal government through the activities of OPM in recruiting and hiring civilian personnel. Example: "Federal Summer Employment" (see **27.006**). Note that only OPM programs provide federal employment as structured programs; the ongoing recruitment activities of other federal agencies are not classified as "domestic programs."

Investigation of complaints: programs through which federal agencies examine or investigate claims of violations of federal laws, policies, or regulatory procedures. The claim must originate outside the federal government. Example: "Shipping—Investigation of Complaints," conducted by the Federal Maritime Commission (see **33.001**).

Sale, exchange, or donation of property and goods: programs featuring the transfer of federally-owned real estate or personal property, commodities, and other goods including equipment, food, drugs, or supplies. Example: "Disposal of Federal Surplus Real Property," administered by GSA (**39.002**).

Specialized services: programs providing federal personnel to perform certain services for communities, individuals, or others. Example: "Planning Assistance to States," administered by the Corps of Engineers-DOD (**12.110**). *(Note that several Corps of Engineers programs provide specialized services involving construction activities; however, these programs are not classified as providing financial assistance, and a portion of total costs for such projects usually must be matched locally.)*

Technical information: programs through which technical information or data are prepared, published, and distributed—often through clearinghouses, libraries, centers, or through electronic media. Example: NIST-USDC's "Standard Reference Materials" (see **11.604**).

Training: programs offering federal agency instruction to persons not employed by the federal government. Example: FEMA's "Emergency Management Institute (EMI)—Resident Educational Program" (see **83.530**).

Use of property, facilities, and equipment: programs providing for the temporary use of or access to federally-owned resources, with or without charge to the user. Example: "National Gallery of Art Extension Service" (see **68.001**).

Not included as a classification, but reflected in the list and included in this book, are "block grants" which may be used for a range of related activities. Block grants usually are awarded as "formula grants" or "project grants." Their permitted uses generally are more flexible than other types of programs. Such programs are cited in the index under the subject heading "Block grant programs."

Many programs offer more than one type of assistance; for example, the second program listed in PART II, **10.025**, offers project grants as well as specialized services, advisory services/counseling, technical information, and training.

The following types of government activities are not defined as domestic programs; they are *not included* in this book:

- *Procurement contracts* for the purchase of goods and services by the federal government. For instance, basic DOD contracting activities do not meet the definition of domestic programs; however, DOD administers several programs classified as providing "domestic assistance." Programs offering assistance to firms wanting to do business with the federal government through its procurement contracts *are included*.
- *U.S. government foreign activities* without a direct benefit in the domestic economy. For instance, most Department of State activities are not domestic programs; however, the state department also administers several domestic programs. The federal government sponsors several programs pertaining to importing and exporting, which *are included* in this book.
- *Employee recruitment programs* of individual federal departments and agencies.
- *Programs benefiting only current or retired military personnel or federal employees.* However, all DVA benefit programs *are included*—although many DVA programs are not classified as providing financial assistance.
- *Ongoing public information services* of federal entities.
- *Basic domestic functions of the federal government* such as operation

and maintenance of services and facilities, collection of taxes, enforcement of federal laws and regulations, judicial processes, etc.

- *Smithsonian Institution programs*, several of which formerly were classified as "domestic programs" (and were included in early *ALMANAC* editions), but are no longer listed in the *Catalog of Federal Domestic Assistance*.

Also not included are various tax incentives offered through the Internal Revenue Code, which are not classified as federal programs. These include so-called tax shelters, tax credits, writeoffs, and the like. Such government benefits to private taxpayers have stimulated activity in the domestic economy in recent years. Their features are the subject of other books dealing with taxes, finance, investment, etc.

Frequently, however, such "non-programs" relate directly to certain structured domestic programs which *are included* in this book. Examples: program **15.904**, "Historic Preservation Fund Grants-in-Aid," can be used to obtain accelerated depreciation of the value of improvements for tax purposes; program **20.812**, "Construction Reserve Fund," relating to merchant vessels, offers tax incentives to participants.

Resources for the Resourceful

GOVERNMENT ASSISTANCE ALMANAC may reveal previously unknown resources available to various types of users—farmers, students, small businesses, investors, entrepreneurs, homemakers, scientists, the elderly, parents, journalists, civic and social organizations, health professionals, guidance counselors, scholars, state and municipal governments, educators, artists and arts sponsors, members of minority groups, veterans and their dependents, community improvement groups, researchers, and others including those interested in the needs of the foregoing groups, as well as persons planning to enter those fields. They may find programs that offer technical information, services, training, or other types of assistance that they did not know existed.

The simplest assistance programs are those meeting a single purpose. For instance, someone seeking resources for an elderly person whose home needs repairs will find that the index cites a number of programs that could provide help. Selecting the most appropriate of the available programs is a matter of finding the programs in the index, carefully reading the program entries in PART II, and pursuing the most promising. The section entitled "Obtaining Federal Assistance: How to Use PART II," beginning on page 15, provides guidance along these lines.

Frequently, assistance will be found for elderly persons with several needs. For instance, in addition to programs providing loan or grant funds to repair property, subsidies are available to help pay fuel bills—even the cost of air conditioning under certain conditions. Also available are programs through which older persons might obtain part-time employment, or meals, or help with home management tasks; dependents of deceased veterans may be entitled to pensions, health care, and burial expenses and grave markers for the deceased veteran.

Seeking federal assistance becomes more challenging when two or more programs are combined to meet more complex needs. For instance, someone interested in obtaining mortgage insurance on a loan covering a multi-unit housing structure in an older declining area through **14.123** may decide to also pursue the rental subsidies available to tenants through **14.855**.

Resourcefulness often is the key to obtaining federal assistance. The successful outcome of creative use of available assistance is illustrated across the country, in virtually all fields—from child care to environmental enhancement to job creation to the performing arts to scientific research.

Often, those who have successfully used public resources are eager to show what they did and how they went about it. Their experience could save prospective applicants countless hours of trial and error. Federal officials also may provide guidance in learning how to use federal programs effectively; their perspective can be unique, an important resource to tap.

The challenge may increase when federal assistance is channeled through a state, municipal, or private organization. The next section, "Who May Obtain Federal Assistance?" addresses the situation. In such instances, the application *process* is usually similar to making federal office contacts. However, the competition for funds help could be stiffer. The award process could be more complicated, requiring a good deal of groundwork at the community level to obtain the assistance. An applicant's resourcefulness usually pays off, just as with federal contacts.

Who May Obtain Federal Assistance?

Eligibility depends on the specific program.

Assistance through many programs is available to the general public—e.g., use of the national libraries, technical information, and similar facilities and services.

Some programs, because of laws or regulations governing their administration, offer assistance only to certain categories of *applicants*— e.g., farmers, states, small businesses, native Americans. Only specified categories of prospective recipients may *apply.*

Other programs may directly *benefit* only certain industries—e.g., shipbuilding or agriculture, or certain population groups such as the elderly, or teenagers, or immigrants from specific countries.

Under still other federal programs, eligible applicants and beneficiaries are the same. Examples include certain veterans, small business, and student programs.

The distinction between programs offering assistance specifically to eligible applicants, eligible beneficiaries, and eligible applicants/beneficiaries is clear in the program entries presented in PART II.

The point to be understood is that the distinction between eligible applicants and eligible beneficiaries is very important to those seeking assistance. Many deserving persons have not obtained assistance to which they were entitled because this distinction was not understood. Being ineligible to *apply* to a federal agency for assistance under certain programs does not necessarily mean that one cannot *benefit* from those programs. The following actual example illustrates the point.

"The Case of the Muffin Machine"

A few years ago, a baker in a small city used his savings to establish a franchised doughnut business. The city was economically depressed; it managed to obtain relatively large sums of federal money for economic development from several federal agencies.

In a relatively short time after starting, the business did well enough for the owner to meet expenses while employing eleven persons, mostly waiters and waitresses for its 24-hour operation.

The owner was notified by the franchise company of a new product, muffins, that was boosting other franchise owners' sales and profits substantially in market test areas. The franchise company offered an $11,000 package that would include the necessary equipment to begin making and selling muffins. The owner's assets were tied up in the business and in keeping it solvent. So, he applied to a bank for an $11,000 loan to finance purchase of the package. The bank told the owner that it would lend him only $5,500 toward the purchase. The owner did not have the $5,500 balance that he needed, nor would any other bank lend him more because his assets were heavily mortgaged.

Meanwhile, the city's success in obtaining federal funds to help in the creation of new jobs was publicized in the local media. The owner phoned the Department of Housing and Urban Development's nearest office for information about obtaining the funds, because he had heard that HUD was the source of much of the money received by the city. Unfortunately, whoever answered the phone at HUD told the owner that only the city could receive that type of funds from HUD.

Several weeks passed before the owner "badmouthed" the HUD program to the right customer. The customer happened to be another small business owner who had obtained some of the HUD funds to finance the expansion of his business. The customer told the owner whom to contact *locally* to apply for funds. Following a short meeting with an official in the city's economic development organization, the baker-owner had an entirely different attitude toward the program he had been complaining about.

Three weeks later, financing had been arranged to purchase the "muffin machine." The bank loaned the small businessman $5,500 at its commercial interest rate. From the city's funds received from HUD, he obtained $4,400 at 5 percent interest. And, he scraped up the remaining $1,100, or 10 percent of the total investment, on his own. One full-time job and two part-time jobs resulted from this loan.

In this particular program (**14.228**) only small cities may *apply* for the available project grants, which may be used for quite a broad range of activities, including revolving loan funds with interest rates established locally. However, as an *eligible beneficiary* of the program the small business owner was able to obtain the assistance; the city accomplished its objectives of creating jobs and "leveraging" private funds through its economic development efforts; and, most important perhaps, three persons received jobs generated by the program.

The importance of this example to persons seeking federal assistance is the distinction between eligible *applicants* and eligible *beneficiaries*. If only certain types of applicants may apply for a program and you are not eligible, but you are eligible to *benefit*—say, under a training program—find out who has obtained funds and apply there for the training. If it cannot be established who has received funds by contacting organizations at the community level, contact the appropriate federal field office listed in PART IV of this book; if there is no field office, contact the program headquarters listed in PART II.

Organization of the Federal Programs in This Book

PART II of *GOVERNMENT ASSISTANCE ALMANAC* uses the same numerical system of listing federal programs followed in the *Catalog of Federal Domestic Assistance*. The system is not totally logical, in that the programs are not listed alphabetically, functionally, or by type of assistance. They are organized according to their administering department or agency; this makes the *ALMANAC*'s MASTER INDEX especially useful in identifying available assistance.

Each program is identified by a five-digit number. The first two digits identify the administrative entity responsible for the program. The last three digits identify the administrative sub-unit, if any, and the program. Using as examples several programs described in PART II, pages 84 to 116 illustrate the numerical system:

DEPARTMENT OF COMMERCE

This administrative entity has responsibility for all programs that begin with the digits "11."

BUREAU OF THE CENSUS

This administrative sub-unit of the Department of Commerce has management responsibility for the programs outlined. **11.001** through **11.006** are the numbers identifying programs managed by the Bureau of the Census.

All programs with "**12**" as their first two digits, beginning on page 117, are administered by the Department of Defense. The system continues throughout PART II and PART III, as well as PART IV which provides field contact information.

PART III. Program Funding Levels—Summary Tables (page 571) lists the departments, agencies, commissions, and other governmental entities in the order in which they are presented in PART II.

Note, however, that PARTS II and III provide headings for administrative sub-units only when such headings also are provided in the *Catalog of Federal Domestic Assistance*. The *ALMANAC*'s AGENCY INDEX lists all administrative units and sub-units alphabetically, and it includes the program numbers within their respective purviews.

(The numerical system originated in the 1960s when the first edition of the *Catalog of Federal Domestic Assistance* was published. It was organized alphabetically by the name of the administering agency. Many numbers were not used, to allow for inclusion of new programs. Through the years, new agencies and programs were established and existing ones were terminated. The new agencies were added to the end of the list, to avoid changing the numerical sequence within the numbering system. Program numbers for terminated agencies or programs were removed altogether, and reserved in case they are reinstated eventually.)

Red Tape—Should You Hire a Consultant?

Federal laws, regulations, statutory provisions, policies, forms, criteria, procedures, processes, standards, deadlines, audits, certifications, documentation, appeals, authorizations, records, credentials, formulas, obligations, guidelines—these terms and many others signify the "red tape" of federal programs.

The terms form an important part of the language used in administering federal programs. Expect to encounter the language in seeking federal assistance. Depending on the program pursued, none, some, or all of the terms may be encountered.

The following general principles concerning "red tape" are understood by persons experienced in applying for federal assistance.

1. *Programs involving financial benefits in any form involve more red tape than other types of assistance.*

2. *The more persons served by a given program, the less red tape to the beneficiaries.* For example, applicants for basic Social Security benefits must produce certain information to enable federal officials to verify their eligibility and to calculate their benefits. Because millions of persons participate in the Social Security program, red tape has been minimized and usually is simple enough to overcome.

3. *Programs providing for one-on-one contacts between federal officials and applicants usually involve less red tape.* Examples: persons applying for some types of farming assistance or fellowships, training, veterans benefits, and similar assistance. In such cases, the applicant/beneficiary usually can easily arrange to provide the required information.

4. *Programs with relatively few participants nationwide and with large benefit amounts require extensive lengths of red tape.* Examples: programs addressing the problem of toxic waste; multi-year intensive research projects; financial assistance programs based on the recipient's promise to perform certain tasks, such as construction projects involving federal mortgage insurance.

5. *Programs with several parties to an application for assistance involve increased red tape.* For example, a housing developer applying for a mortgage guaranty on apartments to receive rental subsidies will be required to produce documents from a lender, attorneys, architects, housing management experts, local housing officials, and others—with each party needing to satisfy various requirements. Such applications must be "packaged" into a single application. Moreover, the approval process requires "sign-off" (i.e., approval) by several officials both outside and within the administering federal agency.

6. *Programs that provide federal assistance to beneficiaries through nonfederal offices may or may not have added red tape.* The five preceding principles apply. Examples: information about drug abuse might be obtained easily through a federally-funded state agency, but obtaining federal funds through the same state agency to establish a local drug abuse program could be more difficult than dealing with a federal office because of complex state requirements *in addition to* federal requirements; a student applying to a college financial aid office for federal educational assistance could have to meet federal, state, *and* the institution's requirements.

For most programs, paid consultants are not needed to apply for federal assistance. Generally, the official receiving the application will guide applicants in meeting requirements. Many programs require that applications be submitted through public administering agencies, private organizations, banks, or similar entities. Personnel in these organizations might well be considered the "consultant" or advocate for the application.

Programs involving complicated applications may require expert assistance to assure favorable action by the funding agency. Applicants without the time or patience to learn about and fulfill all requirements may find it advantageous to hire an experienced consultant.

In selecting a consultant, verify his or her credentials, experience, and record in obtaining federal assistance *of the type to be sought*. Check with the consultant's other clients and with federal offices to confirm that the qualifications are pertinent to the specific program. A consultant's impressive background in one field or with one federal agency is not necessarily a recommendation in another field or with a different federal agency. Most federal offices will provide advice about the need for a consultant's help in applying for given programs.

Keep the red tape in perspective. Try to understand its necessity. Federal requirements are intended to assure the proper use of federal funds. Virtually everyone agrees that many federal programs involve excessive red tape. Separate complaints and constructive recommendations about program requirements from the application process.

Obtaining Federal Assistance: How to Use PART II

Identifying and obtaining federal assistance is a reasonably straightforward process when one proceeds carefully and resourcefully. The previous section commented on the most complicated part of the process: the requirements that must be met to obtain assistance from the federal government. Complications can be minimal if a few basic steps are followed.

STEP ONE: USE THE MASTER INDEX

Thumb through the MASTER INDEX at the end of this book. Each program appears in the index an average of ten times. Together with the cross-references, the index assures that users will be able to identify *all* available assistance programs. Become familiar with the types of headings, sub-headings, and cross references. The index presents:

- subjects (shown in bold face);
- official program titles (in capital letters); bracketed agency identifiers are added to program titles to clarify the federal agency involved in cases where the program title alone is indistinct;
- popular titles of programs;
- miscellaneous (abbreviations, agency names, names of Acts, etc.);

The numbers following the headings refer to the program numbers in PART II where they appear in the left column. *Indexed programs that offer financial assistance are italicized, distinguishing them from programs that do not,* to further assist users in quickly identifying programs most pertinent to their needs.

Finding programs by title, popular name, abbreviation, or administrative entity is a simple procedure of looking in the index alphabetically, and then turning to PART II where the program descriptions are presented in numerical order. The introductory notes preceding the MASTER INDEX may prove useful.

Finding programs by subject involves looking for a main term and then scanning the indented entries under it. Generally, programs *intended* for the benefit of certain groups of people, such as women, youth, Indians, the disadvantaged, the handicapped, etc., are indexed directly under the common name of the group. Many programs are available to group members even though not targeted primarily for them. For example, programs relating to housing for Indians will be found under "Indian housing;" however, programs listed under the more general headings beginning with "Housing," such as "Housing, rental" or "Housing, construction," may also be applicable. To ascertain that every possible available program has been identified, both approaches should be followed.

The MASTER INDEX also includes section and title numbers of certain Acts, as well as the names of the Acts themselves. So if an *ALMANAC* user is interested in "section 109," for example, but does not know or cannot remember the exact name of the Act, in looking under "Section" numerous section numbers will be found with their corresponding program numbers.

Finding programs by administrative entity, such as "Department of Labor," can be done through the MASTER INDEX for all agencies. Or, the AGENCY INDEX might be consulted instead. The AGENCY INDEX also shows programs administered by sub-units. "PART III. Program Funding Levels—Summary Tables" gives the names of all the agencies, arranged by governmental department, in the order in which the programs are presented in PARTS II and IV.

For other programs, the recommended procedure is to check first under the specific term, and then under more general terms. "*See*" and "*see also*" references have been used liberally to direct searches. For example, under "Aquaculture" a "*see also*" reference suggests looking under such other headings as "Farm, nonfarm enterprises," "Fish," and "Fisheries industry" for more entries of possible interest.

Or, if a scholarship to attend podiatry school is sought, users should look first under "Podiatry" where one or more programs will be found; but the *see also* reference directs users to "Health professions" where more general programs will be found that may be of interest; users also will be referred to "Fellowships, scholarships, traineeships" for still other related programs.

The index includes some terms indicating permitted uses of programs, which may not be mentioned in the program entry. These terms are included in the index for programs where it is known that program funds possibly may be used for activities embodied in the indexed term. "Block grant" programs frequently are indexed in this manner.

Often, more than one program will be found providing assistance under a given heading. Read all program entries in PART II carefully, and pursue the most pertinent.

After perusing the index, if no reference is found to a program providing assistance for a specific purpose, it is almost certain that such federal assistance is unavailable. There is one more step that might be taken: contact the federal office most apt to know about assistance available for specific purposes. Many programs can be "stretched" to cover activities that are not found in the program entry or in the index.

STEP TWO: "READ" A FEDERAL PROGRAM

PART II provides outlines of all available domestic programs. Properly "reading" the information on a given program—that is, understanding the program entry—will facilitate decisions on whether to pursue the available assistance. The following explanation of the program entries explains how to "read" the entries to greatest advantage. Program **14.239** on page 154 serves as the example.

① **COMMUNITY PLANNING AND DEVELOPMENT**

② **14.239   HOME INVESTMENT PARTNERSHIPS PROGRAM**
③ **("HOME Program")**
④ **Assistance:** formula grants (100 percent/2-5 years).
⑤ **Purposes:** pursuant to the National Affordable Housing Act, to support partnerships among all levels of government and the private sector, including profit and nonprofit organizations, in the production and operation of affordable housing, particularly rental housing for low- and very-low-income families. Funds may be used for: planning; development of model projects; technical assistance; housing rehabilitation; tenant-based rental assistance; assistance to homebuyers; new construction of housing; site acquisition and improvements, demolition, relocation. Fund may not be used: for public housing modernization; to match funds required for other federal programs; as rental housing operating subsidies; for activities under the Low Income Housing Preservation Act, except for priority purchasers.
⑥ **Eligible applicants:** states, cities, urban counties, or consortia or general local government units; Insular Areas.
⑦ **Eligible beneficiaries:** rental housing—90 percent of funds for families with incomes at 60 percent of area median, and the remainder for families below 80 percent. Homeownership assistance—families with incomes below 80 percent of the area median.
⑧ **Range:** $339,000 to $104,240,000. **Average:** $2,650,000.
⑨ **Activity:** cumulatively, funds committed to 347,000 units, 210,000 units completed; 46,000 tenants receiving rental assistance.
⑩ **HQ:** Director, Office of Affordable Housing Programs, CPD-HUD, 451 Seventh St. SW, Washington, DC 20410. Phone: (202)708-2685.

---

① *Administrative sub-unit* with management responsibility for all programs under the heading.

② *Program number,* and *official program title.*

③ *popular title.*

Many program titles in PART II are followed by one or more *popular titles,* shown within parentheses and quotation marks, as in this illustration. Field office officials and others may know programs only by their popular titles.

④ *Classification of assistance* available through the program. (The fifteen "Types of Federal Assistance Available" are defined beginning on page 4.)

Many programs provide more than one type of assistance. When financial assistance is provided this line indicates the percentage of assistance provided by the federal agency, as well as the usual project term *when the term is other than for one year.* For some programs, the percentage and project term are clarified under "⑤ **Purposes.**"

Project grants usually are awarded either through competitions or solicitations of proposals by the sponsoring federal agency; however, authorizing statutes for some programs allocate funds on the basis of a formula, as in the "HOME Program," in which case the federal administrative agency notifies eligible applicants of the availability of funds. It is mandatory for prospective applicants for competitive, solicited, or unsolicited proposals to remain aware of available programs.

Although the percentage of federal assistance may say "100 percent," most programs have maintenance of effort ("MOE") or "non-supplementation" requirements—meaning that federal funds may not supplant existing nonfederal funding allocated to the effort for which federal funds are sought. Also, some level of cost sharing by the applicant almost always is required—if only through the provision of administrative space and services supporting project activities; such contributions by applicants are known as "in-kind" contributions. *Frequently, the level of "MOE" or of cost sharing by applicants will influence the approval of applications.*

⑤ Description of the *basic objectives* and *permitted uses* of the program, as well as *restrictions* on the use of funds. Examples of funded projects are also included when they help to explain the types of activities that are eligible.

The information on the purposes of program **14.239** should be sufficient to permit a decision on whether to pursue it. Note that many programs include more than a single program purpose. Other program features also are included in program descriptions.

⑥ *Who may apply* for the available assistance.

⑦ *Who may benefit* from the program.

Thus, the headings setting forth the eligibility for program **14.239** indicate that only states, cities, urban counties, or consortia or general local government units, and Insular Areas may apply directly for assistance. However, when program assistance is sought for rental housing, 90 percent of approved funds must benefit families with incomes at 60 percent of area median, and the remainder for families below 80 percent; when assistance is approved for homeownership projects, families with incomes below 80 percent of the area median may benefit.

It follows that someone interested in participating in this program, if not an eligible applicant, should contact appropriate state or local officials to learn more about it. Contact the state or city public information office to find out whom to contact for details; if that fails, contact the nearest HUD Community Planning and Development field office listed in PART IV.

Frequently, there is no distinction between eligible applicants and eligible beneficiaries, because they are one and the same. And, many program descriptions name the intended beneficiaries; those beneficiaries need not apply because services will (or should) be provided to them by the applicants—for instance, programs intended to benefit elderly persons, children and youth, substance abusers, and other general categories of beneficiaries. Such programs have the following eligibility heading:

Eligible applicants/beneficiaries:

Review the section beginning on page 9 entitled "Who May Obtain Federal Assistance?" for a discussion and example of the significance of eligible applicants vs. eligible beneficiaries.

Occasionally a notation in this heading will indicate "same as for" another program (e.g., in program **93.551**). In "reading" program entries, take such a notation to mean that the two programs probably have related purposes—suggesting that, if the one being considered does not meet your needs, perhaps the other will.

⑧   Indicates the *range and average amounts* provided to applicants or, sometimes, to beneficiaries for programs that provide financial assistance. Numbers over 10,000 under this heading are rounded to the nearest 1,000.

Knowing range and average amounts helps in assessing the chances of obtaining a certain sum. Often, applying for a sum that is outside the range shown is pointless, whether the sum sought is below or above the range.

Complementing the "Range" heading are the tables in PART III. *Used together*, the amounts provide a perspective of the funding available nationally for a given activity, and how much an applicant or a beneficiary might expect to obtain through that program.

In "reading" the tables, remember that the U.S. government's fiscal year begins on October 1 and ends on September 30. Fiscal years are expressed in the ending date; thus, FY 00 ends September 30, 2000. On page 580, Table 1 shows the following funding available for program **14.239**:

(FY 97) $1,332,200,000;   (FY 98) $1,438,000,000;   (FY 99) $1,550,300,000 e;   (FY 00) $1,550,300,000 e

Note that amounts are rounded to the nearest $1,000 in Tables 1, 2, and 3.

The information on funding for the four years: (1) indicates the amount available nationally; (2) shows whether, from year to year, a program's funding level remains relatively consistent or if it is increasing or decreasing.

"•" following an amount indicates that the amount is a "credit" rather than an actual outlay of funds. For purposes of the tables, amounts loaned or insured by the government were classified as credits. Program **14.239** provides formula grants and, therefore, is classified as an outlay.

"e" next to an amount indicates that it is *estimated*. In the example, the amounts shown are actual for FY 97 and FY 98; the amounts for FY 99 and FY 00 are estimated.

Estimated amounts could mean that Congress had not approved a specific amount when the information was compiled, or that the amount obligated for a program fluctuates depending on demands for the funds.

Estimates of "$0" may indicate that the program has been proposed for termination.

Amounts shown in the tables must meet demands nationwide. The total often is allocated geographically by government agencies to regions, states, districts, or areas, according to legislative or administrative policy. Therefore, it could be useful to learn the amount available in a given geographical area, from the officials contacted concerning a specific program—for an indication of the extent of competition to be expected.

The tables offer a perspective of government support for agencies and programs, in relation to one another and to other federal domestic activities. The introduction to the tables further discusses their usefulness in "reading" federal programs.

⑨   *Activity within the program* in the most recent period reported by the administering entity, including such information as the number of assistance awards or of persons benefiting. Numbers over 10,000 under this heading are rounded to the nearest 1,000. It is also noted when the program is new—with or without reported activity.

In combination with the information provided under *Range/Average* and in the Tables, "reading" the level of activity provides an indication of the participation nationally in given programs.

⑩   *Program headquarters address and phone number* of the administering agency. FAX and e-mail numbers are included when provided in the source material.

Occasionally, a notation in this heading will indicate "same address/ phone as" another program (e.g., in program **10.028**). In "reading" program entries, such a notation means that the two programs probably have closely related purposes—suggesting that, if the one being considered does not meet certain needs, perhaps the other will.

THE FIRST CONTACT WITH A FEDERAL AGENCY ABOUT A PROGRAM SHOULD ALWAYS BE WITH THE FIELD OFFICE IF ONE EXISTS. The "HQ" entry always indicates when there are no field offices for a given program with "(Note: no field offices for this program.)" following the HQ address. If the notation does not appear, field office contact information is provided in PART IV. For example, the Department of Housing and Urban Development's field offices begin on page 643.

Contacting field offices has advantages for both applicants and federal officials. The nearer a federal office is to applicants, the more probable it is that the officials will be able to provide pertinent information; field office personnel usually are more aware of needs in the area they serve; contacts with them add to this awareness.

Also, they are more apt to know who else in a given area has similar interests; they could provide leads to others experienced with the program. It is important for the field offices to know the extent of interest in the programs that they manage. Generally, headquarters personnel are more involved with "big picture" matters than with handling individual contacts from throughout the country.

PART IV provides contact information for regional, state, and area or district offices. The hierarchy should be followed upwards when deciding which office to contact—that is, if there is a district, branch, or area office, it should be contacted before state or regional offices; state offices should be contacted before regional offices.

When contacting a field office, address the "Director" unless the entry in PART IV suggests otherwise. Include the full name of the agency. For example, correspondence with HUD's Chicago state office, concerning program **14.239**, should be addressed as follows (per the listing on page 647):

> Director, State Office
> Community Planning and Development
> Department of Housing and Urban Development
> Metcalf Federal Bldg.
> 77 W. Jackson Blvd.
> Chicago, IL 60604-3507

PART IV also provides contact information for specialized field service offices such as research centers, laboratories, and testing stations.

STEP THREE: ASK THE RIGHT QUESTIONS

"STEP ONE" and "STEP TWO" involve the selection of programs to pursue. The process of obtaining federal assistance begins when those steps are completed. Hundreds of programs involve very little red tape.

They require little or no additional "homework", especially those involving nonfinancial assistance. For nonfinancial programs, one or two contacts with the right federal official usually will bring the desired assistance.

This "step" is meant for newcomers to federal programs, who decide to pursue the more complicated programs involving awards of funds. All the points discussed will not be pertinent to all the programs, obviously.

Before formally applying for financial assistance under all but the least complicated programs, a preliminary contact with the responsible federal office is always advisable; indeed, some programs require a preapplication conference. An appointment with the responsible official should be requested; when making this request, the eligibility criteria for the program being pursued should be discussed generally. At this first meeting at least the following should be accomplished:

1. *Verify the eligibility of the applicant*—whether as an individual or as an organization. This should have been done verbally when the appointment was made. If the official mentioned credentials required to document eligibility, these should be shown at the meeting. The required credentials could include documents such as a birth certificate, academic certificates, a financial statement, endorsements, a copy of the organization's charter or license, etc. If the required credentials are not ready, evidence that they be can produced should be shown—e.g., publications, sample products, leaflets describing the organization, a good resume.

2. *Explain the applicant's specific need for the assistance in very basic terms.* Prior to the meeting an outline for using the assistance should be prepared, and it should be shown to the official. This will open a discussion of the program, its objectives, the permitted uses of funds, program restrictions, etc. All possible questions about the program should be posed, including the availability of funding. The official should be allowed to do most of the talking—the purpose of the meeting is for the applicant to obtain information, not give it. On the other hand, prospective applicants should answer all questions honestly to reveal potential problems early in the process. If problems do surface, the official's advice should be sought on how to resolve them. *Written* notes should be made, both during and immediately after the meeting.

3. *Obtain all available written information pertaining to the program.* The following could be useful in preparing a thorough application:

- a copy of the law establishing the program;
- policy statements;
- procedural guidelines and instructions to applicants;
- regulations governing the program, including those published in the *Federal Register* and those pertaining mainly to the processing requirements that federal agencies themselves must fulfill—the latter often provide instructions for "scoring" the merits of applications, giving insights into what those reviewing an application will look for;
- statements of application deadlines, if any;
- general literature describing the program and the experiences of others that have obtained funds under the same or similar programs;
- a copy of a sample successful application;
- most important, copies of any pertinent circulars governing the program issued by the Office of Management and Budget, as well as Executive Orders or other regulations issued by federal or state agencies that will coordinate or review applications—e.g., the Environmental Protection Agency;
- lists of requirements for records to be kept and reports to be filed if the application is approved—including copies of pertinent accounting procedures;
- a description of the "appeal process," in case the application is not approved and the decision is appealed.

4. *If the program requires cost sharing or a matching contribution* by the applicant, it should be determined whether any portion of this sum can be provided through "in-kind" services, use of facilities or equipment, or other noncash contributions. Review the explanation of the program description entry heading "Assistance" on page 18 for insights on cost sharing.

5. *Ask to be placed on the office's mailing list* to receive announcements, news releases, notifications of invitations to apply or of awards, changes in regulations or deadlines, and the like.

6. Keep the meeting as brief as possible.

STEP FOUR: COMPLETE YOUR HOMEWORK

Examine carefully all the material obtained in "STEP THREE." Make a list of the most important points. Note especially items that are not readily understood, and follow through on each of them. Follow all instructions carefully. In your application, projecting an ability to adhere carefully and fully to instructions and regulations is all-important. "Dot every i, cross every t."

At this point, the "grantsmanship" process begins. Grantsmanship is a term often used inaccurately to describe *obtaining* federal assistance. Successful grantsmanship necessitates thorough familiarity with program and project planning, development, and operations. A good application will reflect complete understanding of program purposes and requirements, *as well as sound project management capability.* The grantsmanship process is both an art and a science; its productive outcome requires extensive research, discipline, precise work, sound psychology, effective presentation, a good sense of business, and persistence.

The *ALMANAC*'s author/editor and publisher wish users success in their quest, trusting that this book points them in the right direction.

Finding More Information

Several sources might be checked for more information on obtaining federal assistance.

1. Two principal sources provide additional details about the assistance programs outlined in this *ALMANAC*:

    First, the *Catalog of Federal Domestic Assistance*, available by subscription from:

    Superintendent of Documents
    U.S. Government Printing Office
    Washington, DC 20402

    The catalog provides source material for the *ALMANAC*. The main edition is published in June every year, containing some 2,000 pages and mailed unbound for filing in a loose-leaf binder; subscriptions include the *Update to the Catalog of Federal Domestic Assistance*, published in December and numbering several hundred pages.

The catalog contains a brief section with "Suggestions for Proposal Writing and Following Grant Application Procedures," which could be helpful to newcomers to federal programs.

The General Services Administration, which compiles the catalog, distributes copies to:

Members of Congress
Congressional staff
All federal Depository Libraries (see program **40.002**)
Federal offices
Governors
State coordinators of federal-state relations
Directors of state departments of administration
Directors of state agricultural extension services
Directors of state departments of community affairs
Directors of state planning agencies
State budget offices
State municipal leagues
State associations of counties
Chief state school officers
State employment security agencies
Mayors
County chairmen
Chairmen of boards of commissioners
City planners
Some other state and local government agencies and officials

The catalog may be examined at one of the offices listed. *Federal Information Centers* also have copies available for examination; for information on contacting Federal Information Centers, see program **39.008**.

Second, the "Federal Assistance Programs Retrieval System" (FAPRS), a computerized question/answer system, provides access to the information available in the *Catalog of Federal Domestic Assistance*. Searches may be requested from certain state access points, a current list of which is available from:

Federal Domestic Assistance Catalog Staff (MVS)
General Services Administration
Rm. 101 Reporters Bldg.

300 7th Street, SW
Washington, DC 20407
Phone: (202)708-5126

2. *The United States Government Manual* is a useful reference source for persons wanting to better understand the federal government. The manual describes the basic functions and operations of all government agencies, including the judicial, legislative, and executive branches. Most libraries have copies available for reference. The current manual may be purchased from Government Printing Office Bookstores, addresses for which will be found in PART IV, under program **40.002**, or it may be ordered by mail from the Superintendent of Documents.

3. *The Federal Register,* published daily, provides the public with federal agency regulations and other legal documents covering government activities, including *proposed* changes in regulations. Newly authorized programs and the availability of funding also are announced in *The Federal Register.*

   The Federal Register Index, published monthly, consolidates entries appearing in the basic publication, with broad references to the contents.

   Additional *Federal Register* resources include "Weekly Compilation of Presidential Documents" and "The Federal Register: What It Is and How to Use It."

   The *Code of Federal Regulations* ("CFR") codifies the general and permanent rules published in the *The Federal Register* by federal executive departments and agencies. The CFR includes all statutory regulations; it is updated by *The Federal Register.*

   The foregoing publications are available for examination in federal depository libraries and major libraries, or for purchase from the Government Printing Office.

4. *Libraries* are obvious places to look for additional information about government programs, grantsmanship, proposal writing, and similar topics. Larger or more specialized libraries also will have available directories of trade or professional associations and of commercial

publishers specializing in information on various government activities, which might provide assistance or guidance concerning certain federal assistance programs. Directories of consultants and consulting organizations also are available.

5. *Government Phone Book USA—A Comprehensive Guide to Federal, State, County, and Local Government Offices in the United States,* provides standard and e-mail addresses and phone and FAX numbers, totaling some 164,000 listings. Published annually by Omnigraphics, Inc., this comprehensive reference should be available at libraries.

6. *Congressional offices* may or may not be able to provide help in obtaining additional information or actual assistance. Some senators and representatives are more anxious to do so than others, depending on the capacity, interest, and capabilities of their staffs.

Many elected officials respond more quickly to requests for assistance from other elected officials, or from campaign supporters. Keep this in mind when deciding to seek a congressman's intercession. The first contact should be with district or state offices. The Washington addresses for offices of Members of Congress are:

United States Senate   House of Representatives
Washington, DC 20510   Washington, DC 20515

The best source of more information about given programs and obtaining the assistance they provide usually is someone experienced in those programs or similar ones.

less intensive uses such as grasses, legumes, shrubs, trees. Basic program objectives include reducing soil erosion or sedimentation, improving water quality as well as wildlife habitat. Participants must institute approved conservation plans and reduce the aggregate total of acreage bases, allotments, and quotas for the contract period.

Eligible applicants/beneficiaries: individuals, partnerships, associations, tribal corporations, estates, trusts, other businesses or legal entities; states and their political subdivisions; other owners or operators of croplands or certain marginal pastureland.

Range: $50 to $50,000. **Average:** $4,000; contracts, rental rate, $49.20/acre.

Activity: FY 86-98, 29,000,000 acres under active contracts. (Average contract, 97 acres.)

HQ: same address/phone as **10.054**.

10.070   COLORADO RIVER BASIN SALINITY CONTROL PROGRAM ("CRBSCP")

Assistance: direct payments/specified use (to 70 percent/3-10 years).

Purposes: for salinity control activities in the Colorado River basin, toward the improvement of water quality in the U.S. and Mexico. Assistance may be financial or technical, to: identify salt source areas; employ conservation practices to reduce salt loads; conduct research, education, and demonstration projects.

Eligible applicants/beneficiaries: individuals, tribes, partnerships, firms, associations, corporations, joint stock companies, conservation or irrigation districts, estates, trusts, states, or local public or nonpublic entities that are owners, landlords, operators, or tenants of eligible lands.

Range/Average: $20,000.

Activity: varying by project in eligible counties.

HQ: same address as **10.062**. Phone: (202)720-1873.

10.071   FEDERAL-STATE COOPERATION IN WAREHOUSE EXAMINATION AGREEMENT ("Warehouse Examination")

Assistance: direct payments/specified use.

Purposes: for costs of examinations and inspections of warehouses covered by CCC storage agreements and state warehouse licenses. The CCC provides training to applicants prior to approving agreements. No new agreements are being approved currently.

Eligible applicants/beneficiaries: state agencies.

Range: $770 to $406,000. **Average:** $106,000.

Activity: agreements currently in effect in Alabama, Colorado, Idaho, Iowa, Illinois, Indiana, Kansas, Louisiana, Minnesota, Missouri, Nebraska, Ohio, Oklahoma, South Carolina, Washington, and Wisconsin.

HQ: Director, Warehouse and Inventory Division (STOP 0553), FSA-USDA, Washington, DC 20013. Phone: (202)720-4018.

10.072 WETLANDS RESERVE PROGRAM
("WRP")

Assistance: direct payments/specified use (to 100 percent/5 to 30 years).

Purposes: to install necessary restoration practices needed to protect farmed or converted wetlands, riparian areas, and buffer areas. Landowners must: place the wetlands under permanent or long-term easement with USDA; provide an access road to the land to enable easement management and monitoring. Permitted land uses after restoration or protective practices are installed include haying and grazing.

Eligible applicants/beneficiaries: individual landowners, partnerships, associations, corporations, estates, trusts; other businesses or legal entities; states and their political subdivisions; other cropland owners or operators.

Range/Average: N.A.

Activity: FY 99 estimate, 120,000 acres enrolled.

HQ: Watersheds and Wetlands Division, NRCS-USDA, P.O. Box 2890, Washington, DC 20013. Phone: (202)690-0848.

10.153 MARKET NEWS

Assistance: technical information.

Purposes: to report on prices, demand, movement, volume, and quality of major agricultural commodities. Information is disseminated through news media and through printed reports, bulletin boards, phone, facsimile machines, data networks, and telegraph.

Eligible applicants/beneficiaries: anyone may subscribe.

Activity: FY 00 estimate, 1,733 markets covered.

HQ: Associate Administrator, AMS-USDA, Washington, DC 20250. Phone: (202)720-4276.

10.155 MARKETING AGREEMENTS AND ORDERS

Assistance: specialized services; advisory services/counseling.

Purposes: to help maintain adequate prices to producers of agricultural products by issuing federal marketing orders or agreements relating to marketing and economic problems of the commodity or area covered by the federal actions. Marketing orders are issued by USDA only after a public hearing where milk, fruit, and vegetable producers, marketers, and consumers testify, and after farmers vote approval through a referendum. Funds collected are remitted to the CCC to help offset dairy price support costs.

Eligible applicants/beneficiaries: generally, growers of certain fruits, vegetables, and specialty crops (e.g., nuts, raisins, olives, and hops); dairy farmers.

Activity: FY 00 estimate, $15.3 billion in marketings.

HQ: same address/phone as **10.153**. (Note: no field offices for this program.)

10.156 FEDERAL-STATE MARKETING IMPROVEMENT PROGRAM

Assistance: project grants (50 percent/to 3 years).

Purposes: for state pilot marketing service projects to improve the marketability of agricultural products, expand export markets, and improve economic and physical marketing efficiency and competitive trading. Project examples include direct marketing, international trade, alternative crop production, and aquaculture.

Eligible applicants/beneficiaries: state agencies.

Range: $5,000 to $150,000. **Average:** $57,000.

Activity: FY 00 estimate, 24 projects funded.

HQ: Staff Officer, Federal-State Marketing Improvement Programs, AMS-USDA, Washington, DC 20250. Phone: (202)720-2704. (Note: no field offices for this program.)

10.162 INSPECTION GRADING AND STANDARDIZATION ("Agricultural Fair Practices Act")

Assistance: specialized services.

Purposes: to develop and apply standards of quality and condition used by federal inspectors and private dealers, for agricultural commodities including imports; to provide continuous in-plant inspection of all manufacturers of liquid frozen or dried egg products; to conduct quarterly inspection of egg handlers and hatcheries. Commodity classifications are established for cotton, tobacco, dairy and poultry products, fruits and vegetables, livestock.

Eligible applicants/beneficiaries: agricultural commodity owners or dealers with a financial interest in the commodity to be graded; egg hatcheries and shell egg handlers with an annual production from 3000 or more hens, that pack for the retail consumer—located within the U.S. or its territories.

Activity: FY 00 estimates, 15,329,000 bales of cotton classed; 114 tobacco auctions and 2.03 billion pounds of imported and domestic tobacco inspected; 14.2 billion pounds of poultry products graded; 36 billion pounds of meat graded; 1.95 billion dozens of shell eggs graded; 14.3 billion pounds of processed fruit and vegetables graded; 85 billion pounds of fresh fruit and vegetables graded; 30,000,000 pounds of livestock graded; 970 million pounds of dairy products graded.

HQ: same address/phone as **10.153**.

10.163 MARKET PROTECTION AND PROMOTION

Assistance: specialized services; advisory services/counseling; training.

Purposes: to assure a fair and open marketing distribution system through the elimination of deceptive, unfair, or fraudulent trade practices in the processing and marketing of food and agricultural products. Various activities fall under the national dairy promotion research and nutrition education program, the Federal Seed Program, the Plant Variety Protection Program, the Research and Promotion Program, and the Pesticide Data Program.

Eligible applicants/beneficiaries: any state government, public or private organization, business, or individual.

Activity: FY 00 estimates, 2,350 seed samples tested, 275 plant variety certificates of protection issued, 9,000 pesticide data samples collected.

HQ: same address/phone as **10.153**.

10.164   WHOLESALE MARKET DEVELOPMENT

Assistance: advisory services/counseling; training.

Purposes: to provide marketing assistance to food producers through studies on wholesaling, conducted in cooperation with other government agencies and private industry. Project examples: design study of central refrigeration systems in modern food centers; study of wholesale and farmers' market use for distributing produce.

Eligible applicants: government agencies and private industry.

Eligible beneficiaries: producers, processors, marketing agencies, and consumers.

Activity: FY 00 estimate, 13 projects and studies.

HQ: Deputy Administrator, Transportation and Marketing Programs, AMS-USDA, Washington, DC 20250. Phone: (202)690-1300. (Note: no field offices for this program.)

10.165   PERISHABLE AGRICULTURAL COMMODITIES ACT ("PACA")

Assistance: investigation of complaints.

Purposes: to suppress unfair and fraudulent practices in the marketing of perishable agricultural commodities in interstate and foreign commerce, such as dumping or destruction of farm produce.

Eligible applicants/beneficiaries: businesses or individuals may apply for a PACA license.

Activity: FY 00 estimate, 28,000 license actions completed.

HQ: same address/phone as **10.153**.

10.167   TRANSPORTATION SERVICES

Assistance: advisory services/counseling; training.

Purposes: for the development and promotion of agricultural transportation policies and systems, toward improved farm income and expanded exports. Assistance is provided where it is determined that a significant regional impact is at stake or that a significant policy with broad implications is at issue.

Eligible applicants/beneficiaries: any state government, public or private organization, business or industry, individual.

Activity: FY 00 estimate, 4 research projects, 4 publications, 2 workshops to be completed.

HQ: same address/phone as **10.164**. (Note: no field offices for this program.)

10.200   GRANTS FOR AGRICULTURAL RESEARCH, SPECIAL RESEARCH GRANTS ("Special Research Grants")

Assistance: project grants (varying match/1-3 years).

Purposes: for research, extension, and education projects toward breakthroughs in the food and agricultural sciences, and for ongoing state-federal programs.

Current priority areas are water quality, integrated pest management, and rangelands. Project examples: A Spatial Decision Support System for Water Quality Management; Nitrogen and Phosphorus Mineralization in Conifer and Aspen Soils; Ecologically-Based Alternatives for Management of Pecan Scabs.

Eligible applicants/beneficiaries: state agricultural experiment stations, all colleges and universities, federal agencies, private organizations and corporations, individuals.

Range: $3,500 to $1,880,000. **Average:** $154,000.

Activity: not quantified specifically.

HQ: Proposal Services Branch, Office of Extramural Programs, CSREES-USDA, 14th & Independence Ave. SW, Washington, DC 20250-2245. Phone: (202)401-5048. (Note: no field offices for this program.)

10.202 COOPERATIVE FORESTRY RESEARCH ("McIntire-Stennis Act")

Assistance: formula grants.

Purposes: for forestry research and research training at state forestry schools in such categories as reforestation, forest and watershed management, rangeland management, production of wildlife and domestic livestock forage, forest pest control, outdoor recreation, wood products development, and protection against fire, insects, and diseases.

Eligible applicants/beneficiaries: governor-designated state institutions. Available also in Guam, PR, VI, Samoa, Northern Marianas, Micronesia.

Range: $30,000 to $694,000. **Average:** $323,000.

Activity: not quantified specifically.

HQ: Deputy Administrator/Natural Resources and Environment, CSREES-USDA, Washington, DC. 20250. Phone: (202)720-4318. (Note: no field offices for this program.)

10.203 PAYMENTS TO AGRICULTURAL EXPERIMENT STATIONS UNDER THE HATCH ACT ("Hatch Act")

Assistance: formula grants (50 percent).

Purposes: for basic and applied research in broad subject areas at state agricultural experiment stations—to promote efficient production, marketing, distribution, and use of farm products. Funds also may be used to pay for administrative planning and direction, and for such purposes as purchasing or renting land and acquiring or constructing or repairing buildings used for research. The stations may contract with agencies and individuals for research projects.

Eligible applicants/beneficiaries: state agricultural experiment stations. Available also in territories and possessions.

Range: $612,000 to $5,832,000. **Average:** $2,796,000.

Activity: not quantified specifically.

HQ: Deputy Administrator/Partnerships, CSREES-USDA, Washington, DC. 20250-2201. Phone: (202)720-5623. (Note: no field offices for this program.)

10.205   PAYMENTS TO 1890 LAND-GRANT COLLEGES AND TUSKEGEE UNIVERSITY

Assistance: formula grants (50-70 percent).

Purposes: for continuing agricultural research at land grant colleges and Tuskegee University—toward the promotion of efficient production, marketing, distribution, and utilization of farm products, and toward sound agriculture and rural life. Funds may be used to pay for developmental costs, retirement programs, administrative planning and direction, and for such purposes as purchasing or renting land and acquiring or constructing or repairing buildings used for research. Recipients may contract with agencies and individuals.

Eligible applicants/beneficiaries: Tuskegee University and sixteen "1890" land grant colleges, in Alabama, Arkansas, Delaware, Florida, Georgia, Kentucky, Louisiana, Maryland, Mississippi, Missouri, North Carolina, Oklahoma, South Carolina, Tennessee, Texas, and Virginia.

Range: $518,000 to $1,540,000. Average: $1,571,000.

Activity: not quantified specifically.

HQ: same address/phone as 10.203. (Note: no field offices for this program.)

10.206   GRANTS FOR AGRICULTURAL RESEARCH—COMPETITIVE RESEARCH GRANTS
("National Research Initiative Competitive Grants Program")

Assistance: project grants (100 percent/to 3 years).

Purposes: for basic research in food, agriculture, and related areas. Emphasis is on such areas as plant and animal systems, natural resources and environment, nutrition, food quality and health, markets, trade and rural development, and new products and processes.

Eligible applicants/beneficiaries: state agricultural experiment stations; colleges, universities, research institutions and organizations; federal agencies; private organizations or corporations; individuals.

Range: $4,000 to $491,000. Average: $120,000.

Activity: not quantified specifically.

HQ: Chief Scientist, National Research Initiative Competitive Grants Program, CSREES-USDA, 14th & Independence Ave. SW, Washington, DC 20250-2241. Phone: (202)401-5022. (Note: no field offices for this program.)

10.207   ANIMAL HEALTH AND DISEASE RESEARCH

Assistance: formula grants (50 percent matching above base amount).

Purposes: for research on health and disease of food animals and horses. Focus is on: infectious diseases; internal and external parasites; noninfectious diseases, toxins, poisons, transportation losses, predators, and other hazards; diseases and parasites of wildlife and other animals transmissible to food animals, horses, or humans.

Eligible applicants/beneficiaries: public nonprofit schools and colleges of veterinary medicine; state agricultural experiment stations.

Range: $1,586 to $409,000. **Average:** $66,000.

Activity: not quantified specifically.

HQ: Deputy Administrator/Plant and Animal Science, CSREES-USDA, Washington, DC. 20250. Phone: (202)720-4329. (Note: no field offices for this program.)

10.210 FOOD AND AGRICULTURAL SCIENCES NATIONAL NEEDS GRADUATE FELLOWSHIP GRANTS

Assistance: project grants (100 percent/to five years).

Purposes: to support graduate degree candidates and professionals in the food and agricultural sciences. Fellowships are awarded to outstanding students pursuing graduate degrees in fields for which there is a national need for the development of scientific expertise. Doctoral and masters fellows may receive three and two years of support, respectively. The targeted national need areas include animal and plant biotechnology; food science and human nutrition; agribusiness, food, and forest product management and marketing; food, forest, biological and agricultural engineering; and water science.

Eligible applicants: U.S. colleges and universities.

Eligible beneficiaries: graduate students.

Range: N.A.

Activity: not quantified specifically.

HQ: Grant Programs Manager, Higher Education Programs, CSREES-USDA, South Bldg. - Rm.3912, Washington, DC 20250-2251. Phone: (202)720-7854. (Note: no field offices for the program.)

10.212 SMALL BUSINESS INNOVATION RESEARCH ("SBIR Program")

Assistance: project grants (100 percent).

Purposes: for research by small businesses to stimulate technological innovation, mainly in the areas of: forests and related resources; plant, animal production and protection; air, water, and soils; food science and nutrition; rural and community development; aquaculture; industrial applications; marketing and trade. Phase I grants range up to $65,000 for six months of activity; phase II, to $250,000 for up to two years; phase III covers pursuit of commercialization of research products, and receives no federal funding. An objective of SBIR programs is to foster and encourage participation by women-owned and socially disadvantaged firms.

Eligible applicants/beneficiaries: small, U.S. for-profit businesses.

Range: $46,000 to $250,000. **Average:** $95,000.

Activity: not quantified specifically.

HQ: SBIR Director, CSREES-USDA, 14th & Independence Ave. SW, Washington, DC 20250-2243. Phone: (202)401-4002. (Note: no field offices for this program.)

10.215   SUSTAINABLE AGRICULTURE RESEARCH AND EDUCATION

Assistance: project grants (100 percent/1-5 years).

Purposes: for scientific investigations and education to: reduce the use of chemical pesticides, fertilizers, and toxic materials; improve management of farm resources to enhance productivity and competitiveness; promote crop, livestock, and enterprise diversification; facilitate research projects designed to study agricultural production systems located in areas with various soil, climatic, and physical characteristics; study farms that are managed using production practices optimizing on-farm resources and conservation practices. Funds may not be used to pay indirect costs or tuition.

Eligible applicants/beneficiaries: land grant colleges or universities, other universities, state agricultural experiment and cooperative extension stations, nonprofit organizations, individuals, federal or state government entities.

Range: $8,000 to $1,752,000. **Average:** $856,000.

Activity: not quantified specifically.

HQ: Deputy Administrator/Economic and Community Systems, CSREES-USDA, Washington, DC. 20250. Phone: (202)720-7948. (Note: no field offices for the program.)

10.216   1890 INSTITUTION CAPACITY BUILDING GRANTS

Assistance: project grants (100 percent/1-3 years).

Purposes: to build research and teaching capacities at "1890" land grants institutions and Tuskegee University. Teaching grants may support: curricula design and materials development; faculty development; instruction delivery systems; scientific instrumentation; student recruitment and retention; student experiential learning. Research grants may support studies and experimentation in food and agricultural sciences, centralized research support systems, and technology delivery systems. CSREES encourages cost-sharing by grant recipients.

Eligible applicants/beneficiaries: "1890" land grant institutions, Tuskegee University.

Range: teaching grants, $88,000 to $225,000; research, $108,000 to $350,000. **Average:** teaching, $171,000; research, $243,000.

Activity: not quantified specifically.

HQ: same address/phone as **10.210**. (Note: no field offices for this program.)

10.217   HIGHER EDUCATION CHALLENGE GRANTS

Assistance: project grants (50 percent/1-5 years).

Purposes: to increase institutional capacities to respond to state, regional, national, or international educational needs in food and agricultural sciences. Funds may be used for curriculum design and materials development, faculty development, instruction delivery systems, scientific instrumentation, student recruitment and retention. Project examples: graduate discovery programs for minorities; food processing management and computer simulation.

Eligible applicants/beneficiaries: U.S. colleges and universities.

Range: $48,000 to $152,000. **Average:** $89,000.

Activity: not quantified specifically.

HQ: same address/phone as **10.210**. (Note: no field offices for this program.)

10.218 BUILDINGS AND FACILITIES PROGRAM

Assistance: project grants (50 percent).

Purposes: for construction, modernization, or improvement of program facilities used in the food and agricultural sciences. Funds may be used for facilities planning and design, land acquisition, construction, repairs, improvements, extensions, alterations, and purchase and installation of fixed equipment—and not for indirect costs, operating or maintenance expenses, or movable equipment purchases.

Eligible applicants/beneficiaries: only as specified by Congress.

Range: $480,000 to $4,850,000. **Average:** $2,056,000.

Activity: FY 98, 27 grants.

HQ: Deputy Administrator/Competitive Research Grants and Awards Management, CSREES-USDA, Washington, DC 20250. Phone: (202)401-1761. (Note: no field offices for this program.)

10.219 BIOTECHNOLOGY RISK ASSESSMENT RESEARCH

Assistance: project grants (100 percent/1-5 years).

Purposes: for research focusing on environmental effects of biotechnology. Project examples: The Spread and Ecological Impact of Escaped Transgenes in Wild Sunflowers; Ecologically Safe Assessment of Introduction.

Eligible applicants/beneficiaries: any public or private research or educational institution or organization.

Range: $50,000 to $223,000. **Average:** $148,000.

Activity: not quantified specifically.

HQ: same address/phone as **10.218**. (Note: no field offices for this program.)

10.220 HIGHER EDUCATION MULTICULTURAL SCHOLARS PROGRAM ("Minority Scholars Program")

Assistance: project grants (75 percent/5 years).

Purposes: for four-year undergraduate scholarships supporting minority students pursuing baccalaureate degrees in the food and agricultural sciences, including natural resources, forestry, veterinary medicine, home economics, and closely allied disciplines.

Eligible applicants: all U.S. colleges and universities with appropriate baccalaureate or higher degree programs and with significant minority enrollments.

Eligible beneficiaries: full-time undergraduate African-American, Hispanic, Asian, native American, Alaska native, or Pacific Islander students.

Range: $20,000 to $80,000. **Average:** $52,000.

Activity: not quantified specifically.

HQ: same address/phone as **10.210**. (Note: no field offices for this program.)

10.221 TRIBAL COLLEGES EDUCATION EQUITY GRANTS

Assistance: formula grants (1-2 years).

Purposes: pursuant to the Equity in Educational Land-Grant Status Act of 1994 as amended, to enhance educational opportunities at the 30 tribal colleges designated as the "1994 Land-Grant Institutions" by strengthening their teaching programs in the food and agricultural sciences in targeted need areas. Funds may support: curricula design and instructional materials development; faculty development; instruction delivery systems; scientific instrumentation; student experiential learning; student recruitment and retention.

Eligible applicants/beneficiaries: the 30 designated tribal colleges.

Range/Average: $50,000 to each eligible institution.

Activity: new program listing in 1997.

HQ: Science and Education Resources Development, Higher Education Programs, CSREES-USDA, Rm.3912-S, Washington, DC 20250-2251. Phone: (202)720-7854. (Note: no field offices for this program.)

10.222 TRIBAL COLLEGES ENDOWMENT PROGRAM

Assistance: formula grants (100 percent).

Purposes: pursuant to the Equity in Educational Land-Grant Status Act of 1994, to enhance educational opportunities at the 30 tribal colleges designated as the "1994 Land-Grant Institutions" by strengthening their teaching programs in the food and agricultural sciences in targeted need areas. Funds may be used to establish endowments in support of: curricula design and materials development; faculty development; instruction delivery systems; scientific instrumentation; student experiential learning; student recruitment and retention.

Eligible applicants/beneficiaries: same as for **10.221.**

Range: $7,932 to $40,000. **Average:** $15,000.

Activity: new program listing in 1997.

HQ: same address/phone as **10.221.** (Note: no field offices for this program.)

10.223 HISPANIC SERVING INSTITUTIONS EDUCATION GRANTS

Assistance: formula grants (matching/1-3 years).

Purposes: to support activities by consortia of Hispanic serving institutions to enhance educational equity for under-represented students, by strengthening institutional capacities to respond to identified state, regional, national, or international needs in the food and agricultural sciences. Funds may support cooperative initiatives between two or more institutions and units of state government or the private sector, for activities such as: student mentoring beginning at the high school level and continuing with the provision of financial support for students through graduate training; library resources; curricula design and materials development; faculty development; instruction delivery systems; scientific instrumentation; student experiential learning; student recruitment and retention.

Eligible applicants/beneficiaries: Hispanic-serving IHEs with an enrollment of at least 25 percent Hispanic students, and providing an educational program beyond the secondary level for which a two-year associate, baccalaureate, or higher degree is awarded.

Range: $25,000 to $75,000.

Activity: new program in FY 97.

HQ: same address/phone as **10.221**. (Note: no field offices for this program.)

10.224 FUND FOR RURAL AMERICA—RESEARCH, EDUCATION, AND EXTENSION ACTIVITIES

Assistance: project grants (from 50 percent/6 months-4 years).

Purposes: pursuant to the Federal Agriculture Improvement and Reform Act of 1996, for research, education, and extension projects to aid farmers, ranchers, and rural communities in addressing changes resulting from fundamental reforms to federal farm programs. Funded projects are expected to: increase international competitiveness, efficiency, and farm profitability; reduce economic and health risk; conserve and enhance natural resources; develop new crops, crop uses, and agricultural applications of biotechnology; enhance animal agricultural resources; preserve plant and animal germplasm; increase economic opportunities in farming and rural communities; and, expand locally-owned, value-added processing. Funds may support: applied, developmental, and adaptive research; technology transfer; extension and related activities; and, education—with emphasis on biological, physical, and social sciences to address systems-based problems; planning costs toward development of Fund for Rural America (FRA) Centers.

Eligible applicants: federal research agencies; national laboratories; colleges or universities and their research foundations; private research organizations.

Eligible beneficiaries: producers, commodity groups, environmental interests, rural communities.

Range: $25,000 to $600,000. **Average:** standard grants, $271,000; center planning grants, $25,000.

Activity: new program listing in FY 97.

HQ: same address/phone as **10.218**. (Note: no field offices for this program.)

10.225 COMMUNITY FOOD PROJECTS

Assistance: project grants (50 percent/1-3 years).

Purposes: for community food projects designed to provide food to low-income persons; to increase self-reliance in communities; to promote comprehensive responses to local food, farm, and nutrition issues. Funds may support: improving access to affordable food by low-income households; local food systems such as urban gardening and obtaining food from local farms; expanding economic opportunities for community residents through local businesses or other economic development, job training, youth apprenticeships, school-to-work transitions. Projects should link the food sector to community development, economic opportunity, and environmental enhancement.

Eligible applicants/beneficiaries: private nonprofit entities.

Range: $10,000 to $250,000.

Activity: 1998, 25 organizations and 2,500 persons received food production and horticultural instruction at workshops.

HQ: same address/phone as **10.218**. (Note: no field offices for this program.)

10.226   SECONDARY AGRICULTURE EDUCATION GRANTS

Assistance: project grants (50 percent).

Purposes: to promote excellence in agriscience and agribusiness education, and to encourage increased pursuit of undergraduate and higher degrees in the food and agricultural sciences. Funds may be used for such targeted areas as curricula design and materials development, promotion of teaching competencies, student experiential learning, increasing the diversity of students enrolling.

Eligible applicants/beneficiaries: public secondary schools.

Range/Average: $15,000.

Activity: new program in FY 99.

HQ: same address/phone as **10.210**. (Note: no field offices for this program.)

10.240   ALTERNATIVE AGRICULTURAL RESEARCH AND COMMERCIALIZATION PROGRAM ("AARC Corporation")

Assistance: project grants (to 50 percent/1-5 years).

Purposes: to develop new non-food, non-feed products from agricultural commodities, and new processes to produce such products as pharmaceuticals, fine chemicals, encapsulation agents, rubber, etc.—based on the use of starches and carbohydrates, fats and oils, fibers, agricultural and forest materials, animal by-products, and other plant materials. Funds may support: process development and demonstration projects; cooperative development and marketing efforts among manufacturers, private and government laboratories, universities, and financiers; information dissemination. Funds may not be used for acquisition or construction of facilities.

Eligible applicants/beneficiaries: public and private educational and research institutions and organizations, federal agencies, individuals—with preference to private firms that operate in or near rural communities.

Range: $10,000 to $1,000,000. **Average:** $250,000.

Activity: cumulatively since 1993, 76 projects funded.

HQ: Executive Director, Alternative Agricultural Research and Commercialization Corporation, USDA, South Bldg.- Rm.0156, Washington, DC 20250-0401. Phone: (no number provided); FAX (202)690-1655. (Note: no field offices for this program.)

10.250   AGRICULTURAL AND RURAL ECONOMIC RESEARCH

Assistance: technical information.

Purposes: to provide economic and other social science information and analysis related to U.S. and world agriculture, food, natural resources, and rural America. Reports are authored annually by USDA staff, and are available in printed or electronic form. Fees may be charged.

Eligible applicants/beneficiaries: anyone in the U.S. and territories.

Activity: FY 99, 17 active projects; responses to 50,000 requests for information; 250 reports published.

HQ: Director, Extramural Agreement Division, ARS-USDA, Sunnyside Ave. - Rm.5601, Beltsville, MD 20705-5110. Phones: (301)504-1107; *sales,* (800) 999-6779. (Note: no field offices for this program.)

10.350 TECHNICAL ASSISTANCE TO COOPERATIVES

Assistance: advisory services/counseling; technical information.

Purposes: to provide research, technical assistance, and educational programs on the financial, organization, management, legal, social, and economic aspects of farmer cooperatives. Assistance may include publications, training programs, audiovisual materials, computer systems.

Eligible applicants/beneficiaries: rural and farmer cooperatives, groups of farmers and other rural residents, including in the territories.

Activity: FY 98, agency staff participated in 99 technical assistance projects involving 107 cooperatives and producer groups in 38 states.

HQ: Deputy Administrator, RBCS-USDA, Washington, DC 20250-3250. Phone: (202)720-8460. (Note: no field offices for this program.)

10.404 EMERGENCY LOANS

Assistance: direct loans (3.75 percent interest).

Purposes: to repair, restore, or replace damaged or destroyed farm property, required as a result of declared natural disasters; for farm operating expenses and other costs necessary to return disaster victims' farming operations to financially sound condition, including debt refinancing. Loans may cover: 100 percent of the cost of physical loss for up to 40 years; 80 percent of actual production loss for up to 15 years.

Eligible applicants/beneficiaries: established family farmers, ranchers, or aquaculture operators (tenant- or owner-operator) conducting a farming operation at the time of the disaster, as proprietors, partnerships, cooperatives, corporations, or joint operations—and that: are U.S. citizens or legal resident aliens, or entities operated by citizens owning over a 50 percent interest; are unable to obtain necessary credit from other sources to qualify for subsidized loss loans; are capable of managing the operation; have county committee eligibility certification; provide suitable collateral to secure the loan; have crop insurance if available for affected crops; have not caused a loss to FSA, nor have received FSA debt forgiveness on more than one occasion, after 4 April 1996. Available also in most territories when those areas are designated. Prospective applicants should contact FSA county offices immediately after sustaining the loss.

Range: $500 to $500,000. **Average:** $58,000.

Activity: FY 98, 1,569 loans obligated.

HQ: Director, Loan Making Division, FSA-USDA, Ag Box 0522, Washington, DC 20250. Phone: (202)720-1632.

10.405   FARM LABOR HOUSING LOANS AND GRANTS ("Labor Housing" - "Sections 514 and 516")

Assistance: project grants (to 90 percent); guaranteed/insured loans (to 33 years).

Purposes: to construct, repair, or purchase basic year-round or seasonal housing and related support facilities for domestic farm laborers. Funds may be used for land acquisition, recreation areas, central cooking and dining facilities, small infirmaries, laundry facilities, day care centers. Grants are available only when there is a pressing need and when facilities could not be developed otherwise.

Eligible applicants: loans—farmers, family farm partnerships or corporations, associations of farmers. Loans and grants—states and their political subdivisions, PR, VI, broad-based public or private nonprofit organizations, tribes, and nonprofit corporations of farm workers.

Eligible beneficiaries: domestic farm laborers that are U.S. citizens or legal permanent residents receiving a substantial portion of their income as laborers on a U.S. farm.

Range: grants, $135,000 to $2,300,000; initial loans to organizations, $165,000 to $670,000; initial loans to individuals, $20,000 to $200,000. **Average:** grants, $1,104,000; loans/organizations, $293,000; loans/individuals, $34,500.

Activity: FY 98, 419 multifamily and single-family on-farm housing units rehabilitated or developed.

HQ: Multifamily Housing Processing Division, RHS-USDA, Washington, DC 20250. Phone: (202)720-1604.

10.406   FARM OPERATING LOANS

Assistance: direct loans; guaranteed/insured loans (7-22 years).

Purposes: to enable family farm operators to: purchase livestock, poultry, fur-bearing and other farm animals, fish, and bees; purchase farm, forestry, recreation, or nonfarm enterprise equipment and provide funds for operating expenses for such enterprises; meet family subsistence needs; purchase essential home equipment; refinance certain secured and unsecured debts; pay property taxes and property insurance premiums; finance youth projects. The interest rate on guaranteed loans may be subsidized up to 4 percent; direct loans are awarded at one percent interest above the federal borrowing rate.

Eligible applicants/beneficiaries: U.S. citizens or permanent residents with: experience or training to operate a farm; an acceptable credit history; legal capacity to incur a loan obligation; inability to obtain a reasonable loan elsewhere; and, that will become owners or tenants operating family farms through the program; except for youth projects, no history of causing a loss to FSA, nor of receiving FSA debt forgiveness on more than three occasions, after 4 April 1996. Certain corporations, cooperatives, partnerships, and joint operations conducting family farms. Available also in most territories.

Range: direct, to $200,000; guaranteed, to $700,000. **Average:** direct, $43,000; guaranteed, $124,000.

Activity: FY 98, 10,000 direct, 8,161 guaranteed loans.

HQ: same address/phone as **10.404.**

10.407   FARM OWNERSHIP LOANS

Assistance: direct loans; guaranteed/insured loans (to 40 years).

Purposes: to purchase, enlarge, and improve family farms; to provide necessary water and water facilities; to take necessary basic soil treatment and land conservation measures; to construct, repair, or improve buildings needed in family farm operations; provide facilities to produce fish under controlled conditions.

Eligible applicants/beneficiaries: applicants must meet the criteria for **10.406** and: if an individual, not have a combined farm ownership loan, soil and water loan, and recreation loan indebtedness to FSA of more than $200,000 for direct loans, and $700,000 for guaranteed loans, or a total indebtedness against the property securing the loan of more than the market value of the security, whichever is the lesser amount.

Range: direct, to $200,000; guaranteed, to $700,000. **Average:** direct, $83,000; guaranteed, $174,000.

Activity: FY 98, 978 direct, 2,396 guaranteed loans.

HQ: same address/phone as **10.404.**

10.410   VERY LOW TO MODERATE INCOME HOUSING LOANS ("Section 502 Rural Housing Loans")

Assistance: guaranteed loans (to 33 years); direct loans (to 38 years).

Purposes: for below-market-rate loan financing to lower-income rural families to: purchase, construct, improve, or repair housing and related facilities, to be used as a permanent residence; to finance the cost of sewage disposal, water supply facilities, weatherization, and essential household equipment; and, under certain conditions, to refinance housing debts, finance the purchase of manufactured homes and sites for their location. Loans can be subsidized through interest credits to as low as an effective rate of one percent, depending on the loan amount and applicant income and family size; interest subsidies are subject to recapture if property is liquidated. Nonsubsidized funds are also available for subsequent repair and rehabilitation loans, and for the payment of equity in connection with transfers by assumption or credit sales.

Eligible applicants/beneficiaries: U.S. citizens or persons with legal permanent residence or on indefinite parole, with adequate and dependable available income to meet operating and family living expenses, including taxes, insurance, maintenance, and repayments on debts including the proposed loan—without sufficient resources to obtain the necessary housing or related facilities. For direct loans, applicants must be eligible for interest credit, with income not above limits established by HUD. Available in the states, territories, and possessions.

Range: $1,000 to $105,000. **Average:** new construction, $68,000; existing housing, $49,000.

Activity: FY 98, 17,000 direct, 39,000 guaranteed loans.

HQ: Director, Single Family Loan Division, RHS-USDA, Washington, DC 20250. Phone (202)720-1452.

10.411 RURAL HOUSING SITE LOANS AND SELF-HELP HOUSING LAND DEVELOPMENT LOANS
("Section 523 and 524 Site Loans")

Assistance: direct loans (2 years).

Purposes: to buy land and install improvements on housing sites to be sold to low- or very-low-income households. Loans also may cover the costs of water and sewer facilities, walks, driveways, parking areas, landscaping, engineering and legal fees, and closing costs.

Eligible applicants: private or public nonprofit organizations that will provide the developed sites to qualified borrowers without profit, in open country or towns of 10,000 population or less, or in places up to 25,000 population under certain conditions. Available also in PR, VI, Guam, and the Northern Marianas.

Eligible beneficiaries: Section 524—low- and very-low-income families, nonprofit organizations, public agencies, cooperatives. Sites developed under Section 523 must be used for housing built under the self-help method.

Range: to $200,000 (unless with RHS approval). **Average:** Section 523, $9,380; Section 524, $12,000.

Activity: FY 98, 3 loans.

HQ: Director, Single-Family Housing Processing Division, RHS-USDA, Washington, DC 20250. Phone (202)720-1474.

10.415 RURAL RENTAL HOUSING LOANS
("Sections 515 and 521")

Assistance: direct loans.

Purposes: for the purchase, construction, or substantial rehabilitation of rural rental or cooperative housing with two or more family units, including manufactured housing, and certain related uses including recreational and service facilities. Loans may be made in communities with up to 10,000 population, and up to 20,000 under certain conditions. Loans may not cover nursing, special care, or institutional homes.

Eligible applicants: individuals, cooperatives, nonprofit organizations, state or local public agencies, profit corporations, trusts, partnerships, limited partnerships and, except for state or local public agencies, unable to finance the housing either with their own resources or with credit obtained from private sources. Available also in territories.

Eligible beneficiaries: very-low-, low-, and moderate-income households, senior citizens, and handicapped or disabled persons.

Range: individuals, $60,000 to $450,000; organizations, $75,000 to $2,000,000.
Average: individuals, $250,000; organizations, $950,000.

Activity: FY 98, 2,392 units developed.

HQ: same address/phone as **10.405.**

10.417   VERY LOW-INCOME HOUSING REPAIR LOANS AND GRANTS ("Section 504 Rural Housing Loans and Grants")

Assistance: direct loans (1 percent interest/to 20 years); project grants.

Purposes: to provide loans of up to $20,000 at one percent interest, to very low-income rural owner-occupants—and/or grants of up to $7,500 to eligible elderly persons—to repair or modernize their existing homes, including weatherization, and to upgrade water and waste disposal systems.

Eligible applicants/beneficiaries: owner-occupants of homes in rural areas, with sufficient income to repay loans, and that are U.S. citizens or legal residents or on indefinite parole. Applicant's income may not exceed very-low-income limits set forth in USDA instructions—ranging from $6,300 to $22,650, depending on family size and area median income. Grant recipients must be at least age 62 and unable to repay the part of the assistance received as a grant. Available also in territories.

Range/Average: loans, $5,388; grants, $4,547.

Activity: FY 98, 5,516 loans, 5,695 grants.

HQ: same address/phone as **10.411.**

10.420   RURAL SELF-HELP HOUSING TECHNICAL ASSISTANCE ("Section 523 Technical Assistance")

Assistance: project grants (100 percent/2 years).

Purposes: for the organizational, administrative, and basic costs of carrying out mutual self-help housing programs in rural areas. Grant funds may be used to pay the costs of training self-help group members and of purchasing tools and equipment—but not to hire construction personnel, nor to buy real estate or building materials.

Eligible applicants: states or political subdivisions; public or private nonprofit corporations. Available also in PR, VI, Guam, Northern Marianas.

Eligible beneficiaries: very-low- and low-income rural families, usually in groups of 6 to 10 families.

Range: to $204,000.

Activity: FY 98, 54 grants.

HQ: same address/phone as **10.411.**

10.421   INDIAN TRIBES AND TRIBAL CORPORATION LOANS

Assistance: direct loans (100 percent/to 40 years).

Purposes: to buy land within tribal reservations and Alaskan communities. Loan funds may be used to acquire land to round out farming or ranching units or to eliminate fractional heirships. Loan funds may not be used for development, improvements, or operating costs.

Eligible applicants/beneficiaries: tribes and tribal corporations or Alaska communities recognized by the Secretary of the Interior.

Range: $450,000 to $2,000,000. **Average:** $224,000.

Activity: FY 99-00 estimate, 2 loans.

HQ: same address/phone as **10.404.**

10.427   RURAL RENTAL ASSISTANCE PAYMENTS
("Rental Assistance" - "Section 521")

Assistance: direct payments/specified use (5-10 years).

Purposes: to subsidize rents paid by low-income senior citizens, families, and domestic farm laborers whose rents exceed 30 percent of an adjusted annual income figure established for each state.

Eligible applicants: basically, state and local agencies and nonprofit or limited-profit sponsors of certain rural rental housing projects financed by RHS.

Eligible beneficiaries: low- or very-low-income families and handicapped or senior citizens occupying eligible rural rental, cooperative, or farm labor housing.

Range: N.A.

Activity: FY 00 estimate, 44,000 households to be assisted.

HQ: Director, Multifamily Housing Portfolio Management Division, RHS-USDA, Washington, DC 20250. Phone: (202)720-1600.

10.433   RURAL HOUSING PRESERVATION GRANTS
("HPG" - "Section 533")

Assistance: project grants (formula based, 100 percent/to 2 years).

Purposes: to assist low- and very-low-income rural homeowners, rental property owners, and cooperatives to repair or rehabilitate their housing. Generally, assistance is used in conjunction with other federal funding, such as HUD's CDBG or HHS's weatherization programs, or with programs sponsored by states. Revolving loan funds may be established. Applicants may use up 20 percent of funds for project operating costs, including training of project personnel; the remaining 80 percent must be used as loans or grants for housing improvements.

Eligible applicants: authorized public or private nonprofit organizations; city and county agencies, state governments; tribes; territories and possessions; consortia of eligible entities—in communities with up to 10,000 population, or up to 25,000 under certain conditions.

Eligible beneficiaries: very-low- and low-income homeowners, rental property owners, and cooperatives requiring subsidization to improve their housing to minimum code standards.

Range/Average: N.A.

Activity: FY 98, 163 preapplications funded, assisting 2,634 units.

HQ: Multiple Family Housing Processing Division, RHS-USDA, Washington, DC 20250. Phone: (202)720-1660.

10.435 STATE MEDIATION GRANTS

Assistance: project grants (70 percent).

Purposes: to cover state operating and administrative costs in connection with certified agricultural loan mediation programs for producers and their creditors.

Eligible applicants: state governments.

Eligible beneficiaries: agricultural producers and their creditors; others directly affected by USDA actions.

Range: $3,012 to $292,000.

Activity: FY 99, 22 states requested USDA certification.

HQ: FSA-USDA (Stop 0539), Washington, DC 20250. Phones: (202)720-1471; FAX (202)690-0644. (Note: no field offices for this program.)

10.437 INTEREST ASSISTANCE PROGRAM

Assistance: guaranteed/insured loans (to 10 years).

Purposes: to guarantee up to 90 percent of mortgage amounts (to 95 percent in certain cases), and for interest rate buy-downs on behalf of family-sized farms indebted to conventional lenders. Essentially, FSA pays up to four percent of a borrower's interest rate on: (1) farm ownership loans of up to $300,000 to buy, improve, or enlarge farm homes and service buildings, including improvement of on-farm water supplies; (2) operating (chattel) loans of up to $400,000 to pay for items needed for farm operations including livestock, farm and home equipment, feed, seed, fertilizer, fuel, hail and other crop insurance, family living expenses, water system development, hired labor, compliance with OSHA regulations.

Eligible applicants/beneficiaries: individuals, partnerships, joint operations, legal resident aliens, corporations, and cooperatives. Loans may be obtained through lenders or by contacting FSA offices.

Range: to $400,000. **Average:** $150,000.

Activity: FY 98, 1,898 farmers assisted through operating loans. Note: no funds authorized for ownership loans.

HQ: same address/phone as **10.404.**

10.438 SECTION 538 RURAL RENTAL HOUSING GUARANTEED LOANS

Assistance: guaranteed/insured loans.

Purposes: for partnerships between RHS and major lenders including state and local housing finance agencies and bond insurers, resulting in an increased supply of new, affordable, multifamily, rural housing consisting of two or more family units. Projects must provide new forms of credit enhancements for housing development. Nursing, special care, and industrial type housing are ineligible.

Eligible applicants: lenders approved by the Federal National Mortgage Association, Federal Home Loan Mortgage Corporation, HUD, or state housing finance agencies.

Eligible beneficiaries: very-low, low-, or moderate-income households; elderly, handicapped, or disabled persons—residing in rural areas and with income not exceeding 115 percent of the median.

Range/Average: N.A.

Activity: new program in 1997. FY 98, RHS conducted a demonstration program and funded 28 projects.

HQ: same address/phone as **10.404.**

10.441 TECHNICAL AND SUPERVISORY ASSISTANCE GRANTS

Assistance: project grants (100 percent/1-2 years).

Purposes: for housing delivery and counseling projects to assist low-income rural persons obtain adequate rental housing, homeownership, or continued occupancy in existing housing—through technical and supervisory assistance provided by grantees. Project funds may cover such costs as staff salaries, travel, administrative and office expenses, training. Grant funds may not be used for real estate acquisition or improvement, vehicles, equipment, or for financial assistance to families participating in the projects.

Eligible applicants/beneficiaries: public or private nonprofit corporations, organizations, agencies, institutions, tribal governments, and other associations; sponsored organizations including community development, model cities, and community action agencies; IHEs, hospitals.

Range/Average: N.A.

Activity: N.A.

HQ: RHS-USDA, 14th & Independence Ave. SW, Washington, DC 20250. Phone: (202)720-1474.

10.442 HOUSING APPLICATION PACKAGING GRANTS
("Section 509 Grants")

Assistance: project grants.

Purposes: to package applications for single-family housing for very-low- and low-income rural residents wishing to buy, build, or repair houses for their own use—in colonias and designated counties; to package applications for organizations developing rental units for lower-income families. Funds may cover operating, administrative, and coordinating costs.

Eligible applicants/beneficiaries: states, state and local agencies, local government units, private nonprofit housing organizations.

Range/Average: N.A.

Activity: FY 98, 29 grants.

HQ: same address/phone as **10.411.**

10.443 SMALL FARMER OUTREACH TRAINING AND TECHNICAL ASSISTANCE PROGRAM
("Outreach and Assistance for Socially Disadvantaged Farmers and Ranchers")

Assistance: project grants (100 percent/5 years).

Purposes: to provide educational, technical assistance, research, and counseling services to socially disadvantaged farmers and ranchers—toward their ownership and operation of farms and toward their participation in farm programs.

Eligible applicants: "1890/1862" land-grant colleges and Tuskegee University; "1994 Institutions;" tribal community colleges and Alaska native cooperative colleges, Hispanic-serving and other postsecondary educational institutions, and community-based organizations.

Eligible beneficiaries: socially disadvantaged farmers or ranchers including Blacks, women, American Indians, Alaska natives, Hispanics, Asians, and Pacific Islanders.

Range/Average: N.A.

Activity: cumulatively through FY 98, 28 awards assisting 8,686 farmers, outreach to 108,000 constituents.

HQ: Assistant Secretary/Administration, Office of Outreach, USDA, Rm.538-A Whitten Bldg., Washington, DC 20250. Phones: (202)720-6350; FAX (202)720-7489.

10.444   DIRECT HOUSING—NATURAL DISASTER LOANS AND GRANTS ("Section 504 Rural Housing Loans and Grants")

Assistance: direct loans; project grants (100 percent).

Purposes: to meet emergency housing assistance needs of very-low-income owner-occupants, resulting from natural disasters. Funds may be used to repair or replace damaged property, only to the extent that funds are not provided by FEMA.

Eligible applicants/beneficiaries: loans—owner-occupants with incomes ranging from $6,300 to $22,650, with sufficient income to repay the loans. Grants—owner-occupants at least age 62 and unable to repay loans.

Range/Average: loans, $5,046; grants, $5,143.

Activity: new program listing in 1998. FY 98, 35 loans, 65 grants awarded.

HQ: same address/phone as **10.411.**

10.445   DIRECT HOUSING—NATURAL DISASTER ("Section 502 Very Low and Low Income Loans")

Assistance: direct loans.

Purposes: to meet emergency housing assistance needs of lower-income families, resulting from natural disasters. Funds may be used to buy, build, rehabilitate, or improve dwellings in rural areas. Payment subsidies may be available to eligible low- and very-low-income applicants, in the form of payment assistance or interest credits, to effectively reduce interest payments to as low as one percent. Payment subsidies are subject to recapture if the borrower transfers title or ceases to occupy the property. Funds are available only to the extent that funds are not provided by FEMA.

Eligible applicants/beneficiaries: households without adequate resources to obtain housing or related facilities, and unable to secure credit from other sources.

Range/Average: loans, $72,000.

Activity: new program listing in 1998. FY 98, 118 loans.

HQ: same address/phone as **10.411.**

10.450   CROP INSURANCE

Assistance: insurance.

Purposes: pursuant to the Federal Crop Insurance Act, amendments, Federal Agriculture Improvement and Reform Act of 1996, and other legislation, to insure farmers against losses resulting from unavoidable causes and uncontrollable events. Producers must obtain at least the catastrophic level of coverage to be eligible under the price support or production adjustment programs, the Conservation Reserve Program, or farm credit programs. The premium is fully subsidized on catastrophic crop insurance, except for a processing fee. Coverage compensates producers for yield losses exceeding 50 percent, at a price equal to 55 percent of maximum price as of crop-year 1999. Additional protection at higher levels of coverage is also offered. Insurance covers: almonds, apples, apricots, avocados and avocado trees, barley, beans, blueberries, canola, carambola trees, citrus, citrus trees, corn, cotton, cranberries, figs, flax, forage production and seeding, grapes, macadamia nuts and trees, mango trees, millet, nectarines, nursery stock, oats, onions, peaches, peanuts, pears, peas, peppers, plums, popcorn, potatoes, prunes, raisins, rice, rye, safflower, sorghum (grain and seed), soybeans, sugar beets and cane, sunflowers, tobacco, tomatoes, walnuts, and wheat. The program provides for ongoing research to devise and establish crop insurance protection programs, as well as risk management education for producers including futures and options trading. Pilot insurance programs being tested include: Income Protection Program covering avocados, corn, cotton, grain sorghum, soybeans, and wheat; Revenue Assurance Program covering corn and soybeans; Crop Revenue Coverage for corn, cotton, grain sorghum, and rice; Group Risk Plan for corn, cotton, forage, grain sorghum, peanuts, soybeans, and wheat.

Eligible applicants/beneficiaries: any owner or operator of farmland, with an insurable interest in a crop in a county where insurance is offered on that crop. A Noninsured Assistance Program is available in other areas; see **10.451**. Note: applications are to be submitted to companies reinsured by FCIC.

Range/Average: N.A.

Activity: crop year 2000 estimate, 177,900,000 acres covered, with protection of $23.1 billion.

HQ: Administrator, RMA-USDA, Ag Box 0801, Washington, DC 20250. Phone: (202)690-2803.

10.451   NONINSURED CROP DISASTER ASSISTANCE ("NAP")

Assistance: direct payments/unrestricted use.

Purposes: pursuant to the Federal Crop Insurance Reform Act of 1994 and the Federal Agriculture Improvement and Reform Act of 1996, to provide producers with protection comparable to the catastrophic risk protection plan of crop insurance (see **10.450**) and to help reduce production risks faced by crop producers for which federal insurance is not available under the Federal Crop Insurance Act; to reduce financial losses that occur when natural disasters cause catastrophic loss of production or prevent planting of an eligible crop. Payment eligibility is based on an expected yield for the area and the producer's approved yield based on actual production history, or a transitional yield if sufficient records are unavailable. Yields must fall below specified percentages to be eligible for payment. Eligible areas may be located within or outside the continental U.S., as determined by USDA; generally, areas within the continental U.S. are eligible if they have suffered a greater than 35 percent loss of eligible production because of damaging weather or of an adverse natural occurrence. Eligible crops include any commercial agricultural crop (excluding livestock and their by-products), commodity, or acreage of a commodity grown for food or fiber for which catastrophic coverage is unavailable; included also are floriculture, ornamental nursery, Christmas tree crops, turfgrass sod, seed crops, aquaculture including ornamental fish, and industrial crops.

Eligible applicants/beneficiaries: producers (1) with total annual gross revenue not exceeding $2,000,000 for the preceding tax year; (2) not receiving payments in excess of $100,000 per person per crop year; (3) suffering a greater than 50 percent loss of production and, for crop years after 1998, will receive assistance against the loss at 55 percent of the established market price for the crop; and (4) choosing whether to receive other program benefits or benefits under more than one USDA program for the same crop loss (beneficiaries are not eligible for both). NOTE: applicants must file notice of crop loss within 15 calendar days after the disaster occurred or after damage to the crop became obvious; also, crop acreage and harvests must have been reported and certified prior.

Range/Average: N.A.

Activity: new program listing in 1997.

HQ: Emergency and Noninsured Assistance Program Division, FSA-USDA, 1400 Independence Ave. SW, Washington, DC 20250-0526. Phone: (202) 720-3168.

10.452 DISASTER RESERVE ASSISTANCE ("DRAP")

Assistance: direct payments/specified use.

Purposes: to provide emergency feed assistance to livestock owners in areas approved by USDA, where livestock emergencies exist because of disease, insect infestation, flood, drought, fire, hurricane, earthquake, hail storm, hot or cold weather, freeze, snow, ice, winterkill, or other natural disaster. Assistance may be provided for losses of feed grain crops, forage, and grazing. Direct payments are for unrestricted use; feed provided must be fed to the producer's livestock, may not be resold, and must be used during the established feeding period.

Eligible applicants/beneficiaries: U.S. citizens or legal resident aliens, cooperatives, private domestic corporations, partnerships, or joint operations, tribal organizations that: (1) do not have total annual gross revenue in excess of $2,500,000; (2) are actively engaged in farming with at least 10 percent of gross revenue derived from producing grain or livestock; (3) have suffered a 40 percent or greater loss of normal feed production; (4) have insufficient feed for eligible livestock for the duration of the emergency. Applicants must choose whether to receive disaster assistance program benefits or benefits under another USDA program for the same crop loss (applicants are not eligible for both).

Range/Average: N.A.

Activity: new program listing in 1997.

HQ: same address/phone as **10.451.**

10.453   FUND FOR RURAL AMERICA—FARM OWNERSHIP LOANS

Assistance: direct loans (to 40 years).

Purposes: essentially, same as **10.407.**

Eligible applicants/beneficiaries: same as for **10.407.**

Range: to $200,000. **Average:** $83,000.

Activity: new program in FY 97. FY 98, 115 loans.

HQ: same address/phone as **10.404.**

10.454   DAIRY OPTIONS PILOT PROGRAM ("DOPP")

Assistance: direct payments/specified use (80 percent).

Purposes: pursuant to the Federal Agriculture Improvement and Reform Act of 1996 and to the Agricultural Market Transition Act, to educate dairy producers in managing their price risk by purchasing options on milk futures, in selected regions. Payments, including some fee costs, are made to commodities brokers for options contracts purchased by participants. For FY 99 and 00, DOPP costs will be paid by the CCC.

Eligible applicants/beneficiaries: dairy farmers producing at least 100,000 pounds of milk during the consecutive six-month period preceding application—including individuals, entities, or joint operations, owners, operators, landlords, tenants, or sharecroppers.

Range: the farmer pays 20 percent of the premium and any broker fees exceeding $30 per contract.

Activity: new program listing in 1999; 8,400 estimated participating producers in California, Minnesota, New York, Pennsylvania, Texas, Vermont, and Wisconsin.

HQ: RMA-USDA (Stop 0804), 1400 Independence Ave. SW - Rm.6727-S, Washington, DC 20250. Phones: (202)720-4232; FAX (202)690-3604. (Note: no field offices for this program.)

10.475   COOPERATIVE AGREEMENTS WITH STATES FOR INTRASTATE MEAT AND POULTRY INSPECTION ("Meat and Poultry Inspection State Programs")

Assistance: project grants (to 50 percent).

Purposes: to cover cooperating states' costs of meat and poultry inspection programs.

Eligible applicants/beneficiaries: state or territorial agencies administering meat or poultry inspection programs under laws comparable to the Federal Meat and Poultry Products Inspection Acts.

Range: $218,000 to $4,589,000. **Average:** $1,485,000.

Activity: FY 99 estimate, 26 states participating under the Federal Meat Inspection Act, 23 under the Poultry Products Inspection Act; 1.5 billion pounds of products inspected.

HQ: Director, Federal-State Relations Staff, Office of Field Operations, Food Safety and Inspection Service-USDA, Rm.329 West End Court Bldg., Washington, DC 20250-3700. Phone: (202)418-8897.

10.477   MEAT, POULTRY, AND EGG PRODUCTS INSPECTION

Assistance: specialized services.

Purposes: inspection by USDA personnel of the slaughtering, processing, and labeling of meat, poultry, and egg products shipped in commerce. All U.S. plants are required to be under continuous USDA inspection, including in the territories.

Eligible applicants/beneficiaries: any meat or poultry plant engaging in slaughtering or processing meat, poultry, and all egg products processing— for shipment in commerce. Available also in the territories.

Activity: FY 99 estimate, some 87.9 billion pounds of products inspected at some 6,005 establishments.

HQ: Deputy Administrator, Office of Field Operations, Food Safety and Inspection Service-USDA, Washington, DC 20250. Phone: (202)720-8803.

10.500   COOPERATIVE EXTENSION SERVICE

Assistance: formula grants; project grants (matching, 44 percent).

Purposes: pursuant to the Smith-Lever Act and other legislation, for land grant institutions to operate state and county agricultural extension service programs providing educational and technical assistance to: farmers, producers, and marketing firms in applying technical developments ensuing from research; community organizations to develop natural, economic, and human resources; homemakers and youth regarding food and nutrition, home economics, child development, and parent education; 4-H youth programs. "1890" institutions may receive funds to construct, renovate, plan, and develop new facilities and to purchase equipment.

Eligible applicants/beneficiaries: designated state land grant institutions including in the territories; "1890" and Tuskegee extension programs.

Range: $890,000 to $19,962,000. **Average:** $7,210,000.

Activity: not quantified specifically.

HQ: Deputy Administrator/Partnerships, CSREES-USDA, Washington, DC 20250. Phone: (202)720-5623. (Note: no field offices for this program.)

10.501   AGRICULTURAL TELECOMMUNICATIONS PROGRAM

Assistance: project grants (50 percent).

Purposes: to develop and operate an agricultural communications network supporting agricultural extension, resident education and research, and domestic and international marketing of commodities and products. Project examples: the agricultural satellite network (AG*SAT), a nationwide distance-learning consortium of 46 land grant institutions; audio conferences; computer-based instruction (Internet); videotaped programs.

Eligible applicants: IHEs.

Eligible beneficiaries: state extension services, federal and local governments, private organizations and corporations, individuals.

Range: $28,000 to $110,000. **Average:** $85,000.

Activity: not quantified specifically.

HQ: CSREES-USDA, Washington, DC 20250-0901. Phone: (202)720-2810. (Note: no field offices for this program.)

10.550 FOOD DISTRIBUTION
("Food Donation Program")

Assistance: sale, exchange, or donation of property and goods.

Purposes: to provide food without charge for distribution to qualifying outlets, such as emergency feeding organizations, soup kitchens, food banks, child feeding programs, schools, child and adult day care, charitable institutions, nutrition programs for the elderly, nonprofit summer camps and food services for children. Food distributed under the program may be acquired under USDA surplus removal or price support operations.

Eligible applicants/beneficiaries: state, territorial, and federal agencies designated as distributing agencies by the governor, legislature, or other authority; qualifying entities apply to their state agencies; elderly nutrition programs for Indians apply to FNS regional offices.

Activity: not quantified specifically.

HQ: Director, Food Distribution Division, FNS-USDA, Alexandria, VA 22302. Phone: (703)305-2680.

10.551 FOOD STAMPS

Assistance: direct payments/specified use (100 percent).

Purposes: to provide subsidies to low-income households to purchase food. Eligible recipients receive a coupon allotment, varying according to household size and income, to be used to buy food or seeds and plants to produce food for their personal consumption. The maximum allotment is reduced by 30 percent of participants' net income. Coupons may also be used to purchase meals by special categories of recipients, including the elderly, handicapped, homeless, alcoholics and drug addicts participating in rehabilitation programs, disabled or blind, specific categories of noncitizens, and residents of shelters for battered women and children.

Eligible applicants/beneficiaries: state or territorial agencies.

Range/Average: FY 97, $71.34 per person per month.

Activity: FY 98 monthly participation average, 71,090,000 persons.

HQ: Deputy Administrator/Food Stamp Program, FNS-USDA, Alexandria, VA 22302. Phone: (703)305-2026.

10.553   SCHOOL BREAKFAST PROGRAM

Assistance: formula grants.

Purposes: to subsidize the cost of breakfasts for eligible public and private nonprofit school children through the high school grades, through cash grants and food donations. Breakfasts are served free or at a reduced price to children determined by local school authorities to be unable to pay the full price, based on income eligibility guidelines. Reimbursements rates are based on changes in the "Food Away From Home" series of the Consumer Price Index. The maximum reduced price charged for breakfast is 30 cents.

Eligible applicants/beneficiaries: state and territorial agencies; public and nonprofit private schools and residential child care institutions except Job Corps Centers; residential summer camps that participate in the Summer Food Service Program; private foster homes.

Range: FY 97, per meal reimbursement of 19.83 cents to 121.80 cents. **Average:** 101.9 cents per meal.

Activity: FY 98, 1.215 billion breakfasts served.

HQ: Director, Child Nutrition Division, FNS-USDA, Alexandria, VA 22302. Phone: (703)305-2590.

10.555   NATIONAL SCHOOL LUNCH PROGRAM
("School Lunch Program")

Assistance: formula grants (70 percent).

Purposes: to subsidize the cost of school lunches for public and private nonprofit school children through the high school grades, through cash grants and food donations. Eligible schools also may be reimbursed for meal supplements served to children in after-school-hour care programs. Meals are served free or at a reduced price to children determined by local school authorities to be unable to pay the full price, based on income eligibility guidelines. States are reimbursed at a rate based on changes in the "Food Away from Home" series of the Consumer Price Index. The maximum reduced price charge for lunch is 40 cents.

Eligible applicants/beneficiaries: same as for **10.553**.

Range:: FY 97, 4.5 cents for snacks to 198.25 cents per meal. **Average:** cash and commodity assistance, 114.22 cents per lunch.

Activity: FY 98 estimate, 4.5 billion lunches served.

HQ: same address/phone as **10.553**.

10.556   SPECIAL MILK PROGRAM FOR CHILDREN

Assistance: formula grants.

Purposes: to reimburse the cost of milk served to pupils in public and private nonprofit schools and institutions, in high school grades and under. A portion of the cost of the milk is subsidized for non-needy children; the milk is free to students meeting certain income guidelines. Nonprofit schools with split-session kindergartens and pre-kindergartens that do not have access to the meal service program operating in the school may receive milk subsidies. States bear the costs in excess of the federal reimbursement.

Eligible applicants/beneficiaries: any state or territorial agency or public or private nonprofit school or child care institution of high school grade or under, including nursery schools, child-care centers, settlement houses, summer camps, and similar institutions devoted to the care and training of children, except Job Corps Centers—provided they do not participate in a meal service program authorized under the National School Lunch Act or the Child Nutrition Act of 1966.

Range/Average: 1997-98, reimbursement, 12.25-15.85 cents per half-pint.

Activity: FY 98, 140.6 billion half-pints of milk served.

HQ: same address/phone as **10.553**.

10.557   SPECIAL SUPPLEMENTAL NUTRITION PROGRAM FOR WOMEN, INFANTS, AND CHILDREN ("WIC Program")

Assistance: formula grants (100 percent).

Purposes: pursuant to the Child Nutrition Act of 1966, to supply supplemental foods, nutrition education, and health care referrals at no cost to low-income pregnant, postpartum, and breast-feeding women, infants, and children under age five, identified as at nutritional risk. Grants are awarded to state health or comparable agencies and certain tribes or Indian groups; in turn, funds and food are distributed through local public or nonprofit agencies.

Eligible applicants: public or private nonprofit health or human service agencies. Applications must be submitted to the responsible state or territorial agency.

Eligible beneficiaries: pregnant, postpartum, or breast-feeding women, infants and children to age five—determined to be in need of supplemental foods, meeting an income standard or receiving benefits under the Food Stamp, Medicaid, or Temporary Assistance to Needy Families Program, and residents of the state in which they receive benefits.

Range: $69,000 to $688,600,000. **Average:** $45,790,000; $31.68 per person per month.

Activity: participation by 88 state, territorial, and Indian agencies. FY 98 monthly average, 7,409,000 participants.

HQ: Director, Supplemental Food Programs Division, FNS-USDA, Alexandria, VA 22302. Phone: (703)305-2746.

10.558   CHILD AND ADULT CARE FOOD PROGRAM

Assistance: formula grants.

Purposes: to provide funding and commodity foods to food service programs in institutions that serve meals to eligible children, and to elderly or impaired adults receiving care in nonresidential day care facilities.

Eligible applicants: state and territorial educational agencies or other state agencies. In Virginia where the state does not administer the program, institutions may receive funds directly from USDA.

Eligible beneficiaries: public and private nonprofit organizations, including day care centers including outside-school-hour centers, settlement houses, recreation centers, family and group day care home programs, Head Start programs, institutions providing day care services for mentally or physically handicapped children; certain licensed private for-profit centers that receive compensation under Title XX for at least 25 percent of the children, or under Title XIX or XX for at least 25 percent of the adults, enrolled in nonresidential day care services.

Range: 1998 state grants, $165,000 to $179,200,000.

Activity: FY 98, 1.60 billion meals served.

HQ: same address/phone as **10.553**.

10.559   SUMMER FOOD SERVICE PROGRAM FOR CHILDREN

Assistance: formula grants.

Purposes: to provide funding and other donations to nonprofit food service programs for needy children age 18 and under and for disabled persons, when schools are closed for summer vacation or for periods of 15 days or more during the regular school year. Funds are available to institutions conducting regularly scheduled programs for children in areas where at least 50 percent of the children meet the family income eligibility criteria for free and reduced-price lunches. Disbursements equal the full cost of food service operations, but cannot exceed per meal rates.

Eligible applicants: state and territorial agencies; where states do not administer the program, beneficiary agencies may apply directly.

Eligible beneficiaries: public and private nonprofit school food authorities, residential summer camps serving eligible children, and IHEs operating the National Youth Sports Program; units of local, municipal, county, or state government; shelters for homeless children and families; homeless feeding sites regardless of location. Other organizations may participate under certain conditions.

Range/Average: state grants, $16,000 to $42,000,000.

Activity: FY 98, 133.3 billion meals served.

HQ: same address/phone as **10.553**.

10.560   STATE ADMINISTRATIVE EXPENSES FOR CHILD NUTRITION

Assistance: formula grants.

Purposes: to cover the costs of administering various child nutrition programs, including expenses in providing technical assistance to operating agencies. Program funds may be used to purchase supplies, equipment, and services.

Eligible applicants/beneficiaries: state and territorial agencies administering child nutrition programs, and agencies distributing USDA donated commodities to schools.

Range: $229,000 to $13,293,000. **Average:** $2,021,000.

Activity: not quantified specifically.

HQ: same address/phone as **10.553**.

10.561 STATE ADMINISTRATIVE MATCHING GRANTS FOR FOOD STAMP PROGRAM

Assistance: formula grants (from 50 percent).

Purposes: for the administrative costs of operating the food stamp program, including for fraud investigations and for developing computer systems. States also conduct an employment and training program requiring no state matching funds. Reimbursements are made to participants for up to 50 percent their dependent care costs, not exceeding $25 monthly per participant; states also receive 50 percent of case management costs.

Eligible applicants/beneficiaries: state and territorial cooperators.

Range: $1,777,000 to $256,714,000. **Average:** $32,800,000.

Activity: not quantified specifically.

HQ: same address/phone as **10.551.**

10.564 NUTRITION EDUCATION AND TRAINING PROGRAM ("NET Program")

Assistance: formula grants.

Purposes: for nutrition training of educational and food service personnel, including management training; nutrition education activities in schools and child care institutions.

Eligible applicants: state and territorial education agencies or alternate state agencies.

Eligible beneficiaries: public and private nonprofit schools, residential child and adult care institutions, day care centers, institutions offering summer food service programs.

Range: $50,000 to $314,000. **Average:** $67,000.

Activity: FY 98, 98,000 food service personnel, 96,000 teachers, 46,000 schools participated.

HQ: Nutrition and Technical Services Division, FNS-USDA, Alexandria, VA 22302. Phone: (703)305-5285.

10.565 COMMODITY SUPPLEMENTAL FOOD PROGRAM

Assistance: sale, exchange, or donation of property and goods; formula grants.

Purposes: to provide for the donation of supplemental foods to recipients deemed to be at nutritional risk. Grant funds may be used to cover only such administrative costs as are incurred in making the donated goods and nutrition education services available to beneficiaries.

Eligible applicants: state agencies; tribes, bands, or groups recognized by DOI—which distribute funds to local public or nonprofit agencies.

Eligible beneficiaries: infants or children to age 6; pregnant, postpartum, or breast-feeding women; or, elderly persons age 60 or older—certified as income-eligible for benefits under existing federal, state, or local food, health, or welfare programs for low-income persons, and at nutritional risk.

Range: $28,000 to $4,359,000.

Activity: FY 98, 128,000 women, infants, and children, 249,000 elderly persons participated monthly.

HQ: same address/phone as for **10.550**.

10.566 NUTRITION ASSISTANCE FOR PUERTO RICO ("NAP")

Assistance: direct payments/specified use.

Purposes: for low-income Puerto Ricans to purchase food, as an alternative to Food Stamps

Eligible applicants: only the Commonwealth of PR.

Eligible beneficiaries: low-income Puerto Rican individuals and families.

Range/Average: $73.92/person/month.

Activity: FY 98, 1,240,000 persons assisted monthly.

HQ: same address/phone as **10.551**.

10.567 FOOD DISTRIBUTION PROGRAM ON INDIAN RESERVATIONS

Assistance: project grants (75 percent); sale, exchange, or donation of property and goods.

Purposes: to provide food to needy persons living on or near Indian reservations, and funds for the administrative costs incurred by organizations operating the program. Donated foods may be acquired under USDA's surplus removal or price support operations.

Eligible applicants: state agencies; tribal organizations.

Eligible beneficiaries: households living on an Indian reservation; Indian households living near an Indian reservation (or, for Oklahoma, living in Indian country) that has the program—certified by local authorities as having inadequate income and resources. Upper limits of allowable income and resources vary with family size.

Range: $57,000 to $4,458,000.

Activity: FY 98, 125,000 persons participating monthly; 94 tribal organizations and 6 states administering the program for 219 participating reservations.

HQ: same address/phone as for **10.550**.

10.568 EMERGENCY FOOD ASSISTANCE PROGRAM (ADMINISTRATIVE COSTS)

Assistance: formula grants.

Purposes: to cover state and local costs of processing, storage, and distribution of food used to feed needy persons.

Eligible applicants: state agencies.

Eligible beneficiaries: public or private organizations that operate USDA food programs.

Range: $9,211 to $5,736,000. **Average:** $844,000.

Activity: not quantified specifically.

HQ: Director, Food Distribution Division, FNS-USDA, 3101 Park Center Dr. - Rm.502, Alexandria, VA 22302. Phone: (703)305-2680.

10.569   EMERGENCY FOOD ASSISTANCE PROGRAM (FOOD COMMODITIES)

Assistance: formula grants (100 percent).

Purposes: to make food commodities available to needy persons, including for meals served at congregate meal sites.

Eligible applicants: designated state food commodity distributing agencies.

Eligible beneficiaries: needy persons including the unemployed, welfare recipients, and the low-income.

Range: $19,000 to $12,452,000. **Average:** $1,818,000.

Activity: not quantified specifically.

HQ: same address/phone as **10.568.**

10.570   NUTRITION PROGRAM FOR THE ELDERLY (COMMODITIES) ("NPE")

Assistance: formula grants.

Purposes: to provide meals to the elderly and to disabled and handicapped persons, using domestically produced foods acquired under USDA's surplus removal or price support operations. Food is made available for use in nutrition programs in the preparation of congregate or home-delivered meals, for which participants may or may not be asked to contribute voluntarily toward the cost, based on local economic conditions.

Eligible applicants: designated food distributing agencies in states, Trust Territories, and federal agencies.

Eligible beneficiaries: persons at least age 60 and their spouses; disabled or handicapped persons; volunteers providing meals may also receive meals, and they may or may not be asked for voluntary contributions toward the cost.

Range/Average: $60,000 to $13,908,000.

Activity: FY 98, 247,000,000 meals served, using 398,000 pounds of donated foods.

HQ: same address/phone as **10.550.**

10.572   WIC FARMERS' MARKET NUTRITION PROGRAM ("FMNP")

Assistance: formula grants (70 percent; tribal organizations, 70-90 percent).

Purposes: to provide fresh and nutritious unprepared foods (such as fruits and vegetables) from farmers' markets to low-income women, infants, and children at nutritional risk—through the use of FMNP coupons; to expand awareness and use of farmers' markets. States may meet matching fund requirements through state contributions to similar programs.

Eligible applicants: state health, agriculture, and other agencies; federally recognized Indian organizations.

Eligible beneficiaries: WIC program participants (i.e., pregnant, postpartum, or breast-feeding women, infants over age 4 months, children to age 5). At the discretion of the states, WIC program applicants may also participate.

Range: $40,000 to $2,830,000. **Average:** $372,000.

Activity: FY 98, 35 state programs approved.

HQ: Branch Chief, Supplemental Food Programs Division, FCS-USDA, 3101 Park Center Dr. - Rm. 540, Alexandria, VA 22302. Phone: (703)305-2730.

10.573   HOMELESS CHILDREN NUTRITION PROGRAM

Assistance: formula grants.

Purposes: to reimburse participating entities for free meals served to homeless children under age 6, residing in approved emergency shelters.

Eligible applicants/beneficiaries: state, city, local, or county governments; other public entities; private nonprofit organizations operating not more than five food service sites and serving no more than 300 homeless children at each site.

Range: 53.25 cents per supplement to 194.25 cents per lunch and supper; 14.75 cents cash in lieu of commodity assistance.

Activity: FY 98, 87 organizations operating 118 shelters.

HQ: same address/phone as **10.553.**

10.574   TEAM NUTRITION GRANTS
("TN Training Grants")

Assistance: project grants (100 percent/2 years).

Purposes: to establish and enhance sustainable infrastructures for delivery of training and technical assistance to school food service professionals. The program provides start-up money for projects, and may include a cafeteria-classroom link to support nutrition education and healthy food choices. States may use funds to provide a comprehensive, action-oriented delivery of training programs for schools. Project examples: development of training materials including CD-ROM training package on menu management, lesson plans, and videos; resource libraries; Internet connections.

Eligible applicants/beneficiaries: state agencies—applying individually or as coalitions.

Range: $50,000 to $250,000.

Activity: new program listing in 1997. FY 98, 17 grants.

HQ: Grants Management Division, FNS-USDA, Alexandria, VA 22302. Phone: (703)305-2049.

10.600   FOREIGN MARKET DEVELOPMENT COOPERATOR PROGRAM

Assistance: direct payments/specified use (cost sharing/1-3 years).

Purposes: for projects abroad to develop, expand, and maintain long-term export markets for U.S. agricultural products, usually conducted by U.S. nonprofit trade associations or "Cooperators." Funded activities may include trade servicing, market research, and technical assistance to actual or potential foreign purchasers.

Eligible applicants/beneficiaries: nonprofit nationwide or industry-wide U.S. agricultural trade groups.

Range: $11,000 to $7,000,000. **Average:** $1,243,000.

Activity: FY 99, 26 cooperator programs in 100 foreign countries.

HQ: Deputy Administrator, Commodity and Marketing Programs, FAS-USDA, Washington, DC 20250. Phone: (202)720-4761. (Note: no field offices for this program.)

10.601 MARKET ACCESS PROGRAM ("MAP")

Assistance: direct payments/specified use (50-90 percent).

Purposes: for promotional activities abroad to market U.S. agricultural commodities. Projects may involve generic (90 percent funding) or brand-specific (50 percent) promotions. Activities may include consumer advertising, point-of-sale demonstrations, public relations, trade fairs, exhibits, market research, or technical assistance—and are usually conducted outside the U.S. Funding is through CCC reimbursements for authorized activities.

Eligible applicants/beneficiaries: U.S. nonprofit agricultural trade organizations; state regional trade groups; cooperative organizations; state agencies; private firms.

Range: $22,000 to $9,611,000. **Average:** $1,375,000.

Activity: 1999, allocations to 65 groups.

HQ: same address/phone as **10.600**. (Note: no field offices for this program.)

10.652 FORESTRY RESEARCH ("Research Grants & Agreements")

Assistance: project grants (1-5 years).

Purposes: for fundamental research in the management of timber stands, watershed areas, forest ranges, wildlife habitat; also in forest recreation, forest fire protection, insect and disease protection and control, forest products utilization, forest engineering, forest production economics and marketing, forest surveying, and social/cultural influences. Project examples: effects of prescribed fire on nutrient cycling in ponderosa pine forests; experimental system for continuous press drying of paper; biological decay of logging residues.

Eligible applicants/beneficiaries: state agricultural experiment stations, universities and colleges, state and local governments, territories; profit, non-profit, and international organizations; students.

Range: $2,000 to $100,000. **Average:** $25,000.

Activity: FY 98, 600 grants awarded.

HQ: Deputy Chief/Research and Development, Forest Service-USDA, Washington, DC 20090-6090. Phone: (202)205-1075.

10.664 COOPERATIVE FORESTRY ASSISTANCE

Assistance: formula grants; project grants (50-80 percent).

Purposes: for state forest stewardship programs on private, local, state, and other nonfederal forest and rural lands. Programs may involve: timber production: forest insect and disease control; processing of wood products; producing and distributing tree seeds and seedlings, urban forestry; conversion of wood to energy; improvement and maintenance of fish and wildlife habitat; financial and technical assistance for rural firefighting; organizational improvement; technology transfer; acquisition and loan of federal surplus property.

Eligible applicants: states, tribes, municipalities, territories and possessions, nonprofit organizations.

Eligible beneficiaries: owners of nonfederal lands; rural community firefighting forces; urban and municipal governmental and other state, local, and private agencies acting through state foresters or equivalent state officials.

Range: $25,000 to $6,000,000. **Average:** $1,000,000.

Activity: estimated 2000 activities (representative): 19,000 land owners enrolled in forest stewardship programs, covering 2,500,000 acres; 1,800 rural and 8,000 urban communities assisted.

HQ: Deputy Chief, State and Private Forestry, Forest Service-USDA, Washington, DC 20090-6090. Phone: (202)205-1657.

10.665 SCHOOLS AND ROADS—GRANTS TO STATES
("25 Percent Payments to States")

Assistance: formula grants.

Purposes: to return 25 percent of revenues from the national forests to states and U.S. territories, for the benefit of public schools and public roads of the counties in which the forests are located.

Eligible applicants/beneficiaries: states or territories containing national forest land.

Range: $35 to $161,889,000. **Average:** $8,963,000.

Activity: N.A.

HQ: Director/Acquisitions Management, Forest Service-USDA, RPE - Rm. 706, Washington, DC 20090-6090. Phone: (703)605-4662.

10.666 SCHOOLS AND ROADS—GRANTS TO COUNTIES
("Payments to Counties")

Assistance: formula grants.

Purposes: to return 25 percent of revenues from national grasslands and land utilization projects, for the benefit of public schools and roads of the counties in which they are located.

Eligible applicants/beneficiaries: U.S. counties with national grasslands or land utilization projects.

Range: $5 to $1,707,000. **Average:** $69,000.

Activity: N.A.

HQ: Director/Procurement and Property, same address/phone as **10.665.**

10.670 NATIONAL FOREST-DEPENDENT RURAL COMMUNITIES
("Economic Recovery")

Assistance: project grants (80 percent); use of property, facilities, and equipment; training.

Purposes: to provide accelerated assistance to communities with acute economic problems associated with federal, state, or private sector forest management policies. Assistance is coordinated with other USDA agencies and may be provided through a community action team to identify and develop opportunities to promote economic improvement, diversification, and revitalization. Funds may support costs of technical assistance, planning, and community training related to the upgrading of existing industries, and development of new economic activities in industries unrelated to the forests.

Eligible applicants/beneficiaries: general purpose local governments or tribes represented by state-authorized nonprofit corporations, with not more than 10,000 population; counties not within metropolitan statistical areas— located inside or within 100 miles of a national forest, and whose economies are strongly related to activities in the forest.

Range: $1,000 to $30,000.

Activity: FY 99, 850 communities assisted.

HQ: same address/phone as **10.664.**

10.671   SOUTHEAST ALASKA ECONOMIC DISASTER FUND

Assistance: direct payments/specified use (formula based).

Purposes: to counter the effects of the declining timber program of the Tongass National Forest. Funds may be used to employ former timber workers and for related community development projects. Note: this program is scheduled to end in FY 99.

Eligible applicants/beneficiaries: local communities/boroughs named in PL 104-134.

Range: $16,000 to $4,700,000.

Activity: new program listing in 1997.

HQ: Forest Service-USDA, 3301 C St. - Ste.522, Anchorage, AK 99503-3956. Phone: (907)271-2519. (Note: the field office is the headquarters for this program.)

10.700   NATIONAL AGRICULTURAL LIBRARY

Assistance: technical information.

Purposes: to provide agricultural information products and services through traditional library functions and through modern electronic distribution. The facilities are open to the general public; publications are available through interlibrary loan or photo-reproduction.

Eligible applicants/beneficiaries: general public.

Activity: 3,200,000 items available.

HQ: Office of the Director, National Agricultural Library, ARS-USDA, Beltsville, MD 20705-2351. Phone: (301)504-6780. (Note: no field offices for this program.)

10.760   WATER AND WASTE DISPOSAL SYSTEMS FOR RURAL COMMUNITIES

Assistance: project grants; direct loans, guaranteed/insured loans (40 years).

Purposes: to provide low-interest loans and grants for the installation, repair, improvement, or expansion of rural water facilities and waste disposal systems, including the collection and treatment of sanitary, storm, and solid wastes. Funds may be used to pay for distribution lines, well-pumping facilities, and their related costs. Loans have varying interest rates beginning as low as 4.5 percent, depending on area median income. Grants are made only when necessary to reduce the average annual benefited user charges to a reasonable level, with the matching percentage based on the applicant area's median income. Grant funds may not be used to pay loan interest, operation, or maintenance costs, nor to acquire or refinance existing systems. Grant funding for this program includes **10.761** and **10.770**.

Eligible applicants/beneficiaries: municipalities, counties, state political subdivisions such as districts and authorities; associations, cooperatives, and nonprofit corporations; tribes on federal and state reservations and other federally recognized tribes. Authorized also in territories.

Range: direct loans, $5,000 to $7,304,000; grants, $3,000 to $4,148,000. **Average:** loans, $878,000; grants, $677,000.

Activity: FY 99 estimate, 1,068 direct, 20 guaranteed loans; 850 grants.

HQ: Assistant Administrator, Water and Environmental Programs, RUS-USDA, Washington, DC 20250. Phone: (202)690-2670.

10.761 TECHNICAL ASSISTANCE AND TRAINING GRANTS

Assistance: project grants (100 percent).

Purposes: for technical assistance projects to identify and evaluate solutions to rural water problems relating to source, storage, treatment, and waste disposal; to provide training to improve the management, operation, and maintenance of water and waste disposal facilities. Funding for this program is included in **10.760**.

Eligible applicants: tax-exempt nonprofit organizations.

Eligible beneficiaries: state political subdivisions such as counties, municipalities, districts, and authorities; tribes; cooperatives; nonprofit corporations.

Range: $73,000 to $5,940,000. **Average:** $754,000.

Activity: FY 98, 8 grants.

HQ: same address/phone as **10.760**.

10.762 SOLID WASTE MANAGEMENT GRANTS

Assistance: project grants (100 percent).

Purposes: to evaluate landfill conditions to determine threats to water resources in rural areas; to provide technical assistance and training in the operation of landfills, and to reduce the solid waste stream; to provide planning assistance for closing landfill sites and for future uses of such sites.

Eligible applicants/beneficiaries: tax-exempt nonprofit organizations; public bodies including local government-based multijurisdictional organizations.

Range: $40,000 to $642,000. **Average:** $23,000.

Activity: FY 98, 30 grants awarded.

HQ: same address/phone as **10.760**.

10.763 EMERGENCY COMMUNITY WATER ASSISTANCE GRANTS

Assistance: project grants (100 percent).

Purposes: to assist rural areas experiencing a significant decline in quality or quantity of water, in complying with the Safe Drinking Water Act. Funds may be used to: extend or repair water lines on existing systems; construct new lines; construct new wells, reservoirs, transmission lines, treatment plants, storage tanks; and, for similar projects and related activities and costs.

Eligible applicants/beneficiaries: public bodies, private nonprofit corporations, state political subdivisions, tribes—in communities with populations not above 10,000, with a median household income below the statewide nonmetropolitan median.

Range: $10,000 to $500,000. **Average:** $253,000.

Activity: FY 98, 11 grants.

HQ: same address/phone as **10.760**.

10.766 COMMUNITY FACILITIES LOANS AND GRANTS

Assistance: direct loans; guaranteed loans; project grants.

Purposes: to construct, enlarge, extend, or improve public facilities serving rural residents, including child care, food recovery and distribution, assisted living, group homes, mental health clinics, shelters, fire and rescue services, industrial park sites, transportation, access ways, utility extensions.

Eligible applicants/beneficiaries: state agencies, counties, cities, state political and quasi-political subdivisions, tribes, associations including nonprofit corporations. Available also in territories.

Range: direct loans, $50,000 to $2,500,000; guaranteed, $100,000 to $2,500,000; grants, $10,000 to $100,000. **Average:** direct, $448,000; guaranteed, $906,000; grants $35,000.

Activity: FY 00 estimate, 500 direct, 210 guaranteed loans; 234 grants.

HQ: Deputy Administrator, Community Programs, RHS-USDA, Washington, DC 20250-3222. Phone: (202)720-1490.

10.767 INTERMEDIARY RELENDING PROGRAM

Assistance: direct loans (75 percent/1 percent interest/to 30 years).

Purposes: for business facilities or community development in rural areas with under 25,000 population. Successful applicants become intermediary lenders that may make loans to ultimate recipients to finance up to 75 percent of project costs, but not more than $150,000 to any one recipient. Project example: rural transportation project.

Eligible applicants: private nonprofit organizations, state or local governments, federally recognized tribes, cooperatives.

Eligible beneficiaries: individuals, public and private profit or nonprofit organizations.

Range: $250,000 to $2,000,000. **Average:** $774,000.

Activity: FY 98 estimate, 37 loan approvals.

HQ: RBCS-USDA, South Agriculture Bldg. - Rm.6321, Washington, DC 20250-0700. Phone: (202)690-4100.

10.768   BUSINESS AND INDUSTRY LOANS

Assistance: direct loans (75-80 percent); guaranteed/insured loans (to 50-90 percent).

Purposes: for the development or improvement of rural businesses, industry, and employment. Loan funds may cover such costs as business and industrial acquisition, construction, conversion, enlargement, repair, modernization, equipment, machinery, supplies, pollution control and abatement— for 30 years for real estate, up to 15 years for machinery and equipment, and seven years for working capital. Assistance is unavailable for community antenna TV services or facilities, charitable and educational institutions, hotels and tourist facilities, large businesses, or uses other than those that will protect or create jobs, improve existing business and industry, and provide economic stability to rural areas. Project examples: agri-business expansion; radio station start-up; catfish farm operating loan; printing company expansion.

Eligible applicants/beneficiaries: cooperatives, corporations, partnerships, trusts, or other for-profit enterprises; certain nonprofit entities; tribes, municipalities, counties, or other state political subdivisions; individuals. Applicants must be U.S. citizens or legal permanent residents; if corporations, 51 percent ownership must be held by U.S. citizens. Available also in some territories. Projects must be in rural jurisdictions under 50,000 population, with preference to those under 25,000.

Range: direct loans, $35,000 to $10,000,000; guaranteed loans, $35,000 to $25,000,000. **Average:** direct, $383,000; guaranteed, 1,245,000.

Activity: FY 00 estimate, 808 guaranteed, 130 direct loans.

HQ: Administrator, RBCS-USDA, Washington, DC 20250-3201. Phones: (202) 690-4730; FAX (202)690-4737.

10.769   RURAL DEVELOPMENT GRANTS
("RBEG" - "TDG")

Assistance: project grants (formula based).

Purposes: to facilitate the development of small and emerging business, industry, and related employment, toward economic improvement of rural areas. Rural Business Enterprise Grants (RBEG) may be used to establish revolving loan funds, provide operating capital, and finance industrial sites including: land acquisition; construction, conversion, enlargement, repair, or modernization of buildings, plants, machinery, equipment; access streets and roads, parking areas, transportation serving the site; utility extensions; water supply and waste disposal facilities, pollution control and abatement; technical assistance, fees, and refinancing. Television demonstration grants (TDG) may be used for programming demonstrating the effectiveness of providing information on agriculture and other issues of importance to farmers and other rural residents.

Eligible applicants: RBEG—public bodies and nonprofit corporations serving rural areas, such as states, counties, cities, townships, and incorporated towns and villages, boroughs, authorities, districts, and tribes on federal and state reservations serving rural areas. TDG—statewide nonprofit public television systems whose coverage is predominantly rural. For this program, "rural area" is defined as all territory of a state not within the outer boundary of any city with a population over 50,000. Priority is accorded to projects: in areas of under 25,000 population with a large number of low-income persons; designed to save existing or to create new jobs; in areas with high unemployment.

Eligible beneficiaries: private businesses that will employ 50 or fewer new employees, and with under $1,000,000 in projected revenue.

Range: $2,000 to $1,500,000. **Average:** $160,000.

Activity: FY 99 estimate, 325 grants.

HQ: Director, Specialty Lenders Division, RBCS-USDA, Washington, DC 20250-3222. Phone: (202)720-1400.

10.770 WATER AND WASTE DISPOSAL LOANS AND GRANTS ("Section 306C")

Assistance: project grants; direct loans (100 percent).

Purposes: to develop water and waste disposal facilities and services to rural low-income communities facing significant health risks. Funds may be used to: construct, enlarge, extend, or improve community water or sewer systems; to connect residences to community systems; to enable individuals to install plumbing and related fixtures and to construct bathrooms within their dwellings. Funded projects must primarily serve residents of counties with per capita incomes not more than 70 percent of the national average, and with unemployment not less than 125 percent of the national average rate. Grant funds for this program are included in **10.760**—and may be used only in colonias.

Eligible applicants/beneficiaries: local governments, tribes, nonprofit associations, cooperatives—including territories and possessions.

Range/Average: $481,000.

Activity: not quantified specifically.

HQ: same address/phone as **10.760**.

10.771 RURAL COOPERATIVE DEVELOPMENT GRANTS ("RCDG")

Assistance: project grants (75 percent).

Purposes: to establish and operate centers for rural cooperative development to improve economic conditions by promoting the development of new cooperatives and/or the improvement of existing cooperatives. Funds may be used for: applied research, basic feasibility studies; technical assistance, advisory services; research or technical support for individuals, small businesses, cooperatives, or rural industries

Eligible applicants/beneficiaries: nonprofit corporations and IHEs serving rural areas beyond the outer boundary of any city with population 50,000 or more.

Range: $65,000 to $200,000.

Activity: FY 98, 11 grants.

HQ: Assistant Deputy Administrator/Cooperative Services, RBCS-USDA, Washington, DC 20250. Phone: (202)720-8460.

10.772   EMPOWERMENT ZONES PROGRAM
("Empowerment Zones and Enterprise Communities")

Assistance: project grants (100 percent/to 10 years).

Purposes: to establish a limited number of job creation zones in rural areas toward the revitalization of economically distressed areas, for the benefit of the disadvantaged and long-term unemployed. Through national competitions among applicants demonstrating a certain level of distress, designated rural Enterprise Communities become eligible for private activity tax exempt bonding authority to finance qualifying enterprises and facilities, subject to state bond caps and special limits on issue size. Approved Empowerment Zones are eligible for: employer wage credits; accelerated IRS Section 179 expensing for eligible property; priority funding or special consideration under other federal programs, including the National Service and Community Policing Initiatives; empowerment zone/enterprise community social service block grants (EZ/EC-SSBG) from HHS, based on activities identified in strategic plans ($40,000 during Round I held in 1994). Round II designations were made in late 1998; provisions changed slightly. (Urban area programs are described under **14.244**.)

Eligible applicants/beneficiaries: "Rural Zone and Community" applicants—generally, rural areas with pervasive poverty, unemployment, general distress, and with a maximum population of 30,000, no larger than 1,000 square miles, located entirely within no more than three contiguous states, and not including any portion of an Indian reservation. Applications may be submitted on behalf of nominated beneficiaries by state and local governments, regional planning agencies, nonprofit organizations, or community partnerships. Additional details should be obtained from RDA state offices.

Range: $2,970,000 to $40,000,000. **Average:** $6,300,000.

Activity: 1998, 5 Round II Rural Empowerment Zones, 20 Rural Enterprise Communities designations.

HQ: Deputy Administrator, Office of Community Development-USDA, Reporters Bldg. - Rm.701, 300 Seventh St. SW, Washington, DC 20024. Phones: (202)619-7980; Internet, www.ezec.gov

10.773   RURAL BUSINESS OPPORTUNITY GRANTS
("RBOG")

Assistance: project grants (2 years).

Purposes: to promote sustainable economic development in rural communities with exceptional needs. Grants may support technical assistance, training, and planning costs.

Eligible applicants/beneficiaries: public bodies, nonprofit corporations, tribes, cooperatives.

Range/Average: N.A.

Activity: new program in FY 99.

HQ: Specialty Lenders Division, RBCS-USDA, 1400 Independence Ave. SW - Rm.6767, Washington, DC 20250-1521. Phone: (202)720-1400.

10.774   NATIONAL SHEEP INDUSTRY IMPROVEMENT CENTER ("NSIIC")

Assistance: direct loans; guaranteed/insured loans (80 percent/to 40 years); direct payments/specified use (50 percent); project grants.

Purposes: for the sheep and goat industries to strengthen and enhance production and marketing. Funds may support such activities as coordination of marketing systems and public communication programs. A revolving fund supports this program; no appropriations are provided.

Eligible applicants/beneficiaries: public, private, cooperative, and nonprofit organizations; federally-recognized tribes; public and quasi-public agencies.

Range: loans, to $1,000,000.

Activity: new program listing in 1998.

HQ: National Sheep Industry Improvement Center-USDA, Bldg.20 - Rm. A1311, Denver Federal Center, Lakewood, CO 80228-1028. Phones: (303) 236-2858; FAX (303)236-7683. (Note: no field offices for this program.)

10.800   LIVESTOCK, MEAT AND POULTRY MARKET SUPERVISION ("Packers and Stockyards Act")

Assistance: project grants.

Purposes: to protect producers and consumers against unfair, deceptive, discriminatory, and monopolistic practices in the marketing of livestock, meat, and poultry. Reparation awards for money damages may be granted against stockyard owners or operators, livestock commission personnel, or dealers.

Eligible applicants/beneficiaries: anyone may file a complaint alleging an illegal practice by in the marketing, slaughtering, processing, or handling of livestock, poultry, or meat.

Range/Average: N.A.

Activity: FY 00 estimates, 1,250 stockyards posted; 1,800 investigations; 5,800 packers, covered slaughterers, and processors; 6,700 distributors, brokers, dealers; 6,300 market agencies/dealers; 210 poultry firms.

HQ: Deputy Administrator/Packers and Stockyards Programs, USDA, South Bldg. - Rm.3039, Washington, DC 20250. Phone: (202)720-7051.

10.850   RURAL ELECTRIFICATION LOANS AND LOAN GUARANTEES

Assistance: direct loans (to 90 percent/35 years).

Purposes: pursuant to the REA as amended, to supply continuing central station electric service in rural areas—i.e., any farm or nonfarm area not within the boundaries of any urban area. RUS also guarantees loans used primarily for generation and transmission projects.

Eligible applicants/beneficiaries: rural electric cooperatives, public utility districts, power companies, municipalities, and other qualified power suppliers, including in territories.

Range: direct loans, $260,000 to $22,926,000; FFB guarantees, $2,126,000 to $56,833,000. **Average:** direct, $4,401,000; FFB, $10,345,000.

Activity: FY 98, 142 direct and 29 guaranteed loans.

HQ: Administrator, RUS-USDA, Washington, DC 20250-1500. Phone: (202) 720-9540. (Note: no field offices for this program.)

10.851 RURAL TELEPHONE LOANS AND LOAN GUARANTEES

Assistance: direct loans; guaranteed/insured loans.

Purposes: pursuant to the REA 1936 as amended, to improve, expand, construct, acquire, and operate telecommunications systems in rural areas—i.e., any area of the U.S., including territories and possessions, not within the boundaries of any city, village, or borough with over 5,000 population.

Eligible applicants/beneficiaries: telephone companies or cooperatives; nonprofit, limited dividend, or mutual associations; public bodies.

Range: direct loans, $195,000 to $23,944,000; guaranteed, $375,000 to $19,424,000. **Average:** direct, $12,069,000; guaranteed, $9,990,000. (Average loan term, 24 years.)

Activity: FY 98, 45 direct, 6 guaranteed loans.

HQ: Assistant Administrator, same address as **10.850**. Phone: (202)720-9554. (Note: no field offices for this program.)

10.852 RURAL TELEPHONE BANK LOANS

Assistance: direct loans (to 35 years).

Purposes: pursuant to the REA of 1936 as amended, to provide supplemental financing to supply or improve telecommunications services in rural areas—i.e., any area of the U.S., including territories and possessions, not within the boundaries of any city, village, or borough with over 5,000 population.

Eligible applicants/beneficiaries: borrowers with a current RUS loan or loan commitment.

Range: $114,000 to $13,967,000. **Average:** $7,041,000.

Activity: FY 98, 45 loans.

HQ: Assistant Governor, Rural Telephone Bank, USDA, Washington, DC 20250. Phone: (202)720-9554. (Note: no field offices for this program.)

10.854 RURAL ECONOMIC DEVELOPMENT LOANS AND GRANTS

Assistance: direct loans (80 percent, no interest/10 years); project grants (80 percent).

Purposes: pursuant to the REA of 1936 as amended, for rural economic and job development projects, including the costs of feasibility studies, project start-up, and other reasonable expenses. Project examples: business incubators; establishment or expansion of factories or businesses; revolving loan funds.

Eligible applicants/beneficiaries: electric and telephone utilities with current RUS loans.

Range: loans, $10,000 to $750,000; grants, $10,000 to $330,000. **Average:** loans, $375,000; grants, $260,000.

Activity: cumulatively 1989-FY 99, 474 loans, 125 grants approved.

HQ: same address/phone as **10.769**.

10.855 DISTANCE LEARNING AND TELEMEDICINE LOANS AND GRANTS

Assistance: project grants (70 percent/to 2 years); direct loans (90 percent).

Purposes: for telecommunications, computer networks, and other projects that provide educational and/or medical benefits to students, teachers, medical professionals, and rural residents. Ineligible project costs: telecommunications transmission facilities if the local telephone company will provide service through the use of expedited RUS loans; medical or other equipment except that required for encoding and decoding data for telecommunications; salaries of medical or education personnel providing medical or educational services; applicant's salaries or administrative expenses; projects in areas covered by the Coastal Barrier Resources Act.

Eligible applicants/beneficiaries: schools, libraries, hospitals, medical centers, and similar organizations.

Range/Average: N.A.

Activity: cumulatively FY 93-FY 98, 252 projects funded.

HQ: Assistant Administrator/Telecommunications, RUS-USDA, South Bldg. - Rm.4056, 1400 Independence Ave. SW, Washington, DC 20250-1500. Phone: (202)720-9554. (Note: no field offices for this program.)

10.900 GREAT PLAINS CONSERVATION

Assistance: direct payments/specified use (50-80 percent/3-10 years); advisory services/counseling.

Purposes: for technical and financial assistance in the conservation and development of soil and water resources on the Great Plains, including: pollution abatement; enhancement of fish, wildlife, recreational resources; promotion of economic land use.

Eligible applicants/beneficiaries: farmers, ranchers, and others in the 556 designated counties of the ten states in the Great Plains area.

Range: to $35,000 per farm operating unit.

Activity: active contracts cover 9,300,000 acres.

HQ: Deputy Chief/Programs, NRCS-USDA, P.O. Box 2890, Washington, DC 20013. Phone: (202)720-1873.

10.901 RESOURCE CONSERVATION AND DEVELOPMENT

Assistance: project grants (to 75 percent); advisory services/counseling.

Purposes: to encourage and improve capabilities to plan, develop, and execute programs for resource conservation and development, in approved "RC&D" areas. Assistance is available for approved measures for land conservation, water management, community development, and environmental enhancement. Project examples include: promotion of economic development, cluster zoning, land conservation easements, historic preservation; formation of water quality association; use of low-grade timber for housing development; fertilizer development from composting.

Eligible applicants/beneficiaries: authorize state and local governments and nonprofit organizations in multi-jurisdictional areas. Available also in PR, VI, Guam, Northern Marianas.

Range/Average: N.A.

Activity: 41,000 completed projects as of FY 99.

HQ: same address as **10.900**. Phones: (202)720-4527; FAX (202)720-6559.

10.902 SOIL AND WATER CONSERVATION

Assistance: advisory services/counseling.

Purposes: to assist in planning and applying soil and water conservation practices and treatment; to provide technical natural resource conservation information.

Eligible applicants/beneficiaries: general public, state and local government units. Available also in PR, VI, and Western Pacific Trust Territories.

Activity: FY 98 estimate, 742,000 landowners and users received services.

HQ: same address as **10.900**. Phone: (202)720-4527.

10.903 SOIL SURVEY

Assistance: technical information.

Purposes: to maintain updated published soil surveys and related data bases of counties and areas of comparable size for use by environmentalists, engineers, planners, zoning and tax commissions, homeowners, farmers, ranchers, land developers, and others—in selecting and implementing appropriate use and treatment of the soils surveyed.

Eligible applicants/beneficiaries: anyone needing soil surveys.

Activity: FY 00 estimate, 24,000,000 acres surveyed.

HQ: Deputy Chief/Soil Survey and Resource Assessment, NRCS-USDA, P.O. Box 2890, Washington, DC 20013. Phone: (202)690-4616.

10.904 WATERSHED PROTECTION AND FLOOD PREVENTION ("Small Watershed Program" - "PL-566 Operations Phase")

Assistance: project grants (50-100 percent); advisory services/counseling.

Purposes: to plan and execute projects to protect, develop, and utilize land and water resources in small watersheds (250,000 acres or less). Funds may support watershed protection measures, flood prevention, irrigation, drainage, agricultural water management, sedimentation control, and public water-based fish, wildlife, and recreation resources; also, to extend long-term credit to help local interests with their share of costs. Single structure capacity is limited to 25,000 acre-feet of total capacity and 12,500 acre-feet of flood-water detention capacity.

Eligible applicants/beneficiaries: any authorized state agency, county or groups of counties, municipality, town or township, soil and water conservation district, flood prevention or flood control district, tribe or tribal organization, or nonprofit agency. Available also in territories.

Range: to $2,164,000. **Average:** $650,000.

Activity: FY 99 estimate, 13 projects approved for operations; 520 projects under construction; 908 projects completed.

HQ: same address as **10.900**. Phone: (202)720-4527.

10.905   PLANT MATERIALS FOR CONSERVATION

Assistance: specialized services.

Purposes: to assemble, evaluate, select, release, and introduce into commerce the use of new and improved plant materials such as grasses, legumes, forbs, shrubs, and trees for soil, water, and related resource conservation and environmental improvement programs—including erosion control, roadside and stream bank protection, surface-mined land reclamation, and wildlife food and cover. Plant materials are produced only for field testing and to provide commercial producers with breeder and foundation quality seed or propagules. Other plants or seed are not provided to the general public under this program.

Eligible applicants/beneficiaries: cooperating state and federal agencies and cooperators of conservation districts; commercial seed growers and nurseries interested in the production of selected plant materials, including in PR and VI.

Activity: to date, over 450 releases for commercial increase.

HQ: Deputy Chief/Science and Technology, NRCS-USDA, P.O. Box 2890, Washington, DC 20013. Phone: (202)720-4630.

10.906   WATERSHED SURVEYS AND PLANNING
("Small Watershed Program" - "PL-566")

Assistance: specialized services; advisory services/counseling.

Purposes: to assist in the development of coordinated water and related land resource programs in watersheds and river basins to help solve such problems as those involving upstream rural community flooding, agricultural nonpoint source pollution, wetlands preservation, and drought management—through such disciplines as engineering, economics, social sciences, landscape architecture, agronomy, range management, forestry, biology, waste management, hydrology, archaeology. There is special emphasis on assisting communities wishing to adopt floodplain management regulations meeting National Flood Insurance Program requirements, and to assist states in developing a strategic water resource plan.

Eligible applicants/beneficiaries: any local or state water resource agency or other federal agency concerned with water and related land resource development. Available also in territories.

Activity: since 1954 program inception, 1,627 watershed plans, 550 flood insurance studies, 599 flood plain management studies, 461 river basin studies, 171 resource plans completed.

HQ: same address as **10.900**. Phone: (202)720-4527.

10.907   SNOW SURVEY AND WATER SUPPLY FORECASTING

Assistance: technical information.

Purposes: to provide information on forthcoming seasonal water supplies from streams that derive most of their runoff from snowmelt in the mountain states and the far west—assisting farm operators, rural communities, municipalities, and others in planning for and managing water resources. Data are used in the regulation of small and large reservoirs for irrigation, flood control, power generation, recreation, industry, and municipal supplies.

Eligible applicants/beneficiaries: general public, including in the territories.

Activity: daily snow and precipitation data gathered from 630 automated snow telemetry sites and 900 manual snow courses in the U.S. and Alaska; 6,000 forecasts of seasonal volume streamflows at 600 streamgaging points provided to water users.

HQ: same address/phone as **10.905.**

10.910 RURAL ABANDONED MINE PROGRAM ("RAMP")

Assistance: direct payments/specified use (25-100 percent/5-10 years).

Purposes: for conservation practices needed for the reclamation, conservation, and development of abandoned rural coal mine land or lands and waters affected by coal mining activities. Up to 320 acres per owner may be assisted.

Eligible applicants/beneficiaries: individuals, groups, or units of government that own or control the surface or water rights of abandoned coal land or lands and water affected by coal mining practices before August 3, 1977. These areas are ineligible if: (1) reclamation responsibility on the part of the mine operator or the state is continuing; (2) the lands are in federal ownership; and (3) the surface rights are under easement or lease to be remined.

Range/Average: N.A.

Activity: through FY 98, 1,488 contracts awarded to treat 18,000 acres.

HQ: same address as **10.900.** Phone: (202)720-2847.

10.912 ENVIRONMENTAL QUALITY INCENTIVES PROGRAM ("EQIP")

Assistance: direct payments/specified use (to 75 percent/5-10 years).

Purposes: to assist farmers and ranchers to comply with environmental laws and to encourage environmental enhancement by providing technical, educational, and financial assistance to implement structural, vegetative, and land management practices that address soil, water, and related natural resource concerns. Program is funded through the CCC. Fifty percent of available funding must be targeted at practices relating to livestock production.

Eligible applicants/beneficiaries: individual and family farmers and ranchers that are owners, landlords, operators, or tenants of eligible agricultural lands—with special encouragement to apply to limited resource producers, small-scale producers, and minority groups, tribal governments, Alaska natives, and Pacific Islanders.

Range: to $10,000 per person per year, to $50,000 for life of contract. **Average:** $15,000.

Activity: new program listing in 1997. FY 98, 665 priority areas approved.

HQ: same address as **10.900.** Phones: (202)720-1845; FAX (202)720-4265.

10.913 FARMLAND PROTECTION PROGRAM

Assistance: direct payments/specified use (50 percent).

Purposes: to purchase conservation easements or other interests in lands to limit nonagricultural uses of farm land with prime, unique, or other productive soils—with a minimum 30-year duration.

Eligible applicants/beneficiaries: local or state agencies, counties, municipalities, towns, local government units, tribes, soil of water conservation districts—with a farm land protection program. Available also in territories. Individuals apply through local agencies.

Range: $100,000 to $1,900,000. **Average:** $387,000.

Activity: new program listing in 1997. FY 97-98, 41 entities in 18 states acquired easements on 230 farms covering 82,000 acres with a value of $134,000,000.

HQ: Community Assistance and Resource Development Division, NRCS-USDA, P.O. Box 2890, Washington, DC 20013. Phones: (202)720-2847; FAX (202)690-0639.

10.914 WILDLIFE HABITAT INCENTIVE PROGRAM ("WHIP")

Assistance: direct payments/specified use (to 75 percent/5-10 years minimum).

Purposes: to develop habitats for upland and wetland wildlife, threatened and endangered species, and fish. Technical assistance is provided to prepare a Wildlife Habitat Development Plan.

Eligible applicants/beneficiaries: owners, landlords, operators, tenants of eligible lands. Limited resource producers, small-scale producers, and minority groups, tribal governments, Alaska natives, and Pacific Islanders are encouraged to apply.

Range: to $10,000/contract. **Average:** $4,600.

Activity: new program in FY 97. FY 98, 672,000 acres enrolled.

HQ: same address as **10.900**. Phones: (202)720-1845; FAX (202)720-4265.

10.950 AGRICULTURAL STATISTICS REPORTS ("Agricultural Estimates")

Assistance: technical information.

Purposes: to collect and publish statistics related to agriculture, resources, and rural communities. Reports cover crops, agricultural chemical usage, livestock and poultry estimates, prices received by farmers, prices for commodities and services, data on farm employment and wage rates.

Eligible applicants/beneficiaries: farmers and agricultural producers, marketing and processing groups, transportation and handler groups, consumers, state governments, educational institutions, and the general public, including in the territories.

Activity: estimates on some 120 crops and 45 livestock items, published in 400 reports.

HQ: Administrator, National Agricultural Statistics Service-USDA, Washington, DC 20250. Phones: (202)720-2707; Internet, http://www.usda.gov/nass (Note: no field offices for this program.)

10.960 TECHNICAL AGRICULTURAL ASSISTANCE

Assistance: project grants (100 percent/1-2 years).

Purposes: for technical research and assistance projects dealing with international agricultural problems. Current projects include expansion of developing-country agricultural management concepts and technologies, guidance on the development of private enterprise, livestock production and health. Program is conducted in cooperation with the State Department's Agency for International Development.

Eligible applicants/beneficiaries: U.S. IHEs; public and private nonprofit scientific research organizations, including in territories.

Range: $20,000 to $200,000. **Average:** $80,000.

Activity: not quantified specifically.

HQ: Development Resources Division, Office of International Cooperation and Development, FAS-USDA, Washington, DC 20250-1092. Phone: (202)690-1924. (Note: no field offices for this program.)

10.961 SCIENTIFIC COOPERATION PROGRAM
("International Collaborative Research and Scientific Exchanges")

Assistance: project grants (50-100 percent); direct payments/specified use.

Purposes: for research abroad on international agriculture and forestry problems in collaboration with foreign scientists—through short- (to 4 weeks) and long-term (1-3 years) exchanges.

Eligible applicants/beneficiaries: same as for **10.960.**

Range: long-term, to $30,000; visits, to $5,000. **Average:** visits, $2,500.

Activity: 100 ongoing projects in 40 countries.

HQ: Director, Research and Scientific Exchanges Division, Office of International Cooperation and Development, FAS-USDA, Washington, DC 20250-1084. Phones: (202)690-4872; Internet, http://www.fas.usda.gov (Note: no field offices for this program.)

10.962 INTERNATIONAL TRAINING—FOREIGN PARTICIPANT

Assistance: project grants (100 percent).

Purposes: for international research training in food, agricultural, and related subjects, mainly in the areas of course development and evaluation. Funding currently supports projects involving short-term agricultural and trade-related training and orientation for senior and mid-level officials, including marketing and production of forestry and wood products, soybean utilization, rice processing, food safety, and dairy production and livestock management.

Eligible applicants/beneficiaries: U.S. IHEs or nonprofit organizations.

Range: $10,000 to $40,000. **Average:** $19,000.

Activity: not quantified specifically.

HQ: Food Industries Division, Office of International Cooperation and Development, FAS-USDA, Washington, DC 20250-1086. Phone: (202)690-1339. (Note: no field offices for this program.)

DEPARTMENT OF COMMERCE

BUREAU OF THE CENSUS

11.001   CENSUS BUREAU DATA PRODUCTS

Assistance: technical information.

Purposes: to distribute statistical results of censuses, surveys, and other programs. Data cover population, housing, retail and wholesale trade, service and construction industries, transportation, communications, utilities, manufacturing, mineral industries, governments, foreign trade statistics, and financial, insurance, real estate industries. Certain estimates and projections, as well as boundary and code maps, are also available. Various types of geographic areas are covered. Distribution is through printed reports, computer disks and tapes, CD-ROMs, online and other media, statistical compendia, directories, indexes, catalogs, and guides. Data products contain statistical summaries only.

Eligible applicants/beneficiaries: anyone.

Activity: not quantified specifically.

HQ: Customer Services, Bureau of the Census-USDC, Washington, DC 20233. Phones: (301)457-4100; Internet, http://www.census.gov

11.002   CENSUS CUSTOMER SERVICES

Assistance: advisory services/counseling; technical information; training.

Purposes: to assist census data users in the access to and use of census data—through newsletters, technical guides, conferences, training courses, and related activities including development of user-oriented computer programs for processing census files. Staff are available to participate in conferences and workshops on the censuses and other Census Bureau programs.

Eligible applicants/beneficiaries: materials and consultation—anyone. Data user training—officials of federal, state, and local governments, universities, community organizations, the private sector; nominal fees may be charged.

Activity: not quantified specifically.

HQ: same address/phones as **11.001.**

11.003   CENSUS GEOGRAPHY
("Census Mapping and Statistical Areas")

Assistance: specialized services; technical information.

Purposes: to prepare computer-generated maps for use in conducting censuses and surveys; to determine boundaries of statistical areas; to develop geographic code systems; to provide maps and area reports for states and local areas throughout the U.S. including territories and possessions; to develop computer files of area measurements, geographic areas, and map features with address ranges. "TIGER" (Topologically Integrated Geographic Encoding and Referencing), an automated cartographic data base, developed in cooperation with the U.S. Geological Survey, covers the entire U.S. and its possessions; the system generates maps and other geographic products; geographic base files, called TIGER/Line files, are available on computer tape and CD-ROM. Published maps are sold by GPO; unpublished maps are sold directly by the Census Bureau.

Eligible applicants/beneficiaries: anyone.

Activity: not quantified specifically.

HQ: Geography Division, Bureau of the Census-USDC, Washington, DC 20233-7400. Phone: (301)457-1128. *Or,* Customer Services, same address/phones as **11.001**.

11.004   CENSUS INTERGOVERNMENTAL SERVICES
("Intergovernmental Services Program")

Assistance: advisory services/counseling; technical information; training.

Purposes: to provide technical assistance and information on methods of making population estimates and projections. Consultation services are available to local officials to plan and conduct special surveys. Special surveys are taken on a cost reimbursement basis. Assistance is provided to states in establishing and operating State Data Centers and Business/Industry Data Centers.

Eligible applicants/beneficiaries: federal, state, local government officials; community organizations.

Activity: currently, all states, DC, and PR participating in Federal-State Cooperative Program for the preparation of county population estimates; all states participating in the State Data Center Program, along with DC, Guam, Northern Marianas, PR, and the VI; 1,800 state and local governmental agencies, universities, and other organizations participating in the Business/Industry Data Center Program.

HQ: Bureau of the Census-USDC, Washington, DC 20233. Phones: *special censuses*, Office of Special Censuses, (301)457-1429; *population estimates and projections*, Population Division, (301)457-2422; *State Data Center and BIDC Programs*, State and Regional Programs Staff (DUSD), (301)457-1305.

11.005   CENSUS SPECIAL TABULATIONS AND SERVICES

Assistance: technical information; specialized services.

Purposes: to provide customized census tabulations in a variety of output forms to meet user needs and to conduct statistical surveys, on a reimbursable basis.

Eligible applicants/beneficiaries: federal, state, local government officials; community and private organizations; individuals.

Activity: not quantified specifically.

HQ: Director, Bureau of the Census-USDC, Washington, DC 20233. Phones: *demographic and household special surveys*, Office of Special Censuses, (301)457-1429; *special economic surveys*, Chief, Economic Planning and Coordination Division, (301)457-2558; *special tabulations (demographic)*, Population Division, (301)457-2408; *special tabulations (housing)*, Housing and Household Economic Statistics Division, (301)763-3188.

11.006 PERSONAL CENSUS SEARCH
("Age Search")

Assistance: specialized services.

Purposes: to provide data for proof of age, relationship, or citizenship, for such purposes as: qualifying for certain government program benefits (e.g., Medicare, Social Security, pensions); proof of citizenship; qualifying for certain types of employment or for inheritances, annuities, and other rights or benefits. A $40 fee is charged for searches.

Eligible applicants/beneficiaries: personal information from census records of 1930 and later is confidential and may be furnished only upon written request by the person to whom it relates, or, for a proper purpose, to a legal representative of an estate. Information regarding a child not of legal age may be obtained upon written request by either parent. For records of a deceased person, application must be signed by either: (1) a blood relative in the immediate family; (2) the surviving spouse; (3) a beneficiary; or, (4) the administrator or executor of the estate. Appropriate certifications are required.

Activity: annually, 12,500 requests processed.

HQ: Chief, Personal Census Search Branch, Bureau of the Census-USDC, P.O. Box 1545, Jeffersonville, IN 47131. Phone (812)218-3046. (Note: the field office is the headquarters for this program.)

ECONOMICS AND STATISTICS ADMINISTRATION

11.025 MEASURES AND ANALYSES OF THE U.S. ECONOMY

Assistance: technical information.

Purposes: to produce measures and analyses of the national income and product accounts (NIPAs) as summarized by the gross domestic product, as well as a series of related economic data analyses—used to formulate and execute fiscal, financial, international, and other policies. The principal analyses include: corporate profits; personal income series by state and region; U.S. balance of payments; international trade; gross domestic product by industry. Reports are available in the monthly "Survey of Current Business" by subscription through GPO. On-line services include the Economic Bulletin Board; certain reports are available on CD-ROM.

Eligible applicants/beneficiaries: general public.

Activity: publications.

HQ: Public Information Office, Bureau of Economic Analysis (BE-53), USDC, 1441 L St. NW - Rm.1026, Washington, DC 20230. Phones: (202)606-9900; *Order Desk,* (800)704-0415, *or* Web, www.bea.doc.gov ; *Economic Bulletin Board,* (800)782-9972, *or,* Internet, www.stat-usa.gov

11.026   NATIONAL TRADE DATA BANK ("NTDB")

Assistance: technical information.

Purposes: to provide a comprehensive source of international trade and export data from over 50 federal agencies—including the Commercial Service International Contacts (CSIC), an extensive list of foreign companies interested in establishing trade links with U.S. companies. The NTDB contains over 300,000 documents, released monthly and available on CD-ROM and on-line by subscription—and at federal depository libraries (see **40.001**). Funding for this program is derived from revolving fund proceeds from product sales.

Eligible applicants/beneficiaries: general public.

Activity: currently, over 120 program titles including market research, country profiles, export and import statistics, and export "how-to" guides.

HQ: Director, STAT-USA, USDC, HCHB - Rm.4880, Washington, DC 20230. Phones: (202)482-1405; *subscriptions,* 202)482-1986, FAX (202)482-2164, *or,* Internet, http://www.stat-usa.gov (Note: no field offices for this program.)

11.027   ECONOMIC BULLETIN BOARD ("EBB")

Assistance: technical information.

Purposes: to maintain an on-line computer service providing access to over 8,000 files containing trade leads, official economic and financial press releases, and statistical data prepared by numerous federal agencies. Files are continually updated. Annual subscriptions are available from ESA. The EBB may be accessed by 50 users simultaneously. Funding for this program is derived from revolving fund proceeds from product sales.

Eligible applicants/beneficiaries: general public.

Activity: not quantified specifically.

HQ: same address/phones as **11.026**. (Note: no field offices for this program.)

INTERNATIONAL TRADE ADMINISTRATION

11.106   REMEDIES FOR UNFAIR FOREIGN TRADE PRACTICES— ANTIDUMPING AND COUNTERVAILING DUTY INVESTIGATIONS

Assistance: specialized services; investigation of complaints.

Purposes: to protect U.S. industries against economic injury from the sale of foreign merchandise at less than fair value and by unfair subsidies provided by foreign governments—pursuant to the Tariff Act of 1930 as amended and other acts. Import duties are assessed against such merchandise if "dumping" or countervailing subsidies are found to occur, which may be revoked five years after violations of the act have ceased.

Eligible applicants/beneficiaries: any interested party may file a complaint on behalf of an affected U.S. industry.

Activity: not quantified specifically.

HQ: Office of Policy, Import Administration, International Trade Administration-USDC, 14th & Constitution Ave. NW, Washington, DC 20230. Phone: (202)482-4412. (Note: no field offices for this program.)

11.108   COMMERCIAL SERVICE

Assistance: advisory services/counseling.

Purposes: to expand export markets by providing information and guidance on overseas trade markets and opportunities to U.S. firms, through: non-financial assistance in export promotion with displays, trade and industrial exhibits, trade missions, catalog shows, and foreign buyer shows; information on trade statistics, foreign tariffs, customs regulations and procedures; overseas government-to-government advocacy and representation; assistance on sources of export finance available from the U.S. Export-Import Bank, SBA, and the U.S. Agency for International Development—in U.S. Export Assistance Centers.

Eligible applicants/beneficiaries: anyone.

Activity: not quantified specifically.

HQ: International Trade Administration-USDC, 14th & Constitution Ave. NW, Washington, DC 20230. Phone: (no number provided).

11.110   TRADE DEVELOPMENT

Assistance: advisory services/counseling.

Purposes: to provide a central federal source of industry-specific expertise, policy development, industry competitiveness analysis, and international trade promotion assistance. Services include regular statistical reports, economic studies on current policy issues such as international trade and industry competitiveness, forecasts of industry/sector outputs and cost trends, information on technological developments, export promotion events, and foreign market information.

Eligible applicants/beneficiaries: anyone.

Activity: not quantified specifically.

HQ: International Trade Administration-USDC, 14th & Constitution Ave. NW, Washington, DC 20230. Phones: Advocacy Center, (202)482-3896; Technology and Aerospace Industries, (202)482-1872; Basic Industries, (202)482-5023; Environmental Technologies Exports, (202)482-5225; Service Industries and Finance, (202)482-5261; Export Trading Company Affairs, (202)482-5131; Textiles, Apparel, and Consumer Goods Industries, (202)482-3737; Tourism Industries, (202)482-0140; Trade and Economic Analysis, (202)482-5145; Export Promotion Coordination, (202)482-4501; Planning, Coordination and Resource Management, (202) 482-4921; Internet, http//www.doc.ita.gov/itahome/html

11.111   FOREIGN-TRADE ZONES IN THE UNITED STATES

Assistance: specialized services.

Purposes: to assist in establishing and operating foreign trade zones (FTZ) in localities to encourage and streamline import-export trade activities and to stimulate domestic production of export goods. FTZs function like public utilities, subject to U.S. Customs and other requirements, providing access to businesses and manufacturers.

Eligible applicants/beneficiaries: public and private corporations in states with appropriate enabling legislation.

Activity: annually, 70-100 FTZ orders issued, covering zones, sub-zones, and expansion applications.

HQ: Executive Secretary, Foreign-Trade Zones Board, International Trade Administration-USDC, 14th & Pennsylvania Ave. NW - Rm.4008, Washington, DC 20230. Phone: (202)482-2862.

11.112   EXPORT PROMOTION—MARKET DEVELOPMENT COOPERATOR

Assistance: project grants (cost sharing/to 3 years).

Purposes: to develop, maintain, and expand foreign markets for nonagricultural goods and services produced in the U.S. "Cooperators" conduct activities abroad to promote certain industries, including outreach campaigns, conferences, consultative services, exhibitions, training, market research. Project funds support direct costs only. Applicants may charge fees for services provided to companies in the industry being promoted.

Eligible applicants/beneficiaries: nonprofit industry organizations, trade associations, state departments of trade and their regional associations, private industry firms or groups of firms.

Range: $50,000 to $400,000. **Average:** $298,000.

Activity: FY 99, 9 awards.

HQ: Resource Management and Planning Staff, Trade Development/OPCRM, International Trade Administration-USDC, HCHB - Rm.3221, Washington, DC 20230. Phones: (202)482-2969; FAX (202)482-5828. (Note: no field offices for this program.)

11.113   ITA SPECIAL PROJECTS

Assistance: project grants (100 percent).

Purposes: to assist small-/medium-sized businesses specifically identified by Congress to expand exports. Assistance may include contracts, information, and research and development.

Eligible applicants/beneficiaries: organizations or individuals specifically identified by Congress.

Range: $255,000 to $7,500,000.

Activity: not quantified specifically.

HQ: same address (except Rm.3209)/phones as **11.112**. (Note: no field offices for this program.)

11.114   SPECIAL AMERICAN BUSINESS INTERNSHIP TRAINING PROGRAM ("SABIT")

Assistance: project grants (100 percent).

Purposes: to train business executives and scientists from the New Independent States of the former Soviet Union. Mid- to senior-level interns participate in internships with public and private sector companies—in fields including agribusiness, environmental technology, financial services, telecommunications, energy. Project funds reimburse recipients for costs of travel and $30.00 daily stipends for up to six months.

Eligible applicants/beneficiaries: profit or nonprofit U.S. corporations, associations, organizations, or other public or private entities.

Range: to $7,500 per intern for travel and stipends; to $40,000 per project.

Activity: new program listing in 1997. 1,300 interns trained in 900 companies.

HQ: SABIT Program, International Trade Administration-USDC, 14th & Constitution Ave. NW - Rm. 3319, Washington, DC 20230. Phones: (202) 482-0073; FAX (202)482-2443; E-mail, sabitapply@usita.gov ; Internet, www.mac.doc.gov/sabit.html (Note: no field offices for this program.)

11.115   AMERICAN BUSINESS CENTER ("ABC")

Assistance: project grants (50 percent/to 5 years).

Purposes: to help U.S. firms identify opportunities to export and invest in Russia; to provide business training and technical assistance to Russian firms. Services to U.S. firms may include counseling, market research, trade mission and event planning, screening and assessing partners, telecommunications services. Services are available exclusively to U.S. firms on a fee-for-service basis.

Eligible applicants/beneficiaries: U.S. profit firms, nonprofit organizations, nonfederal government agencies, industry and trade associations, educational institutions. Enterprises proposing to include participation by host country citizens are eligible, provided U.S. entities control approved projects.

Range: $650,000 to $4,688,000. **Average:** $1,794,000.

Activity: new program listing in 1998; during first three years, more than 2,000 companies reported over $34,000,000 in sales.

HQ: Russia/NIS Program Office, U.S. and Foreign Commercial Service, ITA-USDC, HCHB - Rm.1235, Washington, DC 20230. Phones: (202)482-2902; FAX (202)482-2456. (Note: no field offices for this program.)

BUREAU OF EXPORT ADMINISTRATION

11.150   EXPORT LICENSING SERVICE AND INFORMATION ("Export Control" - "Exporter Assistance Program")

Assistance: advisory services/counseling.

Purposes: to provide information, training, seminars, and other assistance on export licensing requirements, regulations, and policies; to expedite export applications when priority action is warranted.

Eligible applicants/beneficiaries: anyone.

Activity: FY 00 estimate, 200,000 exporters counseled; processing of 43,000 phone inquiries through the automated System for Tracking Export License Applications (STELA); 204 export licensing seminars.

HQ: Exporter Counseling Division, Office of Exporter Services, Bureau of Export Administration-USDC - Rm.1099, P.O. Box 273, Washington, DC 20044. Phones: *status & trade fair*, (202)482-2753; *regulatory and policy questions*, (202)482-4811; *STELA*, (202)482-2752.

ECONOMIC DEVELOPMENT ADMINISTRATION

11.300   GRANTS FOR PUBLIC WORKS AND INFRASTRUCTURE DEVELOPMENT

Assistance: project grants (50-100 percent).

Purposes: for the construction of public works and development facilities to create or retain permanent jobs in the private sector in areas experiencing substantial economic distress. Projects may involve water and sewer systems, railroad spurs, industrial parks, industrial access roads and other business infrastructure, port facilities, tourism facilities, vocational schools, renovation and recycling of old industrial buildings, business incubator facilities. Projects must be consistent with approved Comprehensive Economic Development Strategies. Grants cover 50 percent of costs; severely depressed areas may receive 80 percent; designated tribes receive 100 percent; projects in redevelopment areas supporting Economic Development Districts may receive 80 percent, and a 10 percent bonus for public works projects.

Eligible applicants/beneficiaries: states, cities, counties, other political subdivisions; IHEs or consortia; tribes; private or public nonprofit organizations or associations; territories and possessions.

Range/Average: $852,000.

Activity: FY 98, 208 projects approved.

HQ: Director, Public Works Division, EDA-USDC, Herbert C. Hoover Bldg. - Rm.H7326, Washington, DC 20230. Phone: (202)482-5265.

11.303   ECONOMIC DEVELOPMENT—TECHNICAL ASSISTANCE
("National, University Center and Local Technical Assistance")

Assistance: project grants (50 percent).

Purposes: to provide technical assistance in developing data and expertise in evaluating and planning specific economic development projects and programs in depressed areas. Technical assistance is provided through: university economic development centers; innovative projects; information dissemination and studies of issues of national significance; feasibility studies and other projects leading to local economic development.

Eligible applicants/beneficiaries: public or private nonprofit groups, educational institutions; tribal, state, municipal, county, and territorial governments.

Range: $6,500 to $200,000. **Average:** university programs, $94,000; national technical assistance projects, $92,000; local projects, $26,000.

Activity: FY 99, 69 university, 61 local, 13 national projects funded.

HQ: Director, Research and National Technical Assistance Division, EDA-USDC, Herbert C. Hoover Bldg. - Rm.H7019, Washington, DC 20230. Phone: (202)482-4085.

11.305   ECONOMIC DEVELOPMENT—STATE AND LOCAL ECONOMIC DEVELOPMENT PLANNING

Assistance: project grants (from 50 percent; tribes, 100 percent).

Purposes: for comprehensive economic development planning activities, including salaries and expenses related to the preparation of studies.

Eligible applicants/beneficiaries: same as for **11.300** (except territories and possessions).

Range: $10,000 to $200,000. **Average:** $55,000.

Activity: FY 98, 437 grants awarded.

HQ: Director, Planning and Development Assistance Division, EDA-USDC, Herbert C. Hoover Bldg. - Rm.H7317, Washington, DC 20230. Phones: (202)482-3027; FAX (202)482-0466.

11.307   ECONOMIC ADJUSTMENT ASSISTANCE

Assistance: project grants (from 50 percent).

Purposes: to design and implement strategies to address problems stemming from serious deterioration of local economies such as actual or anticipated plant or military base closings, defense contract cutbacks, natural disasters, or depletion of natural resources. Strategy Grants may be used for plan development resulting in a Comprehensive Economic Development Strategy. Implementation Grants may be used for development of organizational capacity, business development and financing including through the capitalization of revolving loan funds, infrastructure improvement, and market or industry research and analysis.

Eligible applicants/beneficiaries: same as for **11.300** (except territories and possessions).

Range: no specific minimum or maximum.

Activity: FY 99, 300 projects funded.

HQ: Director, Economic Adjustment Division, EDA-USDC, Herbert C. Hoover Bldg. - Rm.H7327, Washington, DC 20230. Phone: (202)482-2659.

11.312   RESEARCH AND EVALUATION PROGRAM

Assistance: project grants (100 percent/to 15 months).

Purposes: for studies, training, research, and program evaluations to determine the causes of unemployment and under-employment; to develop national, state, and local programs that will raise income levels and relieve unemployment, under-employment, and under-development.

Eligible applicants/beneficiaries: private individuals, firms, colleges, universities, other institutions; profit and nonprofit organizations.

Range: $13,000 to $288,000. **Average:** $169,000.

Activity: FY 98, 4 projects funded.

HQ: same address/phone as **11.303**. (Note: no field offices for this program.)

11.313   TRADE ADJUSTMENT ASSISTANCE ("TAA")

Assistance: project grants (50-100 percent).

Purposes: for trade adjustment assistance to firms and industries adversely affected by increased imports, in the form of technical assistance for which participants must share the expense. Assistance may consist of such detailed aid as industrial engineering, marketing studies, product diversification, and the like. To receive Trade Act certification, firms must demonstrate that increased imports of articles like or directly competitive with those that they produce contributed significantly to declines in sales or production, and to separation or threat of separation of their workers. Firms must submit an acceptable adjustment proposal to be eligible to apply. Industry associations or other organizations must submit evidence demonstrating import competition, and that the industry includes a substantial number of Trade Act-certified firms or workers.

Eligible applicants: intermediary organizations including Trade Adjustment Assistance Centers or industry groups that can demonstrate injury from imports.

Eligible beneficiaries: private firms with Trade Act certification.

Range: to $75,000.

Activity: FY 98, 167 firms certified; 127 adjustment proposals accepted. (No industry-wide funds awarded since FY 96.)

HQ: Planning and Development Assistance Division, EDA-USDC, 14th & Constitution Ave. NW - Rm.H7315, Washington, DC 20230. Phones: (202) 482-2127: FAX (202)482-0466.

NATIONAL OCEANIC AND ATMOSPHERIC ADMINISTRATION

11.400   GEODETIC SURVEYS AND SERVICES (GEODESY AND APPLICATIONS OF THE NATIONAL GEODETIC REFERENCE SYSTEM)

Assistance: project grants (cost sharing).

Purposes: to extend National Geodetic Reference System networks into areas inadequately covered, through Multipurpose Land Information Systems/Geographic Information Systems (MPLIS/GIS) pilot projects. The networks consist of horizontal and vertical geodetic reference monuments at various specified intervals, providing scale, orientation, coordinated positions, and elevations of specific points—for use in surveying, boundary delineation and demarcation, mapping, planning, and development. The system provides the standards of reference on which are based state plane coordinate systems, land and public utility records, and boundary delineations. Funding is limited to projects identified by Congress in appropriations.

Eligible applicants/beneficiaries: state, local, municipal, or regional agencies.

Range/Average: N.A.

Activity: FY 98, 2 pilot projects (Louisiana and South Carolina).

HQ: Grant Program Office, Geodetic Service Division, National Ocean Service, NOAA-USDC, Silver Spring, MD 20910. Phone: (301)713-3228. (Note: no field offices for this program.)

11.405   ANADROMOUS FISH CONSERVATION ACT PROGRAM

Assistance: project grants (50-90 percent/1-3 years).

Purposes: for the conservation, development, and enhancement of anadromous fish stocks and fish in the Great Lakes and Lake Champlain that ascend streams to spawn; to control sea lamprey; for research on migratory east coast striped bass stocks. Permissible uses of funds include: spawning area improvement; installation of fishways; construction of fish protection devices and hatcheries; tagging studies; research to improve anadromous fish resources.

Eligible applicants/beneficiaries: interested persons or organizations, in coordination with state fishery agencies.

Range: $2,000 to $400,000. **Average:** $40,000.

Activity: FY 00 estimate, 15 projects.

HQ: Chief, Staff Office for Intergovernmental and Recreational Fisheries, NMFS-NOAA-USDC, 8484 Georgia Ave., Silver Spring, MD 20910. Phone: (301)427-2014.

11.407   INTERJURISDICTIONAL FISHERIES ACT OF 1986

Assistance: formula grants (75-90 percent).

Purposes: for the management of interjurisdictional fisheries resources. Permissible uses of funds include research, management planning, enforcement; restoration of resources damaged by natural disasters.

Eligible applicants/beneficiaries: state agencies; the Pacific, Atlantic, and Gulf Interstate Marine Fisheries Commissions.

Range: $12,000 to $250,000. **Average:** $100,000.

Activity: FY 00 estimate, 40 projects.

HQ: same address/phone as **11.405.**

11.408   FISHERMEN'S CONTINGENCY FUND
("Title IV")

Assistance: direct payments/unrestricted use.

Purposes: pursuant to the Outer Continental Shelf Lands Act Amendments of 1978, to compensate U.S. commercial fishermen for damage to or loss of fishing gear, and 50 percent of resulting financial loss caused by oil- and gas-related activities in Outer Continental Shelf areas.

Eligible applicants/beneficiaries: U.S. commercial fishermen.

Range: $500 to $54,000. **Average:** $6,000.

Activity: FY 99 estimate, 56 claims paid.

IIQ: Chief, Financial Services Division, NMFS-NOAA-USDC, 1315 East-West Hwy., Silver Spring, MD 20910. Phone: (301)713-2396.

11.413 FISHERY PRODUCTS INSPECTION AND CERTIFICATION ("Inspection and Grading of Fishery Products")

Assistance: specialized services.

Purposes: voluntary inspection, grading, and certification of seafood harvesting and processing operations regarding their hygienic aspects and product identity, condition, quality, and quantity. Fees are charged for the service, in support of program costs.

Eligible applicants/beneficiaries: individuals; federal, state, county, or municipal agencies; carriers with a financial interest in the commodity.

Activity: 1998, over 950,000,000 pounds of fishery products inspected and certified, at 300 plants.

HQ: Inspection Services Division, NMFS-NOAA-USDC, 1315 East-West Hwy., Silver Spring, MD 20910. Phone: (301)713-2355. (Note: no field offices for this program.)

11.415 FISHERIES FINANCE PROGRAM

Assistance: direct loans (to 80 percent/to 25 years).

Purposes: for certain fisheries costs including: purchase or reconstruction of used vessels; refinancing of existing debt; financing or refinancing of shore-side fishery and aquaculture facilities; financing of Community Development Quota (CDQ) groups fisheries investments; long-term fishery buyback financing. Funds may not be used for loans that add to fishing capacity or that over-capitalize the industry.

Eligible applicants/beneficiaries: commercial fishermen, fishery products processors or distributors.

Range: $100,000 to $25,000,000. **Average:** $1,000,000.

Activity: FY 99 estimate, 20 direct, 1 buyback, 3 CDQ loans.

HQ: same address as **11.408**. Phones: (301)713-2390; FAX (301)713-1306.

11.417 SEA GRANT SUPPORT

Assistance: project grants (67-100 percent).

Purposes: for marine resources research, education, training, and advisory services at major university centers—for activities relevant to the oceans, Great Lakes, and the marine environment. Some institutions may obtain coherent area, institutional, and Sea Grant College support. Project examples: cardiovascular, anti-cancer, and central nervous system drugs from marine organisms; marine fouling and corrosion in seawater; marine finfish and shellfish aquaculture; seafood quality and safety; coastal erosion. Funds may not be used to purchase or construct ships or facilities.

Eligible applicants/beneficiaries: universities, colleges, junior colleges, technical schools, institutes, laboratories; any public or private corporation, partnership, or other association or entity; any state or its political subdivisions or agencies; individuals.

Range: $5,000 to $3,595,000.

Activity: FY 98, 802 projects funded.

HQ: Director, National Sea Grant College Program, NOAA-USDC, 1315 East-West Hwy., Silver Spring, MD 20910. Phone: (301)713-2448. (Note: no field offices for this program.)

11.419   COASTAL ZONE MANAGEMENT ADMINISTRATION AWARDS

Assistance: formula grants (cost sharing-to 18 months).

Purposes: to administer various elements of approved Coastal Zone Management programs, including such activities as management and protection of coastal wetlands, natural hazards management, public access improvements, reduction of marine debris, ocean resource planning, siting of coastal energy facilities.

Eligible applicants/beneficiaries: coastal states including those bordering the Great Lakes; territories.

Range: $500,000 to $2,000,000. **Average:** $1,300,000.

Activity: 32 coastal states and U.S. island territories participating.

HQ: Chief, Coastal Programs Division, Office of Ocean and Coastal Resource Management, National Ocean Service, NOAA-USDC, 1305 East-West Hwy., Silver Spring, MD 20910. Phone: (301)713-3102. (Note: no field offices for this program.)

11.420   COASTAL ZONE MANAGEMENT ESTUARINE RESEARCH RESERVES

Assistance: project grants (50 percent).

Purposes: to acquire, develop, and operate national estuarine research reserves; for data gathering, research, and educational purposes.

Eligible applicants/beneficiaries: acquisition, development, operating grants— coastal states including those bordering the Great Lakes; territories. Research or monitoring grants—qualified scientists, educators, students, and entities.

Range: $17,000 to $6,000,000; $5,000,000 maximum per sanctuary. **Average:** $100,000.

Activity: FY 99, 25 designated reserves.

HQ: Chief, Estuarine Reserves Division, Office of Ocean and Coastal Resource Management, National Ocean Service, NOAA-USDC, 1305 East-West Hwy. - 12th floor, Silver Spring, MD 20910. Phone: (301)713-3125. (Note: no field offices for this program.)

11.426   FINANCIAL ASSISTANCE FOR NATIONAL CENTERS FOR COASTAL OCEAN SCIENCE

Assistance: project grants (100 percent/to 5 years).

Purposes: for research to determine the long-term consequences of human activities affecting the coastal and marine environment; to assess the ecological, economic, and social impacts of these activities upon human, physical, and biotic environments; to define and evaluate management alternatives that minimize adverse consequences of human use of marine environments and resources.

Eligible applicants/beneficiaries: universities, colleges, technical schools, institutes, laboratories; public or private profit or nonprofit entities; state and local government agencies; individuals.

Range: $20,000 to $550,000. **Average:** $250,000.

Activity: not quantified specifically.

HQ: National Centers for Coastal Ocean Science (N/SCI), National Ocean Service, NOAA-USDC, 1305 East-West Hwy., Rockville, MD 20910. Phone: (no number provided). (Note: no field offices for this program.)

11.427   FISHERIES DEVELOPMENT AND UTILIZATION RESEARCH AND DEVELOPMENT GRANTS AND COOPERATIVE AGREEMENTS PROGRAM

Assistance: project grants (from 50 percent).

Purposes: pursuant to the Saltonstall-Kennedy Act, for research to develop and strengthen the U.S. fishing industry. Project examples: development of sustainable fisheries and aquaculture systems; studies of by-catch issues.

Eligible applicants/beneficiaries: U.S. citizens or nationals including in the territories and possessions; state and local governments. Federal employees and employees of Regional Fishery Management Councils are ineligible.

Range: $35,000 to $245,000. **Average:** $140,000.

Activity: FY 99, 28 projects recommended for funding.

HQ: Financial Services Division (F/SF2), Office of Sustainable Fisheries, NMFS-NOAA-USDC, 1315 East-West Hwy., Silver Spring, MD 20910. Phones: (301)713-2358; FAX (301)713-1939.

11.428   INTERGOVERNMENTAL CLIMATE—PROGRAM (NESDIS) ("National Environmental Satellite, Data, and Information Service" - "Regional Climate Centers")

Assistance: project grants (100 percent).

Purposes: to establish regional climate centers to supply guidance and data to the private and public sectors, and to perform research on regional climate problems.

Eligible applicants/beneficiaries: states or groups of states, public or private educational institutions, state agencies, and other persons or institutions.

Range: $293,000 for each of 6 centers.

Activity: FY 98, 6 continuation grants awarded.

HQ: National Environmental Satellite, Data, and Information Service, NOAA-USDC, Asheville, NC. Phone: (704)271-4378. (Note: the field office is the headquarters for this program.)

11.429   MARINE SANCTUARY PROGRAM

Assistance: project grants (100 percent).

Purposes: for research and educational programs in the marine sanctuary system; for enforcement activities at sanctuary sites. Project examples:

Baseline Measurements of Spatial Arrangements and Population Dynamics in Marine Sanctuary Reef Communities; Living Marine Microcosms for Public Education and for Management of Coastal Ecosystems: A Cold Water System.

Eligible applicants/beneficiaries: states, local governments, regional and interstate agencies, or other persons; nonprofit organizations for agreements to solicit private donations.

Range: $18,000 to $135,000. **Average:** $50,000.

Activity: currently, 13 designated sanctuaries.

HQ: same address/phone as **11.420**. (Note: no field offices for this program.)

11.430   UNDERSEA RESEARCH

Assistance: project grants (100 percent).

Purposes: for undersea research and development projects. Funds may be used to acquire necessary technology. Examples: Nutrient Cycling and Primary Productivity of Marine Ecosystems; diving safety and physiology research; submarine venting of liquids and gases.

Eligible applicants/beneficiaries: universities, colleges, junior colleges, technical schools, institutes, laboratories; states, political subdivisions, agencies; individuals.

Range: $15,000 to $2,226,000.

Activity: FY 97, 7 grants awarded.

HQ: Director, Office of Undersea Research, NOAA-USDC, 1315 East-West Hwy., Silver Spring, MD 20910. Phone: (301)713-2427. (Note: no field offices for this program.)

11.431   CLIMATE AND ATMOSPHERIC RESEARCH

Assistance: project grants (100 percent).

Purposes: for research and development, advisory services, and operational systems designed to establish a predictive capability for short- and long-term climate fluctuations and trends. Projects funded to date have ranged from some with a global scope to specific activities in the Indian Ocean and the S.W. Tropical Pacific Ocean.

Eligible applicants/beneficiaries: same as for **11.430**.

Range: $10,000 to $220,000. **Average:** $85,000.

Activity: FY 98, 170 grants awarded.

HQ: Director, Office of Global Programs, NOAA-USDC, 1100 Wayne Ave., Silver Spring, MD 20910. Phone: (301)427-2089. (Note: no field offices for this program.)

11.432   OFFICE OF ATMOSPHERIC RESEARCH (OAR) COOPERATIVE INSTITUTES
("OAR Cooperative Institutes")

Assistance: project grants (cost sharing/5 years).

Purposes: for research and development, education, training, advisory services, and operational systems as they relate to specific programs in the environmental sciences. Projects involve research in oceanography, atmospherics, limnology, and the solar, Arctic, near-space environments. Examples of funded projects: Subtropical Atlantic Climate Studies; Fisheries Oceanography Coordinated Investigations; National Ozone Expedition; National Acid Precipitation Assessment Program.

Eligible applicants/beneficiaries: major state universities located near NOAA environmental research laboratories.

Range: individual proposals, $3,000 to $60,000; group proposals, $60,000 to $150,000. **Average:** individual, $25,000; group, $80,000.

Activity: FY 00 estimate, 13 cooperative agreements.

HQ: Deputy Director, Environmental Research Laboratories, NOAA-USDC, 1315 East-West Hwy., Silver Spring, MD 20910. Phone: (301)713-2474, ext. 114.

11.433   MARINE FISHERIES INITIATIVE ("MARFIN")

Assistance: project grants (100 percent/to 3 years).

Purposes: for fisheries research and development projects involving harvest methods, economic analyses, processing methods, and fish stock assessment and enhancement—in the Gulf of Mexico, South Atlantic, and New England fisheries. Funded project examples: red drum population assessment; turtle excluder devices; reduction of the catch of nontarget species in shrimp trawls.

Eligible applicants/beneficiaries: state or local governments, universities, profit and nonprofit entities; individuals.

Range: $14,000 to $144,000. **Average:** $64,000.

Activity: not quantified specifically.

HQ: State/Federal Liaison Office, NMFS-NOAA-USDC, 9721 Executive Center Drive-North, St. Petersburg, FL 33702. Phone: (727)570-5324. *Or*: Northeast Regional Office, NMFS-NOAA-USDC, One Blackburn Drive, Gloucester, MA 01930. Phone: (978)281-9243. (Note: no other field offices for this program.)

11.434   COOPERATIVE FISHERY STATISTICS

Assistance: project grants (100 percent/to 3 years).

Purposes: for cooperative state-federal programs to collect, analyze, and distribute statistics on commercial and recreational fishing in the States' Territorial Sea and the U.S. Exclusive Economic Zone—supporting the Magnuson-Stevens Fishery Conservation and Management Act.

Eligible applicants/beneficiaries: fisheries conservation agencies in the southeast and Gulf states, and PR and VI.

Range: $71,000 to $185,000. **Average:** $95,000.

Activity: not quantified specifically.

HQ: State/Federal Liaison Office, NMFS-NOAA-USDC, 9721 Executive Center Drive-North, St. Petersburg, FL 33702. Phone: (813)570-5324. (Note: the field office is the headquarters for this program.)

11.435 SOUTHEAST AREA MONITORING AND ASSESSMENT PROGRAM ("SEAMAP")

Assistance: project grants (100 percent/to 3 years).

Purposes: to collect and disseminate independent information on marine fisheries, and to participate in inter-jurisdictional fisheries management programs—exclusively in the Gulf of Mexico, South Atlantic, and U.S. Caribbean.

Eligible applicants/beneficiaries: same as for **11.434**.

Range: $71,000 to $211,000. **Average:** $83,000.

Activity: not quantified specifically.

HQ: same address/phone as **11.434**. (Note: no other field offices for this program.)

11.436 COLUMBIA RIVER FISHERIES DEVELOPMENT PROGRAM

Assistance: project grants (100 percent).

Purposes: to develop measures to protect and enhance salmon and steelhead resources in the Pacific Northwest, using the facilities and personnel of state fisheries agencies. Project examples: operation and maintenance of fish hatcheries, fish ladders, fish screens, other fish passages; waterflow planning and input; studies of irrigation screens.

Eligible applicants/beneficiaries: state governments, quasi-public nonprofit organizations.

Range: $11,000,000 to $18,910,000. **Average:** $15,303,000.

Activity: FY 00 estimate, 3 awards.

HQ: Office of Operations, Management and Information, NMFS-NOAA-USDC, 1315 East-West Hwy., Silver Spring, MD 20910. Phone: (301)713-2245.

11.437 PACIFIC FISHERIES DATA PROGRAM

Assistance: project grants (100 percent).

Purposes: pursuant to the Magnuson Fishery Conservation and Management Act as amended, to enhance state fishery data collection and analysis systems to respond to Pacific coastwide fisheries management needs, including projects providing catch, effort, and economic and biological data on federally managed species.

Eligible applicants/beneficiaries: same as for **11.436**, and Guam, Samoa, and Northern Marianas.

Range: $72,000 to $1,659,000. **Average:** $866,000.

Activity: FY 00 estimate, 6 awards.

HQ: Budget Officer, same address/phone as **11.436**.

11.438 PACIFIC SALMON TREATY PROGRAM

Assistance: project grants (100 percent).

Purposes: to fund state fishery agencies to assist the U.S. in fulfilling its administrative, management, and research responsibilities under the Pacific Salmon Treaty Act.

Eligible applicants/beneficiaries: same as for **11.436**.

Range: $631,000 to $2,674,000. **Average:** $551,000.

Activity: FY 00 estimate, 4 awards.

HQ: Budget Officer, same address/phone as **11.436**.

11.439 MARINE MAMMAL DATA PROGRAM

Assistance: project grants (100 percent).

Purposes: pursuant to the Marine Mammal Act of 1972, to collect and analyze information on the abundance and distribution of marine mammals and their interactions with fisheries and other marine resources, toward the conservation of such mammals.

Eligible applicants/beneficiaries: same as for **11.436**.

Range: $288,000 to $1,575,000. **Average:** $459,000.

Activity: FY 00 estimate, 10 awards.

HQ: Budget Officer, same address/phone as **11.436**.

11.440 RESEARCH IN REMOTE SENSING OF THE EARTH AND ENVIRONMENT

Assistance: project grants (100 percent/1-5 years).

Purposes: for applied research and technology development in satellite remote sensing of the earth and the atmosphere. Project examples: climate diagnostics and radiation budget estimates; characteristics and behavior of severe weather systems.

Eligible applicants/beneficiaries: any state university, college, institute, laboratory; any public or private nonprofit institution or consortium.

Range: $20,000 to $2,000,000. **Average:** $700,000.

Activity: FY 00 estimate, 4 cooperative agreements, 15 grants.

HQ: Office of Research and Applications (E/RA), National Environmental Satellite, Data, and Information Service, NOAA-USDC, 5200 Auth Rd. - Rm.701, Camp Springs, MD 20746-4304. Phones: (no number provided); FAX (301)763-8108. (Note: no field offices for this program.)

11.441 REGIONAL FISHERY MANAGEMENT COUNCILS

Assistance: project grants (100 percent).

Purposes: pursuant to the Magnuson-Stevens Fishery Conservation and Management Act as amended, for the eight regional fishery management councils to prepare, monitor, and revise fishery management plans and data collection programs for domestic and foreign fishing within the 200-mile U.S. Exclusive Economic Zone.

Eligible applicants/beneficiaries: Regional Fishery Management Councils (New England, Mid-Atlantic, South Atlantic, Gulf of Mexico, Caribbean, Pacific, North Pacific, and Western Pacific).

Range: $618,000 to $1,399,000. **Average:** $1,070,000.

Activity: FY 98, 30 new fishery management plan amendments.

HQ: Office of Sustainable Fisheries, NMFS-NOAA-USDC, 1315 East-West Hwy., Silver Spring, MD 20910. Phone: (301)713-2334.

11.443 SHORT TERM CLIMATE FLUCTUATIONS

Assistance: project grants (95 percent).

Purposes: for studies relevant to the diagnosis and prediction of short-term climate fluctuations.

Eligible applicants/beneficiaries: public and private educational institutions; qualified institutional personnel.

Range/Average: N.A.

Activity: FY 98, 1 renewal grant.

HQ: Climate Prediction Center. National Centers for Environmental Prediction, National Weather Service NOAA-USDC, World Weather Bldg., 5200 Auth Rd., Camp Springs, MD 20746. Phone: (301)763-8000, ext. 7512. (Note: no field offices for this program.)

11.444 AQUACULTURE PROGRAM

Assistance: project grants (100 percent).

Purposes: to develop commercially feasible technology for high-value marine finfish in the U.S., toward their increased availability for aquaculture and stock enhancement in the U.S.

Eligible applicants: Oceanic Institute.

Eligible beneficiaries: general public.

Range: $452,000 to $750,000. **Average:** $601,000.

Activity: funding restricted to one applicant.

HQ: Southwest Fisheries Science Center, NMFS-NOAA-USDC, 8604 La Jolla Shores Drive, La Jolla, CA 90238-0271. Phones: (619)546-7000; FAX (619)546-7003. (Note: the field office is the headquarters for this program.)

11.445 STOCK ENHANCEMENT OF MARINE FISH IN THE STATE OF HAWAII ("SEMFISH")

Assistance: project grants (100 percent).

Purposes: to develop and test the technology of a marine stock enhancement program in Hawaii, as a management option to protect and enhance some of Hawaii's depleted near-shore fishery resources.

Eligible applicants/beneficiaries: same as for **11.444.**

Range/Average: $475,000.

Activity: funding restricted to one applicant.

HQ: same address/phones as **11.444.** (Note: no other field offices for this program.)

11.449 INDEPENDENT EDUCATION AND SCIENCE PROJECTS AND PROGRAMS
("Practical Hands-on Application to Science Education" - "PHASE")

Assistance: project grants (100 percent).

Purposes: to increase the number of minority students enrolling in college and majoring in math, science, and engineering, and to recruit scientists and engineers to serve as volunteer tutors primarily for girls and minority students. Funds are used for: student stipends, tutoring, and field trips to universities, businesses, and government facilities; advisors training.

Eligible applicants/beneficiaries: only the Colorado Minority Engineering Achievement Association/Mathematics, Engineering, Science Achievement (CMEA/MESA).

Range: grants and contracts, $5,000 to $10,000; cooperative agreements, $45,000 to $60,000.

Activity: funding limited to CMEA/MESA.

HQ: Program Officer, Environmental Research Laboratory (R/EX-4), NOAA-USDC, 325 Broadway, Boulder, CO 80303. Phone: (303)497-6731. (Note: no other field offices for this program.)

11.450   INTEGRATED FLOOD OBSERVING AND WARNING SYSTEMS ("IFLOWS")

Assistance: project grants (to 100 percent).

Purposes: for a joint undertaking by the National Weather Service and participating states to improve flood warning capabilities in the Appalachian region. Funds are used for initial capital, costs of replacement and upgrading of equipment, software development, training of county personnel, development of technical procedures, and costs of implementation personnel.

Eligible applicants/beneficiaries: only New York, Pennsylvania, West Virginia, Virginia, Kentucky, Tennessee, and North Carolina.

Range: $36,000 to $175,000. **Average:** $90,000.

Activity: FY 98, 5 cooperative agreements awarded; 182 associated participating counties.

HQ: IFLOWS Program Manager, Hydrologic Operations Division, Office of Hydrology, National Weather Service (W/OH22), NOAA-USDC, 1325 East-West Hwy., Silver Spring, MD 20910. Phone: (301)713-0006.

11.452   UNALLIED INDUSTRY PROJECTS

Assistance: project grants (to 100 percent).

Purposes: for biological, economic, sociological, public policy, and other research and administration projects benefiting the U.S. fisheries; to develop innovative approaches and methods to ensure the safety, quality, and integrity of fishery products; to develop, test, and apply new technology in molecular biology for use in the management of commercial and recreational marine fisheries, emphasizing the development of molecular genetics techniques. Project funds may support research and management activities for high-priority marine and estuarine resources, especially for species and habitats currently under or proposed for federal or interjurisdictional management.

Eligible applicants/beneficiaries: state and local governments, universities and colleges, territorial agencies, tribal governments, private profit and nonprofit research and conservation organizations, and individuals.

Range: $128,000 to $577,000. **Average:** $214,000.

Activity: not quantified specifically.

HQ: same address/phone as **11.436**.

11.454   UNALLIED MANAGEMENT PROJECTS

Assistance: project grants (to 100 percent).

Purposes: for projects supporting fisheries management and conservation activities by providing economic, sociological, public policy, and other information relating to fishery resources and protected species and their environments—in federal, state, and territorial waters. Activities are intended to benefit high-priority marine and estuarine resources, especially for species and habitats currently under or proposed for federal or interjurisdictional management.

Eligible applicants/beneficiaries: same as for **11.452.**

Range/Average: N.A.

Activity: FY 00 estimate, 2 awards.

HQ: same address/phone as **11.436.**

11.455   COOPERATIVE SCIENCE AND EDUCATION PROGRAMS

Assistance: project grants (to 100 percent).

Purposes: to support partnerships with NMFS for cooperative science and education on marine issues, especially living marine resources and their habitat, confronting local, regional, and national resources managers; to develop innovative approaches and methods for marine and estuarine science and education—through programs including: Cooperative Marine Education and Research Programs (CMER); Joint Institute for Marine Observation (JIMO); Cooperative Unit of Fisheries Education and Research (CUFER); Cooperative Institute of Fishery Oceanography (CIFO); Cooperative Education and Research Program (CERP); Cooperative Institute Agreement (CIA); Cooperative Institute for Marine Resources Studies (CIMRS); Cooperative Institute for Marine and Atmospheric Studies (CIMAS); Cooperative Institute for Arctic Research (CIFAR); Joint Institute for the Study of the Atmosphere and Oceans (JISAO).

Eligible applicants/beneficiaries: state, territorial, and private IHEs; private and public research organizations affiliated with IHEs; national and international organizations.

Range: $50,000 to $300,000. **Average:** $100,000.

Activity: not quantified specifically.

HQ: Senior Scientist, NMFS-NOAA-USDC, 1315 East-West Hwy., Silver Spring, MD 20910. Phone: (301)713-2239.

11.457   CHESAPEAKE BAY STUDIES

Assistance: project grants (to 100 percent).

Purposes: to execute a bay-wide plan for the assessment of commercially, recreationally, and selected ecologically important fish and shellfish resources in the Chesapeake Bay; for fishery habitat and management planning in cooperation with EPA.

Eligible applicants/beneficiaries: state and local governments, IHEs, private profit and nonprofit research and conservation organizations.

Range: $20,000 to $461,000. **Average:** $130,000.

Activity: not quantified specifically.

HQ: Budget Officer, same address/phone as **11.436**.

11.458 ALASKA SALMON ENHANCEMENT

Assistance: project grants (50-100 percent/to 3 years).

Purposes: for the State of Alaska for salmon enhancement efforts supplementing the stock rehabilitation initiative mandated by (1) the Pacific Salmon Treaty (50 percent funding), and (2) by the 1989 and 1990 Understandings between the United States and Canadian Sections of the Pacific Salmon Commission concerning Joint Enhancement of Transboundary River Salmon Stocks (100 percent funding).

Eligible applicants/beneficiaries: only the State of Alaska.

Range/Average: $380,000.

Activity: only Alaska receives funds.

HQ: Budget Officer, same address as **11.436**. Phone: (301)713-2455.

11.459 CLIMATE AND AIR QUALITY RESEARCH

Assistance: project grants (100 percent).

Purposes: for research and development, advisory services, and operational systems designed to establish a predictive capability for short- and long-term climate and air quality fluctuations and trends.

Eligible applicants/beneficiaries: universities, colleges, junior colleges, technical schools, institutes, laboratories; states, political subdivisions, agencies; individuals.

Range: from $2,000.

Activity: 1-3 contracts per year.

HQ: Director, National Acid Precipitation Assessment Program, Office of Oceanic and Atmospheric Research, NOAA-USDC, 1315 East-West Hwy., Silver Spring, MD 20910. Phones: (301)713-0197, ext. 159. (Note: no field offices for this program.)

11.460 SPECIAL OCEANIC AND ATMOSPHERIC PROJECTS

Assistance: project grants (100 percent).

Purposes: for research and development, education and training, advisory services, and operational systems—based on NOAA special announcements relating to oceanic and atmospheric resources.

Eligible applicants/beneficiaries: organizations and individuals specified in NOAA special announcements.

Range/Average: N.A.

Activity: not quantified specifically.

HQ: Director, OAR, Office of Scientific Support, same address/phone as **11.432**.

11.462 HYDROLOGIC RESEARCH

Assistance: project grants (to 100 percent).

Purposes: for research and development on issues relating to the forecasting of surface hydrologic conditions. Project examples: automated calibration of hydrologic models; flash flood guidance procedures and models.

Eligible applicants/beneficiaries: IHEs, state and local government agencies, quasi-public institutions such as water supply or power companies, and hydrologic consultants and companies.

Range: $5,000 to $100,000. **Average:** $25,000.

Activity: FY 98, 8 cooperative agreements.

HQ: Deputy Chief, Hydrologic Research Laboratory, National Weather Service (W/OH1), NOAA-USDC, 1325 East-West Hwy., Silver Spring, MD 20910. Phone: (301)713-0640. (Note: no field offices for this program.)

11.463 HABITAT CONSERVATION

Assistance: project grants (75-100 percent).

Purposes: for biological, economic, sociological, public policy, and other research, and for administration and public education activities relating to marine and estuarine habitats, especially for species currently under or proposed for federal or interjurisdictional management. Funds may be used for related construction and management activities.

Eligible applicants/beneficiaries: same as for **11.452**.

Range/Average: N.A.

Activity: FY 97, 6 awards.

HQ: Office of Habitat Conservation (FHC3), NOAA-USDC, 1315 East-West Hwy., Silver Spring, MD 20910. Phone: (301)713-0174.

11.467 METEOROLOGIC AND HYDROLOGIC MODERNIZATION DEVELOPMENT
("Hydrometeorological Development")

Assistance: formula grants; project grants (to 100 percent); direct payments/specified use; direct payments/unrestricted use; technical information; training.

Purposes: to maintain a cooperative university-federal partnership to conduct meteorological training, education, professional development, and research and development on hydrometeorological issues. Funding supports the Cooperative Program for Operational Meteorology, Education and Training (COMET).

Eligible applicants/beneficiaries: IHEs and consortia, state or local government agencies including school systems, quasi-public institutions, consultants, companies.

Range: $15,000 to $4,000,000. **Average:** $24,000

Activity: FY 98, 14 projects funded; 6 fellowship projects.

HQ: Director, Office of Meteorology, National Weather Service (W/OM), NOAA-USDC, 1325 East-West Hwy., Silver Spring, MD 20910. Phones: (301)713-1970, ext. 194; FAX (301)713-1520. (Note: no field offices for this program.)

11.468 COOPERATIVE INSTITUTE FOR APPLIED METEOROLOGICAL STUDIES (CIAMS) AND COOPERATIVE INSTITUTE FOR TROPICAL METEOROLOGY (CITM)

Assistance: project grants (to 100 percent).

Purposes: for applied meteorological and hydrological research by faculty and students for the National Weather Service, including in the areas of Doppler radar, training, and agriculture. Project examples: training manual for marine forecasters; symposium on marine meteorology; papers on agricultural dew forecasting.

Eligible applicants/beneficiaries: only Texas A&M University and Florida State University.

Range: $120,000 to $150,000. **Average:** $133,000.

Activity: 2 programs funded.

HQ: CIAMS/CITM Program Manager, Southern Region Headquarters, National Weather Service, NOAA-USDC, 819 Taylor St. - Rm.10A26, Fort Worth, TX 76102. Phone: (817)978-2671. (Note: no other field offices for this program.)

11.469 CONGRESSIONALLY IDENTIFIED CONSTRUCTION PROJECTS

Assistance: project grants (to 100 percent).

Purposes: for the construction of facilities to support education, research, and development associated with issues of the atmospheric and marine sciences.

Eligible applicants/beneficiaries: state and local governments, universities and colleges, quasi-governmental agencies, private profit and nonprofit organizations, and individuals.

Range: $140,000 to $14,205,000.

Activity: FY 99, 2 awards.

HQ: Program Officer, Congressionally Identified Construction Projects, (OFA5X1 - SSMC4), NOAA-USDC, 1305 East-West Hwy., Silver Spring, MD 20910. Phone: (301)713-1142. (Note: no field offices for this program.)

11.470 OFFICE OF ADMINISTRATION SPECIAL PROGRAMS

Assistance: project grants (100 percent).

Purposes: to identify, develop, and encourage minority students to pursue graduate degrees and careers in the atmospheric, environmental, and related sciences. Funds may support curriculum and faculty development, student research, and similar activities; scholarships may be awarded.

Eligible applicants/beneficiaries: Historically Black Colleges and Universities.

Range/Average: $225,000.

Activity: not quantified specifically.

HQ: Chief Scientist, NOAA-USDC, Hoover Bldg. - Rm.5128, 14th & Constitution Ave. NW, Washington, DC 20230. Phone: (202)482-2977. (Note: no field offices for this program.)

11.472 UNALLIED SCIENCE PROGRAM

Assistance: project grants (to 100 percent).

Purposes: for biological, socio-economic, and physical science research on the stocks of U.S. fishery and protected resources and their environment, contributing to their optimal management; to develop innovative approaches and methods for marine and estuarine science.

Eligible applicants/beneficiaries: same as for **11.452**.

Range/Average: N.A.

Activity: not quantified specifically.

HQ: same address/phone as **11.436**.

11.473 COASTAL SERVICES CENTER ("CSC")

Assistance: project grants (100 percent/1-3 years).

Purposes: to develop a science-based, multi-dimensional approach allowing for the maintenance or improvement of environmental quality while allowing for economic growth. Funds may be used for: fellowships and apprenticeships; facilitation and mediation activities; training materials development and information dissemination; development of geographic information system and tabular and spatial data bases; commercialization of related advanced environmental technologies; to generate, archive, interpret, and validate aircraft, satellite, and other remotely sensed data and derived products; related purposes.

Eligible applicants/beneficiaries: state and local governments; public institutions and organizations.

Range: $38,000 to $235,000.

Activity: FY 98, 5 grants awarded.

HQ: Assistant Administrator, National Ocean Service, NOAA-USDC, 1305 East-West Hwy., Silver Spring, MD 20910. Phone: (301)713-3074.

11.474 ATLANTIC COAST FISHERIES COOPERATIVE MANAGEMENT ACT

Assistance: project grants (to 100 percent).

Purposes: for the development, implementation, and enforcement of effective interstate conservation and management plans pertaining to Atlantic Coastal fishery resources, and for activities required by such plans including: collection, management, and analysis of fishery data; law enforcement; habitat conservation; fishery research and management planning.

Eligible applicants/beneficiaries: Atlantic States Marine Fisheries Commission; Atlantic Coast state governments; Potomac River Fisheries Commission; DC.

Range/Average: N.A.

Activity: not quantified specifically.

HQ: same address/phone as **11.405**.

11.477   FISHERIES DISASTER RELIEF

Assistance: project grants (75 percent).

Purposes: to assess the effects of commercial fishery failures caused by natural or man-made disasters; to restore fisheries or prevent future failures; to assist communities affected by the failures. Funded activities may not expand assisted commercial fishery failures.

Eligible applicants/beneficiaries: state agencies; fishing communities including vessel owners, operators, crew; fish processors.

Range/Average: N.A.

Activity: new program in FY 99.

HQ: same address/phone as **11.427**.

11.478   COASTAL OCEAN PROGRAM ("COP")

Assistance: project grants (100 percent/1-3 years).

Purposes: to provide a predictive capability for managing coastal ecosystems, including in Great Lakes areas. Funds support research and inter-agency initiatives in coastal ecosystem oceanography, cumulative coastal impacts, and forecasting coastal and natural hazards

Eligible applicants/beneficiaries: same as for **11.459**.

Range: $25,000 to $1,000,000. **Average:** $375,000.

Activity: new program in FY 98.

HQ: Deputy Director, Coastal Ocean Program, NOAA-USDC, 1315 East-West Hwy. - Rm.9608, Silver Spring, MD 20910. Phones: (301)713-3338; FAX (301)713-4044. (Note: no field offices for this program.)

11.480   NATIONAL OCEAN SERVICE INTERN PROGRAM

Assistance: project grants (100 percent/3 years).

Purposes: to establish internship programs providing opportunities for cooperative study, research and development—to increase the number and diversity of skilled engineers, scientists, and managers in the environmental arena, skilled with the techniques and technologies used by the National Ocean Service. Funds may support: recruitment and evaluation of candidates; stipends for a maximum of two years.

Eligible applicants: nonprofit organizations.

Eligible beneficiaries: recent college graduates.

Range: $40,000 to $1,500,000/year to support 1-50 interns.

Activity: new program in FY 99; 7 internships supported.

HQ: Special Projects Office, National Ocean Service, NOAA-USDC, 1305 East-West Hwy. - 9th floor, Silver Spring, MD 20910. Phone: (301)713-3000, ext. 132. (Note: no field offices for this program.)

NATIONAL TELECOMMUNICATIONS AND INFORMATION ADMINISTRATION

11.550   PUBLIC TELECOMMUNICATIONS FACILITIES—PLANNING AND CONSTRUCTION
("PTFP")

Assistance: project grants (75-100 percent/to 2 years).

Purposes: to plan, acquire, install, or modernize public telecommunications facilities. Funds may be used to pay for apparatus needed for production, dissemination, interconnection, and reception of noncommercial educational and cultural radio and television programs—but not for buildings, land, operating, or indirect expenses. Planning grants may cover 100 percent of costs; construction, 75 percent. Special consideration is given to applications for facilities involving ownership, operation, and participation by minorities and women.

Eligible applicants/beneficiaries: public or noncommercial educational broadcast stations; noncommercial telecommunications entities; public telecommunications systems; nonprofit foundations, corporations, institutions, or associations organized primarily for education or cultural purposes; state, local, tribal governmental agencies; state political or special purpose subdivisions. Available also in territories.

Range: $3,000 to $978,000. **Average:** $173,000.

Activity: FY 99, 252 applications filed.

HQ: Director, Public Telecommunications Facilities Program, Office of Telecommunications and Information Applications, NTIA-USDC, 1401 Constitution Ave. NW - Rm.4625, Washington, DC 20230. Phone: (202)482-5802. (Note: no field offices for this program.)

11.552   TELECOMMUNICATIONS AND INFORMATION INFRASTRUCTURE ASSISTANCE PROGRAM
("TIIAP")

Assistance: project grants (50-75 percent/1-3 years).

Purposes: to develop a nationwide, interactive, multimedia telecommunications infrastructure accessible to both urban and rural areas. Funding supports projects that: improve cultural, educational, training, health care, and public health resources; reduce costs; promote public safety services; improve the effectiveness and efficiency of government services; foster communication, resource sharing, and economic development within rural and urban communities.

Eligible applicants/beneficiaries: state, local, and tribal governments; universities and colleges; nonprofit entities.

Range: $46,000 to $625,000. **Average:** $402,000.

Activity: FY 98, 46 grants awarded.

HQ: Director, Telecommunications and Information Infrastructure Assistance Program, Office of Telecommunications and Information Applications,

NTIA-USDC, 1401 Constitution Ave. NW - Rm.4092, Washington, DC 20230. Phone: (202)482-2048. (Note: no field offices for this program.)

NATIONAL INSTITUTE OF STANDARDS AND TECHNOLOGY

11.601 CALIBRATION PROGRAM

Assistance: technical information.

Purposes: to maintain a national consistent system of physical measurements used for assurance of interchangeability and uniformity of manufactured items, for process control, for informational and scientific purposes, and for fairness and objectivity in commerce and regulation. Fees are charged for tests and calibrations.

Eligible applicants/beneficiaries: state and local governments, academic institutions, laboratories, industrial firms, corporations, individuals.

Activity: FY 99 estimate, 12,000 tests conducted for 850 organizations.

HQ: Chief, Calibration Program, NIST-USDC, 100 Bureau Drive, Gaithersburg, MD 20899-2330. Phones: (301)975-2002; FAX (301)869-3548; e-mail, calibrations@nist.gov (Note: no field offices for this program.)

11.603 NATIONAL STANDARD REFERENCE DATA SYSTEM ("NSRDS")

Assistance: technical information; project grants (100 percent/1-2 years).

Purposes: to provide evaluated scientific and technical data on the chemical and physical properties of substances to scientists, engineers, and the general public. Publications and data bases may be purchased, subject to copyright restrictions.

Eligible applicants/beneficiaries: research grants—technical groups in universities, industrial laboratories, research establishments. Data compilations and data bases—general public.

Range: to $400,000.

Activity: annually, some 30 publications and computerized data bases issued.

HQ: Standard Reference Data Program, NIST-USDC, 100 Bureau Drive, Gaithersburg, MD 20899-2310. Phones: (301)975-2200; FAX (301)926-0416; Internet, http://www.nist.gov/srd

11.604 STANDARD REFERENCE MATERIALS ("SRM")

Assistance: technical information.

Purposes: to develop accurate methods of analysis and to calibrate measurement systems, through the certification and dissemination of reference materials used to: facilitate the exchange of goods; institute quality control; determine material performance characteristics; measure materials at state-of-the-art limits; assure the long-term adequacy and integrity of measurement quality assurance programs. Materials are used as primary reference measurement standards for such purposes as: clinical laboratories testing; monitoring of air, water, and low-level radioactive pollution; quality control in the production of basic materials such as steel, rubber, cement, and plastics. Materials may be purchased from NIST.

Eligible applicants/beneficiaries: federal agencies, state and local governments, societies, institutions, firms, corporations, individuals.

Activity: FY 00 estimate, sales of 36,000 units.

HQ: Standard Reference Materials Program, NIST-USDC, Bldg. 202 - Rm. 112, 100 Bureau Dr., Gaithersburg, MD 20899-2320. Phones: (301)975-2021; FAX (301)926-4342; e-mail, srminfo@nist.gov

11.606 WEIGHTS AND MEASURES SERVICE

Assistance: advisory services/counseling; specialized services; technical information.

Purposes: to provide education, publications, technical and other assistance, and training to states, devices and measures manufacturers, the packaging industry, and others—concerning weights and measures operations, development of model laws and regulations, upgrading of state laboratories, administration of device evaluation, and promotion of a uniform national weights and measures system.

Eligible applicants/beneficiaries: states, political subdivisions, private industry, general public.

Activity: not quantified specifically.

HQ: Chief, Weights and Measures Program, NIST-USDC, Gaithersburg, MD 20899. Phone: (301)975-4004. (Note: no field offices for this program.)

11.609 MEASUREMENT AND ENGINEERING RESEARCH AND STANDARDS

Assistance: project grants (100 percent).

Purposes: for scientific research for measurement and engineering research and standards, in such areas as advanced ceramics, fire prevention, building construction, precision measurement, automated manufacturing.

Eligible applicants/beneficiaries: universities, colleges, professional institutes and associations, nonprofit organizations, state and local governments.

Range: N.A.

Activity: FY 00 estimate, 36 grant awards.

HQ: NIST-USDC, Gaithersburg, MD 20899. Phone: (no number provided). (Note: no field offices for this program.)

11.610 NATIONAL CENTER FOR STANDARDS AND CERTIFICATION INFORMATION ("NCSCI")

Assistance: technical information.

Purposes: to serve as an information center and referral service, maintaining a reference collection of standards and specifications, regulations, certification rules, directories, reference books, special publications, copyrights, lending restrictions, and similar data; information relating to foreign trade. NCSCI does not analyze, evaluate, translate, or interpret standards. Published directories, indexes, and bibliographies are available from GPO, NTIS, and NCSCI.

Eligible applicants/beneficiaries: state and local governments; private, public, profit and nonprofit organizations; individuals.

Activity: not quantified specifically.

HQ: Standards Information Program, Office of Standards Services, NIST-USDC, 100 Bureau Dr., Gaithersburg, MD 20899-2150. Phones: (301)975-4040; FAX (301)926-1559; e-mail, ncsci@nist.gov   (Note: no field offices for this program.)

11.611   MANUFACTURING EXTENSION PARTNERSHIP

Assistance: project grants (50 percent); technical information.

Purposes: to establish and maintain extension centers and services for the transfer of advanced manufacturing technology based on NIST's and other research, to smaller U.S. manufacturing firms. Funding may support: demonstrations, technology transfer, and short-term loans of advanced manufacturing equipment especially to firms with fewer than 500 employees; statewide planning and pilot testing projects.

Eligible applicants/beneficiaries: for extension services—U.S. nonprofit institutions, organizations. Planning and pilot services grants—state and local governments, state-affiliated nonprofit organizations, consortia.

Range: planning and testing, $25,000 to $100,000; extension centers, $200,000 to $7,000.000.

Activity: FY 97, 18 grants.

HQ: Director, Manufacturing Extension Partnership, NIST-USDC, 100 Bureau Drive, Gaithersburg, MD 20899-4800. Phone: (301)975-5020. (Note: no field offices for this program.)

11.612   ADVANCED TECHNOLOGY PROGRAM
("ATP")

Assistance: project grants (from 40 percent/3-5 years).

Purposes: to assist U.S. businesses in creating and applying competitive generic technology and research results necessary to rapidly commercialize significant new discoveries and technologies, and to refine manufacturing technologies. Project examples: printed wiring board; flat panel display; magneto-resistive random access memories; deep ultraviolet lasers; high temperature superconducting material processes.

Eligible applicants/beneficiaries: U.S. businesses, joint research and development ventures, certain foreign-owned businesses. Universities, governmental entities, and nonprofit independent research organizations may participate in joint ventures that include at least two profit companies.

Range: $482,000 to $31,500,000. **Average:** $3,200,000.

Activity: since 1990 program inception, 431 awards.

HQ: Director, Advanced Technology Program, NIST-USDC, 100 Bureau Drive, Gaithersburg, MD 20899-4700. Phones: (301)975-5187; FAX (301) 869-1150; *for application kit*, (800)ATP-FUND; e-mail, atp@nist.gov (Note: no field offices for this program.)

11.614   EXPERIMENTAL PROGRAM TO STIMULATE COMPETITIVE TECHNOLOGY ("EPSCoT")

Assistance: project grants (50-75 percent/to 3 years).

Purposes: to build statewide institutional capacity to support commercialization of technology in eligible jurisdictions, through partnerships between state and local governments, community institutions and organizations, and the private sector.

Eligible applicants/beneficiaries: state, local, or tribal governments; community colleges, universities; profit or nonprofit organizations, industry councils, technology centers, business incubators—and combinations of thereof, within Alabama, Arkansas, Idaho, Kansas, Kentucky, Louisiana, Maine, Mississippi, Montana, Nevada, New Hampshire, North Dakota, Oklahoma, South Carolina, South Dakota, Vermont, West Virginia, Wyoming, or Puerto Rico.

Range: $70,000 to $300,000.

Activity: new program listing in 1999.

HQ: Director, EPSCoT, NIST-USDC, 1401 Constitution Ave. NW - Rm.4418, Washington, DC 20230. Phones: (202)482-1320; FAX (202)219-8667; e-mail, epscot@ta.doc.gov ; Web, http://ta/dpc/gov/epscot (Note: no field offices for this program.)

NATIONAL TECHNICAL INFORMATION SERVICE

11.650   NATIONAL TECHNICAL INFORMATION SERVICE ("NTIS")

Assistance: technical information.

Purposes: to serve as the principal source for the sale of federally-sponsored technological and technical information products, services, research and engineering reports, register of research in progress, machine-processable data files, computer programs. NTIS operates the FedWorld Information Network and the Government Information Locator Service which provide government-wide public information retrieval, and the National Audio-visual Center, which distributes videotapes, slide sets, and multimedia kits—covering subjects ranging from foreign languages and history to law enforcement and natural resources. Fees are charged, supporting a revolving fund.

Eligible applicants/beneficiaries: any U.S. and most foreign organizations or individuals.

Activity: FY 98, 1,336,000 products distributed.

IIQ: Director, NTIS-USDC, Forbes - Rm.200, 5285 Port Royal Rd., Springfield, VA 22161. Phones: (703)605-6400; *Sales Division,* (800)553-6847; e-mail, orders@ntis.fedworld.gov (Note: no field offices for this program.)

OFFICE OF THE SECRETARY

11.702 INTERNSHIP PROGRAM FOR POSTSECONDARY STUDENTS

Assistance: project grants (100 percent/3 years).

Purposes: to aid and promote experiential training activities through internships fostering future employment at USDC or the federal government in general—primarily in the Washington, DC area.

Eligible applicants: 2- and 4-year universities and colleges and nonprofit organizations.

Eligible beneficiaries: U.S citizens enrolled as postsecondary students.

Range: $214,000 to $313,000. **Average:** $272,000.

Activity: new program listing in 1999. FY 99, 117 internships.

HQ: Office of Executive Assistance Management, USDC, Washington, DC 20230. Phone: (202)482-1445. (Note: no field offices for this program.)

MINORITY BUSINESS DEVELOPMENT AGENCY

11.800 MINORITY BUSINESS DEVELOPMENT CENTERS ("MBDC")

Assistance: project grants (85 percent/1-3 years).

Purposes: for the operation of MBDCs—i.e., organizations offering management and technical assistance in all phases of business development and management by existing or proposed minority firms. No loans are offered to businesses. Client service fees may be charged.

Eligible applicants/beneficiaries: state and local governments, tribes, educational institutions, nonprofit and profit organizations, individuals.

Range: $165,000 to $1,200,000. **Average:** $233,000.

Activity: FY 98, MBDCs in some 50 locations received grants; assistance provided to 11,000 clients that, in turn, obtained $195,900,000 in financial packages and over $333,600,000 in procurement contracts.

HQ: Chief, Field Coordination Division, MBDA-USDC, 14th & Constitution Ave. NW - Rm.5079, Washington, DC 20230. Phone: (202)482-6022.

11.801 NATIVE AMERICAN PROGRAM ("NAP")

Assistance: project grants (100 percent/1-3 years).

Purposes: for eight Native American Business Development Centers (NABDCs) to provide management and technical assistance of all types to new or existing American Indian businesses. No loans or grants are awarded to businesses under this program; however, businesses may be helped in obtaining financial assistance for their operations.

Eligible applicants/beneficiaries: same as for **11.800**.

Range: $169,000 to $311,000. **Average:** $187,000.

Activity: FY 98, 1,237 clients obtained $26,300,000 in financial packages and $37,900,000 in procurement contracts.

HQ: same address/phone as **11.800**.

11.802   MINORITY BUSINESS DEVELOPMENT

Assistance: project grants (100 percent/1-3 years).

Purposes: for activities advocating the expansion of opportunities for minority business firms, by: identifying and developing private markets and capital sources; expanding business information and business services through trade associations; promoting and supporting the mobilization of resources of federal, state, and local governments at the local level. Some cost-sharing may be required.

Eligible applicants/beneficiaries: established businesses; professional, trade associations; individuals; chambers of commerce.

Range: $5,000 to $550,000. **Average:** $102,000.

Activity: not quantified specifically.

HQ: same address/phone as **11.800**.

PATENT AND TRADEMARK OFFICE

11.900   PATENT AND TRADEMARK TECHNICAL INFORMATION DISSEMINATION

Assistance: technical information.

Purposes: to support the growth of American commerce and technology through the utilization and dissemination of technical information available through patents and trademarks, and for the maintenance of public search centers. The office examines patent and trademark applications, and grants patents and approves trademarks when legal requirements are met. Fees are charged for services.

Eligible applicants/beneficiaries: general public.

Activity: annually (representative), processing of some 900,000 customer requests for general patent and trademark information; 2,000,000 new references filed.

HQ: Patent and Trademark Office-USDC, Washington, DC 20231. *Public search room*: Patent and Trademark Office Headquarters, 2021 South Clark Place, Arlington, VA. Phones: (703)308-4357; (800)786-9199; Web, www.uspto.gov

DEPARTMENT OF DEFENSE

DEFENSE LOGISTICS AGENCY

12.002 PROCUREMENT TECHNICAL ASSISTANCE FOR BUSINESS FIRMS ("PTA")

Assistance: project grants (50-75 percent).

Purposes: to establish and operate new or existing procurement technical assistance programs to assist business firms in selling their goods and services to DOD, other federal agencies, and state and local governments.

Eligible applicants/beneficiaries: state and local governments, private non-profit organizations, and tribal organizations including profit or nonprofit economic enterprises.

Range: $30,000 to $300,000. **Average:** $160,000.

Activity: FY 99 estimate, 66 cooperative agreements.

HQ: Office of Small and Disadvantaged Business Utilization (DDAS), Defense Logistics Agency-DOD, 8725 John J. Kingman Rd. - Ste.2533, Ft. Belvoir, VA 22060-6221. Phone: (703)767-1650. (Note: no field offices for this program.)

DEPARTMENT OF THE ARMY, OFFICE OF THE CHIEF OF ENGINEERS

12.100 AQUATIC PLANT CONTROL

Assistance: specialized services; technical information.

Purposes: to assist in controlling and eradicating obnoxious aquatic plants in rivers, harbors, and allied waters. Localities must provide 50 percent matching funds.

Eligible applicants/beneficiaries: states, political subdivisions or instrumentalities.

Activity: FY 98, planning and control operations in 18 states, PR, and DC.

HQ: Commander, U.S. Army Corps of Engineers - Attn: CECW-ON, DOD, Washington, DC 20314-1000. Phone: (202)272-0247.

12.101 BEACH EROSION CONTROL PROJECTS ("Small Beach Erosion Control Projects")

Assistance: specialized services.

Purposes: to design and construct beach and shore erosion control projects not specifically authorized by Congress. The Corps funds the first $100,000 in planning costs, and 50 percent of additional study costs; cost-sharing is required for construction, with a $2,000,000 maximum federal share.

Eligible applicants/beneficiaries: states, political subdivisions, other authorized local agencies.

Activity: FY 98, 11 construction projects.

HQ: U.S. Army Corps of Engineers - Attn: CECW-PM, DOD, Washington, DC 20314-1000. Phone: (202)761-1975.

12.102 EMERGENCY REHABILITATION OF FLOOD CONTROL WORKS OR FEDERALLY AUTHORIZED COASTAL PROTECTION WORKS ("Public Law 84-99, Code 300 Program")

Assistance: specialized services.

Purposes: to assist in the emergency repair or restoration of flood control works damaged by flood, or federally authorized hurricane flood and shore protection works damaged by extraordinary wind, wave, or water action. Nonfederal sources must provide 20 percent of project costs.

Eligible applicants/beneficiaries: owners of damaged flood protective works, or state and local public entities responsible for their maintenance, repair, and operation.

Activity: 1993 floods resulted in over 200 projects to date.

HQ: Commander, U.S. Army Corps of Engineers - Attn: CECW-OE, DOD, Washington, DC 20314-1000. Phone: (202)272-0251.

12.103 EMERGENCY OPERATIONS FLOOD RESPONSE AND POST FLOOD RESPONSE ("Public Law 84-99 Code 200 Program")

Assistance: specialized services.

Purposes: to provide emergency assistance in all phases of flood fighting, and post-flood response and rescue operations in times of flood or coastal storm.

Eligible applicants/beneficiaries: state or local public agencies.

Activity: annually, 50 to 250 operations.

HQ: same address/phone as **12.102.**

12.104 FLOOD PLAIN MANAGEMENT SERVICES ("FPMS")

Assistance: advisory services/counseling; technical information.

Purposes: to promote recognition of flood hazards in land and water use planning and development, by providing and interpreting historical data maintained by the Corps on floods and flood plains areas subject to flooding and flood losses from streams, lakes, and oceans. Services are available to states and local governments without charge; fees are charged to private parties.

Eligible applicants/beneficiaries: states, political subdivisions, general public.

Activity: annually, 32,000 responses to requests.

HQ: U.S. Army Corps of Engineers - Attn: CECW-PF, DOD, Washington, DC 20314-1000. Phone: (202)761-0169.

12.105 PROTECTION OF ESSENTIAL HIGHWAYS, HIGHWAY BRIDGE APPROACHES, AND PUBLIC WORKS ("Emergency Bank Protection")

Assistance: specialized services.

Purposes: to design and construct projects protecting highways, highway bridges, essential public works, churches, hospitals, schools, and other nonprofit public services endangered by flood-caused erosion. Federal costs may not exceed $1,000,000 per project; local cost sharing usually is required.

Eligible applicants/beneficiaries: states, political subdivisions, other responsible local agencies.

Activity: FY 98, 100 construction projects.

HQ: same address/phone as **12.101**.

12.106 FLOOD CONTROL PROJECTS ("Small Flood Control Projects")

Assistance: specialized services.

Purposes: to design and construct flood control projects not specifically authorized by Congress. The federal cost limit is $5,000,000 per project, with a local cost sharing requirement.

Eligible applicants/beneficiaries: same as for **12.105**.

Activity: FY 98, 56 construction projects.

HQ: same address/phone as **12.101**.

12.107 NAVIGATION PROJECTS ("Small Navigation Projects")

Assistance: specialized services.

Purposes: to design and construct small general navigation projects not specifically authorized by Congress. The federal cost limit is $4,000,000 per project, with a local cost sharing requirement.

Eligible applicants/beneficiaries: same as for **12.105**.

Activity: FY 98, 13 construction projects.

HQ: same address/phone as **12.101**.

12.108 SNAGGING AND CLEARING FOR FLOOD CONTROL ("Section 208")

Assistance: specialized services.

Purposes: to design and construct snagging and clearing projects for flood control. The federal cost limit is $500,000 per project, with a requirement for local cost sharing.

Eligible applicants/beneficiaries: same as for **12.105**.

Activity: FY 98, no construction projects.

HQ: same address/phone as **12.101**.

12.109 PROTECTION, CLEARING AND STRAIGHTENING CHANNELS ("Section 3 Emergency Dredging Projects")

Assistance: specialized services.

Purposes: for the emergency protection, clearing, and straightening of navigation channels in rivers, harbors, and other waterways, including for flood control purposes. Local cost sharing is required.

Eligible applicants/beneficiaries: same as for **12.105**.

Activity: no current projects.

HQ: Commander, U.S. Army Corps of Engineers - Attn: CECW-OD, DOD, Washington, DC 20314-1000. Phone: (202)272-8835.

12.110 PLANNING ASSISTANCE TO STATES ("Section 22")

Assistance: specialized services.

Purposes: to cooperate with states in preparing comprehensive plans for the development, utilization, or conservation of water and related land resources of drainage basins. No state may receive more than $300,000 in assistance in any one year; 50 percent cost sharing is required.

Eligible applicants/beneficiaries: states, tribes, territories.

Activity: FY 98, assistance to 25 states, 5 territories, 3 tribes.

HQ: same address/phone as **12.104**.

12.111 EMERGENCY ADVANCE MEASURES FOR FLOOD PREVENTION ("Public Law 84-99 Code 500 Program")

Assistance: specialized services.

Purposes: to provide assistance when there is an immediate threat of unusual flooding, including such work as removal of waterway obstructions, dam failure prevention, and work necessary to prepare for abnormal snowmelt.

Eligible applicants/beneficiaries: state governors.

Activity: not quantified specifically.

HQ: same address/phone as **12.102**.

12.112 PAYMENTS TO STATES IN LIEU OF REAL ESTATE TAXES

Assistance: formula grants (100 percent).

Purposes: to compensate local taxing units for 75 percent of real estate taxes lost as the result of U.S. acquisition of land for flood control, navigation, hydroelectric power projects, and allied purposes. Funds must be expended for certain public purposes.

Eligible applicants: state governments.

Eligible beneficiaries: state, county governments.

Range/Average: N.A.

Activity: not quantified specifically.

HQ: Headquarters - Attn: CERM-FC, U.S. Army Corps of Engineers, DOD, 20 Massachusetts Ave. NW, Washington, DC 20314-1000. Phone: (202)272-1931. (Note: no field offices for this program.)

12.113   STATE MEMORANDUM OF AGREEMENT PROGRAM FOR THE REIMBURSEMENT OF TECHNICAL SERVICES ("DSMOA")

Assistance: project grants (100 percent/2 years).

Purposes: pursuant to CERCLA, to reimburse states for costs incurred to provide technical services in support of the DOD Environmental Restoration Program, in cleaning up DOD hazardous wastes sites.

Eligible applicants: state, territorial governments.

Eligible beneficiaries: state, local, territorial governments; public, private, nonprofit and profit organizations.

Range: $104,000 to $11,400,000.

Activity: as of FY 98, 44 states and 4 territories participating.

HQ: Corps of Engineers, CEMP-RI, DOD, 20 Massachusetts Ave. NW, Washington, DC 20314. Phone: (202)504-4950. (Note: no field offices for this program.)

12.114   COLLABORATIVE RESEARCH AND DEVELOPMENT ("Construction Productivity Advanced Research Program" - "CPAR")

Assistance: project grants (50 percent).

Purposes: to improve construction productivity through research and development and application of advanced technologies involving collaborative projects, field demonstrations, licensing agreements, and other means of commercialization and technology transfer. Corps laboratories must perform a significant portion of projects.

Eligible applicants/beneficiaries: any U.S. private firm including corporations, partnerships, and industrial development organizations; public and private foundations; nonprofit organizations; units of state or local government; academic institutions; and, others.

Range: $200,000 to $900,000. **Average:** $400,000.

Activity: as of FY 98, 76 projects.

HQ: Headquarters - Attn: CERD-C, U.S. Army Corps of Engineers, DOD, 20 Massachusetts Ave. NW, Washington, DC 20314-1000. Phone: (202)272-1846.

DEPARTMENT OF THE NAVY, OFFICE OF NAVAL RESEARCH

12.300   BASIC AND APPLIED SCIENTIFIC RESEARCH

Assistance: project grants (100 percent).

Purposes: for basic and applied research in the physical, mathematical, environmental, engineering, and life sciences leading to the improvement of naval operations; for programs encouraging careers in those disciplines by supporting outstanding graduate, undergraduate, and high school students; to increase the number of graduates from under-represented minority groups; to assist universities to buy major high-cost research equipment; for symposia.

Eligible applicants/beneficiaries: nonprofit private and public educational institutions and other research organizations.

Range: $1,000 to $15,000,000. **Average:** $111,000.

Activity: FY 99 estimate, 1,200 new grants.

HQ: Office of Naval Research (ONR 22), DOD, 800 N. Quincy St., Arlington, VA 22217-5000. Phone: (703)696-2578. (Note: no field offices for this program.)

DEPARTMENT OF THE NAVY, NAVAL SURFACE WARFARE CENTER

12.301   BASIC AND APPLIED SCIENTIFIC RESEARCH

Assistance: project grants (100 percent).

Purposes: for basic and applied research in the physical, mathematical, environmental, engineering, and life sciences leading to the improvement of naval operations. Project example: chemical and biological sensors.

Eligible applicants/beneficiaries: same as for **12.300**.

Range: $10,000 to $10,000,000. **Average:** $100,000.

Activity: new program listing in FY 99. FY 99-00 estimate, 10-20 grants.

HQ: Dahlgren Division, Naval Surface Warfare Center (NSWCDD-SD13), DOD, 17320 Dahlgren Rd., Dahlgren, VA 22448-5100. Phone: (540)653-7765. (Note: no field offices for this program.)

NATIONAL GUARD BUREAU

12.400   MILITARY CONSTRUCTION, NATIONAL GUARD

Assistance: project grants (75-100 percent).

Purposes: to construct facilities for training and administering Army and Air Force National Guard units. Funds may be used for armories or to provide offices, storage, assembly areas, rifle ranges, and classrooms. For non-armories, funds may provide for maintenance, supply, training, and other logistical and administrative expenses.

Eligible applicants/beneficiaries: states, DC, territories and possessions.

Range: from $300,000.

Activity: FY 98, 20 armory, 74 non-armory projects.

HQ: Director of Engineering (NGB-AEN), National Guard Bureau, ARNG Readiness Center, DOD, 111 S. George Mason Drive, Arlington, VA 22204-1382. Phone: (703)607-7900; DSN 327-7900. (Note: no field offices for this program.)

12.401 NATIONAL GUARD MILITARY OPERATIONS AND MAINTENANCE (O&M) PROJECTS

Assistance: project grants (75-100 percent).

Purposes: for services provided by states for such National Guard activities as real property maintenance and repair, environmental resources management and services, security guard services, electronic security systems, telecommunications services, air traffic control, automated target systems, recruitment, fire protection, and related activities.

Eligible applicants/beneficiaries: states, DC, PR, VI, Guam.

Range: from $100,000.

Activity: not quantified specifically.

HQ: National Guard Bureau, DOD, ARNG Readiness Center, 111 S. George Mason Drive, Arlington, VA 22204-1382. Phones: Real Property O&M Projects, (703)607-7922; Environmental Resources Management, (703)607-7977; Security Guard Activities, (703)607-7158; Electronic Security System, (703)607-7449; Telecommunications, (703)607-7672; Aviation Operations, (703)607-7752; Automated Target Systems, (703)607-7346; Full Time Dining Facility Operations, (703)607-7408; Store Front Recruiting Office Lease, (703)607-7199; Printing and Duplication, (703)681-3758.

DEPARTMENT OF THE ARMY
ARMY MEDICAL RESEARCH AND MATERIAL COMMAND

12.420 MILITARY MEDICAL RESEARCH AND DEVELOPMENT

Assistance: project grants (100 percent/to 5 years).

Purposes: for basic and applied medical research projects that expand the technology base or understanding of biological-medical processes. Early project examples: analysis of investigational drugs in biological fluids; altered response to infection induced by severe injury; breast cancer research. Some grants are available to support conferences and symposia.

Eligible applicants/beneficiaries: public, quasi-public, or private nonprofit institutions and organizations; specialized groups.

Range: $100,000 to $5,000,000. **Average:** $650,000.

Activity: not quantified specifically.

HQ: U.S. Army Medical Research and Material Command, (ATTN: MCMR-ACQ-BA) Fort Detrick, Frederick, MD 21702-5012. Phone: (301)619-7216.

ARMY RESEARCH OFFICE

12.431 BASIC SCIENTIFIC RESEARCH

Assistance: project grants (100 percent/3-5 years).

Purposes: for basic research in the mathematical, physical, engineering, biological, and geosciences related to the improvement of Army programs or operations. Funds may support: programs encouraging careers for outstanding graduate, undergraduate, and high school students; increases in the number of graduates from under-represented minority groups; symposia; purchases of major high-cost research equipment.

Eligible applicants/beneficiaries: educational institutions, nonprofit scientific research organizations.

Range: $25,000 to $1,000,000.

Activity: FY 00 estimate, 500 awards.

HQ: U.S. Army Research Office - ATTN: AMXRO-RT, Research Triangle Park, NC 27709-2211. Phones: (919)549-4204; DSN 832-4204. (Note: no field offices for this program.)

OFFICE OF ASSISTANT SECRETARY/ STRATEGY AND REQUIREMENTS

12.550 INTERNATIONAL EDUCATION—U.S. COLLEGES AND UNIVERSITIES ("National Security Education Program" - "NSEP")

Assistance: project grants (100 percent/1-2 years).

Purposes: to develop and strengthen IHE capabilities in critical language education, area studies, and international fields. International exchanges are ineligible for funding. The National Security Education Trust Fund supports this program.

Eligible applicants/beneficiaries: two- and four-year U.S. IHEs. Others may be included in proposals, but may not receive grants.

Range/Average: to $200,000 for two years.

Activity: 1998, 7 grants, benefiting 42 IHEs.

HQ: National Security Education Program, Under Secretary of Defense/Policy, Assistant Secretary/Strategy and Requirements, DOD, 1101 Wilson Blvd. - Ste.1210, Arlington, VA 22209-2248. Phone: (703)696-1991. (Note: no field offices for this program.)

12.551 NATIONAL SECURITY EDUCATION—SCHOLARSHIPS

Assistance: project grants (100 percent/2 academic terms per year).

Purposes: for undergraduate scholarships in critical languages and world area studies. Recipients must agree to work in a federal organization or in higher education for a time equal to the length of the award. Studies may be conducted abroad. International exchanges are ineligible for funding. The National Security Education Trust Fund supports this program.

Eligible applicants/beneficiaries: U.S. citizens enrolled in public or private two- or four-year IHEs. Students in federal government schools are ineligible.

Range: to $8,000/academic term.

Activity: new program listing in 1998. Since 1993 program inception, 800 awards.

HQ: same address/phone as **12.550**. (Note: no field offices for this program.)

12.552 NATIONAL SECURITY EDUCATION—FELLOWSHIPS

Assistance: project grants (100 percent/2 academic terms per year).

Purposes: for graduate fellowships in critical languages and world area studies. Recipients must agree to work in a federal organization or in higher education for a time equal to the length of the award. Studies may be conducted abroad. International exchanges are ineligible for funding. The National Security Education Trust Fund supports this program.

Eligible applicants/beneficiaries: U.S. citizens enrolled in public or private IHEs. Students in federal government schools are ineligible.

Range: $2,000 to $10,000.

Activity: new program listing in 1998. Since 1993 program inception, 381 awards.

HQ: same address/phone as **12.550**. (Note: no field offices for this program.)

OFFICE OF ECONOMIC ADJUSTMENT

12.600 COMMUNITY ECONOMIC ADJUSTMENT

Assistance: specialized services; advisory services/counseling.

Purposes: for communities, regions, and states to alleviate serious economic impacts resulting from DOD program changes—e.g., base openings or closings, contract changes, personnel increases or reductions. Typically, assistance consists of assessing the impact and formulating strategies to relieve problems, including involving other federal departments; identifying alternative resources and solutions; and developing an action plan.

Eligible applicants/beneficiaries: states and political subdivisions, other public organizations, community leadership groups.

Activity: not quantified specifically.

HQ: Director, Office of Economic Adjustment (DUSD - IA&I), DOD, 400 Army-Navy Dr. - Ste.200, Arlington, VA 22202-2884. Phone: (703)604-6020.

12.607 COMMUNITY ECONOMIC ADJUSTMENT PLANNING ASSISTANCE ("Community Planning Assistance")

Assistance: project grants (75 percent).

Purposes: to prepare military base re-use studies in coordination with communities, concerning military installation closures or realignment. Funds may be used for staffing, operating and administrative costs, studies.

Eligible applicants/beneficiaries: in DOD-approved areas—state and local governments, regional organizations, tribes, DC, PR, Guam.

Range: $300,000 to $1,300,000. **Average:** $500,000.

Activity: FY 98, 57 communities received funds.

HQ: Director, Office of Economic Adjustment (OASD - ES), DOD, same address/phone as **12.600.**

12.610   JOINT LAND USE STUDIES

Assistance: project grants (50 percent/1-2 years).

Purposes: to enable the Army, Navy, Air Force, and Marine Corps to participate in the preparation of joint military/community comprehensive land use plans concerning public or private land development around military installations. The goal is to assure that land uses are compatible with both military operations and plans of non-military jurisdictions.

Eligible applicants/beneficiaries: in DOD-approved areas—state and local governments or regional organizations, tribes.

Range: $50,000 to $100,000.

Activity: FY 98, 3 communities received funds.

HQ: same address as **12.600.** Phone: (703)604-5498.

12.611   COMMUNITY ECONOMIC ADJUSTMENT PLANNING ASSISTANCE FOR REDUCTIONS IN DEFENSE INDUSTRY EMPLOYMENT

Assistance: project grants (75 percent/12-18 months).

Purposes: for communities to undertake economic adjustment planning activities to respond to major reductions in defense industry employment resulting from the cancellation, termination, or failure to proceed with DOD spending under a previously approved program. Funds may be used for planning expenses including staffing, operating and administrative costs, studies.

Eligible applicants/beneficiaries: states on behalf of local governments, local governments, tribes, DC, PR, Guam—if the spending reduction involves the loss of at least: 2,500 full-time contractor employee jobs in a metropolitan statistical area; or 1,000 jobs outside a metropolitan statistical area; or one percent of the total number of jobs in that area.

Range: $100,000 to $200,000.

Activity: FY 98, 8 communities assisted.

HQ: same address as **12.600.** Phone: (703)604-5498.

12.612   COMMUNITY BASE REUSE PLANS
("Community Planning Assistance")

Assistance: project grants (75 percent).

Purposes: to prepare community base reuse plans at closing or realigning military installations—required as part of the Environmental Impact Statement for disposal and reuse of such installations.

Eligible applicants/beneficiaries: same as for **12.607.**

Range: $100,000 to $300,000. **Average:** $220,000.

Activity: FY 98, 4 communities funded.

HQ: same address as **12.600.** Phone: (703)604-5498.

12.613   GROWTH MANAGEMENT PLANNING ASSISTANCE ("Community Planning Assistance")

Assistance: project grants (75 percent).

Purposes: for growth management planning activities to respond to military base opening or expansion resulting in large-scale military-related population growth requiring additional public facilities and services off-base. Funds may support staffing, operating and administrative costs, studies—if expansions involve assignment of more than 2,000 personnel, or if they equal 10 percent or more of existing employment within 15 miles of the installation.

Eligible applicants/beneficiaries: same as for **12.607**.

Range: $100,000 to $150,000. **Average:** $150,000.

Activity: no funding FY 94-99.

HQ: same address as **12.600**. Phone: (703)604-5498.

OFFICE OF THE SECRETARY

12.630   BASIC, APPLIED, AND ADVANCED RESEARCH IN SCIENCE AND ENGINEERING

Assistance: project grants.

Purposes: for multidisciplinary university research in areas that cut across traditional academic disciplines, in mathematical, physical, engineering, environmental, life sciences, and other fields—with long-term potential for contributing to technology for DOD missions; for fellowships and research traineeships for graduate education. Funds may also be used to purchase costly (from $50,000) university research equipment.

Eligible applicants: private and public educational institutions.

Eligible beneficiaries: graduate and undergraduate students in science and engineering disciplines important to defense.

Range: $1,000 to $3,000,000. **Average:** $120,000.

Activity: not quantified specifically.

HQ: contact the executive agents listed under "HQ" for programs **12.300**, **12.431**, **12.800**, or **12.910**. (Note: no field offices for this program.)

DEPARTMENT OF THE ARMY, AVIATION APPLIED TECHNOLOGY DIRECTORATE

12.640   INTEGRATED HELICOPTER DESIGN TOOLS

Assistance: project grants (50 percent/to 3 years).

Purposes: for research and development on technologies important to both defense and commercial application; to integrate defense and commercial bases; for technology transfer. Funds may cover costs of labor, materials, and travel, plus associated indirect costs.

Eligible applicants/beneficiaries: experienced companies and consortia that conduct a significant level of their research, development, engineering, and manufacturing in the U.S.

Range/Average: N.A.

Activity: new program listing in 1998.

HQ: Commander, Aviation Applied Technology Directorate (ATTN: AMSAT-R-TC), DOD, Fort Eustis, VA 23604-5577. Phones: (804)878-4828; DSN 927-4828. (Note: no field offices for this program.)

SECRETARIES OF MILITARY DEPARTMENTS

12.700 DONATIONS/LOANS OF OBSOLETE DOD PROPERTY

Assistance: use of property, facilities, and equipment.

Purposes: donation or loan of obsolete combat materiel and other specified items for historical, ceremonial, or display purposes—including books, manuscripts, models, captured vessels. Recipients must pay packing and handling costs.

Eligible applicants/beneficiaries: veterans' organizations recognized by the Office of the Deputy Under Secretary of Defense (LIMDM); libraries, historical societies, educational institutions, and tax-exempt museums operated and maintained only for education purposes; municipalities; states, territories, and possessions.

Activity: not quantified specifically.

HQ: appropriate military department, DOD, Pentagon, Washington, DC 20301.

DEPARTMENT OF THE AIR FORCE, MATERIEL COMMAND

12.800 AIR FORCE DEFENSE RESEARCH SCIENCES PROGRAM

Assistance: project grants (1-3 years).

Purposes: for research to maintain technological superiority in scientific areas relevant to Air Force needs; to prevent technology surprise to the nation and to create it for adversaries; to maintain a strong research infrastructure composed of Air Force laboratories, industry, and universities; to complement the national research effort. Projects may be in such areas as the aerospace, engineering, chemical and materials, life, environmental, mathematical, and computer sciences.

Eligible applicants/beneficiaries: private and public educational institutions; private and public nonprofit organizations; commercial concerns.

Range: $50,000 to $5,000,000. **Average:** $500,000.

Activity: FY 99 estimate, 600 new grants.

HQ: HQ-Air Force Materiel Command/PKT, DOD, 4375 Childlaw Rd. - Ste.6, Wright-Patterson AFB, OH 45433-5006. Phone: (513)257-8934.

NATIONAL SECURITY AGENCY

12.900   LANGUAGE GRANT PROGRAM

Assistance: project grants (100 percent).

Purposes: to foster language training of Americans. Funded projects have included documentation of low density languages, foreign language reference works, and research in training methods and computer-assisted instruction technologies.

Eligible applicants/beneficiaries: U.S. private or public nonprofit educational institutions and organizations operated primarily for language training.

Range: $5,000 to $500,000.

Activity: not quantified specifically.

HQ: Chief, Language Training, National Security Agency (ATTN: E41), DOD, Fort George Meade, MD 20755-6000. Phone: (410)859-6087. (Note: no field offices for this program.)

12.901   MATHEMATICAL SCIENCES GRANTS PROGRAM

Assistance: project grants (100 percent/to 2 years).

Purposes: to stimulate developments and promote careers in areas of mathematics identified with cryptology, including number theory, discrete mathematics, statistics, probability. Funds may support summer salary (one month maximum), professional travel, publishing costs, graduate or postgraduate student support, conferences.

Eligible applicants/beneficiaries: employees and graduate students at U.S. colleges or universities, that are U.S. citizens, permanent residents, or intending to apply for citizenship.

Range: $5,000 to $60,000. **Average:** $15,000.

Activity: not quantified specifically.

HQ: National Security Agency (ATTN: R51A), DOD, Fort George Meade, MD 20755-6000. Phone: (301)688-0400. (Note: no field offices for this program.)

12.902   INFORMATION SECURITY GRANT PROGRAM
("Information Security University Research Program" - "URP")

Assistance: project grants (100 percent/1-2 years).

Purposes: for research to design, build, and maintain secure computing systems involving unclassified information; to develop and train computer science graduates to be recruited by NSA. Project examples: "Multilevel Secure Distributed Systems Security;" "Computer Misuse and Anomaly Detection." Funds may support summer salary (two months maximum), professional travel, publishing costs, graduate and postdoctoral student support, conferences.

Eligible applicants/beneficiaries: same as **12.901**.

Range: $50,000 to $100,000. **Average:** $80,000.

Activity: 1999, 45 proposals received.

HQ: Program Director, INFOSEC University Research Program, National Security Agency (ATTN: R23), DOD, 9840 O'Brien Rd., Fort George Meade, MD 20755-6000. Phones: (301)688-0847; FAX (301)688-0255; e-mail, urp@tycho.ncsc.mil (Note: no field offices for this program.)

DEFENSE ADVANCED RESEARCH PROJECTS AGENCY

12.910   RESEARCH AND TECHNOLOGY DEVELOPMENT

Assistance: project grants (50 percent/3-5 years).

Purposes: for basic and applied research and development in science and technology; for projects advancing the state of the art or resulting in fundamental changes in technology—in areas that may have military or dual-use applications. Funds may also support: symposia and conferences; programs encouraging careers in science, technology, and engineering, and an increase in the number of graduates from under-represented minority groups; university research instrumentation. Project examples: submicron systems architecture for high performance computing; high band-width, digital compressed video educational network; acoustic communication through real-time channel modeling.

Eligible applicants/beneficiaries: grants—public and private educational institutions and nonprofit organizations. Cooperative agreements—educational institutions, nonprofit organizations, commercial firms.

Range: $100,000 to $100,000,000. **Average:** $1,150,000.

Activity: FY 98 estimate, 30 grant awards and 20 "other transactions."

HQ: Director, Contract Management Office (CMO), Defense Advanced Research Projects Agency, DOD, 3701 N. Fairfax Drive, Arlington, VA 22203. Phones: (703)696-2399; Web, http://www.darpa.mil/cmo (Note: no field offices for this program.)

12.911   DEFENSE TECHNOLOGY CONVERSION, REINVESTMENT, AND TRANSITION ASSISTANCE
("Dual Use Applications Projects - "DUAP")

Assistance: project grants (50 percent/1-4 years).

Purposes: for applied, dual-use technology development, deployment, and education projects stimulating the transition to a growing, integrated, national industrial capability, providing advanced military systems and competitive commercial products. The program also funds Small Business Innovation Research.

Eligible applicants/beneficiaries: commercial profit or nonprofit firms; federal, state, and local government agencies; federal laboratories; nonprofit organizations of two or more state or local governments; existing manufacturing extension programs; regional entities; IHEs.

Range: $90,000 to $10,000,000.

Activity: FY 98 estimate, no grants, 2 "other transactions."

HQ: Technology Reinvestment Project Office, Defense Advanced Research Projects Agency, DOD, 3701 N. Fairfax Drive, Arlington, VA 22203. Phones: (800)382-5873; FAX (703)696-3813; Internet, pa95-04@arpa.mil (Note: no field offices for this program.)

DEPARTMENT OF HOUSING AND URBAN DEVELOPMENT

HOUSING—FEDERAL HOUSING COMMISSIONER

> *NOTE: For most mortgage insurance programs administered by the Federal Housing Commissioner, "Eligible applicants" cited in program descriptions should submit applications to a HUD-approved lender for approval action. Lenders are authorized to act on applications covering single-family housing. Proposed multifamily projects generally require HUD approval of prospective project sponsors; pre-application conferences are held with HUD field offices to determine project feasibility, particularly if housing subsidies are sought.*

14.103 INTEREST REDUCTION PAYMENTS—RENTAL AND COOPERATIVE HOUSING FOR LOWER INCOME FAMILIES ("Section 236")

Assistance: direct payments/specified use; guaranteed/insured loans (40 years).

Purposes: pursuant to the NHA as amended, to subsidize interest costs covering mortgages on rental or cooperative housing developed for the low and moderate income. The program now is inactive except for commitments to existing projects; no projects have been approved since 1992. Subsidies on previously developed projects are paid directly to lenders for the term of the mortgage; payments are adjusted to equal the difference between interest costs at the market rate and as low as one percent, depending on the incomes of tenants who must pay at least 30 percent of their adjusted gross incomes toward rent.

Eligible applicants: eligible mortgagors included nonprofit, cooperative, builder-seller, investor-sponsor, and limited-distribution sponsors. Public bodies were ineligible mortgagors.

Eligible beneficiaries: families and individuals, including the elderly or handicapped or those displaced by government action or natural disaster, within certain locally determined income limits. Families with incomes higher than that eligible for subsidies may occupy apartments, but may not benefit from subsidy payments.

Activity: FY 92 status, 378,000 rental units insured, valued at $6.5 billion.

Note: this program was deleted from the CFDA in 1994, and reinstated in 1999.

HQ: Director, Office of Multifamily Housing Management-HUD, Washington, DC 20410. Phone: (202)708-3730.

14.108   REHABILITATION MORTGAGE INSURANCE ("Section 203(k)")

Assistance: guaranteed/insured loans (30 years).

Purposes: pursuant to the NHA as amended, for existing one- to four-unit residential buildings to cover the cost of rehabilitation, acquisition and rehabilitation, acquisition and relocation from another site and rehabilitation, or rehabilitation and debt refinancing. Rehabilitation cost must be at least $5,000. Certain application fees must be paid by purchasers. FY 98-00 funding for this program is included in **14.133**.

Eligible applicants/beneficiaries: house purchasers or investors (*see NOTE preceding* **14.103**).

Range: $115,200 maximum insurable loans for single-family units; $147,408 for two-family housing, $178,176 for three-family, $221,448 for four-family—which may be increased in high-cost areas.

Activity: FY 98, 14,000 loans insured.

HQ: None. (All contacts are with field offices listed in Part IV.)

14.110   MANUFACTURED HOME LOAN INSURANCE—FINANCING PURCHASE OF MANUFACTURED HOMES AS PRINCIPAL RESIDENCES OF BORROWERS ("Title I")

Assistance: guaranteed/insured loans (to 90 percent/20 years).

Purposes: pursuant to the NHA as amended, for manufactured ("mobile") home purchasers when the units will be used as their principal residence. 5 percent down payments and fees must be provided by purchasers. Funding for this program includes **14.162**.

Eligible applicants/beneficiaries: anyone (*see NOTE preceding* **14.103**).

Range: to $48,600.

Activity: FY 98, 800 loans made.

HQ: Chief, Home Improvement Branch, HUD, 451 Seventh St. SW - Rm.8272, Washington, DC 20410. Phone: (202)708-6396.

14.112   MORTGAGE INSURANCE FOR CONSTRUCTION OR SUBSTANTIAL REHABILITATION OF CONDOMINIUM PROJECTS ("Section 234(d) Condominiums")

Assistance: guaranteed/insured loans (to 90 percent/40 years).

Purposes: pursuant to the NHA and the Housing Act of 1964 as amended, for the construction or substantial rehabilitation of multifamily housing projects by sponsors intending to sell individual units as condominiums; in turn, purchasers may obtain mortgage insurance through **14.133**.

Eligible applicants/beneficiaries: private profit-motivated developers, public bodies, certain others (*see NOTE preceding* **14.103**).

Range/Average: 90 percent of replacement cost within statutory limits.

Activity: no funding available in recent years.

HQ: Office of Business Products, HUD, Washington, DC 20410. Phone: (202) 708-0624.

14.116 MORTGAGE INSURANCE—GROUP PRACTICE FACILITIES ("Title XI")

Assistance: guaranteed/insured loans (to 90 percent/25 years).

Purposes: pursuant to the NHA as amended, for the construction or rehabilitation of group practice facilities providing preventive, diagnostic, and treatment services by medical, dental, optometric, osteopathic, or podiatric groups. Costs may include major movable equipment. Funding for this program is included in **14.128**.

Eligible applicants/beneficiaries: private nonprofit sponsors providing comprehensive health care to members or subscribers on a group practice prepayment or fee-for-service basis, or established to improve the availability of health care in the community—that will make the facility available to an eligible group (*see NOTE preceding* **14.103**).

Range: to 90 percent of replacement cost.

Activity: no mortgages insured in several years.

HQ: same address/phone as **14.112**.

14.117 MORTGAGE INSURANCE—HOMES ("Section 203(b)")

Assistance: guaranteed/insured loans (30 years).

Purposes: pursuant to the NHA as amended, to acquire existing or to construct new one- to four-unit housing. Mortgage indebtedness on existing housing owned by applicants may also be refinanced. Small down payments, certain closing costs, and other expenses must be covered by purchasers. Funding for this program includes **14.119**, **14.121**, **14.159**, **14.163**, **14.172**, and **14.175**.

Eligible applicants/beneficiaries: purchasers that will occupy insured units (*see NOTE preceding* **14.103**).

Range: $115,200 maximum insurable loans for single-family units; $147,408 for two-family housing, $178,176 for three-family, $221,448 for four-family—which may be increased in high-cost areas.

Activity: FY 98, 1,091,000 loans insured.

HQ: None. (All contacts are with field offices listed in Part IV.)

14.119 MORTGAGE INSURANCE—HOMES FOR DISASTER VICTIMS ("Section 203(h)")

Assistance: guaranteed/insured loans (100 percent/30-35 years).

Purposes: pursuant to the NHA as amended, to enable disaster victims to acquire new or reconstructed existing single-family housing. Certain fees must be paid by purchasers. Funding for this program is included in **14.117**.

Eligible applicants/beneficiaries: any victim of a major disaster so designated by the President (*see NOTE preceding* **14.103**).

Range: to 100 per cent of the property value as estimated by HUD.

Activity: N.A.

HQ: None. (All contacts are with field offices listed in Part IV.)

14.120 MORTGAGE INSURANCE—HOMES FOR LOW AND MODERATE INCOME FAMILIES ("Section 221(d)(2)")

Assistance: guaranteed/insured loans (to 97 percent/30-40 years).

Purposes: pursuant to the NHA as amended, for low- and moderate-income families, especially those displaced by disasters or governmental action, to purchase new, existing, or rehabilitated one- to four-family structures. Certain fees must be paid by purchasers; the minimum down payment is $200. FY 98-00 funding for this program is included in **14.133**.

Eligible applicants/beneficiaries: all purchasers are eligible. Certified displaced families qualify for special terms (*see NOTE preceding* **14.103**).

Range: to $31,000 for single-family units, to $36,000 in high-cost areas; $36,000 for a large family (five or more persons), to $42,000 in high-cost areas; higher limits apply for two- to four-family structures.

Activity: N.A.

HQ: None. (All contacts are with field offices listed in Part IV.)

14.121 MORTGAGE INSURANCE—HOMES IN OUTLYING AREAS ("Section 203(i)")

Assistance: guaranteed/insured loans (75 percent/30-35 years).

Purposes: pursuant to the NHA as amended, for new or existing nonfarm houses, or new farm houses on at least 2.5 acres adjacent to an all-weather road, in outlying areas. Small down payments and fees must be paid by purchasers. Funding for this program is included in **14.117**.

Eligible applicants/beneficiaries: purchasers in outlying areas (*see NOTE preceding* **14.103**).

Range: to 75 percent of the maximums for **14.117**.

Activity: N.A.

HQ: None. (All contacts are with field offices listed in Part IV.)

14.122 MORTGAGE INSURANCE—HOMES IN URBAN RENEWAL AREAS ("Section 220 Homes")

Assistance: guaranteed/insured loans (30-35 years).

Purposes: pursuant to the Housing Act of 1954 as amended, for new, existing, or rehabilitated, owner-occupied one- to 11-unit housing acquired or rehabilitated in approved urban renewal or code enforcement areas. Small down payments and fees must be paid by purchasers. FY 98-00 funding for this program is included in **14.133**.

Eligible applicants/beneficiaries: purchasers of houses in approved urban renewal areas (*see NOTE preceding* **14.103**).

Range: same as for **14.117**, plus $9,165 for each unit over four.

Activity: included in report for **14.117**.

HQ: None. (All contacts are with field offices listed in Part IV.)

14.123 MORTGAGE INSURANCE—HOUSING IN OLDER, DECLINING AREAS ("Section 223(e)")

Assistance: guaranteed/insured loans (varying terms).

Purposes: pursuant to the NHA as amended, to provide long-term mortgage insurance on existing, new, or rehabilitated single-family or multifamily housing in older declining areas where conditions are such that certain normal eligibility requirements for mortgage insurance cannot be met. Small down payments and insurance fees may be required of beneficiaries. HUD insures loans under other programs (e.g., **14.135**); claims are paid from the Special Risk Insurance Fund.

Eligible applicants: HUD-approved mortgagees. Multifamily sponsorship is determined by applicable program requirements.

Eligible beneficiaries: for single-family houses, individuals or families.

Range: varies according to program under which mortgage is insured.

Activity: FY 98, no loans insured.

HQ: None. (All contacts are with field offices listed in Part IV.)

14.126 MORTGAGE INSURANCE—COOPERATIVE PROJECTS ("Section 213 Cooperatives")

Assistance: guaranteed/insured loans (90-98 percent/to 35-40 years).

Purposes: pursuant to the NHA as amended and other acts, for existing, new, or rehabilitated cooperative housing consisting of detached, semi-detached, row, walk-up, or elevator structures, with five units minimum. Certain fees must be paid by purchasers. Maximum mortgage term: "management-type" projects, 40 years; "sales-type," 35 years. Funding for this program is included in **14.135.**

Eligible applicants: nonprofit cooperatives; ownership housing corporations or trusts that may sponsor projects directly, sell individual units to cooperative members, or purchase projects from investor-sponsors (*see NOTE preceding* **14.103**).

Eligible beneficiaries: members of cooperatives.

Range: maximum mortgage to investor-sponsor, 90 percent of replacement cost; cooperative member, 98 percent—within statutory maximums for individual units under program **14.117.**

Activity: no projects insured since FY 85. (Most cooperative loans have been insured under **14.135** for new construction or **14.155** for rehabilitation.)

HQ: same address/phone as **14.112.**

14.127 MORTGAGE INSURANCE—MANUFACTURED HOME PARKS ("Section 207(m) Manufactured Home Parks")

Assistance: guaranteed/insured loans (90 percent/40 years).

Purposes: pursuant to the NHA as amended, for manufactured home park development, new or rehabilitated, with five or more spaces. Funding for this program is included in **14.135.**

Eligible applicants: investors, builders, developers (*see NOTE preceding* **14.103**).

Eligible beneficiaries: families or individuals owning manufactured houses and leasing spaces.

Range: to $9,000 per space (higher in high-cost areas).

Activity: FY 98, 3 loans insured.

HQ: same address/phone as **14.112.**

14.128   MORTGAGE INSURANCE—HOSPITALS
(Section 242 Hospitals")

Assistance: guaranteed/insured loans (90 percent/25 years).

Purposes: pursuant to the NHA as amended, for hospital construction or rehabilitation, including the costs of major movable equipment. Funding for this program includes **14.116.**

Eligible applicants/beneficiaries: profit or nonprofit hospitals providing acute care to at least 50 percent of their patient census, and licensed or regulated by the state, municipality, or other political subdivision.

Range: $360,000 to $591,000,000. **Average:** $29,200,000.

Activity: FY 99 estimate, 20 projects insured including new projects, refundings, joint ventures, mergers, and equipment loans.

HQ: Office of Insured Health Care Facilities, HUD, Washington, DC 20410. Phone: (202)708-0599. *Or*: Division of Facilities Loans, HHS, Rockville, MD 20857. Phone: (301)443-5317. (Note: no field offices for this program.)

14.129   MORTGAGE INSURANCE—NURSING HOMES, INTERMEDIATE CARE FACILITIES, BOARD AND CARE HOMES AND ASSISTED LIVING FACILITIES
("Section 232 Nursing Homes")

Assistance: guaranteed/insured loans (varying terms).

Purposes: pursuant to the NHA as amended and other acts, for nursing homes or intermediate care facilities accommodating 20 or more patients, or board and care homes and assisted living facilities with five or more accommodations or units, or a combination of the foregoing types of facilities. Loans may cover the cost of fire safety equipment and major equipment. FY 98-00 funding for this program is included in **14.135.**

Eligible applicants/beneficiaries: investors, builders, developers, public entities, and private nonprofit corporations or associations licensed or regulated by the state for the accommodation of convalescents and persons requiring skilled nursing or intermediate care (*see NOTE preceding* **14.103**).

Range: 40-year mortgage insurance on 90 percent loans for new or substantially rehabilitated facilities (95 percent for nonprofit sponsors); 35 years on 85 percent loans for refinanced existing HUD-insured facilities not requiring substantial rehabilitation (to 90 percent for nonprofit sponsors).

Activity: FY 98, 155 loans insured, with 16,000 beds total.

HQ: same address/phone as **14.112.**

14.130   MORTGAGE INSURANCE—PURCHASE BY HOMEOWNERS OF FEE SIMPLE TITLE FROM LESSORS ("Section 240")

Assistance: guaranteed/insured loans (20 years).

Purposes: pursuant to the NHA as amended, for owners of one- to four-family houses to purchase the fee simple title to property held under long-term leases and on which their houses are located.

Eligible applicants/beneficiaries: owners of houses located on property held under long-term ground leases (*see NOTE preceding* **14.103**).

Range: to $10,000 maximum existing mortgage indebtedness per unit ($30,000 in Hawaii).

Activity: included in report for **14.117.**

HQ: None. (All contacts are with field offices listed in Part IV.)

14.132   MORTGAGE INSURANCE—PURCHASE OF SALES-TYPE COOPERATIVE HOUSING UNITS ("Section 213 Sales")

Assistance: guaranteed/insured loans (30-35 years).

Purposes: pursuant to the NHA as amended and the Housing Act of 1950, for purchases of new dwelling units by members of cooperatives, in projects with at least five units. Small down payments are required. Funding for this program is included in **14.135.**

Eligible applicants/beneficiaries: members of nonprofit cooperative ownership housing corporations or trusts (*see NOTE preceding* **14.103**).

Range: same as for **14.117.**

Activity: included in report for **14.117.**

HQ: None. (All contacts are with field offices listed in Part IV.)

14.133   MORTGAGE INSURANCE—PURCHASE OF UNITS IN CONDOMINIUMS ("Section 234(c)")

Assistance: guaranteed/insured loans (90 percent/30-35 years).

Purposes: pursuant to the NHA as amended and other acts, to purchase new or existing individual units in condominium projects containing four or more dwellings. Units converted from rental to condominiums are insurable, provided: the conversion occurred more than one year prior to the application for insurance; tenant was a tenant of the rental housing; conversion was sponsored by an approved tenants organization. Small down payments and fees must be paid by purchasers. FY 98-00 funding for this program includes **14.108**, **14.120**, **14.122**, **14.165**, **14.166**, and **14.183.**

Eligible applicants/beneficiaries: condominium purchasers (*see NOTE preceding* **14.103**).

Range: same as for **14.117.**

Activity: FY 98, 92,000 units insured.

HQ: None. (All contacts are with field offices listed in Part IV.)

14.134   MORTGAGE INSURANCE—RENTAL HOUSING ("Section 207")

Assistance: guaranteed/insured loans (90 percent/to 40 years).

Purposes: pursuant to the NHA as amended, for the construction or rehabilitation of middle-income rental housing in detached, semi-detached, row, walk-up, or elevator structures, with five units minimum. Funding for this program is included in **14.135**.

Eligible applicants: investors, builders, developers, and others meeting HUD requirements (*see NOTE preceding* **14.103**).

Eligible beneficiaries: renters.

Range: to 90 percent of value.

Activity: no projects insured in several years. (Section 221(d)(4) (**14.135**) is used instead.)

HQ: same address/phone as **14.112**.

14.135   MORTGAGE INSURANCE—RENTAL AND COOPERATIVE HOUSING FOR MODERATE INCOME FAMILIES AND ELDERLY, MARKET INTEREST RATE ("Section 221(d)(3) and (4) Multifamily - Market Rate Housing")

Assistance: guaranteed/insured loans (to 40 years).

Purposes: pursuant to the NHA as amended, for sponsors of new or rehabilitated market-rate rental or cooperative housing developed for moderate-income families, the elderly, and the handicapped, including for "single-room occupancy" (**14.184**). Units may be in detached, semi-detached, row, walk-up, or elevator structures containing five units minimum. Funding for this program includes **14.126, 14.127, 14.129, 14.132, 14.134, 14.139, 14.142, 14.151, 14.155, 14.167,** and **14.188**.

Eligible applicants: public, profit-motivated, limited-distribution, nonprofit, cooperative, builder-seller, investor, and general sponsors (*see NOTE preceding* **14.103**).

Eligible beneficiaries: all households regardless of income.

Range: Section 221(d)(3), to 90 percent of replacement cost for profit-motivated and limited-distribution sponsors; to 100 percent for nonprofit sponsors. Section 221(d)(4), to 90 percent of replacement cost—within statutory maximums

Activity: FY 99 estimate, 40,000 units insured.

HQ: same address/phone as **14.112**.

14.138   MORTGAGE INSURANCE—RENTAL HOUSING FOR THE ELDERLY ("Section 231")

Assistance: guaranteed/insured loans (90-100 percent/40 years).

Purposes: pursuant to the NHA as amended, for rental housing for elderly or handicapped persons—in new or rehabilitated detached, semi-detached, walk-up, or elevator structures with a minimum of five units.

Eligible applicants/beneficiaries: private profit-motivated investors, public bodies, and nonprofit sponsors (*see NOTE preceding* **14.103**).

Range: within statutory maximum per unit costs—nonprofit and public sponsors, 100 percent of replacement cost; other sponsors, 90 percent.

Activity: FY 97-99, no projects insured. (Note: program **14.135** has been used instead of Section 231 during the last several years.)

HQ: same address/phone as **14.112**.

14.139   MORTGAGE INSURANCE—RENTAL HOUSING IN URBAN RENEWAL AREAS
("Section 220 Multifamily")

Assistance: guaranteed/insured loans (90 percent/40 years).

Purposes: pursuant to the NHA as amended, for new or rehabilitated rental housing located in urban renewal, code enforcement, or other approved public program areas including disaster areas; loans may also cover existing properties rehabilitated by a local public agency. Projects must include a minimum of two units, and may involve detached, semi-detached, walk-up, or elevator structures. Funding for this program is included in **14.135**.

Eligible applicants: private profit entities, public bodies, others (*see NOTE preceding* **14.103**).

Eligible beneficiaries: all families.

Range: to 90 percent of replacement cost within statutory maximum.

Activity: FY 98, no projects insured.

HQ: same address/phone as **14.112**.

14.140   MORTGAGE INSURANCE—SPECIAL CREDIT RISKS
("Section 237")

Assistance: guaranteed/insured loans (varying maximums/30-35 years).

Purposes: pursuant to the NHA as amended, for low- and moderate-income purchasers of existing, new, or rehabilitated one- to four-family houses, including condominiums. This program is intended to make home ownership possible for families that cannot meet HUD's normal eligibility requirements. Counseling of purchasers must be provided by a HUD-approved agency.

Eligible applicants/beneficiaries: only families not qualifying for homeownership under regular HUD credit standards (*see NOTE preceding* **14.103**).

Range: $18,000 maximum ($21,000 in high-cost areas).

Activity: units insured included in report for **14.117**.

HQ: None. (All contacts are with field offices listed in Part IV.)

14.142   PROPERTY IMPROVEMENT LOAN INSURANCE FOR IMPROVING ALL EXISTING STRUCTURES AND BUILDING OF NEW NONRESIDENTIAL STRUCTURES
("Title I")

Assistance: guaranteed/insured loans (90 percent/20-30 years).

Purposes: pursuant to the NHA as amended, for property improvement loans for existing single-family or multifamily housing, including the cost of erecting new nonresidential structures that substantially protect or improve the livability or utility of the properties. FY 98-00 funding for this program is included in **14.135**.

Eligible applicants/beneficiaries: owners of properties to be improved; lessees with a lease extending at least six months beyond loan maturity; purchasers under a land installment contract (*see NOTE preceding* **14.103**).

Range: $25,000 maximum for one-family dwelling or nonresidential structure; $12,000 maximum per unit for multifamily structures, not to exceed $60,000.

Activity: FY 98 estimate, 64,000 loans insured.

HQ: None. (All contacts are with field offices listed in Part IV.)

14.149   RENT SUPPLEMENTS—RENTAL HOUSING FOR LOWER INCOME FAMILIES

Assistance: direct payments/specified use (to 40 years).

Purposes: pursuant to the Housing and Urban Development Act of 1965, to subsidize rents paid by lower-income tenants of certain HUD-insured and other housing. Assistance covers the difference between the rent paid by the tenant and up to 70 percent of the market rent, with the tenant paying between 25 and 30 percent of monthly adjusted income. This program is inactive except for commitments to existing projects; all existing HUD-insured projects are being converted to the Section 8 Housing Assistance Payments program (see **14.856**).

Eligible applicants: eligible sponsors included nonprofit, cooperative, builder-seller, investor-sponsor, and limited-distribution mortgagors.

Eligible beneficiaries: families with income within the limits for admission to Section 8 housing (see **14.856**). Families may continue in occupancy if 30 percent of adjusted monthly income exceeds market rents, but subsidy may be adjusted downward or eliminated.

Range: N.A.

Activity: FY 92 cumulative commitments, 19,270 units. Note: this program was deleted from the CFDA in 1994 and reinstated in 1999.

HQ: same address/phone as **14.103**.

14.151   SUPPLEMENTAL LOAN INSURANCE—MULTIFAMILY RENTAL HOUSING
("Section 241(a)")

Assistance: guaranteed/insured loans (90 percent/varying term).

Purposes: pursuant to the NHA as amended, to expand or improve existing multifamily housing, group practice facilities, hospitals, or nursing homes already covered by HUD mortgage insurance—including energy conservation improvements and major movable equipment for health facilities.

Eligible applicants/beneficiaries: owners of multifamily projects or facilities subject to a HUD-insured mortgage (*see NOTE preceding* **14.103**).

Range: to 90 percent of the value of the improvements.

Activity: FY 98, 14 loans insured, with 1,584 units/beds.

HQ: Policies and Procedures Division, Office of Insured Multifamily Housing Development-HUD, Washington, DC 20411. Phone: (202)708-2556.

14.155 MORTGAGE INSURANCE FOR THE PURCHASE OR REFINANCING OF EXISTING MULTIFAMILY HOUSING PROJECTS ("Section 223(f)")

Assistance: guaranteed/insured loans (85 percent/10-35 years).

Purposes: pursuant to the NHA as amended, to purchase or refinance existing rental multifamily housing not requiring substantial rehabilitation. The property must have five or more living units and meet the following criteria: (a) three years elapsed from the later of completion of project construction or substantial rehabilitation, or beginning of occupancy to date of application for mortgage insurance; (b) remaining economic life long enough to permit at least a ten-year mortgage term. Funding for this program is included in **14.135**.

Eligible applicants: private or public mortgagors (*see NOTE preceding* **14.103**).

Eligible beneficiaries: all persons.

Range: repairs, maximum of 15 percent of estimated value after repairs or $6,500 per unit—more in high-cost areas.

Activity: FY 98, 144 loans with 18,000 units insured.

HQ: same address/phone as **14.112**.

14.157 SUPPORTIVE HOUSING FOR THE ELDERLY ("Section 202")

Assistance: direct payments/specified use.

Purposes: pursuant to the Housing Act of 1959 as amended and other acts, for the acquisition, construction, or substantial rehabilitation of rental or cooperative housing with supportive services and related facilities (e.g., central dining) for the very low-income elderly. Resolution Trust Corporation properties may be assisted. Capital advances are provided by HUD to meet development costs; these advances need not be repaid, provided the project is available to the very-low-income elderly for 40 years. HUD Project Rental Assistance contract payments may cover the difference between per-unit operating cost and the rent amount paid by tenants, for a maximum of 20 years.

Eligible applicants/beneficiaries: private nonprofit corporations; consumer cooperatives.

Range: $559,000 to $10,216,000. **Average:** $3,404,000.

Activity: FY 98, 6,563 units assisted.

HQ: same address as **14.112**. Phone: (202)708-2866.

14.159 SECTION 245 GRADUATED PAYMENT MORTGAGE PROGRAM

Assistance: guaranteed/insured loans (30 years).

Purposes: pursuant to the NHA of 1934, later acts, and amendments, for existing or new single-family housing, including condominiums, financed with graduated payment mortgages—allowing homeowners to make smaller monthly payments initially and to increase the amount of the payments over time as their incomes increase. Small down payments are required, and mortgagors must pay certain closing costs. Funding for this program is included in **14.117**.

Eligible applicants/beneficiaries: prospective owner-occupants (*see NOTE preceding* **14.103**).

Range: basically, 97 percent of appraised value and closing costs minus deferred interest during graduated term—with a maximum of $125,000 (more in high-cost areas).

Activity: FY 98, 108 loans insured.

HQ: None. (All contacts are with field offices listed in Part IV.)

14.162   MORTGAGE INSURANCE—COMBINATION AND MANUFACTURED HOME LOT LOANS
("Title I")

Assistance: guaranteed/insured loans (90 percent).

Purposes: pursuant to the NHA as amended, to purchase manufactured homes and lots. The maximum term is 20 years for a single module and lot, 25 years for a double module, and 15 years for a lot only. Funding for this program is included in **14.110**.

Eligible applicants/beneficiaries: purchasers intending to use property as their principal place of residence (*see NOTE preceding* **14.103**).

Range: to $64,800 for a manufactured home and lot; to $16,200 for a developed lot only. Maximums are higher in high-cost areas.

Activity: FY 98, 80 loans insured.

HQ: same address/phone as **14.110**.

14.163   MORTGAGE INSURANCE—SINGLE FAMILY COOPERATIVE HOUSING
("Section 203(n)")

Assistance: guaranteed/insured loans (30 years).

Purposes: pursuant to the NHA as amended, to purchase the Corporate Certificate and Occupancy Certificate for a unit in a HUD-insured cooperative housing project, giving purchasers the right to occupy the unit. Funding for this program is included in **14.117**.

Eligible applicants/beneficiaries: potential owner-occupant mortgagors (*see NOTE preceding* **14.103**).

Range: to the maximum stipulated for **14.117**.

Activity: included in report for **14.117**.

HQ: None. (All contacts are with field offices listed in Part IV.)

14.164   OPERATING ASSISTANCE FOR TROUBLED MULTIFAMILY HOUSING PROJECTS
("Flexible Subsidy Fund" - "Troubled Projects")

Assistance: direct payments/specified use (75 percent/1 year).

Purposes: pursuant to the Housing and Community Development Amendments of 1978, to restore or maintain the physical and financial soundness of HUD-assisted (i.e., subsidized) low- to moderate-income multifamily rental projects—through repairs, augmentation of replacement reserves, or funding of operating deficits. Owners, except nonprofits, must contribute at least 25 percent of the total needed.

Eligible applicants/beneficiaries: nonprofit, profit, limited dividend, cooperative owners. Public bodies are ineligible. Field offices recommend projects to be assisted.

Range/Average: N.A.

Activity: FY 98, 31 Section 202 (see **14.153**) projects assisted.

HQ: Director, Office of Portfolio Management, HUD, Washington, DC 20420. Phone: (202)708-3730.

14.165   MORTGAGE INSURANCE—HOMES—MILITARY IMPACTED AREAS ("Section 238(c)")

Assistance: guaranteed/insured loans (30-35 years).

Purposes: pursuant to the NHA as amended, for the purchase of existing, new, or refinanced one- to four-unit structures in areas impacted by military facilities. Small down payments are required, and mortgagors must pay certain closing costs. FY 98-00 funding for this program is included in **14.133**.

Eligible applicants/beneficiaries: purchasers in approved areas, intending to occupy the housing (*see NOTE preceding* **14.103**).

Range: same as for **14.117**.

Activity: included in report for **14.117**.

HQ: None. (All contacts are with field offices listed in Part IV.)

14.166   MORTGAGE INSURANCE—HOMES FOR MEMBERS OF THE ARMED SERVICES ("Section 222")

Assistance: guaranteed/insured loans (30-35 years).

Purposes: pursuant to the NHA as amended and the Housing Act of 1954, for existing or new single-family homes purchased by members of the armed services on active duty. Small down payments are required, and mortgagors must pay certain closing costs. FY 98-00 funding for this program is included in **14.133**.

Eligible applicants/beneficiaries: military personnel on active duty for two or more years in any branch of the Armed Forces, Coast Guard, or NOAA—including homes located in the states and territories (*see NOTE preceding* **14.103**).

Range: same as for **14.117**.

Activity: included in report for **14.117**.

HQ: Director, Single Family Development Division, Office of Insured Single Family Housing, HUD, Washington, DC 20410. Phone: (202)708-2700.

14.167   MORTGAGE INSURANCE—TWO YEAR OPERATING LOSS LOANS, SECTION 223(D)
("Two Year Operating Loss Loans")

Assistance: guaranteed/insured loans.

Purposes: pursuant to the NHA as amended, to cover operating losses incurred during the first two years of occupancy of HUD-insured multifamily projects, and/or for any other two-year period within 10 years of project completion. Such loans may extend for the unexpired term of the original mortgage.

Eligible applicants/beneficiaries: owners of multifamily projects or facilities subject to a HUD-insured or -held mortgage (*see NOTE preceding* **14.103**). FY 98-00 funding for this program is included in **14.135**.

Range: 2-year loans, essentially, to the maximum loss amount supported by debt service limitations; 10-year loans, 80 percent of unreimbursed funds invested.

Activity: FY 98, 6 loans insured covering 833 units.

HQ: same address as **14.112**. Phone: (202)708-2556.

14.168   LAND SALES—CERTAIN SUBDIVIDED LAND
("Interstate Land Sales Registration Program")

Assistance: technical information; investigation of complaints.

Purposes: pursuant to the Interstate Land Sales Full Disclosure Act as amended, to provide consumer protection through fraud prohibitions and full disclosure requirements concerning subdivision lot sales. The law requires developers that engage in interstate land sales consisting of 100 or more nonexempt lots to register with HUD; prospective purchasers must be given a property report with pertinent facts about the development and the developer. Anti-fraud provisions of the act apply to subdivisions of 25 lots or more.

Eligible applicants: affected land developers are required to submit a filing in compliance with registration requirements.

Eligible beneficiaries: persons buying lots in a covered subdivision.

Activity: FY 98, 453 filings processed.

HQ: Interstate Land Sales/RESPA Division, Office of Consumer and Regulatory Affairs, Housing-HUD, 451 Seventh St. SW, Washington, DC 20410. Phone: (202)708-0502. (Note: no field offices for this program.)

14.169   HOUSING COUNSELING ASSISTANCE PROGRAM

Assistance: project grants (cost sharing).

Purposes: pursuant to the Housing and Urban Development Act of 1968 as amended, to provide counseling services to homeowners, buyers, and tenants in HUD-assisted or -insured housing and other housing—toward the prevention and reduction of mortgage or rental delinquencies, defaults, and foreclosures.

Eligible applicants/beneficiaries: HUD-approved agencies.

Range: $1,500 to $100,000. **Average:** $15,000.

Activity: FY 99 estimate, 350 local agencies, 13 intermediaries, and 30 state housing finance agencies funded.

HQ: Marketing and Outreach Division, Office of Insured Single Family Housing, HUD, 451 Seventh St. SW, Washington, DC 20410. Phone: (202)708-0317.

14.171 MANUFACTURED HOME CONSTRUCTION AND SAFETY STANDARDS

Assistance: technical information; investigation of complaints.

Purposes: to provide consumer protection through enforcement of standards covering the safety, quality, and durability of manufactured homes—through certifications, testing, in-plant inspections, design review, and investigations of complaints against manufacturers or dealers. Siting and other local activity are considered to be under state or local jurisdiction, and are not covered by the program.

Eligible applicants/beneficiaries: purchasers of manufactured homes built since June 15, 1976.

Activity: annually, 360,000 homes produced.

HQ: Office of Consumer and Regulatory Affairs, Manufactured Housing and Construction Standards Division, Office of Single Family Housing, HUD - Rm.9152, Washington, DC 20410-8000. Phones: (202)708-6409, consumer hotline, (800)927-2891 (messages only); FAX (202)708-4213; Internet, mhs@hud.gov (Note: no field offices for this program.)

14.172 MORTGAGE INSURANCE—GROWING EQUITY MORTGAGES ("GEMs" - "Section 245(a)")

Assistance: guaranteed/insured loans (varying term).

Purposes: pursuant to the NHA as amended, to purchase existing, new, or refinanced single-family housing, including condominiums, with growing equity mortgages providing for a rapid principal reduction and shorter mortgage terms, by gradually increasing monthly payments over a 10-year period. Small down payments are required, and mortgagors must pay certain closing costs. Funding for this program is included in **14.117**.

Eligible applicants/beneficiaries: prospective purchasers (*see NOTE preceding* **14.103**).

Range: same as for **14.117**.

Activity: FY 98, 5 loans insured.

HQ: None. (All contacts are with field offices listed in Part IV.)

14.175 ADJUSTABLE RATE MORTGAGES ("ARMs" - "Section 251")

Assistance: guaranteed/insured loans (30 years).

Purposes: pursuant to the NHA as amended and the Housing and Urban-Rural Recovery Act of 1983, for adjustable rate mortgages financing the purchase of new, existing, or refinanced one- to four-family housing, including condominiums—offering lenders more assurance of long-term profitability than fixed rate mortgages. Interest rates may not increase more than one percent per year or five percent over the mortgage term. Small down payments are required, and mortgagors must pay certain closing costs. Funding for this program is included in **14.117**.

Eligible applicants/beneficiaries: prospective owner-occupants (*see NOTE preceding* **14.103**).

Range: same as for **14.117**.

Activity: FY 98, 226,000 loans insured.

HQ: None. (All contacts are with field offices listed in Part IV.)

14.181   SUPPORTIVE HOUSING FOR PERSONS WITH DISABILITIES ("Section 811")

Assistance: direct payments/specified use (100 percent).

Purposes: pursuant to the National Affordable Housing Act, for the construction, acquisition, or rehabilitation of supportive housing and related facilities for persons with disabilities, including group homes, for 40-year projects. Project Rental Assistance Contract payments may be obtained for 5-year periods (renewable), and may cover operating costs not met from project income.

Eligible applicants: "501(c)(3)" nonprofit corporations.

Eligible beneficiaries: very-low-income physically or developmentally disabled or chronically mentally ill persons, age 18 or older.

Range: $213,000 to $1,650,000. **Average:** $821,000.

Activity: FY 98, 1,650 units receiving rental assistance.

HQ: same address as **14.112**. Phone: (202)708-2866.

14.183   HOME EQUITY CONVERSION MORTGAGES ("Section 255")

Assistance: guaranteed/insured loans.

Purposes: pursuant to the NHA as amended and the Housing and Community Development Act of 1987, for "reverse mortgage" loans obtained by elderly homeowners to convert equity in their homes to monthly streams of income or lines of credit. Eligible properties are one- to four-unit dwellings, including condominiums, and manufactured homes. Borrowers must pay loan origination charges and other fees. Funding for this program is included in **14.133**.

Eligible applicants/beneficiaries: homeowners at least age 62 (*see NOTE preceding* **14.103**).

Range: determined by calculating the limit of the principal, established by using a factor corresponding to the age of the borrower, the interest rate, and the value of the property.

Activity: FY 98, 7,898 units insured.

HQ: same address/phone as **14.166**.

14.184   MORTGAGE INSURANCE FOR SINGLE ROOM OCCUPANCY (SRO) PROJECTS
("Section 221(d) Single Room Occupancy")

Assistance: guaranteed/insured loans (90 percent/to 40 years).

Purposes: pursuant to the NHA as amended, for the construction or substantial rehabilitation of multifamily properties with at least five single-room occupancy residential units—intended to provide housing for tenants with income insufficient to enable them to rent a standard apartment. Projects may have no more than 10 percent of total gross floor space dedicated to commercial use (20 percent for substantial rehabilitation).

Eligible applicants: nonprofit entities; builder-sellers with a nonprofit purchaser; limited-distribution, private profit, or public sponsors (*see NOTE preceding* **14.103**).

Eligible beneficiaries: anyone, subject to normal tenant selection procedures.

Range: to 90 percent of replacement cost.

Activity: FY 97-99, no loans insured.

HQ: same address/phone as **14.112**.

14.188   HOUSING FINANCE AGENCIES (HFA) RISK SHARING PILOT PROGRAM
("Section 542(c) Risk Sharing Program")

Assistance: guaranteed/insured loans.

Purposes: pursuant to the Housing and Community Development Act of 1992, for a pilot program providing HUD mortgage insurance to state and local housing finance agencies on their multifamily projects, covering up to 57,000 units through FY 99. Program intent is to assess the feasibility of HUD and HFAs sharing between 10 and 90 percent of the financial risk. Projects may involve acquisitions, new construction, or refinancing of Section 8, elderly, single-room occupancy, or assisted-living projects. FY 98-00 funding for this program is included in **14.135**.

Eligible applicants: state and local housing finance agencies.

Eligible beneficiaries: investors, builders, developers, public entities, private nonprofit corporations or associations. Applications are submitted to qualified housing finance agencies.

Range: $290,000 to $71,000,000 (for projects with 8 to 1,900 units). **Average:** $4,800,000 (408 units).

Activity: through January 1999, 183 projects with 21,000 units insured.

HQ: same address as **14.112**. Phone: (202)708-2556.

14.189   QUALIFIED PARTICIPATING ENTITIES (QPE) RISK SHARING PILOT PROGRAM
("Section 542(b) Risk Sharing Program")

Assistance: guaranteed/insured loans (50 percent).

Purposes: pursuant to the Housing and Community Development Act of 1992, for pilot projects in which HUD provides reinsurance on multifamily housing projects whose loans covering affordable housing are originated, underwritten, serviced, and disposed of by QPEs or approved lenders. In the event of default, the QPE will pay all costs associated with loan disposition, 50 percent of which may be reimbursed by HUD.

Eligible applicants/beneficiaries: HUD-approved lenders and QPEs. Investors, builders, developers, public entities, private nonprofit corporations or associations submit applications to the lender.

Range: $889,000 to $8,000,000 (for projects with 48-397 units). **Average:** $7,300,000 (191 units).

Activity: FY 98, 9 loans insured.

HQ: same address as **14.112**. Phone: (202)708-2556.

14.191   MULTIFAMILY HOUSING SERVICE COORDINATORS

Assistance: project grants (100 percent/to 3 years).

Purposes: pursuant to the National Affordable Housing Act as amended and the Housing and Community Development Act of 1992, to hire multifamily housing service coordinators—to link elderly, especially the frail and disabled, or disabled non-elderly, assisted housing residents to community supportive or medical services; to prevent premature and unnecessary institutionalization; and, to assess individual service needs, determine eligibility for public services, and make resource allocation decisions enabling residents to remain in the community longer. Coordinators are social service staff persons providing such services as: formal case management; resident and management education; monitoring of services; and, resident advocacy. Project funds may not be used to pay coordinators to serve as recreational or activities director, nor to provide supportive services directly or perform project administrative duties.

Eligible applicants: owners/managers of HUD-assisted housing projects including in rural areas, that are under management and current in mortgage payments. Congregate Housing Service Programs, Section 202 Capital Advance, or Section 811 projects are ineligible.

Eligible beneficiaries: residents of approved projects, at least age 62 and frail (unable to perform at least three activities of daily living), disabled, or *at risk* (i.e., deficient in one or two activities of daily living).

Range: $5,500 to $750,000. **Average:** $130,000.

Activity: new program listing in 1997. FY 98, 50 grants awarded.

HQ: Office of Portfolio Management, Office of Multifamily Housing Programs, HUD, 451 Seventh St. SW - Rm.6160, Washington, DC 20410. Phone: (202)708-3944, ext. 2487.

14.193   FEDERALLY ASSISTED LOW-INCOME HOUSING DRUG ELIMINATION

Assistance: project grants (100 percent).

Purposes: pursuant to the Anti-Drug Abuse Act of 1988, National Affordable Housing Act of 1990, and Housing and Community Development Act of

1992, to reduce or eliminate drug-related and other crime problems within or near federally assisted low-income housing, to encourage owners of such housing to develop plans to address the problems, and to provide grants to help them carry out their plans. Funds may be used for such purposes as: physical improvements to enhance security including systems to limit building access to project residents; locks, barriers, lighting, landscaping; drug prevention and reduction programs; intervention activities; on-site drug treatment programs; tenant patrol training; and purchasing communications and related equipment.

Eligible applicants/beneficiaries: owners of HUD-assisted projects.

Range: $27,000 to $125,000. **Average:** $116,000.

Activity: new program listing in 1997. FY 98, 143 grants covering 23,000 housing units.

HQ: same address/phone as **14.191.**

14.195 SECTION 8 HOUSING ASSISTANCE PAYMENTS PROGRAM—SPECIAL ALLOCATIONS
("Project-based Section 8")

Assistance: direct payments/specified use.

Purposes: pursuant to the U.S. Housing Act of 1937, to reduce claims on HUD's insurance fund by aiding insured or Secretary-held projects mortgages with immediate or potentially serious financial difficulties. HUD makes payments to owners of assisted housing on behalf of tenants, representing the difference between the contract and tenant rent. Tenants pay no more than 30 percent or their adjusted monthly income for rent. Assistance is available only on a renewable basis; current projects receive a one-year renewal upon expiration of a Section 8 contract.

Eligible applicants: Section 8 project owners of record, with an expiring Section 8 contract.

Eligible beneficiaries: families currently assisted, with income not exceeding 80 percent of area median income.

Range/Average: N.A.

Activity: new program listing in 1998. FY 98, 1,300,000 units assisted.

HQ: Program Management Division, Office of Multifamily Asset Management and Disposition, HUD, 451 Seventh St. SW, Washington, DC 20410. Phone: (202)708-4162.

14.196 SECONDARY MARKET FOR NON-CONFORMING LOANS TO LOW-WEALTH BORROWERS DEMONSTRATION PROGRAM

Assistance: project grants (100 percent/to 3 years).

Purposes: to enhance homeownership opportunities for "low-wealth borrowers" by providing grant funds to nonprofit intermediaries, including community development financial institutions, enabling them to purchase nonconforming home loans from conventional lenders—encouraging the secondary mortgage market to expand purchases of, or investments in, loans made to low-income homebuyers.

Eligible applicants: experienced tax-exempt organizations.

Eligible beneficiaries: low-income homebuyers.

Range/Average: N.A.

Activity: new program in FY 99; estimate, up to 3 grants.

HQ: same address/phone as **14.166.** (Note: no field offices for this program.)

14.197   MULTIFAMILY ASSISTED HOUSING REFORM AND AFFORDABILITY ACT ("Market-to-Market")

Assistance: direct payments/specified use.

Purposes: to retain affordable housing resources represented by existing FHA-insured Section 8 assisted housing, maintain such housing in good physical and financial condition, and reduce ongoing federal subsidies. HUD works with willing owners and lenders to reduce the Section 8 rents and operating expenses to true market levels, while providing for the project's capital improvement needs. Participating owners must commit to maintaining project affordability for 30 years.

Eligible applicants/beneficiaries: owners of projects subject to

FHA-insured mortgages, supported by Section 8 contracts, with rent levels exceeding comparable market rents.

Range: to the amount of the unpaid principal mortgage balance.

Activity: new program listing in 1999.

HQ: Office of Multifamily Housing Assistance Restructuring, HUD, 1280 Maryland Ave. SW - Ste. 4000, Washington, DC 20040. Phone: (202)708-0001. (Note: no field offices for this program.)

14.198   OFFICER NEXT DOOR SALES PROGRAM

Assistance: sale, exchange, donation of property and goods.

Purposes: to improve security in HUD-designated revitalization

areas, by providing 50 percent discounts to law enforcement officers purchasing homes in those neighborhoods. Officers must agree to occupy the homes as their sole residence for at least 36 months. Available homes are listed on the Internet; purchasers are selected by lottery when more than one officer indicates an interest in a property.

Eligible applicants/beneficiaries: federal, state, county, and municipal law enforcement officers.

Range: to 50 percent discount off list price. **Average:** $60,000.

Activity: new program listing in 1999. As of FY 00, 2,750 purchases in 36 states and DC; FY 00 estimate, 1,500 home sales.

HQ: Office of Assistant Secretary/Housing, HUD, 451 Seventh St. SW, Washington, DC 20410. Phones: (800)217-6970; Officer Next Door Specialists, (202)708-1672—*states in the northeast*, ext. 2306; *mid-continent states*, ext. 5545; *far-western states*, ext. 2303; Web, http://www.hud.gov/local/sams/ctznhome.html (Note: no field offices for this program.)

COMMUNITY PLANNING AND DEVELOPMENT

14.218 COMMUNITY DEVELOPMENT BLOCK GRANTS/ENTITLEMENT GRANTS ("CDBG")

Assistance: formula grants (100 percent).

Purposes: pursuant to the Housing and Community Development Act of 1974 as amended, for a broad range of activities designed to result in housing and suitable living environments, neighborhood revitalization, economic development, and improved community facilities and services. Program policy requires that the "principal benefit" be to low- and moderate-income persons—i.e., at least 70 percent of the grant allocation. Projects may be operated by the locality or through subgrantees, including public or nonprofit agencies, neighborhood-based organizations, local development corporations, small business investment companies, and other groups. Permitted uses of funds include: virtually any aspect of residential or nonresidential rehabilitation, including historic preservation and energy conservation; energy development; grants or loans to businesses; revolving loan funds for rehabilitation or for economic development purposes; real property acquisition; relocation of households or businesses; demolition; redevelopment site clearance and preparation for re-use; improvement or installation of public works; certain social service programs; housing code enforcement; city planning and related studies. Ineligible uses include: facilities for the general conduct of government; community-wide facilities; new housing construction; housing subsidies paid directly to occupants; income maintenance payments. Cities must: include citizen participation in program planning; have an approved comprehensive housing assistance plan. For "entitlement" communities CDBG grant amounts are based on a statutory formula.

Eligible applicants: cities in Metropolitan Statistical Areas with populations over 50,000; qualified urban counties of at least 200,000 (excluding the population in entitlement cities); and cities with populations under 50,000 that are central cities in Metropolitan Statistical Areas. NOTE: small cities obtain CDBG funds under **14.219** or **14.228**.

Eligible beneficiaries: low- and moderate-income residents, including those benefiting from projects sponsored by CDBG subgrantees or others who obtain CDBG funds.

Range: N.A.

Activity: FY 98, 989 eligible local government units.

HQ: Entitlement Communities Division, Office of Block Grant Assistance, CPD-HUD, 451 Seventh St. SW, Washington, DC 20410. Phone: (202)708-1577.

14.219 COMMUNITY DEVELOPMENT BLOCK GRANTS/SMALL CITIES PROGRAM ("Small Cities")

Assistance: project grants (100 percent).

Purposes: pursuant to the Housing and Community Development Act of 1974 as amended, to provide funding with limited maximums, for the same eligible uses as for program **14.218**. Funds may also be used for activities meeting urgent community development needs because existing conditions pose a serious and immediate threat to the community health or welfare. Applicants must compete for available funding.

Eligible applicants: "Small cities" are those with populations under 50,000 and that are not central cities within metropolitan areas; there is no minimum population. Under the CDBG State's Program (**14.228**) each state elects whether to administer the Small Cities Program for the non-entitlement communities within its jurisdiction—i.e, those with population under 50,000. HUD administers the Small Cities Program only in the states of Hawaii and New York where eligible applicants are general local government units (including counties), except metropolitan cities, urban counties or units participating in an urban county's CDBG Program, and tribes eligible for assistance under Section 106(a) of the Act; others should seek funding under **14.228**.

Eligible beneficiaries: same as for **14.218**.

Range/Average: N.A.

Activity: N.A.

HQ: State and Small Cities Division, Office of Block Grant Assistance, CPD-HUD, 451 Seventh St. SW, Washington, DC 20410. Phone: (202)708-1322.

14.225   COMMUNITY DEVELOPMENT BLOCK GRANTS/SPECIAL PURPOSE GRANTS/INSULAR AREA

Assistance: project grants (formula based, 100 percent).

Purposes: pursuant to the Housing and Community Development Act of 1974 as amended, basically, the same as for program **14.218**.

Eligible applicants/beneficiaries: Samoa, Guam, Northern Marianas, Palau, VI. (Note: funding for Palau will be phased out after 1998 because Palau became an independent nation in 1994.)

Range: N.A.

Activity: N.A.

HQ: same address/phone as **14.219**.

14.227   COMMUNITY DEVELOPMENT BLOCK GRANTS/SPECIAL PURPOSE GRANTS/TECHNICAL ASSISTANCE PROGRAM

Assistance: project grants (100 percent/1-2 years); direct payments/specified use.

Purposes: pursuant to the Housing and Community Development Act of 1974 as amended, for technical assistance and training in planning and administering CDBG programs.

Eligible applicants/beneficiaries: states, general local government units, tribes, areawide planning organizations; qualified groups.

Range: $16,000 to $830,000. **Average:** $167,000.

Activity: 50 states, 986 entitlement communities assisted.

HQ: Office of Management and Technical Assistance, CPD-HUD, 451 Seventh St. SW, Washington, DC 20410. Phone: (202)708-3176.

14.228   COMMUNITY DEVELOPMENT BLOCK GRANTS/STATE'S PROGRAM

Assistance: formula grants (100 percent).

Purposes: pursuant to the Housing and Community Development Act of 1974 as amended, funding to small cities for uses permitted in program **14.218**. States may elect to administer program **14.219**, or to leave program administration to HUD; all states except Hawaii and New York administer the program themselves.

Eligible applicants/beneficiaries: state governments. States must distribute the funds to units of general local government in non-entitlement areas.

Range: N.A.

Activity: N.A.

HQ: same address/phone as **14.219**.

14.231   EMERGENCY SHELTER GRANTS PROGRAM ("ESG")

Assistance: formula grants (50 percent/to 2 years).

Purposes: pursuant to the McKinney homeless assistance act, to improve existing or to develop additional emergency shelters, transitional housing, and homeless assistance programs. Funds may be used for: renovation, major rehabilitation, or conversion of existing buildings; essential social services; certain maintenance and operating costs; activities to prevent homelessness.

Eligible applicants/beneficiaries: states, metropolitan cities, territories. Other local government units and nonprofit organizations apply to states for funds rather than to HUD. Grantees may, in turn, subcontract with nonprofit entities to conduct program activities.

Range: $75,000 to $7,868,000.

Activity: FY 98, 368 grants.

HQ: Director, Office of Special Needs Assistance Programs, CPD-HUD, 451 Seventh St. SW - Rm.7266, Washington, DC 20410. Phone: (202)708-4300.

14.235   SUPPORTIVE HOUSING PROGRAM

Assistance: project grants (50 percent/to 3 years); direct payments/specified use.

Purposes: pursuant to the McKinney homeless assistance act, to develop transitional housing and supportive services to assist homeless persons in the transition from homelessness and to enable them to live as independently as possible. Funds may support projects to provide: transitional housing for a 24-month period and up to six months of follow-up services; permanent supportive housing for homeless persons with disabilities to maximize participants' ability to live as independently as possible; innovative supportive housing to develop alternative methods of meeting the immediate and long-term needs of homeless individuals and families; supportive services for homeless persons not in conjunction with supportive housing; safe havens for homeless persons with serious mental illness. Funds are available for: facilities leasing (to three years), acquisition, and rehabilitation costs, as well as limited new construction; operating costs and supportive services (to 75 percent for the first two years, to 50 percent for the third year).

Eligible applicants/beneficiaries: state, local, and other governmental entities; nonprofit organizations; public community mental health associations.

Range: acquisition/rehabilitation, to $200,000 ($400,000 in high-cost areas); new construction, to $400,000.

Activity: N.A.

HQ: same address/phone as **14.231**.

14.237   HISTORICALLY BLACK COLLEGES AND UNIVERSITIES PROGRAM

Assistance: project grants (100 percent/to 5 years).

Purposes: pursuant to the Housing and Community Development Act of 1974 as amended, to assist HBCUs in addressing community needs, including neighborhood revitalization, housing, and economic development. Project examples include development of entrepreneurial training center, local vegetable processing plant, and model for self-sufficiency for public housing residents.

Eligible applicants/beneficiaries: HBCUs.

Range: $250,000 to $380,000.

Activity: FY 98 estimate, 19 grants.

HQ: Office of Grant Programs, CPD-HUD, 451 Seventh St. SW, Washington, DC 20410. Phones: (202)708-1590; FAX (202)401-8939.

14.238   SHELTER PLUS CARE

Assistance: project grants (50 percent/5-10 years).

Purposes: pursuant to the McKinney homeless assistance act as amended, to provide rental assistance in connection with supportive services available through other programs, to homeless persons with disabilities and their families—primarily those with serious mental illness, or with substance addictions, or with AIDS and related diseases. Four program components include: Tenant-based Rental Assistance (TRA); Sponsor-based Rental Assistance (SRA); Project-based Rental Assistance (PRA); Single Room Occupancy for Homeless Individuals (SRO). Funds obtained must be matched by supportive services equal in value to the grant amount.

Eligible applicants/beneficiaries: states, local government units, public housing agencies.

Range: N.A.

Activity: N.A.

HQ: same address (except Rm.7262)/phone as **14.231**.

14.239   HOME INVESTMENT PARTNERSHIPS PROGRAM ("HOME Program")

Assistance: formula grants (100 percent/2-5 years).

Purposes: pursuant to the National Affordable Housing Act, to support partnerships among all levels of government and the private sector, including profit and nonprofit organizations, in the production and operation of affordable housing, particularly rental housing for low- and very-low-income families. Funds may be used for: planning; development of model projects; technical assistance; housing rehabilitation; tenant-based rental assistance; assistance to homebuyers; new construction of housing; site acquisition and improvements, demolition, relocation. Fund may not be used: for public housing modernization; to match funds required for other federal programs; as rental housing operating subsidies; for activities under the Low Income Housing Preservation Act, except for priority purchasers.

Eligible applicants: states, cities, urban counties, or consortia or general local government units; Insular Areas.

Eligible beneficiaries: rental housing—90 percent of funds for families with incomes at 60 percent of area median, and the remainder for families below 80 percent. Homeownership assistance—families with incomes below 80 percent of the area median.

Range: $339,000 to $104,240,000. **Average:** $2,650,000.

Activity: cumulatively, funds committed to 347,000 units, 210,000 units completed; 46,000 tenants receiving rental assistance.

HQ: Director, Office of Affordable Housing Programs, CPD-HUD, 451 Seventh St. SW, Washington, DC 20410. Phone: (202)708-2685.

14.241 HOUSING OPPORTUNITIES FOR PERSONS WITH AIDS ("HOPWA")

Assistance: formula grants; project grants (to 3 years).

Purposes: pursuant to the AIDS Housing Opportunity Act as amended, to develop long-term comprehensive strategies to meet the housing needs of low-income persons with AIDS or related diseases, and their families. Eligible funds uses include: resource identification to establish, coordinate, and develop housing assistance; information services including counseling and referral; acquisition, rehabilitation, conversion, lease, and repair of facilities to provide housing and services; construction of single-room occupancy and community residences; project- or tenant-based rental assistance including for shared housing arrangements; short-term rent, mortgage, and utility payments to prevent the homelessness of a tenant or mortgagor; supportive services including health, mental health, assessment, permanent housing placement, alcohol and drug abuse treatment and counseling, nutritional services, day care, intensive care; housing operating costs; training; technical assistance. Resident rent payments are required.

Eligible applicants: entitlement (formula) grants—states and eligible metropolitan areas with the largest number of AIDS cases (communities in metropolitan areas must designate one unit of local government to serve as the applicant/grantee for the area). Competitive project grants—states, local governments, and nonprofit organizations for projects of national significance; states and localities not qualifying for formula grants.

Eligible beneficiaries: low-income persons with AIDS and related diseases, and their families. Housing information may be provided to all persons with AIDS. Persons living near community residences may receive educational information.

Range: formula grants, $92,000 to $48,668,000; competitive, $348,000 to $1,150,000. **Average:** formula, $2,067,000; competitive, $1,008,000.

Activity: FY 99 estimate, housing assistance to 52,000 persons including family members, in 42,000 housing units; rental assistance covering 8,000 units; 6,500 units of supportive housing to be developed.

HQ: Director, Office of HIV/AIDS Housing, CPD-HUD, 451 Seventh St. SW - Rm.7154, Washington, D.C. 20410. Phones: (202)708-1934, TTY (800) 877-8339; Web, http://www.hud.gov/cpd/hopwahom.html

14.243   OPPORTUNITIES FOR YOUTH—YOUTHBUILD PROGRAM ("Youthbuild Program")

Assistance: project grants (100 percent/30 months).

Purposes: pursuant to the National Affordable Housing Act as amended, to help economically disadvantaged high school dropouts obtain the education and employment skills necessary to achieve economic self-sufficiency, and to develop leadership skills and a commitment to community involvement in low-income communities; to provide on-site training in constructing or rehabilitating housing as a community service; to expand the supply of permanent affordable housing for homeless persons and for low- and very-low-income families. Project funds are intended to support: educational and supportive services including basic skills development, counseling, referral, and support services. Although the following are discouraged, funds may also be used for: architectural and engineering fees; housing acquisition, construction, rehabilitation; operating expenses, replacement reserves, and related costs.

Eligible applicants: public or private nonprofit agencies including community-based organizations, Job Training and Partnership Act agencies, community action agencies, state or local housing development agencies, community development corporations, public or Indian housing authorities, resident management organizations, state and local youth service and conservation corps, and other entities including states, local government units, tribes.

Eligible beneficiaries: very-low-income young adults age 16-24 that have dropped out of high school, with special emphasis on eligible young women. Up to 25 percent of project participants not meeting the foregoing criteria but requiring educational services may be allowed.

Range: from $350,000. **Average:** $500,000.

Activity: FY 98, 70 grants awarded—involving 2,264 participants and 859 housing units.

HQ: Office of Economic Development, HUD, 751 Seventh St. SW - Rm.7134, Washington, DC 20410. Phone: (202)708-2035.

14.244   EMPOWERMENT ZONES PROGRAM ("Empowerment Zones and Enterprise Communities")

Assistance: project grants (100 percent/to 10 years).

Purposes: for competitive programs to establish Empowerment Zones and Enterprise Communities in urban and rural areas—to stimulate the creation of new jobs particularly for the disadvantaged and long-term unemployed and to promote revitalization of distressed areas. Designated areas receive

Social Services Block Grant funds from HHS, special tax benefits to employers, and special consideration in obtaining funds under other federal programs.

Eligible applicants/beneficiaries: urban zones—basically, areas no larger than 20 square miles, with 200,000 maximum population or the greater of 50,000 or 10 percent of the population of the most populous city, with pervasive poverty, unemployment, and general distress. Rural zones are defined by USDA (see **10.772**).

Range: $10,000,000 per year to each Empowerment Zone.

Activity: FY 99, 15 designations.

HQ: CPD-HUD, Washington, DC 20410. Phones: (202)708-6339; *general information*, (800)998-9999.

14.246   COMMUNITY DEVELOPMENT BLOCK GRANTS/ECONOMIC DEVELOPMENT INITIATIVE ("Section 108" - "EDI")

Assistance: project grants (1-2 years).

Purposes: pursuant to the Housing and Community Development Act of 1974 as amended, to enhance the security of loans or improve the viability of projects financed under the Section 108 loan guarantee program (**14.248**)— including: commercial, industrial, and economic development revolving loan funds; qualified "brownfields" projects. Activities must be consistent with local CDBG plans and meet citizen participation requirements.

Eligible applicants/beneficiaries: local government units eligible under the Section 108 loan guarantee program.

Range: $97,000 to $2,000,000. **Average:** $1,120,000.

Activity: FY 99, 25 EDI, 23 Brownfields grants.

HQ: Financial Management Division, Office of Block Grant Assistance, CPD-HUD, 451 Seventh St. SW, Washington, DC 20410. Phone: (202)708-1871.

14.247   SELF-HELP HOMEOWNERSHIP OPPORTUNITY PROGRAM

Assistance: project grants (2 years).

Purposes: pursuant to the Housing Opportunity Program Extension Act of 1996, for innovative projects enabling low-income families to become homeowners under the self-help concept, by contributing "sweat equity" toward the construction of dwellings. Program funds may be used only for land acquisition and infrastructure improvements.

Eligible applicants/beneficiaries: nonprofit national or regional organizations or consortia—excluding affiliates of Habitat for Humanity International which are funded separately.

Range: to $10,500,000. **Average:** $10,000 maximum per dwelling.

Activity: new program listing in 1997. FY 98, cumulative total, 1,600 units completed, 1,800 under development; 4 grants awarded.

HQ: same address as **14.239**. Phone: (202)708-3226. (Note: no field offices for this program.)

14.248   COMMUNITY DEVELOPMENT BLOCK GRANTS—SECTION 108 LOAN GUARANTEES
("Section 108")

Assistance: guaranteed/insured loans (to 20 years).

Purposes: pursuant to the Housing and Community Development Act of 1974 as amended, to provide communities with a source of financing for economic development, housing rehabilitation, public facilities, and large-scale physical development projects—provided the "principal benefit" of such projects: is to low- or moderate-income persons; aids in the elimination or prevention of slums and blight; or, meets urgent community needs.

Eligible applicants/beneficiaries: CDBG entitlement and nonentitlement recipients. The public entity may be the borrower or it may designate a public agency.

Range: $100,000 to $41,000,000 (generally, an amount five times the latest CDBG amount received by the public entity, minus any outstanding Section 108 commitment or principal balances).

Activity: new program listing in 1997. FY 98, 96 loan commitments.

HQ: same address/phone as **14.246.**

14.249   SECTION 8 MODERATE REHABILITATION SINGLE ROOM OCCUPANCY

Assistance: project grants (100 percent/10-year contracts).

Purposes: pursuant to the McKinney homeless assistance act as amended, to provide rental assistance to homeless individuals occupying single-room dwelling units rehabilitated specifically for this purpose.

Eligible applicants/beneficiaries: local public housing agencies and private nonprofit organizations.

Range/Average: N.A.

Activity: new program listing in 1998. Cumulatively as of FY 99, 375 grants totaling $800,000,000.

HQ: same address (except Rm.7262)/phone as **14.231.**

14.250   RURAL HOUSING AND ECONOMIC DEVELOPMENT

Assistance: project grants (100 percent/3 years).

Purposes: to expand the supply of affordable housing and access to economic opportunities in rural areas. Funds may support capacity building, innovative housing and economic development programs, and seed money.

Eligible applicants/beneficiaries: local, rural, and nonprofit community development corporations; tribes. State housing finance, community, and economic development agencies may apply only for Innovative Grants.

Range: $150,000 to $500,000. **Average:** $300,000.

Activity: new program in FY 99.

HQ: Deputy Director/Economic Development and Empowerment Services, CPD-HUD, 451 Seventh St. SW, Washington, DC 20410. Phone: (202)709-2290, ext. 4660. (Note: no field offices for this program.)

OFFICE OF FAIR HOUSING AND EQUAL OPPORTUNITY

14.400   EQUAL OPPORTUNITY IN HOUSING ("Fair Housing")

Assistance: investigation of complaints.

Purposes: to enforce the Fair Housing Act protecting the right to choose housing suited to one's needs and financial ability in areas where one chooses to live, without discrimination because of race, color, religion, sex, family status, handicap, or national origin, in the sale, lease, advertising, financing, or appraisal—including multifamily housing built for occupancy after 13 March 1991 which must comply with accessibility guidelines. Complaints are investigated and conciliated; if discrimination is established and conciliation is unsuccessful, complainants receive legal representation in taking further legal action. Technical assistance is available to attorneys, developers, real estate brokers, and the general public.

Eligible applicants/beneficiaries: aggrieved persons may file a complaint with HUD or with a HUD-approved state or local fair housing agency. Suits may be filed in a federal court, seeking injunctive relief, actual or punitive damages together with court costs and reasonable attorney fees. Litigation may be initiated by the individual, by HUD on behalf of the individual, or, under certain conditions, by the Attorney General.

Activity: FY 98, 1,920 complaints processed by HUD, 3,851 by state and local agencies; $9,500,000 in monetary relief obtained.

HQ: Office of Fair Housing and Equal Opportunity, HUD, 451 Seventh St. SW - Rm.5206, Washington, DC 20410. Phones: (202)708-0836; *complaint lines*, (800)669-9777, TTY (800)927-9275.

14.401   FAIR HOUSING ASSISTANCE PROGRAM—STATE AND LOCAL ("FHAP")

Assistance: project grants (100 percent).

Purposes: pursuant to the Fair Housing Act, for administrative costs, technical assistance, training, education, outreach, data and information systems, and special enforcement efforts—to handle complaints regarding violations of fair housing laws.

Eligible applicants/beneficiaries: state and local enforcement agencies administering state and local fair housing laws and ordinances, certified by HUD as providing substantially equivalent rights and remedies as those provided by the Fair Housing Act.

Range: capacity building, $115,000; complaint processing, training, special enforcement, $15,000 to $1,600,000.

Activity: 1998, 80 jurisdictions funded.

HQ: Office of Fair Housing and Equal Opportunity, HUD, 451 Seventh Street SW, Washington, DC 20410. Phones: (202)708-0800.

14.402   NON-DISCRIMINATION IN FEDERALLY-ASSISTED PROGRAMS (ON THE BASIS OF AGE)

Assistance: investigation of complaints.

Purposes: to enforce the Age Discrimination Act of 1975 as amended, prohibiting discrimination on the basis of age, in programs or activities receiving HUD financial assistance. Complaints are referred to FMCS; investigations are conducted by HUD if complaints cannot be mediated successfully.

Eligible applicants/beneficiaries: aggrieved persons may file a complaint with HUD. A complainant may file a civil action following exhaustion of administrative remedies.

Activity: FY 98, 3 complaints.

HQ: Office of Fair Housing and Equal Opportunity, HUD, 451 Seventh St. SW - Rm.5236, Washington, DC 20410. Phone: (202)708-2333.

14.404   NON-DISCRIMINATION IN FEDERALLY ASSISTED AND CONDUCTED PROGRAMS (ON THE BASIS OF DISABILITY) ("Section 504")

Assistance: investigation of complaints.

Purposes: to enforce Section 504 of the Rehabilitation Act of 1973 as it pertains to discrimination against persons with disabilities, in HUD programs except contracts of insurance and guaranty.

Eligible applicants/beneficiaries: aggrieved persons.

Activity: FY 98, 260 complaints received.

HQ: same address (except Rm.5240)/phone as **14.402**.

14.405   NON-DISCRIMINATION IN FEDERALLY ASSISTED PROGRAMS (ON THE BASIS OF RACE, COLOR, OR NATIONAL ORIGIN) ("Title VI")

Assistance: investigation of complaints.

Purposes: to enforce Title VI of the Civil Rights Act of 1964 as amended, prohibiting discrimination on the basis race, color, or national origin, as it pertains to HUD assistance programs except contracts of insurance and guaranty.

Eligible applicants/beneficiaries: aggrieved persons. Complaints may be filed on behalf of specific groups or individuals.

Activity: FY 98, 92 complaints received.

HQ: same address/phone as **14.402**.

14.406   NON-DISCRIMINATION IN THE COMMUNITY DEVELOPMENT BLOCK GRANT PROGRAM (ON THE BASIS OF RACE, COLOR, NATIONAL ORIGIN, RELIGION, OR SEX) ("Section 109")

Assistance: investigation of complaints.

Purposes: pursuant to Title I of the Housing and Community Act of 1974 as amended, to enforce the nondiscrimination provisions of the CDBG program, on the basis of race, color, national origin, religion, or sex.

Eligible applicants/beneficiaries: aggrieved persons. Complaints may be filed on behalf of specific groups or individuals.

Activity: FY 98, 125 complaints received.

HQ: same address/phone as **14.402.**

14.407 ARCHITECTURAL BARRIERS ACT ENFORCEMENT ("Section 502 Architectural Barriers Act")

Assistance: investigation of complaints.

Purposes: to assure that facilities assisted by the federal government are accessible to physically disabled persons, in programs involving HUD including its leased or owned facilities (e.g., public housing).

Eligible applicants/beneficiaries: aggrieved persons. Complaints may be sent to HUD or to the Architectural and Transportation Barriers Compliance Board.

Activity: FY 98, 6 complaints received.

HQ: same address/phone as **14.404.** (Note: no field offices for this program.)

14.408 FAIR HOUSING INITIATIVES AND ADMINISTRATIVE ENFORCEMENT INITIATIVE PROGRAM ("FHIP & AEI")

Assistance: project grants (100 percent/to 18 months).

Purposes: pursuant to the Housing and Community Development Acts of 1987 and 1992 as amended, to develop, execute, or coordinate specialized programs or activities designed to obtain enforcement of the Fair Housing Act—or state or local laws certified by HUD as providing substantially equivalent rights and remedies for discriminatory housing practices.

Eligible applicants/beneficiaries: state and local fair housing agencies.

Range/Average: N.A.

Activity: no program funding since FY 95.

HQ: Deputy Director/Programs, Office of Fair Housing and Equal Opportunity, HUD, 451 Seventh Street SW - Rm.5234, Washington, DC 20410. Phone: (202)708-0800, ext. 7011.

14.409 FAIR HOUSING INITIATIVES PROGRAM EDUCATION (FHIP) AND OUTREACH INITIATIVE ("FHIP & EOI")

Assistance: project grants (100 percent/18 months).

Purposes: pursuant to the Housing and Community Development Acts of 1987 and 1992 as amended, to develop, execute, and coordinate education and outreach programs informing the public concerning rights and obligations provided by the Fair Housing Act, or substantially equivalent state and local laws. Project examples: public service announcements, posters, brochures; fair housing counseling; training for educational institutions and the housing industry.

Eligible applicants/beneficiaries: state and local governments, public or private nonprofit organizations, and other private entities.

Range/Average: N.A.

Activity: FY 98, 12 awards—1 national project, 5 projects addressing community tensions.

HQ: same address/phone as **14.408.**

14.410 FAIR HOUSING INITIATIVES PROGRAM PRIVATE ENFORCEMENT INITIATIVE
("FHIP & PEI")

Assistance: project grants (100 percent/to 18 months).

Purposes: pursuant to the Housing and Community Development Acts of 1987 and 1992 as amended, for projects conducted by private organizations that formulate or carry out programs to prevent or eliminate discriminatory housing practices—to obtain enforcement of the Fair Housing Act or substantially equivalent state and local laws. Projects may involve testing where there are allegations of discrimination. Funds may not be used for litigation against the U.S. government.

Eligible applicants/beneficiaries: private nonprofit fair housing enforcement organizations.

Range: $160,000 to $350,000.

Activity: FY 98, 30 awards.

HQ: same address/phone as **14.408.**

14.412 EMPLOYMENT OPPORTUNITIES FOR LOWER INCOME PERSONS AND BUSINESSES
("Section 3")

Assistance: investigation of complaints.

Purposes: to enforce provisions of the Housing and Urban Development Act of 1968, requiring development of opportunities for job training and employment to lower-income residents in connection with any HUD-funded project in their neighborhoods—as well as for contract opportunities to local businesses. Section 3 also applies to financial assistance in the form of insurance or guaranty, or assistance to tenant-based organizations.

Eligible applicants/beneficiaries: aggrieved lower-income persons residing, or businesses located, in or substantially owned by persons residing in Section 3 areas.

Activity: FY 97, 8,622 jobs generated.

HQ: Office of Fair Housing and Equal Opportunity, HUD, 451 Seventh Street SW - Rm.5112, Washington, DC 20410. Phone: (202)708-2251.

14.413 FAIR HOUSING INITIATIVES AND FAIR HOUSING ORGANIZATIONS INITIATIVE PROGRAM
("FHIP & FHOI")

Assistance: project grants (to 18 months).

Purposes: pursuant to the Housing and Community Development Acts of 1987 and 1992 as amended, in furtherance of Fair Housing Act purposes, to organize, establish, and build the capacity of fair housing enforcement organizations. Continuation grants may not exceed 50 percent.

Eligible applicants/beneficiaries: fair housing enforcement organizations and nonprofit groups.

Range: $93,000 to $400,000.

Activity: FY 98, 6 awards.

HQ: same address/phone as **14.408**.

14.414 NON-DISCRIMINATION ON THE BASIS OF DISABILITY BY PUBLIC ENTITIES
("Title II of the ADA")

Assistance: investigation of complaints.

Purposes: to enforce the provisions of Title II of the Americans with Disabilities Act of 1990, prohibiting discrimination against persons with disabilities, in all programs, services, and regulatory activities relating to state and local government, public housing, and housing assistance and referral.

Eligible applicants/beneficiaries: aggrieved persons.

Activity: FY 98, 138 complaints received.

HQ: same address (except Rm.5240)/phone as **14.402**.

OFFICE OF POLICY DEVELOPMENT AND RESEARCH

14.506 GENERAL RESEARCH AND TECHNOLOGY ACTIVITY

Assistance: project grants.

Purposes: for research, demonstration, and program evaluation and monitoring in such HUD program-related areas as national housing needs, building technology, government-sponsored enterprises, housing affordability, community and urban economic development.

Eligible applicants/beneficiaries: state and local governments, academic institutions, public and private profit and nonprofit organizations.

Range: $2,870 to $500,000. **Average:** $56,000.

Activity: annually, 25 to 80 awards.

HQ: Budget, Contracts, and Program Control Division, Office of Policy Development and Research, HUD, 451 Seventh St. SW, Washington, DC 20410. Phone: (202)708-1796. (Note: no field offices for this program.)

14.511 COMMUNITY OUTREACH PARTNERSHIP CENTER PROGRAM

Assistance: project grants (outreach, 75 percent; research, 50 percent/3 years).

Purposes: for partnerships among IHEs and communities to solve urban problems through research, outreach, and exchange of information. Projects must focus on housing, economic development, neighborhood revitalization, infrastructure, health care, job training, education, crime prevention, planning, community organization, and similar areas.

Eligible applicants/beneficiaries: IHEs.

Range: $150,000 to $400,000.

Activity: annually, 18 new grants.

HQ: Office of University Partnerships, Office of Policy Development and Research, HUD, 451 Seventh St. SW - Rm.8110, Washington, DC 20410. Phone: (202)708-1537, ext. 5918. *For application kits,* HUD User, P.O. Box 6091, Rockville, MD 20849. Phone: (800)245-2691. (Note: no field offices for this program.)

14.512   COMMUNITY DEVELOPMENT WORK-STUDY PROGRAM

Assistance: project grants (100 percent/2 years).

Purposes: for community development work-study programs for minority and economically disadvantaged college students. Students must be enrolled full-time in graduate programs in community and economic development, community or urban planning or management, public administration, urban economics, or related fields. Such fields as law, economics, psychology, education, or history are excluded.

Eligible applicants/beneficiaries: IHEs; states and areawide planning organizations for programs conducted by two or more IHEs.

Range/Average: $30,000 per student.

Activity: annually, 150 students assisted.

HQ: same addresses/phones as **14.511.** (Note: no field offices for this program.)

14.513   HISPANIC-SERVING INSTITUTIONS WORK-STUDY PROGRAM ("HSI-WSP")

Assistance: project grants (100 percent/2 years).

Purposes: for community development work-study programs at Hispanic-serving institutions, for minority and economically disadvantaged college students. Students must be enrolled full-time in associate degree programs in community or economic development, community or urban planning or management, public administration, urban economics, administration of justice, child development, and human services.

Eligible applicants/beneficiaries: public and private two-year IHEs defined as "Hispanic-Serving Institutions of Higher Education" in the Higher Education Act of 1965, and offering associate degrees in a community building academic discipline.

Range: students, to $26,400/year for two years.

Activity: annually, 120 students assisted.

HQ: same addresses/phones as **14.511.** (Note: no field offices for this program.)

14.514   HISPANIC-SERVING INSTITUTIONS ASSISTING COMMUNITIES

Assistance: project grants (100 percent/to 2 years).

Purposes: for Hispanic-serving IHEs to expand their activities in addressing community development needs in their localities, including neighborhood revitalization, housing, and economic development consistent with the purposes Title I of the Housing and Community Development Act of 1974.

Eligible applicants/beneficiaries: public and private two-year IHEs defined as "Hispanic-Serving Institutions of Higher Education" in the Higher Education Act of 1965.

Range/Average: $400,000.

Activity: new program in FY 99.

HQ: same addresses/phones as **14.511**. (Note: no field offices for this program.)

PUBLIC AND INDIAN HOUSING

14.850 PUBLIC AND INDIAN HOUSING

Assistance: direct payments/specified use.

Purposes: pursuant to the Housing Act of 1937 as amended, for the development and operation of lower-income housing by local public housing agencies. Housing may be developed through: acquisition of existing private units; new construction or rehabilitation; "turnkey" contracts with private firms developing the housing; or, "mixed-finance" from both public and private sources, and ownership of the units by entities other than public housing agencies. Funds also may be used for reconstruction of obsolete existing public housing. For projects approved prior to 1 October 1986, HUD makes "annual contributions" to the local agencies for up to 30 years (to 20 years for modernization) to meet debt service requirements that cannot be paid with rental revenue; HUD pays capital costs for contracts executed after 1 October 1986 for up to 40 years. Also, operating subsidies may be available to achieve and maintain adequate operating and maintenance service and reserves. Housing for larger families, requiring three of more bedrooms, receive priority.

Eligible applicants: local public housing agencies. (Note: per the Native American Housing Assistance and Self Determination Act of 1996, Indian housing authorities now are ineligible.)

Eligible beneficiaries: lower-income families that are U.S. citizens or eligible immigrants. "Families" include families with or without children, the elderly and near-elderly, remaining members of a tenant family, certain single persons, and the handicapped and displaced.

Range/Average: N.A.

Activity: FY 98, no new development (all new or replacement housing financed under **14.852**, **14.859**, or **14.866**.); subsidies provided for 1,295,000 existing public housing units.

HQ: Assistant Secretary/Public and Indian Housing, HUD, Washington, DC 20410. Phone: (202)708-0950.

14.852 PUBLIC HOUSING—COMPREHENSIVE IMPROVEMENT ASSISTANCE PROGRAM
("CIAP" - "Public Housing Modernization")

Assistance: project grants (100 percent/to 3 years).

Purposes: pursuant to the Housing Act of 1937 as amended, for capital improvements, major repairs, management improvements, energy conservation, and planning costs incurred by local public housing agencies to modernize existing public housing. FY 99-00 funding for this program is included in **14.859**.

Eligible applicants/beneficiaries: local public housing agencies operating under an existing annual contributions contract, with fewer than 250 units.

Range: $5,550 to $3,652,000. **Average:** $303,000.

Activity: FY 98, 1,004 awards.

HQ: same address/phone as **14.850**.

14.853 PUBLIC HOUSING—TENANT OPPORTUNITIES PROGRAM ("TOP")

Assistance: project grants (100 percent/to 2 years).

Purposes: pursuant to the Housing Act of 1937 as amended, for resident associations to provide technical assistance and training to encourage increased resident activities in public housing projects, such as tenant patrols, resident businesses, child care centers, and other social services programs.

Eligible applicants/beneficiaries: public housing resident associations including resident management corporations; national, regional, and state resident organizations.

Range: $25,000 to $100,000; intermediary organizations, $250,000.

Activity: cumulatively since 1988, 196 resident management contracts, 124 resident-owned businesses, 281 training programs.

HQ: Office of Community Services and Amenities, Office of Public and Assisted Housing Delivery, Assistant Secretary/Public and Indian Housing-HUD, Washington, DC 20410. Phones: (202)708-3611; TDD (800)955-2232.

14.854 PUBLIC AND INDIAN HOUSING DRUG ELIMINATION PROGRAM ("PHDEP")

Assistance: project grants (100 percent/to 2 years); direct payments/specified use.

Purposes: to plan and execute drug elimination programs in and around public housing projects. Funds may be used to: employ security personnel and investigators; reimburse local law enforcement agencies for additional security and protective services; install physical improvements that enhance security; provide funding to resident management groups to develop security and drug abuse prevention, intervention, treatment, and referral programs.

Eligible applicants/beneficiaries: local public housing agencies and Indian housing authorities.

Range/Average: $376,000.

Activity: FY 98, 532 awards.

HQ: Office of Community Safety and Conservation, Office of Community Relations and Involvement, Public and Indian Housing, HUD, 451 Seventh St. SW - Rm.4116, Washington, DC 20410. Phones: (202)708-1197; TDD

(202)708-0850; Drug Information Strategy Clearinghouse, (800)578-3472, FAX (301)519-5681.

14.855   SECTION 8 RENTAL VOUCHER PROGRAM

Assistance: direct payments/specified use (to 5 years).

Purposes: pursuant to the Housing Act of 1937, other housing acts, and amendments, for subsidies of rents paid by very-low-income families. Through local housing agencies, HUD pays participating housing owners, including private owners, the difference between the standard rent and 30 percent of participating families' adjusted incomes. Families must pay a minimum of ten percent of their gross income. Funding for this program is included in **14.857**.

Eligible applicants: state, county, municipal, or other public housing agencies. (Note: per the Native American Housing Assistance and Self Determination Act of 1996, Indian housing authorities are ineligible after current contracts expire.)

Eligible beneficiaries: owners of housing approved for rental to very-low-income families whose incomes, generally, do not exceed 50 percent of median for a given area (80 percent in exceptional cases).

Range: N.A.

Activity: cumulatively as of FY 99, 394,000 rental vouchers available.

HQ: Office of Public and Assisted Housing Delivery, Public and Indian Housing, HUD, Washington, DC 20410. Phone: (202)708-0477.

14.856   LOWER INCOME HOUSING ASSISTANCE PROGRAM—SECTION 8 MODERATE REHABILITATION
("Section 8 Housing Assistance Payments Program for Very Low Income Families - Moderate Rehabilitation")

Assistance: direct payments/specified use.

Purposes: pursuant to the Housing Act of 1937, other housing acts, and amendments, to pay rent subsidies to property owners to cover the difference between low-income renters' adjusted family income and the market rent for moderately rehabilitated housing. The housing owners coordinate with HUD and/or local agencies to obtain the subsidies for their tenants. Payments to owners may be made for up to 180 months. Families must pay toward the rent the highest of: 30 percent of their adjusted monthly family income; ten percent of gross monthly family income; or, the portion of welfare assistance designated for their monthly housing cost. Funding for this program is included in **14.857**. (Note: this program was deleted from the CFDA in 1998 and reinstated in 1999. The program is inactive; no new projects are being approved.)

Eligible applicants: state, county, municipal, or other authorized public housing agencies.

Eligible beneficiaries: same as for **14.850**.

Range/Average: N.A.

Activity: cumulatively as of FY 96, 100,000 units available for occupancy or receiving subsidies.

HQ: Office of Rental Assistance, Deputy Assistant Secretary/Public and Assisted Housing Operations, HUD, Washington, DC 20410. Phone: (202)708-0477.

14.857 SECTION 8 RENTAL CERTIFICATE PROGRAM

Assistance: direct payments/specified use.

Purposes: pursuant to the Housing Act of 1937, National Affordable Housing Act, McKinney homeless assistance act, other acts, and amendments, to make rental assistance payments to participating housing owners for essentially the same purposes and on the same terms as **14.856**. Primarily, the program permits tenants to obtain units of their choice, provided the housing meets program guidelines. Housing agencies may commit 15 percent of certificate funding to new or rehabilitated units. Funding for this program includes **14.855**.

Eligible applicants: same as for **14.855**.

Eligible beneficiaries: same as for **14.850**.

Range/Average: N.A.

Activity: cumulatively as of FY 98, 1,120,000 certificates in effect.

HQ: same address/phone as **14.855**.

14.859 PUBLIC HOUSING—COMPREHENSIVE GRANT PROGRAM
("CGP" - "Public Housing Modernization")

Assistance: project grants (formula-based, 100 percent/to 3 years).

Purposes: pursuant to the Housing Act of 1937 as amended, to improve the physical condition and to upgrade the management and operation of existing public housing projects. CGPs are used as block grants which may fund planning costs, capital improvements, management improvements, and major repairs—consistent with approved comprehensive plans. FY 99-00 funding for this program includes **14.852**.

Eligible applicants/beneficiaries: same as for **14.852**.

Range: $135,000 to $371,252,000. **Average:** $2,459,000.

Activity: FY 98, 830 housing agencies funded.

HQ: same address/phone as **14.850**.

14.862 INDIAN COMMUNITY DEVELOPMENT BLOCK GRANT PROGRAM

Assistance: project grants (100 percent/to 2 years).

Purposes: basically, the same as for program **14.218**.

Eligible applicants/beneficiaries: any tribe, band, group, or nation, including Alaskan Indians, Aleuts, and Eskimos, and any Alaskan native village eligible for assistance under the Indian Self-Determination and Education Assistance Act or, previously, under the Local Fiscal Assistance Act of 1972.

Range/Average: $510,000.

Activity: FY 98, 112 awards.

HQ: Office of Native American Programs, HUD, 1999 N. Broadway - Ste.3990, P.O. Box 90, Denver, CO 80202. Phone: (303)675-1600.

14.864   ECONOMIC DEVELOPMENT AND SUPPORTIVE SERVICES PROGRAM ("EDSS")

Assistance: project grants (some matching/to 3 years).

Purposes: to enable partnerships between public housing agencies or tribes or tribally-designated housing entities (TDHEs) and nonprofit and profit agencies—to facilitate economic development opportunities and supportive services for public housing residents. Funds may support job training and educational programs, including the employment of services coordinators and case managers; for supportive services to elderly and disabled persons, to help them to live independently and to prevent their premature or unnecessary institutionalization.

Eligible applicants/beneficiaries: public housing agencies and tribes or TDHEs.

Range: $26,000 to $1,000,000.

Activity: new program in FY 97.

HQ: Office of Community Services and Amenities, Office of Public and Assisted Housing Delivery, Assistant Secretary/Public and Indian Housing-HUD, 451 Seventh St. SW - Rm.4224, Washington, DC 20410. Phones: (202)708-4214; TDD (202)708-0850.

14.865   PUBLIC AND INDIAN HOUSING—INDIAN LOAN GUARANTEE PROGRAM
("Loan Guarantees for Indian Housing")

Assistance: guaranteed/insured loans (to 30 years).

Purposes: for native Americans, tribes, and tribally-designated housing entities (TDHEs) to acquire new, existing, or rehabilitated homes on Indian land. Such homes may be sold or rented to families. Individual applicant's total debts should not exceed 41 percent of income, including amount of loan.

Eligible applicants/beneficiaries: native Americans including Alaska natives, tribes, tribally-designated housing entities (TDHEs), and Indian housing authorities.

Range: to 97.75 percent of appraised value if over $50,000; to 98.75 percent if under $50,000. **Average:** $107,000.

Activity: new program listing in 1997. FY 98, 186 guaranteed loans.

HQ: Director, Office of Loan Guaranty, same address(except Rm.3390)/phone as **14.862**.

14.866   DEMOLITION AND REVITALIZATION OF SEVERELY DISTRESSED PUBLIC HOUSING
("HOPE VI")

Assistance: project grants (95-100 percent/to 4 years).

Purposes: to revitalize severely distressed or obsolete public housing through: demolition of obsolete projects or portions thereof; where appropriate, revitalization of demolition sites by developing replacement housing that avoids or lessens concentration of very-low-income families. A portion of grant funds may be used for community and supportive services programs.

Eligible applicants/beneficiaries: public housing agencies that operate housing projects.

Range: revitalization, $7,500,000 to $50,000,000; demolition-only, $110,000 to $10,000,000. **Average:** revitalization, $32,900,000; demolition, $2,000,000.

Activity: new program listing in 1997. FY 98, 35 planning, 104 implementation, 78 demolition-only grants.

HQ: Office of Urban Revitalization, Deputy Assistant Secretary/Public Housing Investments, Public and Indian Housing-HUD, Washington, DC 20410. Phone: (202)708-2822.

14.867 INDIAN HOUSING BLOCK GRANTS

Assistance: formula grants (100 percent/2 years).

Purposes: pursuant to the Native American Housing Assistance and Self-Determination Act of 1996, for affordable housing activities such as: Indian housing assistance; development; housing management services; crime prevention and safety; model activities.

Eligible applicants/beneficiaries: tribes or tribally-designated housing entities (TDHEs).

Range/Average: N.A.

Activity: new program in FY 98.

HQ: same address/phone as **14.862**.

14.868 NEW APPROACH ANTI-DRUG GRANTS

Assistance: project grants (100 percent/to 2 years).

Purposes: to eliminate drug-related and other crime problems in or near low-income housing assisted or supported by public or private entities. Projects are conducted by partnerships of owner-operators of eligible housing with federal and local law enforcement, local government units, and others—using comprehensive coordinated neighborhood or community-based approaches. Funds may support: increased police presence; security services provided by others such as state law enforcement entities, resident-management associations, or private security agencies; reimbursement of local and state prosecuting offices and related public agencies for the prosecution or investigation of crimes; capital improvements to enhance security including police mini-stations, lighting systems, closed-circuit TV.

Eligible applicants/beneficiaries: "assisted housing" owner-operators receiving financial support from local government units or private nonprofit sources. Subgrantees must include the general local government unit, preferably with the local police department and district attorney or prosecutor's office, and other community stakeholders such as residents, neighborhood businesses, nonprofit providers of support services including spiritually-based organizations and their affiliates; and, public housing authorities and tribally-designated housing entities (TDHEs).

Range/Average: N.A.

Activity: new program in FY 98.

HQ: Office of Community Safety and Conservation, HUD, Washington, DC 20410. Phone: (202)708-1197. *Program policy and other guidance,* HUD State Office, 3600 W. Broad St., Richmond, VA 23230-4920. Phone: (804) 278-4504, ext. 3027. *Application materials,* Super NOFA Information Center phones: (800)HUD-8929; TTY (800)HUD-2209; Web, www.HUD.gov

14.869 TITLE VI FEDERAL GUARANTEES FOR FINANCING TRIBAL HOUSING ACTIVITIES

Assistance: guaranteed/insured loans (20 years).

Purposes: pursuant to the Native American Housing Assistance and Self-Determination Act of 1996, to assist tribes or TDHEs to obtain financing where an obligation cannot be completed without such guaranty. Assistance is limited to eligible affordable housing activities listed in Section 202 of the Act.

Eligible applicants/beneficiaries: approved recipients of program **14.867** funds.

Range: to five times the amount of program **14.867** funds received.

Activity: new program in FY 99.

HQ: Director, Office of Loan Guaranty, same address/phone as **14.862**

14.870 RESIDENT OPPORTUNITY AND SUPPORTIVE SERVICES ("ROSS")

Assistance: project grants (some matching/2 years).

Purposes: to assist public housing residents through economic development and supportive services activities, organizational development, mediation—including the employment of service coordinators or case managers.

Eligible applicants/beneficiaries: public and Indian housing agencies, TDHEs, resident management corporations, resident councils.

Range/Average: N.A.

Activity: new program listing in 1999.

HQ: Public and Indian Housing-HUD, 451 Seventh St. SW, Washington, DC 20410. Phones: (202)708-4214; TDD (202)708-0850. (Note: no field offices for this program.)

OFFICE OF LEAD HAZARD CONTROL

14.900 LEAD-BASED PAINT HAZARD CONTROL IN PRIVATELY-OWNED HOUSING

Assistance: project grants (90-100 percent/2-3 years).

Purposes: for programs to identify and control lead-based paint hazards in privately-owned housing occupied by low- or very-low-income families, and to prevent childhood lead poisoning caused by lead-based paint; for research (100 percent funding) on the effectiveness of control methods and techniques, as well as other aspects of lead contamination. Lead Hazard Control Grants (90 percent funding) may support such activities as: risk assessment, inspection, and testing of paint, dust, and soil in housing constructed prior to 1978; abatement of lead-based hazards; use of hazard reduction techniques; temporary relocation of affected families; blood testing of children under age 6 in affected housing—as well as of workers, supervisors, and contractors; air sampling; minimal housing rehabilitation required to abate hazards; pre- and post-hazard reduction testing; interim controls; interim control of hazards in priority housing; community education programs; liability insurance; data collection, analysis, and evaluation and case study preparation; planning and management costs including those involving coordination with or by states and counties; state contractor certification and worker training. Projects must be conducted by certified contractors and workers. Mold and Mildew Control Grants may be used for research in inner-city housing.

Eligible applicants/beneficiaries: Lead Hazard Control Grants—states, tribes, and local general government units. Research grants—academic and non-profit institutions; state and local governments; profit organizations agreeing to participate without fee or profit. Mold and Mildew Control Grants—only state and local governments.

Range: control, $1,000,000 to $4,000,000; research, $103,000 to $1,200,000.

Activity: cumulatively since FY 93 program inception, 28,000 units tested, 15,000 units made lead-safe; 2,700 units undergoing hazard mitigation. FY 99 estimate, 20-25 control, 3-8 research, 1-3 Mold & Moisture Control awards.

HQ: Program Management Division, Office of Lead Hazard Control, HUD, 451 Seventh St. SW - Rm.P-3206, Washington, DC 20410. Phones: *control grants,* (202)755-1785, ext.112; *research, Mold & Moisture Control grants,* Planning and Standards Division, (202)(202)755-1785, ext.115. (Note: no field offices for this program.)

DEPARTMENT OF THE INTERIOR

BUREAU OF INDIAN AFFAIRS

15.020   AID TO TRIBAL GOVERNMENTS

Assistance: direct payments/specified use.

Purposes: pursuant to ISDEAA as amended, to support general tribal government operations, to maintain up-to-date tribal enrollment records, to conduct tribal elections, and to develop tribal policies, legislation, and regulations.

Eligible applicants/beneficiaries: federally recognized tribal governments.

Range: $10,000 to $700,000. **Average:** $80,000.

Activity: new program listing in 1997. Annually, 15 tribes distribute judgment funds; 80-90 tribes revise their constitutions; 50,000 certificates of degree of Indian blood issued.

HQ: Chief, Division of Tribal Government Services (MS 4641-MIB), BIA-DOI, 1849 C St. NW, Washington, DC 20240. Phone: (202)208-4097.

15.022   TRIBAL SELF-GOVERNANCE

Assistance: direct payments/specified use.

Purposes: pursuant to ISDEAA as amended, for such tribal programs as law enforcement, social services, welfare payments, natural resource management and enhancement, housing improvement, road maintenance, college scholarships, economic development and job training—but not for the operation of educational institutions.

Eligible applicants/beneficiaries: federally recognized tribal governments and consortia.

Range: $330,000 to $9,000,000. **Average:** $6,000,000.

Activity: new program listing in 1997. FY 99, 67 agreements covering 209 tribes.

HQ: Director, Office of Self-Governance-OS (MS 2542-MIB), BIA-DOI, 1849 C St. NW, Washington, DC 20240. Phone: (202)219-0240.

15.023   TRIBAL SELF-GOVERNANCE GRANTS

Assistance: project grants (100 percent).

Purposes: pursuant to ISDEAA as amended, to support self-governance planning, legal and budgetary research, negotiations with BIA and other agencies, and related activities; to cover initial management expenses; for self-governance education, training, and dissemination of information.

Eligible applicants/beneficiaries: federally recognized tribal governments and consortia.

Range: $10,000 to $20,000. **Average:** $20,000.

Activity: new program listing in 1997. FY 99 estimate, 10 BIA negotiation grants, 5 advance planning grants.

HQ: same address (except MS 2548-MIB)/phone as **15.022.**

15.024   INDIAN SELF-DETERMINATION CONTRACT SUPPORT ("Contract Support")

Assistance: direct payments/specified use.

Purposes: pursuant to ISDEAA as amended, to cover indirect costs incurred in administering federal programs.

Eligible applicants/beneficiaries: federally recognized tribal governments and authorized organizations.

Range: $10,000 to $8,000,000. **Average:** $190,000.

Activity: new program listing in 1997. Annually, 470 tribal governments and organizations funded.

HQ: Division of Self-Determination Services (MS 4603-MIB), BIA-DOI, 1849 C St. NW, Washington, DC 20240. Phone: (202)208-5727.

15.025   SERVICES TO INDIAN CHILDREN, ELDERLY AND FAMILIES ("Social Services")

Assistance: direct payments/specified use.

Purposes: pursuant to ISDEAA as amended, to administer welfare assistance programs for adults and children including foster care placement; to reduce substance abuse. Funds may support caseworkers and counselors, staffing and operation of emergency shelters, and similar costs.

Eligible applicants/beneficiaries: federally recognized tribal governments.

Range: $10,000 to $4,800,000. **Average:** $100,000.

Activity: new program listing in 1997. Annually, 130 tribes funded.

HQ: Division of Social Services (MS 4641-MIB), BIA-DOI, 1849 C St. NW, Washington, DC 20240. Phone: (202)208-2479.

15.026   INDIAN ADULT EDUCATION

Assistance: direct payments/specified use.

Purposes: pursuant to the Snyder Act of 1921 and ISDEAA as amended, to establish and conduct Indian adult education programs.

Eligible applicants/beneficiaries: federally recognized tribal governments.

Range: $100 to $629,000. **Average:** $25,000.

Activity: new program listing in 1997. Annually, 140 tribes funded.

HQ: Office of Indian Education Programs (MS-3512 MIB), BIA-DOI, 1849 C St. NW, Washington, DC 20240. Phone: (202)219-1129.

15.027   ASSISTANCE TO TRIBALLY CONTROLLED COMMUNITY COLLEGES AND UNIVERSITIES

Assistance: project grants (100 percent).

Purposes: pursuant to the Tribally Controlled College Assistance Act, to operate and improve tribally controlled community colleges, including expansion of their physical resources.

Eligible applicants/beneficiaries: nonprofit, nonsectarian colleges sponsored by federally recognized tribal governments and organizations, offering certificates or associate, baccalaureate, or graduate degrees.

Range: $154,000 to $6,967,000 (based on enrollment). **Average:** $1,222,000.

Activity: new program listing in 1997. Annually, 20,000 Indian students enrolled; 1,000 graduates.

HQ: same address as **15.026**. Phone: (202)219-1127.

15.028   TRIBALLY CONTROLLED COMMUNITY COLLEGE ENDOWMENTS

Assistance: project grants (50 percent).

Purposes: pursuant to the Tribally Controlled College Assistance Act, to establish endowments for tribally controlled community colleges. Interest earned may be used to defray college operating costs, but not to benefit private persons.

Eligible applicants/beneficiaries: colleges chartered by federally recognized tribes, offering certificates or associate, baccalaureate, or graduate degrees.

Range: $27,000 to $52,000. **Average:** $41,000.

Activity: new program listing in 1997. Annually, 24 colleges receive grants

HQ: same address as **15.026**. Phone: (202)219-2127.

15.029 TRIBAL COURTS

Assistance: direct payments/specified use.

Purposes: pursuant to ISDEAA as amended, to operate judicial branches of tribal governments. Funds may support salaries and related expenses of judges, prosecutors, defenders, clerks, probation and juvenile officers, and other court personnel.

Eligible applicants/beneficiaries: federally recognized tribal governments.

Range: $15,000 to $800,000. **Average:** $50,000.

Activity: new program listing in 1997. Annually, 200 tribes operate tribal courts.

HQ: same address as **15.020**. Phone: (202)208-4400.

15.030 INDIAN LAW ENFORCEMENT

Assistance: direct payments/specified use.

Purposes: pursuant to ISDEAA as amended and to the Indian Law Enforcement Act, for tribal governments to operate police departments and detention facilities. Funds may be used for salaries and related expenses of criminal investigators, uniformed officers, detention personnel, radio dispatchers, administrative costs.

Eligible applicants/beneficiaries: federally recognized tribal governments.

Range: $20,000 to $20,000,000. **Average:** $200,000.

Activity: new program listing in 1997. Annually, 200 tribes funded; 32 detention facilities operated.

HQ: Director, Office of Law Enforcement Services, BIA-DOI, 417 Gold SW - Ste.120, P.O. Box 66, Albuquerque, NM 87103. Phone: (505)248-7937.

15.031 INDIAN COMMUNITY FIRE PROTECTION

Assistance: direct payments/specified use.

Purposes: pursuant to ISDEAA as amended, for fire protection services when tribal governments do not receive such services from state or local governments. Funds may cover costs of staff, volunteer firefighters training, equipment purchases and repairs, and to purchase smoke detectors, fire extinguishers, fire escapes, and emergency lighting for public buildings.

Eligible applicants/beneficiaries: federally recognized tribal governments.

Range: $300 to $153,000. **Average:** $33,000.

Activity: new program listing in 1997. Annually, 40 tribes funded.

HQ: Director, Office of Tribal Services (MS 4603-MIB), BIA-DOI, 1849 C St. NW, Washington, DC 20240. Phone: (202)208-3463.

15.032 INDIAN ECONOMIC DEVELOPMENT

Assistance: direct payments/specified use.

Purposes: pursuant to the Snyder Act of 1921, ISDEAA as amended, and other acts, for the administration of revolving loan and loan guaranty programs, including assistance to Indian-owned businesses in obtaining private financing—toward the improvement of tribal economies. Administered programs may include BIA's Loan Guaranty and Insurance Fund, Indian Business Development Program, and Community and Economic Development Program.

Eligible applicants/beneficiaries: federally recognized tribal governments.

Range: $50,000 to $300,000. **Average:** $215,000.

Activity: new program listing in 1997. No specific numbers provided.

HQ: Office of Economic Development (MS 4640), BIA-DOI, 1849 C St. NW, Washington, DC 20240. Phone: (202)501-5324.

15.033 ROAD MAINTENANCE—INDIAN ROADS

Assistance: direct payments/specified use.

Purposes: pursuant to the Federal Highway Act of 1921 and ISDEAA as amended, for limited routine maintenance of roads, bridges, and airstrips serving Indian reservations, emphasizing school bus routes and arterial highways.

Eligible applicants/beneficiaries: federally recognized tribal governments and authorized organizations.

Range: $300 to $500,000. **Average:** $100,000.

Activity: new program listing in 1997. Annually, maintenance of 50,000 miles of roads, 745 bridges, and numerous airstrips, and operation of a ferry.

HQ: Division of Transportation, Office of Trust Responsibilities (MS-4510), BIA-DOI, 1849 C St. NW, Washington, DC 20240. Phone: (202)208-4359.

15.034 AGRICULTURE ON INDIAN LANDS

Assistance: direct payments/specified use; advisory services/counseling; specialized services.

Purposes: pursuant to ISDEAA as amended and to the American Indian Agriculture Resource Management Act, to protect and restore the agronomic and rangeland resources on trust lands; to facilitate the development of renewable agricultural resources following principles of sustained yield management. Noxious weed eradication requires 50 percent local matching funds.

Eligible applicants/beneficiaries: federally recognized tribal governments and authorized organizations.

Range: $200 to $575,000. **Average:** $50,000; noxious weed eradication, $20,000.

Activity: new program listing in 1997. Annually, 28,500 farmers, ranchers, and landowners assisted; 50 noxious weed eradication awards, treating 80,000 acres.

HQ: Branch of Agriculture and Range, Division of Water and Land Resources, Office of Trust Responsibilities (MS 4513-MIB), BIA-DOI, 1849 C St. NW, Washington, DC 20240. Phone: (202)208-3598.

15.035   FORESTRY ON INDIAN LANDS

Assistance: direct payments/specified use; advisory services/counseling; specialized services.

Purposes: pursuant to the Snyder Act of 1921, ISDEAA as amended, and other acts, for Indian forest management activities to maintain, protect, enhance, and develop forest resources. Funds may be used for reforestation, commercial stand improvement, timber sales management, forest planning and inventories.

Eligible applicants/beneficiaries: federally recognized tribal governments and authorized organizations (currently limited to the Intertribal Timber Council).

Range: $10,000 to $1,000,000. **Average:** $100,000.

Activity: new program listing in 1997. FY 98, reforestation on 12,000 acres.

HQ: Division of Forestry, Office of Trust Responsibilities (MS 4513-MIB), BIA-DOI, 1849 C St. NW, Washington, DC 20240. Phone: (202)208-4439.

15.036   INDIAN RIGHTS PROTECTION

Assistance: direct payments/specified use.

Purposes: pursuant to ISDEAA as amended and other acts, to protect Indian rights guaranteed through treaty or statute by obtaining the services or information needed by the federal government to litigate challenges to these rights. Project examples: research and data collection concerning water and land title disputes, hunting and fishing rights, environmental problems.

Eligible applicants/beneficiaries: federally recognized tribal governments and authorized organizations.

Range: $1,000 to $100,000. **Average:** $25,000.

Activity: new program listing in 1997. Not quantified specifically.

HQ: Office of Trust Responsibilities (MS-4510 MIB), BIA-DOI, 1849 C St. NW, Washington, DC 20240. Phone: (202)208-7737.

15.037   WATER RESOURCES ON INDIAN LANDS

Assistance: direct payments/specified use; advisory services/counseling; specialized services.

Purposes: pursuant to the Snyder Act of 1921 and ISDEAA as amended, to assist tribes in the management, planning, and development of their water and related land resources. Water Management, Planning, and Development funds are awarded competitively. Project examples: geographic, hydrologic quantitative and qualitative analysis of water, ground, surface water monitoring; aquifer classification and stream gauging.

Eligible applicants/beneficiaries: federally recognized tribal governments and authorized organizations.

Range: $200 to $750,000. **Average:** $50,000.

Activity: new program listing in 1997. FY 98, 63 studies and investigations.

HQ: same address as **15.034**. Phone: (202)208-6042.

15.038   MINERALS AND MINING ON INDIAN LANDS

Assistance: direct payments/specified use; specialized services; technical information.

Purposes: pursuant to the Snyder Act of 1921 and ISDEAA as amended and to other acts, to assist and support the inventory and development of energy and minerals on Indian lands. Minerals and Mining funds may be used to inventory, develop, and produce nonrenewable resources; Mineral Assessment funds may be used for inventory programs and to develop baseline data. Project examples: feasibility studies; lease compliance; environmental reviews; seismic explorations; mapping systems.

Eligible applicants/beneficiaries: federally recognized tribal governments and authorized organizations.

Range: assessments, $10,000 to $400,000. **Average:** $70,000.

Activity: new program listing in 1997. Annually, 8-10 assessment projects funded.

HQ: Division of Energy and Minerals, Office of Trust Responsibilities, BIA-DOI, 12136 W. Bayaud Ave. - Ste.300, Lakewood, CO 80228. Phone: (303)969-5270, ext. 227.

15.039   FISH, WILDLIFE, AND PARKS PROGRAMS ON INDIAN LANDS ("Wildlife and Parks")

Assistance: direct payments/specified use.

Purposes: pursuant to the Snyder Act of 1921 and ISDEAA as amended, to promote the conservation, development, and utilization of fish, wildlife, and recreational resources for sustenance, cultural enrichment, economic support, and maximum benefit of Indians. Tribes participate in resource planning and management with their state and federal counterparts.

Eligible applicants/beneficiaries: federally recognized tribal governments and authorized organizations.

Range: $5,000 to $800,000; fish hatchery maintenance, $1,500 to $22,000. **Average:** hatcheries, $12,000.

Activity: new program listing in 1997. Awards to 8 intertribal fish and wildlife commissions and authorities, 14 fish-producing tribes, 100 tribal fish hatcheries, 32 individual fish and wildlife resource tribes, 6 tribal fish and wildlife organizations.

HQ: Branch of Fish, Wildlife, and Recreation, Division of Water and Land Resources, Office of Trust Responsibilities (MS 4513-MIB), BIA-DOI, 1849 C St. NW, Washington, DC 20240. Phone: (202)208-4088.

15.040   REAL ESTATE PROGRAMS—INDIAN LANDS

Assistance: direct payments/specified use.

Purposes: pursuant to ISDEAA as amended, the Indian Land Consolidation Act, and other acts, to provide real property management, counseling, and land use planning services to individual Indian allottees and tribal and Alaska native entities owning an interest in the almost 56,000,000 acres of trust land; to provide appraisal services required in processing land transactions; to protect and enhance the Indian leasehold estate by providing individual landowners and tribes with lease compliance activities.

Eligible applicants/beneficiaries: federally recognized tribal governments and authorized organizations; individual American Indians.

Range: services, $1,000 to $500,000; appraisals, $500 to $2,500; lease compliance, $250 to $30,000. **Average:** lease compliance, to $5,000.

Activity: new program listing in 1997. FY 98, 12,000 surface leases approved; 7,800 acquisitions, 4,000 land sales processed; 20,000 appraisals; 25,000 inspections completed on 100,000 leases.

HQ: same address/phone as **15.036.**

15.041   ENVIRONMENTAL MANAGEMENT—INDIAN PROGRAMS

Assistance: direct payments/specified use.

Purposes: pursuant to ISDEAA as amended, CERCLA, and other acts, to determine environmental impacts of federal projects on Indian lands and to identify hazardous waste sites—to determine compliance with the National Environmental Policy Act; to obtain information for compliance with the National Historic Preservation Act and the Archeological Resources Protection Act.

Eligible applicants/beneficiaries: federally recognized tribal governments and authorized organizations.

Range: $5,000 to $250,000. **Average:** $25,000.

Activity: new program listing in 1997. Annually, 3,000 compliance issues addressed.

HQ: Division of Environmental and Cultural Resources, Office of Trust Responsibilities (MS 4516-MIB), BIA-DOI, 1849 C St. NW, Washington, DC 20240. Phone: (202)208-5696.

15.042   INDIAN SCHOOL EQUALIZATION PROGRAM
("ISEP")

Assistance: direct payments/specified use.

Purposes: pursuant to ISDEAA as amended and other acts, for primary and secondary education including residential programs for Indian students not served by public or sectarian schools.

Eligible applicants/beneficiaries: federally recognized tribes or tribal organizations currently served by a BIA-funded school.

Range: $129,000 to $5,890,000. **Average:** $1,325,000 per school.

Activity: new program listing in 1997. Annually, 30,000 students served by 116 tribally operated schools.

HQ: same address/phone as **15.026.**

15.043   INDIAN CHILD AND FAMILY EDUCATION
("Family and Child Education Act" - "FACE")

Assistance: project grants (100 percent); training.

Purposes: pursuant to the Indian Education Amendments of 1978, to conduct early childhood education, adult education, and parenting skills programs. Funds may not support administration costs.

Eligible applicants/beneficiaries: federally recognized tribes or tribal organizations with BIA-funded schools.

Range/Average: $225,000 per site.

Activity: new program listing in 1997. Annually, 1,800 children and 1,700 families receive services.

HQ: same address as **15.026**. Phone: (202)219-1127.

15.044   INDIAN SCHOOLS—STUDENT TRANSPORTATION

Assistance: direct payments/specified use.

Purposes: pursuant to ISDEAA as amended and other laws, to provide round-trip transportation of students between home and schools.

Eligible applicants: federally recognized tribal governments or tribal organizations currently served by a BIA-funded school.

Eligible beneficiaries: Indian children age 5 to 21, enrolled in schools eligible for assistance under **15.042**.

Range: $2,000 to $1,133,000. **Average:** $204,000.

Activity: new program listing in 1997. Annually, 20,000 students served.

HQ: same address/phone as **15.026**.

15.045   ASSISTANCE FOR INDIAN CHILDREN WITH SEVERE DISABILITIES ("Institutionalized Handicapped")

Assistance: direct payments/specified use.

Purposes: pursuant to ISDEAA as amended, IDEA, and other acts, for special education and related services to Indian children with severe disabilities, including: physical, occupational, and speech therapy; counseling; direct academic services; administration and staff development.

Eligible applicants/beneficiaries: members or direct descendants of members of federally recognized tribes, age 5 to 21, determined to need of specialized services available only in residential settings—enrolled in BIA-funded schools.

Range: $140 to $300 per day.

Activity: new program listing in 1997. Annually, institutional services to 170 students requiring 24-hours/day attention.

HQ: same address as **15.026**. Phone: (202)208-6675.

15.046   ADMINISTRATIVE COST GRANTS FOR INDIAN SCHOOLS

Assistance: project grants (100 percent).

Purposes: pursuant to ISDEAA as amended and other acts, to pay school operating costs including administration, property and procurement management, insurance, security, and related expenses.

Eligible applicants/beneficiaries: federally recognized tribal governments or organizations operating BIA-funded schools.

Range: $49,000 to $1,785,000. **Average:** $363,000.

Activity: new program listing in 1997. Annually, funding for 105 tribally operated schools.

HQ: same address/phone as **15.026.**

15.047   INDIAN EDUCATION FACILITIES, OPERATIONS, AND MAINTENANCE

Assistance: direct payments/specified use.

Purposes: pursuant to ISDEAA as amended and other acts, for Indian-controlled schools to pay facilities operations and maintenance costs including personnel, utilities, minor repairs, equipment, and similar costs.

Eligible applicants/beneficiaries: federally recognized tribal governments or organizations currently served by BIA-funded elementary or secondary schools or peripheral dormitories.

Range: $9,600 to $1,326,000. **Average:** $360,000.

Activity: new program listing in 1997. Annually, 100 schools receive funded.

HQ: same address/phone as **15.026.**

15.048   BUREAU OF INDIAN AFFAIRS FACILITIES—OPERATIONS AND MAINTENANCE

Assistance: direct payments/specified use.

Purposes: pursuant to ISDEAA as amended, for basic operating and maintenance services provided to BIA-owned or -operated noneducation facilities, including expenses incurred for personnel, supplies, planning, utility costs, telecommunications equipment, and similar costs.

Eligible applicants/beneficiaries: federally recognized tribal governments with BIA-owned or -operated facilities on their reservations.

Range/Average: N.A.

Activity: new program listing in 1997. Annually, funding for 1,263 buildings, excluding quarters.

HQ: Director, Facilities Management and Construction Center, BIA-DOI, 201 Third St. NW - Ste.500, P.O. Box 1248, Albuquerque, NM 87103. Phone: (505)766-2825.

15.049   IRRIGATION OPERATIONS AND MAINTENANCE ON INDIAN LANDS

Assistance: direct payments/specified use; specialized services; use of property, facilities, and equipment.

Purposes: pursuant to ISDEAA as amended and other acts, to operate and maintain existing Indian irrigation projects and the Indian Dams Safety Maintenance Program.

Eligible applicants/beneficiaries: federally recognized tribal governments and authorized organizations.

Range: $8,000 to $3,000,000.

Activity: new program listing in 1997. Not quantified specifically.

HQ: same address as **15.034.** Phone: (202)208-5480.

15.050   UNRESOLVED INDIAN HUNTING AND FISHING RIGHTS

Assistance: direct payments/specified use.

Purposes: pursuant to the Snyder Act of 1921 and ISDEAA as amended, to assist tribes in negotiations with other fish and wildlife resource management authorities in clarifying and defining their off-reservation hunting, fishing, and gathering rights.

Eligible applicants/beneficiaries: federally recognized tribal governments and authorized organizations.

Range: $50,000 to $320,000.

Activity: new program listing in 1997. Generally, only 1 competitive award annually, supporting 20 tribes; 1-2 competitive awards.

HQ: same address/phone as **15.039.**

15.051   ENDANGERED SPECIES ON INDIAN LANDS

Assistance: direct payments/specified use; technical information; advisory services/counseling.

Purposes: pursuant to the Snyder Act of 1921, ISDEAA as amended, and the Endangered Species Act, to enable compliance with the Endangered Species Act, the Northern Spotted Owl Recovery Plan, and to implement the Cheyenne River Prairie Management Plan on Indian lands. Project examples: water impoundments, cross fencing and vegetative management; owl and habitat surveys.

Eligible applicants/beneficiaries: federally recognized tribal governments and authorized organizations.

Range: $20,000 to $500,000. **Average:** $100,000.

Activity: new program listing in 1997. Annually, 12 tribes funded.

HQ: same address as **15.034.** Phone: (202)208-3607.

15.052   LITIGATION SUPPORT FOR INDIAN RIGHTS

Assistance: direct payments/specified use.

Purposes: pursuant to ISDEAA as amended and other acts, to establish or defend Indian property or treaty rights through judicial, administrative, or settlement actions. Funds may be used to pay for expert witnesses, research, data collection, technical support, and other evidence-gathering activities required to defend such rights issues as: hunting, fishing, and gathering; trespass; titles; allotment claims; mineral entry; Equal Access to Justice Act settlements.

Eligible applicants/beneficiaries: federally recognized tribal governments and authorized organizations.

Range: $2,000 to $220,000. **Average:** $76,000.

Activity: new program listing in 1997. FY 98, 27 projects funded.

HQ: same address as **15.036.** Phone: (202)208-7216.

15.053   ATTORNEY FEES—INDIAN RIGHTS

Assistance: direct payments/specified use.

Purposes: to support tribes in protecting their treaty rights and other rights established through executive order or court action, by providing assistance in obtaining legal representation. Project examples: environmental damage claims; water rights negotiation or litigation; boundary disputes.

Eligible applicants/beneficiaries: federally recognized tribal governments.

Range: $20,000 to $237,000. **Average:** $60,000.

Activity: new program listing in 1997. FY 98, 27 applications funded.

HQ: same address as **15.036**. Phone: (202)208-7216.

15.055 ALASKAN INDIAN ALLOTMENTS AND SUBSISTENCE PREFERENCE— ALASKA NATIONAL INTEREST LANDS CONSERVATION ACT ("ANILCA")

Assistance: direct payments/specified use.

Purposes: pursuant to the Alaska National Interest Lands Conservation Act, ISDEAA as amended, and other acts, to assist Alaska natives in acquiring title to lands they occupy; to study past subsistence uses and conduct population studies on subsistence resources.

Eligible applicants/beneficiaries: federally recognized tribal governments in Alaska and authorized organizations; individual Alaska natives.

Range: allotments, $12,000 to $221,000; subsistence preferences, $15,000 to $40,000.

Activity: new program listing in 1997. Cumulatively, 9,000 parcels finalized, 2,800 parcels awaiting final action.

HQ: same address as **15.036**. Phone: (202)208-5831.

15.057 NAVAJO-HOPI INDIAN SETTLEMENT PROGRAM

Assistance: direct payments/specified use.

Purposes: pursuant to the Navajo-Hopi Settlement Act and ISDEAA as amended, to restore the grazing potential of rangeland within the former Navajo/Hopi Joint Use Area, including: livestock monitoring; issuance of grazing permits; implementation of range management plans and grazing control methods; establishment of range units and grazing capacity; removal of trespass livestock on the Hopi Partitioned Lands; initiation of grazing control on the Navajo Partitioned Lands; natural resources restoration.

Eligible applicants/beneficiaries: federally recognized tribal governments of the Navajo and Hopi tribes and organizations authorized by either tribe.

Range: $5,000 to $150,000. **Average:** $75,000.

Activity: new program listing in 1997. Activities are ongoing.

HQ: same address as **15.036**. Phone: (202)208-3598.

15.058 INDIAN POST SECONDARY SCHOOLS ("Haskell and SIPI")

Assistance: training.

Purposes: pursuant to the Snyder Act of 1921, to enable American Indian students to attend either of the BIA-operated postsecondary schools without charge for tuition or room and board—Haskell Indian Nations University and Southwestern Indian Polytechnic Institute (SIPI).

Eligible applicants/beneficiaries: members of federally recognized tribes.

Activity: new program listing in 1997. Annually, 900 students enrolled at Haskell, 100 graduates; 600 students enrolled at SIPI, 80 graduates.

HQ: Haskell Indian Nations University, 155 Indian Ave., Lawrence, KS 66046. Phone: (913)749-8454. *Or,* SIPI, 9169 Coors Rd. NW, Albuquerque, NM 81774. Phones: (505)897-5362, (800)586-SIPI.

15.059 INDIAN GRADUATE STUDENT SCHOLARSHIPS ("Special Higher Education Scholarships")

Assistance: project grants.

Purposes: pursuant to the Snyder Act of 1921, to provide financial aid to Indian students, enabling them to obtain advanced degrees.

Eligible applicants/beneficiaries: Indian students that are members of federally recognized tribal governments, admitted to a graduate program.

Range: $250 to $4,000. **Average:** $3,200.

Activity: new program listing in 1997. Annually, 325 students assisted.

HQ: American Indian Graduate Center, 4520 Montgomery Blvd. - Ste.1-B, Albuquerque, NM 87109. Phone: (505)881-4584. (Note: no other field offices for this program.)

15.060 INDIAN VOCATIONAL TRAINING—UNITED TRIBES TECHNICAL COLLEGE

Assistance: training; direct payments/specified use.

Purposes: pursuant to the Snyder Act of 1921, ISDEAA as amended, and other acts, to provide vocational training to American Indians through the United Tribes Technical College in Bismarck, North Dakota.

Eligible applicants: the United Tribes Technical College.

Eligible beneficiaries: members of federally recognized tribes, residing on or near reservations under BIA jurisdiction and needing financial assistance.

Range: $500 to $3,000. **Average:** $2,500.

Activity: new program listing in 1997. Annually, 160 students admitted; total enrollment, 337 students; 57 graduates in FY 97.

HQ: Division of Job Placement and Training, Office of Economic Development (MS 4640-MIB), BIA-DOI, 1849 C St. NW, Washington, DC 20240. Phone: (202)208-2671.

15.061 INDIAN JOB PLACEMENT—UNITED SIOUX TRIBES DEVELOPMENT CORPORATION

Assistance: direct payments/specified use; advisory services/counseling.

Purposes: pursuant to the Snyder Act of 1921, ISDEAA as amended, and other acts, to assist Indians in finding employment through job development programs, counseling, and referrals to job training programs—through the United Sioux Tribes Development Corporation in Pierre, South Dakota. Participants receive weekly or monthly stipends.

Eligible applicants: United Sioux Tribes Development Corporation.

Eligible beneficiaries: members of federally recognized tribes, residing on or near reservations under BIA jurisdiction and needing financial assistance.

Range: $500 to $1,200. **Average:** $1,000.

Activity: new program listing in 1997. 1998, 127 individuals served.

HQ: same address/phone as **15.060.**

15.062   REPLACEMENT AND REPAIR OF INDIAN SCHOOLS

Assistance: direct payments/specified use.

Purposes: pursuant to ISDEAA as amended and other acts, for advanced planning, design, and construction of major expansion or replacement projects or improvement and repair projects—involving BIA-owned or -funded education facilities for the direct support of primary and secondary schools and dormitories.

Eligible applicants/beneficiaries: federally recognized tribal governments and organizations, including school boards.

Range: expansion/replacement, $6,000,000 to $25,000,000; improvement/ repair, to $7,000,000.

Activity: new program listing in 1997. Not quantified specifically.

HQ: same address/phone as **15.048.**

15.063   IMPROVEMENT AND REPAIR OF INDIAN DETENTION FACILITIES

Assistance: direct payments/specified use.

Purposes: pursuant to ISDEAA as amended and the Tribal Self-Governance Act of 1994, for advanced planning and design of, and improvements, repair, additions to BIA adult or juvenile detention facilities.

Eligible applicants/beneficiaries: federally recognized tribal governments.

Range: to $4,000,000.

Activity: new program listing in 1997. Not quantified specifically.

HQ: same addresses/phones as **15.030** *or* **15.048.**

15.064   STRUCTURAL FIRE PROTECTION—BUREAU OF INDIAN AFFAIRS FACILITIES
("Fire Protection")

Assistance: direct payments/specified use.

Purposes: pursuant to ISDEAA as amended and other acts, to install fire protection and varied prevention equipment in schools, dormitories, detention centers, and other BIA facilities. Funds also may be used for personnel training, to conduct inventories, and to retrofit equipment.

Eligible applicants/beneficiaries: federally recognized tribal governments and organizations, including school boards.

Range: $5,000 to $250,000. **Average:** $120,000.

Activity: new program listing in 1997. Not quantified specifically.

HQ: Structural Fire Protection Program Manager, same address/phone as **15.048.**

15.065   SAFETY OF DAMS ON INDIAN LANDS

Assistance: direct payments/specified use (100 percent/1-5 years).

Purposes: pursuant to the Snyder Act of 1921, ISDEAA as amended, and other acts, to improve the structural integrity of the 116 dams on Indian lands, including inspection and classification.

Eligible applicants/beneficiaries: federally recognized tribal governments and authorized organizations.

Range: conceptual design, $100,000 to $300,000; final design, $300,000 to $1,000,000; construction, $1,000,000 to $17,000,000.

Activity: new program listing in 1997. FY 98, 1 conception design, 4 final design, 4 repair awards.

HQ: same address as **15.034**. Phone: (202)208-5480.

15.108   INDIAN EMPLOYMENT ASSISTANCE

Assistance: direct payments/specified use.

Purposes: pursuant to the Snyder Act of 1921, ISDEAA as amended, and other acts, for American Indians to obtain vocational training and employment opportunities. Funds may be used for subsistence, tuition, and related training costs. Payments may extend for up to two years—three years for registered nurses training.

Eligible applicants: federally recognized tribal governments and authorized organizations.

Eligible beneficiaries: unemployed or under-employed members of recognized tribes, residing on or near an Indian reservation under BIA jurisdiction—in need of financial assistance.

Range: tribal awards, $7,000 to $350,000; individual awards, $200 to $10,000 per year. **Average:** tribal, $46,000; individuals, $5,100.

Activity: annually, 175 tribal awards assisting 1,500 persons.

HQ: same address/phone as **15.060**.

15.113   INDIAN SOCIAL SERVICES—GENERAL ASSISTANCE

Assistance: direct payments/unrestricted use.

Purposes: pursuant to the Snyder Act of 1921, for cash payments to needy Indians to pay: for food, clothing, shelter, etc.; for adult nonmedical institutional or custodial care; for foster home care; for burial expenses; for emergency assistance—when such assistance is unavailable from state or local public agencies.

Eligible applicants/beneficiaries: needy members of recognized tribes, living on or near reservations.

Range/Average: from several dollars to several hundred dollars monthly, based on family size and needs.

Activity: FY 00 estimate, 48,000 persons assisted monthly.

HQ: same address as **15.025**. Phone: (202)208-2721.

15.114   INDIAN EDUCATION—HIGHER EDUCATION GRANT PROGRAM ("Higher Education")

Assistance: project grants (to 5 years).

Purposes: pursuant to the Snyder Act of 1921, to provide financial assistance to Indian undergraduate college students, supplementing aid packages awarded by colleges.

Eligible applicants/beneficiaries: federally recognized tribal governments and authorized organizations; members of tribes, enrolled in or accepted by an accredited college, and with financial need as determined by the institution's financial aid office.

Range: $300 to $5,000. **Average:** $3,000.

Activity: annually, 9,800 students assisted.

HQ: same address as **15.026**. Phone: (202)208-1127.

15.124   INDIAN LOANS—ECONOMIC DEVELOPMENT ("Loan Guaranty Program")

Assistance: guaranteed/insured loans (80-90 percent/to 30 years).

Purposes: pursuant to the Snyder Act of 1921, ISDEAA as amended, and other acts, for economic development on or near federal Indian reservations, through projects involving business, industry, or agriculture.

Eligible applicants/beneficiaries: federally recognized tribal governments and authorized organizations; individual American Indians.

Range: individuals and tribal enterprises, $2,500 to $500,000; tribes, $10,000 to $5,500,000. **Average:** individuals and tribal enterprises, $125,000; tribes, $1,500,000.

Activity: cumulatively, $230,000,000 in guaranteed loans outstanding.

HQ: same address as **15.032**. Phone: (202)208-5324.

15.130   INDIAN EDUCATION—ASSISTANCE TO SCHOOLS ("Johnson-O'Malley")

Assistance: direct payments/specified use (formula based).

Purposes: pursuant to the Johnson-O'Malley Act of 1934, for supplemental education programs for Indians in public schools. Project examples: home-school coordinators; remedial tutoring; educational field trips; cultural programs.

Eligible applicants: tribal organizations, Indian corporations, school districts, or states with eligible Indian Education Committees.

Eligible beneficiaries: children age 3 through grade 12, of one-fourth or more degree of Indian blood and descendants of members of recognized tribes—with priority to those residing on or near reservations.

Range: $700 to $4,359,000. **Average:** $72,000.

Activity: annually, 272,000 students in 33 states served.

HQ: Chief, Division of Education, Office of Indian Education Programs, BIA-DOI, 1849 C St. NW, Washington, DC 20240. Phone: (202)219-1127.

15.141   INDIAN HOUSING ASSISTANCE

Assistance: project grants (100 percent); technical information; direct payments/specified use.

Purposes: pursuant to ISDEAA as amended, for home improvements, for housing construction in certain situations, and for technical assistance in establishing housing plans. The HHS Indian Health Service may supplement this program by funding water and sanitary systems.

Eligible applicants/beneficiaries: federally recognized tribal governments and organizations; Indians eligible for HIP assistance.

Range: repairs/renovations, to $35,000; temporary repairs, $2,500. **Average:** repairs, $8,000; new housing, $36,000 ($49,000 in Alaska).

Activity: FY 98, 428 homes repaired, 128 units constructed.

HQ: Division of Human Services, Office of Tribal Services (MS 4641-MIB), BIA-DOI, 1849 C St. NW, Washington, DC 20240. Phone: (202)208-2721.

15.144   INDIAN CHILD WELFARE ACT—TITLE II GRANTS

Assistance: project grants (100 percent).

Purposes: pursuant to the Indian Child Welfare Act, for the operation and maintenance of counseling programs and facilities related to child and family services, including: family assistance; protective day and after-school care; recreational activities; foster care subsidies; preparation and administration of child welfare codes, including legal representation; education and training; related services and programs.

Eligible applicants/beneficiaries: federally recognized tribal governments.

Range: $26,000 to $750,000. **Average:** $60,000.

Activity: FY 98, 500 programs funded.

HQ: Division of Social Services, Office of Tribal Services (MS-4603 MIB), BIA-DOI, 1849 C St. NW, Washington, DC 20240. Phone: (202)208-2721.

15.146   IRONWORKER TRAINING PROGRAM

Assistance: project grants (100 percent/to 12 weeks).

Purposes: pursuant to the Snyder Act of 1921, the Indian Adult Vocational Training Act of 1956 as amended, and other acts, to pay stipends to native Americans to permit them to obtain vocational training through apprenticeships as ironworkers at the National Ironworker Training Program in Broadview, Illinois, and to provide job placement assistance.

Eligible applicants/beneficiaries: American Indian members of federally-recognized tribes, at least age 20, with a high school diploma or equivalent certificate, residing on or near an Indian reservation under BIA jurisdiction, and in good physical health.

Range/Average: $175/week.

Activity: annually, 120 participants.

HQ: same address/phone as **15.060**.

BUREAU OF LAND MANAGEMENT

15.214   NON-SALE DISPOSALS OF MINERAL MATERIAL
("Free Use of Mineral Material")

Assistance: sale, exchange, or donation of property and goods.

Purposes: pursuant to the Materials Act of 1947 as amended, to grant free use permits to extract mineral material from BLM lands for use in public projects. Such material may not be bartered or sold.

Eligible applicants/beneficiaries: federal or state agencies, municipalities; nonprofit entities.

Activity: not quantified specifically.

HQ: Team Leader, Use Authorization Team, BLM-DOI, Washington, DC 20240. Phone: (202)452-0350.

15.222 COOPERATIVE INSPECTION AGREEMENTS WITH STATES AND TRIBES ("Section 202 Agreements")

Assistance: project grants (50 percent).

Purposes: pursuant to the Federal Oil and Gas Royalty Act of 1982, for cooperative inspections of oil and gas leases on Indian lands, by state or tribal inspectors.

Eligible applicants/beneficiaries: states or tribes with producing oil and gas leases on Indian lands for which the federal government has trust responsibility.

Range: to $220,000. **Average:** $82,000.

Activity: FY 98, 655 inspections, 394 violations detected.

HQ: Assistant Director, Resource Use and Protection (300), BLM-DOI, Washington, DC 20240. Phone: (202)208-4201.

15.224 CULTURAL RESOURCE MANAGEMENT

Assistance: project grants (100 percent); sale, exchange, donation, of property or goods; use of property, facilities, and equipment; specialized services; advisory services/counseling; technical information; training; investigation of complaints.

Purposes: pursuant to the Federal Land Policy and Management Act of 1982, the Archaeological Resources Protection Act, and the National Historic Preservation Act of 1966 as amended, to manage and protect cultural resources on BLM lands; to increase public awareness of the resources. Project examples: universities conducting management-focused archaeological field schools and scholarly research; production of educational materials.

Eligible applicants/beneficiaries: anyone.

Range: to $75,000. **Average:** $10,000.

Activity: 20 university archaeology field schools participating; 7,000 new cultural properties identified; interpretive signing for 300 properties.

HQ: Group Administrator, Cultural and Recreation Group (WO 340), BLM-DOI, 1849 C St. NW, Washington, DC 20240. Phone: (202)452-0330.

15.225 RECREATION RESOURCE MANAGEMENT

Assistance: project grants (cost sharing); use of property, facilities, and equipment; specialized services; advisory services/counseling; technical information; training.

Purposes: pursuant to the Federal Land Policy and Management Act, to manage and upgrade recreational resources and related facilities on public lands; for related public education. Project examples: promotion of effective cave management; Back Country Byways program; "watchable" wildlife and recreational fishing programs.

Eligible applicants/beneficiaries: anyone.

Range: to $50,000. **Average:** $10,000.

Activity: not quantified specifically.

HQ: Group Manager, Recreation Group (WO 250), BLM-DOI, 1849 C St. NW - 204LS, Washington, DC 20240-9998. Phone: (202)452-5041.

15.226 PAYMENTS IN LIEU OF TAXES ("PILT")

Assistance: direct payments/unrestricted use; direct payments/restricted use.

Purposes: to compensate local governmental taxing units for the loss of taxes from federal lands. Funds may be used for any government purpose.

Eligible applicants/beneficiaries: units of government.

Range/Average: N.A.

Activity: new program listing in 1999.

HQ: PILT Specialist (WO-880), BLM-DOI, 1848 C St. NW, Washington, DC 20240. Phone: (202)452-7721. (Note: no field offices for this program.)

OFFICE OF SURFACE MINING RECLAMATION AND ENFORCEMENT

15.250 REGULATION OF SURFACE COAL MINING AND SURFACE EFFECTS OF UNDERGROUND COAL MINING

Assistance: project grants (50-100 percent); direct payments/specified use.

Purposes: pursuant to the Surface Mining Control and Reclamation Act of 1977, for regulatory activities to control surface impacts of coal mining. Grants may be used to develop state legislation, programs, and regulations, as well as for enforcement activities; also, to provide hydrologic and geologic data for small coal operators.

Eligible applicants/beneficiaries: state governors. Small coal mine operators (annual production under 300,000 tons) may apply for assistance in meeting technical permit application requirements.

Range: $104,000 to $11,788,000. **Average:** $2,100,000.

Activity: currently, 24 states receive grants.

HQ: Chief, Division of Regulatory Support, Office of Surface Mining Reclamation and Enforcement, DOI, 1951 Constitution Ave. NW, Washington, DC 20240. Phone: (202)208-2651.

15.252 ABANDONED MINE LAND RECLAMATION (AMLR) PROGRAM

Assistance: formula grants; project grants (100 percent/3 years).

Purposes: pursuant to the Surface Mining Control and Reclamation Act of 1977, for reclamation projects to correct environmental damage caused or affected by coal and other mining and related practices on eligible lands and waters—occurring prior to 3 August 1977, and certain post-1977 lands and waters beginning 1 October 1991. Subsidence insurance grants, limited to $3,000,000, are also available to states to insure private property against damages caused by underground coal mining.

Eligible applicants/beneficiaries: states and tribes with eligible lands and coal mining operations, and paying reclamation fees.

Range: $100,000 to $26,000,000. **Average:** $5,000,000.

Activity: 23 states and 3 tribes with approved programs.

HQ: Chief, Division of Reclamation Support, Office of Surface Mining, DOI, 1951 Constitution Ave. NW, Washington, DC 20240. Phone: (202)208-5365.

15.253   NOT-FOR-PROFIT AMD RECLAMATION

Assistance: project grants (100 percent/2 years).

Purposes: pursuant to the Surface Mining Control and Reclamation Act of 1977, for local acid mine drainage (AMD) reclamation projects, especially in watershed areas. Eligibility is limited to lands and water where mining and related damage occurred prior to 3 August 1977, and where there is no continuing state or federal legal responsibility.

Eligible applicants/beneficiaries: established nonprofit organizations.

Range: $5,000 to $80,000.

Activity: new program in FY 99.

HQ: same address/phone as **15.252**. (Note: no field offices for this program.)

BUREAU OF RECLAMATION

15.504   RECLAMATION AND WATER REUSE PROGRAM

Assistance: formula grants (25 to 50 percent).

Purposes: pursuant to the Reclamation Wastewater and Groundwater Study and Facilities Act as amended and other acts, for appraisals and feasibility studies (50 percent federal funding) on water reclamation and re-use projects, including from such sources as agricultural drainage, municipal and industrial wastewater, brackish surface and groundwater, and sources containing toxics or other contaminants—only in the 17 western states; for research and demonstration programs (25 percent federal funding); for construction of re-use projects (25 percent federal funding).

Eligible applicants/beneficiaries: projects—irrigation districts, municipalities. Research—colleges, universities; architectural and engineering firms.

Range: to $20,000,000.

Activity: new program listing in 1998.

HQ: Office of the Commissioner, Bureau of Reclamation-DOI, 1849 C St. NW, Washington, DC 20240-0001. Phone: (202)208-4157.

15.506 WATER DESALINATION RESEARCH AND DEVELOPMENT PROGRAM ("Desal R& D Program")

Assistance: project grants (50-100 percent).

Purposes: pursuant to the Water Desalination Act of 1966, for water desalination studies, research, demonstration, development, and related activities.

Eligible applicants/beneficiaries: individuals, academic institutions, commercial and industrial organizations, and other profit, nonprofit and public entities including state, local, and tribal governments.

Range: $10,000 to $125,000. **Average:** $45,000.

Activity: new program listing in 1999. FY 00 estimate, 2 awards.

HQ: Acquisitions Operations Group (D-7810), Bureau of Reclamation-DOI, Federal Center, P.O. Box 25007, Denver, CO 80225. Phone: (303)445-6345. (Note: the field office is the headquarters for this program.)

U.S. FISH AND WILDLIFE SERVICE

15.602 CONSERVATION LAW ENFORCEMENT TRAINING ASSISTANCE

Assistance: training.

Purposes: for state conservation officer training in criminal law and in the principles, techniques, and procedures of wildlife law enforcement.

Eligible applicants/beneficiaries: state agencies.

Activity: not quantified specifically.

HQ: Chief, Office of Law Enforcement, Fish and Wildlife Service-DOI, Arlington, VA 22203-3247. Phone: (703)358-1949.

15.605 SPORT FISH RESTORATION ("Dingell-Johnson Program" - "D-J Program")

Assistance: formula grants (to 75 percent/2 years).

Purposes: to restore and manage sport fish populations for the preservation and improvement of sport fishing and related uses of fisheries resources. Funds may be used for land acquisition, development, research, coordination, and lake and stream rehabilitation.

Eligible applicants/beneficiaries: fish and wildlife agencies in states with laws prohibiting diversion of revenues from fishing licenses to uses other than administration of the agency; territories.

Range: $900,000 to $13,600,000. **Average:** $4,800,000.

Activity: not quantified specifically.

HQ: Chief, Division of Federal Aid, Fish and Wildlife Service-DOI, Washington, DC 20240. Phone: (703)358-2156.

15.608 FISH AND WILDLIFE MANAGEMENT ASSISTANCE

Assistance: specialized services.

Purposes: for the conservation and management of fish and wildlife resources, based on biological, chemical, and physical examinations of land and waters;

stocking of fishes from national fish hatcheries. Services are provided on a cost recoverable basis.

Eligible applicants/beneficiaries: state agencies, native Americans, federal agencies.

Activity: assistance to 100 native American tribes, 254 national wildlife refuges, 150 DOD installations.

HQ: Chief, Division of Fish and Wildlife Management Assistance, Fish and Wildlife Service, DOI, ARLSQ - Rm.840, Washington, DC 20240. Phone: (703)358-1718.

15.611 WILDLIFE RESTORATION
("Pittman-Robertson Program" - "P-R Program")

Assistance: formula grants (75 percent/2 years).

Purposes: to restore or manage wildlife populations and to provide facilities and services for hunter safety programs. Funds may be used for land acquisition, development, research, and coordination.

Eligible applicants/beneficiaries: fish and wildlife agencies in states with laws prohibiting diversion of hunting license revenues to uses other than administration of the agency; territories.

Range: $268,000 to $7,187,000. **Average:** $2,750,000.

Activity: not quantified specifically.

HQ: same address/phone as **15.605**.

15.614 COASTAL WETLANDS PLANNING, PROTECTION AND RESTORATION ACT
("National Coastal Wetlands Conservation Grants")

Assistance: project grants (50-75 percent).

Purposes: for coastal wetlands conservation projects. Funds may be used to acquire interests in lands or waters, and for restoration, enhancement, or management of coastal wetlands ecosystems, including conservation of fish and wildlife.

Eligible applicants/beneficiaries: states bordering the Atlantic, Pacific, Great Lakes, or Gulf coasts (except Louisiana); territories and possessions.

Range: $90,000 to $1,000,000. **Average:** to $495,000.

Activity: FY 98, 240 acres of wetlands restored, 12,000 acres acquired.

HQ: same address/phone as **15.605**.

15.615 COOPERATIVE ENDANGERED SPECIES CONSERVATION FUND

Assistance: project grants (75-90 percent).

Purposes: pursuant to the Endangered Species Act of 1973 as amended, for the conservation of endangered and threatened species of animals and plants. Funds may cover the costs of habitat surveys, research, planning, management, land acquisition, protection, and public education.

Eligible applicants/beneficiaries: states and territories with cooperative agreements with DOI.

Range: $1,000 to $235,000. **Average:** $100,000.

Activity: FY 99, 200 applications expected.

HQ: Chief, Division of Endangered Species, Fish and Wildlife Service-DOI, Washington, DC 20240. Phone: (703)358-2171.

15.616 CLEAN VESSEL ACT
("Clean Vessel Act Pumpout Grant Program")

Assistance: project grants (75 percent).

Purposes: for surveys and plans for installing pumpout/dump stations to protect sensitive areas in the coastal zone from recreational boat sewage; to construct pumpout/dump stations; to develop related education programs.

Eligible applicants/beneficiaries: states bordering the Atlantic, Pacific, or Gulf coasts, or the Great Lakes; territories and possessions.

Range: $1,000 to $900,000. **Average:** $171,000.

Activity: FY 93-97, 2,200 pumpout and 1,400 dump stations constructed in 45 states; education programs implemented in 40 states.

HQ: same address/phone as **15.605.**

15.617 WILDLIFE CONSERVATION AND APPRECIATION
("Partnerships for Wildlife")

Assistance: project grants (33-40 percent).

Purposes: for partnerships among the U.S. Fish and Wildlife Service, states, and private organizations and individuals: for conservation and appreciation projects to conserve fish and wildlife species; to encourage private donations for conservation and appreciation projects under the National Fish and Wildlife Foundation. Project funds may support inventories, monitoring, species and problem identification, conservation actions, and activities promoting nonconsumptive enjoyment of fish and wildlife.

Eligible applicants/beneficiaries: state fish and wildlife agencies, including in insular areas.

Range: $3,330 to $107,000. **Average:** $28,000.

Activity: FY 99, 10 research and survey, 5 educational and recreational, 13 management projects.

HQ: same address/phone as **15.605.**

15.618 ADMINISTRATIVE GRANTS FOR FEDERAL AID IN SPORT FISH AND WILDLIFE RESTORATION

Assistance: project grants (100 percent/to 3 years).

Purposes: to administer sport fish and wildlife restoration projects. Funds may support: administration and execution of the Sport Fish Restoration Act, the Wildlife Restoration Act, and the Migratory Bird Conservation Act; investigations; formulation of interstate compacts for the conservation and management of migratory fishes in marine or fresh waters; education and training; evaluation of new technologies.

Eligible applicants/beneficiaries: nonprofit organizations and individuals.

Range: $45,000 to $615,000. **Average:** $188,000.

Activity: not quantified specifically.

HQ: same address/phone as **15.605**.

15.619 RHINOCEROS AND TIGER CONSERVATION

Assistance: project grants (matching).

Purposes: for rhinoceros and tiger conservation projects including: surveys and monitoring; conservation education; wildlife inspection, law enforcement, and forensic skills; protected area and reserve management; sustainable development in buffer zones surrounding rhinoceros and tiger habitat; management of human behavior and livestock to decrease conflicts; use of substitutes for tiger and rhinoceros products in oriental medicine.

Eligible applicants/beneficiaries: federal, state, and local government agencies; public, private, nongovernmental, and nonprofit organizations; IHEs; others.

Range/Average: $20,000.

Activity: first three program years, 56 grants total.

HQ: Chief, Office of International Affairs, Fish and Wildlife Service-DOI, ARLSQ 730, 4401 N. Fairfax Dr., Arlington, VA 22203. Phone: (703)358-1754; FAX (703)358-2849. (Note: no field offices for this program.)

15.620 AFRICAN ELEPHANT CONSERVATION

Assistance: project grants (50 percent).

Purposes: for African elephant conservation projects including research, conservation, management, and protection activities. Projects are coordinated with foreign governments through the U.S. Department of State. Project examples: meritorious service awards program for game wardens in Africa; training in elephant biology and ecology; providing anti-poaching equipment.

Eligible applicants/beneficiaries: experienced public or private organizations and individuals.

Range: $6,700 to $398,000. **Average:** $83,000.

Activity: not quantified specifically.

HQ: same address/phone as **15.619**. (Note: no field offices for this program.)

15.621 ASIAN ELEPHANT CONSERVATION

Assistance: project grants (matching).

Purposes: for Asian elephant conservation projects including research, conservation, management, and protection activities.

Eligible applicants/beneficiaries: same as for **15.619**.

Range: to $50,000.

Activity: new program in FY 99.

HQ: same address/phone as **15.619**. (Note: no field offices for this program.)

15.622 SPORTFISHING AND BOATING SAFETY ACT
("Boating Infrastructure Grant Program")

Assistance: project grants (75 percent).

Purposes: to construct, renovate, or maintain tie-up facilities for transient, nontrailerable recreational vessels.

Eligible applicants/beneficiaries: states, possessions, and territories.

Range: $10,000 to $1,000,000. **Average:** $300,000.

Activity: new program in FY 00.

HQ: same address/phone as **15.605.**

15.623   NORTH AMERICAN WETLANDS CONSERVATION FUND ("NAWCF")

Assistance: project grants (50 percent/2 years).

Purposes: for wetlands conservation projects including: acquisition of lands or waters for fish and wildlife protection; to restore, manage, or enhance wetland ecosystems and habitats—only in coastal wetlands in coastal states.

Eligible applicants/beneficiaries: any organization or individual recommended by the North American Wetlands Conservation Council and approved by the Migratory Bird Conservation Commission.

Range: $600 to $1,000,000. **Average:** $423,000.

Activity: new program listing in 1999; since program inception, 645 projects.

HQ: Fish and Wildlife Service, DOI, Washington, DC. Phone: (no number provided). *Contact:* Executive Director, North American Wildlife and Wetlands Office, DOI, 4401 N. Fairfax Dr. - Ste.110, Arlington, VA 22203. Phone: (703)358-1784.

U.S. GEOLOGICAL SURVEY

15.805   ASSISTANCE TO STATE WATER RESOURCES RESEARCH INSTITUTES ("Water Research Institute Program")

Assistance: formula grants (50 percent); project grants.

Purposes: for basic and applied research, conferences, studies, student training, and related activities concerning water resources, conducted at water resources research institutes. Projects deal with water quality deterioration, groundwater depletion, and inefficient allocation and use of water resources. Project funds may not support formal instructional activities, general education, or costs of permanent buildings.

Eligible applicants/beneficiaries: university water research institutes in states and territories. Other IHEs may participate in cooperation with the designated state institute.

Range: $20,000 to $312,000.

Activity: FY 00 estimate, 54 formula grants, 10 competitive awards.

HQ: Chief, Office of External Research (MS 424), Geological Survey-DOI, National Center, Reston, VA 20192. Phones: (703)648-6800; FAX (703)648-5070. (Note: no field offices for this program.)

15.807 EARTHQUAKE HAZARDS REDUCTION PROGRAM

Assistance: project grants (cost sharing-to 2 years).

Purposes: for projects to assist in mitigating earthquake losses. Projects may consist of various types of activities, including providing earth science data and assessments, land use planning, engineering design, emergency preparedness systems.

Eligible applicants/beneficiaries: colleges, universities, profit and nonprofit organizations; state and local governments.

Range: $6,000 to $1,100,000. **Average:** $56,000.

Activity: FY 99, 122 awards.

HQ: External Research Program Manager, Earthquakes Hazards Program Office, Geologic Division, Geological Survey-DOI, 905A National Center, Reston, VA 20192. Phones: (703)648-6722; FAX (703)648-6642; Web, http://erp.usgs.gov ; e-mail, erp@usgs.gov (Note: no field offices for this program.)

15.808 U.S. GEOLOGICAL SURVEY—RESEARCH AND DATA ACQUISITION

Assistance: project grants (cost sharing).

Purposes: for a broad range of geological activities which may include: preparing and interpreting geological maps and data; appraising mineral, water, and energy resources; research in hydrology; other earth sciences research projects.

Eligible applicants/beneficiaries: same as for **15.807**.

Range: $4,000 to $300,000. **Average:** $50,000.

Activity: FY 99 estimate, 270 grants and cooperative agreements.

HQ: Assistant Director/Programs (MS-101), Geological Survey-DOI, National Center, 12201 Sunrise Valley Dr., Reston, VA 20192. Phone: (703)648-4460.

15.809 NATIONAL SPATIAL DATA INFRASTRUCTURE COOPERATIVE AGREEMENTS PROGRAM

Assistance: project grants (75 percent).

Purposes: for partnerships in the establishment of a National Geospatial Data Clearinghouse to develop and promulgate the use of standards in data collection, documentation, transfer, and search and query; for educational outreach programs.

Eligible applicants/beneficiaries: state and local government agencies, educational institutions, private firms and foundations, federally- or state-recognized native American tribes or groups.

Range: $35,000 to $40,000. **Average:** $40,000.

Activity: new program listing in 1997. FY 99 estimate, 37 awards.

HQ: Federal Geographic Data Committee Secretariat (MS 590), Geological Survey-DOI, 12201 Sunrise Valley Dr., Reston, VA 20192. Phones: (703) 648-5514; FAX (703)648-5755; Internet, gdc@usgs.gov (Note: no field offices for this program.)

15.810   NATIONAL COOPERATIVE GEOLOGIC MAPPING PROGRAM ("STATEMAP" - "EDMAP")

Assistance: project grants (50 percent/1-2 years).

Purposes: to produce geologic maps of areas in which knowledge of geology is important to the economic, social, or scientific welfare of states. "STATE-MAP" supports projects: (1) producing new geologic maps with attendant explanatory information; (2) compiling existing geologic data in a digital form at a scale of 1 to 100,000 for inclusion in the National Digital Geologic Map Database. "EDMAP") provides funding: (1) for graduate students in academic research programs involving geologic mapping and scientific data analysis as major components; (2) to expand research and educational capacity of graduate programs; (3) for publication and distribution of geologic maps generated in field-based graduate academic research programs.

Eligible applicants/beneficiaries: state geological surveys. State colleges or universities may apply on behalf of the state survey.

Range: STATEMAP, $10,000 to $158,000; EDMAP, $3,000 for 1 student to $31,000 for 3 students ($15,000 maximum per student). **Average:** STATE-MAP, $88,000; EDMAP, $9,389.

Activity: new program listing in 1998. FY 99 estimate, 43 STATEMAP, 45 EDMAP awards.

HQ: National Cooperative Geologic Mapping Program, Geological Survey-DOI, 205A National Center, 12201 Sunrise Valley Dr., Reston, VA 20192. Phone: (703)648-7483. (Note: no field offices for this program.)

INDIAN ARTS AND CRAFTS BOARD

15.850   INDIAN ARTS AND CRAFTS DEVELOPMENT

Assistance: use of property, facilities, and equipment; advisory services/ counseling; investigation of complaints.

Purposes: to provide program planning assistance in promoting the development of American Indian and native Alaskan arts and crafts. Assistance is nonfinancial including: development of innovative educational, promotional, production, and economic concepts related to native culture; investigations of misrepresentation of handicrafts.

Eligible applicants/beneficiaries: American Indian and Alaska native individuals and organizations; federally recognized tribal governments; state and local governments; nonprofit organizations.

Activity: annually, 6,500 native artists and craftsmen served. Also, operation of the Sioux Indian Museum in Rapid City, South Dakota, the Museum of the Plains Indian in Browning, Montana, and the Southern Plains Indian Museum in Anadarko, Oklahoma.

HQ: Director, Indian Arts and Crafts Board, DOI, Main Interior Bldg. - Rm.4004, Washington, DC 20240. Phone: (202)208-3773. (Note: no field offices for this program.)

OFFICE OF INSULAR AFFAIRS

15.875 ECONOMIC, SOCIAL, AND POLITICAL DEVELOPMENT OF THE TERRITORIES AND THE FREELY ASSOCIATED STATES

Assistance: project grants (100 percent).

Purposes: to promote the economic, social, and political development of the U.S. territories and freely associated states, toward their self-government and self-sufficiency. Operational costs and capital improvements may be funded, such as the construction of water systems, roads, schools, hospitals, and power and sewer facilities.

Eligible applicants/beneficiaries: Guam, VI, American Samoa, Northern Mariana Islands, Federated States of Micronesia, Republic of the Marshall Islands.

Range: N.A.

Activity: not quantified specifically.

HQ: Director, Financial Management Division, Office of Insular Affairs-DOI, Washington, DC 20240. Phones: (202)208-4736; Director, Financial Management and Technical Assistance Division, (202)208-6971. (Note: no field offices for this program.)

NATIONAL PARK SERVICE

15.904 HISTORIC PRESERVATION FUND GRANTS-IN-AID

Assistance: formula grants; project grants (60 percent; territories, 100 percent/2 years).

Purposes: for the identification, evaluation, and protection of historic properties listed or eligible for listing in the National Register of Historic Places. Historic properties may include districts, sites, buildings, structures, and objects significant in American history, architecture, archaeology, engineering, and culture, at national, state, and local levels. Grants may finance studies and reports, preservation plans, state staff salaries, equipment, materials, necessary travel, acquisition, or repair. Development projects must involve preservation, restoration, rehabilitation, or non-major reconstruction. Certain tax incentives are available to owners of listed properties.

Eligible applicants/beneficiaries: states and territories operating programs administered by a state historic preservation officer—which may subgrant to public and private parties including local governments, profit and non-profit organizations, or individuals to accomplish program objectives. Tribal Grant Program—tribal governments, Alaska native corporations.

Range: $160,000 to $928,000. **Average:** $532,000.

Activity: FY 98, 59 state grants and, in turn, some 800 subgrants.

HQ: Associate Director, Cultural Resource Stewardships and Partnerships, NPS-DOI, Washington, DC 20240. Phone: (202)343-9654.

15.910 NATIONAL NATURAL LANDMARKS PROGRAM

Assistance: specialized services; technical information.

Purposes: to identify and designate nationally significant natural areas, and to encourage their preservation. Technical assistance is available to landmark owners and administrators. No financial assistance is provided.

Eligible applicants/beneficiaries: anyone may suggest an area for inclusion on the National Registry of Natural Landmarks.

Activity: cumulatively as of 1998, 587 natural landmarks designated.

HQ: Natural Landmarks Program, Natural Systems Management Office (2320), NPS-DOI, Washington, DC 20013-7127. Phone: (202)219-8934.

15.912 NATIONAL HISTORIC LANDMARK

Assistance: advisory services/counseling.

Purposes: to study, identify, and encourage preservation of nationally-significant historic properties. Designation of historic landmarks and registration on the National Register of Historic Places renders them eligible for federal protection, some grants-in-aid programs, and certain tax benefits. Properties of only state or local significance do not qualify.

Eligible applicants/beneficiaries: anyone may suggest properties for inclusion. Property owners may be individuals, governments, or corporate bodies.

Activity: cumulatively as of 2000, 2,277 National Historic Landmarks designated.

HQ: National Historic Landmarks Survey, NRHE-NPS-DOI, 1849 C St. NW - Ste.NC400, Washington, DC 20240. Phone: (202)343-8175.

15.914 NATIONAL REGISTER OF HISTORIC PLACES
("National Register")

Assistance: advisory services/counseling.

Purposes: to expand and maintain the National Register of Historic Places which serves as a planning tool and source of information on sites, buildings, districts, structures, and objects of historical, architectural, engineering, archaeological, and/or cultural significance. Designation of historic landmarks and registration on the National Register of Historic Places renders them eligible for federal protection, some grants-in-aid and loan programs, and certain tax benefits. Federal agencies are required to consider and nominate historic properties within their jurisdiction.

Eligible applicants/beneficiaries: states and territories operating programs administered by state historic preservation officers; tribal preservation officers; federal agencies. Applicants eligible for federal tax benefits include owners of individually listed properties and properties certified by NPS as historic and in a district certified as historic.

Activity: cumulatively as of FY 99, 70,000 properties listed in the National Register, with some 140 entries added monthly; as of FY 00, 28,000 projects representing $20 billion in rehabilitation work had received Tax Reform Act certifications.

HQ: Keeper of the National Register of Historic Places, same address as **15.912**. Phone: (202)343-9536; Internet, http://www.cr.nps.gov/nr

15.915 TECHNICAL PRESERVATION SERVICES

Assistance: advisory services/counseling; specialized services; technical information.

Purposes: to offer technical information pertaining to the treatment and maintenance of historic properties. The program provides for the development of policies and standards and for distribution of publications on the technical and design aspects of preservation and rehabilitation, as well as for monitoring acquisition and development grant awards under **15.904**; the service also provides general technical assistance concerning preservation efforts, including certification for eligibility for tax credits.

Eligible applicants/beneficiaries: federal agencies, state and local governments, and individuals.

Activity: not quantified specifically.

HQ: Chief, Heritage Preservation Services Program, NPS-DOI, 1849 C St. NW - Ste.NC200, Washington, DC 20240. Phone: (202)343-9578.

15.916 OUTDOOR RECREATION—ACQUISITION, DEVELOPMENT AND PLANNING
("Land and Water Conservation Fund Grants")

Assistance: project grants (50 percent/to 3 years).

Purposes: to plan, acquire, and develop public outdoor recreation areas and facilities, including picnic areas, inner city parks, campgrounds, tennis courts, boat launching ramps, bike trails, outdoor swimming pools, roads, water supply, etc.; for studies, surveys, and data collection and analysis related to refinement and improvement of Statewide Comprehensive Outdoor Recreation Plans (SCORPs). Grant funds are not available to cover operating and maintenance costs.

Eligible applicants/beneficiaries: planning grants—only state agencies and territories. Acquisition and development grants—state agencies may apply for direct assistance, or on behalf of other state agencies or political subdivisions, such as cities, counties, and park districts; tribes functioning as general purpose units of government.

Range: $150 to $5,450,000. **Average:** $68,000.

Activity: FY 96-00, no new funding.

HQ: Chief, Recreation Programs, NPS-DOI, 1849 C St. NW - Rm.3624, Washington, DC 20240. Phones: (202)565-1200; FAX (202)565-1130.

15.918 DISPOSAL OF FEDERAL SURPLUS REAL PROPERTY FOR PARKS, RECREATION, AND HISTORIC MONUMENTS
("Surplus Property Program"- "Federal Land-to-Parks Program" - "Historic Surplus Property Program")

Assistance: use of property, facilities, and equipment.

Purposes: to transfer surplus federal real property for public park, recreation, or historic monument use. Recipients must agree to manage the property in the public interest and for public use. Only properties listed on the National Register or so eligible may be transferred through the Historic Monument Program. Examples of new uses include nature study areas, wildlife conservation areas, youth and senior citizen areas, historic monuments; arts and crafts centers.

Eligible applicants/beneficiaries: only states or local government units.

Activity: since 1949, 1,300 properties transferred for park and recreation uses, comprising over 145,000 acres; 130 properties for historic monuments. FY 98, 18 properties (521 acres) transferred.

HQ: National Center for Conservation and Recreation, NPS-DOI, Washington, DC 20013-7127. Phones: *Federal Land-to-Parks Program,* (202)565-1184; *Heritage Preservation Services,* (202)343-9587; *Historic Surplus Property Program,* (202)343-9531.

15.919　URBAN PARK AND RECREATION RECOVERY PROGRAM

Assistance: project grants (50-85 percent/to 3 years).

Purposes: for the rehabilitation of recreation areas and facilities; to demonstrate innovative approaches to improve park system management and recreation opportunities; and development of improved recreation planning. Recovery Action Program grants (50 percent funding) may be used for resource and needs assessments, citizen involvement, and planning. Rehabilitation grants (70 percent funding) may be used to rebuild, remodel, or expand existing facilities. Innovation grants (70 percent funding) may cover costs of personnel, facilities, or services involved in demonstrating innovative and cost effective ways to enhance park and recreation opportunities at the neighborhood level, including promotion of anti-crime activities in parks, special programs for the handicapped and senior citizens.

Eligible applicants/beneficiaries: cities and counties—based on need, economic and physical distress, and the relative quality and condition of urban recreation facilities and systems. Discretionary funds—jurisdictions within SMSAs not on the eligibility listing.

Range: rehabilitation grants, $8,438 to $5,250,000; innovation grants, $7,000 to $1,100,000; recovery action grants, $2,750 to $175,000.

Activity: not quantified specifically.

HQ: same address/phones as **15.916.**

15.921　RIVERS, TRAILS AND CONSERVATION ASSISTANCE ("RTCA")

Assistance: advisory services/counseling.

Purposes: to provide NPS staff assistance to support partnerships between government and citizens to increase the number of rivers and landscapes protected and trails established nationwide.

Eligible applicants/beneficiaries: private nonprofit organizations; federal, state, and local government agencies.

Activity: not quantified specifically.

HQ: Assistant Director/Recreation and Conservation, NPS-DOI, 1849 C St. NW, Washington, DC 20240. Phone: (202)565-1200.

15.922 NATIVE AMERICAN GRAVES PROTECTION AND REPATRIATION ACT ("NAGPRA")

Assistance: project grants (100 percent/to 2 years).

Purposes: for the documentation, inventory, and repatriation of native American human remains and cultural items including sacred objects, objects of cultural patrimony, funerary objects. Funds may be used: to involve specialists including lineal descendants, traditional religious leaders, and other officials; for staff training; for travel costs; to construct appropriate containers to transport finds. Ineligible uses of funds include documentation or repatriation of items from the Smithsonian Institution, care and curation of repatriated items, facilities construction or renovation, or real estate purchases.

Eligible applicants/beneficiaries: museum documentation—any institution or state or local government agency including IHEs with possession of, or control over, native American human remains or cultural items. Tribal documentation and repatriation—recognized tribes, Alaska native villages or corporations, native Hawaiian organizations.

Range: documentation, $5,000 to $75,000; repatriation, $5,000 to $15,000. **Average:** documentation, $58,000; repatriation, $6,575.

Activity: new program listing in 1997. Cumulatively since 1994, 205 museums and tribes received funds.

HQ: Departmental Consulting Archeologist, Archeology & Ethnography Program, NPS-DOI, 1848 C St. NW - Rm.NC340, Washington, DC 20240. Phones: (202)343-8161; FAX (202)343-5260. (Note: no field offices for this program.)

15.923 NATIONAL CENTER FOR PRESERVATION TECHNOLOGY AND TRAINING

Assistance: project grants (100 percent).

Purposes: to develop and distribute preservation and conservation skills and technologies for the identification, evaluation, conservation, and interpretation of prehistoric and historic resources; to develop and train federal, state, and local professional, managerial, maintenance, and other personnel; for technology transfer; and for international cooperation efforts. Funds may support projects involving: information management; training and education in such disciplines as archeology, historic architecture, historic landscapes, object and materials conservation and interpretation; applied and fundamental research; pollutant research and treatment; technology transfer; analytical facilities; conferences; publications. Ineligible projects include: those focused on specific sites, structures, objects, or collections; internships and fellowships when integrated into funded projects; current projects.

Eligible applicants/beneficiaries: universities, colleges; nonprofit organizations including museums, research laboratories, professional societies; Cooperative Park Study Units of the National Park System; federal, state, local, and tribal preservation offices; native Hawaiian organizations; profit organizations, individuals.

Range: $7,856 to $50,000.

Activity: new program listing in 1997. FY 99 estimate, 30 awards.

HQ: Grants Administrator, Heritage Preservation Services Program, National Center for Cultural Resource Stewardship and Partnership, NPS-DOI, Washington, DC 20013-7127. Phone: (202)343-9577.

15.924 HISTORICALLY BLACK COLLEGES AND UNIVERSITIES PRESERVATION INITIATIVE

Assistance: project grants.

Purposes: for the preservation of historically significant structures on HBCU campuses; to conduct surveys and perform condition assessments of buildings listed on the National Register; to complete restoration of historically significant structures.

Eligible applicants/beneficiaries: HBCUs where selected historic buildings are located.

Range: $100,000 to $2,000,000.

Activity: new program listing in 1997; 12 critically threatened buildings selected, and assessments completed.

HQ: same address as **15.923**. Phone: (202)343-9564.

15.925 NATIONAL MARITIME HERITAGE GRANTS

Assistance: project grants (50 percent/to 2 years).

Purposes: to preserve historic maritime resources and increase public awareness and appreciation for the maritime heritage of the U.S. Eligible preservation activities include: acquisition; planning; documentation; protection and stabilization; preservation, restoration, or rehabilitation; maintenance of properties; reporting and publicity projects. Eligible education activities include: enhancement of public access, use, and appreciation for maritime heritage collections; activities focusing on heritage trails and corridors; field programs; preservation of traditional maritime skills; minor construction projects to improve access, use, and appreciation of educational and exhibit spaces; reconstruction or reproduction of well-documented properties. Generally, costs of staff training or professional development are ineligible.

Eligible applicants/beneficiaries: state and local governments, private nonprofit organizations.

Range: $2,500 to $50,000.

Activity: new program in FY 97.

HQ: NPS-DOI, Washington, DC 20013-7127. Phone: (202)343-5969. (Note: no field offices for this program.)

15.926 AMERICAN BATTLEFIELD PROTECTION

Assistance: project grants (100 percent).

Purposes: for the protection and preservation of battlefield lands on American soil by supporting nonacquisition preservation methods such as planning, education, and survey and inventory. Project examples: preparation of Vision and Protection Plan; preparation of National Register nomination; archeological survey. Funds may not be used for such activities as battlefield reenactments, any construction, permanent staff positions, curation, or other ongoing activities.

Eligible applicants/beneficiaries: federal, intrastate, interstate, state and local agencies; public and private nonprofit organizations; federally-recognized tribal governments; territories and possessions; public and private IHEs. Multi-organizational applications are encouraged.

Range: $1,000 to $100,000. **Average:** $20,000.

Activity: new program listing in 1997. FY 92-98, 225 projects funded.

HQ: American Battlefield Protection Program, NPS-DOI, 1849 C St. NW - Rm.330, Washington, DC 20240. Phones: (202)343-1210, -3941; FAX (202)343-1836. (Note: no field offices for this program.)

15.976 MIGRATORY BIRD BANDING AND DATA ANALYSIS

Assistance: technical information.

Purposes: to provide a central repository for all migratory bird banding records in North America; dissemination of ensuing analytical information for use in research and management, as well as in setting hunting seasons and bag limits.

Eligible applicants/beneficiaries: anyone with a serious interest in research or management activities related to migratory birds.

Activity: FY 98, 1,200,000 bandings, 73,000 band recoveries recorded and analyzed.

HQ: Biological Resources Division, Geological Survey, DOI (MS 300), 12201 Sunrise Valley Dr., Reston, VA 20192. Phone: (703)648-4090.

15.978 UPPER MISSISSIPPI RIVER SYSTEM LONG TERM RESOURCE MONITORING PROGRAM ("LTRMP")

Assistance: project grants (100 percent).

Purposes: to maintain the Upper Mississippi River System as a sustainable large river ecosystem—through monitoring of trends and effects related to resources, and through research as specified in the LTRMP Operations Plan.

Eligible applicants/beneficiaries: states, local governments, intra- and interstate agencies, sponsored organizations, private nonprofit organizations.

Range: $8,500 to $895,000. **Average:** $295,000.

Activity: new program listing in 1998. FY 99 estimate, 9 awards.

HQ: Upper Midwest Environmental Sciences Technical Center, Geological Survey-DOI, 2630 Fanta Reed Rd. LaCrosse, WI 54603. Phones: Center Director, (608)781-6221, FAX (608)783-6066; *or,* LTRM Program Manager, (608)783-7550, ext. 51, FAX (608)783-8058; *or,* Management Analyst, (608)783-7550, FAX (608)783-8058. (Note: the field office is the headquarters for this program.)

DEPARTMENT OF JUSTICE

16.001   LAW ENFORCEMENT ASSISTANCE—NARCOTICS AND DANGEROUS DRUGS—LABORATORY ANALYSIS

Assistance: specialized services; advisory services/counseling; technical information.

Purposes: pursuant to the Comprehensive Drug Abuse Prevention and Control Act of 1970, to provide drug evidence analysis, expert court testimony, and technical assistance to law enforcement agencies concerning narcotics and other abused drugs.

Eligible applicants/beneficiaries: state and local governments, law enforcement officials, forensic laboratories.

Activity: FY 98, 7,473 drug samples analyzed.

HQ: Deputy Assistant Administrator, Office of Forensic Sciences, DEA-DOJ, Washington, DC 20537. Phone: (202)307-8866.

16.003   LAW ENFORCEMENT ASSISTANCE—NARCOTICS AND DANGEROUS DRUGS TECHNICAL LABORATORY PUBLICATIONS ("Microgram")

Assistance: technical information.

Purposes: pursuant to the Comprehensive Drug Abuse Prevention and Control Act of 1970, to disseminate scientific information on the detection and analysis of narcotics and dangerous drugs, published monthly in "Microgram."

Eligible applicants/beneficiaries: forensic laboratories, scientists doing work for law enforcement agencies.

Activity: annual distribution, 1,800 copies.

HQ: same address/phone as **16.001**.

16.004   LAW ENFORCEMENT ASSISTANCE—NARCOTICS AND DANGEROUS DRUGS TRAINING

Assistance: training.

Purposes: pursuant to the Comprehensive Drug Abuse Prevention and Control Act of 1970, for DEA training of accredited professional and enforcement personnel in: drug investigations techniques; aspects of physical security in legitimate drug distribution; analysis of evidence; pharmacology, socio-psychology of drug abuse and drug education; managing and supervising drug unit commanders.

Eligible applicants/beneficiaries: state, local, military, and other federal law enforcement and regulatory officials; crime laboratory technicians and forensic chemists.

Activity: FY 98, 4,579 participants.

HQ: Special Agent in Charge, Office of Training, DEA-DOJ, FBI Academy, Quantico, VA 22134-1475. Phone: (703)632-5011.

16.005   PUBLIC EDUCATION ON DRUG ABUSE—INFORMATION

Assistance: specialized services; training; technical information.

Purposes: pursuant to the Comprehensive Drug Abuse Prevention and Control Act of 1970, to coordinate and facilitate the involvement of law enforcement and communities in drug abuse prevention and public education. Video tapes, publications, and other resources are available. Only nonfinancial assisted is provided.

Eligible applicants/beneficiaries: anyone. Law enforcement agencies receive priority.

Activity: FY 98, all 50 states and several foreign countries assisted.

HQ: Demand Reduction Section, Congressional and Public Affairs Staff, DEA-DOJ, Washington, DC 20537. Phone: (202)307-7936.

16.006   COUNTY AND MUNICIPAL AGENCY DOMESTIC PREPAREDNESS EQUIPMENT SUPPORT PROGRAM

Assistance: project grants (100 percent).

Purposes: to equip and prepare municipal fire and emergency service responders for Weapons of Mass Destruction (WMD) domestic terrorist attacks and other explosive incidents—including personal protective, chemical and biological detection, and communications equipment.

Eligible applicants/beneficiaries: municipal jurisdictions designated for DOD training, situated in large metropolitan areas.

Range: $100,000 to $300,000, based on population.

Activity: new program in FY 99.

HQ: Office of Justice Programs-DOJ, 810 Seventh St. NW, Washington, DC 20531. Phone: (202)305-9887. (Note: no field offices for this program.)

16.007   STATE DOMESTIC PREPAREDNESS EQUIPMENT SUPPORT PROGRAM

Assistance: project grants (100 percent).

Purposes: to equip and prepare state and local first responders for Weapons of Mass Destruction (WMD) domestic terrorist attacks. Funds may be used to: plan and execute comprehensive statewide threat and needs assessments, based on three-year plans; to purchase equipment; provide specialized training to emergency medical services, law enforcement agencies, and hazardous materials units.

Eligible applicants/beneficiaries: states and the 157 largest cities and localities.

Range/Average: N.A.

Activity: new program in FY 99.

HQ: same address/phone as **16.006**. (Note: no field offices for this program.)

16.100   DESEGREGATION OF PUBLIC EDUCATION

Assistance: specialized services.

Purposes: to initiate legal processes to assure compliance with the provisions of Title IV of the Civil Rights Act of 1964, the Equal Educational Opportunities Act of 1974, and amendments, concerning equal educational opportunities in public schools and colleges, including those receiving federal financial assistance, for all persons regardless of their race, color, religion, sex, or national origin.

Eligible applicants/beneficiaries: public school parents or groups of parents; public college students or their parents.

Activity: FY 98 (sampling), responses to 230 routine citizen inquiries, 45 Congressional referrals; 15 court-approved consent decrees, 35 favorable decisions secured affecting 59 school districts.

HQ: Chief, Educational Opportunities Litigation Section, Civil Rights Division-DOJ, Washington, DC 20035-5958. Phones: (202)514-4092; Office of Public Affairs, (202)514-2007, TDD (202)514-1888. (Note: no field offices for this program.)

16.101   EQUAL EMPLOYMENT OPPORTUNITY

Assistance: specialized services.

Purposes: to initiate legal processes enforcing the provisions of Title VII of the Civil Rights Act of 1964 and regulations concerning equal employment opportunities, including authorized affirmative action programs—for all persons, regardless of their race, religion, national origin, or sex. Discrimination is forbidden by employers, labor organizations, employment agencies, state and local governments, public agencies, government contractors and subcontractors.

Eligible applicants/beneficiaries: all persons.

Activity: FY 98 (sampling), in employment litigation, $7,200,000 in back pay obtained for 1,200 persons denied employment opportunities by the Arkansas Department of Corrections; $2,000,000 in back pay obtained for 300 persons denied employment opportunities by the Parish of Orleans. In defensive litigation, 5 new challenges filed.

HQ: Chief, Employment Litigation Section, Civil Rights Division-DOJ, Washington, DC 20035-5968. Phones: (202)514-3831, TDD (800)578-5404; Office of Public Affairs, (202)514-2007, TDD (202)514-1888. (Note: no field offices for this program.)

16.103   FAIR HOUSING AND EQUAL CREDIT OPPORTUNITY

Assistance: specialized services.

Purposes: to initiate legal processes assuring enforcement of the provisions of: (1) Title VIII of the Civil Rights Act of 1968 as amended by the Fair Housing Amendments Act of 1988—assuring equal housing opportunities for all in the sale, rental, financing, and related housing activities—regardless of race, color, religion, sex, national origin, family status, or handicap; (2) the Equal Credit Opportunity Act (ECOA) which prohibits discrimination in credit transactions on the basis of race, color, religion, sex, national origin, marital status, or age—because any part of the applicant's income is derived from public assistance, or because the applicant has in good faith exercised a right under the Consumer Credit Protection Act. Since 1988, HUD investigates and attempts conciliation of fair housing cases; if unsuccessful, HUD may file administrative charges; DOJ brings suit in federal court.

Eligible applicants/beneficiaries: all persons.

Activity: FY 98 (sampling), 25 pattern of practice cases filed. $33,000,000 in monetary relief obtained since 1992.

HQ: Chief, Housing and Civil Enforcement, Civil Rights Division-DOJ, Washington, DC 20035-5998. Phones: (202)514-4713; Office of Public Affairs, (202)514-2007, TDD (202)514-1888. (Note: no field offices for this program.)

16.104 PROTECTION OF VOTING RIGHTS

Assistance: specialized services.

Purposes: to enforce the provisions of the Voting Rights Act of 1965, amendments, and related laws, regarding voter registration and voting in local, state, and federal elections. The laws protect the rights of all persons to register and vote, without discrimination based on race, color, membership in a language minority group, age, disability, literacy, or residence overseas.

Eligible applicants/beneficiaries: all U.S. citizens of voting age.

Activity: (sampling) participation in redistricting challenges, changes in voting practices and procedures, polling place monitoring.

HQ: Chief, Voting Section, Civil Rights Division-DOJ, Washington, DC 20035-6128. Phones: (202)307-3143, (800)253-3931; Office of Public Affairs, (202)514-2007, TDD (202)514-1888. (Note: no field offices for this program.)

16.105 CIVIL RIGHTS OF INSTITUTIONALIZED PERSONS
("Equal Enjoyment of Rights in Public Facilities" - "Protection of Rights to Reproductive Health Services")

Assistance: specialized services.

Purposes: to enforce the provisions of the Civil Rights of Institutionalized Persons Act (CRIPA), the Freedom of Access to Clinic Entrances Act (FACE), OCCSSA, and related laws. CRIPA assures the right of equal utilization of any public facility owned or operated by any state or subdivision thereof, without regard to race, religion, or national origin—including facilities for the mentally ill or for the retarded or chronically ill, prisons, jails, pretrial detention facilities, juvenile facilities, and homes for the elderly. FACE authorizes the Attorney General to investigate and, where appropriate, to initiate actions for relief from certain violent, threatening, obstructive, and destructive actions intended to injure, intimidate, or interfere with persons seeking reproductive health services, or deny religious freedom or destruction of property at places of religious worship.

Eligible applicants/beneficiaries: anyone.

Activity: (sampling) CRIPA, compliance monitoring in 70 facilities, new investigations in 34 facilities, cases filed involving 14 facilities; FACE, 3 new cases filed, relief obtained in 4 cases.

HQ: Chief, Special Litigation Section, Civil Rights Division-DOJ, Washington,

DC 20350-6400. Phones: (202)514-6255; Office of Public Affairs, (202) 514-2007, TDD (202)514-1888. (Note: no field offices for this program.)

16.108 AMERICANS WITH DISABILITIES ACT TECHNICAL ASSISTANCE PROGRAM ("ADA")

Assistance: project grants (100 percent); technical information; advisory services/counseling; investigation of complaints.

Purposes: to ensure that public accommodations and commercial facilities and state and local governments learn and understand the requirements of the Americans with Disabilities Act. Publications, conferences, seminars, training, and other educational services and materials are developed and disseminated through technical assistance grants and contracts.

Eligible applicants/beneficiaries: nonprofit organizations including trade and professional associations; state and local government agencies; national and state organizations representing the disabled; individuals.

Range/Average: N.A.

Activity: (sampling), 163,000 calls annually on the ADA telephone information line; direct mailings to 15,000 libraries; 8,000,000 publications distributed; expansion of "911" emergency phone systems to users of TDD.

HQ: Chief, Disability Rights Section, Civil Rights Division-DOJ, Washington, DC 20035-6738. Phones: (800)514-0301, TDD (800)514-0383; Office of Public Affairs, (202)514-2007, TDD (202)514-1888. (Note: no field offices for this program.)

16.109 CIVIL RIGHTS PROSECUTION ("Criminal Section")

Assistance: investigation of complaints.

Purposes: to prosecute cases of national significance involving the deprivation of personal liberties that cannot be or are not sufficiently addressed by state or local authorities. The Criminal Section's jurisdiction includes: acts of racial violence; misconduct by local, state, or federal law enforcement officers; violations of the peonage and involuntary servitude statutes protecting migrant workers and others held in bondage.

Eligible applicants/beneficiaries: all persons.

Activity: FY 98 (sampling), 77 cases charging 189 defendants; 19 trials resulting in 36 convictions and 6 acquittals.

HQ: Chief, Criminal Section, Civil Rights Division-DOJ, Washington, DC 20035-6018. Phones: (202)514-3204; Office of Public Affairs, (202)514-2007, TDD (202)514-1888.

16.110 EDUCATION AND ENFORCEMENT OF THE ANTIDISCRIMINATION PROVISION OF THE IMMIGRATION AND NATIONALITY ACT

Assistance: project grants (100 percent); specialized services; investigation of complaints.

Purposes: to educate employers and workers about their rights and responsibilities under the Immigration and Nationality Act to prevent employment discrimination based on citizenship status or national origin. Eligible project activities: preparation and distribution of videos, brochures, pamphlets; radio and TV service announcements; Internet information; conferences. (NOTE: for charges relating to national origin, the Office of the Special Counsel has jurisdiction only over employers with four to fourteen employees—with respect to the hiring, firing, recruiting, or referral for a fee of protected individuals and aliens authorized to work in the U.S.; employers with 15 or more employees are under the jurisdiction of the Equal Employment Opportunity Commission.)

Eligible applicants/beneficiaries: private nonprofit institutions and organizations; state and local government entities; local, regional, or national ethnic and immigrants' rights advocacy organizations; trade associations; industry groups; professional organizations; or, other entities—providing information and/or services to employers or potential victims of discrimination.

Range: $50,000 to $150,000.

Activity: not quantified specifically.

HQ: Outreach Coordinator, Office of Special Counsel, Civil Rights Division-DOJ, Washington, DC 20038-7728. Phones: (800)225-7688, (202)616-5594; TDD (800)237-2515, (202)616-5525; e-mail, osc.crt@usdoj.gov (Note: no field offices for this program.)

16.200 COMMUNITY RELATIONS SERVICE ("CRS")

Assistance: specialized services.

Purposes: to provide conciliation, mediation, training, and technical services to communities in resolving disputes, disagreements, and difficulties arising from perceived discrimination based on race, ethnicity, or national origin. Resource materials and publications are available.

Eligible applicants/beneficiaries: representatives of groups, communities; federal, state, or local governmental units—seeking to alleviate tensions related to race, color, or national origin.

Activity: FY 98, 1,450 active cases of which 425 were closed.

HQ: Community Relations Service-DOJ, 600 E St. NW - Ste.2000, Washington, DC 20530. Phone: (202)305-2935.

16.201 CUBAN AND HAITIAN ENTRANT RESETTLEMENT PROGRAM

Assistance: project grants (100 percent/1-4 years).

Purposes: for primary resettlement services to eligible Cubans and Haitians paroled into communities by the INS; for Cuban and Haitian entrants living in south Florida and requiring secondary resettlement assistance; to provide residential shelter care and other child care services, including family reunification, to alien unaccompanied minors in INS custody.

Eligible applicants/beneficiaries: public or private nonprofit organizations or agencies; certain profit organizations.

Range: to $2,000,000. **Average:** $1,000,000.

Activity: FY 00 estimate, 8 continuation grants to 3 awardees; 7,000 entrants, 100 unaccompanied minors served.

HQ: Director, Humanitarian Affairs Branch (HQIAO), INS-DOJ, 425 Eye St. NW, Washington, DC 20536. Phone: (202)305-1951. *Grants management information*: Grants Officer, same address/phone.

16.300   LAW ENFORCEMENT ASSISTANCE—FBI ADVANCED POLICE TRAINING
("FBI Academy, Advanced Specialized Courses")

Assistance: training (1-11 weeks).

Purposes: to provide advanced training at the FBI Academy in such topics as criminal law and investigations, behavioral science, forensic science, education, management, fitness and health—emphasizing development of managers and administrators. Specialized advanced courses and seminars include firearms administration, white-collar and computer related crimes, police legal issues, hostage negotiations, executive development, laboratory matters, budgeting, scientific technical analysis, death investigations, bombing and arson investigations, violent crimes against the elderly, sexual exploitation of children. Participants may be reimbursed for round-trip travel costs to Washington, DC; housing, food, laundry and dry cleaning are furnished to students at FBI Academy, Quantico, VA.

Eligible applicants/beneficiaries: regular full-time personnel of municipal, county, or state criminal justice agencies; qualified representatives of federal agencies—meeting age, experience, education, physical, and character requirements.

Activity: FY 00 estimate, 1,080 enrollees at FBI National Academy for 11-week general curriculum.

HQ: Director, FBI-DOJ, Washington, DC 20535. Phone: (202)324-3000.

16.301   LAW ENFORCEMENT ASSISTANCE—FBI CRIME LABORATORY SUPPORT
("FBI Laboratory")

Assistance: specialized services; training.

Purposes: to provide FBI Laboratory facilities and staff assistance in examining evidence in criminal matters and to provide related expert testimony; specialized training in forensic disciplines.

Eligible applicants/beneficiaries: state and local law enforcement agencies in the U.S. or its possessions.

Activity: FY 00 estimate, 102,000 nonfederal scientific examinations.

HQ: same address/phone as **16.300**.

16.302   LAW ENFORCEMENT ASSISTANCE—FBI FIELD POLICE TRAINING
("FBI Field Police Training")

Assistance: training.

Purposes: to provide training courses by FBI instructors for criminal justice personnel, covering such areas as fingerprinting, legal topics, police-community relations, hostage negotiation, white collar crime, organized crime, computer fraud, management techniques, investigative support.

Eligible applicants/beneficiaries: municipal, county, local, and state criminal justice personnel.

Activity: FY 00 estimate, 120,000 personnel to attend.

HQ: same address/phone as **16.300.**

16.303   LAW ENFORCEMENT ASSISTANCE—FBI FINGERPRINT IDENTIFICATION
("FBI Criminal Justice Information Services Division")

Assistance: specialized services.

Purposes: to provide fingerprint and arrest-record services of the FBI. Besides criminal identification, services include locating missing persons and identifying unknown living or deceased persons and victims of major disasters.

Eligible applicants/beneficiaries: criminal justice agencies, federal government, and other authorized governmental and nongovernmental entities.

Activity: FY 00 estimate, 14,100,000 fingerprint cards processed.

HQ: Assistant Director, Criminal Justice Information Services Division, FBI-DOJ, 1000 Custer Hollow Rd., Clarksburg, WV 26306. Phone: (304)625-2222.

16.304   LAW ENFORCEMENT ASSISTANCE—NATIONAL CRIME INFORMATION CENTER
("NCIC")

Assistance: specialized services.

Purposes: to operate the FBI NCIC, complementing the development of similar metropolitan and statewide criminal justice information systems. Located in Washington, D.C., NCIC is a computerized index of crimes and criminals of nationwide interest, serving as a nucleus of a high-speed communications network that includes criminal justice agencies throughout the U.S., Canada, PR, and VI. The service can also be used to locate wanted or missing persons and stolen property. Technical assistance, consultant services, and training are provided to state agencies.

Eligible applicants/beneficiaries: local, state, and federal criminal justice agencies may participate through their individual control terminal agency.

Activity: FY 00 estimate, 899,190,000 transactions.

HQ: same address/phone as **16.300.** (Note: no field offices for this program.)

16.305   LAW ENFORCEMENT ASSISTANCE—UNIFORM CRIME REPORTS

Assistance: technical information.

Purposes: to collect, analyze, and publish nationwide crime statistics providing information on crime trends, offenses known to police, demographic characteristics of arrested persons, police disposition of juveniles arrested, police employee information.

Eligible applicants/beneficiaries: all participating law enforcement agencies including state and local governments receive the annual publication and semiannual releases. Limited copies of semiannual releases are available to any interested individual; the annual publication may be purchased from GPO.

Activity: annually, 25,000 copies of "Crime in the United States" distributed, plus 2,500 CD-ROM copies.

HQ: same address/phone as **16.300**. (Note: no field offices for this program.)

16.307 COMBINED DNA INDEX SYSTEM ("CODIS")

Assistance: project grants (75 percent/to 2 years).

Purposes: pursuant to the DNA Identification Act of 1994, to establish a national data base containing DNA records from persons convicted of crimes and from samples recovered from crime scenes and from unidentified human remains. CODIS software allows storage and matching of DNA records; installation, training, and user support are provided. With the DOJ National Institute of Justice, the FBI jointly administers the Forensic Laboratory Improvement grant program, providing funds for required equipment, supplies, and contractual services.

Eligible applicants/beneficiaries: software and technical assistance—publicly funded state or local forensic science laboratories performing DNA analysis, or private laboratories under contract. DNA grants—units of state or local governments with forensic laboratories.

Range/Average: N.A.

Activity: as of January 1998, 86 laboratories with CODIS in 36 states and DC.

HQ: *CODIS,* Forensic Science Systems Unit, Laboratory Division, FBI-DOJ, Washington, DC 20535. Phone: (202)324-9440. *DNA grants program,* Program Manager, Office of Science and Technology, National Institute of Justice-DOJ, Washington, DC 20531. Phone: (202)307-0648. (Note: no field offices for this program.)

16.308 INDIAN COUNTRY INVESTIGATIONS

Assistance: training.

Purposes: pursuant to VCCLEA, to train BIA and tribal law enforcement officers in conducting investigations in Indian country—in coordination with the Federal Law Enforcement Training Center and the BIA.

Eligible applicants/beneficiaries: BIA investigators, tribal and other law enforcement officers.

Activity: FY 96-98, 1,000 investigators trained.

HQ: FBI-DOJ, 935 Pennsylvania Ave. NW, Washington, DC 20535. Phone: (202)324-3366. (Note: no field offices for this program.)

16.400 CITIZENSHIP EDUCATION AND TRAINING

Assistance: technical information.

Purposes: pursuant to the Immigration and Nationality Act, to provide instruction and training materials in citizenship responsibilities for immigrants interested in naturalization, and in learning English and U.S. history and government. Free federal textbooks on citizenship at various reading levels are provided, including for correspondence courses.

Eligible applicants/beneficiaries: public schools; other educational groups conducting classes under supervision of public schools; public educational institutions.

Activity: FY 98, 9,541 textbooks distributed.

HQ: Director, Business Process and Reengineering, INS-DOJ, 801 Eye St. NW Ste.900, Washington, DC 20536. Phones: (202)305-0539; Web, www.ins. usdoj.gov

16.523   JUVENILE ACCOUNTABILITY INCENTIVE BLOCK GRANTS ("JAIBG")

Assistance: formula grants (90 percent/2 years); project grants (100 percent/1-3 years).

Purposes: to develop programs promoting greater accountability in the juvenile justice system. Formula grant funds may be used for such purposes as: building, expanding, renovating, or operating temporary or permanent juvenile correction or detention facilities, including personnel training; to develop and administer accountability-based sanctions for juvenile offenders; to hire additional judges, probation officers, court-appointed defenders, and prosecutors; to enable prosecutors to address drug, gang, and youth violence problems more effectively; to acquire related technology, equipment, and training; to establish juvenile "gun courts" and "drug courts;" to establish and maintain interagency information-sharing programs involving the juvenile and criminal justice systems, schools, and social services agencies; for programs to protect students and school personnel from drug, gang, and youth violence; to implement a policy of controlled substance testing for appropriate categories of juveniles. Discretionary project grants may be awarded for pertinent research, demonstrations, evaluations, and training and technical assistance.

Eligible applicants/beneficiaries: formula grants—states, territories and possessions (except Palau), and local government units. Discretionary grants—public or private agencies, organizations, individuals.

Range/Average: N.A.

Activity: new program in FY 98; 19 awards.

HQ: OJJDP, Office of Justice Programs-DOJ, 810 Seventh St. NW, Washington, DC 20531. Phones: Assistant Director, State Relations and Assistance Division, (202)307-5924; Director, Research and Program Development Division, (202)307-5929; Director, Training and Technical Assistance Division, (202)307-5940; Director, Special Emphasis Division, (202)307-5914. (Note: no field offices for this program.)

16.524   DOMESTIC VIOLENCE VICTIMS' CIVIL LEGAL ASSISTANCE PROGRAM ("Civil Legal Assistance")

Assistance: project grants (100 percent/to 18 months).

Purposes: to strengthen civil legal assistance available to domestic violence victims, through the development of innovative collaborative programs within the civil legal system—enabling battered women to secure a safe life and home for themselves and their children. Funded projects provide: direct legal services to victims; ongoing training and mentoring to lawyers and legal advocates.

Eligible applicants/beneficiaries: public or private nonprofit organizations providing legal services to domestic violence victims, including state law schools, legal aid or legal services programs, shelters for battered women, Bar associations, tribal governments.

Range: $50,000 to $240,000.

Activity: new program listing in 1999. FY 98, 58 grants.

HQ: Violence Against Women Grants Office, Office of Justice Programs-DOJ, 810 Seventh St. NW, Washington, DC 20531. Phone: (202)307-6026. (Note: no field offices for this program.)

16.525   GRANTS TO COMBAT VIOLENT CRIMES AGAINST WOMEN ON CAMPUSES

Assistance: project grants (100 percent/to 18 months).

Purposes: to develop and strengthen effective security and investigation strategies to combat violent crimes against women on campuses, including domestic violence, sexual assault, and stalking; for victim services programs. Grant recipients must meet strict crime reporting requirements.

Eligible applicants/beneficiaries: IHEs.

Range/Average: N.A.

Activity: new program in FY 99.

HQ: same address/phone as **16.524**. (Note: no field offices for this program.)

16.540   JUVENILE JUSTICE AND DELINQUENCY PREVENTION—ALLOCATION TO STATES
("State Formula Grants")

Assistance: formula grants (50-100 percent/2 years); project grants (to 3 years).

Purposes: pursuant to JJDPA as amended, for state and local programs to prevent juvenile delinquency and improve the juvenile justice system, including: deinstitutionalization of status offenders; separation of adults and juveniles in secure custody; community-based services such as group homes and halfway houses; personnel education and training; monitoring and evaluation; juvenile rehabilitation services. Applicants must have three-year comprehensive plans for meeting program purposes. States must pass through two-thirds of funds to local governments, private nonprofit agencies, and tribes performing law enforcement functions.

Eligible applicants/beneficiaries: formula grants—designated state agencies and territories. Technical assistance contracts—qualified organizations, agencies, and individuals.

Range: minimum—territories, $100,000; states, $600,000.

Activity: FY 98, 54 awards.

HQ: OJJDP, Office of Justice Programs, DOJ, Washington, DC 20531. Phone: (202)307-5924. (Note: no field offices for this program.)

16.541   JUVENILE JUSTICE AND DELINQUENCY PREVENTION—SPECIAL EMPHASIS

Assistance: project grants (50-100 percent/to 18 months); specialized services.

Purposes: pursuant to JJDPA as amended, for programs to design, test, and demonstrate approaches, techniques, and methods of preventing and controlling juvenile delinquency, such as: community-based alternatives to institutional confinement; diverting juveniles from the traditional justice and correctional system; advocacy activities; strengthening of the family unit; prevention and treatment programs for juveniles that commit serious crimes; national law education program. 100 percent funding is provided for programs; 50 percent for facilities construction involving 20 or fewer beds

Eligible applicants/beneficiaries: public and private nonprofit organizations; individuals; state and local government units or combinations thereof.

Range: N.A.

Activity: FY 98, 46 continuation, 18 new Congressional "earmark" awards.

HQ: same address as **16.540**. Phone: (202)307-5914. (Note: no field offices for this program.)

16.542   NATIONAL INSTITUTE FOR JUVENILE JUSTICE AND DELINQUENCY PREVENTION

Assistance: project grants (100 percent/1-3 years).

Purposes: pursuant to JJDPA as amended, to operate the National Institute for Juvenile Justice and Delinquency Prevention to: coordinate and conduct research and evaluation of justice and delinquency prevention activities; serve as a clearinghouse and information center for collecting and distributing information; conduct national training programs and provide technical assistance to federal, state, and local governments, judges and other court personnel, law enforcement executives, correctional administrators, probation officers, and volunteers. Projects may involve such activities as: developing programs addressing high-risk youth; prevention and treatment of drug and alcohol abuse by juveniles; effective parenting strategies for families of high-risk youth; reduction of drugs and crime in schools; longitudinal research on the causes and correlates of delinquency and juvenile court statistics.

Eligible applicants/beneficiaries: public or private agencies, organizations, or individuals.

Range: N.A.

Activity: not quantified specifically.

HQ: National Institute for Juvenile Justice and Delinquency Prevention, OJJDP-DOJ, Washington, DC 20531. Phones: Director, Research and Program Development Division, (202)307-5929; Director, Training and Technical Assistance Division, (202)307-5940. (Note: no field offices for this program.)

16.543   MISSING CHILDREN'S ASSISTANCE

Assistance: project grants (100 percent/1-3 years).

Purposes: pursuant to JJDPA as amended, to coordinate public and private programs related to missing children and to establish and operate a national resource center and clearinghouse to: provide technical assistance and training in locating and recovering missing children; toll-free hotline; disseminate information about innovative and model programs, services, and legislation; conduct national incidence studies. Research, demonstration, or service program contracts may be awarded for public education programs, services to missing children and their families, location and return of adults with Alzheimer's disease, statewide clearinghouses, and related purposes. Project example: Internet Crimes Against Children Task Force Program.

Eligible applicants/beneficiaries: state and local governments, public and private nonprofit organizations; consortia.

Range: N.A.

Activity: not quantified specifically.

HQ: same address as **16.540**. Phone: (202)616-3637. (Note: no field offices for this program.)

16.544   GANG-FREE SCHOOLS AND COMMUNITIES—COMMUNITY-BASED GANG INTERVENTION

Assistance: project grants (100 percent/to 18 months).

Purposes: pursuant to JJDPA as amended, to establish and operate programs and activities involving families and community agencies, designed to: reduce the participation of juveniles in gang-related crimes, especially in elementary and secondary schools; improve adjudicatory, correctional, and treatment systems addressing the problems of juveniles convicted of serious drug and gang-related offenses; provide individual, peer, family, and group counseling, including provision of life skills training and preparation for living independently, and cooperation with social services, welfare, and health care agencies; reduce juvenile participation in gangs, particularly those involving drug distribution; provide education and training to program personnel; accomplish similar program objectives.

Eligible applicants/beneficiaries: public or private nonprofit agencies, organizations; individuals.

Range/Average: N.A.

Activity: not quantified specifically.

HQ: same address as **16.540**. Phone: (202)307-5914. (Note: no field offices for this program.)

16.547   VICTIMS OF CHILD ABUSE
("Judicial Child Abuse Training, Investigation and Prosecution of Child Abuse Through the Criminal Justice System, Court Appointed Special Advocates ("CASA)", and Children's Advocacy Centers")

Assistance: project grants (100 percent/1-3 years).

Purposes: pursuant to the Victims of Child Abuse Act of 1990, to develop model technical assistance and training programs to improve court handling of child abuse and neglect cases; to facilitate the adoption of laws to protect child abuse victims against the potential "second assault" of courtroom proceedings; to address situations in which states have laws and procedures that outpace federal law, leaving children entering the federal system inadequately protected; to address inconsistencies and disparities among pertinent state laws; to train criminal justice system personnel on the latest investigative and prosecuting techniques; to promote a multi-disciplinary approach to coordinating the investigation and prosecution of cases, by limiting the number of pre-trial interviews of child victims and better assuring interview accuracy; to provide technical assistance, information, and support to local CASA programs, and to assist communities in developing new programs; and, for similar projects and programs.

Eligible applicants/beneficiaries: National Court Appointed Special Advocates; National Network of Children's Advocacy Centers. Local nonprofit agencies and organizations and local children's advocacy centers may apply to the national network.

Range: N.A.

Activity: FY 99 (sampling), 150 grants to local children's advocacy centers; 10 national and 45 state training programs.

HQ: Training and Technical Assistance Division, OJJDP-DOJ, Washington, DC 20531. Phone: (202)307-5940. (Note: no field offices for this program.)

16.548 TITLE V—DELINQUENCY PREVENTION PROGRAM

Assistance: formula grants (50 percent/3 years).

Purposes: pursuant to JJDPA as amended, to increase the capacity of state and local governments to support more effective education, training, research, prevention, diversion, treatment, and rehabilitation programs in the prevention of juvenile delinquency and in the improvement of the juvenile justice system.

Eligible applicants: states and territories.

Eligible beneficiaries: local government units.

Range/Average: N.A.

Activity: FY 99, 54 states and territories participated.

HQ: same address/phone as **16.540.** (Note: no field offices for this program.)

16.549 PART E—STATE CHALLENGE ACTIVITIES ("Challenge Grants")

Assistance: formula grants (100 percent/3 years).

Purposes: pursuant to JJDPA as amended, to provide incentives to states to develop, adopt, and approve policies and programs in one or more of the following challenge activities: providing basic health, mental health, and appropriate education services for youth in the juvenile justice system; providing access by juveniles to counsel for consultation before waiving the right to counsel; increasing community-based alternatives to incarceration, and developing and adopting objective criteria for the placement of juveniles in detention and secure confinement; providing secure settings for the placement of violent juvenile offenders by closing traditional training schools and replacing them with secure settings with capacities of no more than 50 offenders with staff ratios assuring adequate supervision and treatment; prohibiting gender bias in treatment and placement; establishing and operating state ombudsman offices for children, youth, and families to investigate and resolve complaints concerning practices adversely affecting the rights of resident children and youth; removing status offenders from the jurisdiction of juvenile courts to prevent the placement in secure detention or correctional facilities of juveniles who are nonoffenders or charged with offenses that would not be criminal if committed by an adult; developing alternatives to suspension and expulsion from school; increasing after-care services for juveniles involved in the system; or, similar activities.

Eligible applicants/beneficiaries: state and territorial agencies participating in the OJJDP Formula Grants Program (**16.548**).

Range: to 10 percent of the state's formula grant allocation (per project).

Activity: FY 98, 53 states and territories participated.

HQ: same address/phone as **16.540**. (Note: no field offices for this program.)

16.550 STATE JUSTICE STATISTICS PROGRAM FOR STATISTICAL ANALYSIS CENTERS
("SACs")

Assistance: project grants (100 percent).

Purposes: pursuant to OCCSSA as amended, to establish and operate Statistical Analysis Centers for the collection, analysis, and dissemination of statistics pertaining to crime and criminal justice.

Eligible applicants/beneficiaries: state agencies.

Range: $50,000 to $150,000. **Average:** $50,000.

Activity: FY 99 estimate, 40 grant and cooperative agreement awards.

HQ: Bureau of Justice Statistics-DOJ, Washington, DC 20531. Phone: (202) 307-0771. (Note: no field offices for this program.)

16.554 NATIONAL CRIMINAL HISTORY IMPROVEMENT PROGRAM
("NCHIP")

Assistance: project grants (100 percent/to 3 years).

Purposes: pursuant to the Brady Handgun Violence Prevention Act, VCCLEA, OCCSSA, Crime Identification Technology Act of 1998, "Megan's Law," and other acts and amendments, for states: to establish or improve computerized criminal history record systems; to collect data on stalking and domestic violence; to improve data accessibility and transmission to the National Instant Criminal Background Check System (NICS). Projects are to permit immediate identification of persons: prohibited from purchasing firearms; subject to domestic violence protective orders; ineligible to hold positions of responsibility involving children, the elderly, or the disabled. Funds may support participation in the Interstate Identification Index (III) and the National Sex Offender Registry through data base automation and record improvements, record flagging, equipment, training, research, and related costs.

Eligible applicants/beneficiaries: designated state agencies, which may allocate funds to other state or local agencies or courts. Private organizations may receive contracts.

Range/Average: N.A.

Activity: not quantified specifically.

HQ: Chief, Criminal History Improvement Programs, Bureau of Justice Statistics-DOJ, Washington, DC 20531. Phone: (202)307-0759. (Note: no field offices for this program.)

16.560 JUSTICE RESEARCH, DEVELOPMENT, AND EVALUATION PROJECT GRANTS

Assistance: project grants (100 percent/to 2 years); technical information.

Purposes: pursuant to OCCSSA as amended and the Anti-Drug Abuse Act of 1988, for research, development, and evaluation projects relating to the causes and control of crime and the improvement of the criminal justice system. Priorities include: violent crime; alcohol- and drug-related crime; community crime prevention; criminal justice system improvement; forensic science research; technology development.

Eligible applicants/beneficiaries: state and local governments, profit and nonprofit organizations, IHEs, tribal governments, qualified individuals, including in the territories.

Range: N.A.

Activity: FY 00 estimate, 400 awards.

HQ: National Institute of Justice-DOJ, 810 Seventh St. NW, Washington, DC 20531. Phones: (202)307-2942; FAX (202)307-6394; Web, www.ojp.usdoj. gov/nij (Note: no field offices for this program.)

16.561 NATIONAL INSTITUTE OF JUSTICE VISITING FELLOWSHIPS

Assistance: project grants (100 percent/6-18 months).

Purposes: pursuant to OCCSSA of 1968 as amended and the Anti-Drug Abuse Act of 1988, to award fellowships to conduct research at the National Institute of Justice, on crime and the criminal justice system including juvenile delinquency, crime causation, crime measurements, criminal justice administration.

Eligible applicants/beneficiaries: experienced practitioners and researchers or their parent agencies or organizations including criminal justice agencies, universities, or colleges. Recipients must have at least a bachelor's degree.

Range: N.A.

Activity: FY 99 estimate, 2 awards.

HQ: same address/phones as **16.560**. (Note: no field offices for this program.)

16.562 CRIMINAL JUSTICE RESEARCH AND DEVELOPMENT—GRADUATE RESEARCH FELLOWSHIPS
("Graduate Research Fellowship Program")

Assistance: project grants (100 percent/to 2 years).

Purposes: pursuant to the OCCSSA as amended and the Anti-Drug Abuse Act of 1988, for fellowships to doctoral candidates to conduct research related to law enforcement, crime, or criminal justice—covering stipends, project costs, and certain university fees.

Eligible applicants/beneficiaries: IHEs.

Range: to $15,000.

Activity: FY 00 estimate, 15 awards.

HQ: same address/phones as **16.560**. (Note: no field offices for this program.)

16.563   CORRECTIONS AND LAW ENFORCEMENT FAMILY SUPPORT

Assistance: project grants (50 percent/12-18 months).

Purposes: pursuant to VCCLEA, for research on the effects of stress on corrections and law enforcement personnel and their families; to identify and evaluate model programs providing support services; for demonstration projects; for technical assistance and training projects to develop stress reduction and family support programs; for dissemination of information and research findings.

Eligible applicants/beneficiaries: state and local agencies; organizations representing law enforcement or correctional personnel in employment matters, including national, state, or local labor unions or associations. IHEs, independent research enterprises, professional associations, health care providers, and others may obtain contracts to provide technical assistance.

Range: agencies, to $100,000; organizations, to $250,000.

Activity: new program listing in 1997. FY 00 estimate, 10 awards.

HQ: National Institute of Justice, Office of Justice Programs-DOJ, 810 Seventh St. NW, Washington, DC 20531. Phones: (202)307-1480; FAX (202)616-9249; *DOJ Response Center,* (800)421-6770. (Note: no field offices for this program.)

16.564   NATIONAL INSTITUTE OF JUSTICE FORENSIC DNA LABORATORY IMPROVEMENT PROGRAM

Assistance: project grants (75 percent).

Purposes: pursuant to OCCSSA and other acts, to increase state and local forensic laboratory capacity to conduct DNA testing. Funds may be used for: laboratory equipment and supplies, outside training; laboratory space modifications; contracted DNA testing services; CODIS equipment. Personnel costs are ineligible.

Eligible applicants/beneficiaries: state or local governments, regional crime laboratories, consortia.

Range/Average: N.A.

Activity: new program listing in 1999. FY 98, 38 grants awarded.

HQ: same address/phones as **16.560**. (Note: no field offices for this program.)

16.565   NATIONAL INSTITUTE OF JUSTICE DOMESTIC ANTI-TERRORISM TECHNOLOGY DEVELOPMENT PROGRAM

Assistance: project grants (100 percent/6-18 months).

Purposes: pursuant to OCCSSA and other acts, to develop counter-terrorism technologies for state and local law enforcement. Project examples: interactive computer-based training tools for bomb technicians; flying plate disrupter technology to disrupt capability of large explosive devices; electro-magnetic portal for detection of concealed weapons.

Eligible applicants/beneficiaries: state, local, tribal governments; public or private nonprofit or profit organizations; IHEs; individuals—including in territories and possessions.

Range/Average: N.A.

Activity: new program listing in 1999; not quantified specifically.

HQ: same address/phones as **16.560**. (Note: no field offices for this program.)

16.566 NATIONAL INSTITUTE OF JUSTICE W.E.B. DUBOIS POST-DOCTORAL FELLOWSHIP PROGRAM

Assistance: project grants (100 percent/6-12 months).

Purposes: pursuant to OCCSSA, for research fellowships concerning justice system administration, delinquency prevention, violence reduction, and related topics. Studies are conducted at the National Institute of Justice.

Eligible applicants/beneficiaries: individuals working in the criminal justice field, or parent agencies or organizations on their behalf. Candidates must have a doctoral-level or legal degree of J.D. or higher.

Range/Average: N.A.

Activity: new program in FY 00.

HQ: same address/phones as **16.560**. (Note: no field offices for this program.)

16.571 PUBLIC SAFETY OFFICERS' BENEFITS PROGRAM

Assistance: direct payments/unrestricted use.

Purposes: pursuant to OCCSSA as amended, to pay disability benefits to officers permanently and totally disabled in the line of duty, or death benefits to survivors of federal, state, or local public safety officers whose death results from a personal injury sustained in the line of duty. Public safety officers include law enforcement officers, firefighters and public rescue squad or ambulance crew members, both paid and volunteer. Law enforcement officers include police, corrections, probation, parole, and judicial officers.

Eligible applicants/beneficiaries: totally and permanently disabled officers or their surviving spouses and children (the parents become eligible if the officer is not survived by a spouse or children). Children include any natural, illegitimate, adopted, or posthumous child, or stepchild 18 years old or younger; children over 18 may be eligible if they are full-time students or incapable of self-support. Available also in territories and possessions.

Range: $143,943 death or disability benefit.

Activity: FY 98, 227 death benefit, 15 disability claims approved.

HQ: Public Safety Officers' Benefits Program, Bureau of Justice Assistance-DOJ, Washington, DC 20531. Phones: (202)307-0635, (888)744-6513. (Note: no field offices for this program.)

16.575 CRIME VICTIM ASSISTANCE

Assistance: formula grants (4 years).

Purposes: pursuant to VOCA, VCCLEA, and other acts, for crime victim assistance programs. Primary program purposes include: to stimulate state participation and support for victim services programs; to promote victim cooperation with law enforcement; to provide direct compensation and services to victims of violent crimes, sexual assault, spousal abuse, or child abuse, or of terrorist acts or mass violence occurring domestically or while they are abroad. Project examples: domestic violence shelter services; rape crisis programs; support groups for survivors of homicide victims and DUI/DWI crash victims.

Eligible applicants: states, all territories and possessions. Funds are subgranted to public agencies and nonprofit organizations.

Eligible beneficiaries: crime victims or their survivors.

Range: base amounts—states, $500,000 minimum; territories, possessions, $200,000 minimum. Additional amounts are based on population.

Activity: annually, 57 awards.

HQ: Director, State Compensation and Assistance Division, Office for Victims of Crime, Office of Justice Programs-DOJ, 810 Seventh St. NW, Washington, DC 20531. Phone: (202)514-4696. (Note: no field offices for this program.)

16.576 CRIME VICTIM COMPENSATION

Assistance: formula grants (100 percent/3 years).

Purposes: pursuant to VOCA, VCCLEA, and other later acts, to match amounts awarded by states to crime victims (other than for property damage excluding damage to prosthetic devices, eyeglasses or corrective lenses, or dental devices) to support victim compensation programs, including survivors, of terrorism, drunk driving, and domestic violence. Purposes of this program include: to stimulate state participation and support for victim services programs; to promote victim cooperation with law enforcement. Compensation may be made for such expenses as medical costs including mental health counseling and care, loss of wages, funeral expenses, costs incurred by nonresidents of the jurisdictions with operating programs.

Eligible applicants: states, territories, and possessions with crime victim compensation programs in effect.

Eligible beneficiaries: victims of crime resulting in death or physical or personal injury.

Range: states receive 40 percent of their prior year payout.

Activity: FY 99, 51 states and territories participating.

HQ: same address as **16.575**. Phone: (202)307-5983. (Note: no field offices for this program.)

16.577   EMERGENCY FEDERAL LAW ENFORCEMENT ASSISTANCE

Assistance: project grants (100 percent).

Purposes: pursuant to the Justice Assistance Act of 1984, for services to state and local governments that experience law enforcement emergencies, enabling response through federal law enforcement assistance. Project examples: emergency aid provided relating to serial arson of 30 churches in Florida, and during Hurricane Andrew.

Eligible applicants/beneficiaries: states, territories, and possessions.

Range: N.A.

Activity: N.A.

HQ: Bureau of Justice Assistance, Office of Justice Programs-DOJ, 810 Seventh St. NW, Washington, DC 20531. Phone: (202)616-3458.

16.578   FEDERAL SURPLUS PROPERTY TRANSFER PROGRAM

Assistance: use of property, facilities, and equipment.

Purposes: pursuant to the Comprehensive Crime Control Act of 1984, to transfer or convey surplus federal real or other property for use in correctional or law enforcement programs and projects involving the care or rehabilitation of criminal offenders.

Eligible applicants/beneficiaries: state, local, and territorial governments; political subdivisions.

Activity: 26 properties conveyed to date.

HQ: Bureau of Justice Assistance, Office of Justice Programs-DOJ, 810 Seventh St. NW - 4th floor, Washington, DC 20531. Phone: (202)616-3214. (Note: no field offices for this program.)

16.579   BYRNE FORMULA GRANT PROGRAM

Assistance: formula grants (base amount plus 75 percent of project costs/3 years; tribes, 100 percent).

Purposes: pursuant to OCCSSA as amended, to reduce and prevent illegal drug activity, crime, and violence; to improve the functioning of the criminal justice system. Funds may support costs of: additional personnel; equipment; facilities including upgraded and additional corrections and law enforcement crime laboratories; personnel training—to increase the apprehension, prosecution, and adjudication of persons that violate state and local laws relating to the production, possession, and transfer of controlled substances.

Eligible applicants/beneficiaries: states, territories, possessions.

Range: $500,000 to $52,000,000.

Activity: not quantified specifically.

HQ: same address as **16.577**. Phone: (202)514-6638. (Note: no field offices for this program.)

16.580   EDWARD BYRNE MEMORIAL STATE AND LOCAL LAW ENFORCEMENT ASSISTANCE DISCRETIONARY GRANTS PROGRAM
("Discretionary Drug and Criminal Justice Assistance Program")

Assistance: project grants (to 100 percent).

Purposes: pursuant to OCCSSA as amended and the Crime Control Act of 1990, to control the use and availability of illegal drugs and to improve the functioning of the criminal justice system, emphasizing violent crime and serious offenders. Funds may be used: for replicable demonstration programs that develop new concepts or strategies; for personnel education and training; national or multi-jurisdictional approaches to violent crime control and community mobilization.

Eligible applicants/beneficiaries: state and local government agencies, public and private nonprofit organizations, tribal governments.

Range: $25,000 to $1,000,000.

Activity: FY 98, 230 awards.

HQ: same address as **16.577**. Phone: (202)514-5943. (Note: no field offices for this program.)

16.582   CRIME VICTIM ASSISTANCE/DISCRETIONARY GRANTS

Assistance: project grants (100 percent/3 years); direct payments/specified use.

Purposes: pursuant to VOCA, VCCLEA, and other acts, for programs to improve the overall quality of services delivered to crime victims, through demonstration projects and technical assistance to and training of those providing such services. Examples of potential projects include those involving local victim witness, family violence, and victim compensation programs, as well as technical assistance in collecting evidence of sexual assault.

Eligible applicants/beneficiaries: states, U.S. Attorneys offices, victim service agencies, private nonprofit agencies, federal training centers; tribes and tribal organizations.

Range/average: $5,000 to $200,000.

Activity: not quantified specifically.

HQ: Director, Federal Crime Victims Division, Office for Victims of Crime, Office of Justice Programs-DOJ, 810 Seventh St. NW, Washington, DC 20531. Phone (202)616-3568. *Training, technical assistance,* Director, Special Projects Division, same address. Phone: (202)616-3585. (Note: no field offices for this program.)

16.583   CHILDREN'S JUSTICE ACT PARTNERSHIPS FOR INDIAN COMMUNITIES

Assistance: project grants (100 percent/1-3 years); direct payments/specified use.

Purposes: pursuant to VOCA, the Children's Justice and Assistance Act of 1986 as amended, VCCLEA, and other acts, for Indian tribes to develop, establish, and operate programs to improve the handling of child abuse cases, particularly cases of sexual abuse, and to improve the investigation and prosecution of such cases.

Eligible applicants/beneficiaries: federally recognized tribal governments, nonprofit Indian organizations.

Range/Average: N.A.

Activity: 38 programs funded.

HQ: Program Specialist, Federal Crime Victims Division, Office for Victims of Crime, Office of Justice Programs-DOJ, 810 Seventh St. NW, Washington, DC 20531. Phone: (202)616-3578. (Note: no field offices for this program.)

16.585   DRUG COURT DISCRETIONARY GRANT PROGRAM

Assistance: project grants (75 percent/to 2 years).

Purposes: pursuant to VCCLEA and OCCSSA, to plan, establish, and improve drug courts to handle cases involving nonviolent adult and juvenile offenders. Program funds may support projects providing early and continuous judicial supervision and integrated administration of sanctions and services, including: mandatory periodic testing for controlled or addictive substance use during any period of supervised release or probation; treatment; diversion, probation, or other supervised release; offender management and after-care services.

Eligible applicants/beneficiaries: states, local government units, state and local courts, tribal governments; joint applicants.

Range: planning, to $30,000; continuations, to $200,000; enhancements, to $100,000 for single- and to $300,000 for multi-jurisdictions.

Activity: FY 98, 75 planning, 52 implementation, 21 enhancement, 12 continuation, and 3 "mini" grants.

HQ: Director, Drug Courts Program Office, Office of Justice Programs-DOJ, Washington, DC 20531. Phones: (202)616-5001; FAX (202)514-6452; *DOJ Response Center,* (800)421-6770, (202)307-1480; *Drug Courts Clearinghouse,* (202)885-2875. (Note: no field offices for this program.)

16.586   VIOLENT OFFENDER INCARCERATION AND TRUTH IN SENTENCING INCENTIVE GRANTS
("Prison Grants")

Assistance: project grants (90 percent/5 years).

Purposes: pursuant to VCCLEA, to construct, renovate, or expand: adult or juvenile correctional facilities for violent offenders; temporary or permanent correctional facilities, including on military bases, prison barges, and "boot camps," for confinement of nonviolent offenders; and, jails. Funds may not be used to pay operating costs.

Eligible applicants/beneficiaries: states; multi-state compacts; territories and possessions. Subgrants may be awarded to local government units.

Range: states, from $1,622,000; VI, Guam, Samoa, Northern Marianas, $108,000 each.

Activity: N.A.

HQ: Chief, Grants Management, Corrections Program Office, Office of Justice Programs-DOJ, 810 Seventh St. NW, Washington, DC 20531. Phone: (800) 848-6325. (Note: no field offices for this program.)

16.587   VIOLENCE AGAINST WOMEN DISCRETIONARY GRANTS FOR INDIAN TRIBAL GOVERNMENTS

Assistance: project grants (75 percent).

Purposes: pursuant to VCCLEA and OCCSSA, to develop and strengthen law enforcement and prosecution strategies to combat violent crimes against women, and to augment victim services. Funding may be used to pay costs of personnel, training, technical assistance, data collection, and equipment.

Eligible applicants/beneficiaries: tribal governments or consortia. Nonprofit nongovernmental victim services agencies may receive contracts.

Range: $50,000 to $84,000.

Activity: FY 98, 61 awards.

HQ: Administrator, Violence Against Women Office, Office of Justice Programs-DOJ, 810 Seventh St. NW, Washington, DC 20531. Phone: (202)307-6026. (Note: no field offices for this program.)

16.588   VIOLENCE AGAINST WOMEN FORMULA GRANTS

Assistance: formula grants (75 percent).

Purposes: pursuant to VCCLEA and OCCSSA, to develop and strengthen law enforcement and prosecution strategies to combat violent crimes against women, and to augment victim services. Grants may support costs of personnel, training, technical assistance, and data collection and other equipment for apprehension, prosecution, and adjudication.

Eligible applicants/beneficiaries: states, territories, and possessions. Subgrants will be awarded to local government units, nonprofit nongovernmental victim services programs, and tribal governments.

Range: base grant, $500,000 per state plus an amount based on population.

Activity: FY 98, 56 grants.

HQ: same address/phone as **16.587**. (Note: no field offices for this program.)

16.589   RURAL DOMESTIC VIOLENCE AND CHILD VICTIMIZATION ENFORCEMENT GRANT PROGRAM

Assistance: project grants (100 percent/to 18 months).

Purposes: pursuant to VCCLEA and OCCSSA, for rural areas to implement, expand, and establish cooperative efforts and projects among law enforcement officers, prosecutors, victim advocacy groups, and others—to: investigate and prosecute incidents of domestic violence and child abuse; provide treatment and counseling to victims; develop community education and prevention strategies.

Eligible applicants/beneficiaries: state agencies, local governments, tribal governments, and public and private entities in rural states—i.e., those with a population density of 52 or fewer persons per square mile, or in which the largest county's population is less than 150,000, including only Alaska, Arkansas, Arizona, Colorado, Idaho, Iowa, Kansas, Maine, Montana, Nebraska, Nevada, New Mexico, North Dakota, Oklahoma, Oregon, South Dakota, Utah, Vermont, and Wyoming.

Range: $50,000 to $750,000.

Activity: FY 98, 79 grants.

HQ: same address/phone as **16.587**. (Note: no field offices for this program.)

16.590   GRANTS TO ENCOURAGE ARREST POLICIES

Assistance: project grants (100 percent/to 18 months).

Purposes: pursuant to VCCLEA and OCCSSA, to implement mandatory arrest or pro-arrest programs and policies in police departments in cases of domestic violence, including for protection order violations; to improve tracking of cases; to centralize and coordinate police enforcement in groups or units of police officers, prosecutors, or judges; to coordinate computer tracking systems; to strengthen legal advocacy service programs for victims; to improve judicial handling or such cases.

Eligible applicants/beneficiaries: states, local government units, and tribal governments.

Range: $50,000 to $2,500,000.

Activity: FY 98, 137 awards

HQ: same address/phone as **16.587**. (Note: no field offices for this program.)

16.592   LOCAL LAW ENFORCEMENT BLOCK GRANTS PROGRAM

Assistance: formula grants (90 percent/2 years).

Purposes: pursuant to the Local Law Enforcement Block Grants Act of 1996, to: (1) hire and train new, additional, permanent law enforcement officers and necessary support personnel, pay overtime to presently employed officers and personnel, and acquire equipment, technology, and other material directly related to basic law enforcement; (2) enhance security measures in and around schools and other high-risk locations; (3) establish and support drug courts; (4) enhance the adjudication of cases involving violent offenders including juveniles; (5) establish multijurisdictional law enforcement task forces to prevent and control crime, particularly in rural areas; (6) establish crime prevention programs involving cooperation among community residents and law enforcement personnel; (7) defray the cost of indemnification insurance of law enforcement officers.

Eligible applicants/beneficiaries: local government units; recognized tribes, Alaska native villages; territories. Recipients may subcontract with private nonprofit entities or community-based organizations.

Range: N.A.

Activity: FY 98, 3,000 awards.

HQ: Director, Local Law Enforcement Block Grants Program, Bureau of Justice Assistance, Office of Justice Programs-DOJ, 810 Seventh St. NW, Washington, DC 20531. Phone: (202)305-2088. (Note: no field offices for this program.)

16.593   RESIDENTIAL SUBSTANCE ABUSE TREATMENT FOR STATE PRISONERS
("RSAT")

Assistance: formula grants (75 percent/3 years).

Purposes: pursuant to OCCSSA, to develop and implement residential substance abuse treatment programs within state and local correctional facilities, including individual and group programs to develop cognitive, behavioral, social, vocational, and other skills—and lasting six to twelve months.

Eligible applicants/beneficiaries: states, possessions and territories. Subgrants may be awarded to state and local government units.

Range: $234,000 to $6,399,000.

Activity: N.A.

HQ: same address/phone as **16.586**. (Note: no field offices for this program.)

16.595   EXECUTIVE OFFICE FOR WEED AND SEED ("Weed and Seed Program")

Assistance: project grants (100 percent); specialized services.

Purposes: in cooperation with several other federal departments and agencies, to implement "Operation Weed and Seed"—a comprehensive, multidisciplinary approach to combat violent crime, drug use, and gang activity in high-crime neighborhoods. The goal is to identify drug activity and then to "seed" the sites with an array of crime and drug prevention programs, along with human service resources to prevent crime from reoccurring. The strategy is to bring together federal, state, and local government, the community, and the private sector in a partnership. Project examples: community policing of public housing; victims training; job development and apprentice programs.

Eligible applicants/beneficiaries: coalitions of community residents, local, county, state, and federal agencies, and the private sector.

Range/Average: $225,000.

Activity: cumulatively, 200 sites involved, with and without DOJ funding.

HQ: Executive Office for Weed and Seed, DOJ, 810 Seventh St. NW, Washington, DC 20531. Phones: (202)616-1152; FAX (202)616-1159. (Note: no field offices for this program.)

16.596   CORRECTIONAL GRANT PROGRAM FOR INDIAN TRIBES

Assistance: project grants (90 percent/2 years).

Purposes: pursuant to VCCLEA, to construct jails on tribal lands for the incarceration of adult or juvenile offenders.

Eligible applicants/beneficiaries: tribes—defined as any Indian or Alaska native tribe, band, nation, pueblo, village, or community recognized by DOI.

Range/Average: N.A.

Activity: FY 97, 2 awards.

HQ: Deputy Director, same address/phone as **16.586**. (Note: no field offices for this program.)

16.597   MOTOR VEHICLE THEFT PROTECTION ACT PROGRAM ("Watch Your Car")

Assistance: project grants (100 percent/to 18 months).

Purposes: pursuant to VCCLEA, to develop a national voluntary motor vehicle theft prevention program as a cooperative initiative among states, local governments, and DOJ. The Watch Your Car program allows owners to voluntarily display decals or devices alerting police that the vehicle normally is not driven between 1:00 a.m. and 5:00 a.m., nor across or in proximity of international borders or ports. Grant funds may be used: to print, purchase, distribute decals, and registration and consent forms; for public information campaigns; for law enforcement personnel training and overtime costs; for computer database upgrading; related costs.

Eligible applicants/beneficiaries: states; local government units (when states do not apply).

Range: $114,000 to $200,000. **Average:** $144,000.

Activity: new program listing in 1997; FY 98, 6 states with active programs.

HQ: Program Manager/Watch Your Car, Bureau of Justice Assistance-DOJ, 810 Seventh St. NW, Washington, DC 20531. Phone: (202)616-3458. (Note: no field offices for this program.)

16.598   STATE IDENTIFICATION SYSTEMS GRANT PROGRAM ("SIS")

Assistance: formula grants (100 percent).

Purposes: pursuant to the Antiterrorism and Effective Death Penalty Act of 1996—to establish, develop, update, or upgrade: (1) computerized identification systems compatible with the NCIC database at the FBI; (2) capabilities to analyze DNA in forensic laboratories, compatible with FBI systems; (3) automated fingerprint identification systems compatible and integrated with the FBI system. Funds may be used for equipment, training, supplies, and services.

Eligible applicants/beneficiaries: states, territories and possessions meeting DOJ criteria. Funds may be awarded to subrecipients.

Range: $57,000 (Northern Marianas) to $173,000 per state.

Activity: new program in FY 97.

HQ: *eligibility matters,* Program Analyst, Forensic Science Systems Unit, FBI Laboratory-DOJ, 935 Pennsylvania Ave. NW - Rm.GRB-3R, Washington, DC 20535-0001. Phone: (202)324-1820. *Applications,* Operations Chief, State and Local Assistance Division, Bureau of Justice Assistance, DOJ, 810 Seventh St. NW, Washington, DC 20531. Phone: (202)514-6638. (Note: no field offices for this program.)

16.601   CORRECTIONS—TRAINING AND STAFF DEVELOPMENT

Assistance: project grants (100 percent); specialized services; technical information; training.

Purposes: pursuant to JJDPA, to upgrade operation of state and local correctional programs through training seminars, workshops, or other programs for law enforcement officers, judges and judicial personnel, probation and parole personnel, corrections personnel, welfare workers, lay ex-offenders, and paraprofessionals—involved in the treatment and rehabilitation of criminal and juvenile offenders; to develop technical training teams.

Eligible applicants/beneficiaries: states, local government units, public and private agencies, educational institutions, organizations, and individuals.

Range: $1,500 to $300,000. **Average:** $100,000.

Activity: FY 98, 75,000 practitioners participated.

HQ: National Institute of Corrections-DOJ, 320 First St. NW - Rm.5007, Washington, DC 20534. Phones: (202)307-3106, (800)995-6423; TDD (202) 307-3156; FAX (202)307-3361.

16.602 CORRECTIONS—RESEARCH AND EVALUATION AND POLICY FORMULATION

Assistance: project grants (100 percent); specialized services; technical information.

Purposes: pursuant to JJDPA, for research and evaluation projects on the corrections system, including the causes, prevention, diagnosis, and treatment of criminal offenders. Project examples: classification systems and methods; community corrections options; communications audits.

Eligible applicants/beneficiaries: same as for **16.601**.

Range: $1,500 to $200,000. **Average:** $75,000.

Activity: not quantified specifically.

HQ: same address/phones as **16.601**.

16.603 CORRECTIONS—TECHNICAL ASSISTANCE/CLEARINGHOUSE

Assistance: project grants (100 percent); specialized services; technical information.

Purposes: pursuant to JJDPA, to upgrade the operation of state and local correctional facilities, programs, and services for criminal and juvenile offenders; to provide consultation to federal, state, and local courts, departments, and agencies. Examples of funded projects: improved programs for female offenders; evaluation of offender classification systems; development of community sanctions.

Eligible applicants/beneficiaries: same as for **16.601**.

Range: $1,500 to $50,000. **Average:** $7,500.

Activity: FY 98, technical assistance responding to 472 requests.

HQ: Technical Assistance Coordinator/Prisons or Community Corrections, same address/phones as **16.601**.

16.606 STATE CRIMINAL ALIEN ASSISTANCE PROGRAM ("SCAAP")

Assistance: direct payments/unrestricted use (100 percent).

Purposes: pursuant to the Immigration and Nationality Act as amended and VCCLEA, to reimburse states and localities for costs incurred to imprison undocumented aliens convicted of felonies or of two or more misdemeanors; to better identify and expedite the transfer of illegal aliens from state and local correctional institutions to federal custody for deportation.

Eligible applicants/beneficiaries: states, DC, PR, Guam, VI; authorized localities and local jurisdictions.

Range/Average: N.A.

Activity: new program listing in 1998. Cumulative 4-year reimbursement of $2.2 billion to 297 jurisdictions.

HQ: SCAAP Coordinator, Bureau of Justice Assistance, Office of Justice Programs-DOJ, 810 Seventh St. NW, Washington, DC 20531. Phone: (202) 514-6638. (Note: no field offices for this program.)

16.607 BULLETPROOF VEST PARTNERSHIP PROGRAM

Assistance: direct payments/specified use (50 percent/to 4 years).

Purposes: to purchase armored vests for law enforcement officers, including costs of vest carriers, attachments, inserts, essential covers, and fitting, shipping, handling, and tax charges.

Eligible applicants/beneficiaries: chief executives of states, local governments units, federally-recognized tribes, territories, possessions.

Range/Average: N.A.

Activity: new program in FY 99.

HQ: Program Manager, National Programs Division, Bureau of Justice Assistance, DOJ, 810 Seventh St. NW - 4th floor, Washington, DC 20531. Phones: (202)514-3447; Justice Response Center, (800)421-6770; Web, http://vests. ojp.gov (Note: no field offices for this program.)

16.608 TRIBAL COURT ASSISTANCE PROGRAM

Assistance: project grants (100 percent/to 18 months).

Purposes: to develop, enhance, and operate tribal courts.

Eligible applicants/beneficiaries: federally-recognized tribal governments.

Range/Average: N.A.

Activity: new program in FY 99.

HQ: Program Development Division, Bureau of Justice Assistance, Office of Justice Programs-DOJ, 810 Seventh St. NW, Washington, DC 20531. Phone: (202)514-5947. (Note: no field offices for this program.)

16.609 PLANNING, IMPLEMENTING, AND ENHANCING STRATEGIES IN COMMUNITY PROSECUTION
("Community Prosecution Program")

Assistance: project grants (100 percent/to 18 months).

Purposes: pursuant to OCCSSA, to establish a mechanism for participation of community leaders and residents in the identification of local priorities, problem solving, and strategic planning for public safety, through: education and training for criminal justice personnel; technical assistance; demonstration programs.

Eligible applicants/beneficiaries: state, county, city, and tribal public prosecutor offices.

Range: $75,000 to $200,000.

Activity: new program in FY 99.

HQ: Senior Advisor, Bureau of Justice Assistance, Office of Justice Programs-DOJ, 810 Seventh St. NW, Washington, DC 20531. Phone: (202)514-5943. (Note: no field offices for this program.)

16.610   REGIONAL INFORMATION SHARING SYSTEMS ("RISS")

Assistance: project grants (100 percent); technical information; training; specialized services.

Purposes: pursuant to OCCSSA, to enhance the ability of state and local criminal justice agencies to identify, target, and remove criminal conspiracies and activities that span interjurisdictional boundaries—by exchanging and sharing information among federal, state, and local law enforcement agencies, pertaining to known or suspected criminals or criminal activity; to provide technical resources, specialized equipment, and training.

Eligible applicants/beneficiaries: Middle Atlantic-Great Lakes Organized Crime Law Enforcement Center, Mid-States Organized Crime Information Center, New England State Police Information Network, Regional Crime Information Center, Rocky Mountain Information Network, and Western States Information Network.

Range/Average: N.A.

Activity: new program listing in 1999.

HQ: same address as **16.607**. Phones: (202)514-6278; Justice Response Center, (800)421-6770. (Note: no field offices for this program.)

16.611   CLOSED-CIRCUIT TELEVISING OF CHILD VICTIMS OF ABUSE ("CCTV")

Assistance: project grants (100 percent).

Purposes: pursuant to the Victims of Child Abuse Act, to provide equipment and personnel training for the closed-circuit televising and videotaping of the testimony of children in criminal proceedings for the violation of laws relating to the abuse of children.

Eligible applicants/beneficiaries: state or local units of government with enabling laws in effect.

Range: $50,000 to $100,000.

Activity: new program listing in 1999; 10-15 grants expected.

HQ: CCTV Program Manager, Program Development Division, Bureau of Justice Assistance, DOJ, 810 Seventh St. NW - 4th floor, Washington, DC 20531. Phone: (202)616-3219; Justice Response Center, (800)421-6770. (Note: no field offices for this program.)

16.612   NATIONAL WHITE COLLAR CRIME CENTER ("NWCCC")

Assistance: training; technical assistance; advisory services/counseling.

Purposes: pursuant to OCCSSA, for the NWCCC, a nationwide support system for the prevention, investigation, and prosecution of economic crime—through research, training, and investigative support services.

Eligible applicants/beneficiaries: state and local law enforcement authorities.

Activity: new program listing in 1999; (sampling) training in disaster fraud and financial investigations; computer training courses such as Cybercop 101 and 102; National Fraud Complaint Management Center under development.

HQ: same address as **16.607**. Phone: Justice Response Center, (800)421-6770. (Note: no field offices for this program.)

16.613 SCAMS TARGETING THE ELDERLY

Assistance: project grants (100 percent/12-18 months).

Purposes: pursuant to VCCLEA, to assist law enforcement in preventing and stopping marketing scams against senior citizens, through: training and technical assistance including a telemarketing fraud task force; state and local demonstration programs; public awareness initiatives and assistance through the National Fraud Information Center.

Eligible applicants/beneficiaries: state and local law enforcement agencies; public and private nonprofit organizations.

Range/Average: N.A.

Activity: new program listing in 1999; 5 demonstration grants.

HQ: same address as **16.608**. Phones: (202)514-6278; Justice Response Center, (800)421-6770. (Note: no field offices for this program.)

16.614 STATE AND LOCAL ANTI-TERRORISM TRAINING ("SLATT")

Assistance: training; technical information; advisory services/counseling.

Purposes: pursuant to the Anti-Terrorism and Effective Death Penalty Act of 1996, to provide specialized multi-agency anti-terrorism preparedness training, covering both domestic and international threats and incidents. Training focus includes crisis and consequence management, anti-terrorist research, operational issues development, and technical assistance and support.

Eligible applicants/beneficiaries: state and local law enforcement and prosecution authorities.

Activity: new program listing in 1999; FY 99 estimate, 41 workshop and training sessions.

HQ: Bureau of Justice Assistance, DOJ, 810 Seventh St. NW - 4th floor, Washington, DC 20531. Phone: (202)514-6278. (Note: no field offices for this program.)

16.615 PUBLIC SAFETY OFFICERS' EDUCATIONAL ASSISTANCE ("PSOEA")

Assistance: direct payments/unrestricted use (100 percent/4 years).

Purposes: to provide financial assistance for higher education for dependents of public safety officers killed or totally disabled in the line of duty.

Eligible applicants/beneficiaries: spouses and surviving children under age 27—of federal, state, or local public safety officers including those who served public agencies with or without compensation in law enforcement, firefighting, or as members of public rescue squads or ambulance crews.

Range/Average: full-time, $404 monthly; half-time, $202 monthly.

Activity: new program listing in 1999.

HQ: same address/phone as **16.614**, and Justice Response Center phone, (800)421-6770. (Note: no field offices for this program.)

16.710   PUBLIC SAFETY PARTNERSHIP AND COMMUNITY POLICING GRANTS ("'Cops' Grants")

Assistance: project grants (75 percent/3 years).

Purposes: pursuant to the OCCSSA and VCCLEA, to increase police presence in communities, to expand and improve cooperation between law enforcement agencies and communities in addressing problems of crime and disorder, and to enhance public safety. Funds may be used to hire or rehire career law enforcement officers and to procure equipment, technology, or support systems. Grants may also cover costs of programs or projects to: increase the number of officers interacting with community members on proactive crime control and prevention; train officers to increase their skills in conflict resolution, mediation, problem solving; increase participation in multidisciplinary early intervention teams; develop new technologies; support similar activities including innovative approaches to fulfilling the duties of police officers.

Eligible applicants/beneficiaries: states, local government units, tribal governments, other public and private entities, and multijurisdictional or regional consortia.

Range: $1,000 to $17,000,000. **Average:** $184,000.

Activity: cumulatively through February 1999, 24,000 awards funding the hiring of 93,000 additional officers.

HQ: Office of Community Oriented Policing Services-DOJ, 1100 Vermont Ave. NW, Washington, DC 20530. Phones: (202)307-1480; DOJ Response Center, (800)421-6770. *Address applications to:* COPS, same address. (Note: no field offices for this program.)

16.711   TROOPS TO COPS

Assistance: project grants (100 percent/1 year).

Purposes: pursuant to the OCCSSA, VCCLEA, and the National Defense Authorization Act, to hire separated members of the armed forces as law enforcement officers. Grants may cover costs of academy, field, and supplementary community policing training, uniforms, and basic issue equipment.

Eligible applicants/beneficiaries: as established by DOJ.

Range: reimbursements, $1,566 to $212,000; to $25,000 per veteran hired; **Average:** $22,000.

Activity: FY 98, 500 veterans trained.

HQ: same address/phone as **16.710**. *Address applications to:* Troops to COPS Control Desk, same address. (Note: no field offices for this program.)

16.712   POLICE CORPS

Assistance: project grants (100 percent).

Purposes: pursuant to VCCLEA, for scholarships and reimbursement of expenses for advanced education and training on community patrol—of police personnel or of students pursuing careers in law enforcement. Assistance to personnel must be attributable to courses leading to a baccalaureate or graduate degree in preparation for police service; recipients must complete the 16-week Police Corps training program and serve for four years as a state or local police officer or sheriff's deputy.

Eligible applicants/beneficiaries: states; U.S. citizens or lawful permanent residents pursuing undergraduate or graduate study. (NOTE: applications should be directed to the state lead agencies in participating states.)

Range: $5,000 to $30,000 per participant cumulatively. **Average:** participants, $6,750 annually; agencies, $40,000 over 4 years.

Activity: FY 98 (cumulatively), 17 states approved, 1,000 participants; 68 scholarships to children of officers killed in the of duty.

HQ: Office of the Police Corps and Law Enforcement Education, Office of Justice Programs-DOJ, 810 Seventh St. NW, Washington, DC 20531. Phones: (202)353-8953; DOJ Response Center, (800)421-6770. (Note: no field offices for this program.)

16.726 JUVENILE MENTORING PROGRAM ("JUMP")

Assistance: project grants (3 years).

Purposes: pursuant to JJDPA, for one-to-one mentoring programs for youth at risk of educational failure or of dropping out of school, by volunteer adult mentors (at least age 21). Special Emphasis Grants cover 100 percent of project costs; construction projects require a 50 percent local match on facilities of 20 beds or less.

Eligible applicants/beneficiaries: LEAs, public or private nonprofit organizations.

Range: to $200,000 for 3-year project period.

Activity: FY 98 (cumulatively), 93 JUMP sites established in 34 states; 4,000 participating youth. FY 99, 25 new sites to be selected.

HQ: same address as **16.523**. Phone: (202)307-5911. (Note: no field offices for this program.)

16.727 ENFORCING UNDERAGE DRINKING LAWS PROGRAM

Assistance: project grants (1-2 years).

Purposes: to enforce state laws prohibiting alcohol purchase, possession, and use by minors—through projects conducted by partnerships among state and local governments, organizations, and agencies. Discretionary funding may be available for training and technical assistance.

Eligible applicants/beneficiaries: states, territories, DC.

Range: from $360,000.

Activity: new program listing in FY 98; 19 awards.

HQ: State Relations and Assistance Division, OJJDP, Office of Justice Programs-DOJ, 810 Seventh St. NW, Washington, DC 20531. Phone: (202)616-3663. (Note: no field offices for this program.)

16.728 DRUG PREVENTION PROGRAM

Assistance: project grants (100 percent/12-18 months).

Purposes: to reduce drug use through projects: promoting multiple approaches to educating and motivating young adolescents to pursue healthy lifestyles; fostering interpersonal and decision making skills to help them choose alternatives to high-risk behaviors; providing the motivation and tools to build constructive lives.

Eligible applicants/beneficiaries: public and private agencies and organizations; states and territories; local governments units.

Range/Average: N.A.

Activity: new program listing in FY 98; funds awarded to the Center for Study of Violence, University of Colorado, for training and technical assistance on the Life Skills Training drug prevention model.

HQ: Office of National Drug Control Policy, Executive Office of the President, Washington, DC 20503. Phone: (202)395-6700. (Note: no field offices for this program.)

16.729 DRUG-FREE COMMUNITIES SUPPORT PROGRAM GRANTS

Assistance: project grants (50 percent).

Purposes: pursuant to the Drug-Free Communities Act of 1997, to increase the capacity of community coalitions to reduce substance abuse among adults; to disseminate state-of-the-art information on practices and initiatives proven to be effective in reducing substance abuse among youths.

Eligible applicants/beneficiaries: nonprofit, charitable, educational community coalitions collaborating with community entities, including government agencies, in a substantial voluntary effort—established for at least six months and with a five-year strategic plan. Note: proposals are submitted to the Office of Justice Programs, and approved by OJJDP and the Office of National Drug Control Policy.

Range/Average: to $100,000.

Activity: new program listing in FY 98; 92 coalitions funded.

HQ: Director, Special Emphasis Division, OJJDP, Office of Justice Programs-DOJ, 810 Seventh St. NW, Washington, DC 20531. Phone: (202)307-5914. (Note: no field offices for this program.)

16.730 REDUCTION AND PREVENTION OF CHILDREN'S EXPOSURE TO VIOLENCE
("Safe Start")

Assistance: project grants (18 months).

Purposes: for a demonstration initiative to create a comprehensive service delivery system to prevent and reduce the impact of family and community violence on young children (primarily from birth to age 6), by expanding existing community partnerships between service providers such as law enforcement, mental health, early childhood education agencies and others. Program grants cover 100 percent of project costs; construction projects require a 50 percent local match on facilities of 20 beds or less.

Eligible applicants/beneficiaries: public agencies applying on behalf of collaboratives including private agencies and organizations.

Range/Average: N.A.

Activity: new program in FY 99.

HQ: same address as **16.540**. Phone: (202)307-5914. (Note: no field offices for this program.)

16.731 TRIBAL YOUTH PROGRAM ("TYP")

Assistance: project grants (100 percent/3 years).

Purposes: to reduce, control, and prevent crime by or against tribal youth; to provide interventions for court-involved tribal youth; to improve tribal juvenile justice systems; to provide prevention programs focusing on alcohol and drugs.

Eligible applicants/beneficiaries: federally-recognized tribes and Alaska native villages, including partnerships.

Range/Average: N.A.

Activity: new program in FY 99.

HQ: same address/phone as **16.540**. (Note: no field offices for this program.)

16.732 NATIONAL EVALUATION OF THE SAFE SCHOOLS/HEALTHY STUDENTS INITIATIVE ("SS/HS National Evaluation")

Assistance: project grants (100 percent).

Purposes: to evaluate the Safe Schools/Healthy Students Initiative.

Eligible applicants/beneficiaries: public or private agencies, organizations, and individuals.

Range/Average: N.A.

Activity: new program in FY 99; 1 award.

HQ: OJJDP, Office of Justice Programs-DOJ, Washington, DC 20531. Phone: (202)307-5929. (Note: no field offices for this program.)

DEPARTMENT OF LABOR

BUREAU OF LABOR STATISTICS

17.002 LABOR FORCE STATISTICS

Assistance: project grants (100 percent); technical information.

Purposes: to develop statistical data and analyses of labor force activities— e.g., employment and unemployment, wages, occupations, layoffs, plant closings. Quarterly and monthly reports are produced, covering national, state, and local statistics. The data and analyses appear in publications such as "Monthly Labor Review," "Unemployment in States and Local Areas," and "Handbook of Labor Statistics" published by BLS.

Eligible applicants/beneficiaries: grants—SESAs. Information—anyone, from SESAs and BLS.

Range: $3,410 (Guam) to $5,879,000 (California). **Average:** $1,200,000.

Activity: cooperative agreements in effect with all states, DC, PR, VI, and Guam. FY 99 (monthly), labor force survey of 50,000 households; 390,000 establishments reporting on employment, hours, and earnings; 400,000 establishments providing occupational employment statistics; 6,800 areas covered by reports on state and local employment statistics.

HQ: Office of Employment and Unemployment Statistics, BLS-DOL, Washington, DC 20212. Phone: (202)606-6400.

17.003   PRICES AND COST OF LIVING DATA

Assistance: technical information.

Purposes: to provide statistical data on consumer, producer, export, and import prices and price changes, and consumer expenditures. The "Consumer Price Index," "Producer Price Index," "International Price Indexes," and "Consumer Expenditure Surveys" are produced, serving as the basis for periodic governmental and other economic analyses.

Eligible applicants/beneficiaries: general public.

Activity: FY 99 (sampling): indexes expanded to include more private sector factors including housing, insurance coverage, retail food stores, radiotelephone communications.

HQ: Office of Prices and Living Conditions, BLS-DOL, Washington, DC 20212. Phone: (202)606-6960.

17.004   PRODUCTIVITY AND TECHNOLOGY DATA

Assistance: technical information.

Purposes: to provide and analyze data and trends on productivity and technology in major sectors of the U.S. economy and specific industries, and in selected countries. Pertinent reports are published—e.g., "Productivity Measures for Selected Industries," "Measuring State and Local Government Labor Productivity: Examples from Eleven Services," consumer price indexes in foreign countries, international comparisons of productivity labor costs, and the labor force and unemployment.

Eligible applicants/beneficiaries: general public.

Activity: FY 98-99 estimate, 29 reports, studies, and articles completed, 4,700 individual statistical series published.

HQ: Associate Commissioner, Office of Productivity and Technology, BLS-DOL, 2 Massachusetts Ave. NE, Washington, DC 20212. Phone: (202)606-5600.

17.005   COMPENSATION AND WORKING CONDITIONS DATA

Assistance: project grants (50 percent); technical information.

Purposes: to develop and publish data on levels and trends in wages, employee benefits, compensation, occupational safety and health, and work stoppages.

Eligible applicants/beneficiaries: cooperative agreements—state and local governments to operate statistical programs concerning occupational health and safety. Technical information—general public.

Range: $5,200 to $571,000. **Average:** $98,000.

Activity: FY 00 estimate, 245 major reports, studies completed.

HQ: Office of Compensation and Working Conditions, BLS-DOL, Washington, DC 20212. Phone: (202)606-6300.

17.006   EMPLOYMENT PROJECTIONS DATA

Assistance: technical information.

Purposes: to analyze and provide data and related studies on current and long-run economic developments affecting employment, including projections of: the labor force by age, sex, race, and Hispanic origin; patterns of growth in the economy; interindustry sales and purchases; demand for labor in various industries; occupational employment by detailed industry.

Eligible applicants/beneficiaries: general public.

Activity: FY 00, revised projections for the year 2008, new edition of "Occupational Outlook Handbook."

HQ: Office of Employment Projections, BLS-DOL, 2 Massachusetts Ave. NE, Washington, DC 20212. Phone: (202)606-5700.

OFFICE OF LABOR-MANAGEMENT STANDARDS

17.140   LABOR ORGANIZATION REPORTS
("Landrum-Griffin Act")

Assistance: advisory services/counseling; technical information; investigation of complaints.

Purposes: to provide for reporting and disclosure of financial transactions and administrative practices of labor organizations, employers, labor consultants, and others required to report under the Landrum-Griffin Act; to provide standards for the election of union officers, administration of trusteeships, fiduciary responsibilities of union officers, and rights of union members; for court enforcement of safeguards pertaining to union organizations.

Eligible applicants/beneficiaries: union officers, members, organizations. All required reports are available for disclosure to the general public.

Activity: FY 99 estimate, 36,000 reports received and processed; 3,180 investigations; 478 audits; 45 supervised elections.

HQ: Office of Labor-Management Standards-DOL, 200 Constitution Ave. NW, Washington, DC 20210. Phones: (202)219-8861; *Public Disclosure Room (N-5610)*, (202)219-7393.

PENSION AND WELFARE BENEFITS ADMINISTRATION

17.150   PENSION AND WELFARE BENEFITS ADMINISTRATION
("PWBA")

Assistance: technical information.

Purposes: pursuant to the Employee Retirement Security Act (ERISA) as amended, to protect the interests of participants in and beneficiaries of private pension and other employee benefit plans, by: requiring reporting and disclosure of plan and financial information; developing and enforcing fiduciary standards; providing technical assistance, advisory and informational services, workshops and conferences; deterring and correcting violations of statutes through education, voluntary compliance, and civil and criminal enforcement actions.

Eligible applicants/beneficiaries: plan administrators, trustees, participants, beneficiaries.

Activity: annually, 150,000 participants, employers, and plan administrators assisted. FY 99, $390,000,000 in monetary recoveries.

HQ: Pension and Welfare Benefits Administration, DOL, 200 Constitution Ave. NW - Rm.N5656, Washington, DC 20210. Phone: (202)219-8776.

EMPLOYMENT AND TRAINING ADMINISTRATION

17.201   REGISTERED APPRENTICESHIP TRAINING

Assistance: advisory services/counseling.

Purposes: pursuant to the National Apprenticeship Act of 1937 as amended, to develop, expand, and improve apprenticeship and training programs in industry; to register apprentices and programs; to provide technical assistance to state councils. (Apprentice wage rates are exempt from prevailing wages requirements of the Davis-Bacon Act and the Service Contract Act when federal and state programs are registered.)

Eligible applicants: employers, associations of employers—with or without union participation.

Eligible beneficiaries: individuals at least age 16 with sufficient ability, aptitude, and education to master the rudiments of the trade or occupation and to satisfactorily complete required theoretical instruction.

Activity: FY 00 estimate, 424,000 apprentices, including in the military, trained in 42,000 registered programs; 105,000 new apprentices registered.

HQ: Director, Bureau of Apprenticeship and Training, ETA-DOL, 200 Constitution Ave. NW - Rm.N-4649, Washington, DC 20210. Phones: (202)219-5921; FAX (202)219-5011.

17.202   CERTIFICATION OF FOREIGN WORKERS FOR TEMPORARY AGRICULTURAL EMPLOYMENT

Assistance: specialized services.

Purposes: pursuant to the Immigration and Nationality Act as amended and the Immigration Reform and Control Act of 1986, to assist agricultural and logging employers in obtaining temporary alien workers for specific seasonal jobs when domestic workers are unavailable. Funding for this program includes **17.203** and **17.252**.

Eligible applicants/beneficiaries: organizations and individuals interested in importing temporary foreign agricultural and logging workers.

Activity: 24,000 foreign workers certified.

HQ: U.S. Employment Service, ETA-DOL, 200 Constitution Ave. NW, Washington, DC 20210. Phone: (202)219-5257.

17.203 LABOR CERTIFICATION FOR ALIEN WORKERS

Assistance: specialized services.

Purposes: pursuant to the Immigration and Nationality Act as amended, to certify aliens seeking nonagricultural employment, provided U.S workers similarly employed will not be adversely affected. Funding for this program is included in **17.202**.

Eligible applicants/beneficiaries: employers unable to find qualified domestic workers to meet their needs; aliens whose category of employment is included in the DOL "Schedule A" list of precertified occupations.

Activity: FY 98, 62,000 permanent, 2,698 temporary applications received.

HQ: Director, same address/phone as **17.202**.

17.207 EMPLOYMENT SERVICE

Assistance: formula grants (100 percent); specialized services; advisory services/counseling.

Purposes: pursuant to the Wagner-Peyser Act of 1933, Social Security Act of 1935, and amendments, for states to provide job finding, counseling, referral, re-employment, and placement services, including a computerized interstate listing of hard-tofill openings, and testing services for job seekers and employers seeking qualified workers—in cooperation with the DOL's U.S. Employment Service nationwide network of public employment offices. Specialized services may be provided for groups such as veterans, migrant and seasonal farm workers, ex-offenders, and the disabled, disadvantaged, youth, minorities, and older workers.

Eligible applicants: states, DC, VI, PR, and Guam.

Eligible beneficiaries: employers seeking workers; persons seeking employment; associated groups. Veterans receive priority, with handicapped veterans receiving preferential treatment.

Range: N.A.

Activity: N.A.

HQ: Director, same address/phone as **17.202**.

17.225 UNEMPLOYMENT INSURANCE

Assistance: formula grants; direct payments/unrestricted use.

Purposes: to administer state programs providing unemployment compensation, trade adjustment assistance, disaster unemployment insurance, and unemployment compensation for federal employees and ex-servicemembers. State unemployment insurance tax collections fund benefit payments; federal unemployment insurance tax collections fund state administrative costs, and reimburse states for one-half the costs of extended benefits paid under the Social Security Act and the Federal Unemployment Tax Act. Trade Adjustment Assistance payments and training costs are paid out of the Federal

Unemployment Benefits and Allowance Appropriation account in the Unemployment Trust Fund. Disaster Unemployment Assistance is paid by FEMA.

Eligible applicants: state unemployment insurance agencies, including in DC, PR, and VI.

Eligible beneficiaries: workers whose wages are subject to state unemployment laws, federal civilian employees, ex-servicemembers, workers whose unemployment resulted from trade imports, workers whose unemployment resulted from a Presidentially declared disaster—all are eligible if they are involuntarily unemployed, able to and available for work, and meet state eligibility and qualifying requirements. Individual state eligibility requirements are available from local employment offices.

Range: $1,500,000 to $500,000,000. **Average:** $44,000,000.

Activity: not quantified specifically.

HQ: Director, Unemployment Insurance Service, ETA-DOL, Washington, DC 20210. Phone: (202)219-7831.

17.235   SENIOR COMMUNITY SERVICE EMPLOYMENT PROGRAM ("SCSEP" - "Older Worker Program")

Assistance: formula grants; project grants (90 percent).

Purposes: pursuant to the Older Americans Act of 1965 as amended, to provide, foster, and promote useful part-time (usually 20 hours weekly) work opportunities for unemployed persons age 55 or over—in community service activities such as schools, hospitals, day care centers, park systems, public housing projects, weatherization and nutrition programs, libraries, etc. Training, counseling, and other supportive services may be provided. The program also assists and promotes the transition of enrollees into unsubsidized employment.

Eligible applicants: states; national public and private nonprofit agencies and organizations other than political parties; territories.

Eligible beneficiaries: adults age 55 or older, with family income at or below 125 percent of the HHS poverty level.

Range: N.A.

Activity: 1998, 61,100 part-time positions supported.

HQ: Office of National Programs, ETA-DOL, 200 Constitution Ave. NW - Rm.N4641, Washington, DC 20210. Phone: (202)219-5500. (Note: no field offices for this program.)

17.245   TRADE ADJUSTMENT ASSISTANCE—WORKERS

Assistance: direct payments/unrestricted use (to 78 weeks); specialized services.

Purposes: pursuant to the Trade Act of 1974 as amended, Omnibus Trade and Competitiveness Act of 1988, North American Free Trade Agreement Act, and other acts, to provide "adjustment assistance" payments to and assistance for workers adversely affected by increased imports—including relocation allowances, job testing, counseling, training, and placement services. Payments may be made only after state unemployment compensation benefits have been exhausted. The maximum number of weeks of state unemployment compensation, extended benefits, and trade readjustment allowances may not exceed 52—except that benefits may be paid for an additional 26 weeks to workers participating in approved training.

Eligible applicants: groups of three of more workers, or their union or authorized representative—including those adversely affected by the North American Free Trade Agreement.

Eligible beneficiaries: unemployed workers certified by DOL as eligible to apply for adjustment assistance, and meeting specific other requirements.

Range: same as weekly amount of state unemployment benefits.

Activity: cumulatively 1975-1998, 15,831 certifications covering 2,249,000 workers.

HQ: Director, Office of Trade Adjustment Assistance, ETA-DOL, 200 Constitution Ave. NW - Rm.C-4318, Washington, DC 20210. Phone: (202)219-5555.

17.246   EMPLOYMENT AND TRAINING ASSISTANCE—DISLOCATED WORKERS

Assistance: formula grants; project grants (100 percent).

Purposes: pursuant to the Job Training Partnership Act of 1982 as amended, for programs to train and provide employment-related services, including job search, relocation assistance, and needsrelated payments—to workers dislocated by mass industry layoffs, environmental protection legislation, defense cutbacks, or natural disasters.

Eligible applicants: states.

Eligible beneficiaries: individuals terminated or laid off or notified of same and not likely to return to their previous industry or occupation, or that are long-term unemployed. Natural Reserve Program—individuals affected by mass lay-offs, natural disasters, or federal government actions.

Range: N.A.

Activity: N.A.

HQ: ETA-DOL, 200 Constitution Ave. NW - Rm.N5426, Washington, DC 20210. Phone: (202)219-5577.

17.247   MIGRANT AND SEASONAL FARMWORKERS

Assistance: formula grants; project grants (100 percent/2-4 years).

Purposes: pursuant to the Job Training Partnership Act of 1982 as amended, for job training, job search, health services, relocation and education assistance, and other supportive services—to migrant and seasonal farm workers and their families suffering chronic unemployment and under-employment in the agricultural industry.

Eligible applicants: public agencies and government units; private nonprofit organizations.

Eligible beneficiaries: individuals who, during any consecutive 12 months in the prior 24-month period, were seasonal or migrant farm workers, and: (a) received at least 50 percent of their total earned income, or (b) were employed at least 50 percent of their total time in farm work, and (c) are members of a family receiving public assistance or whose income does not exceed the poverty level or 70 percent of the lower living standard income level.

Range: $120,000 to $6,893,000.

Activity: 1998, 45,000 persons enrolled; grants to 50 farm worker organizations, 6 housing organizations.

HQ: Division of Seasonal Farmworker Programs, same address/phone as **16.235.**

17.248 EMPLOYMENT AND TRAINING RESEARCH AND DEVELOPMENT PROJECTS

Assistance: project grants (100 percent/1-2 years).

Purposes: pursuant to the Job Training Partnership Act of 1982 as amended, for studies, research and development, and demonstration projects to improve employment and training program techniques and systems.

Eligible applicants/beneficiaries: state colleges and universities; public, private, junior and community colleges; state and local government organizations, including territories; other organizations and individuals.

Range: $10,000 to $1,000,000. **Average:** $175,000.

Activity: FY 99 estimate, 25 new or continued projects.

HQ: Division of Research and Demonstration, ETA-DOL, Washington, DC 20210. Phone: (202)219-5677.

17.249 EMPLOYMENT SERVICES AND JOB TRAINING—PILOT AND DEMONSTRATION PROGRAMS

Assistance: project grants (100 percent).

Purposes: pursuant to the Job Training Partnership Act of 1982 as amended, for national demonstration and pilot projects involving new training, related services, and job opportunity projects especially for groups with particular disadvantages in the labor market, such as displaced homemakers, single parents, offenders, handicapped persons, youth, displaced workers, persons lacking educational skills or with limited English-speaking ability. Project examples: training and apprenticeship; training handicapped persons in the aerospace and machining industry; workplace literacy model; state-local coordination model to train public housing residents.

Eligible applicants/beneficiaries: state and local governments, federal agencies, private nonprofit and profit organizations, educational institutions.

Range: $100,000 to $1,750,000.

Activity: FY 99 estimate, 50 new or continued projects.

HQ: Administrator, Office of Policy and Research, ETA-DOL, 200 Constitution Ave. NW, Washington, DC 20210. Phone: (202)219-5677. (Note: no field offices for this program.)

17.250 JOB TRAINING PARTNERSHIP ACT ("JTPA")

Assistance: formula grants.

Purposes: for job training and related services primarily to the economically disadvantaged, including adults, youth, and others facing significant employment barriers to permanent, selfsustaining employment. Partnerships between the private sector and state and local governments are authorized. A summer youth employment and training component is funded through this program.

Eligible applicants: states.

Eligible beneficiaries: Title II-A—economically disadvantaged adults facing serious barriers to employment, with basic skills deficiencies or who are school dropouts, cash welfare recipients, offenders, disabled, or homeless. Title II-B Summer Jobs Program—economically disadvantaged in-school youth, age 14- or 16-21 (depending on approved plan), with basic skills deficiencies or with educational attainment below grade level, or who are pregnant or parenting, disabled, homeless or run-aways, offenders. Title II-C Summer Jobs Program—economically disadvantaged out-of-school youth age 14-21.

Range: N.A.

Activity: N.A.

HQ: Director, Office of Employment and Training Programs, ETA-DOL, 200 Constitution Ave. NW, Washington, DC 20210. Phone: (202)219-5303, ext.169.

17.251 NATIVE AMERICAN EMPLOYMENT AND TRAINING PROGRAMS

Assistance: formula grants (100 percent/1-3 years).

Purposes: pursuant to the Job Training Partnership Act of 1982 as amended, for employment and training programs and services for native Americans facing serious barriers to employment. Programs may include classroom and on-the-job training, community service employment, work experience, youth employment programs. Grant funds may be used to pay for such services as day care, health care, job search, relocation and transportation allowances.

Eligible applicants/beneficiaries: tribes, bands or groups; Alaska native villages or groups; Hawaiian native communities; consortia of the foregoing groups. Also, public or private nonprofit agencies.

Range: $19,000 to $6,431,000. **Average:** $290,000.

Activity: 1999 estimate, 19,000 participants.

HQ: Division of Indian and Native American Programs, same address/phone as **17.235**. (Note: no field offices for this program.)

17.252 ATTESTATIONS BY EMPLOYERS USING NON-IMMIGRANT ALIENS IN SPECIALTY OCCUPATIONS

Assistance: specialized services.

Purposes: pursuant to the Immigration and Nationality Acts of 1952 and 1990 as amended, to process attestations by employers of the working conditions and wages of aliens to be employed in specialty occupations. Documentation must be available for public inspection at the employer's principal place of business, as well as at the ETA. Funding for this program is included in **17.202**.

Eligible applicants/beneficiaries: employers; aliens to be employed in specialty occupations or as fashion models.

Activity: FY 98, 181,000 attestations received and processed.

HQ: Director, same address/phone as **17.202**.

17.253   WELFARE-TO-WORK GRANTS TO STATES AND LOCALITIES ("WtW Grants")

Assistance: formula grants (67-100 percent/to 3 years).

Purposes: pursuant to the Social Security Act, Personal Responsibility and Work Opportunity Reconciliation Act of 1996, and other acts, to help move hard-to-employ welfare recipients into lasting unsubsidized jobs and achieve self-sufficiency. Formula grants (67 percent funding) and competitive grants (100 percent funding) may be used for community service or work experience programs, job creation through public or private sector employment wage subsidies, on-the-job training, various employment services, job vouchers. At least 70 percent of funds must be expended to assist eligible program beneficiaries.

Eligible applicants: states, which must subgrant 85 percent of formula funds to service delivery area agencies supervised by Private Industry Councils.

Eligible beneficiaries: welfare recipients or noncustodial parents of minors whose custodial parents are welfare recipients—meeting a combination of specific DOL criteria such as low educational skills, requiring substance abuse treatment, poor work history, expiring eligibility for assistance.

Range/Average: N.A.

Activity: new program listing in FY 98.

HQ: Administrator, Office of Job Training Programs, ETA-DOL, 200 Constitution Ave. NW, Washington, DC 20210. Phones: (202)219-0181, ext.141; Web, www.wtw.doleta.gov

17.254   WELFARE-TO-WORK GRANTS TO FEDERALLY RECOGNIZED TRIBES AND ALASKA NATIVES

("Indian and Native American Welfare-to-Work Grant Program" - "INA WtW Grants")

Assistance: formula grants (100 percent/3 years).

Purposes: pursuant to the Social Security Act as amended, to help Indian tribes and Alaska native regional corporations move hardto-employ welfare recipients into lasting unsubsidized jobs and family self-sufficiency. Funds may be used for community service or work experience programs, job creation through public or private sector employment wage subsidies, on-the-job training, various employment services, job vouchers. At least 70 percent of funds must be expended to assist eligible program beneficiaries.

Eligible applicants: federally-recognized tribes and Alaska native regional nonprofit corporations, or consortia.

Eligible beneficiaries: same as for **17.253**.

Range: $2,072 to $1,970,000. **Average:** $136,000.

Activity: new program in FY 98; 100 entities determined eligible, 82 applicants to be allotted funds,

HQ: same address as **17.251**. Phones: (202)219-8502, ext.119; FAX (202)219-

6338; TDD (202)326-2577; Web, www.wdsc.org/dinap   (Note: no field offices for this program.)

17.255 WORKFORCE INVESTMENT ACT ("WIA")

Assistance: formula grants (100 percent).

Purposes: to design a revitalized work force system that provides workers with the information, advice, job search assistance, and training they need to obtain and retain good jobs, and to provide employers with skilled workers. The Act: authorizes the new Workforce Investment System and establishes State Workforce Investment Boards with oversight responsibility for local boards; establishes the design and required partnerships of One-Stop Career Centers and the process for which eligible providers of youth and training activities are identified. Funds may be used: for youth, adult, and dislocated worker employment and training activities; to establish local youth councils; to provide core services, intensive services, and training; for national programs; for technical assistance to states and local areas; for demonstration, pilot, and other special national projects; for emergency grants.

Eligible applicants: Title I formula grants—governors. Native American programs—Indian tribes, tribal organizations, Alaska native entities, native Hawaiian organizations. Migrant and seasonal farm worker programs—experienced entities. Veterans' work force investment programs—public and private nonprofit organizations. Youth opportunity grants—local work force investment boards.

Eligible beneficiaries: youth age 14-21 meeting certain criteria establishing their disadvantaged status; adult and dislocated workers; native Americans; migrant and seasonal farm workers; veterans.

Range/Average: N.A.

Activity: new program listing in 1999.

HQ: Director, Workforce Investment Act Implementation Taskforce, ETA-DOL, 200 Constitution Ave. NW - Rm.S5513, Washington, DC 20210. Phone: (202)219-0316.

17.257 ONE-STOP CAREER CENTER INITIATIVE

Assistance: project grants (some matching/3 years).

Purposes: pursuant to the Wagner-Peyser Act and Social Security Acts as amended, to provide access to all DOL-funded programs within one physical facility or through electronic access. Grants are used: to establish the technical infrastructure and to train professional staff to provide quality services; to develop state and local working partnerships among governmental and nonprofit agencies, to serve job seekers and employers; to maintain and expand an electronic labor exchange and information system, including America's Job Bank, America's Talent Bank, America's Career InfoNet, and America's Learning Exchange.

Eligible applicants/beneficiaries: states, DC, PR, VI, Guam.

Range: $1,000,000 to $8,000,000.

Activity: new program listing in 1999. As of 1999, 54 grants awarded; 1,091 centers opened in 41 states.

HQ: One-Stop Implementation Team, ETA-DOL, Washington, DC 20210. Phones: (202)219-8395; Web, www.ttrc.doleta.gov

EMPLOYMENT STANDARDS ADMINISTRATION

17.301   NON-DISCRIMINATION AND AFFIRMATIVE ACTION BY FEDERAL CONTRACTORS AND FEDERALLY ASSISTED CONSTRUCTION CONTRACTORS
("Office of Federal Contract Compliance Programs" - "OFCCP")

Assistance: investigation of complaints.

Purposes: to enforce nondiscrimination and affirmative action regulations covering employment by federal contractors, including subcontractors and those involved in federally-assisted construction. Complaints alleging employment discrimination on the basis of race, sex, religion, color, national origin, disability, or covered veteran status may be filed with OFCCP. Technical advice and assistance are available to employers.

Eligible applicants/beneficiaries: applicants, employees, and former employees of federal contractors or federally involved contractors performing work in the U.S., Panama Canal Zone, and possessions and territories—including those recruited in the U.S. to perform work abroad.

Activity: FY 98, 294 complaints investigated; $35,491,000 in financial settlements concluded, including $10,524,000 in back pay to 6,306 recipients.

HQ: Deputy Assistant Secretary, OFCCP, Employment Standards Administration-DOL, Washington, DC 20210. Phone: (202)219-9475.

17.302   LONGSHORE AND HARBOR WORKERS' COMPENSATION

Assistance: direct payments/unrestricted use.

Purposes: to replace and supplement income to compensate for permanent disability or death resulting from injury, including occupational disease; to provide benefits for certain medical expenses including hospital care, as well as funeral expenses up to $3,000. Benefits are paid by private insurers or self-insured employers; federal funds are available in certain cases of permanent total disability, and death.

Eligible applicants/beneficiaries: longshore workers, harbor workers, and certain other maritime employees working on U.S. navigable waters and in pier and dock areas; also, employees working on the Outer Continental Shelf, of nonappropriated fund instrumentalities, of private employers working in DC within specified periods or abroad under U.S. government contracts; survivors. PR is not covered.

Range: disability—two-thirds of average weekly wage; death benefits—50 percent of average wages of deceased to widow or widower, plus 16-2/3 percent for each surviving child with a twothirds limit. Benefits are limited to 200 percent of national average weekly wage. Payments are made for the period of total or partial disability, with no monetary limit; death benefits are paid to the spouse until death or remarriage, and to children until age 18—or 23 if qualified as a student.

Activity: FY 99 estimate, 16,000 workers or survivors receiving monthly benefits; 26,000 lost-time injuries reported.

HQ: Division of Longshore and Harbor Workers' Compensation, Office of Workers' Compensation Programs, Employment Standards Administration-DOL, Washington, DC 20210. Phone: (202)219-8721.

17.303 WAGE AND HOUR STANDARDS
("Federal Wage-Hour Laws")

Assistance: advisory services/counseling; investigation of complaints.

Purposes: to develop and enforce standards protecting wages of working persons with respect to minimum rate of pay, overtime pay, prevailing hourly wage rates, fringe benefits, child labor; to protect against discrimination in certain "whistleblower" activities; to enforce wage payment standards for professional performers and related professional employees. Funding for this program includes **17.306** and **17.308**.

Eligible applicants/beneficiaries: any covered employee in the U.S., territories, and possessions.

Activity: FY 98, 272,000 employees found to be underpaid by $197,092,000; 252,000 employees received $163,593,000 in back wages.

HQ: Administrator, Wage and Hour Division, Employment Standards Administration-DOL, Washington, DC 20210. Phone: (202)219-8305.

17.306 CONSUMER CREDIT PROTECTION
("Federal Wage Garnishment Law")

Assistance: advisory services/counseling; investigation of complaints.

Purposes: pursuant to the Consumer Protection Act as amended, to enforce federal restrictions on the amount of a person's income that may be garnished, and prohibiting employers from discharging employees by reason of garnishment for any one indebtedness. Earnings are defined as compensation paid or payable for personal services, whether as wages, salary, commission, bonuses, including periodic payments under a pension or retirement program. Funding for this program is included in **17.303**.

Eligible applicants/beneficiaries: persons with earnings subjected to garnishment, in the U.S. and territories and possessions.

Activity: not quantified specifically.

HQ: same address/phone as **17.303**.

17.307 COAL MINE WORKERS' COMPENSATION
("Black Lung")

Assistance: direct payments/unrestricted use.

Purposes: pursuant to the Federal Mine Safety and Health Amendments Act of 1977 as amended, to pay monthly cash benefits to coal miners totally disabled with black lung disease, and to their surviving dependents.

Eligible applicants/beneficiaries: disabled miners; miners' widows and other surviving dependents. Included are some workers involved in coal transportation in and around mines, and in coal mine construction. Beneficiaries must have become "totally disabled" from coal workers' pneumoconiosis, as defined in the Act. Applicants may work in areas other than coal mines and remain eligible for benefits. Benefits may be reduced on account of excess earnings.

Range: $455.40 monthly for claimant only, to $910.70 for three or more dependents, effective January 1998 (not including medical services). **Average:** $512.32 monthly.

Activity: FY 98, 4,769 claims processed; 71,000 claimants benefiting.

HQ: Director, Division of Coal Mine Workers' Compensation, Office of Workers' Compensation Programs, Employment Standards Administration-DOL, Washington, DC 20210. Phone: (202)219-6692.

17.308   FARM LABOR CONTRACTOR REGISTRATION ("Crew Leader")

Assistance: advisory services/counseling; investigation of complaints.

Purposes: pursuant to the Migrant and Seasonal Agricultural Worker Protection Act as amended, to enforce regulations covering farm labor contractors regarding such factors as wages, records, transportation, health, safety, and housing provided for migrant and seasonal agricultural workers. Funding for this program is included in **17.303**.

Eligible applicants/beneficiaries: contractors and their fulltime or regular employees who recruit, solicit, hire, furnish, or transport migrant or seasonal agricultural workers for employment for a fee in any form must register with DOL.

Activity: FY 98, 2,549 compliance actions.

HQ: same address/phone as **17.303**.

17.309   LABOR ORGANIZATION REPORTS ("Landrum-Griffin Act")

Assistance: advisory services/counseling; technical information; investigation of complaints.

Purposes: same as for **17.140**.

Eligible applicants/beneficiaries: same as for **17.140**.

Activity: new program listing in 1999. Same as for **17.140**.

HQ: same as for **17.140**.

OCCUPATIONAL SAFETY AND HEALTH ADMINISTRATION

17.502   OCCUPATIONAL SAFETY AND HEALTH—SUSAN HARWOOD TRAINING GRANTS

Assistance: project grants (80 percent).

Purposes: pursuant to the Occupational Safety and Health Act, for projects providing occupational safety and health training and education to employees and employers, particularly in the recognition, avoidance, and abatement of workplace hazards.

Eligible applicants/beneficiaries: nonprofit organizations except state and local governments; local-, state-funded IHEs.

Range: $50,000 to $150,000.

Activity: FY 00 estimate, 45 grants.

HQ: Assistant Secretary, OSHA-DOL, Washington, DC 20210. Phones: (202) 639-2000; (847)297-4810.

17.503 OCCUPATIONAL SAFETY AND HEALTH—STATE PROGRAM

Assistance: project grants (50 percent).

Purposes: pursuant to the Occupational Safety and Health Act, for state administration and enforcement of approved occupational safety and health programs.

Eligible applicants/beneficiaries: designated state agencies.

Range: $294,000 to $19,566,000.

Activity: FY 00 estimate, 57,000 state enforcement inspections.

HQ: same address as **17.502**. Phone: (202)693-2426.

17.504 CONSULTATION AGREEMENTS

Assistance: project grants (90 percent).

Purposes: pursuant to the Occupational Safety and Health Act, for consultative workplace safety and health services by states to small employers with hazardous operations.

Eligible applicants: designated state agencies.

Eligible beneficiaries: any private employer.

Range: $143,000 to $3,569,000.

Activity: FY 00 estimate, 27,500 consultation visits.

HQ: same address as **17.502**. Phone: (202)693-2426.

MINE SAFETY AND HEALTH ADMINISTRATION

17.600 MINE HEALTH AND SAFETY GRANTS

Assistance: project grants (80 percent).

Purposes: pursuant to the Federal Mine Safety and Health Amendments Act of 1977 as amended, to develop and enforce laws and regulations related to the health and safety of miners; to improve workmen's compensation and occupational disease laws and programs; for miner training.

Eligible applicants/beneficiaries: any mining state.

Range: $13,000 to $591,000. **Average:** $127,000.

Activity: FY 98, grant awards to most mining states and the Navajo Nation.

HQ: Assistant Secretary/Mine Safety and Health, Mine Safety and Health Administration-DOL, 4015 Wilson Blvd., Arlington, VA 22203. Phones: (703)235-1515, -1400. (Note: no field offices for this program.)

17.601 MINE HEALTH AND SAFETY COUNSELING AND TECHNICAL ASSISTANCE

Assistance: advisory services/counseling; technical information.

Purposes: pursuant to the Federal Mine Safety and Health Amendments Act of 1977 as amended, to establish or improve health and safety conditions in and around coal, metal, and nonmetallic mines and mineral facilities—through equipment testing, special studies, technical advice, investigations.

Eligible applicants/beneficiaries: states, organizations, or individuals.

Activity: not quantified specifically.

HQ: same address as **17.600.** Phones: (202)235-1385, -1580.

17.602 MINE HEALTH AND SAFETY EDUCATION AND TRAINING

Assistance: training.

Purposes: pursuant to the Federal Mine Safety and Health Amendments Act of 1977 as amended, to provide initial and advanced mine safety and health training of federal mine inspectors, miners, and others. Curriculum materials and audiovisual programs are available.

Eligible applicants/beneficiaries: mine operators, miners, or their agents.

Activity: 694 course days of federal employee training; mining industry, 341 days.

HQ: Director, Educational Policy and Development, Mine Safety and Health Administration-DOL, 4015 Wilson Blvd., Arlington, VA 22203. Phones: (703)235-1515, (304)256-3201.

WOMEN'S BUREAU, OFFICE OF THE SECRETARY

17.700 WOMEN'S SPECIAL EMPLOYMENT ASSISTANCE

Assistance: advisory services/counseling; technical information.

Purposes: to develop training and employment policies and programs affecting the employment of women; to expand employment opportunities for women and promote their entry into better paying jobs, especially in new technology and nontraditional occupations; operation of the Women's Bureau Clearinghouse. Project examples: model school-to-work transition program; Work and Family projects; planning for employer-sponsored child care; international programs.

Eligible applicants/beneficiaries: any individual or group.

Activity: not quantified specifically.

HQ: Director, Women's Bureau, Office of the Secretary-DOL, Washington, DC 20210. Phones: (202)219-6611; Office of Information and Support Services (Rm.S3305), (202)219-6606.

OFFICE OF ASSISTANT SECRETARY/VETERANS' EMPLOYMENT AND TRAINING

17.801 DISABLED VETERANS' OUTREACH PROGRAM ("DVOP")

Assistance: formula grants (100 percent).

Purposes: pursuant to the Veterans' Rehabilitation and Education Amendments of 1980, to pay the salaries and expenses of DVOP specialists assigned to meet the employment needs of eligible veterans. Specialists promote jobs, job training, and apprenticeships for disabled and other veterans, through contacts with employers and other outreach programs.

Eligible applicants/beneficiaries: state employment security agencies.

Range: $146,000 to $12,114,000. **Average:** $1,539,000.

Activity: FY 97, 52 awards.

HQ: Assistant Secretary/Veterans' Employment and Training-DOL, 200 Constitution Ave. NW - Rm.S-1316, Washington, DC 20210. Phone: (202)219-9105.

17.802 VETERANS' EMPLOYMENT PROGRAM ("JTPA Title IV - Part C")

Assistance: project grants (100 percent).

Purposes: pursuant to the Job Training Partnership Act of 1982 as amended, to enhance services to veterans in employment and training programs and related services; for outreach and public information programs.

Eligible applicants: governors. Discretionary funds—all applicants.

Eligible beneficiaries: service-connected disabled veterans, Vietnam-era veterans, and those recently separated from military service.

Range: $200,000 to $850,000. **Average:** $487,000.

Activity: 1998, 11 competitive grants.

HQ: same address/phone as **17.801**.

17.803 UNIFORMED SERVICES EMPLOYMENT AND REEMPLOYMENT RIGHTS

Assistance: advisory services/counseling; technical information; investigation of complaints.

Purposes: to assist in the employment and reemployment of noncareer veterans or candidates for the uniformed services. Unresolved complaints are referred to DOJ for representation in federal district courts.

Eligible applicants/beneficiaries: persons (including reservists and National Guard members) that have served on active duty, active duty for training, or training duty with the uniformed services; candidates for duty. Entitlement ceases upon termination service with a bad conduct or dishonorable discharge, or upon separation under other than honorable conditions.

Activity: FY 98, 1,045 new complaint cases processed, 1,055 cases closed; responses to 11,000 public inquiries; 500 staff presentations.

HQ: same address as **17.801**. Phone: (202)219-8611.

17.804   LOCAL VETERANS' EMPLOYMENT REPRESENTATIVE PROGRAM ("LVER Program")

Assistance: formula grants (100 percent).

Purposes: pursuant to the Servicemen's Readjustment Act of 1944, to fund salaries and expenses of Local Veterans' Employment Representatives assigned to assure compliance with federal regulations and standards concerning employment and training opportunities for veterans.

Eligible applicants/beneficiaries: state employment/job service agencies.

Range: $66,000 to $6,350,000. **Average:** $1,454,000.

Activity FY 98, 53 grant awards.

HQ: same address/phone as **17.801**.

17.805   HOMELESS VETERANS REINTEGRATION PROJECT

Assistance: project grants (100 percent).

Purposes: pursuant to the Stewart B. McKinney Homeless Assistance Act of 1987, for demonstration projects to reintegrate homeless veterans into the labor force—through activities including outreach, employment and training services, support services, and linkages with other service providers. Outreach is to be performed by formerly homeless veterans. (NOTE: this program was deleted in 1996 and reinstated in 1998.)

Eligible applicants/beneficiaries: state and local public agencies, private industry councils, nonprofit agencies.

Range/Average: $100,000 to $125,000.

Activity: FY 98 estimate, assistance to 3,200 veterans and placement of 1,600.

HQ: same address/phone as **17.801**.

DEPARTMENT OF STATE

OFFICE OF THE LEGAL ADVISER

19.200   CLAIMS AGAINST FOREIGN GOVERNMENTS ("International Claims")

Assistance: specialized services.

Purposes: to settle legally valid claims of U.S. nationals against foreign governments. Examples of possible claims include takings of property without adequate or prompt payment, acts of mobs, insurgents, or individuals through lack of due diligence by the foreign government's officials. The State Department uses its "good offices" toward settlement on behalf of claimants after all local administrative or judicial remedies have been exhausted.

Eligible applicants/beneficiaries: U.S. nationals at time claim arose, able to show responsibility of the respondent government.

Range: unlimited.

Activity: not quantified specifically.

HQ: Assistant Legal Adviser/International Claims and Investment Disputes, Office of the Legal Adviser, Department of State, South Bldg. - Ste.203, 2340 E St. NW, Washington, DC 20037-2800. Phone: (202)776-8360. (Note: no field offices for this program.)

19.201 PROTECTION OF SHIPS FROM FOREIGN SEIZURE ("Fishermen's Protective Act")

Assistance: insurance (reimbursement).

Purposes: to reimburse fishing vessel owners for fines and other charges paid to secure the release of vessels and crew seized by a foreign country, on the basis of: (1) claims to jurisdictions not recognized by the U.S.; (2) claims to recognized jurisdictions but exercised in a manner inconsistent with international law; or (3) any general claim to exclusive fishery management with certain conditions and restrictions sanctioned by the Department of State.

Eligible applicants/beneficiaries: U.S. citizen-owners of documented and certified private vessels seized by a foreign country.

Range: N.A.

Activity: not quantified specifically.

HQ: same address/phone as **19.200**. (Note: no field offices for this program.)

BUREAU OF PERSONNEL

19.202 SPECIAL DOMESTIC ASSIGNMENTS ("Pearson Program")

Assistance: specialized services.

Purposes: pursuant to the Foreign Service Act of 1980, to assign Foreign Service Officers to provide assistance in management and other functions of special domestic programs. Host organizations must reimburse the State Department $10,000 annually for such assignments. Assignments are expected to relate directly to international affairs.

Eligible applicants/beneficiaries: members of the Foreign Service may be assigned for duty in the U.S. or any territory or possession, with a state or local government, a public or private nonprofit organization (including an educational institution), or a Member or office of the Congress.

Activity: at any one time, approximately 10 Foreign Service Officers assigned.

HQ: Program Coordinator, Office of Career Development and Assignments (PER/CDA/SL/CDT), Bureau of Personnel, Department of State, NS-Rm. 2336, Washington, DC 20520. Phone: (202)647-9526. (Note: no field offices for this program.)

BUREAU OF OCEANS AND INTERNATIONAL ENVIRONMENTAL AND SCIENTIFIC AFFAIRS

19.204   FISHERMEN'S GUARANTY FUND ("Section 7")

Assistance: insurance.

Purposes: pursuant to the Fishermen's Protective Act of 1967 as amended and to other acts, to reimburse U.S. commercial fishing vessel owners for losses resulting from the seizure of the vessel by a foreign country on the basis of rights or claims in territorial waters, or on the high seas not recognized by the U.S. Losses payable generally are limited to the market value of fish caught before seizure, to the market value of the confiscated vessel or gear, and up to 50 percent of gross income lost as a result of seizure. Effective November 28, 1990, the U.S. acknowledges the authority of coastal states to manage highly migratory species, reducing the basis for claims under this program.

Eligible applicants/beneficiaries: U.S. citizen-owners or -charterers of a documented fishing vessel. Claimants must have paid a premium for the year in which the seizure occurs.

Range/Average: N.A.

Activity: FY 99 estimate, 15 guaranty agreements.

HQ: Office of Marine Conservation, Bureau of Oceans and International Environmental and Scientific Affairs, Department of State, Rm.5806, Washington, DC 20520-7818. Phones: (202)647-3941; FAX (202)736-7350. (Note: no field offices for this program.)

BUREAU OF INTELLIGENCE AND RESEARCH

19.300   PROGRAM FOR STUDY OF EASTERN EUROPE AND THE INDEPENDENT STATES OF THE FORMER SOVIET UNION ("Title VIII")

Assistance: project grants (100 percent/to 3 years).

Purposes: pursuant to the Research and Training for Eastern Europe and the Independent States of the Former Soviet Union Act of 1983 as amended, for advanced research, graduate training, language training, and related activities—toward the development of American expertise on the countries of the former Soviet Union and Eastern Europe. Funds may support short-term research projects, fellowships, conferences, travel, and publication costs.

Eligible applicants: nonprofit organizations or IHEs.

Eligible beneficiaries: graduate students, scholars.

Range: $120,000 to $1,000,000. **Average:** $200,000.

Activity: FY 98, 9 grants recommended.

HQ: Executive Director *or*Program Officer, Program for Study of Eastern Europe and the Independent States of the Former Soviet Union (INR/RES), Department of State, 2201 C St. - Rm.6841, Washington, DC 20520-6510. Phones: (202)736-4572; FAX (202)736-4851; Web, www.State.gov/www/regions/nis/grants (Note: no field offices for this program.)

DEPARTMENT OF TRANSPORTATION

U.S. COAST GUARD

20.001   BOATING SAFETY

Assistance: specialized services; technical information; training.

Purposes: for the Coast Guard Auxiliary to provide: boating safety education and training: assistance to boaters in distress; Courtesy Marine Examinations covering safety of equipment, operation, and use of watercraft; publications.

Eligible applicants/beneficiaries: U.S. citizens at least age 17 may join the Auxiliary.

Activity: 1998, 151,000 examinations; 249,000 public school students enrolled in courses; auxiliary—2,247 regatta and 25,000 safety patrols, 4,130 public assists, 481 lives saved.

HQ: Commandant (G-OCX-1), USCG-DOT, 2100 Second St. SW - Rm.3501, Washington, DC 20593-0001 Phone: (202)267-1001.

20.005   BOATING SAFETY FINANCIAL ASSISTANCE

Assistance: formula grants; project grants (50-100 percent/to 3 years).

Purposes: for the development and operation of boating safety programs. Funds may support education, maintenance, and enforcement activities including the cost of facilities, acquisition and construction or repair of access sites, personnel training, administration.

Eligible applicants/beneficiaries: states, territories, and possessions with an approved boating safety program; national nonprofit service organizations.

Range: states, $329,000 to $3,945,000; organizations, $9,000 to $438,000. **Average:** states, $987,000; organizations, $125,000.

Activity: FY 98, 49 states, several territories, possessions, and 22 national organizations funded.

HQ: Commandant, USCG-DOT, Washington, DC 20593-0001. Phones: *states,* (202)267-0857; *national organizations,* (202)267-0950. (Note: no field offices for this program.)

20.006   STATE ACCESS TO THE OIL SPILL LIABILITY TRUST FUND

Assistance: project grants (100 percent).

Purposes: pursuant to the Oil Pollution Act of 1990, to reimburse states for costs incurred in responding to actual or threatened discharges of oil, relating to incidents after August 18, 1990. Eligible expenses include engaged state officials' salaries, personnel and materials transportation, equipment, and similar costs.

Eligible applicants/beneficiaries: states, territories and possessions.

Range: $250,000 maximum per incident.

Activity: N.A.

HQ: Director (cm), USCG National Pollution Funds Center, DOT, 4200 Wilson Blvd. - Ste.1000, Arlington, VA 22203-1804. Phone: (703)235-4756. (Note: no field offices for this program.)

20.007   BRIDGE ALTERATION
("Truman-Hobbs Act")

Assistance: direct payments/specified use (cost sharing).

Purposes: for the alteration of obstructive bridges to render navigation reasonably free, easy, and unobstructed. Project funds may not be used for activities that provide special benefits to bridge owners, nor solely to achieve savings in repair or maintenance costs or to increase carrying capacity.

Eligible applicants/beneficiaries: any state, county, municipality, or other political subdivision, or any corporation, association, partnership, or individual—owning or jointly owning a lawful bridge over U.S. navigable waters used and operated to carry railroad or highway traffic.

Range/Average: N.A.

Activity: FY 98, 1 project approved.

HQ: Commandant (G-OPT), USCG-DOT, 2100 Second St. SW, Washington, DC 20593-0001. Phone: (202)267-1977.

FEDERAL AVIATION ADMINISTRATION

20.100   AVIATION EDUCATION

Assistance: advisory services/counseling.

Purposes: for a broad range of public civil aviation education, career awareness, and related programs, from the elementary through college levels in all regions of the country. Also for: clearinghouse, data gathering and dissemination, communications, teacher training activities; conferences; and, publications on aviation including aviation mathematics, science, technology computer literacy; video services.

Eligible applicants/beneficiaries: state and local school administrators, college and university officials, officers of civil organizations; domestic and international governments; aviation industry, education organizations.

Activity: not quantified specifically.

HQ: Aviation Education Program (AHT-100), Civil Aviation Information Distribution Division, FAA-DOT, 400 7th St. SW (PL100), Washington, DC 20590. Phone: (no number provided).

20.106   AIRPORT IMPROVEMENT PROGRAM
("AIP")

Assistance: project grants (75-90 percent); advisory services/counseling.

Purposes: for planning, construction, or rehabilitation of public-use airports and related facilities and equipment. Eligible expenditures include land acquisition, airport master planning, site preparation, runway and related construction and improvement, noise reduction programs, weather reporting equipment, security and snow-removal equipment, firefighting and rescue equipment, lighting, and projects to comply with the ADA, Clean Air Act, and Federal Water Pollution Control. Ineligible uses of funds include hangar and automobile parking facilities, buildings unrelated to safety, landscaping or artwork, routine maintenance.

Eligible applicants/beneficiaries: development grants for airports listed in the National Plan of Integrated Airport Systems (NPIAS)—states, counties, municipalities, territories and possessions, and other public agencies including tribes or pueblos. Noise compatibility grants—certain local government units. Also: private owners of public-use reliever airports or airports enplaning over 2,500 passengers annually.

Range: $13,000 to $34,354,000. **Average:** $1,172,000.

Activity: FY 98 estimate, 950 grants.

HQ: Airports Financial Assistance Division (APP-500), Office of Airport Planning and Programming, FAA-DOT, 800 Independence Ave. SW, Washington, DC 20591. Phone: (202)267-3831.

20.107   AIRWAY SCIENCE
("AWS")

Assistance: project grants (65 percent); use of property, facilities, and equipment.

Purposes: to acquire or construct buildings, associated facilities, nonexpendable instructional materials, and equipment for use by airway science curriculum students. Examples include classrooms, laboratories, computers, aircraft simulators, electronic equipment. Funds may not be used for salaries, operating costs, aircraft, land acquisition, research and development.

Eligible applicants/beneficiaries: accredited U.S. IHEs with an FAA-recognized airway science curriculum.

Range: to $300,000. **Average:** $225,000.

Activity: not quantified specifically.

HQ: Aviation Education (AHR-15), FAA-DOT, 800 Independence Ave. SW - Rm.515, Washington, DC 20590. Phone: (202)267-3690. (Note: no field offices for this program.)

20.108   AVIATION RESEARCH GRANTS

Assistance: project grants (1 year minimum); use of property, facilities, and equipment.

Purposes: for advanced applied research and development projects in: Capacity and Air Traffic Management Technology; Communications, Navigation, and Surveillance; Aviation Weather; Airport Technology; Aircraft Safety Technology; System Security Technology; Human Factors and Aviation Medicine; Environment and Energy; Systems Science and Operations Research; Commercial Space Transportation.

Eligible applicants/beneficiaries: IHEs, nonprofit institutions. Profit organizations may apply in the area of Aviation Security.

Range: $25,000 to $5,000,000. **Average:** $50,000 to $150,000.

Activity: not quantified specifically.

HQ: Office of Research and Technology Applications (AAR-201), FAA-DOT, Hughes Technical Center, Atlantic City International Airport, NJ 08405. Phones: (609)485-5652; FAX (609)485-6509. (Note: no field offices for this program.)

20.109 AIR TRANSPORTATION CENTERS OF EXCELLENCE ("FAA Centers of Excellence")

Assistance: project grants (50 percent/to 10 years); use of property, facilities, and equipment; specialized services.

Purposes: for centers conducting long-term continuing research in such areas as catastrophic failure of aircraft, airspace and airport planning and design, airport capacity enhancement techniques, human performance, aviation safety and security, air transportation personnel training.

Eligible applicants/beneficiaries: IHEs, which may contract with nonprofit research organizations and others.

Range/Average: $500,000 per year per center.

Activity: not quantified specifically.

HQ: same address as **20.108**. Phones: (609)485-5043; FAX (609)485-6509. (Note: no field offices for this program.)

FEDERAL HIGHWAY ADMINISTRATION

20.205 HIGHWAY PLANNING AND CONSTRUCTION ("Federal-Aid Highway Program")

Assistance: formula grants; project grants (80-100 percent/to 3 years).

Purposes: for highway and related projects in the interstate and national highway systems, and for bridge and safety improvements on nonfederal-aid roads and within federal lands. Eligible fund uses include costs of planning, design, right-of-way acquisition, relocation assistance, construction, reconstruction, repair (but not maintenance), improvement of interstate and primary and secondary highways, bridge repairs, roads, and streets in urban systems, congestion mitigation and air quality improvement, and research. Related projects may involve railroad grade crossings, roadside beautification, bridges, bicycle paths, pedestrian walkways, carpool projects, fringe and corridor parking, wetland mitigation, forest highways, rest areas, scenic and historic highway improvements. In some cases, funds may be used for public mass transit improvements. Funding is derived from the Highway Trust Fund.

Eligible applicants/beneficiaries: state transportation agencies; territories, possessions. Projects related to Indian reservations, parkways and park roads, and public lands highways, certain projects in urban areas or off the state highway systems—tribal governments, counties, other political subdivisions or agencies and federal agencies applying through state agencies.

Range: $78,911,000 to $1,575,721,000. **Average:** $344,772,000.

Activity: FY 98 (representative), 43 disaster areas assisted; improvement of 2,800 deficient bridges.

HQ: Director, Office of Program Administration, FHWA-DOT, 400 Seventh St. SW, Washington, DC 20590-0001. Phones: (202)366-4853; *forest highways, Indian reservation roads, park roads and parkways,* Program Manager, Federal Lands Highways, (202)366-9494.

20.215   HIGHWAY TRAINING AND EDUCATION

Assistance: project grants (80 percent).

Purposes: for training, educational, and technical assistance programs related to federal-aid highway work—in new technological developments and in such subjects as value engineering, stream stability, and bridge inspection. Faculty, graduate, research, and minority fellowships may be awarded under the Eisenhower transportation fellowship program, for periods ranging from two to five years. States may allocate some matching funds from grants obtained under **20.205.**

Eligible applicants/beneficiaries: training—state and local transportation agencies; fellowships—U.S. citizens or citizenship applicants.

Range/Average: N.A.

Activity: FY 98, 125 fellowships; FY 99 estimate, 20,000 participants in 700 training presentations.

HQ: Director, National Highway Institute, FHWA-DOT, 4600 N. Fairfax Dr. - Ste.700, Arlington, VA 22203-1553. Phone: (202)235-0500.

20.217   MOTOR CARRIER SAFETY

Assistance: investigation of complaints; training.

Purposes: for training in and enforcement of motor carrier safety regulations, including those applying to the transport of hazardous materials and incident response.

Eligible applicants/beneficiaries: anyone may file a complaint. Safety and hazardous materials training—state and local police, rescue, and fire fighting units.

Activity: FY 98, 327 training sessions attended by 11,000 federal, state, and local personnel; 4,431 federal, 1,835 state compliance reviews.

HQ: Associate Administrator/Motor Carrier and Highway Safety, FHWA-DOT, 400 Seventh St. SW, Washington, DC 20590. Phone: (202)366-2519.

20.218   NATIONAL MOTOR CARRIER SAFETY ("MCSAP")

Assistance: formula grants (80 percent).

Purposes: for programs involving the development and enforcement of federal regulations and standards concerning commercial motor vehicle safety, including hazardous materials transport and drug interdiction.

Eligible applicants/beneficiaries: states, certain territories and possessions.

Range: implementation grants, $255,000 to $2,831,000.

Activity: FY 98, 9,200 state personnel supported.

HQ: Program Manager, same address/phone as **20.217**.

20.219   RECREATIONAL TRAILS PROGRAM

Assistance: formula grants; project grants (80-95 percent/to 3 years).

Purposes: to provide new and maintain existing recreational trails and related facilities for motorized and nonmotorized uses. Project funds may be used to: develop urban trail linkages near urbanized areas; groom and maintain trails across snow; develop trail-side and trail-head facilities; facilitate access by persons with disabilities; acquire easements identified in state trail plans; acquire fee simple title from willing sellers (but not through condemnation); pay limited administrative and public education costs. Funds may not be used to provide access by motorized users to trails used mainly by nonmotorized users.

Eligible applicants/beneficiaries: state agencies, which may accept applications from private organizations, or city, county, or other governmental organizations including federal agencies. States must have an advisory board representing both motorized and nonmotorized users.

Range: $483,000 to $3,500,000. **Average:** $966,000.

Activity: not quantified specifically.

HQ: Office of Environment and Planning, FHWA-DOT, 400 Seventh St. SW, Washington, DC 20590. Phones: (202)366-5013; FAX (202)366-7660; Web, www.fhwa.dot.gov

FEDERAL RAILROAD ADMINISTRATION

20.301   RAILROAD SAFETY

Assistance: investigation of complaints.

Purposes: to enforce federal railroad safety laws and regulations including those applying to track safety, safety appliance and freight car safety, hazardous materials transport, employee hours of work, and power brake rules.

Eligible applicants/beneficiaries: anyone may file a complaint.

Activity: 1999 estimate, 2,000 requests for investigations assigned.

HQ: Associate Administrator/Safety (MS 25), Federal Railroad Administration-DOT, 400 Seventh St. SW, Washington, DC 20590. Phone: (202)493-6304.

20.303 GRANTS-IN-AID FOR RAILROAD SAFETY—STATE PARTICIPATION
("State Participation in Railroad Safety")

Assistance: project grants (50-100 percent).

Purposes: to subsidize 50 percent of state costs of personnel, equipment, and activities related to enforcement of railroad safety standards, including the inspection of equipment, operating practices, signal and train control, and hazardous materials transport. Classroom training costs for state inspectors are reimbursed at 100 percent.

Eligible applicants/beneficiaries: states.

Range: $2,000 to $16,000 per inspector in FY 88 (no funds available since). **Average:** $9,000.

Activity: FY 98, 32 states participating.

HQ: same address as **20.301.** Phone: (202)493-6300.

20.308 LOCAL RAIL FREIGHT ASSISTANCE
("National Rail Service Continuation Grants")

Assistance: project grants (100 percent).

Purposes: to maintain efficient rail freight services through acquisition of railroad lines; for planning, construction, substitution, rehabilitation, and improvement of rail lines, properties, and services.

Eligible applicants/beneficiaries: state agencies.

Range $36,000 to $660,000. **Average:** $300,000.

Activity: FY 98, 1 planning, 1 project grant approved.

HQ: Office of Railroad Development (MS 20), Federal Railroad Administration-DOT, 400 Seventh St. SW, Washington, DC 20590. Phone: (202)632-3290. (Note: no field offices for this program.)

20.312 HIGH SPEED GROUND TRANSPORTATION—NEXT GENERATION HIGH SPEED RAIL PROGRAM
("HSGT")

Assistance: project grants.

Purposes: to implement high speed passenger rail systems. Projects must benefit research, development, design, or operation of incremental high speed passenger rail systems. Project examples: high speed, high acceleration fossil-fueled locomotives; highway-rail grade crossing sensor and warning systems.

Eligible applicants/beneficiaries: any U.S. private business, educational institution, state or local government or public authority, or federal agency.

Range: $100,000 to $6,000,000. **Average:** $250,000.

Activity: not quantified specifically.

HQ: Office of Railroad Development (RDV-13), Federal Railroad Administration-DOT, 400 Seventh St. SW, Washington, DC 20590. Phone: (no number provided). (Note: no field offices for this program.)

FEDERAL TRANSIT ADMINISTRATION

20.500 FEDERAL TRANSIT—CAPITAL INVESTMENT GRANTS

Assistance: formula grants; project grants (80-90 percent).

Purposes: for urban mass transportation project costs such as acquisition, construction, reconstruction, and improvement of facilities and equipment. Funds may be used to purchase land, buses or other rolling stock, new technological methods and techniques, fixed guideway systems, park-and-ride lots, and for projects to meet the needs of the elderly and the disabled.

Eligible applicants/beneficiaries: public agencies; states; municipalities and other state subdivisions; public agencies and instrumentalities of one or more states; public corporations, boards, and commissions established under state law. Private transportation companies may participate through contracts.

Range: $9,450 to $1,636,000,000. **Average:** $7,000,000.

Activity: not quantified specifically.

HQ: Office of Program Management, FTA-DOT, 400 Seventh St. SW, Washington, DC 20590. Phone: (202)366-1660.

20.502 FEDERAL TRANSIT GRANTS FOR UNIVERSITY RESEARCH AND TRAINING
("University Research and Training")

Assistance: project grants (90 percent).

Purposes: for research, research training, and career training in theoretical and practical problems of urban area transportation. Funding for this program is included in **20.514**.

Eligible applicants/beneficiaries: public and private nonprofit IHEs offering two-year or higher degrees. Participation by HBCUs is strongly encouraged.

Range/Average: to $80,000.

Activity: no funding since FY 93.

HQ: Office of Research, Demonstration and Innovation (TRI-30), FTA-DOT, 400 Seventh St. SW - Rm.4401, Washington, DC 20590. Phone: (202)366-0242. (Note: no field offices for this program.)

20.503 FEDERAL TRANSIT MANAGERIAL TRAINING GRANTS
("Managerial Training Program")

Assistance: project grants (50 percent/individuals, 2 years).

Purposes: for fellowships to train mass transportation managerial, technical, and professional personnel. Funding for this program is included in **20.514**.

Eligible applicants/beneficiaries: state and local public agencies; public transportation operators.

Range: $30,000 to $180,000 ($5,000 maximum for any one employee training activity with a two-year limit). **Average:** $88,000.

Activity: no funding since FY 93.

HQ: same address as **20.502**. Phone: (202)366-0234. (Note: no field offices for this program.)

20.505   FEDERAL TRANSIT—METROPOLITAN PLANNING GRANTS ("Metropolitan Planning")

Assistance: formula grants (80 percent/3 years).

Purposes: to plan, engineer, and design federal transit improvement projects, and for related technical studies. Emphasis is on multimodal transportation improvement programs, long-range plans for refinement of transit elements, and expansion of shortrange planning for improvements of existing systems.

Eligible applicants/beneficiaries: states—for distribution to metropolitan planning organizations.

Range: $20,000 to $5,000,000.

Activity: not quantified specifically.

HQ: Chief, Metropolitan Planning Division, Office of Planning (TPL-12), FTA-DOT, 400 Seventh St. SW, Washington, DC 20590. Phone: (202)366-1944.

20.507   FEDERAL TRANSIT—FORMULA GRANTS ("Urbanized Area Formula Program")

Assistance: formula grants (50-90 percent/3 years).

Purposes: to plan, acquire, lease, construct or reconstruct mass transportation facilities and equipment projects, and for relocation assistance—including projects that increase accessibility of public transportation to bicycles or bring equipment into ADA or Clean Air Act compliance; historic transportation facilities renovation and improvement may also be financed, with related private investment. Grants to subsidize operating costs may not exceed 50 percent.

Eligible applicants/beneficiaries: urbanized areas of 200,000 or

more population—public entities jointly designated by the governor, responsible local officials, and publicly-owned operators of mass transportation services. Urbanized areas of 50,000 to 200,000 population—the governor or his designee.

Range: N.A.

Activity: not quantified specifically.

HQ: Office of Program Management, FTA-DOT, 400 Seventh St. SW, Washington, DC 20590. Phones: (202)366-2053.

20.509   FORMULA GRANTS FOR OTHER THAN URBANIZED AREAS ("Nonurbanized Area Formula Program")

Assistance: formula grants (50-90 percent/2 years).

Purposes: for public transportation systems in nonurbanized areas, for uses similar to **20.507**. Funds may be used for capital and operating expenses, technical assistance, training, research, related support services for rural transportation, and user-side subsidies. Participation by private transit system operators is encouraged.

Eligible applicants/beneficiaries: state agencies; local public bodies and agencies, nonprofit organizations, tribes, and operators of public transportation services, including intercity bus service—in rural and small urban areas. Private operators may receive subcontracts.

Range: N.A.

Activity: annually, over 1,200 operators receive assistance.

HQ: same address/phone as **20.507.**

20.511 HUMAN RESOURCE PROGRAMS

Assistance: project grants (varying match); technical information.

Purposes: for a broad scope of projects involving disadvantaged business enterprises in public transportation, such as employment training, research on public transportation manpower and training needs, and outreach to increase female and minority employment. Funding for this program is included in **20.514.**

Eligible applicants/beneficiaries: state and local transit agencies, local governmental entities, IHEs, nonprofit institutions. Contracts may also be awarded to private profit businesses.

Range: N.A.

Activity: not quantified specifically.

HQ: Director, Office of Civil Rights, FTA-DOT, 400 Seventh St. SW - Rm. 9102, Washington, DC 20590. Phone: (202)366-4018.

20.512 FEDERAL TRANSIT TECHNICAL ASSISTANCE
("Research, Development and Demonstration Project")

Assistance: project grants (cost sharing); technical information; training.

Purposes: to develop, test, and demonstrate innovative technologies, service concepts, techniques, and analytical tools for planning, operating, and managing transit enterprises and improving mobility. Funding for this program is included in **20.514.**

Eligible applicants/beneficiaries: public bodies, nonprofit institutions, state and local agencies, universities, public agencies.

Range: N.A.

Activity: not quantified specifically.

HQ: Associate Administrator/Research, Demonstration and Innovation (TRI-1), FTA-DOT, 400 Seventh St. SW - Rm.9401, Washington, DC 20590. Phones: (202)366-4052, -0184. (Note: no field offices for this program.)

20.513 CAPITAL ASSISTANCE PROGRAM FOR ELDERLY PERSONS AND PERSONS WITH DISABILITIES

Assistance: formula grants (80-90 percent).

Purposes: to cover capital costs of providing specialized transportation services for elderly and handicapped persons. Specially designed vehicles may be purchased with grant funds. Awards favor projects involving private profit operators.

Eligible applicants/beneficiaries: private nonprofit organizations or public bodies.

Range/Average: N.A.

Activity: cumulatively since 1975 program inception, funds to 1,000 organizations to purchase some 2,300 vehicles.

HQ: Office of Program Management, Office of Resource Management and State Programs, FTA-DOT, 400 Seventh St. SW, Washington, DC 20590. Phones: (202)366-2053, 366-1630.

20.514 TRANSIT PLANNING AND RESEARCH
("National Planning and Research Program")

Assistance: project grants; technical information; training.

Purposes: for projects that develop, test, and demonstrate innovative service concepts, techniques, and analytical tools for operating and managing transit enterprises and improve mobility. Funding for this program includes **20.502, 20.503, 20.511,** and **20.512.**

Eligible applicants/beneficiaries: public agencies, state and local agencies, nonprofit institutions, universities, and operators of public transportation services.

Range: N.A.

Activity: not quantified specifically.

HQ: same address)/phones as **20.512.** (Note: no field offices for this program.)

20.515 STATE PLANNING AND RESEARCH

Assistance: formula grants (80-100 percent).

Purposes: to develop cost-effective multimodal transportation improvement programs, including the planning, engineering, and design of federal transit projects and other technical studies and training, within a unified or officially coordinated statewide transportation system. States may authorize use of funds to supplement metropolitan planning funds. This program operates as a block grant program, for projects identified by states to accomplish planning and research objectives.

Eligible applicants/beneficiaries: states.

Range: $45,000 to $1,000,000.

Activity: not quantified specifically.

HQ: Chief, Intermodal/Statewide Planning, Office of Planning (TPL-11), FTA-DOT. 400 Seventh St. SW, Washington, DC 20590. Phones: (202)366-1626.

NATIONAL HIGHWAY TRAFFIC SAFETY ADMINISTRATION

20.600 STATE AND COMMUNITY HIGHWAY SAFETY

Assistance: formula grants (80 percent).

Purposes: for highway traffic safety enforcement program costs, such as police equipment purchases, training, and overtime pay; emergency medical services training and equipment purchases; public education projects. Program priority areas include Alcohol and Other Drug Countermeasures, Police Traffic Services, Occupant Protection, Traffic Records, Emergency Medical Services, Motorcycle Safety, Pedestrian/Bicycle Safety, Speed Control, and Roadway Safety.

Eligible applicants/beneficiaries: states, federally-recognized tribes, territories, possessions.

Range: $340,000 to $13,000,000. **Average:** $2,200,000.

Activity: not quantified specifically.

HQ: Associate Administrator/State and Community Services, National Highway Traffic Safety Administration-DOT, Washington, DC 20590. Phone: (202)366-2121. *Or:* Transportation Specialist, Safety Technology Division, Office of Highway Safety, FHWA-DOT, Washington, DC 20590. Phone: (202)366-6902.

20.601   ALCOHOL TRAFFIC SAFETY AND DRUNK DRIVING PREVENTION INCENTIVE GRANTS

Assistance: project grants (formula based/to 5 years).

Purposes: for state programs to reduce crashes resulting from persons driving under the influence of alcohol and other controlled substances. Grant amounts are based on apportionments by states. Funds may be used: to purchase breath testing devices; to train law enforcement personnel; for public education; to pay for overtime by police personnel.

Eligible applicants/beneficiaries: states, territories, possessions.

Range/Average: $262,000 to $4,500,000.

Activity: not quantified specifically.

HQ: Associate Administrator/State and Community Services, National Highway Traffic Safety Administration-DOT, Washington, DC 20590. Phone: (202)366-2121.

RESEARCH AND SPECIAL PROGRAMS ADMINISTRATION

20.700   PIPELINE SAFETY

Assistance: formula grants (50 percent).

Purposes: to pay personnel, inspection, equipment, training, and research costs related to natural gas and hazardous liquids pipeline safety.

Eligible applicants/beneficiaries: state agencies.

Range: $4,522 to $1,123,000.

Activity: FY 98, 48 grants.

HQ: Research and Special Programs Administration-DOT, 400 Seventh St. SW, Washington, DC 20590. Phone: (202)366-4564.

20.701 UNIVERSITY TRANSPORTATION CENTERS PROGRAM

Assistance: project grants (50 percent/4-6 years).

Purposes: to establish and operate transportation centers to conduct research, education, and technology transfer programs addressing regional and national problems and issues. Undergraduate and graduate level study may be supported.

Eligible applicants/beneficiaries: public and private nonprofit IHEs, with established transportation research programs.

Range/Average: $300,000 to $2,000,000 per center per year.

Activity: not quantified specifically.

HQ: Office of University Research and Education (DRA-2), Research and Special Programs Administration-DOT, 400 Seventh St. SW - Rm.8417, Washington, DC 20590. Phones: (202)366-4434; Web, http://utc.dot.gov (Note: no field offices for this program.)

20.703 INTERAGENCY HAZARDOUS MATERIALS PUBLIC SECTOR TRAINING AND PLANNING GRANTS
("Hazardous Materials Emergency Preparedness Training and Planning Grants" - "HMEP")

Assistance: project grants (80 percent/to 6 years).

Purposes: pursuant to the Federal Hazardous Materials Transportation Law, for the development, improvement, and implementation of emergency response plans to handle hazardous materials accidents and incidents; to enhance implementation of the Emergency Planning and Community Right-to-Know Act of 1986; for related training of public sector employees.

Eligible applicants/beneficiaries: states, tribes, territories.

Range: $2,444 to $443,000. **Average:** $86,000.

Activity: all states, territories, and 32 tribes funded since program inception.

HQ: HMEP Grants Manager (DHM-64), Research and Special Programs Administration-DOT, 400 Seventh St. SW, Washington, DC 20590. Phone: (202)366-0001. (Note: no field offices for this program.)

MARITIME ADMINISTRATION

20.801 DEVELOPMENT AND PROMOTION OF PORTS AND INTERMODAL TRANSPORTATION
("Ports and Domestic Shipping and Intermodal Development")

Assistance: advisory services/counseling; technical information.

Purposes: pursuant to the Merchant Marine Acts and amendments, to promote and plan domestic waterways, ports, port facilities, and intermodal transportation—by conducting studies in cooperation with port authorities and others with related interests. Technical assistance and information may also be provided. No grants are awarded under this program.

Eligible applicants/beneficiaries: state and local government agencies, metropolitan planning organizations, regional development organizations, public port and intermodal authorities, trade associations, private terminal operators.

Activity: not quantified specifically.

HQ: Director, Office of Port and Domestic Shipping, Maritime Administration-DOT, Washington, DC 20590. Phones: (202)366-4357, FAX (202)366-6988; Director, Office of Intermodal Development, (202)366-8888, FAX (202)366-6988.

20.802 FEDERAL SHIP FINANCING GUARANTEES
("Title XI")

Assistance: guaranteed/insured loans (87.5 percent/to 25 years).

Purposes: pursuant to the Merchant Marine Act of 1936 as amended, for: construction, reconstruction, reconditioning, or refinancing of ships built in U.S. shipyards, used in foreign or domestic commerce, in research, or as an ocean thermal energy conversion facility—in coast-wide or intercoastal trade, on the Great Lakes or on bays, sounds, rivers, harbors, inland lakes, or as floating dry-docks; for advanced shipbuilding technology of general shipyard facilities. Vessels must be larger than five net tons—other than towboats, barges, scows, lighters, car floats, canal boats, or tank vessels of less than 25 gross tons.

Eligible applicants/beneficiaries: qualified individuals, U.S. shipyards, U.S. and foreign ship owners.

Range: from less than $1 million to several hundred million.

Activity: FY 98, 12 approvals; 20 applications pending.

HQ: Associate Administrator/Ship Financial Assistance and Cargo Preference, Office of Ship Financing, Maritime AdministrationDOT, Washington, DC 20590. Phone: (202)366-0364.

20.803 MARITIME WAR RISK INSURANCE
("Title XII, MMA, 1936")

Assistance: insurance.

Purposes: pursuant to the Merchant Marine Act of 1936 as amended, to provide war risk insurance binders or policies on vessels in operation or under construction. Insurance is available at nominal cost in peacetime.

Eligible applicants/beneficiaries: owners of U.S. flag vessels and certain foreign flag vessels.

Range: N.A.

Activity: as of FY 99, 270 vessels covered.

HQ: Director, Office of Subsidy and Insurance, Maritime Administration-DOT, 400 Seventh St. SW, Washington, DC 20590. Phone: (202)366-2400.

20.804 OPERATING-DIFFERENTIAL SUBSIDIES
("ODS")

Assistance: direct payments/specified use (to 20 years).

Purposes: pursuant to the Merchant Marine Act of 1936 as amended, to subsidize the development and maintenance of vessels used in U.S. foreign commerce, to equalize the cost of operating a competitive foreign flagship. Note: the Maritime Security Act, enacted in 1996, provides for the wind-up of the program; no new contracts will be issued; previously active contracts will remain in effect (see **20.813**, new program in FY 97).

Eligible applicants/beneficiaries: qualified U.S. citizens.

Range: $5,000 to $10,000 per day subsidy per ship.

Activity: as of 1 January 1999, 7 vessels receiving subsidies.

HQ: same address/phone as **20.803**.

20.805 SHIP SALES

Assistance: sale, exchange, or donation of property and goods.

Purposes: pursuant to the Merchant Marine Act of 1936 and amendments, for sales by competitive bid of surplus merchant ships for dismantling, but not for transporting cargo or passengers. Also, ships may be donated for such purposes as sinking for artificial fish reefs.

Eligible applicants/beneficiaries: sales—those with a need for ships for dismantling purposes. Artificial reefs—states.

Activity: FY 99 estimate, 17 ships sold for scrapping, 1 donation for sinking as artificial fish reef.

HQ: Chief, Division of Vessel Transfer and Disposal, Maritime Administration-DOT, Washington, DC 20590. Phone: (202)366-5821.

20.806 STATE MARINE SCHOOLS

Assistance: direct payments/specified use (50 percent); use of property, facilities, and equipment.

Purposes: for the operation and maintenance of state marine schools; for loans to the schools of training vessels by the federal government, as well as their maintenance and repair; for incentive payments to selected cadets. States must admit out-ofstate students.

Eligible applicants/beneficiaries: states (limited to one academy per state).

Range: states, $200,000 annually; student stipends, $3,000 per academic year for up to four years.

Activity: FY 97, 447 officers graduated.

HQ: Director, Office of Maritime Labor, Training, and Safety, Maritime Administration-DOT, Washington, DC 20590. Phone: (202)366-5755.

20.807 U.S. MERCHANT MARINE ACADEMY
("Kings Point")

Assistance: training.

Purposes: for the operation and maintenance of the maritime academy, including subsistence payments to students training to become merchant marine officers—as well as their quarters, medical care, program travel, and other expenses.

Eligible applicants/beneficiaries: U.S. citizens that are high school graduates; international students.

Range: allowance prescribed for all personnel for uniforms and textbooks.

(During the sea year a midshipman will earn $600 monthly from his/her steamship company employer.)

Activity: 1999 estimate, 182 graduates.

HQ: same address and phone number as **20.806**.

20.808 CAPITAL CONSTRUCTION FUND ("CCF")

Assistance: direct payments/specified use.

Purposes: pursuant to the Merchant Marine Act of 1936 as amended, to provide tax deferment incentives to shipbuilders to acquire, construct, or reconstruct vessels built in the U.S. for use in the U.S. foreign, Great Lakes, or noncontiguous domestic trades, and in the fisheries.

Eligible applicants/beneficiaries: U.S. citizens that own or lease one or more eligible vessels.

Range: N.A.

Activity: as of FY 99, 142 agreements in effect; cumulatively since program inception, over $6.5 billion in tax deferments.

HQ: same address/phone as **20.802**.

20.810 SUPPLEMENTARY TRAINING

Assistance: training.

Purposes: pursuant to the Merchant Marine Act of 1936 as amended, to train seafarers in shipboard firefighting, intermodal freight transportation, maritime defense, and safety-related subjects. Training is provided on a fee-paid basis.

Eligible applicants/beneficiaries: qualified U.S. merchant seafarers; operators of inland waterway, offshore drilling, and mining vessels; maritime academy students; personnel of the NOAA, U.S. Coast Guard, U.S. Army Corps of Engineers and Naval Reserve; qualified representatives of marine industry; state and local governments.

Activity: FY 98, 2,020 participants.

HQ: same address/phone as **20.806**.

20.812 CONSTRUCTION RESERVE FUND ("CRF")

Assistance: direct payments/specified use.

Purposes: pursuant to the Merchant Marine Act of 1936 as amended, to provide tax deferment incentives to shipbuilders to construct, reconstruct, recondition, or acquire vessels necessary for national defense or U.S. commerce.

Eligible applicants/beneficiaries: U.S. citizens that own in whole or in part one or more vessels operating in the foreign or domestic commerce of the U.S. or in the fisheries; any citizen operating such vessel or vessels owned by another individual.

Range: N.A.

Activity: as of FY 99, 11-15 active contracts with deposits totaling $70,900,000.

HQ: Associate Administrator/Maritime Aids, Maritime Administration-DOT, Washington, DC 20590. Phone: (202)366-0364.

20.813 MARITIME SECURITY FLEET PROGRAM

Assistance: direct payments/specified use.

Purposes: pursuant to the Merchant Marine Act of 1936 as amended, to maintain a U.S. flag merchant fleet crewed by U.S. citizens to serve both commercial and national security needs, including container ships, lighter-aboard ships, and roll-on/roll-off vessels.

Eligible applicants/beneficiaries: U.S. citizens and certain specified foreign corporations.

Range/Average: to $2,100,000 per vessel per year.

Activity: new program in FY 97; as of 1998, 47 vessels enrolled.

HQ: Director, Office of Sealift Support, Maritime AdministrationDOT, 400 Seventh St. SW, Washington, DC 20590. Phones: (202)366-2323; FAX (202)493-2180. (Note: no field offices for this program.)

OFFICE OF THE SECRETARY

20.900 TRANSPORTATION—CONSUMER AFFAIRS

Assistance: investigation of complaints.

Purposes: to provide assistance and information to consumers with complaints of all types against airlines, travel agents, tour operators, and freight forwarders.

Eligible applicants/beneficiaries: all users of air transportation.

Activity: 1998, 10,000 complaints and information requests received.

HQ: Aviation Consumer Protection Division (C-75), DOT, 400 Seventh St. SW - Rm.4107, Washington, DC 20590. Phone: (202)366-5957.

20.901 PAYMENTS FOR ESSENTIAL AIR SERVICES

Assistance: direct payments/specified use.

Purposes: to provide air commuter services to communities that would be unserved without subsidies to airlines.

Eligible applicants/beneficiaries: carriers selected by DOT.

Range: for continental U.S., $158,000 to $1,308,000. **Average:** $599,000 annually per point.

Activity: currently, some 100 communities retaining service.

HQ: Director, Office of Aviation Analysis (X-50), DOT, 400 Seventh St. SW, Washington, DC 20590. Phone: (202)366-1030. (Note: no field offices for this program.)

20.903 SUPPORT MECHANISMS FOR DISADVANTAGED BUSINESSES ("Liaison and Outreach Services Program" - "LOSP")

Assistance: project grants (100 percent/6-12 months).

Purposes: for liaison, management, technical assistance, and referral services supporting participation by disadvantaged business enterprises in transportation-related contract opportunities. Lending and bonding assistance may be provided to minority- and women-owned businesses.

Eligible applicants/beneficiaries: minority chambers of commerce, minority trade associations; socially and economically disadvantaged persons and businesses.

Range/Average: $100,000.

Activity: FY 98, 11 new cooperative agreements in effect.

HQ: Office of Small and Disadvantaged Business Utilization (S40), Office of the Secretary-DOT, 400 Seventh St. SW, Washington, DC 20590. Phones: (202)366-1930; (800)532-1169. (Note: no field offices for this program.)

20.904   BONDING ASSISTANCE PROGRAM

Assistance: insurance.

Purposes: to enable disadvantaged business enterprises to obtain bid, performance, and payment bonds for contracts emanating from DOT, its grantees, and recipients, and their contractors and subcontractors—including contracts for maintenance, rehabilitation, restructuring, improvement, or revitalization of any mode of transportation with any public or commercial provider or any federal, state, or local transportation agency.

Eligible applicants/beneficiaries: certified disadvantaged business enterprises, minority- and women-owned enterprises; all SBA "Section 8(a)" firms.

Range/Average: $330,000.

Activity: FY 98, 73 bid and performance bond applications issued.

HQ: same address as **20.903**. Phone: (800)532-1169. (Note: no field offices for this program.)

20.905   DISADVANTAGED BUSINESS ENTERPRISES—SHORT TERM LENDING PROGRAM

Assistance: direct loans.

Purposes: to provide lines of credit to disadvantaged business enterprises to obtain accounts receivable financing for the performance of transportation-related contracts from DOT, its grantees, and recipients, and their contractors and subcontractors—including for maintenance, rehabilitation, restructuring, improvement, or revitalization of any mode of transportation with any public or commercial provider of transportation or any federal, state, or local transportation agency.

Eligible applicants/beneficiaries: same as for **20.904**.

Range: to $500,000.

Activity: FY 98, 33 approvals.

HQ: same address as **20.903**. Phones: (202)366-2852, (800)532-1169. (Note: no field offices for this program.)

20.906   HISPANIC SERVING INSTITUTIONS—ENTREPRENEURIAL TRAINING AND TECHNICAL ASSISTANCE

Assistance: project grants (100 percent).

Purposes: for Hispanic Serving Institutions to design and operate programs to encourage, promote, and assist minority and disadvantaged entrepreneurs and businesses, including women-owned businesses, in obtaining transportation-related contracts, subcontracts, and projects. Funds may also support internships, curriculum development, and faculty fellowships.

Eligible applicants/beneficiaries: public and private nonprofit IHEs with at least a 25 percent enrollment of full-time undergraduate Hispanic students.

Range/Average: $30,000 to $60,000.

Activity: FY 98, 5 cooperative agreement awards.

HQ: Minority Institutions Representative, same address as **20.903**. Phones: (202)366-2852, (800)532-1169. (Note: no field offices for this program.)

20.907 HISTORICALLY BLACK COLLEGES AND UNIVERSITIES—ENTREPRENEURIAL TRAINING AND TECHNICAL ASSISTANCE ("ETTAP")

Assistance: project grants (100 percent).

Purposes: for HBCUs to design and operate programs to encourage, promote, and assist minority and disadvantaged entrepreneurs and businesses, including women-owned businesses, in obtaining transportation-related contracts, subcontracts, and projects. Funds may also support student internships and curriculum development.

Eligible applicants/beneficiaries: HBCUs.

Range/Average: $30,000 to $60,000.

Activity: FY 99, 8 awards.

HQ: same address as **20.903**. Phones: (202)366-2852, (800)532-1169. (Note: no field offices for this program.)

DEPARTMENT OF THE TREASURY

INTERNAL REVENUE SERVICE

21.003 TAXPAYER SERVICE

Assistance: advisory services/counseling; training.

Purposes: to provide information and guidance on income tax matters, including taxpayer obligations and rights. Apart from "800" number services and information offices, IRS offers training for volunteer programs, films, seminars, and other services. Special educational programs are available to assist small businesses, secondary school teachers, adult education classes, and colleges. Special procedures become effective for victims of natural disasters.

Eligible applicants/beneficiaries: individuals, groups.

Activity: annually, 12,000,000 taxpayer contacts.

HQ: Executive Officer/Customer Service, IRS, 1111 Constitution Ave. NW - Rm.2116, Washington, DC 20224. Phones: (202)622-5044; Web, www.irs. ustreas.gov

21.004   EXCHANGE OF FEDERAL TAX INFORMATION WITH STATE TAX AGENCIES
("Agreement on Coordination of Tax Administration")

Assistance: specialized services.

Purposes: to increase taxpayer compliance and to reduce duplication of resources—through the exchange of tax data, models, and extracts with states and municipalities for tax administration purposes.

Eligible applicants/beneficiaries: states, territories, and municipalities with over 250,000 population that impose taxes on income or wages.

Activity: annually, 126 state and municipal agencies participate.

HQ: Director, Governmental Liaison and Disclosure, IRS, 1111

Constitution Ave. NW - Rm.7331, Washington, DC 20224. Phone: (202)622-6200.

21.006   TAX COUNSELING FOR THE ELDERLY

Assistance: direct payments/specified use.

Purposes: to reimburse volunteers for their out-of-pocket expenses in receiving training and in providing tax counseling to elderly taxpayers.

Eligible applicants/beneficiaries: private or public nonprofit organizations. Governmental agencies are ineligible.

Range: N.A.

Activity: annually, 50 sponsors funded; 1,600,000 taxpayers assisted.

HQ: Program Manager, Tax Counseling for the Elderly, IRS, 5000 Ellin Rd., Lanham, MD 20706. Phone: (202)283-0188. (Note: no field offices for this program.)

21.008   LOW-INCOME TAXPAYER CLINICS

Assistance: project grants (50 percent/to 3 years).

Purposes: to enable organizations to represent low-income taxpayers in controversies with the IRS, or to inform individuals with limited English language abilities of their tax rights and responsibilities.

Eligible applicants/beneficiaries: private nonprofit organizations; educational institutions with accredited law, business, or accounting schools.

Range/Average: N.A.

Activity: new program in FY 99.

HQ: Program Manager, Low-Income Taxpayer Clinics, same address as **20.006**. Phone: (202)283-0197. (Note: no field offices for this program.)

COMMUNITY DEVELOPMENT
FINANCIAL INSTITUTIONS FUND

21.020 COMMUNITY DEVELOPMENT FINANCIAL INSTITUTIONS PROGRAM ("CDFI")

Assistance: project grants (50 percent/to 5 years).

Purposes: to provide financial and technical assistance through CDFIs, promoting economic revitalization and community development. Project examples include investments in activities designed to result in: retention and expansion of manufacturing companies and other businesses employing low-income residents of a city empowerment zone; affordable housing development in targeted population areas.

Eligible applicants/beneficiaries: private nonprofit institutions and organizations, profit organizations. Governmental entities are ineligible.

Range: $79,000 to $3,200,000. **Average:** $798,000.

Activity: new program listing in 1998. FY 98, 112 awards.

HQ: Awards Manager, CDFI Fund, Department of the Treasury, 601 13th St. NW - Ste.200 South, Washington, DC 20005. Phones: (202)622-8662; FAX (202)622-7754. (Note: no field offices for this program.)

21.021 BANK ENTERPRISE AWARD PROGRAM ("BEA")

Assistance: project grants (100 percent).

Purposes: to encourage insured depository institutions to increase their level of community development activities in the form of loans, investments, services, and technical assistance within distressed communities; to provide assistance to community development financial institutions through grants, stock purchases, loans, deposits, and other forms of financial and technical assistance. Project example: multifamily housing financing.

Eligible applicants/beneficiaries: Federal Deposit Insurance Corporation-insured depository institutions not currently participating in **21.020**.

Range: $1,100 to $2,500,000. **Average:** $73,000.

Activity: new program listing in 1998. FY 98, 79 awards.

HQ: same address/phones as **20.020**. (Note: no field offices for this program.)

BUREAU OF ALCOHOL, TOBACCO AND FIREARMS

21.052 ALCOHOL, TOBACCO, AND FIREARMS—TRAINING ASSISTANCE

Assistance: training.

Purposes: pursuant to OCCSSA as amended and other acts, to provide training in the enforcement of laws relating to alcohol, tobacco, firearms, arson, explosives, and organized crime. Programs include identification of firearms problems, laboratory capability, interviewing, investigation techniques, case management.

Eligible applicants/beneficiaries: state, county, and local law enforcement agencies. Participation is limited to nonuniformed police personnel.

Activity: annually, 600 officers participate.

HQ: Chief, ATF National Academy, Bureau of Alcohol, Tobacco and Firearms, Department of the Treasury, Bldg. 67 FLETC, Glynco, GA 31524. Phone: (912)267-2251. (Note: no field offices for this program.)

UNITED STATES SECRET SERVICE

21.100   SECRET SERVICE—TRAINING ACTIVITIES

Assistance: training.

Purposes: to provide training in techniques used to detect counterfeit money and documents, and to protect dignitaries. Bank tellers, cashiers, and other money handlers may be briefed in the detection of counterfeit currency, by Secret Service regional offices.

Eligible applicants/beneficiaries: sworn members of police agencies.

Activity: annually, 3,200 participants.

HQ: Office of Training, U.S. Secret Service, 1800 G St. NW, Washington, DC 20223. Phone: (202)435-7100.

APPALACHIAN REGIONAL COMMISSION

23.001   APPALACHIAN REGIONAL DEVELOPMENT (SEE INDIVIDUAL APPALACHIAN PROGRAMS) ("Appalachian Program")

Assistance: project grants.

Purposes: pursuant to the Appalachian Regional Development Act of 1965 as amended, for programs and projects that stimulate public investments in public services, facilities, and institutions in the Appalachian region— through federal-state-local efforts. Priorities are established by the Appalachian Regional Commission, composed of the 13 state governors within the region, or their alternates. All proposed projects must meet the requirements of the state Appalachian plan and the annual state investment program, both of which must be approved annually by the commission. (See individual Appalachian program descriptions). Funding is through the commission's various programs (**23.002 - 23.011**).

Eligible applicants/beneficiaries: only in the Appalachian region—states and, through the states, public bodies and private nonprofit organizations.

Range/Average: see individual programs.

Activity: see individual programs.

HQ: Executive Director, Appalachian Regional Commission, 1666 Connecticut Ave. NW, Washington, DC 20235. Phone: (202)884-7700.

23.002 APPALACHIAN AREA DEVELOPMENT ("Supplemental and Direct Grants")

Assistance: project grants (50-100 percent).

Purposes: to supplement other federal area development project funding or, if other funds are unavailable, to fund projects entirely—in support of physical, human, or business development in the region's most distressed and underdeveloped counties. Project examples include water and sewer systems, industrial parks, entrepreneurship, export promotion, training, vocational education, health care, child development, revolving loan funds, and business incubator projects, in conjunction with private sector commitments.

Eligible applicants/beneficiaries: (Appalachia only) states, state subdivisions and instrumentalities, private nonprofit agencies.

Range: $2,000 to $1,000,000. **Average:** $136,000.

Activity: FY 98, 479 projects funded.

HQ: same address/phone as **23.001.**

23.003 APPALACHIAN DEVELOPMENT HIGHWAY SYSTEM ("Appalachian Corridors")

Assistance: project grants (80 percent).

Purposes: to develop a highway system within the Appalachian region where commerce and communication have been inhibited by inadequate access. Grants may cover preliminary engineering, right-of-way acquisition, and construction costs. In FY 99, additional funding was provided to DOT from the Highway Trust Fund for Appalachian highways.

Eligible applicants/beneficiaries: (Appalachia only) state governments.

Range: N.A.

Activity: FY 98 estimate, 40 miles of construction completed.

HQ: same address/phone as **23.001.**

23.008 APPALACHIAN LOCAL ACCESS ROADS

Assistance: project grants (80 percent).

Purposes: to develop road access to industrial, commercial, educational, recreational, residential, and related facilities with significant development potential. Grants may cover engineering, right-of-way acquisition, relocation, and construction costs.

Eligible applicants/beneficiaries: (Appalachia only) states, public bodies, and private groups.

Range: $19,000 to $218,000. **Average:** $157,000.

Activity: FY 98, 8 new projects approved.

HQ: same address/phone as **23.001.**

23.009   APPALACHIAN LOCAL DEVELOPMENT DISTRICT ASSISTANCE ("LDD")

Assistance: project grants (50 percent).

Purposes: for development planning and activities relating to local economic development. Funds may be used for: administrative expenses including technical services of local development districts; with ARC approval, real estate and vehicle purchases, construction and space improvement.

Eligible applicants/beneficiaries: (Appalachia only) multicounty organizations.

Range: $9,120 to $158,000. **Average:** $64,000.

Activity: FY 99, 71 planning districts assisted.

HQ: same address/phone as **23.001.**

23.011   APPALACHIAN STATE RESEARCH, TECHNICAL ASSISTANCE, AND DEMONSTRATION PROJECTS

Assistance: project grants (50-80 percent).

Purposes: for research and planning projects (50 percent funding), and demonstration and technical assistance projects (100 percent funding)—relating to economic and social development. Priority is on technical assistance projects leading to job creation. Project examples: Appalachian scholar program; study of capital and credit needs; evaluation of the effect of industrial clusters on exports.

Eligible applicants/beneficiaries: Appalachian states, state consortia; local public bodies; state instrumentalities.

Range: $10,000 to $200,000. **Average:** $113,000.

Activity: not quantified specifically.

HQ: same address/phone as **23.001.**

OFFICE OF PERSONNEL MANAGEMENT

27.001   FEDERAL CIVIL SERVICE EMPLOYMENT

Assistance: federal employment.

Purposes: to fill federal job vacancies, usually through competitive exams and without discrimination on any basis. Veterans receive preference. Special programs help place the physically handicapped, the mentally retarded or mentally restored, and the disadvantaged.

Eligible applicants/beneficiaries: U.S. citizens age 18 or older (age 16 in certain cases).

Activity: FY 98, 10,212,000 inquiries received and answered.

HQ: (no address provided). Phones: (202)606-2700; *nation-wide,* TTD (912)

744-2299, USA JOBS Telephone Listing System, (912)757-3000, Federal Job Opportunities Bulletin Board (FJOB), (912)757-3100; Web, www.usa-jobs.opm.gov

27.002   FEDERAL EMPLOYMENT ASSISTANCE FOR VETERANS

Assistance: federal employment.

Purposes: to assist veterans in obtaining federal employment, with preferences according to their discharge status.

Eligible applicants/beneficiaries: nondisabled and disabled veterans, and certain spouses, widows, widowers, and mothers of veterans.

Activity: as of FY 99, 480,000 veterans constituted 26.9 percent of non-postal federal workers.

HQ: *Disabled Veterans Affirmative Action Programs,* Office of Diversity, Employment Service, OPM, 1900 E St. NW -Rm.2445, Washington, DC 20415. Phones: (202)606-1059; *veterans preference and special hiring programs,* Office of Staffing Reinvention, same address (except Rm.6500). Phone: (202)606-0830. (Note: no field offices for this program.)

27.003   FEDERAL STUDENT TEMPORARY EMPLOYMENT PROGRAM

Assistance: federal employment.

Purposes: to provide part-time temporary federal employment for youth during school terms (full-time during extended vacation periods). OPM coordinates this program, but it is effected and funded by other participating federal agencies.

Eligible applicants/beneficiaries: students accepted for or enrolled at least half-time in a secondary school or IHE through the graduate level.

Activity: FY 98, 32,000 participants.

HQ: *information available from personnel offices of the agencies of interest. For inquiries on policy issues,* Staffing Reinvention Office, Employment Service, OPM, 1900 E St. NW, Washington, DC 20415. Phone: (202)606-0830. (Note: no field offices for this program.)

27.005   FEDERAL EMPLOYMENT FOR INDIVIDUALS WITH DISABILITIES ("Selective Placement Program")

Assistance: federal employment.

Purposes: to provide special OPM assistance to federal agencies to assist persons with disabilities in obtaining or retaining federal employment. Federal agencies have coordinators responsible for expanding employment opportunities under this program, to coordinate activities with state vocational rehabilitation agencies, DVA, and other public and private agencies. Funding is by the accounts of individual agencies.

Eligible applicants/beneficiaries: persons with physical, cognitive, or mental disabilities.

Activity: as of FY 98, 127,000 federal employees with targeted and nontargeted disabilities; FY 99, 12,000 full-time position hires.

HQ: *information available from personnel offices of the agencies of interest.*

For inquiries on policy issues, same address/phone as **27.002.** (Note: no field offices for this program.)

27.006   FEDERAL SUMMER EMPLOYMENT ("Summer Jobs in Federal Agencies")

Assistance: federal employment.

Purposes: to provide summer employment primarily for college and high school students, in clerical, craft or trade, administrative, and subprofessional jobs. Summer jobs are filled through agency staffing plans, with funding by the participating agencies.

Eligible applicants/beneficiaries: any U.S. citizen at least age 16 at time of appointment.

Activity: N.A.

HQ: same as **27.001.**

27.011   INTERGOVERNMENTAL PERSONNEL ACT (IPA) MOBILITY PROGRAM

Assistance: specialized services; advisory services/counseling.

Purposes: to permit temporary assignments of professional, administrative, or technical personnel back and forth between federal, state, local, and tribal governments, IHEs, and other organizations. Assignments may be for up to two years, with one two-year extension. Upon completion of assignments, assigned federal employees must serve in the Civil Service for a period equal to that of the assignment. Cost sharing is negotiable.

Eligible applicants/beneficiaries: federal agencies; state, local, and tribal governments; IHEs. Other organizations include: national, regional, state-wide, areawide, or metropolitan organizations of state or local governments; associations of state or local public officials; nonprofit organizations offering professional advisory, research, educational, or development services, or related services to governments or universities concerned with public management.

Activity: annually, 1,400 mobility assignments with participation by all states, PR, VI, Samoa, Guam, Northern Marianas, DC, 519 local governments, 512 universities, 106 tribal governments, and 161 other organizations.

HQ: Office of Merit Systems and Oversight, OPM, 1900 E St. NW -Rm.7463, Washington, DC 20415-0001. Phone: (202)606-1181.

27.013   PRESIDENTIAL MANAGEMENT INTERN PROGRAM

Assistance: federal employment; training; specialized services.

Purposes: to attract graduate students of exceptional potential to the federal service. Two-year internships may be awarded for work in federal agencies (exceptionally, for three years). Awardees may be assigned to work temporarily for state or local governments. Nominations for awards are submitted by deans of graduate level programs.

Eligible applicants/beneficiaries: organizations eligible for **27.011**—for rotational assignments.

Activity: annually, up to 400 interns selected.

HQ: Presidential Management Intern Program, OPM, 600 Arch St., Philadelphia, PA 19106. Phones: (215)597-7136, 597-1920.

COMMISSION ON CIVIL RIGHTS

29.001   CLEARINGHOUSE SERVICES, CIVIL RIGHTS DISCRIMINATION COMPLAINTS

Assistance: technical information.

Purposes: to serve as a national clearinghouse; to provide research, liaison, publications, and public information services to private and public groups and the media; and to process complaints—concerning violations of the civil rights of individuals, entitling them to equal protection of the laws regardless of their race, color, religion, sex, age, handicap, or national origin. Complaints are referred to appropriate federal agencies.

Eligible applicants/beneficiaries: anyone may seek information.

Activity: FY 98, 6,000 complaints processed, 8 publications completed.

HQ: Commission on Civil Rights, 624 Ninth St. NW, Washington, DC 20425. Phones: (202)376-8177, TDD (202)376-8116; *complaints,* (202)376-8582 or (800)552-6843.

EQUAL EMPLOYMENT OPPORTUNITY COMMISSION

30.001   EMPLOYMENT DISCRIMINATION—TITLE VII OF THE CIVIL RIGHTS ACT OF 1964

Assistance: advisory services/counseling; investigation of complaints.

Purposes: to enforce regulations prohibiting discrimination in employment in the public and private sectors, based on race, sex, color, national origin, or religion. Complaints are investigated and, if reasonable cause is found, mediation is offered; if unsuccessful, civil action may be brought against named respondents. If conciliation fails on a charge against a state or local government, EEOC may refer the case to DOJ for further action. Funding for this program includes **30.008, 30.010,** and **30.011.**

Eligible applicants/beneficiaries: any individual or any labor union, association, legal representative, or unincorporated organization—filing on behalf of an individual with reason to believe that an unlawful employment practice has been committed by an employer with more than 15 employees, an employment agency, a labor organization, or a joint labor-management committee controlling apprenticeship or other training activities.

Activity: FY 98 (including **30.008**, **30.010**, and **30.011** for litigation and systemic data), 80,000 charges to process, 61,000 cases resolved with $169,218,000 in benefits to 11,000 persons; 376 suits filed, 293 resolved; 95 appellate briefs filed.

HQ: Public Information Unit, Office of Communications and Legislative Affairs, EEOC, 1801 L St. NW, Washington, DC 20507. Phones: (202)663-4900, (800)669-3362; TTY (202)663-4494, (800)699-6820; Web, http://www.eeoc.gov

30.002 EMPLOYMENT DISCRIMINATION—STATE AND LOCAL FAIR EMPLOYMENT PRACTICES AGENCY CONTRACTS

Assistance: direct payments/specified use (100 percent/1-3 years).

Purposes: for state and local government enforcement and resolution of charges of violation of civil rights laws prohibiting discrimination in employment, based on race, color, national origin, sex, religion, disability, or age. Funding for this program includes **30.009**.

Eligible applicants: designated state and local government agencies.

Eligible beneficiaries: applicants, employees, and former employees covered by Title VII of the Civil Rights Act of 1964, the Age Discrimination in Employment Act of 1967, or the Americans with Disabilities Act of 1990, and amendments.

Range: $18,000 to $2,196,000.

Activity: FY 99, 90 agencies funded to resolve 51,000 charges.

HQ: Director, State and Local Programs, Office of Field Programs, EEOC, 1801 L St. NW -Rm.8030, Washington, DC 20507. Phone: (202)663-4944.

30.005 EMPLOYMENT DISCRIMINATION—PRIVATE BAR PROGRAM

Assistance: specialized services.

Purposes: to assist aggrieved individuals in locating lawyers to represent them in suits involving employment discrimination under provisions of Title VII of the Civil Rights Act of 1964, the Equal Pay Act, the Age Discrimination in Employment Act, or the Americans with Disabilities Act; to provide technical assistance to aggrieved parties and their attorneys.

Eligible applicants/beneficiaries: individuals filing charges.

Activity: N.A.

HQ: Office of General Counsel, EEOC, 1801 L St. NW, Washington, DC 20507. Phone: (202)663-4791.

30.008 EMPLOYMENT DISCRIMINATION—AGE DISCRIMINATION IN EMPLOYMENT

Assistance: advisory services/counseling; investigation of complaints.

Purposes: to enforce regulations concerning arbitrary employment discrimination on the basis of age; to promote the employment of older workers—pursuant to the Age Discrimination Act of 1967. Individuals age 40 or older are protected from discrimination by: private commercial employers with 20 or more employees; federal, state, local governments; employment agencies; labor organizations in an industry affecting commerce, with 25 or more members. Funding for this program is included in **30.001**.

Eligible applicants/beneficiaries: persons age 40 or over.

Activity: FY 98, 12,000 charges received; 16,000 charges resolved with $34,738,000 in benefits to 1,451 persons. (Information on systemic charges and suits filed is included under **30.001**.)

HQ: same address/phones as **30.001**.

30.009 EMPLOYMENT DISCRIMINATION PROJECT CONTRACTS—INDIAN TRIBES

Assistance: direct payments/specified use.

Purposes: for Tribal Employment Rights Offices (TEROs) to protect the employment rights of Indians working or seeking work on or near reservations, pursuant to Title VII of the Civil Rights Act of 1964. Funding for this program is included in **30.002**.

Eligible applicants/beneficiaries: land-based tribes with approved TEROs.

Range/Average: $25,000 to each tribe.

Activity: FY 00 estimate, 64 offices funded.

HQ: same address/phone as **30.002**.

30.010 EMPLOYMENT DISCRIMINATION—EQUAL PAY ACT

Assistance: advisory services/counseling; investigation of complaints.

Purposes: to enforce laws prohibiting discrimination on the basis of sex in the payment of wages to men and women performing equal work in the same establishment, which is illegal for: employers engaged in commerce or in the production of goods; federal, state, and local governments. Also, labor organizations are prohibited from causing or attempting to cause employers to violate the law. Exceptions are permitted only where payments are based on systems recognizing seniority, merit, quantity or quality of production, or differentials based on factors other than sex. Funding for this program is included in **30.001**.

Eligible applicants/beneficiaries: persons believing that they or others have been or are being paid in violation of the Equal Pay Act of 1963 as amended—in any state, territory, or possession.

Activity: FY 98, 883 complaints received; 1,134 complaints resolved with $2,771,000 in benefits to 139 persons. (Information on systemic charges and suits filed is included under **30.001**.)

HQ: same address/phones as **30.001**.

30.011 EMPLOYMENT DISCRIMINATION—TITLE I OF THE AMERICANS WITH DISABILITIES ACT

Assistance: advisory services/counseling; investigation of complaints.

Purposes: to enforce the ADA which prohibits employment discrimination by private employers and state and local governments against qualified individuals with disabilities. The commission investigates complaints and, if reasonable cause is found, attempts conciliation; if unsuccessful, legal action may be taken against named respondents. Funding for this program is included in **30.001**.

Eligible applicants/beneficiaries: same as for **30.001**.

Activity: FY 98, 18,000 charges received; 23,000 charges resolved with $49,114,000 in benefits to 3,131 persons. (Information on systemic charges and suits filed is included under **30.001**.)

HQ: same address/phones as **30.001**.

FEDERAL COMMUNICATIONS COMMISSION

32.001 COMMUNICATIONS INFORMATION AND ASSISTANCE AND INVESTIGATION OF COMPLAINTS

Assistance: technical information; investigation of complaints.

Purposes: for public information, education, and investigation of complaints concerning telephone or telegraph services and radio and television broadcasting, including cable services. FCC services relate to rates, broadcast signal interference, equal time for political candidates, and the presentation of issues (the "Fairness Doctrine").

Eligible applicants/beneficiaries: anyone.

Activity: FY 98, received 23,000 broadcast and cable, 32,000 common carrier, and 30,000 interference complaints; 3,098 comments and information requests received.

HQ: Public Service Division, Federal Communications Commission, 1919 M St. NW -Rm.244, Washington, DC 20554. Phones: *FEES*, (202)418-0220; *CAB*, (202)418-0190.

FEDERAL MARITIME COMMISSION

33.001 SHIPPING—INVESTIGATION OF COMPLAINTS

Assistance: investigation of complaints.

Purposes: pursuant to the Shipping Act of 1984 as amended, to enforce regulations concerning maritime shipping, including complaints about unlawful rates or practices.

Eligible applicants/beneficiaries: anyone.

Activity: FY 98, responses to 1,923 informal inquiries and complaints.

HQ: Director, Complaints and Informal Dockets, Office of Informal Inquiries,

Federal Maritime Commission, 800 N. Capitol St. NW, Washington, DC 20573. Phones: (202)523-5807; FAX (202)523-0014.

FEDERAL MEDIATION AND CONCILIATION SERVICE

34.001 LABOR MEDIATION AND CONCILIATION

Assistance: specialized services; advisory services/counseling.

Purposes: pursuant to the Labor-Management Relations Act of 1947 as amended and other acts, to prevent or minimize work stoppages caused by disputes between labor and management in industries affecting commerce (excluding railroads and airlines)—through mediation of collective bargaining disputes, arbitration assistance, public education, conciliation.

Eligible applicants/beneficiaries: employers involved in interstate commerce, related labor organizations.

Activity: FY 99 estimate, 24,000 arbitration panels submitted.

HQ: Director of Communications *or* Public Affairs Specialist, FMCS, 2100 K St. NW, Washington, DC 20427. Phone: (202)606-8097.

34.002 LABOR-MANAGEMENT COOPERATION

Assistance: project grants (75-90 percent/12-18 months).

Purposes: to establish or expand joint labor-management committees in the public or private sectors at the work site, area, and industry-wide levels—to improve labor-management relations and productivity.

Eligible applicants/beneficiaries: private nonprofit labor-management committees; labor organizations and private companies or public agencies applying jointly; private nonprofit entities.

Range: work site, $10,000 to $50,000; others, $10,000 to $100,000. **Average:** work site, $35,000; others, $70,000.

Activity: annually, 12-18 grants.

HQ: Director of Program Services, Grants Program Office, FMCS, 2100 K St. NW, Washington, DC 20427. Phone: (202)606-8181. (Note: no field offices for this program.)

FEDERAL TRADE COMMISSION

36.001 FAIR COMPETITION COUNSELING AND INVESTIGATION OF COMPLAINTS

Assistance: advisory services/counseling; investigation of complaints.

Purposes: to prevent and eliminate monopolistic practices, unfair methods of competition, and unfair or deceptive practices affecting consumers. The FTC's concerns include price-fixing, boycotts, price discrimination, illegal mergers and acquisitions, false and misleading advertising, consumer credit transactions and reporting, debt collection practices, food and drug advertising, and other practices affecting the consuming public.

Eligible applicants/beneficiaries: anyone.

Activity: FY 98, 737 formal investigations initiated, 630 closed; 66 orders to cease and desist issued; 276 compliance actions completed; no trade regulation promulgated or amended.

HQ: Federal Trade Commission, Sixth & Pennsylvania Ave. NW, Washington, DC 20580. Phones: Director, Bureau of Consumer Protection, (202)326-3430; Director, Bureau of Competition, (202)326-2932.

GENERAL SERVICES ADMINISTRATION

39.001 BUSINESS SERVICES
("Counseling on Doing Business with the Federal Government")

Assistance: advisory services/counseling.

Purposes: to promote business participation in government procurement contracts for products and services, in surplus property sales, concession, and repair and renovation contracts. Services are directed to small, small disadvantaged, and women-owned businesses. GSA contracts for over $10 billion in goods and services annually.

Eligible applicants/beneficiaries: any business concern.

Activity: FY 98, 111,000 business and counseling actions, 412 business opportunity meetings.

HQ: Associate Administrator, Office of Enterprise Development (E), GSA, Washington, DC 20405. Phone: (202)501-1021.

39.002 DISPOSAL OF FEDERAL SURPLUS REAL PROPERTY

Assistance: sale, exchange, or donation of property and goods.

Purposes: to dispose of surplus federal real and related personal property, at discounts of up to 100 percent—through leases, permits, sale, exchange, or donation. Applicants for property coordinate with appropriate other federal agencies. Surplus property not deeded to public bodies is generally offered for sale to the public on a competitive bid basis.

Eligible applicants/beneficiaries: general public. Surplus real property for park, recreation, correctional facility, historic monument, public airport uses, for health, educational, or homeless programs, and for replacement housing and general public purposes—state and local government agencies. Property for wildlife conservation use—states. Property for health, educational, and homeless program uses—tax-supported and nonprofit medical and educational institutions exempt from taxation under IRS Section 501(c)(3).

Activity: FY 00 estimate, value of $375,000,000 for 568 property disposals.

HQ: Assistant Commissioner, Office of Property Disposal, Public Building Service, GSA, Washington, DC 20405. Phone: (202)501-0084.

39.003 DONATION OF FEDERAL SURPLUS PERSONAL PROPERTY

Assistance: sale, exchange, or donation of property and goods.

Purposes: to donate surplus federal personal property to state and local public agencies for public purposes, to qualifying nonprofit entities for tax-exempt activities, or for educational activities of special interest to the armed services. Examples of surplus property include office machines and supplies, furniture, hardware, textiles, special purpose motor vehicles, boats, airplanes, construction equipment. Participation requires prior GSA approval of state plans for distribution to eligible recipients. Items not donated are made available for sale to the general public (see **39.007**).

Eligible applicants/beneficiaries: state and local agencies, departments, instrumentalities, economic development districts, instrumentalities; multijurisdictional substate districts; tribes, bands, groups, pueblos; nonprofit, tax-exempt organizations such as schools, colleges, universities, public libraries, schools for the handicapped, educational radio or TV stations, child care centers, museums, hospitals, health centers, clinics, programs for the elderly or homeless; public airports; private service and educational organizations. **Ineligible** organizations include: private animal hospitals, summer camps, or playgrounds; church and nonprofit public health and educational organizations that provide grants, scholarships, and funds to support public health and educational institutions, but do not themselves operate such programs. Questions concerning eligibility of others should be addressed to the responsible state agency.

Activity: FY 99, $608,200,000 in original acquisition cost of property donated.

HQ: Director, Property Management Division, Office of Transportation and Property Management, Federal Supply Service, GSA, Washington, DC 20406. Phone: (703)305-7240. (*NOTE: for information concerning service educational activities, contact:* Deputy Under Secretary of Defense/Production and Logistics (L/MDM), The Pentagon, Washington, DC 20301.)

39.007 SALE OF FEDERAL SURPLUS PERSONAL PROPERTY

Assistance: sale, exchange, or donation of property and goods.

Purposes: to sell surplus federal personal property on behalf of most federal civil agencies—such as vehicles, aircraft, hardware, electronic and electrical equipment, paper products, office supplies and equipment, scrap goods. Disposal is by competitive bid.

Eligible applicants/beneficiaries: general public.

Activity: FY 00, $43,200,000 in proceeds from sales.

HQ: same address as **39.003**. Phones: (703)305-7240; *scrap paper inquiries,* (202)501-3458; Internet, www.fss.gsa.gov/property.html

39.008 FEDERAL INFORMATION CENTER

Assistance: technical information.

Purposes: to staff central information posts to answer questions and provide referrals to the general public about any federal agency or program.

Eligible applicants/beneficiaries: general public.

Activity: annually, more than 2,300,000 telephone calls.

HQ: Federal Information Center Program, GSA (TSTI), Fairfax, VA 20230-2238. Phones: (800)688-9889; TTY (800)326-2996; Internet *discussions,* http://fic.info.gov ; *orders,* (888)878-3256.

39.009 CONSUMER INFORMATION CENTER

Assistance: technical information.

Purposes: to assist federal agencies in releasing information of interest to consumers through pertinent news releases, media scripts, and publications, including a quarterly catalog of consumer-oriented publications and an annual listing of publications in Spanish. Fees are charged for some products. A revolving fund supports the program.

Eligible applicants/beneficiaries: general public.

Activity: not quantified specifically.

HQ: Director, Consumer Information Center, GSA, Washington, DC 20405. Phones: (202)501-1794; Internet, http://www.pueblo.gsa.gov

GOVERNMENT PRINTING OFFICE

40.001 DEPOSITORY LIBRARIES FOR GOVERNMENT PUBLICATIONS

Assistance: technical information.

Purposes: to provide government publications and other information products for public reference in depository libraries in the U.S. and its possessions.

Eligible applicants: libraries designated by members of Congress (two designations in each congressional district, four Senatorial designations in each state). By law, all state, highest state appellate court, land-grant college, and law school libraries are eligible for designation.

Eligible beneficiaries: general public.

Activity: FY 99, 40,000 titles distributed to 1,355 depository libraries.

HQ: Director, Library Programs Service (Stop SL), Superintendent of Documents, GPO, 732 N. Capitol St., Washington, DC 20402. Phones: (202)512-1002; telnet, fedbbs.access.gpo.gov

40.002 GOVERNMENT PUBLICATIONS SALES AND DISTRIBUTION ("The Government Bookstore")

Assistance: sale, exchange, or donation of property and goods; technical information.

Purposes: to make available some 10,000 government publications, including 500 subscription services, for sale to the general public. Discounts are available to dealers and other purchasers of large quantities. A revolving fund supports this program.

Eligible applicants/beneficiaries: general public.

Activity: FY 99 estimate, 656,000 mail orders processed.

HQ: *mail orders and inquiries*, Superintendent of Documents, GPO, 732 N. Capitol St., Washington, DC 20402. Phones: Order Desk, (202)512-1800.

LIBRARY OF CONGRESS

42.001   BOOKS FOR THE BLIND AND PHYSICALLY HANDICAPPED

Assistance: use of property, facilities, and equipment.

Purposes: to provide library services to blind and physically handicapped persons—consisting of books on cassette, music scores, discs, and instructional materials in braille, large type, and on cassettes and talking book machines, in 57 regional and 83 subregional libraries.

Eligible applicants/beneficiaries: U.S. residents and citizens living abroad, providing a certificate of inability to read or manipulate conventional printed material from a competent authority.

Activity: FY 98, 769,000 blind and physically handicapped readers served, with a collection of 253,000 titles.

HQ: Director, National Library Service for the Blind and Physically Handicapped, LC, 1291 Taylor St. NW, Washington, DC 20542. Phone: (202)707-5100.

42.002   COPYRIGHT SERVICE

Assistance: technical information.

Purposes: to administer the U.S. Copyright Law, including processing of applications, renewals, transfers, searches, and distribution of regulations; registration of compulsory licenses for satellite carriers and cable systems, and collection of royalties. Fees are charged for certain services. Funding for this program also supports **42.008**.

Eligible applicants/beneficiaries: anyone. Registration may be made by authors, their assignees, or their exclusive licensees, and others designated by law, or by their agents.

Activity: FY 98, 559,000 registrations, 127,000 title searches, 7,446 search reports.

HQ: Register of Copyrights, Copyright Office, LC, 101 Independence Ave. SE, Washington, DC 20559-6000. Phones: (202)707-3000; *application forms,* Web, http://www.loc.go/copyright (Note: no field offices for this program.)

42.003 DISTRIBUTION OF LIBRARY OF CONGRESS CATALOGING ("Cataloging Data Distribution")

Assistance: technical information.

Purposes: to distribute cataloguing and bibliographic information in the form of printed catalog cards, Internet data, book catalogs, magnetic tapes, microforms, CD-ROMs, and other technical publications—for adoption by government agencies, libraries, and others. Fees are charged.

Eligible applicants/beneficiaries: institutions or individuals.

Activity: FY 98, 1,592 annual catalog subscriptions, 28,000 technical publications, and 228 magnetic tape and 3,354 CD-ROM subscriptions.

HQ: Chief, Cataloging Distribution Service, LC, Washington, DC 20541-4910. Phone: (202)707-6100. (Note: no field offices for this program.)

42.005 LIBRARY OF CONGRESS PUBLICATIONS

Assistance: technical information.

Purposes: to provide guides to LC collections, bibliographies, literary brochures, book catalogs, collection facsimiles, and other materials in the field of library technology; literary and folk song recordings. These publications serve as guides to the Library's collections, working tools for other libraries, and reference materials for scholars. Most publications are available for sale by the Superintendent of Documents, Government Printing Office, Washington, DC 20402; some are available directly from LC.

Eligible applicants/beneficiaries: general public.

Activity: FY 98, 10 publications issued.

HQ: Publishing Office, Library of Congress, Washington, DC 20540. Phone: (202)707-5093. (Note: no field offices for this program.)

42.006 LIBRARY OF CONGRESS—LIBRARY SERVICES

Assistance: technical information.

Purposes: to provide research and reader services in diverse fields, with respect to all LC resources and other information sources including: bibliographies; direct reference services in person, and by correspondence, electronic mail, and telephone; exhibits, public lectures, symposia. (In deference to the demands on staff, prospective users should exhaust regional, state, and local resources prior to seeking assistance from the Library staff.)

Eligible applicants/beneficiaries: use of the Library is free.

Activity: not quantified specifically.

HQ: National Reference Service, LC, Washington, DC 20540. Phones: (202) 707-5522; *visitors services*, Visitors Orientation and Tours, (202)707-5458. (Note: no field offices for this program.)

42.007 REFERENCE SERVICES IN SCIENCE AND TECHNOLOGY

Assistance: technical information.

Purposes: to provide general and specialized reference and bibliographic services based on library holdings in scientific and technological subjects.

Eligible applicants/beneficiaries: individuals over high school age, or organizations working in the fields of science and technology.

Activity: FY 98, 71,000 direct reference services.

HQ: Science and Technology Division (reference services), LC, Washington, DC 20540-4750. Phones: (202)707-5522; FAX (202)707-1925. (Note: no field offices for this program.)

42.008   SEMICONDUCTOR CHIP PROTECTION SERVICE

Assistance: technical information.

Purposes: to administer the provisions of the Semiconductor Chip Protection Act of 1984. The Copyright Office staff: examines and decides on the acceptability of applications and identifying materials for registration of claims of protection; records and publishes legal facts or data pertaining to registered works; furnishes pertinent information to the public; and, records transfer documents. Fees are charged for some services. Note: program operating costs are absorbed in the budget of the Copyright Office; fees collected are returned to the U.S. Treasury to offset program costs.

Eligible applicants: general public.

Eligible beneficiaries: owners of qualified mask works.

Activity: FY 98, 965 mask work registrations.

HQ: same address as **42.002**. Phone: (202)707-1497. (Note: no field offices for this program.)

NATIONAL AERONAUTICS AND SPACE ADMINISTRATION

43.001   AEROSPACE EDUCATION SERVICES PROGRAM ("Spacemobile")

Assistance: technical information.

Purposes: to support increased instruction and to initiate systemic change in mathematics, science, and technology education—using NASA specialists to provide inservice and preservice workshops for K-12 teachers, lectures, classroom demonstrations, and media broadcasts.

Eligible applicants/beneficiaries: schools, teacher training institutions, colleges, universities, civic groups, museums, and planetaria.

Activity: FY 98, 5,559 programs for 293,000 students, 1,789 teacher workshops with attendance of 19,000 persons; 22 radio and television programs.

HQ: Education Division (Code FE), NASA Headquarters, Washington, DC 20546. Phone: (202)358-1110.

43.002   TECHNOLOGY TRANSFER

Assistance: technical information.

Purposes: to provide information about government-sponsored civilian aerospace research and development, including inventions, discoveries, innovations, and other improvements—through: NASA's "TechTracs" system, via the Internet; publications including "Tech Briefs;" Regional Technology Transfer Centers; commercial technology field center offices.

Eligible applicants/beneficiaries: Tech Briefs subscriptions (no charge)— engineers, domestic enterprise managers, professionals, and others involved in technology transfer. Technical information search and retrieval services and computer programs/documentation—domestic organizations (fees charged for services beyond those available on the Internet); Technology Transfer Projects—those demonstrating a national public need.

Activity: annually, information to 200,000 persons and firms.

HQ: Commercial Technology Division, Office of Aero-Space Technology (Code RW), NASA Headquarters, Washington, DC 20546-0001. Phones: (202)358-2320; Internet, http://ntas.techtracs.org

NATIONAL CREDIT UNION ADMINISTRATION

44.001 CREDIT UNION CHARTER, EXAMINATION, SUPERVISION, AND INSURANCE

Assistance: insurance; specialized services; advisory services/counseling.

Purposes: to assist in establishing and operating chartered federal credit unions; to provide $100,000 deposit insurance on individual accounts. Approval of applications is based on a combination of interests by group, economic feasibility, and other factors. Fees and insurance premiums support this program.

Eligible applicants/beneficiaries: generally, associations, employee groups, and communities with 500 or more potential members. State-chartered credit unions may apply for depositor insurance.

Activity: 1998, 8 new charters granted.

HQ: Board Chairman, NCUA, 1775 Duke St., Alexandria, VA 22314-3428. Phone: (703)518-6300.

44.002 COMMUNITY DEVELOPMENT REVOLVING LOAN PROGRAM FOR CREDIT UNIONS
("CDCU")

Assistance: direct loans (67 percent/1-3 percent interest/to 5 years).

Purposes: to stimulate economic development activities by: increasing income, business ownership, and employment opportunities among the low-income; providing basic financial and related services to community residents, such as financial counseling, membership and participation drives. Loans can also involve housing, including cooperatives and self-help. Funding is derived from a revolving loan fund.

Eligible applicants/beneficiaries: established state- and federally-chartered credit unions serving low-income communities; territories and possessions.

Range: $25,000 to $300,000.

Activity: not quantified specifically.

HQ: Community Development Revolving Loan Program for Credit Unions, NCUA, 1775 Duke St., Alexandria, VA 22314-3428. Phone: (703)518-6610. (Note: no field offices for this program.)

NATIONAL FOUNDATION ON THE ARTS AND THE HUMANITIES

NATIONAL ENDOWMENT FOR THE ARTS

45.024 PROMOTION OF THE ARTS—GRANTS TO ORGANIZATIONS AND INDIVIDUALS

Assistance: project grants (organizations, to 50 percent/to 2 years; individuals, 100 percent/to 2 years).

Purposes: to support organizations in the visual, literary, media, design, and performing arts in projects involving one of more aspects of: heritage and preservation; education; access; creation and presentation; planning and stabilization. Also, to support published writers through fellowships for creative writing, poetry, and literary translations. (NOTES: no FY 00 funding available for the planning and stabilization category; projects with a Millennium focus are encouraged.)

Eligible applicants/beneficiaries: organizations—nonprofit tax-exempt entities such as arts institutions and arts service organizations; local arts agencies; state and local governments; tribal organizations; consortia. Individuals—U.S. citizens or permanent residents with exceptional talent (other than previous NEA literature fellowship recipients).

Range: organizations, $5,000 to $200,000; individuals, $20,000.

Activity: FY 98, organizations—140 heritage/preservation, 265 education/access grants; individuals—32 literature.

HQ: NEA, 1100 Pennsylvania Ave. NW, Washington, DC 20056-0001. Phones: *general NEA information,* (202)682-5400; Web, http://arts.endow.gov *Grants to organizations: arts education (K-12),* (202)682-5563, *dance, design, media arts, museums, visual arts,* (202)682-5452; *folk and traditional arts,* (202)682-5678, -5724, -5726; *literature,* (202)682-5787, -5771; *local arts agencies,* (202)682-5581, -5586; *multidisciplinary,* (202)682-5658; *mu-*

sic, (202)682-5590, -5487; *musical theater,* (202)682-5509; *opera,* (202)682-5438, -5600; *presenting,* (202)682-5591; *theater,* (202)682-5509, -5511, -5020. *Grants to individuals: literature,* (202)682-5428. *Other phones:* voice/TT (202)682-5496; *cassette recordings of guidelines,* (202)682-5532. (Note: no field offices for this program.)

45.025 PROMOTION OF THE ARTS—PARTNERSHIP AGREEMENTS

Assistance: formula grants; project grants (50 percent); advisory services/counseling.

Purposes: for development of basic state arts plans; for elements of state plans addressing arts education and fostering arts in underserved areas; and, to provide basic support through Partnership Agreements for regional arts planning and for presenting and touring. State arts agencies may use funds for inclusive planning, evaluation, involvement of underserved groups, fair decision making, and promotion of public awareness and appreciation of the arts. Some partnership funds are available for national services provided by membership organizations of state and regional arts organizations.

Eligible applicants/beneficiaries: state arts agencies in the states and in six special U.S. jurisdictions; regional arts and national arts organizations.

Range: $257,000 to $887,000. **Average:** $504,000.

Activity: FY 98, 63 Partnership Agreements.

HQ: Director, State and Regional, NEA, 1100 Pennsylvania Ave. NW, Washington, DC 20056-0001. Phones: (202)692-5429; voice/TT (202)682-5496; *cassette recordings of guidelines,* (202)682-5532; Web, http://arts.endow.gov (Note: no field offices for this program.)

45.026 PROMOTION OF THE ARTS—LEADERSHIP INITIATIVES

Assistance: project grants (from 50 percent).

Purposes: for arts projects of national significance or that serve as models in one field or across disciplines. Grant categories include: Folk and Traditional Arts Infrastructure; "ArtsREACH" projects, specifically targeting 20 underrepresented states; National Heritage Fellowships; American Jazz Master awards.

Eligible applicants/beneficiaries: same as for **45.024.**

Range: Folk and Traditional Arts Infrastructure, $10,000 to $50,000; ArtsREACH, $3,000 to $10,000; National Heritage Fellowships, $10,000; American Jazz Masters, $20,000; other, $5,000 to $500,000.

Activity: FY 98, 34 Folk and Traditional Arts Infrastructure, 84 ArtsREACH, 11 National Heritage Fellowships, 3 American Jazz Master, and 56 other awards.

HQ: NEA, 1100 Pennsylvania Ave. NW, Washington, DC 20056-0001. Phones: Leadership Coordinator, (202)682-5487; *ArtsREACH,* (202)682-5700; *folk and traditional arts, heritage fellowships,* (202)682-5428; *jazz masters,* (202)682-5438; voice/TT (202)682-5496; *cassette recordings of guidelines,* (202)682-5532; Web, http://arts.endow.gov (Note: no field offices for this program.)

NATIONAL ENDOWMENT FOR THE HUMANITIES

45.129 PROMOTION OF THE HUMANITIES—FEDERAL/STATE PARTNERSHIP

Assistance: project grants (formula based, 50 percent/3 years).

Purposes: to 56 state and territorial humanities councils for regranting to local groups to conduct local, statewide, and regional humanities projects. Project examples: cultural heritage programs; family reading and literacy programs; residential institutes.

Eligible applicants: state nonprofit citizen councils. If the state matches a certain percentage of the federal grant, the governor may designate the existing council as a state agency.

Eligible beneficiaries: state and local governments, sponsored organizations, public and private nonprofit organizations, federally recognized tribal governments, native American organizations, territories, minority organizations and other specialized groups, quasi-public nonprofit institutions.

Range: $207,000 to $1,231,000.

Activity: grants to 56 nonprofit organizations.

HQ: Federal/State Partnership, NEH, Rm.511, Washington, DC 20506. Phones: (202)606-8254; Web, http://neh.gov (Note: no field offices for this program.)

45.130 PROMOTION OF THE HUMANITIES—CHALLENGE GRANTS

Assistance: project grants (20-25 percent/1-4 years).

Purposes: for educational and cultural institutions and organizations to increase their financial stability and to sustain or improve humanities programs, services, or resources. Principally, project funds are used to establish endowments; also, for library acquisitions, technological enhancement, construction and renovation, or debt retirement. Grants may not fund general operating costs, projects eligible for other NEH support, or undergraduate scholarships.

Eligible applicants/beneficiaries: public or private nonprofit organizations including: two- and four-year colleges; universities; museums; historical or professional societies; research or public libraries; advanced study centers; university presses; media organizations; other similar and related organizations. States, local governments, and territories may apply on their own behalf or on behalf of organizations within their jurisdictions. Individuals and public and private elementary and secondary schools are ineligible.

Range: $20,000 to $600,000. **Average:** $406,000.

Activity: FY 99 estimate, 25 grants.

HQ: Office of Challenge Grants, NEH, Rm.420, Washington, DC 20506. Phone: (202)606-8309. (Note: no field offices for this program.)

45.149 PROMOTION OF THE HUMANITIES—DIVISION OF PRESERVATION AND ACCESS

Assistance: project grants (50-80 percent/to 5 years).

Purposes: for the preservation of library, museum, archival, and other humanities collections including still and moving images and recorded sound collections; for preservation practices and activities including microfilming, archival surveys, cataloguing; for disaster planning for materials preservation; for a national program to catalog and preserve U.S. newspapers; for training; for research; for related uses.

Eligible applicants/beneficiaries: state and local governments, sponsored organizations, public and private nonprofit organizations, federally recognized tribal governments, native American organizations, territories, minority organizations and other specialized groups, quasi-public nonprofit institutions, and U.S. citizens and residents.

Range: $32,000 to $913,000. **Average:** $291,000.

Activity: FY 00 estimate, 307 awards.

HQ: Division of Preservation and Access, NEH, Rm.411, Washington, DC 20506. Phones: (202)606-8570; FAX (202)606-8639; e-mail, PRESERVATION@NEH.FED.US (Note: no field offices for this program.)

45.160   PROMOTION OF THE HUMANITIES—FELLOWSHIPS AND STIPENDS

Assistance: project grants.

Purposes: for six- to twelve-month fellowships and two-month summer stipends to undertake full-time independent research and writing in the humanities; for HBCU faculty graduate study grants to work toward completion of doctoral degrees in the humanities.

Eligible applicants/beneficiaries: fellowships and stipends—college, university, and other institutional faculty and staff, and independent scholars and writers that have completed their professional training; degree candidates are ineligible. Faculty graduate study—HBCU faculty members with at least one year of graduate work completed. All applicants must be U.S. citizens or nationals, or foreign nationals with at least three years of U.S. legal residence.

Range/Average: fellowships, to $30,000 for 9-12 months, $24,000 for 6-8 months; faculty graduate study, $30,000; summer stipends, $4,000.

Activity: FY 00 estimate, 682 awards.

HQ: Fellowships and Stipends, Division of Research, NEH, Rm.318, Washington, DC 20506. Phone: (202)606-8466. (Note: no field offices for this program.)

45.161   PROMOTION OF THE HUMANITIES—RESEARCH

Assistance: project grants (cost sharing/to 3 years).

Purposes: to support collaboration by scholars, and research centers in the humanities. Fellowships may be offered through independent research centers and international research organizations. Grants may cover the costs of salaries, travel, supplies, and appropriate research assistance and consultation.

Eligible applicants: collaborative research—IHEs, nonprofit professional associations, scholarly societies, other nonprofit organizations. Fellowships—independent research centers, scholarly societies, and international research organizations with existing fellowships programs.

Eligible beneficiaries: U.S. citizens and residents, state and local governments, sponsored organizations, public and private nonprofit organizations, federally recognized tribal governments, native American organizations, territories, minority organizations and other specialized groups, quasi-public nonprofit institutions.

Range: $18,000 to $277,000. **Average:** $112,000.

Activity: FY 00 estimate, 92 awards.

HQ: Division of Research and Education, NEH, Rm.318, Washington, DC 20506. Phone: (202)606-8210. (Note: no field offices for this program.)

45.162   PROMOTION OF THE HUMANITIES—EDUCATION DEVELOPMENT AND DEMONSTRATION

Assistance: project grants (to 3 years).

Purposes: for education development and demonstration projects by teachers and educational institutions to engage their students in substantive study in the humanities.

Eligible applicants/beneficiaries: state and local governments, sponsored organizations, public and private nonprofit organizations, federally recognized tribal governments, native American organizations, territories, minority organizations and other specialized groups, quasi-public nonprofit institutions.

Range: focus grants, $10,000 to $25,000; national projects, to $250,000; Millennium planning, $30,000; Millennium projects, to $200,000.

Activity: FY 00 estimate, 163 awards.

HQ: Education Development and Demonstration Program, NEH, Rm.318, Washington, DC 20506. Phone: (202)606-8380. (Note: no field offices for this program.)

45.163   PROMOTION OF THE HUMANITIES—SEMINARS AND INSTITUTES

Assistance: project grants.

Purposes: for summer seminars and national institutes in the humanities. Grants may support salaries, participant stipends, travel, and related direct costs.

Eligible applicants: distinguished humanities scholars and teachers applying through sponsoring institutions to direct a program for teachers.

Eligible beneficiaries: teachers in grades K-12 or colleges.

Range: seminars, $60,000 to $130,000; institutes, $100,000 to $170,000.

Activity: FY 00 estimate, 127 grants.

HQ: Seminars and Institutes, Division of Research and Education, NEH, Rm.318, Washington, DC 20506. Phone: (202)606-8463. (Note: no field offices for this program.)

45.164   PROMOTION OF THE HUMANITIES—PUBLIC PROGRAMS

Assistance: project grants (6 months - 2 years).

Purposes: for planning and implementation costs of humanities programs in museums, historical organizations, libraries, community centers, as well as on public television and radio.

Eligible applicants/beneficiaries: same as for **45.162**.

Range: $10,000 to $800,000. **Average:** $230,000.

Activity: FY 00 estimate, 109 grants.

HQ: Division of Public Programs, NEH, Rm.426, Washington, DC 20506. Phone: (202)606-8267. (Note: no field offices for this program.)

FEDERAL COUNCIL ON THE ARTS AND THE HUMANITIES

45.201   ARTS AND ARTIFACTS INDEMNITY

Assistance: insurance.

Purposes: to provide indemnification against loss or damage to eligible art works, artifacts, and objects exhibited abroad or borrowed from abroad for display in the U.S. Deductibles and maximum amounts apply.

Eligible applicants/beneficiaries: federal, state, and local government entities; nonprofit agencies, institutions; individuals.

Range: $1,000,000 to $5,000,000,000.

Activity: FY 00 estimate, 40 indemnity certificates issued, insuring up to $5 billion.

HQ: Indemnity Administrator, Museum Program, NEA, Washington, DC 20506. Phone: (202)682-5452. (Note: no field offices for this program.)

INSTITUTE OF MUSEUM AND LIBRARY SERVICES

45.301   INSTITUTE OF MUSEUM AND LIBRARY SERVICES—GENERAL OPERATING SUPPORT ("GOS")

Assistance: direct payments/unrestricted use (2 years).

Purposes: to maintain or improve general museum operations. Grants are competitive.

Eligible applicants/beneficiaries: generally, museums in the states, territories or possessions—that have provided museum services for at least two years. A public or private nonprofit agency, such as a municipality, college, or university responsible for operating a museum, may apply on its behalf. Under the IMS definition, a museum is a public or private nonprofit institution organized on a permanent basis for educational or aesthetic purposes, and which: owns or uses and cares for tangible objects, whether animate or inanimate; exhibits them to the general public on a regular basis. "Museums" includes aquariums and zoological parks, botanical gardens and arboreta, and nature centers; art, history (including historic buildings and sites), natural history; children's, general, and specialized museums; science and technology centers; and planetariums. Federal museums are ineligible.

Range/Average: to $113,000.

Activity: FY 98, 186 grants.

HQ: IMLS, 1100 Pennsylvania Ave. NW - Rm.510, Washington, DC 20506. Phones: *general information,* (202)606-5226; Public Affairs, (202)606-4646; *library programs,* (202)606-8539; TTY, (202)606-8636; e-mail, imlsinfo@imls.fed.us (Note: no field offices for this program.)

45.302 MUSEUM ASSESSMENT PROGRAM ("MAP")

Assistance: direct payments/specified use.

Purposes: for assessments of various aspects of museum collections and operations. Applicants must first complete a self-study questionnaire provided by the American Association of Museums (1575 Eye St. NW - Ste.400, Washington, DC 20005; phone (202)289-9118).

Eligible applicants/beneficiaries: same as for **45.301.**

Range/Average: $1,775 to $2,970.

Activity: new program listing in 1998. FY 99, 200 awards.

HQ: same address/phones as **45.301.** (Note: no field offices for this program.)

45.303 CONSERVATION PROJECT SUPPORT ("CP")

Assistance: project grants (50 percent/to 2 years).

Purposes: for projects involving the safekeeping of living and nonliving museum and library collections, including: surveys of collections and environmental conditions; collections treatment; research; staff training.

Eligible applicants/beneficiaries: same as for **45.301.**

Range/Average: $22,000.

Activity: new program listing in 1998. FY 98, 74 awards.

HQ: same address/phones as **45.301.** (Note: no field offices for this program.)

45.304 CONSERVATION ASSESSMENT PROGRAM ("CAP")

Assistance: direct payments/specified use (cost sharing).

Purposes: for overall assessments of the conditions of museum environments and collections to identify their conservation needs and priorities. Applicants must apply through Historic Preservation, Inc. (3299 K St. NW, Washington, DC 20007; phone (202)625-1495, FAX (202)625-1485).

Eligible applicants/beneficiaries: same as for **45.301.**

Range/Average: $6,000.

Activity: new program listing in 1998. FY 98, 156 awards.

HQ: same address/phones as **45.301.** (Note: no field offices for this program.)

45.305 PROFESSIONAL SERVICES PROGRAM ("PSP")

Assistance: direct payments/specified use (to 50 percent/to 2 years).

Purposes: for projects undertaken to strengthen museum services—e.g., publications or training.

Eligible applicants: private nonprofit professional service organizations, institutions, or associations.

Eligible beneficiaries: public or private nonprofit museums.

Range/Average: $30,000.

Activity: new program listing in 1998. FY 98, 10 cooperative agreements.

HQ: same address/phones as **45.301**. (Note: no field offices for this program.)

45.306 MUSEUM LEADERSHIP INITIATIVES ("MLI")

Assistance: project grants (50 percent).

Purposes: for projects designed to develop and implement partnerships between museum and community organizations to develop mutually beneficial relationships.

Eligible applicants: museums, nonprofit organizations, individuals, universities, consortia of museums, schools, or other organizations. (Any organization participating in the collaborative planning relationship may be the applicant.)

Eligible beneficiaries: public or private nonprofit museums.

Range/Average: $30,000.

Activity: new program listing in 1998. FY 98, 14 awards.

HQ: same address/phones as **45.301**. (Note: no field offices for this program.)

45.310 STATE LIBRARY PROGRAM

Assistance: formula grants (66 percent).

Purposes: for states to support a broad range of library and information services, either directly or through subgrants, including: establishing or enhancing electronic linkages among or between libraries and with educational, school, or information services; promoting targeted services to diverse geographic, cultural, and socioeconomic audiences in urban and rural communities; acquiring or sharing computer systems and telecommunications technologies. Recipients must have a state five-year plan meeting requirements of the Library Services and Technology Act.

Eligible applicants/beneficiaries: state library administrative agencies in DC, PR, and outlying areas.

Range/Average: N.A.

Activity: new program in FY 98; 59 awards.

HQ: Office of Library Services, IMLS, 1100 Pennsylvania Ave. NW - Rm.802, Washington, DC 20506. Phones: (202)606-5526; Web, www.//imls.fed.us (Note: no field offices for this program.)

45.311 NATIVE AMERICAN LIBRARY SERVICES

Assistance: project grants.

Purposes: to provide library services to native Americans, including: support of core library operations; technical assistance projects for training tribal library staff; establishing or enhancing electronic linkages among libraries and with educational, school, or information services; acquiring or sharing computer systems and telecommunications technologies; targeted services to those having difficulty using a library and to under-served communities.

Eligible applicants/beneficiaries: federally recognized tribes, organizations primarily serving Hawaii natives.

Range/Average: N.A.

Activity: new program in FY 98; 294 grants.

HQ: same address as **45.310**. Phone: (202)606-5408. (Note: no field offices for this program.)

45.312 INSTITUTE OF MUSEUM AND LIBRARY SERVICES—NATIONAL LEADERSHIP GRANTS

Assistance: project grants (if over $250,000, 50 percent/to 2 years).

Purposes: to enhance the quality of library services nationwide and to provide coordination between libraries and museums. Funded activities may include: education and training in library and information science, including graduate fellowships, traineeships, institutes, and other programs; research and demonstration projects; preservation or digitization of library materials and resources; model cooperative library-museum programs.

Eligible applicants/beneficiaries: libraries, museums, and IHEs applying individually or in partnerships—including with other public, nonprofit, or profit organizations.

Range: $15,000 to $500,000.

Activity: new program in FY 98; 41 grants.

HQ: IMLS, 1100 Pennsylvania Ave. NW, Washington, DC 20506. Phone: (202)606-5419. (Note: no field offices for this program.)

NATIONAL LABOR RELATIONS BOARD

46.001 LABOR-MANAGEMENT RELATIONS
("NLRB")

Assistance: specialized services; investigation of complaints.

Purposes: pursuant to the Labor-Management Relations Act of 1947 as amended, to avoid or minimize industrial strife affecting interstate commerce by providing orderly procedures to protect the rights of employers, employees, labor organizations, and the general public; to prevent unlawful interference with these rights. Services are provided to employee organizations voting on whether to be represented by a labor organization, and to employers or unions regarding unfair labor practices—only after charges or petitions are filed.

Eligible applicants/beneficiaries: any covered employer, employee, labor organization, or person believing that a violation has occurred, or wishing to vote on whether to be represented by a labor organization. "Employees" exclude: agricultural and domestic workers; persons employed by spouse or parent; independent contractors; employees subject to the Railway Labor Act; certain others not covered by the Act. Federal, state, and local governments and most government corporations (except the U.S. Postal Service) are ineligible employers.

Activity: FY 99, 35,000 cases.

HQ: Division of Information, National Labor Relations Board, 1099 14th St. NW, Washington, DC 20570. Phone: (202)273-1991.

NATIONAL SCIENCE FOUNDATION

47.041   ENGINEERING GRANTS
("ENG")

Assistance: project grants (67-100 percent/6 months-3 years).

Purposes: for engineering research and education programs in virtually all phases of engineering science and technological innovation and practice. Funding may support such activities as: research in emerging areas; industry-university cooperative research centers; biomedical engineering research; research equipment and instrumentation grants; undergraduate student research; faculty enhancement; inter-disciplinary studies; small business innovation research. Cost sharing is required except for solicited proposals, conferences, publications, travel, and logistical support. Funds may not support product development or marketing. Most projects are conducted by academic institutions.

Eligible applicants/beneficiaries: public and private IHEs; nonprofit institutions; profit organizations including small businesses; federal, state, and local government agencies; individuals.

Range: $5,000 to $3,000,000. **Average:** $114,000.

Activity: FY 00 estimate, 2,850 grants.

HQ: Senior Advisor/Planning and Evaluation, Directorate for Engineering, NSF, 4201 Wilson Blvd., Arlington, VA 22230. Phones: (703)306-1303; FAX (703)306-0292; e-mail, enginfo@nsf.gov; Web, URL, http://www.eng. nsf.gov/ ; *general inquiries,* enginfo@nsf.gov (Note: no field offices for this program.)

47.049   MATHEMATICAL AND PHYSICAL SCIENCES
("MPS")

Assistance: project grants (to 100 percent/3-5 years).

Purposes: for basic research in physics, chemistry, astronomical and mathematical sciences, and materials, including multidisciplinary research. Grants may support: science and technology centers; institutes; undergraduate student research; developing research opportunities for women, minority, and disabled scientists and engineers; instrumentation; laboratory improvement; research workshops, symposia, and conferences; faculty enhancement; curriculum development. Cost sharing is required, except for symposia, conferences, publications, travel, education, training, or facilities.

Eligible applicants/beneficiaries: public and private IHEs; nonprofit, nonacademic research institutions; private profit organizations; foreign institutions; state and local governments; other federal agencies; certain unaffiliated scientists.

Range: $10,000 to $30,000,000. **Average:** $94,000.

Activity: FY 00 estimate, 4,230 grants.

HQ: Assistant Director, Mathematical and Physical Sciences, NSF, 4201 Wilson Blvd., Arlington, VA 22230. Phones: (703)306-1800; Web, URL, http://www.nsf.gov/ (Note: no field offices for this program.)

47.050 GEOSCIENCES ("GEO")

Assistance: project grants (to 100 percent/1-3 years).

Purposes: for basic research and studies in the atmospheric (e.g., meteorology, climate, paleoclimate), earth, and ocean sciences and in related biological, chemical, and physical disciplines. Grants may support science and technology centers, undergraduate student research, facility enhancement, instrumentation, laboratory equipment, and research opportunities for women, minority, and disabled scientists and engineers. Cost sharing is required, except for symposia, conferences, publications, travel, education, training, facilities, ship operations, or equipment.

Eligible applicants/beneficiaries: public and private IHEs, nonacademic research institutions, private profit organizations, certain unaffiliated scientists.

Range: $1,000 to $60,000,000. **Average:** $140,000.

Activity: FY 00 estimate, 2,800 awards.

HQ: NSF, 4201 Wilson Blvd., Arlington, VA 22230. Phones: *atmospheric sciences*, (703)306-1520, FAX (703)306-0377; *earth sciences*, (703)306-1550, FAX (703)306-0382; *ocean sciences*, (703)306-1580, FAX (703)306-0390; Web, URL, http://www.nsf.gov/ ; geosciences, URL, http://www.geo.nsf.gov/ (Note: no field offices for this program.)

47.070 COMPUTER AND INFORMATION SCIENCE AND ENGINEERING ("CISE")

Assistance: project grants (to 100 percent/6 months-3 years).

Purposes: for research improving the fundamental understanding of computer and information processing; to enhance the training and education of scientists and engineers; and, to provide access to very advanced computing and networking capabilities. Examples of funded projects: estuary pollution modeling; multimodal interaction. Cost sharing is required. Ineligible uses of funds include fellowships, scholarships, product development and marketing. Most funded projects are conducted by academic institutions.

Eligible applicants/beneficiaries: public and private IHEs; nonprofit and profit organizations; small businesses; federal, state, and local government agencies.

Range: $1,000 to $30,000,000. **Average:** $75,000.

Activity: FY 00 estimate, 1,520 awards.

HQ: Assistant Director, Computer and Information Science and Engineering, NSF, 4201 Wilson Blvd., Arlington, VA 22230. Phones: (703)306-1900; Web, URL, http://www.cise.nsf.gov/ (Note: no field offices for this program.)

47.074 BIOLOGICAL SCIENCES ("BIO")

Assistance: project grants (to 100 percent/to 5 years).

Purposes: for basic research in the biological sciences, including cellular and molecular biosciences, integrative biology and neuroscience, environmental biology, and biological infrastructure, and plant genomes. Grants may be used to purchase multi-user scientific equipment and for instrument development; mid-career or professional development; research workshops, symposia, and conferences; postdoctoral fellowships including for minority scientists. Cost sharing is required, except for symposia, conferences, publications, travel, education, or training.

Eligible applicants/beneficiaries: same as for **47.050.**

Range: $4,000 to $3,500,000. **Average:** $80,000.

Activity: FY 00 estimate, 2,950 grants.

HQ: Assistant Director, Biological Sciences, NSF, 4201 Wilson Blvd., Arlington, VA 22230. Phones: (703)306-1400; Web, URL, http://www.nsf.gov/ (Note: no field offices for this program.)

47.075 SOCIAL, BEHAVIORAL, AND ECONOMIC SCIENCES ("SBE")

Assistance: project grants (cost sharing/2-5 years).

Purposes: for basic research in the social, behavioral and economic sciences, including international programs—in such disciplines as: anthropological and geographic sciences; cognitive, psychological, and language science; economic, decision, and management sciences; social and political science; science, technology, and society. Grants may support: science and technology centers; studies abroad including joint research projects; international research workshops, symposia, and conferences; doctoral and postdoctoral fellowships; junior faculty research; graduate traineeships; undergraduate student research; research opportunities for women, minorities, and disabled scientists and engineers.

Eligible applicants/beneficiaries: same as for **47.050.** And, for international cooperative scientific activities—government scientific organizations.

Range: $1,000 to $9,000,000. **Average:** $64,000.

Activity: FY 00 estimate, 1,925 grants.

HQ: Division of International Programs, Directorate for Social, Behavioral, and Economic Sciences, NSF, 4201 Wilson Blvd., Arlington, VA 22230. Phones: (703)306-1710; Division of Science Resources Studies, (703)306-1780; Division of Social and Economic Sciences *and* Division of Behavioral and Cognitive Sciences, (703)306-1760; Web, URL, http://www.nsf.gov (Note: no field offices for this program.)

47.076 EDUCATION AND HUMAN RESOURCES ("EHR")

Assistance: project grants (50-100 percent/to 5 years).

Purposes: for programs improving the effectiveness of science, mathematics, engineering, and technology education, including: systemic reform; elementary, secondary, and informal science education; undergraduate and graduate education; human resource development; and research, evaluation, and dissemination; experimental programs. Grants may support fellowships for up to three years, scholarships, equipment purchases, salaries, and other expenses.

Eligible applicants: public and private two- and four-year IHEs; SEAs and LEAs; nonprofit and private organizations; professional societies; science museums and zoological parks; research laboratories; other educational institutions.

Eligible beneficiaries: elementary, secondary, and undergraduate science, mathematics, and engineering teachers and faculty; secondary, undergraduate, and graduate students.

Range: $2,500 to $4,000,000. **Average:** $118,000.

Activity: FY 00 estimate, 2,400 awards; 100 H1-B Nonimmigrant Petitioner awards for 8,000 scholarships.

HQ: Assistant Director, Education and Human Resources, NSF, 4201 Wilson Blvd. - Rm.805, Arlington, VA 22230. Phones: (703)306-1600; Web, URL, http://www.nsf.gov/ (Note: no field offices for this program.)

47.078 POLAR PROGRAMS ("OPP")

Assistance: project grants (cost sharing/1-3 years).

Purposes: for basic research in the arctic and antarctic regions, focused on the solid earth, glacial and sea ice, terrestrial ecosystems, the oceans, the atmosphere and beyond. Support is available for science and technology centers, undergraduate student research, facility enhancement, instrumentation, laboratory equipment, and research opportunities for women, minority, and handicapped scientists and engineers.

Eligible applicants/beneficiaries: same as for **47.050.**

Range: $1,000 to $1,000,000. **Average:** $90,000.

Activity: new program listing in 1997. FY 00, 550 awards.

HQ: National Science Foundation, 4201 Wilson Blvd., Arlington, VA 22230. Phones: Arctic Sciences, (703)306-1029, FAX (703)306-0648; Antarctic Sciences, (703)306-1033, FAX (703)306-0648; Polar Research, (703)306-

1032; FAX (703)305-0139; Web, URL, http:/www.nsf.gov/ (Note: no field offices for this program.)

PRESIDENT'S COMMITTEE ON EMPLOYMENT OF PEOPLE WITH DISABILITIES

53.001   EMPLOYMENT PROMOTION OF PEOPLE WITH DISABILITIES

Assistance: advisory services/counseling; technical information.

Purposes: to promote employment opportunities for persons with disabilities toward implementation of the ADA, through: promotional campaigns directed toward business leaders, organized labor, and others; training; a Web site; the DOD Workforce Recruitment Program; technical information. The committee also operates the Job Accommodations Network (JAN) a toll-free telephone system providing information about accommodations for employees with disabilities

Eligible applicants/beneficiaries: state governors' committees; national groups; others.

Activity: not quantified specifically.

HQ: Executive Director, President's Committee on Employment of People with Disabilities, 1331 F St. NW, Washington, DC 20004. Phones: (202)376-6200; TDD (202)376-6205; FAX (202)376-6219; e-mail, Info@pcepd.gov

RAILROAD RETIREMENT BOARD

57.001   SOCIAL INSURANCE FOR RAILROAD WORKERS

Assistance: direct payments/unrestricted use.

Purposes: pursuant to the Social Security, Railroad Unemployment Insurance, and Railroad Retirement Acts as amended, to pay benefits to railroad workers and their beneficiaries, including retirement, death, disability, unemployment, or sickness insurance, including "rail social security."

Eligible applicants/beneficiaries: Railroad Retirement Act benefits—for employee, spouse, and survivor benefits, the employee must have had 10 or more years of railroad service; for survivors, the employee must have been insured at death. Railroad Unemployment Insurance Act—employees with certain minimum earnings in railroad wages; new employees must have worked for a railroad at least five months in a calendar (base) year.

Range/Average: age annuities, monthly maximum $2,531, average $1,264; disability, monthly maximum $2,503, average $1,346; employee supplemental annuities, monthly maximum $70, average $43; spouse benefits, monthly maximum $1,206, average $506; widows/widowers, monthly maximum $1,953, average $765; widowed mothers/fathers, monthly maximum $1,613, average $957; children, monthly maximum $1,435, average $646; unemployment and sickness, weekly maximum $230, average $230.

Activity: FY 98, 800,000 total beneficiaries; 38,000 retirement awards; 31,000 unemployment insurance beneficiaries.

HQ: Public Affairs, Railroad Retirement Board, 844 N. Rush St., Chicago, IL 60611-2092. Phone: (312)751-4777.

SECURITIES AND EXCHANGE COMMISSION

58.001 SECURITIES—INVESTIGATION OF COMPLAINTS AND SEC INFORMATION
("Complaints and Inquiries")

Assistance: technical information; investigation of complaints.

Purposes: to provide assistance to or on behalf of securities investors, including educational materials and public educational activities. SEC's public files contain financial and other information about companies, broker-dealers, investment companies, investment advisers, transfer agents, and banks, which may be examined at SEC offices; or, copies may be obtained from the headquarters office from the Public Reference Branch. Investors believing they have been defrauded, or that another party has violated the federal securities laws, may present their complaint and/or information to the SEC. A public action taken by SEC does not necessarily result in monetary benefits to investors; however, an aggrieved investor may find the information disclosed by the commission in its actions helpful in any private action brought to recover losses.

Eligible applicants/beneficiaries: anyone may seek information or file a complaint.

Activity: FY 98, 53,000 complaints and inquiries closed.

HQ: Office of Investor Education and Assistance, Securities and Exchange Commission, 450 Fifth St. NW (MS 2-13), Washington, DC 20549. Phones: (202)942-7040, FAX (202)942-9634, e-mail, help@sec.gov ; Public Reference Branch (MS 1-2), (202)942-8090, FAX (202)628-9001, e-mail, publicinfo@sec.gov ; Web, www.sec.gov

SMALL BUSINESS ADMINISTRATION

> **NOTE:** *In the following SBA program descriptions, "small business" means a business that is independently owned and operated, not dominant in its field, and meets certain size standards—generally: for manufacturers, average employment not exceeding 500; wholesalers, to 100 employees; special trade, revenues not over $7,000,000; retailers and service concerns, revenues not over $5,000,000; agricultural enterprises, to $500,000 in gross sales; general construction, annual revenues not over $17,000,000. Unless otherwise indicated, SBA excludes from its financial assistance programs: nonprofit enterprises (except for disaster loans and sheltered workshops); lending or investment enterprises; gambling enterprises; and, real estate speculators.*

59.002   ECONOMIC INJURY DISASTER LOANS ("EIDL")

Assistance: direct loans (4 percent); guaranteed/insured loans (to 30 years).

Purposes: to help small businesses recover from declared disasters. Funds may be used for debt payments and working capital, but not realty or equipment acquisition or repair. Funding for this program is included in **59.008.**

Eligible applicants/beneficiaries: small business and small agricultural cooperative or nursery victims in declared disaster areas, unable to obtain credit elsewhere, with evidence of the cause and extent of economic injury.

Range: direct loans, to $1,500,000. **Average:** $51,000.

Activity: FY 98, 5,780 loans.

HQ: Office of Disaster Assistance, SBA, 409 Third St. SW, Washington, DC 20416. Phones: (202)205-6734; e-mail, disaster.assistance@sba.gov

59.005   BUSINESS DEVELOPMENT ASSISTANCE TO SMALL BUSINESS

Assistance: advisory services/counseling; technical information; training.

Purposes: to provide advice on management and operation of small businesses, provided through workshops, expertise from the Service Corps of Retired Executives and other volunteer programs, courses, and educational materials.

Eligible applicants/beneficiaries: existing and potential small business persons, veterans, and, in some cases, members of community groups.

Activity: FY 98, 175,000 persons counseled, enrollment of 100,000 in management training.

HQ: Associate Administrator/Business Initiatives, SBA, 409 Third St. SW, Washington, DC 20416. Phones: (202)205-6665; *general information*, electronic bulletin board, SBA On-Line access, (800)697-4636, (900)463-4636, (202)401-9600; Internet, "SBA Online".

59.006   8(A) BUSINESS DEVELOPMENT
("Section 8(a) Program")

Assistance: specialized services.

Purposes: for SBA procurement contracts with other federal agencies and for subcontracts, in turn, with socially and economically disadvantaged businesses. The program incorporates contract, financial, technical, and managerial assistance to participants.

Eligible applicants/beneficiaries: small businesses at least 51 percent owned, controlled, and managed by U.S. citizens determined to be socially and economically disadvantaged, or by disadvantaged tribes, Alaska native corporations, or native Hawaiian organizations.

Activity: FY 97, 32,000 contract actions valued at $6.59 billion.

HQ: Associate Administrator/8(a) Business Development, SBA, 409 Third St. SW, Washington, DC 20416. Phone: (202)205-6421.

59.007   MANAGEMENT AND TECHNICAL ASSISTANCE FOR SOCIALLY AND ECONOMICALLY DISADVANTAGED BUSINESSES
("Section 7(j) Development Assistance Program")

Assistance: project grants (100 percent).

Purposes: for business management and technical assistance services through qualified individuals or public or private organizations, to businesses that are socially and economically disadvantaged, located in areas of high unemployment or low income, or participants in program **59.006**.

Eligible applicants/beneficiaries: state and local governments; educational institutions; public or private organizations and businesses; tribes; qualified individuals.

Range/Average: N.A.

Activity: FY 97, 153 cooperative agreement awards.

HQ: Associate Administrator/Minority Enterprise Development, SBA, 409 Third St. SW, Washington, DC 20416. Phone: (202)205-6410.

59.008   PHYSICAL DISASTER LOANS
("Section 7(b) Loans" - "DL")

Assistance: direct loans (4-8 percent interest/3-30 years); guaranteed/insured loans.

Purposes: for victims of physical disasters to restore or replace damaged or destroyed real or personal property. Loan terms depend on the applicant's access to credit. Funding for this program includes **59.002**.

Eligible applicants/beneficiaries: homeowners, renters, businesses, and charitable and nonprofit organizations. Agricultural enterprises are ineligible.

Range: homes, to $240,000, plus $200,000 in special cases to refinance existing liens, and $48,000 additional for protective measures; businesses, to $1,500,000 with higher amounts available for major source of employment. **Average:** homes, $18,000; businesses, $51,000.

Activity: FY 98, 30,000 loans.

HQ: same address/phone as **59.002.**

59.009   PROCUREMENT ASSISTANCE TO SMALL BUSINESSES

Assistance: specialized services.

Purposes: to assist small businesses in all phases of obtaining and administering government procurement contracts. SBA: advocates small business participation in federal contracts and subcontracts, including application of small business "set-asides;" consults with other federal procuring agencies to optimize small business participation; manages the procurement Marketing and Access Network (PRO-Net), a nationwide Internet database on small businesses interested in obtaining federal contracts or subcontracts.

Eligible applicants/beneficiaries: existing and potential small businesses.

Activity: FY 97, $10.4 billion in set-asides.

HQ: Associate Administrator/Government Contracting, SBA, 409 Third St. SW, Washington, DC 20416. Phone: (202)205-6460.

59.011   SMALL BUSINESS INVESTMENT COMPANIES ("SBIC - SSBIC")

Assistance: direct loans, guaranteed/insured loans (to 10-15 years); advisory services/counseling.

Purposes: for SBA-licensed small business investment companies, including specialized SBICs (SSBICs) that assist socially or economically disadvantaged enterprises, to provide equity capital, in turn, to small businesses—through long-term loans or equity purchases. SBA guarantees debentures issued by the investment companies to maximize leveraging of private funds, by up to 300 percent within maximums established by SBA and for terms of 10 years; participating securities may be guaranteed for up to 15 years. The investment companies provide continuing management and other assistance to firms that obtain the loans.

Eligible applicants: qualified chartered SBICs with combined paid-in capital and surplus of at least $3,000,000.

Eligible beneficiaries: small businesses (single proprietorship, partnership, or corporation) including socially or economically disadvantaged enterprises.

Range: guarantee loans, $50,000 to $90,000,000. **Average:** $3,804,000.

Activity: as of FY 99, 246 SBICs, 75 SSBICs participating.

HQ: Associate Administrator/Investment, Investment Division, SBA, 409 Third St. SW, Washington, DC 20416. Phone: (202)205-6510.

59.012   SMALL BUSINESS LOANS ("Regular Business Loans" - "Section 7(a) Loans")

Assistance: guaranteed/insured loans.

Purposes: to construct, expand, or convert facilities; to purchase equipment or materials; for working capital. (Eligible loan uses include design, manufacture, marketing, installation, or servicing of specific energy measures.) Program components include SBA's: Low Documentation Loan Program

(Low Doc; Cap Line Program; "FA$ TRAK Program" (formerly, Small Loan Express); Women's and Minority Prequalification Program.

Eligible applicants/beneficiaries: small businesses including those owned by low-income or handicapped individuals or located in high unemployment areas; nonprofit sheltered workshops.

Range: guaranty, to $500,000. **Average:** $227,000.

Activity: FY 98, 39,000 loans.

HQ: Loan Policy and Procedures Branch, SBA, 409 Third St. SW, Washington, DC 20416. Phone: (202)205-6570.

59.016 BOND GUARANTEES FOR SURETY COMPANIES ("Surety Bond Guarantee")

Assistance: insurance (70-90 percent).

Purposes: for surety companies for bid, payment, and performance or other bonds provided to small businesses on contracts up to $1,250,000.

Eligible applicants: surety companies holding certificates of authority from the Secretary of the Treasury.

Eligible beneficiaries: small contractors with gross annual receipts of no more than $5,000,000 as averaged for the last three fiscal years; certain manufacturers. (Applications are submitted directly to insurance agents or brokers.)

Range: $475 to $1,250,000. **Average:** contract, $185,000; guarantee, $150,000.

Activity: FY 98, 10,000 bid bonds approved, 2,860 final bond guarantees issued.

HQ: Associate Administrator, Office of Surety Guarantees, SBA, 409 Third St. SW, Washington, DC 20416. Phone: (202)205-6540.

59.026 SERVICE CORPS OF RETIRED EXECUTIVES ("SCORE")

Assistance: advisory services/counseling; training.

Purposes: to operate the SCORE program through which retired or active business executives volunteer their services to counsel and train new and existing small business persons. Out-of-pocket expenses of volunteers may be reimbursed.

Eligible applicants/beneficiaries: existing and potential small businesses.

Activity: 12,400 volunteers serve in the 50 states and in possessions.

HQ: National SCORE Office, SBA, 409 Third St. SW, Washington, DC 20024. Phones: (202)205-6762, (800)634-0245; Web, www.score.org; *Or*, Office of Business Development, same address. Phone: (202)205-7414.

59.037 SMALL BUSINESS DEVELOPMENT CENTER ("SBDC")

Assistance: project grants (formula based, 50 percent); specialized services; advisory services/counseling; technical information.

Purposes: for Small Business Development Centers to provide management counseling, training, and technical assistance to existing or potential small businesses.

Eligible applicants/beneficiaries: public or private IHEs including land grant, community, or junior colleges; certain existing SBDCs.

Range: $500,000 to $5,927,000. **Average:** $1,298,000.

Activity: FY 98, 238,000 individuals counseled, 20,000 training sessions.

HQ: SBDC Office, SBA, 409 Third St. SW - 4th floor, Washington, DC 20416. Phones: (202)205-6766; FAX (202)205-7727.

59.041   CERTIFIED DEVELOPMENT COMPANY LOANS (504 LOANS) ("Section 504 Loans")

Assistance: guaranteed/insured loans (40 percent/10-20 years).

Purposes: to assist small businesses in acquiring fixed assets, through the sale of debentures to private investors. Loans may cover land, buildings, equipment, construction, expansion, renovation, or modernization. Ten percent of project costs must be provided by the small business concern, and 50 percent by a private lender.

Eligible applicants/beneficiaries: nonprofit certified development companies.

Range: to $1,000,000. **Average:** $350,000.

Activity: FY 98, 4,847 loans approved.

HQ: Office of Financial Assistance, SBA, 409 Third St. SW, Washington, DC 20416. Phone: (202)205-6490.

59.043   WOMEN'S BUSINESS OWNERSHIP ASSISTANCE

Assistance: project grants (33-67 percent/to 5 years).

Purposes: to establish women's business centers to assist new or existing small businesses owned and controlled by women, through financial, management, and marketing training and counseling.

Eligible applicants/beneficiaries: private nonprofit organizations.

Range: $75,000 to $150,000. **Average:** $150,000.

Activity: currently, 29 centers.

HQ: Office of Women's Business Ownership, SBA, 409 Third St. SW, Washington, DC 20416. Phones: (202)205-6673; *interactive women's business center,* Internet, www.onlinewbc.org

59.044   VETERANS ENTREPRENEURIAL TRAINING AND COUNSELING ("Veterans Business Outreach Program" - "VBOP")

Assistance: project grants (50 percent/1-5 years).

Purposes: to establish and operate Veterans Business Outreach Centers to provide long-term training, counseling, and mentoring to veterans starting or operating small businesses.

Eligible applicants/beneficiaries: educational institutions; private businesses; veterans nonprofit community-based organizations; federal, state, and local entities.

Range: $350 to $1,500 per client.

Activity: N.A.

HQ: Director, Office of Veterans Affairs, SBA, 409 Third St. SW - 5th Floor, Washington, DC 20416. Phone: (202)205-6773.

59.046 MICROLOAN DEMONSTRATION PROGRAM

Assistance: formula grants; direct loans (to 10 years).

Purposes: to provide loan funds or loan guaranties to eligible intermediary lenders that, in turn, will make short-term, fixed-rate loans of up to $25,000 to newly established or growing small businesses for working capital or for the acquisition of supplies or equipment; to make grants to intermediaries to provide intensive marketing, management, and technical assistance to borrowers; to make grants to nonprofit entities to assist low-income individuals in obtaining private sector financing for their businesses.

Eligible applicants: intermediary lenders meeting SBA requirements.

Eligible beneficiaries: small businesses, minority entrepreneurs, nonprofit entities, women, low-income and other persons.

Range/Average: $10,000.

Activity: N.A.

HQ: Microenterprise Development Branch (MC 7881), Office of Financial Assistance, SBA, 409 Third St. SW - 8th Floor, Washington, DC 20416. Phone: (202)205-6490. (Note: no field offices for this program.)

INTERNATIONAL TRADE COMMISSION

61.001 IMPORT RELIEF (INDUSTRY)
("Escape Clause")

Assistance: specialized services.

Purposes: to provide for the imposition of tariff adjustment and/or import quotas for industries; to provide adjustment assistance (through program **17.245**) to firms and workers in industries adversely affected by imports.

Eligible applicants/beneficiaries: action may be initiated by the President, U.S. Trade Representative, Senate Committee on Finance, House Committee on Ways and Means, or International Trade Commission; or, by a trade association, firm, certified or recognized union, or group of workers representing an industry producing an article like or directly competitive with a foreign article claimed to be imported in quantities causing serious injury or threat to the domestic industry.

Activity: FY 98, no new investigations completed.

HQ: Secretary, U.S. International Trade Commission, 500 E St. SW, Washington, DC 20436. Phone: (202)205-2000. (Note: no field offices for this program.)

TENNESSEE VALLEY AUTHORITY

62.001   TVA ENERGY RESEARCH AND TECHNOLOGY APPLICATIONS

Assistance: use of property, facilities, and equipment; advisory services/counseling.

Purposes: to research, develop, demonstrate, and transfer innovative cost-effective solutions concerning energy and environmental problems including resource threats: technical information and assistance; to award TVA patent licenses.

Eligible applicants/beneficiaries: universities, environmental industry firms, government agencies, professional organizations and institutions, agricultural input suppliers, public and private sectors. Patent licenses—industry. Cooperative R&D contracts—research stations, government agencies, and private industry extension services.

Activity: sampling and analyses for 59 solid waste management units completed; corrective measures study initiated.

HQ: Vice President, Energy Research and Technology Applications, TVA, 35662-1010. Phone: (256)386-2026.

DEPARTMENT OF VETERANS AFFAIRS

NOTE: *In DVA programs providing benefits directly to veterans, general eligibility factors may include all or some of the following: discharge under other than dishonorable conditions; former prisoners of war; award of the Medal of Honor in peacetime and unable to pay the cost of necessary care; wartime service resulting in need of treatment for a full or partial service-connected or nonservice-connected disability, or for a disease; receiving a DVA pension or age 65 or older and with wartime or peacetime active service; discharged for a disability, or receiving compensation for and suffering from a permanent disability, with no adequate means of support; receiving compensation or allowances based on need of regular aid and attendance or housebound. Income limits may apply under some programs. Veterans whose eligibility is based on financial income may receive some services by making a copayment.*

*Details may be obtained from DVA medical centers or outpatient clinics, from DVA Veterans Benefits Administration field offices (see **64.115** or other centers listed in Part IV).*

VETERANS HEALTH ADMINISTRATION

64.005 GRANTS TO STATES FOR CONSTRUCTION OF STATE HOME FACILITIES ("State Home Construction")

Assistance: project grants (65 percent).

Purposes: to acquire or construct state domiciliary or nursing homes for veterans; to expand, remodel, alter, or equip existing buildings to provide domiciliary, nursing home, or hospital care to veterans in state homes.

Eligible applicants/beneficiaries: states.

Range: $141,000 to $27,182,000. **Average:** $2,400,000.

Activity: FY 98, 3 grants, 6 conditional grants approved.

HQ: Chief, State Home Construction Program, Geriatrics and Extended Care Strategic Healthcare Group (114), DVA, Central Office, Washington, DC 20420. Phone: (202)273-8356. (Note: no field offices for this program.)

64.007 BLIND REHABILITATION CENTERS

Assistance: specialized services (4 months).

Purposes: for personal and social adjustment programs and medical or health-related services for blind veterans at DVA medical centers with blind rehabilitation centers.

Eligible applicants/beneficiaries: blind veterans meeting certain general requirements (*see NOTE preceding* **64.005**). Active duty armed forces personnel may be transferred to a center.

Activity: FY 98, 1,730 veterans benefited at the 9 Blind Rehabilitation Centers.

HQ: Blind Rehabilitation Service (117B), Patient Care Services, DVA, Washington, DC 20420. Phone: (202)273-8481, -8482.

64.008 VETERANS DOMICILIARY CARE

Assistance: specialized services.

Purposes: for inpatient medical care and physical, social, and psychological support services for ambulatory veterans disabled by age or illness, and not requiring acute care or skilled nursing services; for rehabilitation services preparing veterans for independent community living, or assisting them in reaching their optimal level of functioning in a protective environment.

Eligible applicants/beneficiaries: veterans meeting specific criteria (*see NOTE preceding* **64.005**).

Activity: FY 98, 50,000 veterans served; average daily census, 11,000.

HQ: Domiciliary Care Program Chief, Geriatrics and Extended Care Strategic Healthcare Group (114A), DVA, Washington, DC 20420. Phone: (202)273-8543, -8545.

64.009 VETERANS MEDICAL CARE BENEFITS ("Hospitalization and Medical Services")

Assistance: specialized services.

Purposes: for hospital outpatient medical, dental, medicine, medical supplies, home health, podiatric, optometric, surgical, and mental health services for enrolled veterans and their dependents, including reimbursement for some travel costs. Services are provided at DVA facilities or under fee-basis hometown care programs when properly authorized.

Eligible applicants/beneficiaries: veterans meeting specific criteria (*see NOTE preceding* **64.005**). Services also may be provided to dependents and survivors that are ineligible for Medicare, CHAMPUS (Civilian Health and Medical Program of the Uniformed Service), or CHAMPVA (Civilian Health and Medical Program, Veterans Affairs).

Activity: FY 98, 35,777,000 visits involving 631,000 patients in VA, state, and contract facilities.

HQ: Director, Health Administration Services (10C3), DVA, Washington, DC 20420. Phone: (202)273-8302, -8303.

64.010 VETERANS NURSING HOME CARE

Assistance: specialized services.

Purposes: for skilled nursing home care in DVA facilities for veterans. Also provided are related medical services, supportive personal care, and individual adjustment services.

Eligible applicants/beneficiaries: veterans requiring skilled nursing care and related medical services, and meeting specific criteria (*see NOTE preceding* **64.005**).

Activity: FY 98, 97,000 patients treated; average daily census, 34,000.

HQ: Nursing Home Care Program Chief, Geriatric and Extended Strategic Health Group (114), DVA, Washington, DC 20420. Phone: (202)273-8544.

64.011 VETERANS DENTAL CARE

Assistance: specialized services.

Purposes: to provide dental services for veterans.

Eligible applicants/beneficiaries: veterans meeting specific criteria (*see NOTE preceding* **64.005**).

Activity: FY 98, 287,000 examinations and 160,000 treatments by DVA staff, 15,000 fee cases.

HQ: same address/phone as **64.009**.

64.012 VETERANS PRESCRIPTION SERVICE
("Medicine For Veterans")

Assistance: sale, exchange, or donation of property and goods.

Purposes: for prescription drugs and expendable medical supplies from DVA pharmacies for veterans and certain dependents and survivors. Prescription drugs may be provided by mail or on a reimbursable basis in areas only in the U.S. where there are no DVA pharmacies.

Eligible applicants/beneficiaries: veterans meeting specific criteria (*see NOTE preceding* **64.005**). Services also may be provided to dependents and survivors under CHAMPVA (Civilian Health and Medical Program, Veterans Affairs)

Activity: N.A.

HQ: Chief Consultant, Pharmacy Benefits Management, DVA, Washington, DC 20420. Phone: (202)273-8429.

64.013   VETERANS PROSTHETIC APPLIANCES

Assistance: sale, exchange, or donation of property and goods.

Purposes: to provide prosthetic and related appliances, equipment, and services to disabled veterans, including artificial limbs, artificial eyes, wheelchairs, aids for the blind, hearing aids, braces, orthopedic shoes, eyeglasses, crutches and canes, automobile adaptive equipment, and medical equipment, implants, and supplies; training in the use of the foregoing.

Eligible applicants/beneficiaries: disabled veterans meeting specific criteria (*see NOTE preceding* **64.005**).

Range: $10 to $25,000. **Average:** $118.

Activity: FY 98, 2,800,000 prosthetic items and services provided.

HQ: Chief Consultant, Prosthetic and Sensory Aids Strategic Health Care Group (113), DVA, Washington, DC 20420. Phones: (202)273-8515; FAX (202)273-9110.

64.014   VETERANS STATE DOMICILIARY CARE

Assistance: formula grants (to 50 percent).

Purposes: to provide domiciliary care services in state homes to veterans disabled by age or illness, to assist them in attaining physical, mental, and social well-being through rehabilitative programs.

Eligible applicants: states.

Eligible beneficiaries: veterans meeting specific criteria (*see NOTE preceding* **64.005**) including state admission requirements.

Range: $5,000 to $3,600,000. **Average:** $427,000.

Activity: FY 98, 5,831 patients in 49 state homes; average daily census, 3,626.

HQ: Chief, State Home Per Diem Program, Assistant Chief Medical Director/Geriatrics and Extended Care (114B), DVA, Washington, DC 20420. Phone: (202)273-8538.

64.015   VETERANS STATE NURSING HOME CARE

Assistance: formula grants (to 50 percent).

Purposes: to provide skilled nursing home care and related medical services to veterans in state veterans homes.

Eligible applicants: states.

Eligible beneficiaries: veterans eligible for care in a DVA facility, needing nursing home care, and meeting other specific criteria (*see NOTE preceding* **64.005**).

Range: $417,000 to $7,879,000. **Average:** $2,410,000.

Activity: FY 98, 21,000 patients in 88 state homes; average daily census, 15,000.

HQ: same address/phone as **64.014**.

64.016   VETERANS STATE HOSPITAL CARE

Assistance: formula grants (to 50 percent).

Purposes: to provide hospital care to veterans in state veterans homes.

Eligible applicants: states.

Eligible beneficiaries: veterans meeting specific criteria (*see NOTE preceding* **64.005**) including state requirements.

Range: $42,000 to $2,900,000. **Average:** $790,000.

Activity: FY 98, 1,620 patients in 5 state homes; average daily census, 234.

HQ: same address/phone as **64.014**.

64.018   SHARING SPECIALIZED MEDICAL RESOURCES

Assistance: specialized services.

Purposes: to provide for exchanges between DVA and communities or mutual use of advanced medical techniques and specialized resources which otherwise might not be available to DVA or to the communities.

Eligible applicants: medical schools; state, local, public or private hospitals; clinics; research centers; blood and organ banks.

Eligible beneficiaries: patients in the DVA or community facilities.

Activity: FY 98, 550 sharing contracts.

HQ: Director, Sharing and Purchasing Office (175), Veterans Health Administration, DVA, 810 Vermont Ave. NW, Washington, DC 20420. Phone: (202) 273-8406.

64.019   VETERANS REHABILITATION—ALCOHOL AND DRUG DEPENDENCE ("Substance Abuse Treatment Program, Mental Health and Behavioral Sciences Service")

Assistance: specialized services.

Purposes: to provide medical, social, and vocational rehabilitation therapies to alcohol- and drug-dependent veterans, in DVA medical centers and clinics. Services include detoxification, substance abuse rehabilitation, individual and group and family therapy, psychotropic medications, psychiatric counseling, social services, vocational rehabilitation.

Eligible applicants/beneficiaries: veterans meeting specific criteria (*see NOTE preceding* **64.005**).

Activity: FY 98, 20,000 inpatients and 132,000 outpatients treated.

HQ: Director, Mental Health and Behavioral Sciences Services (11C), DVA, Washington, DC 20420. Phone: (202)273-8437.

64.022   VETERANS HOME BASED PRIMARY CARE

Assistance: specialized services.

Purposes: to provide primary health care services to veterans in their homes.

Eligible applicants/beneficiaries: veterans requiring intermittent skilled nursing care and related medical services, and meeting specific criteria (*see NOTE preceding* **64.005**).

Activity: FY 98, 6,348 veterans/day received home care.

HQ: Home Based Primary Care Program Coordinator, Geriatrics and Extended Care Strategic Healthcare Group (114), DVA, Washington, DC 20420. Phone: (202)273-6488, -8540. (Note: no field offices for this program.)

64.024   VA HOMELESS PROVIDERS GRANT AND PER DIEM PROGRAM

Assistance: project grants (65 percent).

Purposes: to establish new programs and service centers to provide supportive housing, centers, and services for homeless veterans. Funds may be used to: acquire, renovate, or alter facilities; purchase mobile service centers; purchase a maximum of 20 vans. Per diem payments may be provided on behalf of VA-referred or -authorized veterans. Operating costs may be partially supported with grant funds.

Eligible applicants/beneficiaries: project grants—public or private nonprofit entities. For per diem payments, programs must have been established after 10 November 1992.

Range: $13,000 to $541,000.

Activity: not quantified specifically.

HQ: Program Manager, Homeless Providers Grant and Per Diem Program, Mental Health Strategic Healthcare Group (116E), DVA, 810 Vermont Ave. NW, Washington, DC 20420. Phones: (202)273-8966, -8443; *toll-free*, (877) 322-0334. (Note: no field offices for this program.)

64.025   TRANSITIONAL HOUSING LOAN PROGRAM

Assistance: direct loans (2 years).

Purposes: to provide leased transitional housing exclusively for veterans in substance abuse treatment programs. Loans may cover such costs as residence start-up, furnishings, supplies, utility connection fees. Ineligible costs include major property improvements, new construction, permanent alterations. The interest rate is the rate at which DVA borrows funds from the U.S. Treasury.

Eligible applicants/beneficiaries: qualified nonprofit organizations.

Range/Average: to $4,500 per leased residence.

Activity: no loan awards to date.

HQ: Program Coordinator, Transitional Housing Loan Program, Office of Associate Director/Psychosocial Rehabilitation Services (302/116D), Veterans Affairs Medical Center, DVA, 100 Emancipation Dr., Hampton, VA 23667. Phone: (757)722-9961, ext.3628. (Note: no field offices for this program.)

VETERANS BENEFITS ADMINISTRATION

64.100   AUTOMOBILES AND ADAPTIVE EQUIPMENT FOR CERTAIN DISABLED VETERANS AND MEMBERS OF THE ARMED FORCES

Assistance: direct payments/specified use.

Purposes: to purchase automobiles or other conveyances with adaptive equipment for disabled veterans and servicepersons. Funds also may be used for repairs, replacements, or reinstallation. Adaptive equipment may be provided for no more than two conveyances during any four-year period, unless one of the vehicles becomes unavailable to the veteran.

Eligible applicants/beneficiaries: veterans with honorable service and servicepersons with a service-connected disability caused by loss of use or permanent loss of one or both feet, one or both hands, or a permanent impairment of vision of both eyes to a prescribed degree. Adaptive equipment—service-connected ankylosis of one or both knees or hips.

Range: no maximum for adaptive equipment; $8,000 maximum for automobile or other conveyance.

Activity: FY 98, 779 vehicles purchased.

HQ: DVA, Washington, DC 20420. Phone: (202)273-7210.

64.101 BURIAL EXPENSES ALLOWANCE FOR VETERANS

Assistance: direct payments/specified use.

Purposes: for the plot or internment expenses of certain veterans not buried in a national cemetery; for funeral and burial expenses of veterans whose death results from a service-connected disability; for transportation of the remains of service-connected, disabled veterans to a national cemetery. Headstones or markers and an American flag to drape the casket may also be provided.

Eligible applicants: the person bearing the veteran's burial expense or the funeral director, if unpaid.

Eligible beneficiaries: burial and plot allowances—on behalf of veterans discharged under other than dishonorable conditions and meeting the following criteria: discharged or released from active duty for a disability incurred or aggravated in line of duty; or, at time of death, entitled to compensation or pension or indigent or properly hospitalized at VA expense. In lieu of plot and burial allowances, the service-connected allowance is payable toward the burial expenses of veterans who died of a service-connected cause. Flags—next of kin, friend, or associate.

Range: to $150 for plot or interment expenses; to $300 for burial allowance if death is not service-connected; to $1,500 if death is service-connected.

Activity: FY 98, 84,000 burial allowances; 476,000 flags.

HQ: same address/phone as **64.100**.

64.102 COMPENSATION FOR SERVICE-CONNECTED DEATHS FOR VETERANS' DEPENDENTS
("Death Compensation")

Assistance: direct payments/unrestricted use.

Purposes: for dependents or survivors of veterans whose death resulted from a service-connected disability.

Eligible applicants/beneficiaries: unmarried surviving spouses, unmarried children, and dependent parent(s) of veterans deceased before January 1, 1957; compensation for later deaths is payable under Dependency and Indemnity Compensation (DIC) (see **64.110**).

Range: monthly, $87 for surviving spouses to $121 for widows or widowers with one child, plus $29 for each additional child; dependent parent(s), $75 for one alone, $80 for two—with additional $79 aid and attendance is required.

Activity: FY 98, benefits to 20 widows and 3,402 parents.

HQ: same address/phone as **64.100**.

64.103   LIFE INSURANCE FOR VETERANS ("GI Insurance")

Assistance: direct loans; insurance.

Purposes: to provide life insurance protection for veterans of WW-I and -II, the Korean conflict, and for those with service-connected disabilities, separated from active duty on April 25, 1951 or later; mortgage protection life insurance for veterans receiving specially adapted housing; policy loans at varying interest rates. The programs are closed for new issues except Service-Disabled Veterans Insurance and the Mortgage Protection Life Insurance.

Eligible applicants/beneficiaries: veterans may apply for either type of insurance. However, if the eligible applicant is mentally incompetent, a legal guardian may apply for Service-Disabled Veterans Insurance—benefits of which may also be granted under certain conditions for mentally incompetent veterans who were otherwise eligible for such insurance but, due to their incompetence, died without filing an application.

Range: N.A.

Activity: N.A.

HQ: DVA Regional Office and Insurance Center, P.O. Box 8079, Philadelphia, PA 19101. Phone: (800)669-8477.

64.104   PENSION FOR NON-SERVICE-CONNECTED DISABILITY FOR VETERANS

Assistance: direct payments/unrestricted use.

Purposes: for wartime veterans with total and permanent nonservice-connected disabilities. Income and asset restrictions are prescribed. Pension is not payable to those whose estates are so large that it is reasonable they use the estate for maintenance.

Eligible applicants/beneficiaries: veterans with 90 days or more of honorable active wartime service in the Armed Forces or, if less than 90 days, released or discharged from service because of a service-connected disability, or permanently and totally disabled for reasons not due to service.

Range: $8,778 annually, reduced by countable income for veteran alone ($14,647 if in need of aid and attendance, and $10,729 if housebound); $11,497 for a veteran with one dependent ($17,365 if in need of aid and attendance, and $13,448 if housebound) plus $1,496 for each additional dependent. Also, an additional $1,989 if a veteran of WW-I or Mexican Border Period.

Activity: FY 98, pensions to 397,000 veterans.

HQ: same address/phone as **64.100**.

64.105   PENSION TO VETERANS SURVIVING SPOUSES, AND CHILDREN ("Death Pension")

Assistance: direct payments/unrestricted use.

Purposes: for needy dependents of deceased wartime veterans whose deaths were not due to service. Income restrictions apply; pensions are not payable to those whose estates are so large that it is reasonable they use the estate for maintenance.

Eligible applicants/beneficiaries: unmarried surviving spouses and children of deceased veterans with at least 90 days of honorable active wartime service or, if less than 90 days, discharged for a service-connected disability. A child must be unmarried and under age 18, between 18 and 23 if in school, or disabled before 18 and continuously incapable of self-support.

Range: $5,884 annually, reduced by countable income for a spouse without children ($9,409 if in need of aid and attendance, and $7,194 if housebound), $7,707 for spouse with one child ($11,227 if in need of aid and attendance, and $9,011 if housebound), plus $1,496 for each additional child.

Activity: FY 98, 299,000 cases.

HQ: same address/phone as **64.100**.

64.106   SPECIALLY ADAPTED HOUSING FOR DISABLED VETERANS ("Paraplegic Housing")

Assistance: direct payments/specified use (50 percent).

Purposes: to provide suitable housing with special fixtures and facilities to disabled veterans, including construction, remodeling, or mortgage reduction payments.

Eligible applicants/beneficiaries: veterans with permanent, total, and compensable disabilities.

Range: 50 percent of cost to purchase, construct, or remodel a suitable housing unit, with $43,000 maximum; to $8,250 for special residential adaptations.

Activity: FY 98, 478 grants.

HQ: DVA, Washington, DC 20420. Phone: (202)273-7355.

64.109   VETERANS COMPENSATION FOR SERVICE-CONNECTED DISABILITY

Assistance: direct payments/unrestricted use.

Purposes: for disabled veterans, in amounts reflecting the average impairment in the earning capacity the disability would cause in civilian occupations.

Eligible applicants/beneficiaries: persons suffering disabilities during service in the Armed Forces, incurred in or aggravated by service in the line of duty. Separation from service must have been under other than dishonorable conditions.

Range: monthly, from $96 for a 10 percent degree of disability, to $5,688 for very severe disabilities.

Activity: FY 98, 2,270,000 cases.

HQ: same address/phone as **64.100**.

64.110   VETERANS DEPENDENCY AND INDEMNITY COMPENSATION FOR SERVICE-CONNECTED DEATH ("DIC")

Assistance: direct payments/unrestricted use.

Purposes: for dependents of deceased veterans whose death resulted from a service-connected disability or while on active duty.

Eligible applicants/beneficiaries: unmarried and certain remarried surviving spouses, unmarried children, and parent(s) of veterans deceased on or after January 1, 1957 because of a service-connected disability or while on active duty. Survivors of veterans deceased prior to January 1, 1957 may elect to receive DIC. DIC payments may be authorized for surviving spouse and children of certain veterans totally service-connected disabled at time of death and whose deaths did not result from their service-connected disability. Income restrictions apply for surviving parents.

Range: monthly, from $365 for one child when no spouse is entitled; $861 to $1,966 for a surviving spouse, with $217 additional if in need of aid and attendance, or $105 if housebound; surviving spouse is entitled to an additional $217 monthly for each child under age 18; parents, $5 to $418 depending on income and whether single or married, with $224 additional if in need aid and attendance.

Activity: FY 98, 300,000 cases.

HQ: same address/phone as **64.100**.

64.114   VETERANS HOUSING—GUARANTEED AND INSURED LOANS ("VA Home Loans")

Assistance: guaranteed/insured loans.

Purposes: for housing for veterans, certain service personnel, or their surviving unremarried spouses—covering home construction or purchases, repairs, improvements, or refinancing. Eligible loans include those covering standard single-family units, condominiums, or manufactured homes and lots—for their own use; also, for solar heating or cooling or other energy conservation improvements. Applicants must have sufficient present and prospective income to meet loan repayment terms, and a satisfactory credit record.

Eligible applicants/beneficiaries: veterans meeting specific criteria (*see NOTE preceding* **64.005**). Also, unremarried surviving spouses of eligible veterans deceased in service or as a result of service-connected disabilities.

Range/Average: to 50 percent for loans of $45,000 or less; $22,500 for loans between $45,000 and $56,250; $36,000 or 40 percent, whichever is less, for loans between $56,250 to $144,000; $50,750 or 25 percent, whichever is less, for loans greater than $144,000 or for VA loan refinancing.

Activity: FY 98, 369,000 insured loans.

HQ: DVA, Washington, DC 20420. Phone: (202)273-7390.

64.115   VETERANS INFORMATION AND ASSISTANCE ("Veterans Services")

Assistance: advisory services/counseling.

Purposes: to provide information and assistance to all veterans—including of the PHS, NOAA, and certain WW-II Merchant Marines—relating to the full range of benefits to which they are entitled.

Eligible applicants/beneficiaries: generally, veterans, their dependents or beneficiaries, their representatives or other interested parties.

Activity: FY 98, 10,500,000 contacts.

HQ: same address/phone as **64.100**.

64.116   VOCATIONAL REHABILITATION FOR DISABLED VETERANS

Assistance: direct payments/unrestricted use; direct payments/specified use; direct loans; advisory services/counseling.

Purposes: to provide counseling, no-interest loans, and payments for tuition, fees, related costs, and subsistence for up to four years to disabled veterans and hospitalized service members pending discharge, to obtain vocational training and suitable employment—or to achieve maximum independence in daily living.

Eligible applicants/beneficiaries: veterans of WW-II and later service, with a compensable service-connected disability; certain hospitalized service members pending discharge or release from service, in need of vocational rehabilitation because of an employment handicap.

Range: full cost of tuition, books, fees, supplies, and services; monthly full-time allowances range from $420 for a single veteran to $615 for a veteran with two dependents, plus $45 for each additional dependent; no-interest loans of up to $841 and a work-study allowance not higher than 25 times the minimum hourly wage times the number of weeks of the veteran's period of enrollment.

Activity: FY 98, 53,000 participants, 4,290 loans, 9,289 participants rehabilitated.

HQ: Vocational Rehabilitation and Counseling Service (28), Veterans Benefits Administration, DVA, Washington, DC 20420. Phone: (202)273-7419.

64.117   SURVIVORS AND DEPENDENTS EDUCATIONAL ASSISTANCE

Assistance: direct payments/specified use (to 45 months).

Purposes: for dependents of deceased or disabled veterans, to cover tuition, books, subsistence, etc. Education must be completed within ten years of the date that the disability was incurred, or from the date of death of the veteran.

Eligible applicants/beneficiaries: spouses, surviving spouses, and children between age 18 and 26—of veterans deceased because of service-connected disabilities; of living veterans with service-connected disabilities considered permanently and totally disabling; of those deceased because of any cause while such disabilities were in existence; of service members listed for more than 90 days as missing in action; or, of prisoners of war.

Range: monthly, institutional training—full time, $485; three-quarters time, $365; half-time, $242. Tutorial assistance, to $1,200. Work-study allowances may also be paid.

Activity: FY 93, 43,000 participants.

HQ: Central Office, DVA, Washington, DC 20420. Phone: (202)273-7132.

64.118 VETERANS HOUSING—DIRECT LOANS FOR CERTAIN DISABLED VETERANS

Assistance: direct loans (below-market interest).

Purposes: for disabled veterans to purchase, construct, or improve homes, including farm residences, with specially adapted features and facilities. Loans are coordinated with grants obtained under **64.106**. It must be medically feasible for the veteran to reside in the proposed or existing housing unit, and in the locality; the housing unit must be so adapted as to suit the veteran's needs; it must also be financially feasible for the veteran to acquire it with the assistance provided by the grant.

Eligible applicants/beneficiaries: disabled veterans serving on active duty on or after September 16, 1940.

Range: to $33,000. **Average:** $33,000.

Activity: FY 98, no loans.

HQ: same address/phone as **64.114**.

64.119 VETERANS HOUSING—MANUFACTURED HOME LOANS

Assistance: guaranteed/insured loans (to 95 percent/15-25 years).

Purposes: for manufactured homes, or homes and lots, or lots only—purchased or refinanced for their own use by veterans, service members, and certain unremarried surviving spouses of veterans.

Eligible applicants/beneficiaries: same as for **64.114**.

Range: maximum guaranteed amount, $20,000 or 40 percent of the loan, whichever is less. **Average:** $30,000.

Activity: FY 98, no loans.

HQ: same address/phone as **64.114**.

64.120 POST-VIETNAM ERA VETERANS' EDUCATIONAL ASSISTANCE ("Voluntary-Contributory Matching Program")

Assistance: direct payments/specified use.

Purposes: for educational, vocational, or professional training to persons entering the Armed Services after 31 December 1976 and before 1 July 1985. Payments are provided on the basis of a $2 to $1 match of federal to participant contribution. Enrollments in avocational or recreational courses may not be approved. Participants must have satisfactorily contributed to the program, consisting of monthly deduction of $25 to $100 from military pay, up to a maximum of $2,700, for deposit in a special training fund. Participants may make lump-sum contributions.

Eligible applicants/beneficiaries: basically, veterans serving honorably on active duty for more than 180 days beginning on or after 1 January 1977, or discharged after such date because of a service-connected disability; veterans serving for more than 180 days and continuing on active duty and completing their first period of obligated service (or six years of active duty, whichever comes first). No persons on active duty may initiate contributions to this program after March 31, 1987. The following veterans may elect Montgomery GI Bill benefits (see **64.124**), provided their basic pay was reduced by $1,200: those on active duty on 30 September 1990 or after 29 November 1993 and involuntarily separated from active duty after 2 February 1991; those voluntarily separated after 23 October 1992, under the Voluntary Separation Incentive or the Special Separation Benefit.

Range: $8,100 maximum; $1,200 maximum tutorial assistance. Work study allowances may also be provided.

Activity: FY 98, 6,148 participants.

HQ: same address/phone as **64.117.**

64.123 VOCATIONAL TRAINING FOR CERTAIN VETERANS RECEIVING VA PENSION

Assistance: direct payments/specified use; advisory services/counseling.

Purposes: to assist new pension recipients in obtaining vocational training for up to 24 months. The enrollment period ended 1 January 1996. Following or instead of training, the veteran may receive up to 18 months of employment assistance. Certain veterans may receive an initial supply of goods and commodities to start a business.

Eligible applicants/beneficiaries: veterans pensioned by DVA before 1 January 1996, and for whom vocational training is found feasible. (NOTE: DVA will not process applications received on or after 31 December 1995.)

Range: actual cost of training program, including books, tuition, supplies, and fees (not including pension allowance).

Activity: N.A.

HQ: same address/phone as **64.116.**

64.124 ALL-VOLUNTEER FORCE EDUCATIONAL ASSISTANCE ("Montgomery GI Bill Active Duty" - "MGIB" - "Chapter 30")

Assistance: direct payments/specified use.

Purposes: for the educational expenses of veterans enrolling in approved educational, professional, or vocational programs, including certain flight training. Participants must have agreed to reductions in their military pay while in service, as nonrefundable contributions toward their participation. $100 monthly is deducted from the basic pay for the first twelve months, unless the veteran specifically elects not to participate in the program; such deductions are nonrefundable except in the case of the death of the veteran within a certain time frame. DOD may provide supplementary contributions to participants' funds as inducements to reenlist, paid while they are enrolled in educational programs. Applicants must complete their education within ten years after release from service, with certain exceptions.

Eligible applicants/beneficiaries: basically, veterans with an honorary discharge and military personnel on active duty on or after 1 July 1985, and with a minimum of two years service. Participants without the required obligated service must have been discharged for a service-connected disability, for hardship, for a pre-existing medical or physical or mental condition, or for involuntary separation due to reduction in force. Certain others may also meet eligibility requirements as described in **64.120**; full criteria may be obtained from DVA.

Range: to $19,000 in basic assistance; work-study allowances based on minimum wage rates; tutorial assistance, to $1,200.

Activity: FY 98, 297,000 trainees.

HQ: same address/phone as **64.117.**

64.125 VOCATIONAL AND EDUCATIONAL COUNSELING FOR SERVICEMEMBERS AND VETERANS ("Chapter 36 Counseling")

Assistance: advisory services/counseling.

Purposes: to provide vocational and educational counseling by psychologists to servicemembers or veterans, in the identification of personal objectives including the development of employment plans.

Eligible applicants/beneficiaries: servicemembers applying within 180 days of projected discharge or release from active duty; veterans within one year of discharge or release.

Activity: FY 99, 13,000 participants.

HQ: same address/phone as **64.116.**

64.126 NATIVE AMERICAN VETERAN DIRECT LOAN PROGRAM ("VA Native American Veterans Housing Loan Program")

Assistance: direct loans.

Purposes: for certain native American veterans to purchase, construct, improve, or refinance homes that they will occupy, including manufactured homes, located on trust lands.

Eligible applicants/beneficiaries: qualifying native American veterans so recognized by a federally recognized tribal government, and their surviving unremarried native American spouses.

Range/Average: to $80,000 (more in high-cost areas).

Activity: FY 98, 17 loans.

HQ: DVA, Washington, DC 20420. Phone: (202)273-7377.

64.127 MONTHLY ALLOWANCE FOR CHILDREN OF VIETNAM VETERANS BORN WITH SPINA BIFIDA

Assistance: direct payments/unrestricted use.

Purposes: to provide financial assistance to children of Vietnam veterans, born with spina bifida.

Eligible applicants/beneficiaries: natural children of Vietnam veterans, born with spina bifida, except spina bifida occulta, regardless of age or marital status, conceived after the date on which the veteran first served in Vietnam (between 9 January 1962 and 2 May 1975).

Range: $208 to $1,242 monthly, based on the degree of disability.

Activity: new program in FY 98; 633 children assisted.

HQ: same address/phone as **64.100.**

64.128   VOCATIONAL TRAINING AND REHABILITATION FOR VIETNAM VETERANS' CHILDREN WITH SPINA BIFIDA

Assistance: direct payments/specified use.

Purposes: to provide vocational training and rehabilitation to certain children of Vietnam veterans, born with spina bifida.

Eligible applicants/beneficiaries: same as for **64.127**. DVA must determine that it is feasible for the child to achieve a vocational goal within 2 to 4 years.

Range/Average: N.A.

Activity: new program in FY 98.

HQ: same address/phone as **64.116**.

NATIONAL CEMETERY SYSTEM

64.201   NATIONAL CEMETERIES

Assistance: specialized services.

Purposes: to provide memorial plots or interment of deceased veterans, members of the Armed Forces whose service was terminated other than dishonorably, and certain dependents—in national cemeteries.

Eligible applicants/beneficiaries: next of kin or, if there is no living kin, a friend of the decedent or public assistance officer on their behalf, of deceased: veterans, members of the Armed Forces (Army, Navy, Air Force, Marine Corps, Coast Guard) dying while on active duty; members of the Reserve or Army or Air National Guard dying while on active duty for training; 20-year reservists and certain of their dependents; enlisted personnel entering military duty after September 7, 1980, and/or becoming commissioned officers after October 16, 1981, and serving for a minimum of two years; spouses of eligible veterans or members of the Armed Forces lost or buried at sea or determined to be permanently missing or missing in action; minor children and certain unmarried adult children of eligible veterans; U.S. citizens serving in the Armed Forces of any government allied with the U.S. during any war, and holding U.S. citizenship at time of death; certain commissioned officers of the PHS, NOAA, and others.

Activity: FY 98, 77,000 interments in the 116 national cemeteries under DVA jurisdiction.

HQ: Director, Office of Field Operations (401), National Cemetery System, DVA, 810 Vermont Ave. NW, Washington, DC 20420. Phone: (202)273-5226.

64.202   PROCUREMENT OF HEADSTONES AND MARKERS AND/OR PRESIDENTIAL MEMORIAL CERTIFICATES

Assistance: direct payments/specified use; specialized services.

Purposes: for headstones and markers for the unmarked graves or memorial plots in national, post, and state veterans cemeteries, or for the unmarked graves or memorial plots in private cemeteries—of deceased eligible veterans; also, costs of transportation and installation and maintenance, replacement of illegible markers. Presidential Memorial Certificates may also be provided.

Eligible applicants: private cemetery burials—next of kin or nonmembers of the deceased's family, after ascertaining that the grave is unmarked and that a government monument is preferred over a privately purchased one. Monuments must be of a type permitted on the grave of the deceased. If burial or memorial plot is in a national cemetery or state veterans cemetery, the director of the cemetery orders the headstone or marker, after completion of the interment in the cemetery, or upon need for replacement.

Eligible beneficiaries: deceased veterans of wartime or peacetime service, discharged under conditions other than dishonorable; members of the Reserve and the Army and Air National Guard dying while performing or as a result of performing active duty for training; commissioned officers of the PHS and the NOAA, Merchant Marine Seamen, and certain others participating in wartime activities; veterans of Operation Desert Storm. Qualifying service after September 7, 1980 must be for a minimum of 24 months or completed for special circumstances.

Activity: FY 98, 346,000 applications; 346,000 markers or headstones, and 316,000 Certificates.

HQ: Director, Memorial Programs Service (403), National Cemetery System, DVA, 810 Vermont Ave. NW, Washington, DC 20420-0001. Phones: (202) 565-4200; *application assistance, tracer information, problems with shipments arriving C.O.D., eligibility matters, inscription matters, problems relating to quality of headstones and markers,* (800)697-6947; *Presidential Certificates,* (202)565-4259.

64.203   STATE CEMETERY GRANTS

Assistance: project grants (100 percent/to 3 years).

Purposes: to establish, construct, expand, or improve state veterans cemeteries for the interment of eligible veterans and their dependents.

Eligible applicants/beneficiaries: states.

Range: $3,450 to $11,856,000. **Average:** $672,000.

Activity: FY 00 estimate, 15 to 20 applications.

HQ: Director, State Cemetery Grants Service (401C), National Cemetery System, DVA, 810 Vermont Ave. NW, Washington, DC 20420. Phones: (202)565-6152, -6801; FAX (202)565-6141. (Note: no field offices for this program.)

ENVIRONMENTAL PROTECTION AGENCY

66.001   AIR POLLUTION CONTROL PROGRAM SUPPORT

Assistance: formula grants (to 60 percent).

Purposes: pursuant to the Clean Air Act as amended, to plan, establish, improve, and maintain air pollution prevention and control programs; for personnel training. Construction costs are ineligible for funding.

Eligible applicants/beneficiaries: municipal, intermunicipal, state, recognized tribal, and interstate agencies, including possessions and territories.

Range: $7,500 to $6,000,000. **Average:** $900,000.

Activity: not quantified specifically.

HQ: National Air Grant Coordinator, Office of Air and Radiation (6102A), EPA, Washington, DC 20460. Phone: (202)564-1349.

66.009   AIR INFORMATION CENTER

Assistance: technical information.

Purposes: pursuant to the Clean Air Act as amended, to provide information on the published literature on air pollution control. Literature searches are made.

Eligible applicants/beneficiaries: state and local governmental air pollution control agencies; territories and possessions; nonprofit citizens environmental groups; foreign governments; EPA grantees and on-site contractors.

Activity: annually, 1,500 requests processed.

HQ: Librarian, Library Services Office (MD-35), EPA, Research Triangle Park, NC 27711. Phone: (919)541-2777. (Note: no field offices for this program.)

66.032   STATE INDOOR RADON GRANTS
("SIRG")

Assistance: project grants (50 percent; tribes, 95 percent).

Purposes: pursuant to the Indoor Radon Abatement Act and TSCA, to develop and operate programs and projects to reduce radon risks. Eligible activities include radon surveys, public information and educational materials, radon control programs, purchase and maintenance of analytic equipment, training, administrative costs, data storage and management, mitigation demonstrations, toll-free hotlines, and promotion of environmental justice through outreach to low-income and culturally-diverse populations. Financial assistance may be provided to individuals only if such costs relate to demonstration projects or to the purchase of measurement devices.

Eligible applicants: states, territories and possessions, tribes.

Eligible beneficiaries: local, municipal, district, or areawide organizations; colleges and universities; nonprofit organizations; low-income persons, homeowners.

Range: $5,000 to $500,000. **Average:** $150,000.

Activity: 47 states, 35 tribal nations with radon programs.

HQ: Indoor Environments Division (6604J), Office of Radiation and Indoor Air, EPA, 401 M St. SW, Washington, DC 20460. Phone: (202)564-9439.

66.033   OZONE TRANSPORT

Assistance: project grants (60-100 percent/2 years).

Purposes: to develop or recommend regional air quality control implementation plans, pursuant to Section 106 (interstate pollution) or Section 111 (interstate ozone pollution) of the Clean Air Act of 1963 as amended. Funds may be used to support interstate pollution projects.

Eligible applicants/beneficiaries: governor-designated state agencies or commissions representing affected states and political subdivisions.

Range: $10,000 to $400,000. **Average:** $200,000.

Activity: new program in FY 97.

HQ: Office of Air and Radiation (6102), EPA, 401 M St. SW, Washington, DC 20460. Phone: (202)260-6877.

66.419 WATER POLLUTION CONTROL—STATE AND INTERSTATE PROGRAM SUPPORT
("Section 106 Grants")

Assistance: formula grants (100 percent).

Purposes: pursuant to the Clean Water Act as amended, to prevent and abate surface and ground water pollution from point and nonpoint sources— including planning, monitoring, assessments, permitting, studies, surveillance and enforcement, training, technical assistance, and public information; hazardous materials spills response. Funds may not be used for waste treatment plant construction, operation, or maintenance.

Eligible applicants/beneficiaries: state, interstate, territorial, tribal agencies.

Range: $60,000 to $4,000,000.

Activity: annually, 62 awards.

HQ: Office of Wastewater Management (4201), Office of Water, EPA, Washington, DC 20460. Phones: State and Interstate Coordinator, (202)260-6742; Tribal Coordinator, (202)260-5828.

66.432 STATE PUBLIC WATER SYSTEM SUPERVISION

Assistance: formula grants (75 percent).

Purposes: to develop and implement public water system supervision programs adequate to enforce Safe Drinking Water Act (SDWA) provisions, including program plan development, data management, system inventories, technical assistance, and enforcement.

Eligible applicants/beneficiaries: state agencies, territories and possessions, tribes qualifying as states.

Range: $123,000 to $5,674,000. **Average:** $1,674,000.

Activity: FY 98, 56 grants.

HQ: Office of Ground Water and Drinking Water (4604), Office of Water, EPA, Washington, DC 20460. Phone: (202)260-5551.

66.433 STATE UNDERGROUND WATER SOURCE PROTECTION

Assistance: formula grants (75 percent; tribes, 90 percent).

Purposes: to develop and implement underground injection control programs to implement SDWA provisions. Funds may be used for such purposes as plan development, data management, identification of aquifers, technical assistance, public participation, enforcement activities.

Eligible applicants/beneficiaries: states, tribes qualifying as states.

Range: $32,000 to $996,000. **Average:** $175,000.

Activity: FY 98, funding to 43 states and territories with primary responsibility for 36 full and 7 partial programs.

HQ: Regulatory Implementation Branch, Implementation and Assistance Division, Office of Ground Water and Drinking Water, Office of Water (4606), EPA, 401 M St. SW, Washington, DC 20460. Phone: (202)260-4891.

66.454 WATER QUALITY MANAGEMENT PLANNING ("Section 205(j)(2)")

Assistance: formula grants (100 percent).

Purposes: pursuant to the Clean Water Act as amended, for water quality management planning. States must allocate 40 percent of funds to regional and interstate agencies. Program examples: performing waste load allocations; point and nonpoint source planning.

Eligible applicants/beneficiaries: state agencies.

Range: $100,000 to $2,500,000. **Average:** $250,000.

Activity: FY 98, 57 state and territorial grants awarded.

HQ: Assessment and Watershed Protection Division (4503F), Office of Water, EPA, 401 M St. SW, Washington, DC 20460. Phone: (301)694-7329.

66.456 NATIONAL ESTUARY PROGRAM

Assistance: project grants (75 percent/to 3 years).

Purposes: pursuant to the Clean Water Act as amended, to develop comprehensive conservation and management plans to protect and restore the coastal resources of 28 estuaries holding priority for funding. Funds must be used to develop master environmental plans based on relationships between pollutant loading and ecological impacts. Limited demonstration actions may be funded.

Eligible applicants/beneficiaries: within the priority geographic areas—regional, interstate, state water pollution control agencies; state coastal zone management agencies; public or private nonprofit organizations; individuals.

Range: $10,000 to $795,000. **Average:** $100,000.

Activity: N.A.

HQ: Director, Oceans and Coastal Protection Division, Office of Wetlands, Oceans, and Watersheds Protection (4504F), Office of Water, EPA, Washington, DC 20460. Phone: (202)260-1952.

66.458 CAPITALIZATION GRANTS FOR STATE REVOLVING FUNDS ("State Revolving Fund")

Assistance: formula grants (80 percent).

Purposes: pursuant to the Clean Water Act as amended, to establish state revolving loan funds to finance wastewater treatment facilities and other water quality management activities. Capitalization grants deposited in the revolving funds may be used to provide loans to finance construction of publicly owned wastewater treatment works, to execute a nonpoint source management program, and to develop and execute estuary conservation and management plans.

Eligible applicants: states, territories and possessions, tribes.

Eligible beneficiaries: community, intermunicipal, and interstate agencies.

Range: $10,000,000 to $216,000,000. **Average:** $30,000,000.

Activity: FY 99 estimate, grants to 50 states and PR.

HQ: State Revolving Fund Branch, Municipal Support Division (4204), Office of Wastewater Management, EPA, Washington, DC 20460. Phone: (202)260-7366.

66.460 NONPOINT SOURCE IMPLEMENTATION GRANTS ("Section 319 Program")

Types: formula grants (60 percent; tribes, 90 percent).

Purposes: pursuant to the Clean Water Act, to implement EPA-approved nonpoint source management programs. Project examples: "best management practices" (BMP) installation for animal wastes and sediment, pesticide, and fertilizer control; design and implementation of BMP systems for stream, lake, and estuary watersheds; basin-wide landowner education programs.

Eligible applicants: states, territories and possessions, tribes.

Eligible beneficiaries: community, intermunicipal, interstate, and intrastate agencies; public and private nonprofit organizations.

Range: states, territories, $539,000 to $10,649,000; tribes, $45,000 to $55,000. **Average:** states, territories, $4,000,000; tribes, $50,000

Activity: grants to all states and selected tribes.

HQ: Program Implementation Team, Nonpoint Source Control Branch, Assessment and Watershed Protection Division, Office of Wetlands, Oceans and Watersheds (4503-F), EPA, 401 M St. SW, Washington, DC 20460. Phone: (202)260-7112.

66.461 WETLANDS PROTECTION—DEVELOPMENT GRANTS

Assistance: project grants (75 percent).

Purposes: pursuant to the Clean Water Act as amended, to develop new or enhance existing wetlands protection management and restoration programs. Grant funds may not be used for operating costs.

Eligible applicants/beneficiaries: state, interstate, local, tribal agencies.

Range: $1,500 to $489,000.

Activity: not quantified specifically.

HQ: Wetlands Division, Office of Wetlands, Oceans and Watersheds (4502F), EPA, 401 M St. SW, Washington, DC 20460. Phone: (202)260-6218.

66.463 NATIONAL POLLUTANT DISCHARGE ELIMINATION SYSTEM RELATED STATE PROGRAM GRANTS ("Water Quality Cooperative Agreements")

Assistance: project grants (100 percent/to 2 years).

Purposes: pursuant to the Clean Water Act as amended, to develop, implement, and demonstrate innovative approaches relating to the National Pollutant Discharge Elimination System (NPDES) program, such as watershed approaches for combined sewer overflow and storm water discharge problems, pretreatment and sludge program activities, and alternative ways to measure the effectiveness of point source programs.

Eligible applicants/beneficiaries: state, interstate agencies; tribes.

Range/Average: $25,000 to $500,000.

Activity: not quantified specifically.

HQ: Office of Wastewater Management (4203), EPA, 401 M St. SW, Washington, DC 20460. Phone: (202)260-5854.

66.466   CHESAPEAKE BAY PROGRAM

Assistance: project grants (50-95 percent/to 5 years).

Purposes: pursuant to the Clean Water Act, for research, experiments, investigations, training, demonstrations, surveys, or studies related to reducing pollution and improving the quality of living resources in the Chesapeake Bay (95 percent federal funding); for the implementation of Chesapeake Bay interstate management programs (50 percent funding).

Eligible applicants/beneficiaries: within the Chesapeake Bay basin—state water pollution control agencies, interstate agencies, other public and private nonprofit organizations, individuals.

Range: $25,000 to $2,800,000.

Activity: not quantified specifically.

HQ: Office of Water (4101), EPA, Washington, DC 20460. Phone: (202)260-5700.

66.467   WASTEWATER OPERATOR TRAINING GRANT PROGRAM (TECHNICAL ASSISTANCE)

Assistance: project grants (75 percent/to 3 years).

Purposes: for pilot programs to provide technical assistance to operations and maintenance (O&M) personnel at publicly owned wastewater treatment works.

Eligible applicants/beneficiaries: state agencies; possessions, territories, and tribes; state-designated nonprofit agencies.

Range/Average: $35,000.

Activity: FY 98, 999 facilities assisted

HQ: Municipal Support Branch (4204), Office of Wastewater Management, EPA, 401 M St. SW, Washington, DC 20460. Phone: (202)260-5806.

66.468   CAPITALIZATION GRANTS FOR DRINKING WATER STATE REVOLVING FUND
("Drinking Water State Revolving Fund")

Assistance: formula grants (80 percent).

Purposes: pursuant to SDWA, to capitalize drinking water state revolving funds to finance infrastructure needed to achieve compliance, through loans or other assistance; to establish new programs emphasizing prevention of contamination through source water protection and enhanced water systems management.

Eligible applicants: capitalization grants—states, PR. Direct grants—DC, territories, tribes.

Eligible beneficiaries: loans—public or private nonprofit community drinking water systems.

Range: $7,464,000 to $89,817,000. **Average:** $24,300,000.

Activity: new program in FY 97. FY 99, 51 grants.

HQ: Implementation and Assistance Division, Office of Ground Water and Drinking Water, EPA, Washington, DC 20460. Phones: (202)260-3980; Web, www.epa.gov/safewater/dwsrf.htmp

66.469 GREAT LAKES PROGRAM

Assistance: project grants (to 95 percent/to 2 years); use of property, facilities, and equipment; specialized services; technical information.

Purposes: pursuant to the Clean Water Act, to restore and maintain the chemical, physical, and biological integrity of the Great Lakes Basin Ecosystem. Funds may be used for such activities as contaminated sediment assessment, pollution prevention, habitat protection and restoration, contaminant monitoring of lake and tributary waters, information management.

Eligible applicants/beneficiaries: state, interstate, and other public and private nonprofit agencies; institutions; organizations; individuals.

Range: $5,000 to $500,000.

Activity: new program listing in 1997.

HQ: Great Lakes National Program Office (G-17J), EPA, 77 W. Jackson Blvd., Chicago, IL 60604-3590. Phones: (312)886-4013; Internet, URL, http://www.epa.gov/glnpo/fund/glf.html (Note: the field office is the headquarters for this program.)

66.500 ENVIRONMENTAL PROTECTION—CONSOLIDATED RESEARCH

Assistance: project grants (100 percent/to 5 years).

Purposes: pursuant to the Clean Air Act, SDWA, Resource Conservation and Recovery Act (RCRA), TSCA, Solid Waste Disposal Act (SWDA), CERCLA, and other laws—for research and demonstration projects in pollution control techniques, and pollution control of energy systems including evaluations of the economic, health, social, governmental, and environmental consequences of alternative approaches. The Science to Achieve Results Program (STAR) gives priority to research concerning safe drinking water, air pollutants, human health risk assessments, ecological risk assessment, emerging issues, and new pollution prevention technologies; graduate fellowships in environmental sciences and engineering; environmental research centers; training.

Eligible applicants/beneficiaries: state and local governments, territories and possessions, IHEs, hospitals, laboratories, nonprofit institutions, individuals.

Range: $6,000 to $1,500,000; fellowships, $6,000 to $34,000 annually; new grants, $150,000 to $950,000; new centers, to $1,500,000. **Average:** $260,000.

Activity: annually, 120 fellowships, 175 competitive grants.

HQ: Director, National Center for Environmental Research and Quality Assurance (8701), EPA, Washington, DC 20460. Phones: (800)490-9194; Internet, http://www.epa.gov/ncerqa *Grants management information*: Grants Administration Division (3903F), same address. Phone: (no number provided.)

66.508 SENIOR ENVIRONMENTAL EMPLOYMENT PROGRAM ("SEE")

Assistance: project grants (100 percent/1-3 years).

Purposes: to employ older Americans to provide technical assistance in pollution prevention, abatement, and control projects. Funded project examples: nonagricultural pesticide surveys; monitoring asbestos compliance in schools; research, general administrative, and clerical tasks; review and monitoring of the import car program.

Eligible applicants: nonprofit organizations designated by DOL under provisions of the Older Americans Act of 1965.

Eligible beneficiaries: individuals age 55 or older; federal, state, and local environmental agencies.

Range: $3,000 to $2,296,000. **Average:** $169,000.

Activity: FY 99 estimate, 500 cooperative agreements.

HQ: Director, SEE Program (3641), Human Resources Staff, Office of Administration and Resources Management, EPA, Washington, DC 20460. Phone: (202)260-4331. (Note: no field offices for this program.)

66.600 ENVIRONMENTAL PROTECTION CONSOLIDATED GRANTS— PROGRAM SUPPORT ("Consolidated Program Support Grants")

Assistance: formula grants.

Purposes: to provide an alternative funding mechanism to develop an integrated approach to pollution control programs, by consolidating activities funded under programs **66.001, 66.419, 66.432, 66.433, 66.454, 66.700, 66.801**. Those eligible for two or more of the programs may consolidate applications into a single application and receive a single total award. Funding for this program is the aggregate total of the programs that may be consolidated; it is not appropriated separately.

Eligible applicants/beneficiaries: state and local agencies.

Range: $806,000 to $3,517,000. **Average:** $1,869,000.

Activity: FY 98, 11 consolidated awards.

HQ: Grants Administration Division (PM 3903R), EPA, Washington, DC 20460. Phone: (202)564-5325. (*NOTE: for information on individual programs contact HQ for each respective program.*)

66.604 ENVIRONMENTAL JUSTICE GRANTS TO SMALL COMMUNITY GROUPS ("EJGSC")

Assistance: project grants (100 percent).

Purposes: pursuant to the Clean Air Act, SDWA, TSCA, SWDA, CERCLA, and other laws—for projects to design, demonstrate, or disseminate practices, methods, or techniques related to environmental justice—specifically, for: education and awareness programs; local monitoring and pollution prevention; technical assistance in gathering and interpreting existing justice survey and assessment data; technical assistance to obtain available public information; training; development of education tools and materials, field methods; faculty development.

Eligible applicants/beneficiaries: incorporated community-based nonprofit organizations; tribal governments. Individuals may apply through organizations, institutions, or governments.

Range/Average: to $20,000.

Activity: FY 99, 85 grants.

HQ: Director, Office of Environmental Justice (2201A), EPA, 401 M St. SW, Washington, DC 20460. Phones: (202)564-2515; Environmental Justice Hotline, (800)962-6215.

66.605 PERFORMANCE PARTNERSHIP GRANTS ("PPGs")

Assistance: formula grants; project grants (cost sharing).

Purposes: to provide an alternative assistance delivery mechanism to give grant recipients greater flexibility in addressing environmental priorities; to improve environmental performance; to achieve savings in administrative costs; and, to strengthen partnerships between EPA and grant recipients. For application and administrative purposes, recipients may combine two or more of the 17 available EPA grant programs—e.g., pollution control, hazardous waste management, wetlands development, radon control, lead-based paint activities, pesticides enforcement. Funding for this program is included in the programs that may be consolidated; it is not appropriated separately.

Eligible applicants/beneficiaries: state, interstate, and local agencies; territories; federally recognized tribes.

Range/Average: N.A.

Activity: new program listing in 1997.

HQ: *contact* Regional Grants Management Offices listed in Part IV. Phone: *for regulations,* Internet, http://www.epa.gov/ow/ppgguide.html

66.606 SURVEYS, STUDIES, INVESTIGATIONS AND SPECIAL PURPOSE GRANTS

Assistance: project grants (to 5 years).

Purposes: pursuant to the Clean Air Act, SDWA, TSCA, SWDA, and other laws—for surveys, studies, investigations, and special purpose assistance associated with air quality, acid deposition, drinking water quality, hazardous waste, toxic substances, and pesticides; to develop and demonstrate pollution control techniques; to evaluate the economic and social consequences of alternative mechanisms.

Eligible applicants/beneficiaries: states, tribes, territories, possessions; public and private nonprofit IHEs, hospitals, laboratories, other institutions; individuals; profit organizations.

Range: $1,000 to $500,000.

Activity: new program listing in 1997. FY 98, 1,200 awards.

HQ: *grants information,* Grants Administration Division (3903R), EPA, Washington, DC 20460. Phone: (no number provided). *Program information phones:* Office of Air and Radiation, (202)260-0533; Office of Water, (202) 260-3617; Office of Research and Development, (202)260-2597; Office of Policy, Planning, and Evaluation, (202)260-4332; Office of Environmental Justice, (202)564-2602; Office of Solid Waste and Emergency Response, (202)260-0251; Office of Compliance and Enforcement, (202)564-2488.

66.607   TRAINING AND FELLOWSHIPS FOR THE ENVIRONMENTAL PROTECTION AGENCY

Assistance: project grants (100 percent).

Purposes: pursuant to the Clean Air Act, SDWA, TSCA, SWDA, CERCLA, and other laws—to provide training and fellowship opportunities to students interested in pursuing environmental careers.

Eligible applicants/beneficiaries: same as for **66.606**.

Range: $4,000 to $5,000,000.

Activity: new program listing in 1997. FY 98, 572 training and fellowship grants.

HQ: Grants Administration Division (3903F), EPA, Washington, DC 20460. Phone: (no number provided).

66.608   ONE STOP REPORTING

Assistance: project grants (100 percent/to 3 years).

Purposes: pursuant to CERCLA, the Clean Air Act, and TSCA, to demonstrate "full-scale reinvention" of environmental reporting and data management in order to reduce burden, promote multi-media and place-based problem-solving, and improve public access.

Eligible applicants/beneficiaries: states, territories, and possessions administering EPA programs.

Range: $300,000 to $500,000.

Activity: new program listing in 1997; 21 awards.

HQ: Director, One Stop Reporting (1801), Office of Reinvention, Office of the Administrator, EPA, Washington, DC 20460. Phones: (202)260-8699; FAX (202)260-6738.

66.609   CHILDREN'S HEALTH PROTECTION

Assistance: project grants.

Purposes: pursuant to the Clean Air Act, SDWA, TSCA, SWDA, CERCLA, and other laws—to identify and address environmental health threats to children, through community-based and regional projects that: enhance public outreach and communications; assist families in evaluating risks and making informed consumer choices; leverage private and public investments.

Eligible applicants/beneficiaries: community groups; public and private non-profit organizations; municipal, local, and tribal governments; specialized groups; profit organizations.

Range: $35,000 to $135,000.

Activity: new program listing in 1998; 11 cooperative agreements.

HQ: Office of Children's Health Protection (1107), EPA, Washington, DC 20460. Phone: (no number provided). (Note: no field offices for this program.)

66.651 SUSTAINABLE DEVELOPMENT CHALLENGE GRANTS

Assistance: project grants (80 percent/1-3 years).

Purposes: pursuant to the Clean Air Act, SDWA, TSCA, SWDA, and other laws—to leverage public and private investment in sustainable development activities. Project example: construction materials recovery, transformation, and low-cost resale.

Eligible applicants/beneficiaries: nonprofit organizations, state and local agencies, tribes, territories, possessions.

Range: to $250,000 per project.

Activity: new program listing in 1997.

HQ: Office of Administration, EPA, Washington, DC 20460. Phone: (202)260-6812. (Note: no field offices for this program.)

66.700 CONSOLIDATED PESTICIDE ENFORCEMENT COOPERATIVE AGREEMENTS

Assistance: project grants (100 percent).

Purposes: pursuant to the Federal Insecticide, Fungicide, and Rodenticide Act, for the development and maintenance of pesticide regulations compliance monitoring, inspection, and enforcement activities, including: inspection of production facilities and retailing, and of application practices; civil and criminal prosecution of violations; state management plans for the protection of ground water and of endangered species; worker protection programs. Grant funds may be used to pay for inspection and laboratory equipment and supplies, personnel salaries, other administrative costs.

Eligible applicants/beneficiaries: states, territories and possessions, tribes.

Range: $32,000 to $755,000. **Average:** $250,000.

Activity: as of August 1997, 74 awards.

HQ: Office of Compliance, Office of Enforcement and Compliance Assurance (2222A), EPA, Washington, DC 20460. Phone: (202)564-5033.

66.701 TOXIC SUBSTANCES COMPLIANCE MONITORING COOPERATIVE AGREEMENTS

Assistance: project grants (75-100 percent).

Purposes: pursuant to TSCA as amended, to: develop and enhance comprehensive toxic substance enforcement programs, including PCBs, asbestos, lead-paint; for cooperative surveillance, monitoring, and analytical procedures; to encourage state regulatory activities. Grant funds may cover costs of inspection supplies and equipment, personnel, and administration.

Eligible applicants/beneficiaries: same as for **66.700**.

Range: $21,000 to $187,000. **Average:** $150,000.

Activity: FY 99, 52 awards.

HQ: same address/phone as **66.700**.

66.707   TSCA TITLE IV STATE LEAD GRANTS—CERTIFICATION OF LEAD-BASED PAINT PROFESSIONALS ("State Lead Certification Grants")

Assistance: project grants (100 percent).

Purposes: pursuant to TSCA as amended, to develop and conduct accredited training and certification programs for persons and contractors engaged in lead-based paint activities.

Eligible applicants/beneficiaries: same as for **66.700**.

Range: $16,000 to $400,000.

Activity: as of FY 99, 28 states, several tribes with approved programs.

HQ: Director, Chemical Management Division (7404), Office of Pollution Prevention and Toxics, EPA, 401 M St. SW, Washington, DC 20460. Phone: (202)260-1866.

66.708   POLLUTION PREVENTION GRANTS PROGRAM ("PPIS")

Assistance: project grants (50 percent/to 3 years).

Purposes: pursuant to the Pollution Prevention Act of 1990, for innovative, comprehensive, and coordinated pollution reduction and prevention programs involving pollution of air, land, and water. Projects may involve: technical assistance; data collection and dissemination; education for and outreach to business, government, and academic personnel; training; environmental auditing; technology transfer; demonstrations; planning—or combinations of such activities.

Eligible applicants/beneficiaries: state agencies and universities, tribal governments, territories and possessions. Participation is encouraged through partnerships with private nonprofit or profit organizations or institutions.

Range: $20,000 to $200,000. **Average:** $80,000.

Activity: FY 99, 62 grants.

HQ: Pollution Prevention Division, Office of Pollution Prevention and Toxics (7409), EPA, 401 M St. SW, Washington, DC 20460. Phones: (202)260-3480; Web, http://www.epa.gov/p2/grants

66.710   ENVIRONMENTAL JUSTICE COMMUNITY/UNIVERSITY PARTNERSHIP GRANTS PROGRAM ("EJCUP")

Assistance: project grants (100 percent/1-3 years).

Purposes: pursuant to the Clean Air Act, SDWA, TSCA, SWDA, CERCLA, and other laws—to link community residents and organizations and tribes with nearby academic institutions to forge partnerships to address local environmental and public health concerns. Program funds may be used for projects that promote environmental justice, including community education, community monitoring, and similar activities.

Eligible applicants/beneficiaries: IHEs including HBCUs, Hispanic-serving institutions, tribal colleges, institutions serving Asian Americans and other minority or low-income communities, tribes with partnerships with affected parties, tribal governments.

Range: to $250,000.

Activity: new program listing in 1997. FY 98-99, no funding.

HQ: same address/phones as **66.604.**

66.711   ENVIRONMENTAL JUSTICE THROUGH POLLUTION PREVENTION GRANTS

Assistance: project grants (100 percent/to 2 years).

Purposes: pursuant to the Clean Air Act, SDWA, TSCA, SWDA, and other laws, for replicable innovative projects addressing community environmental justice concerns and that use pollution prevention as the proposed solution. Projects should have a direct impact on the environmental justice community, and may involve: public education; training; demonstrations; public-private partnerships; approaches to develop, evaluate, and demonstrate nonregulatory strategies and technologies.

Eligible applicants/beneficiaries: local and state governments, academic institutions—with preference to community-based nonprofit organizations and state and federally recognized tribal organizations.

Range: $7,000 to $210,000. **Average:** $100,000.

Activity: new program listing in 1999. FY 98, over 250 grants.

HQ: same address as **66.708.** Phone:(703)841-0483. (Note: no field offices for this program.)

66.713   STATE AND TRIBAL ENVIRONMENTAL JUSTICE ("STEJ")

Assistance: project grants (100 percent/1-3 years).

Purposes: pursuant to the Clean Air Act, SDWA, TSCA, SWDA, CERCLA, and other laws—for projects, programs, or activities promoting environmental justice, including: development or enhancement of programs to work directly with communities to improve compliance by states or tribes with Title VI of the Civil Rights Act of 1964; development of state or tribal environmental justice regulations, plans, advisory councils, environmental ombudspersons for community grass-roots groups—to enhance community participation in access to state or tribal advisory boards, data and information, and technical assistance.

Eligible applicants/beneficiaries: state or tribal agencies, including agency partnerships.

Range: to $100,000.

Activity: new program listing in FY 98; 5 grants.

HQ: same address/phones as **66.604.**

66.714   PESTICIDE ENVIRONMENTAL STEWARDSHIP ("PESP Regional Grants")

Assistance: project grants (100 percent/to 2 years).

Purposes: pursuant to the Federal Insecticide, Fungicide, and Rodenticide Act, to reduce risk from the use of pesticides in agricultural and nonagricultural settings—through research, monitoring, demonstration, and related activities.

Eligible applicants/beneficiaries: states, territories, possessions, tribes.

Range: $20,000 to $40,000. **Average:** $38,000.

Activity: new program listing in 1999. FY 98, 13 grants.

HQ: Environmental Stewardship Program, Biopesticides and Pollution Prevention Division (7511-C), EPA, 401 M St. SW, Washington, DC 20460. Phone: (800)972-7717.

66.801   HAZARDOUS WASTE MANAGEMENT STATE PROGRAM SUPPORT

Assistance: formula grants (75 percent).

Purposes: pursuant to RCRA, SWDA, and amendments, to develop and execute waste management programs to control the generation, transportation, treatment, storage, and disposal of hazardous wastes.

Eligible applicants/beneficiaries: state agencies, territories, possessions.

Range/Average: $1,795,000.

Activity: not quantified specifically.

HQ: *state program information*, Office of Solid Waste (5303w), EPA, Washington, DC 20460. Phone: (703)308-8790. *Grants management information*: Grants Administration Division (3903R), EPA, Washington, DC 20460. Phone: (no number provided).

66.802   SUPERFUND STATE SITE-SPECIFIC COOPERATIVE AGREEMENTS ("Superfund")

Assistance: project grants (50-100 percent; tribes, 100 percent).

Purposes: pursuant to CERCLA, to conduct site characterization activities at potential confirmed hazardous waste sites; to undertake remedial planning and implementation at sites on the National Priorities List (NPL) of the National Oil and Hazardous Substances Contingency Plan. Project funds may be used to: conduct nontime-critical removal actions; inspect, assess, investigate, study, and clean up hazardous waste sites; identify responsible parties, conduct settlement negotiations, and take enforcement actions. Matching fund requirements: none if site was privately owned and operated at time of waste disposal prior to development of the NPL, and 10 percent for subsequent activities; 50 percent for sites state or locally operated; 10 percent for infrastructure development.

Eligible applicants/beneficiaries: state and tribal governments; territories and possessions.

Range: $30,000 to $1,000,000. **Average:** $500,000.

Activity: not quantified specifically.

HQ: State, Tribal and Site Identification Center, Office of Emergency and Remedial Response (5203G), EPA, Washington, DC 20460. Phone: (703) 308-8506.

66.804 STATE UNDERGROUND STORAGE TANKS PROGRAM ("UST Program")

Assistance: project grants (75 percent).

Purposes: pursuant to RCRA, SWDA, and amendments, to develop and implement state underground hazardous substances storage tank programs to operate in lieu of the federal program. Funds may be used to: promote effective compliance; ensure routine and correct monitoring by owners and operators; establish state statutory and regulatory authority.

Eligible applicants/beneficiaries: state agencies, territorial governments, tribal nations.

Range: $50,000 to $200,000. **Average:** states, $187,000; territories, $81,000.

Activity: FY 98, 66 awards.

HQ: Implementation Division, Office of Underground Storage Tanks (5401G), OSWER-EPA, 401 M St. SW, Washington, DC 20460. Phone: (703)603-7148.

66.805 LEAKING UNDERGROUND STORAGE TANK TRUST FUND PROGRAM

Assistance: project grants (90 percent).

Purposes: pursuant to RCRA, SWDA, and Superfund amendments, to correct releases of petroleum from underground storage tanks, and to conduct related enforcement and cost recovery activities.

Eligible applicants/beneficiaries: state governments, tribes.

Range: $50,000 to $4,300,000. **Average:** $1,500,000.

Activity: FY 98, 50 states, 6 territories, tribes funded.

HQ: same address/phone as **66.804.**

66.806 SUPERFUND TECHNICAL ASSISTANCE GRANTS FOR CITIZEN GROUPS AT PRIORITY SITES

Assistance: project grants (80 percent/to 6 years).

Purposes: pursuant to CERCLA, for community groups to hire technical advisors to assist in: interpreting technical information concerning the assessment of potential hazards at waste sites; selecting and designing appropriate remedies at sites eligible for clean-up under the Superfund program. Grant funds may not pay the costs of developing new information, underwriting legal actions or political activity, or travel by recipients.

Eligible applicants/beneficiaries: technical assistance—groups affected by an actual or threatened release at any Superfund facility. Funding—incorporated groups demonstrating direct effects from the site, such as actual or potential health or economic injury.

Range/Average: to $50,000.

Activity: cumulatively since 1988 program inception, 212 awards.

HQ: Community Involvement and Outreach Center, Office of Emergency and Remedial Response (5204G), OSWER-EPA, Washington, DC 20460. Phone: (703)603-8889.

66.807 SUPERFUND INNOVATIVE TECHNOLOGY EVALUATION PROGRAM ("SITE")

Assistance: project grants (50 percent).

Purposes: to develop and apply innovative remediation technologies to manage human health and environmental risk in response actions under CERCLA— including separation, detoxification, destruction, stabilization, containment, or handling of hazardous chemical wastes. Assistance is available to developers of technologies at pilot- or full-scale to conduct actual field demonstrations at uncontrolled hazardous waste sites.

Eligible applicants/beneficiaries: agencies, private developers, individuals.

Range: to $3,000,000 per project.

Activity: FY 00 estimate, 5-6 new sites and technologies.

HQ: SITE Program Coordinator, National Risk Management Research Laboratory, EPA, 26 W. Martin Luther King Dr., Cincinnati, OH 45268. Phones: (513)569-7697; Web, www.epa.gov/ORD/SITE (Note: the field office is the headquarters for this program.)

66.808 SOLID WASTE MANAGEMENT ASSISTANCE

Purposes: project grants (95-100 percent/to 3 years).

Assistance: pursuant to RCRA and SWDA as amended, to promote use of integrated solid waste management systems to solve municipal generation and management problems at the local, regional, and national levels. Funds may be used for training, surveys, public education, studies, and demonstrations. Project examples: National Solid Waste Information Clearinghouse; targeted media recycling outreach, involving radio and television commercials; information on scrap-based manufacturing.

Eligible applicants/beneficiaries: federal, state, interstate, and local public authorities; private nonprofit organizations and agencies, institutions, individuals; tribes.

Range: $5,000 to $250,000. **Average:** $76,000.

Activity: FY 99 estimate, 50 project awards.

HQ: *grants management information*, Grants Administration Division (3903F), EPA, Washington, DC 20460. Phone: (202)260-9266.

66.809 SUPERFUND STATE CORE PROGRAM COOPERATIVE AGREEMENTS ("Core Program")

Assistance: project grants (90 percent).

Purposes: to enable states to participate in CERCLA response actions that are not site-specific, including program development, personnel hiring and training, emergency response procedural planning, enforcement, legislative development, voluntary clean-up projects.

Eligible applicants/beneficiaries: states, territories and possessions, tribal governments.

Range: $50,000 to $1,124,000. **Average:** $439,000.

Activity: FY 98, 54 grants.

HQ: same address/phone as **66.802.**

66.810 CEPP TECHNICAL ASSISTANCE GRANTS PROGRAM ("CAA Section 112 and SARA Title III State Grants Program")

Assistance: project grants (75 percent/to 2 years).

Purposes: pursuant to the Clean Air Act and TSCA, for chemical accident emergency preparedness and prevention planning (CEPP) and community right-to-know programs established to prevent or eliminate unreasonable risk to community health and environment. Project funds may be used to develop technical assistance and materials to be used directly or by others. Project examples: educational videos; Hazardous Vulnerability Analysis Plans.

Eligible applicants: states, tribes, PR, VI, Northern Marianas.

Eligible beneficiaries: local emergency planning committees, local emergency responders.

Range: $4,000 to $100,000. **Average:** $50,000.

Activity: FY 98, 34 awards.

HQ: Grant Program Manager, CEPPO, OSWER-EPA (5104), 401 M St. SW, Washington, DC 20460. Phone: (202)260-8247.

66.811 BROWNFIELD PILOTS COOPERATIVE AGREEMENTS

Assistance: project grants (to 100 percent/2 years).

Purposes: pursuant to CERCLA and amendments, to establish self-sustaining independent processes to assess and respond to environmental conditions inhibiting redevelopment of "brownfield sites"—i.e., abandoned, idled, or under-used industrial and commercial facilities where expansion or redevelopment is complicated by real or perceived environmental contamination. Funds may be used: to develop administrative, managerial, and technical models; for demonstrations of site assessment activities to return sites to productive use; to capitalize revolving loan funds for follow-up response actions after assessment activities are completed; for training and evaluations. Funds may not be used for remedial actions or actual development activities, nor at sites contaminated by petroleum products.

Eligible applicants/beneficiaries: states and political subdivisions, territories and possessions, tribal governments. Training and demonstrations— colleges, universities, nonprofit training centers and organizations, state and local governments, tribes.

Range: assessments, training, and demonstrations, to $200,000; revolving funds, to $500,000.

Activity: new program listing in 1997. FY 99, 307 assessment, 21 training and development, 68 revolving fund awards.

HQ: Director, Outreach and Special Projects Staff, OSWER-EPA, Washington, DC 20460. Phone: (202)260-4039.

66.926   INDIAN ENVIRONMENTAL GENERAL ASSISTANCE PROGRAM
("General Assistance Program for Tribes" - "GAP")

Assistance: project grants (100 percent/to 4 years).

Purposes: pursuant to the Indian Environmental General Assistance Program Act of 1992 as amended, to administer environmental regulatory programs on Indian lands; to provide EPA technical assistance in the development of multimedia programs to address environmental issues. Funds may be used: to plan, develop, and establish capacity to implement environmental protection programs including development and implementation of solid and hazardous waste programs; to conduct assessments and monitoring; to foster compliance with federal environmental statutes. Project examples: water quality assessment program; environmental assessment inventory; establishment of environmental codes; radon and underground storage tank projects.

Eligible applicants/beneficiaries: federally recognized tribal governments or consortia.

Range/Average: from $75,000.

Activity: not quantified specifically.

HQ: American Indian Environmental Office (4104), EPA, 401 M St. SW, Washington, DC 20460. Phone: (202)260-7939.

66.930   U.S.-MEXICO BORDER GRANTS PROGRAM

Assistance: project grants (95 percent).

Purposes: pursuant to the Clean Air Act, SDWA, RCRA, TSCA, SWDA, and other laws, to promote community-based and regional approaches to meeting the goals of sustainable development, capacity building, and coordination among key participants in addressing U.S.-Mexico border environmental issues.

Eligible applicants/beneficiaries: educational institutions, local governments, "501(C)3" nongovernmental organizations.

Range: $35,000 to $40,000. **Average:** $37,000.

Activity: new program in FY 97. FY 98, 14 awards.

HQ: U.S.-Mexico Border Grants Program, Office of Western Hemisphere and Bilateral Affairs (2650R), Office of International Activities, EPA, Washington, DC 20460. Phone: (202)564-6424.

66.950   ENVIRONMENTAL EDUCATION AND TRAINING PROGRAM
("EETP")

Assistance: project grants (75 percent/3-5 years).

Purposes: pursuant to the National Environmental Education Act, to train professionals in the development and delivery of environmental education programs. Funds may be used to develop programs involving such activities as: classroom training; demonstration projects; curriculum development; international exchanges involving the U.S., Mexico, and Canada; library acquisitions; conferences; networking.

Eligible applicants/beneficiaries: IHEs, nonprofit institutions, consortia.

Range/Average: $1,400,000 to $2,000,000.

Activity: not quantified specifically.

HQ: Environmental Education Specialist, Office of Environmental Education (1704), EPA, 401 M St. SW, Washington, DC 20460. Phone: (202)260-4951.

66.951 ENVIRONMENTAL EDUCATION GRANTS ("EEG")

Assistance: project grants (75 percent).

Purposes: pursuant to the National Environmental Education Act, to design, demonstrate, or disseminate practices, methods, or techniques related to environmental education and training, including: development of curricula and educational tools and materials; teacher and faculty training programs; international exchanges involving the U.S., Mexico, and Canada; projects to understand and assess specific environmental and ecological issues or problems.

Eligible applicants/beneficiaries: state, local, or tribal education or environmental agencies; colleges, universities, nonprofit organizations; noncommercial broadcasting entities.

Range: $5,000 to $250,000.

Activity: annually, 200 grants.

HQ: Environmental Education Grant Program (1704), Office of Environmental Education, EPA, 401 M St. SW, Washington, DC 20460. Phones: (202)260-8619; Web, www.epa.gov/enviroed

NATIONAL GALLERY OF ART

68.001 NATIONAL GALLERY OF ART EXTENSION SERVICE

Assistance: use of property, facilities, and equipment.

Purposes: to provide educational materials from the National Gallery of Art for use in art and humanities programs. Available audiovisual materials are based on collections of paintings and sculptures and special exhibitions in the gallery, including teaching packets, slide programs, video cassettes, and films; distribution may also be through public educational radio or television. The service is free of charge, except for return mailing costs.

Eligible applicants/beneficiaries: schools, colleges, libraries, museums, clubs, community organizations, and individuals.

Activity: FY 99 estimate, 147,000 showings.

HQ: Extension Programs Section, Department of Education Resources, National Gallery of Art, Washington, DC 20565. Phones: (202)737-4215, (202)842-6273; Web, www.nga.gov/resources (Note: no field offices for this program.)

OVERSEAS PRIVATE INVESTMENT CORPORATION

70.002 FOREIGN INVESTMENT FINANCING

Assistance: guaranteed loans; direct loans (5-15 years).

Purposes: pursuant to the Foreign Assistance Act of 1969, for investments in developing countries and emerging economies. Projects must contribute to the economic and social development of host countries and have a positive impact on the U.S. economy. Examples of funded projects include power generation, cellular telephone network, retail petroleum.

Eligible applicants/beneficiaries: U.S. citizens, corporations, partnerships, other associations, and their foreign subsidiaries. Direct loans are reserved for projects significantly involving U.S. small businesses or cooperatives.

Range: guarantees, $10,000,000 to $200,000,000; direct loans, $1,000,000 to $30,000,000. **Average:** guarantees, $60,000,000; direct loans, $8,000,000.

Activity: FY 98, some 20,000 U.S. jobs resulted from projects.

HQ: Information Officer, OPIC, 1100 New York Ave. NW, Washington, DC 20527. Phones: (202)336-8799; FAX (202)336-8700; e-mail, OPIC/S@opic.gov ; Internet, http://www.opic.gov (Note: no field offices for this program.)

70.003 FOREIGN INVESTMENT INSURANCE
("Political Risk Insurance")

Assistance: insurance (90 percent/to 20 years).

Purposes: to insure U.S. investments in developing countries and emerging markets against certain economic and political risks including inconvertibility, expropriation, and political violence. The investments must contribute to the economic and social development of host countries, and not adversely affect U.S. employment. Special programs insure contractors and exporters against arbitrary drawings of letters of credit posted as bid, performance, or advance payment guarantees.

Eligible applicants/beneficiaries: U.S. citizens, corporations, partnerships, other associations, and their foreign subsidiaries.

Range: $68,000 to $200,000,000.

Activity: during 26-year program life, 230,000 U.S. jobs to be created.

HQ: same address/phones as **70.002**. (Note: no field offices for this program.)

NUCLEAR REGULATORY COMMISSION

77.001   RADIATION CONTROL—TRAINING ASSISTANCE AND ADVISORY COUNSELING

Assistance: advisory services/counseling; technical information; training.

Purposes: pursuant to the Atomic Energy Act of 1954 as amended, to train radiation control personnel to conduct state regulatory functions. Courses are provided in health physics and radiation protection, safety aspects of using radioactive materials, regulatory practices and procedures, compliance inspection.

Eligible applicants: state and local government agencies.

Eligible beneficiaries: state and local government personnel with academic training or experience in a physical or life sciences equivalent to a bachelor's degree.

Activity: FY 98, 35 training programs.

HQ: Office of State Programs, NRC, Washington, DC 20555. Phone: (301)415-2348. (Note: no field offices for this program.)

77.005   FINANCIAL ASSISTANCE FOR NRC LOCAL PUBLIC DOCUMENT ROOMS
("NRC Local Public Document Rooms" - "LPDRs")

Assistance: technical information (to 5 years).

Purposes: pursuant to the Atomic Energy Act of 1954 as amended, to maintain and operate NRC local public document room collections in libraries in the vicinity of nuclear facilities—including information concerning the licensing, hearing, inspection, and enforcement activities at the facilities. Funds may be used for the costs of: maintenance and servicing; shelf and equipment space; filing, reference, and administrative staff time; some overhead expenses.

Eligible applicants/beneficiaries: libraries operated by nonprofit educational or governmental institutions located in the vicinity of nuclear power facilities. Collections may be used by anyone.

Range/Average: $500 to $9,818.

Activity: FY 98, 62 cooperative agreements.

HQ: LPDR Program Staff, Information Management Division, Office of Chief Financial Officer, NRC, Washington, DC 20555-0001. Phone: (800)638-8081. (Note: no field offices for this program.)

COMMODITY FUTURES TRADING COMMISSION

78.004   COMMODITY FUTURES REPARATIONS CLAIMS

Assistance: investigation of complaints.

Purposes: to respond to customer complaints and inquiries concerning commodity futures trading; to conduct hearings and rulings on reparations complaints regarding monetary damages resulting from violations of the Commodity Exchange Act or regulations by persons or firms registered under the Act.

Eligible applicants/beneficiaries: market users and the general public.

Activity: FY 98, 218 reparations complaints accepted.

HQ: Executive Director, Office of Proceedings, Commodity Futures Trading Commission, 1155 21st St. NW, Washington, DC 20581. Phone: (202)418-5250.

DEPARTMENT OF ENERGY

81.003   GRANTING OF PATENT LICENSES
("DOE Patents Available for Licensing")

Assistance: technical information.

Purposes: pursuant to the Atomic Energy Act of 1954 and other laws, to license some 1,200 DOE-owned U.S. and 200 foreign patents. Licenses usually are nonexclusive and revocable, but may be exclusive or partially so under some circumstances such as for commercialization. Copies of patents may be obtained at $3.00 per copy from the U.S. Patent and Trademark Office (see **11.900**).

Eligible applicants/beneficiaries: individuals, firms, or corporations with satisfactory commercialization plans.

Activity: FY 99 estimate, 6 licenses granted.

HQ: Office of Assistant General Counsel/Patents, DOE, Washington, DC 20585. Phone: (202)586-2802. (Note: no field offices for this program.)

81.022   USED ENERGY-RELATED LABORATORY EQUIPMENT GRANTS

Assistance: sale, exchange, or donation of property and goods.

Purposes: pursuant to the Atomic Energy Act of 1954 and other laws, to grant used energy-related laboratory equipment for use in energy-oriented research or instructional programs in the life, physical, and environmental sciences and engineering.

Eligible applicants/beneficiaries: U.S. nonprofit IHEs, hospitals, technical institutes, or museums.

Activity: N.A.

HQ: Office of Science, DOE, 1000 Independence Ave. SW, DOE, Washington, DC 20585. Phones: (202)586-7231; Internet, www.erle.osti.gov/erle (Note: no field offices for this program.)

81.036   ENERGY-RELATED INVENTIONS

Assistance: project grants (cost sharing/2 years); use of property, facilities, and equipment; technical information; advisory services/counseling.

Purposes: pursuant to the Federal Nonnuclear Energy Research and Development Act of 1974, to evaluate inventions contributing to the development of non-nuclear energy technology, and to provide related technical advice in engineering, marketing, and business planning. Some funding may be provided—but not equity capital. Examples of inventions: heat pipe dehumidification unit for air conditioners; molded pulp products dryer.

Eligible applicants/beneficiaries: small businesses, individual inventors, entrepreneurs, universities.

Range/Average: $83,000.

Activity: FY 98 estimate, 22-24 grants.

HQ: Office of Industrial Technologies (EE-23), DOE, 1000 Independence Ave. SW, Washington, DC 20585. Phones: (202)586-3987; Internet, http://www.oit.doe.gov

81.039   NATIONAL ENERGY INFORMATION CENTER ("NEIC")

Assistance: technical information.

Purposes: to operate the NEIC as a comprehensive source and referral service for statistical and analytical energy data, computer models, publications, on-line services, and information. Clearinghouse services are provided.

Eligible applicants/beneficiaries: federal, state, and local governments; academic and other nonprofit institutions; industrial and commercial organizations; general public.

Activity: annually, 25,000 inquiries.

HQ: Team Leader, NEIC, Energy Information Administration, DOE, Forrestal Bldg. - Rm.1F-048, Washington, DC 20585. Phones: (202)586-8800; FAX (202)586-0727; Internet, infoctr@eia.doe.gov ; Web, http://www.eie.doe.gov ; FTP, ftp://ftp.eia.doe.gov (Note: no field offices for this program.)

81.041   STATE ENERGY PROGRAM

Assistance: formula grants; project grants.

Purposes: pursuant to the Energy Policy and Conservation Act and related acts, to develop, implement, or modify state energy conservation plans. The plan must reflect a goal of a ten percent improvement in energy efficiency by the year 2000. Funds may cover costs of technical assistance in developing plans, but not research, demonstrations, subsidies, or tax credits.

Eligible applicants/beneficiaries: states; certain territories, possessions.

Range: $110,000 to $1,630,000. **Average:** $455,000.

Activity: 57 states and territories participate.

HQ: Office of State and Community Programs (EE-44), Office of Energy Efficiency and Renewable Energy, DOE, 1000 Independence Ave. SW, Washington, DC 20585. Phones: (202)586-4074.

81.042   WEATHERIZATION ASSISTANCE FOR LOW-INCOME PERSONS

Assistance: formula grants (100 percent).

Purposes: pursuant to the Energy Policy and Production Act and related acts, for weatherization measures in the homes of low-income households, especially the elderly and the handicapped. Funds may cover such costs as attic insulation, storm windows, furnace and cooling system modifications, replacement furnaces and boilers.

Eligible applicants/beneficiaries: states and certain tribal organizations. If a state does not apply, general purpose local government units, community action agencies, or other nonprofit agencies may apply.

Range: to $2,002 per dwelling unit. **Average:** $2,369,000.

Activity: to date, over 2,600,000 homes weatherized.

HQ: same address/phone as **81.041.**

81.049   OFFICE OF SCIENCE FINANCIAL ASSISTANCE PROGRAM

Assistance: project grants (to 100 percent/3 years).

Purposes: pursuant to the Atomic Energy Act of 1954 and other laws, for fundamental energy research, training, and related activities in all the basic sciences and in advanced technology concepts and assessments in related fields. Funds may be obtained for work in such fields as basic energy sciences, engineering, geosciences, high energy and nuclear physics, fusion energy, biological and health and environmental research, computational and technology research.

Eligible applicants/beneficiaries: IHEs, profit and nonprofit organizations, state and local governments, foreign organizations, unaffiliated individuals.

Range: $10,000 to $2,000,000. **Average:** $200,000.

Activity: not quantified specifically.

HQ: Grants and Contracts Division, Office of Energy Research (SC-64), DOE, 19901 Germantown Rd., Germantown, MD 20874-1290. Phone: (301)903-5212.

81.057   UNIVERSITY COAL RESEARCH

Assistance: project grants (to 100 percent/to 5 years).

Purposes: pursuant to the Atomic Energy Act of 1954 and other laws, for fundamental research on the physics and chemistry involved in the conversion and utilization of coal. Projects must involve teaching faculty and funded student participation.

Eligible applicants/beneficiaries: U.S. colleges and universities.

Range: $75,000 to $425,000. **Average:** $300,000.

Activity: FY 98, 22 grants.

HQ: Office of Advanced Research, Assistant Secretary/Fossil Energy-DOE, Washington, DC 20585. Phone: (301)903-2786.

81.064 OFFICE OF SCIENTIFIC AND TECHNICAL INFORMATION ("OSTI")

Assistance: technical information.

Purposes: for OSTI to conduct its centralized technical information management program for the collection, management, and distribution of domestic and international energy data and research findings in electronic and printed form.

Eligible applicants/beneficiaries: state and local governments, universities that are DOE contractors, and other organizations.

Activity: annually, 1,300,000 users served.

HQ: OSTI, DOE, P.O. Box 62, Oak Ridge, TN 37831. Phones: *operations*, (423)576-2413; FAX (423)241-3826; *input and policy considerations*, (423) 574-0295; Web, http://www.osti.gov (Note: no field offices for this program.)

81.065 NUCLEAR WASTE DISPOSAL SITING

Assistance: direct payments/specified use; project grants (to 100 percent).

Purposes: pursuant to the Nuclear Waste Policy Act, to develop repositories for the disposal of high-level radioactive waste and spent nuclear fuel. Funds may be used to: review potential economic, social, health and safety, and environmental impacts; develop requests for impact and mitigation assistance; engage in monitoring, testing, or evaluation activities; provide information to the public.

Eligible applicants/beneficiaries: the state of Nevada and volunteer states in which DOE is considering nuclear waste disposal activities, including executive agencies and offices of the state legislature; affected local governments and tribes.

Range: $40,000 to $5,000,000.

Activity: 2 grants.

HQ: Office of Civilian Radioactive Waste Management-DOE, Washington, DC 20585. Phone: (202)586-9175.

81.079 REGIONAL BIOMASS ENERGY PROGRAMS

Assistance: project grants (to 100 percent/2 months-1 year).

Purposes: to develop and transfer biomass energy technologies to the scientific and industrial communities; for outreach, public education, and behavioral modification activities. Regional programs are tailored to specific regions— for feedstock production, conversion technologies, and municipal solid waste.

Eligible applicants/beneficiaries: profit and nonprofit organizations; intrastate, interstate, state, local government agencies; universities.

Range: N.A.

Activity: not quantified specifically.

HQ: Manager, Regional Biomass Energy Program (EE-31), Office of Fuels Development, DOE, Washington, DC 20585. Phones: (202)586-1480; FAX (202)586-9815.

81.081 ENERGY TASK FORCE FOR THE URBAN CONSORTIUM

Assistance: project grants (100 percent/18 months).

Purposes: for the Energy Task Force of the Urban Consortium—the latter, an organization of the 50 largest cities and counties, and the former, a subgroup of 20 of its representatives with appropriate expertise—to develop community energy supply and conservation techniques. Project example: plan to reduce carbon dioxide emissions through transportation, land use, use of district cooling loops, and incentives encouraging utility participation in deregulated environment.

Eligible applicants/beneficiaries: cities and counties with population at least 250,000. (Those with populations of 100,000 or more may seek support for technology transfer projects.)

Range/Average: research and development, $75,000; technology transfer, $25,000.

Activity: since 1979, 335 projects funded.

HQ: Project Manager, Office of Building Technology, Office of State and Community Programs, Office of Energy Efficiency and Renewable Energy (EE-44), DOE, 1000 Independence Ave. SW - Rm.5E-066, Washington, DC 20585. Phone: (202)586-4074.

81.082 MANAGEMENT AND TECHNICAL ASSISTANCE FOR MINORITY BUSINESS ENTERPRISES

Assistance: advisory services/counseling.

Purposes: to promote minority- and women-owned and -operated business participation in DOE energy technology procurement contracts, by providing assistance to MBEs in learning of and bidding for DOE contracts.

Eligible applicants/beneficiaries: minority business enterprises.

Activity: not quantified specifically.

HQ: Office of Economic Impact and Diversity (ED-1), DOE, Forrestal Bldg. - Rm.5B-110, Washington, DC 20585. Phone: (202)586-8698. (Note: no field offices for this program.)

81.086 CONSERVATION RESEARCH AND DEVELOPMENT

Assistance: project grants (to 100 percent/to 2 years).

Purposes: pursuant to the Federal Nonnuclear Energy Research and Development Act of 1974, for research in energy conservation technology in buildings, industry, and transportation. Project examples include research on high-performance heat pumps, thermally efficient commercial buildings, vehicle engines, high temperature materials, industrial separation processes.

Eligible applicants/beneficiaries: profit and nonprofit organizations, state and local governments.

Range: $50,000 to $500,000. **Average:** $200,000.

Activity: not quantified specifically.

HQ: Office of Energy Efficiency and Renewable Energy, DOE, Washington, DC 20585. Phones: Office of Building Technology, State and Community Programs, (202)586-2300; Office of Transportation Technologies, (202)586-6715; Office of Industrial Technologies, (202)586-0098; Office of Utility Technologies, (202)586-4142. (Note: no field offices for this program.)

81.087 RENEWABLE ENERGY RESEARCH AND DEVELOPMENT

Assistance: project grants (to 100 percent/2 months-1 year).

Purposes: for research and development projects in the following energy technologies: solar buildings, photovoltaics, solar thermal, biomass, alcohol fuels, urban waste, wind, hydropower and hydrogen, and geothermal.

Eligible applicants/beneficiaries: profit and nonprofit organizations; intrastate, interstate, and local agencies; universities.

Range: $10,000 to $100,000.

Activity: not quantified specifically.

HQ: same address/phones as **81.086**, *and,* Residential, Commercial and Institutional Buildings, (202)586-1660. (Note: no field offices for this program.)

81.089 FOSSIL ENERGY RESEARCH AND DEVELOPMENT

Assistance: project grants.

Purposes: pursuant to the Federal Nonnuclear Energy Research and Development Act of 1974, Energy Policy and Conservation Act, and other acts, for fundamental research and technology development to promote the use of environmentally and economically superior technologies for supply, conversion, delivery, and utilization of fossil fuels.

Eligible applicants/beneficiaries: states, local governments, universities, governmental entities, consortia, nonprofit institutions, commercial corporations, joint federal-industry corporations, territories, individuals.

Range: $16,000 to $2,099,000. **Average:** $510,000.

Activity: FY 99 estimate, 65 awards.

HQ: Fossil Energy Program (FE-122), DOE, Germantown, MD 20874. Phones: (301)903-3514; Web, http://www.pr.doe.gov/gdintro.html

81.104 TECHNOLOGY DEVELOPMENT FOR ENVIRONMENTAL MANAGEMENT

Assistance: project grants (to 100 percent/to 5 years).

Purposes: pursuant to the Atomic Energy Act and other laws, to develop new or improved technologies to: eliminate or reduce known or recognized potential risks to the public and to the environment; reduce overall clean-up costs; develop new clean-up methods. Major remediation and waste management areas include: mixed waste characterization treatment and disposal;

radioactive tank waste remediation; subsurface contaminants; deactivation and decommissioning.

Eligible applicants/beneficiaries: public and quasi-public agencies, private industry, individuals, groups, educational institutions, nonprofit organizations, state and local governments, tribal governments, territories and possessions.

Range: $100,000 to $5,000,000.

Activity: not quantified specifically.

HQ: Office of Science and Technology, Office of Environmental Management, DOE, Washington, DC 20585. Phone: (301)903-7259. (Note: no field offices for this program.)

81.105   NATIONAL INDUSTRIAL COMPETITIVENESS THROUGH ENERGY, ENVIRONMENT, AND ECONOMICS ("NICE3")

Assistance: project grants (50 percent/to 3 years).

Purposes: to develop new strategies, processes, and/or equipment to reduce the generation of high-volume wastes and greenhouse gases in industry, and to conserve energy and energy-intensive feed stocks, including through integration of pollution prevention and recycling approaches. Emphasis is on states with industries with the highest energy consumption and the greatest levels of generation of pollutants—especially chemicals and allied products, petroleum and coal products, paper and allied products, primary metal industries. State funding must include industrial partner monies.

Eligible applicants/beneficiaries: state agencies.

Range: $69,000 to $425,000. **Average:** $310,000.

Activity: not quantified specifically.

HQ: Headquarters (EE-23), DOE, 1000 Independence Ave. SW, Washington, DC 20585. Phone: (202)586-2212. (*Note.* Proposals are to be submitted to: DOE Field Office, Bldg. 17-3, 1617 Cole Blvd., Golden, CO 80401.)

81.106   TRANSPORT OF TRANSURANIC WASTES TO THE WASTE ISOLATION PILOT PLANT: STATES AND TRIBAL CONCERNS, PROPOSED SOLUTIONS

Assistance: project grants (100 percent).

Purposes: to support cooperative efforts among the tribes, states, and DOE on the Waste Isolation Pilot Plant shipping corridors—in developing plans and procedures for the safe transportation of transuranic waste from temporary storage facilities to the plant. Project elements include accident prevention, emergency preparedness, and public information activities

Eligible applicants/beneficiaries: Western Governors' Association, Southern Governors' Association, State of New Mexico, and 10 affected tribal governments.

Range: $25,000 to $1,313,000.

Activity: FY 00 estimate, 2 awards.

HQ: Office of Western Operations, DOE, Washington, DC 20585. Phone: (301)903-8466.

81.108   EPIDEMIOLOGY AND OTHER HEALTH STUDIES FINANCIAL ASSISTANCE PROGRAM

Assistance: project grants (100 percent).

Purposes: pursuant to the Atomic Energy Act, Federal Nonnuclear Energy Research and Development Act of 1974, and other acts and amendments, for basic research, education, conferences, communication, and other activities relating to the health of DOE workers and others potentially exposed to health hazards associated with energy production, transmission, and use. Grant funds may support costs relating to project administration, training, publications, epidemiological studies and research.

Eligible applicants/beneficiaries: IHEs, businesses, nonprofit institutions.

Range: $50,000 to $1,100,000. Average: $225,000.

Activity: new program listing in 1999.

HQ: Office of Epidemiologic Studies (EH-62/270CC), DOE, Germantown, MD 20874-1290. Phone: (301)903-3721. (Note: no field offices for this program.)

81.110   NATIONAL RESOURCE CENTER FOR PLUTONIUM

Assistance: project grants (100 percent).

Purposes: for the State of Texas to establish and maintain a National Resource Center for Plutonium to focus on the storage, disposition, potential utilization, and transportation of plutonium—as a consequence of the dismantling of nuclear warheads. The center will also respond to needs for environmental and health research, and for interpretation of technical and scientific data.

Eligible applicants/beneficiaries: only the State of Texas.

Range/Average: FY 99, 00, $5,000,000 annually.

Activity: the center has been established.

HQ: Office of Defense Programs (DP-24), DOE, Germantown MD 20874. Phone: (301)903-5543.

81.112   STEWARDSHIP SCIENCE GRANT PROGRAM
("Inertial Confinement Fusion" - "ICF")

Assistance: project grants (100 percent).

Purposes: pursuant to the Atomic Energy Act, Federal Nonnuclear Energy Research and Development Act, amendments, and other laws, for basic and applied research in high-energy density science relevant to ICF related to the DOE stockpile stewardship program; to promote inter-action among researchers and scientists at DOE weapons laboratories; to train scientists.

Eligible applicants/beneficiaries: U.S. IHEs, private industry, and nonprofit institutions.

Range: $58,000 to $199,000. Average: $135,000.

Activity: new program in FY 98.

HQ: Office of Inertial Fusion (DP-18), Office of Defense Programs-DOE,

19901 Germantown Rd., Germantown, MD 20874. Phones: (301)903-8059; FAX (301)903-4096.

81.113   NONPROLIFERATION AND NATIONAL SECURITY RESEARCH

Assistance: project grants (100 percent/to 3 years).

Purposes: pursuant to the Atomic Energy Act, Federal Nonnuclear Energy Research and Development Act, amendments, and other laws, for basic and applied research and development on verification technologies needed for effective treaty negotiations and international agreements on the control of special nuclear materials, nuclear weapons, and weapons of mass destruction.

Eligible applicants/beneficiaries: IHEs with postdoctoral programs.

Range: $10,000 to $20,000/year.

Activity: new program in FY 98; 20 grants expected per year.

HQ: Group Leader, Office of Research and Development, Office of Nonproliferation and National Security, DOE, Washington, DC 20585. Phone: (202)586-1766. (Note: no field offices for this program.)

81.114   UNIVERSITY NUCLEAR SCIENCE AND REACTOR SUPPORT

Assistance: project grants (to 100 percent).

Purposes: pursuant to the Atomic Energy Act as amended and other laws, for research design, analysis, and assessments in science and technology in fields related to nuclear energy, including financing plans, market analyses, and technical and related activities. Funds may also be used for nuclear energy engineering education research, fellowships, and scholarships.

Eligible applicants/beneficiaries: individuals, partnerships, corporations, associations, joint ventures, IHEs, nonprofit organizations.

Range: to $20,000,000.

Activity: new program in FY 98.

HQ: Office of Nuclear Energy, Science and Technology (NE-20), DOE, 19901 Germantown Rd., Germantown, MD 20874. Phone: (301)903-1632.

81.116   SCIENCE AND ENGINEERING TRAINING TO SUPPORT DIVERSITY-RELATED PROGRAMS

Assistance: project grants.

Purposes: for special emphasis programs to encourage training of Colorado minority group members, women, and disabled students, toward their pursuit of careers in science, mathematics, engineering, and technology. Activities include support for public-private partnerships, summer camps, employment counseling.

Eligible applicants/beneficiaries: state and local governments; sponsored organizations; public, quasi-public, and private nonprofit organizations; native American organizations. Beneficiaries must be Colorado residents.

Range: $25,000 to $100,000. **Average:** $65,000.

Activity: new program listing in 1998. FY 99 estimate, to 6 grants.

HQ: Civil Rights and Diversity Manager, Rocky Flats Environmental Technology Site, DOE, Golden, CO 80402-0928. Phone: (303)966-2483. (Note: the field office is the headquarters for this program.)

81.117   ENERGY EFFICIENCY AND RENEWABLE ENERGY INFORMATION, DISSEMINATION, OUTREACH, TRAINING AND TECHNICAL ANALYSIS/ASSISTANCE

Assistance: project grants (6 months-4 years).

Purposes: pursuant to the Energy Policy Act of 1992 and other acts, to stimulate increased energy efficiency and use of renewable and alternative energy in transportation, buildings, industry, and the federal sector—through information dissemination, outreach, training, and related technical assistance.

Eligible applicants/beneficiaries: public and private profit and nonprofit organizations, state and local governments, tribal organizations, universities, individuals.

Range: $10,000 to $800,000.

Activity: new program in FY 99; 140 awards.

HQ: Office of Energy Efficiency and Renewable Energy (EE-60), DOE, 1000 Independence Ave, SW, Washington, DC 20585. Phones: (202)586-3835; Web, http//www.ee.doe.gov (Note: no field offices for this program.)

81.118   SOLAR ENERGY PARTNERSHIP SUPPORT AND BARRIER ELIMINATION ("Million Solar Roofs Initiative")

Assistance: project grants.

Purposes: pursuant to the Energy Policy Act of 1992, other acts,

and amendments, to stimulate increased use of solar energy applications in residential, commercial, and federal buildings—through partnerships to provide information dissemination, outreach, training, and related technical assistance.

Eligible applicants/beneficiaries: same as for **81.117**

Range/Average: N.A.

Activity: new program in FY 99; 25-50 awards anticipated.

HQ: same address (except EE-1) as **81.117**. Phones: (202)586-8779; Web, http//www.ee.doe.gov (Note: no field offices for this program.)

UNITED STATES INFORMATION AGENCY

82.001   EDUCATIONAL EXCHANGE—GRADUATE STUDENTS ("Fulbright Program")

Assistance: project grants (100 percent).

Purposes: pursuant to MECEA, for scholarships to graduate students for one year of academic studies abroad, covering costs of tuition, maintenance, transportation, books, insurance. Travel grants may supplement awards obtained from others.

Eligible applicants/beneficiaries: U.S. citizens with: B.A. degree or equivalent, with certain exceptions; no doctoral degree; the majority of their high school and undergraduate college education received at U.S. institutions; language proficiency; good health.

Range: $1,200 to $40,000. **Average:** $21,000.

Activity: FY 99 estimate, 850 grants.

HQ: Institute of International Education, 809 United Nations Plaza, New York, NY 10017. Phone: (no number provided).

82.002   EDUCATIONAL EXCHANGE—UNIVERSITY LECTURERS (PROFESSORS) AND RESEARCH SCHOLARS ("Fulbright-Hays Program")

Assistance: project grants (100 percent).

Purposes: pursuant to MECEA, for lectureships for university lecturers to serve as visiting professors abroad; for research grants for scholars for postdoctoral work abroad—for one full academic year, covering costs of travel for the grantee (and, in some cases, dependents), maintenance, books, and services.

Eligible applicants/beneficiaries: U.S. citizens with foreign language proficiency and, for lecturing—college or university teaching experience. For research—a doctoral degree or, in some fields, recognized professional standing as demonstrated by faculty rank, publications, compositions, exhibition record, concerts, etc. Doctoral and other predoctoral candidates should contact the Institute of International Education (see **82.001**).

Range: $3,500 to $89,000. **Average:** $50,000.

Activity: FY 00 estimate, 800 grants.

HQ: Council for International Exchange of Scholars, 3007 Tilden St. NW - Ste.5M, Washington, DC 20008. Phone: (no number provided). (Note: no field offices for this program.)

82.004   INTERNATIONAL VISITORS PROGRAM ("Fulbright-Hays Program")

Assistance: project grants (cost sharing).

Purposes: pursuant to MECEA, to plan and conduct programs of travel, observation, consultation, study, and practical experience for foreign visitors selected and assigned by USIA—to bring visitors into contact with influential Americans and representative organizations and institutions, and increase communication and mutual understanding between the foreign and domestic parties.

Eligible applicants/beneficiaries: incorporated nonprofit organizations with at least four years experience.

Range: $260,000 to $3,400,000. **Average:** $1,300,000.

Activity: new program listing in 1998. FY 99, 1 grant to an HBCU consortium.

HQ: Community Relations Division, Office of International Visitors, USIA, 301 Fourth St. SW - Rm.266, Washington, DC 20547. Phone: (202)619-5220. (Note: no field offices for this program.)

82.006 AMERICAN COUNCIL OF YOUNG POLITICAL LEADERS ("ACYPL")

Assistance: project grants (60 percent).

Purposes: pursuant to MECEA, to arrange two-way exchanges with emerging U.S. and foreign political leaders, enabling them to experience firsthand the cultural and political dynamics of the countries visited, usually for two-week programs. Grants cover costs of travel, insurance, program activities, and orientation.

Eligible applicants: ACYPL.

Eligible beneficiaries: state and local elected officials, staff and party activists—to age 41, and selected by a Delegate Selection Committee with Democratic and Republican co-chairs.

Range/Average: $700,000.

Activity: new program listing in 1999.

HQ: Youth Programs Division (E/PY), Office of Citizen Exchanges, Bureau of Educational and Cultural Affairs, USIA, 301 Fourth St. SW, Washington, DC 20547. Phone: (202)619-6299; FAX (202)619-5311. (Note: no field offices for this program.)

82.009 PROFESSIONAL DEVELOPMENT—INTERNATIONAL EDUCATORS/ ADMINISTRATORS
("Education and Training Program")

Assistance: project grants (cost sharing/1-3 weeks).

Purposes: pursuant to MECEA, for training and consultation between overseas-based educational advisers and U.S.-based international education professionals. "Linkage" awards support one-week attendance at U.S. regional conferences; "Partnership" awards are for 3-week visits by U.S. professionals at overseas educational advising centers.

Eligible applicants: limited to NAFSA-Association of International Educators.

Eligible beneficiaries: international education administration professionals.

Range/Average: $4,000.

Activity: new program listing in 1997.

HQ: Association of International Educators, 1307 New York Ave. NW, Washington, DC 20005-4701. Phones: NAFSA, (202)737-3699; USIA: E/ASA, (202)619-5434. (Note: no field offices for this program.)

82.010 COLLEGE AND UNIVERSITY PARTNERSHIPS PROGRAM

Assistance: project grants (cost sharing/3 years).

Purposes: pursuant to MECEA, to foster sustainable linkages between academic institutions of the U.S. and New Independent States (NIS), enhancing the objectives of the Freedom Support Act by assisting the transition of the

NIS to democratic, free-market oriented societies. Project funds may support faculty exchanges, curriculum development, and collaborative research.

Eligible applicants/beneficiaries: U.S. postsecondary, degree-granting institutions and recognized foreign institutions.

Range: $100,000 to $300,000.

Activity: new program listing in 1998. FY 98, 24 grants.

HQ: College and University Affiliations Program, Teaching and Specialized Programs Division, Office of Academic Programs Advising, USIA, 301 Fourth St. SW -Rm.349, Washington, DC 20547. Phone: (202)619-4126; FAX (202)401-1433; Internet, affiliat@usia.gov (Note: no field offices for this program.)

82.011   COLLEGE AND UNIVERSITY AFFILIATIONS PROGRAM

Assistance: project grants (cost sharing/3 years).

Purposes: pursuant to MECEA, to foster sustainable linkages between U.S. and foreign academic institutions to advance specific U.S. foreign policies. Funds may support faculty exchanges, curriculum development, and collaborative research with a foreign partner institution.

Eligible applicants/beneficiaries: postgraduate degree-granting institutions.

Range: $90,000 to $120,000.

Activity: new program listing in 1998. FY 98, 12 grants.

HQ: same address as **82.010**. Phones: (202)619-5289; FAX (202)401-1433; Internet, affiliat@usia.gov (Note: no field offices for this program.)

82.012   TEACHER EXCHANGE—NEW INDEPENDENT STATES (NIS)
("Partners in Education")

Assistance: project grants (100 percent).

Purposes: pursuant to MECEA, for five-week teacher exchanges between U.S. and NIS schools.

Eligible applicants: nonprofit organizations that recruit secondary social science educators in Russia, Ukraine, and the NIS and place them in U.S. schools.

Eligible beneficiaries: U.S. school districts willing to host groups of NIS teachers; U.S. teachers wishing to consult in the NIS.

Range/Average: N.A.

Activity: new program listing in 1998. FY 98-99, 250 NIS teachers and administrators hosted in U.S. schools, 50 U.S. educators to visit the NIS.

HQ: Teacher Exchange Branch, USIA, 301 Fourth St. SW -Rm.349, Washington, DC 20547. Phone: (202)619-4556. (Note: no field offices for this program.)

82.013   EDUCATIONAL EXCHANGE—TEACHERS FROM SECONDARY AND
POSTSECONDARY LEVELS
("Fulbright Program")

Assistance: project grants (100 percent/1 year).

Purposes: pursuant to MECEA, to enable U.S. and foreign educators to live and teach in a foreign country. Participants from primary, secondary, or junior/community colleges exchange classroom assignments for one academic year. Generally, participants receive leave with pay and benefits from their respective employers; grants support transportation, maintenance, accident and health insurance, and, as necessary, a "top-off" stipend.

Eligible applicants/beneficiaries: teachers and administrators with at least a B.A., 3 years full-time experience, English and foreign language proficiency, and U.S. citizenship.

Range: $2,000 to $25,000.

Activity: new program listing in 1997. FY 99 estimate, 460 grants.

HQ: Teacher Exchange Branch (E/ASX), USIA, 301 Fourth St. SW, Washington, DC 20547. Phones: (202)619-4556; FAX (202)401-1433; Web, http://www.usia.gov (Note: no field offices for this program.)

82.015 CREATIVE ARTS GRANTS

Assistance: project grants (70 percent/1-3 years).

Purposes: pursuant to MECEA, for cooperative international group projects that introduce American and foreign participants to each other's cultural and artistic life and traditions—including composers, choreographers, playwrights, theater designers, writers, poets, filmmakers, visual artists, and arts administrators. Ineligible projects include those involving youth, speaking tours, research, amateurs or semi-professionals, community-level presentations, or vocational and technical long-term academic study.

Eligible applicants: public or private "501(c)(3)" nonprofit organizations with four years experience.

Eligible beneficiaries: professional artists, arts administrators at least age 25.

Range: $60,000 to $300,000.

Activity: new program listing in 1998. FY 98, 7 grants.

HQ: Creative Arts Exchanges Program, Office of Citizen Exchanges, Bureau of Educational and Cultural Affairs, USIA, 301 Fourth St. SW, Washington, DC 20547. Phone: (202)205-2209; FAX (202)619-5311. (Note: no field offices for this program.)

82.016 EDUCATIONAL EXCHANGE—CONGRESS-BUNDESTAG YOUTH EXCHANGE ("CBYX")

Assistance: projects grants (cost sharing/18 months).

Purposes: pursuant to MECEA, to foster interaction between young people from the U.S. and Germany to promote mutual understanding through reciprocal exchanges of groups of high school students and practical trainees. Grants support costs of travel, insurance, orientation, selection, and administration.

Eligible applicants: organizations with at least four years experience and with a German partner.

Eligible beneficiaries: generally, high school students demonstrating language ability, social skills, academic achievement.

Range/Average: $300,000 (depending on number of students).

Activity: new program listing in 1998. Since 1983 program inception, 10,000 participants as of FY 97.

HQ: same address/phone as **82.006**. (Note: no field offices for this program.)

82.018 EDUCATIONAL EXCHANGE—NIS SECONDARY SCHOOL INITIATIVE

Assistance: project grants (cost sharing/to 2 years).

Purposes: pursuant to MECEA, to foster interaction between young people from the U.S. and the NIS to promote mutual understanding, through: (1) Future Leaders Exchange (FLEX) providing NIS students a full scholarship to live for one academic year with American host families and attend a school; (2) School Linkage Program providing partial support for thematic exchanges of students and educators between American schools and their NIS partners. Grants support costs of travel, stipends, insurance, orientation, selection, administration, and follow-on alumni activities.

Eligible applicants: U.S. private nonprofit organizations and public institutions with at least four years experience.

Eligible beneficiaries: same as for **82.016**.

Range: Linkage grants, $50,000 to $200,000. **Average:** $100,000.

Activity: new program listing in 1998. FY 98, 10 Linkage, 16 FLEX grants.

HQ: same address/phone as **82.006**. (Note: no field offices for this program.)

82.026 EDUCATIONAL EXCHANGE—POSTGRADUATES AND FACULTY ("Regional Scholars Exchange Program with the New Independent States")

Assistance: project grants (cost sharing/to 2 years).

Purposes: pursuant to MECEA (Fulbright-Hays Act), to enable U.S. and NIS university faculty, researchers, or scholars in the social sciences or humanities to conduct research, share perspectives, collaborate, cooperate at a counterpart university in the host country, and participate as part of an electronic community of scholars.

Eligible applicants: private nonprofit organizations with at least four years experience and with offices in the NIS.

Eligible beneficiaries: U.S. or NIS faculty or advanced graduate students in the social sciences or humanities.

Range: $14,000 to $20,000.

Activity: new program listing in 1997. FY 99, 70 fellowships.

HQ: European Programs Branch, Office of Academic Exchanges Division, USIA, 301 Fourth St. SW, Washington, DC 20547. Phones: (202)205-0525; FAX (202)260-7985. (Note: no field offices for this program.)

82.030 CULTURAL EXCHANGE (PERFORMING ARTS)

Assistance: project grants.

Purposes: pursuant to MECEA, for the creative and professional development of U.S. artists, by supporting the presentation of their work at significant international festivals outside the U.S. USIA funding is augmented by the federal NEA, and privately by the Rockefeller Foundation and the Pew Charitable Trust.

Eligible applicants/beneficiaries: creative, interpretive, or traditional performing artists working at a professional level.

Range: organizations, $2,000 to $10,000; individuals, $500 to $2,000.

Activity: new program in FY 98; 100 grants.

HQ: Fund for U.S. Artists, Arts International, Institute of International Education, 809 United Nations Plaza, New York, NY 10017. Phones: (212)984-5370; FAX (212)984-5574; Web, WWW.IIE.ORG (Note: no field offices for this program.)

82.032 CULTURAL EXCHANGE (VISUAL ARTS)

Assistance: project grants.

Purposes: pursuant to MECEA, to help ensure that the excellence, diversity, and vitality of the arts in the U.S. are represented at international visual and performing arts festivals. Grants are awarded to independent curators and nonprofit museums and galleries invited to participate in international festivals around the world. USIA funding is augmented by funding from the federal NEA and privately by the Rockefeller Foundation and the Pew Charitable Trust.

Eligible applicants: nonprofit museums, galleries, artists cooperatives, independent curators.

Eligible beneficiaries: professional painters, sculptors, photographers, printmakers, or artists working with electronic media, installation, or traditional arts.

Range: $40,000 to $300,000.

Activity: new program listing in 1997.

HQ: Office of Citizens Exchanges, USIA, 301 Fourth St. SW, Washington, DC 20547. Phones: (202)619-4806; FAX (202)619-6315; Web, WWW.USIA. ORG *Application information,* same address/phones as **82.030.** (Note: no field offices for this program.)

82.033 PROFESSIONAL EXCHANGE—ANNUAL OPEN GRANT ("Office of Citizen Exchanges")

Assistance: project grants (cost sharing).

Purposes: pursuant to MECEA, to foster, improve, and strengthen U.S. international relations by promoting mutual understanding among the peoples of the world through educational and professional exchanges. Grant funds should support: development of lasting institutional links; establishment of consortia, associations, and information networks; information transfer; development of internships.

Eligible applicants: public and private nonprofit organizations meeting the provisions of IRS regulation 26CFR1.501(c).

Eligible beneficiaries: U.S. citizens and foreign nationals.

Range: to $135,000; developing organizations, to $60,000.

Activity: new program listing in 1997. FY 99 estimate, 30 grants.

HQ: Office of Citizen Exchanges, USIA, 301 Fourth St. SW - Rm.220, Washington, DC 20547. Phone: (202)619-5326. (Note: no field offices for this program.)

82.034 EXCHANGE—ENGLISH TEACHING FELLOWS ("English Language Programs")

Assistance: project grants (100 percent).

Purposes: pursuant to MECEA, to increase American presence abroad, enhance appreciation of American cultural ideas, and improve academic standards at universities, teacher training colleges, binational centers, and other USIA-USIS selected institutions with language programs. Selected Fellows participate for one academic year in such activities at host institutions as materials or test development and teacher training. Grants support costs of participants' travel and related living expenses, as well as a basic stipend.

Eligible applicants/beneficiaries: U.S. citizens with an M.A. in TESL/TEFL or closely related field, obtained within the last 5 years.

Range: $25,000 to $40,000. **Average:** $35,000.

Activity: new program listing in 1997. FY 99 estimate, 35 grants.

HQ: World Learning, Inc., School for International Training, Kipling Rd., Brattleboro, VT 05302-0676. Phone: (802)258-3311. (Note: no field offices for this program.)

82.035 EXCHANGE—ENGLISH AS A FOREIGN LANGUAGE (EFL) FELLOWS ("English Language Programs")

Assistance: project grants (100 percent).

Purposes: pursuant to MECEA, to improve and develop English language capabilities in Eastern and Central Europe, Russia, and China and to contribute to the development of economic reform in the regions. The program places U.S. teacher-trainers and teachers of English for Specific Purposes (ESP) in respective countries at local ministries of education and teacher training institutions to work on such activities as curriculum development, teaching methodology, textbook analysis, and testing. Grants support costs of participants' travel and related living expenses, as well as a basic stipend. Funding is derived from the USIA/USAID Support for Eastern European Democracy (SEED) program.

Eligible applicants/beneficiaries: same as for **82.034**.

Range: $50,000 to $65,000. **Average:** $55,000.

Activity: new program listing in 1997. FY 99 estimate, 25 grants.

HQ: USIA, 301 Fourth St. SW - Rm.304, Washington, DC 20547. Phone: (202)619-5869. (Note: no field offices for this program.)

82.038 EDUCATIONAL EXCHANGE—AMERICAN STUDIES INSTITUTES ("Study of the U.S. Program - Office of Academic Programs")

Assistance: project grants (cost sharing/6-8 months).

Purposes: pursuant to MECEA, to provide foreign educators with a deeper understanding of American society, culture, and institutions, to improve courses and teaching about the U.S. abroad. Participants attend an integrated series of lectures, readings, interactive discussions, research and independent study, faculty mentoring, and site visits. Grant recipients are responsible for institute design and implementation, as well as all logistical program aspects.

Eligible applicants: IHEs or consortia, other nonprofit academic organizations—with four years of pertinent experience.

Eligible beneficiaries: foreign university faculty nominated by a USIS post or Fulbright Commission.

Range: $150,000 to $235,000. **Average:** $170,000.

Activity: new program listing in 1997. FY 98, cooperative agreements with 10 institutions, hosting 200 foreign participants.

HQ: Branch for the Study of the U.S. (E/AAS), USIA, 301 Fourth St. SW - Rm.252, Washington, DC 20547. Phones: (202)619-4578; FAX (202)619-6790; Web, http://usia.gov/education/am study   (Note: no field offices for this program.)

FEDERAL EMERGENCY MANAGEMENT AGENCY

83.007   REIMBURSEMENT FOR FIREFIGHTING ON FEDERAL PROPERTY

Assistance: direct payments/specified use.

Purposes: to reimburse fire service organizations for their direct expenses and losses from fire fighting operations on federal property.

Eligible applicants/beneficiaries: volunteer and paid fire departments of states, territories, possessions, and federal Indian lands.

Range/Average: to $500,000, with no stated limit.

Activity: FY 98, no claims submitted.

HQ: U.S. Fire Administration, FEMA, 16825 S. Seton Ave., Emmitsburg, MD 21727. Phone: (301)447-1080. (Note: no field offices for this program.)

83.009   NATIONAL FIRE ACADEMY TRAINING ASSISTANCE
("Student Stipend Reimbursement Program")

Assistance: direct payment/specified use.

Purposes: for stipends, travel expenses, and lodging costs of attending resident or regional programs the National Fire Academy.

Eligible applicants/beneficiaries: students who are members of fire departments or have significant responsibility for fire prevention and control. Federal and private industry employees and foreign students may attend courses, but are ineligible for payments.

Range/Average: resident courses, $339; regional, $105/one week. (Students pay for their own meals.)

Activity: FY 98, 4,516 stipends paid.

HQ: Educational and Technology Services Branch, National Emergency Training Center, FEMA, 16825 S. Seton Ave., Emmitsburg, MD 21727. Phone: (301)447-1035. (Note: no field offices for this program.)

83.010 NATIONAL FIRE ACADEMY EDUCATIONAL PROGRAM

Assistance: training.

Purposes: to provide training at the National Fire Academy or at off-campus locations, to increase the professional level of the fire service and others responsible for fire prevention and control. Training is provided on specific subjects to specific audiences.

Eligible applicants/beneficiaries: members of fire departments or persons with significant responsibility for fire prevention and control.

Activity: FY 98, 5,316 national facility, 1,538 regional, 8,366 "State Weekend," 50,000 train-the-trainer program participants.

HQ: same address as **83.007**. Phone: (301)447-1000. (Note: no field offices for this program.)

83.011 HAZARDOUS MATERIALS TRAINING PROGRAM FOR IMPLEMENTATION OF THE SUPERFUND AMENDMENT AND REAUTHORIZATION ACT (SARA) OF 1986
("SARA Title III Training Program")

Assistance: project grants (80 percent).

Purposes: pursuant to CERCLA, for training and education programs to improve emergency planning, preparedness, mitigation, response, and recovery capabilities of state, local, and tribal government personnel—with emphasis on hazardous chemicals and related emergencies.

Eligible applicants/beneficiaries: state and tribal governments; territories.

Range: $15,000 to $263,000. **Average:** $84,000.

Activity: N.A.

HQ: EMI-FEMA, 16825 S. Seton Ave., Emmitsburg, MD 21727. Phone: (301) 447-1142.

83.100 FLOOD INSURANCE
("NFIP")

Assistance: insurance.

Purposes: pursuant to the National Flood Insurance Act of 1968, to insure property owners against losses from floods, mudflow, and flood-caused erosion—at or below normal actuarial rates; to promote flood plain management practices. Flood insurance must be purchased as a condition of obtaining any form of federal financial assistance, including disaster assistance and mortgage loan insurance from VA, FmHA, and FHA, when projects are located within flood hazard areas where flood insurance is available. Special program provisions apply for properties within the Coastal Barrier Resource System.

Eligible applicants/beneficiaries: residential, business, and municipal property owners, in states or political subdivisions that have enacted NFIP flood plain management measures.

Range: claims paid: $1 to $100,000. **Average:** $16,000. Maximum amounts of coverage and other requirements apply, according to type and location of structure; details are available from FEMA regional offices or responsible state offices.

Activity: as of November 1998, 18,939 communities participating; 4,114,000 policies in force, representing $483 billion in insurance.

HQ: Federal Insurance Administration, FEMA, Washington, DC 20472. Phone: (202)646-3443.

83.105   COMMUNITY ASSISTANCE PROGRAM—STATE SUPPORT SERVICES ELEMENT ("CAP-SSSE")

Assistance: formula grants (75 percent).

Purposes: pursuant to the National Flood Insurance Act of 1968 and Flood Disaster Protection Act of 1973 as amended, to identify, prevent, and resolve flood plain management issues in communities participating in the NFIP, through the adoption of flood loss reduction measures. Project examples: community assistance visits, ordinance assistance, coordination meetings with FEMA regional offices, community rating system application assistance and review workshops, technical assistance.

Eligible applicants/beneficiaries: states.

Range: $50,000 to $250,000. **Average:** $90,000.

Activity: FY 98 estimate, 46 awards.

HQ: Program Specialist, Program Implementation Division, Mitigation Directorate, FEMA, 500 C St. SW - Rm.417, Washington, DC 20472. Phone: (202)646-3121.

83.505   STATE DISASTER PREPAREDNESS GRANTS ("Disaster Preparedness Improvement Grants")

Assistance: project grants (50 percent).

Purposes: to develop and improve disaster preparedness and prevention systems, including planning, revision of state legislation and regulations, system design, public information and education, training and exercises. Grant funds may not be used for equipment or facilities purchases or repairs.

Eligible applicants/beneficiaries: states, territories, and possessions.

Range: $15,000 to $50,000 annually. **Average:** $49,000.

Activity: not quantified specifically.

HQ: State and Local Division, Preparedness, Training and Exercises Directorate, FEMA, Washington, DC 20472. Phones: (202)646-3492; FAX (202) 646-4279; *24-hour phone service,* (202)566-1600.

83.523   EMERGENCY FOOD AND SHELTER NATIONAL BOARD PROGRAM

Assistance: formula grants (100 percent).

Purposes: pursuant to the McKinney homeless assistance act of 1968 as amended, to supplement and expand ongoing programs providing shelter, food, and supportive services for needy families and individuals; for projects to create more effective and innovative local programs; for minimum reha- bilitation of existing mass shelter or feeding facilities, bringing them into compliance with local building codes. Eligible expenses include: costs of food and its transport, food preparation and serving equipment; mass shelter and other shelter, such as hotels and motels; rent or mortgage payments assistance for one month only; limited facility repairs; utility payments. Ineligible costs include such expenses as rental security or other deposits, cash payments to the homeless, major property improvements.

Eligible applicants/beneficiaries: jurisdictions approved by the Emergency Food and Shelter Program National Board chaired by FEMA, or by State Set-Aside Committees, may award grants to: public or private nonprofit organizations, community action agencies, food banks, food pantries; spe- cialized community groups such as domestic violence centers; native Ameri- can organizations; organizations providing food and shelter to AIDS patients, handicapped persons, the elderly, teenage runaways, and others with emer- gency needs.

Range: $300 to $1,142,000. **Average:** $9,610.

Activity: assistance to 11,000 social service agencies in 2,500 jurisdictions, 25 training sessions with 1,500 participants.

HQ: Preparedness, Training and Exercises Directorate, FEMA, Washington, DC 20472. Phone: (202)646-3107. *Or:* Director, Emergency Food and Shelter Program, FEMA, 701 N. Fairfax St. - Ste.310, Alexandria, VA 22314. Phone: (703)706-9660.

83.526 NATIONAL URBAN SEARCH AND RESCUE (US&R) RESPONSE SYSTEM ("US&R")

Assistance: project grants (50-100 percent/to 3 years).

Purposes: pursuant to the Earthquake Hazards Reduction Act of 1977 as amended, to develop immediately deployable urban search and rescue task forces to locate, extricate, and provide medical treatment to victims of structural collapse during a disaster. Funds may be used for training and to acquire and maintain specialized equipment.

Eligible applicants/beneficiaries: 27 jurisdictions designated by FEMA.

Range/Average: $150,000 per existing grantee.

Activity: 27 annual grants.

HQ: Emergency Services Branch, Operations and Planning Division, Response and Recovery Directorate, FEMA, 500 C St. SW - Rm.609, Washington, DC 20472. Phone: (202)646-4013.

83.527 EMERGENCY MANAGEMENT INSTITUTE—TRAINING ASSISTANCE ("Student Stipend Reimbursement Program" - "SEP")

Assistance: direct payments/specified use.

Purposes: for state and local emergency management personnel to obtain training at the Emergency Management Institute and selected other locations. Programs embody the Comprehensive Emergency Management System by unifying the elements of planning, preparedness, mitigation, response, and recovery. Travel and per diem costs are reimbursed for state and local participants.

Eligible applicants/beneficiaries: state and local emergency management personnel.

Range/Average: $451 stipend. (Students pay for their own meals.)

Activity: FY 98, 6,449 participants; 2,963 stipends paid.

HQ: same address as **83.009**. Phone: (301)447-1000.

83.529 EMERGENCY MANAGEMENT INSTITUTE (EMI)—INDEPENDENT STUDY PROGRAM

Assistance: training.

Purposes: to offer home study courses in emergency management practices. Available courses include: Emergency Program Manager; Radiological Emergency Management; A Citizen's Guide to Disaster Assistance; Building for the Earthquakes of Tomorrow: Engineering Principles and Practices for Retrofitting Flood Prone Residential Buildings; Animals in Disaster; and, refresher and other specialized courses.

Eligible applicants/beneficiaries: general public, emergency management personnel, public officials.

Activity: FY 99 estimate, 60,000 enrollments.

HQ: Independent Study Program, EMI-FEMA, 16825 S. Seton Ave, Emmitsburg, MD 21727. Phone: (301)447-1240.

83.530 EMERGENCY MANAGEMENT INSTITUTE (EMI)—RESIDENT EDUCATIONAL PROGRAM

Assistance: training.

Purposes: to provide training at EMI of federal, state, and local emergency management personnel involved in emergency and disaster response. Training emphasizes planning, mitigation, response, and recovery—embodied in the Comprehensive Emergency Management System.

Eligible applicants/beneficiaries: official emergency management personnel.

Activity: FY 98, 6,449 participants.

HQ: same address as **83.009**. Phone: (301)447-1000.

83.534 EMERGENCY MANAGEMENT—STATE AND LOCAL ASSISTANCE

Assistance: formula grants (50 percent).

Purposes: to fund necessary and essential state and local emergency management personnel and administrative expenses, including the costs of planning, development of response systems, training, equipment purchases, testing and exercises.

Eligible applicants/beneficiaries: states, interstate authorities, territories and possessions. Local governments and tribes participate as subgrantees.

Range: $221,000 to $8,710,000. **Average:** $1,984,000.

Activity: not quantified specifically.

HQ: same address/phones as **83.505.**

83.535   MITIGATION ASSISTANCE

Assistance: project grants (50-75 percent).

Purposes: to develop and maintain state capabilities to implement comprehensive pre- and post-disaster hazard mitigation capabilities. Funds support state hazard mitigation officers and planning, training, public awareness activities.

Eligible applicants/beneficiaries: states and territorial governments.

Range: $54,000 to $1,547,000. **Average:** $110,000.

Activity: new program in FY 97; grants to all 56 states and territories.

HQ: Mitigation Directorate, FEMA, Washington, DC 20472. Phone: (202)646-4090.

83.536   FLOOD MITIGATION ASSISTANCE
("FMA")

Assistance: project grants (base amount plus 75 percent/2 years).

Purposes: for cost-effective measures that reduce or eliminate long-term risks of flood damage to buildings, manufactured homes, and other insurable structures. Funds may support planning, engineering and planning services, and such implementation activities as elevation or dry flood-proofing of structures, minor structural projects, beach nourishment.

Eligible applicants/beneficiaries: planning and project grants—states and communities participating in the NFIP. Technical assistance grants—state agencies.

Range: 5-year planning, to $150,000 to states, $50,000 to communities—with $300,000 maximum to any state; projects, from $100,000.

Activity: new program in FY 97; not quantified specifically.

HQ: Program Support Division, Mitigation Directorate, FEMA, 500 C St. SW, Washington, DC 20472. Phone: (202)646-3619.

83.537   COMMUNITY DISASTER LOANS

Assistance: direct loans (5 years).

Purposes: for local governments that have suffered substantial loss of tax and other revenue and that demonstrate a need for financial assistance. Funds may be used only to maintain existing municipal operating functions.

Eligible applicants/beneficiaries: local governments in disaster areas.

Range: to 25 percent of the applicant's FY operating budget.

Activity: new program listing in 1997.

HQ: Response and Recovery Directorate, FEMA, 500 C St. SW, Washington, DC 20472. Phone: (202)646-3683.

83.538   CORA BROWN FUND

Assistance: direct payments/specified use.

Purposes: to help victims of natural disasters that will not obtain assistance through other government or private programs. The fund was established by the late Cora C. Brown of Kansas City, Missouri, who left a portion of her estate to the U.S. government to help victims of natural disasters not caused by or attributed to war.

Eligible applicants/beneficiaries: individuals, families, and groups in need of disaster-related home repair and rebuilding and other services.

Range/Average: N.A.

Activity: new program listing in 1997.

HQ: Director, Human Services Division, Response and Recovery Directorate, FEMA, Washington, DC 20472. Phone: (202)646-3642.

83.539   CRISIS COUNSELING

Assistance: project grants (100 percents/60 days).

Purposes: to provide immediate crisis counseling services to victims of major natural disasters to relieve mental health problems, at no cost to the victims. Services include screening, diagnostic and counseling techniques, outreach, education, training of providers.

Eligible applicants/beneficiaries: states or public or private agencies designated by the governor.

Range/Average: N.A.

Activity: new program listing in 1997. FY 98, responses to 45 major disasters in 28 states.

HQ: same address/phone as **83.538**.

83.540   DISASTER LEGAL SERVICES

Assistance: specialized services; advisory services/counseling.

Purposes: to provide free legal services to persons affected by natural disasters, including legal advice, counseling, and representation in nonfee-generating cases.

Eligible applicants/beneficiaries: low-income individuals, families, groups.

Activity: new program listing in 1997.

HQ: same address as **83.538**. Phone: (202)646-3685.

83.541   DISASTER UNEMPLOYMENT ASSISTANCE ("DUA")

Assistance: direct payments/specified use (to 26 weeks); specialized services.

Purposes: to provide weekly unemployment benefits to persons left jobless by natural disasters and ineligible for regular unemployment insurance benefits.

Eligible applicants/beneficiaries: disaster victims.

Range/Average: N.A.

Activity: new program listing in 1997.

HQ: same address as **83.538**. Phone: (202)646-3685.

83.542   FIRE SUPPRESSION ASSISTANCE

Assistance: project grants (70-100 percent); use of property, facilities, and equipment; specialized services.

Purposes: for the suppression of any fire on nonfederal public or privately owned forest or grassland that threatens to become a major disaster.

Eligible applicants/beneficiaries: state governments; territories and possessions.

Range/Average: N.A.

Activity: new program listing in 1997. FY 98, 54 grants authorized.

HQ: same address as **83.537**. Phone: (202)646-4535.

83.543 INDIVIDUAL AND FAMILY GRANTS ("IFG")

Assistance: project grants (75 percent).

Purposes: to help meet the necessary expenses and serious needs of disaster victims that cannot be met through other disaster assistance or insurance. Funds may be used for property repairs, personal property replacement, medical and dental costs, funeral expenses, and transportation.

Eligible applicants/beneficiaries: states.

Range: to $13,600 per applicant. **Average:** $1,990.

Activity: new program listing in 1997. FY 98, 283,000 grants approved.

HQ: same address as **83.538**. Phone: (202)646-3685.

83.544 PUBLIC ASSISTANCE GRANTS

Assistance: project grants (75 percent).

Purposes: to provide supplemental assistance in alleviating suffering and hardship resulting from declared major disasters or emergencies. Funds may be used for the removal of wreckage and debris, to take emergency protective measures on public and private land, for emergency transportation or communications, to restore eligible facilities.

Eligible applicants/beneficiaries: state and local governments, other state political subdivisions, territories and possessions, tribal governments, Alaska native villages or organizations, certain nonprofit organizations.

Range/Average: N.A.

Activity: new program listing in 1997. FY 98, 49 disasters, 2 emergencies declared.

HQ: same address as **83.537**. Phone: (202)646-2751.

83.545 DISASTER HOUSING PROGRAM

Assistance: direct payments/specified use (100 percent/1-18 months); specialized services.

Purposes: for households affected by disasters to enable them to address their disaster-created housing needs. Assistance may include funds for transient housing accommodations, home repairs, and rental or mortgage assistance.

Eligible applicants/beneficiaries: disaster victims in designated emergency or major disaster areas.

Range/Average: N.A.

Activity: new program listing in 1997.

HQ: same address as **83.538**. Phone: (202)646-3685.

83.547   FIRST RESPONDER COUNTER-TERRORISM TRAINING ASSISTANCE ("Counter-Terrorism Training" - "ATT")

Assistance: project grants (100 percent).

Purposes: to train first responders in managing the consequences of terrorist acts. Training is provided through individual state fire training systems.

Eligible applicants/beneficiaries: all fire and emergency first responders and law enforcement personnel with operational or incident management responsibilities. Individuals apply to their state fire training office.

Range/Average: N.A.

Activity: new program in FY 97. FY 98, 50 grants.

HQ: Regional Field Training Specialist, National Fire Academy, U.S. Fire Administration-FEMA, 16825 S. Seton Ave., Emmitsburg, MD 21727. Phone: (301)447-1158.

83.548   HAZARD MITIGATION GRANT ("HMPG")

Assistance: project grants (75 percent/2 years).

Purposes: for measures to permanently reduce or eliminate future damages and losses from natural hazards through safer building practices, improving existing structures, and supporting infrastructure. Funds may be used: to acquire, relocate, modify, or demolish structures; for seismic rehabilitation or retrofitting of structures; for initial implementation of vegetation management programs; to provide pertinent training to architects, engineers, building officials, and others; to bring structures into compliance with floodplain management requirements.

Eligible applicants/beneficiaries: state and local governments, other public entities, authorized tribal organizations, Alaska native villages or organizations, certain nonprofit organizations.

Range/Average: N.A.

Activity: new program listing in 1997.

HQ: same address/phone as **83.536**.

83.549   CHEMICAL STOCKPILE EMERGENCY PREPAREDNESS PROGRAM ("CSEPP")

Assistance: projects grants.

Purposes: to enhance emergency preparedness capabilities at the eight chemical agent stockpile facilities maintained by DOD. Funding has paid for operational siren systems, demographic surveys, dedicated radio and telephone systems, public training courses and exercises.

Eligible applicants/beneficiaries: the states of Alabama, Arkansas, Colorado, Illinois, Indiana, Kentucky, Maryland, Oregon, Utah, and Washington. Local governments and tribes may relieve subgrants.

Range: $60,000 to $4,000,000. **Average:** $2,000,000.

Activity: new program listing in 1998.

HQ: Preparedness, Training and Exercises Directorate, FEMA, Washington, DC 20472. Phones: (202)646-3200; FAX (202)646-4321; *24-hour/day EPA phone operator,* (202)566-1600; e-mail, @fema.gov

83.550 NATIONAL DAM SAFETY PROGRAM
("Dam Safety State Assistance Program")

Assistance: project grants (50 percent).

Purposes: to establish, improve, and maintain safety programs covering nonfederal dams. Eligible uses of funds include permitting and approval of project plans, legislative modifications and regulations development, enforcement activities, emergency response, program staffing, public education, and training.

Eligible applicants/beneficiaries: state offices, PR.

Range: $15,000 to $155,000.

Activity: new program listing in 1998.

HQ: Mitigation Directorate, FEMA, Washington, DC 20472. Phone: (202)646-2704.

83.551 PROJECT IMPACT—BUILDING DISASTER RESISTANT COMMUNITIES

Assistance: project grants (75-100 percent/2-5 years).

Purposes: to implement sustained pre-disaster, natural hazard loss mitigation programs. Project funds may be used: to acquire, relocate, elevate, or strengthen structures; for drainage improvement; to develop state or local standards; for training, hazard identification and risk assessment, public education, and related activities.

Eligible applicants/beneficiaries: communities, states or jurisdictions with Project Impact communities; DC, PR.

Range: $300,000 to $500,000. **Average:** $300,000.

Activity: new program listing in 1998; 57 pilot Project Impact communities designated to date.

HQ: Project Impact, Mitigation Directorate, FEMA, Washington, DC 20472. Phone: (202)646-3701.

83.552 EMERGENCY MANAGEMENT PERFORMANCE GRANTS
("EMPG")

Assistance: formula grants; project grants (matching).

Purposes: to develop comprehensive emergency management, including for terrorism consequence, by combining several funding streams into a consolidated grant. The key functional areas are: Laws and Authorities; Hazard Identification and Risk Assessment; Hazard Management; Resource Management; Planning; Direction, Control, and Coordination; Communications and Warning; Operations and Procedures; Logistics and Facilities; Training; Exercises; Public Education and Information; Finance and Administration.

Eligible applicants/beneficiaries: states, territories, possessions.

Range: $50,000 to $9,000,000. **Average:** $2,000,000.

Activity: new program in FY 00.

HQ: Office of Financial Management, FEMA, Washington, DC 20472. Phones: (202)646-7057; FAX (202)646-4268.

DEPARTMENT OF EDUCATION

84.002   ADULT EDUCATION—STATE GRANT PROGRAM

Assistance: formula grants (75 percent/to 27 months; territories, 88 percent).

Purposes: for adult education and literacy services. Portions of grant amounts may be spent for: state leadership activities, professional development, teacher training; correctional education and services to other institutionalized individuals.

Eligible applicants: SEAs. LEAs and other public or private nonprofit organizations may receive subgrants, including libraries, public housing authorities, IHEs.

Eligible beneficiaries: out-of-school adults at least age 16 and lacking mastery of basic educational skills or without a high school diploma or English language proficiency.

Range: $100,000 to $38,791,000.

Activity: FY 98, 59 grants to states and insular areas, 4,000 subgrants;.

HQ: Division of Adult Education and Literacy, OVAE-DOED, Washington, DC 20202-7240. Phone: (202)205-8270. (Note: no field offices for this program.)

84.004   CIVIL RIGHTS TRAINING AND ADVISORY SERVICES

Assistance: project grants (100 percent/3 years).

Purposes: pursuant to the Civil Rights Act of 1964 as amended, Title IV, for educational equity assistance centers to provide technical assistance and training services to school districts, relating to compliance with civil rights laws pertaining to race, gender, and national origin. Project funds may be used for information dissemination, staff and community training, and instruction of students with limited English proficiency relevant to program purposes.

Eligible applicants/beneficiaries: any private nonprofit organization or public agency.

Range/Average: $733,000.

Activity: FY 98, 10 grants to centers.

HQ: Equity and Educational Excellence Division, OESE-DOED, 400 Maryland Ave. SW, Washington, DC 20202-6140. Phone: (202)260-2638. (Note: no field offices for this program.)

84.007   FEDERAL SUPPLEMENTAL EDUCATIONAL OPPORTUNITY GRANTS ("FSEOG" - "SEOG")

Assistance: direct payments/specified use (75 percent).

Purposes: for undergraduate postsecondary study by students in financial need, including for studies abroad. Institutions may receive an administrative cost allowance.

Eligible applicants: public, private nonprofit, postsecondary vocational, and proprietary IHEs.

Eligible beneficiaries: needy undergraduate students meeting citizenship or residency requirements, enrolled or enrolling as regular students, maintaining satisfactory academic progress, in compliance with Selective Service requirements, and neither owing a refund nor in default on a Title IV grant or loan.

Range: $100 to $4,000/year (to $400 additional for study abroad). **Average:** $727.

Activity: 1997-98, 1,116,000 student awards.

HQ: Chief, Grants Branch, Policy Development Division, OSFA-DOED, 400 Maryland Ave. SW, Washington, DC 20202-5446. Phone: (202)708-8242.

84.010   TITLE 1 GRANTS TO LOCAL EDUCATIONAL AGENCIES ("Title 1 Basic, Concentration, and Targeted Grants")

Assistance: formula grants (100 percent).

Purposes: to supplement state and local funding for compensatory instructional activities for children from low-income families, failing to meet academic standards or at-risk.

Eligible applicants/beneficiaries: SEAs; DOI. LEAs and tribal schools are subgrantees.

Range: $16,261,000 to $829,978,000. **Average:** $140,346,000.

Activity: FY 98, 11,000,000 public and nonpublic (3 percent) school children in 14,000 districts and 50,000 schools served.

HQ: Compensatory Education Programs, OESE-DOED, FOB-6 - Rm.3W230, 400 Maryland Ave. SW, Washington, DC 20202-6132. Phone: (202)260-0826. (Note: no field offices for this program.)

84.011   MIGRANT EDUCATION—BASIC STATE GRANT PROGRAM

Assistance: formula grants (100 percent).

Purposes: for comprehensive educational programs for migratory children, including academic, remedial, bilingual, compensatory, multicultural, and vocational instruction; preschool services; health services; career education services.

Eligible applicants: SEAs; consortia.

Eligible beneficiaries: children age 0-21, of migratory agricultural workers or fishers that have moved across school districts during the last 36 months.

Range/Average: $5,759,000.

Activity: 1998, 700,000 eligible children in 3,500 school districts.

HQ: Office of Migrant Education, OESE-DOED, FOB 6 - Rm.3E329, 400 Maryland Ave. SW, Washington, DC 20202-6135. Phone: (202)260-1164. (Note: no field offices for this program.)

84.013   TITLE I PROGRAM FOR NEGLECTED AND DELINQUENT CHILDREN

Assistance: formula grants (100 percent).

Purposes: for education programs and related services for institutionalized neglected or delinquent children, including children under age 21 in state institutions, adult correctional institutions, or state-operated community day schools. Funds may cover supplemental instruction in core academic subjects, tutoring, counseling, services facilitating transition to schools. Juvenile institutions must provide at least 20 hours of instruction per week; adult institutions, at least 15 hours—from nonfederal funds.

Eligible applicants/beneficiaries: SEAs. Related state agencies may receive subgrants.

Range: subgrants, $43,000 to $3,603,000. **Average:** $756,000.

Activity: FY 98, 196,000 children served in 400 state institutions in 50 states, DC, and PR.

HQ: same address/phone as **84.010**. (Note: no field offices for this program.)

84.015   NATIONAL RESOURCE CENTERS AND FELLOWSHIPS PROGRAM FOR LANGUAGE AND AREA OR LANGUAGE AND INTERNATIONAL STUDIES

Assistance: project grants (100 percent/to 3 years).

Purposes: for instruction in modern foreign languages and in area and international studies. National resource center program grants may be awarded for undergraduate training only, or they may be comprehensive involving undergraduate, graduate, and professional training. Funds may support the costs of instruction programs, administration, library resources, lectures and conferences. Fellowships may be awarded for graduate language study combined with area studies and world affairs, covering tuition, fees, and basic subsistence.

Eligible applicants/beneficiaries: U.S. IHEs. Fellowships—graduate students that are U.S. citizens, nationals, or permanent residents; training must be undertaken at a school with a quota of Foreign Language and Area Studies Fellowships (FLAS).

Range/Average: centers, $178,000; fellowships, $106,000.

Activity: FY 98, 109 centers funded; 129 IHEs supported for fellowships.

HQ: Advanced Training and Research Team, OPE-DOED, 400 Maryland Ave. SW, Washington, DC 20202-5331. Phones: *for Canada, Latin America, Caribbean, Inner Asia, Eastern and Western Europe, Russia, North America*, (202)401-9782; *East, South, and Southeast Asia, Middle East, Pacific Islands*, (202)401-9785; *Africa and international*, (202)401-9774. (Note: no field offices for this program.)

84.016 UNDERGRADUATE INTERNATIONAL STUDIES AND FOREIGN LANGUAGE PROGRAMS

Assistance: project grants (50 percent/1-3 years).

Purposes: for undergraduate international studies and foreign language programs and projects. Funds may cover administration, curriculum and faculty development, lectures and conferences, library enhancement, travel.

Eligible applicants/beneficiaries: accredited IHEs, public and private nonprofit agencies and organizations.

Range/Average: new awards $63,000; continuations, $67,000.

Activity: 1998, 56 programs funded.

HQ: International Studies Branch, International Education and Graduate Programs Service, OPE-DOED, 400 Maryland Ave. SW, Washington, DC 20202-5332. Phone: (202)401-9783. (Note: no field offices for this program.)

84.017 INTERNATIONAL RESEARCH AND STUDIES

Assistance: project grants (100 percent/1-3 years).

Purposes: for studies, surveys, research, and development of instructional materials and publications relating to establishing needs for and the improvement and evaluation of education and training in modern foreign languages, area, and other international studies. Funds may not support student or teacher training.

Eligible applicants/beneficiaries: public and private agencies, organizations, institutions, and individuals.

Range/Average: new awards, $106,000; continuations, $88,000.

Activity: 1998, 9 new, 22 continuation grants; 1 SBIR project.

HQ: Advanced Training and Research Team, International Education and Graduate Programs Service, OPE-DOED, 400 Maryland Ave. SW, Washington, DC 20202-5331. Phone: (202)401-9784. (Note: no field offices for this program.)

84.018 INTERNATIONAL: OVERSEAS SEMINARS ABROAD—BILATERAL PROJECTS

Assistance: project grants (100 percent/4-6 weeks).

Purposes: pursuant to MECEA as amended, to pay the travel and tuition costs of educators participating in short-term training seminars abroad, on topics in the social sciences and humanities.

Eligible applicants/beneficiaries: U.S. citizens or permanent residents with appropriate language proficiency and a bachelor's degree, that are: undergraduate faculty members or full-time elementary or junior high school teachers, administrators, or supervisors with at least three years of professional experience in U.S. school systems. (DOED recommends applicants to the Fulbright scholarship board for approval.)

Range/Average: $120,000.

Activity: 1998, 115 participants in 8 projects.

HQ: same address as **84.016**. Phone: (202)401-9798. (Note: no field offices for this program.)

84.019   INTERNATIONAL: OVERSEAS—FACULTY RESEARCH ABROAD

Assistance: project grants (100 percent/3-12 months).

Purposes: pursuant to MECEA as amended, for fellowships for research and study abroad by college faculty members, relevant to a modern foreign language or area specialization that cannot be conducted in the U.S. or for which a foreign country or region provides superior research facilities. The assistance should contribute to the development or improvement of the study of modern foreign languages or area studies in those fields needed for a full understanding of the area, regions, or countries in which the modern foreign languages are commonly used. Generally, grants are unavailable for projects focusing primarily on Western Europe or in countries where the U.S. has no formal diplomatic relations. Awards provide stipends in lieu of salary and cover travel costs, fees to foreign institutions, expenses for expendable materials and supplies, services.

Eligible applicants: IHEs.

Eligible beneficiaries: U.S. citizens, nationals, or permanent residents that: are IHE employees; have been engaged in teaching relevant to the foreign language or area specialization for the previous two years; are not engaged in dissertation research for a Ph.D.; have appropriate language skills. (DOED recommends applicants to the Fulbright scholarship board for approval.)

Range/Average: $48,000.

Activity: FY 98, 17 fellowships.

HQ: same address as **84.017**. Phone: (202)401-9777. (Note: no field offices for this program.)

84.021   INTERNATIONAL: OVERSEAS—GROUP PROJECTS ABROAD

Assistance: project grants (100 percent/5-52 weeks; to 36 months).

Purposes: pursuant to MECEA as amended, for groups of teachers, faculty, and graduate or upper-classmen to conduct studies abroad in modern foreign languages and area studies. Funds may cover travel, rent for instructional facilities, general maintenance allowances, books, teaching materials, clerical, and related costs.

Eligible applicants: IHEs; state departments of education; private nonprofit educational organizations; consortia. (DOED recommends applicants to the Fulbright scholarship board for approval.)

Eligible beneficiaries: U.S. citizens, nationals, or permanent residents that are faculty members or teachers at all levels, or graduate students or upperclassmen planning teaching careers in foreign language or area studies.

Range: $40,000 to $165,000. **Average:** $58,000.

Activity: FY 98, 38 projects with 575 participants.

HQ: same address as **84.017**. Phone: (202)708-7283. (Note: no field offices for this program.)

84.022   INTERNATIONAL: OVERSEAS—DOCTORAL DISSERTATION

Assistance: project grants (100 percent/6-12 months).

Purposes: pursuant to MECEA as amended, for fellowships to graduate students to complete dissertation research abroad in modern foreign languages and area studies—to develop research knowledge and capability in areas not widely included in American curricula. Generally, no grants are available for projects focusing primarily on Western Europe or in countries where the U.S. has no formal diplomatic relations. Grants may cover stipends, travel costs, tuition to host institutions, dependents allowances, insurance, project expenses.

Eligible applicants: IHEs. (DOED recommends applicants to the Fulbright scholarship board for approval.)

Eligible beneficiaries: U.S. citizens, nationals, or permanent residents that are graduate students in good standing, plan teaching careers in the U.S. upon graduation, and have appropriate language skills.

Range: $8,583 to $60,000. **Average:** $24,000.

Activity: FY 98, 81 fellowships.

HQ: same address as **84.017**. Phone: (202)401-9774. (Note: no field offices for this program.)

84.027   SPECIAL EDUCATION—GRANTS TO STATES

Assistance: formula grants (100 percent).

Purposes: pursuant to IDEA as amended, to provide special education and related services to children and youth, age 3-21, with disabilities, including those in private schools.

Eligible applicants/beneficiaries: SEAs; territories and possessions; BIA. LEAs apply to SEAs for funds.

Range: $3,133,000 to $377,133,000.

Activity: FY 98, 6,000,000 children served.

HQ: Division of Monitoring and State Improvement Planning, OSERS-DOED, 400 Maryland Ave. SW, Washington, DC 20202. Phone: (202)205-5547.

84.031   HIGHER EDUCATION—INSTITUTIONAL AID

Assistance: project grants (to 100 percent/to 5 years).

Purposes: to help colleges and universities solve their fiscal and management problems. The Strengthening Institutions Program includes American Indian tribally controlled and Alaska native- and Hawaii native-serving institutions; funds may be used to plan, develop, and implement programs for faculty development, and for administrative expenses, improvement of academic programs, library and equipment purchases, and student services. The Historically Black Colleges and Universities Program provides funds for undergraduate and graduate programs, which may be used: to acquire scientific equipment; to construct, maintain, and improve classroom, library, and other instructional facilities; for faculty exchanges and fellowships; to purchase library materials; to provide tutoring, counseling, and other student services; for administrative management and equipment. Graduate HBCU program funds may be used to establish or maintain endowments. Projects over $1,000,000 require a 50 percent match.

Eligible applicants/beneficiaries: IHEs with a low average educational and general expenditure, substantial percentage of students receiving Pell Grants or other federal need-based financial aid; HBCUs established prior to 1964.

Range: HBCU, from $500,000 **Average:** Strengthening Institutions, $330,000.

Activity: FY 98, 326 grants.

HQ: Institutional Development and Undergraduate Education Service, OPE-DOED, 400 Maryland Ave. SW, Washington, DC 20202-5335. Phone: (202)708-8816. (Note: no field offices for this program.)

84.032   FEDERAL FAMILY EDUCATION LOANS

Assistance: guaranteed/insured loans (5-30 years).

Purposes: to provide federal reinsurance on loans insured by state or private nonprofit guaranty agencies—for vocational, graduate, or undergraduate educational expenses. Loans are obtained from banks, credit unions, savings and loan associations, pension funds, insurance companies, and schools. Repayment of Stafford loans begins six months after termination of at least half-time enrollment; for PLUS loans, repayment begins 60 days after disbursement of the last installment, and generally extends five to ten years, except that consolidation loans may extend up to 30 years. Deferments and forbearance of payment may be granted for certain periods.

Eligible applicants/beneficiaries: Stafford loans—generally, any U.S. citizen, national, or permanent resident enrolled or accepted for at least half-time as an undergraduate, graduate, professional, or vocational student at a participating postsecondary school. PLUS program—parents on behalf of dependent students. Federal Unsubsidized Stafford program—graduate, professional, and independent undergraduate students, including half-time students seeking elementary or secondary teacher certification; exceptionally, dependent undergraduate students. Consolidation loans—graduates including married couples; school enrollment not required. U.S. citizens or nationals may obtain loans to attend eligible foreign postsecondary schools. Applicants for subsidized loans must meet needs criteria. Applicants must maintain satisfactory academic performance, and may neither owe a refund nor be in default on a Title IV grant or loan.

Range: Stafford-undergraduate first academic year, to $2,625; second, to $3,500; to $5,500/year afterwards, with $23,000 maximum total; graduate and professional, to $8,500 annually, with $65,500 maximum including any amounts borrowed as undergraduate. Unsubsidized Stafford, undergraduate first two years, to $4,000/year; to $5,000 for remaining years, with $23,000 aggregate maximum; graduate, $10,000/academic year with $73,000 maximum including undergraduate loans. PLUS-parents may borrow the full cost of education, minus any other financial aid obtained, with no maximum.

Activity: 4,813 participating lenders.

HQ: Policy, Training, and Analysis Service, Division of Policy Development, OPE-DOED, Washington, DC 20202. Phone: (202)708-8242.

84.033   FEDERAL WORK-STUDY PROGRAM ("FWS")

Assistance: direct payments/specified use.

Purposes: to provide part-time jobs to postsecondary students. The program contributes up to 75 percent of student earnings in jobs in public or nonprofit organizations, or 50 percent when a profit organization hires the student—plus administrative cost allowances to the educational institution.

Eligible applicants: public, private nonprofit, postsecondary vocational, and proprietary IHEs.

Eligible beneficiaries: undergraduate, graduate, or professional students meeting citizenship and residency requirements and demonstrating financial need.

Range/Average: students, $1,215 per award.

Activity: 1998, 746,000 student jobs supported.

HQ: same address/phone as **84.007.**

84.037   FEDERAL PERKINS LOAN CANCELLATIONS

Assistance: direct payments/specified/unrestricted use.

Purposes: to reimburse institutions for their share of loans canceled for certain National Defense Student Loan recipients.

Eligible applicants: same as for **84.033.**

Eligible beneficiaries: for current borrowers for loans made July 23, 1992 or after, loan cancellation is available for full-time service as: teachers in designated elementary or secondary schools with a high enrollment of children from low-income families; Head Start Programs staff; members of the Armed Forces in areas of hostilities; volunteers in the Peace Corps or in ACTION programs (Perkins program only); law enforcement or corrections officers serving state, local, or federal agencies; special education teachers of children with disabilities or professional providers of early intervention services; teachers of mathematics, science, foreign languages, bilingual education, or certain other fields; nurses or medical technicians; or, employees of public or private child or family service agencies providing services to high-risk children from low-income communities and their families.

Range/Average: $11,000.

Activity: N.A.

HQ: Chief, Institutional Services Branch, Institutional Financial Management Division, OSFA-DOED, 400 Maryland Ave. SW, Washington, DC 20202-5347. Phone: (202)708-7742.

84.038   FEDERAL PERKINS LOAN PROGRAM—FEDERAL CAPITAL CONTRIBUTIONS

Assistance: direct payments/specified use.

Purposes: for educational institutions to make low-interest loans to needy undergraduate and graduate students to cover their educational expenses. The institutions receive an administrative cost allowance.

Eligible applicants: same as for **84.033.**

Eligible beneficiaries: needy undergraduate, graduate, or professional students meeting citizenship or residency requirements, enrolled as regular students, maintaining satisfactory academic progress, in compliance with Selective Service requirements, and neither owing a refund nor in default on a Title IV grant or loan.

Range: graduate students, to $6,000 annually and $40,000 cumulative maximum—including undergraduate loans; undergraduates, to $4,000 annually and $20,000 cumulative maximum. (Maximums may be 20 percent more for study abroad.) **Average:** $1,564 annual.

Activity: FY 97, 679,000 student awards.

HQ: Chief, Loans Branch, same address/phone as **84.007.**

84.040 IMPACT AID—FACILITIES MAINTENANCE

Assistance: project grants (100 percent).

Purposes: to construct, enlarge, maintain, restore, or improve school facilities owned by DOED and operated by LEAs, and to transfer such facilities to LEAs.

Eligible applicants/beneficiaries: LEAs.

Range/Average: N.A.

Activity: not quantified specifically.

HQ: Impact Aid Program, OESE-DOED, 400 Maryland Ave. SW, Washington, DC 20202-6244. Phone: (202)260-3858. (Note: no field offices for this program.)

84.041 IMPACT AID

Assistance: formula grants (100 percent).

Purposes: for operating costs of LEAs where enrollments or the tax base are adversely affected by federal activities including: federal acquisition of real property; employment of parents on federal property or in the uniformed services; significant numbers of children residing on federal land including Indian lands; sudden increases in school enrollment. Special additional funds are provided based on related enrollments of handicapped children, which must be used for special programs. Payments for construction may be used for construction and renovation, debt service, or other capital fund activities.

Eligible applicants/beneficiaries: LEAs.

Range: N.A.

Activity: 1,700 grants on behalf of 1,400,000 children.

HQ: same address/phone as **84.040.** (Note: no field offices for this program.)

84.042 TRIO—STUDENT SUPPORT SERVICES

Assistance: project grants (100 percent/4-5 years).

Purposes: to provide supportive services to disadvantaged college students to enhance their potential to complete their programs, to facilitate their transition from two-year to four-year programs of study or to graduate and professional programs. Projects may include personal and academic counseling, career guidance, instruction, mentoring, tutoring, and special services to students with limited language proficiency. At least two-thirds of project participants must be physically handicapped or low-income, first-generation college students.

Eligible applicants/beneficiaries: IHEs and consortia.

Range: $170,000 to $300,000. **Average:** $216,000.

Activity: FY 98, 796 continuation awards, 178,000 students served.

HQ: Federal TRIO Programs, OPE-DOED, Portals Bldg. - Ste.600C, 400 Maryland Ave. SW, Washington, DC 20202-5249. Phone: (202)708-4804.

84.044 TRIO—TALENT SEARCH

Assistance: project grants (100 percent/to 5 years).

Purposes: to identify disadvantaged youth with potential for postsecondary education; to encourage them to return to or continue in and graduate from secondary schools and enroll in postsecondary education programs; to publicize the availability of financial aid; to provide special tutoring. Two-thirds of project participants must be low-income, potential first-generation college students.

Eligible applicants: IHEs; public and private agencies and organizations; combinations of IHEs and others; some secondary schools.

Eligible beneficiaries: individuals residing in target areas or attending a target school. Participants must be age 11-27 (exceptions allowed).

Range: $190,000 to $400,000. **Average:** $265,000.

Activity: FY 98, 362 grants; 324,000 individuals served.

HQ: College and University Preparation and Support Team, same address/phone as **84.042**. (Note: no field offices for this program.)

84.047 TRIO—UPWARD BOUND

Assistance: project grants (100 percent/to 5 years).

Purposes: for programs providing academic instruction, personal and academic counseling, tutoring, career guidance, and special instruction—to prepare participants for postsecondary education and for careers in which persons from disadvantaged backgrounds are under-represented. Stipends may be paid to students ($40 monthly during the academic year and $60 monthly during special summer residential programs). Two-thirds of the participants must be low-income, potential first-generation college students.

Eligible applicants: same as for **84.044**.

Eligible beneficiaries: low-income individuals and potential first-generation college students. Except for veterans, eligible regardless of age, participants must be age 13-19 and have completed the eighth grade but not have entered the twelfth grade (exceptions allowed).

Range: $200,000 to $690,000; math/science awards, $200,000 to $300,000. **Average:** $304,000; math/science, $249,000.

Activity: FY 98, 598 awards; 45,000 students served; 81 awards for math/science projects.

HQ: same address (except FOB 6 - Rm.5065)/phone as **84.044**.

84.048 VOCATIONAL EDUCATION—BASIC GRANTS TO STATES

Assistance: formula grants (states, partial matching; outlying areas, 100 percent/27 months).

Purposes: to expand and improve vocational education programs, including special programs for single parents, single pregnant women, displaced homemakers, criminal offenders, and for individuals participating in programs to eliminate sex bias and stereotyping.

Eligible applicants/beneficiaries: states. Subgrants may be awarded to LEAs and postsecondary institutions.

Range: $4,215,000 to $107,278,000.

Activity: all states and outlying areas receive grants.

HQ: Division of Vocational-Technical Education, OVAE-DOED, 600 Independence Ave. SW, Washington, DC 20202-7323. Phone: (202)205-9441. (Note: no field offices for this program.)

84.051 NATIONAL VOCATIONAL EDUCATION RESEARCH

Assistance: project grants (100 percent/to 5 years).

Purposes: to support the National Center for Research in its vocational education and special projects including clearinghouse services, training, and applied and policy research.

Eligible applicants/beneficiaries: universities or university consortia (competition held every five years).

Range/Average: N.A.

Activity: not quantified specifically.

HQ: Division of National Programs, OVAE-DOED, 400 Maryland Ave. SW, Washington, DC 20202-7242. Phones: (202)205-9071, -9673. (Note: no field offices for this program.)

84.060 INDIAN EDUCATION—GRANTS TO LOCAL EDUCATIONAL AGENCIES

Assistance: formula grants; project grants (100 percent/to 5 years).

Purposes: to establish, maintain, and operate supplementary elementary and secondary school projects designed to assist Indian students in achieving state content and student performance standards. Among the types of activities that may be funded are culturally related programs, early childhood and family programs emphasizing school readiness, enrichment programs.

Eligible applicants/beneficiaries: LEAs that enroll at least 10 Indian children or in which Indians constitute at least 25 percent of the total enrollment— except those serving Indian children in Alaska, California, and Oklahoma or located on, or in proximity to, an Indian reservation; BIA-funded schools.

Range: $3,000 to $1,315,000. **Average:** $47,000 ($133 per student).

Activity: FY 98, awards to 1,120 LEAs, 84 BIA grant/contract, and 70 BIA-operated schools, serving 461,000 Indian students.

HQ: Office of Indian Education, OESE-DOED, 400 Maryland Ave. SW, Washington, DC 20202. Phone: (202)260-3774. (Note: no field offices for this program.)

84.063 FEDERAL PELL GRANT PROGRAM
("Pell Grants")

Assistance: direct payments/specified use.

Purposes: for grants to undergraduate postsecondary students demonstrating financial need—to attend public or private nonprofit colleges, universities, hospital schools of nursing, or for-profit proprietary institutions. Award amount reflects family income and assets.

Eligible applicants/beneficiaries: U.S. citizens or eligible noncitizens with a high school diploma, enrolled as undergraduate students and making satisfactory academic progress. Eligible males age 18 or over and born after December 31, 1959 must have registered with the Selective Service. Students may not owe a refund nor be in default on a Title IV grant or loan.

Range: $400 to $3,125 annually. **Average:** $1,935.

Activity: FY 98, 3,811,000 grants awarded.

HQ: same address/phone as **84.007.**

84.066   TRIO—EDUCATIONAL OPPORTUNITY CENTERS

Assistance: project grants (100 percent/to 5 years).

Purposes: to establish and operate educational opportunity centers to provide academic and financial information to qualified adults interested in pursuing postsecondary education, and to assist them in applying for admission. Tutoring and counseling may be provided for participants not enrolled in an Upward Bound or a Student Support Services project. Two-thirds of the participants must be low-income potential first-generation college students.

Eligible applicants: same as for **84.044.**

Eligible beneficiaries: residents of target areas, at least age 19 (exceptions allowed).

Range: $190,000 to $450,000. **Average:** $349,000.

Activity: FY 98, 83 awards assisting 157,000 participants.

HQ: same address/phone as **84.042.** (Note: no field offices for this program.)

84.069   LEVERAGING EDUCATIONAL ASSISTANCE PARTNERSHIP ("LEAP")

Assistance: formula grants (50 percent).

Purposes: to provide scholarships of up to $5,000 to postsecondary students with substantial financial need, enrolled at postsecondary institutions. Grant amounts are reduced for students enrolled less than full time. (This program replaced the State Student Incentives Grants program [SSIG] in the 1999 CFDA.)

Eligible applicants/beneficiaries: state and territorial agencies.

Range: student awards, to $5,000. **Average:** $1,328.

Activity: FY 98, awards to 676,000 students in 48 states and some territories and possessions.

HQ: Policy, Training, and Analysis Service, Division of Policy Development, same address/phone as **84.007.**

84.083   WOMEN'S EDUCATIONAL ACT EQUITY PROGRAM

Assistance: project grants (100 percent/to 4 years).

Purposes: to promote gender equity for women and girls at all levels of education, including their increased participation in such areas as math, science, and computer science courses. Grants are competitive, and may be awarded for implementation projects or for research and development to develop model programs.

Eligible applicants/beneficiaries: public and private nonprofit agencies, institutions, and organizations; student and community groups; individuals.

Range/Average: implementation, $150,000; contracts, $800,000; research, $38,000.

Activity: FY 99 estimate, 1 contract, 1 research and development, 6 implementation awards.

HQ: Equity and Educational Excellence Division, OESE-DOED, 400 Maryland Ave. SW - Rm.3E228, Washington, DC 20202-6246. Phone: (202)260-2502. (Note: no field offices for this program.)

84.101 VOCATIONAL EDUCATION—INDIANS SET-ASIDE

Assistance: project grants (100 percent/to 2 years).

Purposes: to plan, conduct, and administer Indian vocational and technical education programs or portions of programs.

Eligible applicants/beneficiaries: tribes, tribal organizations, native Alaska entities.

Range: $250,000 to $500,000. **Average:** $350,000.

Activity: FY 98, 30 projects funded.

HQ: same address as **84.051**. Phone: (202)205-9270. (Note: no field offices for this program.)

84.103 HIGHER EDUCATION—TRIO STAFF TRAINING PROGRAM ("TRIO Staff Training")

Assistance: project grants (100 percent/1-2 years).

Purposes: to train present or new staff and leadership personnel involved full- or part-time in federal TRIO programs (special programs for students from disadvantaged backgrounds—**84.042, 84.044, 84.047, 84.066, 84.217**). Grants support seminars, workshops, internships, and publications.

Eligible applicants/beneficiaries: IHEs, public and nonprofit private agencies and organizations.

Range: $170,000 to $280,000. **Average:** $221,000.

Activity: FY 98, 17 grants involving 2,955 TRIO programs.

HQ: Higher Education Preparation and Support, same address/phone as **84.042**. (Note: no field offices for this program.)

84.116 FUND FOR THE IMPROVEMENT OF POSTSECONDARY EDUCATION ("FIPSE")

Assistance: project grants (to 100 percent/1-3 years).

Purposes: to develop innovative programs to improve access to and quality of postsecondary education. Examples of funded projects include cooperation between colleges and business, uses of technology, improved access for Blacks, Hispanics, and other minorities.

Eligible applicants/beneficiaries: two- and four-year IHEs, community organizations, libraries, museums, consortia, student groups, local government agencies.

Range: $5,000 to $150,000. **Average:** $70,000.

Activity: FY 98, 115 new, 165 continuation grants.

HQ: FIPSE, OPE-DOED, ROB-3 - Rm.3100, 7th & D Sts. SW, Washington, DC 20202-5175. Phone: (202)708-5175. (Note: no field offices for this program.)

84.120 MINORITY SCIENCE AND ENGINEERING IMPROVEMENT ("MSEIP")

Assistance: project grants (to 100 percent/1-3 years).

Purposes: to improve undergraduate science and engineering education programs at minority institutions to better prepare their students for graduate work or careers. Eligible uses of funds include salaries, purchase of equipment and instructional materials; faculty development; inservice training.

Eligible applicants/beneficiaries: private and public nonprofit two- and four-year IHEs whose enrollments are predominantly American Indian, Alaska native, Black, Hispanic, Pacific Islander, or any combination of these or other under-represented disadvantaged ethnic minorities. Also, nonprofit science-oriented organizations, professional scientific societies, and all accredited IHEs.

Range/Average: institutional, $140,000; cooperative projects, $250,000; design projects, $18,000; special projects, $23,000.

Activity: FY 98, 68 awards.

HQ: Institutional Development and Undergraduate Education Service, OPE-DOED, Washington, DC 20202-5251. Phones: (202)260-9338; FAX (202) 401-7532. (Note: no field offices for this program.)

84.126 REHABILITATION SERVICES—VOCATIONAL REHABILITATION GRANTS TO STATES

Assistance: formula grants (100 percent).

Purposes: for vocational rehabilitation services to persons with mental and/or physical disabilities resulting in employment handicaps, that may reasonably be expected to increase their employability. Services include: assessment; counseling; vocational and other training; reader services for the blind; interpreter services for the deaf; job placement. Also, payments for: medical and related services, prosthetic and orthotic devices; transportation to obtain services; construction and establishment of community rehabilitation facilities; services to families of handicapped persons.

Eligible applicants/beneficiaries: state agencies, territories, possessions.

Range: $52,000 to $217,332,000.

Activity: not quantified specifically.

HQ: Office of Program Operations, Rehabilitation Services Administration, OSERS-DOED, Washington, DC 20202-2574. Phone: (202)205-9406.

84.128 REHABILITATION SERVICES—SERVICE PROJECTS

Assistance: project grants (50-100 percent/3-5 years).

Purposes: for vocational rehabilitation demonstrations and special projects for disabled persons, when proposed projects hold promise of expanding and otherwise improving services over and above those provided by **84.126**. Special programs include recreation projects, migrant and seasonal worker projects.

Eligible applicants/beneficiaries: public and nonprofit organizations, state vocational rehabilitation agencies including territories and possessions.

Range/Average: N.A.

Activity: FY 98, 30 recreational, 14 migrant projects.

HQ: Rehabilitation Services Administration, OSERS-DOED, Switzer Bldg., 330 C St. SW, Washington, DC 20202. Phone: (202)205-8435.

84.129 REHABILITATION LONG-TERM TRAINING

Assistance: project grants (90 percent/to 5 years).

Purposes: for academic training programs for personnel involved in vocational rehabilitation for the disabled, targeted to areas with personnel shortages. Scholarships may cover such specialties as rehabilitation counseling, independent living, rehabilitation medicine, physical and occupational therapy, prosthetics-orthotics, speech-language, pathology and audiology, rehabilitation of the deaf and the blind, rehabilitation technology. At least 75 percent of grant funds must be used for scholarships.

Eligible applicants/beneficiaries: state vocational rehabilitation agencies including territories and possessions, other public or nonprofit agencies and organizations, IHEs.

Range: $70,000 to $100,000. **Average:** $100,000.

Activity: FY 98, 1,200 students supported.

HQ: Rehabilitation Services Administration, OSERS-DOED, 400 Maryland Ave. SW, Washington, DC 20202-2649. Phone: (202)205-8926.

84.132 CENTERS FOR INDEPENDENT LIVING

Assistance: project grants (to 100 percent/5 years).

Purposes: to establish and operate centers for independent living for significantly disabled persons, including training of personnel. The centers provide a broad range of services to residents such as referrals for attendant care, training in independent living skills, referrals in housing and transportation, peer counseling, and individual and systems advocacy. Individuals with disabilities must be employed by and substantially involved in policy direction and management of the centers.

Eligible applicants: principally, previously funded private nonprofit agencies. If funds are available, other centers for independent living and state agencies, including territories and possessions, become eligible.

Eligible beneficiaries: persons with such significant physical, mental cognitive, or sensor impairments that independent living services are needed to attain independence in the home or community.

Range: $27,000 to $640,000. **Average:** $192,000.

Activity: FY 98 estimate, 275 centers supported.

HQ: Rehabilitation Services Administration, OSERS-DOED, Switzer Bldg., 330 C St. SW, Washington, DC 20202-2575. Phones: (202)205-9315; TT (202)205-8352.

84.133 NATIONAL INSTITUTE ON DISABILITY AND REHABILITATION RESEARCH

Assistance: project grants (cost sharing/to 5 years).

Purposes: for research, demonstrations, innovations, dissemination and utilization projects, rehabilitation personnel career training, and research fellowships—involving broad ranges of programs and services for persons of all ages with physical and mental disabilities, especially the severely disabled.

Eligible applicants/beneficiaries: states; public, private, or nonprofit agencies and organizations; IHEs; tribes and tribal organizations. Individuals may obtain fellowships.

Range: contracts, $10,000 to $750,000. **Average:** $150,000; research and training centers, $525,000; engineering research centers, $680,000.

Activity: FY 98, 10 fellowships; 36 continuation, 25 new field-initiated grants; 33 continuation, 9 new rehabilitation research and training center awards; 15 continuation rehabilitation engineering center grants; 18 spinal cord model systems grants; 20 continued, 12 new research and demonstration projects; 6 continuation, 5 new research training awards.

HQ: Director, National Institute on Disability and Rehabilitation Research, OSERS-DOED, 600 Independence Ave. SW, Washington, DC 20202-2572. Phones: *grants and contracts*, (202)205-5880; *fellowships*, (202)205-9800; TDD (202)205-5479. (Note: no field offices for this program.)

84.141 MIGRANT EDUCATION—HIGH SCHOOL EQUIVALENCY PROGRAM ("HEP")

Assistance: project grants (100 percent/to 5 years).

Purposes: to assist migrant students obtain the equivalent of a secondary school diploma and subsequently to gain employment or to attend college or obtain other postsecondary education or training. Program funds may be used to recruit and provide academic and support services and financial assistance to students.

Eligible applicants: IHEs or private nonprofit agencies in cooperation with IHEs.

Eligible beneficiaries: migrant students age 16 or older.

Range/Average: $2,067 per student.

Activity: 1998, 3,600 students served in 20 projects.

HQ: same address (except Rm.3E317) as **84.011**. Phone: (202)260-1396. (Note: no field offices for this program.)

84.144 MIGRANT EDUCATION—COORDINATION PROGRAM

Assistance: project grants (100 percent/to 5 years).

Purposes: to improve interstate and intrastate coordination of migrant education among SEAs and LEAs. Incentive grants may be provided to SEAs that participate in an approved consortium.

Eligible applicants/beneficiaries: SEAs and LEAs, IHEs, other public or nonprofit private entities.

Range: $30,000 to $4,500,000.

Activity: FY 98, 32 consortium incentive grants.

HQ: same address/phone as **84.011.** (Note: no field offices for this program.)

84.145 FEDERAL REAL PROPERTY ASSISTANCE PROGRAM

Assistance: sale, exchange, or donation of property and goods.

Purposes: to convey surplus federal real property for educational purposes, including all educational levels, vocational education or rehabilitation, libraries, central administration facilities, educational radio and television, rehabilitation and training, research, correctional education centers. Examples include: improved or unimproved land; former Nike sites; total military bases.

Eligible applicants/beneficiaries: states and their political subdivisions and instrumentalities; tax-supported, tax-exempt organizations or private nonprofit institutions.

Range: value of property, $726 to $212,000. **Average:** $40,000.

Activity: annually, 10 transfers.

HQ: Federal Real Property Assistance Program, Office of the Administrator/Management Services, DOED, 600 Independence Ave. SW, Washington, DC 20202. Phone: (202)401-0500.

84.149 MIGRANT EDUCATION—COLLEGE ASSISTANCE MIGRANT PROGRAM ("CAMP")

Assistance: project grants (100 percent/to 5 years).

Purposes: to provide supportive and instructional services and other assistance to migrants enrolling in college full-time for the first academic year. Funds may be used to provide tutoring, counseling, and assistance in obtaining financial aid to students, as well as inservice training for project staff.

Eligible applicants: same as for **84.141.**

Eligible beneficiaries: first-year college students engaged, or whose families are engaged, in migrant or other seasonal farm work, or that participated or were eligible to participate in the Chapter 1 Migrant Education Program or JTPA 402.

Range/Average: $5,408 per student.

Activity: 375 students served at 6 institutions.

HQ: same address (except Rm.3E317) as **84.011.** Phone: (202)260-1396. (Note: no field offices for this program.)

84.153 BUSINESS AND INTERNATIONAL EDUCATION

Assistance: project grants (50 percent/1-2 years).

Purposes: for innovations and improvements in international business education curricula. Participating institutions must enter into agreements with businesses or trade organizations engaged in international commerce.

Eligible applicants/beneficiaries: IHEs.

Range/Average: continuations, $74,000; new awards, $76,000.

Activity: FY 98, 49 awards.

HQ: same address as **84.016.** Phone: (202)401-9778. (Note: no field offices for this program.)

84.160   TRAINING INTERPRETERS FOR INDIVIDUALS WHO ARE DEAF AND INDIVIDUALS WHO ARE DEAF-BLIND

Assistance: project grants (cost sharing/to 5 years).

Purposes: to train prospective or improve the skills of present manual, oral, and cued speech interpreters providing services to deaf or deaf-blind persons— through classroom instruction, workshops, seminars, and field placement. Curriculum may include such specialty areas as interpreting in medical, legal, or rehabilitation settings.

Eligible applicants/beneficiaries: public or private nonprofit agencies and organizations; IHEs.

Range: $112,000 to $137,000.

Activity: N.A.

HQ: OSERS-DOED, 400 Maryland Ave. SW, Washington, DC 20202-2736. Phones: (202)205-9152; TDD (202)205-8352. (Note: no field offices for this program.)

84.161   REHABILITATION SERVICES—CLIENT ASSISTANCE PROGRAM ("CAP")

Assistance: formula grants (100 percent).

Purposes: to help persons with disabilities obtain information about and benefits of Rehabilitation Act projects, programs, facilities, and services, whether as clients or applicants for services—and to help them overcome problems with service delivery systems including assistance and advocacy in pursuing legal, administrative, and other appropriate remedies. Grants may not support class action suits.

Eligible applicants/beneficiaries: states and territories, through public or private agencies designated by the governor.

Range: $12,000 to $1,050,000.

Activity: FY 98, 60,000 clients served.

HQ: same address/phone as **84.126.**

84.162   IMMIGRANT EDUCATION

Assistance: formula grants (100 percent).

Purposes: for educational services to immigrant children enrolled in elementary and secondary public and nonpublic schools. Grants may cover costs of supplementary educational services, basic instruction, and inservice training for school personnel.

Eligible applicants: SEAs, territories.

Eligible beneficiaries: LEAs serving at least 500 immigrant children, or three percent of their total enrollment. Children must have been enrolled in U.S. schools for less than three years.

Range: $37,000 to $39,000,000. **Average:** $183 per child.

Activity: FY 98, awards to 40 states, DC, PR; 821,000 children served.

HQ: OBEMLA-DOED, Switzer Bldg. - Rm.5615, 330 C St. SW, Washington, DC 20202. Phone: (202)205-9808. (Note: no field offices for this program.)

84.165 MAGNET SCHOOLS ASSISTANCE

Assistance: project grants (100 percent/to 3 years).

Purposes: for magnet school projects that are part of approved desegregation plans designed to bring together students from different social, economic, racial, and ethnic backgrounds. Funds may be used for planning and conducting projects, including: enhancement of academic instruction; subsidizing teacher and staff salaries; purchasing books, materials, equipment. Funds may not be used for transportation or activities that do not augment academic improvement. Project examples: science and math, performing arts magnet programs; Montessori programs.

Eligible applicants/beneficiaries: LEAs.

Range/Average: $1,692,000.

Activity: FY 98, 57 awards.

HQ: Magnet Schools Assistance Program, School Improvement Programs, OESE-DOED, 400 Maryland Ave. SW - Rm.3E112, Washington, DC 20202-6140. Phone: (202)260-2476. (Note: no field offices for this program.)

84.168 EISENHOWER PROFESSIONAL DEVELOPMENT—FEDERAL ACTIVITIES

Assistance: project grants (100 percent/to 5 years).

Purposes: for projects of national significance to improve K-12 teaching and learning in core academic subjects; for mathematics and science instruction consortia to disseminate exemplary project information; to reform teacher preparation and certification standards; to develop comprehensive performance-based assessment and professional development standards. Project examples: teacher professional development in environmental education and use of technology; operation of the Eisenhower National Clearinghouse for Mathematics and Science Education.

Eligible applicants/beneficiaries: SEAs, LEAs, IHEs, educational service agencies, state agencies for higher education, public and private nonprofit organizations.

Range: $150,000 to $500,000.

Activity: FY 98, 2 grants.

HQ: Office of Reform Assistance and Dissemination, OERI-DOED, Washington, DC 20208-5645. Phone: (202)219-2206. (Note: no field offices for this program.)

84.169   INDEPENDENT LIVING—STATE GRANTS

Assistance: formula grants (50 percent).

Purposes: to promote a philosophy of independent living for significantly disabled persons, incorporating such principles as consumer control, peer support, self-help, self-determination, individual and system advocacy. Funds may be used to: support statewide independent living councils; support center operations; demonstrate ways to expand and improve services; increase the capacities of public or nonprofit organizations and agencies to develop comprehensive approaches and systems; conduct studies and analyses; train the disabled and service personnel; provide outreach to unserved or underserved populations.

Eligible applicants/beneficiaries: state agencies, territories, possessions.

Range: $27,000 to $1,936,000.

Activity: FY 98, 79 state units funded.

HQ: Independent Living Branch Office, Rehabilitation Services Administration, OSERS-DOED, 330 C St. SW, Washington, DC 20202-2741. Phone: (202)205-9362.

84.170   JAVITS FELLOWSHIPS

Assistance: project grants (100 percent/to 4 years).

Purposes: for fellowships to graduate degree candidates demonstrating exceptional promise, intending to pursue doctoral degrees in the arts, humanities, or social sciences.

Eligible applicants/beneficiaries: U.S. citizens, nationals, or permanent residents.

Range/Average: $15,000, plus a $10,000 institutional allowance.

Activity: FY 98, 267 new and continuation awards.

HQ: International Education and Graduate Programs, OPE-DOED, Washington, DC 20202-5247. Phone: (202)260-3574. (Note: no field offices for this program.)

84.173   SPECIAL EDUCATION—PRESCHOOL GRANTS

Assistance: formula grants (100 percent).

Purposes: pursuant to IDEA, for free appropriate public educational programs for preschool children with disabilities, requiring special education and related services. States may also use funds to develop and implement elements of comprehensive statewide service delivery systems.

Eligible applicants: SEAs, DC, PR.

Eligible beneficiaries: children age 3-5 (optionally, age 2 and to reach age 3 during the school year), determined to be mentally retarded, hearing impaired, speech or language impaired, visually handicapped, seriously emotionally disturbed, autistic, orthopedically impaired, other health-impaired.

Range: $236,000 to $37,946,000. **Average:** $7,192,000.

Activity: FY 98, all state, DC, PR agencies funded.

HQ: same address as **84.027**. Phone: (202)205-9097.

84.177 REHABILITATION SERVICES—INDEPENDENT LIVING SERVICES FOR OLDER INDIVIDUALS WHO ARE BLIND

Assistance: project grants (90 percent/to 3 years).

Purposes: to provide independent living services for blind persons age 55 or older, with vision impairments making competitive employment extremely difficult, but for whom independent living in their own homes or communities is feasible. Program funds may be used to pay such costs as: vision correction or modification; eyeglasses or other visual aids; services and equipment to enhance mobility and self-care; training in braille; teaching services in household management; public education activities.

Eligible applicants/beneficiaries: state agencies, territories, possessions.

Range: $190,000 to $251,000. **Average:** $108,000.

Activity: FY 99 estimate, 56 projects.

HQ: Rehabilitation Services Administration, OSERS-DOED, MES Bldg. - Rm. 3416, 330 C St. SW, Washington, DC 20202-2741. Phone: (202)205-9320.

84.181 SPECIAL EDUCATION—GRANTS FOR INFANTS AND FAMILIES WITH DISABILITIES

Assistance: formula grants (100 percent).

Purposes: to plan, develop, and implement statewide, comprehensive, coordinated, multidisciplinary, inter-agency systems to provide early intervention services for handicapped infants and toddlers and their families. Grants may support expanded or improved services.

Eligible applicants/beneficiaries: states, territories, possessions.

Range: $1,714,000 to $46,132,000. **Average:** $6,143,000.

Activity: FY 98, all eligible applicants funded; 197,000 participants served.

HQ: same address as **84.027**. Phone: (202)205-8828. (Note: no field offices for this program.)

84.184 SAFE AND DRUG-FREE SCHOOLS AND COMMUNITIES—NATIONAL PROGRAMS

Assistance: project grants (to 100 percent/1-4 years).

Purposes: for prevention and education activities concerning the illegal use of drugs and violence at all educational levels.

Eligible applicants/beneficiaries: IHEs, public and private and nonprofit organizations, individuals.

Range: N.A.

Activity: FY 98, 20 grants.

HQ: Director, Safe and Drug-Free Schools Program, OESE-DOED, 400 Maryland Ave. SW, Washington, DC 20202-6123. Phone: (202)260-3954. (Note: no field offices for this program.)

84.185 BYRD HONORS SCHOLARSHIPS

Assistance: formula grants (100 percent/to 4 years).

Purposes: for $1,500 annual merit scholarships to recognize and promote student excellence and achievement. Each participating state is allotted at least 10 scholarships, based on population.

Eligible applicants: SEAs including territories and possessions.

Eligible beneficiaries: U.S. citizens or residents that are public or private high school graduates, accepted for enrollment at IHEs, demonstrating promise of continued outstanding academic achievement.

Range: $60,000 to $2,939,000. **Average:** scholarships, $1,500.

Activity: FY 98, 26,000 scholarships.

HQ: Division of Higher Education Incentive Programs, OPE-DOED, The Portals - Ste.C-80, 400 Maryland Ave. SW, Washington, DC 20202-5251. Phone: (202)260-3394. (Note: no field offices for this program.)

84.186 SAFE AND DRUG-FREE SCHOOLS AND COMMUNITIES—STATE GRANTS

Assistance: formula grants (100 percent).

Purposes: to establish alcohol, drug, tobacco, and firearms abuse education and prevention programs in local school systems, coordinated with related federal, state, and community efforts and resources, including parent involvement. At least 20 percent of awarded funds must be distributed to community-based organizations—and at least 10 percent to law enforcement education partnerships.

Eligible applicants: state governors, SEAs, insular areas, native Hawaiian organizations.

Eligible beneficiaries: LEAs, tribal governments, public and private nonprofit organizations including community action agencies, parent groups, and other community-based organizations.

Range: $2,592,000 to $59,536,000. **Average:** $9,968,000.

Activity: not quantified specifically.

HQ: same address as **84.184**. Phone: (202)260-3394. (Note: no field offices for this program.)

84.187 SUPPORTED EMPLOYMENT SERVICES FOR INDIVIDUALS WITH SEVERE DISABILITIES

Assistance: formula grants (100 percent).

Purposes: for time-limited services leading to supported employment for severely handicapped persons whose potential to engage in a training program has been properly evaluated. Funds may be used for most program operating costs including systematic client training, skilled job trainers to accompany workers for intensive on-the-job training, job development, follow-up services.

Eligible applicants/beneficiaries: state vocational rehabilitation agencies, territories and possessions.

Range: states, $300,000 to $4,113,000.

Activity: not quantified specifically.

HQ: same address/phone as **84.126**.

84.191   ADULT EDUCATION—NATIONAL LEADERSHIP ACTIVITIES

Assistance: project grants (100 percent).

Purposes: for the improvement and expansion of adult basic education through applied research, development, demonstration, dissemination, evaluation, and related activities. Project examples: evaluations of "what works" for adult basic education and ESL, the funding set-aside for corrections education, and distance learning initiative.

Eligible applicants/beneficiaries: public or private agencies, institutions, organizations; business concerns; individuals.

Range/Average: N.A.

Activity: not quantified specifically.

HQ: Division of Adult Education and Literacy, OVAE-DOED, 600 Independence Ave. SW, Washington, DC 20202-7242. Phone: (202)205-8270. (Note: no field offices for this program.)

84.194   BILINGUAL EDUCATION SUPPORT SERVICES

Assistance: project grants (100 percent/1-3 years).

Purposes: for SEAs to collect, aggregate, and publish data on persons with limited English proficiency; to provide technical assistance to LEAs; to provide academic excellence grants for the dissemination of model bilingual programs; to support the National Clearinghouse for Bilingual Education.

Eligible applicants/beneficiaries: SEAs. Academic excellence grants—SEAs, LEAs, and IHEs including junior colleges; nonprofit organizations.

Range: $100,000 to $1,180,000. **Average:** $143,000.

Activity: FY 98, 53 SEAs, 1 clearinghouse funded.

HQ: same address (except Rm.5086) as **84.162**. Phones: (202)205-8739, -9907. (Note: no field offices for this program.)

84.195   BILINGUAL EDUCATION—PROFESSIONAL DEVELOPMENT

Assistance: project grants (100 percent/1-5 years).

Purposes: to train new or present bilingual education personnel—including funding for program improvement and, in certain cases, fellowships for students pursuing graduate degrees.

Eligible applicants/beneficiaries: IHEs, LEAs, SEAs; private nonprofit organizations.

Range: $12,000 to $273,000. **Average:** $165,000.

Activity: FY 98, 111 projects, 384 fellowships funded.

HQ: same address (except Rm.5086) as **84.162**. Phone: (202)205-8842. (Note: no field offices for this program.)

84.196   EDUCATION FOR HOMELESS CHILDREN AND YOUTH

Assistance: formula grants (100 percent).

Purposes: pursuant to the McKinney homeless assistance act, to develop and implement plans to coordinate and improve education programs for homeless children and youth. Primary purposes of this program are to identify homeless children and ensure that they enroll in, attend, and achieve success in school. States may provide subgrants to LEAs for direct services to homeless children and youth including tutoring, summer enrichment programs, purchases of supplies, school personnel training.

Eligible applicants/beneficiaries: state departments of education and outlying areas; schools funded by DOI, serving Indian students. LEAs may receive subgrants.

Range: from $100,000. **Average:** states, $458,000.

Activity: awards to 50 states, DC, PR, VI, Guam, Samoa, Palau, Northern Marianas, and BIA.

HQ: OESE-DOED, 400 Maryland Ave. SW, Washington, DC 20202-6132. Phone: (202)260-0994. (Note: no field offices for this program.)

84.200   GRADUATE ASSISTANCE IN AREAS OF NATIONAL NEED ("GAANN")

Assistance: project grants (75 percent/3 years).

Purposes: for graduate fellowships for up to five years that will help sustain and enhance the capacity for teaching and research in academic areas of national need, designated by the Secretary of Education.

Eligible applicants: IHEs.

Eligible beneficiaries: needy graduate students with excellent academic records and planning teaching or research careers. They must be U.S. citizens, nationals, permanent residents, or permanent residents of the Trust Territory of the Pacific Islands or citizens of the Freely Associated States.

Range/Average: continuation grants, $138,000; new grants, $135,000.

Activity: FY 98, 173 awards.

HQ: same address as **84.170**. Phones: (202)260-3608; FAX (202)260-9489. (Note: no field offices for this program.)

84.203   STAR SCHOOLS

Assistance: project grants (50-75 percent/to 5 years).

Purposes: for demonstrations by telecommunications partnerships to encourage improved instruction in mathematics, science, foreign languages, vocational education, literacy skills, and other subjects. Funds may be used: to develop, construct, and acquire telecommunications facilities, equipment, instructional programming; for technical assistance: instructional programming; for teacher training. Priority is given to projects that will meet the needs of traditionally underserved populations.

Eligible applicants/beneficiaries: partnerships organized on a statewide or multistate basis (1) by public agencies or corporations or, (2) that include at least one SEA or LEA, and three or more of the following: LEAs with a significant number of schools eligible for Title 1 funds (or operated by DOI for Indian children); SEAs; adult and family education programs; IHEs or state higher education agencies; teacher training centers; public or private agencies with relevant experience, or public broadcasting entities; or a public or private elementary or secondary school.

Range: to $10,000,000. **Average:** $2,000,000.

Activity: FY 99, 12 grants.

HQ: OERI-DOED, 555 New Jersey Ave. NW, Washington, DC 20208-5644. Phone: (202)219-2186. (Note: no field offices for this program.)

84.206 JAVITS GIFTED AND TALENTED STUDENTS EDUCATION GRANT PROGRAM

Assistance: project grants (100 percent/to 3 years).

Purposes: for programs designed to meet the special educational needs of gifted and talented elementary and secondary students, including: personnel professional development; exemplary programs; innovative learning strategies; SEA leadership and assistance to local entities in planning, operating, and improving programs; research, technical assistance, and information dissemination.

Eligible applicants/beneficiaries: SEAs and LEAs, IHEs, public and private agencies and organizations, including tribes and Hawaii native organizations.

Range: $100,000 to $215,000.

Activity: FY 99, 9 new awards.

HQ: Development and Demonstration Programs Division, OERI-DOED, 555 New Jersey Ave. NW, Washington, DC 20208-5645. Phones: *project grants*, (202)219-2210; *research center*, (202)219-2096. (Note: no field offices for this program.)

84.209 NATIVE HAWAIIAN FAMILY BASED EDUCATION CENTERS

Assistance: direct payments/specified use (100 percent/5 years).

Purposes: to expand the operation of family-based education centers throughout the Hawaiian Islands, including prenatal and preschool programs, follow-up and assessment, and research and development.

Eligible applicants: native Hawaiian organizations.

Eligible beneficiaries: infants to age 3, preschoolers age 4-5—and their parents.

Range/Average: $3,000,000.

Activity: FY 98, 2 continuation grants to operate 20 centers.

HQ: School Improvement Programs, OESE-DOED, 400 Maryland Ave. SW, Washington, DC 20202. Phone: (202)260-2502. (Note: no field offices for this program.)

84.210 NATIVE HAWAIIAN GIFTED AND TALENTED

Assistance: direct payments/specified use (100 percent/to 5 years).

Purposes: for demonstration programs addressing the special needs of native Hawaiian gifted and talented elementary and secondary school students, including: providing for student emotional and psychosocial needs; family support services; research and development.

Eligible applicants/beneficiaries: native Hawaiian educational organizations, educational entities.

Range/Average: N.A.

Activity: FY 98, 1 grant (University of Hawaii/Hilo).

HQ: same address/phone as **84.209**. (Note: no field offices for this program.)

84.213   EVEN START—STATE EDUCATIONAL AGENCIES

Assistance: formula grants (50-90 percent/subgrants to 4 years).

Purposes: to operate family-centered education projects involving low-income parents in the early education of their children from birth-age 7, and to provide literacy training, adult and parenting education. Funds may support participant recruitment and screening, program design and coordination, instruction of children and parents, staff training.

Eligible applicants/beneficiaries: SEAs. Subgrants—partnerships of LEAs and community-based organizations, public agencies, IHEs, or other non-profit organizations, with priority to projects in Empowerment Zones or Enterprise Communities.

Range: $565,000 to $12,433,000. **Average:** $2,175,000.

Activity: 1997-98, 500 projects.

HQ: Compensatory Education Programs, OESE-DOED, 400 Maryland Ave. SW, Washington, DC 20202-6132. Phone: (202)260-0991. (Note: no field offices for this program.)

84.214   EVEN START—MIGRANT EDUCATION

Assistance: project grants (60-90 percent/to 4 years).

Purposes: for family-centered education projects involving parents of migratory children in the early education of their children from birth-age 7, including adult literacy and adult basic and parenting education. Funds may support participant recruitment and screening, program design and coordination, instruction of children and parents, staff training.

Eligible applicants/beneficiaries: SEAs, LEAs, other entities including non-profit community-based organizations.

Range: $110,000 to $270,000. **Average:** $230,000.

Activity: FY 99, 16 projects operating.

HQ: same address/phone as **84.011**. (Note: no field offices for this program.)

84.215   FUND FOR THE IMPROVEMENT OF EDUCATION ("FIE")

Assistance: project grants (100 percent).

Purposes: for projects of national significance to improve the quality of education, to assist all students to meet challenging state content standards, and contribute to the achievement of the National Education Goals. Projects may support a wide range of activities. Competitions are announced annually in the Federal Register.

Eligible applicants/beneficiaries: SEAs, LEAs, IHEs, public and private organizations.

Range/Average: $100,000 to $250,000.

Activity: FY 98, 4 new, 8 continuation grants to SEAs.

HQ: OERI-DOED, 555 New Jersey Ave. NW, Washington, DC 20208-5645. Phone: (202)219-1768. (Note: no field offices for this program.)

84.216 CAPITAL EXPENSES

Assistance: formula grants, project grants (100 percent).

Purposes: to cover increases in capital expenses associated with providing equitable Title 1 services to eligible private school children, in compliance with the Aguilar vs. Felton decision. Funds may be used to cover noninstructional expenses including: purchase, lease, and renovation of classroom space as neutral sites, including portable units; to purchase vans; for transportation costs.

Eligible applicants/beneficiaries: SEAs. LEAs are subgrantees.

Range: $6,000 to $7,053,000. **Average:** $791,000.

Activity: grants to the 50 states, DC, and PR.

HQ: same address/phone as **84.010**. (Note: no field offices for this program.)

84.217 MCNAIR POST-BACCALAUREATE ACHIEVEMENT

Assistance: project grants (100 percent/4-5 years).

Purposes: to prepare low-income, first-generation college students and students from under-represented groups for graduate study. Services may include: opportunities for research and other scholarly activities; summer internships; seminars; tutoring; academic counseling; obtaining admission and financial assistance; mentoring; exposure to cultural events.

Eligible applicants/beneficiaries: IHEs or combinations of IHEs.

Range/Average: $216,000.

Activity: FY 98, 99 grants in effect, serving 2,500 students.

HQ: Higher Education Preparation and Support Team, same address/phone as **84.042**. (Note: no field offices for this program.)

84.220 CENTERS FOR INTERNATIONAL BUSINESS EDUCATION

Assistance: project grants (50-90 percent/3 years).

Purposes: for inter-disciplinary faculty research to promote international competitiveness of U.S. business. Activities must include: center advisory councils to plan and design activities and programs; collaboration in the center's establishment and operation among the business, management, foreign language, international studies, and other professional schools or departments; assurance that the center's programs are open to students concentrating in these areas.

Eligible applicants/beneficiaries: public and nonprofit private IHEs, or combinations thereof.

Range/Average: $287,000.

Activity: FY 98, 25 continuation grants.

HQ: International Studies Branch, Center for International Education, OPE-DOED, 600 Independence Ave. SW, Washington, DC 20202-5332. Phone: (202)401-9780. (Note: no field offices for this program.)

84.221 NATIVE HAWAIIAN SPECIAL EDUCATION

Assistance: project grants (100 percent/to 5 years).

Purposes: for projects addressing the special education needs of native Hawaiian students, including: identification of children that are learning-disabled, mentally or physically handicapped, or require special education services—as well as their individual requirements and those of their families; conducting special education programs, including the use of native language and cultural traditions; research, evaluation, related activities.

Eligible applicants/beneficiaries: state of Hawaii, native Hawaiian organizations.

Range/Average: one award only, $1,600,000.

Activity: 5 demonstration sites; completion of teacher's language handbook.

HQ: OSERS-DOED, 400 Maryland Ave. SW, Washington, DC 20202. Phone: (202)205-9805. (Note: no field offices for this program.)

84.224 ASSISTIVE TECHNOLOGY

Assistance: project grants (100 percent/to 10 years); technical information.

Purposes: to develop and implement comprehensive consumer-responsive statewide programs of technology-related assistance for persons of all ages with disabilities. States may provide assistance directly to individuals or to statewide community-based organizations.

Eligible applicants/beneficiaries: states, possessions, and territories.

Range/Average: first extension grants, $587,000; second, $690,000.

Activity: FY 98, 56 awards.

HQ: same address as **84.133**. Phone: (202)205-5666. (Note: no field offices for this program.)

84.229 LANGUAGE RESOURCE CENTERS

Assistance: project grants (100 percent/to 3 years).

Purposes: to establish and operate foreign language resource centers to improve teaching and learning at IHEs, including the use of advanced educational technology; to develop new teaching materials based on the research; for the development and application of performance testing; for teacher training; to publish instructional materials in the less commonly taught languages; to disseminate project results.

Eligible applicants/beneficiaries: IHEs or combinations of IHEs.

Range/Average: $311,000.

Activity: FY 98, 7 continuation awards.

HQ: same address/phone as **84.017**. (Note: no field offices for this program.)

84.234 PROJECTS WITH INDUSTRY ("PWI")

Assistance: project grants (80 percent/to 5 years).

Purposes: for programs preparing persons with disabilities for employment in the competitive labor market by partnering with private industry to provide job training, placement, and career advancement services.

Eligible applicants/beneficiaries: employers, profit and nonprofit organizations, labor unions, state vocational rehabilitation agencies.

Range/Average: continuations, $215,000.

Activity: FY 99 estimate, 101 awards.

HQ: Rehabilitation Services Administration, OSERS-DOED, 400 Maryland Ave. SW, Washington, DC 20202. Phone: (202)205-7320.

84.235 REHABILITATION SERVICES DEMONSTRATION AND TRAINING—SPECIAL DEMONSTRATION PROGRAMS

Assistance: project grants (100 percent/to 5 years).

Purposes: to expand and improve vocational rehabilitation and related services for the disabled and severely disabled, authorized under the Rehabilitation Act of 1973. Projects may include demonstrations involving such activities as: increasing client choice; service delivery; technical assistance; systems change; special studies and evaluations; supportive employment; services to unserved, underserved, or isolated populations.

Eligible applicants/beneficiaries: states, public and other nonprofit organizations.

Range/Average: N.A.

Activity: not quantified specifically.

HQ: same address as **84.128**. Phones: (202)205-8494, -9361.

84.240 PROGRAM OF PROTECTION AND ADVOCACY OF INDIVIDUAL RIGHTS

Assistance: project grants (100 percent).

Purposes: to establish systems for protection and advocacy of the rights of persons with disabilities—including services upholding their individual legal and human rights beyond the scope of the Client Assistance Program, and for persons ineligible for programs under the Developmental Disabilities Assistance (DDA) and Bill of Rights Act and the Protection and Advocacy for Individuals with Mental Illness Act (PAIMI).

Eligible applicants/beneficiaries: state-designated protection and advocacy agencies, including territories.

Range: $51,000 to $638,000.

Activity: FY 98, 63,000 persons served.

HQ: Rehabilitation Services Administration, OSERS-DOED, MES Bldg. - Rm.3326, 330 C St. SW, Washington, DC 20202-2575. Phones: (202)205-9406; TT, (202)732-1352.

84.243 TECH-PREP EDUCATION

Assistance: formula grants, project grants (100 percent/27 months).

Purposes: for planning and demonstrations by educational consortia to develop and operate four-year programs to provide "tech-prep" education programs leading to two-year associate degrees or certificates, establishing proficiency in mathematics, science, communications, and technologies. The four years must include the two years preceding and following graduation from secondary school, including apprenticeships. Funds may support curriculum development, inservice teacher and counselor training.

Eligible applicants/beneficiaries: state vocational education boards. Subgrants—consortia of LEAs, intermediate education agencies or area vocational education schools serving secondary students, BIA-funded secondary schools, nonprofit and proprietary IHEs offering two-year associate degrees, and two-year apprenticeship programs that follow secondary instruction.

Rang: $138,000 to $10,892,000.

Activity: Tech-Prep consortia in 50 states, DC, PR, and VI.

HQ: Division of Vocational-Technical Education, OVAE-DOED, 600 Independence Ave. SW, Washington, DC 20202-7241. Phone: (202)205-9441. (Note: no field offices for this program.)

84.245 TRIBALLY CONTROLLED POSTSECONDARY VOCATIONAL AND TECHNICAL INSTITUTIONS

Assistance: project grants (100 percent/to 5 years).

Purposes: for the operation and maintenance of tribally controlled postsecondary vocational and technical institutions.

Eligible applicants/beneficiaries: accredited tribally controlled postsecondary vocational institutions that have operated for at least three years, that enroll at least 100 full-time students (a majority of which are Indians), and that meet other requirements.

Range/Average: $1,550,000.

Activity: FY 98, 2 awards.

HQ: same address as **84.051.** Phone: (202)205-9396. (Note: no field offices for this program.)

84.246 REHABILITATION SHORT-TERM TRAINING

Assistance: project grants (cost sharing/1-3 years).

Purposes: for special training seminars, institutes, workshops, and other short-term courses in technical matters relating to the delivery of vocational, medical, social, and psychological services—in fields directly related to the vocational and independent living rehabilitation of persons with disabilities.

Eligible applicants/beneficiaries: same as for **84.129.**

Range: $100,000 to $250,000.

Activity: not quantified specifically.

HQ: same address as **84.129.** Phone: (404)562-6336.

84.250 REHABILITATION SERVICES—AMERICAN INDIANS WITH DISABILITIES

Assistance: project grants (90 percent/to 5 years).

Purposes: to establish and operate tribal vocational rehabilitation service projects serving American Indians with disabilities, residing on reservations.

Eligible applicants/beneficiaries: tribal governments or consortia, on federal or state reservations.

Range/Average: N.A.

Activity: FY 98, 39 projects funded.

HQ: Rehabilitation Services Administration, OSERS-DOED, Washington, DC 20202. Phone: (202)205-8292.

84.252 URBAN COMMUNITY SERVICE

Assistance: project grants (75 percent/to 5 years).

Purposes: for projects encouraging urban IHEs to work with private and civic organizations, providing the assistance of faculty, student, and other institutional resources to address high priority needs identified by the community— especially in Empowerment Zones or Enterprise Communities. Awards may support such activities as applied research, planning services, specialized training, resource exchanges or technology transfers, and other services. Project examples: crime prevention; youth safety; neighborhood revitalization; improving student retention and performance.

Eligible applicants/beneficiaries: urban IHEs or consortia with at least 40 percent of their undergraduate enrollments drawn from the areas in which the institutions are located or from contiguous areas.

Range/Average: $196,000.

Activity: FY 98, 25 continuation awards.

HQ: Institutional Development and Undergraduate Education Services Programs, OPE-DOED, Portals Bldg., 400 Maryland Ave. SW, Washington, DC 20202-5335. Phone: (202)260-3281. (Note: no field offices for this program.)

84.255 LITERACY PROGRAMS FOR PRISONERS

Assistance: project grants (100 percent/to 3 years).

Purposes: to establish and operate programs assist persons incarcerated in prisons, jails, or detention centers to achieve functional literacy; to reduce prisoner recidivism through the development and improvement of their life skills necessary for reintegration into society.

Eligible applicants/beneficiaries: state or local correctional agencies or correctional education agencies.

Range/Average: $345,000.

Activity: FY 98, 13 awards.

HQ: same address as **84.051**. Phone: (202)205-5621. (Note: no field offices for this program.)

84.256 FREELY ASSOCIATED STATES—EDUCATION GRANT PROGRAM

Assistance: project grants (100 percent/3 years).

Purposes: for educational activities consistent with ESEA Title I, including teacher training, curriculum development, instructional materials, general school improvement, and schoolwide reform.

Eligible applicants/beneficiaries: LEAs in Micronesia, Marshall Islands, Palau.

Range/Average: N.A.

Activity: N.A.

HQ: School Improvement Programs, OESE-DOED, 400 Maryland Ave. SW, Washington, DC 20202-6140. Phone: (202)260-2543.

84.257 NATIONAL INSTITUTE FOR LITERACY ("NIL")

Assistance: project grants (100 percent).

Purposes: to enhance the national effort to reach the National Education Goal that all Americans be literate by the year 2000—by coordinating literacy projects across federal agencies, building on existing public and private efforts. Activities include: research and development; developing a data base of current information on policy and practice; providing technical assistance; fellowships; national literacy hotline.

Eligible applicants: public and private nonprofit institutions.

Eligible beneficiaries: state literacy resource centers, individuals, universities, education organizations.

Range/Average: N.A.

Activity: not quantified specifically.

HQ: National Institute for Literacy, 800 Connecticut Ave. NW, Washington, DC 20006. Phone: (202)632-1500. (Note: no field offices for this program.)

84.258 EVEN START—INDIAN TRIBES AND TRIBAL ORGANIZATIONS

Assistance: project grants (50-90 percent/to 4 years).

Purposes: to operate family-centered education projects involving low-income parents in the early education of their children from birth-age 7, and to provide literacy training, adult and parenting education. Funds may support participant recruitment and screening, program design and coordination, instruction of children and parents, staff training.

Eligible applicants/beneficiaries: tribes and tribal organizations.

Range: $75,000 to $200,000.

Activity: FY 98 estimate, 11 grants.

HQ: same address/phone as **84.213**. (Note: no field offices for this program.)

84.259 NATIVE HAWAIIAN VOCATIONAL EDUCATION

Assistance: project grants (100 percent/to 5 years).

Purposes: for vocational education projects conducted by organizations primarily serving and representing Hawaii natives, for programs authorized by the Carl D. Perkins Vocational and Technical Education Act.

Eligible applicants/beneficiaries: organizations primarily serving and representing Hawaii natives.

Range: N.A.

Activity: not quantified specifically.

HQ: same address **84.051**. Phone: (202)205-9962. (Note: no field offices for this program.)

84.263 REHABILITATION TRAINING—EXPERIMENTAL AND INNOVATIVE TRAINING

Assistance: project grants (cost sharing/to 5 years).

Purposes: to develop new and improved methods of training rehabilitation personnel, relating to vocational and independent living services provided to persons with disabilities.

Eligible applicants/beneficiaries: same as for **84.129**.

Range: $90,000 to $110,000. **Average:** $100,000.

Activity: not quantified specifically.

HQ: same address as **84.129**. Phone: (202)205-9561.

84.264 REHABILITATION TRAINING—CONTINUING EDUCATION

Assistance: project grants (cost sharing/to 5 years).

Purposes: for training centers providing continuing education for rehabilitation counselors, administrators, independent living specialists, audiologists, rehabilitation teachers for the blind, and rehabilitation technology specialists— providing vocational, independent living, and client assistance services to the disabled.

Eligible applicants/beneficiaries: same as for **84.129**.

Range: $271,000 to $498,000. **Average:** $384,000.

Activity: not quantified specifically.

HQ: same address as **84.129**. Phone: (202)205-8291.

84.265 REHABILITATION TRAINING—STATE VOCATIONAL REHABILITATION UNIT IN-SERVICE TRAINING

Assistance: project grants (90 percent/to 3 years).

Purposes: for special projects to train state vocational rehabilitation unit personnel. Projects must address: recruitment and retention of professionals; planning needs; issues of leadership development and capacity building; training on the Rehabilitation Act of 1973 and amendments.

Eligible applicants/beneficiaries: state vocational rehabilitation agencies including territories and possessions.

Range: $7,400 to $240,000. **Average:** $70,000.

Activity: FY 95, 13,000 rehabilitation personnel in 80 agencies participating.

HQ: same address/phone as **84.129**.

84.268 FEDERAL DIRECT LOAN

Assistance: direct loans.

Purposes: to provide education loans for any year of school to vocational, undergraduate, and graduate postsecondary students and their parents—

directly from DOED rather than through private lenders. Subsidized loans are based on financial need; unsubsidized loans are not. Standard, extended, consolidate, and graduated repayment plans are available. Generally, repayment begins six months after termination of at least half-time enrollment, with loan terms extending five to 30 years.

Eligible applicants/beneficiaries: generally, any U.S. citizen, national, or permanent resident enrolled or accepted for at least half-time enrollment as an undergraduate, graduate, professional, or vocational student at a participating postsecondary school. Students must maintain satisfactory academic progress, be in compliance with Selective Service requirements, and neither owe a refund nor be in default on a Title IV grant or loan. Parents may borrow for dependent students under the Direct PLUS program. School enrollment is not required for Direct Consolidation Loans which are available to students, married couples, or parents if they are unable to obtain consolidated loans under **84.032**.

Range/Average: N.A.

Activity: FY 99, 1,567 schools participating.

HQ: Federal Direct Loans, OSFA-DOED, Washington, DC 20202. Phone: (202) 708-9951.

84.269   INSTITUTE FOR INTERNATIONAL PUBLIC POLICY

Assistance: project grants (75 percent/5 years).

Purposes: to establish an institute of international public policy to conduct a program to increase the numbers of African Americans and other underrepresented minorities in the international service, including with private international voluntary organizations and the U.S. foreign service. Funds may support a junior year abroad, graduate fellowships, internships, intensive academic programs such as summer institutes, or intensive language training.

Eligible applicants/beneficiaries: a consortium of institutions eligible for assistance under Part B of Title III of the Higher Education Act of 1965 and an IHE serving substantial numbers of African Americans or other underrepresented minority students.

Range/Average: $1,000,000.

Activity: FY 98, 1 continuation award.

HQ: same address as **84.016**. Phone: (202)401-9798. (Note: no field offices for this program.)

84.274   AMERICAN OVERSEAS RESEARCH CENTERS

Assistance: project grants (100 percent/3 years).

Purposes: to establish or operate overseas research centers that are consortia of higher education institutions, to promote postgraduate research, exchanges, and area studies. Funds may cover the costs of: faculty and staff stipends, salaries, travel, and research; student travel; maintenance and operations; teaching and research materials; conferences; publications.

Eligible applicants/beneficiaries: tax-exempt permanent overseas centers receiving over 50 percent of their funding from public or private U.S. sources.

Range/Average: $55,000.

Activity: FY 98, 11 awards.

HQ: same address as **84.015**. Phone: (202)401-9785. (Note: no field offices for this program.)

84.275 REHABILITATION TRAINING—GENERAL TRAINING

Assistance: project grants (100 percent/1-5 years).

Purposes: for education programs for rehabilitation personnel providing services to persons with disabilities through such programs as: vocational, medical, social, and psychological rehabilitation; supported employment; independent living client assistance. Specialties include rehabilitation counselors, administrators, audiologists, teachers of the blind, rehabilitation teachers, and rehabilitation technology specialists.

Eligible applicants/beneficiaries: same as for **84.129**.

Range: $100,000 to $258,000. **Average:** $258,000.

Activity: not quantified specifically.

HQ: same address/phone as **84.129**.

84.276 GOALS 2000—STATE AND LOCAL EDUCATION SYSTEMIC IMPROVEMENT GRANTS

Assistance: formula grants (100 percent/5 years).

Purposes: pursuant to the Goals 2000-Educate America Act, to develop and implement comprehensive reform plans at the state, local, and school levels to improve teaching and learning; for states and localities to establish high standards in their core content areas. At least 90 percent of grant funds must be subgranted to LEAs to implement plans to improve assessments, curriculum, preservice training, and professional development activities. Project examples: charter school development; math and science instruction strengthening.

Eligible applicants/beneficiaries: states, territories and possessions, Alaska Federation of Natives, BIA.

Range: $1,640,000 to $54,798,000.

Activity: not quantified specifically.

HQ: Goals 2000, OESE-DOED, 400 Maryland Ave. SW - Rm.3E241, Washington, DC 20202. Phone: (202)401-0039. (Note: no field offices for this program.)

84.281 EISENHOWER PROFESSIONAL DEVELOPMENT STATE GRANTS

Assistance: formula grants (100 percent).

Purposes: for the improvement of teaching of the core academic subjects in elementary and secondary schools, through professional development activities for teachers, staff, and administrators.

Eligible applicants/beneficiaries: SEAs, state agencies for higher education, BIA, insular areas. (IHEs and nonprofit organizations apply to state agencies; LEAs apply to SEAs.)

Range: $1,530,000 to $33,854,000. **Average:** $5,865,000.

Activity: not quantified specifically.

HQ: same address as **84.256**. Phones: *state agencies for higher education,* (202)260-2456; *SEAs,* (202)260-2516.

84.282   CHARTER SCHOOLS

Assistance: project grants (100 percent/to 3 years).

Purposes: for the design, initial implementation, and evaluation of the effectiveness of charter schools.

Eligible applicants/beneficiaries: SEAs. If SEAs do not participate, authorized public chartering agencies or other public entities may apply.

Range: schools, $75,000 to $100,000. **Average:** SEAs, $2,500,000.

Activity: FY 99, 940 schools supported.

HQ: Charter Schools Program, same address as **84.256**. Phone: (202)260-2671. (Note: no field offices for this program.)

84.283   COMPREHENSIVE REGIONAL ASSISTANCE CENTERS

Assistance: project grants (100 percent/to 5 years); technical information.

Purposes: to coordinate and integrate the implementation of ESEA Title XIII and other federal programs with state and local activities, toward the improvement of teaching and learning. Centers provide training, technical assistance, and direct services in: various aspects of school reform; assisting special needs children; professional development; parent participation projects; bilingual education improvement; creating safe and drug-free learning environments; implementing educational applications of technology; improvement of school governance and management; program evaluation; information dissemination. No direct funding is provided to public or private schools.

Eligible applicants/beneficiaries: public or private nonprofit entities or consortia.

Range/Average: $1,704,000.

Activity: not quantified specifically.

HQ: same address/phone as **84.276**. (Note: no field offices for this program.)

84.286   TELECOMMUNICATIONS DEMONSTRATION PROJECT FOR MATHEMATICS

Assistance: project grants (100 percent/to 5 years).

Purposes: for a national telecommunications-based demonstration project to improve the teaching of mathematics. Projects must: use existing publicly funded telecommunications infrastructure to deliver the service; be conducted in conjunction with appropriate SEAs, LEAs, state, and local profit public telecommunications entities, and a national mathematics education professional association that has developed content standards; benefit schools with a high percentage of children counted for the purpose of ESEA Part A, Title I.

Eligible applicants/beneficiaries: SEAs, LEAs, nonprofit telecommunications entities, or partnership with these entities.

Range/Average: N.A.

Activity: FY 98, 1 continuation award (to the Public Broadcasting Service).

HQ: same address as **84.203**. Phone: (202)219-2181. (Note: no field offices for this program.)

84.287 TWENTY-FIRST CENTURY COMMUNITY LEARNING CENTERS

Assistance: project grants (100 percent/to 3 years).

Purposes: to plan and establish community learning centers to conduct projects meeting educational, health, social service, cultural, and recreational needs of at-risk families in rural and inner city economically depressed areas.

Eligible applicants/beneficiaries: rural and inner city public elementary and secondary schools or consortia.

Range/Average: $365,000; centers, $125,000.

Activity: FY 99, 187 projects funded.

HQ: State and Local Service Division, Office of Reform Assistance and Dissemination, OERI-DOED, Washington, DC 20208-5524. Phone: (202) 219-2128. (Note: no field offices for this program.)

84.288 BILINGUAL EDUCATION—PROGRAM DEVELOPMENT AND IMPLEMENTATION GRANTS

Assistance: project grants (100 percent/3 years).

Purposes: to develop and implement new comprehensive and coherent bilingual education or special alternative instructional programs for students with limited English proficiency, including: programs of early childhood, K-12, gifted and talented, vocational, and applied technology education; family education programs and parent outreach and training activities; acquiring and upgrading curriculum, instructional and educational software; personnel training and salaries including for aides; tutoring and career counseling.

Eligible applicants/beneficiaries: LEAs.

Range: $14,000 to $188,000. Average: $152,000.

Activity: FY 98, 112 projects funded.

HQ: OBEMLA-DOED, 600 Independence Ave. SW, Washington, DC 20202. Phone: (202)205-5576. (Note: no field offices for this program.)

84.289 BILINGUAL EDUCATION—PROGRAM ENHANCEMENT GRANTS

Assistance: project grants (100 percent/to 2 years).

Purposes: for highly focused, innovative projects designed locally to expand or enhance existing bilingual education or special alternative instruction programs for students with limited English proficiency.

Eligible applicants/beneficiaries: LEAs.

Range/Average: $130,000.

Activity: FY 98, 151 projects funded.

HQ: same address/phone as **84.288**. (Note: no field offices for this program.)

84.290 BILINGUAL EDUCATION—COMPREHENSIVE SCHOOL GRANTS

Assistance: project grants (100 percent/5 years).

Purposes: to develop school-wide programs that reform, restructure, and upgrade programs and operations in schools with at least 25 percent of their enrollments comprised of students with limited English proficiency.

Eligible applicants/beneficiaries: LEAs.

Range/Average: $252,000.

Activity: FY 98, 336 projects funded.

HQ: same address as **84.288**. Phone: (202)205-5530. (Note: no field offices for this program.)

84.291   BILINGUAL EDUCATION—SYSTEMWIDE IMPROVEMENT GRANTS

Assistance: project grants (100 percent/5 years).

Purposes: to implement district-wide bilingual education programs to improve, reform, and update relevant programs and operations.

Eligible applicants/beneficiaries: one or more LEAs; one or more LEAs in collaboration with IHEs and community-based organizations; SEAs. LEAs must have enrollments of at least 1,000 students with limited English proficiency, or comprising at least 25 percent of their enrollments.

Range/Average: $478,000.

Activity: FY 98, 80 projects funded.

HQ: same address as **84.288**. Phone: (202)205-5530. (Note: no field offices for this program.)

84.292   BILINGUAL EDUCATION—RESEARCH PROGRAMS

Assistance: project grants (100 percent/to 5 years).

Purposes: for research and program evaluation activities designed to improve bilingual education and special alternative instruction programs for students with limited English proficiency.

Eligible applicants/beneficiaries: SEAs, LEAs, IHEs, nonprofit organizations, or consortia.

Range/Average: N.A.

Activity: N.A.

HQ: same address as **84.288**. Phone: (202)205-8739. (Note: no field offices for this program.)

84.293   FOREIGN LANGUAGE ASSISTANCE

Assistance: project grants (50 percent/3 years).

Purposes: for innovative model programs of foreign language study in public elementary and secondary schools.

Eligible applicants/beneficiaries: SEAs, LEAs.

Range/Average: $78,000.

Activity: FY 98, 64 projects funded.

HQ: same address as **84.288**. Phone: (202)205-9808. (Note: no field offices for this program.)

84.295 READY-TO-LEARN TELEVISION

Assistance: project grants (100 percent/to 5 years).

Purposes: to develop: educational programming for preschool and early elementary school children and their families; educational television, programming, and ancillary materials to increase school readiness for young children with limited English proficiency and family literacy; support materials and services promoting effective use of educational programming.

Eligible applicants/beneficiaries: a qualified nonprofit entity including a public telecommunications entity; the Corporation for Public Broadcasting (CPB).

Range/Average: single grant (CPB).

Activity: CPB and various subgrants.

HQ: National Institute on Early Childhood Development and Education, OERI-DOED, 555 New Jersey Ave. NW, Washington, DC 20208-5524. Phone: (202)219-1596. (Note: no field offices for this program.)

84.296 NATIVE HAWAIIAN COMMUNITY-BASED EDUCATION LEARNING CENTERS

Assistance: project grants (100 percent).

Purposes: for collaborative efforts between community-based native Hawaiian organizations and community colleges to establish and operate at least three community-based education learning centers—coordinating new or existing preschool, after-school, vocational, and adult education programs.

Eligible applicants/beneficiaries: community-based native Hawaiian organizations and community colleges in Hawaii.

Range/Average: $1,000,000.

Activity: FY 98, 1 award.

HQ: same address/phone as **84.209**. (Note: no field offices for this program.)

84.297 NATIVE HAWAIIAN CURRICULUM DEVELOPMENT, TEACHER TRAINING AND RECRUITMENT

Assistance: project grants (100 percent/to 5 years).

Purposes: for native Hawaiian programs of elementary and secondary instruction for math, science, the native Hawaiian language, and other subjects; for curriculum development and teacher recruitment and inservice training.

Eligible applicants/beneficiaries: native Hawaiian education organizations or entities.

Range/Average: $625,000.

Activity: FY 99, 7 awards.

HQ: same address/phone as **84.209**. (Note: no field offices for this program.)

84.298 INNOVATIVE EDUCATION PROGRAM STRATEGIES

Assistance: formula grants (100 percent).

Purposes: for reforms in elementary and secondary education by LEAs and SEAs. Funds may be used for: acquiring instructional materials; related technology and training; improving services to disadvantaged students; meeting the educational needs of gifted and talented students; reform activities associated with "Goals 2000" including parental involvement.

Eligible applicants/beneficiaries: states and insular areas.

Range: $1,737,000 to $41,044,000. **Average:** $6,680,000.

Activity: not quantified specifically.

HQ: same address as **84.256**. Phone: (202)260-2551. (Note: no field offices for this program.)

84.302   REGIONAL TECHNICAL SUPPORT AND PROFESSIONAL DEVELOPMENT CONSORTIA
("Regional Technology in Education Consortia")

Assistance: project grants (100 percent/to 5 years).

Purposes: to establish and operate regional consortia to promote the comprehensive integration of advanced technologies in education settings, including grades K-12, library media centers, adult literacy programs—through technical assistance, professional development, information and resource dissemination, and collaboration activities.

Eligible applicants/beneficiaries: regional consortia of SEAs, IHEs, and nonprofit organizations, including existing regional consortia, educational laboratories, or centers.

Range: $1,200,000 to $2,100,000.

Activity: 6 consortia funded.

HQ: Office of Reform Assistance and Dissemination, OERI-DOED, Washington, DC 20208-5572. Phone: (202)219-8070. (Note: no field offices for this program.)

84.303   TECHNOLOGY INNOVATION CHALLENGE GRANTS

Assistance: project grants (100 percent/to 5 years).

Purposes: for the development, interconnection, implementation, improvement, and maintenance of an educational technology infrastructure, including activities and equipment to provide training for teachers, school library and media personnel, and technical support—with priority to areas with a concentration of disadvantaged children.

Eligible applicants/beneficiaries: consortia of at least one LEA and other LEAs, SEAs, IHEs, business, academic content experts, software designers, museums, libraries, or other entities.

Range: $500,000 to $2,000,000. **Average:** $1,000,000/year.

Activity: 82 grants awarded.

HQ: Team Leader, Challenge Grants for Technology in Education, OERI-DOED, 555 New Jersey Ave. NW, Washington, DC 20208-5544. Phone: (202)208-3882. (Note: no field offices for this program.)

84.304   INTERNATIONAL EDUCATION EXCHANGE

Assistance: project grants (100 percent/to 4 years).

Purposes: for international education exchange activities between the U.S. and eligible countries, in civics, government, and economics education—in Eastern and Central European countries, Lithuania, Latvia, Estonia, Georgia, and the countries of the former Soviet Union recognized by the U.S.

Eligible applicants/beneficiaries: independent nonprofit education organizations experienced in program areas.

Range/Average: N.A.

Activity: FY 98, 2 awards (Center for Civic Education, National Council on Economic Education).

HQ: National Institute on Student Achievement, Curriculum, and Assessment, OERI-DOED, 555 New Jersey Ave. NW, Washington, DC 20208-5573. Phone: (202)219-2079. (Note: no field offices for this program.)

84.305   NATIONAL INSTITUTE ON STUDENT ACHIEVEMENT, CURRICULUM, AND ASSESSMENT

Assistance: project grants (100 percent/1-5 years).

Purposes: to develop and distribute research-based information to teachers, schools, policy-makers, and parents engaged in education reform. Grants support basic and applied research, planning, training surveys, evaluations, and demonstrations. Project examples: reducing and preventing violence in schools; technology to improve teaching and learning.

Eligible applicants/beneficiaries: IHEs, public and private agencies and organizations, institutions, individuals, or consortia.

Range/Average: N.A.

Activity: not quantified specifically.

HQ: same address/phone as **84.304**. (Note: no field offices for this program.)

84.306   NATIONAL INSTITUTE ON THE EDUCATION OF AT-RISK STUDENTS

Assistance: project grants (100 percent/1-5 years).

Purposes: to expand research-based knowledge and strategies promoting excellence and equity in the education of children and youth at risk of education failure. Grants support basic and applied research, planning, training surveys, evaluations, and demonstrations.

Eligible applicants/beneficiaries: same as for **84.305**.

Range/Average: N.A.

Activity: not quantified specifically.

HQ: National Institute on the Education of At-Risk Students, OERI-DOED, 555 New Jersey Ave. NW, Washington, DC 20208-5521. Phone: (202)219-2239. (Note: no field offices for this program.)

84.307   NATIONAL INSTITUTE ON EARLY CHILDHOOD DEVELOPMENT AND EDUCATION

Assistance: project grants (100 percent/1-5 years).

Purposes: for research on societal influences, such as poverty and access to pre- and postnatal health care and quality preschools, and their effect on young children—and on early childhood development and education. Grants support basic and applied research, planning, training surveys, evaluations, and demonstrations.

Eligible applicants/beneficiaries: same as for **84.305**.

Range/Average: N.A.

Activity: not quantified specifically.

HQ: National Institute on Early Childhood Development and Education, OERI-DOED, 555 New Jersey Ave. NW, Washington, DC 20202. Phone: (202)219-1935. (Note: no field offices for this program.)

84.308   NATIONAL INSTITUTE ON EDUCATIONAL GOVERNANCE, FINANCE, POLICYMAKING, AND MANAGEMENT

Assistance: project grants (100 percent/1-5 years).

Purposes: to develop and disseminate information to help guide the design, implement the policy, and formulate management decisions that support high levels of learning by all students. Grants support basic and applied research, planning, training surveys, evaluations, and demonstrations.

Eligible applicants/beneficiaries: same as for **84.305**.

Range/Average: N.A.

Activity: not quantified specifically.

HQ: National Institute on Educational Governance, Finance, Policymaking, and Management, OERI, same address as **84.304**. Phone: (202)219-2032. (Note: no field offices for this program.)

84.309   NATIONAL INSTITUTE ON POSTSECONDARY EDUCATION, LIBRARIES, AND LIFELONG LEARNING

Assistance: project grants (100 percent/1-5 years).

Purposes: to advance the education and training of adults in a variety of contexts, providing knowledge and skills necessary to compete in a global economy and exercise the rights and responsibilities of citizenship. Grants support basic and applied research, planning, training surveys, evaluations, and demonstrations.

Eligible applicants/beneficiaries: same as for **84.305**.

Range/Average: N.A.

Activity: not quantified specifically.

HQ: National Institute on Postsecondary Education, Libraries, and Lifelong Learning, OERI, same address as **84.304**. Phone: (202)219-2229. (Note: no field offices for this program.)

84.310   GOALS 2000: PARENTAL ASSISTANCE PROGRAM

Assistance: project grants (first year, 100 percent/1-4 years).

Purposes: pursuant to the Goals 2000-Educate America Act, to establish parental information and resource centers to: (1) increase parent knowledge of and confidence in child-rearing activities such as teaching and nurturing their young children; (2) strengthen partnerships between parents and professionals in meeting the educational needs of children from birth-age 5, and the working relationships between home and school; (3) enhance the developmental progress of assisted children. At least 50 percent of grant funds must be used to serve areas with high concentrations of low-income families, to serve parents that are severely educationally or economically disadvantaged. After the first year of grant-funded activities, nonfederal cost sharing is required.

Eligible applicants/beneficiaries: nonprofit organizations; nonprofit organizations in consortia with LEAs.

Range: $50,000 to $500,000. **Average:** $350,000.

Activity: grants all states, DC, PR, and outlying areas.

HQ: same address (except Rm.4000)/phone as **84.276**. (Note: no field offices for this program.)

84.314   EVEN START—STATEWIDE FAMILY LITERACY PROGRAM

Assistance: project grants (50 percent/18 months).

Purposes: to plan and implement statewide family literacy initiatives coordinating and integrating existing federal, state, and local resources consistent with the purposes of Even Start and Head Start projects, including projects funded under the Adult Education Act and the Family Support Act of 1988. Grants may support design, implementation, evaluation, and employment and training of project staff.

Eligible applicants/beneficiaries: SEAs.

Range/Average: N.A.

Activity: not quantified specifically.

HQ: same address/phone as **84.213**. (Note: no field offices for this program.)

84.315   CAPACITY BUILDING FOR TRADITIONALLY UNDERSERVED POPULATIONS

Assistance: project grants (100 percent/1-5 years).

Purposes: to enhance the capacity and increase the participation of HBCUs, Hispanic serving institutions, and other IHEs where minority enrollment is at least 50 percent, through competitions for discretionary funds under the Rehabilitation Act. Projects should focus on recruiting minorities into vocational rehabilitation and related service careers.

Eligible applicants/beneficiaries: states; public and nonprofit agencies; profit organizations.

Range: $150,000 to $250,000. **Average:** $200,000.

Activity: not quantified specifically.

HQ: Rehabilitation Services Administration, OSERS-DOED, Washington, DC 20202. Phone: (202)205-9481.

84.316   NATIVE HAWAIIAN HIGHER EDUCATION PROGRAM

Assistance: project grants (100 percent/1-5 years).

Purposes: for full or partial fellowships to native Hawaiian students for undergraduate or postgraduate work, with priority for professions underrepresented in the native Hawaiian community. Institutions may also use funds: to provide counseling and support services to fellowship recipients; for college preparation and guidance counseling at the secondary level for fellowship candidates; for research and evaluation; for faculty development programs. Fellowship recipients are obliged to provide professional services to the native Hawaiian community either during the fellowship period or upon its completion.

Eligible applicants: native Hawaiian education organizations or entities with experience in developing or operating native Hawaiian programs.

Eligible beneficiaries: native Hawaiians enrolled or enrolling in two- or four-year postsecondary institutions.

Range/Average: $1,000,000.

Activity: FY 98, 2 grants.

HQ: Higher Education Programs, OPE-DOED, 600 Independence Ave. SW, Washington, DC 20202. Phone: (202)260-3439. (Note: no field offices for this program.)

84.318 TECHNOLOGY LITERACY CHALLENGE FUND GRANTS

Assistance: formula grants (100 percent).

Purposes: to develop and implement systemic technology plans at the state, local, and school levels to improve teaching and learning. At least 95 percent of grant funds to SEAs must be subgranted to LEAs to: apply technology to support school reform; support projects that improve student learning; acquire hardware and software; access telecommunications networks; support ongoing professional development in the integration of technology into curriculum improvements; provide better educational services for adults and families.

Eligible applicants/beneficiaries: states, territories and possessions, BIA.

Range: $2,125,000 to $46,549,000. **Average:** $8,000,000.

Activity: new program listing in 1998.

HQ: same address/phone as **84.276**. (Note: no field offices for this program.)

84.319 EISENHOWER REGIONAL MATHEMATICS AND SCIENCE EDUCATION CONSORTIA

Assistance: project grants (80 percent/to 5 years).

Purposes: to establish and operate regional mathematics and science education consortia—to disseminate exemplary curriculum materials, to provide technical assistance to implement teaching methods and assessment tools for K-12 students, teachers, and administrators.

Eligible applicants/beneficiaries: SEAs, LEAs, elementary or secondary schools, IHEs, nonprofit organizations, regional education laboratories, or combinations of such entities.

Range: $1,500,000 to $1,750,000.

Activity: new program listing in 1997. FY 98, 10 continuations funded.

HQ: same address as **84.168**. Phone: (202)219-2087. (Note: no field offices for this program.)

84.320 ALASKA NATIVE EDUCATIONAL PLANNING, CURRICULUM DEVELOPMENT, TEACHER TRAINING, AND RECRUITMENT PROGRAM ("ANE")

Assistance: direct payments/specified use.

Purposes: to operate programs reflecting Alaska native cultural diversity and contributions, or elementary and secondary instruction programs in the Alaska native language, for such purposes as: consolidating existing education plans, recommendations, and research into implementation methods and strategies; curriculum development including innovative programs, pilots, and demonstrations; teacher recruitment, pre-teacher and inservice training.

Eligible applicants/beneficiaries: experienced Alaska native organizations or educational entities, or partnerships.

Range/Average: $402,000.

Activity: new program listing in 1997. FY 98, 10 grants awarded.

HQ: School Improvement Programs, OESE-DOED, 400 Maryland Ave. SW - Rm.3C124, Washington, DC 20202-6140. Phone: (202)260-1541. (Note: no field offices for this program.)

84.321 ALASKA NATIVE HOME BASED EDUCATION FOR PRESCHOOL CHILDREN ("ANE")

Assistance: direct payments/specified use.

Purposes: to implement home instruction programs for Alaska native youngsters age 0-5, by developing and involving parents as educators, including such elements as: training, education, and support in teaching parents skills in observation, reading readiness, story telling, and critical thinking; parent-infant and preschool programs; continued research and development; long-term follow-up and assessment.

Eligible applicants/beneficiaries: same as for **84.320**.

Range/Average: $394,000.

Activity: new program listing in 1997. FY 98, 8 grants awarded.

HQ: same address/phone as **84.320**. (Note: no field offices for this program.)

84.322 ALASKA NATIVE STUDENT ENRICHMENT PROGRAM ("ANE")

Assistance: direct payments/specified use.

Purposes: for science and mathematics education enrichment programs for Alaska native students from rural areas, preparing to enter village high schools, including support services to their parents.

Eligible applicants/beneficiaries: same as for **84.320**.

Range/Average: $241,000.

Activity: new program listing in 1997. FY 98, 3 grants awarded.

HQ: same address as **84.320**. Phone: (202)260-1431. (Note: no field offices for this program.)

84.323 SPECIAL EDUCATION—STATE PROGRAM IMPROVEMENT GRANTS FOR CHILDREN WITH DISABILITIES

Assistance: project grants (100 percent/1-5 years).

Purposes: pursuant to IDEA as amended, to reform and improve systems for providing educational, early intervention, and transitional services to infants, toddlers, and children with disabilities and their families—including professional development, technical assistance, and dissemination of knowledge about best practices to improve results.

Eligible applicants/beneficiaries: SEAs.

Range: $500,000 to $2,000,000 per year; outlying areas, from $80,000.

Activity: new program in FY 98. FY 99 estimate, 7 new grants.

HQ: same address as **84.027**. Phone: (202)205-5390. (Note: no field offices for this program.)

84.324 SPECIAL EDUCATION—RESEARCH AND INNOVATION TO IMPROVE SERVICES AND RESULTS FOR CHILDREN WITH DISABILITIES

Assistance: project grants (to 100 percent/1-5 years).

Purposes: for applied research to improve services provided and results achieved under IDEA, for infants, toddlers, and children with disabilities—including educational and early intervention services and professional practices.

Eligible applicants/beneficiaries: SEAs, LEAs, IHEs, public agencies, private nonprofit organizations, tribes and tribal organizations, profit organizations, outlying areas.

Range: $150,000 to $700,000 per year.

Activity: new program in FY 98. FY 99 estimate, 116 new awards.

HQ: Division of Research to Practice, OSERS-DOED, 400 Maryland Ave. SW, Washington, DC 20202. Phone: (202)205-8522. (Note: no field offices for this program.)

84.325 SPECIAL EDUCATION—PERSONNEL PREPARATION TO IMPROVE SERVICES AND RESULTS FOR CHILDREN WITH DISABILITIES

Assistance: project grants (to 100 percent/1-5 years).

Purposes: pursuant to IDEA as amended, to prepare personnel to serve infants, toddlers, and children with disabilities—in special and regular education, related services, and early intervention. Projects must emphasize use of skills and knowledge derived from research and experience.

Eligible applicants/beneficiaries: same as for **84.324**.

Range: $200,000 to $400,000 per year.

Activity: new program in FY 98. FY 99 estimate, 100 awards.

HQ: same address as **84.324**. Phone: (202)401-7659. (Note: no field offices for this program.)

84.326 SPECIAL EDUCATION—TECHNICAL ASSISTANCE AND DISSEMINATION TO IMPROVE SERVICES AND RESULTS FOR CHILDREN WITH DISABILITIES

Assistance: project grants (to 100 percent/1-5 years).

Purposes: pursuant to IDEA as amended, to provide technical information and disseminate information supporting capacity building to improve early intervention, education, and transitional services and results for infants, toddlers, and children with disabilities and their families.

Eligible applicants/beneficiaries: same as for **84.324.**

Range: $500,000 to $4,000,000 per year.

Activity: new program in FY 98. FY 99 estimate, 15 awards.

HQ: same address as **84.324.** Phone: (202)205-9864. (Note: no field offices for this program.)

84.327 SPECIAL EDUCATION—TECHNOLOGY AND MEDIA SERVICES FOR INDIVIDUALS WITH DISABILITIES

Assistance: project grants (to 100 percent/1-5 years).

Purposes: pursuant to IDEA as amended, for the development, demonstration, and utilization of technology and for educational media activities designed to be of educational value to infants, toddlers, and children with disabilities and their families.

Eligible applicants/beneficiaries: same as for **84.324.**

Range: $150,000 to $600,000 per year.

Activity: new program in FY 98. FY 99 estimate, 42 new awards.

HQ: same address as **84.324.** Phone: (202)205-8883. (Note: no field offices for this program.)

84.328 SPECIAL EDUCATION—TRAINING AND INFORMATION FOR PARENTS OF CHILDREN WITH DISABILITIES

Assistance: project grants (to 100 percent/1-5 years).

Purposes: pursuant to IDEA as amended, to ensure that parents of children with disabilities: receive training and information on their rights under the Act; can participate effectively in planning and decision-making in system-change activities.

Eligible applicants/beneficiaries: parent organizations as defined in IDEA.

Range: $100,000 to $400,000 per year.

Activity: new program in FY 98. FY 99 estimate, 23 new awards.

HQ: same address/phone as **84.324.** (Note: no field offices for this program.)

84.329 SPECIAL EDUCATION—STUDIES AND EVALUATIONS

Assistance: project grants (to 100 percent/1-5 years).

Purposes: to evaluate progress in implementing IDEA. Projects cover state and local efforts to provide a free appropriate public education to children with disabilities and early intervention services to infants and toddlers that would be at risk of having substantial development delays without such services.

Eligible applicants/beneficiaries: same as for **84.324.**

Range: $100,000 to $1,000,000 per year.

Activity: new program in FY 98. FY 99 estimate, 6 new awards.

HQ: same address as **84.324.** Phone: (202)205-8883. (Note: no field offices for this program.)

84.330   ADVANCED PLACEMENT INCENTIVE PROGRAM

Assistance: project grants (100 percent/to 2 years).

Purposes: to cover part or all of the cost of Advanced Placement Test Fees for low-income persons enrolled in an advanced placement class, or planning to take a test. Grant recipients must publicize the availability of such payments to eligible persons through school teachers and guidance counselors.

Eligible applicants/beneficiaries: SEAs, territories and possessions.

Range: $1,000 to $400,000.

Activity: new program in FY 98. FY 99, 83,000 student participants.

HQ: OESE-DOED, Portals Bldg. - Rm.500, 400 Maryland Ave. SW, Washington, DC 20202-6140. Phone: (202)260-2669. (Note: no field offices for this program.)

84.331   GRANTS TO STATES FOR INCARCERATED YOUTH OFFENDERS

Assistance: formula grants (100 percent/2 years).

Purposes: to assist and encourage incarcerated youth offenders to acquire postsecondary education and vocational training, and to provide them with employment counseling and related services during their incarceration and pre-release periods, and subsequently.

Eligible applicants: state correctional education agencies, territories and possessions.

Eligible beneficiaries: persons age 25 or younger incarcerated in state prisons including pre-release facilities or alternative programs such as boot camps, eligible for release or parole within five years, and possessing a secondary school diploma or equivalent.

Range: $18,000 to $1,713,000. **Average:** $300,000.

Activity: new program in FY 98.

HQ: same address as **84.051.** Phone: (202)205-5621. (Note: no field offices for this program.)

84.332   COMPREHENSIVE SCHOOL REFORM DEMONSTRATION ("CSRD")

Assistance: formula grants (100 percent).

Purposes: to substantially improve student achievement, particularly in Title I schools, through implementation of comprehensive school reform programs that are based on reliable research and effective practices and emphasize basic academics and parental involvement. Funded projects must also include: comprehensive schools designs with aligned components; professional development; external technical support and assistance; evaluation strategies; coordination of resources.

Eligible applicants/beneficiaries: SEAs. Subgrants—LEAs.

Range: $318,000 to $16,294,000. **Average:** $2,733,000.

Activity: new program listing in 1999.

HQ: CSRD, OESE-DOED, Portals Bldg. - Rm.6202, 600 Independence Ave. SW, Washington, DC 20202. Phone: (202)205-4292. (Note: no field offices for this program.)

84.333 DEMONSTRATION PROJECTS TO ENSURE STUDENTS WITH DISABILITIES RECEIVE A HIGHER EDUCATION

Assistance: project grants (100 percent/3 years).

Purposes: for model demonstration projects providing technical assistance or professional development for higher education faculty, to provide students with disabilities a quality postsecondary education.

Eligible applicants/beneficiaries: IHEs of which at least two provide professional development for students with learning disabilities.

Range/Average: $200,000.

Activity: new program in FY 99.

HQ: Higher Education Programs, OPE-DOED, Portals Bldg. - Ste.600, 600 Independence Ave. SW, Washington, DC 20202. Phones: (202)708-8596; FAX (202)708-9046. (Note: no field offices for this program.)

84.334 GAINING EARLY AWARENESS AND READINESS FOR UNDERGRADUATE PROGRAMS ("GEAR-UP")

Assistance: project grants (50 percent/to 5 years).

Purposes: to assist low-income students with a secondary diploma in obtaining the financial assistance necessary to attend an IHE; to provide supportive services to elementary, middle, and secondary students at risk of becoming school drop-outs; to provide outreach and relevant information to students and their parents. Services are provided under the Early Intervention Component. Federal grants may be provided under the Scholarship Component to students participating in the Early Intervention component or in a TRIO program.

Eligible applicants/beneficiaries: states; partnerships of LEAs, IHEs, community organizations including businesses, professional associations, philanthropic organizations, state agencies, parent groups.

Range/Average: N.A.

Activity: new program in FY 99.

HQ: same address/phones as **84.333**. (Note: no field offices for this program.)

84.335 CHILD CARE ACCESS MEANS PARENTS IN SCHOOL

Assistance: project grants (4 years).

Purposes: to support participation of low-income parents in postsecondary education by providing campus-based child care services. Grants may be used to support or establish child care programs—but not for construction other than minor renovations. Grant amounts may not exceed one percent of the total amount of Pell grants awarded by the IHE for the preceding year.

Eligible applicants/beneficiaries: IHEs that awarded $350,000 or more in Pell grants for the preceding year.

Range/Average: N.A.

Activity: new program in FY 99.

HQ: same address as **84.333**. Phone: (202)260-4015. (Note: no field offices for this program.)

84.336 TEACHER QUALITY ENHANCEMENT GRANTS FOR STATES AND PARTNERSHIPS

Assistance: project grants (50-75 percent/3-5 years).

Purposes: for projects to reform teacher preparation programs and certification and licensure requirements, to provide alternatives to traditional preparation for teaching, and to develop and implement effective mechanisms for teacher recruitment, pay, removal, and social promotion.

Eligible applicants/beneficiaries: states and partnerships with LEAs with high percentages of households below the poverty line, secondary teachers not teaching within their specialty, and teacher turn-over. IHEs must demonstrate specific teacher training performance standards.

Range: state grants, $1,700,000 to $2,500,000. **Average:** partnerships, $2,800,000; teacher recruitment, $500,000.

Activity: new program in FY 99; 20 state, 12 partnership, 15 teacher recruitment awards.

HQ: same address/phone as **84.333**. (Note: no field offices for this program.)

84.337 TECHNOLOGICAL INNOVATION AND COOPERATION FOR FOREIGN INFORMATION ACCESS

Assistance: project grants (67 percent).

Purposes: to develop innovative techniques or programs using new electronic technologies to collect, organize, preserve, and disseminate information on world regions and countries other than the U.S.—addressing U.S. teaching and research needs in international education and foreign languages.

Eligible applicants/beneficiaries: IHEs, public or nonprofit private libraries, or consortia.

Range/Average: $200,000.

Activity: new program in FY 99.

HQ: same address as **84.016**. Phone: (202)401-9780. (Note: no field offices for this program.)

84.338 READING EXCELLENCE

Assistance: project grants (100 percent/to 3 years).

Purposes: to provide children with the readiness skills and support they need in early childhood to learn to read when they enter school; to teach every child to read by the end of the third grade; to improve instructional practices in elementary schools.

Eligible applicants: SEAs, territories and possessions.

Eligible beneficiaries: LEAs with at least one school in Title I improvement status; districts with the highest or second highest percentages of poverty or number of poor children in the state.

Range: $100,000 to $28,000,000.

Activity: new program in FY 99.

HQ: OESE-DOED, 400 Maryland Ave. SW - Rm.5C141, Washington, DC 20202. Phone: (202)260-8228. (Note: no field offices for this program.)

84.339   LEARNING ANYTIME ANYWHERE PARTNERSHIPS ("LAAP")

Assistance: project grants (50 percent/to 5 years).

Purposes: to enhance the delivery, quality, and accountability of postsecondary education and career-oriented lifelong learning through technology and related innovations. Projects may include: development and assessment of model distance learning programs or innovative software; methodologies to identify and measure skill competence; innovative student support services.

Eligible applicants/beneficiaries: partnerships with two or more independent agencies, organizations, or institutions including IHEs, community organizations, and other public and private entities.

Range: $100,000 to $500,000.

Activity: new program in FY 99.

HQ: same address as **84.116.** Phone: (202)708-5750. (Note: no field offices for this program.)

84.340   CLASS SIZE REDUCTION

Assistance: project grants (100 percent/to 3 years).

Purposes: to hire highly qualified teachers to reduce class size, particularly in early grades, to improve educational achievement for regular and special needs children.

Eligible applicants/beneficiaries: SEAs. LEAs are subgrantees.

Range: $5,623,000 to $129,178,000.

Activity: new program in FY 99.

HQ: same address/phone as **84.338.** (Note: no field offices for this program.)

84.341   COMMUNITY-BASED TECHNOLOGY CENTERS

Assistance: project grants (100 percent/to 3 years).

Purposes: to develop model community technology centers, demonstrating their educational effectiveness in rural and urban areas and economically distressed communities.

Eligible applicants/beneficiaries: SEAs, LEAs, IHEs, other public and private nonprofit and profit agencies and organizations, or groups of same.

Range: $75,000 to $300,000.

Activity: new program in FY 99; 40 awards anticipated.

HQ: same address/phone as **84.002**. (Note: no field offices for this program.)

84.342 PREPARING TOMORROW'S TEACHERS TO USE TECHNOLOGY ("Teacher Training in Technology")

Assistance: project grants (50 percent/to 3 years).

Purposes: for partnerships of teacher preparation programs to ensure that teachers master the instructional strategies, learning styles, and content applications enabled by modern learning technologies. Funds may support faculty development, curriculum resign, and cross-disciplinary partnerships among academic departments and between IHEs and the preschool and high school community.

Eligible applicants/beneficiaries: IHEs in collaboration with schools of education; nonprofit organizations applying on behalf of consortia of SEAs, community colleges, school districts, private schools, and other agencies and organizations including businesses, foundation, and others.

Range/Average: $230,000.

Activity: new program in FY 99; 325 awards anticipated.

HQ: Higher Education Programs Office, OPE-DOED, 400 Maryland Ave. SW, Washington, DC 20202. Phone: (202)708-1365. (Note: no field offices for this program.)

84.343 ASSISTIVE TECHNOLOGY—STATE GRANTS FOR PROTECTION AND ADVOCACY

Assistance: project grants (100 percent/to 6 years).

Purposes: for protection and advocacy services related to assistive technology services and devices for persons with disabilities—as provided in the Developmental Disabilities Assistance and Bill of Rights Act.

Eligible applicants/beneficiaries: designated protection and advocacy agencies in states and outlying areas.

Range: $20,000 to $40,000.

Activity: new program in FY 99.

HQ: National Institute on Disability and Rehabilitation Research, OSERS-DOED, 400 Maryland Ave. SW, Washington, DC 20202. Phone: (202)205-5666. (Note: no field offices for this program.)

SCHOLARSHIP AND FELLOWSHIP FOUNDATIONS

HARRY S TRUMAN SCHOLARSHIP FOUNDATION

85.001 HARRY S TRUMAN SCHOLARSHIP PROGRAM

Assistance: direct payments/specified use.

Purposes: for scholarships for full-time students pursuing careers in public service, financed by a permanent trust fund endowment.

Eligible applicants/beneficiaries: U.S. citizens or nationals in their college junior year, nominated by their IHEs. Applicants must rank in the upper quarter of their class, and their studies should permit admission to a graduate or professional program leading to a public service career.

Range: $3,000 to $13,500/year. **Average:** $6,510/year.

Activity: since 1977, 1,938 scholarships.

HQ: Executive Secretary, Harry S Truman Scholarship Foundation, 712 Jackson Pl. NW, Washington, DC 20006. Phones: (202)395-4831; Internet, http://www.truman.gov (Note: no field offices for this program.)

CHRISTOPHER COLUMBUS FELLOWSHIP FOUNDATION

85.100 CHRISTOPHER COLUMBUS FELLOWSHIP PROGRAM

Assistance: project grants; direct payments/specified-unrestricted use.

Purposes: for research, study, and labor designed to produce new discoveries in all fields. Program purposes generally are accomplished in conjunction with such cooperating entities as *DISCOVER Magazine*, Christopher Columbus Discovery Institute, and the Bayer/National Science Foundation Award for Community Innovations.

Eligible applicants/beneficiaries: U.S. citizens.

Range: $50,000 to $350,000.

Activity: new program listing in 1997.

HQ: Executive Director, Christopher Columbus Scholarship Foundation, Crystal Plaza One - Ste.804, 2001 Jefferson Davis Hwy., Arlington, VA 22202. Phones: (703)305-7700; FAX (703)305-7692. (Note: no field offices for this program.)

BARRY M. GOLDWATER SCHOLARSHIP AND EXCELLENCE IN EDUCATION FOUNDATION

85.200 BARRY M. GOLDWATER SCHOLARSHIP PROGRAM

Assistance: direct payments/specified use.

Purposes: for scholarships to outstanding students to pursue careers in mathematics, the natural sciences, and engineering—financed by a permanent trust fund endowment.

Eligible applicants/beneficiaries: U.S. citizens, nationals, or lawful resident aliens that are full-time college sophomores and juniors at two- and four-year IHEs, ranking in the upper fourth of their class. Nominations must be submitted by accredited institutions.

Range: $300 to $7,500/year. **Average:** $6,800.

Activity: new program listing in 1997. Since 1988 program inception, 2,712 scholars selected.

HQ: President, Barry M. Goldwater Scholarship Foundation, 6225 Brandon Ave. - Ste.315, Springfield, VA 22150-2519. Phones: (703)756-6012; Internet, http://www.act.org/goldwater ; E-mail, goldh2o@erols.com (Note: no field offices for this program.)

WOODROW WILSON INTERNATIONAL CENTER FOR SCHOLARS

85.300 WOODROW WILSON CENTER FELLOWSHIPS IN THE HUMANITIES AND SOCIAL SCIENCES

Assistance: project grants (4-9 months).

Purposes: to foster scholarships and promote nonpartisan exchange of views between scholars and decision makers. The Center sponsors research, meetings, and publications in such areas as history, economics, politics, international relations, the environment, literature, art history. Fellows are in residence at the Center's main offices in Washington, D.C., where they receive office space, use of special libraries and personal computers, part-time research assistance, and publications services.

Eligible applicants/beneficiaries: citizens of any country, with backgrounds in government, business, the professions, or academia—with English language proficiency. For academic participants, eligibility is limited to the postdoctoral level. Degree candidates are ineligible.

Range: stipends, to $69,000. **Average:** $47,200 including travel, support for dependents, health insurance.

Activity: new program listing in 1997. 1998-99, 21 fellows.

HQ: Woodrow Wilson International Center for Scholars, 1300 Pennsylvania Ave. NW, Washington, DC 20523. Phones: (202)691-4001; Fellowships Office, (202)691-4170; Internet, http://wwics.si.edu (Note: no field offices for this program.)

MORRIS K. UDALL SCHOLARSHIP AND EXCELLENCE IN NATIONAL ENVIRONMENTAL POLICY FOUNDATION

85.400 MORRIS K. UDALL SCHOLARSHIP PROGRAM

Assistance: direct payments/specified use.

Purposes: for internships, scholarships, and fellowships to develop increased opportunities for young Americans to prepare for careers related to the environment; for native Americans and Alaska natives intending to pursue careers in health care and tribal public policy. The program is financed by a permanent trust fund endowment.

Eligible applicants/beneficiaries: U.S. citizens, nationals, or permanent resident aliens that are college sophomores or juniors.

Range: $2,500 to $5,000/year.

Activity: new program listing in 1997. FY 98, 75 scholarships.

HQ: Director, Morris K. Udall Foundation, 110 S. Church St. - Ste.3350, Tucson, AZ 85701. Phones: (520)670-5608; FAX (520)670-5530.

85.401   MORRIS K. UDALL FELLOWSHIP PROGRAM

Assistance: direct payments/specified use.

Purposes: same generally as for **85.400**.

Eligible applicants/beneficiaries: U.S. citizens and permanent residents that are full-time doctoral degree candidates in their final year of writing their dissertation in environmental public policy and conflict resolution.

Range/Average: $24,000/year.

Activity: new program listing in 1997. FY 98, 2 fellowships.

HQ: Morris K. Udall Foundation, 2001 N. Dodge, P.O. Box 168, Iowa City, IA 55243. Phones: (319)337-1707; FAX (319)337-1204. (Note: no field offices for this program.)

85.402   MORRIS K. UDALL NATIVE AMERICAN CONGRESSIONAL INTERNSHIP PROGRAM

Assistance: direct payments/specified use.

Purposes: same generally as for **85.400**. Interns receive round-trip air fare to Washington, D.C., lodging, a per diem for meals and incidentals, and a $1,200 stipend at the conclusion of the internship.

Eligible applicants/beneficiaries: enrolled members of recognized tribes or Alaska natives that are matriculated college seniors or graduate or law students with a minimum 3.2 GPA, and interested in tribal government and policy.

Range/Average: $3,200 per intern per 10-week program.

Activity: new program listing in 1997. FY 99, 12 interns completed 10-week internships in various Congressional offices and the White House.

HQ: same address/phone as **85.400**.

JAMES MADISON MEMORIAL FELLOWSHIP FOUNDATION

85.500   JAMES MADISON MEMORIAL FELLOWSHIP PROGRAM

Assistance: direct payments/specified use.

Purposes: for fellowships to future and current secondary school American history, government, or social studies teachers—to strengthen teaching and learning of the principles, framing, and development of the U.S. Constitution. Recipients are obligated to perform one year of teaching for each year of study supported by a fellowship. Payments cover actual costs of tuition, room and board, fees, and books.

Eligible applicants/beneficiaries: Junior Fellows (2-year maximum)—college seniors or college graduates; Senior Fellows (5-year maximum)—experienced, full-time teachers of grades 7-12, pursuing a Master's level degree. All candidates must be U.S. citizens or nationals.

Range: to $12,000 for one year; $24,000 maximum total award.

Activity: new program listing in 1997. Since 1992 program inception, 480 fellowship awards; 97 active junior, 180 active senior fellowships.

HQ: Director of Administration and Finance, James Madison Foundation, 2000 K St. NW - Ste.303, Washington, DC 20006. Phones: (202)653-8700; FAX (202)653-6045. (Note: no field offices for this program.)

PENSION BENEFIT GUARANTY CORPORATION

86.001   PENSION PLAN TERMINATION INSURANCE ("ERISA")

Assistance: insurance.

Purposes: pursuant to the Employee Retirement Income Security Act (ERISA) and other acts, to insure voluntary private pension plans; to provide for uninterrupted payment of pension benefits. Insurance coverage is mandatory for any pension plan established or maintained by an employer or an employee organization engaged in or affecting commerce, except such plans as those covering: individual accounts; federal, state, local employees; church employees; nonresident aliens; select groups of management or highly compensated employees; professional service employers with fewer than 25 participants; other specific groups.

Eligible applicants/beneficiaries: private businesses and organizations that maintain defined benefit plans; participants in such plans.

Range: $10 to $3,051.14 monthly per retiree. **Average:** $332 monthly.

Activity: 44,000 plans insured with 42,000,000 participants; FY 98, 209,000 participants received benefits.

HQ: Pension Benefit Guaranty Corporation, 1200 K St. NW, Washington, DC 20005-4026. Phone: (202)326-4000.

ARCHITECTURAL AND TRANSPORTATION BARRIERS COMPLIANCE BOARD

88.001 ARCHITECTURAL AND TRANSPORTATION BARRIERS COMPLIANCE BOARD ("ATBCB")

Assistance: technical information.

Purposes: pursuant to the ADA, Telecommunications Act, Architectural Barriers Act, and other laws, to enforce federal laws requiring accessibility for physically handicapped persons in federally funded buildings and facilities; to establish guidelines and requirements; to provide technical assistance on design and construction problems; to conduct pertinent research.

Eligible applicants/beneficiaries: federal, state, and local agencies; private organizations; individuals.

Activity: FY 98 (representative), 7,120 persons trained; 85 barriers act complaint cases opened; 106 investigations completed; 2 research projects completed.

HQ: Director, Office of Technical and Information Services, ATBCB, 1331 F St. NW - Ste.1000, Washington, DC 20004-1111. Phones: (202)272-5434; TTY (202)272-5449; FAX (202)272-5447; Computer Bulletin Board *(modem)*, (202)272-5448; *technical assistance,* (800)872-2253, TTY (800)993-2822; e-mail,info@access-board.gov ; Web, www.access-board.gov (Note: no field offices for this program.)

NATIONAL ARCHIVES AND RECORDS ADMINISTRATION

89.001 NATIONAL ARCHIVES REFERENCE SERVICES—HISTORICAL RESEARCH

Assistance: use of property, facilities, and equipment; advisory services/counseling; technical information.

Purposes: to provide reference services to the public and researchers in obtaining access to records and historical materials of the federal government in the National Archives, Presidential Libraries, and Regional Records Services. Conferences, workshops, and other outreach activities may be conducted. Restrictions apply to records subject to the Freedom of Information Act.

Eligible applicants/beneficiaries: general public.

Activity: FY 98 (aggregate of all sources), 7,905,000 reference services.

HQ: Office of Records Services, National Archives and Records Administration, Washington, DC 20408. Phone: (301)713-7000. Office of Regional Records Services, National Archives and Records Administration, College Park, MD 20740-6001. Phone: (301)713-7200.

89.003   NATIONAL HISTORICAL PUBLICATIONS AND RECORDS GRANTS

Assistance: project grants (varying terms).

Purposes: for preservation, publication, and use of documentary sources relating to the history of the U.S. Projects may involve: cooperative efforts with the states, including training; publication in book, microform, or electronic editions of papers and documents of national historical significance.

Eligible applicants/beneficiaries: state and local governments, territorial agencies, federal- and state-recognized tribes; educational and other nonprofit institutions including IHEs, libraries, historical societies, museums, university presses, archives; individuals.

Range: $1,000 to $425,000. **Average:** $73,000.

Activity: FY 00 estimate, 105 grants.

HQ: National Historical Publications and Records Commission, National Archives and Records Administration, National Archives Bldg., Washington, DC 20408. Phone: (202)501-5610. (Note: no field offices for this program.)

UNITED STATES INSTITUTE OF PEACE

91.001   INTERNATIONAL PEACE AND CONFLICT MANAGEMENT—RESEARCH AND EDUCATION

Assistance: project grants (100 percent).

Purposes: for education, training, research, and public information projects in international peace and conflict resolution. Unsolicited grant awards may support: research by scholars; curricula and materials development for secondary through postgraduate programs; media programming, including materials for television and radio; development of library programs, data bases, bibliographies, collections.

Eligible applicants/beneficiaries: domestic or foreign nonprofit organizations, official public institutions; individuals, including U.S. citizens and foreign nationals.

Range/Average: $38,000.

Activity: since FY 89, 901 awards.

HQ: Unsolicited Grant Program, U.S. Institute of Peace, 1200 17th St. NW - Ste.200, Washington, DC 20036-3006. Phones: (202)429-3842; E-mail, grant-program@usip.org (Note: no field offices for this program.)

91.002 INTERNATIONAL PEACE AND CONFLICT MANAGEMENT—ARTICLES AND MANUSCRIPTS

Assistance: project grants (100 percent).

Purposes: for competitive grants to support education, training, research, and public information on international peace and conflict resolution and on themes and topics identified by the Institute.

Eligible applicants/beneficiaries: same as for **91.001**.

Range/Average: $35,000.

Activity: since 1989, 260 awards.

HQ: Solicited Grant Program, same address/phone as **91.001**. (Note: no field offices for this program.)

NATIONAL COUNCIL ON DISABILITY

92.001 NATIONAL COUNCIL ON DISABILITY ("NCD")

Assistance: project grants (100 percent).

Purposes: to make recommendations to the President and Congress on issues affecting the disabled; for research studies to review and collect data on the status of various systems and programs for persons with disabilities. Project examples: quality of education for students with disabilities; financing of assistive technological devices and services; ADA monitoring.

Eligible applicants/beneficiaries: public and private nonprofit institutions; individuals.

Range: $25,000 to $210,000.

Activity: 6 contracts completed.

HQ: Executive Director, National Council on Disability, 1331 F St. NW - Ste.1050, Washington, DC 20004-1107. Phone: (202)272-2004. (Note: no field offices for this program.)

DEPARTMENT OF HEALTH AND HUMAN SERVICES

NOTE: *In HHS programs:*

"NRSA" *refers to National Research Service Awards available to institutions, individuals, or both. Only domestic nonprofit organizations may apply for insti-*

tutional awards. Individual applicants must: be U.S. citizens, noncitizen nationals, or lawful permanent residents; arrange sponsorship by a public or private nonprofit institution with appropriate staff and facilities; have a professional or scientific degree (M.D., Ph.D., D.D.S., D.V.M., Sc.D., D.Eng., or equivalent domestic or foreign degree); comply with applicable service or payback requirements. Predoctoral awards may be available; recipients usually must have a baccalaureate degree and some work completed toward a graduate degree.

"SBIR" refers to the Small Business Innovation Research program; "STTR" refers to the Small Business Technology Transfer program. Under either program contracts must involve domestic small businesses—i.e., for-profit, independently owned, not dominant in the field, and with no more than 500 employees— conducting research in the U.S. or its possessions. Participation by minority, women-owned, and socially and economically disadvantaged businesses is fostered and encouraged.

SBIR grants fund the development of technological innovations that may lead to commercialization of products and processes. Phase I contracts, usually up to $100,000 covering six months of research activity, are to establish technical merit and feasibility. Phase II funding, ranging to $750,000 for up to two years, is for continuation of Phase I activities. Primary employment of the principal investigator named in the firm's proposal must be with the small business.

STTR Phase I grants, up to $100,000 for one year of activity, fund cooperative research and development by small businesses and research institutions—to determine scientific, technical, and commercial merit and feasibility. Phase II funding, up to $500,000 for two years, reflects results of Phase I research. At least 40 percent of project activities must be performed by the small business concern, and at least 30 percent by the research institution.

93.001 CIVIL RIGHTS COMPLIANCE ACTIVITIES

Assistance: investigation of complaints; technical information.

Purposes: to ensure nondiscrimination on any basis against applicants for or beneficiaries of HHS assistance through any program or in any HHS-assisted facility; to encourage compliance with nondiscrimination regulations by providing technical assistance to recipients of HHS assistance, through workshops, designing model compliance plans, and training responsible state and local officials.

Eligible applicants/beneficiaries: anyone believing that they have been discriminated against in any HHS program, as well as under the Americans with Disabilities Act, Multiethnic Placement Act, or other acts, or wanting information or technical assistance to assure compliance with applicable laws.

Activity: (representative) FY 98, 1,548 discrimination complaints filed, 1,644 complaint actions completed; 227 post-grant compliance reviews and investigations completed.

HQ: Director, Policy and Special Projects Staff, HHS, HHH Bldg. - Rm.502-E, 200 Independence Ave. SW, Washington, DC 20201. Phone: (202)619-0671. Director, Office for Civil Rights, OS-HHS, HHH Bldg. - Rm.515-F, same address. Phones: (202)619-0403; *Hotlines,* (800)368-1019, TDD (800)537-7697.

93.003   PUBLIC HEALTH AND SOCIAL SERVICES EMERGENCY FUND

Assistance: project grants (100 percent).

Purposes: to provide supplemental funding for public health and social service emergencies resulting from natural disasters. Funds may be used for: repairs or replacement of property used for federally assisted programs; HHS-type services to persons directly affected by the disaster; activities authorized by the HHS Secretary.

Eligible applicants/beneficiaries: federal agencies, state and local governments, service providers in disaster areas.

Range/Average: N.A.

Activity: not quantified specifically.

HQ: Director, Division of Financial Management, SAMHSA-HHS, Parklawn Bldg., 5600 Fishers Lane, Rockville, MD 20857. Phone: (301)443-3846. Deputy Director, Financial Management Office, CDCP-HHS, 1600 Clifton Rd., Atlanta, GA 30333. Phone: (404)639-7400. Director, Office of Financial Management, ACF-HHS, Aerospace Bldg. - 6th floor, 370 L'Enfant Promenade SW, Washington, DC 20447. Phone:(202)401-9238. Director, Office of Management, AOA-HHS, Cohen Bldg. - Rm.4650, 330 Independence Ave. SW, Washington, DC 20201. Phone: (202)619-0641. (Note: no field offices for this program.)

93.004   COOPERATIVE AGREEMENTS TO IMPROVE THE HEALTH STATUS OF MINORITY POPULATIONS

Assistance: project grants (100 percent/to 5 years).

Purposes: for activities to improve the health status of members of racial and ethnic minority groups. Project examples: training and technical assistance center on cultural competence for community-based organizations serving Hispanics; partnerships development to address public health problems in the Mississippi Delta region. Funds may not be used to provide health care, for construction, or to supplant ongoing project activities.

Eligible applicants/beneficiaries: public and private nonprofit entities.

Range: $18,000 to $4,900,000. **Average:** $402,000.

Activity: new program listing in 1997. FY 99, 7 new, 27 continuation awards.

HQ: Director, Division of Program Operations, Office of Minority Health, Office of Public Health and Science, OS-HHS, Rockwall II Bldg. - Ste.1000, 5515 Security Lane, Rockville, MD 20852. Phone: (301)594-0769. *Grants management information*: Grants Management Officer, Office of Minority

Health, same address. Phone: (301)594-0758. (Note: no field offices for this program.)

93.005   PROJECT GRANTS FOR FACILITIES TO IMPROVE THE HEALTH STATUS OF MINORITY POPULATIONS

Assistance: project grants (100 percent).

Purposes: to construct, expand, renovate, or modernize facilities to improve the health status of underserved minority communities and populations.

Eligible applicants/beneficiaries: public and private nonprofit entities.

Range/Average: from $1,000,000.

Activity: new program listing in 1997. FY 99 estimate, 1 award.

HQ: Deputy Director, Office of Minority Health, same address as **93.004**. Phone: (301)443-5084. *Grants management information*: same address/ phone as **93.004**. (Note: no field offices for this program.)

93.006   STATE AND TERRITORIAL MINORITY HIV/AIDS DEMONSTRATION PROGRAM

Assistance: project grants (100 percent/to 3 years).

Purposes: for partnerships between state and territorial entities, health care facilities, and minority community-based organizations—to develop and implement HIV/AIDS-related education and prevention strategies and to increase access to services and treatment for minorities. Funds may not be used to provide health care, for construction, or to supplant ongoing project activities.

Eligible applicants/beneficiaries: state and territorial offices of minority health or their equivalent.

Range: to $150,000.

Activity: new program in FY 99. FY 00 estimate, 20 continuation grants.

HQ: same addresses/phones as **93.004**. (Note: no field offices for this program.)

93.041   SPECIAL PROGRAMS FOR THE AGING—TITLE VII, CHAPTER 3— PROGRAMS FOR PREVENTION OF ELDER ABUSE, NEGLECT, AND EXPLOITATION
("Elder Abuse Prevention")

Assistance: formula grants (100 percent/2-4 years).

Purposes: pursuant to the Older Americans Act, to develop, coordinate, and enhance programs for the prevention and treatment of abuse, neglect, and exploitation of older persons. States must submit a plan covering 2-4 years. Project examples: public education and outreach; counseling; technical assistance and training for professionals and paraprofessionals.

Eligible applicants/beneficiaries: states and territories with state agencies on aging, designated by the governors.

Range: $2,156 to $449,000. **Average:** $82,000.

Activity: not quantified specifically.

HQ: Director, Office of Program Operations and Development, AOA-HHS, Washington, DC 20201. Phone: (202)619-1828.

93.042 SPECIAL PROGRAMS FOR THE AGING—TITLE VII, CHAPTER 2—LONG-TERM CARE OMBUDSMAN SERVICES FOR OLDER INDIVIDUALS
("State Grants for Long-Term Care Ombudsman Services")

Assistance: formula grants (100 percent/2-4 years).

Purposes: pursuant to the Older Americans Act, to establish and operate ombudsman services for older persons living or seeking to live in long-term care facilities, to: provide for the investigation and resolution of complaints by or on behalf of residents; promote policies and practices to improve the quality of life and care; prevent resident abuse and Medicare and Medicaid fraud.

Eligible applicants/beneficiaries: same as for **93.041.**

Range: $2,021 to $422,000. **Average:** $77,000.

Activity: 1995, 162,000 persons filed 218,000 complaints—75 percent of which were resolved fully or partially.

HQ: AOA-HHS, Washington, DC 20201. Phone: (202)619-0011.

93.043 SPECIAL PROGRAMS FOR THE AGING—TITLE III, PART F—DISEASE PREVENTION AND HEALTH PROMOTION SERVICES
("State Grants for Disease Prevention and Health Promotion")

Assistance: formula grants (85 percent/2-4 years).

Purposes: pursuant to the Older Americans Act, to develop or strengthen programs for preventive health services and health promotion ineligible for reimbursement under Medicare, at senior centers or alternative sites. States must submit plans covering 2-4 years. Project examples: routine health and nutrition screening; group exercise programs; coordination of community mental health services; gerontological counseling; referrals and follow-ups.

Eligible applicants/beneficiaries: same as for **93.041.**

Range: $1,934 to $1,588,000. **Average:** $283,000.

Activity: not quantified specifically.

HQ: Director, Office of State and Community Programs, AOA-HHS, Washington, DC 20201. Phone: (202)619-2617.

93.044 SPECIAL PROGRAMS FOR THE AGING—TITLE III, PART B—GRANTS FOR SUPPORTIVE SERVICES AND SENIOR CENTERS

Assistance: formula grants (75-85 percent/2-4 years).

Purposes: pursuant to the Older Americans Act, to provide comprehensive and coordinated supportive services and to operate multipurpose facilities for older persons, including senior centers—developed according to approved 2-4 year state plans. Special emphasis is given to management improvements geared to maintain and increase service levels. Funds may also cover acquisition, construction, or renovation costs.

Eligible applicants/beneficiaries: same as for **93.041**.

Range: $35,000 to $27,820,000. **Average:** $5,242,000.

Activity: annually, 6,500,000 persons served.

HQ: same address/phone as **93.043**.

93.045   SPECIAL PROGRAMS FOR THE AGING—TITLE III, PART C— NUTRITION SERVICES

Assistance: formula grants (85 percent/2-4 years).

Purposes: pursuant to the Older Americans Act, to provide meals, nutrition education, and related services for the elderly—including at least one hot or other appropriate meal per day, five or more days per week (except in rural areas). Meals may be served in a congregate setting or delivered to the home.

Eligible applicants: all states and territories.

Eligible beneficiaries: persons age 60 and over and their spouses; some disabled or handicapped persons under age 60.

Range: congregate services, $239,000 to $34,679,000; home services, $70,000 to $10,623,000. **Average:** congregate, $6,661,000; home, $2,000,000.

Activity: N.A.

HQ: same address/phone as **93.043**.

93.046   SPECIAL PROGRAMS FOR THE AGING—TITLE III, PART D—IN-HOME SERVICES FOR FRAIL OLDER INDIVIDUALS
("In-Home Services for Frail Older Individuals")

Assistance: formula grants (85 percent/2-4 years).

Purposes: pursuant to the Older Americans Act, for in-home services to frail older persons, including supportive services for victims of Alzheimer's disease and related disorders with neurological and organic brain dysfunctions, and to their families. States must submit plans covering 2-4 years. Projects must take into account age, greatest economic needs, non-economic factors contributing to frailty, and non-economic and non-health factors.

Eligible applicants/beneficiaries: same as for **93.041**.

Range: $1,057 to $962,000. **Average:** $172,000.

Activity: N.A.

HQ: same address/phone as **93.043**.

93.047   SPECIAL PROGRAMS FOR THE AGING—TITLE VI-PART A, INDIAN PROGRAMS—GRANTS TO INDIAN TRIBES AND PART B, GRANTS TO NATIVE HAWAIIANS

Assistance: project grants (formula-based - 100 percent).

Purposes: pursuant to the Older Americans Act, for supportive services to older Indians and Alaska and Hawaii natives, including nutrition services, multipurpose center improvements and staffing, transportation, and information and referral assistance.

Eligible applicants: tribal organizations, public or nonprofit private organizations—serving at least 50 clients.

Eligible beneficiaries: Indians age 60 or older and, for nutrition services, their spouses; certain others under age 60.

Range: $51,000 to $125,000. **Average:** $64,000.

Activity: FY 98, 1 native Hawaiian, 222 tribal organizations funded.

HQ: Director, Office of American Indian, Alaskan Native, and Native Hawaiian Programs, AOA-HHS, 330 Independence Ave. SW - Rm.4743, Washington, DC 20201. Phone: (202)619-2713.

93.048 SPECIAL PROGRAMS FOR THE AGING—TITLE IV—TRAINING, RESEARCH AND DISCRETIONARY PROJECTS AND PROGRAMS

Assistance: project grants (75 percent/to 5 years).

Purposes: pursuant to the Older Americans Act, for personnel training, education, and demonstration programs in the field of aging—to develop knowledge of the problems and needs of the elderly. Project examples: statewide senior legal hotlines; Volunteer Opportunities for Senior Adults; Intergenerational Home Care Model Project.

Eligible applicants/beneficiaries: public or nonprofit private agencies, organizations, and institutions.

Range: $50,000 to $500,000. **Average:** $150,000.

Activity: not quantified specifically.

HQ: Office of Program Development, AOA-HHS, Cohen Bldg. - Rm.4737, 330 Independence Ave. SW, Washington, DC 20201. Phone: (202)619-3032.

93.049 SPECIAL PROGRAMS FOR THE AGING—TITLE VII, CHAPTER 6— ALLOTMENTS FOR VULNERABLE ELDER RIGHTS PROTECTION PROGRAMS
("Benefits Counseling")

Assistance: formula grants (55-75 percent/2 years).

Purposes: pursuant to the Older Americans Act, to develop and operate state programs for outreach, counseling, and assistance programs for insurance and pension and other public benefits available to vulnerable elders, in accordance with official 2-4 year state plans.

Eligible applicants/beneficiaries: same as for **93.041**.

Range/Average: N.A.

Activity: N.A.

HQ: same address/phone as **93.041**.

93.051 NEW DEMONSTRATION GRANTS TO STATES WITH RESPECT TO ALZHEIMER'S DISEASE

Assistance: project grants (55-75 percent/2 years).

Purposes: to plan, establish, and operate programs for persons with Alzheimer's disease and related disorders, their families, and care-givers, including: home health and personal care, companion services, short-term care in health facilities, other respite care; legal counseling and education services; outreach particularly to racial and ethnic groups and rural populations; dissemination of information on available assistance; related services.

Eligible applicants/beneficiaries: state agencies.

Range: $217,000 to $490,000. **Average:** $340,000.

Activity: new program listing in 1999. FY 99, 15 states funded. Cumulatively, first five years of program, 8,000 client families served.

HQ: Immediate Office of Assistant Secretary/Aging, AOA-HHS, HHH Bldg. - Rm.309-F, 200 Independence Ave. SW, Washington, DC 20201. Phone: (202)401-4547, -4634.

93.101   GRANTS FOR RESIDENTIAL TREATMENT PROGRAMS FOR PREGNANT AND POSTPARTUM WOMEN
("Pregnant and Postpartum Women")

Assistance: project grants (75-90 percent/1-5 years).

Purposes: for alcohol and drug abuse treatment services for pregnant and postpartum women, their infants, and children, delivered in residential settings, coupled with primary health, mental health, and social services—to improve their overall treatment outcomes. Projects should: decrease substance abuse; improve physical health, promote safe and healthy pregnancies and perinatal outcome, and reduce patient/client morbidity and mortality—especially incidence of HIV, sero-prevalence, tuberculosis, and sexually transmitted diseases; improve psychiatric, psychological, and emotional health and well-being; improve family-social functioning in a drug- and alcohol-free environment, in concert with other agencies; enhance the socio-economic well-being of women and the family unit by improving employment status, accessibility to housing, and human services; decrease involvement in and exposure to crime, inter-personal violence, child abuse and neglect, and sexual abuse; enhance the cognitive and educational development of infants and children with inter-uterine exposure to alcohol and other drugs. Grant funds may not be used for construction or facility acquisition costs; renovations and alterations require prior approval.

Eligible applicants/beneficiaries: state alcohol and drug abuse agencies, including in territories and possessions; public and private nonprofit agencies; tribal authorities.

Range: $536,000 to $1,215,000.

Activity: FY 99 estimate, 2 continuation awards.

HQ: Chief, Clinical Interventions Branch, Division of Practice and Systems Development, CSAT, SAMHSA-HHS, Rockwall II Bldg. - 7th floor, 5600 Fishers Lane, Rockville, MD 20857. Phone: (301)443-8802. *Grants management information*: Grants Management Officer, Office of Program Support, SAMHSA-HHS, Rockwall II Bldg. - 6th floor, 5600 Fishers Lane, Rockville, MD 20857. Phone: (301)443-9666. (Note: no field offices for this program.)

93.102   DEMONSTRATION GRANTS FOR RESIDENTIAL TREATMENT FOR WOMEN AND THEIR CHILDREN
("Residential Women and Children")

Assistance: project grants (100 percent/to 5 years).

Purposes: for demonstration projects to improve upon services similar to **93.101**, provided in residential settings for women, their infants, and children.

Eligible applicants/beneficiaries: same as for **93.101**.

Range: $650,000 to $800,000.

Activity: FY 99 estimate, 8 continuation awards.

HQ: same addresses/phones as **93.101**. (Note: no field offices for this program.)

93.103 FOOD AND DRUG ADMINISTRATION—RESEARCH

Assistance: project grants (100 percent/to 5 years).

Purposes: for research, demonstration, and public education activities in a broad range of areas, including health problems associated with tobacco products, AIDS, biologics, blood and blood products, therapeutics, vaccine and allergenic projects, drug hazards, human and veterinary drugs, medical devices and diagnostics products, and radiation-emitting devices and materials; food safety and additives. SBIR awards are made (*see Note preceding 93.001*).

Eligible applicants/beneficiaries: public or private nonprofit IHEs, institutions, state and local governments, hospitals, laboratories, commercial and nonprofit organizations, SBIR firms.

Range: $5,000 to $2,000,000. **Average:** $206,000.

Activity: FY 00 estimate, 60 new grants; 2-3 SBIR awards.

HQ: Grants Management Officer, Division of Contracts and Procurement Management (OFACS), FDA-PHS-HHS (HFA-520), 5630 Fishers Lane - Rm.2129, Rockville, MD 20852. Phones: (301)827-7184; FAX (301)827-7103; *SBIR information,* (301)827-7102. (Note: no field offices for administration of this program; however, district offices are listed in Part IV for information purposes.)

93.104 COMPREHENSIVE COMMUNITY MENTAL HEALTH SERVICES FOR CHILDREN WITH SERIOUS EMOTIONAL DISTURBANCES (SED) ("CMHS Child Mental Health Service Initiative")

Assistance: project grants (33-75 percent/to 5 years).

Purposes: to provide community-based care systems for children and adolescents with serious emotional disturbances, and their families—ensuring that: services are provided collaboratively across child-serving systems; each child or adolescent served receives an individualized service plan developed with the participation of the family and, where appropriate, of the child; each plan designates a case manager; funding is provided for the required mental health services. Project funds may be used to pay: administrative costs including staff salaries, travel, supplies, communications, and space and equipment rental; for pertinent training including in providing therapeutic foster or group home care, intensive home-based or intensive day treatment services. Ineligible expenses include real estate-related costs, residential care or services in centers serving more than 10 children, unrelated training, non-mental health services including medical and educational services, and protection and advocacy.

Eligible applicants: states and their political subdivisions, tribal governments.

Eligible beneficiaries: children under age 22 with diagnosed SED or serious behavioral or mental disorders.

Range: $200,000 to $3,500,000. **Average:** $1,850,000.

Activity: FY 00 estimate, 50 continuation awards.

HQ: Chief, Child Adolescent and Family Branch, Division of Knowledge Development and Systems Change, CMHS, SAMHSA-HHS, Parklawn Bldg.- Rm.18-49, 5600 Fishers Lane, Rockville, MD 20857. Phone: (301) 443-1333. *Grants management information*: same address/phone as **93.101**. (Note: no field offices for this program.)

93.105 BILINGUAL/BICULTURAL SERVICE DEMONSTRATION PROJECTS IN MINORITY HEALTH

Assistance: project grants (100 percent/3 years).

Purposes: for bilingual/bicultural assistance in providing health services to members of minority groups whose native language is other than English, including staff training and hiring interpreters and translators—but not providing health care services or augmentation of ongoing project activities.

Eligible applicants/beneficiaries: public or private nonprofit minority community-based organizations.

Range: $90,000 to $100,000. **Average:** $100,000.

Activity: FY 00 estimate, 15 new, 12 continuation awards.

HQ: same addresses/phones as **93.004**. (Note: no field offices for this program.)

93.106 MINORITY INTERNATIONAL RESEARCH TRAINING GRANT IN THE BIOMEDICAL AND BEHAVIORAL SCIENCES

Assistance: project grants (100 percent/3 years).

Purposes: for qualified minority undergraduate or graduate students and faculty members to participate in international biomedical and behavioral research programs. Grants may be awarded: to undergraduates for 8-12 weeks abroad for language training and research experience; to predoctoral candidates or faculty for 3-12 months abroad.

Eligible applicants/beneficiaries: domestic two- or four-year IHEs; consortia.

Range: institutional, $62,000 to $396,000; stipends, $1,000/month for students, $3,000/month for faculty—plus up to $1,000 and $2,000 monthly, respectively, for living expenses; health insurance, foreign tuition and fees, $500 monthly; foreign institutional support, $500 monthly per student. **Average:** institutional, $200,000.

Activity: FY 99 estimate, 10 new, 8 continuation awards.

HQ: Division of International Training and Research, NIH-HHS, Fogarty International Center, Bldg.31 - Rm.B2C32, Bethesda, MD 20892-2220. Phones: (301)496-1653. *Grants management information*: Grants Management Officer, NIH-HHS, Fogarty International Center, Bldg.31 - Rm.B2C39, Bethesda, MD 20892-2220. Phone: (301)496-1653. (Note: no field offices for this program.)

93.107 MODEL STATE-SUPPORTED AREA HEALTH EDUCATION CENTERS

Assistance: formula grants (50 percent/to 3 years).

Purposes: for model Area Health Education Centers (see **93.824**) to encourage regionalization of health professions schools, through collaborative partnerships of university health centers with local planning, educational, and clinical resources. Emphasis is on recruitment and community-based training of primary care students, residents, and providers.

Eligible applicants/beneficiaries: schools of allopathic medicine or osteopathy operating AHECs and not receiving assistance under **93.824**.

Range: $76,000 to $687,000. **Average:** $365,000.

Activity: FY 00 estimate, 23 grants.

HQ: Chief, AHEC Branch, Division of Medicine, Bureau of Health Professions, HRSA-HHS, Parklawn Bldg. - Rm.9A05, 5600 Fishers Lane, Rockville, MD 20857. Phone: (301)443-6950. *Grants management information*: Grants Management Officer, Bureau of Health Professions, HRSA-HHS, Parklawn Bldg. - Rm.8C26, 5600 Fishers Lane, Rockville, MD 20857. Phone: (301)443-6880. (Note: no field offices for this program.)

93.108 HEALTH EDUCATION ASSISTANCE LOANS ("HEAL")

Assistance: guaranteed/insured loans (10-33 years).

Purposes: to insure loans obtained from eligible lenders, covering the educational expenses of students enrolled for full-time study in health professions programs at participating institutions. Repayment begins nine months after recipient no longer maintains full-time student, internship, or residency status. Deferment of principal and interest payments may be allowed during certain periods. Approved lenders may include banks, credit unions, savings and loan associations, pension funds, insurance companies, and educational institutions.

Eligible applicants/beneficiaries: U.S. citizens, nationals, or lawful permanent residents. NOTE: effective October 1, 1995 no first-time HEAL borrowers—i.e., only previous borrowers remain eligible.

Range/Average: for allopathic medicine, osteopathy, dentistry, veterinary medicine, optometry, and podiatry—to $20,000 annually; maximum aggregate, $80,000. For pharmacy, public health, chiropractic, clinical psychology, graduate health administration—to $12,500 annually; maximum aggregate, $50,000.

Activity: FY 98, 6,587 loans.

HQ: Associate Director, HEAL Program, Division of Student Assistance, Bureau of Health Professions, HRSA-HHS, 5600 Fishers Lane - Rm.8-37, Rockville, MD 20857. Phone: (301)443-1540. (Note: no field offices for this program.)

93.110 MATERNAL AND CHILD HEALTH FEDERAL CONSOLIDATED PROGRAMS
("Special Projects of Regional and National Significance" - "SPRANS")

Assistance: project grants (100 percent).

Purposes: pursuant to the Social Security Act, for special projects of regional or national significance involving training, services, research, and demonstrations in special maternal and child health services, including: genetic disease testing, counseling, and information dissemination; operation of centers providing comprehensive hemophilia diagnosis and treatment. Depending on appropriation level, services may also include home visitations, increased participation of obstetricians and pediatricians, maternal and child health centers for women and infants, rural health services, community-based services for children with special health care needs.

Eligible applicants/beneficiaries: training grants—public or private nonprofit IHEs. Research grants—public or private nonprofit IHEs, agencies, and organizations. Hemophilia and genetics grants and other special project grants—any public or private entity.

Range: $50,000 to $1,500,000. **Average:** $182,000.

Activity: FY 99 estimate, 600 projects.

HQ: Director, Maternal and Child Health Bureau, HRSA-HHS, 5600 Fishers Lane - Rm.18-05, Rockville, MD 20857. Phone: (301)443-2170. *Grants management information*: Grants Management Branch, Maternal and Child Health Bureau, HRSA-HHS, Parklawn Bldg. - Rm.18-12, 5600 Fishers Lane, Rockville, MD 20857. Phone: (301)443-1440.

93.111 ADOLESCENT FAMILY LIFE RESEARCH GRANTS

Assistance: project grants (100 percent/to 3 years).

Purposes: for research and information dissemination activities concerning societal causes and consequences of adolescent sexual activity, contraceptive use, pregnancy and child rearing, adoption versus parenting.

Eligible applicants/beneficiaries: state and local government agencies; private nonprofit and profit organizations; IHEs.

Range: $108,000 to $151,000. **Average:** $145,000

Activity: FY 00 estimate, 6 continuation, 1 new project awards.

HQ: Office of Adolescent Pregnancy Programs, Office of Population Affairs, HHS, 4350 East-West Hwy. - Ste.200, Bethesda, MD 20814. Phone: (301) 594-4008. *Grants management information*: Grants Management Officer, Office of Grants Management, Office of Population Affairs, same address. Phone: (301)594-4012. (Note: no field offices for this program.)

93.113 BIOLOGICAL RESPONSE TO ENVIRONMENTAL HEALTH HAZARDS

Assistance: project grants (100 percent/to 5 years).

Purposes: for research and research training on the chemical and physical causes of pathological changes in molecules, cells, tissues, and organs, toward the prevention of neurological, behavioral, and developmental abnormalities, and respiratory diseases, cancer, and other disorders. Grants also support studies of toxicity in metals, natural and synthetic chemicals, pesticides, asbestos and silica, and natural toxins—and their effects on human organ systems, metabolism, endocrine and immune systems, and other biological functions. The Environmental Health Sciences Education Program may fund projects costing up to $100,000, to improve student understanding of environmental health issues and to expand career awareness in health sciences research and services occupations, by developing educational materials for grades K-12. Mentored Research Scientist Development Awards, Mentored Clinical Scientist Development Awards, Academic Career Awards, and Children's Environmental Health Research Centers may also be funded. SBIR and STTR awards are made (*see Note preceding* **93.001**).

Eligible applicants/beneficiaries: research grants and cooperative agreements, science education grants, independent scientist awards, mentored clinical scientist awards, academic career awards—IHEs, hospitals, state or local governments, nonprofit research institutions, or profit organizations for research by a named principal investigator. Candidates for academic career development awards must have a clinical or research doctoral degree and peer-reviewed independent research support, and they must devote at least 75 percent effort. Candidates for mentored clinical scientist awards must have clinical training; those holding a Ph.D. degree are ineligible, as are researchers that have served as principal investigators on PHS-supported research projects.

Range: research grants, $62,000 to $1,125,000; independent scientist, mentored research scientist development, and academic career awards provide institutional grants to $50,000 for salary plus fringe benefits and 8 percent indirect costs, plus $10,000 to $20,000 for research support. **Average:** projects, $236,000.

Activity: FY 00 estimate, 459 awards.

HQ: Division of Extramural Research and Training, NIEHS, NIH-HHS, P.O. Box 12233, Research Triangle Park, NC 27709. Phones: Director, Office of Program Development, (919)541-0797; Chief, Organ and Systems Toxicology Branch, (919)541-3289; *science education grants,* Program Administrator, Chemical Exposures and Molecular Biology Branch, (919)541-4943; *cooperative agreements, individual awards, SBIR, STTR,* Program Administrator, Organ and Systems Toxicology Branch, (919)541-7825. *Grants management information*: Chief, Grants Management Branch, Division of Extramural Research and Training, same address. Phone: (919)541-7628. (Note: no field offices for this program.)

93.114   APPLIED TOXICOLOGICAL RESEARCH AND TESTING
("Bioassay of Chemicals and Test Development")

Assistance: project grants (100 percent/to 5 years).

Purposes: to develop scientific information about potentially toxic and hazardous chemicals through research, testing and test development, and validation efforts. Program goals include the development and validation of existing and emerging methodologies that can be employed successfully to predict human response to toxic agents. SBIR and STTR awards are made (*see Note preceding* **93.001**). Awards for individuals are in the categories and amounts described under "**Range**" in **93.113**.

Eligible applicants/beneficiaries: same as for **93.113**.

Range: projects, $86,000 to $558,000. **Average:** $252,000.

Activity: FY 00 estimate, 75 awards.

HQ: same addresses/phones as **93.113**, *and,* Program Administrator, Organ and Systems Toxicology Branch, (919)541-0781. (Note: no field offices for this program.).

93.115 BIOMETRY AND RISK ESTIMATION—HEALTH RISKS FROM ENVIRONMENTAL EXPOSURES

Assistance: project grants (100 percent/to 5 years).

Purposes: for research and research training in statistics, biomathematics, epidemiology, and risk estimation, toward the estimation of probable health risks of cancer, reproductive and neurological effects, and other adverse effects—from various environmental hazards including air and water pollution. Major emphasis is on refining methods for estimating human risk from data derived from studying laboratory animals, and on examining the quantitative issues involved in designing short-term tests and interpreting the data from the tests. Examples of funded projects: acid aerosol exposure effects on respiratory morbidity; health effects of lead on child development. The Environmental Health Sciences Education Program funds one- to three-year projects costing up to $100,000, to improve student understanding of environmental health issues and to expand career awareness in health sciences research and services occupations, by developing educational materials for grades K-12. SBIR and STTR awards are made (*see Note preceding* **93.001**). Awards for individuals are in the categories and amounts described under "**Range**" in **93.113**.

Eligible applicants/beneficiaries: same as for **93.113**.

Range: projects, $56,000 to $589,000. **Average:** $242,000.

Activity: FY 00 estimate, 54 awards.

HQ: same addresses/phones as **93.113**. (Note: no field offices for this program.).

93.116 PROJECT GRANTS AND COOPERATIVE AGREEMENTS FOR TUBERCULOSIS CONTROL PROGRAMS

Assistance: projects grants (to 100 percent/to 5 years).

Purposes: for tuberculosis control activities. Funds may cover such costs as outreach activities, morbidity surveillance, personnel, equipment, supplies, program assessment, and services. Costs of construction and inpatient care are ineligible uses of project funds.

Eligible applicants/beneficiaries: official public health agencies of state and local governments, territories and possessions.

Range: $52,000 to $27,200,000. **Average:** $1,500,000.

Activity: FY 99, 68 continuation awards.

HQ: National Center for HIV, STD, and TB Prevention, CDCP-HHS, 1600 Clifton Rd. NE, Atlanta, GA 30333. Phone: (404)639-8125. *Grants management information*: Grants Management Officer, Procurement and Grants Office, CDCP-HHS, 255 E. Paces Ferry Rd. NE, Atlanta, GA 30305. Phone: (404)842-6517. (Note: no field offices for this program.)

93.117   GRANTS FOR PREVENTIVE MEDICINE
("Preventive Medicine")

Assistance: project grants (100 percent).

Purposes: to plan, develop, maintain, or improve postgraduate training programs in preventive medicine. Financial assistance may be provided to residency trainees. Grants may not used for construction or patient services.

Eligible applicants/beneficiaries: public or private schools of medicine, osteopathy, or public health.

Range: $39,000 to $218,000. **Average:** $116,000.

Activity: FY 99 estimate, 11 continuation awards.

HQ: Public Health and Dental Education Branch, Division of Associated, Dental and Public Health Professions, Bureau of Health Professions, HRSA-HHS, Parklawn Bldg. - Rm.8C-09, 5600 Fishers Lane, Rockville, MD 20857. Phone: (301)443-6896. *Grants management information*: same address/phone as **93.107**. (Note: no field offices for this program.)

93.118   ACQUIRED IMMUNODEFICIENCY SYNDROME (AIDS) ACTIVITY

Assistance: project grants (100 percent/to 5 years).

Purposes: to develop and implement HIV prevention programs of public education and information, through cooperative agreements.

Eligible applicants/beneficiaries: public and private organizations, both nonprofit and profit; IHEs, research institutions; state and local governments, territories and possessions; small and minority- and women-owned businesses.

Range: $20,000 to $2,750,000. **Average:** $300,000.

Activity: not quantified specifically.

HQ: Chief, Grants Management Branch, Procurement and Grants Office, CDCP-HHS, 255 E. Paces Ferry Rd. NE, Atlanta, GA 30305. Phone: (404)842-6655. (Note: no field offices for this program.)

93.121   ORAL DISEASES AND DISORDERS RESEARCH

Assistance: project grants (100 percent/to 5 years).

Purposes: for research and research training in the oral health sciences, in such areas as craniofacial, oral, and dental health promotion and disease prevention, diagnostics, and therapeutics. Grant programs support basic, clinical, and transitional research from molecular biology to patient-oriented and community-based clinical investigations—including etiology, pathogenesis, epidemiology, prevention, diagnosis, and treatment—within overlapping programs: Inherited Diseases and Disorders (e.g., cleft lip and palate, other craniofacial birth defects, developmentally related disorders, as well as occlusion defects acquired through trauma); Infectious Diseases such as dental caries, periodontitis, oral manifestations of HIV/AIDS, herpes, hepatitis, and other diseases; Neoplastic Diseases; Chronic Disabling Diseases; Biomaterials, Biomimetics and Tissue Engineering; Behavior, Health Promotion and Environment. Also supported are: Comprehensive Oral Research Centers of Discovery; Research Training and Careers; Diversity in Research;

Clinical Trials and Clinical Core Centers; and Technology Transfer. NRSA, SBIR, and STTR awards are available (*see Note preceding* **93.001**).

Eligible applicants/beneficiaries: research grants—scientists at universities, hospitals, laboratories, other public, private, nonprofit, or profit institutions. Career development award candidates must comply with requirements similar to those applying to the NRSA program.

Range: projects, $2,000 to $1,279,000; NRSA, $9,000 to $379,000. **Average:** projects, $218,000; NRSA, $92,000.

Activity: FY 00 estimate, 392 noncompeting, 130 competing research grants; 18 research centers; 93 career development, 274 NRSA positions; 10 other research grants.

HQ: Division of Extramural Research, National Institute of Dental Research, NIH-HHS, Bethesda, MD 20892. Phones: Inherited Diseases and Disorders, and Osteoporosis and Related Bone Disorders, (301)594-2425; Infectious Diseases - General, and Other Systemic Diseases, (301)594-2421; HIV Infection and AIDS, and Auto-immune Diseases, and Biomimetics, Tissue Engineering and Biomaterials, (301)594-2427; Neoplastic Diseases, (301) 594-2419; Chronic Disabling Diseases - General, Temporomandibular Joint Disorders and Neurodegenerative Diseases, (301)594-5095; Behavior, Health Promotion, and Environment, (301)594-2095; Comprehensive Centers of Recovery, (301)594-2419; Career Development and Training, (301)594-2618; Diversity Programs, and Clinical Trials and Clinical Core Centers, (301)594-2089; Technology Development, (301)594-2088; Contracts Management, (301)594-0652. *Grants management information*: same address. Phone: (301)594-4800. (Note: no field offices for this program.)

93.122 COOPERATIVE AGREEMENTS FOR SUBSTANCE ABUSE TREATMENT AND RECOVERY SYSTEMS FOR RURAL, REMOTE AND CULTURALLY DISTINCT POPULATIONS ("RRCD")

Assistance: project grants (100 percent/to 5 years).

Purposes: to design model systems of substance abuse and/or dependence intervention, treatment, and recovery services for rural, remote, and culturally distinct populations including native Americans, Alaska natives, native Hawaiians, recent immigrants residing in farm worker communities. Program objectives include enhancing access to services for target populations, and coordination among assessment, treatment and recovery programs and related health, housing, welfare, training, criminal justice, and other social programs and institutions. Project funds may support health and allied health care workers to staff intake units, to conduct clinical case reviews and case management, and for evaluation expertise, quality assurance oversight, and technical assistance. Funds may not be used to support routine costs or primary or preventive medical care in primary health care settings.

Eligible applicants/beneficiaries: federally recognized tribal authorities, and state agencies for alcohol and drug abuse—applying on behalf of consortia of tribal, state, and local officials and public or nonprofit private entities.

Range: $350,000 to $1,000,000. **Average:** $749,000.

Activity: FY 98, 3 continuation awards; FY 99, no awards.

HQ: Chief, Organization of Services Branch, CSAT, SAMHSA-HHS, Rockwall II Bldg.- Ste.740, 5600 Fishers Lane, Rockville, MD 20857. Phone: (301)443-8802. *Grants management information*: same address/phone as **93.101**. (Note: no field offices for this program.)

93.123   HEALTH PROFESSIONS PREGRADUATE SCHOLARSHIP PROGRAM FOR INDIANS

Assistance: project grants (100 percent).

Purposes: for four-year scholarships to American Indians and Alaska natives to complete pregraduate education leading to a baccalaureate degree in pre-medicine or pre-dentistry. Part-time attendance may be supported for a maximum of eight years.

Eligible applicants/beneficiaries: American Indians or Alaska natives accepted or enrolled in a pregraduate program.

Range: $12,000 to $27,000. **Average:** $17,000.

Activity: FY 99-00, 100 awards.

HQ: IHS Scholarship Program, IHS-HHS, Twinbrook Metro Plaza - Ste.100A, 12300 Twinbrook Pkwy., Rockville, MD 20852. Phone: (301)443-6197. *Grants management information*: Grants Management Officer, Division of Acquisition and Grants Operations, IHS-HHS, Twinbrook Metro Bldg. - Ste.100, 12300 Twinbrook Pkwy., Rockville, MD 20852. Phone: (301)443-0243. (Note: no field offices for this program.)

93.124   NURSE ANESTHETIST TRAINEESHIPS

Assistance: project grants (formula based, 100 percent).

Purposes: for nurse anesthetist traineeships for up to 18 months of full-time study by registered nurses. Students may receive stipends of up to $8,800 plus tuition and other expenses.

Eligible applicants: accredited public and private nonprofit institutions.

Eligible beneficiaries: financially needy U.S. citizens or permanent residents with 12 months of completed nurse anesthetist training.

Range: institutions, $5,471 to $85,000.

Activity: FY 99 estimate, 70 grants supporting 1,000 candidates.

HQ: Division of Nursing, Bureau of Health Professions, HRSA-HHS, Parklawn Bldg. - Rm.9-36, 5600 Fishers Lane, Rockville, MD 20857. Phone: (301)443-5763. *Grants management information*: same address/phone as **93.107**. (Note: no field offices for this program.)

93.125   MENTAL HEALTH PLANNING AND DEMONSTRATION PROJECTS

Assistance: project grants (to 100 percent/to 5 years).

Purposes: to develop and improve community support systems for the long-term mentally ill including inappropriately institutionalized persons, mentally disturbed children and youth, and homeless persons. Project examples include service and research demonstration projects on supported housing, comprehensive systems, consumer-operated alternatives, case management services, psycho-social rehabilitation, crisis response.

Eligible applicants/beneficiaries: state and their political subdivisions, private nonprofit agencies, tribes and tribal organizations.

Range: $1,572 to $2,515,000. **Average:** $243,000.

Activity: FY 99, 9 continuation awards.

HQ: Division of Knowledge Development and Systems Change, CMHS, SAMHSA-HHS, Parklawn Bldg., 5600 Fishers Lane, Rockville, MD 20857. Phones: Chief, Community Support Programs Branch (Rm.11C22), *and* Chief, Child, Adolescent and Family Services Branch (Rm.18-49), *and* *Research Demonstrations,* Director, Child and Adolescent Studies Program—(301)443-3653; *ACCESS grants for the homeless mentally ill,* Chief, Homeless Program Section (Rm.11C-05), (301)443-3706. *Grants management information*: same address/phone as **93.101**. (Note: no field offices for this program.)

93.127   EMERGENCY MEDICAL SERVICES FOR CHILDREN ("EMS for Children")

Assistance: project grants (100 percent/to 3 years).

Purposes: for demonstration projects to expand and improve emergency medical services for children needing critical care or treatment for trauma—with priority to projects targeted to populations with special needs, including native Americans, minorities, and the disabled.

Eligible applicants/beneficiaries: state governments, schools of medicine.

Range: $125,000 to $400,000. **Average:** $219,000.

Activity: FY 98, 20 new, 52 continuation projects.

HQ: EMSC Program Director, Maternal and Child Health Bureau, HRSA-HHS, Parklawn Bldg. - Rm.18A-38, 5600 Fishers Lane, Rockville, MD 20857. Phone: (301)443-6192. *Or:* Traffic Safety Program, Office of Emergency Enforcement Services, National Highway Traffic Safety Administration-DOT (NTS-42), 400 Seventh St. SW, Washington, DC 20590. Phone: (202)366-5440. *Grants management information*: same address/phone as **93.110**. (Note: no field offices for this program.)

93.129   TECHNICAL AND NON-FINANCIAL ASSISTANCE TO HEALTH CENTERS AND NATIONAL HEALTH SERVICE CORPS (NHSC) DELIVERY SITES

Assistance: project grants (100 percent/to 5 years).

Purposes: to provide technical assistance to health centers, assisting them in: developing collaborative activities on state, regional, or area issues; involving state agencies in providing primary care to medically underserved populations including the homeless, public housing residents, farm workers, and rural residents; providing training, recruitment, and retention of primary care providers; developing shared services and joint purchasing arrangements; managing and maximizing nonfederal resources.

Eligible applicants/beneficiaries: private nonprofit entities including state and regional primary care associations; some public agencies.

Range/Average: $125,000 to $200,000.

Activity: FY 99 estimate, 51 associations funded.

HQ: Director, Office of State and External Affairs, Bureau of Primary Health Care, HRSA-HHS, 4350 East-West Hwy. - 3rd floor, Bethesda, MD 20814. Phone: (301)594-4488. *Grants management information*: Office of Grants Management, Bureau of Primary Health Care, HRSA-HHS, 4350 East-West Hwy. - 11th floor, Bethesda, MD 20814. Phone: (301)594-4235.

93.130 PRIMARY CARE SERVICES—RESOURCE COORDINATION AND DEVELOPMENT—PRIMARY CARE OFFICES

Assistance: project grants (100 percent/to 5 years).

Purposes: to coordinate local, state, and federal primary care planning and resources to meet the needs of medically under-served populations—through community-based and migrant health centers and other community-based providers. Emphasis is on the coordination of Medicaid and other health care financing services, maternal and child health, health systems development, National Health Service Corps monitoring, and recruitment and retention of primary care practitioners.

Eligible applicants/beneficiaries: states, state agencies, statewide public or nonprofit entities.

Range/Average: $100,000 to $150,000.

Activity: FY 99-00 estimate, 52 projects.

HQ: same addresses/phones as **93.129**.

93.134 GRANTS TO INCREASE ORGAN DONATIONS

Assistance: project grants (100 percent).

Purposes: to increase the number of organ donors.

Eligible applicants/beneficiaries: only private nonprofit organ procurement and transplantation organizations.

Range/Average: N.A.

Activity: FY 98, no awards.

HQ: Deputy Director, Division of Organ Transplantation, Office of Special Programs, HRSA-HHS, 5600 Fishers Lane - Rm.7-29, Rockville, MD 20857. Phone: (301)443-7577. *Grants management information*: Grants Management Officer, Office of Program Support, HIV/AIDS Bureau, HRSA-HHS, 5600 Fishers Lane - Rm.7-27, Rockville, MD 20857. Phone: (301)443-2280. (Note: no field offices for this program.)

93.135 CENTERS FOR RESEARCH AND DEMONSTRATION FOR HEALTH PROMOTION AND DISEASE PREVENTION
("Prevention Research Centers")

Assistance: project grants (100 percent/1-5 years).

Purposes: to establish, maintain, and operate academic-based centers for research and demonstration programs in health promotion and disease prevention; to establish linkages between ongoing basic and applied research; for field testing and evaluation of new methods and strategies; to streamline the development and delivery of new techniques.

Eligible applicants/beneficiaries: schools of medicine, osteopathy, and public health.

Range: $500,000 to $600,000. **Average:** $500,000.

Activity: FY 99-00, 19 grants.

HQ: Program Director, National Center for Chronic Disease Prevention and Health Promotion (K-30), CDCP-HHS, 4770 Buford Hwy., Atlanta, GA 30333. Phone: (404)488-5395. *Grants management information*: Grants Management Officer, Procurement and Grants Office, CDCP-HHS, 2920 Brandywine Rd. - Rm.3000, Atlanta, GA 30341. Phones: (770)448-2730. (Note: no field offices for this program.)

93.136   INJURY PREVENTION AND CONTROL RESEARCH AND STATE AND COMMUNITY BASED PROGRAMS

Assistance: project grants (100 percent/1-5 years).

Purposes: for injury prevention and control research and demonstrations; to integrate aspects of engineering, public health, behavioral sciences, medicine, and other disciplines; for injury control research centers in academic institutions to develop improved approaches to research and training; for public health programs for injury control. Grants also are available to states and communities to develop and evaluate existing and new methods and techniques of injury surveillance, and to develop, expand, or improve injury control programs to reduce morbidity, mortality, severity, disability, and cost from injuries.

Eligible applicants/beneficiaries: research grants—nonprofit and profit organizations. State and community program grants—official state public health agencies; territories and possessions; jurisdictions of more than 1,000,000 population; public and private nonprofit and profit organizations.

Range: centers, $500,000 to $1,750,000; research projects, $60,000 to $300,000; state, community-based projects, $175,000 to $350,000; youth violence prevention programs, $125,000 to $425,000; violence against women prevention, $250,000 to $350,000; traumatic brain injury research, $100,000 to $150,000; surveillance and brain injury follow-up registry, $350,000. **Average:** centers, $1,125,000; projects, $200,000; surveillance, $175,000; state, community-based, $300,000; youth violence prevention, $250,000; violence against women, $300,000; traumatic brain injury research, $125,000.

Activity: FY 98-99 estimate, continuation of current grants.

HQ: National Center for Injury Prevention and Control (K-58), CDCP-HHS, Atlanta, GA 30341-3724. Phones: *research projects*, (707)488-4824; *centers*, (707)448-4823; *state, community-based*, (707)488-4538. *Grants management information*: Grants Management Officer, Procurement and Grants Office, CDCP-HHS, 255 E. Paces Ferry Rd. NE, Atlanta, GA 30305. Phones: (404)842-6630. (Note: no field offices for this program.)

93.137   MINORITY COMMUNITY HEALTH COALITION DEMONSTRATION

Assistance: project grants (100 percent/3 years).

Purposes: for projects conducted by minority community health coalitions, involving unique and intensified health education efforts to modify behavioral or environmental conditions that affect the health of minority groups—including AIDS, cancer, cardiovascular disease and stroke, chemical dependency, diabetes, homicide, suicide, unintentional injuries, infant mortality. No health care services are provided under this program.

Eligible applicants/beneficiaries: public or private nonprofit organizations that involve Asian/Pacific islanders, African Americans, Hispanics, native Americans, Alaska natives, native Hawaiians, or subgroups.

Range: $145,000 to $150,000. **Average:** $149,000.

Activity: FY 99-00, 13-15 continuation awards.

HQ: same addresses/phones as **93.004**. (Note: no field offices for this program.)

93.138   PROTECTION AND ADVOCACY FOR INDIVIDUALS WITH MENTAL ILLNESS

Assistance: formula grants (100 percent/2 years).

Purposes: to plan, establish, administer, and expand programs to protect and advocate the rights of the mentally ill, and to investigate incidents of their abuse and neglect. Up to 10 percent of funds may be used for staff training and technical assistance.

Eligible applicants: state and local government agencies, public or private organizations designated by governors.

Eligible beneficiaries: mentally ill persons while inpatients or residents in care or treatment facilities, and for 90 days following their discharge.

Range: $139,000 to $1,940,000. **Average:** $384,000.

Activity: FY 99-00, 56 grants (to all states and territories).

HQ: Program Officer, Protection and Advocacy Program, Division of State and Community Systems Development, CMHS, SAMHSA-HHS, Parklawn Bldg. - Rm.15C-26, 5600 Fishers Lane, Rockville, MD 20857. Phone: (301)443-3667. *Grants management information*: Grants Management Officer, Division of Grants Management, SAMHSA-HHS, Parklawn Bldg. - Rm.15C-05, 5600 Fishers Lane, Rockville, MD 20857. Phone: (301)443-4456. (Note: no field offices for this program.)

93.139   FINANCIAL ASSISTANCE FOR DISADVANTAGED HEALTH PROFESSIONS STUDENTS ("FADHPS")

Assistance: project grants (100 percent).

Purposes: for annual scholarships to disadvantaged students of exceptional financial need, to obtain a degree in medicine, osteopathy, or dentistry. Scholarship recipients must fulfill a service obligation.

Eligible applicants: public or private nonprofit schools of medicine, osteopathy, or dentistry.

Eligible beneficiaries: disadvantaged U.S. citizens, nationals, or permanent residents of territories or possessions.

Range/Average: $19,000.

Activity: FY 99 estimate, 159 schools funded.

HQ: Division of Student Assistance, Bureau of Health Professions, HRSA-HHS, Parklawn Bldg. - Rm.8-34, 5600 Fishers Lane, Rockville, MD 20857. Phone: (301)443-4776. (Note: no field offices for this program.)

93.140   INTRAMURAL RESEARCH TRAINING AWARD ("IRTA Program")

Assistance: project grants (100 percent).

Purposes: to provide developmental training and practical research experience at the NIH for pre- or post-doctoral participants, in disciplines related to biomedical and medical library research and related fields. IRTA components include: postdoctoral (1-5 years), for physicians and other doctoral researchers; predoctoral (1 month-3 years), for students enrolled in doctoral degree programs in biomedical sciences, or accepted into graduate, doctoral, or medical degree programs; postbaccalaureate (1-2 years), for recent college graduates, particularly minorities, women, and persons with disabilities; technical (2-3 years), for training of professionals; student (1 month-1 year), for promising high school and undergraduate students. Funding is provided by the individual NIH component entities.

Eligible applicants/beneficiaries: postdoctoral awards—candidates with a Ph.D., M.D., D.D.S., D.M.D., D.V.M., or equivalent degree and not more than five years of postdoctoral research experience; predoctoral awards—students applying for, enrolled in, or accepted into graduate, doctoral, or medical degree programs; postbaccalaureate—candidates that graduated no more than one year prior to activation of the traineeship and intending to apply to graduate or medical school in biomedical research within one year; technical—candidates that graduated from a U.S. college or university with a bachelor's or master's degree in any discipline; student—candidates at least age 16 and enrolled at least half-time in high school, or accepted for or enrolled in an accredited U.S. college or university. All recipients must be U.S. citizens or resident aliens.

Range: postdoctoral stipends, $25,000 to $50,000; predoctoral, $17,600 to $25,100; postbaccalaureate, $17,600; technical, $16,000 to $26,200; student, $990 to $2,200.

Activity: FY 98, 2,949 awards.

HQ: Associate Director/Intramural Affairs, NIH-HHS, Shannon Bldg. - Rm. 140, Bethesda, MD 20892. Phone: (301)496-4920. (Note: no field offices for this program.)

93.142   NIEHS HAZARDOUS WASTE WORKER HEALTH AND SAFETY TRAINING ("Superfund Worker Training Program")

Assistance: project grants (100 percent/to 5 years).

Purposes: to develop and administer model education and training programs in worker health and safety practices for persons involved in hazardous waste generation, treatment, storage, removal, disposal, containment, transportation, or emergency response. Direct costs of classroom and practical training may he supported. Funds for this program are provided to NIEHS by EPA based on CERCLA provisions, and by DOE.

Eligible applicants/beneficiaries: public or private nonprofit entities.

Range: $174,000 to $5,330,000. **Average:** $1,298,000.

Activity: FY 00 estimate, 26 continuation grants.

HQ: Program Director, Superfund Worker Training and Education Program, NIEHS, NIH-HHS, P.O. Box 12233, Research Triangle Park, NC 27709. Phone: (919)541-0217. *Grants management information*: Grants Management Officer, Grants Management Branch, Division of Extramural Research and Training, NIEHS, same address. Phone: (919)541-2749. (Note: no field offices for this program.)

93.143   NIEHS SUPERFUND HAZARDOUS SUBSTANCES—BASIC RESEARCH AND EDUCATION

Assistance: project grants (100 percent/to 5 years).

Purposes: to establish innovative linkages between biomedical research and related engineering, geoscience, and ecological research. Funds may support basic research and advanced or graduate training activities on an interdisciplinary, multi-project basis, covering: advanced techniques for the detection, assessment, and evaluation of the effects of hazardous substances on humans; environmental and occupational health and safety and the engineering aspects of hazardous waste control; related graduate training in the geosciences. Funds for this program are provided to NIEHS by EPA, based on CERCLA provisions.

Eligible applicants/beneficiaries: IHEs. Subcontracts are permitted with state and local governments, public or private organizations, or persons or organizations involved with the generation, assessment, treatment of hazardous substances, or operation or ownership of facilities containing hazardous substances.

Range: $594,000 to $3,100,000. **Average:** $1,835,000.

Activity: FY 99 estimate, 18 grants.

HQ: Director, Superfund Hazardous Substance Basic Research and Training Program, Division of Extramural Research and Training, NIEHS-NIH-HHS, P.O. Box 12233, Research Triangle Park, NC 27709. Phone: (919)541-0797. *Grants management information*: same as **93.142**. (Note: no field offices for this program.)

93.144   DEMONSTRATION GRANTS FOR THE PREVENTION OF ALCOHOL AND DRUG ABUSE AMONG HIGH-RISK POPULATIONS

Assistance: project grants (100 percent/3-5 years).

Purposes: to demonstrate effective community-based models for the prevention and early intervention of drug, tobacco, and alcohol abuse among high-risk youth. Projects should be designed to: decrease incidence and prevalence; identify and reduce risk factors in individuals, parents and extended family, peer groups, and neighborhoods; increase resilience and protective factors.

Eligible applicants/beneficiaries: public or private nonprofit entities.

Range: $100,000 to $500,000. **Average:** $350,000.

Activity: FY 99 estimate, 3 continuation grants.

HQ: Division of Knowledge Development and Evaluation, CSAP, SAMHSA-HHS, Rockwall II Bldg., 5600 Fishers Lane, Rockville, MD 20857. Phone: (301)443-9110. *Grants management information*: same address/phone as **93.101**. (Note: no field offices for this program.)

93.145   AIDS EDUCATION AND TRAINING CENTERS

Assistance: project grants (100 percent/3 years).

Purposes: for the education and training of primary care providers and others on the treatment and prevention of AIDS; to provide updated information about HIV infection, to primary and secondary health care providers; to support area health professionals through hotlines, clearinghouses, and referral activities.

Eligible applicants/beneficiaries: public and private nonprofit entities, schools, and academic health science centers.

Range: $492,000 to $2,083,000. **Average:** $1,086,000.

Activity: FY 98, 15 noncompetitive awards for training of some 155,000 personnel.

HQ: Division of Training and Technical Assistance/AIDS, HIV/AIDS Bureau, HRSA-HHS, 5600 Fishers Lane - Rm.9A-39, Rockville, MD 20857. Phones: (301)443-6364; FAX (301)443-9887. *Grants management information*: same address/phone as **93.134**.

93.150   PROJECTS FOR ASSISTANCE IN TRANSITION FROM HOMELESSNESS ("PATH")

Assistance: formula grants (75 percent; territories, 100 percent).

Purposes: pursuant to the McKinney homeless assistance act and other acts, for services to homeless persons with serious mental illness, with serious mental illness and substance abuse, or at imminent risk of so becoming. Funds may support such services as: outreach; community mental health; screening and diagnosis; habilitation and rehabilitation; referrals to housing, primary health, job training, and substance abuse treatment; staff training; case management; supportive and supervisory services in residential settings. Funds may not be used for emergency shelters or construction, inpatient services, cash payments to recipients of mental health or substance abuse services.

Eligible applicants/beneficiaries: states, territories, possessions. Subgrants must be provided to political subdivisions and private nonprofit entities including veterans and other community-based organizations.

Range: $50,000 to $1,680,000. **Average:** $347,000.

Activity: FY 00 estimate, 56 grants and, in turn, 380 subgrants.

HQ: PATH Program, Homeless Programs Branch, Division of Knowledge

Development and Systems Change, SAMHSA-HHS, Parklawn Bldg. - Rm. 11C-05, 5600 Fishers Lane, Rockville, MD 20857. Phone: (301)443-3706. *Grants management information*: same address/phone as **93.138**. (Note: no field offices for this program.)

93.151   HEALTH CENTER GRANTS FOR HOMELESS POPULATIONS

Assistance: project grants (to 100 percent/to 5 years).

Purposes: for primary health and substance abuse services to homeless persons (defined as those lacking housing, including persons in temporary shelters or in transitional housing). Funds may be used for such activities or services as: primary care; substance abuse treatment; 24-hour emergency services; referrals to mental health and medical facilities; systems for inpatient referrals, outreach, and aid in establishing eligibility for assistance through entitlement programs.

Eligible applicants/beneficiaries: public or private nonprofit entities, state and local governmental agencies—with agreements under state Medicaid programs, Title XIX of the Social Security Act.

Range: $62,000 to $2,000,000. **Average:** $285,000.

Activity: FY 98, 128 grantees funded in 48 states, DC, and PR.

HQ: Director, Division of Programs for Special Populations, Bureau of Primary Health Care, HRSA-HHS, 4350 East-West Hwy. - 9th floor, Bethesda, MD 20814. Phone: (301)594-4420. *Grants management information*: same address/phone as **93.129**.

93.153   HIV DEMONSTRATION PROGRAM FOR CHILDREN, ADOLESCENTS, AND WOMEN

Assistance: project grants (100 percent/to 3 years).

Purposes: for projects to improve and expand the system of comprehensive care services for children, youth, women, and families with HIV/AIDS or at risk, and to link systems with clinical research. Project elements include: case management; preventive, medical, social, psycho-social, and family support services.

Eligible applicants/beneficiaries: public and private nonprofit entities providing primary care.

Range: $167,000 to $2,000,000. **Average:** $605,000.

Activity: FY 99 estimate, 58 projects.

HQ: Division of Community Based Programs/Title IV, HIV-AIDS Bureau, HRSA-HHS, 5600 Fishers Lane - Rm.7-90, Rockville, MD 20857. Phone: (301)443-0127. *Grants management information*: same address as **93.134**. Phone: (301)443-2728. (Note: no field offices for this program.)

93.154   SPECIAL INTERNATIONAL POSTDOCTORAL RESEARCH PROGRAM IN ACQUIRED IMMUNODEFICIENCY SYNDROME

Assistance: project grants (100 percent/5 years).

Purposes: for collaborative research activities and cooperation between U.S.

and foreign scientists in the epidemiology, diagnosis, prevention, and treatment of AIDS. Funds may be used for stipends, travel, training costs, program director's and faculty salary, administrative support.

Eligible applicants: U.S. nonprofit institutions.

Eligible beneficiaries: doctoral level biomedical and behavioral scientists.

Range/Average: $250,000 per award.

Activity: FY 99 estimate, 4 supplemental awards.

HQ: Director, Division of International Training and Research, NIH-HHS, Fogarty International Center, Bethesda, MD 20892. Phone: (301)496-2516. *Grants management information*: same address/phone as **93.106**. (Note: no field offices for this program.)

93.155   RURAL HEALTH RESEARCH CENTERS

Assistance: project grants (100 percent/to 4 years).

Purposes: to operate rural health research centers to provide an information base and policy analysis capability on the full range of rural health issues, including financing, recruitment and retention of health professionals, access to care, and rural delivery systems.

Eligible applicants/beneficiaries: public and private nonprofit and profit entities including IHEs, research organizations, and foundations.

Range: $400,000 to $600,000. **Average:** $490,000.

Activity: FY 99 estimate, 5 continuation awards.

HQ: Director, Office of Rural Health Policy, Office of the Administrator, HRSA-HHS, Parklawn Bldg. - Rm.9-05, 5600 Fishers Lane, Rockville, MD 20857. Phone: (301)443-0835. *Grants management information*: same address/phone as **93.129**. (Note: no field offices for this program.)

93.156   GERIATRIC TRAINING REGARDING PHYSICIANS AND DENTISTS ("Geriatric Fellowships")

Assistance: project grants (100 percent).

Purposes: for the operation of postdoctoral training programs for current and future faculty in geriatric medicine and dentistry. Funds may support: one-year retraining programs for physician faculty members in departments of internal or family medicine, gynecology, geriatrics, and psychiatry, and dentist faculty members at schools of dentistry or hospital departments of dentistry; two-year fellowships for physicians and dentists with relevant advanced training or experience in medical or dental education.

Eligible applicants/beneficiaries: public or private nonprofit schools of medicine or osteopathy, teaching hospitals, graduate medical education programs.

Range: $191,000 to $374,000. **Average:** $322,000

Activity: FY 98, 8 awards; FY 99, no awards.

HQ: Coordinator, Faculty Training Projects in Geriatric Medicine and Dentistry, Division of Associated, Dental, and Public Health Professions, Bureau of Health Professions, HRSA-HHS, Parklawn Bldg. - Rm.8-103, 5600 Fishers Lane, Rockville, MD 20857. Phone: (301)443-6887. *Grants man-*

agement information: same address/phone as **93.107**. (Note: no field offices for this program.)

93.157   CENTERS OF EXCELLENCE

Assistance: project grants (100 percent/1-5 years).

Purposes: to establish, strengthen, or expand programs to enhance the academic performance of minority students in the health professions. Funds may be used for such costs as: faculty recruitment, training, and retention through financial support and preceptorship programs; library resource development and enhancement; student recruitment and academic performance enhancement programs, curriculum development; facilitating faculty and student research on issues particularly affecting minority groups; updating facilities and equipment.

Eligible applicants/beneficiaries: schools of medicine, osteopathy, dentistry, pharmacy, podiatry, chiropractic, veterinary medicine, optometry, allied health; private nonprofit schools with graduate training programs in behavioral and mental health; physician assistants training programs; certain HBCUs.

Range: $416,000 to $3,370,000. **Average:** $906,000.

Activity: FY 00 estimate, 20 continuation, 4 new grants.

HQ: Chief, Centers of Excellence Section, Division of Disadvantaged Assistance, Bureau of Health Professions, HRSA-HHS, Parklawn Bldg. - Rm.8A-09, 5600 Fishers Lane, Rockville, MD 20857. Phones: (301)443-2100. *Grants management information*: same address as **93.107**. Phone: (301)443-6857. (Note: no field offices for this program.)

93.161   HEALTH PROGRAM FOR TOXIC SUBSTANCES AND DISEASE REGISTRY

Assistance: project grants (100 percent/1-5 years).

Purposes: pursuant to CERCLA, to reduce or eliminate illness, disability, and death resulting from public or worker exposure to toxic substances at spill and waste disposal sites. Services may include: health assessments; health effects studies; exposure and disease registries; technical assistance; consultation; information dissemination; consultation; specialized services and assistance in responding to public health emergencies; training.

Eligible applicants/beneficiaries: states and their political subdivisions; state IHEs, hospitals, and research institutions; state and local health departments; national organizations; federally recognized tribal governments.

Range: $50,000 to $500,000. **Average:** $250,000.

Activity: FY 00 estimate, 23 continuation, 5 new grants.

HQ: Office of Program Operations and Management, Agency for Toxic Substances and Disease (MS E60), HHS, 1600 Clifton Rd. NE, Atlanta, GA 30333. Phones: (404)639-5011; FAX (404)639-0560. *Grants management information*: Grants Management Branch, Procurement and Grants Office, CDCP-HHS, 2920 Brandywine Rd., Atlanta, GA 30341. Phones: (770)488-2710; FAX (770)488-2777. (Note: no field offices for this program.)

93.162   NATIONAL HEALTH SERVICE CORPS LOAN REPAYMENT PROGRAM ("NHSC Loan Repayment Program")

Assistance: project grants (100 percent).

Purposes: for the repayment of NHSC participants' qualified government and commercial health professions education loans. Up to $25,000 per year may be awarded during the first two years of practice at selected NHSC service sites, and up to $35,000 in the third and subsequent years—plus a 39 percent tax assistance payment. Priority currently is given to primary care physicians, dentists, certified nurse-midwives and nurse practitioners, physician assistants, clinical psychologists, clinical social workers, psychiatric nurse specialists, marriage and family therapists, dental hygienists.

Eligible applicants/beneficiaries: U.S. citizens with a degree in health professions or in professional practice, licensed in a state, and eligible for appointment in the PHS or the civil service. Applicants may not: be in default on any federal debt; have a court judgment against them; have an existing service obligation.

Range: physician awards, $10,000 to $70,000. **Average:** $60,000.

Activity: FY 98, 440 new awards.

HQ: Chief, Loan Repayment Programs Branch, Division of Scholarships and Loan Repayments, Bureau of Primary Health Care, HRSA-HHS, 4350 East-West Hwy. - 10th floor, Bethesda, MD 20814. Phones: (301)594-4400; *public information*, (800)435-6464. (Note: no field offices for this program.)

93.164   INDIAN HEALTH SERVICE EDUCATIONAL LOAN REPAYMENT ("IHS Loan Repayment Program")

Assistance: project grants (100 percent).

Purposes: for payments of up to $30,000 annually toward participants' health professions education loans during each year of service at IHS priority sites or certain other sites—plus up to 31 percent for tax liability on the grant award. A minimum of two years of service is required. Eligible specialties include nursing, nurse practitioner, nurse midwife, mental health professional, anesthesiology, general surgery, dentistry, otolaryngology/otorhinolaryngology, obstetrics/gynecology, ophthalmology, orthopedic surgery, psychiatry, radiology, emergency medicine.

Eligible applicants/beneficiaries: students enrolled in their final year in a program leading to a degree, or graduate students enrolled in approved programs—in allopathic or osteopathic medicine or other health profession; or, degreed and state-licensed professionals in those fields, eligible for a PHS appointment or civil service in the IHS; or employees of a tribal or urban Indian health program.

Range: $3,000 to $79,000 for a two-year service obligation.

Activity: FY 99-00 estimate, 260 new, 47 continuation awards.

HQ: Chief, Loan Repayment Program, IHS-HHS, 12300 Twinbrook Pkwy. - Ste.100A, Rockville, MD 20852. Phones: (301)443-3369.

93.165 GRANTS FOR STATE LOAN REPAYMENT
("State Loan Repayment Program")

Assistance: project grants (50 percent/to 5 years).

Purposes: for state educational loan repayment programs for health professionals agreeing to serve full-time for a minimum of two years in a health manpower shortage area. State programs must be similar to **93.162**. Applicants must have a degree in allopathic medicine or osteopathy. Dentists, psychiatrists, nurse midwives and practitioners, physician assistants, and other specialists may also qualify for assistance.

Eligible applicants/beneficiaries: state governments.

Range: $20,000 to $1,000,000. **Average:** $250,000.

Activity: FY 99 estimate, 40 awards.

HQ: Director, Division of Scholarships and Loan Repayments, Bureau of Primary Health Care, same address/phone as **93.162**. *Grants management information*: same address/phone as **93.129**. (Note: no field offices for this program.)

93.168 INTERNATIONAL COOPERATIVE BIODIVERSITY GROUPS PROGRAM
("ICBG")

Assistance: project grants (100 percent/5 years).

Purposes: to establish international multidisciplinary groups to conduct biodiversity research projects: (1) to discover, isolate, and evaluate agents from natural sources to treat or prevent cancer, infectious diseases including AIDS, cardiovascular diseases, mental disorders, and other diseases or medical conditions of primary concern to developing countries; (2) to undertake inventories of biological diversity and develop collection practices compatible with conserving biodiversity, and document and disseminate collected material in the form of museum catalogs, publications, or data bases; (3) to support research training of scientists—including in systematics, ethnobiology, ethno-medicine, chemistry, cell biology, biotechnology, pharmaceutical development. Grant funds may support activities designed to meet program objectives, including: development and implementation of project strategies including workable approaches to conducting projects within traditional cultures; development of long-term ecological and economic strategies to ensure the sustainable harvesting of targeted organisms; scientific infrastructure development in host countries; training and education, including in taxonomy; employment of systematists, ecologists, anthropologists, economists, sociologists, and biological and physical scientists.

Eligible applicants/beneficiaries: public and private nonprofit institutions, governments and their agencies, foreign institutions. Profit institutions may participate as an "Associate Program."

Range/Average: $350,000 per award.

Activity: FY 99-00 estimate, 7 continuation awards.

HQ: Division of International Training and Research, NIH-HHS, Fogarty International Center, 31 Center Dr., Bethesda, MD 20892-2220. Phone: (301)496-1653. *Grants management information*: Grants Management Officer, same address/phone. (Note: no field offices for this program.)

93.169   DEMONSTRATION GRANTS ON MODEL PROJECTS FOR PREGNANT AND POSTPARTUM WOMEN AND THEIR INFANTS (SUBSTANCE ABUSE)

Assistance: project grants (100 percent/to 5 years).

Purposes: to demonstrate effective community-based models for the prevention, early-intervention education, treatment, and rehabilitation among pregnant and postpartum women that abuse drugs and alcohol, and their infants.

Eligible applicants/beneficiaries: public, private, nonprofit or profit organizations including IHEs, hospitals, community-based organizations, state or local governments.

Range/Average: $350,000.

Activity: FY 98-00, no awards.

HQ: same address as **93.144**. Phone: (301)443-4564. *Grants management information*: same address/phone as **93.101**. (Note: no field offices for this program.)

93.172   HUMAN GENOME RESEARCH

Assistance: project grants (100 percent/1-5 years).

Purposes: for research to obtain genetic and physical maps and to determine the deoxyribonucleic acid (DNA) sequences of the genomes of humans and model organisms to be used as resources in biomedical research, medicine, and biotechnology—including consideration of the ethical, legal, and social implications. NRSA, SBIR, and STTR awards are available (*see Note preceding* **93.001**).

Eligible applicants/beneficiaries: research projects—public or private, profit or nonprofit IHEs, institutions, state and local governments, hospitals, laboratories, SBIR firms, individuals.

Range: $24,000 to $11,760,000. **Average:** $698,000.

Activity: FY 00 estimate, 33 competing research project grants; 15 research center, 11 research career, 23 other research-related, and 107 full-time research trainee position awards.

HQ: National Human Genome Research Institute, NIH-HHS, Bethesda, MD 20892. Phones: (301)402-5407; *ethical, legal, and social implications*, 402-4997; *research centers, SBIR*, (301)496-7531. *Grants management information*: Grants Management Officer, same address. Phone: (301)402-0733. (Note: no field offices for this program.)

93.173   RESEARCH RELATED TO DEAFNESS AND COMMUNICATION DISORDERS

Assistance: project grants (100 percent/to 7 years).

Purposes: to investigate solutions to problems of patients with deafness or disorders of human communication such as hearing, balance, voice, speech, language, and the senses of taste, touch, and smell. Focus may be on etiology, pathology, detection, treatment, and prevention. Project activities may include basic research in anatomy, audiology, biochemistry, bioengineering, epidemiology, genetics, immunology, microbiology, molecular biology, the neurosciences, otolaryngology, psychology, pharmacology, physiology, speech and language pathology, and other scientific disciplines. Funds may support research centers, Research Career Development and Clinical Investigator Development Awards, other training and education programs for physicians, scientists, and other health professionals, public information programs. Stipends may be paid to trainees. NRSA, SBIR, and STTR awards are available (*see Note preceding* **93.001**).

Eligible applicants/beneficiaries: research and centers grants—public, private, nonprofit, or profit institutions; SBIR firms; individuals.

Range: $72,000 to $458,000. **Average**: $200,000.

Activity: FY 00 estimate, 891 grants.

HQ: National Institute on Deafness and Other Communication Disorders, NIH-HHS, Executive Plaza South - Rm.400-C, Bethesda, MD 20892-7180. Phone: (301)496-5061. *Grants management information*: same address. Phone: (301)402-0909. (Note: no field offices for this program.)

93.178 NURSING EDUCATION OPPORTUNITIES FOR INDIVIDUALS FROM DISADVANTAGED BACKGROUNDS

Assistance: project grants (100 percent/to 3 years).

Purposes: to increase nursing education opportunities for disadvantaged persons. Funds may be used for project personnel salaries, student stipends, consultant fees, supplies and equipment, travel, and related costs.

Eligible applicants/beneficiaries: public and private nonprofit schools of nursing and other nonprofit private entities.

Range: $73,000 to $253,000. **Average**: $167,000.

Activity: FY 99 estimate, 22 grants.

HQ: same address (except Rm.9-35)/phone as **93.124**. *Grants management information*: same address/phone as **93.107**. (Note: no field offices for this program.)

93.181 PODIATRIC RESIDENCY IN PRIMARY CARE

Assistance: project grants (100 percent/to 3 years).

Purposes: for preventive and primary care residency training programs for podiatrists, including financial assistance to residents.

Eligible applicants/beneficiaries: public and private nonprofit hospitals or accredited schools of podiatric medicine.

Range $66,000 to $176,000. **Average**: $109,000.

Activity: FY 99 estimate, 6 continuation awards.

HQ: Chief, Primary Care Medical Education Branch, Division of Medicine, Bureau of Health Professions, HRSA-HHS, Parklawn Bldg. - Rm.9A-27, 5600 Fishers Lane, Rockville, MD 20857. Phone: (301)443-1467. *Grants management information*: same address/phone as **93.107**. (Note: no field offices for this program.)

93.184 DISABILITIES PREVENTION

Assistance: project grants (to 100 percent/3-4 years).

Purposes: to provide a national focus for the prevention of secondary conditions in persons with disabilities, including their mobility, personal care, communication, and learning—through cooperative agreements and research projects designed to: build state capacity to coordinate prevention and education activities and to conduct surveillance; provide related technical assistance to communities; employ epidemiological methods to set priorities and target interventions; conduct research on the disabled and their physical, medical, cognitive, emotional, or psychosocial conditions; establish and support a National Limb Loss Information Center to serve as an information clearinghouse and to conduct peer education and training sessions with hospitals and limb loss support groups.

Eligible applicants/beneficiaries: cooperative agreements—state health departments or other state agencies, including in territories or possessions. Research grants—public and private nonprofit entities including state health departments or other state agencies, universities, nonprofit medical centers, rehabilitation hospitals, disability service organizations, tribal governments. National Limb Loss Information Center—the existing center.

Range/Average: state capacity projects, $334,000; research, $273,000; center, $800,000.

Activity: FY 99-00, 14 state capacity continuation grants; 11 continuation grants; 1 center continuation award.

HQ: Secondary Conditions Prevention Branch, National Center for Environmental Health, CDCP-HHS (MS F-29), Bldg. 101, 4770 Buford Hwy., Atlanta, GA 30341. Phone: (770)488-7082; FAX (770)488-7075. *Grants management information*: same address/phone as **93.161**. (Note: no field offices for this program.)

93.185 IMMUNIZATION RESEARCH, DEMONSTRATION, PUBLIC INFORMATION AND EDUCATION—TRAINING AND CLINICAL SKILLS IMPROVEMENT PROJECTS

Assistance: project grants (100 percent/1-5 years).

Purposes: for research, demonstration, and information dissemination projects on vaccine-preventable diseases and conditions. Funds may be used to conduct project activities including, in certain circumstances, purchasing vaccine.

Eligible applicants/beneficiaries: states and their political subdivisions, other public and private nonprofit entities.

Range: $30,000 to $1,581,000. **Average:** $308,000.

Activity: FY 99-00 estimate, 40 projects.

HQ: Director, Immunization Services Division, National Immunization Program (MS E-52), CDCP-HHS, 1600 Clifton Rd. NE, Atlanta, GA 30333. Phones: (404)639-8208; FAX (404)639-8627; Associate Director/Management and Operations, (404)639-8201, FAX (404)639-8626. *Grants management information*: same address/phone as **93.116**. (Note: no field offices for this program.)

93.186   NATIONAL RESEARCH SERVICES AWARDS ("NRSAs")

Assistance: project grants (100 percent/3-5 years).

Purposes: for postdoctoral research training programs in primary medical care. Individuals receiving awards incur one month of service obligation for each of the first 12 months of the NRSA support (*see Note preceding* **93.001**).

Eligible applicants/beneficiaries: domestic public or private nonprofit organizations; state or local governments and territories. Individuals must be U.S. citizens, noncitizen nationals, or lawful permanent residents.

Range: $57,000 to $552,000. **Average:** $136,000.

Activity: FY 99 estimate, 27 continuation awards.

HQ: same address (except Rm.9A-20)/phone as **93.181**. *Grants management information:* same address/phone as **93.107**. (Note: no field offices for this program.)

93.187   UNDERGRADUATE SCHOLARSHIP PROGRAM FOR INDIVIDUALS FROM DISADVANTAGED BACKGROUNDS ("NIH Undergraduate Scholarship Program" - "UGSP")

Assistance: project grants (100 percent/to 4 years).

Purposes: for scholarships to persons from disadvantaged backgrounds, pursuing undergraduate education preparing them for professions in the biomedical and bio-behavioral sciences and other fields needed by NIH. Recipients must agree: to serve full-time for at least ten consecutive weeks as an NIH employee during each year of the scholarship period; within 60 days of obtaining a degree, to serve one year as a full-time NIH employee for each year of scholarship assistance received unless deferred.

Eligible applicants/beneficiaries: U.S. citizens, nationals, or permanent residents from disadvantaged backgrounds, enrolled or accepted at IHEs, and maintaining good academic standing.

Range/Average: $16,000.

Activity: FY 99-00, 15 awards.

HQ: Office of Loan Repayment and Scholarship, NIH-HHS, Federal Bldg. - Rm.604, 7550 Wisconsin Ave., Bethesda, MD 20892-9121. Phones: (800) 528-7689; FAX (301)480-5481. (Note: no field offices for this program.)

93.188   PUBLIC HEALTH TRAINING CENTERS

Assistance: project grants (100 percent/3-5 years).

Purposes: to plan, develop, demonstrate, operate, and evaluate graduate or specialized public health educational programs in preventive medicine, and in health promotion and disease prevention—to improve access to and quality of health care in medically underserved communities, and to reduce the incidence of domestic violence. Funds may not be used for undergraduate programs, for traineeships, for construction activities, for activities related to research.

Eligible applicants/beneficiaries: accredited schools of public health.

Range: $110,000 to $551,000. **Average:** $181,000.

Activity: FY 99, 12 continuation grants.

HQ: same addresses/phones as **93.117**. (Note: no field offices for this program.)

93.189   HEALTH EDUCATION AND TRAINING CENTERS ("HETC")

Assistance: project grants (100 percent/to 3 years).

Purposes: to plan, develop, establish, maintain, and operate Health Education and Training Centers, in rural and inner-city communities, in Florida, and in U.S.-Mexico border areas. Funds must be expended mainly in the service area of the recipient's program.

Eligible applicants/beneficiaries: public or private nonprofit schools of allopathic or osteopathic medicine; consortia.

Range: border-HETC, $90,000 to $705,000; non-border, $195,000 to $527,000. **Average:** border, $312,000; non-border, $395,000.

Activity: FY 00 estimate, 10 new, 3 continuation awards.

HQ: Division of Medicine, same addresses/phones as **93.107**. (Note: no field offices for this program.)

93.191   ALLIED HEALTH PROJECTS

Assistance: project grants (100 percent).

Purposes: to improve and strengthen training in the allied health and mental health professions, expand enrollments in these professions, strengthen curriculum in areas of special need, expand or establish interdisciplinary and community-based allied health training programs, and to link academic centers to rural clinical centers. Funds may be used for the costs of personnel, equipment, consultants, space rental, or renovation—but not for construction, land acquisition, financial support to students.

Eligible applicants/beneficiaries: schools, universities, state or local governments, public or private nonprofit entities.

Range: $34,000 to $181,000. **Average:** $105,000.

Activity: FY 99, 23 continuation, 15 new awards.

HQ: Division of Associated, Dental and Public Health Professions, Bureau of Health Professions, HRSA-HHS, Parklawn Bldg. - Rm.8C-02, 5600 Fishers Lane, Rockville, MD 20857. Phone: (301)443-1346. *Grants management information*: same address as **93.107**. Phone: (301)443-6857. (Note: no field offices for this program.)

93.192   QUENTIN N. BURDICK PROGRAMS FOR RURAL INTERDISCIPLINARY TRAINING

Assistance: project grants (100 percent/to 3 years).

Purposes: to promote recruitment and retention of health professionals in rural areas, through interdisciplinary training projects in rural health care settings. Grants may be used for student stipends, postdoctoral fellowships, faculty training, and purchase or rental of transportation and telecommunications equipment.

Eligible applicants/beneficiaries: health professions schools; academic health centers; state or local governments; public and private nonprofit entities. Applications must be submitted jointly by at least two eligible applicants.

Range: $148,000 to $241,000. **Average:** $192,000.

Activity: FY 00, 12 continuation, 13 competitive awards.

HQ: Interdisciplinary, Geriatrics and Allied Health Branch, same address as **93.191**. Phone: (301)443-6867. *Grants management information*: same address/phone as **93.107**. (Note: no field offices for this program.)

93.193   URBAN INDIAN HEALTH SERVICES

Assistance: project grants (100 percent/to 5 years).

Purposes: for health-related services to Indians residing in urban areas, including: alcohol and substance abuse prevention, treatment, rehabilitation, and education; mental health needs assessment; health promotion and disease prevention; immunization; child abuse prevention and treatment.

Eligible applicants/beneficiaries: urban Indian organizations.

Range: $36,000 to $521,000. **Average:** $250,000.

Activity: FY 00 estimate, 31 continuation grants.

HQ: Director of Urban Programs, IHS-HHS, Parklawn Bldg. - Rm.6-12, 5600 Fishers Lane, Rockville, MD 20857. Phone: (301)443-4680. *Grants management information*: Grants Management Officer, Division of Acquisition and Grants Operations, IHS-HHS, Twinbrook Metro Bldg. - Ste.100, 12300 Twinbrook Pkwy., Rockville, MD 20852. Phone: (301)443-5204. (Note: no field offices for this program.)

93.194   COMMUNITY PREVENTION COALITIONS (PARTNERSHIP) DEMONSTRATION GRANT

Assistance: project grants (100 percent/3-5 years).

Purposes: to promote and evaluate model community partnerships in the development of long-range, comprehensive, multi-disciplinary, community-wide alcohol and other substance abuse prevention programs. The partnerships should be structured from both public and private organizations, including ethnic and geographic community sub-sets or groups—to plan and coordinate improved prevention programs at the local level. Funds may be used mainly to identify needs and service gaps in target communities, and to leverage public and private resources to augment early intervention and prevention programs.

Eligible applicants/beneficiaries: local governments and private nonprofit organizations in partnerships or coalitions consisting of at least seven organizations or agencies.

Range: $150,000 to $450,000. **Average:** $300,000.

Activity: FY 00 estimate, 2 continuation awards.

HQ: Division of State and Community Systems Development, CSAP, SAM-HSA-HHS, Rockwall II Bldg., 5600 Fishers Lane, Rockville, MD 20857.

Phone: (301)443-0369. *Grants management information*: same address/ phone as **93.101**. (Note: no field offices for this program.)

93.196   COOPERATIVE AGREEMENTS FOR DRUG ABUSE TREATMENT IMPROVEMENT PROJECTS IN TARGET CITIES ("Target Cities")

Assistance: project grants (100 percent/to 3 years).

Purposes: to improve drug treatment services in targeted cities through projects providing high quality, patient-oriented, coordinated, and accessible treatment that can be replicated by other cities. Funds are intended to augment existing programs and to provide "seed money" for activities that eventually will be financed by other sources.

Eligible applicants/beneficiaries: states on behalf of only one city with a population over 266,000 based on 1986 data. Applicants' programs must have existed for at least two years.

Range: $1,469,000 to $4,503,000. **Average:** $3,631,000.

Activity: FY 98, 2 awards. FY 99-00, no awards.

HQ: Public Health Advisor, Systems Development and Integration Branch, Division of Practice and Systems Development, CSAT, SAMHSA-HHS, Rockwall II Bldg.- Ste.740, 5600 Fishers Lane, Rockville, MD 20857. Phone: (301)443-6574. *Grants management information*: same address/ phone as **93.101**.(Note: no field offices for this program.)

93.197   CHILDHOOD LEAD POISONING PREVENTION PROJECTS—STATE AND COMMUNITY-BASED CHILDHOOD LEAD POISONING PREVENTION AND SURVEILLANCE OF BLOOD LEVELS IN CHILDREN ("CLPPP")

Assistance: project grants (100 percent/to 3 years).

Purposes: for childhood lead poisoning prevention projects in communities with demonstrated high-risk populations. Funds are to be used: for screening and testing; to identify sources of lead exposure; to monitor medical and environmental management of cases, including follow-up; for public and technical education activities, including training of program staff; to develop an efficient information management system compatible with CDCP data guidelines; to establish state-based surveillance systems. Ineligible uses of funds include medical care or treatment, remediation of lead sources.

Eligible applicants/beneficiaries: state health or other departments or agencies; local governments with 500,000 population or more; territories and possessions; tribal governments; consortia of the foregoing.

Range: prevention, $75,000 to $1,500,000; surveillance only, $60,000 to $75,000. **Average:** prevention, $520,000; surveillance, $70,000.

Activity: FY 98, 44 grants.

HQ: Lead Poisoning Prevention Branch, Division of Environmental Hazards and Health Effects, National Center for Environmental Health, CDCP-HHS (MS F-42), 4770 Buford Hwy., Atlanta, GA 30341. Phones: (770)488-7330; FAX (770)448-7557. *Grants management information*: Procurement and

Grants Office, CDCP-HHS, 255 E. Paces Ferry Rd. NE, Atlanta, GA 30305. Phones: (404)842-6564; FAX (404)842-6513. (Note: no field offices for this program.)

93.204 SURVEILLANCE OF HAZARDOUS SUBSTANCE EMERGENCY EVENTS

Assistance: project grants (100 percent/1-5 years).

Purposes: pursuant to CERCLA, to develop a state-based surveillance system for monitoring hazardous substance emergency events, to enable states to: assess the burden of adverse health effects created by unexpected, sudden releases; describe the situations and persons most likely impacted; define the risk factors; and, work with appropriate agencies to implement prevention activities. Funds may cover the costs of personnel, travel, supplies, and services.

Eligible applicants/beneficiaries: official state public health departments, possessions and territories.

Range: $60,000 to $80,000. **Average:** $70,000.

Activity: FY 99-00 estimate, 13 awards.

HQ: Division of Health Studies, Agency for Toxic Substances and Disease Registry, CDCP-HHS (MS E-31), 1600 Clifton Rd. NE, Atlanta, GA 30333. Phone: (404)639-5114; FAX (404)639-6220. *Program technical assistance*: Chief, Epidemiology and Surveillance Branch, Division of Health Studies, same address. Phone: (404)639-6203. *Grants management information*: same address/phone as **93.161**. (Note: no field offices for this program.)

93.206 HUMAN HEALTH STUDIES—APPLIED RESEARCH AND DEVELOPMENT

Assistance: project grants (100 percent/1-3 years).

Purposes: pursuant to CERCLA, for research on human health effects of hazardous substances identified at hazardous waste sites, as identified by the Agency for Toxic Substances and Disease Registry, including: birth defects and reproductive disorders; cancers; immune function disorders; kidney and liver dysfunction; lung and respiratory diseases; neurotoxic disorders.

Eligible applicants/beneficiaries: same as for **93.204**, and other approved state research institutions and IHEs; federally-recognized tribal governments.

Range: $200,000 to $300,000. **Average:** $250,000.

Activity: FY 00, 2 continuation awards.

HQ: same address/phone as **93.204**. *Program technical assistance*: Director, Division of Health Studies, same address as **93.204**. Phone: (404)639-6220. *Grants management information*: same address/phones as **93.161**. (Note: no field offices for this program.)

93.208 GREAT LAKES HUMAN HEALTH EFFECTS RESEARCH

Assistance: project grants (100 percent/1-3 years).

Purposes: pursuant to CERCLA, for research on the impact on human health of fish consumption in the Great Lakes Region, focusing on populations identified as having a higher risk of long-term adverse health effects from exposure to contaminants—especially native Americans and other minority groups, sport anglers, the urban poor, the elderly. The research is intended to study the effects of contaminants on human reproductive and developmental, behavioral, neurological, and endocrinological health.

Eligible applicants/beneficiaries: in the Great Lakes states—state and local health agencies, state IHEs and research institutions, and tribal governments.

Range: $148,000 to $801,000. **Average:** $300,000.

Activity: FY 99-00 estimate, 10 continuation grants.

HQ: Division of Toxicology, Agency for Toxic Substances and Disease Registry, HHS (MS E-29), 1600 Clifton Rd. NE, Atlanta, GA 30333. Phones: (404)639-6300, -6306; FAX (404)639-6315. *Grants management information*: same address/phones as **93.161**. (Note: no field offices for this program.)

93.209 CONTRACEPTION AND INFERTILITY LOAN REPAYMENT PROGRAM ("CIR-LRP")

Assistance: direct payments/specified use (to 4 years).

Purposes: to provide incentives to health professionals to work in reproductive research related to contraceptive development or infertility diagnosis and treatment, by providing assistance in repaying their education loans. Participants must agree to commit to a period of obligated service of at least two years.

Eligible applicants/beneficiaries: U.S. citizens, nationals, or permanent residents that are health and allied health professionals, including physicians, scientists, nurses, physician assistants, or graduate students and postgraduate research fellows.

Range/Average: to $20,000 of loan principal and interest for each year of service commitment, not to exceed one-half of remaining loan balance—plus 39 percent to offset tax liability.

Activity: FY 00 estimate, 10 application approvals.

HQ: Health Scientist Administrator, CIR-LRP, Center for Population Research, National Institute of Child Health and Human Development, NIH-HHS, Bldg.61E - Rm.8B01, Bethesda, MD 20892-7510. Phones: (301)496-6515; FAX (301)496-0962. (Note: no field offices for this program.)

93.210 TRIBAL SELF-GOVERNANCE DEMONSTRATION PROGRAM: PLANNING AND NEGOTIATION COOPERATIVE AGREEMENTS AND IHS COMPACTS

Assistance: project grants (100 percent/10 years).

Purposes: to plan, establish, and operate programs to provide planning and negotiation resources to tribes interested in participating in the Self-Governance Demonstration Program—enabling them to enter into compacts to assume program services and functions of the IHS, HHS, and DOI that are otherwise available to Indians or tribes.

Eligible applicants/beneficiaries: federally-recognized tribes that have successfully operated two or more mature contracts.

Range: cooperative agreements, $20,000 to $50,000. **Average:** compacts, $7,455,000.

Activity: N.A.

HQ: Director, Office of Tribal Self-Governance, IHS-HHS, Parklawn Bldg. - Rm.5A-55, 5600 Fishers Lane, Rockville, MD 20857. Phone: (301)443-7821. *Grants management information:* same address/phone as **93.193**. (Note: no field offices for this program.)

93.211   RURAL TELEMEDICINE GRANTS

Assistance: project grants (100 percent/to 3 years).

Purposes: for demonstration projects to establish and operate rural telemedicine networks that provide consultative services, including preventive and emergency services. Up to 40 percent of grant funds may be used for equipment (non-transmission).

Eligible applicants/beneficiaries: public or private nonprofit health care providers or consortia, including for-profit entities, that are members of an existing or proposed telemedicine network.

Range/Average: $400,000.

Activity: FY 98, 18 continuation awards.

HQ: Office for the Advancement of Telehealth, HRSA-HHS, 5600 Fishers Lane - Rm.11A-55, Rockville, MD 20857. Phone: (301)443-0447. *Grants management information:* same address/phone as **93.129**. (Note: no field offices for this program.)

93.212   CHIROPRACTIC DEMONSTRATION PROJECTS

Assistance: project grants (100 percent/to 3 years).

Purposes: for demonstration projects in which chiropractors and medical doctors collaborate to identify and treat spinal and lower-back conditions. Project funds may be used for personnel, equipment, supplies, domestic travel, consultants and guest lecturers, rent, renovations, and other direct project costs—but not for land acquisition, facilities construction, foreign travel, or student support.

Eligible applicants/beneficiaries: public or private nonprofit schools, colleges, and universities of chiropractic medicine.

Range: $216,000 to $280,000. **Average:** $247,000.

Activity: FY 99, 3 continuation awards.

HQ: same address as **93.191**. Phone: (301)443-6763. *Grants management information:* same address/phone as **93.107**. (Note: no field offices for this program.)

93.213   RESEARCH AND TRAINING IN ALTERNATIVE MEDICINE

Assistance: project grants (100 percent/to 5 years).

Purposes: for basic, applied, and clinical intramural and extramural research and research training of complementary and alternative treatment, diagnostic and prevention modalities, disciplines, and systems. Grants may support costs of personnel, consultants, equipment, supplies, patient costs, animals, and fellowships.

Eligible applicants/beneficiaries: IHEs, hospitals, public agencies, nonprofit research institutions, profit concerns.

Range: projects and centers, $250,000 to $1,000,000; investigator-initiated, $250,000 to $375,000; training, $14,000 to $44,000; cooperative agreements, $165,000 to $750,000. **Average:** career development, $82,000;

Activity: FY 98 (sampling), 14 centers funded; 18 investigator-initiated research grants; 1 predoctoral, 3 NRSA postdoctoral fellowship awards.

HQ: National Center for Complementary and Alternative Medicine, NIH-HHS, Bldg. 31 - Rm.5B-38, 9000 Rockville Pike, Bethesda, MD 20892. Phones: (301)402-2466; FAX (301)402-4741. (Note: no field offices for this program.)

93.215   HANSEN'S DISEASE NATIONAL AMBULATORY CARE PROGRAM

Assistance: project grants (100 percent/to 3 years).

Purposes: to provide ambulatory care, treatment, screening, and testing services to patients with Hansen's disease.

Eligible applicants/beneficiaries: existing health centers.

Range: $35,000 to $375,000.

Activity: FY 98, 10 centers funded; FY 99, one additional award.

HQ: Grants Management Officer, Bureau of Primary Health Care, HRSA-HHS, 4350 East-West Hwy. - 11th floor, Bethesda, MD 20814. Phone: (301)594-4235.

93.216   HIV/AIDS MENTAL HEALTH SERVICES DEMONSTRATION PROGRAM

Assistance: project grants (100 percent/4 years).

Purposes: to develop, expand, and evaluate mental health services programs involving individuals, families, and others experiencing serious psychological reactions resulting from HIV/AIDS antibody testing—and to provide them with mental health services.

Eligible applicants/beneficiaries: public or private nonprofit organizations.

Range: $250,000 to $350,000. **Average:** $300,000.

Activity: FY 98-00, no awards.

HQ: HIV/AIDS Program, CMHS, SAMHSA-HHS, Parklawn Bldg. - Rm.15-89, 5600 Fishers Lane, Rockville, MD 20857. Phone: (301)443-7817. *Grants management information*: same address/phone as **93.101**. (Note: no field offices for this program.)

93.217   FAMILY PLANNING—SERVICES

Assistance: project grants (from 90 percent/3-5 years).

Purposes: for educational, counseling, and comprehensive medical and social services involving family planning, with priority to the low-income. Grants may be used for contraceptive, infertility, and special services to adolescents. Funds may not be used in programs where abortion is a method of family planning, nor for personnel salaries paid from other federal funds, nor for building construction.

Eligible applicants/beneficiaries: city, county, local, regional, or state governmental or private nonprofit entities in states, territories, and possessions.

Range: $54,000 to $10,321,000. **Average:** $2,170,000.

Activity: FY 00 estimate, 5,500,000 persons served.

HQ: Director, Office of Family Planning, Office of Population Affairs, same address as **93.111**. Phone: (301)594-4000. *Grants management information*: same address/phone as **93.111**.

93.219 MATCHING GRANTS FOR HEALTH PROFESSIONS SCHOLARSHIPS TO INDIAN TRIBES
("Health Professions Scholarships")

Assistance: project grants (80 percent).

Purposes: for scholarships to Indians to serve as health professionals in Indian communities. Scholarship recipients must: maintain satisfactory academic standing; meet service requirements equal to the number of years covered by the scholarships but not less than two years.

Eligible applicants/beneficiaries: federally-recognized tribes or tribal organizations.

Range: $42,000 to $70,000.

Activity: FY 99-00, 4 continuation awards.

HQ: same address/phone as **93.123**. *Grants management information*: same address/phone as **93.193**. Phone: (301)443-5204. (Note: no field offices for this program.)

93.220 CLINICAL RESEARCH LOAN REPAYMENT PROGRAM FOR INDIVIDUALS FROM DISADVANTAGED BACKGROUNDS
("NIH Clinical Research Loan Repayment Program" - "CR-LRP")

Assistance: project grants (100 percent/2 years minimum).

Purposes: for repayment of extant educational loans incurred by persons from disadvantaged backgrounds, engaged in clinical research as employees of the NIH.

Eligible applicants/beneficiaries: U.S. citizens, nationals, or permanent residents from disadvantaged backgrounds, with: an M.D., Ph.D., D.O., D.D.S., D.M.D., B.S.N./A.D.N., or equivalent degree; qualified undergraduate or graduate educational loan debt exceeding 20 percent of their NIH salary; a contract commitment of at least two years of service to NIH; no existing service obligation to federal, state, or other entities.

Range: to $35,000 per year, plus $13,650 annually for tax reimbursements. **Average:** $23,835, and $9,296 in tax reimbursements.

Activity: FY 99-00, 8 awards.

HQ: same address/phones as **93.187**. (Note: no field offices for this program.)

93.222 CENTERS FOR MEDICAL EDUCATION RESEARCH

Assistance: project grants (75 percent/to 3 years).

Purposes: for research in medical education, focussing on federal policies and programs and their impact on improvements in the training of health professionals and on meeting national health work force goals. Research covers: (a) the extent to which the education debt of medical students detrimentally affects their decisions to enter primary care specialties; (b) the effects of federally-funded educational initiatives for minority or disadvantaged individuals; (c) state effectiveness in protecting the public health through disciplinary actions against health care providers; (d) specific issues related to primary care.

Eligible applicants/beneficiaries: public and private nonprofit entities.

Range/Average: $275,000.

Activity: FY 98, no awards.

HQ: Director, Office of Research and Planning, Bureau of Health Professions, HRSA-HHS, Parklawn Bldg. - Rm.8-47, 5600 Fishers Lane, Rockville, MD 20857. Phone: (301)443-6936. *Grants management information*: same address/phone as **93.107**. (Note: no field offices for this program.)

93.223   DEVELOPMENT AND COORDINATION OF RURAL HEALTH SERVICES

Assistance: project grants (100 percent/3 years).

Purposes: to develop and disseminate information to assist rural communities and rural health care organizations in developing and coordinating rural health care services—including information from federal and state agencies, health publications, research reports, and reports from national health care associations.

Eligible applicants/beneficiaries: nonprofit private organizations representing national, state, and local rural health constituencies.

Range/Average: N.A.

Activity: FY 99, 1 award.

HQ: same addresses/phones as **93.155**. (Note: no field offices for this program.)

93.224   COMMUNITY HEALTH CENTERS

Assistance: project grants (to 100 percent/to 5 years).

Purposes: to develop and operate community health centers providing preventive and primary care services, supplemental health and support services, and environmental health services to medically underserved populations.

Eligible applicants/beneficiaries: public or private nonprofit agencies, institutions, or organizations; some state and local governments.

Range: $15,000 to $8,500,000. **Average:** $952,000.

Activity: FY 98, 750 centers funded at 3,000 sites.

HQ: Director, Division of Community and Migrant Health, Bureau of Primary Health Care, HRSA-HHS, 4350 East-West Hwy. - 7th floor, Bethesda, MD 20814. Phones: (301)594-4300; Web, www.bphc.hrsa.dhhs.gov *Grants management information*: same address/phone as **93.129**.

93.225   NATIONAL RESEARCH SERVICE AWARDS—HEALTH SERVICES RESEARCH TRAINING

Assistance: project grants (100 percent/to 3-5 years).

Purposes: for fellowships for full-time pre- or postdoctoral training in health services research, and grants to institutions providing the training (*see Note preceding* **93.001**). Training is in epidemiology, biostatistics, geriatrics, health administration and public health, medical information sciences, health policy and management, organizational behavior. Fellowship recipients must meet service payback requirements.

Eligible applicants/beneficiaries: domestic public or private nonprofit organizations including state and local governments and territories—with existing training programs.

Range: individuals, $10,000 to $35,000; institutions, $30,000 to $290,000. **Average:** individuals, $23,000; institutions, $160,000.

Activity: FY 99 estimate, 5 fellowships, 26 training grants.

HQ: Grants Management Officer, Agency for Health Care Policy and Research-HHS, 2101 E. Jefferson St. - Ste.601, Rockville, MD 20852. Phone: (301) 594-1844. (Note: no field offices for this program.)

93.226 HEALTH CARE SYSTEMS COST AND ACCESS RESEARCH AND DEVELOPMENT GRANTS

Assistance: project grants (100 percent/to 5 years).

Purposes: for research to develop new options for health services delivery and health policy. Major issue categories include consumer decision making, managed care and the health care marketplace, primary care, rural health services, and AIDS.

Eligible applicants/beneficiaries: federal, state, or local government agencies; federally-recognized tribal governments; territories and possessions; sponsored organizations; public or private nonprofit organizations; minority groups; IHEs; individuals.

Range: $18,000 to $900,000. **Average:** $200,000.

Activity: N.A.

HQ: same address/phone as **93.225**. (Note: no field offices for this program.)

93.227 SURVEILLANCE OF THE COMPLICATIONS OF HEMOPHILIA ("Hemophilia Surveillance")

Assistance: project grants (100 percent/1-3 years).

Purposes: to reduce morbidity, mortality, and costs of hemophilia and its complications, through epidemiology projects characterizing its impact among: (a) patients that access traditional treatment and comprehensive services; (b) those not receiving care or remaining undiagnosed; (c) patients receiving care elsewhere. Project funds may cover costs of staff, travel, supplies, computer hardware, acquisition of additional data base information needed to augment surveillance.

Eligible applicants/beneficiaries: public health agencies of states, territories, possessions, and tribal governments.

Range: $11,000 to $569,000. **Average:** $213,000.

Activity: not quantified specifically.

HQ: National Center for Infectious Diseases, CDCP-HHS (MS E64), 1600 Clifton Rd., Atlanta, GA 30333. Phones: (404)639-4027; FAX (404)639-3991. *Grants management information*: same address as **93.161**. Phones: (770)488-2745; FAX (770)488-2777. (Note: no field offices for this program.)

93.228 INDIAN HEALTH SERVICE—HEALTH MANAGEMENT DEVELOPMENT PROGRAM

Assistance: project grants (100 percent).

Purposes: to increase the capability of American Indians and native Alaskans to operate IHS health care programs involving curative, preventive, and rehabilitative health services. Funds may be used for feasibility studies, planning, tribal health management structure development, evaluation, injury prevention services, technical assistance, and federal programs analysis.

Eligible applicants/beneficiaries: federally-recognized tribes and tribal organizations.

Range: management, $65,000; services projects, $85,000 to $185,000; injury prevention, $25,000.

Activity: FY 99-00 estimate, 35 tribal management, 20 health services, 13 injury prevention continuation awards.

HQ: *management programs,* Chief, Loan Repayment Program, Office of Management Support, IHS-HHS, Twinbrook Metro Plaza - Ste.100A, 12300 Twinbrook Pkwy., Rockville, MD 20852. Phone: (301)443-3396. *Injury prevention programs,* Division of Community and Environmental Health, Office of Public Health, IHS-HHS, Twinbrook Metro Plaza - Ste. 450, 12300 Twinbrook Pkwy., Rockville, MD 20852. Phone: (301)443-1054. *Grants management information:* same address/phone as **93.193**.

93.229 DEMONSTRATION COOPERATIVE AGREEMENTS FOR DEVELOPMENT AND IMPLEMENTATION OF CRIMINAL JUSTICE TREATMENT NETWORKS

Assistance: project grants (100 percent/to 5 years).

Purposes: for integrated criminal justice treatment networks of consortia of criminal justice, substance abuse treatment, primary health and mental health care, and allied social services and job placement agencies—involved with adult male or female offenders and juvenile justice populations. Each network must develop strategies to link existing partnerships into a comprehensive continuum of services, with the pivotal points of referral and supervision either in the courts or community corrections agencies.

Eligible applicants/beneficiaries: state alcohol and drug abuse agencies applying on behalf of consortia state and local officials and public and nonprofit private entities. If the state does not apply, consortia may submit applications through nonprofit entities, in coordination with state agencies.

Range: $1,100,000 to $1,250,000. **Average:** $1,171,000.

Activity: FY 99 estimate, 7 continuation awards.

HQ: same address as **93.101**. Phone: (301)443-6533. *Grants management information:* same address as **93.101**. Phone: (301) 443-9667. (Note: no field offices for this program.)

93.230 CONSOLIDATED KNOWLEDGE DEVELOPMENT AND APPLICATION (KD&A) PROGRAM
("KD&A")

Assistance: project grants (100 percent/3 years).

Purposes: to provide and disseminate immediately usable knowledge to services providers on the efficacy of substance abuse and mental health services in crucial selected areas—based on questions arising from consumers and their families, providers, and public and private agencies and organizations including at state and federal policymaking and legislative levels. Activities are undertaken in service settings. Dissemination occurs through multiple channels including technology. Specific study topics are announced annually.

Eligible applicants/beneficiaries: state and local governments, private nonprofit and profit entities such as community-based organizations, IHEs, and hospitals.

Range: $163,000 to $1,200,000. **Average:** $352,000.

Activity: FY 00 estimate, 319 CMHS, 256 CSAP, 331 CSAT awards.

HQ: *general address,* SAMHSA, 5600 Fishers Lane, Rockville, MD 20857. Program contacts: CSAP, Rockwall II Bldg. - Rm.9D-18. Phone: (301)443-1584. CSAT, Rockwall II Bldg. - Rm.615. Phone: (301)443-8387. CMHS, Parklawn Bldg. - Rm.11C26. Phone: (301)443-3606. *Grants management contact:* same address/phone as **93.101**. (Note: no field offices for this program.)

93.231 EPIDEMIOLOGY COOPERATIVE AGREEMENTS

Assistance: project grants (100 percent/to 3 years).

Purposes: to develop and operate epidemiology centers and public health infrastructure to coordinate and participate in disease surveillance and prevention projects, as well as investigations and studies of national scope. Project activities include convening of meetings, technical assistance and consultation, and training.

Eligible applicants/beneficiaries: tribes; tribal, urban tribal organizations; consortia.

Range: $125,000 to $155,000. **Average:** $140,000.

Activity: FY 99-00, 7 continuation projects.

HQ: Epidemiology Branch, IHS Headquarters West, HHS, 5300 Homestead Rd. NE, Albuquerque, NM 87110. Phone: (505)837-4226. *Grants management information:* same address/phone as **93.193**. (Note: no field offices for this program.)

93.232 LOAN REPAYMENT PROGRAM FOR GENERAL RESEARCH ("NIH General Loan Repayment Program" - "GR-LRP")

Assistance: project grants (100 percent/3 years).

Purposes: for repayment of extant educational loans incurred by professionals engaged in laboratory or clinical research as employees of the NIH for a minimum of three years.

Eligible applicants/beneficiaries: U.S. citizens, nationals, or permanent residents with: an M.D., Ph.D., D.O., D.D.S., D.M.D., or equivalent degree; undergraduate or graduate educational loan debt exceeding 20 percent of their NIH salary; at least a three-year employment contract to engage in NIH clinical research; no service obligation to federal, state, or other entities.

Range: to $35,000 per year, plus $13,650 annually for tax reimbursements. **Average:** $15,026, and $5,860 in tax reimbursements.

Activity: FY 00 estimate, 21 awards.

HQ: same address/phones as **93.187**. (Note: no field offices for this program.)

93.233   NATIONAL CENTER ON SLEEP DISORDERS RESEARCH

Assistance: project grants (100 percent/1-5 years).

Purposes: for research, training, information dissemination, and other activities relating to sleep disorders, including biological and circadian rhythm research, basic understanding of sleep, chronological and other sleep related research; to coordinate center activities with other federal agencies and with public and nonprofit organizations. NRSA, SBIR, and STIR funding is available (*see Note preceding* **93.001**).

Eligible applicants/beneficiaries: nonprofit and profit organizations; individuals.

Range: $50,000 to $1,115,000. **Average:** $252,000.

Activity: new program listing in 1997. FY 99 estimate, 86 grants.

HQ: Director, National Center on Sleep Disorders Research, National Heart, Lung, and Blood Diseases Institute, NIH-HHS, Bethesda, MD 20892. Phones: (301)435-0199; Administrative Office, (301)435-6373; *SBIR*, Deputy Director, Division of Extramural Affairs, (301)435-0266. *Grants management information*: Grants Management Officer, Grants Operations Branch, Office of Program Policy and Procedures, National Heart, Lung, and Blood Diseases Institute, NIH-HHS, Bethesda, MD 20892. Phones: (301) 435-0144. (Note: no field offices for this program.)

93.234   TRAUMATIC BRAIN INJURY
("TBI")

Assistance: project grants (67 percent).

Purposes: for expanded studies and innovative programs concerning traumatic brain injury. Planning grants support development of four state-level core capacity components to provide TBI services. Implementation grants are for states with the four core capacity components in place.

Eligible applicants/beneficiaries: state governments.

Range: planning, $20,000 to $75,000; implementation, to $200,000.

Activity: new program in FY 97. FY 99, 27 projects supported.

HQ: Director, Division of Maternal, Child, and Adolescent Health, same address as **93.127**. Phone: (301)443-2250. *Grants management information*: same address/phone as **93.110**. (Note: no field offices for this program.)

93.235   ABSTINENCE EDUCATION

Assistance: formula grants.

Purposes: for abstinence education and, when appropriate, mentoring, counseling, and adult supervision to promote abstinence from sexual activity outside of marriage—focussing on groups most likely to bear children out of wedlock.

Eligible applicants/beneficiaries: states and insular areas.

Range: $14,000 to $5,764,000. Average: $847,000.

Activity: new program in FY 97. FY 98, 53 grants.

HQ: Office of State and Community Health, Maternal and Child Health Bureau, HRSA-HHS, 5600 Fishers Lane - Rm.18-31, Rockville, MD 20857. Phone: (301)443-2204. *Grants management information*: same address/phone as **93.110**. (Note: no field offices for this program.)

93.236   GRANTS FOR DENTAL PUBLIC HEALTH
("Dental Public Health Specialty Training Grants")

Assistance: project grants (100 percent).

Purposes: to plan and develop new dental public health residency training programs; to provide financial assistance to trainees. Grants may not be used for construction or for direct patient services.

Eligible applicants/beneficiaries: public or private schools of public health or dentistry.

Range/Average: $70,000.

Activity: new program listing in 1998; 7 continuation awards.

HQ: same addresses/phones as **93.117**. (Note: no field offices for this program.)

93.237   SPECIAL DIABETES PROGRAM FOR INDIANS—PREVENTION AND
TREATMENT SERVICES

Assistance: project grants (100 percent/to 5 years).

Purposes: for primary, secondary, and tertiary diabetes prevention and treatment services, and related data collection—among American Indians and native Alaskans.

Eligible applicants/beneficiaries: Indian tribes, tribal and urban Indian organizations—operating IHS health programs.

Range: $46,000 to $5,000,000.

Activity: new program in FY 98.

HQ: Director, Diabetes Program, IHS-HHS, 5300 Homestead Rd. NE, Albuquerque, NM 87110. Phones: (505)248-4182; FAX (505)248-4188. *Grants management information*: same address/phone as **93.193** *and* FAX (301) 443-9602. (Note: no field offices for this program.)

93.238   COOPERATIVE AGREEMENTS FOR STATE TREATMENT OUTCOMES
AND PERFORMANCE PILOT STUDIES ENHANCEMENT
("TOPPS II")

Assistance: project grants (100 percent/3 years).

Purposes: to collect information on Substance Abuse Pilot Treatment Block Grants; to monitor common substance abuse treatment effectiveness data across various state management information systems; for evaluation programs to design or enhance state management information systems or outcome management systems that examine treatment effectiveness and costs through standardized performance and outcome measures while incorporating such common data measures on interstate projects. Project funds may not be used for services unrelated to the research.

Eligible applicants/beneficiaries: projects—single state authorities. Technical assistance centers—domestic nonprofit and profit entities including community-based organizations, IHEs, and hospitals.

Range: $300,000 to $500,000.

Activity: new program in FY 98. FY 99 estimate, 17 awards.

HQ: Division for State and Community Assistance, CSAT, SAMHSA-HHS, Rockwall II Bldg. - Ste.880, 5600 Fishers Lane, Rockville, MD 20857. Phone: (301)443-3820. *Grants management information*: same address/phone as **93.101**. (Note: no field offices for this program.)

93.239 POLICY RESEARCH AND EVALUATION GRANTS

Assistance: project grants (to 100 percent).

Purposes: for analyses, experiments, data systems development, and pilot projects covering: issues of long-term care, disability, and personal assistance services including personal care giving; health care delivery issues including financing; welfare service delivery issues and policies affecting children and youth; management coordination of HHS-wide policy development and policy support activities; science policy development.

Eligible applicants/beneficiaries: nonprofit entities, government agencies, individuals, some profit organizations.

Range: $50,000 to $1,500,000. **Average:** $150,000.

Activity: new program listing in 1998. FY 98, 10 new cooperative agreements.

HQ: Grants Officer, Office of Assistant Secretary/Planning and Evaluation, OS-HHS, HHH Bldg. - Rm.405F, 200 Independence Ave. SW, Washington, DC 20201. Phone: (202)690-8794. (Note: no field offices for this program.)

93.240 STATE CAPACITY BUILDING
("Site Specific Activities Cooperative Agreement Program")

Assistance: project grants (100 percent/to 5 years).

Purposes: to fulfill the mandates of CERCLA and SARA, for public health agency capacity building, in coordination with the Agency for Toxic Substances and Disease Registry, to conduct: health consultations and assessments; exposure investigations; community involvement; health education and studies.

Eligible applicants/beneficiaries: state public health agencies including possessions and territories, federally-recognized tribal governments.

Range: $80,000 to $1,000,000. **Average:** $475,000.

Activity: new program listing in 1999. FY 99-00 estimate, 29 continuation awards.

HQ: Funding Resource Specialist, Program Support Branch, same address as **93.161**. Phones: (404)639-0559; FAX (404)639-0569. *Grants management information*: same address/phones as **93.161**. (Note: no field offices for this program.)

93.241 STATE RURAL HOSPITAL FLEXIBILITY PROGRAM

Assistance: project grants (100 percent).

Purposes: for states to work with rural communities and hospitals to develop and implement a rural health plan and integrated care networks, to improve emergency medical services, and to designate criteria access hospitals.

Eligible applicants/beneficiaries: states with rural health plans previously submitted to HCFA. Other states submit applications to HCFA regional offices.

Range: $200,000 to $700,000.

Activity: new program in FY 99. FY 00, 5 new, 43 continuation awards.

HQ: same addresses/phones as **93.155**. (Note: no field offices for this program.)

93.242 MENTAL HEALTH RESEARCH GRANTS

Assistance: project grants (100 percent/to 5 years).

Purposes: for research on mental and behavioral disorders, employing theoretical, laboratory, clinical, methodological, and field studies involving clinical, subclinical, and normal subjects and populations of all age ranges, as well as animal, computational, and mathematical models. Areas eligible for support include HIV/AIDS behavior, neurosciences including molecular genetics, behavioral sciences, epidemiology, clinical assessment, etiology, treatment, prevention, and services. The Minority Research Infrastructure Support Program provides awards to institutions with substantial enrollments of racial ethnic minority students. Research project grants support clearly defined projects or small groups of related research activities, and research conferences. Program Project and Center grants support large-scale, broad-based interdisciplinary research programs. Small grants (to $50,000 for two years) support small-scale exploratory and pilot studies or exploration of an unusual research opportunity. SBIR and STTR awards are made (*see Note preceding* **93.001**).

Eligible applicants/beneficiaries: public, private, profit, or nonprofit agencies including state and local governments, federal agencies, IHEs, hospitals, academic or research institutions.

Range: $17,000 to $4,885,000. **Average:** $301,000.

Activity: FY 00 estimate, 1,901 grants.

HQ: NIMH, NIH-HHS, 5600 Fishers Lane, Rockville, MD 20857. Phones: Director, Division of Basic and Clinical Neuroscience Research, *and Human Brain Project, SBIR/STTR,* (301)443-3563; Director, Division of Mental Disorders, Behavioral Research and AIDS, (301)443-7281; Director, Division of Services and Treatment Research, (301)443-3648; *AIDS-related SBIR/STTR,* (301)443-3175; Director, Office of Rural Mental Health Research, (301)443-3664; Associate Director/Special Populations, (301)443-2847. *Grants management information:* Grants Management Officer, NIMH, NIH-HHS, Parklawn Bldg. - Rm.7C-08, 5600 Fishers Lane, Rockville, MD 20857. Phone: (301)443-2811. (Note: no field offices for this program.)

93.244 MENTAL HEALTH CLINICAL AND AIDS SERVICE-RELATED TRAINING GRANTS

Assistance: project grants (100 percent/to 5 years).

Purposes: for training programs in the mental health professions, including administrative costs, trainee stipends, and other allowances to trainees—with payback agreements required in some instances. Specific program objectives are to increase the number of qualified minority personnel in the field, and the number of personnel trained to deal with the special problems of children, adolescents, the elderly, the seriously mentally ill, and rural populations. Eligible disciplines include: psychiatry, psychology, social work, psychiatric nursing, and marriage and family therapy. Awards may be made to faculty scholars and for state human resource development.

Eligible applicants: public or private nonprofit institutions and organizations, state and local government agencies.

Eligible beneficiaries: U.S. citizens, nationals, lawful permanent residents.

Range: institutional, $11,000 to $262,000; predoctoral trainees, $10,000; post-doctoral, $19,600 to $32,300; faculty scholars, salary support and $25,000 in educational expenses. **Average:** institutional, $92,000.

Activity: FY 98, 11 project grants. FY 00, 1 grant.

HQ: Human Resource Planning and Development Branch, CMHS, SAMHSA-HHS, Parklawn Bldg. - Rm.15C-18, 5600 Fishers Lane, Rockville, MD 20857. Phones: (301)443-5850; *AIDS training,* (301)443-7817. *Grants management information*: same address/phone as **93.101**. (Note: no field offices for this program.)

93.245 NEW PILOT INNOVATIVE FOOD SAFETY PROJECTS

Assistance: project grants (100 percent).

Purposes: for nationally significant projects enhancing food safety programs and reducing food-borne illness, through development, demonstration, education, and dissemination activities.

Eligible applicants/beneficiaries: city, county, and state regulatory health agencies.

Range: $38,000 to $50,000. **Average:** $44,000.

Activity: new program in FY 99; 6-8 awards.

HQ: Chief Grants Management Officer, Division of Contracts and Procurement Management (OFACS), FDA-PHS-HHS (HFA-520), 5630 Fishers Lane - Rm.2141, Rockville, MD 20852. Phones: (301)827-7185; FAX (301)827-7103. (Note: no field offices for this program.)

93.246 HEALTH CENTERS GRANTS FOR MIGRANT AND SEASONAL FARMWORKERS

Assistance: project grants (100 percent).

Purposes: to develop and operate health centers and programs providing primary health care and supplemental and environmental health services for migrant and seasonal agricultural workers and their families. Funds may support: planning, development, and operating costs; implementation and enforcement of environmental and occupational health standards, including sanitation in migrant labor camps; studies.

Eligible applicants/beneficiaries: public or private nonprofit entities, with priority to community-based organizations.

Range: $30,000 to $1,300,000. **Average:** $300,000.

Activity: FY 99 estimate, 122 awards.

HQ: Chief, Migrant Health Branch, Bureau of Primary Health Care, HRSA-HHS, 4350 East-West Hwy. - 7th floor, Bethesda, MD 20814. Phone: (301) 594-4303. *Grants management information*: same address/phone as **93.129**.

93.260 FAMILY PLANNING—PERSONNEL TRAINING

Assistance: project grants (100 percent/to 3 years).

Purposes: to train paramedical and paraprofessional personnel in family planning services, particularly in rural areas. Programs where abortion as a method of family planning are ineligible for assistance.

Eligible applicants/beneficiaries: city, county, local, regional, or state governments and private nonprofit entities in states, territories, and possessions.

Range: $296,000 to $676,000. **Average:** $484,000.

Activity: FY 99-00 estimate, 22,000 trainees.

HQ: Director, Office of Family Planning, Office of Population Affairs, same address/phone as **93.111**. *Grants management information*: same address/phone as **93.111**.

93.262 OCCUPATIONAL SAFETY AND HEALTH RESEARCH GRANTS

Assistance: project grants (100 percent/1-5 years).

Purposes: for research in occupational disease and injury prevention, including projects involving new or improved procedures, methods, techniques, or systems. SBIR awards are made (*see Note preceding* **93.001**).

Eligible applicants/beneficiaries: domestic and foreign public or private profit and nonprofit organizations; state and local governments; tribal governments; IHEs; research institutions; hospitals; individuals.

Range: $30,000 to $400,000. **Average:** $220,000.

Activity: FY 00 estimate, 75 new, 97 continuation grants.

HQ: Director, Research Grants Office, NIOSH (MS-D30), CDCP-HHS, Building 1 - Rm.3053, 1600 Clifton Rd. NE, Atlanta, GA 30333. Phone: (404)639-3343. *Grants management information*: same address/phone as **93.161**. (Note: no field offices for this program.)

93.263 OCCUPATIONAL SAFETY AND HEALTH—TRAINING GRANTS

Assistance: project grants (100 percent/1-5 years).

Purposes: to train specialized professional and paraprofessional personnel in occupational medicine, nursing, safety, and in industrial hygiene and related disciplines. Grants may be used for: educational resource centers to provide primarily graduate multidisciplinary training; long-term training programs for undergraduate, graduate, technical, or professional trainees toward careers in research, teaching, or practice. Stipends may be paid to trainees.

Eligible applicants/beneficiaries: private or public educational institutions or agencies.

Range: centers, $400,000 to $800,000; other, $20,000 to $500,000. **Average:** centers, $600,000; other, $55,000.

Activity: FY 00 estimate, 21 new, 36 continuation grants.

HQ: NIOSH (MS D-40), CDCP-HHS, 1600 Clifton Rd., Atlanta, GA 30333. Phones: (404)639-3525; FAX (404)639-0035. *Grants management information*: same address/phone as **93.161**. (Note: no field offices for this program.)

93.268   IMMUNIZATION GRANTS
("Section 301 and 317, Public Health Service Act")

Assistance: project grants (to 100 percent).

Purposes: to plan, organize, and conduct immunization programs for the control of vaccine-preventable diseases; to purchase vaccine; and for assessment, surveillance, outbreak control, information and education, and volunteer activities. Vaccine purchased with grant funds may be given to private practitioners but may not be sold to patients.

Eligible applicants/beneficiaries: states and, in consultation with state health authorities, political subdivisions and other public entities.

Range: $39,000 to $19,560,000. **Average:** $3,630,000.

Activity: FY 99-00 estimate, 64 grants.

HQ: same address/phones as **93.185**. *Grants management information*: same address/phone as **93.161**. (Note: no field offices for this program.)

93.271   ALCOHOL RESEARCH CAREER DEVELOPMENT AWARDS FOR SCIENTISTS AND CLINICIANS
("Research Career Awards" - "'K' Awards")

Assistance: project grants (100 percent/5 years).

Purposes: for research training related to alcohol abuse and alcoholism prevention, treatment, and rehabilitation. Funds may support five-year fellowships (ranging from $45,000 to $75,000 annually) and some research costs, including work by senior investigators.

Eligible applicants/beneficiaries: Mentored Research Scientist Development, Mentored Clinical Scientist Development, Independent Scientist, Senior Scientist, and Academic Career Awards—research centers, medical schools, departments of psychiatry, nonmedical academic departments, psychiatric hospitals or hospitals with psychiatric services, community mental health centers, biomedical research institutes, and departments of behavioral science. Researchers must have scholastic degree and previous training, and they must be U.S. citizens, nationals, or lawful permanent residents.

Range: $40,000 to $162,000. **Average:** $103,000.

Activity: FY 00 estimate, 68 grants.

HQ: NIAAA, NIH-HHS, 6000 Executive Blvd., Bethesda, MD 20892-7003. Phones: Director, Division of Basic Research, (301)443-2530; Director, Division of Clinical and Prevention Research, (301)443-1206; Director, Division of Biometry and Epidemiology, (301)443-4897. *Grants management information:* Grants Management Officer, NIAAA, NIH-HHS, Willco Bldg. - Ste.504, 6000 Executive Blvd., Bethesda, MD 20892-7003. Phone: (301)443-4704. (Note: no field offices for this program.)

93.272 ALCOHOL NATIONAL RESEARCH SERVICE AWARDS FOR RESEARCH TRAINING

Assistance: project grants (100 percent/to 6 years).

Purposes: for NRSA programs providing training in clinical research, treatment assessment research, problems of health promotion and alcoholism prevention, and basic biological and behavioral processes (*see Note preceding* **93.001**). Individual grants may cover up to five years for predoctoral or up to three years of postdoctoral full-time research training; M.D. and Ph.D. fellowships are for up to 6 years; senior fellowships are for up to two years. Predoctoral stipend awards are $11,748; postdoctoral, from $21,000 to $33,012. Special predoctoral fellowships are available for students with disabilities and for minority students. Recipients must meet payback requirements through a period of research and/or teaching after training is completed.

Eligible applicants/beneficiaries: domestic public or private nonprofit organizations. Predoctoral applicants must be enrolled in a doctoral degree program. Postdoctoral applicants must have a doctoral degree. All individual applicants must be U.S. citizens, nationals, or lawful permanent residents.

Range: $11,000 to $448,000. **Average:** $79,000.

Activity: FY 00 estimate, 44 fellowships; 28 institutional grants.

HQ: same addresses/phones as **93.271**, except for Division of Basic Research, *contact* Deputy Director. Phone: (301)443-2531. (Note: no field offices for this program.)

93.273 ALCOHOL RESEARCH PROGRAMS

Assistance: project grants (100 percent/to 5 years).

Purposes: for research on alcoholism and alcohol-related problems in such disciplines and subject areas as biomedical and genetic factors, psychological and environmental factors, medical disorders, health services, and prevention and treatment. Research Project Grants support clearly defined projects or small groups of related research activities, and research conferences. Program Project grants support large-scale, broad-based interdisciplinary research programs. Small Grants, limited to $50,000 for up to two years, are for small-scale exploratory and pilot studies or exploration of an unusual research opportunity. Exploratory/Developmental Grants are for treatment assessment, collaborative international or minority projects, or for research on the etiology of alcoholism—limited to $70,000 per year for two years. SBIR and STTR awards are made (*see Note preceding* **93.001**).

Eligible applicants/beneficiaries: public, private profit and nonprofit agencies including state, local, or regional government agencies, IHEs, hospitals, academic or research institutions.

Range: $10,000 to $773,000. **Average:** $238,000.

Activity: FY 00 estimate, 595 grants.

HQ: same addresses/phones as **93.271**, except for Division of Basic Research, *contact* Deputy Director. Phone: (301)443-2531. *And,* for SBIR, phone: (301)443-6107. (Note: no field offices for this program.)

93.274 CLINICAL TRAINING GRANT FOR FACULTY DEVELOPMENT IN ALCOHOL AND DRUG ABUSES

Assistance: project grants (100 percent/3-5 years).

Purposes: for clinical training of academically-based faculty in alcohol and drug abuse personnel training programs. Funds may be used to pay stipends and other allowances to trainees, and for institutional program costs.

Eligible applicants/beneficiaries: graduate schools of medicine, osteopathy, nursing, social work, or psychology. Trainees must be U.S. citizens, nationals, or lawful permanent residents.

Range: $50,000 to $200,000. **Average:** $135,000.

Activity: FY 99-00 estimate, 8 continuation awards.

HQ: Office of the Director, CSAP, SAMHSA-HHS, Rockwall II Bldg. - Rm.9012, Rockville, MD 20852. Phone: (301)443-9351. *Grants management information*: same address/phone as **93.101**. (Note: no field offices for this program.)

93.277 DRUG ABUSE SCIENTIST DEVELOPMENT AWARDS, RESEARCH SCIENTIST DEVELOPMENT AWARDS, AND RESEARCH SCIENTIST AWARDS
("Career Development Awards" - "'K' Awards")

Assistance: project grants (100 percent/to 5 years).

Purposes: to support individuals training for research on drug abuse and addiction. Awards are made to institutions on behalf of ultimate individual recipients. Salary support is from $45,000 to $75,000 annually, plus fringes. Limited research costs are allowable.

Eligible applicants/beneficiaries: research centers, medical schools, departments of psychiatry, nonmedical academic departments, psychiatric hospitals or hospitals with psychiatric services, community mental health centers, biomedical research institutes, and departments of behavioral science. Researchers must have scholastic degree and previous training, and they must be U.S. citizens, nationals, or lawful permanent residents.

Range: $44,000 to $469,000. **Average:** $114,000.

Activity: FY 99 estimate, 173 awards.

HQ: National Institute on Drug Abuse, NIH-HHS, Parklawn Bldg., 5600 Fishers Lane, Rockville, MD 20857. Phones: Director, Division of Basic Research, (301)443-1887; Director, Division of Clinical and Services Research, (301)443-6697; Director, Medications Development Division, (301)

443-6270; Director, Division of Epidemiology and Prevention Research, (301)443-6504; Research Training and Research Scientist Development Coordinator, (301)443-6071; Minority Research Programs, (301)443-6480. *Grants management information*: National Institute on Drug Abuse, same address. Phone: (301)443-6710. (Note: no field offices for this program.)

93.278 DRUG ABUSE NATIONAL RESEARCH SERVICE AWARDS FOR RESEARCH TRAINING

Assistance: project grants (100 percent/to 5 years).

Purposes: for NRSA programs providing training in the drug abuse field, including: basic and applied studies in the life sciences; behavioral and societal factors and epidemiology; experimental design methodology (*see Note preceding* **93.001**). The grants are directed toward young scientists at the predoctoral (annual stipend to $11,748 for up to five years) or postdoctoral (annual stipend of $21,000 to $33,012 for up to three years) levels for full-time work.

Eligible applicants/beneficiaries: same as for **93.272**.

Range: institutional, $92,000 to $529,000. **Average:** $253,000; predoctoral, $14,688; postdoctoral, $34,422.

Activity: FY 98, 101 fellowships, 38 institutional grants.

HQ: same addresses/phones as **93.277** *except:* Director, Division of Epidemiology and Prevention Research, (301)443-6071; Research Training Coordinator, (301)443-6036. (Note: no field offices for this program.)

93.279 DRUG ABUSE RESEARCH PROGRAMS

Assistance: project grants (100 percent/to 5 years).

Purposes: for epidemiology, basic, clinical, and applied research on the etiology, treatment, prevention, and consequences of drug addiction, including HIV/AIDS. Research project grants support clearly defined projects or small groups of related research activities, and research conferences. Program project and center grants support large-scale, broad-based interdisciplinary research programs. Small grants (up to $50,000 for up to two years) support less experienced investigators, testing of new methods and techniques, small-scale exploratory and pilot studies or exploration of an unusual research opportunity. First Independent Research Support and Transition Awards (FIRST) are for physicians, clinician-scientists, and researchers to develop their interest in research careers. SBIR and STTR awards are made (*see Note preceding* **93.001**).

Eligible applicants/beneficiaries: public, private, profit and nonprofit, foreign or domestic agencies, including state, local or regional government agencies, IHEs, hospitals, academic or research institutions.

Range: $10,000 to $4,438,000. **Average:** $339,000.

Activity: FY 99 estimate, 1,239 grants.

HQ: same addresses/phones as **93.277**, except for Director, Medications Development Division, phone (301)443-6173. *And,* SBIR: Phone: (301)443-6710. (Note: no field offices for this program.)

93.281   MENTAL HEALTH RESEARCH CAREER/SCIENTIST DEVELOPMENT AWARDS
("Career Development Awards" - "'K' Awards")

Assistance: project grants (100 percent/to 5 years).

Purposes: for research training in the problems of mental illness and mental health, through Mentored Research Scientist, Mentored Clinical Scientist, Mentored Scientist Development for New Minority Faculty, Independent Scientist, and Senior Scientist Awards. Fellowships range up to $75,000 annually. Some research costs may be supported.

Eligible applicants/beneficiaries: same as for **93.277**.

Range: $58,000 to $802,000. **Average:** $116,000.

Activity: FY 00 estimate, 373 awards.

HQ: NIMH, NIH-HHS, 5600 Fishers Lane, Rockville, MD 20857. Phones: Associate Director/Research Training and Research Development, Office of Science Policy and Program Planning, (301)443-4335; Director, Division of Neuroscience and Basic Behavioral Science, (301)443-3563; Director, Division of Mental Disorders, Behavioral Research and AIDS, (301)443-9700; Director, Division of Services and Treatment Research, (301)443-3266; Director/Special Populations, (301)443-2847. *Grants management information*: same address/phone as **93.242**. (Note: no field offices for this program.)

93.282   MENTAL HEALTH NATIONAL RESEARCH SERVICE AWARDS FOR RESEARCH TRAINING

Assistance: project grants (100 percent/to 6 years).

Purposes: for NRSA programs providing research training in mental health problems (*see Note preceding* **93.001**). Included are: basic biomedical, clinical neuroscience, and behavioral research; epidemiology of mental disorders; etiology, description, diagnosis, and pathogenesis of mental disorders; treatment development, assessment, and evaluation; public health intervention and prevention approaches. Grants for up to six years are directed toward young scientists at the predoctoral or postdoctoral level for full-time work. Career Opportunities in Research (COR) Honors Undergraduate grants are available to minority trainees competing successfully for entry into Ph.D. degree programs. Postdoctoral students receiving support for less than 12 months must meet payback requirements through an equivalent period of research and/or teaching after training is completed.

Eligible applicants/beneficiaries: training grants—domestic public or private nonprofit organizations. Applicants for predoctoral support must have completed at least two years of graduate work and be enrolled in a doctoral degree program. Postdoctoral applicants must have a Ph.D., Psy.D., M.D., D.D.S., Sc.D., D.N.S., D.O., D.S.W., or equivalent degree. COR Honors Undergraduate program awards—four-year IHEs or health professional schools whose enrollment is drawn substantially from ethnic groups.

Range: postdoctoral, $20,292 to $32,300; **Average:** predoctoral stipends, $11,496; COR honors undergraduate, $8,796.

Activity: FY 00 estimate, 295 individual, 196 institutional grants.

HQ: same addresses/phones as **93.242** (*no SBIR component*). (Note: no field offices for this program.)

93.283   CENTERS FOR DISEASE CONTROL AND PREVENTION— INVESTIGATIONS AND TECHNICAL ASSISTANCE

Assistance: project grants (100 percent/1-3 years).

Purposes: for state and local disease prevention and control programs, including communicable and chronic diseases such as tuberculosis, childhood immunization, and sexually transmitted diseases. Services include investigations, epidemic assistance, consultation, personnel training, responses to public health emergencies.

Eligible applicants/beneficiaries: states and their political subdivisions, local health authorities, and organizations with specialized health interests.

Range/Average:: N.A.

Activity: not quantified specifically.

HQ: Chief, Grants Management Branch, Procurement and Grants Office, CDCP-HHS, 2920 Brandywine Rd. - Rm.3000, Atlanta, GA 30341. Phone: (770)488-2700. (Note: no field offices for this program.)

93.288   NATIONAL HEALTH SERVICE CORPS SCHOLARSHIP PROGRAM ("NHSC Scholarship Program")

Assistance: project grants (100 percent/1-4 years).

Purposes: for scholarships to full-time students in the health professions. Disciplines include: allopathic and osteopathic medicine; nurse practitioners; nurse midwifery; primary care physician assistants; and, other disciplines needed by the NHSC. Scholarship recipients must perform one year of service in a federally-designated health manpower shortage area for each year of support received, or a minimum of two years; however, service deferments may be granted to complete residencies in family practice, internal medicine, pediatrics, and OB/GYN. Service sites also may be located in the territories or possessions.

Eligible applicants/beneficiaries: U.S. citizens or nationals.

Range: $935 monthly stipend plus tuition and other fees.

Activity: FY 99 estimate, 326 first-time awards.

HQ: Chief, Scholarship Programs Branch, Division of Scholarships and Loan Repayments, Bureau of Primary Health Care, HRSA-HHS, 4350 East-West Hwy. - 10th floor, Bethesda, MD 20814. Phones: *public information,* (301) 594-4410; *toll-free from outside Maryland,* (800)638-0824. (Note: no field offices for this program.)

93.289   PRESIDENT'S COUNCIL ON PHYSICAL FITNESS AND SPORTS

Assistance: technical information.

Purposes: to provide professional assistance in the design, development, improvement, and implementation of physical fitness programs, as well as expanded exercise and sports participation opportunities for all age groups. This is accomplished through publications and media campaigns, and in coordination with school systems, government agencies, employee and industrial organizations, recreation and park departments, communications media, etc.—not with organizations with a commercial interest in physical fitness. No funding is provided.

Eligible applicants/beneficiaries: general public.

Activity: annually, responses to 50,000 requests.

HQ: Executive Director, President's Council on Physical Fitness and Sports, Office of Public Health and Science, OS-HHS, 200 Pennsylvania Ave. NW - Ste.738H, Washington, DC 20201-0004. Phones: (202)690-5187; Director of Communications, (202)690-9000; FAX (202)690-5211. (Note: no field offices for this program.)

93.291 SURPLUS PROPERTY UTILIZATION
("Federal Property Assistance Program")

Assistance: sale, exchange, or donation of property and goods.

Purposes: to convey or lease surplus federal real property needed and usable in health programs including research—e.g., land and buildings for use as hospitals, clinics, public health administration, water and sewer systems, rehabilitation programs, and facilities for the homeless. Discounts of up to 100 percent of value may be granted. Deed restrictions apply for 30 years for land, and lesser periods for improvements.

Eligible applicants/beneficiaries: states, political subdivisions and instrumentalities; public and nonprofit health institutions.

Activity: FY 98, over $11,355,000 in real property transferred.

HQ: Director, Division of Property Management, Program Support Center, HHS, Parklawn Bldg. - Rm.5B-41, 5600 Fishers Lane, Rockville, MD 20857. Phones: (301)443-2265; FAX (202)443-0084. (Note: no field offices for this program.)

93.298 NURSE PRACTITIONER AND NURSE MIDWIFERY EDUCATION PROGRAMS

Assistance: project grants (100 percent/to 3 years).

Purposes: for nursing education programs including training of family, pediatric, geriatric, and adult nurse practitioners and nurse midwife trainees.

Eligible applicants/beneficiaries: public or private nonprofit schools of nursing or other entities.

Range: $36,000 to $502,000. **Average:** $244,000.

Activity: FY 99, 32 awards.

HQ: same address as **93.124**. Phone: (301)443-6333. *Grants management information*: same address/phone as **93.107**. (Note: no field offices for this program.)

93.299 ADVANCED NURSE EDUCATION

Assistance: project grants (100 percent/to 5 years).

Purposes: for programs for the advanced training of registered nurses at the master's and doctoral levels, preparing them to serve as nurse educators, public health nurses, or in clinical nurse specialties.

Eligible applicants/beneficiaries: public and private nonprofit collegiate schools of nursing.

Range: $116,000 to $361,000. **Average:** $217,000.

Activity: FY 99 estimate, 60 awards.

HQ: same address as **93.124**. Phone: (301)443-6333. *Grants management information*: same address/phone as **93.107**. (Note: no field offices for this program.)

93.306   COMPARATIVE MEDICINE

Assistance: project grants (100 percent/1-5 years).

Purposes: for research and resource projects enabling biomedical scientists to use animals and other research models, including marine invertebrates and vertebrates, in research on human health problems. Grants support the Regional Primate Research Centers (RPRC), the Biological Models and Materials Research (BMMR), and Laboratory Animal Science (LAS) programs—involving biotechnology, normative biology, and animal disease, animal welfare, and mammalian and nonmammalian models. Special Emphasis Research Center Awards (SERCA) support laboratory animal science by candidates with three years of postdoctoral experience. NRSA, SBIR, and STTR awards are available (*see Note preceding* **93.001**).

Eligible applicants/beneficiaries: IHEs, hospitals, other nonprofit and profit institutions and organizations, and individuals.

Range: RPRCs, $5,355,000 to $10,429,000; animal resources, $71,000 to $1,166,000; research projects, $83,000 to $691,000; SERCA, $60,000 to $92,000; training, fellowships, $25,000 to $272,000. **Average**: RPRCs, $7,231,000; animal resources, $401,000; research, $276,000; SERCA, $83,000; training, $162,000.

Activity: FY 00 estimate, 7 RPRC, 64 animal resources, 106 research project, 25 SERCA, 19 training and fellowship grants.

HQ: Director, Comparative Medicine, National Center for Research Resources, NIH-HHS, Bethesda, MD 20892. Phone: (301)435-0744. *Grants management information*: Grants Management Officer, Office of Grants and Contracts Management, National Center for Research Resources, NIH-HHS, Bethesda, MD 20892. Phone: (301)435-0844. (Note: no field offices for this program.)

93.333   CLINICAL RESEARCH

Assistance: project grants (100 percent/2-5 years).

Purposes: for research-based development of lifesaving drugs, devices, and therapies that protect human health—by providing research, research training, and infrastructure for clinical investigators. General Clinical Research Centers (GCRC) are supported to operate as discrete multi-departmental and multi-categorical inpatient and outpatient units where scientists correlate their laboratory studies with controlled clinical investigations and analyses. National Gene Vector Laboratories (NGVL) are supported through a cooperative agreement between the National Center for Research Resources, National Cancer Institute, National Heart, Lung, and Blood Institute, and National Institute of Diabetes, Digestive and Kidney Diseases. Training programs include Clinical Associate Physicians, Minority Clinical Associate Physicians, and Clinical Research Scholars programs. SBIR and STTR awards are available (*see Note preceding* **93.001**).

Eligible applicants/beneficiaries: medical schools, research hospitals, and other institutions.

Range: GCRCs, $373,000 to $4,913,000; NGVLs, $705,000 to $875,000. **Average:** GCRSs, $2,205,000; NGVLs, $809,000.

Activity: FY 99-00 estimate, 77 GCRCs, 3 NGVL awards; FY 00, 95 Clinical Associate Physician, 7 Minority Clinical Associate Physician, 1 Clinical Research Scholar awards.

HQ: Director, Clinical Research, National Center for Research Resources, NIH-HHS, Bethesda, MD 20892-7965. Phone: (301)435-0790. *Grants management information*: same address/phone as **93.306**. (Note: no field offices for this program.)

93.342 HEALTH PROFESSIONS STUDENT LOANS, INCLUDING PRIMARY CARE LOANS/LOANS FOR DISADVANTAGED STUDENTS ("HPSL/PCL/LDS")

Assistance: direct loans (90 percent).

Purposes: for long-term, loans to full-time students in financial need or from disadvantaged backgrounds, preparing for the health professions. Students may borrow the cost of tuition and $2,500 per academic year. Payback service provisions apply. Third- and fourth-year medical and osteopathic medicine students may borrow additional funds to repay earlier educational loans; they must agree to enter and complete a primary health care residency training program not later than four years after graduating, and to practice primary health care until the loan is paid in full. The loan interest rate is 5 percent.

Eligible applicants: accredited public or nonprofit private schools located in states, territories, or possessions, providing a course of study leading to a degree of doctor of medicine, dentistry, osteopathy, pharmacy, optometry, podiatry, or veterinary medicine, or B.S. in pharmacy—or an equivalent degree. For LDS, applicant schools must have student recruitment and retention programs, minority health issues curricula, clinic services for minority groups, and mentor programs.

Eligible beneficiaries: full-time students in need of a loan, enrolled or accepted in an eligible course of study—that are U.S. citizens, nationals, or permanent residents of a state or territories or possessions.

Range: $25,000 to $150,000. **Average:** $48,000.

Activity: not quantified specifically.

HQ: same address/phone as **93.139**. (Note: no field offices for this program.)

93.358 PROFESSIONAL NURSE TRAINEESHIPS
("Nurse Traineeships" - "Traineeships for Registered Nurses")

Assistance: project grants (100 percent).

Purposes: for stipends to nurses at the master's or doctoral level, preparing full-time for careers as nurse educators, specialists, practitioners, or mid-wives, or public health nurses.

Eligible applicants: public or private nonprofit entities, providing full-time advanced education.

Eligible beneficiaries: U.S. citizens licensed as registered nurses, enrolled full-time in graduate courses toward a master's degree or doctoral program.

Range: $6,803 to $323,000; stipends, to $8,800 plus tuition and other expenses.

Activity: FY 99, 267 awards.

HQ: same address as **93.124**. Phone: (301)443-6193. *Grants management information*: same address/phone as **93.107**. (Note: no field offices for this program.)

93.359 NURSING—SPECIAL PROJECTS

Assistance: project grants (25-90 percent/to 5 years).

Purposes: for specified nursing education programs such as continuing education, increasing nursing skills in underserved areas, and providing long-term care fellowships for certain paraprofessionals.

Eligible applicants/beneficiaries: public and private nonprofit schools of nursing and other entities.

Range: $90,000 to $288,000. **Average:** $167,000.

Activity: FY 99 estimate, 12 new, 41 continuation grants.

HQ: same address as **93.124**. Phone: (301)443-9964. *Grants management information*: same address/phone as **93.107**. (Note: no field offices for this program.)

93.361 NURSING RESEARCH

Assistance: project grants (100 percent/to 5 years).

Purposes: for clinical and basic research to establish a scientific basis for the care of individuals across the life span—from management of patients during illness and recovery to the reduction of risks for disease and disability and the promotion of healthy lifestyles, and extending to: patients, families, and care givers; special needs of at-risk and underserved populations; improving clinical care settings; translating scientific advances into cost-effective health care; bioethical issues. The Centers Program: promotes interdisciplinary research; supports research training and career development activities; concentrates research resources on selected research areas through Core Centers for Nursing Research. NRSA, SBIR, and STTR awards are available (*see Note preceding* **93.001**).

Eligible applicants/beneficiaries: research—any corporation, public or private institution or agency, SBIR firm, or other legal entity whether profit or nonprofit; individuals. NRSA applicants must be registered professional nurses with a baccalaureate or master's degree in nursing or a related field.

Range: research, $31,000 to $806,000; NRSA, $16,000 to $806,000. **Average:** research, $276,000; NRSA, $24,000.

Activity: FY 00 estimate, 198 competing and noncompeting awards.

HQ: National Institute of Nursing Research, NIH-HHS, Bldg.45 - Rm.3AN-12, 45 Center Drive, Bethesda, MD 20892-6300. Phone: (301)594-6906. *Grants management information*: Grants Management Officer, National Institute of Nursing Research, NIH-HHS, Bldg.45 - Rm.3AN-32, 45 Center Drive, Bethesda, MD 20892-6301. Phone: (301)594-6869. (Note: no field offices for this program.)

93.364   NURSING STUDENT LOANS
("NSL")

Assistance: direct loans (90 percent).

Purposes: to capitalize revolving loans funds for nursing schools, to be used, in turn, for 5 percent long-term loans to students with financial needs. The maximum loan in any one year is $2,500, except $4,000 for each of the final two years of study; the total borrowed may not exceed $13,000.

Eligible applicants/beneficiaries: accredited public and private nonprofit schools of nursing.

Range: $500 to $4,000. **Average:** $1,830.

Activity: FY 99 estimate, 200 awards.

HQ: same address/phone as **93.139**. (Note: no field offices for this program.)

93.371   BIOMEDICAL TECHNOLOGY
("BTR")

Assistance: project grants (100 percent/3-5 years).

Purposes: to develop innovative technologies for biomedical research. Grants are intended to provide sophisticated research tools for research and training, to be shared and very large-scale, serving major multi-disciplinary, multi-categorical programs. Both centers and individual researchers are supported. Shared Instrument Grants (SIG) in amounts from $100,000 to $400,000 support acquisition of new or updating of existing state-of-the-art instruments used in biomedical research. Small grants are available for one-year pilot projects. SBIR and STTR awards are available (*see Note preceding* **93.001**).

Eligible applicants/beneficiaries: Biomedical Technology Resource grants (BTR)—nonprofit health professional schools, other academic institutions, state and local health agencies, hospitals, research organizations. SIG awards—institutions: that received at least three PHS biomedical or health-related behavioral research grants or cooperative agreements totaling at least $200,000 during the previous fiscal year; whose investigators have at least three NIH-funded required grants.

Range: BTR, $280,000 to $2,019,000 ($650,000/year limit); research projects, $50,000 to $544,000. **Average:** BTR, $901,000; research, $237,000.

Activity: FY 00 estimate, 63 BTR, 70 research project, 30 exploratory, 142 SIG, 72 SBIR and STTR grants.

HQ: Director, Biomedical Technology, National Center for Research Resources, NIH-HHS, Bethesda, MD 20892. Phones: (301)435-0755. *Grants management information*: same address/phone as **93.306**. (Note: no field offices for this program.)

93.375 MINORITY BIOMEDICAL RESEARCH SUPPORT ("MBRS")

Assistance: project grants (100 percent/4 years).

Purposes: to increase the number of minority faculty, students, and investigators engaged in biomedical research, by funding institution-based, health-related research and enrichment activities involving students with faculty. Grant programs include Support of Continuous Research Excellence (SCORE), Research Initiative for Scientific Enhancement (RISE), and Initiative for Minority Student Development (IMSD).

Eligible applicants/beneficiaries: two- and four-year IHEs and health professional schools with over 50 percent minority enrollment, or with significant but not necessarily over 50 percent minority enrollment if they have a history of encouragement and assistance to minorities; tribal governments; Alaskan Regional Corporations.

Range: $75,000 to $1,500,000 per year for 3-4 years.

Activity: FY 00 estimate, 131 grants.

HQ: Chief, MBRS Branch, National Institute of General Medical Sciences, NIH-HHS, 45 Center Drive, Bethesda, MD 20892-6200. Phone: (301)594-3900. *Grants management information*: Chief Grants Management Officer, National Institute of General Medical Sciences, same address. Phone: (301) 594-5135. (Note: no field offices for this program.)

93.379 GRANTS FOR GRADUATE TRAINING IN FAMILY MEDICINE ("Family Medicine Residency")

Assistance: project grants (100 percent).

Purposes: to develop and operate residency training programs in the practice of family medicine. Funds may not be used for construction, patient services, or student assistance.

Eligible applicants/beneficiaries: public and private nonprofit hospitals, schools of medicine or osteopathy, or health or educational entities.

Range: $8,155 to $296,000. **Average:** $120,000.

Activity: FY 00 estimate, no awards.

HQ: same addresses/phones as **93.181**.

93.389 RESEARCH INFRASTRUCTURE

Assistance: project grants (50-100 percent/1-5 years).

Purposes: for predominantly minority health professional and health-related sciences schools and graduate institutions to strengthen and augment their human and physical resources to conduct biomedical and/or behavioral research. In addition to faculty expansion and enhancement, funds may be used: to improve physical facilities; to renovate laboratories and animal facilities; to acquire research equipment; for faculty recruitment; for pilot research projects. Program objectives are accomplished through a variety of programs including: Research Centers in Minority Institutions (RCMI); Clinical Research Infrastructure Initiative (RCRII); Research Infrastructure in Minority Institutions Initiative (RIMI); Science Education Partnership Awards (SEPA), directed toward K-12 teachers and high school teachers to increase pupil interest in biomedical research careers and health professions; Institutional Development Awards (IDeA); Animal Facilities Improvement; and, NIH construction grants.

Eligible applicants/beneficiaries: RCMI—institutions in the U.S. and territories, with more than 50 percent minority enrollment, offering an M.D., D.D.S., D.V.M., or other doctoral degree in the health professions, or a Ph.D. in health-related sciences. RCRII—RCMI-eligible institutions affiliated with medical schools. RIMI—institutions with nearly 50 percent minority enrollment, offering baccalaureate or masters degrees (but not doctorates) in health-related fields. SEPA and IDeA—public and private nonprofit and profit institutions, including universities, colleges, school systems, professional organizations, science museums. NIH construction and Animal Facilities Improvement—nonprofit public and private entities.

Range: RCMI, $725,000 to $2,231,000 and to $1,000,000 in direct costs for core programs (with additional funding for AIDS-related activities and other special initiatives); RCRII, $639,000 to $1,066,000; SEPA, $73,000 to $261,000; NIH construction, $403,000 to $1,500,000; Animal Facilities Improvement, $192,000 to $700,000; IDeA, $61,000 to $339,000. **Average:** RCMI, $1,325,000; RCRII, $918,000; SEPA, $208,000, construction, $949,000; Animal Facilities, $526,000; IDeA, $253,000.

Activity: FY 00 estimate, RCMI, 17 grants and 2 dental research faculty and infrastructure awards; 6 clinical research awards; 32 SEPA awards; Animal Facilities Improvement, 18 awards; IDeA, 60 awards.

HQ: Director, Research Infrastructure, National Center for Research Resources, NIH-HHS, Bethesda, MD 20892. Phone: (301)435-0788. *Grants management information*: same address/phone as **93.306**. (Note: no field offices for this program.)

93.390 ACADEMIC RESEARCH ENHANCEMENT AWARD ("AREA")

Assistance: project grants (100 percent/to 3 years).

Purposes: for small-scale health-related research projects, including feasibility or pilot studies, at educational institutions that are not major participants in other NIH programs.

Eligible applicants/beneficiaries: educational institutions granting baccalaureate and higher degrees in the health sciences, and their faculty—with no major active awards from NIH.

Range: to $75,000.

Activity: FY 98, 150 grants.

HQ: Office of Extramural Programs, Office of Extramural Research, NIH-HHS, Bethesda, MD 20892-7910. Phones: (301)435-2691; FAX (301)4480-8443. (Note: no field offices for this program.)

93.392 CANCER CONSTRUCTION

Assistance: project grants (50 percent).

Purposes: to renovate existing or build new cancer research facilities to meet basic research or clinical space requirements, or laboratory safety, biohazard containment, and animal care standards. Proposed facilities must be part of an existing or developing cancer research program, and used for grant purposes for at least 20 years.

Eligible applicants/beneficiaries: public or private nonprofit agencies, institutions, corporations, organizations, or associations—in the states, possessions, or territories.

Range: $551,000 to $910,000. **Average:** $731,000.

Activity: FY 00 estimate, 2 awards.

HQ: Chief, Research Facilities Branch, Office of Centers, Training and Resources, National Cancer Institute (EPS-638), NIH-HHS, 6120 Executive Blvd., Bethesda, MD 20892. Phone: (301)496-8534. *Grants management information*: Grants Management Officer, National Cancer Institute (EPS-234), NIH-HHS, Bethesda, MD 20892. Phone: (301)496-7753. (Note: no field offices for this program.)

93.393 CANCER CAUSE AND PREVENTION RESEARCH

Assistance: project grants (100 percent/to 5 years).

Purposes: for research into the causes of cancer and to develop prevention mechanisms. Programs include: epidemiology; chemical, physical, and biological carcinogenesis; nutrition; immunology; field studies and statistics; organ site. Grant funds may be used for personnel and consultants, equipment, patient costs, laboratory animals, alterations, and renovations. SBIR and STTR awards are made (*see Note preceding* **93.001**).

Eligible applicants/beneficiaries: IHEs, hospitals, public agencies, nonprofit research institutions, or profit organizations.

Range: $13,000 to $4,006,000. **Average:** $336,000.

Activity: FY 00 estimate, 1,533 grants.

HQ: Director, Division of Cancer Control and Population Science, National Cancer Institute, NIH-HHS, 6130 Executive Blvd., Bethesda, MD 20892. Phone: (301)496-9600. *Grants management information*: same address/phone as **93.392**. (Note: no field offices for this program.)

93.394 CANCER DETECTION AND DIAGNOSIS RESEARCH

Assistance: project grants (100 percent/to 5 years).

Purposes: for research to improve cancer screening, early detection, and diagnostic techniques and methods. Grant funds may be used for patient costs, laboratory animals, equipment, renovations, alterations, personnel and consultant costs. SBIR and STTR awards are made (*see Note preceding* **93.001**).

Eligible applicants/beneficiaries: same as for **93.393**.

Range: $34,000 to $1,661,000. **Average:** $300,000.

Activity: FY 00 estimate, 524 awards.

HQ: Associate Director, Cancer Diagnosis Program, Division of Cancer Treatment, Diagnosis, and Centers, National Cancer Institute (EPN-700), NIH-HHS, 6130 Executive Blvd., Bethesda, MD 20892. Phone: (301)496-8639. *Grants management information*: same address/phone as **93.392**. (Note: no field offices for this program.)

93.395   CANCER TREATMENT RESEARCH

Assistance: project grants (100 percent/to 5 years).

Purposes: for fundamental, applied, and clinical cancer treatment research in all modes of therapy including surgery, radiotherapy, chemotherapy, and biological therapy. Supportive approaches include nutrition, stem cell and bone marrow transplantation, blood component replacement, toxicology, pharmacology. Grant funds may be used for patient costs, laboratory animals, alterations, renovations, personnel and consultant costs. SBIR and STTR awards are made (*see Note preceding* **93.001**).

Eligible applicants/beneficiaries: same as for **93.393**.

Range: $26,000 to $5,586,000. **Average:** $310,000.

Activity: FY 00 estimate, 1,277 grants.

HQ: Division of Cancer Treatment, Diagnosis, and Centers, National Cancer Institute, NIH-HHS, Bldg.31/3A44, 9000 Rockville Pike, Bethesda, MD 20892. Phone: (301)496-4291. *Grants management information*: same as address/phone **93.392**. (Note: no field offices for this program.)

93.396   CANCER BIOLOGY RESEARCH

Assistance: project grants (100 percent/to 5 years).

Purposes: for cancer biology research, including in the areas of nutrition, tumor biology, genetics, and immunology—toward the prevention, detection, diagnosis, and treatment of neoplastic diseases. Grant funds may be used for patient costs, laboratory animals, renovations, alterations, personnel and consultant costs. SBIR and STTR awards are made (*see Note preceding* **93.001**).

Eligible applicants/beneficiaries: same as for **93.393**.

Range: $38,000 to $244,000. **Average:** $258,000.

Activity: FY 00 estimate, 1,527 grants.

HQ: Deputy Director, Division of Cancer Biology, National Cancer Institute, NIH-HHS, 6130 Executive Blvd., Bethesda, MD 20892. Phone: (301)496-8636. *Grants management information*: same address/phone as **93.392**. (Note: no field offices for this program.)

93.397   CANCER CENTERS SUPPORT

Assistance: project grants (100 percent/to 5 years).

Purposes: to provide core funding for comprehensive and specialized cancer centers, supporting the coordination of interdisciplinary programs ranging from basic research to clinical investigation to population science. Funds may be used for professional staff, centralized shared resources and services, and recruitment. Generally, research projects are not supported as such; rather, grants enhance ongoing research.

Eligible applicants/beneficiaries: nonprofit research institutions with a peer-reviewed research base of $3,000,000.

Range: $20,000 to $6,400,000. **Average:** $2,290,000.

Activity: FY 00 estimate, 59 full center, 15 planning awards.

HQ: Chief, Cancer Centers Branch, Division of Cancer Treatment, Diagnosis, and Centers, NIH-HHS (EPN-502), 6130 Executive Blvd., Bethesda, MD 20892. Phone: (301)496-8531. *Grants management information*: same address/phone as **93.392**. (Note: no field offices for this program.)

93.398   CANCER RESEARCH MANPOWER

Assistance: project grants (100 percent/to 5 years).

Purposes: for biomedical training programs in basic, clinical, and cancer prevention research, and for fellowships to trainees under the NRSA program (*see Note preceding* **93.001**). Cancer Education Grants are also available to promote cancer education programs. Various career awards provide short-term support for students.

Eligible applicants/beneficiaries: IHEs, hospitals, public agencies, or non-profit research institutions; U.S. citizens or permanent residents. Cancer Education Grants, career awards—profit organizations.

Range: $6,787 to $739,000. **Average:** $111,000.

Activity: FY 00 estimate, 1,075 awards.

HQ: Chief, Cancer Training Branch, Division of Cancer Treatment, Diagnosis, and Centers, National Cancer Institute (EPN 520), NIH-HHS, 6130 Executive Blvd., Bethesda, MD 20892. Phone: (301)496-8580. *Grants management information*: same address/phone as **93.392**. (Note: no field offices for this program.)

93.399   CANCER CONTROL

Assistance: project grants (100 percent/to 5 years).

Purposes: for basic and applied research in cancer interventions. Programs include chemo-prevention, diet and nutrition, screening and early detection, community oncology and rehabilitation and pain management, special populations research, public health applications, and surveillance research. Grant funds may be used for patient costs, renovations, alterations, personnel and consultant costs, and laboratory animals. SBIR and STTR awards are made (*see Note preceding* **93.001**).

Eligible applicants/beneficiaries: same as for **93.393**.

Range: $11,000 to $2,686,000. **Average:** $356,000.

Activity: FY 00 estimate, 198 awards.

HQ: Deputy Director, Division of Cancer Prevention and Control, National Cancer Institute, NIH-HHS, Bldg. 31/10A49, 9000 Rockville Pike, Bethesda, MD 20892. Phone: (301)496-9569. Director, Division of Cancer Control and Population Science, National Cancer Institute (EPN 242), NIH-HHS, 6130 Executive Blvd., Bethesda, MD 20892. Phone: (301)496-6756. *Grants management information*: same address/phone as **93.392**. (Note: no field offices for this program.)

93.550   TRANSITIONAL LIVING FOR HOMELESS YOUTH

Assistance: project grants (90 percent/3 years).

Purposes: to provide long-term shelters and services assisting older homeless youth, age 16-21, in making a successful transition toward productive adulthood and self-sufficiency.

Eligible applicants/beneficiaries: state, local, tribal governments; territories, possessions; private nonprofit organizations.

Range: $100,000 to $200,000. **Average:** $150,000.

Activity: FY 9, 78 projects funded.

HQ: Associate Commissioner, Family and Youth Services Bureau, ACF-HHS, 330 C St, SW, Washington, DC 20447. Phone: (202)205-8102. (Note: no field offices for this program.)

93.551   ABANDONED INFANTS

Assistance: project grants (90 percent/to 4 years).

Purposes: to prevent the abandonment of infants and young children, especially those with HIV or drug-affected, and to provide them with appropriate services; to find homes for them, whether with their natural families, adoptive parents, or in foster care; to conduct residential programs; to provide respite care for families and care givers; to recruit and train service providers, from foster parents to case management staff to hospital staff.

Eligible applicants/beneficiaries: same as for **93.550**.

Range/Average: $100,000 to $450,000.

Activity: FY 98, 31 grants.

HQ: Children's Bureau, ACF-HHS, P.O. Box 1182, Washington, DC 20013. Phone: (202)205-8657. (Note: no field offices for this program.)

93.556   FAMILY PRESERVATION AND SUPPORT SERVICES

Assistance: formula grants (75 percent).

Purposes: pursuant to the Social Security Act, amendments, and other laws, for community-based family support programs promoting the well-being of children and families—by enhancing family functioning and child development; for family preservation services for those at risk or in crisis, including reunification, adoption promotion and support, preplacement and prevention, follow-up after foster or respite care, and improving parenting skills.

Eligible applicants/beneficiaries: states, territories, and certain tribes.

Range/Average: N.A.

Activity: FY 98, 102 grants.

HQ: Deputy Associate Commissioner, Children's Bureau, ACF-HHS, P.O. Box 1182, Washington, DC 20013. Phone: (202)205-8618.

93.557 EDUCATION AND PREVENTION TO REDUCE SEXUAL ABUSE OF RUNAWAY, HOMELESS AND STREET YOUTH ("Street Outreach Program")

Assistance: project grants (90 percent/3 years).

Purposes: pursuant to VCCLEA and other laws, to provide education and prevention services to runaway, homeless, and street youth that have been subjected to or are at risk of sexual exploitation or abuse, including—outreach, emergency shelter, survival aid, case management, treatment and counseling, information and referral, crisis intervention, and follow-up support.

Eligible applicants/beneficiaries: only private nonprofit agencies.

Range: $100,000 per year to $300,000 for three years.

Activity: new program listing in 1999. FY 98, 139 grants.

HQ: same address/phone as **93.550**.

93.558 TEMPORARY ASSISTANCE FOR NEEDY FAMILIES ("TANF")

Assistance: formula grants (to 5 years).

Purposes: pursuant to the Social Security Act as amended and PRWORA, to provide cash grants, work opportunities, and other services to needy families so that their children can be cared for in their own homes; to reduce dependency by promoting job preparation, work, and marriage; to reduce and prevent out-of-wedlock pregnancies; and, to encourage the formation and maintenance of two-parent families. Permitted uses of funds are flexible, based on state plans developed in consultation with local governments and private organizations, including: assistance to low-income households in meeting home heating and cooling costs; uses permitted predecessor Aid to Families with Dependent Children (AFDC), Job Opportunities and Basic Skills Training (JOBS), and Emergency Assistance (EA) programs; transferring limited amounts to the Child Care and Development Block Grant (CCDBG) and Social Services Block Grant (SSBG) programs; to meet contingencies. "High Performance Bonus" and "Decrease in Illegitimacy Bonus" funds may be awarded. States must meet specific maintenance-of-effort requirements, relating to superseded programs.

Eligible applicants/beneficiaries: states, specified tribes, territories.

Range: $21,781,000 to $3,733,818,000.

Activity: new program in FY 97. FY 98, all states, 15 tribal programs funded.

HQ: Director, Office of Family Assistance, ACF-HHS, Aerospace Bldg. - 5th floor, 370 L'Enfant Promenade SW, Washington, DC 20447. Phone: (202) 401-9275. *Tribal grants,* Director, Office of Community Services, same address. Phone: (no number provided).

93.559   FEDERAL LOANS FOR STATE WELFARE PROGRAMS ("TANF Loans to States")

Assistance: direct loans (to 3 years).

Purposes: pursuant to the Social Security Act as amended and PRWORA, to enable states to meet the family self-sufficiency goals of the TANF program (**93.558**). Loan funds may be used for the same purposes as the TANF program, including for welfare anti-fraud activities and to provide assistance to Indian families that have moved from tribal service areas. Loans bear interest at the current average market yield rate.

Eligible applicants/beneficiaries: same as for **93.558**.

Range/Average: N.A.

Activity: new program in FY 97. FY 98, no loans.

HQ: Office of Administration, ACF-HHS, P.O. Box 1182, Washington, DC 20013. Phone: (202)401-5069. (Note: no field offices for this program.)

93.560   FAMILY SUPPORT PAYMENTS TO STATES—ASSISTANCE PAYMENTS

Assistance: formula grants (varying match).

Purposes: to provide the federal share of Aid to Families with Dependent Children (AFDC) and of assistance to aged, blind or disabled persons in Guam, PR, and VI—enabling recipients to pay for food, shelter, clothing, and other daily living needs; to provide child care enabling recipients to participate in education and employment training programs, and to hold jobs; to provide temporary emergency assistance and special services; and to cover state administrative expenses. The federal grant ranges from 50 to 83 percent, depending on whether the state has a federally approved Medicaid Plan.

Eligible applicants/beneficiaries: state and local welfare agencies; territories, possessions.

Range: $2,613,000 to $2,387,080,000. **Average:** $192,952,000; monthly payments, $365.52 per family.

Activity: program ended June 30, 1997, superseded by **93.558**.

HQ: same address/phone as **93.558**.

93.563   CHILD SUPPORT ENFORCEMENT

Assistance: formula grants (66-100 percent).

Purposes: pursuant to the Social Security Act as amended, to enforce the collection of child support obligations of absent parents—and to locate absent parents, establish paternity, and obtain child, spousal, and medical support. (The federal share of collected sums are not applied directly toward child support payments.)

Eligible applicants: state agencies, DC, PR, VI, and Guam.

Eligible beneficiaries: all AFDC, foster care maintenance, and Medicaid payments applicants or recipients assigning support rights to the states; all ceasing to receive AFDC payments; individuals authorizing the continuation of support enforcement services; other individuals applying for services.

Range: $440,000 to $119,040,000. **Average:** $17,010,000.

Activity: FY 98, 54 grants.

HQ: Office of Child Support Enforcement, ACF-HHS, 370 L'Enfant Promenade SW - 4th floor, Washington, DC 20447. Phone: (202)401-9386.

93.564   CHILD SUPPORT ENFORCEMENT RESEARCH ("OCSE Research")

Assistance: project grants (95 percent/to 2 years).

Purposes: pursuant to the Social Security Act as amended, for innovative research and demonstration projects of regional and national significance to improve the administrative and services delivery aspects of child support payment enforcement programs.

Eligible applicants/beneficiaries: states; nonprofit and profit organizations.

Range: $29,000 to $909,000.

Activity: not quantified specifically.

HQ: Chief, Planning and Evaluation Branch, Policy and Planning Division, Office of Child Support Enforcement, ACF-HHS, 370 L'Enfant Promenade SW - 4th floor, Washington, DC 20447. Phone: (202)401-5368.

93.566   REFUGEE AND ENTRANT ASSISTANCE—STATE ADMINISTERED PROGRAMS

Assistance: direct payments/unrestricted use (100 percent).

Purposes: for resettlement assistance to eligible refugees from foreign countries including Cuban and Haitian entrants, including payments for up to eight months, medical and social services, English language training, case management, employment services. States may contract with other providers to offer such services.

Eligible applicants/beneficiaries: designated state agencies.

Range: $77,000 to $49,000,000.

Activity: FY 98, 75,000 refugees authorized; 46 states and DC with approved plans; 34 states and jurisdictions serving Cuban and Haitian entrants.

HQ: Office of Refugee Resettlement, ACF-HHS, 370 L'Enfant Promenade SW - 6th floor, Washington, DC 20447. Phone: (202)401-4732. (Note: no field offices for this program.)

93.567   REFUGEE ASSISTANCE—VOLUNTARY AGENCY PROGRAMS

Assistance: project grants (to 80 percent/3 years).

Purposes: to assist refugees in becoming self-supporting. The federal share is up to $1,400 per refugee. Funds may be used for transitional assistance, job training, English language training, case management, social services, and medical support.

Eligible applicants/beneficiaries: private nonprofit agencies with a Reception and Placement Grant from the Department of State.

Range: $410,000 to $23,782,000.

Activity: FY 98, 25,000 refugees assisted.

HQ: same address as **93.566**. Phone: (202)401-4559. (Note: no field offices for this program.)

93.568   LOW-INCOME HOME ENERGY ASSISTANCE ("LIHEAP")

Assistance: project grants (100 percent).

Purposes: for Energy Assistance Block Grants to states, enabling them to make payments to or on behalf of eligible low-income households for their home energy costs—either heating or cooling. Recipients may also receive energy crisis and weatherization assistance. Funds may support training and technical assistance to state and other jurisdictions administering the program, involving conferences, workshops, clearinghouses, and similar activities. Supplemental funds may be allocated to grantees that leverage nonfederal resources with their LIHEAP funds, under the Residential Energy Assistance Challenge Program (REACH).

Eligible applicants/beneficiaries: block grants—states, DC, tribal governments, specified territories. Training and technical assistance grants—states, tribes, tribal organizations, territories, public agencies, private nonprofit organizations, businesses applying jointly with private nonprofit organizations.

Range/Average: training and technical assistance, $250,000; block grants, $197 in individual payments.

Activity: FY 98, 5,500,000 households assisted.

HQ: Director, Division of Energy Assistance, Office of Community Services, ACF-HHS, 370 L'Enfant Promenade SW, Washington, DC 20447. Phones: (202)401-9351; FAX (202)401-5718. (Note: no field offices for this program.)

93.569   COMMUNITY SERVICES BLOCK GRANT ("CSBG")

Assistance: formula grants (100 percent).

Purposes: for community-based anti-poverty programs and projects toward the elimination of poverty, including employment services, elderly services, housing, educational services, health care, emergency health and food assistance, services to migrant and seasonal farm workers, coordination of various governmental and private services.

Eligible applicants: states, territories, tribes, tribal organizations.

Eligible beneficiaries: locally-based nonprofit community anti-poverty agencies and other eligible entities providing services to low-income individuals and families.

Range: $2,617,000 to $43,696,000.

Activity: FY 98, 163 grants.

HQ: Division of State Assistance, Office of Community Services, ACF-HHS, 370 L'Enfant Promenade SW, Washington, DC 20447. Phone: (202)401-9343. (Note: no field offices for this program.)

93.570   COMMUNITY SERVICES BLOCK GRANT—DISCRETIONARY AWARDS

Assistance: direct payments/specified use (100 percent/1-5 years).

Purposes: for nationally or regionally significant projects to alleviate the causes of poverty in distressed communities. Eligible activities include those that: promote full-time permanent jobs; provide income or ownership opportunities for community members; address needs for urban and rural housing repair and rehabilitation, or water and waste-water treatment; provide character-building activities for youth, including sports and physical fitness; involve significant new combinations or resources.

Eligible applicants/beneficiaries: economic development projects—private, locally initiated and governed nonprofit community development corporations. Other projects—states, cities, counties, private nonprofit organizations.

Range: $75,000 to $500,000. **Average:** $350,000.

Activity: FY 99, 134 awards.

HQ: Division of Community Discretionary Programs, Office of Community Services, ACF-HHS, 370 L'Enfant Promenade SW, Washington, DC 20447. Phone: (202)401-9345. (Note: no field offices for this program.)

93.571 COMMUNITY SERVICES BLOCK GRANT DISCRETIONARY AWARDS—COMMUNITY FOOD AND NUTRITION

Assistance: formula grants (100 percent); direct payments/specified use (100 percent/to 17 months).

Purposes: for community food and nutrition initiatives for low-income persons, which must be subgranted to eligible agencies. Competitive grants may be awarded for innovative approaches, including outreach and public education activities to inform unserved or underserved target groups of available nutrition services.

Eligible applicants/beneficiaries: formula grants—states, territories, possessions. Direct grants—state and local public and private nonprofit agencies.

Range: formula grants, $389 to $143,000; direct grants, $22,000 to $50,000. **Average:** formula, $27,000.

Activity: FY 98, 90 grants.

HQ: Office of Community Services, ACF-HHS, 370 L'Enfant Promenade SW, Washington, DC 20447. Phones: *formula grants,* Chief, CSBG Branch, (202)401-9343; *direct grants,* Division of Community Discretionary Programs, (202)401-9345. (Note: no field offices for this program.)

93.575 CHILD CARE AND DEVELOPMENT BLOCK GRANT

Assistance: formula grants (100 percent).

Purposes: to develop and provide child care policies and services mainly for working low-income families. Activities must include: comprehensive consumer education to parents and the public; increasing parental choice; resource and referral services; infant and toddler, and school-age services.

Eligible applicants: states, territories, possessions; tribal governments and organizations, Alaska native and native Hawaiian organizations.

Eligible beneficiaries: children under age 13 (19 if disabled), residing with a family with income not above 85 percent of the state median, in which at least one parent has a job or attends a job training or educational program, or needing or receiving protective services.

Range/Average: N.A.

Activity: FY 99 estimate, 310 grants.

HQ: Child Care Bureau, ACF-HHS, 330 C St. SW, Washington, DC 20447. Phone: (202)690-6782.

93.576 REFUGEE AND ENTRANT ASSISTANCE—DISCRETIONARY GRANTS

Assistance: project grants (to 100 percent/to 5 years).

Purposes: for projects promoting refugee self-sufficiency or addressing their special needs. Project examples: relocation from high welfare dependency areas to communities with favorable employment prospects; vocational training and employment services; micro-loans for start-up businesses.

Eligible applicants/beneficiaries: state and local governments, private non-profit organizations.

Range: $5,000 to $19,000,000.

Activity: FY 98 (representative), 67 community and family strengthening grants, 13 grants for micro-enterprise loans, 26 targeted assistance grants, 8 preferred community (relocation) grants.

HQ: same address as **93.566**. Phone: (202)401-4557. (Note: no field offices for this program.)

93.579 U.S. REPATRIATION PROGRAM

Assistance: direct loans (to 90 days).

Purposes: pursuant to the Social Security Act, to provide repayable temporary assistance, care, and treatment to persons returning to the U.S. from foreign travel—required because of physical or mental illness, destitution, or because of war, threat of war, or a similar crisis. Assistance may include money for food, shelter, clothing, transportation, and special services such as medical and psychiatric care and guidance counseling.

Eligible applicants/beneficiaries: U.S. citizens certified by the Department of State, referred to HHS.

Range/Average: N.A.

Activity: FY 98, 200 citizens assisted; 278 received group reception services.

HQ: same address as **93.566**. Phone: (202)401-4851. (Note: no field offices for this program.)

93.581 IMPROVING THE CAPABILITY OF INDIAN TRIBAL GOVERNMENTS TO REGULATE ENVIRONMENTAL QUALITY

Assistance: project grants (80 percent/1-3 years).

Purposes: to plan, develop, and implement tribal environmental regulatory programs pertaining to Indian lands, including: environmental protection regulations, ordinances, and laws; technical and operating capacity relating to both tribal and federal requirements; employee training and education; monitoring and enforcement; tribal court enforcement systems.

Eligible applicants/beneficiaries: federally-recognized tribes; incorporated nonfederally-recognized tribes; Alaska native villages; tribal governments; consortia.

Range: $50,000 to $250,000.

Activity: FY 98, 20 grants.

HQ: Administration for Native Americans, ACF-HHS, 370 L'Enfant Promenade SW - Rm.HHH-348-F, Washington, DC 20447. Phone: (202)690-6326. (Note: no field offices for this program.)

93.582 MITIGATION OF ENVIRONMENTAL IMPACTS TO INDIAN LANDS DUE TO DEPARTMENT OF DEFENSE ACTIVITIES

Assistance: project grants (95 percent/1-3 years).

Purposes: to identify DOD environmental impacts to tribal lands and Alaska native villages, and to plan, develop, and implement mitigation programs.

Eligible applicants/beneficiaries: federally-recognized tribes; incorporated nonfederally-recognized and state-recognized tribes; Alaska native villages, tribes, or tribal governing bodies; nonprofit Alaska native regional associations or corporations or native organizations with village-specific projects; other tribal or village organizations or consortia.

Range: $50,000 to $1,000,000.

Activity: FY 98, 17 grants awarded.

HQ: same address as **93.581**. Phone: (202)690-6420. (Note: no field offices for this program.)

93.583 REFUGEE AND ENTRANT ASSISTANCE—WILSON/FISH PROGRAMS

Assistance: project grants (100 percent).

Purposes: for demonstration projects promoting early employment and self-sufficiency of refugees, including Amerasian immigrants and Cuban and Haitian entrants—developed as alternative approaches to the state-administered program (**93.566**), emphasizing one or more of the following: (1) preclusion of refugees otherwise eligible for public assistance, with cash and medical assistance provided instead through specially designed alternatives programs; (2) elimination or modification of work disincentives, such as the 100-hour rule in AFDC-UP programs; (3) "front-loaded" services providing intensive services in the early months after arrival, constantly emphasizing early employment; (4) integration of case management, cash assistance, and employment services, generally under a single agency that works specifically with refugees.

Eligible applicants/beneficiaries: states, voluntary and other resettlement organizations.

Range: $385,000 to $2,931,000.

Activity: FY 98, 3 projects funded.

HQ: same address as **93.566**. Phone: (202)401-4559. (Note: no field offices for this program.)

93.584 REFUGEE AND ENTRANT ASSISTANCE—TARGETED ASSISTANCE

Assistance: formula grants (100 percent).

Purposes: for employment-related and other social services for refugees and entrants in areas of high concentrations and high welfare rates, including:

job development and placement; on-the-job training; business and employer incentives; job-related and vocational English language training.

Eligible applicants: state agencies providing assistance to counties and similar areas.

Eligible beneficiaries: refugees, Cuban and Haitian entrants, and certain Amerasians from Vietnam and their accompanying family members. (Refugees admitted under the private sector initiative are ineligible while covered under the sponsoring agency's agreement with the Department of State.)

Range: $195,000 to $8,389,000.

Activity: FY 98, 47 grants.

HQ: same address as **93.566**. Phone: (202)401-9246. (Note: no field offices for this program.)

93.586 STATE COURT IMPROVEMENT PROGRAM

Assistance: formula grants (75 percent).

Purposes: to improve the performance of state courts in their role in the continuum of care provided for families and children at risk, and to develop and implement alternative court systems. Funds may be used to assess areas in need of correction or added attention and to implement reforms.

Eligible applicants/beneficiaries: the highest state court in each state and DC.

Range/Average: N.A.

Activity: FY 98, 48 grants.

HQ: Children's Bureau, ACF-HHS, 330 C St. SW, Washington, DC 20447. Phone: (202)205-8709.

93.587 PROMOTE THE SURVIVAL AND CONTINUING VITALITY OF NATIVE AMERICAN LANGUAGES

Assistance: project grants (80 percent/1-3 years).

Purposes: to plan and implement programs to assure the survival and continuing vitality of native American languages. Project examples: development of specialized school curricula and language training programs including language immersion camps and master/apprentice programs; compilation and transcription of oral narratives.

Eligible applicants/beneficiaries: same as for **93.582** and incorporated nonprofit multipurpose community-based Indian organizations; urban Indian centers; public and private nonprofit agencies, tribally controlled community colleges, postsecondary vocational institutions, and IHEs serving native Hawaiians or native peoples from Guam, Samoa, Palau, or Northern Marianas; national or regional incorporated native American organizations.

Range: from $50,000 for planning to $125,000 for implementation.

Activity: FY 98, 48 grants.

HQ: Program Operations Division, same address as **93.581**. Phone: (202)690-6504. (Note: no field offices for this program.)

93.590 COMMUNITY-BASED FAMILY RESOURCE AND SUPPORT GRANTS

Assistance: formula grants (100 percent/3 years).

Purposes: pursuant to the Child Abuse Prevention and Treatment Act, to establish or expand statewide networks of community-based family resource services.

Eligible applicants: states, territories and possessions.

Eligible beneficiaries: children, families; organizations dealing with family resource programs.

Range/Average: N.A.

Activity: FY 98, 58 formula, 4 discretionary grants.

HQ: Office on Child Abuse and Neglect, ACF-HHS, 330 C St. SW, Washington, DC 20447. Phone: (202)205-0749. (Note: no field offices for this program.)

93.591 FAMILY VIOLENCE PREVENTION AND SERVICES/GRANTS FOR BATTERED WOMEN'S SHELTERS—GRANTS TO STATE DOMESTIC VIOLENCE COALITIONS

Assistance: formula grants (100 percent).

Purposes: pursuant to the Child Abuse Prevention and Treatment Act, VCCLEA, and other acts, for prevention and intervention activities conducted by state domestic violence coalitions, including: program coordination with and technical assistance to local programs and services providers; encouraging appropriate responses to domestic violence cases by judicial and law enforcement agencies; public education campaigns; training; related activities.

Eligible applicants/beneficiaries: statewide nonprofit coalitions in states, territories and possessions.

Range/Average: states, $164,000; territories and insular areas, $33,000.

Activity: FY 98, 53 grants.

HQ: Office of Community Services, ACF-HHS, 370 L'Enfant Promenade SW, Washington, DC 20447. Phone: (202)401-5529. (Note: no field offices for this program.)

93.592 FAMILY VIOLENCE PREVENTION AND SERVICES/GRANTS FOR BATTERED WOMEN'S SHELTERS—DISCRETIONARY GRANTS

Assistance: project grants (75 percent/1-5 years).

Purposes: pursuant to VCCLEA and other acts, to prevent family violence through projects intended to improve the design, delivery, and coordination of services addressing the problem. Project activities may involve information gathering, research, demonstrations, evaluation, establishing specialized national resource centers, a national hotline, and public education.

Eligible applicants/beneficiaries: public and private nonprofit or profit agencies, federally-recognized tribes, Alaska native villages or regional corporations.

Range/Average: N.A.

Activity: FY 99, 14 grants to organizations, 8 to HBCUs.

HQ: same address/phone as **93.591**. (Note: no field offices for this program.)

93.593   JOB OPPORTUNITIES FOR LOW-INCOME INDIVIDUALS ("JOLI Program")

Assistance: project grants (to 100 percent/to 5 years).

Purposes: to promote the financial self-sufficiency of welfare recipients and others with incomes below the official poverty level—through demonstration and evaluation projects that will create new jobs, self-employment, micro-enterprises, and business employment opportunities; and, technical and financial assistance to private community employers.

Eligible applicants: nonprofit Section 501(c)(3) or (4) organizations including community development corporations.

Eligible beneficiaries: TANF recipients and other low-income individuals.

Range/Average: $500,000.

Activity: not quantified specifically.

HQ: Division of Community Demonstration Programs, Office of Community Services, ACF-HHS, 370 L'Enfant Promenade SW, Washington, DC 20447. Phone: (202)401-5282. (Note: no field offices for this program.)

93.594   TRIBAL WORK GRANTS

Assistance: formula grants.

Purposes: to allow tribes to operate work programs available to their members.

Eligible applicants/beneficiaries: tribes or Alaska native organizations that conducted JOBS programs in FY 95.

Range: $5,187 to $1,753,000. **Average:** $98,000.

Activity: new program listing in 1997. FY 99, 78 grants.

HQ: Director, Office of Community Services, ACF-HHS, 370 L'Enfant Promenade SW - 5th floor, Washington, DC 20447. Phone: (202)401-9333.

93.595   WELFARE REFORM RESEARCH, EVALUATIONS, AND NATIONAL STUDIES

Assistance: project grants (75-100 percent/1-5 years).

Purposes: for research on the benefits, effects, and costs of various welfare reform interventions; for studies on the effects of different programs on welfare dependency, illegitimacy, teen pregnancy, employment rates, child well-being, and related areas; for demonstrations; for analyses and evaluations.

Eligible applicants/beneficiaries: governmental entities, IHEs, nonprofit and profit organizations.

Range: $10,000 to $2,000,000.

Activity: new program in FY 97. Not quantified specifically.

HQ: Office of Planning, Research and Evaluation, ACF-HHS, Aerospace Bldg. - 7th floor, 370 L'Enfant Promenade SW, Washington, DC 20447. Phones: (202)401-4535; FAX (202)205-3598.

93.596   CHILD CARE MANDATORY AND MATCHING FUNDS OF THE CHILD CARE AND DEVELOPMENT FUND

Assistance: formula grants (matching/2 years).

Purposes: pursuant to the Social Security Act as amended and PRWORA, to assist low-income families with child care by assisting states to: develop flexible child care programs and policies; promote choices by working parents in selecting suitable child care; provide education to help parents make informed child care choices; to implement state health, safety, licensing, and registration standards. At least 70 percent of grant funds must be used to provide child care assistance to families: receiving assistance under a state TANF program; attempting to work to "transition" off temporary assistance programs through work activities, or at risk of becoming dependent on temporary assistance programs. The matching rate is the same as under the Medicaid program.

Eligible applicants: states, DC, tribal governments and organizations, Alaska native corporations.

Eligible beneficiaries: same as for **93.575**.

Range/Average: amounts similar to federal payments received under previous programs—e.g., AFDC, transitional child care, at-risk child care programs.

Activity: new program in FY 97. FY 99 estimate, 304 grants.

HQ: same address/phone as **93.575**.

93.597   GRANTS TO STATES FOR ACCESS AND VISITATION PROGRAMS

Assistance: project grants (90 percent).

Purposes: pursuant to the Social Security Act as amended, for programs that support and facilitate access and visitation by noncustodial parents with their children. Eligible project activities include mediation, counseling, education, development of parenting plans, visitation enforcement, and development of guidelines for visitation and alternative custody arrangements.

Eligible applicants/beneficiaries: states, DC, PR, VI, Guam.

Range/Average: N.A.

Activity: new program in FY 97.

HQ: same address as **93.563**. Phone: (202)401-5364.

93.600   HEAD START

Assistance: project grants (80-100 percent).

Purposes: to operate Head Start Programs offering comprehensive health, education, nutrition, social, and other services to economically disadvantaged preschool children, including children of migratory workers and on Indian reservations; to involve parents in the program. Training and technical assistance grants may be awarded to Head Start agencies and to agencies providing services. At least 90 percent of project enrollment must be from families at or below OMB poverty guidelines or from AFDC families; at least 10 percent must be available for children with disabilities.

Eligible applicants: local governments, federally-recognized tribes, public or private nonprofit agencies. Subcontracts with other agencies are permitted.

Eligible beneficiaries: children from birth until their entry into school systems.

Range: $114,000 to $115,323,000. **Average:** $2,350,000.

Activity: FY 98, 1,630 grants awarded, 830,000 children enrolled.

HQ: Head Start, ACF-HHS, P.O. Box 1182, Washington, DC 20013. Phone: (202)205-8572.

93.601   CHILD SUPPORT ENFORCEMENT DEMONSTRATIONS AND SPECIAL PROJECTS

Assistance: project grants (100 percent/to 17 months).

Purposes: pursuant to the Social Security Act as amended and PRWORA, to improve the effectiveness of child support enforcement efforts on the regional and national levels, advancing the requirements of PRWORA.

Eligible applicants/beneficiaries: state human services umbrella and local public agencies; nonprofit organizations; Indian tribes and tribal organizations; consortia.

Range: $20,000 to $150,000.

Activity: new program listing in 1999. FY 99 estimate, 13 grants.

HQ: Special Assistant to the Director, Division of State and Local Assistance, Office of Child Support Enforcement, ACF-HHS, 370 L'Enfant Promenade SW - 4th floor, Washington, DC 20447. Phone: (202)401-4849.

93.602   NEW ASSETS FOR INDEPENDENCE DEMONSTRATION PROGRAM

Assistance: project grants (50 percent/5 years).

Purposes: for demonstration projects to establish and evaluate the effect of providing incentives to individuals and families to save a portion of their earned income specifically to obtain a postsecondary education, to purchase first homes, or to capitalize small businesses. 90.5 percent of federal and matching funds must be used to match deposits in Individual Development Accounts (IDAs) by participants; the maximum federal contribution is $2,000 per individual and $4,000 per household.

Eligible applicants: tax-exempt nonprofit organizations; state agencies; tribal organizations applying jointly with nonprofit organizations.

Eligible beneficiaries: individuals and members of households eligible for TANF or with adjusted incomes not exceeding the earned income amount specified in Section 32 of the Internal Revenue Code. Maximum net worth provisions apply.

Range/Average: $250,000.

Activity: new program in FY 99; 30 grants awarded.

HQ: Office of Community Services, ACF-HHS, 370 L'Enfant Promenade SW, Washington, DC 20447. Phone: (no number provided). (Note: no field offices for this program.)

93.603   ADOPTION INCENTIVE PAYMENTS

Assistance: formula grants (100 percent).

Purposes: pursuant to the Social Security Act as amended and the Adoption and Safe Families Act of 1997, to provide incentives to states to increase the number of foster child and special needs adoptions. Funds may also be used for post-adoption services to children.

Eligible applicants/beneficiaries: states.

Range/Average: $4,000 per foster child adoption, $2,000 per special needs child adoption—above the state base numbers of adoptions.

Activity: new program in FY 99.

HQ: Director, Division of Program Implementation, Children's Bureau, ACF-HHS, 330 C St. SW, Washington, DC 20202. Phone: (202)205-6733.

93.612   NATIVE AMERICAN PROGRAMS

Assistance: project grants (80-100 percent/1-3 years); direct loans.

Purposes: pursuant to Older Americans Act amendments and other acts, to improve the social and economic conditions of native Americans within their communities. Funds may be used for: governance projects; environmental regulatory enhancement; economic development projects; native language preservation and enhancement; social development projects; training and technical assistance; research and demonstration projects.

Eligible applicants/beneficiaries: public and private nonprofit agencies including governing bodies of tribes on federal and state reservations, Alaskan native villages and regional corporations, agencies serving Hawaii natives, organizations in urban or rural non-reservation areas, native American Pacific Islanders.

Range: tribal grants, $50,000 to $1,200,000; urban grants, $30,000 to $210,000. **Average:** tribal, $125,000; urban, $100,000.

Activity: FY 98 estimate, 225 grants.

HQ: Program Operations, same address as **93.581**. Phone: (202)690-6320. (Note: no field offices for this program.)

93.613   MENTAL RETARDATION—PRESIDENT'S COMMITTEE ON MENTAL RETARDATION

Assistance: technical information.

Purposes: to provide information services pertaining to mental retardation, including studies and coordination of federal, state, and local efforts.

Eligible applicants/beneficiaries: general public.

Activity: not quantified specifically.

HQ: Executive Director, President's Committee on Mental Retardation, ACF-HHS, Washington, DC 20201. Phone: (202)619-0634. (Note: no field offices for this program.)

93.623   RUNAWAY AND HOMELESS YOUTH

Assistance: project grants (to 90 percent/to 5 years).

Purposes: to establish and operate local centers for runaway and homeless youth and their families. Grants may fund: centers operated in a manner outside the law enforcement, child welfare, mental health, and juvenile justice systems—providing such services as counseling, food, clothing, after-care assistance, a national toll-free communication system, personnel training, research, demonstration, and service projects.

Eligible applicants/beneficiaries: public and private nonprofit agencies, and coordinated networks of such agencies.

Range: $200,000 to $350,000.

Activity: FY 99, 363 grants.

HQ: same address/phone as **93.550**.

93.630   DEVELOPMENTAL DISABILITIES BASIC SUPPORT AND ADVOCACY GRANTS

Assistance: formula grants (75-100 percent).

Purposes: to plan and provide comprehensive and coordinated services to developmentally disabled persons, enabling them to reach their maximum potential in the community and to assure the protection of their legal and human rights. Funds may support state and local costs of planning and administration of services.

Eligible applicants: state agencies, territories and possessions.

Eligible beneficiaries: persons age 5 or older with developmental disabilities attributable to a mental and/or physical impairment manifested before age 22, resulting in functional limitations and reflecting lifelong need for services in at least three of seven functional areas—including self-care, receptive and expressive language, learning, mobility, self-direction, capacity for independent living, economic self-sufficiency; infants and children under age 5, showing high probability of a developmental disability.

Range: from $350,000.

Activity: not quantified specifically.

HQ: Director, Program Operations Division, Administration on Developmental Disabilities, ACF-HHS, 370 L'Enfant Promenade SW, Washington, DC 20447. Phone: (202)690-5962.

93.631   DEVELOPMENTAL DISABILITIES PROJECTS OF NATIONAL SIGNIFICANCE

Assistance: project grants (varying match).

Purposes: to increase and support the independence, productivity, and integration into communities of developmentally disabled persons. Grants support such nationally significant projects as those involving education of policy makers, data collection and analysis, federal inter-agency initiatives, technical assistance including for developing information and referral systems, improved supportive services, services to minorities with disabilities, transitional services for youth.

Eligible applicants/beneficiaries: state, local, public, or private nonprofit agencies and organizations.

Range: $75,000 to $200,000.

Activity: FY 99, 26 grants.

HQ: Program Development Division, same address as **93.630**. Phone: (202) 690-7693.

93.632   DEVELOPMENTAL DISABILITIES UNIVERSITY AFFILIATED PROGRAMS

Assistance: project grants (75-90 percent).

Purposes: to administer and operate university- or college-related programs for the developmentally disabled, including: interdisciplinary personnel training; technical assistance; information dissemination; or community demonstration projects including direct services to developmentally disabled persons—e.g., family and individual support, educational and vocational services; project feasibility studies.

Eligible applicants/beneficiaries: public or nonprofit entities associated with IHEs.

Range/Average: core support, $200,000; training, $83,000.

Activity: FY 98, 60 training, 61 core support grants.

HQ: same address/phone as **93.631**. (Note: no field offices for this program.)

93.643   CHILDREN'S JUSTICE GRANTS TO STATES

Assistance: formula grants (100 percent/2 years).

Purposes: pursuant to VOCA and other laws, to develop, establish, and operate improved response to and investigation and prosecution of child abuse and neglect cases, particularly cases of sexual abuse—including experimental, model, and demonstration programs, and legal and procedural reforms.

Eligible applicants/beneficiaries: states, territories, possessions.

Range: N.A.

Activity: FY 99, grants to 46 states, 5 territories.

HQ: same address as **93.590**. Phone: (202)205-8788. (Note: no field offices for this program.)

93.645   CHILD WELFARE SERVICES—STATE GRANTS

Assistance: formula grants (75 percent).

Purposes: pursuant to the Social Security Act, amendments, and other laws, for state and local child welfare services to enable children to remain in their own homes or to provide alternative permanent homes. Grants may cover costs of: personnel providing protective services; licensing and standard-setting for private child care organizations; return of runaway children; prevention and reunification services; homemaker services.

Eligible applicants/beneficiaries: state agencies, certain territories and possessions.

Range: $118,000 to $21,465,000. **Average:** $4,352,000.

Activity: FY 99, 179 grants awarded.

HQ: same address/phone as **93.556**.

93.647   SOCIAL SERVICES RESEARCH AND DEMONSTRATION

Assistance: project grants (75-100 percent/1-3 years).

Purposes: pursuant to the Social Security Act as amended, for innovative research projects to test, demonstrate, and evaluate new concepts in social services for children and families. Project examples: evaluation of welfare-to-work strategies; TANF implementation studies; "Responsible Fatherhood" demonstration.

Eligible applicants/beneficiaries: governmental entities, IHEs, nonprofit or profit organizations.

Range: $30,000 to $1,000,000.

Activity: not quantified specifically.

HQ: same address as **92.595**. Phones: (202)205-4829; FAX (202)205-3598.

93.648   CHILD WELFARE SERVICES TRAINING GRANTS

Assistance: project grants (100 percent).

Purposes: pursuant to the Social Security Act as amended, for programs to train child welfare program personnel. Previous projects examples include child welfare fellowships, tenured faculty development.

Eligible applicants/beneficiaries: IHEs.

Range/Average: $75,000.

Activity: FY 99, 57 grants.

HQ: Children's Bureau, ACF-HHS, 330 C St. SW, Washington, DC 20447. Phone: (202)205-8405.

93.652   ADOPTION OPPORTUNITIES

Assistance: project grants (100 percent/1-5 years).

Purposes: for demonstration projects to improve adoption practices, including methods, training, and information gathering. Funds support resource centers, the National Adoption Exchange, adoptive parent groups.

Eligible applicants/beneficiaries: grants—state or local governments, nonprofit IHEs and organizations. Contracts—public and private nonprofit agencies and organizations.

Range: $50,000 to $500,000.

Activity: FY 99, 108 grants.

HQ: same address as **93.648**. Phone: (202)205-8914. (Note: no field offices for this program.)

93.658   FOSTER CARE—TITLE IV-E

Assistance: formula grants (50-83 percent).

Purposes: pursuant to the Social Security Act as amended and other laws, for state and local foster child programs, including payments on behalf of the children, and training and administrative costs.

Eligible applicants: states, DC.

Eligible beneficiaries: children that are (or would be) eligible under AFDC, need foster care, and cared for by state agencies.

Range/Average: N.A.

Activity: FY 99, 339,000 children receiving monthly benefits.

HQ: same address/phone as **93.556**.

93.659   ADOPTION ASSISTANCE

Assistance: formula grants (varying rates).

Purposes: pursuant to the Social Security Act, amendments, and other laws, for adoption subsidy payments for adopted children with special needs. The subsidies are available from the time of adoption placement to age 18 (or older for certain handicaps).

Eligible applicants: states, DC.

Eligible beneficiaries: children that: are recipients of or eligible for AFDC, AFDC-FC, or SSI; have special needs, e.g., handicapped so as to require adoption assistance for placement.

Range: N.A.

Activity: FY 98, 170,000 children assisted monthly.

HQ: same address/phone as **93.556.**

93.667   SOCIAL SERVICES BLOCK GRANT

Assistance: formula grants (100 percent).

Purposes: pursuant to the Social Security Act, amendments, and other laws, to provide social services to: prevent, reduce, or eliminate dependency; achieve or maintain self-sufficiency; prevent neglect, abuse, or exploitation of persons; prevent or reduce inappropriate institutional care; enable individuals to secure admission or referral for institutional care when other forms of care are inappropriate. Funds may be used for activities relating to preventive health, mental health, substance abuse, and maternal and child health, as well as low-income home energy assistance. Ineligible uses include cash payments for subsistence or for room and board, medical care, health or prison facility social services, educational services, and most real estate costs—unless specifically approved by HHS.

Eligible applicants/beneficiaries: states, certain territories and possessions.

Range: $97,000 to $333,169,000. **Average:** $50,000,000.

Activity: FY 99, 57 grants.

HQ: same address as **93.571.** Phone: (202)401-2333. (Note: no field offices for this program.)

93.669   CHILD ABUSE AND NEGLECT STATE GRANTS

Assistance: formula grants (100 percent/5 years).

Purposes: pursuant to JJDPA amendments and other acts, to operate, improve, and augment state child protective systems, including such activities as: reporting, investigation, management, legal representation, and prosecution of cases of child abuse and neglect; research; treatment of and services to abused children and their families; personnel training; public education and information; community-based programs.

Eligible applicants/beneficiaries: same as for **93.667.**

Range/Average: N.A.

Activity: FY 99, 57 grants.

HQ: same address as **93.648.** Phone: (202)205-2629.

93.670 CHILD ABUSE AND NEGLECT DISCRETIONARY ACTIVITIES

Assistance: project grants (varying match/to 5 years).

Purposes: for research, demonstration service improvement, information dissemination, and technical assistance projects—toward the prevention, assessment, and treatment of child abuse and neglect, including child sexual abuse.

Eligible applicants/beneficiaries: states, local governments, nonprofit organizations.

Range: $10,000 to $300,000. **Average:** $150,000.

Activity: FY 99, 68 grants.

HQ: same address as **93.648**. Phone: (202)205-6814. (Note: no field offices for this program.)

93.671 FAMILY VIOLENCE PREVENTION AND SERVICES/GRANTS FOR BATTERED WOMEN'S SHELTERS—GRANTS TO STATES AND INDIAN TRIBES

Assistance: formula grants (100 percent).

Purposes: pursuant to VCCLEA and other laws, to assist states and tribes in the prevention of family violence; to provide immediate shelter and other assistance to victims and their dependents. The program emphasizes community-based projects that provide shelter, counseling, advocacy, and self-help services to victims and their children. Funds may not be used to make payments to victims.

Eligible applicants/beneficiaries: states, territories and possessions, certain federally-recognized tribes.

Range: states, $440,000 to $2,101,000; tribes, $18,000 to $166,000.

Activity: FY 98, 230 grants to states and tribes.

HQ: same address/phone as **93.591**. (Note: no field offices for this program.)

93.674 INDEPENDENT LIVING

Assistance: formula grants.

Purposes: pursuant to the Social Security Act as amended and other laws, for state and local programs designed to assist youth receiving foster care maintenance payments, in making the transition to independent living. Funds may be used for skill development, education, or training related to program purposes. States receiving more than $25,000,000 must match the amount exceeding that sum.

Eligible applicants: states, DC.

Eligible beneficiaries: children age 16 and over, receiving foster care payments, until they reach age 21.

Range: $13,000 to $12,482,000.

Activity: FY 99-00 estimate, 51 grants.

HQ: same address as **93.556**. Phone: (202)205-8740.

93.767   STATE CHILDREN'S INSURANCE PROGRAM ("CHIP")

Assistance: formula grants (to 85 percent).

Purposes: for states to initiate and expand child health assistance to uninsured low-income children, including under state Medicaid programs. Coverage may not discriminate on the basis of diagnosis nor pre-existing condition—and must be coordinated with other public and private programs. Abortions may be provided only to save the life of the mother or if the pregnancy resulted from rape or incest.

Eligible applicants: states and territories with HHS-approved state plans.

Eligible beneficiaries: targeted low-income children whose family income exceeds Medicaid limits by no more than 50 percent, ineligible for Medicaid and not covered by other health insurance—not including families eligible for a state health benefits plan through employment with a state public agency.

Range: $118,000 (territories) to $858,921,000.

Activity: new program in FY 98.

HQ: Center for Medicaid and State Operations, HCFA-HHS, 7500 Security Blvd., Baltimore, MD 21244. Phone: (410)786-3870.

93.773   MEDICARE—HOSPITAL INSURANCE

Assistance: direct payments/specified use.

Purposes: pursuant to the Social Security Act as amended and other acts, to provide insurance coverage for treatment in hospitals and other care facilities for covered services to persons age 65 or over, to certain disabled persons, and to those with chronic renal disease. Benefits may be paid to participating and emergency hospitals, skilled nursing facilities, home health agencies, and hospice agencies—for inpatient hospital services and post-hospital extended care services incurred during a benefit period. For 1998, the beneficiary is responsible for a $768 inpatient hospital deductible, and varying coinsurance amounts according to the type and length of care received. Home health services are paid in full.

Eligible applicants/beneficiaries: persons age 65 or over and certain disabled persons. Nearly everyone that reached 65 before 1968 is eligible, including persons ineligible for cash Social Security benefits. Those reaching age 65 in 1968 or after and ineligible need some work credit to qualify for hospital insurance benefits, the amount of which depends on their age. Hospital insurance is also available to persons age 65 or over and otherwise ineligible, through payment of a monthly premium. Certain federal, state, and local government employees are also eligible, as are most persons with chronic kidney disease and requiring dialysis or transplant.

Range/Average: N.A.

Activity: FY 99 estimate, 38,964,000 persons insured.

HQ: Director, Center for Beneficiary Services, HCFA-HHS, 7500 Security Blvd. - Rm.C5-19-07, Baltimore, MD 21244. Phone: (410)786-2744.

93.774   MEDICARE—SUPPLEMENTARY MEDICAL INSURANCE

Assistance: direct payments/specified use.

Purposes: pursuant to the Social Security Act as amended and other acts, to provide medical insurance supplementing benefits obtainable under **93.773**. Benefits include payment of the reasonable fees for covered services furnished by physicians and other suppliers of medical services to elderly or disabled persons and to those with chronic renal disease, including services provided by hospitals and home health agencies. The beneficiary is responsible for an annual $100 deductible before benefits may begin; thereafter, Medicare pays 80 percent of the reasonable charges for covered services. The enrollee pays a monthly premium ($45.50 in 1999). Some states and other third-parties pay the premium on behalf of qualifying individuals.

Eligible applicants/beneficiaries: all persons age 65 and over, and those under age 65 eligible for hospital insurance benefits (see **93.773**)—voluntarily enrolled for supplementary medical insurance. Eligibility is available to U.S. citizen-residents or lawful permanent residents residing in the U.S. continuously for the previous five years.

Range/Average: N.A.

Activity: FY 98, payments on behalf of 36,639,000 enrollees; FY 99 estimate, 36,866,000 enrollees.

HQ: same address/phone as **93.774**.

93.775   STATE MEDICAID FRAUD CONTROL UNITS

Assistance: formula grants (75-90 percent).

Purposes: pursuant to the Social Security Act as amended, to investigate and prosecute fraud in state Medicaid programs.

Eligible applicants/beneficiaries: state government entities separate and distinct from the state Medicaid agency.

Range: $262,000 to $25,917,000. **Average:** $1,962,000.

Activity: currently, 47 states certified.

HQ: Director, State Medicaid Oversight and Policy Staff, Office of Inspector General, OS-HHS, Cohen Bldg. - Rm.5453, 330 Independence Ave. SW, Washington, DC 20201. Phones: (202)619-3557, (202)619-3557. (Note: no field offices for this program.)

93.777   STATE SURVEY AND CERTIFICATION OF HEALTH CARE PROVIDERS AND SUPPLIERS

Assistance: formula grants (100 percent).

Purposes: pursuant to the Social Security Act as amended, to monitor health care providers and suppliers to assure their compliance with federal regulatory health and safety standards and conditions of participation in Medicare and Medicaid programs.

Eligible applicants/beneficiaries: state agencies.

Range: Title XVIII, $16,000 to $20,600,000; Title XIX, $233,000 to $22,300,000.

Activity: FY 97, monitoring of 56,000 certified providers and suppliers.

HQ: Director, Disabled and Elderly Health Program Group, HCFA-HHS, 7500 Security Blvd., Baltimore, MD 21244. Phone: (410)786-6763.

93.778 MEDICAL ASSISTANCE PROGRAM
("Medicaid" - "Title XIX")

Assistance: formula grants (50-83 percent).

Purposes: pursuant to the Social Security Act as amended, for medical assistance payments on behalf of recipients of cash assistance, children, pregnant women, the elderly, and other eligible groups. States must provide: hospital in- and outpatient care; rural health clinic care; federally qualified health center services; other laboratory and X-ray services; nursing facility services; home health services for persons over age 21; pediatric or family nurse practitioner services; family planning services; early and periodic screening, diagnosis, and treatment for persons under age 21; nurse-midwife services. States may use funds to pay for Medicare premiums, copayments, and deductibles of eligible beneficiaries.

Eligible applicants: state and local welfare agencies.

Eligible beneficiaries: low-income persons over age 65 or blind or disabled, members of families with dependent children, low-income children and pregnant women; certain Medicare beneficiaries; in some states, medically-needy persons may apply to a state or local welfare agency for medical assistance.

Range: FY 99, $1,810,000 to $16,546,937,000. **Average:** $1,810,338,000.

Activity: FY 99 estimate, 33,200,000 medical assistance recipients.

HQ: Director, same address/phone as **93.767.**

93.779 HEALTH CARE FINANCING RESEARCH, DEMONSTRATIONS AND EVALUATIONS
("HCFA Research")

Assistance: project grants (to 95 percent/to 2 years).

Purposes: pursuant to the Social Security Act as amended, for analyses, experiments, demonstrations, and pilot projects to resolve major health care financing issues or to improve the administration of the Medicare and Medicaid programs. Priority areas for funding include: Medicare enrollment, delivery, and payment systems; measures of health care outcomes; improved access for vulnerable populations; improving consumer choice and health status.

Eligible applicants/beneficiaries: private nonprofit or profit organizations; public agencies including state Medicaid agencies.

Range: $25,000 to $1,000,000. **Average:** $235,000.

Activity: FY 98, 27 new cooperative agreement, 20 contract awards.

HQ: Director, Office of Strategic Planning Research and Demonstrations, HCFA-HHS, Central Bldg. - Rm.C-3-20-11, 7500 Security Blvd., Baltimore, MD 21244-1850. Phone: (410)786-6507.

93.820   SCHOLARSHIPS FOR STUDENTS OF EXCEPTIONAL FINANCIAL NEED ("EFN Scholarship")

Assistance: project grants (100 percent).

Purposes: for scholarships for full-time health professions students of exceptional financial need. The scholarships carry a service obligation, or penalties for failure to serve.

Eligible applicants: public or private nonprofit schools of medicine, dentistry, or osteopathy.

Eligible beneficiaries: U.S. citizens, nationals, or lawful permanent residents, including territories or possessions.

Range/Average: $19,000 per student per year.

Activity: FY 99 estimate, 179 participating schools.

HQ: same address/phone as **93.139.** (Note: no field offices for this program.)

93.821   CELL BIOLOGY AND BIOPHYSICS RESEARCH

Assistance: project grants (100 percent/to 5 years).

Purposes: for research on the structure and function of cells, cellular components, and their biological macromolecules—toward the prevention, treatment, and cure of diseases that result from disturbed or abnormal cellular activity; to develop and improve instruments, devices, and methodologies; to apply modern techniques of molecular structure analysis to develop anti-viral drugs for the treatment of AIDS. NRSA, SBIR, and STTR awards are available (*see Note preceding* **93.001**).

Eligible applicants/beneficiaries: public or private, profit or nonprofit IHEs, institutions, state and local governments, hospitals, laboratories, small businesses, individuals.

Range: $21,000 to $1,445,000. **Average:** $192,000.

Activity: FY 00 estimate, 1,759 grants.

HQ: Director, Division of Cell Biology and Biophysics, National Institute of General Medical Sciences, NIH-HHS, 45 Center Drive, Bethesda, MD 20892-6200. Phones: (301)594-0828; *SBIR/STTR information*, Deputy Associate Director/Extramural Affairs, (301)594-3910. *Grants management information*: same address/phone as **93.375.** (Note: no field offices for this program.)

93.822   HEALTH CAREERS OPPORTUNITY PROGRAM

Assistance: project grants (100 percent/to 3 years).

Purposes: to assist students from disadvantaged backgrounds to undertake education preparing them to enter a health or allied health profession. The program provides preparatory services, including recruitment, counseling, mentoring, preliminary education, information on financial aid, primary care exposure activities, scholarships, and stipends.

Eligible applicants/beneficiaries: public or private nonprofit health or educational entities including schools of medicine, osteopathy, public health, dentistry, veterinary medicine, optometry, pharmacy, allied health, chiropractic, podiatry; schools offering graduate programs in clinical psychology.

Range: $62,000 to $681,000. **Average:** $213,000.

Activity: FY 00 estimate, 101 awards.

HQ: Project Officer, Program Coordination Branch, Division of Disadvantaged Assistance, Bureau of Health Professions, same address/phone as **93.157**. *Grants management information*: same address as **93.107**. Phone: (301)443-6857. (Note: no field offices for this program.)

93.824   BASIC/CORE AREA HEALTH EDUCATION CENTERS ("AHEC")

Assistance: project grants (75 percent).

Purposes: to improve the distribution, quality, utilization, and efficiency of personnel in the health service delivery system, and to regionalize the educational responsibilities of health professions schools. Program funds may be used to initiate, expand, or maintain preceptorships, community-based primary care residency programs, continuing education for health professionals, recruitment and career awareness programs among minority and other elementary and secondary students—but not for construction, patient services, or student assistance.

Eligible applicants/beneficiaries: center cooperative agreements—public or nonprofit schools of medicine or osteopathy, consortia. Special initiatives grants—previously funded medical and osteopathic schools.

Range: $260,000 to $2,200,000. **Average:** $1,184,000.

Activity: FY 00 estimate, 10 continuation, 6-8 new or renewal awards.

HQ: Deputy Branch Chief, same addresses/phones as **93.107**. (Note: no field offices for this program.)

93.837   HEART AND VASCULAR DISEASES RESEARCH

Assistance: project grants (100 percent/1-5 years).

Purposes: for research and research training in prevention, education, and control activities related to heart and vascular diseases. Project funds may support salaries, equipment, and patient hospitalization costs required to perform the research effort. NRSA, SBIR, and STTR awards are available (*see Note preceding* **93.001**).

Eligible applicants/beneficiaries: nonprofit and profit organizations engaged in biomedical research.

Range: $5,000 to $2,748,000. **Average:** $312,000.

Activity: FY 00 estimate, 2,472 research grants, 306 NRSAs; 52 Phase I, 21 Phase II SBIR awards.

HQ: Deputy Director, Division of Heart and Vascular Diseases, National Heart, Lung, and Blood Institute, NIH-HHS, Bethesda, MD 20892. Phone: (301) 435-0477. *SBIR information*: Deputy Director, Division of Extramural Affairs, same address. Phone: (301)435-0266. *Grants management information*: same address/phone as **93.233**. (Note: no field offices for this program.)

93.838   LUNG DISEASES RESEARCH

Assistance: project grants (100 percent/to 5 years).

Purposes: for research and research training concerning lung diseases, and to improve their prevention and treatment. Project funds may support animal research, salaries, equipment, and patient hospitalization costs required to perform the research effort. NRSA, SBIR, and STTR awards are available (*see Note preceding* **93.001**).

Eligible applicants/beneficiaries: same as for **93.837**.

Range: $2,000 to $1,944,000. **Average:** $291,000.

Activity: FY 00 estimate, 991 research grants, 100 NRSAs.

HQ: Director, Division of Lung Diseases, National Heart, Lung, and Blood Institute, NIH-HHS, Bethesda, MD 20892. Phones: (301)435-0233; *SBIR information:* Deputy Director, Division of Extramural Affairs, same address. Phone: (301)435-0266. *Grants management information:* same address/ phone as **93.233**. (Note: no field offices for this program.)

93.839   BLOOD DISEASES AND RESOURCES RESEARCH

Assistance: project grants (100 percent/to 5 years).

Purposes: for research and research training toward the improved diagnosis, treatment, and prevention of blood diseases; to improve the availability, safety, and use of blood and blood products. Project funds may support salaries, equipment, and patient hospitalization costs required to perform the research effort. NRSA, SBIR, and STTR awards are available (*see Note preceding* **93.001**).

Eligible applicants/beneficiaries: same as for **93.837**.

Range: $4,965 to $2,498,000. **Average:** $351,000.

Activity: FY 00 estimate, 720 research grants, 74 NRSAs.

HQ: Director, Division of Blood Diseases and Resources, National Heart, Lung, and Blood Institute, NIH-HHS, Bethesda, MD 20892. Phones: (301) 435-0080; *SBIR information:* Deputy Director, Division of Extramural Affairs, same address. Phone: (301)435-0266. *Grants management information:* same address/phone as **93.233**. (Note: no field offices for this program.)

93.846   ARTHRITIS, MUSCULOSKELETAL AND SKIN DISEASES RESEARCH

Assistance: project grants (100 percent/to 5 years).

Purposes: for basic research, research training, and clinical investigations concerning all aspects and forms of arthritis and musculoskeletal and skin diseases. NRSA, SBIR, and STTR awards are available (*see Note preceding* **93.001**).

Eligible applicants/beneficiaries: individuals, public and private nonprofit or profit institutions proposing to establish, expand, and improve research activities in health sciences and related fields.

Range: research, $10,000 to $1,500,000; NRSA, $15,000 to $236,000. **Average:** research, $239,000; NRSA, $67,000.

Activity: FY 99 estimate, 941 research grants, 118 awards for 252 NRSAs, 40 SBIR awards.

HQ: Director, Extramural Program, National Institute of Arthritis and Musculoskeletal and Skin Diseases, NIH-HHS, Natcher Bldg. - Rm.5AS-13F,

45 Center Drive, Bethesda, MD 20892-6500. Phone: (301)594-2463. *SBIR and grants management information*: Grants Management Officer, Extramural Program, same address (*except,* Rm.5AS-49F). Phone: (301)594-3535. (Note: no field offices for this program.)

93.847 DIABETES, ENDOCRINOLOGY AND METABOLISM RESEARCH

Assistance: project grants (100 percent/to 5 years).

Purposes: for basic and clinical biomedical research and research training: in diabetes and related complications and in metabolic processes of diseases, including their causes, prevention, and treatment; and, in endocrinology. NRSA, SBIR, and STTR awards are available (*see Note preceding* **93.001**).

Eligible applicants/beneficiaries: same as for **93.846**.

Range: research, $17,000 to $2,098,000; NRSA, $3,000 to $264,000. **Average:** research, $180,000; NRSA, $62,000.

Activity: FY 00 estimate, 1,357 research grants; 144 awards for 402 NRSAs; 50 SBIR grants.

HQ: Director, Division of Diabetes, Endocrinology, and Metabolic Diseases, National Institute of Diabetes and Digestive and Kidney Diseases, NIH-HHS, 31 Center Drive, Bethesda, MD 20892-2560. Phones: (301)496-7348; SBIR, (301)594-8842. *Grants management information*: Grants Management Officer, Division of Extramural Activities, National Institute of Diabetes and Digestive and Kidney Diseases, NIH-HHS, 45 Center Drive, Bethesda, MD 20892-6600. Phone: (301)594-8854. (Note: no field offices for this program.)

93.848 DIGESTIVE DISEASES AND NUTRITION RESEARCH

Assistance: project grants (100 percent/to 5 years).

Purposes: for basic and clinical biomedical research and research training concerning digestive diseases and nutrition, including obesity, anorexia, bulimia, and other eating disorders. NRSA, SBIR, and STTR awards are available (*see Note preceding* **93.001**).

Eligible applicants/beneficiaries: same as for **93.846**.

Range: research, $27,000 to $1,439,000; NRSA, $19,000 to $215,000. **Average:** research, $165,000; NRSA, $72,000.

Activity: FY 00 estimate, 751 research grants, 101 awards for 282 NRSAs; 36 SBIR awards.

HQ: Director, Division of Digestive Diseases and Nutrition, National Institute of Diabetes and Digestive and Kidney Diseases, same address as **93.847**. Phones: (301)496-1333; SBIR, (301)594-8842. *Grants management information*: same address/phone as **93.847**. (Note: no field offices for this program.)

93.849 KIDNEY DISEASES, UROLOGY AND HEMATOLOGY RESEARCH

Assistance: project grants (100 percent/to 5 years).

Purposes: for basic and clinical biomedical research and research training concerning kidney diseases, urology, and hematology. NRSA, SBIR, STTR awards are available (*see Note preceding* **93.001**).

Eligible applicants/beneficiaries: same as for **93.846**.

Range: research, $15,000 to $1,647,000; NRSA, $9,168 to $220,000. **Average:** research, $171,000; NRSA, $74,000.

Activity: FY 00 estimate, 856 research awards; 93 awards for 238 NRSAs; 34 SBIR grants.

HQ: Director, Division of Kidney, Urologic and Hematologic Diseases, National Institute of Diabetes and Digestive and Kidney Diseases, same address as **93.847**. Phones: (301)496-6325; SBIR, (301)594-8842. *Grants management information*: same address/phone as **93.847**. (Note: no field offices for this program.)

93.853   CLINICAL RESEARCH RELATED TO NEUROLOGICAL DISORDERS

Assistance: project grants (100 percent/to 5 years).

Purposes: for clinical and basic research and research training concerning neurological disorders and stroke, and their diagnosis, prevention, epidemiology, and treatment through development of drugs and neural prostheses. The Division of Stroke, Trauma, and Neurodegenerative Disease supports research on stroke, traumatic brain and spinal cord injuries, Parkinson's and Alzheimer's diseases, brain tumors. The focus of the Division of Fundamental Neuroscience and Developmental Disorders is on cellular, molecular, and systems neuroscience, developmental neurobiology and disorders, and neurogenetics. The Division of Convulsive, Infectious, and Immune disorders supports research in areas including epilepsy, multiple sceloris, AIDS, and sleep and pain disorders. Clinical investigator and research career development awards are available to institutions for up to five years, for the development of young scientists for careers in independent research. "Re-Entry into the Neurological Sciences" awards are made to scientists that have been away from research for a least three years, to re-establish their skills. Special programs, including the Ernest Everett Just Faculty Research Career Development Award, support research and faculty development at minority institutions. NRSA, SBIR, and STTR awards are available (*see Note preceding* **93.001**).

Eligible applicants/beneficiaries: research grants—any public or private nonprofit or profit institution. Career program awards—U.S. citizens or permanent residents nominated and sponsored by a public or private nonprofit institution.

Range: research, $20,000 to $3,000,000; clinical investigator awards, $54,000 to $80,000; research career development awards, $40,000 to $70,000; NRSA institutional, $20,000 to $235,000; NRSA individual, $25,000 to $37,000. **Average:** research, $470,000; investigator, $70,000; research career, $60,000; NRSA institutional, $140,000; NRSA individual, $29,000.

Activity: FY 98-99 estimate, 117 competing research grants, 20 NRSAs.

HQ: National Institute of Neurological Disorders and Stroke, NIH-HHS, Federal Bldg. - Rm.1016, Bethesda, MD 20892. Phones: *training and special programs,* (301)496-4188; *fundamental neurosciences and development disorders,* (301)436-5745; *convulsive, infectious and immune disorders,* (301)496-6541; *stroke, trauma, and neurogenerative disease,* (301)496-

2581. *Grants management information*: Grants Management Officer, National Institute of Neurological Disorders and Stroke, NIH-HHS, Federal Bldg. - Rm.1012, Bethesda, MD 20892. Phone: (301)496-9231. (Note: no field offices for this program.)

93.855 ALLERGY, IMMUNOLOGY AND TRANSPLANTATION RESEARCH

Assistance: project grants (100 percent/to 7 years).

Purposes: to establish, expand, and improve biomedical research and research training in allergic and immunologic diseases, including asthma, AIDS, transplantation biology, and related areas including genetics. Research Career Development Awards are available to institutions for up to five years, to train young scientists for careers of independent research. NRSA, SBIR, and STTR awards are available (*see Note preceding* **93.001**).

Eligible applicants/beneficiaries: same as for **93.821**.

Range: research projects, $1,000 to $919,000; NRSA, $2,837 to $679,000. **Average:** projects, $226,000; NRSA, $122,000.

Activity: FY 00 estimate, 1,207 awards.

HQ: Director, Division of Extramural Activities, National Institute of Allergy and Infectious Diseases, NIH-HHS, Bethesda, MD 20892. Phone: (301)496-7291. *Grants management information*: Grants Management Officer, Grants Management Branch, same address. Phone: (301)496-7075. (Note: no field offices for this program.)

93.856 MICROBIOLOGY AND INFECTIOUS DISEASES RESEARCH

Assistance: project grants (100 percent/to 7 years).

Purposes: for biomedical research and research training related to microbiology and infectious diseases. Program aims include the control of disease caused by infectious or parasitic agents including AIDS. Studies are supported on the mechanisms of antibiotics, as well as epidemiological observations in hospitalized patients or community populations. Research Career Development Awards are available to institutions for up to five years, to train young scientists for careers in independent research. NRSA, SBIR, and STTR awards are available (*see Note preceding* **93.001**).

Eligible applicants/beneficiaries: same as for **93.821**.

Range: research, $1,000 to $15,305,000; NRSA, $4,000 to $429,000. **Average:** research, $299,000; NRSA, $82,000.

Activity: FY 99 estimate, 2,687 grants.

HQ: same addresses/phones as **93.855**. (Note: no field offices for this program.)

93.859 PHARMACOLOGY, PHYSIOLOGY, AND BIOLOGICAL CHEMISTRY RESEARCH

Assistance: project grants (100 percent/to 5 years).

Purposes: for research and research training in chemistry, biochemistry, pharmacology, physiology, and biotechnology—to improve the understanding of biological processes at the molecular level, and to discover approaches to their control. Supported research areas include the mechanisms and actions of drugs and anesthetics drug discoveries, natural products synthesis, biological catalysis, physiologic processes induced by trauma and brain injury. NRSA, SBIR, and STTR awards are available (*see Note preceding* **93.001**).

Eligible applicants/beneficiaries: same as for **93.821**.

Range: $21,000 to $1,445,000. **Average:** $198,000.

Activity: FY 00 estimate, 1,411 research, center, and NRSA awards.

HQ: Director, Division of Pharmacology, Physiology, and Biological Chemistry, National Institute of General Medical Sciences, same address as **93.821**. Phones: (301)594-3827; *SBIR/STTR information*, Deputy Associate Director/Extramural Affairs, (301)594-3910. *Grants management information*: same address/phone as **93.375**. (Note: no field offices for this program.)

93.862 GENETICS AND DEVELOPMENTAL BIOLOGY RESEARCH

Assistance: project grants (100 percent/to 5 years).

Purposes: for research and research training aimed at the diagnosis, prevention, therapy, and cure of human genetic and developmental disorders. Development, gene regulation and structure, DNA replication, and control mechanisms for genetic expression for a range of organisms from viruses and bacteria to humans are studied. NRSA, SBIR and STTR awards are available (*see Note preceding* **93.001**).

Eligible applicants/beneficiaries: same as for **93.821**.

Range: $21,000 to $1,445,000. **Average:** $202,000.

Activity: FY 00 estimate, 1,479 research grants and NRSAs.

HQ: Director, Division of Genetics and Developmental Biology, National Institute of General Medical Sciences, same address as **93.821**. Phones: (301)594-0943; *SBIR/STTR information*, Deputy Associate Director/Extramural Affairs, (301)594-3910. *Grants management information*: same address/phone as **93.375**. (Note: no field offices for this program.)

93.864 POPULATION RESEARCH

Assistance: project grants (100 percent/to 5 years).

Purposes: for biomedical research and research training in the fundamental problems of reproductive processes; to develop safer and more effective contraceptives; to improve understanding of how population structure and change affect the health and well-being of individuals and society—including behavioral and demographic studies. NRSA, SBIR, and STTR awards are available (*see Note preceding* **93.001**).

Eligible applicants/beneficiaries: same as for **93.821**.

Range: research, $16,000 to $1,900,000. **Average:** research, $217,000; NRSA basic stipend first year beyond the doctoral degree, $22,000.

Activity: FY 99 estimate, 489 research grants, 225 NRSAs.

HQ: Director, Center for Population Research, National Institute of Child

Health and Human Development, NIH-HHS, Bldg. 61E - Rm.8B07, Bethesda, MD 20892-7510. Phones: (301)496-1101; FAX (301)496-0962. *Grants management information*: Chief, Grants Management Branch, National Institute of Child Health and Human Development, NIH-HHS, Bldg. 61E, Bethesda, MD 20892-7510. Phones: (301)496-5001; FAX (301)496-0915. (Note: no field offices for this program.)

93.865   CENTER FOR RESEARCH FOR MOTHERS AND CHILDREN

Assistance: project grants (100 percent/to 5 years).

Purposes: for fundamental and clinical, biomedical, and behavioral research and research training concerning the normal development of mothers and children from conception to maturity. Research supported includes: advance knowledge about fetal development, pregnancy, birth; prerequisites of optimal growth and development through infancy, childhood, and adolescence; prevention and treatment of mental retardation, developmental disabilities, and other childhood and adolescent problems. NRSA, SBIR, and STTR awards are available (*see Note preceding* **93.001**).

Eligible applicants/beneficiaries: IHEs; medical, dental, nursing, and public health schools; state and local health departments; hospitals; laboratories; other public or private profit or organizations; individuals.

Range: research, $50,000 to $5,000,000. **Average:** research, $311,000; NRSA basic stipend first year beyond the doctoral degree, $28,000.

Activity: FY 00, 867 research grants, 452 NRSAs.

HQ: Director, Center for Research for Mothers and Children, National Institute of Child Health and Human Development, NIH-HHS, Bldg. 61E - Rm.4B05, Bethesda, MD 20892-7510. Phones: (301)496-5097; FAX (301)480-7773. *Grants management information*: same address/phone as **93.864**. (Note: no field offices for this program.)

93.866   AGING RESEARCH

Assistance: project grants (100 percent/to 5 years).

Purposes: for biomedical, social, and behavioral research and research training concerning the aging process and the diseases, special problems, and needs people as they age—including geriatric research and research into genetic diseases and Alzheimer's, and social aspects of care and aging. NRSA, SBIR, and STTR awards are available (*see Note preceding* **93.001**).

Eligible applicants/beneficiaries: same as for **93.865**.

Range: research, $3,276 to $3,933,000; institutional NRSA, $3,386 to $428,000. **Average:** research, $297,000; institutional NRSA, $153,000; individual NRSA, basic stipend first year beyond doctoral degree, $21,000.

Activity: FY 00 estimate, 387 competing research grants, 22 competing NRSAs.

HQ: National Institute on Aging, NIH-HHS, Bethesda, MD 20892. Phones: *biology of aging*, (301)496-4996; *geriatrics and clinical research*, (301) 496-6761; *behavioral and social research*, (301)496-3136; *neuroscience and neuro-psychology*, (301)496-9350; *SBIR information*, (301)496-9322. *Grants management information*: Grants Management Officer, Office of

Extramural Affairs, National Institute on Aging, NIH-HHS, Bethesda, MD 20892. Phone: (301)496-1472. (Note: no field offices for this program.)

93.867 VISION RESEARCH

Assistance: project grants (100 percent/to 8 years for NRSA institutional award).

Purposes: for basic and applied research and research training projects addressing the leading causes of blindness and impaired vision, including retinal and corneal diseases, diabetic retinopathy, macular degeneration, cataract, glaucoma, strabismus, and amblyopia; for related projects including enhancement of the rehabilitation, training, and quality of life of persons who are partially-sighted or blind. Conference grants, core grants, mentored clinical scientist development awards, clinical vision research development awards, clinical study planning grants, and small grants for data analysis may be offered. NRSA, SBIR, and STTR awards are available (*see Note preceding* **93.001**).

Eligible applicants/beneficiaries: research grants, cooperative agreements, career development awards—IHEs, hospitals, laboratories, federal institutions; other public or private nonprofit and profit organizations including small businesses; state and local governments. Foreign institutions may apply for research grants only.

Range: research grants and cooperative agreements, $762 to $3,716,000; NRSA institutional, $1,080 to $316,000; NRSA individual, $3,964 to $66,000. **Average:** research, $238,000; institutional NRSA, $146,000; NRSA individual, $29,000.

Activity: FY 00 estimate, 1,316 grants including 278 NRSAs, 41 SBIR and STTR awards.

HQ: Research Resources Officer, National Eye Institute, NIH-HHS (EPS 350), 6120 Executive Blvd., Bethesda, MD 20892-7164. Phones: (301)496-5301; Internet, www.nei.nih/gov *Grants management information*: Chief, Grants Management Branch, same address. Phone: (301)596-5884. (Note: no field offices for this program.)

93.879 MEDICAL LIBRARY ASSISTANCE

Assistance: project grants (100 percent/to 5 years).

Purposes: for training programs for professional medical library personnel; for fellowships; to expand or improve existing medical libraries; for biomedical publications; for research in medical informatics and related sciences; for similar uses, including computer and telecommunications technology. SBIR and STTR awards are made (*see Note preceding* **93.001**).

Eligible applicants/beneficiaries: information access grants—public or private nonprofit institutions that maintain or plan to establish library and information services to clientele in the health professions. Information systems grants—nonprofit institutions whose primary function is the acquisition, preservation, dissemination, and/or processing of information relating to the health sciences. Internet connections grants—domestic, public or private nonprofit institutions engaged in health sciences administration, education, research, and/or clinical care. Integrated Advanced Information Management Systems grants—public or private nonprofit health sciences institutions or organizations. Scientific publication grants—appropriate public or private nonprofit IHEs may apply on behalf of the principal investigator for the project; in unusual circumstances, individuals may apply directly. Research grants—institutions with research capabilities in health information fields or in medical informatics. Training grants—nonfederal public and nonprofit private institutions. Fellowships—pre- or postdoctoral candidates. Trainees or fellows must be U.S. citizens, nationals, or lawful permanent residents.

Range: $12,000 to $1,800,000. **Average:** $30,000.

Activity: FY 99 estimate, 87 new and competing, 84 continuation grants.

HQ: Extramural Programs, National Library of Medicine, NIH-HHS, Bethesda, MD 20894. Phones: (301)496-4621, (301)594-4882; Web, www. nlm.nih/gov/ep/extramural.html *Grants management information*: Grants Management Officer, same address. Phones: (301)496-4221; Scientific Review Administrator, (301)496-4253. (Note: no field offices for this program.)

93.880   MINORITY ACCESS TO RESEARCH CAREERS ("MARC")

Assistance: project grants (100 percent/to 5 years).

Purposes: to assist minority institutions in supporting traineeships for undergraduate honors students, and for graduate and postdoctoral students preparing to become biomedical scientists and teachers in health-related fields. NRSAs are available (*see Note preceding* **93.001**). Faculty fellowships and visiting scientist awards may be granted.

Eligible applicants/beneficiaries: any nonfederal public or private nonprofit four-year university or college with substantial enrollment of ethnic minority students; individuals.

Range: $17,000 to $706,000. **Average:** $121,000.

Activity: FY 99 estimate, 207 NRSAs.

HQ: Chief, MARC Branch, National Institute of General Medical Sciences, same address/phone as **93.375**. *Grants management information*: same address/phone as **93.375**. (Note: no field offices for this program.)

93.884   GRANTS FOR RESIDENCY TRAINING IN GENERAL INTERNAL MEDICINE AND/OR GENERAL PEDIATRICS ("Primary Care Training")

Assistance: project grants (100 percent).

Purposes: for graduate education programs leading to the practice of general internal medicine or general pediatrics. Grants may not be used for construction, patient services, or student assistance.

Eligible applicants/beneficiaries: accredited public or private nonprofit schools of medicine or osteopathy, hospitals, or other entities.

Range: $108,000 to $295,000.

Activity: FY 99, 39 awards.

HQ: same address/phone as **93.181**. *Grants management information*: same address/phone as **93.107**.

93.886   PHYSICIAN ASSISTANT TRAINING IN PRIMARY CARE ("Physician Assistant Training Program")

Assistance: project grants (100 percent).

Purposes: to plan, develop, and operate or maintain training programs for physician assistants, including faculty training. Grants may not be used for construction, patient services, or student assistance.

Eligible applicants/beneficiaries: state and local government entities; private nonprofit health or educational institutions.

Range: $52,000 to $299,000. **Average:** $141,000.

Activity: FY 99, 42 continuation, 5 new grants. FY 00, no awards.

HQ: same addresses/phones as **93.181**. (Note: no field offices for this program.)

93.887   PROJECT GRANTS FOR RENOVATION OR CONSTRUCTION OF NON-ACUTE HEALTH CARE FACILITIES AND OTHER FACILITIES ("Section 1610(b) Program")

Assistance: project grants (80-100 percent).

Purposes: to renovate, expand, repair, equip, or modernize non-acute health care facilities, including for AIDS patients.

Eligible applicants/beneficiaries: public or private nonprofit entities.

Range from $100,000. **Average:** $5,000,000.

Activity: FY 99, 38 grants.

HQ: Director, Division of Facilities Compliance and Recovery, Office of Special Programs, HRSA-HHS, Twinbrook Metro Plaza Bldg. Ste. 520, 12300 Twinbrook Pkwy., Rockville, MD 20857. Phone: (301)443-4303. *Grants management information*: same address as **93.134**. Phone: (301)443-2385. (Note: no field offices for this program.)

93.891   ALCOHOL RESEARCH CENTER GRANTS

Assistance: project grants (100 percent/5 years).

Purposes: for core support of alcohol research centers, focusing multidisciplinary attention on the problems of alcohol use and alcoholism. The activities of investigators from biomedical, behavioral, and social sciences are coordinated at such centers.

Eligible applicants/beneficiaries: state and local governments; domestic, public or private nonprofit institutions—for centers affiliated with an institution such as a university, medical center, or research center with resources to sustain long-term coordinated research programs.

Range: $1,416,000 to $1,700,000. **Average:** $1,607,000.

Activity: FY 00 estimate, 15 grants.

HQ: Deputy Director, Division of Basic Research, NIAAA, same address as **93.271**. Phone: (301)443-2351. *Grants management information*: same address/phone as **93.271**. (Note: no field offices for this program.)

93.894 RESOURCE AND MANPOWER DEVELOPMENT IN THE ENVIRONMENTAL HEALTH SCIENCES ("Core Centers and Research Training Program")

Assistance: project grants (100 percent/to 5 years).

Purposes: for multidisciplinary research and research training on environmental health problems, at environmental health sciences centers and marine and freshwater biomedical sciences centers—consisting primarily of core support. NRSAs support individual pre- and postdoctoral training in environmental toxicology, pathology, mutagenesis, or epidemiology/biostatistics (*see Note preceding* **93.001**).

Eligible applicants/beneficiaries: centers—university-based, nonprofit research institutions, or profit organizations.

Range: centers, $237,000 to $1,617,000; NRSA, $12,000 to $700,000. **Average:** centers, $968,000; NRSA, $101,000.

Activity: FY 00 estimate, 21 center, 5 marine and freshwater biomedical center, and 51 individual and 62 institutional NRSA awards.

HQ: same address as **93.113**. Phones: *Centers Program,* Chemical Exposures and Molecular Biology Branch, (919)541-4943; *Research Training,* Organ and Systems Toxicology Branch, (919)541-7825. *Grants management information:* same address/phone as **93.113**. (Note: no field offices for this program.)

93.895 GRANTS FOR FACULTY DEVELOPMENT IN FAMILY MEDICINE

Assistance: project grants (100 percent).

Purposes: to increase the number of physician faculty teaching family medicine, and to enhance the pedagogical skills of present faculty. Fellowships (to two years) for faculty and workshops may be supported. Funds may not be used for construction, patient services, or student assistance.

Eligible applicants/beneficiaries: public or private nonprofit hospitals, schools of medicine or osteopathy, health or educational institutions.

Range: $48,000 to $311,000. **Average:** $171,000.

Activity: FY 99, 66 awards; FY 00, no awards.

HQ: Program Specialist, same address/phone as **93.181**. *Grants management information:* same address/phone as **93.107**.

93.896 GRANTS FOR PREDOCTORAL TRAINING IN FAMILY MEDICINE ("Predoctoral Training")

Assistance: project grants (100 percent).

Purposes: to plan, develop, operate, and maintain professional predoctoral training programs in family medicine. Grants may not pay for construction, patient services, or student assistance.

Eligible applicants/beneficiaries: nonprofit schools of medicine or osteopathy.

Range: $43,000 to $236,000. **Average:** $114,000.

Activity: FY 99 estimate, 64 continuation, 24 new awards.

HQ: same addresses/phones as **93.181**. (Note: no field offices for this program.)

93.897   RESIDENCIES AND ADVANCED EDUCATION IN THE PRACTICE OF GENERAL DENTISTRY

Assistance: project grants (100 percent/to 3 years).

Purposes: to plan, develop, and operate residency or advanced educational programs in the general practice of dentistry, including: personnel costs; financial assistance to trainees or residents; general program support costs; space renovation; equipment purchases.

Eligible applicants/beneficiaries: public or private nonprofit schools of dentistry or postgraduate dental training institutions in the states, territories, or possessions.

Range: $22,000 to $338,000. **Average:** $104,000.

Activity: FY 99 estimate, 19 continuation, 20 new awards.

HQ: same address as **93.117.** Phone: (301)443-4832. *Grants management information:* same address/phone as **93.107.** (Note: no field offices for this program.)

93.900   GRANTS FOR FACULTY DEVELOPMENT IN GENERAL INTERNAL MEDICINE AND/OR GENERAL PEDIATRICS
("GIM/GP Faculty Development")

Assistance: project grants (100 percent).

Purposes: to develop faculty skills in physicians (full- or part-time, volunteer, fellows, and/or residents) teaching or planning to teach in general internal medicine and/or general pediatrics training programs—emphasizing primary care. Grants may not be used for costs of construction, patient services, or student assistance.

Eligible applicants/beneficiaries: same as for **93.884.**

Range: $85,000 to $260,000. **Average:** $143,000.

Activity: FY 99 estimate, 20 continuation, 11 new awards.

HQ: same addresses/phones as **93.181.**

93.905   INDIAN HEALTH SERVICE RESEARCH

Assistance: project grants (100 percent).

Purposes: for research and development projects in various areas of concern within the functional health care responsibilities of the IHS. Projects may involve studies such as: basic epidemiology, preventive strategies and treatment alternatives involving chronic diseases, alcohol and substance abuse, mental health; health care for the elderly and estimates of demand for extended care services; involvement of professional nursing in reproductive health care, infant care, patient education; intervention alternatives for family dysfunction problems; health care delivery services systems.

Eligible applicants/beneficiaries: federally-recognized tribes or tribal organizations contracting with IHS; IHS components including service units and area offices.

Range: $9,000 to $50,000. **Average:** $30,000.

Activity: FY 99 estimate, 3 grants.

HQ: Program Coordinator, IHS Research Program, IHS-HHS, Headquarters West, 5300 Homestead Rd. NE, Albuquerque, NM 87110. Phone: (505)248-4141. *Grants management information*: same as **93.193**. (Note: no field offices for this program.)

93.906 RURAL HEALTH MEDICAL EDUCATION DEMONSTRATION PROJECTS

Assistance: direct payments/specified use (100 percent/3 years).

Purposes: to reimburse participating rural hospitals for the costs of graduate medical education projects conducted under the Social Security Act's Medicare provisions—involving medical residents, to enable physicians to develop clinical experience in rural areas. (Note: no funds are appropriated for this program; reimbursements are paid from the HI Trust Fund as they are approved.)

Eligible applicants/beneficiaries: public, private, nonprofit, or profit teaching hospitals that train medical residents in family medicine, osteopathic general practice, primary care internal medicine, or primary care pediatrics—and that currently receive payments for graduate medical education costs as defined under Medicare.

Range/Average: N.A.

Activity: no new awards anticipated.

HQ: same address (except Rm.9A-20)/phone as **93.181**. *Financial matters information*, HCFA-HHS, (301)966-5400. (Note: no field offices for this program.)

93.907 GRANTS FOR NURSE ANESTHETIST FACULTY FELLOWSHIPS

Assistance: project grants (to 100 percent).

Purposes: for fellowships to certified registered nurse anesthetist faculty members or adjunct faculty, for advanced education relevant to their teaching functions. Funds may not be granted for part-time study, nor to those employed on full-time salary.

Eligible applicants/beneficiaries: public or private nonprofit institutions.

Range: $4,236 to $144,000. **Average:** $32,000.

Activity: FY 98, 8 awards. FY 99, no awards.

HQ: same address as **93.124**. Phone: (301)443-6193. *Grants management information*: same address/phone as **93.107**. (Note: no field offices for this program.)

93.908 NURSING EDUCATION LOAN REPAYMENT PROGRAM FOR REGISTERED NURSES ENTERING EMPLOYMENT AT ELIGIBLE HEALTH FACILITIES

Assistance: project grants (100 percent).

Purposes: to repay education loans on behalf of nurses entering full-time employment at IHS or native Hawaiian health centers, public hospitals, migrant or rural health clinics, or certain other health facilities with critical shortages of nurses. Repayment agreements are made for not less than two consecutive years of service; amounts range from 30 percent of the unpaid initial principal and interest of qualified loans in return for the first year of service, to 85 percent for three years.

Eligible applicants/beneficiaries: licensed or license-eligible registered nurses that: will have received a diploma or academic degree in nursing prior to October 1 of the current fiscal year; will begin employment for two or three years at an eligible health facility; have unpaid educational loans obtained for their nursing education on the date their employment begins.

Range: $737 to $18,000. **Average:** $9,787.

Activity: FY 00 estimate, 200 contracts.

HQ: same address/phone as **93.162**. (Note: no field offices for this program.)

93.910   FAMILY AND COMMUNITY VIOLENCE PREVENTION PROGRAM ("Family Life Centers")

Assistance: project grants (100 percent/3 years).

Purposes: to establish a family and community violence consortium to prevent minority-related violence and to improve health and human services to minorities. Project examples: data base and resource directory on viable violence and substance abuse services and resources; establishment of positive education experiences for youth and families; community outreach services. Funds may not be used to cover real property costs.

Eligible applicants/beneficiaries: an IHE representing a consortium of HBCUs and predominantly Black colleges and universities.

Range/Average: cooperative agreement, $4,900,000.

Activity: FY 00, 1 continuation award.

HQ: same addresses/phones as **93.004**. (Note: no field offices for this program.)

93.912   RURAL OUTREACH—RURAL NETWORK DEVELOPMENT PROGRAM

Assistance: project grants (100 percent).

Purposes: to expand access to and improve rural primary health care services; to integrate and coordinate services among rural populations, including staff development; to foster linkages among eligible grant recipients—including mental health services, emergency services, prenatal care, free clinical services, prevention services.

Eligible applicants/beneficiaries: public or private nonprofit entities in rural areas, applying in conjunction with three or more entities.

Range: $50,000 to $200,000. **Average:** $175,000.

Activity: FY 99 estimate, 75 new, 100 continuation awards.

HQ: Senior Grant Programs Administrator, same address as **93.155**. Phone: (301)443-7529. *Grants management information*: same address/phone as **93.129**. (Note: no field offices for this program.)

93.913   GRANTS TO STATES FOR OPERATION OF OFFICES OF RURAL HEALTH

Assistance: project grants (25-75 percent/3 years).

Purposes: to improve health care in rural areas by establishing state offices of rural health. Funds must support information clearinghouses, coordination of state and federal programs, and technical assistance.

Eligible applicants/beneficiaries: states.

Range: $50,000 to $70,000.

Activity: FY 98, 50 noncompeting continuation grants.

HQ: Director, State Office of Rural Health Grant Programs, Office of Rural Health Policy, same address (except Rm.9A-55)/phone as **93.155**. *Grants management information*: same address/phone as **93.129**. (Note: no field offices for this program.)

93.915 HIV EMERGENCY RELIEF FORMULA GRANTS

Assistance: formula grants (100 percent).

Purposes: to develop, organize, and operate outpatient and ambulatory HIV-related health care and support services for patients and their families, including case management and comprehensive treatment services, substance abuse treatment, and mental health treatment; for inpatient case management services to prevent unnecessary hospitalization or to expedite discharge.

Eligible applicants/beneficiaries: metropolitan areas with populations of 500,000 or more, reporting more than 2,000 cases of AIDS during the most recent five years, per CDCP data.

Range/Average: N.A.

Activity: N.A.

HQ: Director, Division of Service Systems, HIV/AIDS Bureau, HRSA-HHS, 5600 Fishers Lane - Rm.7A-55, Rockville, MD 20857. Phones: (301)443-6745. *Grants management information*: same address/phone as **93.134** (Note: no field offices for this program.)

93.916 NURSE ANESTHETIST EDUCATION PROGRAMS

Assistance: project grants (100 percent/to 3-5 years).

Purposes: to develop and operate, maintain or expand nurse anesthetist education programs.

Eligible applicants/beneficiaries: public or private nonprofit institutions.

Range: $55,000 to $315,000. **Average:** $165,000.

Activity: FY 99, 5 continuation, 2 competing grants.

HQ: same address as **93.124**. Phone: (301)443-6193. *Grants management information*: same address/phone as **93.107**. (Note: no field offices for this program.)

93.917 HIV CARE FORMULA GRANTS

Assistance: formula grants (100 percent).

Purposes: to improve the quality, availability, and organization of health care and support services for persons with HIV disease and their families. Funds may be used: to develop or enhance outpatient and ambulatory health and support services, including case management and comprehensive treatment services, substance abuse treatment, and mental health treatment; for inpatient case management services to prevent unnecessary hospitalization or to expedite discharge; to establish and operate consortia; to provide home and community-based care services; to assure the continuity of health insurance coverage.

Eligible applicants/beneficiaries: states, territories and possessions.

Range: $11,000 to $87,884,000. **Average:** $9,631,000.

Activity: FY 98 estimate, grants to all states, DC, PR, 2 territories.

HQ: same addresses/phones as **93.915**. (Note: no field offices for this program.)

93.918 GRANTS TO PROVIDE OUTPATIENT EARLY INTERVENTION SERVICES WITH RESPECT TO HIV DISEASE

Assistance: project grants (100 percent/to 3 years).

Purposes: to improve the availability, accessibility, and organization of ambulatory services to persons infected with HIV or at high risk, and to offer early intervention services, including: counseling and testing; partner involvement in risk reduction; transmission prevention; primary care diagnosis and treatment; case management. Funds may not be used to acquire real property or to provide inpatient or residential care.

Eligible applicants/beneficiaries: public or private nonprofit: community health centers; family planning grantees under PHS Section 1001, other than states; comprehensive programs of primary health care; comprehensive hemophilia diagnostic and treatment centers.

Range: $100,000 to $650,000; planning, to $50,000. **Average:** $350,000.

Activity: 181 programs funded currently. FY 98, 10 new awards.

HQ: Director, HIV-AIDS Bureau, Division of Community Based Programs, HRSA-HHS, 5600 Fishers Lane - Rm.7-47, Rockville, MD 20857. Phone: (301)443-0759. *Grants management information*: same address as **93.134**. Phone: (301)443-2728. (Note: no field offices for this program.)

93.919 COOPERATIVE AGREEMENTS FOR STATE-BASED COMPREHENSIVE BREAST AND CERVICAL CANCER EARLY DETECTION PROGRAMS

Assistance: project grants (75 percent/1-5 years).

Purposes: to develop comprehensive breast and cervical cancer early detection programs; to increase screening and follow-up among all groups of women, especially those that are low-income, uninsured, under-insured, minority, or native Americans. Funds may be used for public education and outreach, referrals and follow-up services, staff training, project monitoring and evaluation—but not for treatment services.

Eligible applicants/beneficiaries: state health agencies, territories and possessions, tribes and tribal organizations.

Range: $125,000 to $5,000,000.

Activity: FY 98, 50 states, DC, 15 American Indian and Alaska native tribes, 5 territories funded.

HQ: Division of Cancer Prevention and Control, National Center for Chronic Disease Prevention and Health Promotion (MS K57), CDCP-HHS, 4770 Buford Hwy. NE, Atlanta, GA 30341. Phone: (404)488-4880. *Grants management information*: same address as **93.135**. Phone: (404)842-6817. (Note: no field offices for this program.)

93.923 DISADVANTAGED HEALTH PROFESSIONS FACULTY LOAN REPAYMENT AND FELLOWSHIP PROGRAM

Assistance: direct payments/specified use.

Purposes: to repay educational loans owed by health professionals from disadvantaged backgrounds, serving for at least two years on the full-time faculty of a school of medicine, nursing, osteopathy, dentistry, pharmacy, podiatry, optometry, veterinary medicine, public health, allied health, or graduate clinical psychology. Payments cover principal and interest up to $20,000 per year on government or commercial loans; unless waived, schools are required to pay 50 percent of the amount due for each year of service.

Eligible applicants/beneficiaries: health professionals from disadvantaged backgrounds with degrees or enrolled in approved graduate training programs, or enrolled as full-time students in their final course of study.

Range: $17,000 to $107,000. **Average:** $51,000.

Activity: FY 00 estimate, 20 awards.

HQ: *Disadvantaged faculty program,* Program Analysis Officer, same address as **93.139**. Phone: (301)443-1700. *Minority faculty fellowship program,* Program Specialist, Analysis and Evaluation Branch, Division of Disadvantaged Assistance, Bureau of Health Professions, HRSA-HHS, Parklawn Bldg. - Rm.8A-09, 5600 Fishers Lane, Rockville, MD 20857. Phone: (301) 443-1503. (Note: no field offices for this program.)

93.924 RYAN WHITE HIV/AIDS DENTAL REIMBURSEMENTS

Assistance: direct payments/specified use.

Purposes: to reimburse the uncompensated costs incurred by dental schools and postdoctoral dental education programs, for oral health services to patients with HIV/AIDS.

Eligible applicants/beneficiaries: public or private nonprofit schools of dentistry or postgraduate dental education programs in the states, territories, and possessions.

Range: $150 to $659,000. **Average:** $81,000.

Activity: FY 00 estimate, 100 awards.

HQ: Primary Care Services Branch, Division of Community Based Programs, HRSA-HHS, Parklawn Bldg. - Rm.774, 5600 Fishers Lane, Rockville, MD 20857. Phone: (301)443-1434. (Note: no field offices for this program.)

93.925 SCHOLARSHIPS FOR HEALTH PROFESSIONS STUDENTS FROM DISADVANTAGED BACKGROUNDS ("SDS")

Assistance: project grants (100 percent).

Purposes: for annual scholarships to full-time students from disadvantaged backgrounds, awarded by health professions schools that maintain special programs for enrollees, including: recruiting and retaining racial and ethnic minority faculty as well as students; instruction concerning minority health issues; mentor programs; arrangements with health clinics to provide services by the students to the disadvantaged; arrangements with secondary schools and undergraduate institutions to prepare targeted students to enter the health professions. At least 30 percent of funds must be allocated for nursing scholarships.

Eligible applicants: same as for **93.822.**

Eligible beneficiaries: U.S. citizens, nationals, or lawful permanent residents of states, territories, or possessions.

Range/Average: N.A.

Activity: FY 00 estimate, grants to 400 schools.

HQ: same address/phone as **93.139.** (Note: no field offices for this program.)

93.926 HEALTHY START INITIATIVE
("Targeted Infant Mortality Initiative")

Assistance: project grants (100 percent/to 5 years).

Purposes: for programs to reduce infant mortality and improve maternal and infant health, by targeting 15 high-rate communities and directing resources and interventions to improve access to, utilization of, and full participation in comprehensive service projects. Funds may be used to: develop outreach and case management programs to bring pregnant women into prenatal care early; increase the number of available primary care and obstetrical providers; link health departments, community health centers, state programs, and community residents in a joint effort to meet program objectives.

Eligible applicants/beneficiaries: in urban and rural communities with infant mortality rates of at least 15.7 per 1,000 live births—local or state health departments, publicly supported or nonprofit organizations, tribal organizations, or consortia. Applications must be approved by the chief elected officials, and endorsed by the state governor.

Range: $1,000,000 to $3,000,000.

Activity: FY 99-00 estimate, 98 grants.

HQ: Director, Division of Healthy Start, Maternal and Child Health Bureau, HRSA-HHS, Parklawn Bldg. - Rm.11A-05, 5600 Fishers Lane, Rockville, MD 20857. Phone: (301)443-0543. *Grants management information*: same address/phone as **93.110.**

93.927 HEALTH CENTERS GRANTS FOR RESIDENTS OF PUBLIC HOUSING

Assistance: project grants (100 percent/to 5 years).

Purposes: to improve the availability, accessibility, and provision of primary health services including comprehensive perinatal care for public housing residents. Funds may be used for health screening, counseling, and education—but not for inpatient services, cash payments to services recipients, real property costs, or motor vehicles.

Eligible applicants/beneficiaries: public and private nonprofit entities near public housing sites.

Range: $125,000 to $500,000.

Activity: FY 98, 21 continuation awards; FY 99, no new awards.

HQ: same addresses/phones as **93.151.**

93.928 SPECIAL PROJECTS OF NATIONAL SIGNIFICANCE ("SPNS")

Assistance: project grants (100 percent/5 years).

Purposes: to advance knowledge and skills in the delivery of health and support services to persons with HIV disease. Funds support innovative projects: for which implementation, costs, utilization, and outcomes can be evaluated rigorously; providing models unlikely to exist without SPNS support; that extend the care model to previously underserved or unserved populations.

Eligible applicants/beneficiaries: state and local public and private nonprofit entities including health departments, hospitals, IHEs, community-based organizations; national service provider organizations.

Range: $142,000 to $1,418,000. **Average:** $400,000.

Activity: FY 99-00 estimate, 50 continuation, 8 new awards.

HQ: Deputy Director, Office of Science and Epidemiology, HIV/AIDS Bureau, HRSA-HHS, Parklawn Bldg. - Rm.7A-08, 5600 Fishers Lane, Rockville, MD 20857. Phone: (301)443-7136. *Grants management information*: same address as **93.134**. Phone: (301)443-2385. (Note: no field offices for this program.)

93.929 CENTER FOR MEDICAL REHABILITATION RESEARCH ("CMRR")

Assistance: project grants (100 percent/to 5 years).

Purposes: for research and training in medical rehabilitation related to impairments, disabilities, and handicaps resulting from illnesses, injuries, or developmental processes. The program focuses on improvement in human functioning—physical, cognitive, behavioral, and social—through the application of new knowledge to the development of medical, behavioral, psychological, social, and technological interventions. NRSA, SBIR, and STTR awards are also available (*see Note preceding* **93.001**).

Eligible applicants/beneficiaries: IHEs; medical, dental, nursing, and public health schools; laboratories; hospitals; state and local health departments; public or private nonprofit or profit organizations; individuals.

Range: research projects, $37,000 to $800,000. **Average:** research projects, $245,000; fellowships (first-year postdoctoral stipend), $22,000.

Activity: FY 00 estimate, 77 project grants, 94 NRSAs.

HQ: National Center for Medical Rehabilitation Research, National Institute of Child Health and Human Development, NIH-HHS, 6000 Executive Blvd. - Rm.2A03, Bethesda, MD 20892-7510. Phones: (301)402-4221; FAX (301)402-0832. *Grants management information*: same address/phones as **93.864**. (Note: no field offices for this program.)

93.931 DEMONSTRATION GRANTS TO STATES FOR COMMUNITY SCHOLARSHIPS

Assistance: project grants (40 percent/to 3 years).

Purposes: for scholarship programs in urban and rural health professions shortage areas, to match contributions by both states and community organizations to health professions students. Scholarship recipients must agree to provide primary health care in the community organization's area for the greater of the number of years equal to the scholarship period or two years; however, communities may require a longer period.

Eligible applicants: states, DC.

Eligible beneficiaries: residents of health professions shortage areas, enrolled full-time in health professions schools.

Range: $5,000 to $100,000. **Average:** $39,000.

Activity: FY 99 estimate, 2 new awards.

HQ: same address/phone as **93.162**. *Grants management information:* same address/phone as **93.129**.

93.932   NATIVE HAWAIIAN HEALTH SYSTEMS

Assistance: project grants (83.3 percent/3 years).

Purposes: for programs raising the health status of native Hawaiians living in Hawaii, by providing comprehensive health promotion and disease prevention and primary health care services. Outreach, case management, and referral components should integrate traditional health concepts with western medicine, employing existing health resources as much as possible.

Eligible applicants/beneficiaries: public or nonprofit native Hawaiian health centers or organizations, as specifically defined by HHS regulations.

Range: $300,000 to $660,000.

Activity: FY 99-00 estimate, no new grants.

HQ: same addresses/phones as **93.151**.

93.933   RESEARCH AND DEMONSTRATION PROJECTS FOR INDIAN HEALTH

Assistance: project grants (100 percent/to 5 years).

Purposes: to promote improved health care among American Indians and Alaska natives, through research studies and demonstration projects addressing such issues as elder care, women's health care, and child protection and child abuse prevention.

Eligible applicants/beneficiaries: federally recognized tribes, tribal organizations, nonprofit inter-tribal or urban Indian organizations, public or private nonprofit health and education entities, state and local health agencies.

Range: $27,000 to $300,000. **Average:** $115,000.

Activity: FY 00 estimate, 25 projects.

HQ: *management,* same address/phone as **93.228**. *Programs address:* IHS-HHS, Parklawn Bldg., 5600 Fishers Lane, Rockville, MD 20857. Phones: *elder care initiative,* Senior Public Health Advisor (Rm.6A-55), (301)443-3024; *women's health demonstration,* Chief, Principal Nursing Consultant (Rm.6A-44), (301)443-1840. *Grants management information:* same address/phone as **93.193**. (Note: no field offices for this program.)

93.934   FOGARTY INTERNATIONAL RESEARCH COLLABORATION AWARD ("FIRCA")

Assistance: project grants (100 percent/to 3 years).

Purposes: for collaborative research efforts between U.S. and foreign scientists that will enhance the NIH-supported program of the U.S. principal investigator, while benefiting that of the collaborating foreign scientist. Funds may be used to cover costs of supplies, small equipment, travel.

Eligible applicants: U.S. institutions employing U.S. principal investigators.

Eligible beneficiaries: scientists and researchers. Foreign collaborators must hold a position at a public or private nonprofit institution in a developing country, and, for cancer-related research, Sub-Saharan Africa; for HIV or AIDS studies, the foreign collaborator may be located in most any country.

Range: $35,000.

Activity: FY 00 estimate, 28 competing, 105 noncompeting awards.

HQ: same addresses/phones as **93.106.** (Note: no field offices for this program.)

93.936 NATIONAL INSTITUTES OF HEALTH ACQUIRED IMMUNODEFICIENCY SYNDROME RESEARCH LOAN REPAYMENT PROGRAM ("AIDS-LRP")

Assistance: project grants (100 percent/from 2 years).

Purposes: for partial repayment of educational loans owed by physicians, registered nurses, and scientists employed by NIH in AIDS research. Recipients must have qualified educational debt exceeding 20 percent of their annual salary, and they must engage in research for a minimum of two years. Continuation contracts are available.

Eligible applicants/beneficiaries: AIDS researchers with an M.D., Ph.D., D.D.S., D.O., D.M.D., D.V.M., A.D.N., B.S.N., R.N., or equivalent degree, that: are U.S. citizens, nationals, or permanent residents; have no existing service obligation to federal, state, or other entities.

Range: per annum, to $20,000 for loan repayment, and to $7,800 for tax reimbursements. Maximum, $35,000; tax, $13,650. **Average:** loan, $24,000; tax, $9,296.

Activity: FY 00 estimate, 13 awards.

HQ: NIH Loan Repayment Program/AIDS Research, same address/phones as **93.187.** (Note: no field offices for this program.)

93.938 COOPERATIVE AGREEMENTS TO SUPPORT COMPREHENSIVE SCHOOL HEALTH PROGRAMS TO PREVENT THE SPREAD OF HIV AND OTHER IMPORTANT HEALTH PROBLEMS ("SHEPSA")

Assistance: project grants (100 percent/to 5 years).

Purposes: to develop and implement health education programs for HIV and other health problems for school-age populations (elementary through college), parents, and school, health, and education personnel. Funds may support costs of planning and conducting programs including personnel salaries, training, related travel, supplies, services, data collection, monitoring, preparation and dissemination of information including audiovisuals, technical assistance. Funds may not be used for research, surveys, computer and office equipment purchases, office space costs, construction or renovation—unless specifically approved.

Eligible applicants/beneficiaries: states, territories and possessions; large urban school districts with high HIV-AIDS rates; nonprofit organizations.

Range: $175,000 to $900,000. **Average:** $250,000.

Activity: FY 97-99, cooperation agreements in effect with 50 SEAs, territories and possessions, 18 LEAs. FY 98, new competitive awards to national organizations.

HQ: Program Development and Services Branch, Division of Adolescent and School Health, National Center for Chronic Disease Prevention and Health Promotion (MS K31), CDCP-HHS, 4770 Buford Hwy., Atlanta, GA 30341. Phones: (770)488-3252; FAX (770)488-3112. *Grants management information*: same address/phone as **93.135**. (Note: no field offices for this program.)

93.939 HIV PREVENTION ACTIVITIES—NON-GOVERNMENTAL ORGANIZATION BASED

Assistance: project grants (to 100 percent/to 5 years).

Purposes: to promote coordination for primary and secondary HIV prevention efforts among community-based organizations, HIV education and prevention service agencies, and national and regional nonprofit organizations, including local and state health departments and substance abuse agencies. Project examples: street outreach programs; risk reduction programs; community intervention programs.

Eligible applicants/beneficiaries: nongovernmental public and private entities.

Range: $75,000 to $300,000. **Average:** $250,000.

Activity: FY 00 estimate, 120 awards.

HQ: same address as **93.116** (MS E-27). Phone: (404)639-5200. *Grants management information*: same address as **93.116**. Phone: (404)842-6634. (Note: no field offices for this program.)

93.940 HIV PREVENTION ACTIVITIES—HEALTH DEPARTMENT BASED

Assistance: project grants (to 100 percent/1-5 years).

Purposes: to support, develop, implement, and evaluate primary and secondary HIV prevention programs by state and local health departments. Project activities may include: health education and risk reduction for drug users; public information; minority initiatives; counseling, testing, referral, and partner notification.

Eligible applicants/beneficiaries: states and political subdivisions, territories and possessions.

Range: $61,000 to $23,255,000. **Average:** $3,480,000.

Activity: FY 99-00, 65 continuation awards.

HQ: National Center for Prevention Services (MS D-21), CDCP-HHS, 1600 Clifton Rd. NE, Atlanta, GA 30333. Phone: (404)639-5200. *Grants management information*: same address as **93.135**. Phone: (770)488-2720. (Note: no field offices for this program.)

93.941 **HIV DEMONSTRATION, RESEARCH, PUBLIC AND PROFESSIONAL EDUCATION PROJECTS**

Assistance: project grants (to 100 percent/1-5 years).

Purposes: for research to develop, test, and disseminate improved HIV prevention strategies at the community level. Applicants are encouraged to involve research groups in the program.

Eligible applicants/beneficiaries: states and political subdivisions, other public and private nonprofit entities.

Range: $150,000 to $1,000,000. **Average:** $225,000.

Activity: FY 99-00 estimate, 90 awards.

HQ: same address/phone as **93.940**. *Grants management information*: same address as **93.135**. Phone: (770)488-2720. (Note: no field offices for this program.)

93.942 **RESEARCH, TREATMENT AND EDUCATION PROGRAMS ON LYME DISEASE IN THE UNITED STATES ("Lyme Disease")**

Assistance: project grants (100 percent/to 3 years).

Purposes: to develop and implement improved measures for the primary and secondary prevention of Lyme disease, including: surveillance activities; ecological and epidemiological studies; diagnostic tests; public education; use of primate models.

Eligible applicants/beneficiaries: public and private nonprofit organizations able to provide services in areas where Lyme disease is found, including IHEs, research institutions, state and local health departments.

Range: $23,000 to $269,000. **Average:** $112,000.

Activity: FY 99 estimate, 32 continuation grants.

HQ: National Center for Infectious Diseases, CDCP-HHS, P.O. Box 2087, Fort Collins, CO 80522. Phones: (970)221-6426; FAX (970)221-6476. *Grants management information*: same address/phone as **93.135**. (Note: no field offices for this program.)

93.943 **EPIDEMIOLOGIC RESEARCH STUDIES OF ACQUIRED IMMUNODEFICIENCY SYNDROME (AIDS) AND HUMAN IMMUNODEFICIENCY VIRUS (HIV) INFECTION IN SELECTED POPULATION GROUPS**

Assistance: project grants (100 percent/1-3 years).

Purposes: for research of HIV-related epidemiologic issues concerning risks of transmission, the natural history and transmission of the disease in certain populations, and development and evaluation of behavioral recommendations to reduce AIDS and HIV infection—particularly as they affect minority populations.

Eligible applicants/beneficiaries: states and their political subdivisions, agents, or instrumentalities; public or private nonprofit or profit organizations.

Range: $5,000 to $3,500,000. **Average:** $600,000.

Activity: FY 00 estimate, 50 cooperative agreements.

HQ: Chief of Operations, Epidemiology Branch, Division of HIV/AIDS Prevention/Surveillance and Epidemiology, National Center for HIV, STD, and TB Prevention (MS E-45), CDCP-HHS, 1600 Clifton Rd. NE, Atlanta, GA 30333. Phone: (404)639-6130. *Grants management information:* same address as **93.135.** Phone: (770)488-2720. (Note: no field offices for this program.)

93.944 HUMAN IMMUNODEFICIENCY VIRUS (HIV)/ACQUIRED IMMUNODEFICIENCY SYNDROME (AIDS) SURVEILLANCE

Assistance: project grants (100 percent/1-5 years).

Purposes: to continue and strengthen HIV/AIDS surveillance programs; to effect, maintain, measure, and evaluate the extent of incidence and prevalence throughout the U.S. and its territories; to provide information for targeting and implementing prevention activities. Funds may support staffing costs, purchase of computer hardware and software, laboratory costs.

Eligible applicants/beneficiaries: state and local governments including territories and possessions currently receiving HIV/AIDS surveillance cooperative agreements.

Range: $2,000 to $3,500,000. **Average:** $800,000.

Activity: FY 00 estimate, 65 new awards.

HQ: Division of HIV/AIDS Prevention, National Center for HIV, STD, and TB Prevention, CDCP-HHS, 1600 Clifton Rd. NE, Atlanta, GA 30333. Phone: (404)639-0902. *Grants management information:* same address as **93.135.** Phone: (770)488-2720. (Note: no field offices for this program.)

93.946 COOPERATIVE AGREEMENTS TO SUPPORT STATE-BASED INFANT HEALTH INITIATIVE PROGRAMS
("Infant Health Initiative")

Assistance: project grants (100 percent/5 years).

Purposes: for: (1) Pregnancy Risk Assessment and Monitoring Systems (PRAMS) to establish and maintain state-specific, population-based surveillance of selected maternal behaviors that occur during pregnancy and early infancy, and to generate state-specific data for planning and assessing perinatal health programs; (2) Maternal and Child Health Epidemiology Programs (MCHEP) to develop state multidisciplinary teams to assist states in using epidemiological and surveillance data to address the health problems of women, infants, and children.

Eligible applicants/beneficiaries: state and territorial public health agencies designated as vital U.S. registration areas; New York City public health agency; federally recognized tribal governments.

Range: PRAMS, $60,000 to $120,000; MCHEP, $32,000 to $147,000. **Average:** PRAMS, $100,000; MCHEP, $86,000.

Activity: FY 98, 5 continuation PRAMS, 7 MCHEP awards.

HQ: *PRAMS,* Division of Reproductive Health, National Center for Chronic

Disease Prevention and Health Promotion (MS-K22), CDCP-HHS, 4770 Buford Hwy. NE, Atlanta, GA 30341. Phone: (404)488-5613. *MCHEP, Pregnancy and Infant Health Branch, National Center for Chronic Disease Prevention and Health Promotion* (MS-K23), CDCP-HHS, 1600 Clifton Rd. NE, Atlanta, GA 30333. (404)488-5157. *Grants management information*: same address/phone as **93.135**. (Note: no field offices for this program.)

93.947   TUBERCULOSIS DEMONSTRATION, RESEARCH, PUBLIC AND PROFESSIONAL EDUCATION

Assistance: project grants (to 100 percent/1-5 years).

Purposes: for research into prevention and control of tuberculosis, especially concerning strains resistant to drugs; for demonstration projects; for public information and education programs; for education, training, and clinical skills improvement for health professionals including allied health personnel.

Eligible applicants/beneficiaries: states, political subdivisions; public and private nonprofit entities.

Range: $50,000 to $150,000. **Average:** $100,000.

Activity: FY 99 estimate, 1 award.

HQ: same address as **93.116**. Phone: (404)639-8120. *Grants management information*: same address as **93.135**. Phone: (770)488-2720. (Note: no field offices for this program.)

93.948   PILOT CLINICAL PHARMACOLOGY TRAINING

Assistance: project grants (100 percent/1-5 years).

Purposes: to establish a clinical pharmacology training program at a college of medicine currently without such a program.

Eligible applicants/beneficiaries: IHEs with established colleges of medicine.

Range: $60,000 to $225,000.

Activity: FY 99 estimate, 2 supplementary awards, 2 extensions issued.

HQ: Grants Management Specialist, same address as **93.103**. Phones: (301) 827-7120; FAX (301)827-7106. (Note: no field offices for this program.)

93.951   DEMONSTRATION GRANTS TO STATES WITH RESPECT TO ALZHEIMER'S DISEASE

Assistance: project grants (55-75 percent/to 3 years).

Purposes: for demonstration projects concerning Alzheimer's disease and related disorders, involving planning, establishment, and operation of programs. Principal project activities: (1) coordination with public and private organizations in the development and operation of diagnosis, treatment, care management, respite care, legal counseling, and education services within the state; (2) delivery of services including home health care, personal care, day care, companion services, short-term care in health facilities, other respite care; (3) dissemination of information on services and sources of assistance available to patients, their families, and care-provider organizations.

Eligible applicants/beneficiaries: state governments.

Range: $217,000 to $490,000. **Average:** $340,000.

Activity: FY 98, continuation grants only, to 15 states.

HQ: same addresses/phones as **93.151**. (Note: no field offices for this program.)

93.954   TRIBAL RECRUITMENT AND RETENTION OF HEALTH PROFESSIONALS INTO INDIAN HEALTH PROGRAMS

Assistance: project grants (100 percent).

Purposes: to establish and operate programs designed to recruit for and retain health professionals in Indian health programs and facilities, including those operated by IHS.

Eligible applicants/beneficiaries: federally recognized tribes or Indian health organizations, with preference to proposed participants in the IHS Loan Repayment Program (**93.164**).

Range: $60,000 to $100,000.

Activity: FY 00 estimate, 7 continuation grants.

HQ: Director, Health Professions Support Team, Office of Management Support, IHS-HHS, 12300 Twinbrook Pkwy. - Ste.100A, Rockville, MD 20852. Phone: (301)443-4242. *Grants management information*: same address/ phone as **93.193**. (Note: no field offices for this program.)

93.955   HEALTH AND SAFETY PROGRAMS FOR CONSTRUCTION WORK

Assistance: project grants (100 percent/3-5 years).

Purposes: to reduce occupational injuries and illnesses in the construction industry. Project funds may be used to: establish health and safety programs for construction workers; develop interventions; establish a prevention center.

Eligible applicants/beneficiaries: profit and nonprofit organizations, IHEs, research institutions, hospitals, state or local health departments, other public and private organizations; small minority- and women-owned businesses.

Range: $255,000 to $3,500,000.

Activity: FY 99-00 estimate, 1 continuation award.

HQ: Director, NIOSH (MS-D40), CDCP-HHS, 1600 Clifton Rd., Atlanta, GA 30333. Phone: (404)639-2376. *Grants management information*: same address/phone as **93.161**. (Note: no field offices for this program.)

93.956   AGRICULTURAL HEALTH AND SAFETY PROGRAMS

Assistance: project grants (100 percent/3-5 years).

Purposes: to establish Centers for Agricultural Health and Safety Programs to address research, education, and disease and injury prevention interventions unique to agriculture; to develop, implement, and maintain a model program for the diagnosis, evaluation, and rehabilitation of persons with occupational respiratory disease and musculoskeletal disorders, and to disseminate findings including education and training information to state health officials, health care providers, workers, management, unions, and employers; for Community Partners for Healthy Farming (CPHF) projects funding the placement of specialized public health and occupational health nurses in agricultural communities, to practice nursing while maintaining coordinating disease and injury reporting systems with other local health care providers. Also, the Deep-South Center for Agricultural Disease and Injury Research, Education, and Prevention conducts activities unique to the deep-south.

Eligible applicants/beneficiaries: centers—state and private universities, non-profit university-affiliated medical centers. CPHF—same as for **93.955**.

Range: centers, $225,000 to $1,000,000; CPHF, $45,000 to $175,000. **Average:** centers, $613,000; CPHF, $95,000; Deep-South Center, $350,000.

Activity: FY 99-00, continuation of 1 Deep-South Center, 16 CPHF awards.

HQ: *centers,* Division of Respiratory Disease Studies (MS PO4/18), NIOSH, CDCP-HHS, 1095 Willowdale Rd., Morgantown, WV 26505-2888. Phones: (304)285-5711; *Occupational Respiratory Disease Evaluation and Rehabilitation,* same address (MS 122), (304)285-5726. *CPHF,* Division of Surveillance, Hazard Evaluation and Field Studies, (MS P03/R21), NIOSH, CDCP-HHS, 5555 Ridge Ave., Cincinnati, OH 45213. Phone: (513)841-4353. *Grants management information*: same address/phone as **93.161**. (Note: no field offices for this program.)

93.957 OCCUPATIONAL HEALTH AND SURVEILLANCE FATALITY ASSESSMENT AND CONTROL EVALUATION ("FACE")

Assistance: project grants (100 percent/to 5 years).

Purposes: to recognize new hazards, define the magnitude of the problem, follow trends in incidence, target exceptional hazardous workplaces for intervention, and evaluate prevention efforts—toward the prevention of fatal work injuries. Cooperative agreements may be contracted in the areas of "SENSOR," "FACE," and "Blood Lead."

Eligible applicants/beneficiaries: appropriate state departments; territories.

Range: SENSOR, $100,000 to $200,000; FACE, $60,000 to $100,000; Blood Lead, $25,000 to $35,000. **Average:** SENSOR, $150,000; FACE, $80,000; Blood Lead, $30,000.

Activity: FY 99-00 estimate, 50 continuation projects.

HQ: *SENSOR,* NIOSH (MS-D28), CDCP-HHS, Bldg. 1, 1600 Clifton Rd., Atlanta, GA 30303. Phone: (404)639-1528. *Blood Lead,* Division of Surveillance, Hazard Evaluation and Field Studies (MS R21), Robert A. Taft Laboratory, NIOSH, CDCP-HHS, 4676 Columbia Pkwy., Cincinnati, OH 45226. Phone: (513)841-4353. *FACE,* Division of Safety Research (MS 180), NIOSH, CDCP-HHS, 944 Chestnut Ridge Rd., Morgantown, WV 26505. Phone: (304)285-6016. *Health Promotion,* Division of Safety Research (MS-1174), NIOSH, CDCP-HHS, 944 Chestnut Ridge Rd., Morgantown, WV 26505-2888. Phone: (304)284-5704. *Grants management information*: same address/phone as **93.161**. (Note: no field offices for this program.)

93.958 BLOCK GRANTS FOR COMMUNITY MENTAL HEALTH SERVICES ("CMHS Block Grant")

Assistance: formula grants (100 percent).

Purposes: to provide comprehensive community mental health services to adults with a serious mental illness and to children with serious emotional disturbance; for program monitoring; for technical assistance in related planning and implementation. Services must be provided through qualified community programs including community mental health centers or child mental health, psycho-social rehabilitation, mental health peer-support, or mental health primary consumer-directed programs. Funds may not be used for inpatient services, cash payments to patients, most real estate or major equipment costs.

Eligible applicants/beneficiaries: state and territory governments.

Range: $50,000 to $33,244,000. **Average:** $4,435,000.

Activity: FY 99-00 estimate, 59 awards.

HQ: State Planning and System Development Branch, CMHS, SAMHSA-HHS, Parklawn Bldg. - Rm.15C-26, 5600 Fishers Lane, Rockville, MD 20857. Phone: (301)443-4257. *Grants management information:* same address/phone as **93.138**. (Note: no field offices for this program.)

93.959 BLOCK GRANTS FOR PREVENTION AND TREATMENT OF SUBSTANCE ABUSE
("Prevention and Treatment Block Grant" - "SAPT")

Assistance: formula grants (100 percent).

Purposes: to develop and implement prevention, treatment, and rehabilitation activities directed to the diseases of alcohol and drug abuse. At least 20 percent of funds allocated must support education and counseling programs concerning alcohol and substance abuse and tobacco use, for persons not requiring treatment; at least 5 percent of funds must increase treatment services for pregnant women and women with dependent children. States must require treatment programs for intravenous drug abusers, stipulating prompt admittance of such individuals into treatment. States must provide tuberculosis services such as counseling, testing, treatment, and early intervention for substance abusers at risk for HIV disease—either directly or through public or nonprofit entities.

Eligible applicants/beneficiaries: state and territory governments; tribes or tribal organizations.

Range: $61,000 to $177,000,000.

Activity: FY 00 estimate, 60 awards.

HQ: same address/phone as **93.238**. *Grants management information:* Grants Management Branch, Office of Resource Management, SAMHSA-HHS, Rockwall II Bldg. - Ste.618, 5600 Fishers Lane, Rockville, MD 20857. Phone: (301)443-4456. (Note: no field offices for this program.)

93.960 SPECIAL MINORITY INITIATIVES

Assistance: project grants (100 percent/to 5 years).

Purposes: to increase the number of minority students trained for careers in biomedical sciences research, through: NRSAs to such students (*see Note preceding* **93.001**); Institutional Education Projects ("Bridges Program") targeting students in IHEs offering only M.S. degrees in biomedical sciences and in two-year institutions, to participate in partnership programs established to increase their academic competitiveness and facilitate their transition into the next stage of preparing for research careers; technical assistance workshops concerning research conducted by minority students and investigators.

Eligible applicants/beneficiaries: NRSA—minority students. Bridges Program—partnerships of domestic private or public educational institutions appropriate to the program. Technical assistance workshops—public or private nonprofit agencies or organizations including state and local government agencies, IHES, and academic or research institutions.

Range: $16,000 to $360,000. **Average:** $35,000

Activity: FY 99-00 estimate, 71 NRSAs; FY 98, 26 Bridges Program awards.

HQ: same address as **93.375**. Phones: *predoctoral NRSA,* (301)594-3900; *Bridges Program,* (301)496-0943; *technical assistance workshops,* (301) 594-3833. *Grants management information*: same address/phone as **93.375**. (Note: no field offices for this program.)

93.962   HEALTH ADMINISTRATION TRAINEESHIPS AND SPECIAL PROJECTS PROGRAM

Assistance: formula grants (100 percent).

Purposes: for traineeships for graduate students enrolled in health program or hospital administration, or health policy analysis and planning.

Eligible applicants: public or private nonprofit educational entities (excluding schools or programs of public health).

Eligible beneficiaries: enrolled U.S. citizens or permanent residents, with priority to students demonstrating a commitment to public or nonprofit employers.

Range: $5,460 to $56,000. **Average:** traineeships, $17,000; special projects, $25,000.

Activity: FY 99 estimate, 42 continuation grants.

HQ: same address/phone as **93.117**. *Grants management information*: same address/phone as **93.107**. (Note: no field offices for this program.)

93.964   PUBLIC HEALTH TRAINEESHIPS

Assistance: formula grants (100 percent/to 3 years).

Purposes: for traineeships for graduate students of public health. Training should be in: biostatistics; epidemiology; environmental health; toxicology; public health nutrition; maternal and child health.

Eligible applicants: schools of public health; other accredited public and private nonprofit institutions.

Eligible beneficiaries: U.S. citizens or permanent residents.

Range: $9,876 to $207,000. **Average:** $73,000.

Activity: FY 98 estimate, 32 continuation grants.

HQ: same address as **93.117**. Phone: (301)443-6041. *Grants management information*: same address/phone as **93.107**. (Note: no field offices for this program.)

93.965   COAL MINERS RESPIRATORY IMPAIRMENT TREATMENT CLINICS AND SERVICES
("Black Lung Clinics")

Assistance: project grants (100 percent).

Purposes: for broad support of coal miners respiratory impairment treatment clinics and services, including patient and family member education to maximize the patient's ability for self-care.

Eligible applicants/beneficiaries: state and local government agencies, private nonprofit agencies.

Range: $50,000 to $350,000 for local programs (more for state or area programs).

Activity: FY 99-00, 14 grants supporting 62 clinics serving 35,000 patients.

HQ: same address/phone as **93.151**. *Grants management information*: same address as **93.129**. Phone: (301)594-4237.

93.969   GRANTS FOR GERIATRIC EDUCATION CENTERS

Assistance: project grants (100 percent/to 3 years).

Purposes: to develop educational resource centers focused on strengthening multi-disciplinary training of health professionals in geriatric health care, including faculty training and retraining; to establish new affiliations with health care facilities including nursing homes, chronic and acute care hospitals, ambulatory care centers, and senior centers—to provide students with clinical training. Funds may not be used for trainee costs or for land acquisition or construction activities.

Eligible applicants/beneficiaries: health professions schools; schools of allied health; physician assistant training programs; schools of nursing; graduate programs in health administration, clinical psychology, or clinical social work, or marriage and family therapy.

Range: $75,000 to $317,000. **Average:** $202,000.

Activity: FY 99 estimate, 26 continuation, 4 new awards.

HQ: Coordinator, Geriatrics Education Centers Program, Division of Associated, Dental and Public Health Professions, same address as **93.156**. Phone: (301)443-6763. *Grants management information*: same address/phone as **93.107**. (Note: no field offices for this program.)

93.970   HEALTH PROFESSIONS RECRUITMENT PROGRAM FOR INDIANS

Assistance: project grants (100 percent).

Purposes: to establish and operate programs to recruit American Indians and Alaska natives into education or training programs in health or allied health professions schools; to increase the number of nurses, nurse midwives, nurse practitioners, and nurse anesthetists delivering health care services to Americans Indians and Alaska natives; to place health professional residents for short-term assignments at IHS facilities.

Eligible applicants/beneficiaries: public or private nonprofit health or educational entities; tribes or tribal organizations.

Range: $50,000 to $400,000. **Average:** $225,000.

Activity: FY 99-00 estimate, 16 continuation projects.

HQ: same addresses/phones as **93.954**. (Note: no field offices for this program.)

93.971 HEALTH PROFESSIONS PREPARATORY SCHOLARSHIP PROGRAM FOR INDIANS

Assistance: project grants (100 percent).

Purposes: for compensatory pre-professional health education scholarships to American Indians and Alaska natives, covering up to two years of full-time study. Eligible disciplines are pre-nursing, -pharmacy, -medical technology, -physical therapy, -engineering, and pre-sanitation.

Eligible applicants/beneficiaries: persons of American Indian or Alaska native descent, with high school completed and accepted into an eligible program.

Range: $13,000 to $26,000. **Average:** $15,000.

Activity: FY 99-00 estimate, 95 continuation awards.

HQ: Scholarship Branch, Division of Health Professions Support, same addresses/phones as **93.123**.

93.972 HEALTH PROFESSIONS SCHOLARSHIP PROGRAM

Assistance: project grants (100 percent/to 4 years).

Purposes: for scholarships to American Indians and Alaska natives enrolling full- or part-time in health professions schools, to prepare them for careers serving Indians in: allopathic or osteopathic medicine; dentistry; nursing; graduate public health nutrition; graduate medical social work; graduate speech pathology/audiology; optometry; pharmacy; health care administration. Grantees must serve one year in the IHS or an Indian health organization for each year of support received through the program, with a minimum of two years—with deferments for certain types of advanced training.

Eligible applicants/beneficiaries: native American Indians or Alaskans enrolled as members of a federally-recognized tribe, accepted for study at a U.S. educational institution in a medical/health career education program deemed necessary by the IHS; eligible for or holding an appointment to the PHS or for civilian service in the IHS.

Range: $12,000 to $38,000. **Average:** $20,000.

Activity: FY 99-00 estimate, 380 new and continuation scholarships.

HQ: Scholarship Branch, Division of Health Professions Support, same addresses/phones as **93.123**.

93.974 FAMILY PLANNING—SERVICE DELIVERY IMPROVEMENT RESEARCH GRANTS
("SDI")

Assistance: project grants (100 percent).

Purposes: for research studies to improve family planning services. Funds may not be used in programs where abortion is a method of family planning.

Eligible applicants/beneficiaries: public or private nonprofit entities including in territories and possessions.

Range: $150,000 to $510,000. **Average:** $190,000.

Activity: FY 99 estimate, 4 new, 1 continuation grants; 10 continuation, 5 new male involvement grants.

HQ: Office of Population Affairs, same addresses/phones as **93.111.** (Note: no field offices for this program.)

93.977 PREVENTIVE HEALTH SERVICES—SEXUALLY TRANSMITTED DISEASES CONTROL GRANTS

Assistance: project grants (to 100 percent/1-5 years).

Purposes: for sexually transmitted disease prevention activities including surveillance, reporting, screening, case follow-up including notification of sex partners; interstate epidemiological referral; personnel education and training; demonstrations; development of control strategies and activities.

Eligible applicants/beneficiaries: any state, and in consultation with state authorities, political subdivisions.

Range: $20,000 to $5,400,000. **Average:** $1,170,000.

Activity: FY 98-99 estimate, 65 grants.

HQ: Director, Division of STD Prevention (MS E-02), CDCP-HHS, 1600 Clifton Rd. NE, Atlanta, GA 30333. Phone: (404)639-8260. *Grants management information*: same address as **93.161.** Phone: (770)488-2720. (Note: no field offices for this program.)

93.978 PREVENTIVE HEALTH SERVICES—SEXUALLY TRANSMITTED DISEASES RESEARCH, DEMONSTRATIONS, AND PUBLIC INFORMATION AND EDUCATION GRANTS

Assistance: project grants (100 percent/1-5 years).

Purposes: for applied research, demonstration, personnel training, and public education activities concerning the prevention and control of sexually transmitted diseases.

Eligible applicants/beneficiaries: states, political subdivisions, public or private nonprofit institutions.

Range: $35,000 to $311,000. **Average:** $185,000.

Activity: FY 99-00 estimate, 10 continuation center grants.

HQ: same addresses/phones as **93.977.** (Note: no field offices for this program.)

93.982 MENTAL HEALTH DISASTER ASSISTANCE AND EMERGENCY MENTAL HEALTH

Assistance: project grants (100 percent/9-12 months).

Purposes: for supplemental emergency mental health counseling services to victims of major disasters; training of workers to provide such counseling.

Eligible applicants/beneficiaries: state or local nonprofit agencies recommended by the state governor.

Range: $47,000 to $3,705,000. **Average** $1,876,000.

Activity: FY 99 estimate, 10 grants.

HQ: Chief, Emergency Services and Disaster Relief Branch, CMHS, SAM-

HSA-HHS, 5600 Fishers Lane - Rm.16C-26, Rockville, MD 20857. Phones: (301)443-4735; FAX (301)443-8030. *Grants management information*: same address/phone as **93.138**.

93.984 ACADEMIC ADMINISTRATIVE UNITS IN PRIMARY CARE ("Family Medicine Departments")

Assistance: project grants (100 percent).

Purposes: to establish, maintain, or improve family medicine academic administrative units to provide clinical instruction. Funds may not be used for construction, patient services, or student assistance.

Eligible applicants/beneficiaries: public or private nonprofit schools of medicine or osteopathy.

Range: $64,000 to $281,000. **Average:** $163,000.

Activity: FY 99 estimate, 56 continuation, 24 new grants.

HQ: same address/phone as **93.181**. *Grants management information*: same address/phone as **93.107**.

93.988 COOPERATIVE AGREEMENTS FOR STATE-BASED DIABETES CONTROL PROGRAMS AND EVALUATION OF SURVEILLANCE SYSTEMS

Assistance: project grants (80 percent/5 years).

Purposes: to plan, develop, and evaluate state-based diabetes control programs including: defining the nature, extent, and causes of diabetes; developing new approaches to prevention and treatment; establishing partnerships to prevent diabetes problems; increasing public awareness of prevention and control opportunities. Direct curative or rehabilitative services to patients may not be provided with grant funds.

Eligible applicants/beneficiaries: official state health agencies, including territories and possessions

Range: core capacity program, $75,000 to $350,000; comprehensive programs, $300,000 to $800,000. **Average:** core capacity, $230,000; comprehensive, $500,000.

Activity: FY 99, new 5-year program awards.

HQ: Division of Diabetes Translation, National Center for Chronic Disease Prevention and Health Promotion, CDCP-HHS, 1600 Clifton Rd. NE, Atlanta, GA 30333. Phone: (770)488-5046. *Grants management information*: same address as **93.116**. Phone: (404)842-6640. (Note: no field offices for this program.)

93.989 SENIOR INTERNATIONAL FELLOWSHIPS

Assistance: project grants (100 percent/3-12 months).

Purposes: for fellowships in the biomedical and behavioral sciences, toward the international exchange of ideas and information about the latest advances. Fellowships may support stipends, foreign living allowances, travel, and minimal other costs required to perform research in a foreign laboratory.

Eligible applicants/beneficiaries: U.S. citizens or permanent residents with at least five years experience in biomedical research, teaching, or other relevant professional experience in the medical and biological sciences beyond the doctorate or equivalent professional medical degree, and invited by a nonprofit foreign institution—holding full-time appointments on the staff of the U.S. nominating institution which must be a nonfederal or private nonprofit research, clinical, or educational institution. Applicants may not be recipients of more than one previous Senior International Fellowship award. Federal employees are ineligible.

Range: $9,500 to $46,000. **Average:** $27,000.

Activity: FY 00 estimate, 21 competing grants.

HQ: same addresses/phones as **93.106**. (Note: no field offices for this program.)

93.990   NATIONAL HEALTH PROMOTION

Assistance: project grants (100 percent/to 3 years).

Purposes: for national organizations to participate in the National Health Promotion Program to educate the public about good health habits and programs designed to prevent disease and disability. Funds may be used to develop promotion programs and materials to be used by schools, medical treatment sites, work sites, and community health promotion programs; to identify the needs of special population groups. Incorporation of the "Year 2000 Health Objectives for the Nation" is expected.

Eligible applicants/beneficiaries: public or private nonprofit organizations.

Range: $50,000 to $300,000.

Activity: FY 99 estimate, 2 continuation awards.

HQ: Director, Office of Disease Prevention and Health Promotion, Office of Public Health and Science-HHS, 200 Independence Ave. SW, Washington, DC 20201. Phone: (202)401-6295. *Grants management information*: Grants Management Specialist, Administrative Operations Service, HHS, Parklawn Bldg.- Rm.5C13, Rockville, MD 20857. Phone: (301)443-8826. (Note: no field offices for this program.)

93.991   PREVENTIVE HEALTH AND HEALTH SERVICES BLOCK GRANT ("PHHS Block Grants")

Assistance: formula grants (100 percent/2 years).

Purposes: for state preventive health service programs including emergency medical services program improvement planning, health incentive activities, hypertension programs, rodent control, fluoridation programs, health education, risk reduction programs, home health services, services for victims of sex offenses, and other services related to the accomplishment of "Year 2000" objectives.

Eligible applicants/beneficiaries: state and territorial governments, certain tribes.

Range: $32,000 to $10,239,000. **Average:** $1,410,000.

Activity: FY 00, 61 states and territories, two tribes to receive funds.

HQ: National Center for Chronic Disease Prevention and Health Promotion (K30), CDCP-HHS, 4770 Buford Hwy. NE, Atlanta, GA 30341-3724.

Phone: (404)488-5645. *Grants management information*: same address/phone as **93.135**. (Note: no field offices for this program.)

93.994   MATERNAL AND CHILD HEALTH SERVICES BLOCK GRANT TO THE STATES

Assistance: formula grants (57 percent).

Purposes: for a broad range of health and related services including preventive and primary care services to pregnant women, mothers, infants, and children including children with special health needs. Funds may support such costs as program planning, administration, education, and evaluation. Ineligible uses of funds are most inpatient services, cash payments for health services, major equipment purchases, construction costs—or research or training other than by public or nonprofit entities.

Eligible applicants/beneficiaries: states and insular areas.

Range: $155,000 to $41,903,000. **Average:** $9,738,000.

Activity: annually, 59 block grants.

HQ: same address/phone as **93.235**. *Grants management information*: same address/phone as **93.110**. (Note: no field offices for this program.)

93.995   ADOLESCENT FAMILY LIFE—DEMONSTRATION PROJECTS

Assistance: project grants (to 70 percent/to 5 years).

Purposes: to establish innovative, comprehensive, and integrated approaches to the delivery of care services to pregnant and parenting adolescents, especially those under age 17; for family-centered approaches to the problem of out-of-wedlock pregnancy by encouraging abstinence from premarital sexual relations. Funds may support costs of: care and prevention services; coordination of services among local providers; appropriate supplemental services.

Eligible applicants/beneficiaries: public organizations including city, county, regional, and state governments; private nonprofit organizations.

Range: $150,000 to $250,000.

Activity: FY 00 estimate, 110 continuation grants.

HQ: Director, same address as **93.111**. Phone: (202)594-2799. *Grants management information*: same address/phone as **93.111**. (Note: no field offices for this program.)

CORPORATION FOR NATIONAL AND COMMUNITY SERVICE

94.002   RETIRED AND SENIOR VOLUNTEER PROGRAM ("RSVP")

Assistance: project grants (70-90 percent).

Purposes: pursuant to the Domestic Volunteer Service Act of 1973 as amended and National and Community Service Trust Act of 1993, for operating costs of programs involving retired persons participating as volunteers in community service projects—e.g., intergenerational activities, in-home care, consumer education, public safety, and health and human service activities. Volunteers are reimbursed only for their out-of-pocket expenses, mainly for transportation.

Eligible applicants: state and local government agencies, private nonprofit organizations.

Eligible beneficiaries: persons at least age 55.

Range: $2,500 to $84,000. **Average:** $49,000.

Activity: FY 98, 450,000 volunteers serving in 58,000 local organizations, contributing 74,000,000 hours of volunteer service.

HQ: National Senior Service Corps, RSVP, CNCS, 1201 New York Ave. NW, Washington, DC 20525. Phones: (202)606-5000, ext. 189; (800)424-8867.

94.003 STATE COMMISSIONS

Assistance: project grants (varying match).

Purposes: pursuant to the National and Community Service Trust Act of 1993, to plan and establish independent, bipartisan state commissions to oversee funded AmeriCorps programs. Commissions generally include 15 to 25 members appointed by governors.

Eligible applicants/beneficiaries: states, DC, PR.

Range: $125,000 to $750,000.

Activity: N.A.

HQ: CNCS, 1201 New York Ave. NW, Washington, DC 20525. Phone: (202) 606-5000, ext. 474.

94.004 LEARN AND SERVE AMERICA—SCHOOL AND COMMUNITY BASED PROGRAMS

Assistance: project grants (50-90 percent/to 3 years).

Purposes: pursuant to the National and Community Service Trust Act of 1993, to encourage elementary and secondary schools, school teachers, and community-based agencies to create, develop, and offer service-learning opportunities for school-age youth—in such areas as health, education, public safety, and environment. Funds may be used for: planning and capacity building; program operating costs including grants to local partnerships; programs involving adult volunteers; training and technical assistance.

Eligible applicants: SEAs, State Commissions on National Service, territories, tribes, public or private nonprofit entities.

Eligible beneficiaries: school-based programs—elementary or secondary school students. Community-based programs—participants age 5-17.

Range: $20,000 to $2,376,000. **Average:** $241,000.

Activity: FY 98, 800,000 youth involved.

HQ: same address as **94.003**. Phone: (202)606-5000, ext. 117.

94.005   LEARN AND SERVE AMERICA—HIGHER EDUCATION

Assistance: project grants (50 percent/to 3 years).

Purposes: pursuant to the National and Community Service Trust Act of 1993, for service learning projects engaging college students in meeting community needs while enhancing their academic and civic learning; to build capacity and strengthen the service infrastructure of IHEs. Eligible project activities include tutoring, mentoring, health outreach and education, primary and preventive health care, conflict resolution, neighborhood clean-up and revitalization, and prevention of gang violence and substance abuse activities.

Eligible applicants: IHEs; consortia of IHEs and nonprofit organizations or public agencies including states.

Eligible beneficiaries: graduate and undergraduate students, faculty members.

Range: $40,000 to $320,000. **Average:** $167,000.

Activity: FY 99, 57 continuation grants supporting some 30,000 students participating at 300 IHEs.

HQ: same address as **94.003**. Phone: (202)606-5000, ext. 117.

94.006   AMERICORPS

Assistance: project grants (67-85 percent).

Purposes: pursuant to the National and Community Service Trust Act of 1993, to plan or operate national and community service programs addressing community education, public safety, human, and environmental needs, by encouraging volunteers to serve part- or full-time. AmeriCorps members serve for one year, and receive education awards for postsecondary education or to pay off student loans. Examples include volunteers serving: as mentors, tutors, teaching assistants, role models—in after-school, immunization, low-income housing renovation, "crime watch", environmental projects.

Eligible applicants/beneficiaries: states, tribes, territories, national nonprofit organizations, professional corps, and multi-state organizations.

Range: $200,000 (state programs) to $3,000,000 (national programs).

Activity: FY 99 estimate, 45,000 AmeriCorps members.

HQ: same address as **94.003**. Phone: (202)606-5000, ext. 474.

94.007   PLANNING AND PROGRAM DEVELOPMENT GRANTS

Assistance: project grants (50-85 percent/to 3 years).

Purposes: pursuant to the National and Community Service Trust Act of 1993, for planning and program development grants ensuring participation of the disabled as AmeriCorps members; for demonstration projects.

Eligible applicants/beneficiaries: demonstration grants—state and local government agencies, nonprofit organizations. Planning and development—disabled persons participating in programs operated by state commissions, IHEs, nonprofit organizations and governments.

Range: demonstration grants, $25,000 to $500,000; disability grants, $5,000 to $50,000; disaster grants, $300,000 to $1,000,000.

Activity: FY 00, 60 AmeriCorps Promise Fellowships grants.

HQ: same address as **94.003**. Phone: (202)606-5000, ext. 260.

94.009   TRAINING AND TECHNICAL ASSISTANCE

Assistance: project grants (100 percent).

Purposes: pursuant to the National and Community Service Trust Act of 1993, for training and technical assistance services to CNCS grantees in such areas as program and financial management, fund raising, membership development and training, community analysis, and program evaluation. Services are provided through workshops, publications, on-site consultations.

Eligible applicants/beneficiaries: federal, state, local agencies; tribes; IHEs; nonprofit organizations; profit companies.

Range: $100,000 to $1,500,000.

Activity: not quantified specifically.

HQ: same address as **94.003**. Phone: (202)606-5000, ext. 139.

94.011   FOSTER GRANDPARENT PROGRAM
("FGP")

Assistance: project grants (90 percent).

Purposes: pursuant to the Domestic Volunteer Service Act of 1973 as amended and National and Community Service Trust Act of 1993, to provide supportive services to infants, children, or youth with special or exceptional needs—including the abused and neglected, terminally ill, juvenile offenders, pregnant teenagers, boarder babies, runaway youth, and the physically handicapped. Programs may be conducted in the children's homes or in residential or nonresidential facilities including preschools. Grant funds may be used to pay stipends to low-income foster grandparents serving as volunteers, and to provide their transportation, physical exams, and meals; for staff salaries and travel, equipment, and space costs.

Eligible applicants: state and local government agencies, private nonprofit organizations.

Eligible beneficiaries: persons at least age 60, low-income, and physically, mentally, and emotionally capable of serving clients on a person-to-person basis; non-low-income individuals may serve as volunteers without stipends.

Range: $12,000 to $1,722,000. **Average:** $269,000.

Activity: FY 98, 288 community-based projects funded, 20,000 volunteer service years by foster grandparents serving 89,000 children.

HQ: Foster Grandparent Program, CNCS, 1201 New York Ave. NW, Washington, DC 20525. Phones: (202)606-5000, ext. 189; (800)424-8867.

94.013   VOLUNTEERS IN SERVICE TO AMERICA
("AmeriCorps-VISTA")

Assistance: specialized services.

Purposes: pursuant to the Domestic Volunteer Service Act of 1973 as amended, to provide volunteers from all walks of life and age groups, working in projects addressing the problems of poverty such as health, illiteracy, substance abuse prevention and education, hunger, homelessness, housing, unemployment. Volunteers may be recruited locally or referred by CNCS; they serve full-time for a full year, living at subsistence levels of support among the people they serve.

Eligible applicants/beneficiaries: federal, state, or local government agencies or private nonprofit organizations.

Activity: FY 99 estimate, 5,000 volunteer service years, 1,200 projects in 50 states, PR, DC.

HQ: Director, VISTA, CNCS, 1201 New York Ave. NW, Washington, DC 20525. Phones: (202)606-5000; (800)424-8867.

94.016   SENIOR COMPANION PROGRAM ("SCP")

Assistance: project grants (90 percent).

Purposes: pursuant to the Domestic Volunteer Service Act of 1973 as amended and National and Community Service Trust Act of 1993, for the operating costs of the Senior Companion Program, including stipends, transportation, physical exams, insurance, and meals for low-income older volunteers. SCP participants serve as companions to other adults, primarily older persons with special needs. Services to the adults may be provided in their homes or in residential or nonresidential facilities, including such activities as helping hospital patients during their recuperation, arranging for community social services, working with the terminally ill. Respite care services, including to Alzheimer's patients and their families, are also provided.

Eligible applicants/beneficiaries: same as for **93.011**.

Range: $13,000 to $427,000. **Average:** $211,000.

Activity: FY 98, 8,100 service-years provided through 147 funded and 44 nonfunded projects supporting 2,800 volunteer service years, serving some 46,000 clients.

HQ: Senior Companion Program, same address/phone as **94.002**.

SOCIAL SECURITY ADMINISTRATION

96.001   SOCIAL SECURITY—DISABILITY INSURANCE

Assistance: direct payments/unrestricted or specified use.

Purposes: pursuant to the Social Security Act of 1935 as amended, to replace part of the earnings lost because of a physical or mental impairment preventing a person from working. Disability is defined as a medically determined physical or mental impairment that has lasted or is expected to last at least 12 months, or to result in death. There is a five-month waiting period. Costs of vocational rehabilitation are eligible.

Eligible applicants/beneficiaries: disabled workers under age 65 if they have worked for a sufficient period of time and made sufficient contributions into Social Security. Certain family members of disabled workers also are eligible for benefits, including: unmarried children under age 18, or 19 for elementary and secondary students; disabled unmarried children under age 22; spouse caring for child under age 16 or disabled, receiving benefits on worker's Social Security record; spouses age 62 or over; divorced spouses age 62 or over, married to the worker for at least 10 years. Benefits are subject to an earnings test, and may be reduced by amounts received under other programs. Certain restrictions apply for impairments based on drug addiction or alcoholism. Applicants should contact local Social Security offices for additional details.

Range: 1999, to $1,646 monthly for a disabled worker; to $2,470 for a family. **Average:** individual, $733; family, $1,217.

Activity: FY 99 estimate, 6,387,000 monthly benefit recipients (average).

HQ: Office of Public Inquiries, Social Security Administration, Annex - Rm. 4100, Baltimore, MD 21235. Phone: (410)965-2736.

96.002   SOCIAL SECURITY—RETIREMENT INSURANCE

Assistance: direct payments/unrestricted use.

Purposes: pursuant to the Social Security Act of 1935 as amended, to pay monthly cash benefits to retired workers and their "auxiliaries," that have contributed to the Social Security system.

Eligible applicants/beneficiaries: retired workers age 62 and over that have worked the required number of years under Social Security. Certain family members also are eligible for benefits, including: a spouse age 62 or over; a spouse at any age if caring for a disabled child under age 16, entitled based on the worker's eligible earnings; unmarried children under age 18, or 19 for elementary and secondary students; disabled unmarried children under age 22; divorced spouses age 62 or over, married to the retired worker for at least 10 years; and, under other circumstances. Benefit payments to eligible workers applying between age 62 and 65 are reduced permanently; benefits also are reduced for persons aged 62 through 69 if their earnings exceed certain limits. Applicants should contact local Social Security offices for additional details and restrictions.

Range: to $1,373 monthly for an individual retiring at age 65; to $2,402 for a family receiving benefits. **Average:** as of 31 December 1998, individual, $780 monthly; retired worker and eligible spouse, $1,310 monthly.

Activity: FY 98, 30,631,000 monthly benefit recipients (average).

HQ: same address/phone as **93.001.**

96.003   SOCIAL SECURITY—SPECIAL BENEFITS FOR PERSONS AGED 72 AND OVER

Assistance: direct payments/unrestricted use.

Purposes: pursuant to the Tax Adjustment Act of 1966 as amended, to pay monthly cash benefits to persons age 72 and over who did not earn protection under the Social Security program during their working years. Payments are not made for any month during which payments are received under the

Supplemental Security Income program; benefits are reduced by the amount of most other governmental pensions, retirement benefits, or annuities.

Eligible applicants/beneficiaries: persons that reached age 72 before 1968 need no work credits under Social Security. Those that reached age 72 in 1968-1971 need some work credits to be eligible. The amount of work credit needed increases gradually each year for persons reaching age 72 in 1968-1971.

Range/Average: as of December 1998, $206 monthly.

Activity: FY 00 estimate, monthly benefits to fewer than 103 persons.

HQ: same address/phone as **93.001.**

96.004 SOCIAL SECURITY—SURVIVORS INSURANCE

Assistance: direct payments/specified or unrestricted uses.

Purposes: pursuant to the Social Security Act of 1935 as amended, to pay monthly cash benefits to a deceased worker's dependents if the deceased was insured for survivors' insurance protection.

Eligible applicants/beneficiaries: widows or widowers age 60 or over; surviving divorced spouses age 60 or over, married to the deceased worker for at least 10 years; survivors with a child in their care under age 16 or disabled; disabled widows, widowers, or divorced spouses age 50-59; unmarried children under age 18, or under 19 if in elementary or secondary school, or age 18 or older if disabled before age 22; dependent parents age 62 or over. Earnings tests and benefit limits apply, except for beneficiaries age 70 or over. Under certain conditions, a lump-sum death payment of $255 is payable to survivors. Applicants should contact local Social Security offices for additional details.

Range: to $1,373 monthly. **Average:** for an aged widow or widower alone, $749 monthly; with two eligible children, $1,542 monthly.

Activity: FY 98, monthly benefits to 7,149,000 survivors (average).

HQ: same address/phone as **93.001.**

96.005 SPECIAL BENEFITS FOR DISABLED COAL MINERS
("Black Lung")

Assistance: direct payments/unrestricted uses.

Purposes: to pay monthly cash benefits to coal miners disabled by black lung or other chronic lung disease, and to their dependents or survivors.

Eligible applicants/beneficiaries: disabled miners; under prescribed circumstances—their widows, surviving divorced wife, children, parents, brothers, and sisters.

Range: as of January 1999, $469.50 to $939 monthly.

Activity: FY 98, monthly benefits to 116,000 miners and dependents.

HQ: same address/phone as **93.001.**

96.006 SUPPLEMENTAL SECURITY INCOME
("SSI")

Assistance: direct payments/unrestricted or specified uses.

Purposes: pursuant to the Social Security Act of 1935 as amended, to provide supplemental income to persons aged 65 and over and to blind or disabled persons with incomes and financial resources below specified levels.

Eligible applicants/beneficiaries: persons age 65 or over or blind or disabled.

Range: 1999, to $500 monthly for individuals; to $751 for an individual with an eligible spouse. **Average:** $368 monthly.

Activity: FY 97, monthly benefits to 6,302,000 persons (average).

HQ: same address/phone as **93.802.**

96.007   SOCIAL SECURITY—RESEARCH AND DEMONSTRATION

Assistance: project grants (75-95 percent/to 3 years).

Purposes: pursuant to the Social Security Act of 1935 as amended, for social, economic, and demographic research and demonstration projects and experiments to improve the management, administration, and effectiveness of facets of SSA programs.

Eligible applicants/beneficiaries: state and local governments, educational institutions, hospitals, public and private nonprofit organizations. Profit organizations may apply, but grant funds may not be paid as profit to any grant recipient.

Range: $100,000 to $1,250,000.

Activity: FY 99, 16 continuation awards.

HQ: Grants Management Officer, Office of Operations Contracts and Grants, Office of Acquisition and Grants, DCFAM, SSA, 1-E-4 Gwynn Oak Bldg., 1710 Gwynn Oak Ave., Baltimore, MD 21207-5279. Phone: (410)965-9503. (Note: no field offices for this program.)

PART III

Program Funding Levels

Summary Tables

Four tables are presented:

- *Table 1. Estimated Outlays/Credits for Domestic Assistance Programs, by Federal Administrative Entity* (FY 97, 98, 00), beginning on page 573.
- *Table 2. Summary of Estimated Outlays/Credits, by Federal Department or Agency* (FY 97, 98, 99, 00), beginning on page 606.
- *Table 3. The Fifty Largest Domestic Assistance Programs in FY 1999, by Funds Outlayed and/or Credited* (page 611).
- *Table 4. The Fifty Smallest Domestic Assistance Programs in FY 1999, by Funds Outlayed and/or Credited* (page 612).

The tables are based on information in the *Catalog of Federal Domestic Assistance 1999* published in June 1999, its December 1999 "Update," and the prior edition. The tables offer a general perspective of government funding for specific programs and agencies, in relation to one another and to other federal activities. Such a perspective can be useful in several ways to persons or organizations interested in certain programs and in government assistance, including:

- Having identified programs meeting given needs, prospective applicants can use the tables to compare relative funding levels.
- Tables 1 and 2 show funding levels for four federal fiscal years. To our knowledge tables compiled specifically for the domestic assistance programs exist nowhere else—i.e., apart from the costs of other administering agency functions. Perhaps such a compilation adds a new dimension to perspectives of federal domestic assistance.
- Tables 3 and 4 answer some questions frequently posed to the editor.

Important Notes on the Tables, Footnotes

Certain inconsistencies in the source material cannot be corrected. Therefore, *the tables should be used only as a general guide to the availability of funding.*

In Table 2, the first two digits in the five-digit number preceding the name of the administering agency correspond to the program number series identifying programs in Part II—e.g., 11.000 preceding DEPARTMENT OF COMMERCE encompasses all department programs including administrative sub-units.

The following footnotes are employed:

*   amount shown is a "credit" rather than an actual cash outlay. In the tables, amounts loaned or insured by the government are classified as credits.

(a)   funding for the program cannot be separately identified from other agency expenses.

e   amount was estimated in the source material, the significance of which is discussed on page 21, following the heading **Range**.

\i   includes funding for this and for one or more other programs; program descriptions in Part II explain such cases.

(n)   program did not exist during the reported fiscal year.

(o)   funding is included in an amount reported for another program, as noted in the Part II program descriptions.

\p   includes value of property or goods awarded; such amounts are not necessarily appropriated in the reported fiscal year.

\r   program supports or is supported by a revolving fund account.

\t   program includes support from or is supported by a federal trust fund.

\u   user charges, fees, or other income help support the program, including loan repayments; amounts shown are not necessarily or entirely appropriated funds.

Table 1.   Estimated Outlays/Credits for All Domestic Assistance Programs, by Administrative Entity

Program number	ADMINISTRATIVE ENTITY/SUB-UNIT Program Title (abridged)	FY 1997 In $thousands	FY 1998 In $thousands	FY 1999 In $thousands	FY 2000 In $thousands
	DEPARTMENT OF AGRICULTURE				
10.001	Agricultural Research	7,503	13,653	11,643 e	11,643 e
10.025	Plant, Animal Disease, Pest Control \ t	455,028	54,579 e	53,450 e	42,050 e
10.028	Wildlife Services	37,974	1,814	1,850 e	1,350 e
10.051	Commodity Loans, Deficiency Payments \ u	26,508	289,985	2,749,121 e	3,342,240 e
		5,333,116*	7,189,199*	8,264,827*e	12,162,622*e
10.053	Dairy Indemnity	257	417	418 e	650 e
10.054	Emergency Conservation	38,084	28,503	84,095 e	0 e
10.055	Production Flexibility Payments \ u	6,320,138	5,671,770	5,544,453 e	5,042,431 e
10.062	Water Bank Program	0	0	597 e	0 e
10.064	Forestry Incentives	6,515	6,470	16,456 e	0 e
10.069	Conservation Reserve Program	1,670,686	1,746,688	1,528,639 e	1,577,972 e
10.070	Colorado River Salinity Control	0	0	648 e	0 e
10.071	Warehouse Examination	1,500	1,500	0 e	0 e
10.072	Wetlands Reserve	99,308	254,228	131,888 e	209,065 e
10.153	Market News	22,341	22,262	22,166 e	23,843 e
10.155	Marketing Agreements and Orders \ u	10,488	10,189	10,998 e	12,443 e
10.156	Federal-State Marketing Improvement	1,200	1,200	1,200 e	1,200 e
10.162	Inspection Grading, Standardization \ t	157,656	162,143	172,880 e	172,880 e
10.163	Market Protection and Promotion	4,913	13,566	15,880 e	25,233 e
10.164	Wholesale Market Development	2,306	2,261	2,235 e	2,556 e
10.165	Perishable Agricultural Commodities \ u	7,907	8,289	8,607 e	8,718 e
10.167	Transportation Services	2,559	2,519	2,522 e	2,522 e
10.200	Agricultural Research, Special	70,397	74,719	85,652 e	33,789 e
10.202	Cooperative Forestry Research	19,373	19,374	20,733 e	18,803 e
10.203	Agricultural Experiment Stations	159,600	159,606	170,774 e	145,565 e
10.205	1890 Land-Grant Colleges	26,208	26,210	28,045 e	26,230 e
10.206	Agricultural Research—Competitive	87,877	90,751	111,433 e	187,200 e
10.207	Animal Health and Disease Research	4,449	4,455	4,770 e	4,469 e
10.210	Food, Sciences—Fellowships	2,910	2,910	2,910 e	2,910 e
10.212	Small Business Innovation Research	10,020	11,673	13,309 e	12,849 e
10.215	Sustainable Agriculture Research	7,566	7,566	7,488 e	7,956 e
10.216	1890 Institution Capacity Building	8,809	8,812	8,722 e	8,722 e
10.217	Higher Education Challenge	3,880	4,220	4,176 e	4,176 e
10.218	Buildings and Facilities	59,743	59,743	0 e	0 e
10.219	Biotechnology Risk Assessment	1,537	1,404	1,358 e	1,358 e
10.220	Minority Scholars Program	970	970	960 e	960 e
10.221	Tribal Colleges Education Equity	1,450	1,450	1,552 e	1,500 e
10.222	Tribal Colleges Endowment	451	451	674 e	1,104 e
10.223	Hispanic Serving Institutions	1,450	2,425	2,736 e	3,056 e
10.224	FRA—Research, Education, Extension	1,679	34,202	0 e	30,000 e
10.225	Community Food Projects	2,500	2,500	2,500 e	2,500 e
10.226	Secondary Agriculture Education	(n)	(n)	480 e	0 e
10.240	Alternative Agricultural Research \ r, u	6,697	4,077	3,500 e	10,000 e
10.250	Agricultural, Rural Research	58,936	76,427	69,366 e	62,028 e
10.350	Assistance/Cooperatives	(o)	(o)	(o)	(o)
10.404	Emergency Loans \ u	144,800*	59,093*	25,000*e	53,000*e
10.405	Farm Labor Housing \ u, r	8,445	12,520	13,500 e	15,000 e
		15,604*	14,600*	20,000*e	25,001*e
10.406	Farm Operating Loans \ u	1,344,377*	1,310,858*	1,832,083*e	2,197,842*e
10.407	Farm Ownership Loans \ u	604,368*	508,466*	510,682*e	559,422*e
10.410	Very Low/Moderate Income Housing \ u	3,394,640*	3,830,180*	3,965,313*e	4,300,000*e
10.411	Rural Site/Self-Help Loans \ u	1,192*	358*	10,152*e	10,152*e
10.415	Rural Rental Housing Loans \ u	156,571*	149,353*	114,321*e	100,000*e
10.417	Housing Repair Loans, Grants \ u	16,732	25,689	20,195 e	30,000 e
		30,251*	30,233*	25,001*e	32,396*e
10.420	Rural Self-Help Housing	26,163	26,687	26,000 e	30,000 e
10.421	Tribal Corporation Loans \ u	224*	500*	1,003*e	1,028*e
10.427	Rural Rental Assistance Payments	523,060	545,247	583,397 e	640,000 e

Please see "Important Notes on the Tables, Footnotes," page 572.

Table 1. (continued)

Program number	ADMINISTRATIVE ENTITY/SUB-UNIT Program Title (abridged)	FY 1997 in $thousands	FY 1998 in $thousands	FY 1999 in $thousands	FY 2000 in $thousands
10.433	Rural Housing Preservation Grants	7,587	11,052	7,000 e	9,000 e
10.435	State Mediation Grants	2,000	2,000	2,000 e	4,000 e
10.437	Interest Assistance Program \ u	216,183*	226,570*	541,704*e	97,442*e
10.438	Section 538 Rural Rental Housing	13,316*	39,687*	74,839*e	100,000*e
10.441	Technical, Supervisory Assistance	781	861	1,264 e	0 e
10.442	Housing Application Packaging	1,894	182	1,405 e	495 e
10.443	Small Farmer Outreach	1,000	3,000	3,000 e	10,000 e
10.444	Housing—Disaster Loans, Grants \ u	781	833	2 e	0 e
		633*	297*	418*e	0*e
10.445	Housing—Disaster Loans \ u	11,804*	7,800*	10,077*e	0*e
10.450	Crop Insurance \ u	945,024	937,514	1,207,863 e	882,737 e
		1,076,104*	2,045,210*	2,037,450*e	1,778,713*e
10.451	Noninsured Crop Disasters \ u	51,713	22,941	66,822 e	88,872 e
10.452	Disaster Reserve Assistance	40,452	7,455	2,409,300 e	4,000 e
10.453	FRA—Farm Ownership Loans	9,510*	9,510*	0*e	0*e
10.454	Dairy Options Pilot Program \ u	(n)	502	0 e	0 e
10.475	Intrastate Meat, Poultry Inspection	41,528	40,552	40,655 e	41,701 e
10.477	Meat, Poultry and Egg Inspection \ t	575,243	593,540	621,301 e	665,021 e
10.500	Cooperative Extension Service	403,027	401,383	415,139 e	386,240 e
10.501	Agricultural Telecommunications Program	1,074	873	0 e	0 e
10.550	Food Distribution \ p, u	59,630	139,615	0 e	0 e
10.551	Food Stamps	19,668,073	17,062,258	17,936,166 e	18,414,551 e
10.553	School Breakfast Program	1,212,745	1,299,556	1,336,723 e	1,410,199 e
10.555	School Lunch Program \ p	5,728,648	5,743,638	5,916,238 e	6,153,837 e
10.556	Special Milk Program	18,008	16,955	17,164 e	16,674 e
10.557	Nutrition/Women, Infants, Children	3,934,724	3,879,145	3,964,000 e	4,102,000 e
10.558	Child, Adult Care Food Program \ p	1,648,223	1,551,098	1,643,497 e	1,755,668 e
10.559	Summer Food Service \ p	259,821	261,604	290,404 e	316,746 e
10.560	State Expenses/Child Nutrition	104,079	110,426	114,858 e	117,839 e
10.561	State Grants/Food Stamp Program	1,950,026	2,075,443	2,150,369 e	1,880,930 e
10.564	Nutrition Education, Training	3,741	3,750	3,750 e	3,750 e
10.565	Commodity Supplemental Food \ p	92,603	89,127	96,176 e	90,215 e
10.566	Nutrition Assistance/Puerto Rico	1,174,000	1,174,000	1,204,000 e	1,236,000 e
10.567	Food Distribution/Indian \ p	71,799	74,995	75,000 e	75,000 e
10.568	Emergency Food—Administrative	47,713	46,434	45,000 e	45,000 e
10.569	Emergency Food—Commodities	130,290	99,974	90,000 e	100,000 e
10.570	Nutrition Program/Elderly \ p	145,618	141,245	140,013 e	150,000 e
10.572	WIC Farmers' Market Nutrition	7,279	12,651	15,000 e	20,000 e
10.573	Homeless Children Nutrition	2,075	2,075	3,400 e	3,700 e
10.574	Team Nutrition Grants	4,008	4,008	4,000 e	4,000 e
10.600	Foreign Market Development	27,500	28,000	27,500 e	27,500 e
10.601	Market Access Program	90,000	90,000	90,000 e	90,000 e
10.652	Forestry Research	14,722	17,724	18,000 e	18,000 e
10.664	Cooperative Forestry Assistance	91,629	91,629	104,159 e	104,793 e
10.665	Schools and Roads—States \ u	234,322	229,035	242,943 e	242,462 e
10.666	Schools and Roads—Counties \ u	4,645	6,093	4,794 e	6,016 e
10.670	Forest-Dependent Communities	5,000	3,000	3,100 e	5,200 e
10.671	Southeast Alaska Economic Disaster	20,000	20,000	20,000 e	0 e
10.700	National Agricultural Library	3,483	3,243	3,340 e	3,351 e
10.760	Water, Waste Disposal Systems \ i, u	518,599	514,915	522,763 e	503,000 e
		836,084*	801,720*	798,632*e	975,000*e
10.761	Technical Assistance, Training	(o)	(o)	(o)	(o)
10.762	Solid Waste Management	2,445	2,587	2,715 e	2,746 e
10.763	Community Water Assistance	936	34	18 e	0 e
10.766	Community Facilities Loans, Grants \ u	6,400	9,475	6,500 e	8,237 e
		194,043*	276,404*	379,476*e	460,000*e
10.767	Intermediary Relending Program \ u	37,639*	37,639*	37,156*e	35,000*e
10.768	Business and Industry Loans \ u	827,400*	827,400*	1,050,000*e	1,050,000*e
10.769	Rural Development Grants	47,728	47,728	38,193 e	40,300 e
10.770	Water, Waste Disposal	(o)	(o)	(o)	(o)
10.771	Rural Cooperative Development	1,700	1,700	1,700 e	1,700 e
10.772	Empowerment Zones Program	(o)	(o)	(o)	(o)
10.773	Rural Business Opportunity Grants	(n)	(n)	500 e	5,000 e
10.774	Sheep Industry Improvement \ r, u	(n)	(n)	(o)	(o)

Please see "Important Notes on the Tables, Footnotes," page 572.

Table 1. (continued)

Program number	ADMINISTRATIVE ENTITY/SUB-UNIT Program Title (abridged)	FY 1997 in $thousands	FY 1998 in $thousands	FY 1999 in $thousands	FY 2000 in $thousands
10.800	Market Supervision \ u	12,442	13,159	16,062 e	14,928 e
10.850	Rural Electrification Loans \ u	824,350*	925,000*	1,066,503*e	600,000*e
10.851	Rural Telephone Loans \ u	495,000*	397,164*	495,005*e	470,000*e
10.852	Rural Telephone Bank Loans \ u	99,800*	168,100*	157,509*e	175,000*e
10.854	Economic Development Loans, Grants \ r, u	11,107	11,107	11,315 e	11,000 e
		12,275*	12,275*	25,000*e	15,000*e
10.855	Distance Learning, Telemedicine	6,500	21,081	12,500 e	20,000 e
		(n)*	4,969*	150,000*e	200,000*e
10.900	Great Plains Conservation	463	0	1,984 e	0 e
10.901	Resource Conservation, Development	29,312	34,852	35,677 e	35,265 e
10.902	Soil and Water Conservation	524,528	534,557	557,251 e	582,548 e
10.903	Soil Survey	75,663	76,853	79,405 e	80,565 e
10.904	Watershed Protection	86,417	90,718	86,849 e	74,423 e
10.905	Plant Materials for Conservation	8,225	8,820	9,862 e	9,238 e
10.906	Watershed Surveys and Planning	12,286	10,855	10,232 e	11,596 e
10.907	Snow Survey, Water Forecasting	5,516	5,906	6,385 e	6,124 e
10.910	Rural Abandoned Mine Program \ u	250	712	459 e	0 e
10.912	Environmental Quality Incentives	196,167	200,000	174,000 e	200,000 e
10.913	Farmland Protection Program	2,000	0	0 e	50,000 e
10.914	Wildlife Habitat Incentive	(n)	26,112	23,888 e	0 e
10.950	Agricultural Statistics Reports	110,364	127,055	113,587 e	110,159 e
10.960	Technical Agricultural Assistance	3,543	5,850	6,000 e	6,200 e
10.961	Scientific Cooperation Program	3,331	1,100	1,100 e	1,100 e
10.962	International Training	1,436	1,750	1,500 e	2,000 e
	DEPARTMENT TOTAL: OUTLAYS	50,477,639	47,542,459	53,599,766	52,018,597
	CREDITS*	15,679,284*	18,872,585*	21,592,151*	25,397,618*

DEPARTMENT OF COMMERCE

BUREAU OF THE CENSUS

Program number	Program Title	FY 1997	FY 1998	FY 1999	FY 2000
11.001	Census Bureau Data Products	314,086	645,399	1,317,822 e	3,080,438 e
11.002	Census Customer Services	7,299	7,940	7,940 e	7,940 e
11.003	Census Geography	43,836	43,162	42,679 e	33,406 e
11.004	Intergovernmental Services	740	800	800 e	800 e
11.005	Census Special Tabulations	153,389	171,009	184,159 e	184,094 e
11.006	Personal Census Search	350	465	357 e	422 e
	Subtotal: Outlays	519,700	868,775	1,553,757	3,307,100
	Credits*	0*	0*	0*	0*

ECONOMICS AND STATISTICS ADMINISTRATION

Program number	Program Title	FY 1997	FY 1998	FY 1999	FY 2000
11.025	Measures and Analyses	40,750	47,499	48,490 e	55,123 e
11.026	National Trade Data Bank \ r, u	841	0	0	0
11.027	Economic Bulletin Board \ r, u	335	0	0	0
	Subtotal: Outlays	41,926	47,499	48,490	55,123
	Credits*	0*	0*	0*	0*

INTERNATIONAL TRADE ADMINISTRATION

Program number	Program Title	FY 1997	FY 1998	FY 1999	FY 2000
11.106	Antidumping Duty	20,555	21,200	22,800 e	24,000 e
11.108	Commercial Service	152,282	190,336	181,690 e	183,198 e
11.110	Trade Development	47	59	60 e	50 e
11.111	Foreign-Trade Zones/U.S.	614	708	800 e	850 e
11.112	Export Promotion	2,972	2,489	2,500 e	2,500 e
11.113	ITA Special Projects	11,228	12,405	11,245 e	0 e
11.114	American Business Internship	497	1,000	2,000 e	1,000 e
11.115	American Business Center	650	1,720	700 e	0 e
	Subtotal: Outlays	188,845	229,917	221,795	211,598
	Credits*	0*	0*	0*	0*

Please see "Important Notes on the Tables, Footnotes," page 572.

Table 1. (continued)

Program number	ADMINISTRATIVE ENTITY/SUB-UNIT Program Title (abridged)	FY 1997 in $thousands	FY 1998 in $thousands	FY 1999 in $thousands	FY 2000 in $thousands
	BUREAU OF EXPORT ADMINISTRATION				
11.150	Licensing Services, Information	1,123	1,344	1,432 e	1,439 e
	Subtotal: Outlays	1,123	1,344	1,432	1,439
	Credits*	0*	0*	0*	0*
	ECONOMIC DEVELOPMENT ADMINISTRATION				
11.300	Public Works, Economic Development	164,802	177,905	205,850 e	191,178 e
11.303	Technical Assistance	9,203	9,221	9,100 e	11,601 e
11.305	Economic Development Planning	3,486	24,024	24,000 e	29,670 e
11.307	Economic Adjustment Assistance	161,242	181,460	139,617 e	129,929 e
11.312	Research and Evaluation	500	507	500 e	500 e
11.313	Trade Adjustment Assistance \ i	8,500	9,500	9,500 e	17,000 e
	Subtotal: Outlays	347,733	402,617	388,567	379,878
	Credits*	0*	0*	0*	0*
	NATIONAL OCEANIC AND ATMOSPHERIC ADMINISTRATION				
11.400	Geodetic Surveys and Services	1,843	764	485 e	485 e
11.405	Anadromous Fish Conservation	2,054	2,000	2,000 e	2,000 e
11.407	Interjurisdictional Fisheries	3,342	3,750	3,750 e	3,750 e
11.408	Fishermen's Contingency Fund \ u	238	311	350 e	500 e
11.413	Fishery Products Inspection \ u	12,954	11,314	12,528 e	12,600 e
11.415	Fisheries Finance Program \ u	27,000*	105,000*	145,800*e	23,800*e
11.417	Sea Grant Support	61,814	64,357	54,700 e	48,950 e
11.419	Coastal Zone Management	48,505	49,700	57,600 e	92,700 e
11.420	Estuarine Research Reserves	7,225	13,860	5,800 e	5,800 e
11.426	Coastal Ocean Science	417	2,156	3,268 e	3,268 e
11.427	Fisheries Development \ u	8,411	2,004	3,073 e	1,000 e
11.428	Intergovernmental Climate—NESDIS	1,467	2,500	2,495 e	2,495 e
11.429	Marine Sanctuary Program \ p	339	369	1,800 e	1,800 e
11.430	Undersea Research	11,193	14,154	13,500 e	8,000 e
11.431	Climate, Atmospheric Research	28,720	27,664	31,375 e	27,800 e
11.432	Oceanic, Atmospheric Research	45,114	20,310	22,000 e	24,000 e
11.433	Marine Fisheries Initiative	1,663	1,327	1,000 e	1,000 e
11.434	Cooperative Fishery Statistics	1,482	1,182	997 e	997 e
11.435	Southeast Area Monitoring	911	911	911 e	911 e
11.436	Columbia River Fisheries	15,648	18,910	16,000 e	11,000 e
11.437	Pacific Fisheries	5,068	3,385	4,070 e	4,000 e
11.438	Pacific Salmon Treaty Program	5,089	5,089	5,305 e	5,305 e
11.439	Marine Mammal Data Program	2,387	2,866	2,331 e	3,000 e
11.440	Remote Sensing/Earth, Environment	3,275	5,452	5,069 e	3,850 e
11.441	Fishery Management Councils	10,451	11,927	13,000 e	13,300 e
11.443	Short-Term Climate Fluctuations	200	200	227 e	187 e
11.444	Aquaculture Program	1,234	0	904 e	452 e
11.445	Marine Fish/Hawaii	950	0	949 e	475 e
11.449	Independent Education and Science	168	98	90 e	105 e
11.450	Flood Observing, Warning System	295	295	466 e	450 e
11.452	Unallied Industry Projects	41,264	220	1,282 e	0 e
11.454	Unallied Management Projects	1,217	3,019	3,061 e	2,059 e
11.455	Cooperative Science, Education	3,485	3,412	3,019 e	2,029 e
11.457	Chesapeake Bay Studies	1,815	1,815	1,700 e	1,700 e
11.458	Alaska Salmon Enhancement	380	380	391 e	391 e
11.459	Climate and Air Quality Research	0	0	50 e	0 e
11.460	Oceanic and Atmospheric Projects	0	7,800	9,800 e	0 e
11.462	Hydrologic Research	533	533	140 e	227 e
11.463	Habitat Conservation	6,547	6,547	4,500 e	5,000 e
11.467	Meteorologic, Hydrologic Projects	3,000	4,934	4,611 e	3,788 e
11.468	Applied Meteorological Studies	1,096	600	500 e	500 e
11.469	Congressionally Identified Projects	12,700	15,000	19,500 e	2,000 e
11.470	Special Programs	400	300	300 e	0 e
11.472	Unallied Science Program	4,115	2,981	2,571 e	2,571 e
11.473	Coastal Services Center	2,064	1,800	2,400 e	2,000 e
11.474	Atlantic Coastal Fisheries	3,725	4,547	4,797 e	5,300 e

Please see "Important Notes on the Tables, Footnotes," page 572.

Table 1. (continued)

Program number	ADMINISTRATIVE ENTITY/SUB-UNIT Program Title (abridged)		FY 1997 in $thousands	FY 1998 in $thousands	FY 1999 in $thousands	FY 2000 in $thousands
11.477	Fisheries Disaster Relief		(n)	(n)	7,000 e	37,000 e
11.478	Coastal Ocean Program		(n)	8,400	8,400 e	9,000 e
11.480	Ocean Service Intern Program		(n)	(n)	500 e	500 e
	Subtotal:	Outlays	364,798	329,143	340,565	354,245
		Credits*	27,000*	105,000*	145,800*	23,800*

NATIONAL TELECOMMUNICATIONS AND INFORMATION ADMINISTRATION

11.550	Public Telecommunications		14,622	19,944	21,000 e	31,555 e
11.552	Telecommunications, Infrastructure		20,902	18,511	17,200 e	17,000 e
	Subtotal:	Outlays	35,524	38,455	38,200	48,555
		Credits*	0*	0*	0*	0*

NATIONAL INSTITUTE OF STANDARDS AND TECHNOLOGY

11.601	Calibration Program \ r		7,356	7,082	7,046 e	7,000 e
11.603	Standard Reference Data System \ r		491	470	390 e	390 e
11.604	Standard Reference Materials \ r		10,448	9,847	10,625 e	10,000 e
11.606	Weights and Measures Service \ r		2,625	2,463	2,683 e	2,677 e
11.609	Measurement, Engineering Research \ r		19,069	27,562	17,521 e	16,369 e
11.610	Standards and Certification \ r		678	709	770 e	775 e
11.611	Manufacturing Extension Partnership		85,698	100,637	110,958 e	83,456 e
11.612	Advanced Technology Program		216,769	140,852	189,152 e	209,931 e
11.614	Competitive Technology		(n)	(n)	3,696 e	0 e
	Subtotal:	Outlays	343,134	289,622	342,841	330,598
		Credits*	0*	0*	0*	0*

NATIONAL TECHNICAL INFORMATION SERVICE

11.650	National Technical Information \ r, u		38,233	35,318	40,987 e	35,000 e
	Subtotal:	Outlays	38,233	35,318	40,987	35,000
		Credits*	0*	0*	0*	0*

OFFICE OF THE SECRETARY

11.702	Postsecondary Internships		(n)	1,362	1,362 e	1,362 e
	Subtotal:	Outlays	0	1,362	1,362	1,362
		Credits*	0*	0*	0*	0*

MINORITY BUSINESS DEVELOPMENT AGENCY

11.800	Minority Business Development		6,688	7,100	9,600 e	9,600 e
11.801	Native American Program		709	693	1,702 e	1,702 e
11.802	Minority Business Development		1,448	1,453	1,722 e	1,722 e
	Subtotal:	Outlays	8,845	9,246	13,024	13,024
		Credits*	0*	0*	0*	0*

PATENT AND TRADEMARK OFFICE

11.900	Patent and Trademark Information		38,078	34,990	36,431 e	39,916 e
	Subtotal:	Outlays	38,078	34,990	36,431	39,916
		Credits*	0*	0*	0*	0*
	DEPARTMENT TOTAL:	OUTLAYS	1,927,939	2,288,288	3,027,451	4,777,838
		CREDITS*	27,000*	105,000*	145,800*	23,800*

DEPARTMENT OF DEFENSE

DEFENSE LOGISTICS AGENCY

12.002	Procurement Technical Assistance		17,300	17,300	12,000 e	12,000 e
	Subtotal:	Outlays	17,300	17,300	12,000	12,000
		Credits*	0*	0*	0*	0*

Please see "Important Notes on the Tables, Footnotes," page 572.

Table 1. (*continued*)

Program number	ADMINISTRATIVE ENTITY/SUB-UNIT Program Title (abridged)		FY 1997 in $thousands	FY 1998 in $thousands	FY 1999 in $thousands	FY 2000 in $thousands
	DEPARTMENT OF THE ARMY, OFFICE OF THE CHIEF OF ENGINEERS					
12.100	Aquatic Plant Control		9,500	9,500	0 e	0 e
12.101	Beach Erosion Control Projects		1,544	3,795	3,000 e	3,200 e
12.102	Emergency Flood Control Works		10,000	10,000	5,000 e	0 e
12.103	Emergency Flood Response		15,000	15,000	5,000 e	0 e
12.104	Flood Plain Management		8,847	8,847	6,441 e	8,000 e
12.105	Essential Highways, Public Works		12,500	8,974	10,000 e	11,000 e
12.106	Flood Control Projects		25,000	34,954	34,000 e	34,000 e
12.107	Navigation Projects		4,000	10,376	8,600 e	8,600 e
12.108	Snagging and Clearing		200	402	1,400 e	600 e
12.109	Protection, Clearing Channels		50	50	50 e	0 e
12.110	Planning Assistance to States		2,000	2,000	6,000 e	0 e
12.111	Flood Prevention		500	500	1,000 e	0 e
12.112	Payments to States/Taxes \ u		5,125	5,125	5,000 e	0 e
12.113	Reimbursements/Technical Services		27,546	27,546	41,453 e	43,545 e
12.114	Collaborative Research, Development \ u		4,660	4,660	5,306 e	6,000 e
	Subtotal:	Outlays	126,472	141,729	132,250	114,945
		Credits*	0*	0*	0*	0*
	DEPARTMENT OF THE NAVY, OFFICE OF NAVAL RESEARCH					
12.300	Basic, Applied Scientific Research		484,943	484,943	470,395 e	0 e
12.301	Basic, Applied Scientific Research		(n)	(n)	10,000 e	0 e
	Subtotal:	Outlays	484,943	484,943	480,395	0
		Credits*	0*	0*	0*	0*
	NATIONAL GUARD BUREAU					
12.400	Military Construction		118,700	118,700	65,800 e	18,400 e
12.401	National Guard Operations		844,000	844,000	900,000 e	0 e
	Subtotal:	Outlays	962,700	962,700	965,800	18,400
		Credits*	0*	0*	0*	0*
	DEPARTMENT OF THE ARMY, U.S. ARMY MEDICAL COMMAND					
12.420	Military Medical Research		137,380	137,380	56,530 e	140,000 e
	Subtotal:	Outlays	137,380	137,380	56,530	140,000
		Credits*	0*	0*	0*	0*
	U.S. ARMY MATERIEL COMMAND					
12.431	Basic Scientific Research		144,759	144,759	150,000 e	150,000 e
	Subtotal:	Outlays	144,759	144,759	150,000	150,000
		Credits*	0*	0*	0*	0*
	ASSISTANT SECRETARY (STRATEGY AND REQUIREMENTS)					
12.550	International Education \ t		2,000	2,000	2,000 e	2,000 e
12.551	National Security—Scholarships \ t		2,000	2,000	2,000 e	2,000 e
12.552	National Security—Fellowships \ t		2,000	2,000	2,000 e	2,000 e
	Subtotal:	Outlays	6,000	6,000	6,000	6,000
		Credits*	0*	0*	0*	0*
	ASSISTANT SECRETARY (ECONOMIC SECURITY)					
12.600	Community Economic Adjustment		(a)	(a)	(a)	(a)
12.607	Community Economic Planning \ t		26,579	26,579	26,579 e	40,000 e
12.610	Joint Land Use Studies \ t		273	273	126 e	300 e
12.611	Community Planning Assistance \ t		1,998	1,998	1,204 e	1,500 e
12.612	Community Base Reuse Plans		572	572	328 e	500 e
12.613	Growth Management Planning		0	0	0 e	150 e
	Subtotal:	Outlays	29,422	29,422	28,237	42,450
		Credits*	0*	0*	0*	0*

Please see "Important Notes on the Tables, Footnotes," page 572.

Table 1. (continued)

Program number	ADMINISTRATIVE ENTITY/SUB-UNIT Program Title (abridged)		FY 1997 in $thousands	FY 1998 in $thousands	FY 1999 in $thousands	FY 2000 in $thousands
	OFFICE OF THE SECRETARY					
12.630	Research/Science, Engineering		224,196	224,196	220,000 e	215,000 e
	Subtotal:	Outlays	224,196	224,196	220,000	215,000
		Credits*	0*	0*	0*	0*
	DEPARTMENT OF THE ARMY, AVIATION APPLIED TECHNOLOGY DIRECTORATE					
12.640	Integrated Helicopter Design		800	800	800 e	800 e
	Subtotal:	Outlays	800	800	800	800
		Credits*	0*	0*	0*	0*
	SECRETARIES OF MILITARY DEPARTMENTS					
12.700	Obsolete DOD Property \ p		2,500	2,500	2,750 e	0 e
	Subtotal:	Outlays	2,500	2,500	2,750	0
		Credits*	0*	0*	0*	0*
	DEPARTMENT OF THE AIR FORCE, MATERIAL COMMAND					
12.800	Air Force Defense Research Sciences		263,000	263,000	260,000 e	275,000 e
	Subtotal:	Outlays	263,000	263,000	260,000	275,000
		Credits*	0*	0*	0*	0*
	NATIONAL SECURITY AGENCY					
12.900	Language Grant Program		50	50	50 e	0 e
12.901	Mathematical Sciences Grants		2,900	2,900	2,600 e	0 e
12.902	Information Security		1,400	1,400	1,000 e	2,000 e
	Subtotal:	Outlays	4,350	4,350	3,650	2,000
		Credits*	0*	0*	0*	0*
	ADVANCED RESEARCH PROJECTS AGENCY					
12.910	Research and Technology		519,551	519,551	170,000 e	160,000 e
12.911	Defense Technology Conversion		212,914	212,914	195,000 e	250,000 e
	Subtotal:	Outlays	732,465	732,465	365,000	410,000
		Credits*	0*	0*	0*	0*
	DEPARTMENT TOTAL:	OUTLAYS	3,136,287	3,151,544	2,683,412	1,386,595
		CREDITS*	0*	0*	0*	0*

DEPARTMENT OF HOUSING AND URBAN DEVELOPMENT

HOUSING—FEDERAL HOUSING COMMISSIONER

		FY 1997	FY 1998	FY 1999	FY 2000
14.103	Interest Reduction—Housing \ u	(n)	(a)	(a) e	(a) e
		(n)*	(a)*	(a)*e	(a)*e
14.108	Rehabilitation Mortgage Insurance \ u	1,675,746*	(o)*	(o)*	(o)*
14.110	Manufactured Home Loan Insurance \ i, u	67,948*	23,000*	21,000*e	15,000*e
14.112	Construction, Rehab/Condominiums \ u	0*	0*	0*e	0*e
14.116	Group Practice Facilities \ u	(o)*	(o)*	(o)*	(o)*
14.117	Mortgage Insurance—Homes \ i, u	61,175,418*	90,518,000*	86,398,000*e	96,167,000*e
14.119	Homes for Disaster Victims \ u	(o)*	(o)*	(o)*	(o)*
14.120	Mortgage Insurance—Low/Moderate \ u	70,595*	(o)*	(o)*	(o)*
14.121	Mortgage Insurance—Outlying Areas \ u	(o)*	(o)*	(o)*	(o)*
14.122	Mortgage Insurance—Renewal Areas \ u	3,077*	(o)*	(o)*	(o)*
14.123	Mortgage Insurance—Declining Areas \ u	(o)*	(o)*	(o)*	(o)*
14.126	Mortgage Insurance—Cooperatives \ u	(o)*	(o)*	(o)*	(o)*
14.127	Manufactured Home Parks \ u	(o)*	(o)*	(o)*	(o)*

Please see "Important Notes on the Tables, Footnotes," page 572.

Table 1. *(continued)*

Program number	ADMINISTRATIVE ENTITY/SUB-UNIT Program Title (abridged)	FY 1997 in $thousands	FY 1998 in $thousands	FY 1999 in $thousands	FY 2000 in $thousands
14.128	Mortgage Insurance—Hospitals \ i, u	98,110*	108,000*	1,000,000*e	1,030,000*e
14.129	Mortgage Insurance—Nursing Homes \ u	984,661*	(o)*	(o)*	(o)*
14.130	Fee Simple Title \ u	(o)*	(o)*	(o)*e	(o)*e
14.132	Sales/Cooperative Housing \ u	(o)*	(o)*	(o)*	(o)*
14.133	Mortgage Insurance—Condominiums \ i, u	4,759,368*	9,663,000*	11,047,000*e	9,070,000*e
14.134	Mortgage Insurance—Rental Housing \ u	(o)*	(o)*	(o)*	(o)*
14.135	Mortgage Insurance—Market Rate \ i, u	1,164,429*	4,251,000*	4,071,000*e	4,999,000*e
14.138	Mortgage Insurance—Elderly \ u	0*	0*	0*e	0*e
14.139	Rental Housing/Renewal Areas \ u	(o)*	(o)*	(o)*	(o)*
14.140	Mortgage Insurance—Credit Risks \ u	0*	0*	0*e	0*e
14.142	Property Improvement Loans \ u	1,407,907*	(o)*	(o)*	(o)*
14.149	Rent Supplements, Housing	(n)*	(a)*	(a)*	(a)*
14.151	Supplemental Loan Insurance \ u	81,056*	(o)*	(o)*	(o)*
14.155	Existing Multifamily Projects \ u	1,511,717*	(o)*	(o)*	(o)*
14.157	Supportive Housing/Elderly \ u	888,932	1,128,490	736,683 e	660,000 e
14.159	Graduated Payment Mortgage \ u	(o)*	(o)*	(o)*	(o)*
14.162	Manufactured Home Lot Loans \ u	(o)*	(o)*	(o)*	(o)*
14.163	Single Family Cooperative Housing \ u	(o)*	(o)*	(o)*	(o)*
14.164	Operating Assistance/Multifamily \ u	17,900	9,392	34,632 e	0 e
14.165	Homes—Military Impacted Areas \ u	22,108*	(o)*	(o)*	(o)*
14.166	Mortgage Insurance—Armed Services \ u	2,045*	(o)*	(o)*	(o)*
14.167	Operating Loss Loans \ u	(o)*	(o)*	(o)*	(o)*
14.168	Land Sales \ u	654	642	1,100 e	1,100 e
14.169	Housing Counseling Assistance	15,000	20,000	18,000 e	20,000 e
14.171	Manufactured Home Standards \ u	13,890	16,604	17,401 e	17,889 e
14.172	Growing Equity Mortgages \ u	(o)*	(o)*	(o)*	(o)*
14.175	Adjustable Rate Mortgages \ u	(o)*	(o)*	(o)*	(o)*
14.181	Supportive Housing/Disabilities \ u	323,123	305,247	220,807 e	194,000 e
14.183	Home Equity Conversion Mortgages \ u	(o)*	(o)*	(o)*	(o)*
14.184	Mortgages/Single Room Occupancy \ u	0*	0*	0*e	0*e
14.188	HFA Risk Sharing Pilot Program \ u	397,338*	(o)*	(o)*	(o)*
14.189	QPE Risk Sharing \ u	7,875*	(o)*	(o)*	(o)*
14.191	Multifamily Housing Coordinators	5,000	0	0 e	0 e
14.193	Low-Income Housing Drug Elimination	17,262	16,489	33,555 e	16,250 e
14.195	Section 8—Special Allocations	8,445,531	16,113,717	15,593,773 e	16,444,140 e
14.196	Non-Conforming Loans/Low-Wealth	(n)	(n)	10,000 e	0 e
14.197	Multifamily Housing Reform \ u	(n)	21,000	348,000 e	685,000 e
14.198	Officer Next Door Sales Program \ p, u	(n)	90,000	75,000 e	90,000 e
	Subtotal: Outlays	9,727,292	17,721,581	17,088,951	18,128,379
	Credits*	73,429,398*	104,563,000*	102,537,000*	111,281,000*

COMMUNITY PLANNING AND DEVELOPMENT

Program number	Program Title	FY 1997	FY 1998	FY 1999	FY 2000
14.218	CDBG/Entitlement \ i	3,017,280	2,936,640	2,952,740 e	3,043,250 e
14.219	CDBG/Small Cities	60,941	59,034	59,042 e	61,328 e
14.225	CDBG/Insular Area	7,000	7,000	7,000 e	7,000 e
14.227	CDBG/Technical Assistance	9,000	4,000	7,500 e	7,500 e
14.228	CDBG/State	1,232,179	1,199,526	1,205,918 e	1,242,922 e
14.231	Emergency Shelter Grants	115,000	165,000	150,000 e	150,000 e
14.235	Supportive Housing Program	618,200	595,900	561,250 e	593,864 e
14.237	Historically Black Colleges	6,500	6,500	9,000 e	6,500 e
14.238	Shelter Plus Care	60,400	116,900	230,000 e	241,100 e
14.239	HOME Investment Partnerships	1,332,200	1,438,000	1,550,300 e	1,550,300 e
14.241	Housing/Persons with AIDS	196,000	204,000	225,000 e	240,000 e
14.243	Youthbuild Program	30,000	33,000	42,500 e	75,000 e
14.244	Empowerment Zones Program	0	5,000	45,000 e	150,000 e
14.246	CDBG/Economic Development	0	63,000	60,000 e	175,000 e
14.247	Self-Help Homeownership	0	16,700	27,500 e	0 e
14.248	CDBG—Section 108 Loans	1,300,000*	1,261,000*	1,261,000*e	1,261,000*e
14.249	Section 8—SRO	25,290	10,140	20,000 e	21,000 e
14.250	Rural Development	(n)	(n)	32,000 e	20,000 e
	Subtotal: Outlays	6,709,990	6,860,340	7,184,750	7,584,764
	Credits*	1,300,000*	1,261,000*	1,261,000*	1,261,000*

Please see "Important Notes on the Tables, Footnotes," page 572.

Table 1. (continued)

Program number	ADMINISTRATIVE ENTITY/SUB-UNIT Program Title (abridged)		FY 1997 in $thousands	FY 1998 in $thousands	FY 1999 in $thousands	FY 2000 in $thousands
	OFFICE OF FAIR HOUSING AND EQUAL OPPORTUNITY					
14.400	Equal Opportunity in Housing		(a)	(a)	(a)	(a)
14.401	FHAP—State, Local		11,377	14,702	23,959 e	20,000 e
14.402	Non-Discrimination/Age		(a)	(a)	(a)	(a)
14.404	Non-Discrimination/Disability		(a)	(a)	(a)	(a)
14.405	Non-Discrimination/Race, Color		(a)	(a)	(a)	(a)
14.406	Non-Discrimination/CDBG		(a)	(a)	(a)	(a)
14.407	Architectural Barriers		(a)	(a)	(a)	(a)
14.408	FHIP Administrative		0	0	0 e	0 e
14.409	FHIP Education, Outreach		2,084	0	8,960 e	15,750 e
14.410	FHIP Private Enforcement		18,400	86	25,745 e	7,750 e
14.412	Employment/Lower Income		(a)	(a)	(a)	(a)
14.413	FHIP/Organizations		2,982	86	38,500 e	27,000 e
14.414	Non-Discrimination/Disabilities		(a)	(a)	(a)	(a)
	Subtotal:	Outlays	34,843	14,874	97,164	70,500
		Credits*	0*	0*	0*	0*
	OFFICE OF POLICY DEVELOPMENT AND RESEARCH					
14.506	General Research and Technology		34,000	27,982	59,018 e	50,100 e
14.511	Community Outreach Partnership		7,500	7,982	14,518 e	15,000 e
14.512	CD Work-Study Program		3,500	3,125	3,517 e	3,000 e
14.513	Hispanic/Work-Study		1,500	3,284	397 e	0 e
14.514	Hispanic-Serving Institutions		(n)	(n)	6,500 e	6,500 e
	Subtotal:	Outlays	46,500	42,373	83,950	74,600
		Credits*	0*	0*	0*	0*
	PUBLIC AND INDIAN HOUSING					
14.850	Public and Indian Housing		2,990,090	2,973,971	2,858,697 e	3,003,000 e
14.852	Public Housing—CIAP		305,361	304,664	(o)	(o)
14.853	Public Housing—Tenants		0	0	10,014 e	(o)
14.854	Public Housing Drug Elimination		22,188	214,075	533,730 e	263,750 e
14.855	Section 8 Rental Voucher		(o)	(o)	(o)	(o)
14.856	Section 8 Moderate Rehabilitation		(n)	(n)	(n)	(a)
14.857	Section 8 Rental Certificates \ i		7,830,273	7,930,592	7,818,597 e	8,535,324 e
14.859	Comprehensive Grant Program \ i		2,121,954	2,121,003	2,950,360 e	2,555,000 e
14.862	Indian CDBG		67,000	67,503	67,000 e	67,000 e
14.864	Economic Development/Services		29,670	55,000	55,000 e	55,000 e
14.865	Indian Housing Loans		46,796*	22,975*	144,946*e	71,956*e
14.866	Distressed Public Housing		506,662	562,091	638,336 e	612,500 e
14.867	Indian Housing Block Grants		(n)	576,438	623,533 e	609,000 e
14.868	Anti-Drug Grants		(n)	(n)	40,000 e	20,000 e
14.869	Tribal Housing Activities		(n)*	(n)*	98,200*e	45,200*e
14.870	Residents—Supportive Services		(n)	27,800	100,800 e	55,000 e
	Subtotal:	Outlays	13,873,198	14,833,137	15,696,067	15,775,574
		Credits*	46,796*	22,975*	243,146*	117,156*
	OFFICE OF LEAD-BASED PAINT ABATEMENT AND POISONING PREVENTION					
14.900	Lead-Based Paint Hazards		65,000	56,194	138,652 e	80,000 e
	Subtotal:	Outlays	65,000	56,194	138,652	80,000
		Credits*	0*	0*	0*	0*
	DEPARTMENT TOTAL:	OUTLAYS	30,456,823	39,528,499	40,289,534	41,713,817
		CREDITS*	74,776,194*	105,846,975*	104,041,146*	112,659,156*
	DEPARTMENT OF THE INTERIOR					
15.020	Aid to Tribal Governments		19,358	96,894	86,100 e	86,900 e
15.022	Tribal Self-Governance		169,898	184,213	168,448 e	164,353 e

Please see "Important Notes on the Tables, Footnotes," page 572.

Table 1. *(continued)*

Program number	ADMINISTRATIVE ENTITY/SUB-UNIT Program Title (abridged)	FY 1997 in $thousands	FY 1998 in $thousands	FY 1999 in $thousands	FY 2000 in $thousands
15.023	Self-Governance Grants	2,676	2,375	250 e	250 e
15.024	Indian Self-Determination	53,138	73,381	76,000 e	88,000 e
15.025	Children, Elderly, Families	13,784	14,596	14,500 e	14,500 e
15.026	Indian Adult Education	2,341	2,256	2,160 e	2,215 e
15.027	Tribally Controlled Colleges	27,420	29,958	31,381 e	38,515 e
15.028	Community College Endowments	977	977	977 e	977 e
15.029	Tribal Courts	7,731	8,051	7,744 e	9,300 e
15.030	Indian Law Enforcement	44,159	44,338	57,200 e	82,700 e
15.031	Indian Community Fire Protection	1,037	1,292	1,200 e	1,100 e
15.032	Indian Economic Development	3,075	1,464	1,500 e	1,500 e
15.033	Road Maintenance	8,553	6,765	7,000 e	7,200 e
15.034	Agriculture on Indian Lands	3,449	3,769	3,400 e	3,500 e
15.035	Forestry on Indian Lands	11,321	11,880	12,000 e	12,000 e
15.036	Indian Rights Protection	449	373	437 e	440 e
15.037	Water Resources on Indian Lands	9,723	10,186	10,000 e	12,000 e
15.038	Minerals, Mining/Indian Lands	741	527 e	542 e	500 e
15.039	Fish, Wildlife, Parks/Indian Lands	24,805	24,805	27,226 e	26,405 e
15.040	Real Estate Programs-Indian Lands	1,883	1,665	2,200 e	2,000 e
15.041	Environmental Management	173	906	3,800 e	5,800 e
15.042	Indian School Equalization	133,073	158,971	166,000 e	174,000 e
15.043	Indian Child and Family Education	3,125	3,482	3,500 e	3,500 e
15.044	Indian Schools—Transportation	15,423	20,689	22,000 e	25,000 e
15.045	Indian Children/Severe Disabilities	3,732	3,737	3,740 e	3,747 e
15.046	Administrative Costs/Indian Schools	35,409	43,672	42,160 e	47,690 e
15.047	Indian Education Facilities	35,409	35,340	36,000 e	38,000 e
15.048	BIA Facilities	1,091	1,093	1,100 e	1,100 e
15.049	Irrigation Operations, Maintenance	3,055	3,140	2,700 e	3,000 e
15.050	Indian Hunting, Fishing Rights	212	212	213 e	220 e
15.051	Endangered Species/Indian Lands	1,567	1,807	1,800 e	2,700 e
15.052	Litigation Support/Indian Rights	792	1,536	1,500 e	1,500 e
15.053	Attorney Fees-Indian Rights	689	1,009	1,100 e	1,100 e
15.055	Alaskan Indian Allotments	583	343	167 e	170 e
15.057	Navajo-Hopi Settlement	292	247	250 e	475 e
15.058	Indian Post Secondary Schools	(a)	(a)	(a)	(a)
15.059	Graduate Student Scholarships	1,337	1,337	1,337 e	1,337 e
15.060	United Tribes Technical College	1,810	2,352	2,310 e	2,381 e
15.061	Sioux Tribes Development Corp.	107	108	108 e	0 e
15.062	Replacement, Repair—Schools	24,295	36,753	41,400 e	84,600 e
15.063	Improvement—Detention Facilities	265	9,948 e	2,176 e	1,400 e
15.064	Fire Protection-BIA Facilities	528	644	650 e	650 e
15.065	Safety of Dams/Indian Lands	19,739	14,625	16,000 e	17,500 e
15.108	Indian Employment Assistance	10,040	8,965	8,500 e	8,300 e
15.113	Indian Social Services—General	64,194	70,270	69,500 e	70,800 e
15.114	Indian—Higher Education	18,504	18,445	18,500 e	18,000 e
15.124	Indian Loans—Economic \ u	5,000*	5,000*	5,001*e	5,008*e
15.130	Indian Education—Schools	14,616	12,379	12,200 e	11,800 e
15.141	Indian Housing Assistance	12,963	13,470	13,500 e	13,100 e
15.144	Indian Child Welfare Act	14,092	14,235	12,945 e	12,627 e
15.146	Ironworker Training Program	524	524	524 e	0 e
15.214	Disposals of Mineral Material \ p	(a)	(a)	(a)	(a)
15.222	Inspection Agreements	204	225	410 e	350 e
15.224	Cultural Resource Management \ p	(a)	(a)	(a)	(a)
15.225	Recreation Resource Management	(a)	(a)	(a)	(a)
15.226	Payments in Lieu of Taxes	(n)	118,824	123,000 e	123,000 e
15.250	Surface Coal Mining	54,316	51,676	52,156 e	52,156 e
15.252	Abandoned Mine Land Reclamation \ u	142,000	142,322	145,252 e	169,252 e
15.253	Not-for-Profit AMD Reclamation	(n)	(n)	750 e	1,750 e
15.504	Reclamation and Water Re-use	38,100	49,700	39,100 e	31,500 e
15.506	Desalination Research, Development	(n)	2,017	1,055 e	100 e
15.602	Conservation Law Training	372	443	469 e	491 e
15.605	Sport Fish Restoration \ t	254,472	291,348	212,429 e	259,515 e
15.608	Fish and Wildlife Management	1,800	1,554	1,632 e	1,670 e
15.611	Wildlife Restoration \ u	219,324	193,875	165,353 e	178,480 e
15.614	Coastal Wetlands \ t	13,621	10,266	9,439 e	11,269 e
15.615	Endangered Species Fund \ u	11,844	20,981	13,520 e	76,520 e

Please see "Important Notes on the Tables, Footnotes," page 572.

Table 1. (continued)

Program number	ADMINISTRATIVE ENTITY/SUB-UNIT Program Title (abridged)	FY 1997 in $thousands	FY 1998 in $thousands	FY 1999 in $thousands	FY 2000 in $thousands
15.616	Clean Vessel Act \ t	7,625	2,626	9,400 e	9,400 e
15.617	Wildlife Conservation \ u	1,195	951	768 e	768 e
15.618	Fish, Wildlife—Administration \ t, u	2,399	4,334	3,765 e	4,000 e
15.619	Rhinoceros, Tiger Conservation \ u	372	388	821 e	970 e
15.620	African Elephant Conservation \ t	652	921	1,500 e	970 e
15.621	Asian Elephant Conservation	(n)	(n)	485 e	970 e
15.622	Sportfishing, Boating Safety \ t	(n)	(n)	(n)	7,520 e
15.623	Wetlands Conservation \ u	(n)	42,741	48,619 e	45,000 e
15.805	State Water Resources Research	4,320	4,301	4,818 e	4,818 e
15.807	Earthquake Hazards Reduction	11,973	10,050	10,900 e	10,500 e
15.808	Geological Survey—Research, Data	16,650	29,000	27,900 e	27,200 e
15.809	National Spatial Data	1,225	2,178	1,400 e	1,600 e
15.810	National Geologic Mapping Program	4,080	4,164	4,226 e	4,226 e
15.850	Indian Arts, Crafts Development	962	967	974 e	1,164 e
15.875	Economic, Social Development	283,015	291,865	282,270 e	295,580 e
15.904	Historic Preservation \ u	36,212	40,812	42,412 e	80,512 e
15.910	National Natural Landmarks	916	932	943 e	965 e
15.912	National Historic Landmarks	373	321	327 e	357 e
15.914	National Register/Historic Places	1,357	1,436	1,500 e	1,564 e
15.915	Technical Preservation Services	3,050	1,500	1,500 e	1,500 e
15.916	Outdoor Recreation \ u	0	0	0 e	0 e
15.918	Federal Surplus Real Property	405	392	392 e	392 e
15.919	Urban Park, Recreation Recovery	0	0	0 e	4,000 e
15.921	Rivers, Trails Conservation	7,068	7,159	7,035 e	10,460 e
15.922	Native American Graves Protection	2,290	2,496	2,496 e	2,496 e
15.923	Preservation Technology, Training	624	746	865 e	800 e
15.924	HBCU Preservation Initiative \ u	1,400	5,622	8,422 e	15,022 e
15.925	National Maritime Heritage \ u	716	0	30 e	50 e
15.926	American Battlefield Protection	611	740	591 e	700 e
15.976	Migratory Bird Banding	1,350	1,340	1,440 e	1,440 e
15.978	Upper Mississippi Monitoring	2,913	2,208	2,711 e	2,900 e
	DEPARTMENT TOTAL: OUTLAYS	1,953,963	2,343,425	2,229,020	2,548,749
	CREDITS*	5,000*	5,000*	5,001*	5,008*

DEPARTMENT OF JUSTICE

Program number	Program Title (abridged)	FY 1997	FY 1998	FY 1999	FY 2000
16.001	Narcotics, Drugs—Laboratory	1,658	1,658	1,881 e	2,004 e
16.003	Narcotics, Drugs/Publications	13	13	13 e	13 e
16.004	Narcotics, Drugs Training	5,025	5,025	3,445 e	3,471 e
16.005	Public Education on Drug Abuse	806	806	903 e	1,011 e
16.006	Municipal Domestic Preparedness	(n)	(n)	16,000 e	0 e
16.007	State Domestic Preparedness	(n)	0	69,500 e	79,000 e
16.100	Desegregation of Public Education	2,714	2,828	2,968 e	3,175 e
16.101	Equal Employment Opportunity	5,644	5,644	5,682 e	6,101 e
16.103	Fair Housing and Equal Credit	9,978	9,742	10,063 e	10,624 e
16.104	Protection of Voting Rights	7,732	8,000	8,281 e	8,781 e
16.105	Institutionalized Persons	3,488	3,782	3,967 e	4,224 e
16.108	Disabilities Act Assistance	9,337	9,490	10,785 e	11,563 e
16.109	Civil Rights Prosecution	4,523	5,345	6,690 e	7,035 e
16.110	Education, Enforcement—Immigration	5,403	5,367	5,517 e	5,817 e
16.200	Community Relations Service	5,319	5,319	7,319 e	8,899 e
16.201	Cuban and Haitian Entrant	4,130	6,608	9,764 e	10,500 e
16.300	FBI Advanced Police Training	16,978	12,755	14,372 e	14,781 e
16.301	FBI Crime Laboratory	117,392	108,755	121,968 e	141,562 e
16.302	FBI Field Police Training	22,900	30,106	23,390 e	24,844 e
16.303	FBI Fingerprint Identification	244,888	239,593	216,565 e	174,531 e
16.304	National Crime Information Center	9,504	11,326	17,695 e	18,777 e
16.305	Uniform Crime Reports	9,610	6,374	9,522 e	10,105 e
16.307	DNA Index System \ i	8,750	9,500	8,100 e	7,000 e
16.308	Indian Country Investigations	1,125	141	1,309 e	1,215 e
16.400	Citizenship Education, Training \ u	50	28	30 e	30 e
16.523	Juvenile Incentive Block Grants	(n)	240,428	250,408 e	0 e
16.524	Domestic Violence—Legal	(n)	11,654	23,346 e	23,000 e

Please see "Important Notes on the Tables, Footnotes," page 572.

Table 1. *(continued)*

Program number	ADMINISTRATIVE ENTITY/SUB-UNIT Program Title (abridged)	FY 1997 in $thousands	FY 1998 in $thousands	FY 1999 in $thousands	FY 2000 in $thousands
16.525	Crimes Against Women/Campuses	(n)	(n)	10,000 e	0 e
16.540	Juvenile Justice—States	79,064	93,516	90,370 e	89,000 e
16.541	Juvenile Justice—Special	8,575	13,746	23,869 e	21,000 e
16.542	National Institute/Juvenile Justice	21,323	29,778	28,381 e	25,750 e
16.543	Missing Children's Assistance	7,688	12,934	17,641 e	17,168 e
16.544	Gang-Free Schools	11,370	10,879	16,945 e	12,000 e
16.547	Victims of Child Abuse	11,389	13,643	15,922 e	15,812 e
16.548	Delinquency Prevention Program	19,315	19,727	47,803 e	55,000 e
16.549	State Challenge Activities	10,378	9,727	10,906 e	10,000 e
16.550	State Justice Statistics Program	1,426	2,391	2,200 e	2,200 e
16.554	Criminal History Improvement	45,596	47,419	49,254 e	0 e
16.560	Justice Research Grants	35,078	63,181	67,178 e	42,948 e
16.561	Visiting Fellowships	376	446	200 e	300 e
16.562	Graduate Research Fellowships	79	136	200 e	200 e
16.563	Corrections, Law Enforcement Support	674	1,034	1,945 e	1,440 e
16.564	DNA Laboratory Improvement	(n)	12,292	15,000 e	15,000 e
16.565	Domestic Anti-Terrorism Technology	(n)	12,526	10,000 e	10,000 e
16.566	Dubois Post-Doctoral Fellowship	(n)	(n)	(n)	100 e
16.571	Public Safety Officers' Benefits	23,529	31,001	31,809 e	32,541 e
16.575	Crime Victim Assistance \ u	397,059	275,671	238,136 e	177,025 e
16.576	Crime Victim Compensation \ u	74,128	67,428	66,966 e	177,025 e
16.577	Emergency Federal Law Enforcement	809	0	0 e	0 e
16.578	Federal Surplus Property Transfer	55	56	57 e	58 e
16.579	Byrne Formula Grant Program	496,752	462,482	508,371 e	383,960 e
16.580	Byrne Law Enforcement Assistance	62,107	58,945	59,203 e	57,546 e
16.582	Victim Assistance/Discretionary \ u	10,254	24,963	25,268 e	10,950 e
16.583	Children's Justice/Indian \ u	1,358	1,213	2,373 e	1,500 e
16.585	Drug Court Program	31,044	35,841	39,669 e	47,995 e
16.586	Violent Offender Incarceration	796,686	509,149	483,187 e	0 e
16.587	Violence Against Women/Indian	5,560	6,960	9,189 e	8,270 e
16.588	Violence Against Women	133,170	135,901	138,407 e	138,407 e
16.589	Rural Domestic Violence	6,916	22,812	28,577 e	24,477 e
16.590	Arrest Policies	48,758	66,260	36,833 e	33,288 e
16.592	Law Enforcement Block Grants	499,914	467,478	574,264 e	0 e
16.593	Substance Abuse Treatment/Prisoners	30,611	60,675	63,852 e	62,489 e
16.595	Weed and Seed Program	26,642	43,260	36,568 e	32,412 e
16.596	Correctional Grant/Tribes	2,678	2,042	36,958 e	34,000 e
16.597	Motor Vehicle Theft Protection Act	868	776	1,424 e	1,248 e
16.598	State Identification Systems	8,118	9,908	8,974 e	0 e
16.601	Corrections—Training	2,245	3,284	2,875 e	2,961 e
16.602	Corrections—Research	0	1,826	4,759 e	1,500 e
16.603	Corrections—Technical Assistance	4,750	4,962	5,869 e	6,045 e
16.606	Criminal Alien Assistance	497,695	492,038	1,148,334 e	479,948 e
16.607	Bulletproof Vest Partnership	(n)	(n)	23,800 e	0 e
16.608	Tribal Court Assistance	(n)	(n)	4,900 e	4,799 e
16.609	Community Prosecution Program	(n)	(n)	5,000 e	0 e
16.610	Regional Information Sharing	(n)	19,978	20,027 e	20,000 e
16.611	Closed-Circuit TV/Child Abuse	(n)	1,051	1,087 e	1,000 e
16.612	National White Collar Crime Center	(n)	5,350	7,350 e	9,250 e
16.613	Scams Targeting the Elderly	(n)	3,809	2,573 e	2,000 e
16.614	State/Local Anti-Terrorism Training	(n)	2,000	2,000 e	2,000 e
16.615	Public Safety Educational Assistance	(n)	36	2,433 e	0 e
16.710	Public Safety, Community Policing	1,219,910	1,437,987	1,462,818 e	1,177,268 e
16.711	Troops to Cops	(n)	(n)	5,600 e	5,700 e
16.712	Police Corps	1,519	5,127	83,346 e	30,000 e
16.726	Juvenile Mentoring Program	10,408	12,451	20,426 e	12,000 e
16.727	Enforcing Underage Drinking Laws	(n)	25,000	25,000 e	0 e
16.728	Drug Prevention Program	(n)	5,000	10,000 e	10,000 e
16.729	Drug-Free Communities Support	(n)	9,520	20,000 e	20,000 e
16.730	Safe Start	(n)	(n)	10,000 e	10,000 e
16.731	Tribal Youth Program	(n)	(n)	10,000 e	20,000 e
16.732	Safe Schools/Healthy Students	(n)	(n)	1,500 e	0 e
	DEPARTMENT TOTAL: OUTLAYS	5,142,841	5,395,902	6,527,079	3,933,643
	CREDITS*	0*	0*	0*	0*

Please see "Important Notes on the Tables, Footnotes," page 572.

Table 1. *(continued)*

Program number	ADMINISTRATIVE ENTITY/SUB-UNIT Program Title (abridged)		FY 1997 in $thousands	FY 1998 in $thousands	FY 1999 in $thousands	FY 2000 in $thousands
	DEPARTMENT OF LABOR					
	BUREAU OF LABOR STATISTICS					
17.002	Labor Force Statistics		221,396	232,282	240,986 e	244,394 e
17.003	Prices and Cost of Living Data		100,134	106,886	120,069 e	131,032 e
17.004	Productivity and Technology Data		7,263	7,186	7,518 e	8,988 e
17.005	Compensation, Working Conditions		61,613	63,759	66,300 e	74,863 e
17.006	Employment Projections Data		4,640	4,719	4,873 e	5,058 e
	Subtotal:	Outlays	395,046	414,832	439,746	464,335
		Credits*	0*	0*	0*	0*
	OFFICE OF LABOR-MANAGEMENT STANDARDS					
17.140	Labor Organization Reports		25,489	25,489	29,224 e	27,648 e
	Subtotal:	Outlays	25,489	25,489	29,224	27,648
		Credits*	0*	0*	0*	0*
	PENSION AND WELFARE BENEFITS ADMINISTRATION					
17.150	Pension and Welfare Benefits		70,812	79,000	90,393 e	101,831 e
	Subtotal:	Outlays	70,812	79,000	90,393	101,831
		Credits*	0*	0*	0*	0*
	EMPLOYMENT AND TRAINING ADMINISTRATION					
17.201	Registered Apprenticeship Training		16,271	16,434	17,485 e	19,580 e
17.202	Certification/Agricultural \ i		31,300	31,300	31,300 e	31,300 e
17.203	Certification/Alien Workers \ i		(o)	(o)	(o)	(o)
17.207	Employment Service \ t		761,735	761,735	761,735 e	761,735 e
17.225	Unemployment Insurance \ t		23,386,458	22,563,458	25,371,358 e	28,144,458 e
17.235	Senior Community Service		435,000	444,000	440,000 e	440,000 e
17.245	Trade Adjustment Assistance		307,000	314,300	318,900 e	0 e
17.246	Training—Dislocated Workers		1,091,900	1,286,200	1,350,510 e	1,450,510 e
17.247	Migrant, Seasonal Farmworkers		69,285	69,285	71,517 e	71,017 e
17.248	Employment, Training Research		9,196	9,196	10,196 e	0 e
17.249	Employment Services, Training		27,100	27,100	23,717 e	0 e
17.250	Job Training Partnership Act		1,892,672	1,892,672	1,955,965 e	1,955,965 e
17.251	Native American Employment		52,502	52,502	53,815 e	53,815 e
17.252	Attestations/Alien Specialty \ i		(o)	(o)	(o)	(o)
17.253	Welfare-to-Work Grants		(n)	(n)	1,488 e	1,388 e
17.254	Welfare-to-Work/Tribes		(n)	(n)	15,000 e	15,000 e
17.255	Workforce Investment Act		(n)	(n)	(n)	5,280,798 e
17.257	One-Stop Career Center Initiative		(n)	150,000	146,000 e	0 e
	Subtotal:	Outlays	28,080,419	27,618,182	30,568,986	38,225,566
		Credits*	0*	0*	0*	0*
	EMPLOYMENT STANDARDS ADMINISTRATION					
17.301	Federal, Construction Contractors		58,910	62,251	65,297 e	76,417 e
17.302	Longshore and Harbor Workers		3,377	3,501	4,000 e	4,000 e
17.303	Minimum Wage, Hour Standards \ i		119,787	121,128	129,269 e	151,042 e
17.306	Consumer Credit Protection		(o)	(o)	(o)	(o)
17.307	Coal Mine Workers' Compensation \ t		478,369	452,194	453,725 e	430,546 e
17.308	Farm Labor Contractors		(o)	(o)	(o)	(o)
17.309	Labor Organization Reports		(n)	26,673	28,085 e	29,308 e
	Subtotal:	Outlays	660,443	665,747	680,376	691,313
		Credits*	0*	0*	0*	0*
	OCCUPATIONAL SAFETY AND HEALTH ADMINISTRATION					
17.502	Susan Harwood Training		2,414	4,800	4,920 e	8,523 e

Please see "Important Notes on the Tables, Footnotes," page 572.

Table 1. (*continued*)

Program number	ADMINISTRATIVE ENTITY/SUB-UNIT Program Title (abridged)		FY 1997 in $thousands	FY 1998 in $thousands	FY 1999 in $thousands	FY 2000 in $thousands
17.503	State Program		77,169	77,941	80,084 e	83,501 e
17.504	Consultation Agreements		34,477	35,373	40,943 e	40,943 e
	Subtotal:	Outlays	114,060	118,114	125,947	132,967
		Credits*	0*	0*	0*	0*
	MINE SAFETY AND HEALTH ADMINISTRATION					
17.600	Mine Health and Safety Grants		5,718	5,718	5,861 e	6,013 e
17.601	Mine Health, Safety Counseling		21,233	23,747	25,312 e	25,840 e
17.602	Mine Health, Safety Education		9,068	7,285	6,956 e	6,825 e
	Subtotal:	Outlays	36,019	36,750	38,129	38,678
		Credits*	0*	0*	0*	0*
	OFFICE OF THE SECRETARY-WOMEN'S BUREAU					
17.700	Women's Special Assistance		7,743	7,762	7,802 e	8,369 e
	Subtotal:	Outlays	7,743	7,762	7,802	8,369
		Credits*	0*	0*	0*	0*
	ASSISTANT SECRETARY FOR VETERANS' EMPLOYMENT AND TRAINING					
17.801	Disabled Veterans Outreach \ t		81,993	81,993	80,040 e	80,040 e
17.802	Veterans Employment Program		7,300	7,300	7,300 e	6,000 e
17.803	Uniformed Services/Rights \ t		(a)	(a)	(a)	(a)
17.804	Local Veterans Employment \ t		75,125	75,125	77,078 e	77,078 e
17.805	Homeless Veterans Reintegration \ t		3,000	0	3,000 e	3,000 e
	Subtotal:	Outlays	167,418	164,418	167,418	166,118
		Credits*	0*	0*	0*	0*
	DEPARTMENT TOTAL:	OUTLAYS	29,557,449	29,130,294	32,148,021	39,856,825
		CREDITS*	0*	0*	0*	0*
	DEPARTMENT OF STATE					
	OFFICE OF THE LEGAL ADVISOR					
19.200	Claims/Foreign Governments		(a)	(a)	(a)	(a)
19.201	Protection of Ships \ u		12	0	5 e	5 e
	Subtotal:	Outlays	12	0	5	5
		Credits*	0*	0*	0*	0*
	BUREAU OF PERSONNEL					
19.202	Special Domestic Assignments		(a)	(a)	(a)	(a)
	Subtotal:	Outlays	0	0	0	0
		Credits*	0*	0*	0*	0*
	BUREAU OF OCEANS & INTERNATIONAL ENVIRONMENTAL & SCIENTIFIC AFFAIRS					
19.204	Fishermen's Guaranty Fund \ u		186	0	500 e	500 e
	Subtotal:	Outlays	186	0	500	500
		Credits*	0*	0*	0*	0*
	BUREAU OF INTELLIGENCE AND RESEARCH					
19.300	Study/Eastern Europe		4,200	4,800	4,800 e	4,800 e
	Subtotal:	Outlays	4,200	4,800	4,800	4,800
		Credits*	0*	0*	0*	0*
	DEPARTMENT TOTAL:	OUTLAYS	4,398	4,800	5,305	5,305
		CREDITS*	0*	0*	0*	0*

Please see "Important Notes on the Tables, Footnotes," page 572.

Table 1. (*continued*)

Program number	ADMINISTRATIVE ENTITY/SUB-UNIT Program Title (abridged)		FY 1997 in $thousands	FY 1998 in $thousands	FY 1999 in $thousands	FY 2000 in $thousands
	DEPARTMENT OF TRANSPORTATION					
	UNITED STATES COAST GUARD					
20.001	Boating Safety		9,200	9,100	9,100 e	9,000 e
20.005	Boating Safety Financial \ t		44,438	53,739	58,000 e	58,000 e
20.006	Oil Spill Trust Fund \ t		35	0	25 e	50 e
20.007	Bridge Alteration		16,000	17,000	14,000 e	11,000 e
	Subtotal:	Outlays	69,673	79,839	81,125	78,050
		Credits*	0*	0*	0*	0*
	FEDERAL AVIATION ADMINISTRATION					
20.100	Aviation Education		131	131	125 e	125 e
20.106	Airport Improvement Program \ t		1,460,001	1,661,000	1,950,000 e	1,600,000 e
20.107	Airway Science		0	0	0 e	0 e
20.108	Aviation Research \ t		30,000	30,000	30,000 e	20,000 e
20.109	Air Transportation Centers \ t		500	500	1,000 e	1,000 e
	Subtotal:	Outlays	1,490,632	1,691,631	1,981,125	1,621,125
		Credits*	0*	0*	0*	0*
	FEDERAL HIGHWAY ADMINISTRATION					
20.205	Highway Planning, Construction \ t		21,361,532	20,976,136	26,571,639 e	28,345,813 e
20.215	Highway Training, Education \ t		4,269	240	280 e	285 e
20.217	Motor Carrier Safety \ t		48,950	51,000	55,375 e	55,418 e
20.218	Motor Carrier Safety \ t		76,399	84,000	100,000 e	105,000 e
20.219	Recreational Trails \ t		16,500	14,691	40,000 e	50,000 e
	Subtotal:	Outlays	21,507,650	21,126,067	26,767,294	28,556,516
		Credits*	0*	0*	0*	0*
	FEDERAL RAILROAD ADMINISTRATION					
20.301	Railroad Safety		51,338	57,082	64,140 e	63,860 e
20.303	Grants/Railroad Safety		0	0	0 e	0 e
20.308	Local Rail Freight Assistance		0	33	0 e	0 e
20.312	High Speed Transportation \ t		24,755	20,395	21,000 e	12,000 e
	Subtotal:	Outlays	76,093	77,510	85,140	75,860
		Credits*	0*	0*	0*	0*
	FEDERAL TRANSIT ADMINISTRATION					
20.500	Capital Investment Grants \ t		1,699,147	1,656,000	2,819,000 e	2,962,000 e
20.502	University Research, Training		(o)	(o)	(o)	(o)
20.503	Managerial Training		(o)	(o)	(o)	(o)
20.505	Metropolitan Planning Grants		41,083	40,934	43,842 e	49,632 e
20.507	Urbanized Area Formula Grants \ t		1,983,690	2,052,026	3,033,792 e	3,420,000 e
20.509	Nonurbanized Areas		131,922	129,450	177,857 e	203,164 e
20.511	Human Resource Programs		(o)	(o)	(o)	(o)
20.512	Technical Assistance		(o)	(o)	(o)	(o)
20.513	Elderly, Persons with Disabilities		53,483	58,557	67,136 e	76,930 e
20.514	Transit Planning, Research \ i		24,376	33,463	27,500 e	33,500 e
20.515	State Planning and Research \ t		8,798	8,318	9,257 e	10,368 e
	Subtotal:	Outlays	3,942,499	3,978,748	6,178,384	6,755,594
		Credits*	0*	0*	0*	0*
	NATIONAL HIGHWAY TRAFFIC SAFETY ADMINISTRATION					
20.600	State, Community Highway Safety \ t		140,200	147,845	150,000 e	153,000 e
20.601	Drunk Driving Prevention \ t		25,500	34,500	35,000 e	36,000 e
	Subtotal:	Outlays	165,700	182,345	185,000	189,000
		Credits*	0*	0*	0*	0*

Please see "Important Notes on the Tables, Footnotes," page 572.

Table 1. (continued)

Program number	ADMINISTRATIVE ENTITY/SUB-UNIT Program Title (abridged)		FY 1997 in $thousands	FY 1998 in $thousands	FY 1999 in $thousands	FY 2000 in $thousands
	RESEARCH AND SPECIAL PROGRAMS ADMINISTRATION					
20.700	Pipeline Safety \ u		13,200	13,600	14,500 e	16,000 e
20.701	University Transportation Centers \ t		13,600	31,650	31,650 e	33,250 e
20.703	Hazardous Materials Training \ u		7,372	6,400	6,700 e	12,000 e
	Subtotal:	Outlays	34,172	51,650	52,850	61,250
		Credits*	0*	0*	0*	0*
	MARITIME ADMINISTRATION					
20.801	Ports, Intermodal Transportation		1,778	702	756 e	686 e
20.802	Federal Ship Financing \ u		13,018*	9,259*	56,582*e	6,000*e
20.803	Maritime War Risk Insurance \ u		250	67	1,000 e	1,000 e
20.804	Operating—Differential Subsidies		148,430	51,030	0 e	0 e
20.805	Ship Sales \ p		243	384	1,000 e	1,000 e
20.806	State Marine Schools		7,532	7,122	6,750 e	7,161 e
20.807	U.S. Merchant Marine Academy		30,900	31,590	32,298 e	34,073 e
20.808	Capital Construction Fund		208	156	112 e	114 e
20.810	Supplementary Training		1,375	190	190 e	190 e
20.812	Construction Reserve Fund		9	9	7 e	7 e
20.813	Maritime Security Fleet Program		49,925	84,331	97,640 e	98,700 e
	Subtotal:	Outlays	240,650	175,581	139,753	142,931
		Credits*	13,018*	9,259*	56,582*	6,000*
	OFFICE OF THE SECRETARY					
20.900	Transportation—Consumer Affairs		679	567	463 e	463 e
20.901	Essential Air Services \ t		23,531	44,972	50,000 e	50,000 e
20.903	Support/Disadvantaged Businesses		1,164	1,100	1,100 e	1,100 e
20.904	Bonding Assistance Program		14,445*	10,000*	17,000*e	0*e
20.905	Disadvantaged—Short-Term Lending		7,885*	8,000*	8,000*e	0*e
20.906	Hispanic Serving Institutions		300	300	300 e	300 e
20.907	Entrepreneurial Training		480	480	480 e	480 e
	Subtotal:	Outlays	26,154	47,419	52,343	52,343
		Credits*	22,330*	18,000*	25,000*	0*
	DEPARTMENT TOTAL:	OUTLAYS	27,553,223	27,410,790	35,523,014	37,532,669
		CREDITS*	35,348*	27,259*	81,582*	6,000*

	DEPARTMENT OF THE TREASURY					
	INTERNAL REVENUE SERVICE					
21.003	Taxpayer Service		267,396	382,800	393,400 e	420,800 e
21.004	Federal Tax Information/States		134	133	133 e	133 e
21.006	Tax Counseling/Elderly		3,700	3,700	3,700 e	3,700 e
21.008	Low-Income Taxpayer Clinics		(n)	(n)	2,000 e	6,000 e
	Subtotal:	Outlays	271,230	386,633	399,233	430,633
		Credits*	0*	0*	0*	0*
	UNDER SECRETARY/DOMESTIC FINANCE					
21.020	Community Development Program		37,494	46,000	76,200 e	61,500 e
21.021	Bank Enterprise Award		16,494	27,977	29,300 e	34,400 e
	Subtotal:	Outlays	53,988	73,977	105,500	95,900
		Credits*	0*	0*	0*	0*
	BUREAU OF ALCOHOL, TOBACCO AND FIREARMS					
21.052	Training Assistance		132	135	135 e	135 e
	Subtotal:	Outlays	132	135	135	135
		Credits*	0*	0*	0*	0*

Please see "Important Notes on the Tables, Footnotes," page 572.

Table 1. (continued)

Program number	ADMINISTRATIVE ENTITY/SUB-UNIT Program Title (abridged)		FY 1997 in $thousands	FY 1998 in $thousands	FY 1999 in $thousands	FY 2000 in $thousands
	UNITED STATES SECRET SERVICE					
21.100	Training Activities		335	337	337 e	337 e
	Subtotal:	Outlays	335	337	337	337
		Credits*	0*	0*	0*	0*
	DEPARTMENT TOTAL:	OUTLAYS	325,685	461,082	505,205	527,005
		CREDITS*	0*	0*	0*	0*
	APPALACHIAN REGIONAL COMMISSION					
23.001	Appalachian Regional Development		(o)	(o)	(o)	(o)
23.002	Appalachian Area Development		60,152	77,970	97,172 e	55,329 e
23.003	Highway System		94,796	111,629	24,607 e	0 e
23.008	Local Access Roads		2,497	1,103	2,000 e	2,000 e
23.009	Development District Assistance		4,436	5,565	5,474 e	5,400 e
23.011	Research, Technical Assistance		900	900	900 e	900 e
	DEPARTMENT TOTAL:	OUTLAYS	162,781	197,167	130,153	63,629
		CREDITS*	0*	0*	0*	0*
	OFFICE OF PERSONNEL MANAGEMENT					
27.001	Federal Civil Service		(a)	(a)	(a)	(a)
27.002	Employment Assistance/Veterans		(a)	(a)	(a)	(a)
27.003	Federal Student Employment		(a)	(a)	(a)	(a)
27.005	Federal Employment/Disabled		(a)	(a)	(a)	(a)
27.006	Federal Summer Employment		(a)	(a)	(a)	(a)
27.011	Intergovernmental Mobility		(a)	(a)	(a)	(a)
27.013	Presidential Management Intern \ r		(a)	(a)	(a)	(a)
	DEPARTMENT TOTAL:	OUTLAYS	0	0	0	0
		CREDITS*	0*	0*	0*	0*
	COMMISSION ON CIVIL RIGHTS					
29.001	Clearinghouse Services		8,500	8,500	8,740 e	8,740 e
	DEPARTMENT TOTAL:	OUTLAYS	8,500	8,500	8,740	8,740
		CREDITS*	0*	0*	0*	0*
	EQUAL EMPLOYMENT OPPORTUNITY COMMISSION					
30.001	Title VII/Civil Rights \ i		239,477	214,176	279,000 e	312,000 e
30.002	Fair Employment Agencies \ i		27,488	27,490	27,086 e	29,000 e
30.005	Private Bar Program		(a)	(a)	(a)	(a)
30.008	Age Discrimination		(o)	(o)	(o)	(o)
30.009	Indian Tribes		(o)	(o)	(o)	(o)
30.010	Equal Pay Act		(o)	(o)	(o)	0
30.011	Title I ADA, Investigations		(o)	(o)	(o)	0
	DEPARTMENT TOTAL:	OUTLAYS	266,965	241,666	306,086	341,000
		CREDITS*	0*	0*	0*	0*
	FEDERAL COMMUNICATIONS COMMISSION					
32.001	Information, Investigation		(a)	(a)	(a)	(a)
	DEPARTMENT TOTAL:	OUTLAYS	0	0	0	0
		CREDITS*	0*	0*	0*	0*
	FEDERAL MARITIME COMMISSION					
33.001	Shipping—Complaints		188	162	184 e	193 e
	DEPARTMENT TOTAL:	OUTLAYS	188	162	184	193
		CREDITS*	0*	0*	0*	0*

Please see "Important Notes on the Tables, Footnotes," page 572.

Table 1. *(continued)*

Program number	ADMINISTRATIVE ENTITY/SUB-UNIT Program Title (abridged)		FY 1997 in $thousands	FY 1998 in $thousands	FY 1999 in $thousands	FY 2000 in $thousands
	FEDERAL MEDIATION AND CONCILIATION SERVICE					
34.001	Labor Mediation, Conciliation		32,525	34,120	34,620 e	36,834 e
34.002	Labor Management Cooperation		1,732	1,764	1,776 e	1,776 e
	DEPARTMENT TOTAL:	OUTLAYS	34,257	35,884	36,396	38,610
		CREDITS*	0*	0*	0*	0*
	FEDERAL TRADE COMMISSION					
36.001	Fair Competition Counseling		102,018	106,085	116,679 e	133,368 e
	DEPARTMENT TOTAL:	OUTLAYS	102,018	106,085	116,679	133,368
		CREDITS*	0*	0*	0*	0*
	GENERAL SERVICES ADMINISTRATION					
39.001	Business Services \ r		1,910	1,881	1,910 e	1,920 e
39.002	Real Property Disposal \ p		12,122	16,678	27,137 e	25,795 e
39.003	Personal Property Donation \ p		11,494	10,003	10,370 e	10,370 e
39.007	Personal Property Sale \ p		13,269	14,013	15,637 e	16,352 e
39.008	Federal Information Center		3,203	3,455	3,700 e	3,700 e
39.009	Consumer Information Center \ r, u		2,753	3,106	3,460 e	3,463 e
	DEPARTMENT TOTAL:	OUTLAYS	44,751	49,136	62,214	61,600
		CREDITS*	0*	0*	0*	0*
	GOVERNMENT PRINTING OFFICE					
40.001	Depository Libraries		29,077	29,077	29,264 e	29,986 e
40.002	Government Publications Sales \ p, r		70,498	60,557	60,500 e	60,500 e
	DEPARTMENT TOTAL:	OUTLAYS	99,575	89,634	89,764	90,486
		CREDITS*	0*	0*	0*	0*
	LIBRARY OF CONGRESS					
42.001	Books for the Blind		44,792	46,288	48,824 e	48,033 e
42.002	Copyright Service \ i, u		28,856	29,986	34,891 e	37,639 e
42.003	LC Cataloging \ u		6,394	5,511	7,400 e	7,400 e
42.005	LC Publications \ u		225	225	225 e	225 e
42.006	Library Services		124,000	126,000	132,900 e	137,000 e
42.007	Science and Technology		1,759	1,790	1,510 e	1,560 e
42.008	Semiconductor Chip Protection \ u		(o)	(o)	(o)	(o)
	DEPARTMENT TOTAL:	OUTLAYS	206,026	209,800	225,750	231,857
		CREDITS*	0*	0*	0*	0*
	NATIONAL AERONAUTICS AND SPACE ADMINISTRATION					
43.001	Aerospace Education Services		5,926	6,564	6,649 e	6,780 e
43.002	Technology Transfer		32,952	45,000	45,900 e	35,000 e
	DEPARTMENT TOTAL:	OUTLAYS	38,878	51,564	52,549	41,780
		CREDITS*	0*	0*	0*	0*
	NATIONAL CREDIT UNION ADMINISTRATION					
44.001	Credit Union Charter \ u		265,000*	271,000*	312,000*e	331,000*e
44.002	Revolving Loan Program \ u		2,261*	2,965*	3,200*e	3,700*e
	DEPARTMENT TOTAL:	OUTLAYS	0	0	0	0
		CREDITS*	267,261*	273,965*	315,200*	334,700*

Please see "Important Notes on the Tables, Footnotes," page 572.

Table 1. (continued)

Program number	ADMINISTRATIVE ENTITY/SUB-UNIT Program Title (abridged)		FY 1997 in $thousands	FY 1998 in $thousands	FY 1999 in $thousands	FY 2000 in $thousands
	NATIONAL FOUNDATION ON THE ARTS AND THE HUMANITIES					
	NATIONAL ENDOWMENT FOR THE ARTS					
45.024	Organizations and Individuals		54,650	39,535 e	39,675 e	(a)
45.025	Partnership Agreements		31,237	33,426	34,838 e	34,638 e
45.026	Leadership Initiatives		8,639	9,481	9,274 e	(a)
	Subtotal:	Outlays	94,526	82,442	83,787	34,638
		Credits*	0*	0*	0*	0*
	NATIONAL ENDOWMENT FOR THE HUMANITIES					
45.129	Federal-State Partnership		28,123	29,089	28,000 e	39,130 e
45.130	Challenge Grants		9,910	9,910	9,900 e	10,000 e
45.149	Preservation and Access		18,044	18,392	18,000 e	22,945 e
45.160	Fellowships and Stipends		5,648	5,698	6,050 e	7,070 e
45.161	Research		7,052	7,737	5,380 e	8,620 e
45.162	Education Development		3,988	4,649	4,875 e	7,560 e
45.163	Seminars and Institutes		6,329	6,107	6,465 e	8,750 e
45.164	Public Programs		10,738	10,935	11,230 e	16,725 e
	Subtotal:	Outlays	89,832	92,517	89,900	120,800
		Credits*	0*	0*	0*	0*
	FEDERAL COUNCIL ON THE ARTS AND THE HUMANITIES					
45.201	Arts and Artifacts Indemnity		0*	0*	0*e	0*e
	Subtotal:	Outlays	0	0	0	0
		Credits*	0*	0*	0*	0*
	INSTITUTE OF MUSEUM SERVICES					
45.301	General Operating Support		15,736	15,610	15,610 e	15,610 e
45.302	Museum Assessment Program		441	450	450 e	450 e
45.303	Conservation Project Support		2,299	2,310	2,310 e	2,310 e
45.304	Conservation Assessment Program		825	820	820 e	820 e
45.305	Professional Services Program		389	650	510 e	1,000 e
45.306	Museum Leadership Initiatives		249	709	700 e	1,000 e
45.310	State Library Program		(n)	135,486	135,367 e	138,118 e
45.311	Native American Library Services		(n)	2,561	2,908 e	2,616 e
45.312	National Leadership Grants		(n)	5,488	25,000 e	10,606 e
	Subtotal:	Outlays	19,939	164,084	183,675	172,530
		Credits*	0*	0*	0*	0*
	DEPARTMENT TOTAL:	OUTLAYS	204,297	339,043	357,362	327,968
		CREDITS*	0*	0*	0*	0*
	NATIONAL LABOR RELATIONS BOARD					
46.001	Labor-Management Relations		174,595	174,617	184,938 e	210,193 e
	DEPARTMENT TOTAL:	OUTLAYS	174,595	174,617	184,938	210,193
		CREDITS*	0*	0*	0*	0*
	NATIONAL SCIENCE FOUNDATION					
47.041	Engineering Grants		349,411	343,140	368,550 e	378,530 e
47.049	Mathematical, Physical Sciences		693,453	687,240	734,400 e	753,970 e
47.050	Geosciences		444,325	438,020	472,980 e	485,480 e
47.070	Computer, Information Science		272,957	269,091	298,680 e	422,530 e

Please see "Important Notes on the Tables, Footnotes," page 572.

Table 1. *(continued)*

Program number	ADMINISTRATIVE ENTITY/SUB-UNIT Program Title (abridged)		FY 1997 in $thousands	FY 1998 in $thousands	FY 1999 in $thousands	FY 2000 in $thousands
47.074	Biological Sciences		324,266	355,700	390,860 e	408,620 e
47.075	Social, Behavioral, Economic		122,614	126,580	137,230 e	143,010 e
47.076	Education and Human Resources		619,140	633,160	689,000 e	711,000 e
47.078	Polar Programs		224,230	223,010	245,070 e	250,630 e
	DEPARTMENT TOTAL:	OUTLAYS	3,050,396	3,075,941	3,336,770	3,553,770
		CREDITS*	0*	0*	0*	0*

PRESIDENT'S COMMITTEE ON EMPLOYMENT OF PEOPLE WITH DISABILITIES

Program number			FY 1997	FY 1998	FY 1999	FY 2000
53.001	Employment Promotion		4,321	4,321	4,421 e	6,750 e
	DEPARTMENT TOTAL:	OUTLAYS	4,321	4,321	4,421	6,750
		CREDITS*	0*	0*	0*	0*

RAILROAD RETIREMENT BOARD

Program number			FY 1997	FY 1998	FY 1999	FY 2000
57.001	Social Insurance/Railroad Workers \t		8,289,000	8,315,000	8,366,000 e	8,428,000 e
	DEPARTMENT TOTAL:	OUTLAYS	8,289,000	8,315,000	8,366,000	8,428,000
		CREDITS*	0*	0*	0*	0*

SECURITIES AND EXCHANGE COMMISSION

Program number			FY 1997	FY 1998	FY 1999	FY 2000
58.001	Investigation of Complaints		308,591	316,000	358,000 e	363,000 e
	DEPARTMENT TOTAL:	OUTLAYS	308,591	316,000	358,000	363,000
		CREDITS*	0*	0*	0*	0*

SMALL BUSINESS ADMINISTRATION

Program number			FY 1997	FY 1998	FY 1999	FY 2000
59.002	Economic Injury Disaster Loans		(o)*	(o)*	(o)*	(o)*
59.005	Business Development Assistance		0	1,245	1,280 e	1,406 e
59.006	8(a) Business Development		19,546	4,583	4,077 e	4,563 e
59.007	Management, Technical Assistance		2,600	2,850	2,600 e	5,000 e
59.008	Physical Disaster Loans \ i		960,809*	728,109*	1,100,000*e	934,000*e
59.009	Procurement Assistance		13,017	13,529	16,930 e	14,129 e
59.011	Small Business Investment Companies		667,387*	972,443*	1,400,000*e	2,400,000*e
59.012	Small Business Loans		8,955,854*	8,998,224*	10,000,000*e	9,000,000*e
59.016	Bond Guarantees \ u		1,767,000*	523,945*	1,672,000*e	1,672,000*e
59.026	Service Corps of Retired Executives		3,300	3,500	3,500 e	3,500 e
59.037	Small Business Development Center		72,875	71,563	90,296 e	62,000 e
59.041	Certified Development Company Loans		2,650*	1,779,000*	3,000,000*e	3,500,000*e
59.043	Women's Business Ownership		4,000	8,000	9,000 e	9,000 e
59.044	Veterans Entrepreneurial Training		44	0	600 e	600 e
59.046	Microloan Demonstration Program		12,949	10,000	12,000 e	12,000 e
			43,052*	44,086*	71,995*e	76,000*e
	DEPARTMENT TOTAL:	OUTLAYS	128,331	115,270	140,283	112,198
		CREDITS*	12,396,752*	13,045,807*	17,243,995*	17,582,000*

INTERNATIONAL TRADE COMMISSION

Program number			FY 1997	FY 1998	FY 1999	FY 2000
61.001	Import Relief		77	77	77 e	81 e
	DEPARTMENT TOTAL:	OUTLAYS	77	77	77	81
		CREDITS*	0*	0*	0*	0*

TENNESSEE VALLEY AUTHORITY

Program number			FY 1997	FY 1998	FY 1999	FY 2000
62.001	Energy Research, Technology \ u		15,000	15,000	3,411 e	5,500 e
	DEPARTMENT TOTAL:	OUTLAYS	15,000	15,000	3,411	5,500
		CREDITS*	0*	0*	0*	0*

Please see "Important Notes on the Tables, Footnotes," page 572.

Table 1. (continued)

Program number	ADMINISTRATIVE ENTITY/SUB-UNIT Program Title (abridged)	FY 1997 in $thousands	FY 1998 in $thousands	FY 1999 in $thousands	FY 2000 in $thousands
	DEPARTMENT OF VETERANS AFFAIRS				
	VETERANS HEALTH ADMINISTRATION				
64.005	Construction/State Homes	37,164	89,474	90,367 e	40,000 e
64.007	Blind Rehabilitation Centers	56,398	56,192	58,333 e	60,555 e
64.008	Veterans Domiciliary Care	292,060	325,526	372,275 e	398,613 e
64.009	Veterans Medical Care Benefits	14,262,579	14,350,455	14,980,002 e	14,813,080 e
64.010	Veterans Nursing Home Care	1,750,615	1,780,117	1,978,934 e	2,118,456 e
64.011	Veterans Dental Care	6,360,744	11,558	13,940 e	15,333 e
64.012	Veterans Prescription Service \ p	1,337,457	1,548,424	1,825,261 e	1,898,271 e
64.013	Veterans Prosthetic Appliances \ p	353,399	419,701	498,437 e	523,366 e
64.014	Veterans State Domiciliary Care	20,966	23,931	27,224 e	30,573 e
64.015	Veterans State Nursing Homes	201,805	205,340	241,696 e	285,050 e
64.016	Veterans State Hospital Care	3,955	5,776	3,912 e	4,514 e
64.018	Specialized Medical Resources	75,000	145,500	185,500 e	200,000 e
64.019	Alcohol and Drug Dependence	468,550	396,450	411,553 e	427,230 e
64.022	Home Based Primary Care	49,889	52,844	54,857 e	90,447 e
64.024	Homeless Providers Grants	3,714	5,886	20,000 e	31,653 e
64.025	Transitional Housing \ t	(n)*	(n)*	68*e	68*e
	Subtotal: Outlays	25,274,295	19,417,174	20,762,291	20,937,141
	Credits*	0*	0*	68*	68*
	VETERANS BENEFITS ADMINISTRATION				
64.100	Automobiles, Adaptive Equipment	27,509	27,420	23,094 e	38,194 e
64.101	Burial Expenses Allowance	113,033	116,640	129,259 e	122,543 e
64.102	Compensation/Deaths	4,186	3,468	2,835 e	2,324 e
64.103	Life Insurance \ t, u	2,181	2,129	2,105 e	2,069 e
		120,612*	105,810*	110,010*e	109,510*e
64.104	Pension/Non-Service Connected	2,276,226	2,292,030	2,366,613 e	2,419,078 e
64.105	Pension/Survivors	768,604	761,693	717,596 e	697,470 e
64.106	Specially Adapted Housing	14,723	15,864	19,373 e	19,373 e
64.109	Service-Connected Disability	13,004,077	13,790,668	14,796,699 e	15,119,868 e
64.110	Dependency, Indemnity Compensation	3,231,197	3,316,635	3,467,507 e	3,568,206 e
64.114	Veterans Housing—Loans \ u	24,286,692*	39,861,939*	32,634,956*e	31,236,909*e
64.115	Veterans Information, Assistance	(a)	(a)	(a)	(a)
64.116	Vocational Rehabilitation \ u	401,467	405,975	403,206 e	405,855 e
		2,309*	2,154*	2,401*e	2,531*e
64.117	Dependents Educational Assistance	104,716	106,763	132,182 e	136,574 e
64.118	Housing—Disabled Veterans \ u	0*	0*	33*e	33*e
64.119	Manufactured Home Loans \ u	184*	0*	0*e	0*e
64.120	Post-Vietnam Era Educational \ t	86,622	37,695	37,493 e	34,345 e
64.123	Vocational Training	211	104	42 e	23 e
64.124	All-Volunteer Force Educational	781,296	795,266	904,665 e	896,804 e
64.125	Vocational, Educational Counseling	6,000	6,000	6,000 e	6,000 e
64.126	Native American Direct Loan \ u	2,245*	2,733*	10,559*e	21,431*e
64.127	Allowance/Spina Bifida	(n)	7,432	7,463 e	7,684 e
64.128	Training/Spina Bifida	(n)	2	2 e	2 e
	Subtotal: Outlays	20,822,048	21,685,784	23,016,134	23,476,412
	Credits*	24,412,042*	39,972,636*	32,757,959*	31,370,414*
	NATIONAL CEMETERY SYSTEM				
64.201	National Cemeteries	77,007	81,062	88,874 e	94,033 e
64.202	Headstones, Markers, Certificates	32,915	33,496	35,942 e	37,053 e
64.203	State Cemetery Grants	4,521	6,088	14,086 e	11,000 e
	Subtotal: Outlays	114,443	120,646	138,902	142,086
	Credits*	0*	0*	0*	0*
	DEPARTMENT TOTAL: OUTLAYS	46,210,786	41,223,604	43,917,327	44,555,639
	CREDITS*	24,412,042*	39,972,636*	32,758,027*	31,370,482*

Please see "Important Notes on the Tables, Footnotes," page 572.

Table 1. *(continued)*

Program number	ADMINISTRATIVE ENTITY/SUB-UNIT Program Title (abridged)		FY 1997 in $thousands	FY 1998 in $thousands	FY 1999 in $thousands	FY 2000 in $thousands
	ENVIRONMENTAL PROTECTION AGENCY					
66.001	Air Pollution Control Support		159,072	146,254	144,798 e	156,155 e
66.009	Air Information Center		47	47	42 e	51 e
66.032	State Indoor Radon Grants		8,158	8,158	8,158 e	8,158 e
66.033	Ozone Transport		650	650	650 e	650 e
66.419	Water Pollution—State, Interstate		80,679	95,529	115,529 e	115,529 e
66.432	Public Water System Supervision		89,215	93,781	93,781 e	93,781 e
66.433	Underground Water Source Protection		9,551	10,500	10,500 e	10,500 e
66.454	Water Quality Management Planning		14,300	14,300	14,200 e	9,500 e
66.456	National Estuary Program		11,400	12,600	12,600 e	12,600 e
66.458	State Revolving Funds \ t		2,073,500	1,240,300	1,329,000 e	800,000 e
66.460	Nonpoint Source Implementation		100,000	105,000	200,000 e	200,000 e
66.461	Wetlands Protection		15,000	15,000	15,000 e	15,000 e
66.463	Pollutant Discharge Elimination		18,498	19,000	19,000 e	19,000 e
66.466	Chesapeake Bay Program		17,000	16,000	15,800 e	16,000 e
66.467	Wastewater Operator Training		1,794	1,794	1,794 e	294 e
66.468	Drinking Water/Revolving Fund \ r		1,275,000	725,000	775,000 e	825,000 e
66.469	Great Lakes Program		6,000	5,800	5,700 e	4,600 e
66.500	Consolidated Research		134,683	112,654	110,000 e	110,000 e
66.508	Senior Environmental Employment		49,500	63,900	53,000 e	53,000 e
66.600	Consolidated Grants		(o)	(o)	(o)	(o)
66.604	Environmental Justice Grants		2,700	2,490	2,000 e	2,000 e
66.605	Performance Partnership Grants		(o)	(o)	(o)	(o)
66.606	Surveys, Studies, Investigations		150,000	376,932	300,000 e	300,000 e
66.607	Training and Fellowships		10,000	37,649	35,000 e	35,000 e
66.608	One Stop Reporting		5,000	4,000	4,000 e	4,000 e
66.609	Children's Health Protection		1,800	2,000	2,000 e	2,000 e
66.651	Sustainable Development		5,000	5,000	4,700 e	4,700 e
66.700	Pesticide Enforcement		16,134	17,512	19,512 e	19,912 e
66.701	Toxic Substances Compliance		6,486	7,364	7,364 e	7,364 e
66.707	TSCA State Lead Grants		12,500	12,500	13,712 e	13,712 e
66.708	Pollution Prevention Grants		4,940	5,117	4,995 e	5,000 e
66.710	Environmental Justice/Partnership		1,750	0	0 e	0 e
66.711	Environmental Justice/Pollution		(n)	4,000	4,000 e	4,000 e
66.713	State, Tribal Environmental Justice		(n)	500	500 e	500 e
66.714	Pesticide Environmental Stewardship		(n)	499	499 e	499 e
66.801	Hazardous Waste Management		98,298	97,593	101,529 e	98,598 e
66.802	Superfund State Site \ t		126,500	135,000	135,000 e	135,000 e
66.804	State Underground Storage Tanks		10,545	10,686	10,633 e	11,945 e
66.805	Underground Storage Trust Fund \ t		50,309	55,250	58,990 e	57,750 e
66.806	Superfund Technical Assistance		700	1,516	1,000 e	2,000 e
66.807	Superfund Innovative Technology		6,006	6,006	6,006 e	6,006 e
66.808	Solid Waste Management Assistance		3,800	3,800	1,600 e	1,600 e
66.809	Superfund State Core Program		30,000	18,000	20,000 e	25,000 e
66.810	Technical Assistance		1,800	1,800	1,100 e	1,210 e
66.811	Brownfield Pilots \ t		8,310	42,000	51,000 e	57,000 e
66.926	Indian Environmental Assistance		28,000	28,000	38,585 e	42,585 e
66.930	U.S.-Mexico Border Grants		500	0	500 e	300 e
66.950	Environmental Education, Training		1,950	1,950	1,625 e	1,625 e
66.951	Environmental Education Grants		3,000	3,000	2,400 e	2,800 e
	DEPARTMENT TOTAL:	OUTLAYS	4,650,075	3,566,431	3,752,802	3,291,924
		CREDITS*	0*	0*	0*	0*
	NATIONAL GALLERY OF ART					
68.001	Art Extension Service		669	681	706 e	728 e
	DEPARTMENT TOTAL:	OUTLAYS	669	681	706	728
		CREDITS*	0*	0*	0*	0*
	OVERSEAS PRIVATE INVESTMENT CORPORATION					
70.002	Foreign Investment Financing \ u		18,000	27,000	50,000 e	24,000 e
			709,000*	635,000*	1,000,000*e	1,200,000*e

Please see "Important Notes on the Tables, Footnotes," page 572.

Table 1. (continued)

Program number	ADMINISTRATIVE ENTITY/SUB-UNIT Program Title (abridged)		FY 1997 in $thousands	FY 1998 in $thousands	FY 1999 in $thousands	FY 2000 in $thousands
70.003	Foreign Investment Insurance \ u		3,732,000*	4,842,000*	5,000,000*e	6,000,000*e
	DEPARTMENT TOTAL:	OUTLAYS	18,000	27,000	50,000	24,000
		CREDITS*	4,441,000*	5,477,000*	6,000,000*	7,200,000*

	NUCLEAR REGULATORY COMMISSION					
77.001	Radiation Control—Training		56	56	100 e	100 e
77.005	NRC Local Public Document Rooms		159	159	151 e	0 e
	DEPARTMENT TOTAL:	OUTLAYS	215	215	251	100
		CREDITS*	0*	0*	0*	0*

	COMMODITY FUTURES TRADING COMMISSION					
78.004	Commodity Futures Reparations		54,746	58,099	61,000 e	67,655 e
	DEPARTMENT TOTAL:	OUTLAYS	54,746	58,099	61,000	67,655
		CREDITS*	0*	0*	0*	0*

	DEPARTMENT OF ENERGY					
81.003	Granting of Patent Licenses		(a)	(a)	(a)	(a)
81.022	Energy-Related Laboratory Equipment \ p		(a)	(a)	(a)	(a)
81.036	Energy-Related Inventions		1,700	2,100	2,900 e	0 e
81.039	National Energy Information Center		(a)	(a)	(a)	(a)
81.041	State Energy Program		29,000	30,250	37,000 e	0 e
81.042	Weatherization Assistance		120,845	124,845	154,100 e	0 e
81.049	Office of Science		573,000	515,000	515,000 e	515,000 e
81.057	University Coal Research		2,837	2,839	2,907 e	3,000 e
81.064	Scientific, Technical Information		10,838	10,100	8,600 e	8,600 e
81.065	Nuclear Waste Disposal Siting \ u		728	733	9,383 e	14,324 e
81.079	Regional Biomass Programs		3,325	2,985	3,500 e	0 e
81.081	Urban Consortium		1,576	1,600	1,600 e	0 e
81.082	Minority Business Enterprises		380	570	542 e	542 e
81.086	Conservation Research, Development		(a)	(a)	(a)	(a)
81.087	Renewable Energy Research		(a)	(a)	(a)	(a)
81.089	Fossil Energy Research, Development		15,500	13,500	7,000 e	7,500 e
81.104	Technology Development		106,000	102,000	90,000 e	80,000 e
81.105	National Industrial Competitiveness		5,800	5,800	6,000 e	7,000 e
81.106	Transport/Transuranic Wastes		2,637	3,841	4,090 e	5,672 e
81.108	Epidemiology, Health Studies		(n)	1,200	0 e	0 e
81.110	Center for Plutonium		10,000	10,000	5,000 e	5,000 e
81.112	Stewardship Science		(n)	2,000	3,470 e	4,000 e
81.113	Nonproliferation Research		(n)	680	465 e	465 e
81.114	University Nuclear Science		(n)	7,000	11,000 e	11,345 e
81.116	Diversity-Related Programs		400	300	325 e	300 e
81.117	Energy Efficiency—Renewable		(n)	(n)	15,000 e	15,000 e
81.118	Solar Energy Partnership		(n)	(n)	1,500 e	2,000 e
	DEPARTMENT TOTAL:	OUTLAYS	884,566	837,343	879,382	679,748
		CREDITS*	0*	0*	0*	0*

	UNITED STATES INFORMATION AGENCY					
82.001	Educational Exchange—Graduate		14,255	14,350	14,500 e	15,100 e
82.002	Lecturers and Research Scholars		20,196	21,180	21,250 e	21,675 e
82.004	International Visitors Program		356	8,600	8,800 e	8,800 e
82.006	Young Political Leaders		(n)	792	974 e	700 e
82.009	Professional Development		27	27	18 e	45 e
82.010	College, University Partnerships		1,100	5,300	8,850 e	8,850 e
82.011	College, University Affiliations		2,365	1,850	1,538 e	1,500 e
82.012	Teacher Exchange—NIS		725	970	1,550 e	1,800 e
82.013	Exchange—Secondary, Postsecondary		2,059	2,059	2,338 e	2,888 e
82.015	Creative Arts Grants		844	844	425 e	0 e

Please see "Important Notes on the Tables, Footnotes," page 572.

Table 1. (continued)

Program number	ADMINISTRATIVE ENTITY/SUB-UNIT Program Title (abridged)		FY 1997 in $thousands	FY 1998 in $thousands	FY 1999 in $thousands	FY 2000 in $thousands
82.016	Exchange—Bundestag Youth		2,400	2,388	2,400 e	2,800 e
82.018	Exchange—NIS Secondary		10,000	11,900	12,735 e	13,000 e
82.026	Exchange—Postgraduates, Faculty		1,500	2,000	1,000 e	1,000 e
82.030	Exchange (Performing Arts)		(n)	607	607 e	607 e
82.032	Exchange (Visual Arts) \ u		450	450	450 e	450 e
82.033	Professional Exchange		8,200	6,300	5,500 e	5,500 e
82.034	Exchange—Teaching Fellows		950	1,008	1,008 e	1,007 e
82.035	Exchange—EFL Fellows		925	700	1,375 e	1,000 e
82.038	American Studies Institutes		1,800	2,010	2,626 e	2,626 e
	DEPARTMENT TOTAL:	OUTLAYS	68,152	83,335	87,944	89,348
		CREDITS*	0*	0*	0*	0*

	FEDERAL EMERGENCY MANAGEMENT AGENCY					
83.007	Firefighting/Federal Property		(a)	(a)	(a)	(a)
83.009	National Fire Academy Training		1,590	1,609	1,500 e	1,600 e
83.010	Educational Program		7,005	8,360	8,922 e	13,576 e
83.011	Hazardous Materials Training		4,348	4,305	4,295 e	4,348 e
83.100	Flood Insurance \ u		1,207,862*	1,279,549*	1,371,232*e	1,445,729*e
83.105	Community Assistance Program \ u		4,928	5,255	5,000 e	5,000 e
83.505	State Disaster Preparedness		2,839	2,832	2,900 e	2,900 e
83.523	Emergency/Food, Shelter		100,000	100,000	100,000 e	100,000 e
83.526	National Urban Search, Rescue		2,500	2,500	2,489 e	4,050 e
83.527	EMI—Training Assistance		1,329	1,414	1,400 e	1,400 e
83.529	EMI—Independent Study		(a)	(a)	(a)	(a)
83.530	EMI—Resident Education		5,227	5,227	5,427 e	5,427 e
83.534	State and Local Assistance		106,868	105,904	104,307 e	0 e
83.535	Mitigation Assistance		10,306	11,008	10,384 e	10,407 e
83.536	Flood Mitigation Assistance \ u		(n)	14,134	26,678 e	20,000 e
83.537	Community Disaster Loans \ u		(a)*	(a)*	(a)*	(a)*
83.538	Cora Brown Fund \ t		(a)	(a)	(a)	(a)
83.539	Crisis Counseling		(a)	(a)	(a)	(a)
83.540	Disaster Legal Services		(a)	(a)	(a)	(a)
83.541	Disaster Unemployment Assistance		(a)	(a)	(a)	(a)
83.542	Fire Suppression Assistance		(a)	(a)	(a)	(a)
83.543	Individual and Family Grants		(a)	(a)	(a)	(a)
83.544	Public Assistance Grants		(a)	(a)	(a)	(a)
83.545	Disaster Housing Program		(a)	(a)	(a)	(a)
83.547	Counter-Terrorism Training		2,500	2,000	4,000 e	4,000 e
83.548	Hazard Mitigation Grant		(a)	(a)	(a)	(a)
83.549	Chemical Stockpile Emergency		28,000	32,176	79,391 e	70,330 e
83.550	Dam Safety		1,000	1,000	2,048 e	4,000 e
83.551	Disaster Resistant Communities		2,682	26,050	17,604 e	25,000 e
83.552	Emergency Management Performance		(n)	(n)	(n)	141,951 e
	DEPARTMENT TOTAL:	OUTLAYS	281,122	323,774	376,345	413,989
		CREDITS*	1,207,862*	1,279,549*	1,371,232*	1,445,729*

	DEPARTMENT OF EDUCATION					
84.002	Adult Education—State Grant		340,339	345,339	365,000 e	468,000 e
84.004	Civil Rights Training		7,334	7,334	7,334 e	7,334 e
84.007	Educational Opportunity Grants		583,407	614,000	619,000 e	631,000 e
84.010	Title I Grants		7,295,323	7,375,232	7,676,020 e	7,996,020 e
84.011	Migrant Education		299,475	299,475	346,189 e	372,000 e
84.013	Neglected and Delinquent Children		39,311	39,311	40,311 e	42,000 e
84.015	Language, Area Studies		33,115	33,213	35,900 e	36,320 e
84.016	Undergraduate International Studies		3,713	3,672	4,300 e	4,350 e
84.017	International Research and Studies		2,855	3,039	3,790 e	3,975 e
84.018	International—Bilateral Projects		1,001	962	1,125 e	1,193 e
84.019	International—Faculty Research		745	822	900 e	968 e
84.021	International—Group Projects		1,809	2,090	2,325 e	2,325 e
84.022	International—Dissertation		1,638	1,802	2,072 e	2,072 e
84.027	Special Education—State Grants		3,107,522	3,807,700	4,310,700 e	4,314,000 e

Please see "Important Notes on the Tables, Footnotes," page 572.

Table 1. (continued)

Program number	ADMINISTRATIVE ENTITY/SUB-UNIT Program Title (abridged)	FY 1997 in $thousands	FY 1998 in $thousands	FY 1999 in $thousands	FY 2000 in $thousands
84.031	Higher Education—Institutional Aid	175,240	185,945 e	222,750 e	210,325 e
84.032	Family Education Loans	22,999,000*	22,327,000*	23,577,000*e	25,006,000*e
84.033	Work-Study Program	830,000	830,000	870,000 e	934,000 e
84.037	Perkins Loan Cancellations	20,000	30,000	30,000 e	30,000 e
84.038	Perkins Loans	158,000*	135,000*	100,000*e	100,000*e
84.040	Impact Aid—Facilities Maintenance	0	3,000	5,000 e	5,000 e
84.041	Impact Aid	707,500	774,000	824,000 e	724,000 e
84.042	TRIO—Student Support Services	166,000	172,129	178,782 e	182,715 e
84.044	TRIO—Talent Search	81,545	98,668	98,368 e	100,532 e
84.047	TRIO—Upward Bound	198,548	201,895	258,853 e	264,573 e
84.048	Vocational Education—States	998,056	1,009,852	1,010,522 e	1,010,522 e
84.051	Vocational Education Research	13,497	4,500	4,500 e	4,500 e
84.060	Indian Education—LEAs	58,050	59,750	62,000 e	62,000 e
84.063	Pell Grant Program	5,919,000	7,344,934	7,704,000 e	7,463,000 e
84.066	TRIO—Educational Opportunity	26,000	28,998	29,794 e	30,450 e
84.069	Leveraging Educational Assistance	50,000	25,000	25,000 e	25,000 e
84.083	Women's Educational Equity	2,000	3,000	3,000 e	3,000 e
84.101	Vocational Education—Indians	12,952	13,013	12,883 e	12,883 e
84.103	Higher Education—Trio Staff	3,313	3,750	4,430 e	5,000 e
84.116	Fund/Postsecondary Education	18,000	25,200	50,000 e	27,500 e
84.120	Minority Science, Engineering	5,255	5,255	7,500 e	8,500 e
84.126	Rehabilitation Services—State	2,164,038	2,231,528	2,287,128 e	2,315,587 e
84.128	Rehabilitation Services—Projects	7,207	5,896	5,896 e	4,946 e
84.129	Rehabilitation Training	15,387	17,413	19,914 e	20,000 e
84.132	Centers for Independent Living	42,876	42,205	46,109 e	50,886 e
84.133	Disability, Rehabilitation Research	69,990	76,800	81,000 e	90,964 e
84.141	Migrant Education—High School	7,441	7,634	9,000 e	15,000 e
84.144	Migrant Education—Coordination	6,000	6,000	8,500 e	8,500 e
84.145	Federal Real Property Assistance \ p	(a)	(a)	(a)	(a)
84.149	Migrant Education—College	2,028	2,081	4,000 e	7,000 e
84.153	Business, International Education	3,650	3,691	3,900 e	4,125 e
84.160	Training Interpreters for Deaf	2,105	2,105	2,105 e	2,105 e
84.161	Rehabilitation—Client Assistance	10,392	10,714	10,928 e	10,928 e
84.162	Immigrant Education	100,000	150,000	150,000 e	150,000 e
84.165	Magnet Schools	92,000	101,000	104,000 e	114,000 e
84.168	Eisenhower Professional Development	13,342	23,300	23,300 e	30,000 e
84.169	Independent Living	21,859	21,859	22,296 e	22,296 e
84.170	Javits Fellowships	5,877	6,075	7,148 e	8,200 e
84.173	Special Education—Preschool	360,409	373,985	373,985 e	402,400 e
84.177	Rehabilitation Services—Blind	9,952	10,950	11,169 e	11,392 e
84.181	Infants, Families/Disabilities	315,754	350,000	370,000 e	390,000 e
84.184	Drug-Free Schools—National	25,000	25,000	90,000 e	90,000 e
84.185	Byrd Honors Scholarships	29,117	39,288	39,288 e	39,859 e
84.186	Safe/Drug-Free Schools—State	530,978	531,000	441,000 e	439,000 e
84.187	Supported Employment	38,152	38,152	38,152 e	38,152 e
84.191	Adult Education—Evaluation	4,998	4,998	14,000 e	101,000 e
84.194	Bilingual Education Support	10,000	14,000	14,000 e	14,000 e
84.195	Bilingual Education/Professional	5,000	25,000	50,000 e	75,000 e
84.196	Homeless Children, Youth	25,000	28,800	28,000 e	31,700 e
84.200	Graduate Assistance/National Need	20,056	23,925	23,852 e	32,800 e
84.203	Star Schools	30,000	34,000	45,000 e	45,000 e
84.206	Javits Gifted/Talented Students	5,000	6,500	6,500 e	6,500 e
84.209	Hawaiian Education Centers	6,100	6,000	7,200 e	7,200 e
84.210	Hawaiian Gifted, Talented	1,500	2,000	2,000 e	2,000 e
84.213	Even Start—State	95,523	113,080	125,250 e	134,750 e
84.214	Even Start—Migrant	3,060	3,720	3,450 e	3,500 e
84.215	Improvement of Education	40,000	180,100	147,000 e	139,500 e
84.216	Capital Expenses	41,119	41,119	24,000 e	0 e
84.217	McNair Post-Baccalaureate	20,367	20,774	23,509 e	32,080 e
84.220	International Business Education	7,026	7,026	7,800 e	8,000 e
84.221	Hawaiian Special Education	1,600	2,000	2,000 e	2,000 e
84.224	Assistive Technology	36,109	36,109	26,250 e	26,250 e
84.229	Language Resource Centers	2,426	2,176	2,450 e	2,600 e
84.234	Projects with Industry	22,071	22,071	22,071 e	22,071 e
84.235	Rehabilitation Services Demonstration	18,942	15,942	14,942 e	14,942 e

Please see "Important Notes on the Tables, Footnotes," page 572.

Table 1. (continued)

Program number	ADMINISTRATIVE ENTITY/SUB-UNIT Program Title (abridged)	FY 1997 in $thousands	FY 1998 in $thousands	FY 1999 in $thousands	FY 2000 in $thousands
84.240	Protection and Advocacy	7,657	9,894	10,894 e	10,894 e
84.243	Tech-Prep Education	100,000	103,000	106,000 e	111,000 e
84.245	Tribal Vocational/Technical	2,919	3,100	4,100 e	4,100 e
84.246	Rehabilitation Short-Term Training	1,498	450	450 e	450 e
84.250	Rehabilitation—Indians/Disabilities	12,000	15,360	17,628 e	17,628 e
84.252	Urban Community Service	9,200	4,900	4,637 e	0 e
84.255	Literacy for Prisoners	4,723	4,723	4,723 e	0 e
84.256	Freely Associated States—Education	(a)	(a)	(a)	(a)
84.257	Institute for Literacy	4,491	5,491	6,000 e	6,000 e
84.258	Even Start—Indian	1,530	1,860	2,025 e	2,025 e
84.259	Hawaiian Vocational Education	2,590	2,603	2,577 e	2,577 e
84.263	Rehabilitation Training—Innovative	1,298	498	0 e	0 e
84.264	Rehabilitation Training—Continuing	9,449	9,449	9,449 e	9,449 e
84.265	Rehabilitation Training—State Unit	5,944	5,944	5,944 e	5,944 e
84.268	Federal Direct Loan	11,271,000*	12,831,000*	16,232,000*e	16,155,000*e
84.269	International Public Policy	1,000	1,000	1,000 e	1,022 e
84.274	Overseas Research Centers	524	600	650 e	700 e
84.275	Rehabilitation Training—General	790	258	258 e	258 e
84.276	Goals 2000 State Grants	476,000	466,000	461,000 e	461,000 e
84.281	Eisenhower State Grants	310,000	335,000	335,000 e	335,000 e
84.282	Charter Schools	50,987	80,000	100,000 e	130,000 e
84.283	Assistance Centers	25,554	27,054	28,000 e	32,000 e
84.286	Math Telecommunications	1,035	2,035	5,000 e	2,000 e
84.287	Community Learning Centers	1,000	40,000	200,000 e	600,000 e
84.288	Bilingual Education—Development	11,657	17,017	16,512 e	27,512 e
84.289	Bilingual Education—Enhancement	20,535	19,677	16,512 e	16,512 e
84.290	Bilingual Education—Comprehensive	69,927	84,521	90,625 e	88,763 e
84.291	Bilingual Education—Improvement	39,131	38,235	42,062 e	31,617 e
84.292	Bilingual Education—Research	1,318	1,127	1,200 e	1,200 e
84.293	Foreign Language Assistance	5,050	5,000	6,000 e	6,000 e
84.295	Ready-To-Learn TV	7,000	7,000	11,000 e	7,000 e
84.296	Hawaiian Learning Centers	1,000	1,000	1,000 e	1,000 e
84.297	Hawaiian Curriculum, Teacher	2,500	3,995	4,800 e	4,800 e
84.298	Innovative Education	310,000	350,000	375,000 e	0 e
84.302	Regional Consortia	10,000	10,000	10,000 e	10,000 e
84.303	Technology Challenge Grants	56,965	106,000	115,100 e	110,000 e
84.304	International Education Exchange	5,000	5,000	7,000 e	7,000 e
84.305	Student Achievement, Curriculum	14,672	15,500	19,093 e	25,093 e
84.306	At-Risk Students	14,672	15,500	19,093 e	25,093 e
84.307	Early Childhood Development	8,028	7,432	7,827 e	10,227 e
84.308	Educational Governance	7,574	7,250	8,002 e	10,602 e
84.309	Postsecondary Education	9,054	8,100	9,769 e	12,369 e
84.310	Goals 2000: Parental Assistance	15,000	25,000	30,000 e	30,000 e
84.314	Even Start—Family Literacy	0	994	0 e	0 e
84.315	Underserved Populations	2,679	1,948	2,000 e	2,000 e
84.316	Hawaiian Higher Education	1,999	2,700	2,700 e	2,700 e
84.318	Technology Literacy	200,000	425,000	425,000 e	450,000 e
84.319	Eisenhower Mathematics, Science	15,000	15,000	15,000 e	17,500 e
84.320	Alaska Educational Planning	3,721	4,023	5,025 e	5,020 e
84.321	Alaska Home Based Education	3,155	3,072	3,832 e	3,837 e
84.322	Alaska Student Enrichment	725	905	1,128 e	1,128 e
84.323	Special Education—State	(n)	35,200	35,200 e	45,200 e
84.324	Special Education—Research	(n)	64,508	64,508 e	64,548 e
84.325	Special Education—Personnel	(n)	82,139	82,139 e	82,139 e
84.326	Special Education—Assistance	(n)	44,438	44,556 e	44,556 e
84.327	Special Education—Technology	(n)	34,023	34,523 e	34,523 e
84.328	Special Education—Training	(n)	18,535	18,535 e	22,535 e
84.329	Special Education—Studies	(n)	6,700	9,700 e	13,000 e
84.330	Advanced Placement Incentive	(n)	3,000	4,000 e	4,000 e
84.331	Incarcerated Youth	(n)	12,000	12,000 e	12,000 e
84.332	Comprehensive School Reform	(n)	145,000	145,000 e	160,000 e
84.333	Disabilities—Higher Education	(n)	(n)	5,000 e	5,000 e
84.334	Awareness, Readiness—Undergraduate	(n)	(n)	120,000 e	240,000 e
84.335	Child Care/Parents in School	(n)	(n)	5,000 e	5,000 e

Please see "Important Notes on the Tables, Footnotes," page 572.

Table 1. (continued)

Program number	ADMINISTRATIVE ENTITY/SUB-UNIT Program Title (abridged)		FY 1997 in $thousands	FY 1998 in $thousands	FY 1999 in $thousands	FY 2000 in $thousands
84.336	Teacher Quality Enhancement		(n)	(n)	75,000 e	115,000 e
84.337	Technology/Foreign Access		(n)	(n)	1,000 e	1,000 e
84.338	Reading Excellence		(n)	(n)	260,000 e	286,000 e
84.339	Learning Anytime Anywhere		(n)	(n)	10,000 e	20,000 e
84.340	Class Size Reduction		(n)	(n)	1,200,000 e	1,400,000 e
84.341	Community Technology Centers		(n)	(n)	10,000 e	65,000 e
84.342	Tomorrow's Teachers/Technology		(n)	(n)	75,000 e	75,000 e
84.343	Assistive Technology/Protection		(n)	(n)	2,370 e	2,370 e
	DEPARTMENT TOTAL:	OUTLAYS	27,138,545	30,764,654	34,318,586	35,287,181
		CREDITS*	34,428,000*	35,293,000*	39,909,000*	41,261,000*

SCHOLARSHIP AND FELLOWSHIP FOUNDATIONS

HARRY S TRUMAN SCHOLARSHIP FOUNDATION

85.001	Truman Scholarship Program \ t		3,177	3,187	3,187 e	3,187 e
	Subtotal:	Outlays	3,177	3,187	3,187	3,187
		Credits*	0*	0*	0*	0*

CHRISTOPHER COLUMBUS FELLOWSHIP FOUNDATION

85.100	Columbus Fellowship Program \ t		553	553	808 e	926 e
	Subtotal:	Outlays	553	553	808	926
		Credits*	0*	0*	0*	0*

BARRY M. GOLDWATER SCHOLARSHIP AND EXCELLENCE IN EDUCATION FOUNDATION

85.200	Goldwater Scholarship Program \ t		2,428	2,634	3,000 e	3,000 e
	Subtotal:	Outlays	2,428	2,634	3,000	3,000
		Credits*	0*	0*	0*	0*

WOODROW WILSON INTERNATIONAL CENTER FOR SCHOLARS

85.300	Wilson Fellowships		5,840	5,840	5,840 e	6,040 e
	Subtotal:	Outlays	5,840	5,840	5,840	6,040
		Credits*	0*	0*	0*	0*

MORRIS K. UDALL SCHOLARSHIP FOUNDATION

85.400	Udall Scholarship Program		350	350	350 e	350 e
85.401	Udall Fellowship Program		48	48	48 e	48 e
85.402	Udall Congressional Internships		91	91	100 e	100 e
	Subtotal:	Outlays	489	489	498	498
		Credits*	0*	0*	0*	0*

JAMES MADISON MEMORIAL FELLOWSHIP FOUNDATION

85.500	Madison Fellowship Program \ t		679	963	996 e	1,030 e
	Subtotal:	Outlays	679	963	996	1,030
		Credits*	0*	0*	0*	0*
	DEPARTMENT TOTAL:	OUTLAYS	13,166	13,666	14,329	14,681
		CREDITS*	0*	0*	0*	0*

PENSION BENEFIT GUARANTY CORPORATION

86.001	Pension Plan Termination Insurance \ u		794,982	852,847	1,290,950 e	1,057,704 e
	DEPARTMENT TOTAL:	OUTLAYS	794,982	852,847	1,290,950	1,057,704
		CREDITS*	0*	0*	0*	0*

Please see "Important Notes on the Tables, Footnotes," page 572.

Table 1. (continued)

Program number	ADMINISTRATIVE ENTITY/SUB-UNIT Program Title (abridged)		FY 1997 in $thousands	FY 1998 in $thousands	FY 1999 in $thousands	FY 2000 in $thousands
	ARCHITECTURAL AND TRANSPORTATION BARRIERS COMPLIANCE BOARD					
88.001	Compliance Board		3,540	3,644	3,847 e	4,633 e
	DEPARTMENT TOTAL:	OUTLAYS	3,540	3,644	3,847	4,633
		CREDITS*	0*	0*	0*	0*
	NATIONAL ARCHIVES AND RECORDS ADMINISTRATION					
89.001	Historical Research		39,855	33,367	36,108 e	40,163 e
89.003	National Historical Publications		5,476	6,219	6,000 e	6,000 e
	DEPARTMENT TOTAL:	OUTLAYS	45,331	39,586	42,108	46,163
		CREDITS*	0*	0*	0*	0*
	UNITED STATES INSTITUTE OF PEACE					
91.001	Research and Education		2,366	2,366	1,985 e	1,900 e
91.002	Articles and Manuscripts		802	802	893 e	1,000 e
	DEPARTMENT TOTAL:	OUTLAYS	3,168	3,168	2,878	2,900
		CREDITS*	0*	0*	0*	0*
	NATIONAL COUNCIL ON DISABILITY					
92.001	National Council on Disability		326	302	593 e	619 e
	DEPARTMENT TOTAL:	OUTLAYS	326	302	593	619
		CREDITS*	0*	0*	0*	0*
	DEPARTMENT OF HEALTH AND HUMAN SERVICES					
93.001	Civil Rights Compliance		19,914	19,621	20,652 e	22,159 e
93.003	Health, Social Services Emergency		1,675	0	124,000 e	74,000 e
93.004	Health Status/Minority Populations		3,523	7,939	7,839 e	7,839 e
93.005	Facilities/Minority Populations		11,500	4,470	1,000 e	0 e
93.006	Minority HIV/AIDS Demonstration		(n)	(n)	3,000 e	3,000 e
93.041	Aging—Prevention of Abuse, Neglect		4,732	4,732	4,732 e	4,732 e
93.042	Aging—Long-Term Care Ombudsman		4,449	4,449	4,449 e	4,449 e
93.043	Aging—Disease Prevention		15,623	16,123	16,123 e	16,123 e
93.044	Aging—Senior Centers		282,194	300,319	300,319 e	310,082 e
93.045	Aging—Nutrition Services		469,874	486,412	486,412 e	521,412 e
93.046	Aging—In-Home Services		9,263	9,263	9,763 e	9,763 e
93.047	Aging—Indian, Native Hawaiian		16,057	18,457	18,457 e	18,457 e
93.048	Aging—Training, Research, Programs		4,000	10,000	18,000 e	22,000 e
93.049	Elder Rights Protection		9,181	0	0 e	12,181 e
93.051	Alzheimer's Disease		(n)	5,970	5,970 e	5,970 e
93.101	Residential/Pregnant, Postpartum		19,962	2,894	2,500 e	0 e
93.102	Residential/Women, Children		24,215	13,804	8,000 e	0 e
93.103	FDA—Research		18,993	21,642	21,000 e	21,000 e
93.104	CMHS/Serious Emotional Disturbances		63,444	58,568	86,784 e	86,784 e
93.105	Bilingual/Bicultural Service		1,322	2,689	2,689 e	2,689 e
93.106	Minority International/Sciences		3,500	2,700	2,700 e	2,700 e
93.107	Model Area Health Education Centers		6,500	7,041	8,400 e	9,091 e
93.108	Health Education Assistance \ u		139,632*	85,000*	0*e	0*e
93.110	Maternal, Child Health Programs		110,235	109,401	114,546 e	114,546 e
93.111	Adolescent Family Life Research		626	1,008	1,000 e	900 e
93.113	Biological Response/Health Hazards		89,807	94,158	110,582 e	108,627 e
93.114	Toxicological Research, Testing		15,121	18,392	23,000 e	24,852 e
93.115	Biometry, Risk/Environmental		8,699	10,415	13,250 e	13,683 e
93.116	Tuberculosis Control Programs		98,690	95,286	95,972 e	93,000 e
93.117	Preventive Medicine		2,161	1,755	1,808 e	0 e
93.118	AIDS Activity		58,673	27,373	27,373 e	27,373 e
93.121	Oral Diseases Research		135,319	145,425	161,736 e	164,351 e
93.122	Substance Abuse/Rural, Remote		4,518	2,019	0 e	0 e

Please see "Important Notes on the Tables, Footnotes," page 572.

Table 1. (continued)

Program number	ADMINISTRATIVE ENTITY/SUB-UNIT Program Title (abridged)	FY 1997 in $thousands	FY 1998 in $thousands	FY 1999 in $thousands	FY 2000 in $thousands
93.123	Pregraduate Scholarship/Indians	1,703	1,703	1,703 e	1,703 e
93.124	Nurse Anesthetist Traineeships	1,604	1,291	1,043 e	0 e
93.125	Mental Health Planning	31,216	6,083	3,942 e	0 e
93.127	Emergency Medical Services/Children	12,500	12,941	15,000 e	15,000 e
93.129	Health Centers, NHSC Sites	11,500	12,500	13,500 e	13,500 e
93.130	Primary Care Services	10,500	10,500	11,000 e	11,000 e
93.134	Organ Donations	0	0 e	0 e	0 e
93.135	Centers/Health Promotion	7,368	7,650	7,650 e	7,650 e
93.136	Injury Prevention, Control Research	31,929	37,127	37,651 e	37,651 e
93.137	Minority Community Health Coalition	1,993	2,541	5,041 e	5,041 e
93.138	Advocacy/Mentally Ill	21,518	21,518	22,498 e	22,498 e
93.139	Assistance/Disadvantaged Students	6,584	6,602	6,728 e	6,728 e
93.140	Intramural Research Training	49,626	23,400	32,000 e	35,200 e
93.142	Hazardous Waste Worker Training \ u	28,658	33,755	32,600 e	32,600 e
93.143	Hazardous Substances Research \ u	30,350	33,030	34,015 e	34,015 e
93.144	Alcohol, Drug Abuse/High-Risk	41,429	17,015	2,114 e	0 e
93.145	AIDS Education, Training Centers	16,287	16,253	19,000 e	19,000 e
93.150	Transition from Homelessness	19,437	22,310	25,221 e	30,071 e
93.151	Health Centers/Homeless	69,345	71,330	72,596 e	81,722 e
93.153	HIV/Children, Women	36,000	36,916	43,900 e	46,300 e
93.154	International Research/AIDS	863	750	750 e	750 e
93.155	Rural Health Research Centers	2,500	2,592	2,776 e	2,500 e
93.156	Geriatric/Physicians, Dentists	2,574	2,350	0 e	0 e
93.157	Centers of Excellence	24,718	23,379	24,219 e	33,142 e
93.161	Toxic Substances, Disease Registry \ t	7,443	7,348	9,155 e	9,155 e
93.162	NHSC Loan Repayment	36,352	35,388	37,554 e	37,961 e
93.164	IHS Loan Repayment	11,119	11,119	11,234 e	11,234 e
93.165	State Loan Repayment	6,134	6,337	6,000 e	8,000 e
93.168	International/Biodiversity Groups	1,402	1,757	2,070 e	2,070 e
93.169	Women, Infants (Substance Abuse)	883	0 e	0 e	0 e
93.172	Human Genome Research	140,683	165,547	218,623 e	214,853 e
93.173	Deafness, Communication Disorders	152,209	201,255	231,620 e	237,171 e
93.178	Nursing Education/Disadvantaged	3,394	3,559	3,036 e	0 e
93.181	Podiatric Residency	624	653	724 e	0 e
93.184	Disabilities Prevention	8,405	9,977	9,597 e	9,100 e
93.185	Immunization Research, Demonstration	14,189	13,628	13,000 e	13,000 e
93.186	National Research Services Awards	4,179	3,802	5,049 e	0 e
93.187	Undergraduate Scholarships	732	430	359 e	503 e
93.188	Public Health Training Centers	2,809	3,077	1,984 e	0 e
93.189	Health Education, Training Centers	3,511	3,538	3,425 e	3,765 e
93.191	Allied Health Projects	3,417	3,372	4,280 e	0 e
93.192	Rural Interdisciplinary Training	3,832	3,843	4,276 e	4,545 e
93.193	Urban Indian Health Services	8,003	7,500	7,500 e	7,500 e
93.194	Community Prevention Coalitions	43,829	8,318	6,422 e	473 e
93.196	Drug Abuse/Target Cities	27,779	1,276	0 e	0 e
93.197	Childhood Lead Poisoning Prevention	26,837	27,228	26,350 e	26,700 e
93.204	Hazardous Substance Emergency \ t	900	1,000	1,000 e	1,000 e
93.206	Health Studies/Research \ t	928	843	668 e	668 e
93.208	Great Lakes Health \ t	2,200	2,299	2,313 e	2,313 e
93.209	Contraception, Infertility LRP	69	69	475 e	500 e
93.210	Tribal Self-Governance	350,300	411,050	441,050 e	441,050 e
93.211	Rural Telemedicine Grants	5,800	5,906	5,057 e	5,000 e
93.212	Chiropractic Demonstration Projects	747	740	740 e	0 e
93.213	Alternative Medicine	8,282	13,646	40,245 e	40,745 e
93.215	Hansen's Disease	1,519	1,439	1,500 e	1,500 e
93.216	HIV/AIDS Mental Health Services	1,678	0 e	0 e	0 e
93.217	Family Planning—Services	182,263	186,349	190,000 e	194,000 e
93.219	Scholarships/Indians	252	252	252 e	252 e
93.220	Loan Repayment/Disadvantaged	152	842	928 e	928 e
93.222	Medical Education Research	442	0	0 e	0 e
93.223	Rural Health Centers	670	415	600 e	600 e
93.224	Community Health Centers	631,548	669,964	681,651 e	767,224 e
93.225	Health Services Research Training	4,179	4,298	4,300 e	4,400 e
93.226	Health Cost Research	19,662	52,920	71,300 e	99,903 e

Please see "Important Notes on the Tables, Footnotes," page 572.

Table 1. *(continued)*

Program number	ADMINISTRATIVE ENTITY/SUB-UNIT Program Title (abridged)	FY 1997 in $thousands	FY 1998 in $thousands	FY 1999 in $thousands	FY 2000 in $thousands
93.227	Hemophilia Surveillance	1,798	1,277	0 e	0 e
93.228	IHS—Health Management	3,039	6,247	5,304 e	5,304 e
93.229	Criminal Justice Treatment	7,967	8,148	8,200 e	0 e
93.230	Knowledge Development, Application	125,639	203,234	260,000 e	247,000 e
93.231	Epidemiology Agreements	1,082	1,082	1,082 e	1,082 e
93.232	Loan Repayment/General Research	1,026	1,202	1,353 e	1,472 e
93.233	Sleep Disorders Research	18,721	18,721	19,507 e	21,249 e
93.234	Traumatic Brain Injury	2,857	2,991	5,000 e	5,000 e
93.235	Abstinence Education	(n)	49,748	50,000 e	50,000 e
93.236	Dental Public Health	483	500	500 e	500 e
93.237	Diabetes Program/Indians	(n)	(n)	30,000 e	30,000 e
93.238	Treatment Outcomes Studies	(n)	(n)	5,000 e	5,000 e
93.239	Policy Research	2,984	6,584	4,300 e	4,100 e
93.240	State Capacity Building \ t	(n)	11,022	11,000 e	11,000 e
93.241	State Rural Hospital Flexibility	(n)	(n)	25,000 e	25,000 e
93.242	Mental Health Research	480,892	509,481	579,959 e	599,368 e
93.244	Mental Health Clinical, AIDS	2,899	2,232	402 e	0 e
93.245	Innovative Food Safety	(n)	(n)	300 e	300 e
93.246	Health Centers/Migrant, Seasonal	66,403	70,598	71,851 e	80,871 e
93.260	Family Planning—Personnel	7,261	5,164	6,000 e	6,400 e
93.262	Occupational Safety—Research	17,500	19,112	27,000 e	32,000 e
93.263	Occupational Safety—Training	11,092	12,234	13,430 e	13,930 e
93.268	Immunization Grants	298,984	233,317	252,000 e	310,000 e
93.271	Alcohol Research Career Awards	5,868	6,169	7,590 e	7,590 e
93.272	Alcohol National Research Training	5,803	5,867	6,791 e	6,791 e
93.273	Alcohol Research Programs	136,292	137,014	153,777 e	159,990 e
93.274	Training/Alcohol, Drug Abuse	2,779	800	900 e	900 e
93.277	Drug Abuse Scientist Awards	15,769	17,219	19,802 e	19,802 e
93.278	Drug Abuse Research Training	11,700	11,912	14,720 e	14,720 e
93.279	Drug Abuse Research	366,287	398,843	443,692 e	454,109 e
93.281	Mental Health/Development Awards	34,962	38,974	44,072 e	44,072 e
93.282	Mental Health Research Training	34,010	36,041	43,214 e	43,214 e
93.283	Disease Control—Investigations	165,125	199,028	199,028 e	199,028 e
93.288	NHSC Scholarship	30,290	30,066	28,521 e	28,521 e
93.289	Physical Fitness and Sports	998	996	1,005 e	1,097 e
93.291	Surplus Property Utilization \ p	311	316	284 e	284 e
93.298	Nurse, Nurse-Midwifery Education	17,280	16,889	17,178 e	0 e
93.299	Advanced Nurse Education	12,099	11,953	11,714 e	0 e
93.306	Comparative Medicine	87,252	95,624	112,201 e	117,846 e
93.333	Clinical Research	155,277 e	170,312	204,529 e	207,029 e
93.342	Health Professions Student Loans	5,468*	6,600*	7,000*e	7,000*e
93.358	Professional Nurse Traineeships	15,663	15,627	15,586 e	0 e
93.359	Nursing—Special Projects	10,187	9,959	9,009 e	10,968 e
93.361	Nursing Research	49,229	52,236	58,130 e	59,703 e
93.364	Nursing Student Loans \ r	2,387*	2,462*	3,000*e	3,000*e
93.371	Biomedical Technology	94,310	103,742	134,118 e	139,118 e
93.375	Minority Biomedical Research	38,185	40,888	50,888 e	51,957 e
93.379	Training in Family Medicine	13,616	12,848	11,781 e	0 e
93.389	Research Infrastructure	58,845	64,293	85,917 e	85,917 e
93.390	Academic Research Enhancement	14,092	15,027	16,600 e	17,100 e
93.392	Cancer Construction	1,410	1,461	1,500 e	1,500 e
93.393	Cancer Cause, Prevention	435,542	451,011	478,950 e	484,772 e
93.394	Cancer Detection, Diagnosis	98,286	113,745	136,869 e	138,112 e
93.395	Cancer Treatment Research	304,750	342,382	377,271 e	385,968 e
93.396	Cancer Biology Research	288,050	321,078	393,078 e	403,477 e
93.397	Cancer Centers Support	160,713	164,891	182,092 e	186,092 e
93.398	Cancer Research Manpower	74,679	84,392	111,633 e	113,633 e
93.399	Cancer Control	70,013	63,760	99,671 e	101,671 e
93.550	Transitional Living/Homeless Youth	14,949	14,922	14,944 e	19,949 e
93.551	Abandoned Infants	12,251	12,229	12,247 e	12,251 e
93.556	Family Preservation, Support	230,000	228,737	265,000 e	285,000 e
93.557	Street Outreach Program	(n)	14,973	15,000 e	15,000 e
93.558	Temporary Assistance/Families	13,402,837	16,666,712	16,844,882 e	16,848,262 e
93.559	TANF Loans	(n)	*	2,102*	0*e

Please see "Important Notes on the Tables, Footnotes," page 572.

Table 1. *(continued)*

Program number	ADMINISTRATIVE ENTITY/SUB-UNIT Program Title (abridged)	FY 1997 in $thousands	FY 1998 in $thousands	FY 1999 in $thousands	FY 2000 in $thousands
93.560	AFDC Assistance Payments	4,497,496	654,599	208,500 e	39,000 e
93.563	Child Support Enforcement	2,846,066	3,956,076	4,369,800 e	4,626,000 e
93.564	Child Support Enforcement Research	(o)	1,800	1,800 e	1,800 e
93.566	Refugee and Entrant Assistance	260,457	203,000	220,560 e	257,000 e
93.567	Refugee Assistance—Voluntary	33,126	30,855	43,409 e	39,000 e
93.568	Low-Income Home Energy Assistance	1,215,250	1,160,000	1,200,000 e	1,200,000 e
93.569	Community Services Block Grant	489,600	489,685	499,841 e	500,000 e
93.570	CSBG—Discretionary	37,332	47,475	48,552 e	0 e
93.571	CSBG—Community Food, Nutrition	4,000	3,993	4,997 e	0 e
93.575	Child Care, Development Block Grant	19,120	1,002,140	1,000,000 e	1,182,672 e
93.576	Refugee, Entrant—Discretionary	60,856	73,534	86,852 e	94,264 e
93.579	U.S. Repatriation Program	935*	816*	1,000*e	1,000*e
93.581	Indian/Environmental Quality	2,125	2,946	3,350 e	2,946 e
93.582	Environmental Impacts/Indian Lands	3,333	2,422	1,001 e	1,500 e
93.583	Refugee, Entrant Assistance	2,583	4,706	5,000 e	5,000 e
93.584	Refugee, Entrant—Targeted	35,371	35,371	49,447 e	49,447 e
93.586	State Court Improvement	10,000	10,000	10,000 e	10,000 e
93.587	Native American Languages	3,021	4,090	2,207 e	4,090 e
93.590	Community-Based Family Resources	32,835	32,775	32,825 e	32,835 e
93.591	Domestic Violence Coalitions	7,280	8,664	8,880 e	10,230 e
93.592	Family Violence—Discretionary	7,280	9,093	8,880 e	10,230 e
93.593	Job Opportunities/Low-Income	5,500	5,499	5,500 e	5,000 e
93.594	Tribal Work Grants	7,633	7,633	7,633 e	7,633 e
93.595	Welfare Reform Research	30,500	24,000	24,000 e	15,000 e
93.596	Child Care and Development	1,967,000	2,070,387	2,167,000 e	2,367,000 e
93.597	Access and Visitation Programs	10,000	9,950	10,000 e	10,000 e
93.600	Head Start	3,980,546	4,347,433	4,658,516 e	5,267,000 e
93.601	Child Support Enforcement	(n)	1,023	1,003 e	1,500 e
93.602	New Assets for Independence	(n)	(n)	9,996 e	20,000 e
93.603	Adoption Incentive Payments	(n)	(n)	19,994 e	20,000 e
93.612	Native American Programs \ r	34,933	34,869	34,922 e	34,933 e
		1,000*	1,000*	1,000*e	1,000*e
93.613	Committee/Mental Retardation	736	720	756 e	794 e
93.623	Runaway and Homeless Youth	43,653	43,574	43,639 e	43,653 e
93.630	Developmental Disabilities/Basic	91,521	91,521	91,521 e	91,521 e
93.631	Developmental Disabilities/Projects	5,250	5,042	10,250 e	10,250 e
93.632	Developmental Disabilities/University	17,461	17,461	17,461 e	17,461 e
93.643	Children's Justice Grants \ u	8,500	8,500	8,500 e	8,500 e
93.645	Child Welfare Services	291,989	291,458	291,896 e	291,989 e
93.647	Social Services Research	44,000	25,953	26,991 e	6,000 e
93.648	Child Welfare Services Training	4,000	5,989	6,998 e	7,000 e
93.652	Adoption Opportunities	13,000	22,958	24,985 e	27,363 e
93.658	Foster Care	3,777,143	3,540,276	3,982,700 e	4,537,200 e
93.659	Adoption Assistance	597,888	700,700	868,800 e	1,020,100 e
93.667	Social Services Block Grant	2,500,000	2,299,000	1,909,000 e	2,380,000 e
93.669	Child Abuse, Neglect State Grants	21,026	20,988	21,026 e	21,026 e
93.670	Child Abuse, Neglect Discretionary	14,154	14,128	14,149 e	14,154 e
93.671	Family Violence/States, Indians	58,240	68,885	71,040 e	81,840 e
93.674	Independent Living	70,000	70,000	70,000 e	110,000 e
93.767	Children's Insurance	(n)	4,235,000	4,247,000 e	4,215,000 e
93.773	Medicare—Hospital Insurance \ t	136,010,147	134,320,035	135,604,000 e	138,053,000 e
93.774	Medicare—Supplementary \ t	71,114,395	75,781,748	81,359,000 e	98,274,000 e
93.775	Medicaid Fraud Control	82,000	87,000	92,200 e	97,700 e
93.777	State Survey/Providers, Suppliers	288,985	321,100	339,000 e	340,940 e
93.778	Medicaid	97,497,990	104,495,484	110,515,810 e	114,964,089 e
93.779	Health Care Financing Research	43,601	51,236	50,000 e	55,000 e
93.820	Scholarships/Exceptional Need	10,962	11,034	11,350 e	11,350 e
93.821	Cell Biology, Biophysics Research	330,757	359,448	401,431 e	411,438 e
93.822	Health Careers Opportunity Program	26,779	25,366	27,799 e	35,299 e
93.824	Area Health Education Centers	20,131	19,569	28,587 e	28,587 e
93.837	Heart, Vascular Diseases Research	623,223	687,062	778,680 e	802,956 e
93.838	Lung Diseases Research	243,276	256,500	290,702 e	299,763 e
93.839	Blood Diseases, Resources Research	216,108	224,753	255,023 e	262,974 e
93.846	Arthritis/Skin Diseases Research	216,602	233,486	260,047 e	265,782 e

Please see "Important Notes on the Tables, Footnotes," page 572.

Table 1. (continued)

Program number	ADMINISTRATIVE ENTITY/SUB-UNIT Program Title (abridged)	FY 1997 in $thousands	FY 1998 in $thousands	FY 1999 in $thousands	FY 2000 in $thousands
93.847	Diabetes, Endocrinology, Metabolism	312,464	327,893	375,963 e	386,258 e
93.848	Digestive Diseases, Nutrition	172,963	185,857	213,321 e	219,101 e
93.849	Kidney Diseases, Urology, Hematology	189,311	209,443	240,091 e	246,681 e
93.853	Research/Neurological Disorders	222,144	222,144	241,304 e	261,372 e
93.855	Allergy, Immunology, Transplantation	242,913	260,625	338,939 e	345,580 e
93.856	Microbiology, Infectious Diseases	653,597	653,597	705,497 e	767,897 e
93.859	Pharmacology, Physiology/Chemistry	279,196	297,252	332,292 e	342,719 e
93.862	Genetics, Developmental Biology	296,953	307,217	333,788 e	339,509 e
93.864	Population Research	139,432	150,824	168,966 e	172,822 e
93.865	Research/Mothers and Children	296,516	317,886	358,651 e	367,101 e
93.866	Aging Research	408,985	429,295	492,504 e	504,376 e
93.867	Vision Research	278,197	308,284	348,074 e	351,374 e
93.879	Medical Library Assistance	26,902	28,065	29,563 e	29,600 e
93.880	Minority Access/Research Careers	18,748	18,901	21,541 e	21,541 e
93.884	Internal Medicine, Pediatrics	10,289	10,146	8,257 e	0 e
93.886	Physician Assistant Training	6,268	5,935	5,679 e	0 e
93.887	Renovation/Care Facilities	12,902	27,282	65,000 e	0 e
93.891	Alcohol Research Center Grants	22,069	22,626	24,275 e	24,275 e
93.894	Environmental Health Sciences	35,233	36,356	42,044 e	42,044 e
93.895	Family Medicine Faculty	7,987	9,231	11,097 e	0 e
93.896	Family Medicine Predoctoral	10,856	9,469	6,602 e	0 e
93.897	Residency, Education/Dentistry	3,720	3,624	4,200 e	0 e
93.900	Internal Medicine, Pediatrics	5,641	4,801	6,437 e	0 e
93.905	Indian Health Service Research	0	0	0 e	100 e
93.906	Rural Health Medical Education \ t	(a)	(a)	(a)	(a)
93.907	Nurse Anesthetist Faculty	224	226	0 e	0 e
93.908	Nursing Education Loan Repayment	2,205	2,205	2,279 e	2,279 e
93.910	Family Life Centers	5,389	4,900	6,400 e	6,400 e
93.912	Rural Outreach	25,172	29,898	30,000 e	31,400 e
93.913	Offices of Rural Health	2,643	2,520	3,000 e	3,000 e
93.915	HIV Emergency Relief Grants	227,734	0	0 e	0 e
93.916	Nurse Anesthetist Education	853	1,155	1,564 e	0 e
93.917	HIV Care Formula Grants	397,895	520,074	709,904 e	744,416 e
93.918	Outpatient Early Intervention/HIV	69,568	70,174	90,050 e	125,497 e
93.919	Breast, Cervical Cancer Detection	111,979	142,779	159,071 e	159,071 e
93.923	Disadvantaged Health Faculty Loan	1,042	1,037	1,061 e	1,061 e
93.924	HIV/AIDS Dental Reimbursements	7,260	7,551	7,538 e	7,840 e
93.925	Health Professions Scholarships	18,127	18,261	37,000 e	37,000 e
93.926	Healthy Start Initiative	92,813	95,526	105,000 e	105,000 e
93.927	Health Centers/Public Housing	9,806	10,086	10,265 e	11,555 e
93.928	Projects of National Significance	25,000	25,000	25,000 e	25,000 e
93.929	Medical Rehabilitation Research	24,703	24,377	26,974 e	27,622 e
93.931	States/Community Scholarships	388	163	0 e	0 e
93.932	Hawaiian Health Systems	3,105	3,105	3,500 e	3,285 e
93.933	Indian Health Demonstrations	2,457	2,457	2,457 e	2,457 e
93.934	Fogarty International Award	3,354	3,449	4,268 e	4,268 e
93.936	AIDS Research Loan Repayment	582	496	657 e	701 e
93.938	School Health Programs/HIV	36,145	36,125	28,769 e	36,125 e
93.939	HIV Prevention—Non-Governmental	25,000	28,501	46,000 e	46,000 e
93.940	HIV Prevention—Health Department	240,000	253,700	250,000 e	255,000 e
93.941	HIV Demonstration, Research	19,000	10,750	13,000 e	13,000 e
93.942	Research, Treatment/Lyme Disease	2,703	4,179	4,559 e	4,600 e
93.943	Epidemiologic Research/AIDS, HIV	22,000	22,751	23,700 e	23,700 e
93.944	HIV/AIDS Surveillance	50,000	46,870	47,000 e	48,000 e
93.946	Infant Health Initiative	1,894	1,894	1,594 e	1,936 e
93.947	Tuberculosis Demonstration	1,291	308	246 e	300 e
93.948	Clinical Pharmacology Training	1,710	0	0 e	3,000 e
93.951	Alzheimer's Disease	6,000	5,999	(o)	e
93.954	Tribal Recruitment/Health	570	580	580 e	580 e
93.955	Health, Safety/Construction	5,275	5,229	4,879 e	0 e
93.956	Agricultural Health, Safety	8,590	8,146	7,962 e	7,962 e
93.957	Occupational Health, Surveillance	4,021	3,937	3,937 e	0 e
93.958	Block Grants/Mental Health	261,649	261,649	274,375 e	340,875 e
93.959	Block Grants/Substance Abuse	1,234,107	1,294,602	1,505,750 e	1,534,250 e

Please see "Important Notes on the Tables, Footnotes," page 572.

Table 1. (continued)

Program number	ADMINISTRATIVE ENTITY/SUB-UNIT Program Title (abridged)		FY 1997 in $thousands	FY 1998 in $thousands	FY 1999 in $thousands	FY 2000 in $thousands
93.960	Special Minority Initiatives		5,901	6,195	10,870 e	10,999 e
93.962	Health Administration Traineeships		1,000	1,048	1,045 e	0 e
93.964	Public Health Traineeships		2,326	2,325	2,295 e	0 e
93.965	Coal Miners Respiratory Impairment		4,000	4,976	4,884 e	5,000 e
93.969	Geriatric Education Centers		5,852	6,051	7,845 e	0 e
93.970	Health Professions/Indians		2,871	2,871	2,871 e	2,871 e
93.971	Health Preparatory/Indians		1,355	2,000	2,000 e	2,000 e
93.972	Health Professions Scholarship		7,717	7,300	7,300 e	7,300 e
93.974	Family Planning—Service Research		3,103	3,843	9,000 e	12,000 e
93.977	STD Control		88,000	84,071	91,896 e	92,000 e
93.978	STD Research		11,021	11,844	14,000 e	16,000 e
93.982	Mental Health Disaster Assistance		8,882	5,643	10,000 e	10,000 e
93.984	Administrative/Primary Care		12,603	12,046	12,600 e	0 e
93.988	Diabetes Control Programs		13,815	19,193	21,408 e	21,825 e
93.989	Senior International Fellowships		904	611	611 e	611 e
93.990	National Health Promotion		700	350	350 e	350 e
93.991	Health Services Block Grant		182,540	182,540	183,987 e	190,694 e
93.994	Maternal, Child Health Block Grant		567,988	563,927	576,227 e	576,391 e
93.995	Adolescent Family Life		11,617	13,352	14,131 e	5,750 e
	DEPARTMENT TOTAL:	OUTLAYS	358,638,159	375,210,265	391,413,262	417,989,096
		CREDITS*	149,422*	97,980*	12,000*	23,000*

CORPORATION FOR NATIONAL AND COMMUNITY SERVICE

Program number	ADMINISTRATIVE ENTITY/SUB-UNIT Program Title (abridged)		FY 1997 in $thousands	FY 1998 in $thousands	FY 1999 in $thousands	FY 2000 in $thousands
94.002	Retired, Senior Volunteer Program		35,286	35,286	39,509 e	42,530 e
94.003	State Commissions		8,698	8,698	11,000 e	11,000 e
94.004	Learn and Serve/School, Community		32,250	32,250	32,250 e	37,500 e
94.005	Learn and Serve/Higher Education		10,750	10,750	10,750 e	12,500 e
94.006	AmeriCorps		215,000	215,000	237,000 e	237,000 e
94.007	Planning, Program Development		10,938	11,410	10,000 e	16,500 e
94.009	Training, Technical Assistance		12,528	12,528	16,000 e	16,000 e
94.011	Foster Grandparent Program		76,905	76,905	87,272 e	93,841 e
94.013	Volunteers in Service to America		41,117	65,235	73,000 e	81,000 e
94.016	Senior Companion Program		31,003	31,003	35,175 e	35,175 e
	DEPARTMENT TOTAL:	OUTLAYS	474,475	499,065	551,956	583,046
		CREDITS*	0*	0*	0*	0*

SOCIAL SECURITY ADMINISTRATION

Program number	ADMINISTRATIVE ENTITY/SUB-UNIT Program Title (abridged)		FY 1997 in $thousands	FY 1998 in $thousands	FY 1999 in $thousands	FY 2000 in $thousands
96.001	Social Security—Disability \ t		45,367,000	47,681,000	50,204,000 e	54,116,000 e
96.002	Social Security—Retirement \ t		254,506,200	250,826,700	257,717,100 e	267,019,400 e
96.003	Special Benefits/Age 72, Over \ t		1,374	815	500 e	257 e
96.004	Survivors Insurance \ t		55,784,100	73,484,300	75,201,100 e	78,106,200 e
96.005	Disabled Coal Miners		623,220	584,815	552,000 e	520,000 e
96.006	Supplemental Security Income		26,639,569	27,390,000	28,161,000 e	28,852,000 e
96.007	Research and Demonstration \ t		1,104	8,638	10,500 e	9,500 e
	DEPARTMENT TOTAL:	OUTLAYS	382,922,567	399,976,268	411,846,200	428,623,357
		CREDITS*	0*	0*	0*	0*
	GRAND TOTAL:	OUTLAYS	985,877,384	1,024,085,897	1,078,928,050	1,131,052,277
		CREDITS*	167,825,165*	220,296,756*	223,475,134*	237,308,493*
	GRAND TOTAL: OUTLAYS + CREDITS		1,153,702,549	1,244,382,653	1,302,403,184	1,368,360,770

Please see "Important Notes on the Tables, Footnotes," page 572.

Table 2.   Summary of Estimated Outlays/Credits, by Federal Department or Agency (FY 97, 98, 99, 00)

Program Series	DEPARTMENT OR AGENCY	FY 1997 in $thousands	FY 1998 in $thousands	FY 1999 in $thousands	FY 2000 in $thousands
10.000	**DEPARTMENT OF AGRICULTURE**				
	Total Outlays	50,477,639	47,542,459	53,599,766	52,018,597
	Total Credits	15,679,284	18,872,585	21,592,151	25,397,618
	TOTAL OUTLAYS + CREDITS	66,156,923	66,415,044	75,191,917	77,416,215
11.000	**DEPARTMENT OF COMMERCE**				
	Total Outlays	1,927,939	2,288,288	3,027,451	4,777,838
	Total Credits	27,000	105,000	145,800	23,800
	TOTAL OUTLAYS + CREDITS	1,954,939	2,393,288	3,173,251	4,801,638
12.000	**DEPARTMENT OF DEFENSE**				
	Total Outlays	3,136,287	3,151,544	2,683,412	1,386,595
	Total Credits	0	0	0	0
	TOTAL OUTLAYS + CREDITS	3,136,287	3,151,544	2,683,412	1,386,595
14.000	**DEPARTMENT OF HOUSING AND URBAN DEVELOPMENT**				
	Total Outlays	30,456,823	39,528,499	40,289,534	41,713,817
	Total Credits	74,776,194	105,846,975	104,041,146	112,659,156
	TOTAL OUTLAYS + CREDITS	105,233,017	145,375,474	144,330,680	154,372,973
15.000	**DEPARTMENT OF THE INTERIOR**				
	Total Outlays	1,953,963	2,343,425	2,229,020	2,548,749
	Total Credits	5,000	5,000	5,001	5,008
	TOTAL OUTLAYS + CREDITS	1,958,963	2,348,425	2,234,021	2,553,757
16.000	**DEPARTMENT OF JUSTICE**				
	Total Outlays	5,142,841	5,395,902	6,527,079	3,933,643
	Total Credits	0	0	0	0
	TOTAL OUTLAYS + CREDITS	5,142,841	5,395,902	6,527,079	3,933,643
17.000	**DEPARTMENT OF LABOR**				
	Total Outlays	29,557,449	29,130,294	32,148,021	39,856,825
	Total Credits	0	0	0	0
	TOTAL OUTLAYS + CREDITS	29,557,449	29,130,294	32,148,021	39,856,825
19.000	**DEPARTMENT OF STATE**				
	Total Outlays	4,398	4,800	5,305	5,305
	Total Credits	0	0	0	0
	TOTAL OUTLAYS + CREDITS	4,398	4,800	5,305	5,305
20.000	**DEPARTMENT OF TRANSPORTATION**				
	Total Outlays	27,553,223	27,410,790	35,523,014	37,532,669
	Total Credits	35,348	27,259	81,582	6,000
	TOTAL OUTLAYS + CREDITS	27,588,571	27,438,049	35,604,596	37,538,669
21.000	**DEPARTMENT OF THE TREASURY**				
	Total Outlays	325,685	461,082	505,205	527,005
	Total Credits	0	0	0	0
	TOTAL OUTLAYS + CREDITS	325,685	461,082	505,205	527,005
23.000	**APPALACHIAN REGIONAL COMMISSION**				
	Total Outlays	162,781	197,167	130,153	63,629
	Total Credits	0	0	0	0
	TOTAL OUTLAYS + CREDITS	162,781	197,167	130,153	63,629

Please see "Important Notes on the Tables, Footnotes," page 572.

Table 2. (continued)

Program Series	DEPARTMENT OR AGENCY	FY 1997 in $thousands	FY 1998 in $thousands	FY 1999 in $thousands	FY 2000 in $thousands
27.000	**OFFICE OF PERSONNEL MANAGEMENT**				
	Total Outlays	0	0	0	0
	Total Credits	0	0	0	0
	TOTAL OUTLAYS + CREDITS	0	0	0	0
29.000	**COMMISSION ON CIVIL RIGHTS**				
	Total Outlays	8,500	8,500	8,740	8,740
	Total Credits	0	0	0	0
	TOTAL OUTLAYS + CREDITS	8,500	8,500	8,740	8,740
30.000	**EQUAL EMPLOYMENT OPPORTUNITY COMMISSION**				
	Total Outlays	266,965	241,666	306,086	341,000
	Total Credits	0	0	0	0
	TOTAL OUTLAYS + CREDITS	266,965	241,666	306,086	341,000
32.000	**FEDERAL COMMUNICATIONS COMMISSION**				
	Total Outlays	0	0	0	0
	Total Credits	0	0	0	0
	TOTAL OUTLAYS + CREDITS	0	0	0	0
33.000	**FEDERAL MARITIME COMMISSION**				
	Total Outlays	188	162	184	193
	Total Credits	0	0	0	0
	TOTAL OUTLAYS + CREDITS	188	162	184	193
34.000	**FEDERAL MEDIATION AND CONCILIATION SERVICE**				
	Total Outlays	34,257	35,884	36,396	38,610
	Total Credits	0	0	0	0
	TOTAL OUTLAYS + CREDITS	34,257	35,884	36,396	38,610
36.000	**FEDERAL TRADE COMMISSION**				
	Total Outlays	102,018	106,085	116,679	133,368
	Total Credits	0	0	0	0
	TOTAL OUTLAYS + CREDITS	102,018	106,085	116,679	133,368
39.000	**GENERAL SERVICES ADMINISTRATION**				
	Total Outlays	44,751	49,136	62,214	61,600
	Total Credits	0	0	0	0
	TOTAL OUTLAYS + CREDITS	44,751	49,136	62,214	61,600
40.000	**GOVERNMENT PRINTING OFFICE**				
	Total Outlays	99,575	89,634	89,764	90,486
	Total Credits	0	0	0	0
	TOTAL OUTLAYS + CREDITS	99,575	89,634	89,764	90,486
42.000	**LIBRARY OF CONGRESS**				
	Total Outlays	206,026	209,800	225,750	231,857
	Total Credits	0	0	0	0
	TOTAL OUTLAYS + CREDITS	206,026	209,800	225,750	231,857
43.000	**NATIONAL AERONAUTICS AND SPACE ADMINISTRATION**				
	Total Outlays	38,878	51,564	52,549	41,780
	Total Credits	0	0	0	0
	TOTAL OUTLAYS + CREDITS	38,878	51,564	52,549	41,780
44.000	**NATIONAL CREDIT UNION ADMINISTRATION**				
	Total Outlays	0	0	0	0
	Total Credits	267,261	273,965	315,200	334,700
	TOTAL OUTLAYS + CREDITS	267,261	273,965	315,200	334,700

Please see "Important Notes on the Tables, Footnotes," page 572.

Table 2. (continued)

Program Series	DEPARTMENT OR AGENCY	FY 1997 in $thousands	FY 1998 in $thousands	FY 1999 in $thousands	FY 2000 in $thousands
45.000	**NATIONAL FOUNDATION ON THE ARTS AND THE HUMANITIES**				
	Total Outlays	204,297	339,043	357,362	327,968
	Total Credits	0	0	0	0
	TOTAL OUTLAYS + CREDITS	204,297	339,043	357,362	327,968
46.000	**NATIONAL LABOR RELATIONS BOARD**				
	Total Outlays	174,595	174,617	184,938	210,193
	Total Credits	0	0	0	0
	TOTAL OUTLAYS + CREDITS	174,595	174,617	184,938	210,193
47.000	**NATIONAL SCIENCE FOUNDATION**				
	Total Outlays	3,050,396	3,075,941	3,336,770	3,553,770
	Total Credits	0	0	0	0
	TOTAL OUTLAYS + CREDITS	3,050,396	3,075,941	3,336,770	3,553,770
53.000	**PRESIDENT'S COMMITTEE ON EMPLOYMENT OF PEOPLE WITH DISABILITIES**				
	Total Outlays	4,321	4,321	4,421	6,750
	Total Credits	0	0	0	0
	TOTAL OUTLAYS + CREDITS	4,321	4,321	4,421	6,750
57.000	**RAILROAD RETIREMENT BOARD**				
	Total Outlays	8,289,000	8,315,000	8,366,000	8,428,000
	Total Credits	0	0	0	0
	TOTAL OUTLAYS + CREDITS	8,289,000	8,315,000	8,366,000	8,428,000
58.000	**SECURITIES AND EXCHANGE COMMISSION**				
	Total Outlays	308,591	316,000	358,000	363,000
	Total Credits	0	0	0	0
	TOTAL OUTLAYS + CREDITS	308,591	316,000	358,000	363,000
59.000	**SMALL BUSINESS ADMINISTRATION**				
	Total Outlays	128,331	115,270	140,283	112,198
	Total Credits	12,396,752	13,045,807	17,243,995	17,582,000
	TOTAL OUTLAYS + CREDITS	12,525,083	13,161,077	17,384,278	17,694,198
61.000	**INTERNATIONAL TRADE COMMISSION**				
	Total Outlays	77	77	77	81
	Total Credits	0	0	0	0
	TOTAL OUTLAYS + CREDITS	77	77	77	81
62.000	**TENNESSEE VALLEY AUTHORITY**				
	Total Outlays	15,000	15,000	3,411	5,500
	Total Credits	0	0	0	0
	TOTAL OUTLAYS + CREDITS	15,000	15,000	3,411	5,500
64.000	**DEPARTMENT OF VETERANS AFFAIRS**				
	Total Outlays	46,210,786	41,223,604	43,917,327	44,555,639
	Total Credits	24,412,042	39,972,636	32,758,027	31,370,482
	TOTAL OUTLAYS + CREDITS	70,622,828	81,196,240	76,675,354	75,926,121
66.000	**ENVIRONMENTAL PROTECTION AGENCY**				
	Total Outlays	4,650,075	3,566,431	3,752,802	3,291,924
	Total Credits	0	0	0	0
	TOTAL OUTLAYS + CREDITS	4,650,075	3,566,431	3,752,802	3,291,924
68.000	**NATIONAL GALLERY OF ART**				
	Total Outlays	669	681	706	728
	Total Credits	0	0	0	0
	TOTAL OUTLAYS + CREDITS	669	681	706	728

Please see "Important Notes on the Tables, Footnotes," page 572.

Table 2. (continued)

Program Series	DEPARTMENT OR AGENCY	FY 1997 in $thousands	FY 1998 in $thousands	FY 1999 in $thousands	FY 2000 in $thousands
70.000	**OVERSEAS PRIVATE INVESTMENT CORPORATION**				
	Total Outlays	18,000	27,000	50,000	24,000
	Total Credits	4,441,000	5,477,000	6,000,000	7,200,000
	TOTAL OUTLAYS + CREDITS	4,459,000	5,504,000	6,050,000	7,224,000
77.000	**NUCLEAR REGULATORY COMMISSION**				
	Total Outlays	215	215	251	100
	Total Credits	0	0	0	0
	TOTAL OUTLAYS + CREDITS	215	215	251	100
78.000	**COMMODITY FUTURES TRADING COMMISSION**				
	Total Outlays	54,746	58,099	61,000	67,655
	Total Credits	0	0	0	0
	TOTAL OUTLAYS + CREDITS	54,746	58,099	61,000	67,655
81.000	**DEPARTMENT OF ENERGY**				
	Total Outlays	884,566	837,343	879,382	679,748
	Total Credits	0	0	0	0
	TOTAL OUTLAYS + CREDITS	884,566	837,343	879,382	679,748
82.000	**UNITED STATES INFORMATION AGENCY**				
	Total Outlays	68,152	83,335	87,944	89,348
	Total Credits	0	0	0	0
	TOTAL OUTLAYS + CREDITS	68,152	83,335	87,944	89,348
83.000	**FEDERAL EMERGENCY MANAGEMENT AGENCY**				
	Total Outlays	281,122	323,774	376,345	413,989
	Total Credits	1,207,862	1,279,549	1,371,232	1,445,729
	TOTAL OUTLAYS + CREDITS	1,488,984	1,603,323	1,747,577	1,859,718
84.000	**DEPARTMENT OF EDUCATION**				
	Total Outlays	27,138,545	30,764,654	34,318,586	35,287,181
	Total Credits	34,428,000	35,293,000	39,909,000	41,261,000
	TOTAL OUTLAYS + CREDITS	61,566,545	66,057,654	74,227,586	76,548,181
85.000	**SCHOLARSHIP AND FELLOWSHIP FOUNDATIONS**				
	Total Outlays	13,166	13,666	14,329	14,681
	Total Credits	0	0	0	0
	TOTAL OUTLAYS + CREDITS	13,166	13,666	14,329	14,681
86.000	**PENSION BENEFIT GUARANTY CORPORATION**				
	Total Outlays	794,982	852,847	1,290,950	1,057,704
	Total Credits	0	0	0	0
	TOTAL OUTLAYS + CREDITS	794,982	852,847	1,290,950	1,057,704
88.000	**ARCHITECTURAL AND TRANSPORTATION BARRIERS COMPLIANCE BOARD**				
	Total Outlays	3,540	3,644	3,847	4,633
	Total Credits	0	0	0	0
	TOTAL OUTLAYS + CREDITS	3,540	3,644	3,847	4,633
89.000	**NATIONAL ARCHIVES AND RECORDS ADMINISTRATION**				
	Total Outlays	45,331	39,586	42,108	46,163
	Total Credits	0	0	0	0
	TOTAL OUTLAYS + CREDITS	45,331	39,586	42,108	46,163
91.000	**UNITED STATES INSTITUTE OF PEACE**				
	Total Outlays	3,168	3,168	2,878	2,900
	Total Credits	0	0	0	0
	TOTAL OUTLAYS + CREDITS	3,168	3,168	2,878	2,900

Please see "Important Notes on the Tables, Footnotes," page 572.

Table 2. (continued)

Program Series	ADMINISTRATIVE ENTITY/SUB-UNIT DEPARTMENT OR AGENCY	FY 1997 in $thousands	FY 1998 in $thousands	FY 1999 in $thousands	FY 2000 in $thousands
92.000	**NATIONAL COUNCIL ON DISABILITY**				
	Total Outlays	326	302	593	619
	Total Credits	0	0	0	0
	TOTAL OUTLAYS + CREDITS	326	302	593	619
93.000	**DEPARTMENT OF HEALTH AND HUMAN SERVICES**				
	Total Outlays	358,638,159	375,210,265	391,413,262	417,989,096
	Total Credits	149,422	97,980	12,000	23,000
	TOTAL OUTLAYS + CREDITS	358,787,581	375,308,245	391,425,262	418,012,096
94.000	**CORPORATION FOR NATIONAL AND COMMUNITY SERVICE**				
	Total Outlays	474,475	499,065	551,956	583,046
	Total Credits	0	0	0	0
	TOTAL OUTLAYS + CREDITS	474,475	499,065	551,956	583,046
96.000	**SOCIAL SECURITY ADMINISTRATION**				
	Total Outlays	382,922,567	399,976,268	411,846,200	428,623,357
	Total Credits	0	0	0	0
	TOTAL OUTLAYS + CREDITS	382,922,567	399,976,268	411,846,200	428,623,357
	GRAND TOTAL: OUTLAYS	**985,877,384**	**1,024,085,897**	**1,078,928,050**	**1,131,052,277**
	CREDITS	**167,825,165**	**220,296,756**	**223,475,134**	**237,308,493**
	GRAND TOTAL: OUTLAYS + CREDITS	**1,153,702,549**	**1,244,382,653**	**1,302,403,184**	**1,368,360,770**

Please see "Important Notes on the Tables, Footnotes," page 572.

Table 3.   The Fifty Largest Domestic Assistance Programs in FY 1999, by Funds Outlayed or Credited

Program number	PROGRAM TITLE (abridged)	Outlays In $thousands	Credits In $thousands	Totals In $thousands	Rank
96.002	Social Security—Retirement \ t	257,717,100	0	257,717,100	1
93.773	Medicare—Hospital Insurance \ t	135,604,000	0	135,604,000	2
93.778	Medicaid	110,515,810	0	110,515,810	3
14.117	Mortgage Insurance—Homes \ i, u	0	86,398,000	86,398,000	4
93.774	Medicare—Supplementary \ t	81,359,000	0	81,359,000	5
96.004	Survivors Insurance \ t	75,201,100	0	75,201,100	6
96.001	Social Security—Disability \ t	50,204,000	0	50,204,000	7
64.114	Veterans Housing—Loans \ u	0	32,634,956	32,634,956	8
96.006	Supplemental Security Income	28,161,000	0	28,161,000	9
20.205	Highway Planning, Construction \ t	26,571,639	0	26,571,639	10
17.225	Unemployment Insurance \ t	25,371,358	0	25,371,358	11
84.032	Family Education Loans	0	23,577,000	23,577,000	12
10.551	Food Stamps	17,936,166	0	17,936,166	13
93.558	Temporary Assistance/Families	16,844,882	0	16,844,882	14
84.268	Federal Direct Loan	0	16,232,000	16,232,000	15
14.195	Section 8—Special Allocations	15,593,773	0	15,593,773	16
64.009	Veterans Medical Care Benefits	14,980,002	0	14,980,002	17
64.109	Service-Connected Disability	14,796,699	0	14,796,699	18
14.133	Mortgage Insurance—Condominiums \ i, u	0	11,047,000	11,047,000	19
10.051	Commodity Loans, Deficiency Payments \ u	2,749,121	8,264,827	11,013,948	20
59.012	Small Business Loans	0	10,000,000	10,000,000	21
57.001	Social Insurance/Railroad Workers \ t	8,366,000	0	8,366,000	22
14.857	Section 8 Rental Certificates \ i	7,818,597	0	7,818,597	23
84.063	Pell Grant Program	7,704,000	0	7,704,000	24
84.010	Title I Grants	7,676,020	0	7,676,020	25
10.555	School Lunch Program \ p	5,916,238	0	5,916,238	26
10.055	Production Flexibility Payments \ u	5,544,453	0	5,544,453	27
70.003	Foreign Investment Insurance \ u	0	5,000,000	5,000,000	28
93.600	Head Start	4,658,516	0	4,658,516	29
93.563	Child Support Enforcement	4,369,800	0	4,369,800	30
84.027	Special Education—State Grants	4,310,700	0	4,310,700	31
93.767	Children's Insurance	4,247,000	0	4,247,000	32
14.135	Mortgage Insurance—Market Rate \ i, u	0	4,071,000	4,071,000	33
93.658	Foster Care	3,982,700	0	3,982,700	34
10.410	Very Low/Moderate Income Housing \ u	0	3,965,313	3,965,313	35
10.557	Nutrition/Women, Infants, Children	3,964,000	0	3,964,000	36
64.110	Dependency, Indemnity Compensation	3,467,507	0	3,467,507	37
10.450	Crop Insurance \ u	1,207,863	2,037,450	3,245,313	38
20.507	Urbanized Area Formula Grants \ t	3,033,792	0	3,033,792	39
59.041	Certified Development Company Loans	0	3,000,000	3,000,000	40
14.218	CDBG/Entitlement \ i	2,952,740	0	2,952,740	41
14.859	Comprehensive Grant Program \ i	2,950,360	0	2,950,360	42
14.850	Public and Indian Housing	2,858,697	0	2,858,697	43
20.500	Capital Investment Grants \ t	2,819,000	0	2,819,000	44
10.452	Disaster Reserve Assistance	2,409,300	0	2,409,300	45
64.104	Pension/Non-Service Connected	2,366,613	0	2,366,613	46
84.126	Rehabilitation Services—State	2,287,128	0	2,287,128	47
93.596	Child Care and Development	2,167,000	0	2,167,000	48
10.561	State Grants/Food Stamp Program	2,150,369	0	2,150,369	49
64.010	Veterans Nursing Home Care	1,978,934	0	1,978,934	50

Please see "Important Notes on the Tables, Footnotes," page 572.

Table 4.   The Fifty Smallest Domestic Assistance Programs in FY 1999, by Funds Outlayed or Credited*

Program number	PROGRAM TITLE (abridged)	Outlays In $actual	Credits In $actual	Totals In $actual	Rank
64.128	Training/Spina Bifida	2,000	0	2,000	1
19.201	Protection of Ships \ u	5,000	0	5,000	2
20.812	Construction Reserve Fund	6,720	0	6,720	3
16.003	Narcotics, Drugs/Publications	13,000	0	13,000	4
10.763	Community Water Assistance	17,500	0	17,500	5
82.009	Professional Development	18,000	0	18,000	6
20.006	Oil Spill Trust Fund \ t	25,000	0	25,000	7
15.925	National Maritime Heritage \ u	30,000	0	30,000	8
16.400	Citizenship Education, Training \ u	30,000	0	30,000	9
64.118	Housing—Disabled Veterans \ u	0	33,000	33,000	10
64.123	Vocational Training	42,000	0	42,000	11
66.009	Air Information Center	42,400	0	42,400	12
85.401	Udall Fellowship Program	48,000	0	48,000	13
11.459	Climate and Air Quality Research	50,000	0	50,000	14
12.109	Protection, Clearing Channels	50,000	0	50,000	15
12.900	Language Grant Program	50,000	0	50,000	16
16.578	Federal Surplus Property Transfer	57,000	0	57,000	17
11.110	Trade Development	59,990	0	59,990	18
64.025	Transitional Housing \ t	0	68,000	68,000	19
61.001	Import Relief	77,000	0	77,000	20
11.449	Independent Education and Science	90,000	0	90,000	21
77.001	Radiation Control—Training	100,000	0	100,000	22
85.402	Udall Congressional Internships	100,000	0	100,000	23
15.061	Sioux Tribes Development Corp.	108,000	0	108,000	24
20.808	Capital Construction Fund	112,100	0	112,100	25
20.100	Aviation Education	125,000	0	125,000	26
12.610	Joint Land Use Studies \ t	126,000	0	126,000	27
21.004	Federal Tax Information/States	133,000	0	133,000	28
21.052	Training Assistance	135,000	0	135,000	29
11.462	Hydrologic Research	140,000	0	140,000	30
77.005	NRC Local Public Document Rooms	151,000	0	151,000	31
15.055	Alaskan Indian Allotments	167,000	0	167,000	32
33.001	Shipping—Complaints	184,000	0	184,000	33
20.810	Supplementary Training	190,000	0	190,000	34
16.561	Visiting Fellowships	200,000	0	200,000	35
16.562	Graduate Research Fellowships	200,000	0	200,000	36
15.050	Indian Hunting, Fishing Rights	213,000	0	213,000	37
42.005	LC Publications \ u	225,000	0	225,000	38
11.443	Short-Term Climate Fluctuations	227,000	0	227,000	39
93.947	Tuberculosis Demonstration	246,000	0	246,000	40
15.023	Self-Governance Grants	250,000	0	250,000	41
15.057	Navajo-Hopi Settlement	250,000	0	250,000	42
93.219	Scholarships/Indians	252,000	0	252,000	43
84.275	Rehabilitation Training—General	257,710	0	257,710	44
20.215	Highway Training, Education \ t	279,617	0	279,617	45
93.291	Surplus Property Utilization \ p	283,900	0	283,900	46
11.470	Special Programs	300,000	0	300,000	47
20.906	Hispanic Serving Institutions	300,000	0	300,000	48
93.245	Innovative Food Safety	300,000	0	300,000	49
81.116	Diversity-Related Programs	324,986	0	324,986	50

*Excluding programs without allocations when data were compiled

Please see "Important Notes on the Tables, Footnotes," page 572.

PART IV

Field Office Contacts

NOTE: Field offices manage specific programs, or they may provide information about programs. However, if the program description in Part II states "Note: no field offices for this program," contacts should be with the headquarters office. "PART I - Obtaining Federal Assistance" offers observations concerning field office contacts, especially in the discussion of the entry heading "⑩ *Program headquarters address and phone number*" on pages 22-23.

DEPARTMENT OF AGRICULTURE

AGRICULTURAL RESEARCH SERVICE

10.001   REGIONAL OFFICES

> **BELTSVILLE**—Bldg. 003 - Rm.203, BARC-West, Beltsville, MD 20705. Phone: FTS (301)504-7019.
>
> **MIDSOUTH**—Delta States Research Center, P.O. Box 225, Stoneville, MS 38776. Phone: FTS (601)686-5345.
>
> **MIDWEST**—Northern Regional Research Center, 1815 N. University St., Peoria, IL 61604. Phone: FTS (700)360-4618.
>
> **NORTH ATLANTIC**—Eastern Regional Research Center, 600 E. Mermaid Lane, Philadelphia, PA 19118. Phone: FTS (215)233-6551.
>
> **NORTHERN PLAINS**—1201 Oakridge Dr. - Ste.150, Ft. Collins, CO 80525-5526. Phone: FTS (303)229-5513.
>
> **PACIFIC WEST**—Western Regional Research Center, 800 Buchanan St., Albany, CA 94710. Phone: FTS (510)559-6016.
>
> **SOUTH ATLANTIC**—Russell Research Center, College Station Rd., Athens, GA 30604-5677. Phone: FTS (706)546-3532.
>
> **SOUTHERN PLAINS**—7607 Eastmark Dr. - Ste.230, College Station, TX 77840. Phone: FTS (409)260-9444.

ANIMAL AND PLANT HEALTH INSPECTION SERVICE

**10.025
and
10.028   REGIONAL OFFICES**

Plant Protection and Quarantine

> **CENTRAL** *(Arkansas, Iowa, Kansas, Louisiana, Missouri, Nebraska, North Dakota, Oklahoma, South Dakota, Texas)*—3505 Boca Chica Blvd. - Ste.360, Brownsville, TX 78521-4065. Phone: (956)504-4150.

10.025
and
10.028
(cont.)

EASTERN *(Connecticut, Delaware, District of Columbia, Illinois, Indiana, Maine, Maryland, Massachusetts, Michigan, Minnesota, New Hampshire, New Jersey, New York, Ohio, Pennsylvania, Rhode Island, Vermont, Virginia, West Virginia, Wisconsin)*—Blason II - 2nd fl., 505 S. Lenola Rd., Moorestown, NJ 08057-1549. Phone: (609)968-4970.

SOUTHEAST *(Alabama, Florida, Georgia, Kentucky, Mississippi, North Carolina, Puerto Rico, South Carolina, Tennessee, Virgin Islands)*—Bldg. 1, 3505 25th Ave., Gulfport, MS 39501. Phone: (601)863-1813.

WESTERN *(Alaska, Arizona, California, Colorado, Guam, Hawaii, Idaho, Montana, Nevada, New Mexico, Oregon, Utah, Washington, Wyoming)*—9580 Micron Ave. - Ste.I, Sacramento, CA 95827. Phone: (916)857-6065.

Veterinary Services

CENTRAL *(Arkansas, Iowa, Kansas, Louisiana, Missouri, Nebraska, North Dakota, Oklahoma, South Dakota, Texas)*—100 W. Pioneer Pkwy. - Ste.100, Arlington, TX 76010. Phone: (817)276-2201.

NORTHERN *(Illinois, Indiana, Maryland, Massachusetts, Michigan, Minnesota, New Jersey, New York, Ohio, Pennsylvania, Virginia, West Virginia, Wisconsin)*—1 Winner's Circle - Ste.100, Albany, NY 12205. Phone (518)453-0103.

SOUTHEAST *(Alabama, Florida, Georgia, Kentucky, Mississippi, North Carolina, Puerto Rico, South Carolina, Tennessee)*—500 E. Zack St. - Ste.410, Tampa, FL 33602-3945. Phone: (813)228-2952.

WESTERN *(Alaska, Arizona, California, Colorado, Hawaii, Idaho, Montana, Nevada, New Mexico, Oregon, Utah, Washington, Wyoming)*—384 Inverness Dr. S. - Ste.150, Englewood, CO 80112. Phone (303)784-6202.

Wildlife Service

EASTERN *(Alabama, Arkansas, Connecticut, Delaware, District of Columbia, Florida, Georgia, Illinois, Indiana, Iowa, Louisiana, Kentucky, Maine, Maryland, Massachusetts, Michigan, Minnesota, Mississippi, Missouri, New Hampshire, New Jersey, New York, North Carolina, Ohio, Pennsylvania, Puerto Rico, Rhode Island, South Carolina, Tennessee, Vermont, Virginia, Virgin Islands, West Virginia, Wisconsin)*—3322 West End Ave. - Ste.301, Nashville, TN 37203. Phone: (615)736-2007.

WESTERN *(Alaska, Arizona, California, Colorado, Guam, Hawaii, Idaho, Kansas, Montana, Nebraska, Nevada, New Mexico, North Dakota, Oklahoma, Oregon, South Dakota, Texas, Utah, Washington, Wyoming)*—12345 W. Alameda Pkwy. - Ste.204, Lakewood, CO 80228. Phone: (303)969-6560.

• National Wildlife Research Center, 1201 Oakridge Dr., Ft. Collins, CO 80525. Phone: (970)223-1588.

FARM SERVICE AGENCY

10.051
thru
10.055

STATE OFFICES

Alabama—4121 Carmichael Rd. - Ste.600, Montgomery, AL 36106-5013. Phone: (334)279-3500. *For mail:* Montgomery, AL 36123-5013.

Alaska—800 W. Evergreen - Ste.216, Palmer, AK 99645-6389. Phone: (907)745-7982.

Arizona—77 E. Thomas Rd. - Ste.240, Phoenix, AZ 85012-3318. Phone: (602)640-5200.

Arkansas—Federal Bldg. - Rm.5416, 700 W. Capitol Ave., Little Rock, AR 72201-3225. Phone: (501)301-3000.

California—430 G St. - Ste.4161, Davis, CA 95616-4161. Phone: (530)792-5538.

Caribbean Area—Cobian's Plaza - Ste.309, 1607 Ponce DeLeon Ave., Santurce, PR

00909-0001. Phone: (809)729-6872. *For mail:* Fernandez Junzos Station, P.O. Box 11188, San Juan PR 00910.

Colorado—655 Parfet St. - Ste.E-305, Lakewood, CO 80215-5517. Phone: (303)236-2866.

Connecticut—88 Day Hill Rd., Windsor, CT 06095. Phone: (860)285-8483.

Delaware—1201 College Park Dr. - Ste.101, Dover, DE 19904-8713. Phone: (302)678-2547.

Florida—440 NW 25th Place - Ste.1, Gainesville, FL 32606. Phone: (352)379-4500.

Georgia—Federal Bldg. - Rm.102, 355 E. Hancock Ave., Athens, GA 30603-1907. Phone: (706)546-2266.

Hawaii—300 Ala Moana Blvd. - Rm.5106, P.O. Box 50008, Honolulu, HI 96850. Phone: (808)541-2644.

Idaho—9173 W. Barners - Ste.B, Boise, ID 83705-1511. Phone: (208)378-5650.

Illinois—3500 W Avenue, P.O. Box 19273, Springfield, IL 62794-9273. Phone: (217) 241-6600.

Indiana—5981 Lakeside Blvd., Indianapolis, IN 46278. Phone: (317)290-3030, ext. 317.

Iowa—10500 Buena Vista Ct., Des Moines, IA 50322. Phone: (515)254-1540, ext.600.

Kansas—3600 Anderson Ave., Manhattan, KS 66502-2511. Phone: (785)539-3531.

Kentucky—771 Corporate Dr. - Ste.100, Lexington, KY 40503-5478. Phone: (606)224-7601.

Louisiana—3737 Government St., Alexandria, LA 71302-3395. Phone: (318)473-7721.

Maine—444 Stillwater Ave. - Ste.1, Bangor, ME 04402-0406. Phone: (207)990-9140.

Maryland—River Center - Ste.E, 8335 Guilford Rd., Columbia, MD 21046. Phone: (410)381-4550.

Massachusetts—445 West St., Amherst, MA 01002-2957. Phone: (413)256-0232.

Michigan—3001 Coolidge Rd. - Ste.100, East Lansing, MI 48823-6321. Phone: (517) 337-6659, ext.1201.

Minnesota—400 Farm Credit Service Bldg., 375 Jackson St., St. Paul, MN 55101-1852. Phone: (612)602-7700.

Mississippi—6310 I-55 North, Jackson, MS 39211. Phone: (601)965-4300. *For mail:* P.O. Box 14995, Jackson, MS 39236-4995.

Missouri—Parkade Plaza, 601 Business Loop 70 West - Ste.225, Columbia, MO 65203. Phone: (573)876-0925.

Montana—10 E. Babcock - Rm.557, Bozeman, MT 59715. Phone: (406)587-6872. *For mail:* Bozeman, MT 59771-0670.

Nebraska—7131 A St., Lincoln, NE 68510-7975. Phone: (402)437-5581. *For mail:* Lincoln, NE 68505-7975.

Nevada—1755 E. Plumb Lane - Ste.202, Reno, NV 89502-3207. Phone: (702)784-5411.

New Hampshire—22 Bridge St. - 4th fl., P.O. Box 1388, Concord, NH 03302-1338. Phone: (603)224-7941.

New Jersey—Mastoris Professional Plaza, Bldg. 2 - Ste.E, 163 Rt. 130, Bordentown, NJ 08505-2249. Phone: (609)298-3446.

New Mexico—6200 Jefferson St. NE, Albuquerque, NM 87109. Phone: (505)761-4900.

New York—441 S. Salina St. - (5th fl.) Ste.356, Syracuse, NY 13202-2455. Phone: (315)477-6303.

North Carolina—4407 Bland Rd. - Ste.175, Raleigh, NC 27609-6296. Phone: (919) 875-4800.

10.051
thru
10.055
(cont.)

North Dakota—1025 28th St. SW, Fargo, ND 58103-3046. Phone: (701)239-5205. *For mail:* P.O. Box 3046, Fargo, ND 58108.

Ohio—Federal Bldg. - Rm.540, 200 N. High St., Columbus, OH 43215. Phone: (614)469-6735.

Oklahoma—100 USDA - Ste.102, Farm Rd. and McFarland St., Stillwater, OK 74074-2653. Phone: (405)742-1130.

Oregon—7620 SW Mohawk, P.O. Box 1300, Tualatin, OR 97062-8121. Phone: (503) 692-6830.

Pennsylvania—One Credit Union Pl. - Ste.320, Harrisburg, PA 17110-2994. Phone: (717)237-2113.

Rhode Island—West Bay Office Complex - Rm.40, 60 Quaker Lane, Warwick, RI 02886-0111. Phone: (401)828-8232.

South Carolina—1927 Thurmond Mall - Ste.100, Columbia, SC 29201-2375. Phone: (803)806-3830.

South Dakota—Federal Bldg. - Rm.308, 200 4th St. SW, Huron, SD 57350-2478. Phone: (605)352-1160.

Tennessee—U.S. Courthouse - Rm.579, 801 Broadway, Nashville, TN 37203-3816. Phone: (615)736-5555.

Texas—Commerce National Bank Bldg. - 2nd fl., 2405 Texas Ave. S., College Station, TX 77840. Phone: (409)260-9207. *For mail:* P.O. Box 2900, College Station, TX 77841-0001.

Utah—125 S. State St. - Rm.4239, Salt Lake City, UT 84138-1189. Phone: (801)524-5013. *For mail:* P.O. Box 11350, Salt Lake City, UT 84147-0350.

Vermont—Executive Square Office Bldg., 346 Shelburne St., Burlington, VT 05401-4995. Phone: (802)658-2803.

Virginia—Culpeper Bldg. - Ste.138, 1606 Santa Rosa Rd., Richmond, VA 23229. Phone: (804)287-1500.

Washington—Rock Pointe Tower - Ste.568, 316 W. Boone Ave., Spokane, WA 99201-2350. Phone: (509)323-3000.

West Virginia—New Federal Bldg. - Rm.239, 75 High St., Morgantown, WV 26505. Phone: (304)291-4351. *For mail*: Morgantown, WV 26507-1049.

Wisconsin—6515 Watts Rd. - Rm.100, Madison, WI 53719-2797. Phone: (608)276-8732, ext.100.

Wyoming—951 Werner Ct. - Ste.130, Casper, WY 82601-1307. Phone: (307)261-5231.

10.062
and
10.064

Listed under **10.900.**

10.069   Listed under **10.051.**

10.070   Listed under **10.900.**

10.071   Chief, Warehouse Examination Division, Kansas City Commodity Office, USDA, P.O. Box 419205, Kansas City, MO 64141-0205. Phone: (816)926-6843.

10.072   Listed under **10.900.**

AGRICULTURAL MARKETING SERVICE

10.153
thru
10.163

COTTON DIVISION

Grading, Marketing Services (including Market News)

3275 Appling Rd., Memphis, TN 38133. Phone: (901)384-3000.

Standardization and Quality Assurance Branch

3275 Appling Rd., Memphis, TN 38133. Phone: (901)384-3015.

DAIRY DIVISION

Dairy Inspection, Grading Branch and Laboratory

Bldg. A - Ste.370, 800 Roosevelt Rd., Glen Ellyn, IL 60137. Phone: (708)790-6920.

Market News Service

2811 Agricultural Dr., Madison, WI 53704-6777. Phone: (608)224-5080.

FRUIT AND VEGETABLE DIVISION

Fresh and Processed Products

Alabama—1557 Reeves St., P.O. Box 1368, Dothan, AL 36302. Phone: (334)792-5185.

Arizona—1688 W. Adams - Rm.415, Phoenix, AZ 85007. Phone: (602)542-0880.

California—1320 E. Olympic Ave. - Rm.212, Los Angeles, CA 90021. Phones: (213) 894-2489, -6553.

▪ 1220 N St. - Rm.A-270, Sacramento, CA 95814. Phones: (916)654-0810, -0813, -0815. *For mail:* P.O. Box 942871, Sacramento, CA 94271-0001.

Colorado—2331 W. 31st Ave., Denver, CO 80211. Phones: (303)844-4570, 477-0093.

Connecticut—Connecticut Regional Market, 101 Reserve Rd. - Rm.5, Hartford, CT 06114. Phone: (860)240-3446.

Delaware—2320 S. DuPont Hwy., Dover, DE 19901. Phone: (302)736-4811.

District of Columbia/Maryland—Baltimore-Washington Terminal Market Office, 8610 Baltimore-Washington Blvd. - Ste.212, Jessup, MD 20794. Phones: (301)317-4387, -4587.

Florida—Techniport Bldg. - Rm.556, 5600 NW 36th St., Miami, FL 33122. Phone: (305)870-9542.

Georgia—Administration Bldg. - Rm.205, 16 Forest Pkwy., Forest Park, GA 30050. Phone: (404)366-7522.

Hawaii—1428 S. King St., Honolulu, HI 96814. Phone: (808)973-9566. *For mail*: P.O. Box 22159, Honolulu, HI 96823-2159.

Idaho—2270 Old Penitentiary Rd., Boise, ID 83712. Phone: (208)332-8670.

Indiana—Greenfield, IN 46140-0427. Phone: (317)462-5897.

Kentucky—No. 1 Produce Terminal, Louisville, KY 40218. Phones: (502)595-4266, -4278.

Louisiana—U.S. Postal Service Bldg. - Rm.11036, 701 Loyola Ave., New Orleans, LA 70113. Phones: (504)589-6741, -6742.

Maine—744 Main St. - Ste.4, P.O. Box 1058, Presque Isle, ME 04769. Phone: (207)764-2100.

Massachusetts—Boston Market Terminal Bldg. - Rm.1, 34 Market St., Everett, MA 02149. Phones: (617)389-2480, -2481.

Michigan—90 Detroit Union Produce Union Terminal, 7201 W. Fort St., Detroit, MI 48209. Phones:(313)226-6059, -6225.

Minnesota—90 W. Plato Blvd., St. Paul, MN 55107. Phones: (612)296-8557, -0593.

Missouri—Gumble Bldg. - Rm.502, 801 Walnut St., Kansas City, MO 64106. Phone: (816)374-6273.

▪ Unit 1 Produce Row - (1st fl.) Rm.100, St. Louis, MO 63102. Phone: (314)425-4514, -4515.

10.153
thru
10.163
(cont.)

New Jersey—Federal Bldg. - Rm.1430, 970 Broad St., Newark, NJ 07102. Phone: (201)645-2636.

New York—Division of Food Safety and Inspection Service, Capital Plaza - Bldg. 2 (2nd fl.), 1 Winners Circle, Albany, NY 12235. Phones: (518)457-1211, -2090, -1982.

▪ 465B Hunts Point Market, Bronx, NY 10474. Phones: (718)991-7665, -7669.

Ohio—3716 Croton Ave., Cleveland, OH 44115. Phone: (216)522-2135.

▪ Division of Food, Dairy and Drugs, Bldg. 2, 8995 E. Main St., Reynoldsburg, OH 43068. Phone: (614)728-6350.

Oklahoma—2800 N. Lincoln Blvd., Oklahoma City, OK 73105. Phone: (405)521-3864.

Oregon—635 Capitol St. NE, Salem, OR 97310-0110. Phone: (503)986-4629.

Pennsylvania—2301 N. Cameron St. - Rm.112, Harrisburg, PA 17110. Phones: (717) 787-5107, -5108.

▪ 210 Produce Bldg., 3301 S. Galloway St., Philadelphia, PA 19148. Phones: (215)336-0845, -0846.

▪ Pittsburgh Produce Terminal Bldg. - Rm.206, 2100 Smallman St., Pittsburgh, PA 15222. Phones: (412)261-6435.

Puerto Rico—Federal-State Inspection, GSA Service Center, 651 Federal Dr. - Ste.103-05, Guaynabo, PR 00965. Phones: (787)783-2230, -4116.

Tennessee—3211 Alcoa Hwy., Knoxville, TN 37920. Phone: (423)577-2633.

▪ Melrose Station, P.O. Box 40627, Nashville, TN 37204. Phone: (615)360-0169.

Texas—1301 W. Expressway, Alamo, TX 78516. Phones: (210)787-4091, -6881. *For mail:* P.O. Box 107, San Juan, TX 78589.

▪ 1406 Parker St. - Ste.203, Dallas, TX 75215. Phones: (214)767-5337, -5338.

▪ 8001 E N. Mesa - Ste.303, El Paso, TX 79932. Phone: (505)589-3753.

▪ 3100 Produce Row - Rm.1A, Houston, TX 77023. Phones: (713)923-2557, -2558.

▪ Administration Bldg. - Rm.244, 1500 S. Zarzamora St., San Antonio, TX 78207. Phone: (210)222-2751.

Utah—350 N. Redwood Rd. - Rm.217, Salt Lake City, UT 84116. Phone: (801)538-7187.

Washington—National Resources Bldg. - 2nd fl., 1111 Washington St., Olympia, WA 98504-2560. Phone: (360)902-1831.

Market News Branch

Arizona—522 N. Central Ave. - Rm.106, Phoenix, AZ 85004. Phone: (602)379-3066.

California—2202 Monterey St. - Ste.104-A, Fresno, CA 93721. Phone: (209)487-5178.

▪ 1320 E. Olympic Blvd. - Ste.212, Los Angeles, CA 90021-1907. Phone: (213)894-3077.

▪ 630 Sansome St. - Rm.727, San Francisco, CA 94111. Phone: (415)705-1300.

Colorado—Greeley Producers Bldg., 711 "O" St., Greeley, CO 80631. Phones: (970) 351-7097, -8256.

Florida (*Seasonal*)—775 Warner Ln., Orlando, FL 32803. Phone: (407)897-5950.

▪ Brickell Plaza Bldg. - Ste.424, 909 SE 1st Ave., Miami, FL 33131. Phone: (305)373-2955.

Georgia—203 Administration Bldg., 16 Forest Pkwy., Forest Park, GA 30050. Phones: (404)763-7297, 361-1376.

▪ Georgia State Farmers Market - Stall 39, 502 Smith Ave., U.S. Hwy. 84, P.O. Box 1447, Thomasville, GA 31799. Phone: (912)228-1208.

Idaho—1820 E. 17th St. - Ste.130, Idaho Falls, ID 83404. Phone: (208)526-0166.

Illinois—Kluczynski Bldg. - Rm.512, 230 S. Dearborn St., Chicago, IL 60604. Phone: (312)353-0111.

Maryland—Maryland Wholesale Produce Market, Bldg. B - Rm.101, 7460 Conowingo

Ave., Jessup, MD 20794. Phones: (410)799-4840, -4841; Washington DC only: (301)621-1261.

Massachusetts—Boston Market Terminal - Rm.10, 34 Market St., Everett, MA 02149. Phones: (617)387-4498, -4615, -4681.

Michigan—Federal Bldg. - Rm.201, 175 Territorial Rd., P.O. Box 1204, Benton Harbor, MI 49023. Phones: (616)925-3270, -3271.

▪ Union Produce Terminal - Rm.53, 7201 W. Fort St., Detroit, MI 48209. Phone: (313)841-1111.

Missouri—Unit 1, Produce Row - Rm.101, St. Louis, MO 63102-1418. Phone: (314) 425-4520.

New York—5A NYC Terminal Market, Halleck St. at Edgewater Rd., Bronx, NY 10474-7355. Phone: (718)542-2225.

Pennsylvania—3301 S. Galloway St. - Rm.261, Philadelphia, PA 19148. Phone: (215) 597-4536.

▪ 2100 Smallman St. - Rm.207, Pittsburgh, PA 15222. Phone: (412)644-5847.

Texas—1406 Parker - Rm.201, Dallas, TX 75215. Phones: (214)767-5375, -5376, -5377.

Washington—Interwest Savings Bank - Ste.302, 15111 8th Ave. SW, Seattle, WA 98148-0099. Phones: (206)764-3753, -3804.

▪ Agricultural Service Center - Rm.4, 2015 S. 1st St., Yakima, WA 98903. Phones: (509)575-2492, -2493.

Marketing Field Service

California—2202 Monterey St. - Ste.102-B, Fresno, CA 93721. Phone: (209)487-5901.

Florida—301 3rd St. NW - Ste.206, P.O. Box 2276, Winterhaven, FL 33881. Phone: (941)299-4770, -4886.

Oregon—1220 SW 3rd Ave. - Rm.369, Portland, OR 97204. Phones: (503)326-2724, -2725.

Texas—1313 E. Hackberry, McAllen, TX 78501. Phone: (956)682-2833.

Processed Products Branch

EASTERN—Regional Director, Bldg. A - Ste.380, 800 Roosevelt Rd., Glen Ellyn, IL 60137-5875. Phone: (630)790-6957.

Florida—6966 NW 36th Ave., Miami, FL 33147-6506. Phone: (305)835-7626.

▪ 98 3rd St. SW, Winter Haven, FL 33880-2909. Phone: (941)294-7416.

Georgia—1555 St. Joseph Ave., East Point, GA 30344-2591. Phone: (404)763-7495.

Indiana—4318 Technology Dr., South Bend, IN 46628-9752. Phone: (219)287-5407.

Louisiana (*Inspection Point of East Point, GA*)—Commerce Bldg. - Ste.3, 1942 Williams Blvd., Kenner, LA 70062-6285. Phone: (504)466-0343.

Maine—165 Lancaster St., Portland, ME 04101-2499. Phone: (207)772-1588.

Maryland (*Inspection Point of Hunt Valley, MD*)—102 Maryland Ave., Easton, MD 21601-3409. Phone: (410)822-3383.

▪ Hunt Valley Professional Bldg., 9 Schilling Rd., Hunt Valley, MD 21031-1106. Phone: (410)962-4946.

Michigan (*Inspection Point of South Bend, IN*)—c/o Vroom Cold Storage, Russell Rd., Hart, MI 49420-0113. Phone: (616)873-5654.

Minnesota (*Inspection Point of Ripon, WI*)—2126 Hoffman Rd., Mankato, MN 56001-5863. Phone: (507)387-6101.

New Jersey—Park Plaza, Professional Bldg. - Ste.304, 622 Georges Rd., North Brunswick, NJ 08902-3313. Phone: (908)545- 0939.

New York (*Inspection Point of North Brunswick, NJ*)—Genesee Valley Regional Mar-

**10.153
thru
10.163
(cont.)**

ket, 900 Jefferson Rd. - Rm.110, Rochester, NY 14623-3289. Phones: (716)424-2092, -2096.

Oklahoma (*Inspection Point of Weslaco, TX*)—716 S. 2nd St. - Ste.106, Stillwater, OK 74960-4806. Phone: (918)696-6333.

Puerto Rico—GSA Center, 651 Federal Dr. - Ste.103-05, Guaynabo, PR 00965-1030. Phones: (809)783-2230, -4116.

Texas—Federal Bldg. - Rm.1011, 2320 La Branch St., Houston, TX 77004-1036. Phone: (713)659-3836.

▪ (*Inspection Point of Weslaco, TX*)—319 Market St., Laredo, TX 78040-8529. Phone: (210)726-2258.

▪ 117 S. Westgate, Weslaco, TX 78596-2701. Phones: (210)968-2772, -2126.

Virginia—No.1 N. 14th St. - Rm.332, Richmond, VA 23219-3691. Phone: (804)786-0930.

Wisconsin—742 E. Fond du Lac St., Ripon, WI 54971-9555. Phone: (414)748-2287.

WESTERN—Regional Director, 2202 Monterey St. - Ste.102-C, Fresno, CA 93721-3175. Phone: (209)487-5891.

California—2202 Monterey St. - Ste.102-A, Fresno, CA 93721-3129. Phone: (209)487-5210.

▪ (*Inspection Point of Fresno*)—45-116 Commerce St. - Ste.15, Indio, CA 92201-3440. Phone: (619)347-1057.

▪ 1320 E. Olympic Rd. - Rm.212, Los Angeles, CA 90021-1948. Phone: (213)894-3173.

Hawaii—State of Hawaii Department of Agriculture, 1428 S. King St., Honolulu, HI 96814. Phone: (808)973-9566. *For mail:* P.O. Box 22159, Honolulu, HI 96823-2159.

Oregon (*Inspection Point of Yakima, WA*)—111 S. Main St., Milton-Freewater, OR 97862-1342. Phone: (541)938-3251.

▪ 340 High St. NE, Salem, OR 97301-3631. Phone: (503)399-5761.

Washington—32 N. 3rd St. - Rm.212, Yakima, WA 98901-2791. Phone: (509)575-5869.

LIVESTOCK DIVISION

Livestock and Grain Market News Branch

Alabama—1445 Federal Dr. - Rm.107, P.O. Box 3336, Montgomery, AL 36109-0336. Phone: (334)223-7488.

Arizona—Stockyards Bldg. - Rm.102, 5001 E. Washington St., Phoenix, AZ 85034-2010. Phone: (602)379-4376.

Arkansas—2301 S. University - Rm.110-B, Little Rock, AR 72203-3910. Phone: (501)671-2203.

Colorado—711 "O" St., Greeley, CO 80631-9540. Phone: (970)353-9750.

Florida—775 Warner Lane, Orlando, FL 32803. Phone: (407)897-2708.

Georgia—Georgia State Farmers Market, 502 Smith Ave. - Stall 38, Thomasville, GA 31792-0086. Phone: (912)226-2198.

Illinois—Illinois Department of Agriculture, Division of Marketing, State Fairgrounds, P.O. Box 19281, Springfield, IL 62794-9281. Phone: (217)782-4925.

Iowa—210 Walnut St. - Rm.767, Des Moines, IA 50309-2106. Phone: (515)284-4460.

▪ 800 Cunningham Dr. - Rm.225, Sioux City, IA 51107-2437. Phone: (712)252-3286.

Kansas—100 Military Ave. - Ste.217, Dodge City, KS 67801-4945. Phone: (316)227-8881.

Kentucky—1321 Story Ave., Louisville, KY 40206-1884. Phone: (502)582-5287.

Louisiana—Capitol Station, 5825 Florida Blvd., Baton Rouge, LA 70821-3334. Phone: (504)922-1328.

Minnesota—New Livestock Exchange Bldg. - Ste.208, S. St. Paul, MN 55075-5598. Phone: (612)451-1565.

Missouri—601 Illinois Ave. - Rm.210, St. Joseph, MO 64504-1396. Phone: (816)238-0678.

Montana—Public Auction Yards Bldg. - Rm.206, 112 S. 18th and Minnesota Ave., Billings, MT 59103-1191. Phone: (406)657-6285.

Nebraska—213 Livestock Exchange Bldg., 29th and O St., Omaha, NE 68107-2603. Phone: (402)731-4520.

New Mexico—2507 N. Telshor Blvd. - Ste.4, Las Cruces, NM 88001. Phone: (505)521-4928.

Oklahoma—Livestock Exchange Bldg. - Rm.140, 2501 Exchange Ave., Oklahoma City, OK 73108-2477. Phone: (405)232-5425.

Oregon—1220 SW 3rd Ave. - Rm.1772, Portland, OR 97204-2899. Phone: (503)326-2237.

Pennsylvania—c/o New Holland Sales Stables, 101 W. Fulton St., P.O. Box 155, New Holland, PA 17557. Phone: (717)354-2391.

South Carolina—Youngblood Bldg., 1001 Bluff Rd., Columbia, SC 29201-3405. Phone: (803)737-4491.

South Dakota—803 E. Rice St. - Rm.103, Sioux Falls, SD 57103-0193. Phone: (605)338-4061.

Tennessee—Melrose Station, Ellington Agriculture Center, Hogan Rd., Nashville, TN 37204-0627. Phone: (615)781-5406.

Texas—Livestock Exchange Bldg. - 1st fl., 101 S. Manhattan St., P.O. Box 30217, Amarillo, TX 79104-0217. Phone: (806)372-6361.

 • Producers Livestock Auction Bldg., San Angelo, TX 76903-0160. Phone: (915)653-1778.

Washington—988 Juniper St., Moses Lake, WA 98837-2250. Phone: (509)765-3611.

Wyoming—1834 E. A St., Torrington, WY 82240-1813. Phone: (307)532-4146.

Meat Grading and Certification

Colorado—400 Livestock Exchange Bldg., Denver, CO 80216-2139. Phone: (303)294-7676.

Illinois—Bldg. A - Ste.330, 800 Roosevelt Rd., Glen Ellyn, IL 60137-5832. Phone: (708)790-6905.

Iowa—210 Walnut St. - Rm.575-A, Des Moines, IA 50309-2106. Phone: (515)284-7166.

Nebraska—204 Livestock Exchange Bldg., 29th and O St., Omaha, NE 68107-2603. Phone: (402)733-4833.

Texas—Livestock Exchange Bldg., 101 S. Manhattan St., Amarillo, TX 79104. Phone: (806)373-7111. *For mail:* P.O. Box 30217, Amarillo, TX 79120-0217.

POULTRY DIVISION

Poultry Grading Branch

EAST MIDWEST *(Alabama, Arkansas, Louisiana, Mississippi, Oklahoma, Tennessee, Texas)*—1 Natural Resources Dr. - Rm.110, Little Rock, AR 72215-8521. Phone: (501)324-5955.

EASTERN *(Connecticut, Delaware, District of Columbia, Florida, Georgia, Maine, Maryland, Massachusetts, New Hampshire, New Jersey, New York, North Carolina, Pennsylvania, Puerto Rico, Rhode Island, South Carolina, Vermont, Virgin Islands, Virginia, West Virginia)*—635 Cox Rd. - Ste.G, Gastonia, NC 28054-3441. Phone: (704)867-3871.

**10.153
thru
10.163
(cont.)**   WEST MIDWEST *(Illinois, Indiana, Iowa, Kentucky, Kansas, Michigan, Minnesota, Missouri, Nebraska, North Dakota, Ohio, South Dakota, Wisconsin)*—Federal Bldg. - Rm.777, 210 Walnut St., Des Moines, IA 50309-2100. Phone: (515)284-4581.

WESTERN *(Alaska, Arizona, California, Colorado, Hawaii, Idaho, Montana, New Mexico, Nevada, Oregon, Utah, Washington, Wyoming)*—2909 Coffee Rd. - Ste.4, Modesto, CA 95355-3188. Phone: (209)522-5251.

Poultry Market News Branch

California—Bldg. 6 - Section E, 5600 Rickenbacker Rd., Bell, CA 90201-6418. Phones: (213)269-4154; *Recorded messages 24 hrs./day*: (213)260-4676.

Connecticut—Connecticut Department of Agriculture, Marketing Division, State Office Bldg. - Rm.263, 165 Capital Ave., Hartford, CT 06106-1688. Phone: (860)566-3671.

District of Columbia—AMS-USDA, PY Division, South Bldg. - Rm.3960, Washington, DC 20090-6456. Phone: (202)720-6911.

Georgia—60 Forsyth St. SW - Rm.6M80, Atlanta, GA 30303. Phones: FTS (404)562-5830, -5856.

Iowa—210 Walnut St. - Rm.951, Des Moines, IA 50309-2103. Phone: (515)284-4545 *(recorded messages 24 hrs./day)*.

Louisiana—Louisiana Department of Agriculture, Wilson Bldg., Baton Rouge, LA 70821-3334. Phone: (504)922-1328.

Mississippi—352 E. Woodrow Wilson, Jackson, MS 39296-4629. Phone: (601)965-4662.

North Carolina—North Carolina Department of Agriculture, State Agriculture Bldg. - Rm.402, 2 W. Edenton St., P.O. Box 27647, Raleigh, NC 27611-7647. Phone: (919)733-7252.

Texas—Texas Department of Agriculture, Capitol Station, 1700 N. Congress Ave., Austin, TX 78711-2847. Phones: (512)463-7628; (toll-free within state, 1-800-252-3407).

Virginia—Virginia Department of Agriculture and Consumer Services, 116 Reservoir St., Harrisonburg, VA 22801-4232. Phone: (540)434-0779.

SCIENCE DIVISION

Alabama—Supervisory Chemist, Aflatoxin Laboratories, 3119 Wesley Way, Dothan, AL 36301-2020. Phone: (334)794-5070.

▪ Laboratory Supervisor, 1557 Reeves St., P.O. Box 1368, Dothan, AL 36302. Phone: (334)792-5185.

Florida—Supervisory Chemist, Eastern Laboratories, 98 3rd St. SW - Ste.211, Winter Haven, FL 33880-2909. Phone: (941)299-7958.

Georgia—Laboratory Supervisor, 1211 Schley Ave., Albany, GA 31707. Phone: (912)430-8490.

▪ Laboratory Supervisor, P.O. Box 488, Ashburn, GA 31714. Phone: (912)567-3703.

▪ Laboratory Supervisor, 610 N. Main St., Blakely, GA 31723. Phone: (912)723-4570.

▪ Laboratory Supervisor, P.O. Box 272, Dawson, GA 31742. Phone: (912)995-7257.

Illinois—Midwestern Laboratory, 3570 N. Avondale Ave., Chicago, IL 60618-5391. Phone: (312)353-6525.

North Carolina—Laboratory Supervisor, 301 W. Pearl St., P.O. Box 279, Aulander, NC 27805. Phone: (919)345-1661, ext.156.

▪ Laboratory Director, Eastern Laboratory, 2311-B Aberdeen Blvd., Gastonia, NC 28054-0614. Phone: (704)867-3873.

▪ Laboratory Address, 645 Cox Rd., Gastonia, NC 28054-0614. Phone: (704)867-1882.

Oklahoma—Laboratory Supervisor, 107 S. 4th St., Madill, OK. 73446. Phone: (405)795-5615.

Virginia—Pesticide Records Branch, 8700 Centreville Rd. - Ste.200, Manassas, VA 22110-0031, Phones: (703)330-7826; Residue Branch, (703)330-2300.

- Laboratory Supervisor, 308 Culloden St., P.O. Box 1130, Suffolk, VA 23434. Phone: (757)925-2286.

TOBACCO DIVISION

Tobacco Inspection and Market News

LEXINGTON REGION *(Indiana, Kentucky, Maryland, Missouri, North Carolina, Ohio, Tennessee, Virginia, West Virginia (burley), and Connecticut, Massachusetts, Pennsylvania, Wisconsin cigar areas)*—771 Corporate Dr. - Ste.500, Lexington, KY 40503. Phone: (606)224-1088.

RALEIGH REGION *(Alabama, Florida, Georgia, North Carolina, South Carolina, Virginia(Flue-cured, Tobacco and Naval Stores Inspection))*—1306 Annapolis Dr. - Rm.205, Raleigh, NC 27608-0001. Phone: (919)856-4584.

10.165   **REGULATORY BRANCH REGIONAL OFFICES**
(Perishable Agricultural Commodities Act)

Arizona—Federal Bldg. - Rm.7, 300 W. Congress St., P.O. Box FB30, Tucson, AZ 85701-1319. Phone: (520)670-4793.

Illinois—Bldg. A - Ste.360, 800 Roosevelt Rd., Glen Ellyn, IL 60137-5832. Phone: (630)790-6929.

New Jersey—622 Georges Rd. - Ste.303, North Brunswick, NJ 08902-3303. Phone: (908)846-8222.

Texas—1200 E. Copeland Rd. - Ste.404, Arlington, TX 76011-4938. Phone: (817)885-7805.

Virginia—8700 Centerville Rd. - Ste.206, Manassas, VA 22110. Phone: (703)330-4455.

10.404   Listed under **10.051**.

RURAL ECONOMIC AND COMMUNITY DEVELOPMENT
(Rural Housing Service — Rural Business-Cooperative Service)

10.405   **STATE OFFICES**

Alabama—Sterling Center - Ste.601, 4121 Carmichael Rd., Montgomery, AL 36106-3683. Phone: (334)279-3400.

Alaska—800 W. Evergreen - Ste.201, Palmer, AK 99645-6539. Phone: (907)745-2176.

Arizona—3003 N. Central Ave. - Ste.900, Phoenix, AZ 85012-2906. Phone: (602)280-8700.

Arkansas—700 W. Capitol Ave. - Rm.3416, P.O. Box 2778, Little Rock, AR 72201-3325. Phone: (501)301-3200.

California—430 G St. - Agency 4169, Davis, CA 95616-4169. Phone: (530)792-5800.

Colorado—655 Parfet St. - Rm.E-100, Lakewood, CO 80215. Phone: (303)236-2801.

Delaware *(Delaware, Maryland)*—5201 S. Dupont Hwy., P.O. Box 400, Camden, DE 19934-9998. Phone: (302)697-4300.

Florida *(Florida, Virgin Islands)*—Federal Bldg., 4440 NW 25th Place, Gainesville, FL 32614-7010. Phone: (352)338-3400.

Georgia—Stephens Federal Bldg., 355 E. Hancock Ave., Athens, GA 30601-2768. Phone: (706)546-2162.

10.405
(cont.)

Hawaii—Federal Bldg. - Rm.311, 154 Waianuenue Ave., Hilo, HI 96720. Phone: (808)933-3000.

Idaho—9173 W. Barnes Dr. - Ste.A1, Boise, ID 83709. Phone: (208)378-5600.

Illinois—Illini Plaza - Ste.103, 1817 S. Neil St., Champaign, IL 61820. Phone: (217) 398-5235.

Indiana—5975 Lakeside Blvd., Indianapolis, IN 46278. Phone: (317)290-3100.

Iowa—Federal Bldg. - Rm.873, 210 Walnut St., Des Moines, IA 50309. Phone: (515) 284-4663.

Kansas—1200 SW Executive Dr., P.O. Box 4653, Topeka, KS 66605. Phone: (785)271-2700.

Kentucky—771 Corporate Plaza - Ste.200, Lexington, KY 40503. Phone: (606)224-7300.

Louisiana—3727 Government St., Alexandria, LA 71302. Phone: (318)473-7920.

Maine—444 Stillwater Ave. - Ste.2, Bangor, ME 04402-0405. Phone: (207)990-9106.

Massachusetts (*Connecticut, Massachusetts, Rhode Island*)—451 West St., Amherst, MA 01002. Phone: (413)253-4300.

Michigan—3001 Coolidge Rd. - Ste.200, East Lansing, MI 48823. Phone: (517)337-6635.

Minnesota—410 Agribank Bldg., 375 Jackson St., St. Paul, MN 55101-1853. Phone: (651)602-7800.

Mississippi—Federal Bldg. - Ste.831, 100 W. Capitol St., Jackson, MS 39269. Phone: (601)965-4316.

Missouri—Parkade Center - Ste.235, 601 Business Loop - 70 West, Columbia, MO 65203. Phone: (573)876-0976.

Montana—900 Technology Blvd. - (Unit 1) Ste.B, P.O. Box 850, Bozeman, MT 59715. Phone: (406)585-2580.

Nebraska—Federal Bldg. - Rm.152, 100 Centennial Mall North, Lincoln, NE 68508. Phone: (402)437-5551.

Nevada—1390 S. Curry St., Carson City, NV 89703-9910. Phone: (702)887-1222.

New Jersey—Tarnsfield Plaza - Ste.22, 790 Woodlane Rd., Mt. Holly, NJ 08060. Phone: (609)265-3600.

New Mexico—6200 Jefferson St. NE - Rm.255, Albuquerque, NM 87109. Phone: (505)761-4950.

New York—The Galleries of Syracuse, 441 S. Salina St. - Ste.357, Syracuse, NY 13202-2541. Phone: (315)477-6400.

North Carolina—4405 Bland Rd. - Ste.260, Raleigh, NC 27609. Phone: (919)873-2000.

North Dakota—Federal Bldg. - Rm.208, 220 E. Rosser, Bismarck, ND 58502-1737. Phone: (701)250-4781.

Ohio—Federal Bldg. - Rm.507, 200 N. High St., Columbus, OH 43215-2477. Phone: (614)469-5606.

Oklahoma—100 USDA - Ste.108, Stillwater, OK 74074-2654. Phone: (405)742-1000.

Oregon—101 SW Main St. - Ste.1410, Portland, OR 97204-3222. Phone: (503)414-3300.

Pennsylvania—One Credit Union Pl. - Ste.330, Harrisburg, PA 17110-2996. Phone: (717)237-2299.

Puerto Rico—New San Juan Office Bldg. - Rm.501, 159 Carlos E. Chardon St., Hato Rey, PR 00918-5481. Phone: (787)766-5095.

South Carolina—Thurmond Federal Bldg. - Rm.1007, 1835 Assembly St., Columbia, SC 29201. Phone: (803)765-5163.

South Dakota—Huron Federal Bldg. - Rm.210, 200 4th St. SW, Huron, SD 57350. Phone: (605)352-1100.

Tennessee—3322 West End Ave. - Ste.300, Nashville, TN 37203-1084. Phone: (615) 783-1300.

Texas—Federal Bldg. - Ste.102, 101 S. Main, Temple, TX 76501. Phone: (254)742-9700.

Utah—Federal Bldg. - Rm.4311, 125 S. State St., P.O. Box 11350, Salt Lake City, UT 84147-0350. Phone: (801)524-4063.

Vermont *(New Hampshire, Vermont)*—City Center - 3rd fl., 89 Main St., Montpelier, VT 05602. Phone: (802)828-6010.

Virginia—Culpeper Bldg. - Ste.238, 1606 Santa Rosa Rd., Richmond, VA 23229. Phone: (804)287-1550.

Washington—1835 Black Lake Blvd. SW - Ste.B, Olympia, WA 98512-5715. Phone: (360)704-7740.

West Virginia—Federal Bldg. - Rm.320, 75 High St., Morgantown, WV 26505-7500. Phone: (304)291-4791.

Wisconsin—4949 Kirschling Court, Stevens Point, WI 54481. Phone: (715)345-7600.

Wyoming—Federal Bldg. - Rm.1005, 100 E. B St., P.O. Box 820, Casper, WY 82602. Phone: (307)261-6300.

10.406 and 10.407	Listed under **10.051**.
10.410 thru 10.420	Listed under **10.405**.
10.421	Listed under **10.051**.
10.427 and 10.433	Listed under **10.405**.
10.437	Listed under **10.051**.
10.438 thru 10.442	Listed under **10.405**.
10.443	Contact appropriate office listed under **10.051**, **10.405**, or **10.900**.
10.444 and 10.445	Listed under **10.405**.

RISK MANAGEMENT AGENCY
(Federal Crop Insurance Corporation)

10.450   **REGIONAL SERVICE OFFICES**

REGION 1 *(Connecticut, Delaware, Maine, Maryland, Massachusetts, New Hampshire, New Jersey, New York, North Carolina, Pennsylvania, Rhode Island, Vermont, Virginia, West Virginia)*—4407 Bland Rd. - Ste.160, Raleigh, NC 27609. Phone: (919)875-4880.

REGION 2 *(Alabama, Florida, Georgia, Puerto Rico, South Carolina, Virgin Islands)*—106 S. Patterson St. - Ste.250, Valdosta, GA 31601-5609. Phone: (912)242-3044.

REGION 3 *(Arkansas, Kentucky, Louisiana, Mississippi, Tennessee)*—8 River Bend Place, Jackson, MS 39208. Phone: (601)965-4771.

10.450
(cont.)   REGION 4 *(Illinois, Indiana, Michigan, Ohio)*—3500 W. Wabash - Ste.B, Springfield, IL 62707. Phone: (217)241-6600.

REGION 5 *(Iowa, Minnesota, Wisconsin)*—Minnesota World Trade Center, 30 E. 7th St. - Ste.910, St. Paul, MN 55101-4901. Phone: (651)290-3304.

REGION 6 *(Montana, North Dakota, South Dakota, Wyoming)*—2110 Overland Ave. - Ste.106, Billings, MT 59102-6440. Phone: (406)657-6447.

REGION 7 *(Colorado, Kansas, Missouri, Nebraska)*—3401 SW Van Buren St., Topeka, KS 66611-2227. Phone: (785)266-0248.

REGION 8 *(New Mexico, Oklahoma, Texas)*—205 NW 63rd St. - Ste.170, Oklahoma City, OK 73116-8209. Phone: (405)879-2700.

REGION 9 *(Arizona, California, Hawaii, Nevada, Utah)*—430 G St. - Ste.4168, Davis, CA 95616-4168. Phone: (530)792-5870.

REGION 10 *(Alaska, Idaho, Oregon, Washington)*—112 N. University Rd. - Ste.205, Spokane, WA 99206-5295. Phone: (509)353-2147.

COMPLIANCE FIELD OFFICES

California—430 G St. - Ste.4167, Davis, CA 95616-4167. Phone: (530)792-5850.

Indiana—6905 Corporate Circle, Indianapolis, IN 46278. Phone: (317)290-3050.

Minnesota—3440 Federal Dr. - Ste.200, Eagan, MN 55122-1301. Phone: (612)725-3730.

Missouri—9435 Holmes Rd., Kansas City, MO 64131. Phone: (816)926-7963.

North Carolina—4407 Bland Rd. - Ste.280, Raleigh, NC 27609. Phone: (919)875-4930.

Texas—1111 W. Mockingbird Lane - Ste. 280, Dallas, TX 75247-5016. Phone: (214) 767-7700.

10.451
thru
10.453   Listed under **10.051**.

FOOD SAFETY AND INSPECTION SERVICE

MEAT, POULTRY, AND EGG PRODUCTS INSPECTION

10.475
and
10.477   ## DISTRICT OFFICES

Arkansas *(DISTRICT 35: Arkansas, Louisiana, Oklahoma)*—Country Club Center - Ste.201, 4700 S. Thompson Bldg. B, Springdale, AR 72764. Phone: (501)751-8412.

California *(DISTRICT 5: California)*—Bldg. 2C, 620 Central Ave., Alameda, CA 94501. Phone: (303)497-5411.

Colorado *(DISTRICT 15: Arizona, Colorado, New Mexico, Nevada, Utah)*—665 S. Broadway - Ste.B, Boulder, CO 80303. Phone: (303)497-5411.

Georgia *(DISTRICT 85: Florida, Georgia)*—Bldg. 1924 - Ste.3R90, 100 Alabama St. SW, Atlanta, GA 30303. Phone: (404)562-5900.

Illinois *(DISTRICT 50: Illinois, Indiana)*—1919 S. Highland Ave. - Ste.115C, Lombard, IL 60148. Phone: (630)620-7474.

Iowa *(DISTRICT 25: Iowa, Nebraska)*—11338 Auroa Ave., Des Moines, IA 50322. Phone: (515)727-8960.

Kansas *(DISTRICT 30: Kansas, Missouri)*—4920 W. 15th St., Lawrence, KS 66049. Phone: (785)841-5600.

Maryland *(DISTRICT 75: Delaware, Maryland, Virginia, Washington D.C.)*—5601 Sunnyside Ave. - Ste.1-2288B, Beltsville, MD 20705-5200. Phone: (301)504-2136.

Massachusetts *(DISTRICT 50: Connecticut, Maine, Massachusetts, New Hampshire,*

Puerto Rico, Vermont, Virgin Islands)—Bldg. 3 - Ste.331, 411 Waverly Oaks Rd., Waltham, MA 02452-8405. Phone: (781)736-1843.

Minnesota *(DISTRICT 20: Minnesota, Montana, North Dakota)*—Butler Square West - Ste.989C, 100 N. 6th St., Minneapolis, MN 55403. Phone: (612)370-2400.

Mississippi *(DISTRICT 90: Alabama, Mississippi, Tennessee)*—715 S. Pear Orchard Rd. - Ste.101, Ridgeland, MS 39157. Phone: (601)965-4312.

New York *(DISTRICT 65: New Jersey, New York)*—230 Washington Ave., Albany, NY 12203-6870. Phone: (518)452-6870.

North Carolina *(DISTRICT 80: North Carolina, South Carolina)*—6020 Six Forks Rd., Raleigh, NC 27609. Phone: (919)844-8400.

Ohio *(DISTRICT 55: Kentucky, Ohio, West Virginia)*—155 E. Columbus St., Pickerton, OH 43147. Phone: (614)833-1045.

Oregon *(DISTRICT 10: Alaska, American Samoa, Guam, Hawaii, Idaho, Oregon, Washington)*—530 Center St. NW, Salem, OR 97301. Phone: (503)399-5831.

Pennsylvania *(DISTRICT 60: Pennsylvania)*—Mellon Independence Center - 2-B South, Philadelphia, PA 19106-1576. Phone: (215)597-4219, ext.104.

Texas *(DISTRICT 40: Texas)*—1100 Commerce - Rm.5F41, Dallas, TX 75242-0598. Phone: (214)767-9124.

Wisconsin *(DISTRICT 45: Michigan, Wisconsin)*—2810 Crossroads Dr. - Ste.3500, Madison, WI 53718-7969. Phone: (608)240-4080.

FOOD AND NUTRITION SERVICE

10.550 thru 10.574

REGIONAL OFFICES

MID-ATLANTIC *(Delaware, District of Columbia, Maryland, New Jersey, Pennsylvania, Puerto Rico, Virgin Islands, Virginia, West Virginia)*—Mercer Corporate Park, Corporate Blvd. - CN 02150, Trenton, NJ 08650. Phone: (609)259-5025.

MIDWEST *(Illinois, Indiana, Michigan, Minnesota, Ohio, Wisconsin)*—77 W. Jackson Blvd - 20th fl., Chicago, IL 60604-3507. Phone: (312)353-6664.

MOUNTAIN PLAINS *(Colorado, Iowa, Kansas, Missouri, Montana, Nebraska, North Dakota, South Dakota, Utah, Wyoming)*—1244 Speer Blvd. - Ste.903, Denver, CO 80204. Phone: (303)844-0300.

NORTHEAST *(Connecticut, Maine, Massachusetts, New Hampshire, New York, Rhode Island, Vermont)*—10 Causeway St. - Rm.501, Boston MA 02222-1068. Phone: (617)565-6370.

SOUTHEAST *(Alabama, Florida, Georgia, Kentucky, Mississippi, North Carolina, South Carolina, Tennessee)*—Martin Luther King, Jr. Federal Annex - (1st fl.) Ste.112, 77 Forsythe St. SW, Atlanta, GA 30303. Phone: (404)730-2565.

SOUTHWEST *(Arkansas, Louisiana, New Mexico, Oklahoma, Texas)*—1100 Commerce St. - Rm.5-C-30, Dallas, TX 75242. Phone: (214)767-0222.

WESTERN *(Alaska, American Samoa, Arizona, California, Guam, Hawaii, Idaho, Nevada, Northern Marianas, Oregon, Washington, Freely Associated States of the Pacific)*—550 Kearny St. - Rm.400, San Francisco, CA 94108. Phone: (415)705-1310.

FOREST SERVICE

10.652

RESEARCH HEADQUARTERS - Forest and Range Experiment Stations

INTERMOUNTAIN *(Idaho, Montana, Nevada, Utah, Wyoming-western one-third)*— 324 25th St., Ogden, UT 84401. Phone: (801)625-5421.

NORTH CENTRAL *(Illinois, Indiana, Iowa, Michigan, Minnesota, Missouri, Wisconsin)*—1992 Folwell Ave., St. Paul, MN 55108. Phone: (612)649-5252.

10.652
(cont.)

NORTHEASTERN *(Connecticut, Kentucky, Maine, Massachusetts, New Hampshire, New Jersey, New York, Ohio, Pennsylvania, Vermont, West Virginia)*—5 Radnor Corporate Center - Ste.200, Radnor, PA 19087-4585. Phone: (610)975-4207.

PACIFIC NORTHWEST *(Alaska, Oregon, Washington)*—Portland, OR 97208-3890. Phone: (503)326-5644.

PACIFIC SOUTHWEST *(California, Hawaii)*—Berkely, CA 94701-0245. Phone: (510)559-6317.

ROCKY MOUNTAIN *(Arizona, Colorado, Kansas, Nebraska, New Mexico, North Dakota, Panhandle, South Dakota, Texas-western, Wyoming-eastern two-thirds)*—240 W. Prospect Rd., Ft. Collins, CO 80526-2098. Phone: (970)498-1139.

SOUTHERN *((Alabama, Arkansas, Florida, Georgia, Louisiana, Mississippi, North Carolina, Oklahoma-except Panhandle, Puerto Rico, South Carolina, Tennessee, Texas-eastern, Virginia)*—200 Weaver Blvd., P.O. Box 2680, Asheville, NC 28802. Phone: (704)257-4301.

Forest Products Laboratory: One Gifford Pinchot Dr., Madison, WI 53705-2398. Phone: (608)231-9315.

10.664
thru
10.671

REGIONAL OFFICES

Note: to contact local Forest Supervisor or Ranger District Offices, consult telephone directory under USDA, or the appropriate regional office, following.

REGION 1 *(Idaho-northern, Montana, North Dakota, South Dakota-northwestern corner)*—Federal Bldg., P.O. Box 7669, Missoula, MT 59807. Phone: (406)329-3280.

REGION 2 *(Colorado, Kansas, Nebraska, South Dakota-except northwestern corner, Wyoming-eastern two-thirds)*—740 Simms St., P.O. Box 25127, Lakewood, CO 80255. Phone: (303)275-5741.

REGION 3 *(Arizona, New Mexico)*—P.O. Box 1689, Santa Fe, NM 87504. Phone: (505)842-3344.

REGION 4 *(Idaho-southern, Nevada, Utah, Wyoming-western one-third)*—Federal Office Bldg., 324 25th St., Ogden, UT 84401. Phone: (801)625-5239.

REGION 5 *(California, Hawaii)*—1323 Club Dr., Vallego, CA 94592. Phone: (707) 562-8910.

REGION 6 *(Oregon, Washington)*—333 SW 1st St., Portland, OR 97208-3623. Phone: (503)808-2355, -2348.

REGION 8 *(Alabama, Arkansas, Florida, Georgia, Kentucky, Louisiana, Mississippi, North Carolina, Oklahoma, Puerto Rico, South Carolina, Tennessee, Texas, Virginia, Virgin Islands)*—1720 Peachtree Rd. NW, Atlanta, GA 30367. Phone: (404)347-7486.

REGION 9 *(Connecticut, Delaware, Illinois, Indiana, Iowa, Maine, Maryland, Massachusetts, Michigan, Minnesota, Missouri, New Hampshire, New Jersey, New York, Ohio, Pennsylvania, Rhode Island, Vermont, West Virginia, Wisconsin)*—5 Radnor Corporate Center - Ste.200, P.O. Box 6775, Radnor, PA 19087-4555. Phone: (610) 975-4103.

REGION 10 *(Alaska)*—3301 C St. - Ste.522, Anchorage, AK 99503-3956. Phone: (907)271-2519.

State and Private Forestry Areas

NORTHEASTERN AREA *(Covers states listed under Region 9, foregoing)*—5 Radnor Corporate Center, P.O. Box 6775, Radnor, PA 19087-8775. Phone: (610)975-4103.

10.760
thru
10.773

Listed under **10.405**.

GRAIN INSPECTION, PACKERS AND STOCKYARD ADMINISTRATION

10.800   ## REGIONAL OFFICES

California *(Alaska, Arizona, California, Hawaii, Idaho, Nevada, Oregon, Washington)*—9550 Micron Ave. - Ste.D, Sacramento, CA 95827. Phone: (916)857-6055.

Colorado *(Colorado, Montana, New Mexico, Utah, Wyoming)*—307 Livestock Exchange Bldg, 4701 Marion St., Denver, CO 80216. Phone: (303)294-7050.

Georgia *(Alabama, Florida, Georgia, South Carolina)*—100 Alabama St., NW - Ste. 5R10, Atlanta, GA 30303-5R10. Phone: (404)562-5840.

Indiana *(Indiana, Kentucky, Michigan, Ohio, Illinois)*—Federal Bldg. and U.S. Courthouse - Rm.434, 46 E. Ohio St., Indianapolis, IN 46204. Phone: (317)226-6424.

Kansas *(Kansas, Missouri)*—Corporate Oaks Bldg. - Ste.200, 12351 W. 96th Terr., Lenexa, KS 66215. Phone: (913)438-1091.

Minnesota *(Minnesota, North Dakota, South Dakota, Wisconsin)*—208 Post Office Bldg., Box 8, S. St. Paul, MN 55075. Phone: (612)290-3876.

Nebraska *(Iowa, Nebraska)*—2900 "O" Plaza - Ste.208, Omaha, NE 68107-2671. Phone: (402)221-3391.

Pennsylvania *(Connecticut, Maine, Massachusetts, New Hampshire, New Jersey, New York, Pennsylvania, Rhode Island, Vermont)*—1860 Charter Lane - Ste.205, Lancaster, PA 17601. Phone: (717)299-6313.

Tennessee *(Arkansas, Louisiana, Mississippi, Tennessee)*—7777 Walnut Grove Rd. - Ste.OM-37, Box 06, Memphis, TN 38120. Phone: (901)544-0231.

Texas *(Oklahoma, Texas)*—Federal Bldg. - Rm.8A36, 819 Taylor St., Ft. Worth, TX 76102. Phone: (817)978-3286.

Virginia *(Delaware, District of Columbia, Maryland, North Carolina, Virginia, West Virginia)*—Turnpike Rd. and Rt. 460W, P.O. Box 1027, Bedford, VA 24523. Phone: (540)857-2830.

10.854   Listed under 10.405.

NATURAL RESOURCES CONSERVATION SERVICE

10.900 thru 10.914   ## REGIONAL OFFICES

EAST—1400 Wilson Blvd. - Ste.1100, Arlington, VA 22209. Phone: (703)312-7282.

MIDWEST—One Gifford Pinchot Dr. - Rm.204, Madison, WI 53705-3210. Phone: (608)264-5281.

NORTHERN PLAINS—100 Centennial Mall North - Rm.152, Lincoln, NE 68508. Phone: (402)437-5315.

SOUTH CENTRAL—Bldg. 23, 501 Felix St., P.O. Box 6459, Ft. Worth, TX 76115. Phone: (817)334-5224, ext.3700.

SOUTHEAST—1720 Peachtree Rd. NW - Ste.716-N, Atlanta, GA 30367. Phone: (404)347-6105.

WEST—650 Capitol Mall - Rm.6072, Sacramento, CA 95600. Phone: (916)498-5284.

STATE OFFICES

Alabama—3381 Skyway Dr., Auburn, AL 36830. Phone: (334)887-4500.

Alaska—949 E. 36 Ave. - Ste.400, Anchorage, AK 99508-4302. Phone: (907)271-2424.

**10.900
thru
10.914
(cont.)**

Arizona—3003 N. Central Ave. - Ste.800, Phoenix, AZ 85012-2945. Phone: (602)280-8808.

Arkansas—Federal Bldg. - Rm.5404, 700 W. Capitol Ave., P.O. Box 2323, Little Rock, AR 72201-3228. Phone: (501)324-5445.

California—2121-C 2nd St. - Ste.102, Davis, CA 95616-5475. Phone: (916)757-8215.

Colorado—655 Parfet St. - Rm.E200C, Lakewood, CO 80215-5517. Phone: (303)236-2886, ext.202.

Connecticut—16 Professional Park Rd., Storrs, CT 06268-1299. Phone: (203)487-4014.

Delaware—1203 College Park Dr. - Ste.101, Dover, DE 19904-8713. Phone: (302)678-4160.

Florida—2614 NW 43rd St., Box 141510, Gainesville, FL 32606-6611. Phone: (904) 338-9500.

Georgia—Federal Bldg., 355 E. Hancock Ave., P.O. Box 13, Athens, GA 30601-2769. Phone: (706)546-2272.

Hawaii—300 Ala Moana Blvd. - Rm.4316, P.O. Box 50004, Honolulu, HI 96850-0002. Phone: (808)541-2601.

Idaho—3244 Elder St. - Rm.124, Boise, ID 83705-4711. Phone: (208)378-5700.

Illinois—1902 Fox Dr., Champaign, IL 61820-7335. Phone: (217)398-5267.

Indiana—6013 Lakeside Blvd., Indianapolis, IN 46278-2933. Phone: (317)290-3200.

Iowa—Federal Bldg. - Ste.693, 210 Walnut St., Des Moines, IA 50309-2180. Phone: (515)284-6655.

Kansas—760 S. Broadway, Salina, KS 67401. Phone: (913)823-4565.

Kentucky—771 Corporate Dr. - Ste.110, Lexington, KY 40503-5479. Phone: (606)224-7350.

Louisiana—3737 Government St., Alexandria, LA 71302-3727. Phone: (318)473-7751.

Maine—5 Godfrey Dr., Orono, ME 04473. Phone: (207)866-7241.

Maryland—John Hansen Business Center - Ste.301, 339 Busch's Frontage Rd., Annapolis, MD 21401-5534. Phone: (410)757-0861.

Massachusetts—451 West St., Amherst, MA 01002-2995. Phone: (413)253-4351.

Michigan—1405 S. Harrison Rd. - Rm.101, East Lansing, MI 48823-5243. Phone: (517)337-6701, ext.1201.

Minnesota—600 Farm Credit Bldg., 375 Jackson St., St. Paul, MN 55101-1854. Phone: (612)290-3675.

Mississippi—Federal Bldg. - Ste.1321, 100 W. Capital St., Jackson, MS 39269-1399. Phone: (601)965-5205.

Missouri—Parkade Center - Ste.250, 601 Business Loop - 70 West, Columbia, MO 65203-2546. Phone: (573)876-0901.

Montana—Federal Bldg. - Rm.443, 10 E. Babcock St., Bozeman, MT 59715-4704. Phone: (406)587-6813.

Nebraska—Federal Bldg. - Rm.152, 100 Centennial Mall N., Lincoln, NE 68508-3866. Phone: (402)437-5327.

Nevada—Bldg. F - Ste.201, 5301 Longley Lane, Reno, NV 89511-1805. Phone: (702)784-5863.

New Hampshire—Federal Bldg., 2 Madbury Rd., Durham, NH 03824-1499. Phone: (603)433-0505.

New Jersey—1370 Hamilton St., Somerset, NJ 08873-3157. Phone: (908)246-1205.

New Mexico—6200 Jefferson NE - Rm.305, Albuquerque, NM 87109-3734. Phone: (505)761-4400.

New York—441 S. Salina St. - (Ste.354) Rm.520, Syracuse, NY 13202-2450. Phone: (315)477-6504.

North Carolina—4405 Bland Rd. - Ste.205, Raleigh, NC 27609-6293. Phone: (919) 873-2102.

North Dakota—Federal Bldg. - Rm.270, 220 E. Rosser Ave. and 3rd St., Bismarck, ND 58502-1458. Phone: (701)250-4421.

Ohio—Federal Bldg. - Rm.522, 200 N. High St., Columbus, OH 43215-2478. Phone: (614)469-6962.

Oklahoma—100 USDA - Ste.203, Stillwater, OK 74074-2624. Phone: (405)742-1204.

Oregon—Federal Bldg. - (16th fl.) Ste.1300, 101 SW Main St. Portland, OR 97204-3221. Phone: (503)414-3201.

Pacific Basin Area—FHB Bldg. - Ste.301, 400 Route 9, Guam 96927. Phone: (9-011-671)472-7490.

Pennsylvania—One Credit Union Place - Ste.340, Harrisburg, PA 17110-2993. Phone: (717)782-2202.

Puerto Rico—IBM Bldg. - Ste.604, 654 Munoz Rivera Ave., Hato Rey, PR 00918-4123. Phone: (no number provided).

Rhode Island—60 Quaker Lane - Ste.46, Warwick, RI 02886-0111. Phone: (401)828-1300.

South Carolina—Thurmond Federal Bldg. - Rm.950, 1835 Assembly St., Columbia, SC 29201-2489. Phone: (803)765-5681.

South Dakota—Federal Bldg., 200 4th St. SW, Huron, SD 57350-2475. Phone: (605) 352-1200.

Tennessee—675 U.S. Courthouse, 801 Broadway, Nashville, TN 37203-3878. Phone: (615)736-5471.

Texas—Poage Federal Bldg., 101 S. Main St., Temple, TX 76501-7682. Phone: (817) 774-1214.

Utah—Bennett Federal Bldg. - Rm.4402, 125 S. State St., Salt Lake City, UT 84147. Phone: (801)524-5050.

Vermont—69 Union St., Winooski, VT 05404-1999. Phone: (802)951-6795.

Virginia—Culpeper Bldg. - Ste.209, 1606 Santa Rosa Rd., Richmond, VA 23229-5014. Phone: (804)287-1691.

Washington—W. 316 Boone Ave. - Ste.450, Spokane, WA 99201-2348. Phone: (509) 323-2900.

West Virginia—75 High St. - Rm.301, Morgantown, WV 26505. Phone: (304)291-4153.

Wisconsin—6515 Watts Rd. - Ste.200, Madison, WI 53719-2726. Phone: (608)264-5577.

Wyoming—Federal Office Bldg. - Rm.3124, 100 E. B St., Casper, WY 82601. Phones: (307)261-5201, -1911.

DEPARTMENT OF COMMERCE

BUREAU OF THE CENSUS

11.001 thru 11.005

REGIONAL OFFICES

California—15350 Sherman Way - Ste.300, Van Nuys, CA 91406-4224. Phone: (818) 904-6393.

11.001
thru
11.005
(cont.)

Colorado—6900 W. Jefferson Ave., Denver, CO 80235-2032. Phone: (303)969-6750.

Georgia—101 Marietta St. NW - Ste.3200, Atlanta, GA 30303-2700. Phone: (404)730-3832.

Illinois—2255 Enterprise Dr. - Ste.5501, Westchester, IL 60154-5800. Phone: (708)562-1350.

Kansas—Gateway Tower II - Ste.600, 400 State Ave., Kansas City, KS 66101-2410. Phone: (913)551-6728.

Massachusetts—2 Copley Place - Ste.301, Boston, MA 02117-9108. Phone: (617)424-0500.

Michigan—1395 Brewery Park Blvd., Detroit, MI 48232-5405. Phone: (313)259-1158.

New York—FOB - Rm.37-130, 26 Federal Plaza, New York, NY 10278-0044. Phone: (212)264-3860.

North Carolina—901 Center Park Dr. - Ste.106, Charlotte, NC 28217-2935. Phone: (704)334-6142.

Pennsylvania—1601 Market St. - 21st fl., Philadelphia, PA 19105-2395. Phone: (215) 656-7550.

Texas—6303 Harry Hines Blvd. - Ste.210, Dallas, TX 75235-5269. Phone: (214)640-4400.

Washington—Key Tower - Ste.5100, 700 5th Ave., Seattle, WA 98104-5018. Phone: (206)553-5837.

11.006   **Personal Census Records Service**—Chief, Personal Census Search Unit, P.O. Box 1545, Jeffersonville, IN 47131. Phone: (812)218-3046.

11.025   ## USDC REGIONAL AND DISTRICT OFFICES
(including Export Assistance Centers)

Alabama—Medical Forum Bldg. - 7th fl., 950 22nd St. N., Birmingham, AL 35203. Phones: (205)731-1331; FAX (205)731-0076.

Alaska—3601 C St. - Ste.700, Anchorage, AK 99503. Phones: (907)271-6237; FAX (907)271-6242.

Arizona—Tower One - Ste.970, 2901 N. Central Ave., Phoenix, AZ 85012. Phones: (602)640-2513; FAX (602)640-2518.

- 166 W. Alameda, Tucson, AZ 85726. Phones: (520)670-5540; FAX (520)791-5413.

Arkansas—425 W. Capitol Ave. - Ste.700, Little Rock, AR 72201. Phones: (501)324-5794; FAX (501)324-7380.

California—390-B Fir Ave., Clovis, CA 93611. Phones: (209)325-1619; FAX (209) 325-1647.

- One World Trade Center - Ste.1670, Long Beach, CA 90831. Phones: (310)980-4450; FAX (310)980-4561.

- 11150 Olympic Blvd. - Ste.975, Los Angeles, CA 90064. Phones: (310)235-7104; FAX (310)235-7220.

- 350 S. Figueroa St. - Ste.172, Los Angeles, CA 90071. Phones: (213)894-8784; FAX (213)894-8789.

- c/o Center for Trade Commercial Diplomacy, 411 Pacific St. - Ste.200, Monterey, CA 93940. Phones: (408)641-9850; FAX (408)641-9849.

- Orange County Export Assistance Center, 3300 Irvine Ave. - Ste.305, Newport Beach, CA 92660. Phones: (949)660-1668; FAX (949)660-8039.

- 330 Ignacio Blvd. - Ste.102, Novato, CA 94949. Phones: (415)883-1966; FAX (415)883-2711.

- 530 Water St. - Ste.740, Oakland, CA 94607. Phones: (510)273-7350; FAX (510)251-7352.

- Inland Empire Export Assistance Center, 2940 Inland Empire Blvd. - Ste.121, Ontario, CA 91764. Phones: (909)466-4134; FAX (909)466-4140.
- 300 Esplanade Dr. - Ste.2090, Oxnard, CA 93030. Phones: (805)981-8150; FAX (805)988-1855.
- 917 7th St. - 2nd fl., Sacramento, CA 95814. Phones: (916)498-5155; FAX (916)498-5923.
- 6363 Greenwich Dr. - Ste.230, San Diego, CA 92122. Phones: (619)557-5395; FAX (619)557-6176.
- 250 Montgomery St. - 14th fl., San Francisco, CA 94104. Phones: (415)705-2300; FAX (415)705-2297.
- 101 Park Center Plaza - Ste.1001, San Jose, CA 95113. Phones: (408)271-7300; FAX (408)271-7307.
- 5201 Great American Pkwy. - Ste.456, Santa Clara, CA 95054. Phones: (408)970-4610; FAX (408)970-4618.

Colorado—1625 Broadway - Ste.680, Denver, CO 80202. Phones: (303)844-6622; FAX (303)844-5651.

Connecticut—213 Court St. - Rm.903, Middletown, CT 06457-3346. Phones: (860) 638-6950; FAX (860)638-6970.

Delaware—*See* **Pennsylvania**, Philadelphia office.

Florida—1130 Cleveland St., Clearwater, FL 33755. Phones: (727)441-1742; FAX (727)449-2889.
- 200 E. Las Olas Blvd. - Ste.1600, Ft. Lauderdale, FL 33301. Phones: (954)356-6640; FAX (954)356-6644.
- 5600 NW 36th St. - Ste.617, Miami, FL 33166. Phones: (305)526-7425; FAX (305)526-7434. *For mail:* P.O. Box 590570, Miami, FL 33159.
- 200 E. Robinson St. - Ste.1270, Orlando, FL 32801. Phones: (407)648-6235; FAX (407)648-6756.
- The Capitol - Ste.2001, Tallahassee, FL 32399-0001. Phones: (850)488-6469; FAX (850)487-3014.

Georgia—285 Peachtree Center Ave, NE - Ste.200, Atlanta, GA 30303-1229. Phones: (404)657-1900; FAX (404)657-1970.
- 6001 Chatham Center Dr. - Ste.100, Savannah, GA 31405. Phones: (912)652-4204; FAX (912)652-4241.

Hawaii—Pacific Tower - Ste.1140, Bishop Square, 1001 Bishop St., P.O. Box 50026, Honolulu, HI 96813. Phones: (808)522-8040; FAX (808)522-8045.

Idaho (*Portland, OR district*)—700 W. State St. - 2nd fl., Boise, ID 83720. Phones: (208)334-3857; FAX (208)334-2783.

Illinois—Xerox Center - Rm.2440, 55 W. Monroe St., Chicago, IL 60603. Phones: (312)353-8045; FAX (312)353-8120.
- 610 Central Ave. - Ste.150, Highland Park, IL 60035. Phones: (847)681-8010; FAX (847)681-8012.
- 515 N. Court St., P.O. Box 1747, Rockford, IL 61103. Phones: (815)987-8123; FAX (815)963-7943.

Indiana—Indianapolis Export Assistance Center, Pennwood One - Ste.106, 11405 N. Pennsylvania St., Carmel, IN 46032. Phones: (317)582-2300; FAX (317)582-2301.

Iowa—601 Locust St. - Ste.100, Des Moines, IA 50309-3739. Phones: (515)288-8614; FAX (515)288-1437.

Kansas—(*Kansas City, MO district*)—209 E. William - Ste.300, Wichita, KS 67202-4012. Phones: (316)269-6111; FAX (316)683-7326.

Kentucky—601 W. Broadway - Rm.634B, Louisville, KY 40202. Phones: (502)582-5066; FAX (502)582-6573.
- 2292 S. Hwy. 27 - Ste.240, Somerset, KY 42501. Phones: (606)677-6160; FAX (606)677-6161.

11.025
(cont.)

Louisiana—Delta Export Assistance Center, 365 Canal St. - Ste.2150, New Orleans, LA 70130. Phones: (504)589-6546; FAX (504)589-2337.

- 7100 W. Park Dr., Shreveport, LA 71129. Phones: (318)676-3064; FAX (318)676-3063.

Maine (*Boston, MA District*)—511 Congress St., Portland, ME 04101. Phones: (207) 541-7400; FAX (207)541-7420.

Maryland—World Trade Center - Ste.2432, 401 E. Pratt St., Baltimore, MD 21202. Phones: (410)962-4539; FAX (410)962-4529.

Massachusetts—World Trade Center - Ste.307, 164 Northern Ave., Boston, MA 02210-2071. Phones: (617)424-5990; FAX (617)424-5992.

- 100 Granger Blvd. - Unit 102, Marlborough, MA 01752. Phones: (508)624-6000; FAX (508)624-7145.

Michigan—425 S. Main St. - Ste.103, Ann Arbor, MI 48104. Phones: (313)741-2430; FAX (313)741-2432.

- 211 W. Fort St. - Ste.2220, Detroit, MI 48226. Phones: (313)226-3650; FAX (313) 226-3657.

- 301 W. Fulton St. - Ste.718-S, Grand Rapids, MI 49504. Phones: (616)458-3564; FAX (616)458-3872.

- Oakland Pointe Office Bldg. - Ste.1300 West, 250 Elizabeth Lake Rd., Pontiac, MI 48341. Phones: (248)975-9600; FAX (248)975-9606.

Minnesota—45 S. 7th St. - Ste.2240, Minneapolis, MN 55402. Phones: (612)348-1638; FAX (612)348-1650.

Mississippi—705 E. Main St., Raymond, MS 39154. Phones: (601)857-0128; FAX (601)857-0026.

Missouri—2345 Grand - Ste.650, Kansas City, MO 64108. Phones: (816)410-9201; FAX (816)410-9208.

- 8182 Maryland Ave. - Ste.303, St. Louis, MO 63105. Phones: (314)425-3302; FAX (314)425-3381.

Montana—University of Montana, Gallagher Business Bldg. - Ste.257, Missoula, MT 59812. Phones: (406)243-2098; FAX (406)243-5259.

Nebraska—11135 "O" St., Omaha, NE 68137. Phones: (402)221-3664; FAX (402)221-3668.

Nevada—1755 E. Plumb Lane - Ste.152, Reno, NV 89502. Phones: (702)784-5203; FAX (702)784-5343.

New Hampshire (*Boston, MA district*)—17 New Hampshire Ave., Portsmouth, NH 03801-2838. Phones: (603)334-6074; FAX (603)334-6110.

New Jersey—One Gateway Center - 9th fl., Newark, NJ 07102. Phones: (973)645-4682; FAX (973)645-4783.

- Bldg.4 - Ste.105, 3131 Princeton Pike, Trenton, NJ 08648. Phones: (609)989-2100; FAX (609)989-2395.

New Mexico (*Dallas, TX District*)—c/o New Mexico Department of Economic Development, 1100 St. Francis Dr., Santa Fe, NM 87503. Phones: (505)827-0350; FAX (505)827-0263.

New York—111 W. Huron St. - Rm.1304, Buffalo, NY 14202. Phones: (716)551-4191; FAX (716)551-5290.

- 1550 Franklin Ave. - Rm.207, Mineola, NY 11501. Phones: (516)739-1765; FAX (516)739-3310.

- Harlem Export Assistance Center, 163 W. 125th St. - Ste.904, New York, NY 10027. Phones: (212)860-6200; FAX (212)860-6203.

- 6 World Trade Center - Rm.635, New York, NY 10048. Phones: (212)466-5222; FAX (212)264-1356.

- Westchester Export Assistance Center, 707 W. Chester Ave. - Ste.209, White Plains, NY 10604. Phones: (914)682-6712; FAX (914)682-6698.

North Carolina—521 E. Morehead St. - Ste.435, Charlotte, NC 28202. Phones: (704)333-4886; FAX (704)332-2681.

- 400 W. Market St. - Ste.400, Greensboro, NC 27401. Phones: (336)333-5345; FAX (336)333-5158.

North Dakota—*See* **Minneapolis, MN** Export Assistance Center.

Ohio—36 E. 7th St. - Ste.2650, Cincinnati, OH 45202. Phones: (513)684-2944; FAX (513)684-3227.

- Bank One Center - Ste.700, 600 Superior Ave. E., Cleveland, OH 44114. Phones: (216)522-4750; FAX (216)522-2235.

- Two Nationwide Plaza - Ste.1400, Columbus, OH 43215. Phones: (614)365-9510; FAX (614)365-9598.

- 300 Madison Ave., Toledo, OH 43604. Phones: (419)241-0683; FAX (419)241-0684.

Oklahoma—301 NW 63rd St. - Ste.330, Oklahoma City, OK 73116. Phones: (405)608-5302; FAX (405)608-4211.

- 700 N. Greenwood Ave. - Ste.1400, Tulsa, OK 74106. Phones: (918)581-7650; FAX (918)581-6263.

Oregon—1445 Willamette St. - Ste.13, Eugene, OR 97401-4003. Phones: (541)465-6575; FAX (541)465-6704.

- One World Trade Center - Ste.242, 121 SW Salmon St., Portland, OR 97204. Phones: (503)326-3001; FAX (503)326-6351.

Pennsylvania—One Commerce Square, 228 Walnut St. - Ste.850, P.O. Box 11698, Harrisburg, PA 17108-1698. Phones: (717)221-4510; FAX (717)221-4505.

- Scranton Export Assistance Center, One Montage Mountain Rd. - Ste.B, Moosic, PA 18507. Phones: (717)969-2530; FAX (717)969-2539.

- 615 Chestnut St. - Ste.1501, Philadelphia, PA 19106. Phones: (215)597-6101; FAX (215)597-6123.

- Federal Bldg. - Rm.2002, 1000 Liberty Ave., Pittsburgh, PA 15222. Phones: (412)395-5050; FAX (412)395-4875.

Puerto Rico *(Hato Rey)*—525 F.D. Roosevelt Ave. - Ste.905, San Juan, PR 00918. Phones: (787)766-5555; FAX (787)766-5692.

Rhode Island *(Hartford, CT district)*—One West Exchange St., Providence, RI 02903. Phones: (401)528-5104; FAX (401)528-5067.

South Carolina—Charleston Trident Chamber of Commerce, 81 Mary St., Charleston, SC 29403 Phones: (843)727-4051; FAX (843)727-4052. *For mail:* P.O. Box 975, Charleston, SC 29402.

- Thurmond Federal Bldg. - Ste.172, 1835 Assembly St., Columbia, SC 29201. Phones: (803)765-5345; FAX (803)253-3614.

- Upstate Export Assistance Center, Park Central Office Park - Bldg. 1 (Ste.109), 555 N. Pleasantburg Dr., Greenville, SC 29607. Phones: (864)271-1976; FAX (864)271-4171.

South Dakota—Siouxland Export Assistance Center, Augustana College - Rm.SS-44, 2001 S. Summit Ave. Sioux Falls, SD 57197. Phones: (605)330-4264; FAX (605)330-4266.

Tennessee—c/o Centre for Enterprise, Buckman Hall - 3rd fl.(Ste.348), 650 E. Parkway S., Memphis, TN 38104. Phones: (901)323-1543; FAX (901)320-9128.

- Old Historic City Hall - Ste.300, 600 W. Summit Hill Dr., Knoxville, TN 37902-2011. Phones: (423)545-4637; FAX (423)545-4435.

- Parkway Towers - Ste.114, 404 James Robertson Pkwy., Nashville, TN 37219-1505. Phones: (615)736-5161; FAX (615)736-2454.

Texas—1700 Congress - 2nd fl., Austin, TX 78701. Phones: (512)916-5939; FAX (512)916-5940. *For mail:* P.O. Box 12728, Austin, TX 78711.

11.025
(cont.)

- 2050 N. Stemmons Fwy. - Ste.170, Dallas, TX 75207. Phones: (214)767-0542; FAX (214)767-8240. *For mail:* Dallas, TX 75342-0069.
- 711 Houston St., Ft. Worth, TX 76102. Phones: (817)212-2673; FAX (817)978-0178.
- 500 Dallas - Ste.1160, Houston, TX 77002. Phones: (713)718-3062; FAX (713)718-3060.
- c/o City of San An IAD, 203 S. St. Mary St. - 3rd fl., San Antonio, TX 78205. Phones: (210)228-9878; FAX (210)228-9874. *For mail:* P.O. Box 839966, San Antonio, TX 78283-3966.

Utah—324 S. State St. - Ste.221, Salt Lake City, UT 84111. Phones: (801)524-5116; FAX (801)524-5886.

Vermont—National Life Bldg., Drawer 20, Montpelier, VT 05620-0501. Phones: (802)828-4508; FAX (802)828-3258.

Virginia—1616 N. Ft. Myer Dr. - Ste.1300, Arlington, VA 22209. Phones: (703)524-2885; FAX (703)524-2649.

- 400 N. 8th St. - Ste.540, P.O. Box 10026, Richmond, VA 23240-0026. Phones: (804)771-2246; FAX (804)771-2390.

Washington—2001 6th Ave. - Ste.650, Seattle, WA 98121. Phones: (206)553-5615; FAX (206)553-7253.

- 801 W. Riverside Ave. - Ste.400, Spokane, WA 99201. Phones: (509)353-2625; FAX (509)353-2449.
- 950 Pacific Ave. - Ste.410, Tacoma, WA 98402. Phones: (253)593-6736; FAX (253) 383-4676.

West Virginia—405 Capitol St. - Ste.807, Charleston, WV 25301. Phones: (304)347-5123; FAX (304)347-5408.

- Wheeling Jesuit University, 316 Washington Ave., Wheeling, WV 26003. Phones: (304)243-5493; FAX (304)243-5494.

Wisconsin—517 E. Wisconsin Ave. - Rm.596, Milwaukee, WI 53202. Phones: (414) 297-3473; FAX (414)297-3470.

Wyoming—*See* Denver, **Colorado** Export Assistance Center.

INTERNATIONAL TRADE ADMINISTRATION

11.108
thru
11.111

Contact Export Assistance Center offices listed under **11.025**.

11.150   Bureau of Export Administration

California—3300 Irvine Ave. - Ste.345, Newport Beach, CA 92660-3198. Phone: (714) 660-0144.

- 101 Park Center Plaza - Ste.1001, San Jose, CA 95113. Phone: (408)998-7402.

ECONOMIC DEVELOPMENT ADMINISTRATION

11.300
thru
11.313

REGIONAL OFFICES

ATLANTA *(Alabama, Florida, Georgia, Kentucky, Mississippi, North Carolina, South Carolina, Tennessee)*—401 W. Peachtree St. NW - Ste.1820, Atlanta, GA 30308-3510. Phone: (404)730-3002.

AUSTIN *(Arkansas, Louisiana, New Mexico, Oklahoma, Texas)*—327 Congress Ave. - Ste.200, Austin, TX 78701-5595. Phone: (512)916-5463.

CHICAGO *(Illinois, Indiana, Michigan, Minnesota, Ohio, Wisconsin)*—111 N. Canal St. - Ste.855, Chicago, IL 60606-7204. Phone: (312)353-8143.

DENVER *(Colorado, Iowa, Kansas, Missouri, Montana, Nebraska, North Dakota, South Dakota, Utah, Wyoming)*—1244 Speer Blvd. - Rm.670, Denver, CO 80204. Phone: (303)844-4715.

PHILADELPHIA *(Connecticut, Delaware, District of Columbia, Maine, Maryland, Massachusetts, New Hampshire, New Jersey, New York, Pennsylvania, Puerto Rico, Rhode Island, Vermont, Virgin Islands, Virginia, West Virginia)*—Independence Square West - Ste.140 South, Philadelphia, PA 19106. Phone: (215)597-4603.

SEATTLE *(Alaska, American Samoa, Arizona, California, Guam, Hawaii, Idaho, Marshall Islands, Micronesia, Nevada, Northern Mariana Islands, Oregon, Washington)*—Jackson Federal Bldg. - Ste.1856, 915 2nd Ave., Seattle, WA 98174. Phone: (206)220-7660.

NATIONAL OCEANIC AND ATMOSPHERIC ADMINISTRATION

11.405 thru 11.427

REGIONAL OFFICES

ALASKA—Juneau, AK 99802-1668. Phone: (907)586-7280.

NORTHEAST—One Blackburn Dr., Gloucester, MA 01930-2298. Phone: (978)281-9243.

NORTHWEST—7600 Sand Point Way NE, Seattle, WA 98115. Phone: (206)526-6150.

SOUTHEAST—9721 Executive Center Dr. N., St. Petersburg, FL 33702. Phone: (727)570-5324.

SOUTHWEST—501 W. Ocean Blvd. - Ste.4200, Long Beach, CA 90802-4213. Phone: (310)980-4001.

▪ **Southwest Fisheries Science Center**, La Jolla, CA 92038-0271. Phone: (619)546-7081.

FIELD AREAS

Virginia—Atlantic Marine Center, 439 W. York St., Norfolk, VA 23510-1114. Phone: (757)441-6776.

Washington—Pacific Marine Center, 1801 Fairview Ave. E., Seattle, WA 98102. Phone: (206)553-7656.

11.432 Program Manager, Environmental Research Laboratories, c/o NOAA/GLERL, 2205 Commonwealth Blvd., Ann Arbor, MI 48105. Phone: (734)741-2041.

11.433 thru 11.435 State/Federal Liason Office, NMFS, 9721 Executive Center Dr. N., St. Petersburg, FL 33702. Phone: (727)570-5324.

Northeast Regional Office, NMFS, One Blackburn Dr., Gloucester, MA 01930. Phone: (978)281-9267; e-mail, Grants.Information@noaa.gov

11.436 Environmental and Technical Services Division, NMFS-NOAA, 525 NE Oregon Ave. - Rm.500, Portland, OR 97232-2737. Phone: (503)231-2009.

11.437 ALASKA—NMFS, Juneau, AK 99802-1668. Phone: (907)586-7280.

NORTHWEST—NMFS-NOAA, 7600 Sand Point Way NE, Seattle, WA 98115. Phone: (206)526-6140.

SOUTHWEST—NMFS-NOAA, 501 W. Ocean Blvd. - Ste.4200, Long Beach, CA 90802-4213. Phone: (310)980-4034.

WESTERN PACIFIC—NMFS-NOAA, Pacific Islands Area Office, 1601 Kapiolani Blvd. - Ste.1110, Honolulu, HI 96814-4700. Phone: (808)973-2935, ext.207.

11.438   ALASKA—NMFS, Juneau, AK 99802-1668. Phone: (907)586-7280.

NORTHWEST—NMFS-NOAA, 7600 Sand Point Way NE, Seattle, WA 98115. Phone: (206)526-6187.

11.439   Alaska Regional and Northwest Regional Offices, *same addresses/phones as* **11.437**.

11.441   Listed under **11.405**.

11.444 and 11.445   Southwest Fisheries Science Center, NMFS, 8604 La Jolla Shores Dr., La Jolla, CA 92038-0271. Phones: (858)546-7000; FAX (858)546-7003.

11.449   NOAA/Environmental Research Laboratories, R/EX-4, 325 Broadway, Boulder, CO 80303. Phone: (303)497-6731.

11.450   IFLOWS Operations Manager, Hydrologic Services Division, National Weather Service Eastern Region (W/ER2), Airport Corporate Center, 630 Johnson Ave., Bohemia, NY 11716. Phone: (516)244-0112.

11.452   NORTHEAST—Chief, State, Federal and Constituent Programs Office, One Blackburn Dr., Gloucester, MA 01930-2298. Phone: (978)281-9243.

SOUTHEAST—Cooperative Programs Division, 9721 Executive Center Dr. N., St. Petersburg, FL 33702. Phone: (727)570-5324.

SOUTHWEST—Grants Coordinator, 501 W. Ocean Blvd., Long Beach, CA 90802-4213. Phone: (310)980-4036.

11.454   ALASKA—NMFS, Juneau, AK 99802-1668. Phone: (907)586-7280; FAX (907)586-7255.

NORTHEAST—State, Federal and Constituent Programs Office, One Blackburn Dr., Gloucester, MA 01930-2298. Phone: (978)281-9243.

SOUTHEAST—State/Federal Liaison Staff, 9721 Executive Center Dr. N., St. Petersburg, FL 33702. Phone: (727)570-5324.

SOUTHWEST—Grants Coordinator, 502 W. Ocean Blvd. - Ste.4200, Long Beach, CA 90802-4213. Phone: (310)980-4001.

11.455   ALASKA—Director, Alaska Fisheries Science Center, BIN C15700 - Bldg. 4, 7600 Sand Point Way NE, Seattle, WA 98115-0070. Phone: (206)526-4004.

NORTHEAST—Deputy Director, Northeast Fisheries Science Center, Woods Hole, MA 02453. Phone: (508)495-2365.

NORTHWEST—Deputy Director, Northwest Fisheries Science Center, 2725 Montlake Blvd. E, Seattle, WA 98112-2097. Phones: (206)860-3200; FAX (206)860-3217.

SOUTHEAST—Director, Southeast Fisheries Science Center, 75 Virginia Beach Dr., Miami, FL 33149. Phones: (305)361-4285; FAX (305)361-4219.

SOUTHWEST—Director, Southwest Fisheries Science Center, La Jolla, CA 92038-0271. Phone: (619)546-7067.

11.457   Chesapeake Bay Division, NMFS-NOAA, 410 Severn Ave. - Ste.107A, Annapolis, MD 21403. Phone: (410)267-5676; FAX (410)267-5666.

Northeast Regional Office, State, Federal and Constituent Programs, NMFS, One Blackburn Dr., Gloucester, MA 01930. Phone: (978)281-9330; e-mail, Grants.Information@noaa.gov

11.458   Alaska Regional Office, NMFS, Juneau, AK 99802-1668. Phone: (907)586-7280; FAX (907)586-7255.

11.463   NORTHEAST—Chief, State, Federal and Constituent Programs Division, One Blackburn Dr., Gloucester, MA 01930-2298. Phone: (508)281-9243.

NORTHWEST—7600 Sand Point Way NE, Seattle, WA 98115. Phone: (206)526-6187.

SOUTHEAST—Cooperative Programs Division, 9721 Executive Center Dr., St. Petersburg, FL 33702. Phone: (813)570-5324.

SOUTHWEST—Grants Coordinator, 501 W. Ocean Blvd. - Ste.4200, Long Beach, CA 90802-4213. Phone: (310)980-4001.

11.472   Listed under **11.454**.

11.473   Program Manager, Coastal Services Center, NOAA, 2234 S. Hobson Ave., Charleston, SC 29405-2413. Phone: (843)740-1200.

11.474   NORTHEAST—State, Federal and Constituent Programs Division, NMFS, One Blackburn Dr., Gloucester, MA 01930. Phone: (978)281-9243; FAX (978)281-9117; e-mail, Grants-Information@noaa.gov

SOUTHEAST—State/Federal Liaison Office, 9721 Executive Center Dr. N., St. Petersburg, FL 33702. Phone: (727)570-5324.

11.477   Listed under **11.405**

NATIONAL INSTITUTE OF STANDARDS AND TECHNOLOGY

11.603   Listed under **11.025**.
and
11.604

MINORITY BUSINESS DEVELOPMENT AGENCY

11.800   **REGIONAL AND DISTRICT OFFICES**
thru
11.802   **REGIONS I, II, AND III** *(Connecticut, Delaware, District of Columbia, Maine, Maryland, Massachusetts, New Hampshire, New Jersey, New York, Pennsylvania, Puerto Rico, Rhode Island, Vermont, Virgin Islands, West Virginia)*—26 Federal Plaza - Rm.3720, New York, NY 10278. Phone: (212)264-3262.

Massachusetts—10 Causeway St. - Rm.418., Boston, MA 02222-1041. Phone: (617)565-6850.

Pennsylvania—Federal Office Bldg. - Rm.10128, 600 Arch St., Philadelphia, PA 19106. Phone: (215)597-9236.

REGION IV *(Alabama, Florida, Georgia, Kentucky, Mississippi, North Carolina, South Carolina, Tennessee)*—401 W, Peachtree St. NW - Rm.1715, Atlanta, GA 30308-3516. Phone: (404)730-3300.

Florida—Federal Bldg. - Rm.1314, 51 SW 1st Ave., P.O. Box 25, Miami, FL 33130. Phone: (305)536-5054.

REGIONS V AND VII *(Illinois, Indiana, Iowa, Kansas, Michigan, Minnesota, Missouri, Nebraska, Ohio, Wisconsin)*—55 E. Monroe St. - Ste.1406, Chicago, IL 60603. Phone: (312)353-0182.

REGIONS VI AND VIII *(Arkansas, Colorado, Louisiana, Montana, New Mexico, North Dakota, Oklahoma, South Dakota, Texas, Utah, Wyoming)*—1100 Commerce St. - Rm.7B23, Dallas, TX 75242. Phone: (214)767-8001.

REGIONS IX AND X *(Alaska, American Samoa, Arizona, California, Guam, Hawaii, Idaho, Nevada, Oregon, Washington)*—221 Main St. - Rm.1280, San Francisco, CA 94105. Phone: (415)744-3001.

California—9660 Flair Dr. - Ste.455, El Monte, CA 91731. Phone: (818)453-8636.

PATENT AND TRADEMARK OFFICE

11.900   Listed under **11.025**.

DEPARTMENT OF DEFENSE

DEPARTMENT OF THE ARMY, CORPS OF ENGINEERS

12.100
thru
12.111

Alabama *(Mobile District)*—P.O. Box 2288, Mobile, AL 36628. Phone: (205)690-2511.

Alaska *(Alaska District)*—P.O. Box 898, Anchorage, AK 99506. Phone: (907)752-5233.

Arkansas *(Little Rock District)*—P.O. Box 867, Little Rock, AR 72203. Phone: (501) 378-5531.

California *(Los Angeles District)*—P.O. Box 2711, Los Angeles, CA 90053. Phone: (213)688-5300.

▪ *(Sacramento District)*—650 Capitol Mall, Sacramento, CA 95814. Phone: (916)448-2232.

▪ *(San Francisco District)*—211 Main St., San Francisco, CA 94105. Phone: (415)974-0358.

▪ *(South Pacific Division)*—630 Sansome St. - Rm.720, San Francisco, CA 94111. Phone: (415)556-0914.

District of Columbia—CDR, USACA/CEMP-RI, 20 Massachussetts Ave. NW, Washington, DC 20314. Phone: (202)504-4950.

Florida *(Jacksonville District)*—P.O. Box 4970, Jacksonville, FL 32232. Phone: (904) 791-2241.

Georgia *(Savannah District)*—P.O. Box 889, Savannah, GA 31402. Phone: (912)944-5224, ext.224.

▪ *(South Atlantic Division)*—510 Title Bldg., 30 Pryor St. SW, Atlanta, GA 30335. Phone: (404)221-6711.

Hawaii *(Pacific Ocean Division)*—Ft. Shafter, HI 96858. Phone: (808)438-1500.

Illinois *(Chicago District)*—219 S. Dearborn St., Chicago, IL 60604. Phone: (312)353-6400.

▪ *(North Central Division)*—536 S. Clark St., Chicago, IL 60605. Phone: (312)353-6310.

▪ *(Rock Island District)*—Clock Tower Bldg., P.O. Box 2004, Rock Island, IL 61204. Phone: (309)788-6361.

▪ Constitution Engineering Research Laboratory, Champaign, IL 61820-1305. Phone: (217)373-6789.

Kentucky *(Louisville District)*—P.O. Box 59, Louisville, KY 40201. Phone: (502)582-5601.

Louisiana *(New Orleans District)*—P.O. Box 60267, New Orleans, LA 70160. Phone: (504)838-1121.

Maryland *(Baltimore District)*—P.O. Box 1715, Baltimore, MD 21203. Phone: (301) 962-4545.

Massachusetts *(New England Division)*—424 Trapelo Rd., Waltham, MA 02254. Phone: (617)647-8220.

Michigan *(Detroit District)*—P.O. Box 1027, Detroit, MI 48231. Phone: (313)226-6762.

Minnesota *(St. Paul District)*—1135 USPO and Custom House, St. Paul, MN 55101. Phone: (612)725-7501.

Mississippi *(Lower Mississippi Valley Division)*—P.O. Box 80, Vicksburg, MS 39180. Phone: (601)634-5750.

▪ *(Vicksburg District)*—P.O. Box 60, Vicksburg, MS 39180. Phone: (601)634-5010.

▪ Waterways Experiment Station, Vicksburg, MS 39180-0631. Phone: (601)634-2424.

Missouri *(Kansas City District)*—700 Federal Bldg., Kansas City, MO 64106. Phone: (816)374-3201.

▪ *(St. Louis District)*—210 N. Tucker Blvd., St. Louis, MO 63101. Phone: (314)263-5660.

Nebraska *(Missouri River Division)*—Downtown Station, P.O. Box 103, Omaha, NE 68101. Phone: (402)221-7201.

▪ *(Omaha District)*—USPO and Courthouse - Rm.6014, Omaha, NE 68102. Phone: (402)221-3900.

New Hamphire—Cold Regions Research and Engineering Laboratory, Hanover, NH 03755-1290. Phone: (603)646-4390.

New Mexico *(Albuquerque District)*—P.O. Box 1580, Albuquerque, NM 87103. Phone: (505)766-2732.

New York *(Buffalo District)*—1776 Niagara St., Buffalo, NY 14207. Phone: (716)876-5454, ext.2200.

▪ *(New York District)*—26 Federal Plaza, New York, NY 10278. Phone: (212)264-0100.

▪ *(North Atlantic Division)*—90 Church St., New York, NY 10007. Phone: (212)264-7101.

North Carolina *(Wilmington District)*—P.O. Box 1890, Wilmington, NC 28402. Phone: (919)343-4501.

Ohio *(Ohio River Division)*—P.O. Box 1159, Cincinnati, OH 45201. Phone: (513)221-6000.

Oklahoma *(Tulsa District)*—P.O. Box 61, Tulsa, OK 74121. Phone: (918)581-7311.

Oregon *(North Pacific Division)*—P.O. Box 2870, Portland, OR 97208. Phone: (503) 221-3700.

▪ *(Portland District)*—P.O. Box 2946, Portland, OR 97208. Phone: (503)221-6000.

Pennsylvania *(Philadelphia District)*—U.S. Custom House, 2nd and Chestnut St., Philadelphia, PA 19106. Phone: (215)597-4848.

(Pittsburgh District)—Federal Bldg., 1000 Liberty Ave., Pittsburgh, PA 15222. Phone: (412)644-6800.

South Carolina *(Charleston District)*—P.O. Box 919, Charleston, SC 29402. Phone: (803)724-4229.

Tennessee *(Memphis District)*—B-202 Clifford Davis Federal Bldg., Memphis, TN 38103. Phone: (901)521-3221.

▪ *(Nashville District)*—P.O. Box 1070, Nashville, TN 37202. Phone: (615)251-5626.

Texas *(Ft. Worth District)*—P.O. Box 17300, Ft. Worth, TX 76102. Phone: (817)334-2300.

▪ *(Galveston District)*—P.O. Box 1229, Galveston, TX 77553. Phone: (409)766-3006.

▪ *(Southwestern Division)*—1114 Commerce St., Dallas, TX 75242. Phone: (214)767-2500.

Virginia *(Norfolk District)*—803 Front St., Norfolk, VA 23510. Phone: (804)441-3601.

▪ Humphreys Engineer Center Support Activity, Ft. Belvoir, VA 22060-5580. Phone: (202)355-2153.

▪ Topographic Engineering Center, Ft. Belvoir, VA 22060-5546. Phone: (202)355-2659.

Washington *(Seattle District)*—P.O. Box C-3755, Seattle, WA 98124. Phone: (206)764-3690.

▪ *(Walla Walla District)*—City-County Airport - Bldg. 602, Walla Walla, WA 99362. Phone: (509)522-6506.

West Virginia *(Huntington District)*—502 8th St., Huntington, WV 25721. Phone: (304)529-5395.

12.114   **Research and Development Laboratories**
(Environmental Restoration Program)

USAE Hydrologic Engineering Center, 609 2nd St., Davis, CA 95616-4887. Phone: (916)756-1104.

USA Construction Engineering Research Laboratory, 2902 Newmark Dr., Champaign, IL 61821-1075. Phones: (800)872-2375, (800)252-7122.

USAE Waterways Experiment Station, 3909 Falls Ferry Rd., Vicksburg, MS 39180-6199. Phones: (601)634-2512, (800)522-6937.

USA Cold Regions Research and Engineering Laboratory, 72 Lynn Rd., Hanover, NH 03755-1290. Phone: (603)646-4445.

USA Topographic Engineering Center, Cude Bldg. No. 2592, Ft. Belvoir, VA 22060-5546. Phone: (703)355-3133.

USAE Institute for Water Resources, Casey Bldg. No. 2594, Ft. Belvoir, VA 22060-5586. Phone: (703)355-3084.

DEPARTMENT OF THE ARMY, U.S. ARMY MEDICAL COMMAND

12.420   Commander, Army Medical Research Acquisition Activity, DOD, Attn: SGRD-RMA-RC, Ft. Detrick, Frederick, MD 21702-5014. Phone: (301)619-2036.

OFFICE OF THE SECRETARY (ECONOMIC SECURITY)

12.600   WESTERN REGION—Office of Economic Adjustment, OASD(FM&P), 1325 J St. -
thru   Ste.1500, Sacramento, CA 95814. Phone: (916)567-7365.
12.613

SECRETARIES OF MILITARY DEPARTMENTS

12.700   *Contact nearest military installation. Consult local phone directory.*

DEPARTMENT OF THE AIR FORCE, MATERIAL COMMAND

12.800   Air Force Office of Scientific Research, Bolling AFB - Ste.B115, 110 Duncan Ave., Washington, DC 20332-4990. Phone: (no number provided).

Armstrong Laboratory, 8005 9th St., Brooks AFB, TX 78235-5353. Phone: (no number provided).

Phillips Laboratory, 3651 Lowry Ave. SE, Kirkland AFB, NM 87117-5777. Phone: (505)846-4979.

Rome Laboratory, 26 Electronics Pkwy., Griffins AFB, NY 13441-4514. Phone: (315) 330-7746.

Wright Laboratory, Bldg. 7, 2530 C St., Wright-Patterson AFB, OH 45433-7607. Phone: (513)255-4813.

DEPARTMENT OF HOUSING AND URBAN DEVELOPMENT

HOUSING - FEDERAL HOUSING COMMISSIONER

14.103 thru 14.195

FIELD OFFICES

GREAT PLAINS *(Iowa, Kansas, Missouri, Nebraska)*:

Iowa State Office—Federal Bldg.- Rm.239, 210 Walnut St., Des Moines, IA 50309-2155. Phones: (515)284-4512; FAX (515)284-4743.

Kansas-Missouri State Office—Gateway Tower II, 400 State Ave., Kansas City, KS 66101-2406. Phones: (913)551-5462; FAX (913)551-5416.

- **St. Louis Area Office**—Young Federal Bldg. - 3rd fl., 1222 Spruce St., St. Louis, MO 63103-2836. Phones: (314)539-6583; FAX (314)539-6575.

Nebraska State Office—Executive Tower Centre, 10909 Mill Valley Rd., Omaha, NE 68154-3955. Phones: (402)492-3100; FAX (402)492-3150.

MID ATLANTIC *(Delaware, District of Columbia, Maryland, Pennsylvania, Virginia, West Virginia)*:

Delaware State Office—824 Market St. - Ste.850, Wilmington, DE 19801-3016. Phones: (302)573-6300; FAX (302)573-6259.

District of Columbia Office—820 1st St. NE - Ste.450, Washington, DC 20002-4205. Phones: (202)275-9200; FAX (202)275-0779.

Maryland State Office—City Crescent Bldg. - 5th fl., 10 S. Howard St., Baltimore, MD 21201-2505. Phones: (410)962-2520; FAX (410)962-0668.

Pennsylvania State Office—The Wanamaker Bldg., 100 Penn Square East, Philadelphia, PA 19107-3380. Phones: (215)656-0600; FAX (215)656-3433.

- **Pittsburgh Area Office**—339 6th Ave. - 6th fl., Pittsburgh, PA 15222-2515. Phones: (412)644-6428; FAX (412)644-6499.

Virginia State Office—The 3600 Centre, 3600 W. Broad St., Richmond, VA 23230-4920. Phones: (804)278-4539; FAX (804)278-4603.

West Virginia State Office—Kanawha Valley Bldg. - Ste.708, 405 Capitol St., Charleston, WV 25301-1795. Phones: (304)347-7000; FAX (304)347-7050.

MIDWEST *(Illinois, Indiana, Michigan, Minnesota, Ohio, Wisconsin)*:

Illinois State Office—Metcalfe Federal Bldg., 77 W. Jackson Blvd., Chicago, IL 60604-3507. Phones: (312)353-5680; FAX (312)353-0121.

Indiana State Office—151 N. Delaware St., Indianapolis, IN 46204-2526. Phones: (317)226-6303; FAX (317)226-6317.

Michigan State Office—McNamara Federal Bldg., 477 Michigan Ave., Detroit, MI 48226-2592. Phones: (313)226-7900; FAX (313)226-5611.

- **Flint Area Office**—Federal Bldg. - Ste.200, 605 N. Saginaw St., Flint, MI 48502-2043. Phones: (810)766-5108; FAX (810)766-5122.

- **Grand Rapids Area Office**—Trade Center Bldg. - 3rd fl., 50 Louis St. NW, Grand Rapids, MI 49503-2648. Phones: (616)456-2100; FAX (616)456-2187.

Minnesota State Office—220 2nd St. S., Minneapolis, MN 55401-2195. Phones: (612)370-3000; FAX (612)370-3220.

Ohio State Office—200 N. High St., Columbus, OH 43215-2499. Phones: (614)469-5737; FAX (614)469-2432.

14.103
thru
14.195
(cont.)

- **Cincinnati Area Office**—525 Vine St. - 7th fl., Cincinnati, OH 45202-3188. Phones: (513)684-3451; FAX (513)684-6224.
- **Cleveland Area Office**—Renaissance Bldg. - Ste.500, 1350 Euclid Ave., Cleveland, OH 44115-1815. Phones: (216)522-4065; FAX (216)522-2975.

Wisconsin State Office—Reuss Federal Plaza - Ste.1380, 310 W. Wisconsin Ave., Milwaukee, WI 53203-2289. Phones: (414)297-3214; FAX (414)297-3947.

NEW ENGLAND *(Connecticut, Maine, Massachusetts, New Hampshire, Rhode Island, Vermont)*:

Connecticut State Office—One Corporate Center - 19th fl., Hartford, CT 06103-3220. Phones: (860)240-4800; FAX (860)240-4850.

Maine State Office—Smith Federal Bldg. - Rm.101, 2020 Harlow St., Bangor, ME 04401-4925. Phones: (207)945-0467; FAX (207)945-0533.

Massachusetts State Office—O'Neill Jr. Federal Office Bldg. - Rm.375, 10 Causeway St., Boston, MA 02222-1092. Phones: (617)565-5234; FAX (617)565-5168.

New Hampshire State Office—Cotton Federal Bldg., 275 Chestnut St., Manchester, NH 03101-2487. Phones: (603)666-7681; FAX (603)666-7736.

Rhode Island State Office—10 Weybosset St. - 6th fl., Providence, RI 02903-2808. Phones: (401)528-5230; FAX (401)528-5312.

Vermont State Office—Federal Bldg. - Rm.237, 11 Elmwood Ave., Burlington, VT 05402-0879. Phones: (802)951-6290; FAX (802)951-6298.

NEW YORK/NEW JERSEY:

Albany Area Office—52 Corporate Circle, Albany, NY 12203-5121. Phones: (518)464-4200; FAX (518)464-4300.

Buffalo Area Office—Lafayette Court - 5th fl., 465 Main St., Buffalo, NY 14203-1780. Phones: (716)551-5755; FAX (716)551-5752.

Camden Area Office—Hudson Bldg. - 2nd fl., 800 Hudson Square, Camden, NJ 08102-1156. Phones: (609)757-5081; FAX (609)757-5373.

New Jersey State Office—One Newark Center - 13th fl., Newark, NJ 07102-5260. Phones: (973)622-7900; FAX (973)645-6239.

New York State Office—26 Federal Plaza, New York, NY 10278-0068. Phones: (212)264-6500; FAX (212)264-0246.

NORTHWEST/ALASKA *(Alaska, Idaho, Oregon, Washington)*:

Alaska State Office—University Plaza Bldg. - Ste.401, 949 E. 36th Ave., Anchorage, AK 99508-4135. Phones: (907)271-4170; FAX (907)271-3667.

Idaho State Office—Plaza IV - Ste.220, 800 Park Blvd., Boise, ID 83712-7743. Phones: (208)334-1990; FAX (208)334-9648.

Oregon State Office—400 SW 6th Ave. - Ste.700, Portland, OR 97204-1632. Phones: (503)326-2561; FAX (503)326-3097.

Washington State Office—Seattle Federal Office Bldg. - Ste.200, 909 1st Ave., Seattle, WA 98104-1000. Phones: (206)220-5101; FAX (206)220-5133.

- **Spokane Area Office**—US Courthouse Bldg. - Rm.588, 920 W. Riverside, Spokane, WA 99201-1010. Phones: (509)353-0674; FAX (509)353-0682.

PACIFIC/HAWAII (*Arizona, California, Hawaii, Nevada)*:

Arizona State Office—Two Arizona Center - Ste.1600, 400 N. 5th St., Phoenix, AZ 85004-2361. Phones: (602)379-4434; FAX (602)379-3985.

- **Tucson Area Office**—Security Pacific Bank Plaza, 33 N. Stone Ave. - Ste.700, Tucson, AZ 85701-1467. Phones: (602)670-6237; FAX (602)670-6207.

California State Office—Burton Federal Bldg. and Courthouse, 450 Golden Gate Ave., P.O. Box 36003, San Francisco, CA 94102-3448. Phones: (415)436-6550; FAX (415)436-6510; TDD (415)436-6594.

- **Fresno Area Office**—2135 Fresno St. - Ste.100, Fresno, CA 93721-1718. Phones: (209)487-5032; FAX (209)487-5344; TTY (209)487-5033.

Los Angeles Area Office—AT&T Center - Ste.800, 611 W. 6th St., Los Angeles, CA 90017-3127. Phones: (213)894-8000; FAX (213)894-8096; TTY (213)894-8133.

- **Sacramento Area Office**—925 L St., Sacramento, CA 95814-2601. Phones: (916) 498-5220; FAX (916)498-5262; TDD (916)498-5959.

San Diego Area Office—Mission City Corporate Center - Ste.300, 2365 Northside Dr., San Diego, CA 92108-2712. Phones: (619)557-5310; FAX (619)557-6296.

- **Santa Ana Area Office**—World Trade Tower, 1000 N. Broadway, Santa Ana, CA 92706-3927. Phones: (888)827-5605; FAX (714)796-1285.

Hawaii State Office—7 Waterfront Plaza - Ste.500, 500 Ala Moana Blvd., Honolulu, HI 96813-4918. Phones: (808)522-8175; FAX (808)522-8194.

Nevada State Office—Atrium Bldg. - Ste.700, 333 N. Rancho Dr. Las Vegas, NV 89106-3714. Phones: (702)388-6525; FAX (702)388-6737.

- **Reno Area Office**—3702 S. Virginia Ave., Reno, NV 89502-0034. Phones: (702)784-5383; FAX (702)784-5066.

ROCKY MOUNTAINS *(Colorado, Montana, North Dakota, South Dakota, Utah, Wyoming)*:

Colorado State Office—First Interstate Tower North, 633 17th St., Denver, CO 80202-3607. Phones: (303)672-5440; FAX (303)672-5061.

Montana State Office—Federal Bldg. - Rm.340 (Drawer 100095), 301 S. Park, Helena, MT 59626-0095. Phones: (406)441-1298; FAX (406)441-1292.

North Dakota State Office—Federal Bldg. - Rm.366, 653 2nd Ave., Fargo, ND 58108-2483. Phones: (701)239-5136; FAX (701)239-5249.

South Dakota State Office—2400 W. 49th St. - Ste.I-201, Sioux Falls, SD 57105-6558. Phones: (605)330-4223; FAX (605)330-4465.

Utah State Office—257 Tower Bldg. - Ste.550, 257 E. 200 South, Salt Lake City, UT 84111-2048. Phones: (801)524-3323; FAX (801)588-3439.

Wyoming State Office—Federal Bldg. - Rm.4229, 100 E. B St., Casper, WY 82602-1918. Phones: (307)261-6250; FAX (307)261-6245.

SOUTHEAST/CARIBBEAN *(Alabama, Caribbean, Florida, Georgia, Kentucky, Mississippi, North Carolina, Panama Canal Zone, Puerto Rico, South Carolina, Tennessee, Virgin Islands)*:

Alabama State Office—Beacon Ridge Tower, 600 Beacon Pkwy. W. - Ste.300, Birmingham, AL 35209-3144. Phones: (205)290-7617; FAX (205)290-7593.

Caribbean Office—New San Juan Office Bldg., 247 Carlos E. Chardon Ave., San Juan, PR 00918-1804. Phones: (787)766-5400; FAX (787)766-5995.

Florida State Office—Brickell Plaza Bldg., 909 SE 1st Ave., Miami, FL 33131-3028. Phones: (305)536-4456; FAX (305)536-4698.

- **Jacksonville Area Office**—Southern Bell Tower - Ste.2200, 301 W. Bay St., Jacksonville, FL 32202-5121. Phones: (904)232-1777; FAX (904)232-3759.

- **Orlando Area Office**—Langley Bldg. - Ste.270, 3751 Maguire Blvd., Orlando, FL 32803-3032. Phones: (407)648-6441; FAX (407)648-6310.

- **Tampa Area Office**—Timberlake Federal Bldg. Annex - Ste.700, 501 E. Polk St., Tampa, FL 33602-3945. Phones: (813)228-2501; FAX (813)228-2431.

Georgia State Office—Five Points Plaza, 40 Marietta St., Atlanta, GA 30303-2806. Phones: (404)331-5136; FAX (404)730-2365.

Kentucky State Office—601 W. Broadway, Louisville, KY 40201-1044. Phones: (502)582-5251; FAX (502)582-6074.

Mississippi State Office—McCoy Federal Bldg. - Rm.910, 100 W. Capitol St., Jackson, MS 39269-1096. Phones: (601)965-4738; FAX (601)965-4773.

14.103 thru 14.195 (cont.)

North Carolina State Office—Koger Bldg., 2306 W. Meadowview Rd., Greensboro, NC 27407-3707. Phones: (910)547-4000; FAX (910)547-4015.

South Carolina State Office—Thurmond Federal Bldg., 1835 Assembly St., Columbia, SC 29201-2480. Phones: (803)765-5592; FAX (803)765-5515.

Tennessee State Office—251 Cumberland Bend Dr. - Ste.200, Nashville, TN 37228-1803. Phones: (615)736-5213; FAX (615)736-2018.

• **Knoxville Area Office**—Duncan Federal Bldg. - 3rd fl., 710 Locust St., Knoxville, TN 37902-2526. Phones: (423)545-4384; FAX (423)545-4569.

• **Memphis Area Office**—One Memphis Place - Ste.1200, 200 Jefferson Ave., Memphis, TN 38103-2335. Phones: (901)544-3367; FAX (901)544-3697.

SOUTHWEST *(Arkansas, Louisiana, New Mexico, Oklahoma, Texas)*:

Arkansas State Office—TCBY Tower, 425 W. Capitol Ave. - Ste.900, Little Rock, AR 72201-3488. Phones: (501)324-5931; FAX (501)324-5900.

Louisiana State Office—Boggs Federal Bldg. - 9th fl., 501 Magazine St., New Orleans, LA 70130-3099. Phones: (504)589-7201; FAX (504)589-6619.

• **Shreveport Area Office**—401 Edwards St. - Ste.1510, Shreveport, LA 71101-3289. Phones: (318)676-3385; FAX (318)676-3407.

New Mexico State Office—625 Silver Ave. SW - Ste.100, Albuquerque, NM 87102-3185. Phones: (505)262-6463; FAX (505)262-6604.

Oklahoma State Office—500 W Main St. - Ste.400, Oklahoma City, OK 73102-2233. Phones: (405)553-7401; FAX (405)553-7588.

• **Tulsa Area Office**—50 E. 15th St., Tulsa, OK 74119-4030. Phones: (918)581-7434; FAX (918)581-7722.

Texas State Office—1600 Throckmorton, Ft. Worth, TX 76113-2905. Phones: (817) 978-9000; FAX (817)978-9289; TTY (817)978-9273.

• **Dallas Area Office**—525 Griffin St. - Rm.860, Dallas, TX 75202-5007. Phones: (214)767-8359; FAX (214)767-8973.

• **Houston Area Office**—Norfolk Tower - Ste.200, 2211 Norfolk, Houston, TX 77098-4096. Phones: (713)313-2274; FAX (713)313-2319.

• **Lubbock Area Office**—Mahon Federal Bldg. and U.S. Courthouse, 1205 Texas Ave., Lubbock, TX 79401-4093. Phones: (806)472-7265; FAX (806)472-7275.

• **San Antonio Area Office**—Washington Square, 800 Dolorosa St., San Antonio, TX 78207-4563. Phones: (210)472-6800; FAX (210)472-6804.

OFFICE OF NATIVE AMERICAN PROGRAMS

Alaska—949 E. 36th Ave. - Ste.401, Anchorage, AK 99508-4399. Phones: (907)271-4633; FAX (907)271-3667.

Eastern/Woodlands *(Iowa, all states east of Mississippi River)*—77 W. Jackson Blvd. - 24th fl., Chicago, IL 60604-3507. Phones: (312)353-1282, (800)735-3239; FAX (312)353-8936.

Northern Plains *(Colorado, Montana, Nebraska, North Dakota, South Dakota, Utah, Wyoming)*—First Interstate Tower North, 633 17th St., Denver, CO 80202-3607. Phones: (303)672-5462; FAX (303)672-5003.

Northwest *(Idaho, Oregon, Washington)*—Seattle Federal Office Bldg. - Ste.300, 909 1st Ave., Seattle, WA 98104-1000. Phones: (206)220-5270; FAX (206)220-5234.

Southern Plains *(Arkansas, Kansas, Louisiana Missouri, Oklahoma,Texas)*—500 W. Main St - Ste.400., Oklahoma City, OK 73102-2233. Phones: (405)553-7400; FAX (405)231-4403.

Southwest *(Arizona, California, Nevada, New Mexico)*—400 N. 5th St. - Ste.1650, Phoenix, AZ 85004-2361. Phones: (602)379-4156; FAX (602)379-3101.

COMMUNITY PLANNING AND DEVELOPMENT

14.218
thru
14.249

Office of Community Planning and Development. Addresses are listed under **14.103**.

FAIR HOUSING AND EQUAL OPPORTUNITY

14.400
thru
14.414

Director, Office of Fair Housing and Equal Opportunity, HUD Regional Office. Addresses are listed under **14.103**.

PUBLIC AND INDIAN HOUSING

14.850
thru
14.867

Office of Public Housing. Addresses are listed under **14.103**.

14.868

For application materials: Contact the Super-NOFA Information Center at 1-800-HUD-8929; TTY 1-800-2209.

For program policy or other guidance: 3600 W. Broad St., Richmond, VA 23230-4920. Phone: (804)278-4504, ext.3027.

14.869

Director of the Office of Loan Guarantee, National Office of Native American Programs, Denver, CO. Phone: (303)675-1660.

DEPARTMENT OF THE INTERIOR

BUREAU OF INDIAN AFFAIRS

15.020
thru
15.025

AREA OFFICES

Alaska—Juneau, AK 99802-5520. Phone: (907)586-7177.

Arizona—Two Arizona Center - 12th fl., MS-100, Phoenix, AZ 85001-0010. Phone: (602)379-6600.

California—Federal Office Bldg., 2800 Cottage Way, Sacramento, CA 95825-1846. Phone: (916)979-2600. *See also* **Arizona**—(Phoenix).

District of Columbia—Deputy Commissioner of Indian Affairs, 1849 C St. NW, (MS-4140 MIB), Washington, DC 20240. Phone: (202)208-5116.

Minnesota—331 S. 2nd Ave., Minneapolis, MN 55401-2241. Phone: (612)373-1000, ext.1020.

Montana—316 N. 26th St., Billings, MT 59101-1397. Phone: (406)247-7943.

Navajo Area Office—P.O. Box 1060, Gallup, NM 87305. Phone: (505)863-8314.

New Mexico—615 1st St., P.O. Box 26567, Albuquerque, NM 87125-6567. Phone: (505)346-7590. *See also* **Navajo Area Office**.

New York—*See* **Virginia**—Eastern Area Office.

North Carolina—*See* **Virginia**—Eastern Area Office.

North Dakota—*See* **South Dakota**.

Oklahoma—Anadarko, OK 73005-0368. Phone: (405)247-6673, ext.257.

15.020
thru
15.025
(cont.)

▪ 101 N. 5th St., Muskogee, OK 74401-6206. Phone: (918)687-2297.

Oregon——911 NE 11th Ave., Portland, OR 97232-4169. Phone: (503)231-6702. *See also* **Arizona(Phoenix).**

South Dakota—115 4th Ave. SE, Aberdeen, SD 57401-4382. Phone: (605)226-7343.

Utah—*See* **Arizona, Navajo Area Office,** and **Oregon.**

Virginia—Eastern Area Office, 3701 N. Fairfax Dr. - Ste.260, Arlington, VA 22203. Phone: (703)235-3006.

Washington—*See* **Oregon.**

Wisconsin—*See* **Minnesota.**

Wyoming—*See* **Montana.**

FIELD AGENCIES

Alaska—Anchorage Agency, 1675 C St., Anchorage, AK 99501-5198. Phone: (907) 271-4088.

▪ Bethal Agency, 1675 C St, Anchorage, AK 99501-5198. Phone: (907)271-4086.

▪ Fairbanks Agency, 101 12th Ave. - Rm.168, Fairbanks, AK 99701-6270. Phone: (907)456-0222.

▪ Metlakatla Field Station, P.O. Box 450, Metlakatla, AK 99926. Phone: (907)886-3791.

Arizona—Chinle Agency, P.O. Box 7-H, Chinle, AZ 86503. Phone: (520)674-5100.

▪ Colorado River Agency, Rt.1 - Box 9-C, Parker, AZ 85344. Phone: (520)669-7111.

▪ Ft. Apache Agency, P.O. Box 560, Whiteriver, AZ 85941. Phone: (520)338-5353.

▪ Ft. Defiance Agency, P.O. Box 619, Ft. Defiance, AZ 86504. Phone: (520)729-7213, -7218.

▪ Ft. Yuma Agency, P.O. Box 11000, Yuma, AZ 85366-1000. Phone: (760)572-0248.

▪ Hopi Agency, P.O. Box 158, Keams Canyon, AZ 86034. Phone: (520)738-2228.

▪ Papago Agency, P.O. Box 578, Sells, AZ 85634. Phone: (520)383-3286.

▪ Pima Agency, P.O. Box 8, Sacaton, AZ 85247. Phone: (520)562-3326.

▪ Salt River Agency, 10000 E. McDowell Rd., Scottsdale, AZ 85256. Phone: (602)640-2168.

▪ San Carlos Agency, P.O. Box 209, San Carlos, AZ 85550. Phone: (520)475-2321.

▪ Truxton Canon Agency, P.O. Box 37, Valentine, AZ 86437. Phone: (520)769-2286.

▪ Western Navajo Agency, P.O. Box 127, Tuba City, AZ 86045. Phone: (520)283-2254, -2252.

California—Central California Agency, 1824 Tribute Rd. - Ste.J, Sacramento, CA 95815. Phone: (916)566-7121.

▪ Northern California Agency, 1900 Churn Creek Rd. - Ste.300, Redding, CA 96002. Phone: (530)246-5141.

▪ Palm Springs Area Field Station, 650 E. Tahquitz Canyon Way - Ste.A, P.O. Box 2245, Palm Springs, CA 92262. Phone: (760)416-2133.

▪ Southern California Agency, 2038 Iowa Ave. - Ste.101, Riverside, CA 92507-0001. Phone: (909)276-6624.

Colorado—Southern Ute Agency, P.O. Box 315, Ignacio, CO 81137. Phone: (970)563-4511.

▪ Ute Mountain Ute Agency, Towaoc, CO 81334. Phone: (970)565-8473.

Florida—Seminole Agency, 6075 Stirling Rd., Hollywood, FL 33024. Phone: (954)356-7288.

Idaho—Ft. Hall Agency, P.O. Box 220, Ft. Hall, ID 83203. Phone: (208)238-2301.

▪ Northern Idaho Agency, P.O. Drawer 277, Lapwai, ID 83540. Phone: (208)843-2300.

▪ Plummer Field Office, 850 A St., P.O. Box 408, Plummer, ID 83851. Phone: (208)686-1887.

Kansas—Haskell Indian Nations University, 155 Indian Ave., Lawrence, KS 66046. Phone: (913)749-8404.

- Horton Agency, P.O. Box 31, Horton, KS 66439. Phone: (785)486-2161.

Michigan—Michigan Agency, 2901.5 I-75 Business Spur, Sault Ste. Marie, MI 49783. Phone: (906)632-6809.

Minnesota—Minnesota Agency, Federal Bldg. - Rm.418, 522 Minnesota Ave. NW, Bemidgi, MN 56601-3062. Phone: (218)335-6913.

- Red Lake Agency, Red Lake, MN 56671. Phone: (218)679-3361.

Mississippi—Choctaw Agency, 421 Powell St., Philadelphia, MS 39350. Phone: (601) 656-1522.

Montana—Blackfeet Agency, P.O. Box 880, Browning, MT 59417. Phone: (406)338-7544.

- Crow Agency, P.O. Box 69, Crow Agency, MT 59022. Phone: (406)638-2672.
- Flathead Agency, P.O. Box A, Pablo, MT 59855-5555. Phone: (406)675-0242.
- Ft. Belknap Agency, R.R. 1 - P.O. Box 980, Harlem, MT 59526. Phone: (406)353-2901, ext.23.
- Ft. Peck Agency, P.O. Box 637, Poplar, MT 59255. Phone: (406)768-5312.
- Northern Cheyenne Agency, P.O. Box 40, Lame Deer, MT 59043. Phone: (406)477-8242.
- Rocky Boy's Agency, R.R. 1 - P.O Box 542, Box Elder, MT 59521. Phone: (406)395-4476.

Nebraska—Winnebago Agency, P.O. Box 18, Winnebago, NE 68071. Phone: (402)878-2502.

Nevada—Eastern Nevada Agency, 1555 Shoshone Circle, Elko, NV 89801. Phone: (775)738-0569.

- Western Nevada Agency, 1677 Hot Springs Rd., Carson City, NV 89706. Phone: (775)887-3500.

New Mexico—Eastern Navajo Agency, P.O. Box 328, Crownpoint, NM 87313. Phone: (505)786-6100.

- Jicarilla Agency, P.O. Box 167, Dulce, NM 87528. Phone: (505)759-3951.
- Laguna Agency, P.O. Box 1448, Laguna, NM 87026. Phone: (505)552-6001.
- Mescalero Agency, P.O. Box 189, Mescalero, NM 88340. Phone: (505)671-4423.
- Northern Pueblos Agency, Fairview Station, P.O. Box 4269, Espanola, NM 87533. Phone: (505)753-1400.
- Ramah-Navajo Agency, Rt.2 - Box 14, Ramah, NM 87321. Phone: (505)775-3235.
- Shiprock Agency, P.O. Box 966, Shiprock, NM 87420. Phone: (505)368-3300.
- Southern Pueblos Agency, P.O. Box 1667, Albuquerque, NM 87103. Phone: (505) 346-2424.
- Zuni Agency, P.O. Box 369, Zuni, NM 87327. Phone: (505)782-5591.

New York—New York Field Office, Syracuse, NY 13261-7366. Phone: (315)448-0620.

North Carolina—Cherokee Agency, Cherokee, NC 28719. Phone: (704)497-9131.

North Dakota—Ft. Berthold Agency, P.O. Box 370, New Town, ND 58763. Phone: (701)627-4707.

- Ft. Totten Agency, P.O. Box 270, Ft. Totten, ND 58335. Phone: (701)766-4545.
- Standing Rock Agency, P.O. Box E, Ft. Yates, ND 58538. Phone: (701)854-3433.
- Turtle Mountain Agency, P.O. Box 60, Belcourt, ND 58316. Phone: (701)477-3191.

Oklahoma—Anadarko Agency, P.O. Box 309, Anadarko, OK 73005. Phone: (405)247-6677.

- Chickasaw Agency, 1500 N. Country Club Rd., P.O. Box 2240, Ada, OK 74821. Phone: (580)436-0784.
- Concho Agency, El Reno, OK 73036-0068. Phone: (405)262-7481.

15.020 thru 15.025 (cont.)

- Okmulgee Agency, P.O. Box 370, Okmulgee, OK 74447. Phone: (918)756-3950.
- Osage Agency, P.O. Box 1539, Pawhuska, OK 74056. Phone: (918)287-1032.
- Miami Agency, P.O. Box 391, Miami, OK 74355. Phone: (918)542-3396.
- Pawnee Agency, Pawnee, OK 74058-0440. Phone: (918)762-2585.
- Shawnee Agency, 624 W. Independence - Ste.114, Shawnee, OK 74801. Phone: (405)273-0317.
- Talihina Agency, Drawer H, Talihina, OK 74561. Phone: (918)567-2207.
- Wewoka Agency, P.O. Box 1060, Wewoka, OK 74884. Phone: (405)257-6259.

Oregon—Siletz Agency, P.O. Box 569, Siletz, OR 97380. Phone: (541)444-2679.

- Umatilla Agency, P.O. Box 520, Pendleton, OR 97801. Phone: (541)278-3786.
- Warm Springs Agency, P.O. Box 1239, Warm Springs, OR 97761. Phone: (541)553-2411.

South Dakota—Cheyenne River Agency, P.O. Box 325, Eagle Butte, SD 57625. Phone: (605)964-6611.

- Crow Creek Agency, P.O. Box 139, Ft. Thompson, SD 57339. Phone: (605)245-2311.
- Lower Brule Agency, P.O. Box 190, Lower Brule, SD 57548. Phone: (605)473-5512.
- Pine Ridge Agency, P.O. Box 1203, Pine Ridge, SD 57770. Phone: (605)867-5125.
- Rosebud Agency, P.O.Box 550, Rosebud, SD 57570. Phone: (605)747-2224.
- Sisseton Agency, P.O. Box 688, Agency Village, SD 57262. Phone: (605)698-3001.
- Yankton Agency, P.O. Box 577, Wagner, SD 57380. Phone: (605)384-3651.

Utah—Uintah and Ouray Agency, P.O. Box 130, Ft. Duchesne, UT 84026. Phone: (435)722-4300.

- Southern Paiate Field Station, P.O. Box 720, St. George, UT 84771. Phone: (435)674-9720.

Washington—Colville Agency, Nespelem, WA 99155-0111. Phone: (509)634-2316.

- Makah Agency, P.O. Box 115, Neah Bay, WA 98357. Phone: (360)645-3232.
- Olympic Peninsula Agency, P.O. Box 48, Aberdeen, WA 98520. Phone: (360)533-9100.
- Puget Sound Agency, 2707 Colby Ave. - Ste.1101, Everett, WA 98201. Phone: (425)258-2651.
- Spokane Agency, P.O. Box 389, Wellpinit, WA 99040. Phone: (509)258-4561.
- Yakima Agency, P.O. Box 632, Toppenish, WA 98948. Phone: (509)865-5121.

Wisconsin—Great Lakes Agency, 615 Main St. W., Ashland, WI 54806-0273. Phone: (715)682-4527.

Wyoming—Wind River Agency, P.O. Box 158, Ft. Washakie, WY 82514. Phone: (307)332-7810.

15.026 thru 15.028

EDUCATION LINE OFFICES

Alaska—Anchorage Education Field Office, 1675 C St., Anchorage, AK 99501. Phone: (907)271-4115.

Arizona—Chinle Agency-Education, Navajo Rt. 7, P.O. Box 6003, Chinle, AZ 86503. Phone: (520)674-5130, ext.201.

- Ft. Apache Agency-Education, Hwy. 73 and Elm St., P.O. Box 920, White River, AZ 85941. Phone: (520)338-5441.
- Ft. Defiance Agency-Education, Bldg. 38, Blue Canyon Hwy., Ft. Defiance, AZ 86504-0110. Phone: (520)729-7251.
- Hopi Agency-Education, Hwy. 264, P.O. Box 568, Keams Canyon, AZ 86034. Phone: (520)738-2262.
- Papago Agency-Education, South Bldg. 49, P.O. Box 38, Sells, AZ 85634. Phone: (520)383-3292.

- Pima Agency-Education, 400 N. 5th St., P.O. Box 10, Phoenix, AZ 85001. Phone: (602)379-3944.
- Western Navajo Agency-Education, Bldg. 407, Hwy. 160 and Warrior Dr., P.O. Box 746, Tuba City, AZ 86045. Phone: (520)283 2218.

California—Sacramento Area Education Office, 2800 Cottage Way, Sacramento, CA 95825. Phone: (916)979-2560, ext.234.

Kansas—Haskell Indian Nations University, 155 Indian Ave. - #1305, Lawrence, KS 66046-4800. Phone: (785)749-8404.

Minnesota—Minneapolis Area Education Office, 331 S. 2nd Ave., Minneapolis, MN 55401-2241. Phone: (612)373-1000, ext.1090.

Montana—Billings Area Education Office, 316 N. 26th St., Billings, MT 59101-1397. Phone: (406)247-7953.

New Mexico—Eastern Navajo Agency Education, Bldg. 222, 1 Main St., P.O. Box 328, Crownpoint, NM 87313. Phone: (505)786-6150.

- Northern Pueblos Agency-Education, Fairview Station, 1 Mile N. of Espanola - Hwy. 68, P.O. Box 4269, Espanola, NM 87533. Phone: (505)753-1465.
- Shiprock Agency-Education, Hwy. 666N, Shiprock, NM 87420-3239. Phone: (505) 368-4427, ext.360.
- Southern Pueblos Agency-Education, 1000 Indian School Rd. NW, P.O. Box 1667, Albuquerque, NM 87103. Phone: (505)346-2431.
- Southwestern Indian Polytechnic Institute, 9169 Coors Rd. NW, P.O. Box 10146-9196, Albuquerque, NM 87184. Phone: (505)346-2343.

North Dakota—Standing Rock Agency-Education, Main St. off Hwy. 106, Agency Ave., P.O. Box E, Ft. Yates, ND 58538. Phone: (701)854-3497.

- Turtle Mountain Agency-Education, School St., P.O. Box 30, Belcourt, ND 58316. Phone: (701)477-6471, ext.211.

Oklahoma—Oklahoma Education Office, 4149 Highline Blvd. - Ste.380, Oklahoma City, OK 73108. Phone: (605)945-6051, ext.301, (405)605-6057.

Oregon—Portland Area Education Office, 911 NE 11th Ave., Portland, OR 97232-4169. Phone: (503)872-2743.

South Dakota—Cheyenne River Agency-Education, 100 N. Main, P.O. Box 2020, Eagle Butte, SD 51625. Phone: (605)964-8722.

- Crow Creek/Lower Brule Agency-Education, 140 Education Ave., P.O. Box 139, Ft. Thompson, SD 57339. Phone: (605)245-2398.
- Pine Ridge Agency-Education, 101 Main St., P.O. Box 333, Pine Ridge, SD 57770. Phone: (605)867-1306.
- Rosebud Agency-Education, 1001 Ave. D, P.O. Box 669, Mission, SD 57555. Phone: (605)856-4478, ext.261.

Virginia—South and Eastern States Agency-Education, 3701 N. Fairfax Dr. - Ste.260, Arlington, VA 22203. Phone: (703)235-3233.

15.029 thru 15.041   Listed under **15.020**.

15.042 thru 15.046   Listed under **15.026**.

15.047 thru 15.058   Listed under **15.020**.

15.060.   Contact BIA agency office listed under **15.020**, *or* United Tribes Technical College, 3315 University Dr., Bismarck, ND 58504. Phone: (701)255-3285, ext.218.

15.061   United Sioux Tribes Development Corp., 1830 Lombardy Dr., Rapid City, SD 57701. Phone: (605)348-3426.

15.062
thru
15.113   Listed under **15.020.**

15.114   Listed under **15.026.**

15.124   Listed under **15.020.**

15.130   Listed under **15.026.**

15.141
and
15.144   Listed under **15.020.**

15.146   Contact BIA agency office listed under **15.020,** *or* Director, National Ironworkers Training Program for American Indians, 1819 Beach St., Broadview, IL 60153. Phone: (708)345-2344.

BUREAU OF LAND MANAGEMENT

15.214
thru   **STATE OFFICES**
15.225
Alaska—6881 Abbott Loop Rd., Anchorage, AK 99507. Phone: (907)267-1323.

Arizona—3707 N. 7th St., P.O. Box 16563, Phoenix, AZ 85011. Phone: (602)650-0266.

California—2135 Butano Dr., Sacramento, CA 95825. Phone: (916)979-2828.

Colorado—2850 Youngfield St., Lakewood, CO 80215. Phone: (303)239-3677.

District of Columbia - Branch of Procurement Management *(For bureauwide inquiries)*—1849 C St. NW (MS 1075-LS), Washington, DC 20240. Phone: (202) 452-5170.

Idaho—1387 S. Vinnell Way, Boise, ID 83709. Phone: (208)373-3909.

Montana—Granite Tower, 222 N 32nd St., P.O. Box 36800, Billings, MT 59107. Phone: (406)255-2746.

Nevada—1340 Financial Blvd, P.O. Box 12000, Reno, NV 89520-0006. Phone: (702) 861-6417.

New Mexico—435 Montano NE, Albuquerque, NM 87107. Phone: (505)761-8994.

Oregon—1515 SW 5th Ave., P.O. Box 2965, Portland, OR 97208. Phone: (503)952-6220.

Utah—Coordinated Financial Center, 324 S. State St., Salt Lake City, UT 84111-2303. Phone: (801)539-4172.

Virginia-Eastern States Office—7450 Boston Blvd., Springfield, VA 22153. Phone: (703)440-1596.

Wyoming—5353 Yellowstone Rd., P.O. Box 1828, Cheyenne, WY 82009. Phone: (307)775-6058.

OFFICE OF SURFACE MINING RECLAMATION AND ENFORCEMENT

15.250
and   **FIELD OFFICES**
15.253
Alabama—135 Gemini Circle - Ste.215, Homewood, AL 35209. Phone: (205)290-7282.

District of Columbia—1951 Constitution Ave. NW, Washington, DC 20240. Phone: (202)208-4006.

Indiana—575 N. Pennsylvania St. - Rm.301, Indianapolis, IN 46204. Phone: (317)226-6700.

Kentucky—2675 Regency Rd., Lexington, KY 40503-2922. Phone: (606)233-2494.

New Mexico—505 Marquette Ave. NW - Ste.1200, Albuquerque, NM 87102. Phone: (505)248-5070.

Oklahoma—5100 E. Skelly Dr. - Ste.470, Tulsa, OK 74135. Phone: (918)581-6430.

Pennsylvania—Harrisburg Transportation Center - Ste.3C, 415 Market St., Harrisburg, PA 17101. Phone: (717)782-4036.

Tennessee—530 Gay St. SW - Ste.500, Knoxville, TN 37902. Phone: (423)545-4103.

Virginia—Powell Valley Square Shopping Center, 1941 Neeley Rd. - Ste.201 (Compartment 116), Big Stone Gap, VA 24219. Phone: (540)523-4303.

West Virginia—1027 Virginia St. E., Charleston, WV 25301. Phone: (304)347-7162.

Wyoming—Federal Bldg. - Rm.2128, 100 E. "B" St., Casper, WY 82601-1918. Phone: (307)261-6541.

REGIONAL COORDINATING CENTERS

Appalachian Region—Three Parkway Center, Pittsburgh, PA 15220. Phone: (412)937-2828.

Mid-Continent Region—Alton Federal Bldg., 501 Belle St. - Rm.216, Alton, IL 62002. Phone: (618)463-6460.

Western Region—1999 Broadway - Ste.3320, Denver, CO 80202-5733. Phone: (303)844-1401.

BUREAU OF RECLAMATION

15.504   ## REGIONAL OFFICES

Great Plains—P.O. Box 36900, Billings, MT 59107-6900. Phone: (406)247-7600.

Lower Colorado—Boulder City, NV 89006-1470. Phone: (702)293-8411.

Mid-Pacific—Federal Office Bldg., 2800 Cottage Way, Sacramento, CA 95825-1898. Phone: (916)978-5000.

Pacific Northwest—1150 N. Curtis Rd., Boise, ID 83706-1234. Phone: (208)378-5012.

Reclamation Service Center—Denver Federal Center, P.O. Box 25007, Denver, CO 80225-0007. Phone: (303)445-2692.

Upper Colorado—125 S. State St. - Rm.6107, Salt Lake City, UT 84138-1102. Phone: (801)524-3600.

U.S. FISH AND WILDLIFE SERVICE

15.602   Federal Law Enforcement Training Center, Bldg. 69 - Rm.100, Glynco, GA 31524. Phone: (912)267-2370.

15.605   ## REGIONAL OFFICES
thru
15.623   REGION I *(California, Hawaii, Idaho, Nevada, Oregon, Washington)*—911 NE 11th Ave., Portland, OR 97232-4181. Phone: (503)231-6118.

REGION II *(Arizona, New Mexico, Oklahoma, Texas)*—500 Gold Ave. SW - Rm.3018, P.O. Box 1306, Albuquerque, NM 87102. Phone: (505)248-6282.

REGION III *(Illinois, Indiana, Iowa, Michigan, Minnesota, Missouri, Ohio, Wisconsin)*—Federal Bldg., 1 Federal Dr., Ft. Snelling, MN 55111-4056. Phone: (612)725-3563.

15.605
and
15.623
(cont.)

REGION IV *(Alabama, Arkansas, Florida, Georgia, Kentucky, Louisiana, Mississippi, North Carolina, Puerto Rico, South Carolina, Tennessee, Virgin Islands)*—1875 Century Blvd., Atlanta, GA 30345. Phone: (404)679-4000.

REGION V *(Connecticut, Delaware, District of Columbia, Maine, Maryland, Massachusetts, New Hampshire, New Jersey, New York, Pennsylvania, Rhode Island, Vermont, Virginia, West Virginia)*—300 Westgate Center Dr., Hadley, MA 01035-9589. Phone: (413)253-8300.

REGION VI *(Colorado, Kansas, Montana, Nebraska, North Dakota, South Dakota, Utah, Wyoming)*—Denver Federal Center, P.O. Box 25486, Denver, CO 80025. Phone: (303)236-7920.

REGION VII *(Alaska)*—1011 E. Tudor Rd., Anchorage, AK 99503. Phone: (907)786-3542.

U.S. GEOLOGICAL SURVEY

15.808   **REGIONAL OFFICES**

Biological Resources Division

CENTRAL *(Arkansas, Colorado, Iowa, Kansas, Louisiana, Minnesota, Missouri, Montana, Nebraska, New Mexico, North Dakota, Oklahoma, South Dakota, Texas, Wyoming)*—Regional Chief Biologist, DFC Bldg.020 - Rm.A1419, P.O. Box 25046, MS-300, Denver, CO 80225. Phone: (303)236-2739.

EASTERN *(Alabama, Connecticut, Delaware, Florida, Georgia, Illinois, Indiana, Kentucky, Maine, Maryland, Massachusetts, Michigan, Mississippi, New Hampshire, New Jersey, New York, North Carolina, Ohio, Pennsylvania, Puerto Rico, Rhode Island, South Carolina, Tennessee, Vermont, Virgin Islands, Virginia, West Virginia, Wisconsin)*—Acting Regional Chief Biologist, National Center - Rm.4A100, 12201 Sunrise Valley Dr., MS-300, Reston, VA 20192. Phone: (703)648-4060.

WESTERN *(Alaska, Arizona, California, Hawaii, Idaho, Nevada, Oregon, Utah, Washington)*—Regional Chief Biologist, 909 1st Ave. - Ste.800, Seattle, WA 98104. Phone: (206)220-4600.

Geologic Division

CENTRAL—Federal Center (MS-911), Denver, CO 80225. Phone: (303)236-5435.

EASTERN—953 National Center, Reston, VA 20192. Phone: (703)648-6662.

WESTERN—345 Middlefield Rd. (MS-919), Menlo Park, CA 94025. Phone: (415) 650-5102.

National Mapping Division

Mapping Application Center—National Center (MS-567), Reston, VA 20192. Phone: (703)648-6002.

Midcontinent Mapping Center—1400 Independence Rd. (MS-300), Rolla, MO 65401. Phone: (573)308-3800.

Rocky Mountain Mapping Center—Denver Federal Center, Bldg. 810 (MS 508), Denver, CO 80225-0046. Phone: (303)202-4040.

South Dakota - Earth Resources Observation Systems Data Center—Mundt Federal Bldg., Sioux Falls, SD 57198. Phone: (605)594-6123.

Western Mapping Center—345 Middlefield Rd. (MS-531), Menlo Park, CA 94025-3591. Phone: (415)329-4254.

Water Resources Division

CENTRAL *(Colorado, Iowa, Kansas, Minnesota, Montana, Nebraska, New Mexico, North Dakota, Oklahoma, South Dakota, Texas, Wyoming)*—Regional Hydrologist,

Denver Federal Center, Bldg. 25 (MS 406), Box 25046, Lakewood, CO 80225-0046. Phone: (303)236-5950, ext.0.

NORTHEAST *(Connecticut, Delaware, Illinois, Indiana, Kentucky, Maine, Maryland, Massachusetts, Michigan, New Hampshire, New Jersey, New York, Ohio, Pennsylvania, Rhode Island, Vermont, Virginia, West Virginia, Wisconsin)*—Regional Hydrologist, 433 National Center (MS-433), Reston, VA 22092. Phone: (703)648-5813.

SOUTHEAST *(Alabama, Arkansas, Florida, Georgia, Louisiana, Mississippi, Missouri, North Carolina, Puerto Rico, South Carolina, Tennessee, Virgin Islands)*—Regional Hydrologist, Spalding-Woods Office Park - Ste.160, 3850 Holcomb Bridge Rd., Norcross, GA 30092-2202. Phone: (404)409-7701.

WESTERN *(Alaska, American Samoa, Arizona, California, Guam, Hawaii, Idaho, Nevada, Oregon, other Pacific Islands, Utah, Washington)*—Regional Hydrologist, 345 Middlefield Rd. (MS-470), Menlo Park, CA 94025-3591. Phone: (415)329-4414.

NATIONAL PARK SERVICE

15.904
thru
15.921
For financial assistance information contact the State Historic Preservation Officer in your state, or the appropriate regional office, following. For information on National Trust subgrants contact: Office of Financial Services, National Trust for Historic Preservation, 1785 Massachusetts Ave. NW, Washington, DC 20036.

NATIONAL HEADQUARTERS

National Park Service—Professional Services, 1849 C St. NW, Washington, DC 20240. Phone: (202)208-3264.

REGIONAL OFFICES

ALASKA—2525 Gambell St., Anchorage, AK 99503-2892. Phone: (907)257-2690.

INTERMOUNTAIN—Intermountain System Support Office, 12795 W. Alameda Pkwy., Denver, CO 80225-0287. Phone: (303)969-2800.

MIDWEST—Professional Services and Legislation, 1709 Jackson St., Omaha, NE 68102. Phone: (402)221-3084.

NATIONAL CAPITAL—Programs and Budget Office, 1100 Ohio Dr. SW, Washington, DC 20242. Phone: (202)619-7309.

NORTHEAST—Resource Stewardship/Partnership, U.S. Custom House, 200 Chestnut St. - 3rd fl., Philadelphia, PA 19106. Phone: (215)597-9195.

SOUTHEAST—Atlanta Federal Center - 1924 Building, 100 Alabama St. SW, Atlanta, GA 30303. Phone: (404)562-3100.

PACIFIC WEST—Resources, Stewardship and Partnership, 600 Harrison St. - Ste.600, San Francisco, CA 94107-1372. Phone: (415)427-1321.

SERVICE CENTERS

Denver Service Center—P.O. Box 25287, Denver, CO 80225. Phone: (303)969-2100.

Harpers Ferry Center—Harpers Ferry, WV 25425-0050. Phone: (304)535-6058.

15.923   PTT Grants, NCPTT, NSU, Box 5682, Natchitoches, LA 71497. Phones: (318)357-6464; FAX (318)357-6421; e-mail, ncptt@ncptt.nps.gov

15.924   HBCU Coordinator, Southeast Field Office, NPS, 1924 Bldg., 100 Alabama St. SW, Atlanta, GA 30303. Phone: (404)562-3171.

15.976   Chief, Bird Banding Laboratory, USGS Patuxent Wildlife Research Center, 12100 Beach Forest Rd., Laurel, MD 20708-4037. Phone: (301)497-5790.

DEPARTMENT OF JUSTICE

DRUG ENFORCEMENT ADMINISTRATION

16.001
thru
16.005

FIELD OFFICES (No phone numbers provided)

Atlanta—75 Spring St. SW - Rm.740, Atlanta, GA 30303.

Boston—JFK Federal Bldg. - Rm.E-400, 15 Sudbury St., Boston, MA 02203-0402.

Chicago—500 Kluczynski Federal Bldg. - Ste.1200, 230 S. Dearborn St., Chicago, IL 60604.

Dallas—1880 Regal Row, Dallas, TX 75235.

Denver—115 Inverness Dr. E., Denver, CO 80112-5116.

Detroit—431 Howard St., Detroit, MI 48226.

El Paso—DEA/EPIC, Biggs Army Airfield - Federal Bldg. 11339, SSG Sims St., Ft. Bliss, El Paso, TX 79908-8098.

Houston—1433 W. Loop South - Ste.600, Houston, TX 77027-9506.

Los Angeles—Royal Federal Bldg. - 20th fl., 255 E. Temple St., Los Angeles, CA 90012.

Miami—8400 NW 53rd St., Miami, FL 33166.

Newark—80 Mulberry St., Newark, NJ 07102.

New Orleans—Three Lakeway Center - Ste.1800, 3838 N. Causeway Blvd., Metairie, LA 70002.

New York—99 10th Ave., New York, NY 10011.

Philadelphia—600 Arch St. - Rm.10224, Philadelphia, PA 19106.

Phoenix—3010 N. 2nd St. - Ste.301, Phoenix, AZ 85012.

San Diego—4560 Viewridge Ave., San Diego, CA 92123-1672.

San Francisco—450 Golden Gate Ave., P.O. Box 36035, San Francisco, CA 94102.

San Juan District—Casa Lee Bldg., 2432 Loiza St., Santurce, PR 00913.

Seattle—220 W. Mercer St. - Ste.104, Seattle, WA 98119.

St. Louis—7911 Forsyth Blvd. - Ste.500, St. Louis, MO 63105.

Washington, D.C.—801 Eye St. NW - Ste.500, Washington, DC 20001.

Office of Training

Drug Enforcement Administration, FBI Academy, Quantico, VA 22134-1475.

CIVIL RIGHTS DIVISION

CRIMINAL SECTION

16.109   Contact local U.S. Attorney's Office, or FBI (addresses listed under **16.300**).

COMMUNITY RELATIONS SERVICE

16.200   **REGIONAL OFFICES**

REGION I *(Connecticut, Maine, Massachusetts, New Hampshire, Rhode Island, Vermont)*—99 Summer St. - Ste.1820, Boston, MA 02110-0220. Phone: (617)424-5715.

REGION II *(New Jersey, New York, Puerto Rico, Virgin Islands)*—26 Federal Plaza - Rm.36-118, New York, NY 10278. Phone: (212)264-0700.

REGION III *(Delaware, District of Columbia, Maryland, Pennsylvania, Virginia, West Virginia)*—2nd and Chestnut St. - Rm.208, Philadelphia, PA 19106-2902. Phone: (215)597-2344.

REGION IV *(Alabama, Florida, Georgia, Kentucky, Mississippi, North Carolina, South Carolina, Tennessee)*—Citizens Trust Co. Bank Bldg. - Rm.900, 75 Piedmont Ave. NE, Atlanta, GA 30303. Phone: (404)331-6883.

REGION V *(Illinois, Indiana, Michigan, Minnesota, Ohio, Wisconsin)*—55 W. Monroe St. - Rm.420, Chicago, IL 60603. Phone: (312)353-4391.

REGION VI *(Arkansas, Louisiana, New Mexico, Oklahoma, Texas)*—1420 Mockingbird Ln. - Ste.250, Dallas, TX 75247. Phone: (214)655-8175.

REGION VII *(Iowa, Kansas, Missouri, Nebraska)*—1100 Main St. - Ste.1320, Kansas City, MO 64105. Phone: (816)426-7434.

REGION VIII *(Colorado, Montana, North Dakota, South Dakota, Utah, Wyoming)*—1244 Speer Blvd. - Ste.650, Denver, CO 80204-3584. Phone: (303)844-2973.

REGION IX *(Arizona, California, Guam, Hawaii, Nevada)*—33 New Montgomery St. - Ste.1840, San Francisco, CA 94105. Phone: (415)744-6565.

REGION X *(Alaska, Idaho, Oregon, Washington)*—915 2nd Ave. - Rm.1808, Seattle, WA 98174. Phone: (206)220-6700.

FIELD OFFICES

Detroit—211 W. Fort St. - Rm.1404, Detroit, MI 48226. Phone: (313)226-4010.

Houston—515 Rusk Ave. - Rm.12605, Houston, TX 77002-2601. Phone: (713)718-4861.

Los Angeles—888 S. Figueroa St. - Ste.1880, Los Angeles, CA 90017. Phone: (213)894-2941.

Miami—51 SW 1st Ave. - Rm.424, Miami, FL 33130. Phone: (305)536-5206.

16.201   INS/HQIAQ/HAB, 51 1st Ave. SW - Rm.424, Miami, FL 33130. Phone: (305)536-4262.

FEDERAL BUREAU OF INVESTIGATION

16.300
thru
16.303

FIELD OFFICES (Special Agent in Charge)

REGION I *(Connecticut, Maine, Massachusetts, New Hampshire, Rhode Island, Vermont)*:

- Federal Office Bldg. - Rm.535, 150 Court St., New Haven, CT 06510-2020. Phones: (203)777-6311, 503-7000.
- 1 Center Plaza - Ste.600, Boston, MA 02108-1801. Phones: (617)742-5533, 223-6000.

REGION II *(New Jersey, New York, Puerto Rico, Virgin Islands)*:

- One Gateway Center - 22nd fl., Newark, NJ 07102-9889. Phones: (973)877-1999, 622-5613.
- Foley Bldg., 200 McCarty Ave., Albany, NY 12209-2095. Phones: (518)465-7551, 431-4800.
- One FBI Plaza, Buffalo, NY 14202-2698. Phones: (716)856-7800, 843-4300.
- Javits Federal Office Bldg., 26 Federal Plaza, New York, NY 10278-0004. Phone: (212)384-1000.
- U.S. Courthouse and Federal Office Bldg. - Rm.526, 150 Carlos Chardon, Hato Rey, PR 00918-1716. Phones: (787)754-6000, -3292.

REGION III *(Delaware, District of Columbia, Maryland, Pennsylvania, Virginia, West Virginia)*:

16.300
thru
16.303
(cont.)

- Washington Metropolitan Field Office, 601 4th St. NW, Washington, DC 20535-0002. Phone: (202)278-2000.
- 7142 Ambassador Rd., Baltimore, MD 21244-2754. Phones: (410)265-8080, 281-0198.
- Federal Office Bldg. - 8th fl., 600 Arch St., Philadelphia, PA 19106-1675. Phones: (215)418-4500, -4000.
- U.S. Post Office - Ste.300, 700 Grant St., Pittsburgh, PA 15219-1906. Phones: (412)471-2000, 456-9100.
- 150 Corporate Blvd., Norfolk, VA 23502-4999. Phones: (757)455-0100, -0123.
- 111 Greencourt Rd., Richmond, VA 23228-4948. Phones: (804)261-1044, (700)923-2000.

REGION IV *(Alabama, Florida, Georgia, Kentucky, Mississippi, North Carolina, South Carolina, Tennessee)*:

- 2121 8th Ave. N. - Rm.1400, Birmingham, AL 35203-2396. Phones: (205)715-0300; FAX (205)715-0232.
- St. Louis Centre - 3rd fl., 1 St. Louis St., Mobile, AL 36602-3930. Phones: (334)438-3674, (700)222-9111.
- 7820 Arlington Expressway - Ste.200, Jacksonville, FL 32211-7499. Phones: (904) 721-1211.
- 16320 NW 2nd Ave., North Miami Beach, FL 33169-6508. Phones: (305)944-9101, 787-6100.
- Federal Office Bldg. - Rm.610, 500 Zack St., Tampa, FL 33602-3917. Phones: (813)273-4566, 272-8000.
- 2635 Century Pkwy. NE - Ste.400, Atlanta, GA 30345-3112. Phones: (404)679-9000, -6100.
- Federal Office Bldg. - Ste.500, 600 Martin Luther King Place, Louisville, KY 40202-2231. Phones: (502)583-3941.
- Federal Office Bldg. - Ste.1553, 100 W. Capitol St., Jackson, MS 39269-1601. Phones: (601)948-5000, 360-7550.
- Wachovia Bldg. - Ste.900, 400 S. Tyron, Charlotte, NC 28285. Phone: (704)377-9200.
- 151 W. Park Blvd., Columbia, SC 29210-3857. Phones: (803)551-4200, 988-0600.
- 710 Locust St. - Ste.600, Knoxville, TN 37902-2537. Phones: (423)544-0751, -3500.
- Eaglecrest Bldg. - Ste.3000, 225 N. Humphreys Blvd., Memphis, TN 38120-2107. Phones: (901)747-4300, -9739.

REGION V *(Illinois, Indiana, Michigan, Minnesota, Ohio, Wisconsin)*:

- Dirksen Federal Office Bldg. - Rm.905, 219 S. Dearborn St., Chicago, IL 60604-1702. Phones: (312)431-1333, 786-2500.
- 400 W. Monroe St. - Ste.400, Springfield, IL 62704-1800. Phones: (217)522-9675, 535-4400.
- Federal Office Bldg. - Rm.679, 575 N. Pennsylvania St., Indianapolis, IN 46204-1585. Phones: (317)639-3301, 321-6100.
- McNamara Federal Office Bldg. - 26th fl., 477 Michigan Ave., Detroit, MI 48226-2598. Phones: (313)965-2323, 237-4355.
- 111 Washington Ave. S. - Ste.1100, Minneapolis, MN 55401-2176. Phones: (612)376-3200.
- Federal Office Bldg. - Rm.9000, 550 Main St., Cincinnati, OH 45202-8501. Phones: (513)421-4310, 562-5600.
- Federal Office Bldg. - Rm.3005, 1240 E. 9th St., Cleveland, OH 44199-9912. Phones: (216)522-1400, 622-6600.
- 330 E. Kilbourn Ave. - Ste.600, Milwaukee, WI 53202-6627. Phones: (414)276-4684, 291-4899.

REGION VI *(Arkansas, Louisiana, New Mexico, Oklahoma, Texas)*:

- Two Financial Centre - Ste.200, 10825 Financial Centre Pkwy., Little Rock, AR 72211-3552. Phones: (501)221-9100, 228-8400.
- 2901 Leon C. Simon Blvd., New Orleans, LA 70126-1061. Phones: (504)522-4671, 592-8199.
- 415 Silver St. SW - Ste.300, Albuquerque, NM 87102. Phone: (505)224-2000.
- 3301 W. Memorial Rd., Oklahoma City, OK 73134. Phones: (405)290-7770, -3875.
- 1801 N. Lamar - Ste.300, Dallas, TX 75202-1795. Phones: (214)720-2200, 922-7475.
- 600 S. Mesa Hills Dr. - Ste.3000, El Paso, TX 79912-5533. Phone: (915)832-5000.
- 2500 E. T.C. Jester, Houston, TX 77008-1300. Phones: (713)693-3999, 803-3525.
- Old Post Office and Courthouse Bldg. - Ste.200, 615 E. Houston St., San Antonio, TX 78205-9998. Phones: (210)693-5000, 693-3800.

REGION VII *(Iowa, Kansas, Missouri, Nebraska)*:
- U.S. Courthouse - Rm.300, 1300 Summit, Kansas City, MO 64105-1362. Phones: (816)221-6100, 512-8200.
- 2222 Market St. - Rm.2704, St. Louis, MO 63103-2516. Phones: (314)231-4324, 589-2500.
- Federal Office Bldg., 10755 Burt St., Omaha, NE 68114-2000. Phones: (402)493-8688, 492-3700.

REGION VIII *(Colorado, North Dakota, South Dakota, Utah, Wyoming)*:
- Federal Office Bldg. - Ste.1823 (18th fl.), 1961 Stout St., Denver, CO 80294-1823. Phones: (303)629-7171, 628-3000.
- 257 Towers Bldg. - Ste.1200, 257 E. 200 S., Salt Lake City, UT 84111-2048. Phones: (801)579-1400, -4400.

REGION IX *(American Samoa, Arizona, California, Guam, Hawaii, Nevada)*:
- Midtowne Business Centre II - Ste.400, 201 E. Indianola Ave., Phoenix, AZ 85012-2080. Phones: (602)279-5511, 650-3300.
- Federal Office Bldg. - Ste.1700, 11000 Wilshire Blvd., Los Angeles, CA 90024-3672. Phones: (310)477-6565, 996-5000.
- 4500 Orange Grove Ave., Sacramento, CA 95841-4205. Phones: (916)481-9110, 977-2200.
- Federal Office Bldg., 9797 Aero Dr., San Diego, CA 92123-1800. Phones: (619)565-1255, 514-5500.
- 450 Golden Gate Ave. - 13th fl., San Francisco, CA 94102-9523. Phones: (415)553-7400, -2000.
- Kalanianaole Federal Office Bldg. - Rm.4-230, 300 Ala Moana Blvd., Honolulu, HI 96850-0053. Phones: (808)521-1411, 538-0034.
- John Lawrence Bailey Bldg., 700 E. Charleston Blvd., Las Vegas, NV 89101-1545. Phones: (702)385-1281, (700)545-0110.

REGION X *(Alaska, Idaho, Oregon, Washington)*:
- 101 E. 6th Ave., Anchorage, AK 99501-2523. Phones: (907)258-5322, 276-4441.
- Crown Plaza Bldg. - Ste.400, 1500 SW 1st Ave., Portland, OR 97201-5828. Phones: (503)224-4181, 423-9790.
- Federal Office Bldg. - Rm.710, 915 2nd Ave., Seattle, WA 98174-1096. Phones: (206)622-0460, (700)391-8760.

Office of the Inspector General

FIELD INSTALLATIONS

Arizona—*Investigations,* 10 E. Broadway - Ste.105, Tucson, AZ 85701. Phones: (520)670-5243; FAX (520)670-5246. *For mail:* Tucson, AZ 85702-0471.

California—*Investigations,* 321 S. Waterman Ave. - Rm.108, El Centro, CA 92243. Phones: (760)335-3549; FAX(760)335-3534.

16.300
thru
16.303
(cont.)

▪ *Investigations*, 330 N. Brand St. - Ste.655, Glendale, CA 91203. Phones: (818)543-1172; FAX (818)637-5082.

▪ 1200 Bayhill Dr. - Ste.220 *(investigations)*, Ste.201 *(audits)*, San Bruno, CA 94066. Phones: *investigations*, (650)876-9058; FAX (650)876-9083; *audits*, (650)876-9220, FAX (650)876-0902.

▪ *Investigations*, 701 "B" St. - Ste.560, San Diego, CA 92101. Phones: (619)557-5970; FAX(619)557-6518.

Colorado—*Investigations*, Plaza of the Rockies, 111 S. Tejon St. - Ste.312, Colorado Springs, CO 80903. Phones: (719)635-2366; FAX (719)635-4769.

▪ *Audits*, The Chancery Bldg. - Ste.1603, 1120 Lincoln St., Denver, CO 80203. Phones: (303)864-2000; FAX (303)864-2004.

District of Columbia—1425 New York Ave. NW - Ste.6000 *(audits)*, Ste.7100 *(investigations and fraud detection unit)*, Washington, DC 20530. Phones: *audits*, (202)616-4688; FAX (202)616-4581; *investigations and fraud detection unit*, (202)616-4760; FAX (202)616-9881. *For mail(investigations)*: P.O. Box 27718, Washington, DC 20038-7718.

Florida—*Investigations*, 3800 Inverrary Blvd. - Ste.312, Ft. Lauderdale, FL 33319. Phones: (954)356-7142; FAX (954)356-7446.

Georgia—*Audits*, 75 Spring St. - Ste.1130, Atlanta, GA 30303. Phones: (404)331-5928; FAX (404)331-5046. *Investigations*, 60 Forsyth St. SW - Ste.8M45, Atlanta, GA 30303. Phones: (404)562-1980; FAX (404)562-1960.

Illinois—Citicorp Center, 500 W. Madison Blvd. - Ste.3510 *(audits)*, Ste.3510B *(investigations)*, Chicago, IL 60661. Phones: *audits*, (312)353-1203, FAX (312)886-0513; *investigations*, (312)886-7050, FAX (312)886-7065. *For mail (investigations):* Chicago, IL 60690-1802.

Massachusetts—*Investigations*, 1003 U.S. Courthouse - Rm.9200, 1 Courthouse Way, Boston, MA 02210. Phones: (617)748-3218; FAX (617)748-3965. *For mail:* Boston, MA 02106-2134.

New York—*Investigations*, JFK Airport, Bldg. 77 - Penthouse no. 2, N. Boundary Rd., Jamaica, NY 11430. Phones: FTS (718)553-7520; FAX (718)553-7533. *For mail:* JFK Airport, Jamaica, NY 11430-0999.

Pennsylvania—*Audits*, 701 Market St. - Ste.201, Philadelphia, PA 19106. Phones: (215)580-2111; FAX (215)597-1348.

Texas—207 S. Houston St. - Rm.575 (Box 4) *(audits)*, Rm.551 (Box 4) *(investigations)*, Dallas, TX 75202-4724. Phones: *audits*, (214)655-5000, FAX (214)655-5025; *investigations*, (214)655-5076, FAX (214)655-5071.

▪ *Investigations*, 4050 Rio Bravo - Ste.200, El Paso, TX 79902. Phones: (915)577-0102; FAX (915)577-9012.

▪ *Investigations*, Casey Federal Courthouse - Ste.3307, 515 Rusk Ave., Houston, TX 77002. Phones: (713)718-4888; FAX (713)718-4706. *For mail:* P.O. Box 610071, Houston, TX 77208-9998.

▪ *Investigations*, Bentsen Tower - Ste.510, 1701 W. Business Hwy.83,, McAllen, TX 78501. Phones: (956)618-8145; FAX (956)618-8151.

Washington—*Investigations*, 620 Kirkland Way - Ste.104, Kirkland, WA 98033-6021. Phones: (425)828-3998; FAX (425)827-2183.

IMMIGRATION AND NATURALIZATION SERVICE

16.400   FIELD OFFICES

Alabama—Mobile Border Patrol, 951 Government St. - Rm.405, P.O. Box 1526, Mobile, AL 36633. Phones: (334)441-6139.

- Mobile Port of Entry, P.O. Box 1526, Mobile, AL 36601. Phones: (205)690-2136, -2139.

Alaska—Anchorage District Office, 620 E. 10th Ave. - Ste.102, Anchorage, AK 99501-3708. Phone: (907)271-3524.

- Anchorage International Airport, 4601 Satellite Dr., Anchorage, AK 99502. Phone: (no number provided).

- Anchorage, AK 99519-0688. Phone: (907)243-1400.

- Dutch Harbor Port of Entry, 2315 Airport Beach Rd. - Rm.205, P.O. Box 750, Dutch Harbor, AK 99692. Phone: (907)581-4114.

- Eagle Port of Entry, c/o Postmaster - Box 1, Eagle, AK 99738. Phone: (907)547-2211.

- Fairbanks Port of Entry, 6450 Old Airport Way, Fairbanks, AK 99709. Phone: (907)474-0307.

- Gambell Port of Entry, P.O. Box 1, Gambell, AK 99742. Phone: (907)985-5211.

- Dalton's Cache Port of Entry, Haines Hwy. - Mile 40, Haines, AK 99827-1509. Phone: (907)767-5580.

- Ketchikan Port of Entry, 111 Main St., Ketchikan, AK 99840. Phone: (907)225-2380.

- Alaska Marine Hwy. Terminal, Prince Rupert, BC Canada, c/o 111 Main St., Ketchikan, AK 99840. Phone: (604)624-3833.

- Nome Port of Entry, P.O. Box 281, Nome, AK 99762. Phone: (907)443-2065.

- Skagaway Port of Entry, Klondike Hwy. Border Station, Skagaway, AK 99840-0475. Phone: (907)983-3144.

- Turner Port of Entry, P.O. Box 1221, Tok, AK 99780. Phone: (907)774-2242.

Arizona—Ajo Border Patrol, 850 N. Tucson - Ajo Hwy. 86, P.O. Drawer J, Ajo/Highway, AZ 85321. Phone: (520)387-7002.

- 1784 N. Pinal Ave., P.O. Box 11230, Casa Grande, AZ 85230-1230. Phone: (602)836-7812.

- Douglas Border Patrol, 1051 Lawrence St., P.O. Box 1175, Douglas, AZ 85608. Phone: (520)364-3991.

- Douglas Port of Entry, Pan American Ave. and 1st St., Douglas, AZ 85607. Phones: (520)364-5532, -6479.

- Eloy Processing Center, 4465 E. Hanna Rd. - Ste.343, Eloy, AZ 85231. Phone: (520)466-2000.

- Florence Processing Center, 3250 N. Pinal Pkwy. Ave., Florence, AZ 85232. Phone: (520)868-5862.

- Lukeville Port of Entry, Highway 85, P.O. Box D, Lukeville, AZ 85341. Phone: (520)387-6047.

- Naco Border Patrol, 2136 Naco Hwy., P.O. Box 695, Naco, AZ 85620. Phone: (520)432-5121.

- Naco Border Patrol, 106 "D" St., P.O. Box 277, Naco, AZ 85620. Phones: (520)432-3111, -2791.

- Nogales Border Patrol, 1500 W. La Quinto Rd., Nogales, AZ 85621. Phone: (520)377-6000.

- Phoenix Border Patrol, 3006 W. Claredon Ave., Phoenix, AZ 85017. Phone: (520)670-6865.

- Phoenix Sky Harbor Airport, P.O. Box 63673, Phoenix, AZ 85082-2673. Phones: (602)275-7745, -7763, -7785.

- Phoenix District Office, 2035 N. Central Ave., Phoenix, AZ 85004-1548. Phone: (602)514-7799.

- San Luis Port of Entry, Hwy. 95, P.O. Box 448, San Luis, AZ 85349. Phone: (520)627-3591.

- Sasabe Port of Entry, Federal Inspection Bldg., Sasabe, AZ 85633-0326. Phone: (520)823-4230.

16.400
(cont.)

- Sonoita Port of Entry, Hwy. 82 and 83, Sonoita, AZ 85637-0037. Phone: (520)455-5051.
- Tucson Border Patrol, 2010 Ajo Way, Tucson, AZ 85713. Phones: (520)670-6865.
- Tucson Border Patrol Sector Hdqtrs., 1970 Ajo Way, Tucson, AZ 85713. Phone: (520)670-6871, -6880.
- Wellton Border Patrol, 29820 Frontage Rd., P.O. Box 128, Wellton, AZ 85356. Phone: (520)785-9364.
- Willcox Border Patrol, 200 W. Downen St., Willcox, AZ 85644-0909. Phone: (520) 384-2412.
- Yuma Border Patrol, 12122 S. Ave. A, Yuma, AZ 85366-2708. Phone: (520)726-8731.
- Yuma Border Patrol Sector Hdqtrs., 350 W. 1st St., Yuma, AZ 85366-2708. Phone: (520)782-9548.

Arkansas—P.O. Box 934, North Little Rock, AR 72115. Phone: (501)324-6504, -5501.

Bahamas—Freeport Bahamas Sub-Office, P.O. Box F-2664, Freeport, Grand Bahama, BAHAMAS. Phone:(242)352-5586.
- U.S. Immigration-Nassau, Miami, FL 33159-9009. Phone: (242)377-7125.

California—Bakersfield Processing Center, 17635 Industrial Farm Rd., Bakersfield, CA 93380. Phone: (805)861-4465.
- Bakersfield Satellite Investigations, 800 Truxton Ave. - Rm.317, Bakersfield, CA 93301. Phone: (805)861-4478.
- Western Form Center, Bldg. 701 - Bay A, 5600 Rickenbacker Rd., Bell, CA 90201. Phone: (213)526-7404.
- Blythe Border Patrol, 16870 W. Hobsonway, P.O. Box 836, Blythe, CA 92226. Phone: (619)922-6715.
- Boulevard Border Patrol, 39701 Avenue de Robles Verde, P.O. Box 1320, Boulevard, CA 92005. Phone: (619)766-4542.
- 1150 Birch, Calexico, CA 92231. Phone: (619)357-2441.
- Calexico Port of Entry, 200 E. 1st St., P.O. Box 1780, Calexico, CA 92231. Phones: (619)357-1189, -7968, -1143.
- Calexico East Port of Entry, 1699 E. Carr Rd., Calexico, CA 92231. Phone: (619)768-2450.
- Oxnard Border Patrol, 275 Skyway Dr., P.O. Box 88, Camarillo, CA 93011. Phone: (805)482-8997.
- Campo Border Patrol, 3 Forest Gate Rd., P.O. Box 68, Campo, CA 91906. Phone: (619)557-6144.
- 311 Athey St., P.O. Box 2506, Chula Vista, CA 91912. Phone: (619)662-7233.
- Livermore Border Patrol Station and Sector Hdqtrs., 6102 9th St., Dublin, CA 94568. Phones: (825)828-3770, (510)828-0371.
- El Cajon Border Patrol, 225 Kenney St., El Cajon, CA 92020. Phone: (619)557-5072.
- El Centro Processing Center, 1115 N. Imperial Ave., El Centro, CA 92243-1739. Phone: (619)353-2170.
- El Centro Border Patrol Sector Hdqtrs., 1111 N. Imperial Ave., El Centro, CA 92243-1795. Phone: (619)352-3241.
- El Centro Border Patrol Station, 1081 N. Imperial Ave., El Centro, CA 92243. Phone: (619)353-0541.
- Fresno Border Patrol Station, 4367 N. Golden State Blvd., Fresno, CA 93722. Phone: (209)487-5506.
- Fresno Sub-Office, 865 Fulton Mall, Fresno, CA 93721-2816. Phone: (209)487-5126.
- Imperial Beach Border Patrol, 1802 Saturn Way, Imperial Beach Beach, CA 91933-0068. Phone: (619)662-7149.
- Indio Border Patrol, 45-620 Commerce St., Indio, CA 92201. Phone: (760)347-3658.
- Western Region Operations, 24000 Avila Rd., P.O. Box 30080, Laguna Niguel, CA 92607-0080. Phone: (714)643-4236.

- Long Beach Seaport Unit, 501 W. Ocean Blvd. - Ste.6300, Long Beach, CA 90802. Phone: (310)980-3400.
- Los Angeles District Office, 300 N. Los Angeles St., Los Angeles, CA 90012. Phone: (213)894-4627.
- Los Angeles International Airport, Tom Bradley International Terminal - Lower Level, 380 Worldway, P.O. Box N-20, Los Angeles, CA 90045. Phones: (310)215-2104, ext.107; (310)215-3101, ext.103.
- Oakland International Airport, International Terminal, 1 Airport Dr., Oakland, CA 94621. Phone: (510)273-7390.
- Ontario Airport, 222 E. Airport Dr., Ontario, CA 91761. Phones: (909)395-8668, -8673.
- Riverside Border Patrol, 2060 Chicago Ave. - Ste.A2, Riverside, CA 92507. Phone: (909)686-4100.
- Sacramento Border Patrol Station, Bldg. 500 - Ste.575, 7000 Franklin Blvd., Sacramento, CA 95823. Phone: (916)391-9087.
- Sacramento Sub-Office, 711 "J" St., Sacramento, CA 95814. Phone: (916)498-6469.
- Salinas Border Patrol, 1636 E. Alisal St., P.O. Box 218, Salinas, CA 93902. Phone: (408)754-0633.
- San Clemente Border Patrol, I-5 Northbound Traffic Checkpoint, P.O. Box 3188, San Clemente, CA 92674. Phone: (619)557-5272.
- San Diego District Office, 880 Front St. - Ste.1234, San Diego, CA 92101-8834. Phone: (619)557-5645.
- Brown Field Border Patrol, 7560 Britannia St., San Diego, CA 92173. Phone: (619)661-3154.
- Ota Mesa Port of Entry, 2500 Paseo International, San Diego, CA 92143-9018. Phones: (619)661-3249, -3231.
- San Diego International Airport, Lindbergh Field Airport, 3665 N. Harbor Dr., San Diego, CA 92101. Phone: (619)298-2612.
- San Ysidro Port of Entry, 720 San Ysidro Blvd., San Diego, CA 92143-9018. Phones: (619)662-7314, -7240.
- San Francisco International Airport, Central Terminal - Lower Level, Customs Area, P.O. Box 280551, San Francisco, CA 94128. Phone: (415)876-2876.
- San Francisco District Office, 630 Sansome St., San Francisco, CA 94111-2280. Phone: (415)705-3102.
- San Jose International Airport, c/o P.O. Box 280551, Central Terminal - Lower Level, Customs Area, San Jose, CA 95110. Phone: (408)291-7209.
- 280 S. 1st St. - Rm.1150, San Jose, CA 95113. Phone: (408)535-5174.
- San Luis Obispo Border Patrol Station, 1170 Calle Joaquin, P.O. Box 1486, San Luis Obispo, CA 93406. Phone: (805)543-9490.
- San Marcos Border Patrol, 126 S. Pacific, P.O. Box 5099, San Marcos, CA 92069. Phone: (619)557-5589.
- San Pedro Processing Center, Terminal Island, 2001 Seaside Ave., San Pedro, CA 90731. Phone: (310)732-0777.
- Stockton Border Patrol, P.O. Box 2047, Stockton, CA 95201. Phones: (209)946-6211, -6284.
- Tecate Port of Entry, Tecate, CA 92080-0219. Phone: (619)478-5029.
- Temecula Border Patrol, 43136 Rancho Way, P.O. Box 38, Temecula, CA 92593. Phone: (909)676-6871.
- Andrade Port of Entry, 235 Andrade Rd., Winterhaven, CA 92283. Phones: (619)572-3550, -5184.

Colorado—Denver District Office, Albrook Center, 4730 Paris St., Denver, CO 80239-2804. Phone: (303)371-0986.

- Grand Junction Port of Entry, 255 Main St., Grand Junction, CO 81501. Phone: (303)243-5141.

16.400
(cont.)

- Pueblo Port of Entry, P.O. Box 1879, Pueblo, CO 81002. Phone: (719)544-9369.

Connecticut—Ribicoff Federal Bldg., 450 Main St., Hartford, CT 06103-3060. Phone: (203)240-3050.

- Bradley International Airport, C/O USINS, 450 Main St., Hartford, CT 06103-3606. Phone: (203)240-3113.

District of Columbia—Dulles International Airport, P.O. Box 17775, Washington, DC 20041. Phone: (703)661-5100.

- INS Headquarters, 425 I St. NW, Washington, DC 20536. Phone: (202)514-4316.

Florida—Canaveral Port of Entry, P.O. Box 1911, Cape Canaveral, FL 32920. Phones: (407)868-7134.

- Jacksonville Port of Entry, Federal Bldg - Rm.G-18, 400 W. Bay St., Jacksonville, FL 32202. Phone: (904)232-2164.

- Key West Port of Entry and Sub-Office, Federal Bldg. - Rm.224, 301 Simontown St., P.O. Box 86, Key West, FL 33040. Phones: (305)296-2233, 536-4274, 293-9150.

- Miami International Airport - Concourse E (3rd fl.), Miami, FL 33299-7895. Phones: (305)526-2612, -2626, -2851, -2930.

- Krome North Service Processing Center, Snapper Creek Station, 18201 SW 12th St., P.O. Box 160327, Miami, FL 33194. Phone: (305)552-1845.

- Miami District Office, 7880 Biscayne Blvd., Miami, FL 33138. Phone: (305)530-7657.

- U.S. Immigration - Nassau, Miami, FL 33159-9009. Phone: (242)377-7125.

- Orlando International Airport, P.O. Box 620848, Orlando, FL 32863. Phone: (407) 648-6869.

- Orlando Border Patrol, 1215 W. Fairbanks Ave., Orlando, FL 32804. Phone: (no number provided).

- Miami Border Patrol Sector Hdqtrs., 7201 Pembroke Rd., Pembroke Pines, FL 33023. Phones: (954)963-9807.

- West Palm Beach Port of Entry, 4 E. Port Rd. - Rm.410, Riviera Beach, FL 33419. Phone: (407)845-6898.

- West Palm Beach Sub-Office, 54 E. Port Rd. - Rm.129, Riviera Beach, FL 33404. Phone: (561)844-1377.

- Tampa Border Patrol, 1821B E. Sahlman Dr., Tampa, FL 33605. Phone: (813)228-2156, -2160.

- Orlando Border Patrol, Winter Park, FL 32790-0440. Phone: (407)648-6081.

Georgia—Atlanta District Office, 77 Forsyth St. SW, Atlanta, GA 30303-0253. Phone: (404)331-0253.

- Hartsfield International Airport Port of Entry, P.O. Box 45527, Atlanta, GA 30320. Phone: (404)763-7816.

- Savannah Port of Entry, 33 Bull St. - Ste.505, Savannah, GA 31401. Phones: (912)232-9666.

Guam—Guam International Airport, Pacific News Bldg. - Rm.801, 238 Archbishop Flores St., Agana, GU 96910. Phones: (200)550-7410, -7358.

Hawaii—Honolulu District Office, 595 Ala Moana Blvd., Honolulu, HI 96813. Phones: (808)532-3748, -3746.

- Honolulu International Airport, 300 Rogers Blvd., Terminal Box 50, Honolulu, HI 96819. Phones: (808)861-8401, -8406, -8400, -8409.

Idaho—4620 Overland Rd. - Rm.108, Boise, ID 83705. Phone: (208)334-1822.

- Bonners Ferry Border Patrol, 1st and W. Kootenai St. - Rm.214, P.O. Box 697, Bonners Ferry, ID 83805. Phones: (208)267-2734, -7645.

- Eastport Port of Entry, Hwy. 95, P.O. Box 8, Eastport, ID 83826. Phones: (208)267-2183, -3745.

- Porthill Port of Entry, Hwy. 1, P.O. Box 40, Porthill, ID 83853. Phones: (208)267-5309.

- 2496 Addison Ave. E., P.O. Box 263, Twin Falls, ID 83301. Phone: (208)734-4369.

Illinois—Chicago District Office, 10 W. Jackson Blvd. - Ste.600, Chicago, IL 60604. Phone: (312)385-1900.

Indiana—Indianapolis Sub-Office, Gateway Plaza - Rm.400, 950 N. Meridan St., Indianapolis, IN 46204. Phone: (217)226-7891.

Kentucky—Louisville Sub-Office, Snyder Courthouse - Rm.604, 601 W. Broadway, Louisville, KY 40202. Phone: (502)582-6526.

Kansas—Garden City Port of Entry, 1404 E. Fulton, Box 1239, Garden City, KS 67846. Phone: (316)275-1054.

- Wichita Port of Entry, 625 N. Winterset, Wichita, KS 67212. Phone: (316)266-6093.

Louisiana—Baton Rouge Port of Entry, 9522 Brookline Dr., P.O. Box 338, Baton Rouge, LA 70821. Phones: (504)389-0231.

- New Orleans International Airport, 900 Airline Hwy., Kenner, LA 70062. Phone: (504)589-3949.

- Lake Charles Border Patrol, P.O. Box 868, Lake Charles, LA 70601. Phone: (318)477-9245.

- 321 Common St., P.O. Box 868, Lake Charles, LA 70601. Phones: (318)437-7218, -7287.

- New Orleans District Office, Postal Services Bldg. - Rm.T-8011, 701 Loyola Ave., New Orleans, LA 70113. Phone: (504)589-6521.

- New Orleans Border Patrol Sector Hdqtrs., 3819 Patterson Dr., P.O. Box 6218, New Orleans, LA 70174. Phones: (504)589-6107.

- Oakdale Processing Center, 207 E. 5th Ave., P.O. Box 5095, Oakdale, LA 71463. Phone: (318)335-0713.

Maine—Bangor Port of Entry, 267A Godfrey Blvd., Bangor, ME 04402-0677. Phone: (207)945-0334.

- Bar Harbor Port of Entry, Marine Atlantic Ferry Terminal, Eden St., Bar Harbor, ME 04609. Phone: (207)288-4675.

- Bridgewater Port of Entry, RFD Rt. 1 - Box 42, Boundary Line Rd., Bridgewater, ME 04735. Phone: (207)425-4502.

- Calais Border Patrol, One Main St., P.O. Box 245, Calais, ME 04619. Phone: (207)454-3613.

- Calais Port of Entry, Border Inspection Station, One Main St. - P.O. Drawer 421, Calais, ME 04619. Phone: (207)454-2546.

- Coburn Gore Port of Entry, Star Rt. 73, P.O. Box 35, Eustis, ME 04936. Phone: (207)297-2771.

- Ft. Fairfield Border Patrol, 205 Main St., P.O. Box 410, Ft. Fairfield, ME 04742. Phone: (207)472-5041.

- Ft. Fairfield Port of Entry, Rural Rt. 1 - Box 217, Ft. Fairfield, ME 04742. Phone: (207)473-7396.

- Ft. Kent Port of Entry, 98 W. Main St., Ft. Kent, ME 04743-1016. Phone: (207)834-3223.

- Houlton Border Patrol Sector Hdqtrs. and Border Station, Rt. 1 - Calais Rd., P.O. Box 706, Houlton, ME 04730. Phones: (207)532-9061, -6521, -6522 (24 hours).

- Houlton Port of Entry, Interstate 95, P.O. Box 189, Houlton, ME 04730. Phone: (207)532-2906.

- Jackman Border Patrol, Nickels Rd., P.O. Box 608, Jackman, ME 04945. Phone: (207)668-3151 (24 hours).

- Jackman Port of Entry, Star Rt. 76 - Box 629, Jackman, ME 04945. Phone: (207)668-3771.

- Limestone Port of Entry, R.F.D. 1, Box 258, Limestone, ME 04750-9729. Phone: (207)325-4760.

- Lubec Port of Entry, Federal Bldg., U.S. Post Office and Border Station, Washington St. and Campobello Bridge, Lubec, ME 04652. Phone: (207)733-4960.

16.400
(cont.)

- Madawska Port of Entry, 2 Bridge St., Madawaska, ME 04756-1230. Phone: (207) 728-4565.
- 739 Warren Ave., Portland, ME 04103. Phone: (207)780-3399.
- Vanceboro Port of Entry, USINS, Water St., P.O. Box C, Vanceboro, ME 04491. Phone: (207)788-7813.
- Van Buren Port of Entry, International Bridge, Bridge St., P.O. Box 116, Van Buren, ME 04785. Phones: (207)868-2202, -3900.
- Van Buren Border Patrol, Main St., P.O. Box 26, Van Buren, ME 04785. Phone: (207)868-7900.
- Hamlin Port of Entry, H.C. 62 - Box 63, Van Buren, ME 04785. Phone: (207)868-0966.

Maryland—Baltimore District Office, Equitable Tower - 12th fl., 100 S. Charles St., Baltimore, MD 21201. Phone: (410)962-2010.

Massachusetts—Boston District Office, Kennedy Federal Bldg. - Rm.1700, Government Center, Boston, MA 02203. Phone: (617)565-4214.

- Boston Service Processing Center, 427 Commercial St., Boston, MA 02109. Phones: (617)223-3090, -3089, -3088.

Michigan—Algonac Port of Entry, 202 Fruit St., Algonac, MI 48001. Phone: (810)794-3321.

- Federal Bldg., 333 Mount Elliott St., P.O. Box 32639, Detroit, MI 48232. Phones: (313)568-6061, -6062.
- Detroit District Office, Federal Bldg., 333 Mount Elliot St., Detroit, MI 48207-4381. Phone: (313)568-6000.
- District/Canada Tunnel, 150 E. Jefferson Ave., Detroit, MI 48226. Phone: (313)568-6019.
- Detroit International Bridge, 3033 Porter, Detroit, MI 48216. Phone: (313)963-4408.
- Detroit City Airport, 11499 Conner - Rm.138C, Detroit, MI 48213. Phone: (313)521-8430.
- Grand Rapids Border Patrol, 100 W. 7th St., Holland, MI 49422-1678. Phone: (616)392-4070.
- Port Huron Border Patrol, 2112 River Rd., Marysville, MI 48040. Phone: (313)364-6041.
- Port Huron Port of Entry, 2322 Pinegrove Ave., Port Huron, MI 48060. Phone: (810)942-0493.
- Detroit Metro Airport, International Terminal, Romulus, MI 48242. Phone: (313)955-6293.
- Sault Ste. Marie Port of Entry and Border Patrol, International Bridge Plaza, P.O. Box 141, Sault Ste. Marie, MI 49783. Phone: (906)632-3383, -8822.
- Trenton Border Patrol, 23100 W. Rd., P.O. Box 206, Trenton, MI 48183. Phone: (313)676-2972.

Minnesota—Baudette Port of Entry, International Bridge, P.O. Box 487, Baudette, MN 56623. Phone: (218)634-2661.

- St. Paul District Office, 2901 Metro Dr. - Ste.100, Bloomington, MN 55425. Phone: (612)335-2211.
- Crane Lake Port of Entry, 7544 Gold Coast Rd., Crane Lake, MN 55725. Phone: (218)993-2321.
- Duluth Port of Entry and Border Patrol, U.S. Courthouse and Custom House, Federal Bldg., 515 W. 1st St., Duluth, MN 55802. Phones: (218)720-5207, -5465.
- Ely Port of Entry, P.O. Box 28, Ely, MN 55731. Phone: (218)365-3262.
- Grand Marais Border Patrol, Hwy. 61 East - P.O. Box 685, Grand Marais, MN 55604. Phone: (218)387-1770.
- Grand Portage Port of Entry, Hwy. 61, Grand Portage, MN 55605. Phone: (218)475-2494.

- International Falls Border Patrol, 1412 Hwy. 11-71 West, International Falls, MN 56649. Phone: (218)283-2461.
- No.2 2nd Ave., International Falls, MN 56649-2328. Phone: (218)283-8611.
- Lancaster Port of Entry, Rt. 1 Box 138 - Hwy. 59, Lancaster, MN 56735. Phone: (218)762-4100.
- Noyes Port of Entry, Rural Rt. 1 - Box 110, Noyes, MN 56740. Phone: (218)823-6291.
- Perbina Border Patrol, Rural Rt. 1 - P.O. Box 106, Noyes, MN 56740. Phones: (218)823-6528, -6594.
- Pine Creek Port of Entry, Hwy. 89, Star Rt. 5, Roseau, MN 56751. Phone: (218)463-1952.
- Roseau Port of Entry, Rt. 1 Box 31 - Hwy. 310 N., Roseau, MN 56751. Phone: (218)463-2054.
- Warroad Port of Entry, H.C. 02, P.O. Box 245, Warroad, MN 56763. Phone: (218)386-1676.
- Warroad Border Patrol, P.O. Box 24, Hwy. 11, Warroad, MN 56763. Phone: (218)386-1802.

Mississippi—Gulfport Border Patrol, P.O. Box 4273, Gulfport, MS 39502. Phone: (601)864-3029.

- Gulfport Port of Entry, P.O. Box 4273, Gulfport, MS 39501. Phone: (601)864-3029.

Missouri—Kansas City District Office, 9747 N. Conant Ave., Kansas City, MO 64153. Phone: (816)891-0864.

- Young Federal Bldg. - Rm.100, 1222 Spruce St., St. Louis, MO 63103-2815. Phone: (314)539-2516.
- St. Louis International Airport, Lambert Field, P.O. Box 10406, St. Louis, MO 63145. Phone: (314)425-7179.

Montana—Piegan Port of Entry, P.O. Box 109, Babb, MT 59411. Phone: (406)732-9297.

- Chief Mountain Port of Entry, P.O. Box 376, Chief Mountain, MT 59411 via Babb, MT 59411. Phone: (406)732-4576.
- Billings Border Patrol, 2601 1st Ave. N., P.O. Box 2298, Billings, MT 59103. Phones: (406)247-7563.
- Del Bonita Port of Entry, Del Bonita Star Rt., Cut Bank, MT 59427. Phone: (406)336-2130.
- Eureka Border Patrol, Hwy. 93 (JB Shopping Center), P.O. Box 909, Eureka, MT 59917. Phone: (406)296-2938.
- Roosville Port of Entry, 8395 Hwy. 93 N., Eureka, MT 59917-9331. Phone: (406)889-3737.
- Havre Border Patrol Sector Hdqtrs., 2605 5th Ave. SE, P.O. Box 112, Havre, MT 59501. Phone: (406)265-6781.
- Wild Horse Port of Entry, Havre, MT 59501. Phone: (406)394-2371.
- Willow Creek Port of Entry, Simpson Rt., Havre, MT 59501. Phone: (406)398-5512.
- Havre Port of Entry, Simpson Rt., Willow Creek Station, Havre, MT 59501. Phone: (406)265-6781.
- Loring Port of Entry, Port of Morgan, HC82 - Box 9250, Loring, MT 59537-9600. Phone: (406)674-5248.
- Malta Border Patrol, P.O. Box 36, Malta, MT 59538. Phone: (406)654-2711.
- Opheim Port of Entry, P.O. Box 317, Opheim, MT 59250. Phone: (406)724-3212.
- Plentywood Border Patrol, P.O. Box 434, Plentywood, MT 59254. Phone: (406)765-1852.
- Raymond Border Patrol, P.O. Box 158, Raymond, MT 59256. Phone: (406)895-2620.
- Scobey Border Patrol, P.O. Box 820, Scobey, MT 59263. Phone: (406)487-2621.
- Scobey Port of Entry, P.O. Box 2300, Scobey, MT 59263. Phone: (406)783-5372.

16.400
(cont.)

- Shelby Border Patrol, 906 Oilfield Ave., P.O. Box 653, Shelby, MT 59474. Phone: (406)434-5588.
- Sweetgrass Port of Entry, P.O. Box 165 - Interstate 15, Sweetgrass, MT 59484. Phone: (406)335-2911.
- Whitefish Border Patrol, 1295 Hwy. 93 W., P.O. Box 400, Whitefish, MT 59937. Phone: (406)862-2561.
- Whitetail Port of Entry, U.S. Border Inspection Station, P.O. Box 38, Whitetail, MT 59276. Phone: (406)779-3531.

Nebraska—Nebraska Service Center, 850 S. St., P.O. Box 82521, Lincoln, NE 68501-2521. Phone: (402)437-5464.

- Omaha District Office, 3736 S. 132nd St., Omaha, NE 68144. Phone: (402)697-9152.

Nevada—Boulder City Border Patrol, Boulder City, NV 89006-0928. Phone: (702)293-8507.

- Las Vegas Sub-Office, 3373 Pepper Lane, Las Vegas, NV 89120. Phone: (702)388-6640.
- Las Vegas Mecarren International Airport, 5757 Wayne Newton Blvd., Las Vegas, NV 89111. Phone: (702)388-6024.
- Reno Sub-Office, 1351 Corporate Blvd., Reno, NV 89502. Phone: (702)784-5186.

New Hampshire—Pittsburg Port of Entry, Rt. 3, P.O. Box 277, Pittsburg, NH 03592. Phone: (819)656-2261.

New Jersey—Newark District Office, Federal Bldg., 970 Broad St., Newark, NJ 07102. Phone: (201)645-4421.

- Newark International Airport, Terminal B (SAT 3), Newark, NJ 07114. Phone: (201)645-6589.

New Mexico—Alamagordo Border Patrol, 1997 Hwy. 54 S., Alamagordo, NM 88310-7377. Phone: (505)437-6960.

- 517 Gold Ave. SW - Rm.1010, P.O. Box 567, Albuquerque, NM 87103. Phone: (505)766-2690.
- Columbus Port of Entry, Pershing Rd. - P.O. Box 307, Columbus, NM 88029. Phones: (505)531-2694, -2695, -2696.
- Deming Border Patrol, P.O. Box 230, Deming, NM 88031. Phone: (505)546-9036.
- Las Cruces Border Patrol, 3120 N. Main, Las Cruces, NM 88001. Phone: (505)527-6895.
- Las Cruces Patrol Training Center, 2320 Temple St., Las Cruces, NM 88001. Phone: (505)524-4730.
- Lordsburg Border Patrol, 441 Duncan Hwy., P.O. Box 459, Lordsburg, NM 88045. Phone: (505)542-3221.
- Truth or Consequences Border Patrol, P.O. Box 72, Truth or Consequences, NM 87901. Phone: (505)744-5235.

New York—Albany Sub-Office, U.S. Post Office and Customhouse - Rm.220, 445 Broadway, Albany, NY 12207. Phone: (518)431-0320.

- Thousand Island Bridge and Cape Vincent Ports of Entry, 46735 U.S. Interstate Rt. 81, Alexandria Bay, NY 13607-9796. Phones: (315)482-2681, -2065, 654-2781.
- Buffalo District Office, 130 Delaware Ave., Buffalo, NY 14202. Phone: (716)846-4741.
- Burke Border Patrol, Burke, NY 12917-0125. Phone: (518)483-5941.
- Champlain Port of Entry, Border Inspection Station, 234 W. Service Rd., Champlain, NY 12919. Phones: (518)298-3221, -8433, -2526.
- Champlain Border Patrol, P.O. Box 1228, Ridge Rd., Champlain, NY 12919. Phone: (518)298-2531.
- Chateaugay Port of Entry, Border Inspection Station, Star Rt. 374, Chateaugay, NY 12920. Phone: (518)497-6772.

- Trout River Port of Entry, State Rt. 30, Via Constable, NY 12926. Phone: (518)483-5021.
- Ft. Covington Port of Entry, Border Inspection Station, Water St., Ft. Covington, NY 12937. Phone: (518)358-2231.
- Fulton Border Patrol Station, 215 S. 1st St. - Rm.228, Fulton, NY 13069-0070. Phone: (315)598-8510.
- Office of Inspector General, JFK Airport Station, P.O. Box 999, Jamaica, NY 11430. Phone: (718)553-7520.
- JFK International Airport, Bldg. 50 - International Arrivals, Jamaica, NY 11430. Phones: (718)553-1688, -1689.
- Lewiston Port of Entry, 1 Lewiston Queenston Bridge, Lewiston, NY 14092-1980. Phone: (716)285-1676.
- Mooers Port of Entry, Border Inspection Station, State Rt. 22, Mooers, NY 12958. Phone: (518)236-7116.
- New York District Office, 26 Federal Plaza, New York, NY 10278. Phone: (212)264-5942.
- Service Processing Center, 201 Varrick St. - 4th fl., New York, NY 10014. Phone: (212)620-3441.
- Niagara Falls Port of Entry, Rainbow Bridge, Niagara Falls, NY 14303. Phone: (716)282-3141.
- Niagara Falls Border Patrol, 1708 Lafayette Ave., Niagara Falls, NY 14305-0281. Phone: (716)285-6444.
- Ogdensburg Border Patrol, 127 N. Water St., Ogdensburg, NY 13669. Phones: (315)393-1150, -0100.
- Massena Port of Entry, P.O. Box 195, Roosevelt, NY 13683. Phones: (315)764-0310, -0677.
- Rouse Point Port of Entry, U.S. Rt. 9B, Rouse Point, NY 12979. Phone: (518)297-7521.
- Buffalo Border Patrol Sector Hdqtrs., 231 Grand Island Blvd., Tonawanda, NY 14150-6502. Phones: (716)551-4101.
- Watertown Border Patrol, Post Office Bldg., 153 Arsenal St., Watertown, NY 13601-0280. Phone: (315)482-7556.

North Carolina—Charlotte Sub-Office, 6 Woodlawn Green - Rm.138, Charlotte, NC 28217. Phone: (704)344-6313.
- Raleigh-Durham International Port of Entry, P.O. Box 80216, Raleigh, NC 27623. Phone: (919)840-5577.
- Wilmington Port of Entry, Lennon Federal Bldg. - Rm.105, 2 Princess St., Wilmington, NC 28401. Phone: (910)343-4876.

North Dakota—Ambrose Port of Entry, State Hwy 42, Rt. HC-1 - Box 202, Ambrose, ND 58833. Phone: (701)982-3211.
- Antler Port of Entry, Rural Rt. 1 - Box 7, Antler, ND 58711. Phone: (701)267-3321.
- Bottineau Border Patrol, P.O. Box 6, Bottineau, ND 58318. Phone: (701)228-3179.
- Carbury Port of Entry, Rural Rt. 1 - Souris, ND, Carbury, ND 58783. Phone: (701)228-2540.
- Dunseith Port of Entry, Rural Rt. 1 - Box 117, Dunseith, ND 58329. Phones: (701)263-4513, -4460.
- Northgate Port of Entry, Flaxton, ND 58737. Phone: (701)596-3805.
- Fortuna Port of Entry, Hwy. 85N - P.O. Box 37, Fortuna, ND 58844. Phone: (701) 834-2493.
- Grand Forks Border Patrol Sector Hdqtrs., 2320 S. Washington St., P.O. Box 12669, Grand Forks, ND 52801. Phone: (701)775-6259.
- Grand Forks International Airport, Rural Rt. 2 - Box 72, 2787 Airport Dr., Hwy. 2 W., Grand Forks, ND 58203. Phone: (701)772-3301.
- Hannah Port of Entry, Hannah, ND 58239. Phone: (701)283-5271.

16.400
(cont.)

- Hansboro Port of Entry, Box 237, Hansboro, ND 58339. Phone: (701)266-5633.
- Maida Port of Entry, Hwy. 1, Maida, ND 58255. Phone: (701)256-5087.
- Neche Port of Entry, Hwy. 18, Neche, ND 58265. Phone: (701)886-7744.
- Noonan Port of Entry, Noonan, ND 58765. Phone: (701)926-5615.
- Pembina Port Of Entry, Rural Rt. 1 - P.O. Box 110, Noyes, Pembina, ND 58271. Phone: (701)825-6722.
- Portal Border Patrol, P.O. Box 298, Portal, ND 58772. Phone: (701)926-4111.
- Portal Port of Entry, P.O. Box 8, Portal, ND 58772. Phone: (701)926-4221.
- Sherwood Port of Entry, Rural Rt. 2 - Box 1D, Sherwood, ND 58782. Phone: (701)459-2250.
- St. John Port of Entry, Box 15 - Rt. 1, St. John, ND 58369. Phone: (701)447-3140.
- P.O. Box 67 - Rt. 1, 6 miles from Village of Sarles, ND 58372. Phone: (701)697-5177.
- Walhalla Port of Entry, Rural Rt. 2 - Box 145, Walhalla, ND 58282-9459. Phone: (701)549-3233.

Ohio—Cleveland District Office, Celebreeze Federal Bldg. - Rm.1917, 1240 E. 9th St., Cleveland, OH 44199. Phone: (216)522-4766.

- Toledo Port of Entry, Federal Office Bldg. - Rm.713, 234 Summit St., Toledo, OH 43604-1536. Phone: (419)259-6474.

Oklahoma—4149 Highline Blvd. - Ste.300, Oklahoma City, OK 73108. Phone: (405) 231-5928.

Oregon—Astoria Port of Entry, P.O. Box 236, Astoria, OR 97103. Phone: (503)325-3054.

- Coos Bay Port of Entry, P.O. Box 209, Coos Bay, OR 97420. Phone: (503)242-4785.
- Portland District Office, 511 NW Broadway, Portland, OR 97209. Phone: (503)326-3962.
- Portland International Airport, P.O. Box 55067, Portland, OR 97238-5067. Phone (503)326-3409.
- Roseburg Border Patrol, 1036 SE Douglas, P.O. Box 1728, Roseburg, OR 97470. Phone: (503)440-4518.

Pennsylvania—Philadelphia District Office, 1600 Callowhill St., Philadelphia, PA 19130. Phone: (215)656-7150.

- Pittsburg Sub-Office, 2130 Federal Bldg., 1000 Liberty Ave., Pittsburgh, PA 15222. Phone; (412)644-3360.

Puerto Rico—Aquadilla Service Processing Center, P.O. Box 250480, Aquadilla, PR 00604-0408. Phones: (787)882-3565, -3567, -3568.

- Deferred Inspections, U.S. Federal Bldg. - Rm.380, Chardon St., Hato Rey, PR 00918. Phone: (809)766-5000.
- District Director's Office, New Federal Bldg. - 3rd fl., Carlos Chardon St., Hato Rey, PR 00918. Phone: (no number provided).
- San Juan International Airport, P.O. Box 37900, Isle Verde, PR 00937-0900. Phone: (809)253-4525.
- Mayaguez Port of Entry, Marina Station, Mayaguez, PR 00709-2990. Phone: (809) 831-3440.
- Ponce Port of Entry, Playa Station, P.O. Box 173, Ponce, PR 00734-3173. Phone: (809)843-3220.
- P.O. Box 365068, San Juan, PR 00936. Phones: (809)766-5329, -5380.

Rhode Island—Providence Sub-Office, Federal Bldg., 200 Dyer St., Providence, RI 02903-3993. Phone: (401)528-5528.

South Carolina—Charleston Port of Entry, Federal Bldg. - Rm.110, 334 Meeting St., Charleston, SC 29403. Phone: (803)727-4421.

Tennessee—245 Wagner Place - Ste.250, Memphis, TN 38103-3815. Phone: (901)544-4108.

Texas—Abilene Border Patrol, 555 Walnut St., Abilene, TX 79604-3076. Phone: (915) 673-3010.

- Alpine Border Patrol, P.O. Box 958, Alpine, TX 79831. Phone: (915)837-3550.
- Amarillo Border Patrol, P.O. Box 2887, Amarillo, TX 79105. Phone: (806)324-2278.
- Austin Sub-Office, 3708 S. 2nd St., P.O. Box 6496, Austin, TX 78704. Phones: (512)482-7901, -7904.
- Big Bend Peak Border Patrol, Big Bend, TX 79834-0067. Phone: (915)477-2287.
- Brackettville Border Patrol, 802 W. Spring St., P.O. Box 216, Brackettville, TX 78832. Phones: (830)563-2477.
- Brownsville Port of Entry, 1500 E. Elizabeth St. - Rm.203, Brownsville, TX 78520. Phone: (210)546-1675.
- Brownsville International Airport, Brownsville, TX 78520. Phone: (210)542-8296.
- Brownsville Border Patrol, P.O. Box 5076, Brownsville, TX 78520. Phone: (956)542-3585.
- Carrizo Springs Border Patrol, Hwy. 85 E., P.O. Box 194, Carrizo Springs, TX 78834. Phone: (830)876-3557.
- Corpus Christi Border Patrol, 6809 Leopard St., P.O. Box 10344, Corpus Christi, TX 78460-0344. Phone: (512)289-0552.
- Comstock Border Patrol, Hwy. 85 W. - P.O. Box 700, Comstock, TX 78837. Phones: (915)292-4450, -4680.
- Cotulla Border Patrol, 602 N. Main, Cotulla, TX 78014. Phone: (830)879-3051.
- Dallas District Office, 8101 N. Stemmons Freeway, Dallas, TX 75247. Phone: (214)655-3011.
- Dallas/Ft. Worth Port of Entry, P.O. Box 610365, Dallas-Ft. Worth, TX 75261. Phone: (214)574-2141.
- Del Rio Border Patrol Sector Hdqtrs. and Border Station, Qualia Dr. - P.O. Box 2020, Del Rio, TX 78841-2020. Phones: (210)703-2100.
- Amistad Dam Port of Entry, Del Rio, TX 78841-4060. Phone: (210)775-7213.
- Eagle Pass Port of Entry, International Bridge, P.O. Box 4280, Eagle Pass, TX 78852. Phones: (210)773-9205, -9206.
- El Paso District Office, 1545 Hawkins - Ste.167, El Paso, TX 79925. Phones: (915)540-1700, -1701.
- Processing Center, 8915 Montana Ave., El Paso, TX 79925. Phone: (915)540-7343.
- Office of Inspector General, 3 Butterfield Trail Blvd. - Ste.120, El Paso, TX 79906. Phone: (915)534-7370.
- El Paso Border Patrol Sector Hdqtrs., 8901 Montana Ave., P.O. Box 9578, El Paso, TX 79986. Phone: (915)540-7850.
- Intelligence Center, 11339 SSG Sims St., El Paso, TX 79908-8098. Phone: (915)564-2031.
- El Paso Port of Entry, Paso Del Norte Bridge, El Paso, TX 79901. Phone: (915)534-6767.
- Yselta Station, P.O. Box 9398, El Paso, TX 79917. Phone: (915)540-3130.
- Yselta Border Patrol, Yselta Station, 12245 Pine Springs Dr., El Paso, TX 79936. Phones: (915)859-6454, -6380.
- Dallas Border Patrol, 2800 S. Pipeline Rd., Euless, TX 79604. Phone: (817)540-0150.
- Fabens Border Patrol and Port of Entry, 802 E. Main, P.O. Box 908, Fabens, TX 79838. Phones: (915)764-2417, -2419.
- Falfurrias Border Patrol, P.O. Box 479, Falfurrias, TX 78355. Phone: (512)325-5616.
- Ft. Hancock Border Patrol, P.O. Box 218, Ft. Hancock, TX 79839. Phone: (915)769-3978.
- Ft. Hancock Port of Entry, P.O. Box 235, Ft. Hancock, TX 79839. Phone: (915)769-3810.

16.400
(cont.)

- Ft. Stockton Border Patrol, P.O. Box 607, Ft. Stockton, TX 79735. Phone: (915)336-2468.

- Freer Border Patrol, P.O. Box "W", Freer, TX 78357. Phone: (512)394-7613.

- Galveston Port of Entry, P.O. Box 388, Galveston, TX 77550. Phone: (409)766-3581.

- Harlingen District Office, 2102 Teege Rd., Harlingen, TX 78550. Phone: (210)427-8691.

- Harlingen Border Patrol, 901 Rangerville Rd., P.O. Box 642, Harlingen, TX 78551. Phone: (956)427-8511.

- Hebbronville Border Patrol, 802 N. Sigrid St., Hebbronville, TX 78361. Phone: (512)527-3256.

- Pharr Port of Entry, c/o Hidalgo POE, International Bridge St., Hidalgo, TX 78557. Phones: (210)783-4739, -4758.

- Hidalgo Port of Entry, International Bridge, Hidalgo, TX 78557-3019. Phones: (210)843-2201, -2202.

- Houston International Airport, P.O. Box 60457, Houston, TX 77205. Phone: (713) 233-3700.

- Kingsville Border Patrol, Navel Air Station - Bldg.3731, Kingsville, TX 78363. Phone: (512)592-3284.

- Laredo Border Patrol Sector Hdqtrs., 207 W. Del Mar Blvd., Laredo, TX 78041. Phone: (210)723-4367.

- Laredo South Border Patrol Station, Rural Rt. 3 - P.O. Box USBP-SLS/L, Laredo, TX 78043. Phones: (210)727-0644.

- Administrative Offices - Bldg. 2, 700 Zaragoza St., P.O. Box 179, Laredo, TX 78042-0179. Phone: (210)722-3283.

- Juerz-Lincoln International Bridge 2, Bldg. 3 - 700 Zaragoza St., Laredo, TX 78042. Phone: (210)722-5440.

- Gateway to the Americas International Bridge 1, 100 Convent St., Laredo, TX 78040. Phone: (210)722-2484.

- Llano Border Patrol, 211 E. Tarrant, P.O. Box 134, Llano, TX 78643. Phone: (915)247-4912.

- Los Ebanos Port of Entry, International Ferry, P.O. Box 399, Los Ebanos, TX 78565. Phone: (512)485-2721.

- Port Isabel Service Processing Center, Rt. 3 - Box 341, Los Fresnos, TX 78566. Phone: (210)233-4431.

- Port Isabel Border Patrol, Rt. 3 - Box 340, Los Fresnos, TX 78566. Phone: (210)233-9554.

- Port Isabel Port of Entry, Alien Processing Center (PIC), Rt. 3 - Box 341, Buena Vista Rd., Los Fresnos, TX 78566. Phone: (210)233-4431.

- Lubbock Border Patrol, 1205 Texas Ave., P.O. Box 1632, Lubbock, TX 79408. Phones: (806)742-7355.

- Marfa Border Patrol Sector Hdqtrs., 300 Madrid St., P.O. Box 1, Marfa, TX 79843. Phone: (915)729-4353.

- McAllen Border Patrol Sector Hdqtrs., 2301 S. Main St., McAllen, TX 78503. Phone: (210)686-5496.

- McAllen Border Patrol, 4201 W. Military Hwy., McAllen, TX 78503. Phone: (210) 618-8163.

- Mercedes Border Patrol, 623 International Blvd., P.O. Box 125, Mercedes, TX 78570. Phone: (956)968-0602.

- Mercedes Border Patrol Station, P.O. Box 60405, Midland, TX 79711. Phone: (915)561-8911.

- Presidio Border Patrol, P.O. Box 929, Presidio, TX 79845. Phone: (915)229-3330.

- Presidio Port of Entry, International Bridge, P.O. Box 937, Presidio, TX 79845. Phones: (915)229-3265, -3663.

- Port Arthur Port of Entry, 4550 Jimmy Johnson Blvd. - Ste.3, Port Arthur, TX 77642. Phone: (409)727-3375.
- Port Arthur Port of Entry, 2875 75th St. - Rm.106, Port Arthur, TX 77640. Phone: (409)727-3375.
- Rio Grande City Border Patrol, 233 E. Hwy., P.O. Box 481, Rio Grande City, TX 78582. Phone: (956)487-2700.
- Rocksprings Border Patrol, 404 W. Austin, P.O. Box 576, Rocksprings, TX 78880. Phone: (830)683-2255.
- Falcon Heights Port of Entry, International Dam, P.O. Box 278, Roma, TX 78584. Phone: (210)848-5221.
- Rio Grande City Port of Entry, International Bridge, P.O. Box 278, Roma, TX 78584. Phones: (210)487-2200, 849-1676.
- San Angelo Border Patrol, P.O. Box 61106, San Angelo, TX 76906. Phone: (915)949-0139.
- San Antonio District Office, 8940 Four Winds Dr., San Antonio, TX 78239. Phone: (210)871-7000.
- San Antonio Border Patrol, 5000 Industrial Dr., San Antonio, TX 78268. Phones: (210)521-7926.
- San Antonio International Airport, 9800 Airport Blvd., Terminal 1, San Antonio, TX 78216. Phone: (210)826-6261.
- Sanderson Border Patrol, P.O. Box 628, Sanderson, TX 78268. Phone: (915)345-2972.
- Uvalde Border Patrol, Industrial Park #30, Uvalde, TX 78801. Phone: (830)278-7133.
- Van Horn Border Patrol, 700 NW Access Rd., P.O. Box 368, Van Horn, TX 79854. Phone: (915)283-2795.
- Pregreso Port of Entry, International Bridge Rt. 2, Box 600, Westlaco, TX 78596. Phone: (210)565-6304.
- Zapata Border Patrol, Lot C-2015, U.S. Hwy. 83 S., Zapata, TX 78076-0685. Phone: (210)765-6395

Utah—5272 S. College Dr. - Ste.100, Salt Lake City, UT 84123. Phone: (801)265-8807.

Vermont—Alburg Springs Port of Entry, Rural Rt. 2, Alburg, VT 05440. Phone: (802)796-3704.

- Alburg Port of Entry, U.S. Border Station, State Rt. 225, Alburg, VT 05440. Phone: (802)796-3703.
- Beebe Plain Port of Entry, Beebe Plain, VT 05823. Phone: (802)873-3151.
- Beecher Falls Border Patrol, P.O. Box 215, Beecher Falls, VT 05902. Phones: (802)266-3035.
- Beecher Falls Port of Entry, Border Inspection, Route 102, Beecher Falls VT 05902. Phone: (802)266-3320.
- Canaan Port of Entry, Border Inspection Station, State Rt. 114, P.O. Box 129, Canaan, VT 05903. Phone: (802)266-8994.
- Derby Line Port of Entry, Rt. 91 - P.O. Box 367, Derby Line, VT 05830. Phone: (802)873-3316.
- East Richford Port of Entry, RFD 1 - P.O. Box 1690, East Richford, VT 05476. Phone: (802)848-3001.
- West Berkshire Port of Entry, RFD 1 - Box 1110, Enosburg Falls, VT 05450. Phone: (802)933-2301.
- Morses Lane Port of Entry, RFD 1, Morses Lane, VT 05457. Phone: (802)285-2214.
- Newport Border Patrol, P.O. Box 815, Newport, VT 05855. Phone: (802)334-6722.
- North Troy Port of Entry, State Rt. 105, North Troy, VT 05859. Phone: (802)988-2633.
- Norton Port of Entry, Border Inspection Station, State Rt. 114, P.O. Box 117, Norton, VT 05907. Phone: (802)822-5222.

16.400
(cont.)
- Richford Border Patrol, Main St., P.O. Box 67, Richford, VT 05476. Phone: (802)848-7713.
- Pinnacle Port of Entry, R.D. 1 - Box 300, Richford, VT 05476. Phone: (802)848-3319.
- Richford Port of Entry, Border Inspection Station, RFD 1 - Box 40, Richford, VT 05476. Phone: (802)848-7766.
- Eastern Region Operations and Administrative Center, 70 Kimball Ave., South Burlington, VT 05403-6813. Phone: (802)660-1111, 951-5000.
- St. Albans Sub-Office, Federal Bldg., P.O. Box 328, St. Albans, VT 05478. Phone: (802)527-3191.
- Eastern Service Center, 75 Lower Welden St., St. Albans, VT 05479-0001. Phone: (802)527-3100.
- Swanton Border Patrol Sector Hdqtrs., Grand Ave., P.O. Box 705, Swanton, VT 05488. Phone: (802)868-3361.
- Highgate Springs Port of Entry, Border Inspection Station, U.S. Rt. 7, RFD Swanton, VT 05488. Phone: (802)868-3349.
- Swanton Border Patrol Station, Rt. 78 - P.O. Box 209, Swanton, VT 05488. Phone: (802)868-3229, -3320 (24 hours).
- Eastern Form Center, Williston, VT 05495-0567. Phone: (802)951-6225.

Virgin Islands—Federal District Court Bldg., P.O. Box 610, Charlotte Amalie, St. Thomas, VI 00801. Phone: (809)774-1390.
- Christiansted Port of Entry, P.O. Box 1270 Kingshill, Christiansted, St. Croix, VI 00851. Phones: (809)778-6559, -6300.
- Cruz Bay Port of Entry, P.O. Box 27, St. John, VI 00831. Phone: (809)776-1390.

Virginia—Washington District Office, 4420 N. Fairfax Dr., Arlington, VA 22203. Phone: (202)307-1504.
- Norfolk Federal Bldg. - Rm.439, 200 Granby Mall, Norfolk, VA 23510-1882. Phone: (804)441-3095.

Washington—2745 McLeod Rd., Bellingham, WA 98225. Phone: (360)733-8420.
- Bellingham Border Patrol Sector Hdqtrs., 104 W. Magnolia and Cornall St. - Rm.207, P.O. Box 2055, Bellingham, WA 98227. Phone: (360)676-8411.
- Blaine Border Patrol Sector Hdqtrs., 1590 H St., P.O. Box 3529, Blaine, WA 98231. Phones: (360)332-7707, -7919.
- Blaine Border Patrol, 1580 H St., P.O. Box 3529, Blaine, WA 98231. Phone: (360)332-4205.
- Pacific Hwy. Port of Entry, 9950 Pacific Hwy., Blaine, WA 98230. Phones: (360)332-6091, -7237.
- Blaine Port of Entry, Peace Arch POE, P.O. Box 3749, Blaine, WA 98230. Phone: (360)332-8511.
- Colville Border Patrol, 209 E. Juniper Ave., P.O. Box 146, Colville, WA 99114. Phone: (509)684-6272.
- Boundary Port of Entry, 5338 N. Port Juanita Rd., Colville, WA 99114. Phone: (509)732-6674.
- Ferry Port of Entry, 3559 Toroda Customs Bridge Rd., Curlew, WA 99118-9715. Phone: (509)779-4655.
- 3184 Hwy. 21 N., Rt. 21 - P.O. Box 28, Danville, WA 99121-9701. Phone: (509)779-4862.
- Friday Harbor Port of Entry, 202 Front St. N., P.O. Box 1907, Friday Harbor, WA 98250. Phone: (206)378-2080.
- Laurier Port of Entry, Hwy. 395 - P.O. Box 40, Laurier, WA 99146. Phone: (509)684-2100.
- Longview Port of Entry, P.O. Box 1027, Longview, WA 98632. Phone: (206)423-5550.
- Nighthawle Port of Entry, Star Rt., Loomis, WA 98827. Phone: (509)476-2125.

- Lynden Border Patrol, 8334 Guide Meridian Rd., P.O. Box 708, Lynden, WA 98264. Phone: (360)354-4118.
- Lynden Port of Entry, 9949 Guide Meridian Rd., Lynden, WA 98264. Phone: (360) 354-6661.
- Metaline Falls Port of Entry, P.O. Box 631, Metaline Falls, WA 99153. Phone: (509)446-2572.
- Frontier Port of Entry, 4939 Hwy. 25 N., Northport, WA 99157. Phone: (509)732-4418.
- Oroville Port of Entry, Rt. 1 - Box 130, Oroville, WA 98844. Phones: (509)476-2454, -3132.
- Oroville Border Patrol, 1105 Main St., P.O. Box 99, Oroville, WA 98844-9726. Phone: (509)476-3622.
- Vancouver-BC Canada, Point Roberts, WA 98281-0450. Phones: (604)278-3360, -3986, -2520.
- Port Angeles Border Patrol, 138 W. 1st St., Port Angeles, WA 98362. Phone: (360) 452-5970.
- Port Townsend Port of Entry, 1322 Washington, P.O. Box 951, Port Townsend, WA 98368-0004. Phone: (360)385-3777.
- Seattle District Office and Sea Inspections, 815 Airport Way S., Seattle, WA 98134. Phones: (206)553-1246, -0070.
- Seattle-Tacoma International Airport, S. 178 and Pacific Hwy., Seattle, WA 98158. Phones: (206)553-0466, -2299.
- Spokane Airport, 691 U.S. Courthouse Bldg., Spokane, WA 99201. Phone: (509)353-2761, -4699.
- Spokane Border Patrol, N. 10710 Newport Hwy., Spokane, WA 99218. Phone: (no number provided).
- Sumas Port of Entry, 109 Cherry St., P.O. Box 99, Sumas, WA 98295. Phone: (360)988-4781.
- Tacoma Port of Entry, 3600 Port Tacoma Rd. - Ste.303, P.O. Box 1296, Tacoma, WA 98401. Phone: (206)922-0848.
- Wenatchee Border Patrol, McQuaig Bldg., 93 Eastmont, P.O. Box 1825, Wenatchee, WA 98807. Phone: (509)884-8893.
- Yakima Port of Entry, 417 E. Chestnut, P.O. Box 49, Yakima, WA 98907. Phone: (509)575-5944.

Wisconsin—Federal Bldg. - Rm.186, 517 E. Wisconsin Ave., Milwaukee, WI 53202. Phone: (414)297-3161.

NATIONAL INSTITUTE OF CORRECTIONS

16.601 thru 16.603   NIC Academy, 1960 Industrial Circle - Ste.A, Longmont, CO 80501. Phones: (303)682-0382, (800)995-6429; FAX (303)682-0469.

DEPARTMENT OF LABOR

BUREAU OF LABOR STATISTICS

17.002 thru 17.006   ## REGIONAL OFFICES

REGION I *(Connecticut, Maine, Massachusetts, New Hampshire, Rhode Island, Vermont)*—JFK Federal Bldg. - E310, Boston, MA 02203. Phone: (617)565-2324.

17.002
thru
17.006
(cont.)

REGION II *(Canal Zone, New Jersey, New York, Puerto Rico, Virgin Islands)*—201 Varick St. - Rm.808, New York, NY 10014-4811. Phone: (212)337-2410.

REGION III *(Delaware, District of Columbia, Maryland, Pennsylvania, Virginia, West Virginia)*—Gateway Bldg. - Rm.8000, 3535 Market St., Philadelphia, PA 19104-3309. Phone: (215)596-1157 *(Public Information)*.

REGION IV *(Alabama, Florida, Georgia, Kentucky, Mississippi, North Carolina, South Carolina, Tennessee)*—AFC - Rm.7T50, 61 Forsyth St. SW, Atlanta, GA 30303. Phone: (404)562-2466.

REGION V *(Illinois, Indiana, Michigan, Minnesota, Ohio, Wisconsin)*—Federal Office Bldg. - 9th fl., 230 S. Dearborn St., Chicago, IL 60604-1595. Phone: (312)353-7200, ext.229.

REGION VI *(Arkansas, Louisiana, New Mexico, Oklahoma, Texas)*—A. Maceo Federal Bldg. - Ste.221, 525 Griffin St., Dallas, TX 75202-5028. Phone: (214)767-9379.

REGIONS VII and VIII *(Colorado, Iowa, Kansas, Missouri, Montana, Nebraska, North Dakota, South Dakota, Utah, Wyoming)*—City Center Square - Ste.600, 1100 Main St., Kansas City, MO 64105-2112. Phone: (816)426-3176.

REGIONS IX and X *(Alaska, American Samoa, Arizona, California, Guam, Hawaii, Idaho, Nevada, Oregon, Washington, Trust Territory of the Pacific Islands)*—71 Stevenson St. - 6th fl., San Francisco, CA 94105. *For mail:* San Francisco, CA 94119-3766. Phone: (415)975-4403.

OFFICE OF LABOR-MANAGEMENT STANDARDS

17.140   ## FIELD OFFICES

California—3660 Wilshire Blvd. - Ste.708, Los Angeles, CA 90010. Phone: (213)252-7508.

▪ 71 Stevenson Pl. - Ste.725, San Francisco, CA 94105. Phone: (415)975-4020.

Colorado—1801 California St. - Ste.940, Denver, CO 80202-2614. Phone: (303)844-1261.

Connecticut—2 Whitney Ave. - Ste.301, New Haven, CT 06510. Phone: (203)773-2130.

District of Columbia—Riddell Bldg. - Ste.558, 1730 K St. NW, Washington, DC 20006. Phone: (202)254-6510.

Florida—Washington Square Bldg. - Ste.503, 111 NW 183rd St. Miami, FL 33169. Phone: (305)653-7414.

Georgia—61 Forsyth St. SW - Rm.8B85, Atlanta, GA 30303. Phone: (404)562-2083.

Illinois—Federal Office Bldg. - Ste.774, 230 S. Dearborn St., Chicago, IL 60604. Phone: (312)353-7264.

Louisiana—701 Loyola Ave. - Ste.13009, New Orleans, LA 70113. Phone: (504)589-6174.

Massachusetts—JFK Federal Bldg. - Rm.E-365, Boston, MA 02203. Phone: (617)565-9880.

Michigan—211 W. Fort St. - Ste.1313, Detroit, MI 48226. Phone: (313)226-6200.

Missouri—1222 Spruce St. - Ste.9.109E, St. Louis, MO 63103. Phone: (314)539-2667.

New York—Federal Bldg. - Ste.1310, 111 W. Huron St., Buffalo, NY 14202. Phone: (716)551-4976.

▪ 201 Varick St. - Ste.878,, New York, NY 10014. Phone: (212)337-2580.

Ohio—525 Vine St. - Ste.950, Cincinnati, OH 45202. Phone: (513)684-6840.

▪ Federal Office Bldg. - Ste.831, 1240 E. 9th St., Cleveland, OH 44199. Phone: (216)522-3855.

Pennsylvania—Green Federal Bldg. - Rm.415, 801 Arch St., Philadelphia, PA 19107. Phone: (215)597-4960.

- Federal Office Bldg. - Ste.801, 1000 Liberty Ave., Pittsburgh, PA 15222. Phone: (412)395-6925.

Tennessee—233 Cumberland Bend Dr. - Ste.238, Nashville, TN 37228. Phone: (615) 736-5906.

Texas—525 Griffin Square Bldg. - Ste.300, Griffin and Young St., Dallas, TX 75202. Phone: (214)767-6834.

Washington—Federal Office Bldg. - Ste.880, 1111 3rd Ave., Seattle, WA 98101-3212. Phone: (206)553-5216.

Wisconsin—517 E. Wisconsin Ave. - Ste.118, Milwaukee, WI 53202-4504. Phone: (414)297-1501.

PENSION AND WELFARE BENEFITS ADMINISTRATION

17.150   **FIELD OFFICES**

California—790 E. Colorado Blvd. - Ste.514, Pasadena, CA 91101. Phones: (818)583-7862; FAX (818)583-7845.

- 71 Stevenson St. - Ste.915, San Francisco, CA 94119-0250. Phones: (415)975-4600; FAX (415)975-4588.

District of Columbia—Riddell Bldg. - Rm.556, 1730 K St. NW, Washington, DC 20006. Phones: (202)254-7013; FAX (202)254-3378.

Florida—Bldg. H - Site 104, 8040 Peters Rd., Plantation, FL 33324. Phones: (954)424-4022; FAX (954)424-0548.

Georgia—61 Forsyth St. - Ste.7B54, Atlanta, GA 30303. Phones: (404)562-2156; FAX (404)562-2168.

Illinois—200 W. Adams St. - Ste.1600, Chicago, IL 60606. Phones: (312)353-0900; FAX (312)353-1023.

Kentucky—Ft. Wright Executive Bldg. - Ste.210, 1885 Dixie Hwy., Ft. Wright, KY 41011-2664. Phones: (606)578-4680; FAX (606)578-4688.

Massachusetts—JFK Bldg. - Rm.575, Boston, MA 02203. Phones: (617)565-9600; FAX (617)565-9666.

Michigan—211 W. Fort St. - Ste.1310, Detroit, MI 48226-3211. Phones: (313)226-7450; FAX (313)226-4257.

Missouri—City Center Square - Ste.1200, 1100 Main St., Kansas City, MO 64105-2112. Phones: (816)426-5131; FAX (816)426-5511.

- 815 Olive St. - Rm.338, St. Louis, MO 63101-1559. Phones: (314)539-2691; FAX (314)539-2697.

New York—US Custom House, 6 World Trade Center - Rm.625, New York, NY 10048. Phones: (212)637-6000; FAX (212)637-0512.

Pennsylvania—Gateway Bldg. - Rm.12400, 3535 Market St., Philadelphia, PA 19104-5025. Phones: (215)596-1134; FAX (215)596-4475.

Texas—Federal Office Bldg. - Rm.707, 525 Griffin St., Dallas, TX 75202-5025. Phones: (214)767-6831; FAX (214)767-1055.

Washington—Midcom Tower - Rm.860, 1111 3rd St., Seattle, WA 98101-3212. Phones: (206)553-4244; FAX (206)553-0913.

EMPLOYMENT AND TRAINING ADMINISTRATION

BUREAU OF APPRENTICESHIP AND TRAINING (BAT)

17.201   **REGIONAL OFFICES**

REGION I *(Connecticut, Maine, Massachusetts, New Hampshire, Rhode Island, Ver-*

17.201   *mont)*—JFK Federal Bldg. - Rm.E-370, Boston, MA 02203. Phones: (617)565-2288;
(cont.)   FAX (617)565-9171.

REGION II *(New Jersey, New York, Puerto Rico, Virgin Islands)*—201 Varick St. -
Rm.602, New York, NY 10014. Phones: (212)337-2313; FAX (212)337-2317.

REGION III *(Delaware, Maryland, Pennsylvania, Virginia, West Virginia)*—3535
Market St. - Rm.13240, Philadelphia, PA 19104. Phones: (215)596-6417; FAX
(215)596-0192.

REGION IV *(Alabama, Florida, Georgia, Kentucky, Mississippi, North Carolina, South
Carolina, Tennessee)*—61 Forsyth St. NW - Rm.6T71, Atlanta, GA 30303. Phones:
(404)562-2335; FAX (404)562-2329.

REGION V *(Illinois, Indiana, Michigan, Minnesota, Ohio, Wisconsin)*—230 S. Dearborn St. - Rm.708, Chicago, IL 60604. Phones: (312)353-7205; FAX (312)353-5506.

REGION VI *(Arkansas, Louisiana, New Mexico, Oklahoma, Texas)*—Federal Bldg. -
Rm.311, 525 Griffin St. Dallas, TX 75202. Phones: (214)767-4993; FAX (214)767-
4995.

REGION VII *(Iowa, Kansas, Missouri, Nebraska)*—1100 Main St. - Ste.1040, Kansas
City, MO 64105-2112. Phones: (816)426-3856; FAX (816)426-3664.

REGION VIII *(Colorado, Montana, North Dakota, South Dakota, Utah, Wyoming)*—
U.S. Custom House - Rm.465, 721 19th St., Denver, CO 80202. Phones: (303)844-
4791; FAX (303)844-4701.

REGION IX *(Arizona, California, Hawaii, Nevada)*—Federal Bldg. - Rm.815, 71
Stevenson St., San Francisco, CA 94105. Phones: (415)975-4007; FAX (415)975-
4010.

REGION X *(Alaska, Idaho, Oregon, Washington)*—1111 3rd Ave. - Rm.925, Seattle,
WA 98101-3212. Phones: (206)553-5286; FAX (206)553-1689.

17.203   ## ETA REGIONAL OFFICES
thru
17.257   *Contact the nearest office of the state employment service in your area, or the appropriate regional office following:*

REGION I *(Connecticut, Maine, Massachusetts, New Hampshire, Rhode Island, Vermont)*—JFK Federal Bldg. - Rm.E-350, Boston, MA 02203. Phones: (617)565-3630;
FAX (617)565-2229.

REGION II *(Canal Zone, New Jersey, New York, Puerto Rico, Virgin Islands)*—201
Varick St. - Rm.755, New York, NY 10014. Phones: (212)337-2139; FAX (212)337-
2144.

REGION III *(Delaware, District of Columbia, Maryland, Pennsylvania, Virginia, West
Virginia)*—P.O. Box 8796, Philadelphia, PA 19104. Phones: (215)596-6336; FAX
(215)596-0329.

REGION IV *(Alabama, Florida, Georgia, Kentucky, Mississippi, North Carolina, South
Carolina, Tennessee)*—Atlanta Federal Center - Rm.6M12, 61 Forsyth St. SW,
Atlanta, GA 30303. Phones: (404)562-2092; FAX (404)562-2149.

REGION V *(Illinois, Indiana, Michigan, Minnesota, Ohio, Wisconsin)*—230 S. Dearborn St. - Rm.628, Chicago, IL 60604. Phones: (312)353-0313; FAX (312)353-4474.

REGION VI *(Arkansas, Louisiana, New Mexico, Oklahoma, Texas)*—525 Griffin St. -
Rm.317, Dallas, TX 75202. Phones: (214)767-8263; FAX (214)767-5113.

REGION VII *(Iowa, Kansas, Missouri, Nebraska)*—City Center Square - Ste.1050,
1100 Main St., Kansas City, MO 64105. Phones: (816)426-3796; FAX (816)426-
2729.

REGION VIII *(Colorado, Montana, North Dakota, South Dakota, Utah, Wyoming)*—
1999 Broadway - Ste.1780, Denver, CO 80202-5716. Phones: (303)844-1650; FAX
(303)844-1685.

REGION IX *(American Samoa, Arizona, California, Guam, Hawaii, Micronesia,*

Nevada, Northern Mariana Islands, Palau)—71 Stevenson St. - Rm.830, San Francisco, CA 94119-3767. Phones: (415)975-4610; FAX (415)975-4612.

REGION X *(Alaska, Idaho, Oregon, Washington)*—1111 3rd Ave. - Ste.900, Seattle, WA 98101-3212. Phones: (206)553-7700; FAX (206)553-0098.

EMPLOYMENT STANDARDS ADMINISTRATION

17.301   OFFICE OF FEDERAL CONTRACT COMPLIANCE PROGRAMS

REGIONAL OFFICES

REGION I *(Connecticut, Maine, Massachusetts, New Hampshire, Rhode Island, Vermont)*—JFK Federal Bldg. - Rm.E-235, One Congress St., Boston, MA 02203. Phone: (617)565-2055.

REGION II *(New Jersey, New York, Puerto Rico, Virgin Islands)*—201 Varick St. - Rm.750, New York, NY 10014-4811. Phone: (212)337-2007.

REGION III *(Delaware, District of Columbia, Maryland, Pennsylvania, Virginia, West Virginia)*—Gateway Bldg. - Rm.15340, 3535 Market St., Philadelphia, PA 19104. Phone: (215)596-6168.

REGION IV *(Alabama, Florida, Georgia, Kentucky, Mississippi, North Carolina, South Carolina, Tennessee)*—Atlanta Federal Center - Rm.7B75, 61 Forsyth St. SW, Atlanta, GA 30303. Phone: (404)562-2424.

REGION V *(Illinois, Indiana, Iowa, Kansas, Michigan, Minnesota, Missouri, Nebraska, Ohio, Wisconsin)*—Kluczynski Federal Bldg. - Rm.570, 230 S. Dearborn St., Chicago, IL 60604. Phone: (312)353-0335.

REGION VI *(Arkansas, Colorado, Louisiana, Montana, New Mexico, North Dakota, Oklahoma, South Dakota, Texas, Utah, Wyoming)*—Federal Bldg. - Ste.840, 525 S. Griffin St., Dallas, TX 75202-5007. Phone: (214)767-2804.

REGION IX *(Arizona, California, Guam, Hawaii, Nevada)*—71 Stevenson St. - Ste. 1700, San Francisco, CA 94105-2614. Phone: (415)975-4720.

REGION X *(Alaska, Idaho, Oregon, Washington)*—Federal Office Bldg. - Ste.610, 1111 3rd Ave., Seattle, WA 98101-3212. Phone: (206)553-4508.

DISTRICT AND AREA OFFICES

Alabama—Medical Forum Bldg. - Ste.660, 905 22nd St. N., Birmingham, AL 35203. Phone: (205)731-0820.

Arizona—3221 N. 16th St. - Ste.303, Phoenix, AZ 85016. Phone: (602)640-2960.

Arkansas—TCBY Tower - Ste.735, 425 W. Capitol Ave., Little Rock, AR 72201. Phone: (501)324-5436.

California—11000 Wilshire Blvd. - Ste.8103, Los Angeles, CA 90024. Phone: (310) 235-6800.

- 1301 Clay St. - Ste.1080N, Oakland, CA 94612. Phone: (510)637-2938.
- 5675 Ruffin Rd. - Ste.320, San Diego, CA 92123-5378. Phone: (619)557-6489.
- 60 S. Market St. - Ste.410, San Jose, CA 95113-2328. Phone: (408)291-7384.
- 34 Civic Center Plaza - Ste.406, P.O. Box 12800, Santa Ana, CA 92712-2800. Phone: (714)836-2784.

Colorado—1244 Spee Blvd. - Rm.620, Denver, CO 80204-3584. Phone: (303)844-4481.

Connecticut—135 High St. - Rm.311, Hartford, CT 06103. Phone: (860)240-4277.

District of Columbia—Reporter's Bldg. - Rm.203, 300 7th St. SW, Washington, DC 20407. Phone: (202)401-8807.

17.301 **Florida**—1851 Executive Center Dr. - Ste.201, Jacksonville, FL 32207. Phone: (904)
(cont.)   232-3073.

• Brickell Plaza Federal Bldg. - Ste.722, 909 SE 1st Ave., Miami, FL 33131. Phone:
(305)536-5670.

• Commodore Bldg. - Ste.160, 3444 McCrory Pl., Orlando, FL 32803-3712. Phone:
(407)648-6181.

Georgia—61 Forsyth St. - Rm.7B65, Atlanta, GA 30367. Phone: (404)562-2444.

Hawaii—300 Ala Moana Blvd. - Rm.7326, P.O. Box 50149, Honolulu, HI 96850.
Phone: (808)541-2933.

Illinois—230 S. Dearborn St. - Rm.434, Chicago, IL 60604. Phone: (312)353-0806.

Indiana—429 N. Pennsylvania St. - Rm.308, Indianapolis, IN 46204. Phones: (317)
226-5860.

Kentucky—Heyburn Bldg. - Ste.1600, 332 W. Broadway, Louisville, KY 40202. Phone:
(502)582-6275.

Louisiana—701 Loyola Ave. - Rm.13029, New Orleans, LA 70113. Phone: (504)589-
6575.

Maryland—Appraiser's Store Bldg. - Rm.202, 103 S. Gay St., Baltimore, MD 21202.
Phone: (410)962-3572.

Massachusetts—JFK Federal Bldg. - Rm.E-235, Boston, MA 02203. Phone: (617)565-
2055.

Michigan—McNamara Federal Bldg. - Rm.1320, 211 W. Fort St., Detroit, MI 48226.
Phone: (313)226-3728.

• Northbrook Office Park - Rm.102, 2920 Fuller Ave. NE, Grand Rapids, MI 49505.
Phone: (616)456-2166.

Minnesota—Bridgeplace Bldg. - Rm.102, 220 2nd St. S., Minneapolis, MN 55401.
Phone: (612)370-3177.

Mississippi—Millsaps Bldg. - Ste.700, 201 W. Capitol St., Jackson, MS 39201. Phone:
(601)965-4668.

Missouri—801 Walnut St. - Ste.201, Kansas City, MO 64106. Phone: (816)374-6035.

Nebraska—106 S. 15th St. - Rm.808, Omaha, NE 68116. Phone: (402)221-3381.

New Jersey—Bldg. 5 - Rm.203, 3131 Princeton Pike, Lawrenceville, NJ 08648. Phone:
(609)989-2380.

• Diamond Head Bldg. - Rm.102, 200 Sheffield Dr., Mountainside, NJ 07092. Phone:
(201)645-6104.

New Mexico—505 Marquette Ave. NW - Ste.810, Albuquerque, NM 87102. Phone:
(505)248-5015.

New York—O'Brien Federal Bldg. - Rm.740, 19 Aviation Rd., Albany, NY 12205.
Phone: (518)435-0323.

• Six Fountain Plaza - Ste.300, Buffalo. NY 14202. Phone: (716)551-5065.

• 825 E. Gate Blvd. - Rm.202, Garden City, NY 11530. Phone: (516)227-3104.

• 26 Federal Plaza - Rm.36-116, New York, NY 10278. Phone: (212)264-8165.

North Carolina—Mart Office Bldg. - Rm.BB-401, 800 Briar Creek Rd., Charlotte, NC
28205. Phone: (704)344-6113.

• 300 Fayetteville Street Mall - Ste.121, Raleigh, NC 27601. Phone: (919)856-4058.

Ohio—55 Erie View Plaza - Rm.520, 1350 Euclid St. - Ste.350, Cleveland, OH 44114.
Phone: (216)522-7472.

• 200 N. High St. - Rm.409, Columbus, OH 43215-2488. Phone: (614)469-5831.

Oklahoma—51 Yale Bldg. - Rm.304, 5110 S. Yale, Tulsa, OK 74135. Phone: (918)496-
6772.

Oregon—Federal Office Bldg. - Ste.1020, 111 SW Columbia St., Portland, OR 97201.
Phone: (503)326-4112.

Pennsylvania—9th and Market St., Philadelphia, PA 19107-0000. Phone: (215)597-4121.

▪ Federal Bldg. - Rm.2012, 1000 Liberty Ave., Pittsburgh, PA 15222. Phone: (412)395-6330.

Puerto Rico—New San Juan Office Bldg. - Rm.103, 159 Chardon Ave., Hato Rey, PR 00918. Phone: (787)766-5081.

South Carolina—Thurmond Federal Bldg. - Ste.608, 1835 Assembly St., Columbia, SC 29201. Phone: (803)765-5244.

Tennessee—167 N. Main St. - Ste.101, Memphis, TN 38103. Phone: (901)544-3458.

▪ 1321 Murfreesboro Rd., Ste.301, Nashville, TN 37217. Phone: (615)781-5395.

Texas—Federal Office Bldg. - Rm.512, 525 Griffin St., Dallas, TX 75202-5007. Phone: (214)767-2911.

▪ 2320 La Branch St. - Rm.1103, Houston, TX 77004. Phone: (713)718-3800.

▪ 800 Dolorosa St. - Rm.200, San Antonio, TX 78207. Phone: (210)472-5835.

Utah—10 W. Broadway - Ste.305, Salt Lake City, UT 84101. Phone: (801)524-4470.

Virginia—700 Centre - Ste.570, 700 E. Franklin St., Richmond, VA 23219. Phone: (804)771-2136.

Washington—Federal Office Bldg. - Ste.745, 1111 3rd Ave., Seattle, WA 98101. Phone: (206)553-7182.

Wisconsin—Federal Bldg. - Ste.1115, 310 W. Wisconsin Ave., Milwaukee, WI 53203. Phone: (414)297-3821.

OFFICE OF WORKERS' COMPENSATION PROGRAMS

REGIONAL OFFICES

California—71 Stevenson St. - Ste.1705, San Francisco, CA 94105. Phone: (415)975-4160.

Colorado—1801 California St. - Ste.920, Denver, CO 80202-2614. Phone: (303)844-1223.

Florida—214 N. Hogan St. - Ste.1026, Jacksonville, FL 32202. Phone: (904)357-4725.

Illinois—230 S. Dearborn St. - Rm.800, Chicago, IL 60604. Phone: (312)886-5883.

Massachusetts—JFK Federal Bldg. - Rm.E-260, Boston, MA 02203. Phone: (617)565-2102.

Missouri—City Center Square - Ste.750, 1100 Main St., Kansas City, MO 64105. Phone: (816)426-2196.

New York—201 Varick St. - Rm.740, New York, NY 10014. Phone: (212)337-2033.

Pennsylvania—3535 Market St. - Rm.15200, Philadelphia, PA 19104. Phone: (215) 596-1180.

Texas—525 S. Griffin St. - Rm.407, Dallas, TX 75202. Phone: (214)767-4713.

Washington—1111 3rd Ave. - Ste.615, Seattle, WA 98101-3212. Phone: (206)553-0074.

17.302   ### Longshore and Harbor Workers' Compensation

DISTRICT OFFICES

DISTRICT 1 *(Connecticut, Maine, Massachusetts, New Hampshire, Rhode Island, Vermont)*—JFK Federal Bldg. - Rm.E-260, Boston, MA 02203. Phone: (617)565-2103.

DISTRICT 2 *(New Jersey, New York, Puerto Rico, Virgin Islands)*—201 Varick St. - Rm.750, New York, NY 10014-0249. Phone: (212)337-2030.

DISTRICT 3 *(Delaware, Pennsylvania, West Virginia)*—Gateway Bldg. - Rm.13180, 3535 Market St., Philadephia, PA 19104. Phone: (215)596-5568.

17.302
(cont.)

DISTRICT 4 *(District of Columbia, Maryland)*—300 W. Pratt St. - Ste.240, Baltimore, MD 21201. Phone: (410)962-3677.

DISTRICT 5 *(Virginia)*—200 Granby Mall - Rm.212, Norfolk, VA 23510. Phone: (757)441-3071.

DISTRICT 6 *(Alabama, Florida, Georgia, Kentucky, Mississippi, North Carolina, South Carolina, Tennessee)*—214 N. Hogan St. - Ste.1040, Jacksonville, FL 32202. Phone: (904)357-4788.

DISTRICT 7 *(Arkansas, Louisiana)*—701 Loyola Ave. - Rm.13032, New Orleans, LA 70113. Phone: (504)589-2671.

DISTRICT 8 *(Oklahoma, New Mexico, Texas)*—8866 Gulf Freeway - Ste.140, Houston, TX 77017. Phone: (713)943-1605.

DISTRICT 10 *(Illinois, Indiana, Iowa, Kansas, Michigan, Minnesota, Missouri, Nebraska, Ohio, Wisconsin)*—230 S. Dearborn St. - Rm.578, Chicago, IL 60604. Phone: (312)353-8883.

DISTRICT 13 *(Arizona, California-northern, Nevada)*—71 Stevenson St. - Rm.1705, San Francisco, CA 94119-3770. Phone: (415)975-4274.

DISTRICT 14 *(Alaska, Colorado, Idaho, Montana, Oregon, North Dakota, South Dakota, Utah, Washington, Wyoming)*—1111 3rd Ave. - Ste.620, Seattle, WA 98111. Phone: (206)553-4471.

DISTRICT 15 *(Hawaii, Pacific Area to 60 east longitude)*—300 Ala Moana Blvd. - Rm.5-135, P.O. Box 50209, Honolulu, HI 96850 *(via air mail)*. Phone: (808)541-1983.

DISTRICT 18 *(Southern California)*—401 E. Ocean Blvd. - Ste.720, Long Beach, CA 90802. Phone: (562)980-3578.

17.303
and
17.306

Wage and Hour Division

REGIONAL OFFICES

REGION I—JFK Federal Bldg. - Rm.525, Boston, MA 02203. Phone: (617)565-2066.

REGION II—201 Varick St. - Rm.750, New York, NY 10014. Phone: (212)337-2000.

REGION III—Gateway Bldg. - Rm.15210, 3535 Market St., Philadelphia, PA 19104. Phone: (215)596-1185.

REGION IV—Atlanta Federal Center - Rm.7M40, 61 Forsyth St. SW, Atlanta, GA 30303. Phone: (404)562-2202.

REGION V—230 S. Dearborn St. - Rm.820, Chicago, IL 60604-1591. Phone: (312) 353-7280. *For mail*: Chicago, IL 60690-2638

REGION VI—Federal Bldg. - Rm.800, 525 S. Griffin St., Dallas, TX 75202-5007. Phone: (214)767-6895.

REGION VII—City Center Square - Ste.700, 1100 Main St., Kansas City, MO 64105-2112. Phone: (816)426-5386.

REGION VIII—71 Stevenson St. - Ste.930, San Francisco, CA 94105. Phone: (415) 975-4510.

DISTRICT OFFICES

Alabama—Medical Forum Bldg. - Ste.656, 950 22nd St. N., Birmingham, AL 35203-3711. Phone: (205)731-0066.

▪ Aronov Bldg. - Rm.708, 474 S. Court St., Montgomery, AL 36104-4158. Phone: (304)223-7641.

Arizona—3221 N. 16th St. - Ste.301, Phoenix, AZ 85016-7103. Phone: (602)640-2990.

Arkansas—TCBY Tower - Ste.725, 425 W. Capitol Ave., Little Rock, AR 72201. Phones: (501)324-5586.

California-Los Angeles—300 S. Glendale Ave. - Ste.400, Glendale, CA 91205-1752. Phones: (818)240-5274, -5275.

▪ 2981 Fulton Ave., Sacramento, CA 95821. Phones: (916)979-2040, -2041, -2042.

▪ 5675 Ruffin Rd. - Ste.320, San Diego, CA 92123-1362. Phone: (619)557-5606.

▪ 455 Market St. - Ste.800, San Francisco, CA 94105. Phone: (415)744-5590.

Colorado—1801 California St. - Ste.935, P.O. Drawer 3505, Denver, CO 80202. Phone: (303)844-4405.

Connecticut—135 High St. - Rm.310, Hartford, CT 06103-1595. Phone: (860)240-4160.

Florida—Federal Bldg. - Rm.408, 299 E. Broward Blvd., Ft. Lauderdale, FL 33301-1976. Phone: (954)356-6896.

▪ 3728 Phillips Hwy. - Ste.219, Jacksonville, FL 32207-0880. Phone: (904)232-2489.

▪ Sunset Center - Rm.255, 10300 Sunset Dr., Miami, FL 33173-3038. Phones: (305) 598-6607; FAX (305)279-8393.

▪ Austin Laurel Bldg. - Ste.300, 4905 W. Laurel Ave., Tampa, FL 33607-3838. Phone: (813)288-1242.

Georgia—Atlanta Federal Center - Rm.7M10, 61 Forsyth St. SW, Atlanta, GA 30303. Phone: (404)562-2201.

▪ Low Federal Bldg. Complex - Ste.B-120, 124 Barnard St., Savannah, GA 31401. Phones: (912)652-4221, -4229.

Illinois—230 S. Dearborn - Rm.412, Chicago, IL 60604-1595. Phone: (312)353-7197.

▪ 509 W. Capitol Ave. - Ste.205, Springfield, IL 62704. Phone: (217)492-4060.

Indiana—429 N. Pennsylvania St. - Rm.403, Indianapolis, IN 46204-1873. Phones: (317)226-6801, -6783.

▪ River Glen Plaza - Ste.160, 501 E. Monroe St., South Bend, IN 46601-1615. Phones:(219)236-8331, -8332.

Iowa—Federal Bldg. - Rm.643, 210 Walnut St., Des Moines, IA 50309. Phone: (515) 284-4625.

Kansas—Gateway Tower II - Ste.706, 400 State Ave., Kansas City, KS 66101. Phone: (913)551-5721.

Kentucky—Snyder U.S. Courthouse and Custom House - Rm.31, 601 W. Broadway, Louisville, KY 40202-9570. Phone: (502)582-5226.

Louisiana—701 Loyola Ave. - Rm.13028, New Orleans, LA 70113-1931. Phones: (504)589-6171, -6172.

Maryland—1100 N. Eutaw St. - Rm.607, Baltimore, MD 21201. Phone:(410)767-2357.

Massachusetts—Kennedy Federal Bldg. - Rm.525, Boston, MA 02203. Phone: (617) 565-2066.

Michigan—2920 Fuller Ave. NE - Ste.100, Grand Rapids, MI 49505-3409. Phone: (616)456-2004.

Minnesota—Bridge Place - Rm.106, 220 S. 2nd St., Minneapolis, MN 55401-2104. Phone: (612)370-3371.

Mississippi—One Jackson Place - Ste.1020, 188 E. Capitol St., Jackson, MS 39201-2126. Phones: (601)965-4347, -4348.

Missouri—Gateway Tower II - Ste.706, 400 State Ave., Kansas City, KS 66101. Phone: (913)551-5721.

▪ 1222 Spruce St. - Rm.9102B, St. Louis, MO 63103. Phones: (314)539-2706, -3014.

Nebraska—Federal Bldg. - Rm.715, 106 S. 15th St., Omaha, NE 68102. Phone: (402)221-4682.

New Hampshire—2 Wall St. - 1st fl., Manchester, NH 03101. Phones: (603)666-7716; FAX (603)666-7600.

New Jersey—Bldg. 5 - Rm.216, 3131 Princeton Pike, Lawrenceville, NJ 08648. Phones: (609)989-2247, -2368.

17.303 and 17.306 (cont.)

- 200 Sheffield St. - Ste.102, Mountainside, NJ 07092. Phones: (201)645-2279, -2473, -2541, -2604.

New Mexico—Western Bank Bldg. - Ste.840, 505 Marquette NW, Albuquerque, NM 87102-2160. Phone: (505)248-5118.

New York—O'Brien Federal Bldg. - Rm.822, Albany, NY 12207. Phone: (518)431-4278.

- 825 E. Gate Blvd. - Rm.202, Garden City, NY 11530. Phone: (516)227-3100.
- 26 Federal Plaza - Rm.3838, New York, NY 10278. Phone: (212)264-8185.

North Carolina—800 Briar Creek Rd. - Ste.CC-412, Charlotte, NC 28205-6903. Phone: (704)344-6298.

- Somerset Park Bldg. - Ste.260, 4407 Bland Rd., Raleigh, NC 27609-6296. Phones: (919)790-2741, -2742.

Ohio—525 Vine St. - Ste.880, Cincinnati, OH 45202-3268. Phone: (513)684-2908.

- Federal Bldg. - Rm.817, 1240 E. 9th St., Cleveland, OH 44199-2054 Phones: (216)522-3892, -3893.
- 646 Federal Bldg., 200 N. High St., Columbus, OH 43215-2475. Phones: (614)469-5677; FAX (614)469-5677.

Oklahoma—5110 S. Yale St., Tulsa, OK 74135-7438. Phone: (918)581-6794.

Oregon—1515 SW 5th Ave. - Ste.1040, Portland, OR 97201-5842. Phone: (503)326-3052.

Pennsylvania—U.S. Customs House - Rm.402, 2nd and Chestnut St., Philadelphia, PA 19106. Phone: (215)597-4950.

- Federal Bldg. - Rm.313, 1000 Liberty Ave., Pittsburgh, PA 15222. Phone: (412)395-4996.
- Stegmaier Bldg. - Ste.373-M, 7 N. Wilkes-Barre Blvd., Wilkes-Barre, PA 18702. Phone: (717)826-6316.

Puerto Rico—New San Juan Office Bldg. - Rm.102, 159 Carlos Chardon St., Hato Rey, PR 00918. Phone: (787)766-5263.

South Carolina—Federal Bldg. - Rm.1072, 1835 Assembly St., Columbia, SC 29201-2449. Phone: (803)765-5981.

Tennessee—Executive Plaza - Bldg.511, 1321 Murfreesboro Rd., Nashville, TN 37217-2648. Phones: (615)781-5343, -5345.

Texas—Smith Federal Bldg. - Rm.507, 525 S. Griffin St., Dallas, TX 75202-5007. Phone: (214)767-6294.

- 9990 Richmond Ave. - Ste.202, Houston, TX 77042-4546. Phone: (713)339-5575.
- Northchase I Office Bldg. - Ste.140, 10127 Morocco St., San Antonio, TX 78216. Phones: (210)229-4515, -4516, -4517.

Utah—10 W. Broadway - Ste.307, Salt Lake City, UT 84101. Phone: (801)524-5706.

Virginia—The 700 Center - Ste.560, 700 E. Franklin St., Richmond, VA 23219. Phone: (804)771-2995.

Washington—1111 3rd Ave. - Ste.755, Seattle, WA 98101-3212. Phone: (206)553-4482.

West Virginia—2 Hale St. - Ste.301, Charleston, WV 25301-2834. Phone: (304)347-5206.

Wisconsin—Federal Center Bldg. - Rm.309, 212 E. Washington Ave., Madison, WI 53703-2878. Phone: (608)264-5221.

17.307   ## Division of Coal Mine Workers' Compensation

DISTRICT OFFICES

Contact nearest Social Security office or appropriate CMWC office listed below.

Colorado *(Western United States)*—1801 California St. - Ste.925, Denver, CO 80202-2614. Phone: (1-800-366-4612).

Kentucky *(Kentucky)*—334 Main St. - 5th fl., Pikeville, KY 41501. Phone: (1-800-366-4599).

▪ *(Alabama, Florida, Georgia, Mississippi, North Carolina, South Carolina, Tennessee)*—500 Springdale Plaza, Spring St., Mt. Sterling, KY 40353. Phone: (1-800 366-4628).

Ohio *(Illinois, Indiana, Michigan, Minnesota, Ohio, Wisconsin)*—274 Marconi Blvd. - 3rd fl., Columbus, OH 43215. Phone: (1-800-347-3771).

Pennsylvania *(Connecticut, Delaware, District of Columbia, Maine, Massachusetts, New Hampshire, New Jersey, New York, Pennsylvania-eastern, Rhode Island, Vermont)*—S. Main Towers, 105 N. Main St. - Ste.100, Wilkes-Barre, PA 18701. Phone: (1-800-347-3755).

▪ *(Maryland, Pennsylvania-western)*—Wellington Square - Ste.405, 1225 S. Main St., Greensburg, PA 15601. Phone: (1-800-347-3753).

▪ *(Pennsylvania-central, Virginia)*—Penn Traffic Bldg. - 2nd fl., 319 Washington St., Johnstown, PA 15901. Phone: (1-800-347-3754).

West Virginia *(West Virginia-northern)*—425 Juliana St., Parkersburg, WV 26101. Phone: (1-800-347-3751).

▪ *(West Virginia-southern)*—2 Hale St. - Ste.304, Charleston, WV 25301. Phone: (1-800-347-3749).

17.308   *Contact the nearest office of the state employment service in your area, or nearest Wage and Hour Division Office listed under **17.303**.*

17.309   *Contact the Office of Labor-Management Standards field office listed under **17.140**.*

OCCUPATIONAL SAFETY AND HEALTH ADMINISTRATION

17.502 thru 17.504

REGIONAL OFFICES

REGION I *(Connecticut, Maine, Massachusetts, New Hampshire, Rhode Island, Vermont)*—JFK Federal Bldg. - Low Rise Bldg. (Rm.E-340), Boston, MA 02203. Phone: (617)565-9860.

REGION II *(New Jersey, New York, Puerto Rico)*—201 Varick St. - Ste.670, New York, NY 10014. Phone: (212)337-2378.

REGION III *(Delaware, District of Columbia, Maryland, Pennsylvania, Virginia, West Virginia)*—Gateway Bldg. - Ste.2100, 3535 Market St., Philadelphia, PA 19104. Phone: (215)596-1201.

REGION IV *(Alabama, Florida, Georgia, Kentucky, Mississippi, North Carolina, South Carolina, Tennessee)*—Atlanta Federal Center, 100 Alabama St. SW, Atlanta, GA 30303. Phone: (404)562-2300.

REGION V *(Illinois, Indiana, Minnesota, Michigan, Ohio, Wisconsin)*—230 S. Dearborn St. - 32nd fl. (Rm.3244), Chicago, IL 60604. Phone: (312)353-2220.

REGION VI *(Arkansas, Louisiana, New Mexico, Oklahoma, Texas)*—525 Griffin Square Bldg. - Rm.602, Dallas, TX 75202. Phone: (214)767-4731.

REGION VII *(Iowa, Kansas, Missouri, Nebraska)*—City Center Square - Ste.800, 1100 Main St., Kansas City, MO 64105. Phone: (816)426-5861.

REGION VIII *(Colorado, Montana, North Dakota, South Dakota, Utah, Wyoming)*—1999 Broadway St. - Rm.1690, Denver, CO 80202-5716. Phone: (303)844-1600.

REGION IX *(American Samoa, Arizona, California, Guam, Hawaii, Nevada, Trust Territory of the Pacific Islands)*—71 Stevenson St. - Rm.420, San Francisco, CA 94105. Phone: (415)975-4310.

REGION X *(Alaska, Idaho, Oregon, Washington)*—1111 3rd Ave. - Ste.715, Seattle, WA 98101-3212. Phone: (206)553-5930.

AREA OFFICES

Alabama—Todd Mall, 2047 Canyon Rd., Birmingham, AL 35216-1981. Phone: (205) 731-1534.

- 3737 Government Blvd. - Ste.100, Mobile, AL 36693-4309. Phone: (334)441-6131.

Alaska—301 W. Northern Lights Blvd. - Rm.407, Anchorage, AK 99503-7571. Phone: (907)271-5152.

Arizona—3221 N. 16th St. - Ste.100, Phoenix, AZ 85016. Phone: (602)640-2007.

Arkansas—TCBY Bldg. - Ste.450., 425 W. Capitol Ave., Little Rock, AR 72201. Phone: (501)324-6291.

California—Resource Center - Ste.105, 105 El Camino Blvd., Sacramento, CA 95815. Phone: (916)566-7470.

- Resource Center, 5675 Ruffin Rd. - Ste.330, San Diego, CA 92123. Phone: (619)569-9071.

- Resource Center, 71 Stevenson St. - Ste.415, San Francisco, CA 94105. Phone: (415)975-4348.

Colorado—1391 Speer Blvd. - Ste.210, Denver, CO 80204-2552. Phone: (303)844-5285.

- 7935 E. Prentice Ave. - Ste.209, Englewood, CO 80111-2714. Phone: (303)843-4500.

Connecticut—One Lafayette Square - Ste.202, Bridgeport, CT 06604. Phone: (203) 579-5580.

- Federal Bldg. - Rm.613, 450 Main St., Hartford, CT 06103. Phone: (860)240-3152.

Delaware—One Rodney Square - Ste.402, 920 King St., Wilmington, DE 19801. Phone: (302)573-6115.

District of Columbia—820 1st St. NE - Ste.440, Washington, DC 20002. Phone: (202)523-1452.

Florida—Bldg. H100, 8040 Peters Rd., Ft. Lauderdale, FL 33324. Phone: (954)424-0242.

- Ribault Bldg. - Ste.227, 1851 Executive Center Dr., Jacksonville, FL 32207. Phone: (904)232-2895.

- 5807 Breckenridge Pkwy. - Ste.A, Tampa, FL 33610. Phone: (813)626-1177.

Georgia—La Vista Perimeter Office Park, Bldg. 7 - Ste.110,, Tucker, GA 30084-4184. Phone: (770)493-8419.

- 450 Mall Blvd. - Ste.J, Savannah, GA 31406-1418. Phone: (912)652-4393.

Hawaii—Resource Center - Ste.S-146, 450 Ala Moana Blvd., Honolulu, HI 96850. Phone: (808)541-2685.

Idaho—3050 N. Lakenharbor - Ste.134, Boise, ID 83703. Phone: (208)321-2960.

Illinois—1600 167th St. - Ste.12, Calumet City, IL 60409. Phone: (708)891-3800.

- 2360 E. Devon Ave. - Ste.1010, Des Plaines, IL 60018. Phone: (847)803-4800.

- 11 Executive Dr. - Ste.11, Fairview Heights, IL 62208. Phone: (618)632-8612.

- 344 Smoke Tree Business Park, North Aurora, IL 60542. Phone: (630)896-8700.

- 2918 W. Willow Knolls Rd., Peoria, IL 61614. Phone: (309)671-7033.

Indiana—U.S. Post Office and Courthouse - Rm.423, 46 E. Ohio St., Indianapolis, IN 46204. Phone: (317)226-7290.

Iowa—210 Walnut St. - Rm.815, Des Moines, IA 50309. Phone: (515)284-4794.

Kansas—8600 Farley - Ste.105, Overland Park, KS 66212-4677. Phone: (913)385-7380.

- 300 Epic Center, 301 N. Main St., Wichita, KS 67202. Phone: (316)269-6644.

Kentucky—Watts Federal Bldg. - Rm.108, 330 W. Broadway, Frankfort, KY 40601-1922. Phone: (502)227-7024.

Louisiana—Hoover Annex - Ste.200, 2156 Wooddale Blvd., Baton Rouge, LA 70806. Phone: (504)389-0474.

Maine—U.S. Federal Bldg. - Rm.608, 40 Western Ave., Augusta, ME 04330. Phone: (207)622-8417, ext.417.

- 202 Harlow St. - Rm.211, Bangor, ME 04401-4906. Phone: (207)941-8177.

Maryland—Federal Bldg. - Rm.280, 300 W. Pratt St. Baltimore, MD 21201. Phone: (410)962-2840.

Massachusetts—639 Granite St. - 4th fl., Braintree, MA 02184. Phone: (617)565-6924.

- Valley Office Park - 1st fl., 13 Branch St., Methuen, MA 01844. Phone: (617)565-8110.

- 1145 Main St. - Ste.108, Springfield, MA 01103-1493. Phone: (413)785-0123.

Michigan—801 S. Waverly Rd. - Ste.306, Lansing, MI 48917-4200. Phone: (517)377-1892.

Minnesota—110 S. 4th St. - Rm.116, Minneapolis, MN 55401. Phone: (612)348-1994.

Mississippi—3780 I-55N. - Ste.210., Jackson, MS 39211-6323. Phone: (601)965-4606.

Missouri—6200 Connecticut Ave. - Ste.100, Kansas City, MO 64120. Phone: (816)483-9531.

- 911 Washington Ave. - Rm.420, St. Louis, MO 63101. Phone: (314)425-4249.

Montana—2900 4th Ave. N. - Ste.303, Billings, MT 59101. Phone: (406)247-7494.

Nebraska—Overland-Wolf Bldg. - Rm.100, 6910 Pacific St., Omaha, NE 68106. Phone: (402)221-3182.

Nevada—Federal Bldg. - Rm.204, 705 North Plaza, Carson City, NV 89701. Phone: (702)885-6963.

New Hampshire—79 Pleasant St. - Rm.201, Concord, NH 03301. Phone: (603)225-1629.

New Jersey—Plaza 35 - Ste.205, 1030 St. Georges Ave., Avenel, NJ 07001 Phone: (908)750-3270.

- 500 Rt. 17 S. - 2nd fl., Hasbrouck Heights, NJ 07604. Phone: (201)288-1700.

- Marlton Executive Park, South Bldg. 2 - Ste.120, 701 Rt. 73, Marlton, NJ 08053. Phone: (609)757-5181.

- 299 Cherry Hill Rd.- Ste.304, Parsippany, NJ 07054. Phone: (201)263-1003.

New Mexico—505 Marquette Ave. - Ste.820, Albuquerque, NM 87102. Phone: (505) 248-5302.

New York—Tomich Federal Bldg. - Ste.330, 401 New Karner Rd., Albany, NY 12205-3809. Phone: (518)464-6742.

- 42-40 Bell Blvd., Bayside, NY 11361. Phone: (718)279-9060.

- 5360 Genessee St., Bowmansville, NY 14026. Phone: (716)684-3891.

- 6 World Trade Center - Rm.881, New York, NY 10048. Phone: (212)466-2481.

- 3300 Vickery Rd., North Syracuse, NY 13212. Phone: (315)451-0808.

- 660 White Plains Rd. - 4th fl., Tarrytown, NY 10591-5107. Phone: (914)524-7510.

- 990 Westbury Rd., Westbury, NY 11590. Phone: (516)334-3344.

North Carolina—Century Station, Federal Bldg. - Rm.438, 300 Fayetteville Mall, Raleigh, NC 27601-9998. Phone: (919)856-4770.

North Dakota—220 3rd and Rosser - Rm.348, P.O. Box 2439, Bismarck, ND 58502. Phone: (701)250-4521.

Ohio—Federal Bldg. - Rm.4028, 36 Triangle Park Dr., Cincinnati, OH 45246. Phone: (513)841-4132.

- Federal Bldg. - Rm.899, 1240 E. 9th St., Cleveland, OH 44199. Phone: (216)522-3818.

- Federal Bldg. - Rm.620, 200 N. High St., Columbus, OH 43215. Phone: (614)469-5582.

- Federal Bldg. - Rm.734, 234 N. Summit St., Toledo, OH 43604. Phone: (419)259-7542.

17.502
thru
17.504
(cont.)

Oklahoma—420 W. Main St. - Ste.300, Oklahoma City, OK 73102. Phone: (405)231-5351.

Oregon—1220 SW 3rd St. - Rm.640, Portland, OR 97204. Phone: (503)326-2251.

Pennsylvania—850 N. 5th St., Allentown, PA 18102. Phone: (610)776-0592.

- 3939 W. Ridge Rd. - Ste.B-12, Erie, PA 16506. Phone: (814)833-5758.
- Progress Plaza, 49 N. Progress Ave., Harrisburg, PA 17109. Phone: (717)782-3902.
- U.S. Customs House - Rm.242, 2nd and Chestnut St., Philadelphia, PA 19106. Phone: (215)597-4955.
- Federal Bldg. - Rm.1428, 1000 Liberty Ave., Pittsburgh, PA 15522. Phone: (412)395-4903.
- Stegmaier Bldg. - Ste.410, 7 N. Wilkes-Barre Blvd., Wilkes-Barre, PA 18702. Phone: (717)826-6538.

Puerto Rico—BBY Plaza Bldg. - Ste.5B, 1510 F.D. Roosevelt Ave., Guaynabo, PR 00968. Phone: (787)277-1560.

Rhode Island—380 Westminster Mall - Rm.243, Providence, RI 02903. Phone: (401)528-4669.

South Carolina—1835 Assembly St. - Rm.1468, Columbia, SC 29201. Phone: (803)765-5904.

Tennessee—2002 Richard Jones Rd. - Ste.C-205, Nashville, TN 37215-2809. Phone: (615)781-5423.

Texas—903 San Jacinto Blvd. - Ste.319, Austin, TX 78701. Phone: (512)482-5783.

- Wilson Plaza West - Ste.700, 606 N. Carancahua, Corpus Christi, TX 78476. Phone: (512)888-3420.
- 834 East R.L. Thornton Fwy. - Ste.420, Dallas, TX 75228. Phone: (214)320-2400.
- Commons Bldg. C - Rm.C119, 4171 N. Mesa, El Paso, TX 79902. Phone: (915)534-7004.
- North Star II - Ste.302, 8713 Airport Fwy., Ft. Worth, TX 76180-7604. Phone: (817)428-2470.
- 17625 El Camino Real - Ste.400, Houston, TX 77058. Phone: (713)286-0583.
- 350 N. Sam Houston Pkwy. - Ste.120, Houston, TX 77060. Phone: (713)591-2438.
- Federal Bldg. - Rm.806, 1205 Texas Ave., Lubbock, TX 79401. Phone: (806)743-7681.

Utah—1781 South 300 W., P.O. Box 65200, Salt Lake City, UT 84165-0200. Phones: (801)487-0267, -0680.

Virginia—200 Granby Mall - Rm.835, Norfolk, VA 23510. Phone: (757)441-3820.

Washington—505 106th Ave. NE - Ste.302, Bellevue, WA 98004. Phone: (360)553-7520.

West Virginia—405 Capitol St. - Ste.407, Charleston, WV 25301. Phone: (304)347-5937.

Wisconsin—2618 N. Ballard Rd., Appleton, WI 54911-8664. Phone: (414)734-4521.

- Federal Bldg. and Courthouse - Rm.B-9, 500 Barstow St., Eau Claire, WI 54701. Phone: (715)832-9019.
- Reuss Bldg. - Ste.1180, 310 Wisconsin Ave., Milwaukee, WI 53203. Phone: (414)297-3315.

MINE SAFETY AND HEALTH ADMINISTRATION

17.601
and
17.602

Coal Mine Safety and Health

DISTRICT OFFICES

DISTRICT NO. 1 *(Connecticut, Delaware, Maine, Massachusetts, New Hampshire, New Jersey, New York, Pennsylvania (counties east of and including Susquehanna,*

Sullivan, Columbia, Montour, Northumberland, Dauphin, York), Rhode Island, Vermont)—Stegmaier Bldg. - Ste.034, 7 N. Wilkes-Barre Blvd., Wilkes-Barre, PA 18702. Phone: (717)826-6321.

DISTRICT NO. 2 *(Pennsylvania counties west of and including Bradford, Lycoming, Union, Snyder, Juniata, Perry, Cumberland, Adams)*—Rural Rt.1 - Box 736, Hunter PA 15639. Phone: (412)925-5150, ext.111.

DISTRICT NO. 3 *(Maryland, Ohio, West Virginia counties north of and including Jackson, Roane, Calhoun, Braxton, Randolph, Pendleton)*—5012 Mountaineer Mall, Morgantown, WV 26505. Phone: (304)291-4277.

DISTRICT NO. 4 *(West Virginia counties south of and including Mason, Putnam, Kanawha, Clay, Nicholas, Webster, Greenbrier, Pocahontas)*—100 Bluestone Rd., Mt. Hope, WV 25880. Phone: (304)877-3900, ext.125.

DISTRICT NO. 5 *(Virginia)*—P.O. Box 560, Norton, VA 24273. Phone: (540)679-0230.

DISTRICT NO. 6 *(Kentucky counties east of and including Mason, Robertson, Fleming, Rowan, Menifee, Morgan, Magoffin, Floyd, Pike, Letcher)*—159 N. Mayo Trail, Pikeville, KY 41501-3249. Phone: (606)432-0943, ext.116.

DISTRICT NO. 7 *(Alabama (counties north and east of, and including, Jackson, Marshall, Etowah, Cherokee), Georgia (counties north of, and including, Polk, Bartow, Cherokee, Forsyth, Hall, Jackson, Madison, Elbert), Kentucky (counties east of and including Boone, Grant, Scott, Woodford, Jessamine, Garrard, Lincoln, Pulaski, Clinton up to District 6 boundary), North Carolina, South Carolina, Tennessee)*—HC 66-Box 1699, Barbourville, KY 40906. Phone: (606)546-5123.

DISTRICT NO. 8 *(Illinois, Indiana, Iowa, Michigan, Minnesota, Missouri counties north of the Missouri River, Wisconsin)*—2300 Old Decker Rd. - Ste.200, Vincennes, IN 47591. Phone: (812)882-7617.

DISTRICT NO. 9 *(All states west of the Mississippi River including Alaska and Hawaii, except Minnesota, Iowa and all counties of Missouri south of the Missouri River)*—Denver Federal Center, Denver, CO 80225-0367. Phone: (303)231-5458.

DISTRICT NO. 10 *(Kentucky counties west of and including Gallatin, Owen, Franklin, Anderson, Mercer, Boyle, Casey, Russell, Cumberland)*—100 YMCA Dr., Madisonville, KY 42431-9019. Phone: (502)821-4180.

DISTRICT NO. 11 *(Alabama and Georgia (counties south and west of the District 7 boundary) Florida, Mississippi, Puerto Rico, Virgin Islands)*—135 Gemini Circle - Ste.213, Birmingham, AL 35209. Phone: (205)290-7300.

Metal and Nonmetal Mine Safety and Health

DISTRICT OFFICES

Alabama *(Southeastern: Alabama, Florida, Georgia, Kentucky, Mississippi, North Carolina, Puerto Rico, South Carolina, Tennessee, Virgin Islands)*—135 Gemini Circle - Ste.212, Birmingham, AL 35209. Phone: (205)290-7294.

California *(Western: Alaska, California, Hawaii, Idaho, Nevada, Oregon, Washington)*—2060 Peabody Rd. - Ste.610, Vacaville, CA 95687-6696. Phone: (707)447-9844.

Colorado *(Rocky Mountain: Arizona, Colorado, Kansas, Montana, Nebraska, North Dakota, South Dakota, Utah, Wyoming)*—Denver, CO 80225-0367. Phone: (303)231-5465.

Minnesota *(North Central: Illinois, Indiana, Iowa, Michigan, Minnesota, Ohio, Wisconsin)*—515 W. 1st St. - #333, Duluth, MN 55802-1302. Phone: (218)720-5448.

Pennsylvania *(Northeastern: Connecticut, Delaware, District of Columbia, Maine, Maryland, Massachusetts, New Hampshire, New Jersey, New York, Pennsylvania, Rhode Island, Vermont, Virginia, West Virginia)*—230 Executive Dr. - Ste.2, Cranberry Township, PA 16066-6415. Phone: (724)772-2333.

17.601
and
17.602
(cont.)

Texas *(South Central: Arkansas, Louisiana, Missouri, New Mexico, Oklahoma, Texas)*—1100 Commerce St. - Rm.4C50, Dallas, TX 75242-0499. Phone: (214)767-8401.

TECHNICAL SUPPORT FIELD CENTERS

Pennsylvania—Safety and Health Technology Center, Cochrans Mill Rd., P.O. Box 18233, Pittsburgh, PA 15236. Phone: (412)386-6902.

West Virginia—Approval and Certification Center, Industrial Park Rd., Rural Rt. 1 - Box 251, Triadelphia, WV 26059. Phone: (304)547-2029.

National Mine Health and Safety Academy

1301 Airport Rd., Beaver, WV 25813-9426. Phone: (304)256-3200.

OFFICE OF THE SECRETARY, WOMEN'S BUREAU

17.700   **REGIONAL OFFICES**

REGION I *(Connecticut, Maine, Massachusetts, New Hampshire, Rhode Island, Vermont)*—One Congress St. - 11th fl., Boston, MA 02114. Phone: (617)565-1988.

REGION II *(New Jersey, New York, Puerto Rico, Virgin Islands)*—201 Varick St. - Rm.601, New York, NY 10014. Phone: (212)337-2389.

REGION III *(Delaware, District of Columbia, Maryland, Pennsylvania, Virginia, West Virginia)*—Gateway Bldg. - Rm.2450, 3535 Market St., Philadelphia, PA 19104. Phone: (215)596-1184.

REGION IV *(Alabama, Florida, Georgia, Kentucky, Mississippi, North Carolina, South Carolina, Tennessee)*—1371 Peachtree St. NE - Rm.323, Atlanta, GA 30367. Phone: (404)562-2336.

REGION V *(Illinois, Indiana, Michigan, Minnesota, Ohio, Wisconsin)*—230 S. Dearborn St. - Rm.1022, Chicago, IL 60604. Phone: (312)353-6985.

REGION VI *(Arkansas, Louisiana, New Mexico, Oklahoma, Texas)*—Federal Bldg. - Ste.735, 525 Griffin St., Dallas, TX 75202. Phone: (214)767-6985.

REGION VII *(Iowa, Kansas, Missouri, Nebraska)*—City Center City Square - Ste. 1230, 1100 Main St., Kansas City, MO 64106. Phone: (816)426-6108.

REGION VIII *(Colorado, Montana, North Dakota, South Dakota, Utah, Wyoming)*—Federal Office Bldg. - Ste.905 (Rm.1452), 1801 California St., Denver, CO 80202-2614. Phone: (303)844-1286.

REGION IX *(Arizona, California, Hawaii, Nevada)*—71 Stevenson St. - Rm.927, San Francisco, CA 94105. Phone: (415)975-4750.

REGION X *(Alaska, Idaho, Oregon, Washington)*—1111 3rd Ave. - Rm.885, Seattle, WA 98101-3211. Phone: (206)553-1534.

OFFICE OF THE ASSISTANT SECRETARY FOR VETERANS' EMPLOYMENT AND TRAINING

17.801
thru
17.805

REGIONAL AND STATE OFFICES

REGION I *(Connecticut, Maine, Massachusetts, New Hampshire, Rhode Island, Vermont, Virgin Islands)*—Connecticut Department of Labor Bldg., 200 Folly Brook Blvd., Wethersfield, CT 06109. Phone: (860)263-6490.

▪ JFK Federal Bldg. - Government Center (Rm.E-315), Boston, MA 02203. Phone: (617)565-2080.

- Hurley Bldg. - 2nd fl., ES Operations Section, 19 Staniford St., Boston, MA 02114. Phone: (617)626-6690.
- 522 Lisbon St., P.O. Box 3106, Lewiston, ME 04243. Phone: (207)783-9090.
- 143 N. Main St. - Rm.208, Concord, NH 03301. Phone: (603)225-1424.
- 57 Spruce St., Westerly, RI 02891. Phone: (401)528-5134.
- Post Office Bldg. - Rm.303, 87 State St., P.O. Box 603, Montpelier, VT 05602. Phone: (802)828-4441.

REGION II *(New Jersey, New York, Puerto Rico, Virgin Islands)*—Labor Bldg. - 11th fl. (CN058), Trenton, NJ 08625. Phone: (609)292-2930.
- Harriman State Campus - Bldg. 12 (Rm.518), Albany, NY 12240-0099. Phone: (518)457-7465.
- 201 Varick St. - Rm.766, New York, NY 10014. (212)337-2211.
- 198 Calle Guayama - 20th fl., Hato Rey, PR 00917. Phone: (787)754-5391.

REGION III *(Delaware, District of Columbia, Maryland, Pennsylvania, Virginia, West Virginia)*—500 C St. NW - Rm.108, Washington, DC 20001. Phone: (202)724-7005.
- 4425 N. Market St. - Rm.420, Wilmington, DE 19809-0828. Phone: (302)761-8138.
- 1100 N. Eutaw St. - Rm.210, Baltimore, MD 21201. Phone: (410)767-2110.
- Labor and Industry Bldg. - Rm.1108,, 7th and Forster St., Harrisburg, PA 17121. Phone: (717)787-5834.
- U.S. Customs House - Rm.802, 2nd and Chestnut St., Philadelphia, PA 19106. Phone: (215)597-1664.
- 703 E. Main St. - Rm.118, Richmond, VA 23219. Phone: (804)786-7269.
- Capitol Complex - Rm.205, 112 California Ave., Charleston, WV 25305-0112. Phone: (304)558-4001.

REGION IV *(Alabama, Florida, Georgia, Kentucky, Mississippi, North Carolina, South Carolina, Tennessee)*—649 Monroe St. - Rm.543, Montgomery, AL 36131-6300. Phone: (334)223-7677.
- Tallahassee, FL 32302-1527. Phone: (850)942-8800.
- Atlanta Federal Center - Rm.6-T85, 61 Forsyth St. SW, Atlanta, GA 30303. Phone: (404)562-2305.
- Sussex Place - Ste.504, 148 International Blvd. NE, Atlanta, GA 30303-1751. Phone: (404)656-3127.
- c/o Department for Employment Services, 275 E. Main St., Frankfort, KY 40621-2339. Phone: (502)564-7062.
- 1520 W. Capitol St., Jackson, MS 39215-1699. Phone: (601)965-4204.
- P.O. Box 27625, Raleigh, NC 27611-1154. Phones: (919)733-7402, -7407.
- Columbia, SC 29202-1755. Phone: (803)765-5195.
- Nashville, TN 37219-8587. Phone (615)736-7680.

REGION V *(Illinois, Indiana, Michigan, Minnesota, Ohio, Wisconsin)*—230 S. Dearborn - Rm.1064, Chicago, IL 60604. Phone: (312)353-0970.
- 401 S. State St. - 7 North, Chicago, IL 60605. Phone: (312)793-3433.
- 10 N. Senate Ave. - Rm.SE-103, Indianapolis, IN 46204. Phone: (317)232-6804.
- 7310 Woodward Ave. - Ste.407, Detroit, MI 48202. Phone: (313)876-5613.
- 390 Robert St. N. - 1st fl., St. Paul, MN 55101. Phone: (612)290-3028.
- P.O. Box 1618, Columbus, OH 43216. Phone: (614)469-2330.
- Madison, WI 53708-8310. Phone: (608)266-3110.

REGION VI *(Arkansas, Louisiana, New Mexico, Oklahoma, Texas)*—P.O. Box 128, Little Rock, AR 72203. Phone: (501)682-3786.
- P.O. Box 94094, Rm.184, Baton Rouge, LA 70804-9094. Phone: (504)389-0339.
- P.O. Box 25085, Albuquerque, NM 87125-5085. Phone: (505)766-2113.
- Will Rogers Memorial Office Bldg. - Rm.301, P.O. Box 52003, Oklahoma City, OK 73152-2003. Phone: (405)231-5088.

17.801
thru
17.805
(cont.)

- P.O. Box 1468, Austin, TX 78767. Phone: (512)463-2814.
- 525 Griffin St. - Rm.858, Dallas, TX 75202. Phone: (214)767-4987.

REGION VII *(Iowa, Kansas, Missouri, Nebraska)*—150 Des Moines St., Des Moines, IA 50309-5563. Phone: (515)281-9061.

- 401 Topeka Blvd., Topeka, KS 66612. Phone: (913)296-5032.
- 421 E. Dunklin St., P.O. Box 59, Jefferson City, MO 65104. Phone: (573)751-3921.
- City Center Square - Ste.850, 1100 Main St., Kansas City, MO 64105-2112. Phone: (816)426-7151.
- 550 S. 16th St., P.O. Box 94600, Lincoln, NE 68509. Phone: (402)437-5289.

REGION VIII *(Colorado, Montana, North Dakota, South Dakota, Utah, Wyoming)*— 1801 California St. - Ste.910, Denver, CO 80202-2614. Phone: (303)844-1175.

- 2 Park Central - Ste.400, 1515 Arapahoe St., Denver, CO 80202-2117. Phone: (303) 844-2151.
- 1215 8th Ave., Helena, MT 59601-4144. Phone: (406)449-5431.
- 1000 E. Divide Ave., Bismarck, ND 58502-1632. Phone: (701)328-2865.
- 420 S. Roosevelt St., Aberdeen, SD 57402-4730. Phone: (605)626-2325.
- 140 E. 300 South, Salt Lake City, UT 84111-2333. Phone: (801)524-5703.
- 100 W. Midwest Ave., Casper, WY 82602-2760. Phone: (307)261-5454.

REGION IX *(Arizona, California, Hawaii, Nevada)*—1400 W. Washington St., P.O. Box 6123-SC760E, Phoenix, AZ 85005. Phone: (602)379-4961.

- 800 Capitol Mall - Rm.W-1142, P.O. Box 826880, Sacramento, CA 94280-0001. Phone: (916)654-8178.
- 71 Stevenson St. - Ste.705, San Francisco, CA 94105. Phone: (415)975-4700.
- P.O. Box 3680, Honolulu, HI 96811. Phone: (808)522-8216.
- 1923 N. Carson St. - Rm.205, Carson City, NV 89702. Phone: (702)687-4632.

REGION X *(Alaska, Idaho, Oregon and Washington)*—1111 W. 8th St., Juneau, AK 99802-5509. Phone: (907)465-2723.

- P.O. Box 2697, Boise, ID 83701. Phone: (208)334-6163.
- 312 Employment Division Bldg. - Rm.108, 875 Union St. NE, Salem, OR 97311-0100. Phone: (503)378-3338.
- Olympia, WA 98507-0165. Phone: (360)438-4600.
- 1111 3rd Ave. - Ste.800, Seattle, WA 98101-3212. Phone: (206)553-4831.

DEPARTMENT OF TRANSPORTATION

U.S. COAST GUARD

20.001   **DISTRICT OFFICES**

ATLANTIC *(Alabama, Arkansas, Colorado, Connecticut, Delaware, District of Columbia, Florida, Georgia, Illinois, Indiana, Iowa, Kansas, Kentucky, Louisiana, Maine, Maryland, Massachusetts, Michigan, Minnesota, Mississippi, Missouri, Nebraska, New Hampshire, New Jersey, New Mexico, New York, North Carolina, North Dakota, Ohio, Oklahoma, Panama Canal Zone, Pennsylvania, Puerto Rico, Rhode Island, South Carolina, South Dakota, Tennessee, Texas, Vermont, Virgin Islands, Virginia, West Virginia, Wisconsin, Wyoming)*—Commander (md), Maintenance and Logistics Command (Atlantic), 300 E. Main St. - Ste.800, Norfolk, VA 23510. Phone: (757)628-4280.

PACIFIC *(Alaska, Arizona, California, Hawaii, Idaho, Montana, Nevada, Oregon, U.S.*

Pacific Island Possessions, Utah, Washington)—Commanding Officer (md), Maintenance and Logistics Command (Pacific), Coast Guard Island, Bldg. 52, Alameda, CA 94501-5100. Phone: (510)437-3474.

20.007   District Bridge Administrator:

First Coast Guard District (obr), 408 Atlantic Ave., Boston, MA 02210-2209. Phones: (617)223-8364; FAX (617)223-8073.

▪ Battery Park Bldg. (obr), New York, NY 10004-5073. Phones: (212)668-7165; FAX (212)668-7967.

Western River Directorate (ob), 1222 Spruce St., St. Louis, MO 63103-2398. Phones: (314)539-3900; FAX (314)539-3755.

Fifth Coast Guard District (Aowb), Federal Bldg., 431 Crawford St., Portsmouth, VA 23704-5004. Phones: (757)398-6557; FAX (757)398-6334.

Seventh Coast District (oan), Brickell Plaza, 909 SE 1st Ave., Miami, FL 33130-3050. Phones: (305)536-4521; FAX (305)530-7655.

Eighth Coast Guard District (ob), Boggs Federal Bldg., 501 Magazine St., New Orleans, LA 70130-3396. Phones: (504)589-2965; FAX (504)589-3063.

Ninth Coast Guard District (obr), 1240 E. 9th St., Cleveland, OH 44199-2060. Phones: (216)902-6085; FAX (216)902-6088.

Eleventh Coast Guard District (oan), Bldg. 10 - Rm.50-6, Alameda, CA 94501-5100. Phones: (510)437-3514: FAX (510)437-5836.

Thirteenth Coast Guard District (oan), Federal Bldg., 915 2nd Ave., Seattle, WA 98174-1067. Phones: (206)220-7270; FAX (206)220-7285.

Fourteenth Coast Guard District (oan), Federal Bldg. - Rm.9139, 300 Ala Moana Blvd., Honolulu, HI 96850-4982. Phones: (808)541-2315; FAX (808)541-2309.

Seventeenth Coast Guard District (mon), Juneau, AK 99802-5517. Phones: (907)463-2268; FAX (907)463-2273.

FEDERAL AVIATION ADMINISTRATION

20.100   ## Aviation Information Distribution Program

REGIONAL OFFICES

Aviation Education:

ALASKA—(AAL-5B), 222 W. 7th Ave., Box 14, Anchorage, AK 99513-7587. Phone: (907)271-5293.

CENTRAL *(Iowa, Kansas, Missouri, Nebraska)*—(ACE-10), Federal Bldg. - Rm.1501, 601 E. 12th St., Kansas City, M0 64106. Phone: (816)426-3046.

EASTERN *(Delaware, District of Columbia, Maryland, New Jersey, New York, Pennsylvania, Virginia, West Virginia)*—(ACM-100), Technical Center, Human Resource Management Division, Atlantic City International Airport, Atlantic City, NJ 08405. Phone: (609)484-6630.

▪ (AEA-61), JFK International Airport, Federal Bldg., Jamaica, NY 11430. Phone: (718)553-1056.

GREAT LAKES *(Illinois, Indiana, Michigan, Minnesota, North Dakota, Ohio, South Dakota, Wisconsin)*—(AGL-14B), O'Hare Lake Office Center, 2300 E. Devon Ave., Des Plaines, IL 60018. Phone: (708)294-7042.

NEW ENGLAND *(Connecticut, Maine, Massachusetts, New Hampshire, Rhode Island, Vermont)*—(ANE-45), 12 New England Executive Park, Burlington, MA 01803. Phone: (617)238-7378.

NORTHWEST MOUNTAIN *(Colorado, Idaho, Montana, Oregon, Utah, Washington,*

20.100   *Wyoming)*—(ANM-14A), 1601 Lind Ave. SW, Renton, WA 98055-4056. Phone:
(cont.)   (206)227-2079.

SOUTHERN *(Alabama, Florida, Georgia, Kentucky, Mississippi, North Carolina, Puerto Rico, South Carolina, Tennessee, Virgin Islands)*—(ASO-17.4), 1701 Columbia Ave., College Park, GA 30337. Phone: (404)305-5386. *For mail:* P.O. Box 20636, Atlanta, GA 30320-0631.

SOUTHWEST *(Arkansas, Louisiana, New Mexico, Oklahoma, Texas)*—(AMC-5), Aeronautical Center, Headquarters Bldg. - Rm.356, P.O. Box 25082, Oklahoma City, OK 73125. Phone: (405)954-7500.

▪ (ASW-5), 2601 Meacham Blvd., Ft. Worth, TX 76137-4298. Phone: (817)222-5804.

WESTERN PACIFIC *(Arizona, California, Nevada, Hawaii)*—(AWP-17F), Worldway Postal Center, P.O. Box 92007, Los Angeles, CA 90009. Phone:(310)297-0556.

20.106   REGIONAL OFFICES

Same addresses as **20.100**.

ALASKA—Phone: (907)271-5438

CENTRAL—(ACE-600), Phone: (816)426-4698

EASTERN—(AEA-600), Phone: (718)553-3331

GREAT LAKES—(AGL-600), Phone: (847)294-7272

NEW ENGLAND—(ANE-600), Phone: (617)238-7600

NORTHWEST MOUNTAIN—(ANM-600), Phone: (206)227-2600

SOUTHERN—(ASO-600), Phone: (404)305-6700

SOUTHWEST—(ASW-600), Phone: (817)222-5600

WESTERN PACIFIC—(AWP), Phone: (310)725-3600

FEDERAL HIGHWAY ADMINISTRATION

20.205
thru
20.219

DIVISION OFFICES

Alabama—500 Eastern Blvd. - Ste.200, Montgomery, AL 36117-2018. Phone: (334) 223-7370.

Alaska—709 W. 9th St. - Rm.851, Juneau, AK 99802-1648. Phone: (907)586-7180.

Arizona—234 N. Central Ave. - Ste.330, Phoenix, AZ 85004. Phone: (602)379-3646.

Arkansas—700 W. Capitol Ave. - Rm.3130, Little Rock, AR 72201-3298. Phone: (501)324-5625.

California—980 9th St. - Ste.400, Sacramento, CA 95814-2724. Phone: (916)498-5014.

Colorado—555 Zang St. - Rm.250, Lakewood, CO 80228-1097. Phone: (303)969-6730.

Connecticut—628-2 Hebron Ave. - Ste.303, Glastonbury, CT 06033-5007. Phone: (860)659-6703, ext.3009.

Delaware—300 S. New St. - Rm.2101, Dover, DE 19901-6726. Phone: (302)734-5323.

District of Columbia—Union Center Plaza - Ste.750, 820 1st St. NE, Washington, DC 20002-4237. Phone: (202)523-0163.

Florida—227 N. Bronough St. - Rm.2015, Tallahassee, FL 32301-1330. Phone: (850) 942-9582.

Georgia—61 Forsyth St. SW - Ste.17T100, Atlanta, GA 30303-3104. Phone: (404)562-3630.

Hawaii—Kalanianaole Federal Bldg. - Rm.3202, 300 Ala Moana Blvd., P.O. Box 50206, Honolulu, HI 96850-5000. Phone: (808)541-2700.

Idaho—3050 Lakeharbor Lane - Ste.126, Boise, ID 83703-6243. Phone: (208)334-1690.

Illinois—3250 Executive Park Dr., Springfield, IL 62703-4514. Phone: (217)492-4640.

Indiana—575 N. Pennsylvania St. - Rm.254, Indianapolis, IN 46204-1576. Phone: (317)266-7475.

Iowa—105 6th St., Ames, IA 50010-0627. Phone: (515)233-7300.

Kansas—3300 S. Topeka Blvd. - Ste.1, Topeka, KS 66611-2237. Phone: (913)267-7281.

Kentucky—330 W. Broadway, Frankfort, KY 40601-1922. Phone: (502)223-6720.

Louisiana—750 Florida St. - Rm.255, Baton Rouge, LA 70801. Phone: (504)389-0244.

Maine—Muskie Federal Bldg. - Rm.614, 40 Western Ave., Augusta, ME 04330-6014. Phone: (207)622-8487.

Maryland—711 W. 40th St. - Ste.220, Baltimore, MD 21211-2140. Phone: (410)962-4440.

Massachusetts—55 Broadway - 10th fl., Cambridge, MA 02142-1093. Phone: (617) 494-3657.

Michigan—315 W. Allegan St. - Rm.211, Lansing, MI 48933-1528. Phone: (517)377-1844.

Minnesota—Goltier Plaza - Ste.500 (Box 75), 175 E. 5th St., St. Paul, MN 55101-2904. Phone: (612)291-6100.

Mississippi—666 North St. - Ste.105, Jackson, MS 39202-3199. Phone: (601)965-4215.

Missouri—209 Adams St., Jefferson City, MO 65101-3203. Phone: (573)636-7104.

Montana—2880 Skyway Dr., Helena, MT 59602-1230. Phone: (406)449-5303.

Nebraska—100 Centennial Mall N. - Rm.220, Lincoln, NE 68508-3851. Phone: (402)437-5521.

Nevada—705 N. Plaza St. - Ste.220, Carson City, NV 89701-0602. Phone: (775)687-1204.

New Hampshire—Federal Bldg. - Rm.204, 279 Pleasant St., Concord, NH 03301-2509. Phone: (603)225-1605.

New Jersey—840 Bear Tavern Rd. - Ste.310, West Trenton, NJ 08628-1019. Phone: (609)637-4200.

New Mexico—604 W. San Mateo Rd., Santa Fe, NM 87505-3920. Phone: (505)820-2021.

New York—O'Brien Federal Bldg. - 9th fl., Clinton Ave. and N. Pearl St., Albany, NY 12207. Phone: (518)431-4127.

North Carolina—310 New Bern Ave - Ste.410, Raleigh, NC 27601-1418. Phone: (919)856-4346.

North Dakota—1471 Interstate Loop, Bismarck, ND 58501-0567. Phone: (701)250-4204.

Ohio—200 N. High St. - Rm.328, Columbus, OH 43215. Phone: (614)280-6896.

Oklahoma—300 N. Meridan - Ste.1005, Oklahoma City, OK 73107-6560. Phone: (405)605-6173.

Oregon—530 Center St. NE - Ste.100, Salem, OR 97301-3776. Phone: (503)399-5749.

Pennsylvania—228 Walnut St. - Rm.558, Harrisburg, PA 17101-1720. Phone: (717) 221-3461.

Puerto Rico—Degetau Federal Bldg. and U.S. Courthouse - Rm.329, Carlos Chardon St., Hato Rey, PR 00918-1755. Phone:(787)766-5600.

Rhode Island—380 Westminster Mall - Ste.5, Providence, RI 02903-3239. Phone: (401)528-4541.

20.205
thru
20.219
(cont.)

South Carolina—1835 Assembly St. - Ste.758, Columbia, SC 29201-2459. Phone: (803)765-5194.

South Dakota—116 E. Dakota Ave., Pierre, SD 57501-3110. Phone: (605)224-8033.

Tennessee—640 Grassmere Park Rd. - Ste.112, Nashville, TN 37211-3658. Phone: (615)781-5770.

Texas—Federal Office Bldg. - Rm.826, 300 E. 8th St., Austin, TX 78701-3276. Phone: (512)916-5511.

Utah—2520 W. 4700 S. - Ste.9A, Salt Lake City, UT 84118-1847. Phone: (801)963-0182.

Vermont—87 State St., Montpelier, VT 05602-2954. Phone: (802)828-4423.

Virginia—1504 Santa Rosa Rd. - Ste.205, Richmond, VA 23229-5109. Phone: (804) 281-5100.

Washington—711 S. Capitol Way - Ste.501, Olympia, WA 98501-1284. Phone: (360) 753-9480.

West Virginia—700 Washington St. E. -Ste.200, Charleston, WV 25301. Phone: (304) 347-5928.

Wisconsin—567 D'Onofrio Dr., Madison, WI 53719-2814. Phone: (608)829-7500.

Wyoming—1916 Evans, Cheyenne, WY 82001-3764. Phone: (307)772-2101.

Federal Lands Highway Division Offices

CENTRAL—555 2nd St., Lakewood, CO 80228-1010. Phone: (303)716-2000.

EASTERN—Loudoun Technical Center, 21400 Ridgetop Circle, Sterling, VA 20166-6511. Phone: (703)285-0001.

WESTERN—610 E. 5th St., Vancouver, WA 98661-3893. Phone: (206)696-7700.

FEDERAL RAILROAD ADMINISTRATION

20.301
and
20.303

REGIONAL OFFICES

Regional Director/Railroad Safety:

REGION I - Northeastern *(Connecticut, Maine, Massachusetts, New Hampshire, New Jersey, New York, Rhode Island, Vermont)*—55 Broadway - Rm.1077, Cambridge, MA 02142. Phone: (617)494-2302.

REGION II - Eastern *(Delaware, District of Columbia, Pennsylvania, Maryland, Virginia, West Virginia, Ohio)*—Scott Plaza Two - Ste.550, Philadelphia, PA 19113. Phone: (610)521-8200.

REGION III - Southern *(Alabama, Florida, Georgia, Kentucky, Mississippi, North Carolina, South Carolina, Tennessee)*—Atlanta Federal Center - Ste.16T20, 61 Forsyth St. SW, Atlanta, GA 30303-3104. Phone: (404)562-3800.

REGION IV - Central *(Illinois, Indiana, Michigan, Minnesota, Wisconsin)*—111 N. Canal St. - Ste.655, Chicago, IL 60606. Phone: (312)353-6203.

REGION V - Southwestern *(Arkansas, Louisiana, New Mexico, Oklahoma, Texas)*—8701 Bedford Euless Rd. - Ste.425, Hurst, TX 76053. Phone: (817)284-8142.

REGION VI - Midwestern *(Colorado, Iowa, Kansas, Missouri, Nebraska)*—110 Main St. - Ste.1130, Kansas City, MO 64105-2095. Phone: (816)426-2497.

REGION VII - Western *(Arizona, California, Nevada, Utah)*—801 "I" St. - Ste.466, Sacramento, CA 95814. Phone: (916)498-6540.

REGION VIII - Northwestern *(Alaska, Idaho, Montana, North Dakota, Oregon, South Dakota, Washington, Wyoming)*—Murdock Executive Plaza - Ste.650, 703 Broadway, Vancouver, WA 98660. Phone: (360)696-7536.

FEDERAL TRANSIT ADMINISTRATION

20.500
thru
20.515

REGIONAL OFFICES

REGION I *(Connecticut, Maine, Massachusetts, New Hampshire, Rhode Island, Vermont)*—c/o Volpe National Transportation Systems Center, Kendall Square - Ste.920, 55 Broadway, Cambridge, MA 02142-1093. Phone: (617)494-2055.

REGION II *(New Jersey, New York, Virgin Islands)*—Metropolitan Office - Ste.428, One Bowling Green, New York, NY 10004-1415. Phone: (212)668-2201.

REGION III *(Delaware, District of Columbia, Maryland, Pennsylvania, Virginia, West Virginia)*—1760 Market St. - Ste.500, Philadelphia, PA 19103-4124. Phone: (215) 656-7100.

REGION IV *(Alabama, Florida, Georgia, Kentucky, Mississippi, North Carolina, Puerto Rico, South Carolina, Tennessee)*—61 Forsyth St. SW - Ste.17T50, Atlanta, GA 30303-8917. Phone: (404)562-3000.

REGION V *(Illinois, Indiana, Michigan, Minnesota, Ohio, Wisconsin)*—200 W. Adams St. - Ste.2410, Chicago, IL 60606-5232. Phone: (312)353-2789.

REGION VI *(Arkansas, Louisiana, New Mexico, Oklahoma, Texas)*—Lanham Federal Bldg. - Ste.8A36, 819 Taylor St., Ft. Worth, TX 76102. Phone: (817)978-0550.

REGION VII *(Iowa, Kansas, Missouri, Nebraska)*—6301 Rockhill Rd. - Ste.303, Kansas City, MO 64131-1117. Phone: (816)523-0204.

REGION VIII *(Note grant making activity for Arizona and Nevada falls under Region VIII) (Colorado, Montana, North Dakota, South Dakota, Utah, Wyoming)*—216 Sixteenth St. - Ste.650, Denver, CO 80202-5120. Phone: (303)844-3242.

REGION IX *(American Samoa, Arizona, California, Guam, Hawaii, Nevada)*—201 Mission St. - Ste.2210, San Francisco, CA 94105-1839. Phone: (415)744-3133.

REGION X *(Alaska, Idaho, Oregon, Washington)*—Jackson Federal Bldg. - Ste.3142, 915 2nd Ave., Seattle, WA 98174-1002. Phone: (206)220-7954.

NATIONAL HIGHWAY TRAFFIC SAFETY ADMINISTRATION

20.600
and
20.601

REGIONAL OFFICES

REGION I *(Connecticut, Maine, Massachusetts, New Hampshire, Rhode Island, Vermont)*—Transportation System Center, Kendall Square (Code 903), Cambridge, MA 02142. Phone: (617)494-3427.

REGION II *(New Jersey, New York, Puerto Rico, Virgin Islands)*—222 Mamaroneck Ave. - Ste.204, White Plains, NY 10605. Phone: (914)682-6162.

REGION III *(Delaware, District of Columbia, Maryland, Pennsylvania, Virginia, West Virginia)*—Crescent Bldg. - Ste.4000, 10 S. Howard St., Baltimore, MD 21201. Phone: (410)962-0077.

REGION IV *(Alabama, Florida, Georgia, Kentucky, Mississippi, North Carolina, South Carolina, Tennessee)*—61 Forsyth St. SW - Ste.17T30, Atlanta, GA 30303-3104. Phone: (404)562-3739.

REGION V *(Illinois, Indiana, Michigan, Minnesota, Ohio, Wisconsin)*—19900 Governors Dr. - Ste.201, Olympia Fields, IL 60461. Phone: (708)503-8822.

REGION VI *(Arkansas, Indian Nations, Louisiana, New Mexico, Oklahoma, Texas)*— 819 Taylor St. - Rm.8A38, Ft. Worth, TX 76102-6177. Phone: (817)978-3653.

REGION VII *(Iowa, Kansas, Missouri, Nebraska)*—P.O. Box 412515, Kansas City, MO 64141. Phone: (816)822-7233.

20.600
and
20.601
(cont.)

REGION VIII *(Colorado, Montana, North Dakota, South Dakota, Utah, Wyoming)*— 555 Zang St. - Rm.430, Denver, CO 80228. Phone: (303)969-6917.

REGION IX *(American Samoa, Arizona, California, Guam, Hawaii, Mariana Islands, Nevada)*—201 Mission St. - Ste.2230, San Francisco, CA 94105. Phone: (415)744-3089.

REGION X *(Alaska, Idaho, Oregon, Washington)*—3140 Jackson Federal Bldg., 915 2nd Ave., Seattle, WA 98174. Phone: (206)220-7640.

RESEARCH AND SPECIAL PROGRAMS ADMINISTRATION

20.700   **REGIONAL OFFICES**

CENTRAL *(Illinois, Indiana, Iowa, Kansas, Michigan, Minnesota, Missouri, Nebraska, North Dakota, Ohio, South Dakota, Wisconsin)*—1100 Main St. - Rm.1120, Kansas City, MO 64105. Phones: (816)426-2654; FAX (816)426-2598.

EASTERN *(Connecticut, Delaware, District of Columbia, Maine, Maryland, Massachusetts, New Hampshire, New Jersey, New York, Pennsylvania, Rhode Island, Vermont, Virginia, West Virginia)*—400 7th St. SW - Rm.2108, Washington, DC 20590. Phones: (202)366-4580; FAX (202)366-3274.

SOUTHERN *(Alabama, Arkansas, Florida, Georgia, Kentucky, Mississippi, North Carolina, Puerto Rico, South Carolina, Tennessee)*—61 Forsyth St. - Ste.16T15, Atlanta, GA 30303. Phones: (404)562-3530; FAX (404)562-3569.

SOUTHWEST *(Arizona, Louisiana, New Mexico, Oklahoma, Texas)*—2320 La Branch - Rm.2100, Houston, TX 77004. Phones: (713)718-3746; FAX (713)718-3724.

WESTERN *(Alaska, California, Colorado, Hawaii, Idaho, Montana, Nevada, Oregon, Utah, Washington, Wyoming)*—Golden Hills Centre - Ste.A250, 12600 W. Colfax Ave., Lakewood, CO 80215. Phones: (303)231-5701; FAX (303)231-5711.

MARITIME ADMINISTRATION

20.801
thru
20.805

REGIONAL OFFICES

CENTRAL *(Alabama, Arkansas, Colorado, Florida-western half, Louisiana, Mississippi, New Mexico, Oklahoma, Tennessee, Texas)*—501 Magazine St. - Rm.1223, New Orleans, LA 70130-3394. Phone: (504)589-2000.

GREAT LAKES *(Illinois, Indiana, Iowa, Kansas, Kentucky, Michigan, Minnesota, Missouri, Nebraska, New York-lake coastal area, North Dakota, Ohio, Pennsylvania-lake coastal area, South Dakota, West Virginia (western third), Wisconsin)*—2860 S. River Rd. - Ste.185, Des Plaines, IL 60018-2413. Phone: (847)298-4535.

NORTH ATLANTIC *(Connecticut, Delaware, Maine, Maryland, Massachusetts, New Hampshire, New Jersey, New York-except Great Lakes coastal area, Pennsylvania-except Great Lakes coastal area, Rhode Island, Vermont)*—26 Federal Plaza - Rm. 3737, New York, NY 10278. Phone: (212)264-1300.

SOUTH ATLANTIC *(Florida-eastern half, Georgia, North Carolina, Puerto Rico, South Carolina, Virginia, West Virginia-eastern two-thirds)*—Bldg. 4D - Rm.211, 7737 Hampton Blvd., Norfolk, VA 23505. Phone: (757)441-6393.

WESTERN *(Alaska, Arizona, California, Hawaii, Idaho, Montana, Nevada, Oregon, Utah, Washington, Wyoming)*—201 Mission St. - Ste.2200, San Francisco, CA 94105. Phone: (415)744-3125.

FIELD OFFICE

New York—U.S. Merchant Marine Academy, Kings Point, NY 11024-1699. Phone: (516)773-5000.

20.806   No field offices. Direct contact with HQ. See main entry. *Information for prospective students may be obtained from:*

- California Maritime Academy, Vallejo, CA 94591.
- Great Lakes Maritime Academy, Traverse City, MI 49684.
- Maine Maritime Academy, Castine, ME 04421.
- Massachusetts Maritime Academy, Buzzards Bay, MA 02532.
- State University of New York Maritime College, Ft. Schuyler, NY 10465.
- Texas State Maritime Program, Galveston, TX 77550.

20.807 thru 20.812   Listed under **20.801**.

OFFICE OF THE SECRETARY

20.900   Alaska Aviation Statistics Field Office, DOT, 801 B St. - Rm.506, Anchorage, AK 99501-23657. Phone: (907)271-5147.

DEPARTMENT OF THE TREASURY

INTERNAL REVENUE SERVICE

21.003   *Consult local phone directory under "U.S. Government - Internal Revenue Service."* Toll-free phones: (800)829-1040; hearing impaired, (800)829-4059.

21.004   *Contact:* District Director, Attn: Disclosure Officer, in local IRS offices. *Consult local phone directory under "U.S. Government - Internal Revenue Service."*

UNITED STATES SECRET SERVICE

21.100   *Regional or local field offices are located in the following U.S. cities. Consult local phone directory for addresses and phone numbers, or contact headquarters office directly (see main entry).*

Alabama—Birmingham, Mobile, Montgomery

Alaska—Anchorage

Arizona—Phoenix, Tucson

Arkansas—Little Rock

California—Bakersfield, Fresno, Los Angeles, Riverside, Sacramento, San Diego, San Francisco, San Jose, Santa Ana, Santa Barbara

Colorado—Denver

Connecticut—New Haven

District of Columbia—Washington

Delaware—Wilmington

Florida—Jacksonville, Miami, Orlando, Pensacola (McAllen Resident Agency, Florida Domicile), Tampa, West Palm Beach

21.100 **Georgia**—Albany, Atlanta, Savannah, White Plains
(cont.) **Hawaii**—Honolulu
Idaho—Boise
Illinois—Chicago, Springfield
Indiana—Indianapolis
Iowa—Des Moines
Kansas—Wichita
Kentucky—Lexington, Louisville
Louisiana—Baton Rouge, New Orleans, Shreveport
Maine—Portland
Maryland—Baltimore, Kent Island (Eastern Domicile)
Massachusetts—Boston
Michigan—Detroit, Grand Rapids, Saginaw
Minnesota—Minneapolis
Mississippi—Jackson
Missouri—Kansas City, St. Louis, Springfield
Montana—Great Falls
Nebraska—Omaha
Nevada—Las Vegas, Reno
New Hampshire—Concord
New Jersey—Atlantic City, Newark
New Mexico—Albuquerque
New York—Albany, Buffalo, Melville, New York, Rochester, Syracuse
North Carolina—Charlotte, Raleigh, Wilmington
North Dakota—Bismarck
Ohio—Canton, Cincinnati, Cleveland, Columbus, Dayton, Toledo
Oklahoma—Oklahoma City, Tulsa
Oregon—Portland
Pennsylvania—Harrisburg, Philadelphia, Pittsburgh, Scranton
Puerto Rico—San Juan
Rhode Island—Providence
South Carolina—Charleston, Columbia, Greenville
South Dakota—Sioux Falls
Tennessee—Chattanooga, Knoxville, Memphis, Nashville
Texas—Austin, Corpus Christi, Dallas, El Paso, Houston, Lubbock, San Antonio, Tyler
Utah—Salt Lake City
Vermont—Rutland (Vermont Domicile)
Virginia—Norfolk, Richmond, Roanoke
Washington—Seattle, Spokane
West Virginia—Charleston
Wisconsin—Madison, Milwaukee
Wyoming—Cheyenne

England—London
France—Paris

Germany—Bonn
Italy—Rome
Thailand—Bangkok

APPALACHIAN REGIONAL COMMISSION

23.001 thru 23.011 **STATE ALTERNATES OFFICES**

Alabama—Director, Department of Economic and Community Affairs, 401 Adams Ave., Montgomery, AL 36104-5690. Phone: (334)242-8672.

Georgia—Director, Intergovernmental Relations, Office of the Governor, 270 Washington St., Atlanta, GA 30334. Phone: (404)651-7768.

Kentucky—Director, Intergovernmental Relations, Office of the Governor, Capital Bldg. - Rm.100, Frankfort, KY 40601. Phone: (502)564-2611.

Maryland—Director, Maryland Office of Planning, 301 W. Preston St. - Rm.1101, Baltimore, MD 21201. Phone: (410)767-4510.

Mississippi—Governor's Alternate, Office of the Governor, Box 139, Jackson, MS 39205. Phone: (601)359-3150.

New York—Secretary of State, 41 State St., Albany, NY 12231. Phone: (518)474-0050.

North Carolina—Director, North Carolina Washington Office, 441 N. Capitol St. - Ste.332, Washington DC 20001-1512. Phone: (202)624-5830.

Ohio—Director, Governor's Office of Appalachia, 77 S. High St. - 28th fl., Columbus, OH 43266-1001. Phone: (614)644-9228.

Pennsylvania—Deputy Secretary/Community Affairs and Development, Department of Community and Economic Development, 313 Forum Bldg., Harrisburg, PA 17120. Phone: (717)787-5053.

South Carolina—Director, S.C. Washington Office, 444 N. Capitol St. - Ste.203, Washington, DC 20001. Phone: (202)624-7784.

Tennessee—Director/Grants and Loans, Department of Economic and Community Development, Jackson State Office Bldg., 320 6th Ave. N., Nashville, TN 37243-0405. Phone: (615)741-6201.

Virginia—Director, Virginia Liaison Office, 444 N. Capitol St. NW - Ste.214, Washington, DC 20001. Phone: (202)783-1769.

West Virginia—Director/Community Development Division, West Virginia Development Office, State Capitol Complex - Bldg. 6 (Rm.553), Charleston, WV 25305. Phone: (304)558-4010.

OFFICE OF PERSONNEL MANAGEMENT

27.001 thru 27.013 **SERVICE CENTERS**

REGION I

Connecticut, Delaware, Maine, Maryland, Massachusetts, New Hampshire, New

27.001
thru
27.013
(cont.)

Jersey, New York, Pennsylvania, Rhode Island, Vermont—Green Federal Bldg. - Rm.3400, 600 Arch St., Philadelphia, PA 19106-1596. Phone: (215)597-7670.

Puerto Rico—Plaza Laz American Tower - Rm.1100, 525 Roosesvelt Ave., Hato Rey, PR 00918. Phone: (809)766-5620.

REGION II

Alabama, Arkansas, Mississippi, Tennessee—520 Wynn Dr. NW, Huntsville, AL 35816-3426. Phone: (205)837-1271.

Florida, Georgia—Russell Federal Bldg. - Ste.956, 75 Spring St. SW, Atlanta, GA 30303-3109. Phone: (404)331-4588.

North Carolina, South Carolina—Somerset Park - Ste.200, 4407 Bland Rd., Raleigh, NC 27609-6296. Phone: (919)790-2817.

Virginia—Federal Bldg. - Rm.500, 200 Granby St., Norfolk, VA 23510-1886. Phone: (804)441-3373.

REGION III

Illinois—Kluzynski Federal Bldg. - DPN30-3, 230 S. Dearborn St., Chicago, IL 60604-1687. Phone: (312)353-6234.

Indiana, Kentucky, Michigan, northern Ohio—477 Michigan Ave. - Rm.594, Detroit, MI 48226-2574. Phone: (313)226-2095.

Iowa, Kansas, Missouri, Nebraska—Federal Bldg. - Rm.131, 601 E. 12th St., Kansas City, MO 64106-2826. Phone: (816)426-5706.

Minnesota, North Dakota, South Dakota, Wisconsin—Whipple Federal Bldg. - Rm.503, One Federal Dr., Ft. Snelling, MN 55111-4007. Phone: (612)725-3437.

Ohio, Indiana, Kentucky, West Virginia—U.S. Courthouse and Federal Bldg. - Rm.507, 200 W. 2nd St., Dayton, OH 45402-0001. Phone: (513)225-2576.

REGION IV

Arkansas, Louisiana, Nevada, Oklahoma, Texas—8610 N. Broadway - Rm.305, San Antonio, TX 78217-0001. Phone: (210)805-2423.

Arizona, Colorado, Montana, New Mexico, Utah, Wyoming—12345 W. Alameda Pkwy. - Rm.316, P.O. Box 25167, Denver, CO 80225-0001. Phone: (303)969-6931.

REGION V

Alaska, Hawaii (*Honolulu and Island of Oahu*), Pacific Overseas)—Federal Bldg., 300 Ala Moana Blvd., P.O. Box 50028, Honolulu, HI 96850-0001. Phone: (808)541-2795.

California, Nevada—120 Howard St. - Rm.735, San Francisco, CA 94105-0001. Phone: (415)281-7074.

Idaho, Oregon, Washington—700 5th Ave. - Ste.5950, Seattle, WA 98104-5012. Phone: (206)553-0870.

COMMISSION ON CIVIL RIGHTS

29.001   ## REGIONAL OFFICES

CENTRAL—Gateway Tower II - Ste.908, 400 State Ave., Kansas City, KS 66101. Phones: (913)551-1400, TDD (913)551-1414.

EASTERN—624 9th St. NW - Ste.500, Washington, DC 20425. Phones: (202)376-7533, TDD (202)376-8116.

MIDWESTERN—55 W. Monroe St. - Ste.410, Chicago, IL 60603. Phones: (312)353-8311, TDD (312)353-8362.

ROCKY MOUNTAIN—1700 Broadway - Ste.710, Denver, CO 80290. Phones: (303) 866-1040, TDD (303)866-1049.

SOUTHERN—61 Alabama St. SW - Ste.1840T, Atlanta, GA 30303. Phones: (404)562-7000, TDD (404)562-7004.

WESTERN—3660 Wilshire Blvd. - Ste.810, Los Angeles, CA 90010. Phones: (213) 894-3437, TDD (213)894-3435.

EQUAL EMPLOYMENT OPPORTUNITY COMMISSION

30.001 thru 30.011

DISTRICT OFFICES

Alabama—1900 3rd Ave. N. - Ste.101, Birmingham, AL 35203-2397. Phone: (205)731-1359.

Arizona—Norwest Tower - Ste.690, 3300 N. Central Ave., Phoenix, AZ 85012-2504. Phone: (602)640-5000.

California—255 E. Temple Ave. - 4th fl., Los Angeles, CA 90012. Phone: (213)894-5980.

▪ 901 Market St. - Ste.500, San Francisco, CA 94103. Phone: (415)356-5100.

Colorado—303 E. 17th Ave. - Ste.510, Denver, CO 80203-9634. Phone: (303)866-1300.

District of Columbia—1400 L St. NW - Ste.200, Washington, DC 20005. Phone: (202)275-7377.

Florida—One Biscayne Tower, 2 S. Biscayne Blvd. - Ste.2700, Miami, FL 33131. Phone: (305)536-4491.

Georgia—100 Alabama St. - Ste.4R30., Atlanta, GA 30303. Phone: (404)562-6930.

Illinois—500 W. Madison St. - Ste.2800, Chicago, IL 60661. Phone: (312)353-2713.

Indiana—Federal Bldg. - Ste.900, 101 W. Ohio St., Indianapolis, IN 46204-4203. Phone: (317)226-7212.

Louisiana—701 Loyola Ave. - Ste.600, New Orleans, LA 70113-9936. Phone: (504) 589-2329.

Maryland—City Crescent Bldg. - 3rd fl., 10 S. Howard St., Baltimore, MD 21201. Phone: (410)962-3932.

Michigan—McNamara Federal Bldg. - Ste.865, 477 Michigan Ave., Detroit, MI 48226-9704. Phone: (313)226-4600.

Missouri—1222 Spruce St. - Rm.8100, St. Louis, MO 63103. Phone: (314)539-7800.

New Mexico—505 Marquette Ave. NW - Ste.900, Albuquerque, NM 87102-2189. Phone: (505)248-5201.

New York—7 World Trade Center - 18th fl., New York, NY 10048-1102. Phone: (212)748-8500.

North Carolina—129 W. Trade St. - Ste.400, Charlotte, NC 28202. Phone: (704)344-6682.

Ohio—Tower City, Skylight Office Tower - Ste.850, 1660 W. 2nd St., Cleveland, OH 44113-1454. Phone: (216)522-2001.

Pennsylvania—Bourse Bldg. - Ste.400, 21 S. 5th St., Philadelphia, PA 19106-2515. Phone: (215)451-5800.

Tennessee—1407 Union Ave. - Ste.621, Memphis, TN 38104. Phone: (901)544-0115.

Texas—207 S. Houston St. - 3rd fl., Dallas, TX 75202-4726. Phone: (214)655-3355.

30.001
thru
30.011
(cont.)

- 1919 Smith St. - 7th fl., Houston, TX 77002. Phone: (713)209-3320.
- Mockingbird Plaza II - Ste.200, 5410 Fredericksburg Rd., San Antonio, TX 78229-3555. Phone: (210)281-7600.

Washington—909 1st Ave. - Ste.400, Seattle, WA 98104-1061. Phone: (206)220-6883.

Wisconsin—310 W. Wisconsin Ave. - Ste.800, Milwaukee, WI 53203-2292. Phone: (414)297-1111.

AREA OFFICES

Arkansas—Sauers Bldg. - Ste.625, 425 W. Capitol Ave., Little Rock, AR 72201. Phone: (501)324-5060.

California—410 B St. - Ste.1550, San Diego, CA 92101. Phone: (619)557-7235.

Florida—501 E. Polk St. - Rm.1020, Tampa, FL 33602. Phone: (813)228-2310.

Kansas—400 State Ave. - Ste.905, Kansas City, KS 66101. Phone: (913)551-5655.

Kentucky—U.S. Post Office and Courthouse - Rm.268, 600 Martin Luther King Jr. Place, Louisville, KY 40202. Phone: (502)582-6082.

Massachusetts—One Congress St. - Rm.1001, Boston, MA 02114. Phone: (617)565-3200.

Minnesota—330 S. 2nd Ave. - Ste.430, Minneapolis, MN 55401-2224. Phone: (612) 335-4040.

Mississippi—Cross Road Plaza Complex, 207 W. Amite St., Jackson, MS 39201. Phone: (601)965-4537.

New Jersey—One Newark Center - 21st fl., Newark, NJ 07102-5233. Phone: (973)645-6383.

North Carolina—1309 Annapolis Dr., Raleigh, NC 27608-2129. Phone: (919)856-4064.

Ohio—525 Vine St. - Rm.810, Cincinnati, OH 45202-3122. Phone: (513)684-2851.

Oklahoma—Oklahoma Tower - Ste.1350, 210 Park Ave., Oklahoma City, OK 73102-2265. Phone: (405)231-4911.

Pennsylvania—Federal Bldg. - Ste.300, 1000 Liberty Ave., Pittsburgh, PA 15222-4187. Phone: (412)644-3444.

Tennessee—50 Vantage Way - Ste.202, Nashville, TN 37228. Phone: (615)736-5820.

Texas—The Commons Bldg. C - Ste.100, 4171 N. Mesa St., El Paso, TX 79902. Phone: (915)534-6550.

Virginia—World Trade Center - Ste.4300, 101 S. Main St., Norfolk, VA 23510. Phone: (757)441-3470.

- 3600 W. Broad St. - Rm.229, Richmond, VA 23230. Phone: (804)278-4651.

LOCAL OFFICES

California—1265 W. Shaw Ave. - Ste.103, Fresno, CA 93711. Phone: (209)487-5793.

- 1301 Clay St. - Ste.1170-N, Oakland, CA 94612-5217. Phone: (510)637-3230.
- 96 N. 3rd St. - Ste.200, San Jose, CA 95112. Phone: (408)291-7353.

Georgia—10 Mall Blvd. - Ste.G, Savannah, GA 31406-4821. Phone: (912)652-4234.

Hawaii—300 Ala Moana Blvd. - Ste.7123-A, P.O. Box 50082, Honolulu, HI 96850-0051. Phone: (808)541-3120.

New York—6 Fountain Plaza - Ste.350, Buffalo, NY 14202. Phone: (716)551-4441.

North Carolina—801 Summit Ave., Greensboro, NC 27405-7813. Phone: (910)333-5174.

South Carolina—15 S. Main St. - Rm.530, Greenville, SC 29601. Phone: (803)241-4400.

FEDERAL COMMUNICATIONS COMMISSION

32.001 **REGIONAL OFFICES**

California—3777 Depot Rd. - Rm.420, Hayward, CA 94545-2756. Phone: (510)732-9046.

Illinois—Park Ridge Office Center - Rm.306, 1550 Northwest Hwy., Park Ridge, IL 60608-1460. Phone: (708)298-5405.

Missouri—Brywood Office Tower - Rm.320, 8800 E. 63rd St., Kansas City, MO 64133-4895. Phone: (816)353-9035.

DISTRICT OFFICES

Alaska—6721 Raspberry Rd., Anchorage, AK 99502-1896. Phone: (907)243-2153.

California—18000 Studebaker Rd. - Rm.660, Cerritos, CA 90701-3684. Phones: (310)809-2096; (310)865-0598.

- 3777 Depot Rd. - Rm.420, Hayward, CA 94545-2725. Phone: (510)732-9046.

- Interstate Office Park, 4542 Ruffner St. - Rm.370, San Diego, CA 92111-2216. Phone: (619)467-0549.

Colorado—165 S. Union Blvd. - Ste.860, Lakewood, CO 80228-2213. Phones: (303) 969-6497, 776-8026.

Florida—Rochester Bldg. - Rm.310, 8390 NW 53rd St., Miami, FL 33166-4668. Phone: (305)526-7420.

- 2203 N. Lois Ave. - Rm.1215, Tampa, FL 33607-2356. Phone: (813)348-1502.

Georgia—Koger Center-Gwinnett - Rm.320, 3575 Koger Blvd., Duluth, GA 30136-4958. Phone: (404)279-4621.

- Powder Springs, GA 30073-0085. Phones: (770)943-5420, 242-0165.

Hawaii—Waipahu, HI 96797-1030. Phone: (808)677-3318.

Illinois—Park Ridge Office Center - Rm.306, 1550 Northwest Hwy., Park Ridge, IL 60068-1460. Phones: (708)298-5401, -5402.

Louisiana—800 W. Commerce St. - Rm.505, New Orleans, LA 70123-3333. Phone: (504)589-2095.

Maine—Belfast, ME 04915-0470. Phone: (207)338-4088.

Maryland—P.O. Box 250, Columbia, MD 21045-9998. Phone: (301)725-3474.

Massachusetts—One Batterymarch Park, Quincy, MA 02169-7495. Phone: (617)770-4023.

Michigan—P.O. Box 89, Allegan, MI 49010-9437. Phone: (616)673-2063.

- 24897 Hathaway St., Farmington Hills, MI 48335-1552. Phones: (810)471-5605; *recorded information,* 471-0052.

Minnesota—2025 Sloan Pl. - Ste.31, Maplewood, MN 55117-2058. Phone: (612)774-5175.

Missouri—Brywood Office Tower - Rm.320, 8800 E. 63rd St., Kansas City, MO 64133-4895. Phone: (816)353-3773.

Nebraska—Grand Island, NE 68802-1588. Phone: (308)382-4296 (*recorded information at night*).

New York—1307 Federal Bldg., 111 W. Huron St., Buffalo, NY 14202-2398. Phone: *recorded information,* (716)551-4511.

32.001
(cont.)
▪ 201 Varick St., New York, NY 10014-4870. Phones: (212)620-3437, -3438; *recorded information,* (212)620-3435, 660-3436, 660-3437.

Oregon—1782 Federal Bldg., 1220 SW 3rd Ave., Portland, OR 97204-2898. Phones: (503)326-4114, -4115.

Puerto Rico—Federal Bldg. - Rm.747, Hato Rey, PR 00918-1731. Phone: (809)766-5567.

Texas—Kingsville, TX 78363-0632. Phone: (512)592-2531.

Washington—11410 NE 122nd Way - Ste.312, Kirkland, WA 98034-6927. Phone: (206)821-9037.

Equipment Construction and Installation Branch

3600 Hiram-Lithia Spring Rd. SW, P.O. Box 65, Powder Springs, GA 30073. Phone: (404)943-6425.

FOB Monitoring Assistance

Watch Officer, Signal Analysis Branch, Enforcement Division, 1919 M St. NW - Rm.749, Washington, DC 20554. Phone: (202)418-1180.

Field Operations Bureau

Chief, 1919 M St. NW - Rm.734, Washington, DC 20554-0001. Phone: (202)418-1100.

FEDERAL MARITIME COMMISSION

33.001   **DISTRICT OFFICES**

LOS ANGELES—Terminal Island Station/U.S. Custom House Bldg. - Rm.1018, 300 S. Ferry St., P.O. Box 3164, San Pedro, CA 90731. Phones: (310)514-4905; FAX (310)514-3931.

MIAMI—Customs Management Center - Rm.736, 909 SE 1st Ave., Miami, FL 33131. Phones: (305)536-4316; FAX (305)536-4317.

NEW ORLEANS—U.S. Customs House - Rm.303, 423 Canal St., New Orleans, LA 70130. Phones: (504)589-6662; FAX (504)589-6663.

SEATTLE—U.S. Customs, 7 S. Nevada St. - Ste.100, Seattle, WA 98134. Phones: (206)553-0221; FAX (206)553-0222.

FEDERAL MEDIATION AND CONCILIATION SERVICE

34.001   **REGIONAL OFFICES**

MIDWESTERN—6161 Oak Tree Blvd. - Ste.100, Independence, OH 44131. Phones: (216)522-4800; FAX (216)522-4815.

NORTHEASTERN—One Newark Center - 16th fl., Newark, NJ 17102. Phones: (973)645-2200; FAX (973)297-4860.

SOUTHERN—401 W. Peachtree St. NW - Ste.472, Atlanta, GA 30308. Phones: (404)331-3995; FAX (404)331-4017.

UPPER MIDWESTERN—Broadway Place West - Ste.3950, 1300 Godward St., Minneapolis, MN 55413. Phones: (612)370-3300; FAX (612)370-3104.

WESTERN—Glendale Financial Square - Ste.610, 225 W. Broadway, Glendale, CA 91204. Phones: (213)965-3814; FAX (213)965-3804.

FEDERAL TRADE COMMISSION

36.001   REGIONAL OFFICES

California—10877 Wilshire Blvd. - Ste.700, Los Angeles, CA 90024. Phone: (310)824-4343.

- 901 Market St. - Ste.570, San Francisco, CA 94103. Phone: (415)356-5270.

Colorado—1961 Stout St. - Ste.1523, Denver, CO 80294-0101. Phone: (303)844-2272.

Georgia—Midrise Bldg. - Ste.5M35, 60 Forsyth St. SW, Atlanta, GA 30303. Phone: (404)656-1390.

Illinois—55 E. Monroe St. - Ste.1860, Chicago, IL 60603-5701. Phone: (312)960-5634.

Massachusetts—101 Merrimac St. - Rm.810, Boston, MA 02114-4719. Phone: (617) 424-5960.

New York—150 William St. - Ste.1300, New York, NY 10038. Phone: (212)264-8290.

Ohio—Eaton Center - Ste.200, 1111 Superior Ave., Cleveland, OH 44114-2507. Phone: (216)263-3455.

Texas—1999 Bryan St. - Ste.2150, Dallas, TX 75201-6808. Phone: (214)979-9350.

Washington—915 2nd Ave. - Ste.2896, Seattle, WA 98174. Phone: (206)220-6350.

GENERAL SERVICES ADMINISTRATION

39.001   Business Service Centers

California—300 N. Los Angeles St. - Rm.3108, Los Angeles, CA 90012. Phone: (213)894-3210.

- Office of Enterprise Development, Burton FOB and Courthouse, 450 Golden Gate Ave. - Rm.5-6514, San Francisco, CA 94102-3400. Phone: (415)522-2700.

Colorado—Denver Federal Center, Bldg. 41 (Rm.145), Denver, CO 80225-0006. Phone: (303)236-7408.

District of Columbia—Program Support Division, 7th and D St. SW - Rm.1050, Washington, DC 20407. Phone: (202)708-5804.

Georgia—Office of Enterprise Development, 401 W. Peachtree St. - Rm.2832, Atlanta, GA 30365-2550. Phone: (404)331-5103.

Illinois—230 S. Dearborn St. - Rm.3718, Chicago, IL 60604. Phone: (312)353-5383.

Massachusetts—Office of Enterprise Development, O'Neill Federal Office Bldg., 10 Causeway St. - Rm.290, Boston, MA 02222. Phone: (617)565-8100.

39.001 **Missouri**—Office of Enterprise Development, Enterprise Development Staff, 1500 E.
(cont.) Bannister Rd. - Rm.1160, Kansas City, MO 64131. Phone: (816)926-7203.

New York—Program Service Division, Javits Federal Bldg. - Rm.18-130, 26 Federal Plaza, New York, NY 10278. Phone: (212)264-1234.

Pennsylvania—Program Service Division, Wanamaker Bldg. - Rm.808, 100 Penn Square E., Philadelphia, PA 19107. Phone: (215)656-5525.

Texas—819 Taylor St. - Rm.11AO9, Ft. Worth, TX 76102. Phone: (817)978-3284.

Washington—Office of Enterprise Development, GSA Center - Rm.1001, 400 15th St. SW, Auburn, WA 98001. Phone: (253)931-7956.

39.002 **Offices of Property Sales**

REGION I *(Connecticut, Illinois, Indiana, Maine, Massachusetts, Michigan, Minnesota, New Hampshire, New Jersey, New York, Ohio, Puerto Rico, Rhode Island, Vermont, Virgin Islands, Wisconsin)*—10 Causeway St., Boston, MA 02222. Phone: (617)565-5700.

REGION IV *(Alabama, Delaware, District of Columbia, Florida, Georgia, Kentucky, Maryland, Mississippi, North Carolina, Pennsylvania, South Carolina, Tennessee, Virginia, West Virginia)*—401 W. Peachtree St., Atlanta, GA 30365-2550. Phone: (404)331-5133.

REGION VII *(Arkansas, Colorado, Iowa, Kansas, Louisiana, Missouri, Montana, Nebraska, New Mexico, North Dakota, Oklahoma, South Dakota, Texas, Utah)*—819 Taylor St., Ft. Worth, TX 76102. Phone: (817)978-2331.

REGION IX *(American Samoa, Alaska, Arizona, California, Guam, Hawaii, Idaho, Oregon, Nevada, Trust Territory of the Pacific Islands, Washington)*—450 Golden Gate Ave. - 4th fl. E., San Francisco, CA 94102-3429. Phone: (415)522-3429.

39.003 **Federal Supply Service/Property Management Offices**

GREAT LAKES REGION *(Illinois, Indiana, Michigan, Minnesota, Ohio, Wisconsin)*—230 S. Dearborn St. - DPN 34-6 (Rm.3400), Chicago, IL 60604-1696. Phone: (312)886-8992.

GREATER SOUTHWEST REGION *(Arkansas, Louisiana, New Mexico, Oklahoma, Texas)*—819 Taylor St. - Rm.7A07, Ft. Worth, TX 76102-6105. Phone: (817)978-3794.

HEARTLAND REGION *(Iowa, Kansas, Missouri, Nebraska)*—1500 E. Bannister Rd. - Rm.1102, Kansas City, MO 64131. Phone: (816)823-3719.

MID-ATLANTIC REGION *(Delaware, Maryland, Virginia, Pennsylvania, West Virginia (except those areas in the National Capital Region))*—Wannamaker Bldg., 100 Penn Square E., Philadelphia, PA 19107-3396. Phone: (215)656-3922.

NATIONAL CAPITAL REGION *(District of Columbia, the counties of Montgomery and Prince Georges in Maryland, the cities of Alexandria, Fairfax, and Falls Church and the counties of Arlington, Fairfax, Loudoun, and Prince William in Virginia)*— 470 L'Enfant Plaza East SW - Ste.8100, Washington, DC 20407. Phone: (202)619-8990.

■ Central Office, GSA-FSS, 1941 Jefferson Davis Hwy. - Rm.812, Washington, DC 20406. Phone: (703)305-7420.

NEW ENGLAND REGION *(Connecticut, Maine, Massachusetts, New Hampshire, Rhode Island, Vermont)*—10 Causeway St. - Rm.347 (3rd fl.), Boston, MA 02222-1076. Phone: (617)565-7319.

NORTHEAST AND CARIBBEAN REGION *(New Jersey, New York, Puerto Rico, Virgin Islands)*—26 Federal Plaza - Rm.20-112, New York, NY 10278. Phone: (212)264-2034.

NORTHWEST/ARCTIC REGION *(Alaska, Idaho, Oregon, Washington)*—400 15th St. SW, Auburn, WA 98001-6599. Phone: (206)931-7311.

PACIFIC RIM REGION *(American Samoa, Arizona, California, Guam, Hawaii, Nevada, Northern Mariana Islands)*—450 Golden Gate Ave., San Francisco, CA 94102-3434. Phone: (415)522-3030.

ROCKY MOUNTAIN REGION *(Colorado, Montana, North Dakota, South Dakota, Utah, Wyoming)*—Denver Federal Center - Bldg. 41, P.O. Box 25506, Denver, CO 80225-0506. Phone: (303)236-7700.

SOUTHEAST SUNBELT REGION *(Alabama, Florida, Georgia, Kentucky, Mississippi, North Carolina, South Carolina, Tennessee)*—401 W. Peachtree St. - Rm.2600, Atlanta, GA 30365-2550. Phone: (404)331-4039.

39.007   *Contact offices listed under* **39.003**, *or for DOD surplus property, contact:* Defense Reutilization and Marketing Service, National Sales Office, 74 Washington Ave. N, Battle Creek, MI 49017-3092. Phone: (no number provided); Internet, http://www.fss. gsa.gov/property.html

39.008   **Federal Information Centers**

Federal Information Centers provide general information about the federal government, assisting persons with questions about federal services and programs. FIC information specialists either answer inquiries directly or refer the inquirer to the expert best able to help. Residents of metropolitan areas may phone the following toll-free number workdays from 9:00a.m. to 8:00p.m. EST: **(800)688-9889**.

If you use a text telephone (TTY/TDD) anywhere in the U.S., dial: **(800)326-2996**.

GOVERNMENT PRINTING OFFICE

40.001   *No field offices. There are 1,355 depository libraries in the U.S., with GPO publications on file; consult local phone directory or local librarian for the nearest depository library.*

40.002   **GPO Bookstores**

Alabama—O'Neill Bldg., 2021 3rd Ave. N., Birmingham, AL 35203. Phones: (205) 731-1056; FAX (205)731-3444.

California—ARCO Plaza - C Level, 505 S. Flower St., Los Angeles, CA 90071. Phones: (213)239-9844; FAX (213)239-9848.

- Marathon Plaza - Rm.141-S, 303 2nd St., San Francisco, CA 94107. Phones: (415) 512-2270; FAX (415)512-2276.

Colorado—1660 Wynkoop St. - Ste.130, Denver, CO 80202. Phones: (303)844-3964; FAX (303)844-4000.

- Norwest Banks Bldg., 201 W. 8th St., Pueblo, CO 81003. Phones: (719)544-3142; FAX (719)544-6719.

District of Columbia—U.S. Government Printing Office, 710 N. Capitol St. NW, Washington, DC 20401. Phones: (202)512-0132; FAX (202)512-1355.

- 1510 H St. NW, Washington, DC 20005. Phones: (202)653-5075; FAX (202)376-5055.

Florida—100 W. Bay St. - Ste.100, Jacksonville, FL 32202. Phones: (904)353-0569; FAX (904)353-1280.

Georgia—First Union Plaza - Ste.120, 999 Peachtree St. NE, Atlanta, GA 30309-3964. Phones: (404)347-1900; FAX (404)347-1897.

Illinois—One Congress Center - Ste.124, 401 S. State St., Chicago, IL 60605. Phones: (312)353-5133; FAX (312)353-1590.

40.002   **Maryland**—Warehouse Sales Outlet, 8660 Cherry Lane, Laurel, MD 20707. Phones:
(cont.)   (301)953-7974, 792-0262; FAX (301)498-9109.

Massachusetts—O'Neill Federal Bldg. - Rm.169, 10 Causeway St., Boston, MA 02222.
Phones: (617)720-4180; FAX (617)720-5753.

Michigan—Federal Bldg. - Ste.160, 477 Michigan Ave., Detroit, MI 48226. Phones:
(313)226-7816; FAX (313)226-4698.

Missouri—120 Bannister Mall, 5600 E. Bannister Rd., Kansas City, MO 64137. Phones:
(816)765-2256; FAX (816)767-8233.

New York—Federal Bldg. - Rm.120, 26 Federal Plaza, New York, NY 10278. Phones:
(212)264-3825; FAX (212)264-9318.

Ohio—Federal Bldg. - Rm.1653, 1240 E. 9th St., Cleveland, OH 44199. Phones:
(216)522-4922; FAX (216)522-4714.

▪ Federal Bldg. - Rm.207, 200 N. High St., Columbus, OH 43215. Phones: (614)469-
6956; FAX (614)469-5374.

Oregon—1305 SW 1st Ave., Portland, OR 97201-5801. Phones: (503)221-6217; FAX
(503)225-0563.

Pennsylvania—Robert Morris Bldg., 100 N. 17th St., Philadelphia, PA 19103. Phones:
(215)636-1900; FAX (215)636-1903.

▪ Federal Bldg. - Rm.118, 1000 Liberty Ave., Pittsburgh, PA 15222. Phones: (412)395-
5021; FAX (412)395-4547.

Texas—Federal Bldg. - Rm.1C50, 1100 Commerce St., Dallas, TX 75242. Phones:
(214)767-0076; FAX (214)767-3239.

▪ Texas Crude Bldg. - Ste.120, 801 Travis St., Houston, TX 77002. Phones: (713)228-
1187; FAX (713)228-1186.

Washington—Federal Bldg. - Rm.194, 915 2nd Ave., Seattle, WA 98174. Phones:
(206)553-4270; FAX (206)553-6717.

Wisconsin—Reuss Federal Plaza - Ste.150, 310 W. Wisconsin Ave., Milwaukee, WI
53203. Phones: (414)297-1304; FAX (414)297-1300.

LIBRARY OF CONGRESS

42.001   *There are 57 regional and 83 subregional libraries in the U.S. Each state has an agency
that distributes talking book machines. Local public libraries have information available. Consult local phone directories. Otherwise, contact headquarters office.*

NATIONAL AERONAUTICS AND SPACE ADMINISTRATION

43.001   ## FIELD CENTERS

Education Officer:

Alabama—Marshall Space Flight Center, Huntsville, AL 35812.

California—Ames Research Center, Moffett Field, CA 94035.

▪ Dryden Flight Research Center, Edwards, CA 93523.

Florida—John F. Kennedy Space Center, Kennedy Space Center, FL 32899.

Maryland—Goddard Space Flight Center, Greenbelt, MD 20771.

Mississippi—Stennis Space Center, Stennis Space Center, MS 39529.

Ohio—Lewis Research Center, 21000 Brookpark Rd., Cleveland, Ohio 44135.

Texas—Johnson Space Center, Houston, TX 77058.

Virginia—Langley Research Center, Langley Station, Hampton, VA 23365.

43.002   TECHNOLOGY UTILIZATION CENTERS

Technology Transfer Officer:

Alabama—Marshall Space Flight Center (MS: LA01), Marshall Space Flight Center, AL 35812. Phone: (205)544-4266.

California—Ames Research Center (MS: 202A-3), Moffett Field, CA 94035-1000. Phone: (650)604-0893.

- Dryden Flight Research Center (MS: D-2014), Edwards, CA 93253-0273. Phone: (805)258-3720.

- NASA Management Office-JPL (MS: 301-350), 4800 Oak Grove Dr., Pasadena, CA 91109-8099. Phone: (818)354-2577.

District of Columbia—NASA Headquarters, Office of Aeronautics and Space Transportation Technology (MS: Code RW), Washington, DC 20546-0001. Phone: (202) 358-2320.

Florida—Kennedy Space Center (MS: DE-TPO), Kennedy Space Center, FL 32899-0001. Phone: (407)867-6624.

Maryland—Goddard Space Flight Center (MS: 702), Greenbelt Rd., Greenbelt, MD 20771-0001. Phone: (301)286-5810.

Mississippi—Stennis Space Center (MS: JAOO), Stennis Space Center, MS 39529-6000. Phone: (601)688-1914.

Ohio—Lewis Research Center (MS: 3-7), 21000 Brookpark Rd., Cleveland, OH 44135. Phone: (216)433-5398.

Texas—Johnson Space Center (MS: HA), 2101 NASA Road 1, Houston, TX 77058-3696. Phone: (281)483-0474.

Virginia—Langley Research Center (MS: 118), 11 Langley Blvd., Hampton, VA 23681-0001. Phone: (757)864-6006.

REGIONAL TECHNOLOGY TRANSFER CENTERS

(Persons or organizations desiring comprehensive technical information may contact the Central Network at (800)642-2872) or the following Regional affiliates.)

FAR WEST—3716 S. Hope St. - Ste.200, Los Angeles, CA 90007-4344. Phone: (213)743-2353.

MID-ATLANTIC Mid-Atlantic Technology Application Center, University of Pittsburgh, 823 William Pitt Union, Pittsburgh, PA 15260. Phone: (412)383-2500.

MID-CONTINENT—Texas Engineering Extension Service, Texas A and M University System, 301 Tarrow, College Station, TX 77843-8000. Phone: (409)845-2907.

MIDWEST—Great Lakes Industrial Technology Center, Battelle Memorial Institute, 25000 Great Northern Corporate Center - Ste.260, Cleveland, OH 44070-5310. Phone: (440)734-0094.

NATIONAL RTTC—Wheeling Jesuit College, 316 Washington Ave., Wheeling, WV 26003. Phone: (800)678-6882.

NORTHEAST—Center for Technology Commercialization, Massachusetts Technology Park, 100 North Dr., Westborough, MA 01581. Phone: (508)870-0042.

SOUTHEAST—Southern Technology Applications Center, University of Florida, 1900 SW 34th St. - Ste.206, Gainesville, FL 32608. Phone: (352)294-7822.

NATIONAL CREDIT UNION ADMINISTRATION

44.001   REGIONAL OFFICES

California—2300 Clayton Rd. - Ste.1350, Concord, CA 94520. Phone: (925)363-6200.

Georgia—7000 Central Pkwy. - Ste.1600, Atlanta, GA 30328. Phone: (678)443-3000.

Illinois—4225 Naperville Rd. - Ste.125, Lisle, IL 60532-3658. Phone: (630)955-4100.

New York—9 Washington Square, Washington Ave. Extension, Albany, NY 12205. Phone: (518)862-7400.

Texas—4807 Spicewood Spring Rd. - Ste.5200, Austin, TX 78759-8490. Phone: (512) 342-5600.

Virginia—1775 Duke St. - Ste.4206, Alexandria, VA 22314-3437. Phone: (703)519-6400.

Asset Management Assistance Center

4807 Spicewood Spring Rd. - Ste.5100, Austin, TX 78759-8490. Phone: (512)231-7900.

NATIONAL LABOR RELATIONS BOARD

46.001   REGIONAL, SUBREGIONAL, AND RESIDENT OFFICES

Information Officer:

Alabama—Massey Bldg. - 3rd fl., 1900 3rd Ave. N., Birmingham, AL 35203-3502. Phone: (205)731-1492.

Alaska—Federal Office Bldg. - Ste.21, 222 W. 7th St., Anchorage, AK 99513-3546. Phone: (907)271-5015.

Arizona—Security Bldg. - Ste.440, 234 N. Central Ave., Phoenix, AZ 85004-2212. Phone: (602)379-3361.

Arkansas—425 W. Capitol St. - Ste.375, Little Rock, AR 72201-3489. Phone: (501) 324-6311.

California—888 Figueroa St. - 9th fl., Los Angeles, CA 90017-5455. Phone: (213)894-5200.

- 11150 E. Olympic Blvd. - Ste.700, Los Angeles, CA 90064-1824. Phone: (310)575-7352.
- 1301 Day St. - Rm.300-N, Oakland, CA 94612-5211. Phone: (510)637-3000.
- 555 W. Beech St. - Ste.418, San Diego, CA 92101-2939. Phone: (619)557-6184.
- 901 Market St. - Ste.400, San Francisco, CA 94103-1735. Phone: (415)356-5130.

Colorado—North Tower - 7th fl., 600 17th St., Denver, CO 80202-5433. Phone: (303)844-3551.

Connecticut—One Commercial Plaza - 21st fl., Hartford, CT 06103-3599. Phone: (203)240-3522.

District of Columbia—1099 14th St. NW - Ste.5530, Washington, DC 20570-0001. Phone: (202)208-3000.

Florida—400 W. Bay St. - Rm.214, Box 35091, Jacksonville, FL 32202-4412. Phone: (904)232-3768.

- Federal Bldg. - Rm.1320, 51 SW 1st Ave., Miami, FL 33130-1608. Phone: (305)536-5391.

- 201 E. Kennedy Blvd. - Ste.530, Tampa, FL 33602-5824. Phone: (813)228-2641.

Georgia—233 Peachtree St. NE - Ste.1000, Atlanta, GA 30303-1504. Phone: (404)331-2896.

Hawaii—300 Ala Moana Blvd. - Rm.7318, Honolulu, HI 96850-4980. Phone: (808) 541-2814.

Illinois—200 W. Adams St. - Ste.800, Chicago, IL 60606-5208. Phone: (312)353-7570.

- 300 Hamilton Blvd. - Ste.200, Peoria, IL 61602-1246. Phone: (309)671-7080.

Indiana—575 N. Pennsylvania St. - Rm.238, Indianapolis, IN 46204-1577. Phone: (317)226-7430.

Iowa—210 Walnut St. - Ste.439, Des Moines, IA 50309-2116. Phone: (515)284-4391.

Kansas—8600 Farley St. - Ste.100, Overland Park, KS 66212-4677. Phone: (913)967-3000.

Louisiana—1515 Poydras St. - Rm.610, New Orleans, LA 70112-3723. Phone: (504) 589-6361.

Maryland—103 S. Gay St. - 8th fl., Baltimore, MD 21202-4026. Phone: (410)962-2822.

Massachusetts—10 Causeway, St. - 6th fl., Boston, MA 02222-1072. Phone: (617)565-6700.

Michigan—477 Michigan Ave. - Rm.300, Detroit, MI 48226-2569. Phone: (313)226-3200.

- 82 Ionia NW - Rm.330, Grand Rapids, MI 49503-3022. Phone: (616)456-2679.

Minnesota—110 S. 4th St. - Rm.330, Minneapolis, MN 55401-2221. Phone: (612)348-1757.

Missouri—611 N. 10th St. - Ste.400, St. Louis, MO 63101-1214. Phone: (314)425-4167.

Nevada—600 Las Vegas Blvd. S. - Ste.400, Las Vegas, NV 89101-6637. Phone: (702)388-6416.

New Jersey—20 Washington Place - 5th fl., Newark, NJ 07102-2570. Phone: (973)645-2100.

New Mexico—505 Marquette Ave. NW - Rm.1820, Albuquerque, NM 87102-2181. Phone: (505)248-5125.

New York—Clinton Ave. at N. Pearl St. - Rm.342, Albany, NY 12207-2350. Phone: (518)431-4156.

- Jay St. and Myrtle Ave. - 10th fl., Brooklyn, NY 11201-4201. Phone: (718)330-7713.

- 111 W. Huron St. - Rm.901, Buffalo, NY 14202-2387. Phone: (716)551-4931.

- 26 Federal Plaza - Rm.3614, New York, NY 10278-0104. Phone: (212)264-0300.

North Carolina—4035 University Pkwy. - Ste.200, Winston- Salem, NC 27106-3325. Phone: (919)631-5201.

Ohio—550 Main St. - Rm.3003, Cincinnati, OH 45202-3271. Phone: (513)684-3686.

- 1240 E. 9th St. - Rm.1695, Cleveland, OH 44199-2086. Phone: (216)522-3715.

Oklahoma—224 S. Boulder Ave. - Rm.318, Tulsa, OK 74103-4214. Phone: (918)581-7951.

Oregon—222 SW Columbia St. - Rm.401, Portland, OR 97201-6604. Phone: (503)326-3085.

Pennsylvania—615 Chestnut St. - 7th fl., Philadelphia, PA 19016-4404. Phone: (215) 597-7601.

- 1000 Liberty Ave. - Rm.1501, Pittsburgh, PA 15222-4173. Phone: (412)395-4400.

46.001 **Puerto Rico**—525 F.D. Roosevelt Ave. - Ste.1002, Hato Rey, PR 00918-1002. Phone:
(cont.)   (809)766-5347.

Tennessee—1407 Union Ave. - Ste.800, Memphis, TN 38104-3627. Phone: (901)544-0018.

- 801 Broadway - 3rd fl., Nashville, TN 37203-3816. Phone: (615)736-5921.

Texas—700 E. San Antonio Ave. - Ste.C403, El Paso, TX 79901-7020. Phone: (915)534-6434.

- 819 Taylor St. - Rm.8-A-24, Ft. Worth, TX 76102-6178. Phone: (817)978-2921.

- 1919 Smith St. - Ste.1545, Houston, TX 77002-2649. Phone: (713)209-4888.

- 615 E. Houston St. - Rm.565, San Antonio, TX 78205-2040. Phone: (210)229-6140.

Washington—915 2nd Ave. - Rm.2948, Seattle, WA 98174-1078. Phone: (206)220-6300.

Wisconsin—310 W. Wisconsin Ave. - Ste.700, Milwaukee, WI 53203-2211. Phone: (414)297-3861.

PRESIDENT'S COMMITTEE ON EMPLOYMENT OF PEOPLE WITH DISABILITIES

53.001   *Contact governor's committees, headquartered in every state capitol.*

RAILROAD RETIREMENT BOARD

57.001 **REGIONAL OFFICES**

Colorado—1999 Broadway - Ste.3300 (Box 7), Denver CO 80202-5737. Phone: (303)844-0800.

Georgia—401 W. Peachtree St. - Ste.1703, Atlanta, GA 30365-2550. Phone: (404)331-2691.

Pennsylvania—NIX Federal Bldg. - Ste.304, 9th and Market St., Philadelphia, PA 19107-4228. Phone: (215)597-2646.

SECURITIES AND EXCHANGE COMMISSION

58.001 **REGIONAL OFFICES**

California—5670 Wilshire Blvd. - 11th fl., Los Angeles, CA 90036-3648. Phone: (213)965-3998.

Colorado—1801 California St. - Ste.4800, Denver, CO 80202-2648. Phone: (303)391-6821.

Florida—1401 Brickell Ave. - Ste.200, Miami, FL 33131. Phone: (305)982-6301.

Illinois—Citicorp Center - Rm.1400, 500 W. Madison St., Chicago, IL 60661-2511. Phone: (312)353-7390.

New York—7 World Trade Center - Ste.1300, New York, NY 10048. Phone: (212)748-8051.

DISTRICT OFFICES

California—44 Montgomery St. - Ste.1100, San Francisco, CA 94104. Phone: (415) 705-2500.

Georgia—3475 Lenox Rd. NE - Ste.1000, Atlanta, GA 30326-1232. Phone: (404)842-7600.

Massachusetts—73 Tremont St., Boston, MA 02108-3912. Phone: (617)424-5900.

Pennsylvania—The Curtis Center - Ste.1005-E, Independence Square West, 601 Walnut St., Philadelphia, PA 19106. Phone: (215)597-2278.

Texas—801 Cherry St. - Ste.800, Ft. Worth, TX 76102. Phone: (817)978-6465.

Utah—Key Bank Tower - Ste.500, 50 S. Main St., Box 79, Salt Lake City, UT. 84144-0402. Phone: (801)524-5796.

SMALL BUSINESS ADMINISTRATION

59.002   ## DISASTER AREA OFFICES

AREA 1 (Regions I and II)—360 Rainbow Blvd. S. - 3rd fl., Niagara Falls, NY 14303-1192. Phone: (716)282-4612.

AREA 2 (Regions III, IV, and V)—One Baltimore Place - Ste.300, Atlanta, GA 30308. Phone: (404)347-3771.

AREA 3 (Regions VI and VII)—4400 Amon Carter Blvd. - Ste.102, Ft. Worth, TX 76155. Phone: (817)885-7600.

AREA 4 (Regions VIII, IX, and X)—1825 Bell St. - Ste.208, Sacramento, CA 95825. Phone: (916)556-7240.

59.005 thru 59.007   ## REGIONAL AND DISTRICT OFFICES

REGION I *(Connecticut, Maine, Massachusetts, New Hampshire, Rhode Island, Vermont)*—10 Causeway St. - Ste.812, Boston, MA 02222. Phone: (617)565-8415.

Connecticut—Federal Bldg., 330 Main St. - 2nd fl., Hartford, CT 06106. Phone: (203)240-4700.

Maine—Federal Bldg. - Rm.512, 40 Western Ave., Augusta, ME 04330. Phone: (207) 622-8378.

Massachusetts—10 Causeway St. - Rm.265, Boston, MA 02222-1093. Phone: (617) 565-5590.

• 1441 Main St. - Ste.410, Springfield, MA 01103. Phone: (413)785-0268.

New Hampshire—143 N. Main St. - Ste.202, Concord, NH 03301-1257. Phone: (603)225-1400.

Rhode Island—380 Westminster Mall - 5th fl., Providence, RI 02903. Phone: (401)528-4561.

59.005
thru
59.007
(cont.)

Vermont—Federal Bldg. - Rm.205, 87 State St., Montpelier, VT 05602. Phone: (802) 828-4422.

REGION II *(New Jersey, New York, Puerto Rico, Virgin Islands)*—26 Federal Plaza - Ste.3108, New York, NY 10278. Phone: (212)264-1450.

New Jersey—2 Gateway Center - 15th fl., Newark, NJ 07102. Phone: (973)645-2434.

New York—Federal Bldg. - Rm.1311, 111 W. Huron St., Buffalo, NY 14202. Phone: (716)551-4301.

- 333 E. Water St. - 4th fl., Elmira, NY 14901. Phone: (607)734-8130.
- 35 Pinelawn Rd. - Ste.207W, Melville, NY 11747. Phone: (516)454-0750.
- 26 Federal Plaza - Rm.3100, New York, NY 10278. Phone: (212)264-2454.
- 100 State St. - Ste.410, Rochester, NY 14614. Phone: (716)263-6700.
- 401 S. Salina St. - 5th fl., Syracuse, NY 13202. Phone: (315)471-9393.

Puerto Rico and Virgin Islands—Degatau Federal Bldg. - Ste.201, 252 Ponce DeLeon Blvd., Hato Rey, PR 00918. Phone: (787)766-5272.

REGION III *(Delaware, District of Columbia, Maryland, Pennsylvania, Virginia, West Virginia)*—900 Market St. - 5th fl., Philadelphia, PA 19107. Phone: (215)580-2SBA.

Delaware Branch Office—824 N. Market St. - Ste.610, Wilmington, DE 19801. Phone: (302)573-6294.

District of Columbia—1110 Vermont Ave. NW - Ste.900, Washington, DC 20005. Phone: (202)606-4000.

Maryland—10 S. Howard St. - Ste.6220, Baltimore, MD 21201-2565. Phone: (410) 962-4392.

Pennsylvania—900 Market St. - 5th fl., Philadelphia, PA 19406. Phone: (215)580-2SBA.

- 100 Chestnut St. - Rm.108, Harrisburg, PA 17101. Phone: (717)782-3840.
- 1000 Liberty Ave. - Rm.1128, Pittsburgh, PA 15222. Phone: (412)395-6560.
- 7 N. Wilkes-Barre Blvd., Wilkes-Barre, PA 18702. Phone: (570)826-6497.

Virginia—400 N. 8th St. - Ste.1150, Richmond, VA 23240-0126. Phone: (804)771-2400.

West Virginia—West Pike St. - Ste.330, Clarksburg, WV 26301. Phone: (304)623-5631.

REGION IV *(Alabama, Florida, Georgia, Kentucky, Mississippi, North Carolina, South Carolina, Tennessee)*—1720 Peachtree St. NW - Ste.496, Atlanta, GA 30309-2482. Phone: (404)347-4999.

Alabama—2121 8th Ave. N. - Ste.200, Birmingham, AL 35203-2398. Phone: (205)731-1344.

Florida—100 S. Biscayne Blvd. - 7th fl., Miami FL 33131. Phone: (305)536-5521.

- 7825 Baymeadows Way - Ste.100-B, Jacksonville, FL 32256-7504. Phone: (904)443-1900.

Georgia—1720 Peachtree Rd. NW - 6th fl., Atlanta, GA 30309. Phone: (404)347-4147.

Kentucky—Federal Bldg. - Rm.188, 600 Martin Luther King Jr. Pl., Louisville, KY 40202. Phone: (502)582-5971.

Mississippi—2909 13th St. - Ste.203, Gulfport, MS 39501. Phone: (228)863-4449.

- 101 W. Capitol St. - Ste.400, Jackson, MS 39201. Phone: (601)965-4378.

North Carolina—200 N. College St. - Ste.A2015, Charlotte, NC 28202-2137. Phone: (704)344-6563.

South Carolina—1835 Assembly St. - Rm.358, Columbia, SC 29201. Phone: (803)765-5377.

Tennessee—50 Vantage Way - Ste.201, Nashville, TN 37228-1500. Phone: (615)736-5881.

REGION V *(Illinois, Indiana, Michigan, Minnesota, Ohio, Wisconsin)*—Federal Bldg. - Ste.1240, 500 W. Madison St., Chicago, IL 60661-2511. Phone: (312)353-0357.

Illinois—500 W. Madison St. - Rm.1250, Chicago, IL 60661-2511. Phone: (312)353-4528.

- 511 W. Capitol Ave. - Ste.302, Springfield, IL 62704. Phone: (217)492-4416.

Indiana—429 N. Pennsylvania St. - Ste.100, Indianapolis, IN 46204-1873. Phone: (317)226-7272.

Minnesota—100 N. 6th St. - Ste.610, Minneapolis, MN 55403-1563. Phone: (612)370-2324.

Michigan—477 Michigan Ave. - Rm.515, Detroit, MI 48226. Phone: (313)226-6075.

- 501 S. Front St., Marquette, MI 49885. Phone: (906)225-1108.

Ohio—1111 Superior Ave. - Ste.630, Cleveland, OH 44144-2507. Phone: (216)522-4180.

- 525 Vine St. - Ste.870, Cincinnati, OH 45202. Phone: (513)684-2814.

- 2 Nationwide Plaza - Ste.1400, Columbus, OH 43215-2592. Phone: (614)469-6860.

Wisconsin—740 Regent St. - Ste.100, Madison, WI 53715. Phone: (608)264-5263.

- 310 W. Wisconsin Ave. - Ste.400, Milwaukee, WI 53202. Phone: (414)297-3941.

REGION VI *(Arkansas, Louisiana, New Mexico, Oklahoma, Texas)*—4300 Amon Carter Blvd. - Ste.108, Ft. Worth, TX 76155. Phone: (817)885-6581.

Arkansas —2120 Riverfront Dr. - Ste.100, Little Rock, AR 72202. Phone: (501)324-5871.

Louisiana—365 Canal St. - Ste.2250, New Orleans, LA 70130. Phone: (504)589-6685.

New Mexico—625 Silver Ave. SW, - Ste.320, Albuquerque, NM 87102. Phone: (505) 346-7909.

Oklahoma—210 Park Ave. - Ste.1300, Oklahoma City, OK 73102. Phone: (405)231-5521.

Texas—606 N. Caranchahua - Ste.1200, Corpus Christi, TX 78476. Phone: (361)888-3331.

- 10737 Gateway West - Ste.320, El Paso, TX 79935. Phone: (915)633-7001.

- 4300 Amon Center Blvd. - Ste.114, Ft. Worth, TX 76155. Phone: (817)885-6500.

- Lower Rio Grande Valley District Office, 222 E. Van Buren St. - Rm.500, Harlingen, TX 78550. Phone: (956)427-8533.

- 9301 SW Freeway - Ste.550, Houston, TX 77074-1591. Phone: (713)773-6500.

- 1205 Texas Ave., Lubbock, TX 79401-2693. Phone: (806)472-7462.

- 727 E. Durango - Rm.A-527, San Antonio, TX 78206. Phone: (210)472-5900.

REGION VII *(Iowa, Kansas, Missouri, Nebraska)*—323 W. 8th St. - Ste.307, Kansas City, MO 64105-1500. Phone: (816)374-6380.

Iowa—215 4th Ave. SE - Ste.200, Cedar Rapids, IA 52401-1806. Phone: (319)362-6405.

- New Federal Bldg. - Rm.749, 210 Walnut St., Des Moines, IA 50309. Phone: (515)284-4422.

Kansas—100 E. English St. - Ste.510, Wichita, KS. 67202 Phone: (316)269-6616.

Missouri—323 W. 8th St. - Ste.501, Kansas City, MO 64105. Phone: (816)374-6708.

- 620 S. Glenstone St. - Ste.110, Springfield, MO 65802. Phone: (417)864-7670.

- 815 Olive St. - Rm.242, St. Louis, MO 63101. Phone: (314)539-6600.

Nebraska—11145 Mill Valley Rd., Omaha, NE 68154. Phone: (402)221-4691.

REGION VIII *(Colorado, Montana, North Dakota, South Dakota, Utah, Wyoming)*— 721 19th St. - Ste.400, Denver, CO 80202-2599. Phone: (303)844-0500.

Colorado—721 19th St. - Rm.426, Denver, CO 80202-2599. Phone: (303)844-2607.

Montana—301 S. Park Ave. - Rm.334, Helena, MT 59626. Phone: (406)441-1081.

59.005
thru
59.007
(cont.)

North Dakota—Federal Bldg. - Rm.219, 657 2nd Ave. N., Fargo, ND 58108-3086. Phone: (701)239-5131.

South Dakota—110 S. Phillips Ave. - Ste.200, Sioux Falls, SD 57104-6727. Phone: (605)330-4243.

Utah—Federal Bldg. - Rm.2231, 125 S. State St., Salt Lake City, UT 84138-1195. Phone: (801)524-5804.

Wyoming—Federal Bldg. - Rm.4001, 100 E. "B" St., Casper, WY 82602-2839. Phone: (307)261-6500.

REGION IX *(Arizona, California, Hawaii, Nevada, Pacific Islands)*—455 Market St. - Ste.2200, San Francisco, CA 94105. Phone: (415)744-2118.

Arizona—2828 N. Central Ave. - Ste.800, Phoenix, AZ 85004-1093. Phone: (602)745-7200.

California—2719 N. Air Fresno Dr. - Ste.200, Fresno, CA 93727-1547. Phone: (559)487-5791.

- 330 N. Brand Blvd. - Ste.200, Glendale, CA 91203-2304. Phone: (818)552-3210.
- 660 J St. - Ste.215, Sacramento, CA 95814. Phone: (916)498-6410.
- 500 W. C St. - Ste.550, San Diego, CA 92101-3540. Phone: (619)557-7250.
- 455 Market St. - 6th fl., San Francisco, CA 94105. Phone: (415)744-6820.
- 200 W. Santa Ana Blvd. - Ste.700, Santa Ana, CA 92701. Phone: (714)550-7420.

Hawaii—300 Ala Moana Blvd. - Rm.2-235, Honolulu, HI 96850-4981. Phone: (808)541-2990.

Guam—400 Route 8, Mongmong, GU 96927. Phone: (671)471-7419.

Nevada—300 Las Vegas Blvd. S. - Ste.1100, Las Vegas, NV 89101. Phone: (702)388-6611.

REGION X *(Alaska, Idaho, Oregon, Washington)*—1200 6th Ave. - Ste.1805, Seattle, WA 98101-1128. Phone: (206)553-5676.

Alaska—222 W. 8th Ave. - Rm.A36, Anchorage, AK 99513-7559. Phone: (907)271-4022.

Idaho—1020 Main St. - Ste.290, Boise, ID 83702-5745. Phone: (208)334-1696.

Oregon—1515 SW 5th Ave. - Ste.1050, Portland, OR 97201-5494. Phone: (503)326-2682.

Washington—1200 6th Ave. - Ste.1700, Seattle, WA 98101-1128. Phone: (206)553-7310.

- 801 W. Riverside Ave. - Ste.200., Spokane, WA 99201-0901. Phone: (509)353-2809.

59.008   Listed under **59.002**

59.009
thru   Listed under **59.005**
59.044

TENNESSEE VALLEY AUTHORITY

62.001   TVA Energy Research and Technology Applications, Muscle Shoals, AL 35662-1010. Phone: (256)386-2026.

DEPARTMENT OF VETERANS AFFAIRS

VETERANS HEALTH ADMINISTRATION

**64.007
thru
64.019**

VETERANS MEDICAL FACILITIES

Alabama—700 S. 19th St., Birmingham, AL 35233. Phone: (205)933-8101.
- 215 Perry Hill Rd., Montgomery, AL 36109-3798. Phone: (334)272-4670.
- Tuscaloosa, AL 35404. Phone: (205)554-2000.
- Tuskegee, AL 36083. Phone: (304)727-0550.

Alaska—Medical/Regional Office Center, 235 E. 8th Ave., Anchorage, AK 99508-2989. Phone: (907)257-4700.

Arizona—7th St. at Indian School Rd., Phoenix, AZ 85012. Phone: (602)277-5551.
- Prescott, AZ 86313-5000. Phone: (520)445-4860.
- Tucson, AZ 85723-0001. Phone: (520)792-1450.

Arkansas—Fayetteville, AR 72703. Phone: (501)443-4301.
- 300 E. Roosevelt Rd., Little Rock, AR 72205. Phone: (501)660-1202.

California—2615 E. Clinton Ave., Fresno, CA 93703-2223. Phone: (209)225-6100.
- Livermore, CA 94550. Phone: (510)447-2560.
- 11201 Benton St., Loma Linda, CA 90822-5201. Phone: (909)825-7084.
- 5901 E. 7th St., Long Beach, CA 90822-5201. Phone: (310)494-2611.
- 3801 Miranda Ave., Palo Alto, CA 94304-1207. Phone: (415)493-5000.
- 2800 Contra Costa Blvd., Pleasant Hill, CA 94523-3961. Phone: (510)372-2000.
- 3350 La Jolla Village Dr., San Diego, CA 92161-0001. Phone: (619)552-8585.
- 4150 Clement St., San Francisco, CA 94121-1598. Phone: (415)221-4810.
- Sepulveda, CA 91343-2099. Phone: (818)891-7711.
- 11301 Wilshire Blvd., West Los Angeles, CA 90073-1002. Phone: (310)478-3711.

Colorado—1055 Clermont St., Denver, CO 80220-0166. Phone: (303)399-8020.
- Ft. Lyon, CO 81038-5000. Phone: (719)384-3100.
- Grand Junction, CO 81501-6499. Phone: (303)242-0731.

Connecticut—55 Willard Ave., Newington, CT 06111. Phone: (860)666-6951.
- West Spring St., West Haven, CT 06516. Phone: (203)932-5711.

Delaware—1601 Kirkwood Hwy., Wilmington, DE 19805. Phone: (302)994-2511.

District of Columbia—50 Irving St. NW, Washington, DC 20422. Phone: (202)745-8000.

Florida—Bay Pines, FL 33744. Phone: (813)398-6661.
- Archer Rd., Gainesville, FL 32608-1197. Phone: (325)376-1611.
- Lake City, FL 32055-5898. Phone: (904)755-3016.
- 1201 NW 16th St., Miami, FL 33125. Phone: (305)324-4455.
- Bruce B. Downs Blvd., Tampa, FL 33612. Phone: (813)972-2000.
- West Palm Beach, FL 33420-3207. Phone: (561)882-6700.

Georgia—1670 Clairmont Rd., Atlanta, GA 30033. Phone: (404)321-6111.
- 2460 Wrightsboro Rd., Augusta, GA 30904-6285. Phone: (706)733-0188.
- 2460 Wrightsboro Rd., Dublin, GA 31021. Phone: (912)272-1210.

Idaho—5th and Fort St., Boise, ID 83702-4598. Phone: (208)336-5100.

Illinois—333 E. Huron St., Chicago, IL 60611. Phone: (312)943-6600.
- 820 S. Damen Ave., Chicago, IL 60612. Phone: (312)666-6500.

64.007
thru
64.019
(cont.)

- Danville, IL 61832-5198. Phone: (217)442-8000.
- Hines, IL 60141-5000. Phone: (708)343-7200.
- 2401 W. Main St., Marion, IL 62959. Phone: (618)997-5311.
- North Chicago, IL 60064. Phone: (847)688-1900.

Indiana—1600 Randallia Dr., Ft. Wayne, IN 46805-5100. Phone: (219)426-5431.
- 1481 W. 10th St., Indianapolis, IN 46202-2884. Phone: (317)635-7401.
- 46952 E. 38th St., Marion, IN 46953-4589. Phone: (317)674-3321.

Iowa—30th and Euclid Ave., Des Moines, IA 50310-5774. Phone: (515)699-5999.
- Highway 6 W., Iowa City, IA 52246-2208. Phone: (319)338-0581.
- 1515 W. Pleasant St., Knoxville, IA 50138-3399. Phone: (515)842-3101.

Kansas—4201 S. 4th St. Traffic Way, Leavenworth, KS 66048. Phone: (913)682-2000.
- 2200 Gage Blvd., Topeka, KS 66622. Phone: (913)272-3111.
- 5500 E. Kellogg, Wichita, KS 67218. Phone: (316)685-2221.

Kentucky—Leestown Rd., Lexington, KY 40511-1093. Phone: (606)233-4511.
- 800 Zorn Ave., Louisville, KY 40206-1499. Phone: (502)895-3401.

Louisiana—Shreveport Hwy., Alexandria, LA 71301. Phone: (318)473-0010.
- 1601 Perdido St., New Orleans, LA 70146. Phone: (504)568-0811.
- 510 E. Stoner Ave., Shreveport, LA 71101-4295. Phone: (318)221-8411.

Maine—Rt. 17 E., Togus, ME 04330. Phone: (207)623-8411.

Maryland—Baltimore, Ft. Howard and Point Perry Divisions, 3900 Lock Raven Blvd., Baltimore, MD 21201. Phone: (410)605-7000.

Massachusetts—200 Spring Rd., Bedford, MA 01730. Phone: (617)275-7500.
- 150 S. Huntington Ave., Boston, MA 02130. Phone: (617)232-9500.
- 940 Belmont St., Brockton, MA 02401. Phone: (508)583-4500.
- N. Main St., Northampton, MA 01060-1288. Phone: (413)584-4040.
- 1400 Veterans of Foreign Wars Pkwy., West Roxbury, MA 02401. Phone: (508)583-4500.

Michigan—2215 Fuller Rd., Ann Arbor, MI 48105-2300. Phone: (313)769-7100.
- 5500 Armstrong Rd., Battle Creek, MI 49016-0544. Phone: (616)966-5600.
- Detroit, MI 48201-1932. Phone: (313)576-1000.
- Iron Mountain, MI 49801. Phone: (906)779-3150.
- 1500 Weiss St., Saginaw, MI 48602-5298. Phone: (517)793-2340.

Minnesota—54th St. and 48th Ave. S., Minneapolis, MN 55417. Phone: (612)725-2000.
- 8th St., N. 44th Ave., St. Cloud, MN 56303. Phone: (612)252-1670.

Mississippi—Pass Rd., Biloxi, MS 39531. Phone: (601)388-5541.
- 1500 E. Woodrow Wilson Dr., Jackson, MS 39216. Phone: (601)362-4471.

Missouri—800 Stadium Rd., Columbia, MO 65201. Phone: (573)443-2511.
- 4801 Linwood Blvd., Kansas City, MO 64128. Phone: (816)861-4700.
- Hwy. 67 N., Poplar Bluff, MO 63901. Phone: (573)686-4151.
- Jefferson Barracks, St. Louis, MO 63125. Phone: (314)487-0400.
- 915 N. Grand Blvd., St. Louis, MO 63106. Phone: (314)652-4100.

Montana—William St. and Hwy. 12 W., Ft. Harrison, MT 59636-1500. Phone: (406)447-7900
- 210 S. Winchester, Miles City, MT 59301-4798. Phone: (406)232-3060.

Nebraska—2201 N. Broad Well, Grand Island, NE 68803-2153. Phone: (308)382-3660.
- 600 S. 70th St., Lincoln, NE 68510-2493. Phone: (402)489-3802.
- 4101 Woolworth Ave., Omaha, NE 68105-1873. Phone: (402)346-8800.

Nevada—1703 Charleston Blvd., Las Vegas, NV 89102-2395. Phone: (702)385-3700.
- 1000 Locust St., Reno, NV 89520-0111. Phone: (702)786-7200.

New Hampshire—718 Smyth Rd., Manchester, NH 02104. Phone: (603)624-4366.

New Jersey—Tremont Ave. and S. Center, East Orange, NJ 07018. Phone: (201)676-1000.

- Valley and Knollcroft Rd., Lyons, NJ 07939. Phone: (201)647-0180.

New Mexico—2100 Ridgecrest Dr. SE, Albuquerque, NM 87108-5138. Phone: (505)256-2843.

New York—113 Holland Ave., Albany, NY 12208. Phone: (518)462-3311.

- Redfield Pkwy., Batavia, NY 14020. Phone: (716)343-7500.
- Medical Center, Argonne Ave., Bath, NY 14810. Phone: (607)776-2111.
- 130 W. Kingsbridge Rd., Bronx, NY 10468. Phone: (718)584-9000.
- 800 Poly Pl., Brooklyn, NY 11209. Phone: (718)630-3521.
- 3495 Bailey Ave., Buffalo, NY 14215. Phone: (716)834-9200.
- Ft. Hill Ave., Canandaigua, NY 14424. Phone: (716)394-2000.
- Castle Point, NY 12511. Phone: (914)831-2000.
- Old Albany Post Rd., Montrose, NY 10548. Phone: (914)737-1216.
- 1st Ave. at E. 24th St., New York, NY 10010. Phone: (212)951-5959.
- Long Island-Middleville Rd., Northport, NY 11768. Phone: (516)261-4400.
- Irving Ave. at University Place, Syracuse, NY 13210. Phone: (315)477-7461.

North Carolina—Asheville, NC 28805. Phone: (704)299-7431.

- 508 Fulton St., Durham, NC 27705. Phone: (919)286-0411.
- 2300 Ramsey St., Fayetteville, NC 28301. Phone: (910)822-7059.
- 1601 Brenner Ave., Salisbury, NC 28144. Phone: (704)638-9000.

North Dakota—2101 Elm St., Fargo, ND 58102. Phone: (701)232-3241.

Ohio—17273 State Rt. 104, Chillicothe, OH 45601. Phone: (614)773-1141.

- 3200 Vine St., Cincinnati, OH 45220. Phone: (513)475-6300.
- 10701 East Blvd., Cleveland, OH 44106-3800. Phone: (216)791-3800.
- Medical Center Nursing Home and Domiciliary, 4100 W. 3rd St., Dayton, OH 45428. Phone: (513)262-2170.

Oklahoma—125 S. Main St., Muskogee, OK 74401. Phone: (918)683-3261.

- 921 NE 13th St., Oklahoma City, OK 73104. Phone: (405)270-0501.

Oregon—3710 SW U.S. Veterans Hospital Rd., Portland, OR 97207-1034. Phone: (503)220-8262.

- New Garden Valley Blvd., Roseburg, OR 97470-6153. Phone: (541)440-1000.
- Domiciliary, White City, OR 97503-3207. Phone: (541)826-2111.

Pennsylvania—Pleasant Valley Blvd., Altoona, PA 16602-4377. Phone: (814)943-8164.

- New Castle Rd., Butler, PA 16001-2480. Phone: (412)287-4781.
- Coatesville, PA 19320. Phone: (610)384-7711.
- 135 E. 38th St., Erie, PA 16504. Phone: (814)868-8661.
- S. Lincoln Ave., Lebanon, PA 17042. Phone: (717)272-6621.
- University and Woodland Ave., Philadelphia, PA 19104. Phone: (215)823-5800.
- Highland Dr., Pittsburgh, PA 15206. Phone: (412)363-4900.
- University Dr., Pittsburgh, PA 15240. Phone: (412)688-6000.
- 1111 East End Blvd., Wilkes-Barre, PA 18711-0026. Phone: (717)824-3521.

Puerto Rico—Barrio Monacillos, Rio Piedras, PR 00927-5800. Phone: (787)758-7575.

Rhode Island—380 Westminster Mall, Providence, RI 02908-4799. Phone: (401)273-7100.

South Carolina—109 Bee St., Charleston, SC 29401-5799. Phone: (803)577-5011.

- 1801 Assembly St., Columbia, SC 29201-1639. Phone: (803)776-4000.

South Dakota—I-90 and Hwy. 34, Ft. Meade, SD 57741. Phone: (605)745-2000.

**64.007
thru
64.019
(cont.)**

- 5th St., Hot Springs, SD 57757. Phone: (605)745-2000.
- 2501 W. 22nd St., Sioux Falls, SD 57117. Phone: (605)336-3230.

Tennessee—1030 Jefferson Ave., Memphis, TN 38104-2193. Phone: (901)523-8990.
- Mountain Home, TN 37684. Phone: (423)926-1171.
- 3400 Lebanon Rd., Murfreesboro, TN 37129-1236. Phone: (615)893-1360.
- 1310 24th Ave. S., Nashville, TN 37212-2637. Phone: (615)327-4751.

Texas—6010 Amarillo Blvd. W., Amarillo, TX 79106. Phone: (806)355-9703.
- 2400 S. Gregg St., Big Spring, TX 79720. Phone: (915)263-7361.
- Sam Rayburn Memorial Veterans Center, Bonham, TX 75418. Phone: (903)583-2111.
- 4500 S. Lancaster Rd., Dallas, TX 75216. Phone: (214)376-5451.
- 5919 Brook Hollow Dr., El Paso, TX 79925. Phone: (915)564-6100.
- 2002 Holcombe Blvd., Houston, TX 77030. Phone: (713)479-1414.
- Memorial Blvd., Kerrville, TX 78028. Phone: (210)896-2020.
- 1016 Ward St., Marlin, TX 76661. Phone: (817)883-3511.
- 7400 Merton Minter Blvd., San Antonio, TX 78284. Phone: (210)617-5300.
- 1901 S. 1st St., Temple, TX 76504. Phone: (817)778-4811.
- 4800 Memorial Dr., Waco, TX 76711. Phone: (817)752-6581.

Utah—500 Foothill Blvd., Salt Lake City, UT 84148-0001. Phone: (801)582-1565.

Vermont—White River Junction, VT 05001-0001. Phone: (802)295-9363.

Virginia—Emancipation Dr., Hampton, VA 23667. Phone: (804)722-9961.
- 1201 Broad Rock Rd., Richmond, VA 23249. Phone: (804)230-0001.
- 1970 Roanoke Blvd., Salem, VA 24153. Phone: (540)982-2463.

Washington—American Lake, WA 98493. Phone: (206)762-1010.
- 1660 S. Columbian Way, Seattle, WA 98108. Phone: (206)762-1010.
- North 4816 Assembly St., Spokane, WA 99205-6197. Phone: (509)328-4521.
- 77 Wainwright Dr., Walla Walla, WA 99362-3975. Phone: (509)525-5200.

West Virginia—200 Veterans Ave., Beckley, WV 25801. Phone: (304)255-2121.
- Milford and Chestnut St., Clarksburg, WV 26301. Phone: (304)623-3461.
- 1540 Spring Valley Dr., Huntington, WV 25704. Phone: (304)429-6741.
- Rt. 9, Martinsburg, WV 25401-9809. Phone: (304)263-0811.

Wisconsin—2500 Overlook Terrace, Madison, WI 53705. Phone: (608)256-1901.
- 5000 W. National Ave., Milwaukee, WI 53295. Phone: (414)384-2000.
- Tomah, WI 54660. Phone: (608)372-3971.

Wyoming—2360 E. Pershing Blvd., Cheyenne, WY 82001-5392. Phone: (307)778-7300.
- Fort Rd., Sheridan, WY 82801-8320. Phone: (307)672-1675.

VETERANS BENEFITS ADMINISTRATION

**64.100
thru
64.102**

FIELD OFFICES

Note: In addition to the following field offices, DVA provides toll-free telephone service throughout the 50 states, Washington DC, and Puerto Rico: (800)827-1000.

Alabama—345 Perry Hill Rd., Montgomery, AL 36109-3798.

Alaska—2925 DeBarr Rd., Anchorage, AK 99508-2989.

Arizona—3225 N. Central Ave., Phoenix, AZ 85012-2405.

Arkansas—Ft. Roots - Bldg. 65, North Little Rock, AR 72115-1280.

California—Oakland Federal Bldg., 1301 Clay St., Oakland, CA 94612-5209.
- Federal Bldg., 11000 Wilshire Blvd., Los Angeles, CA 90024-3602.

- 8810 Rio San Diego Dr., San Diego, CA 92108-1508.

Colorado—155 Van Gordon St., Lakewood, CO 80228-1709.

Connecticut—450 Main St., Hartford, CT 06103-3077.

Delaware—1601 Kirkwood Hwy., Wilmington, DE 19805-4988.

District of Columbia—1120 Vermont Ave. NW, Washington, DC 20421-1111.

Florida—1833 Blvd. - Rm.3109, Jacksonville, FL 32206.

- Federal Bldg. - Rm.120, 51 SW 1st Ave., Miami, FL 33130.

- 5201 Raymond St. - Rm.1704, Orlando, FL 32806.

- 312 Kenmore Rd. - Rm.IG250, Pensacola, FL 32503-7492.

- 144 1st Ave. S., St. Petersburg, FL 33701.

Georgia—730 Peachtree St. NE, Atlanta, GA 30365-1232.

Hawaii—PJKK Federal Bldg., 300 Ala Moana Blvd., P.O. Box 50188, Honolulu, HI 96850.

Idaho—805 W. Franklin St., Boise, ID 83702-5560.

Illinois—536 S. Clark St., P.O. Box 8136, Chicago, IL 60605-1523.

Indiana—575 N. Pennsylvania St., Indianapolis, IN 46204-1526.

Iowa—210 Walnut St. - Rm.1063, Des Moines, IA 50309-9825.

Kansas—5500 E. Kellogg, Wichita, KS 67218-1698.

Kentucky—545 S. 3rd St., Louisville, KY 40202-3835.

Louisiana—701 Loyola Ave. - Rm.4210, New Orleans, LA 70113-1912.

Maine—475 Stevens Ave., Portland, ME 04103.

- 1 VA Center, Togus, ME 04330-6795.

Maryland—Federal Bldg. - Rm.233, 1 Hopkins Plaza, Baltimore, MD 21201-0001.

Massachusetts—JFK Federal Bldg., Government Center - Rm.1265, Boston, MA 02203-0393.

Michigan—McNamara Federal Bldg. - Rm.1400, 477 Michigan Ave., Detroit, MI 48226-2591.

Minnesota—Federal Bldg., Ft. Snelling, St. Paul, MN 55111-4050.

Mississippi—1600 E. Woodrow Wilson Ave., Jackson, MS 39216-5102.

Missouri—601 E. 12th St. - Rm.120, Kansas City, MO 64106-0199.

- 400 S. 18th St., St. Louis, MO 63103-2676.

Montana—Ft. Harrison, MT 59636-9999.

Nebraska—5631 S. 48th St., Lincoln, NE 68516-4198.

Nevada—1201 Terminal Way, Reno, NV 89520-0118.

New Hampshire—Cotton Federal Bldg., 275 Chestnut St., Manchester, NH 03101-2489.

New Jersey—20 Washington Pl., Newark, NJ 07102-3174.

New Mexico—Chavez Federal Bldg. and U.S. Courthouse, 500 Gold Ave. SW, Albuquerque, NM 87102-3118.

New York—O'Brien Federal Bldg., Clinton Ave. and N. Pearl St., Albany, NY 12207.

- Federal Bldg., 111 W. Huron St., Buffalo, NY 14202-2368.

- 245 W. Houston St., New York, NY 10014-4805.

- Federal Office Bldg. and Courthouse, 100 State St., Rochester, NY 14614. Phone: (800)827-0619.

- 344 W. Genesee St., Syracuse, NY 13202.

North Carolina—Federal Bldg., 251 N. Main St., Winston-Salem, NC 27155-1000.

North Dakota—2101 Elm St., Fargo, ND 58102-2417.

Ohio—801-B W. 8th St., Cincinnati, OH 45203-2001.

64.100
thru
64.102
(cont.)

- 1240 E. 9th St., Cleveland, OH 44199-2001.
- Federal Bldg. - Rm.309, 200 N. High St., Columbus, OH 43215.

Oklahoma—Federal Bldg., 125 S. Main St., Muskogee, OK 74401-7025.
- 215 Dean A. McGee Ave. - Rm.276, Oklahoma City, OK 73102.

Oregon—Federal Bldg. - Rm.1217, 1220 SW 3rd Ave., Portland, OR 97204-2825.

Pennsylvania—5000 Wissahickon Ave., Philadelphia, PA 19101-8079.
- 1000 Liberty Ave., Pittsburgh, PA 15222-4004.
- 1111 East End Blvd., Wilkes-Barre, PA 18711.

Philippines—Manila Regional Office and Outpatient Clinic, FPO AP 96515-1100.

Puerto Rico—U.S. Courthouse and Federal Bldg., Carlos E. Chardon St., Hato Rey, San Juan, PR 00936-4867. Phone: (809)766-5510.

Rhode Island—380 Westminster Mall, Providence, RI 02903-3246.

South Carolina—1801 Assembly St., Columbia, SC 29201-2495.

South Dakota—2501 W. 22nd St., Sioux Falls, SD 57117-5046.

Tennessee—U.S. Courthouse Federal Office Bldg., 110 9th Ave. S., Nashville, TN 37203-3817.

Texas—U.S. Courthouse and Federal Office Bldg., 1114 Commerce St., Dallas, TX 75242.
- 6900 Almeda Rd., Houston, TX 77030-4200.
- 4902 34th St. - Ste.10 (Rm.134), Lubbock, TX 79410-0001.
- 3601 Bluemel Rd., San Antonio, TX 78229-2041.
- One Veteran Plaza, 701 Clay Ave., Waco, TX 76799-0001.

Utah—Federal Bldg., 125 S. State St., P.O. Box 11500, Salt Lake City, UT 84147-0500.

Vermont—215 Main St., White River Junction, VT 05009-0001.

Virginia—210 Franklin Rd. SW, Roanoke, VA 24011-2204.

Washington—Federal Bldg., 915 2nd Ave., Seattle, WA 98174-1060.

West Virginia—640 4th Ave., Huntington, WV 25701-1340.

Wisconsin—Bldg. 6, 5000 W. National Ave., Milwaukee, WI 53295-0006.

Wyoming—2360 E. Pershing Blvd., Cheyenne, WY 82001-5356.

64.103   *For all states, contact:* Department of Veterans Affairs, P.O. Box 8079, Philadelphia, PA 19101. *This office should also be contacted about Mortgage Protection Life Insurance.*

64.104   Listed under **64.100**.
thru
64.128

NATIONAL CEMETERY SYSTEM

64.201   ## AREA OFFICES

Colorado—P.O. Box 25126, Denver, CO 80225. Phone: (303)914-5700.

District of Columbia—Memorial Programs Processing Site, National Cemetery Administration, 810 Vermont Ave. NW, Washington DC 20420. Phone: (202)565-4257.

Georgia—730 Peachtree St. NE, Atlanta, GA 30365. Phone: (404)347-2121.

Kansas—Memorial Programs Processing Site, Ft. Leavenworth National Cemetery, 395 Biddle Blvd., Ft. Leavenworth, KS 66077-2307. Phone: (no number provided).

Pennsylvania—Memorial Programs Processing Site, Indiantown Gap National Cemetery, R.R. #2, P.O. Box 484A, Annville, PA 17003-9618. Phone: (no number provided).

▪ P.O. Box 11720, Philadelphia, PA 19101. Phone: (215)381-3787.

Tennessee—Memorial Programs Processing Site, Nashville National Cemetery, 1420 Gallatin Rd., Madison, TN 37115-4619. Phone: (615)736-2840.

Virginia—Centralized Contracting Division, 5101 Russell Rd., Quantico, VA 22134-3903. Phone: (703)441-3088.

ENVIRONMENTAL PROTECTION AGENCY

66.001   **Regional Grants Management Contacts**

REGION I *(Connecticut, Maine, Massachusetts, New Hampshire, Rhode Island, Vermont)*—Grants Information and Management Section, (PAS-205), JFK Federal Bldg. - 10th fl., Boston, MA 02203. Phones: (617)918-1791; FAX (617)918-1929.

REGION II *(New Jersey, New York, Puerto Rico, Virgin Islands)*—Grants Administration Branch, (OPM-GRA), 290 Broadway, New York, NY 10007-1866. Phones: (212)637-3402; FAX (212)637-3518.

REGION III *(Delaware, District of Columbia, Maryland, Pennsylvania, Virginia, West Virginia)*—Grants Management Section, Office of the Comptroller, (3PM70), 1650 Arch St., Philadelphia, PA 19103. Phones: (215)814-5410; FAX (215)814-5271.

REGION IV *(Alabama, Florida, Georgia, Kentucky, Mississippi, North Carolina, South Carolina, Tennessee)*—Grants and Contracts Administration Section, Management Division, 345 Courtland St. NE, Atlanta, GA 30303. Phones: (404)562-8371; FAX (404)562-8370.

REGION V *(Illinois, Indiana, Michigan, Minnesota, Ohio, Wisconsin)*—Acquisition and Assistance Branch, (MC-10J), 77 W. Jackson Blvd., Chicago, IL 60604. Phones: (312)886-2400; FAX (312)353-9096.

REGION VI *(Arkansas, Louisiana, New Mexico, Oklahoma, Texas)*—Grants Audit Section, (6M-PG), Management Division, First International Bldg., 1445 Ross Ave., Dallas, TX 75202. Phones: (214)665-6510; FAX (214)665-7284.

REGION VII *(Iowa, Kansas, Missouri, Nebraska)*—Grants Administration Branch, 726 Minnesota Ave., Kansas City, KS 66101. Phones: (913)551-7739; FAX (913)551-7579.

REGION VIII *(Colorado, Montana, North Dakota, South Dakota, Utah, Wyoming)*—Grants Administration Branch, (8PM-GFM), 999 18th St. - Ste.500, Denver, CO 80202-2405. Phones: (303)312- 6305; FAX (303)312-6685.

REGION IX *(American Samoa, Arizona, California, Guam, Hawaii, Nevada, Trust Territories of Pacific Islands, Wake Island)*—Grants and Finance Branch, 75 Hawthorne St., San Francisco, CA 94105. Phones: (415)744-1693; FAX (415)744-1678.

REGION X *(Alaska, Idaho, Oregon, Washington)*—Grants Administration Unit, 1200 6th Ave., Seattle, WA 98101. Phones: (206)533-2722; FAX (206)553-4957.

Chemical Emergency Preparedness and Prevention Office (CEPP)

Regional Offices

REGION I—One Congress St. - Ste.1100., (MC: SPP), Boston, MA 02114-2023. Phones: (617)918-1804, -1835; FAX (617)918-1810.

REGION II—2890 Woodbridge Ave., (MC: 211), Edison, NJ 08837-3679. Phones: (908)906-6194, 321-6620; FAX (908)321-4425.

66.001   REGION III—1650 Arch St./34S33, (MC: 3HW33), Philadelphia, PA 19103. Phones:
(cont.)   (215)814-3293, 566-3302; FAX(215)814-3254.

REGION IV—Federal Center, 61 Forsyth St., Atlanta, GA 30303. Phones: (404)562-9188, -9121; FAX (404)562-9163.

REGION V—77 W. Jackson Blvd., (MC: SC-9J), Chicago, IL 60604. Phones: (312) 353-9045; FAX (312)886-6064.

REGION VI—Fountain Place - Ste.1200, (MC: 6E-E), Dallas, TX 75202-2733. Phones: (214)665-2292, -2277; FAX (214)665-7447.

REGION VII—726 Minnesota Ave., (MC: ARTD/TSPP), Kansas City, KS 66101. Phones: (913)551-7876, -7540; FAX (913)551-7065.

REGION VIII—One Denver Place, (MC: EPR-ER), 999 18th St. - Ste.500, Denver, CO 80202-2405. Phones: (303)312-6837, -6760; FAX (303)312-6071.

REGION IX—75 Hawthorne St., San Francisco, CA 94105. Phones: (415)744-2337, -2230; FAX (415)744-1917.

REGION X—1200 6th Ave., (MC: HW-093), Seattle, WA 99101. Phones: (206)553-2674, -0383; FAX (206)553-0175.

Municipal Solid Waste Primary Contacts

REGION I—One Congress St. - Ste.1100, (MC: SPP-SPP), Boston, MA 02114-2023. Phones: (617)918-1813; FAX (617)918-1810.

REGION II—290 Broadway, (MC: 2DEPP-RPB), New York, NY 10007-1866. Phones: (212)637-4125; FAX (212)637-4437.

REGION III—1650 Arch St, (MC: 3WC21/3HW60), Philadelphia, PA 19103. Phones: (215)814-3298; FAX (215)814-3163.

REGION IV—Atlanta Federal Center, 61 Forsyth St., (MC: 4WD-RPB/RSS), Atlanta, GA 30303-3104. Phones: (404)562-8449; FAX (404)562-8439.

REGION V—77 W. Jackson Blvd., (MC: DRP-8J), Chicago, IL 60604-3590. Phones: (312)886-0976; FAX (312)353-4788.

REGION VI—1445 Ross Ave., (MC: 6PD-U), Dallas, TX 75202-2733. Phones: (214) 665-6760; FAX (214)665-7263.

REGION VII—726 Minnesota Ave., (MC: ARTD/TSPP), Kansas City, KS 66101. Phones: (913)551-7523; FAX (913)551-7947.

REGION VIII—999 18th St. - Ste.500, (MC: 8P2-P2), Denver, CO 80202-2466. Phones: (303)312-6390; FAX (303)312-6741.

REGION IX—75 Hawthorne St., (MC: WST-7), San Francisco, CA 94105. Phones: (415)744-1284; FAX (415)744-1044.

REGION X—1200 6th Ave., (MC: WCM-128), Seattle, WA 98101. Phones: (206)553-6117; FAX (206)553-8509.

Pollution Prevention Contacts

REGION I—JFK Federal Bldg. - Rm.2203 (SPN), Boston, MA 02203. Phones: (617)918-1817; FAX (617)918-4939.

REGION II—290 Broadway - 25th fl. (2-OPM-PPI),DEPP, New York, NY 10007-1866. Phones: (212)637-3742; FAX (212)637-3771.

REGION III—1650 Arch St. (3RA20), Philadelphia, PA 19103-2029. Phones: (215) 814-2761; FAX (215)566-2782.

REGION IV—Air and Pesticide Center, 61 Forsyth St. SW, Atlanta, GA 30303. Phones: (404)562-9430; FAX (404)562-9066.

REGION V—Waste, Pesticide and Toxics Division, 77 W. Jackson Blvd. (DRP-8J), Chicago, IL 60604-3590. Phones: (312)353-4669; FAX (312)353-4788.

REGION VI—Compliance Assurance and Enforcement Division, 1445 Ross Ave. -

Ste.1200 (6EN-XP), Dallas, TX 75202. Phones: (214)665-2119; FAX (214)665-7446.

REGION VII—Air, RCRA and Toxics Division, 726 Minnesota Ave., (ARTD/TSPP), Kansas City, KS 66101. Phones: (913)551-7517; FAX (913)551-7065.

REGION VIII—Office of P2, State and Tribal Assistance, 999 18th St.- Ste.500 (8P2-P2), Denver, CO 80202-2466. Phones: (303)312-6385; FAX (303)312-6339.

REGION IX—Waste Division, 75 Hawthorne St. (WST-1-1), San Francisco, CA 94105. Phones: (415)744-2192; FAX (415)744-1796.

REGION X—Office of Innovation, 1200 6th Ave., Seattle, WA 98101. Phones: (206) 553-4072; FAX (206)553-6647.

RCRA and Superfund

REGION I—Office of Ecosystem Protection (MC-HHA) and/or Office of Site Remediation and Restoration, One Congress St., Boston, MA 02114-2023. Phones: (617) 918-1501, -1201, -1203.

REGION II—Division of Environmental Planning and Protection, 26 Federal Plaza - Rm.1000 (2AWM-SW), New York, NY 10278. Phone: (212)637-3772.

- Emergency and Remedial Response Division, 290 Broadway, New York, NY 10007. Phones: (212)637-4439, -4363, -4392.

REGION III—Waste Chemical Management Division, 841 Chestnut Bldg. (3HWOO), Philadelphia, PA 19107. Phones: (215)814-3110, -3114.

- Hazardous Site Cleanup Division, 1650 Arch St., Philadelphia, PA 19106. Phone: (215)813-3000.

REGION IV—Waste Management Division, 61 Forsyth St., Atlanta, GA 30303. Phones: (404)562-8628, -8651.

REGION V—Waste, Pesticides and Toxics Division, 77 W. Jackson Blvd., Chicago, IL 60604-3507. Phones: (312)353-2024, 886-0653.

- Superfund Division, Metcalfe Federal Bldg., 77 W. Jackson Blvd., Chicago, IL 60604. Phone: (312)353-9773.

REGION VI—Multimedia Planning and Permitting Division and/or Superfund Division, Fountain Place - Ste.1200, 1445 Ross Ave., Dallas, TX 75202-2733. Phones: (214)665-7200, -6701, -7263.

REGION VII—Air/RCRA Toxics Division and/or Superfund Division, 726 Minnesota Ave., Kansas City, KS 66101. Phones: (913)551-7020, -7050.

REGION VIII—Hazardous Waste Program, Denver Place - Ste.500, (MC-8P2-SA), 999 18th St., Denver, CO 80202-2466. Phones: (303)312-7081, -6064.

- Office of Ecosystems Protection and Remediation, 999 18th St. - Ste.500, Denver, CO 80202. Phone: (303)312-6598.

REGION IX—Waste Division and/or Hazardous Waste Management Division, 75 Hawthorne St., San Francisco, CA 94105. Phones: (415)744-2138, -1750, -2199, -2120.

REGION X—Office of Waste and Chemical Management and/or Office of Environmental Cleanup, 1200 6th Ave., Seattle, WA 98101. Phones: (206)553-4198, -1261, -0455.

Radon Regional Program Office Contacts

(No phone numbers provided.)

REGION I—JFK Federal Bldg. - Rm.ATR, Boston, MA 02203.

REGION II—Radiation Branch (AWM-RAD), 26 Federal Plaza - Rm.1005A, New York, NY 20278.

REGION III—Air Programs Branch (3AT12), 841 Chestnut St., Philadelphia, PA 19107.

66.001
(cont.)

REGION IV—Office of Radiation, 345 Courtland St. NE, Atlanta, GA 30365.

REGION V—77 W. Jackson Blvd., (AT-18J), Chicago, IL 60604-3590.

REGION VI—Air Enforcement Branch (6T-E), 1445 Ross Ave., Dallas, TX 75202.

REGION VI—726 Minnesota Ave., Kansas City, KS 66101.

REGION VII—999 18th St. - Ste.8ART-RP, Denver, CO 80202-2405.

REGION IX—Radon Coordinator (A-1-1), 75 Hawthorne St., San Francisco, CA 94105.

REGION X—1200 6th Ave. (AT-082), Seattle, WA 98101.

66.032   Regional Radon Program Representative. *Use addresses listed under* **66.001**. (No phone numbers provided.)

66.033   *Use general addresses listed under* **66.001**.

OFFICE OF WATER

66.419
thru
66.456

REGION I—Water Quality Policy Division, Boston, MA 02203. Phone: (617)918-1511.

REGION II—Environmental Planning and Protection Division, 26 Federal Plaza, New York, NY 10278. Phone: (212)637-3724.

REGION III—Environmental Services Division, 1650 Arch St., Philadelphia, PA 19106. Phone: (215)815-2710.

REGION IV—Water Management Division, 61 Forsyth St. SW, Atlanta, GA 30303. Phone: (404)562-9355.

REGION VI—Water Quality Protection Division, 1445 Ross Ave., Dallas, TX 75270. Phone: (214)655-7101.

REGION IX—Water Management Division, 75 Hawthorne St., San Francisco, CA 94105. Phone: (415)744-1860.

REGION X—Office of Ecosystems and Communication, 1200 6th Ave., Seattle, WA 98101. Phone: (206)553-4181.

66.458
and
66.460   Listed under **66.001**.

66.461   Wetlands Protection Section:

REGION I—Boston, MA 02203. Phone: (617)565-3602.

REGION II—New York, NY 10278. Phone: (212)637-3810.

REGION III—Environmental Services Division, Philadelphia, PA. 19107. Phone: (215)814-2715.

REGION IV—Atlanta, GA 30365. Phone: (404)562-9369.

REGION V—Chicago, IL 60604. Phone: (312)886-0241.

REGION VI—Dallas, TX 75202. Phone: (214)655-8185.

REGION VII—Water Resources Protection Branch, Kansas City, KS 66101. Phone: (913)551-7320.

REGION VIII—Denver, CO 80202. Phone: (303)312-6946.

REGION IX—Water Management Division, San Francisco, CA 94105. Phone: (415)974-1974.

REGION X—Aquatic Resources Unit, Seattle, WA 98101. Phone: (206)553-6221.

66.463   *Use general addresses listed under* **66.001**.

66.466   Chesapeake Bay Program Office, EPA, 410 Severn Ave. - Ste.109, Annapolis, MD 21403. Phone: (410)267-5700.

66.467
and
66.468   *Use general addresses listed under* **66.419.**

66.500
thru
66.608   Listed under **66.001.**

66.700
thru
66.714   Listed under **66.001.**

OFFICE OF SOLID WASTE
AND EMERGENCY RESPONSE

66.801   Listed under **66.001.**

66.802   ## Superfund TAG ("Technical Assistance Grant") Coordinators

REGION I—One Congress St., Boston, MA 02114-2023. Phones: (617)918-1428; FAX (617)918-1291.

REGION II—290 Broadway - 26th fl., (MC: OEP), New York, NY 10007-1866. Phones: (212)637-3420; FAX (212)637-4445.

REGION III—1650 Arch St., (MC: 3HS43), Philadelphia, PA 19103. Phones: (215) 566-5522; FAX (215)566-5518.

REGION IV—Atlanta Federal Center, 61 Forsyth St., Atlanta, GA 30303. Phones: (404)562-8866; FAX (404)562-8788.

REGION V—Metcalfe Federal Bldg., 77 W. Jackson Blvd., (MC: PS19-J), Chicago, IL 60604-3507. Phones: (312)886-1325; FAX (312)353-1155.

REGION VI—Fountain Place - Ste.1200, 1445 Ross Ave., (MC: 6HMC), Dallas, TX 75202-2733. Phones: (214)665-8157; FAX (214)665-6660.

REGION VII—726 Minnesota Ave., (MC: PBAF), Kansas City, KS 66101. Phones: (913)551-7762; FAX (913)551-7066.

REGION VIII—999 18th St. - Ste.500, (MC: 8OEA/PA1), Denver, CO 80202-2466. Phones: (303)312-6688; FAX (303)312-6961.

REGION IX—75 Hawthorne St., (MC: H-1-1), San Francisco, CA 94105. Phones: (415)744-2179; FAX (415)744-1796.

REGION X—1200 6th Ave., (MC: ECO-081), Seattle, WA 98101. Phones: (206)553-6919; FAX (206)553-6984.

HEADQUARTERS—401 M. St. SW, (MC: 5204G), Washington D.C. 20460. Phone: (703)603-8889; FAX (703)603-9100.

66.804
and
66.805   ## Underground Storage Tank Regional Program Managers

REGION I—One Congress St. - Ste.1100, Boston, MA 02114-2023. Phone: (617)918-1311.

REGION II—Water Compliance Branch, 290 Broadway, (2DECA-WCB-GWCS), New York, NY 10007-1866. Phone: (212)637-4232.

REGION III—State Programs Branch, 1650 Arch St., (3WC21), Philadelphia, PA 19103. Phone: (215)814-3231.

REGION IV—Atlanta Federal Center, 61 Forsyth St. SW, (MC:GW-PB-15), Atlanta, GA 30303-3104. Phone: (404)562-9441.

REGION V—Underground Storage Tanks, 77 W. Jackson Blvd., (DRU-7J), Chicago, IL 60604-3590. Phone: (312)886-6136.

66.804
and
66.805
(cont.)

REGION VI—1st Interstate Bank Tower - Ste.1200., 1445 Ross Ave., (6PD-U), Dallas, TX 75202-2733. Phone: (214)665-6760.

REGION VII—726 Minnesota Ave., (ART-GUTS), Kansas City, KS 66101. Phone: (913)551-7651.

REGION VIII—999 18th St. - Ste.500, (8P2-W-GW), Denver, CO 80202-2466. Phone: (303)312-6137.

REGION IX—75 Hawthorne St. - 10th fl., (H-W-4), San Francisco, CA 94105. Phone: (415)744-2079.

REGION X—1200 6th Ave., (WD-133), Seattle, WA 98101. Phone: (206)553-2857.

66.806 Contact TAG coordinators listed under **66.802**.

66.808 Listed under **66.001**.
and
66.809

66.810 Contact CEPP offices listed under **66.001**.

66.811 Contact Brownfield Coordinators at offices listed under **66.001**.

OFFICE OF FEDERAL ACTIVITIES

66.926 Regional Indian Program Coordinator:

REGION I—JFK Federal Bldg., One Congress St. - Ste.1100, Boston, MA 02114-2023. Phone: (617)918-1672.

REGION II—26 Federal Plaza, New York, NY 10278. Phone: (212)637-3564.

REGION IV—345 Courtland St. NE, Atlanta, GA 30365. Phone: (404)562-9639.

REGION V—77 W. Jackson Blvd., Chicago, IL 60604-3507. Phone: (312)353-1394.

REGION VI—1445 Ross Ave.- Ste.1200, Dallas, TX 75202-2733. Phone: (214)665-7454.

REGION VII—726 Minnesota Ave., Kansas City, KS 66101. Phone: (913)551-7539.

REGION VIII—999 18th St. - Ste.500, Denver, CO 80202-2405. Phone: (303)312-6343.

REGION IX—75 Hawthorne St., San Francisco, CA 94105. Phone: (415)744-1607.

REGION X—1200 6th Ave., Seattle, WA 98101. Phone: (206)553-6200.

66.930 EPA - El Paso U.S.- Mexico Border Liaison Office:

▪ 4050 Rio Bravo - Ste.100, El Paso, TX 79902. Phones: (915)533-7273; FAX (915) 533-2327.

EPA - San Diego U.S. - Mexico Border Liaison Office:

▪ 610 W. Ash St. - Ste.703, San Diego, CA 92101. Phones: FAX (619)235-4771.

OFFICE OF ENVIRONMENTAL EDUCATION

66.950 Listed under **66.001**.
and
66.951

COMMODITY FUTURES TRADING COMMISSION

78.004   REGIONAL OFFICES

CENTRAL—300 S. Riverside Plaza. - Ste.1600 N., Chicago, IL 60606. Phone: (312) 353-9000.

- 510 Grain Exchange Bldg., Minneapolis, MN 55415. Phone: (612)370-3255.

EASTERN—One World Trade Center - Ste.3747, New York, NY 10048. Phone: (212)466-2071.

SOUTHWESTERN—4900 Main St. - Ste.721, Kansas City, MO 64112. Phone: (816)931-7600.

WESTERN—10900 Wilshire Blvd. - Ste.400, Los Angeles, CA 90024. Phone: (310) 235-6783.

DEPARTMENT OF ENERGY

81.022   FIELD OFFICES - OPERATIONS

California—Oakland Operations Office, 1301 Clay St., Oakland, CA 94612-5208. Phone: (510)637-1802.

Colorado—Rocky Flats Office, Golden, CO 80402-0928. Phone: (303)966-6314.

Idaho—Idaho Operations Office, 2050 Energy Dr. - MS 1221., Idaho Falls, ID 83401-1536. Phone: (208)526-0111.

Illinois—Chicago Operations Office, 9800 S. Cass Ave., Argonne, IL 60439-4899. Phone: (630)252-2001.

New Mexico—Albuquerque Operations Office, Albuquerque, NM 87185-5400. Phone: (505)845-4154.

Nevada—Nevada Operations Office, P.O. Box 98518, Las Vegas, NV 89193-8518. Phone: (702)295-1212.

Ohio—Miamisburg, OH 45343-3020. Phone: (513)865-3997.

Pennsylvania—Federal Energy Technology Center, P.O. Box 10940, Pittsburgh, PA 15236-0940. Phone: (412)892-6000.

South Carolina—Savannah River Operations Office, P.O. Box A, Aiken, SC 29801. Phone: (803)725-6211.

Tennessee—Oak Ridge Operations Office, P.O. Box 2001, Oak Ridge, TN 37831. Phone: (423)576-5454.

Washington—Richland Operations Office, 825 Jadwin Ave., P.O. Box 550, Richland, WA 99352. Phone: (509)376-7411.

West Virginia—Federal Energy Technology Center, 3610 Collins Ferry Rd., Morgantown, WV 26507-0880. Phone: (304)291-4764.

81.036   Golden Field Office, 1717 Cole Blvd., Golden, CO 80401. Phones: (303)275-4764, -4744; FAX (303)275-4788.

81.041 STATE ENERGY OFFICES

Alabama—Energy Division, Economic and Community Affairs, Department of Economic and Community Affairs, Montgomery, AL 36103-5690. Phone: (205)242-5292.

Alaska—Housing Finance Corp., 520 E. 34th Ave., Anchorage, AK 99503. Phone: (907)561-1900.

American Samoa—Power Authority Energy Division, American Samoa Government, P.O. PPB, Pago Pago, AS 96799. Phone: (684)699-1101.

Arizona—3800 N. Central Ave.- Ste.1200, Phoenix, AZ 85012. Phone: (602)280-1402.

Arkansas—One State Capitol Mall - Ste.4B-215, Little Rock, AR 72201. Phone: (501)682-7377.

California—Energy Commission, 1516 9th St., (MS-1), Sacramento, CA 95814. Phone: (916)654-4996.

Colorado—Office of Energy Conservation, 1675 Broadway - Ste.1300, Denver, CO 80202-4613. Phone: (303)620-4292.

Connecticut—Policy Development and Planning, Office of Policy and Management, 80 Washington St., Hartford, CT 06106. Phone: (203)566-4298.

Delaware—Division of Facilities Management/Energy, P.O. Box 1401, Dover, DE 19903. Phone: (302)739-5644.

District of Columbia—613 G St. NW - Rm.500, Washington, DC 20001. Phone: (202)673-6750.

Florida—Department of Community Affairs, 2740 Centerview Dr., Tallahassee, FL 32399-2100. Phone: (904)488-6764.

Georgia—Environmental Facilities Authority, Equitable Bldg. - Ste.2080, 100 Peachtree St. NW, Atlanta, GA 30303-1901. Phone: (404)656-5176.

Guam—P.O. Box 2950, Agana, GU 96910. Phone: (671)477-0538.

Hawaii—Department of Business Economic Development and Tourism, 335 Merchant St. - Rm.109, Honolulu, HI 96813. Phone: (808)587-3812.

Idaho—Energy Division, Department of Water Resources, 1301 N. Orchard, Boise, ID 83706. Phone: (208)327-7900.

Illinois—Department of Energy and Natural Resources, 325 W. Adams St. - Rm.300, Springfield, IL 62704-1892. Phone: (217)785-2002.

Indiana—Office of Energy Policy, Department of Commerce, One N. Capitol - Ste.700, Indianapolis, IN 46204-2288. Phone: (317)232-8940.

Iowa—Energy Bureau, Department of Natural Resources, Wallace State Office Bldg., Des Moines, IA 50319-0034. Phone: (515)281-8681.

Kansas—Energy Programs Section, Corporation Commission, 1500 SW Arrowhead Rd., Topeka, KS 66604-4027. Phone: (913)271-3100.

Kentucky—Division of Energy, 691 Teton Trail - 2nd fl., Frankfort, KY 40601. Phone: (502)564-7192.

Louisiana—Energy Division, Department of Natural Resources, P.O. Box 94396, Baton Rouge, LA 70804-9396. Phone: (504)342-5054.

Maine—Department of Economic and Community Development, State House Station #59, 193 State St., Augusta, ME 04333. Phone: (207)624-6802.

Maryland—Energy Administration, 45 Calvert St. - 4th fl., Annapolis, MD 21401. Phone: (301)974-3755.

Massachusetts—Division of Energy Resources, Saltonstall Bldg. - Rm.1500, 100 Cambridge St., Boston, MA 02202. Phone: (617)727-4732.

Michigan—Public Service Commission, P.O. Box 30221, Lansing, MI 48909. Phone: (517)334-6270.

Minnesota—Department of Public Service, 121 7th Place E. - Ste.200, St. Paul, MN 55101. Phone: (612)296-6025.

Mississippi—Energy Division, Department of Economic and Community Development, P.O. Box 850, Jackson, MS 39202-3096. Phone: (601)359-6600.

Missouri—Division of Energy, Department of Natural Resources, P.O. Box 176, Jefferson City, MO 65102. Phone: (314)751-4000.

Montana—Energy Division, Department of Natural Resources and Conservation, 1520 E. 6th Ave., Helena, MT 59620-2301. Phone: (406)444-6754.

Nebraska—Lincoln, NE 68509-5085. Phone: (402)471-2867.

Nevada—1050 E. William - Ste.435, Carson City, NV 89710. Phone: (702)687-4910.

New Hampshire—Office of Energy and Community Services, 57 Regional Dr., Concord, NH 03301-8519. Phone: (603)271-2611.

New Jersey—Office of Planning and Conservation, Board of Public Utility, 2 Gateway Center, Neward, NJ 07102. Phone: (201)648-2129.

New Mexico—Energy Conservation and Management Division, Department of Energy, Minerals and Natural Resources, 2040 S. Pacheco St., Santa Fe, NM 87505. Phone: (505)827-7122.

New York—Energy Research and Development Authority, 2 Rockefeller Plaza, Albany, NY 12223. Phone: (518)465-6251.

North Carolina—Energy Division, Department of Commerce, 430 N. Salisbury St., Raleigh, NC 27611. Phone: (919)733-2230.

North Dakota—Office of Intergovernmental Assistance, State Capitol Bldg. - 14th fl., 600 E. Boulevard Ave., Bismarck, ND 58505-0170. Phone: (701)328-2094.

Northern Mariana Islands—Division of Energy, Department of Public Works, Saipan, CM 96950. Phone: (670)322-9229.

Ohio—Office of Energy Efficiency, Department of Development, 77 S. High St. - 26th fl., Columbus, OH 43215. Phone: (614)466-3465.

Oklahoma—Division of Community Affairs and Development, Department of Commerce, Oklahoma City, OK 73126-0980. Phone: (405)841-9326.

Oregon—Conservation Resources Division, Department of Energy, 625 Marion St. NE, Salem, OR 97310-0831. Phone: (503)378-4040.

Pennsylvania—116 Pine St., Harrisburg, PA 17101-1227. Phone: (717)783-9981.

Puerto Rico—Energy Affairs Administration, Department of Natural Resources and Economics, P.O. Box 5887, Puerta de Terra, PR 00906. Phone: (809)723-3636.

Rhode Island—Office of Management and Administrative Services, State House - Rm.111, Providence, RI 02903-5872. Phone: (401)277-2850, ext.321.

South Carolina—1201 Main St. - Ste.820, Columbia, SC 29201-3227. Phone: (803) 737-8030.

South Dakota—Office of Economic Development, 711 E. Wells Ave., Pierre, SD 57501. Phone: (605)733-5032.

Tennessee—Energy Division, Department of Economic and Community Development, Rachel Jackson Bldg. - 6th fl., 320 6th Ave. N., Nashville, TN 37219-5308. Phone: (615)741-2994.

Texas—Energy Conservation Office, Capitol Station - Ste.200, 221 E. 11th St., P.O. Box 13047, Austin, TX 78711. Phone: (512)463-1931.

Utah—Division of Community Development, 324 S. State St. - Ste.230, Salt Lake City, UT 84111. Phone: (801)538-5428.

Vermont—Department of Public Services, 112 State St. - Drawer 20, Montpelier, VT 05620-2601. Phone: (802)828-2811.

Virgin Islands—Old Customs House, Frederiksted, St. Croix, U.S. Virgin Islands 00840. Phone: (809)772-2616.

81.041
(cont.)

Virginia—Division of Energy, Department of Mines, Minerals and Energy, 202 N. 9th St. - 8th fl., Richmond, VA 23219. Phone: (804)692-3219.

Washington—Olympia, WA 98504-3165. Phone: (360)956-2001.

West Virginia—Energy Efficiency Program, Development Office, Capitol Bldg. 6 - Rm.553, Charleston, WV 25305-0311. Phone: (304)558-4010.

Wisconsin—Division of Energy and Intergovernmental Relations, Department of Administration, Madison, WI 53707-7868. Phone: (608)266-8234.

Wyoming—Economic and Community Development Division, Barrett Bldg. - 4th fl., 2301 Central Ave., Cheyenne, WY 82002. Phone: (307)777-6436.

81.042   *Contact may be made at the following phone numbers:*

- Boston, MA. Phone: (617)565-9710.
- Philadelphia, PA. Phone: (215)656-6954.
- Atlanta, GA. Phone:(404)347-2888.
- Chicago, IL. Phone: (312)886-8575.
- Denver, CO. Phone: (303)275-4801.
- Seattle, WA. Phone: (206)553-1132.

81.049   Listed under **81.022**.

81.057   Project Office, Federal Energy Technology Ctr., P.O. Box 10940, Pittsburgh, PA 15236. Phone: (412)892-5700.

81.065   Yucca Mountain Project Office, Las Vegas, NV. Phone: (702)794-1300.

81.079   **Alabama**—Southeast Regional Biomass Energy Program, Tennessee Valley Authority, Muscle Shoals, AL 35662. Phone: (205)386-3086.

Colorado—Western Regional Biomass Energy Program, Denver Regional Support Office, 1617 Cole Blvd., Golden, CO 80401. Phone: (303)275-4821.

District of Columbia—Northeast Regional Biomass Energy Program, Coalition of Northeast Governors, 400 N. Capitol St. NW, Washington, DC 20001. Phone: (202)624-8450.

Illinois—Great Lakes Regional Biomass Energy Program, Council of Great Lakes Governors, 35 E. Wacker Dr., Chicago, IL 60601. Phone: (312)407-0177.

Nebraska—Western Regional Biomass Energy Program, Nebraska Energy Office, 1200 N. St., Lincoln, NE 68508. Phone: (402)471-2867.

Washington—Northwest Regional Biomass Energy Program, Seattle Regional Support Office, 800 5th Ave. - Ste.3950, Seattle, WA 98104. Phone: (206)553-2079.

81.081   Chicago Operations Office, 9800 S. Cass Ave., Argonne, IL 60439. Phone: (630)252-2667.

81.089   Federal Energy Technology Center Supervisor (FE-UPC/AD21), P.O. Box 10940 (MS 921-143), Cochrans Mill Rd., Pittsburgh, PA 15276. Phone: (412)892-4524.

81.105   **SUPPORT OFFICES**

Colorado—Denver Regional Support Office, 1617 Cole Blvd. - Bldg.17-2, Golden, CO 80401. Phone: (303)275-4816.

- Golden Field Office, 1617 Cole Blvd, Golden, CO 80401. Phone: (303)275-4744.

Georgia—730 Peachtree St. NE - Ste.876, Atlanta, GA 30308-1212. Phone: (404)347-7141.

Illinois—One S. Wacker Dr. - Ste.2380, Chicago, IL 60606-4616. Phone: (312)886-8579.

Massachusetts—One Congress St. - 11th fl., Boston, MA 02114-2023. Phone: (617)565-9732.

Pennsylvania—1880 JFK Blvd. - 5th fl., Philadelphia, PA 19102. Phone: (215)656-6964.

Washington—800 5th Ave. - Ste.3950, Seattle, WA. 98104-3122. Phone: (206)553-2153.

81.106 Institutional Relations Manager, Area Office, DOE, P.O. Box 3090, Carlsbad, NM 88221-3090. Phone: (505)234-7335.

81.110 Program Manager, Amarillo Area Office and Albuquerque Operations Office. Phone: (806)477-3125.

81.112 Listed under **81.022**.

81.114 Director, Support Division, Acquisition and Assistance Group, Chicago Operations Office. Phone: (630)252-2115.

81.116 Civil Rights and Diversity Manager, Rocky Flats Environmental Technology Site, Golden, CO 80402-0928. Phone: (303)966-2483.

UNITED STATES INFORMATION AGENCY

82.001 *Contact Fulbright program advisor at local college, or write to the nearest Institute of International Education, following (no phone numbers provided):*

California—41 Sutter St. - Ste.510, San Francisco, CA 94108.

Colorado—700 Broadway - Ste.112, Denver, CO 80203.

Illinois—401 N. Wabash Ave. - Ste.722, Chicago, IL 60611.

New York—809 United Nations Plaza, New York, NY 10017.

Texas—515 Post Oak Blvd. - Ste.150, Houston, TX 77027.

82.006 American Council of Young Political Leaders, 1612 K St. NW - Ste.300, Washington, DC 20006. Phone: (202)857-0999.

FEDERAL EMERGENCY MANAGEMENT AGENCY

83.011
thru
83.552

REGIONAL OFFICES

REGION I (Boston)—McCormack Post Office and Courthouse - Rm.442, Boston, MA 02109-4595. Phone: (617)223-9540.

REGION II (New York)—26 Federal Plaza - Rm.1337, New York, NY 10278-0002. Phone: (212)225-7209.

REGION III (Philadelphia)—Liberty Square Bldg. - 2nd fl., 105 S. 7th St., Philadelphia, PA 19106-3316. Phone: (215)931-5608.

REGION IV (Atlanta)—3003 Chamblee-Tucker Rd., Atlanta, GA 30341. Phone: (770)220-5200.

REGION V (Chicago)—175 W. Jackson Blvd. - 4th fl., Chicago, IL 60604-2698. Phone: (312)408-5501.

REGION VI (Dallas)—Federal Regional Center, 800 N. Loop 288, Denton, TX 76201-3698. Phone: (940)898-5104.

REGION VII (Kansas City)—2323 Grand Blvd. - Ste.900, Kansas City, MO 64108-2670. Phone: (816)283-7061.

83.011
and
83.552
(cont.)

REGION VIII (Denver)—Federal Center - Bldg. 710, Denver, CO 80225-0267. Phone: (303)235-4812.

REGION IX (San Francisco)—Presidio of San Francisco - Bldg. 105, San Francisco, CA 94129-1250. Phone: (415)923-7100.

REGION X (Seattle)—Federal Regional Center, 130 - 228th St. SW, Bothell, WA 98021-9796. Phone: (425)487-4604.

DEPARTMENT OF EDUCATION

84.007   ## REGIONAL ADMINISTRATORS/STUDENT FINANCIAL AID

Students should contact their educational institution. Educational institutions should contact:

REGION I—McCormack Post Office and Courthouse - Rm.502, 5 Post Office Square (MS 01-0070), Boston, MA 02109. Phone: (617)223-9328.

REGION II—Institutional Review Branch, 75 Park Place - 12th fl., New York, NY 10007. Phone: (212)637-6423.

REGION III—3535 Market St. - Rm.16200 (MS 03-2080), Philadelphia, PA 19104. Phone: (215)596-1018.

REGION IV—P.O. Box 1692, Atlanta, GA 30301. Phone: (404)331-0556.

REGION V—401 S. State St. - Rm.700-D (MS 05-4080), Chicago, IL 60605. Phone: (312)353-0375.

REGION VI—1200 Main Tower Bldg. - Rm.2150 (MS 06-5080), Dallas, TX 75202. Phone: (214)767-3811.

REGION VII—Institutional Review Branch, 10220 N. Executive Hills Blvd. - 9th fl., Kansas City, MO 64153. Phone: (816)880-4054.

REGION VIII—Institutional Review Branch, 1244 Speer Blvd. - Rm.322, Denver, CO 80204. Phone: (303)844-3676.

REGION IX—50 United Nations Plaza - Rm.227 (MS 09-8080), San Francisco, CA 94102-4987. Phone: (415)556-8382.

REGION X—1000 2nd Ave. - Rm.1200, Seattle, WA 98174-1099. Phone: (206)227-1770.

84.027   *Potential applicants should contact their state department of education.*

84.032   Listed under **84.007**. *(Each state with an operating guarantee agency maintains an office; obtain list from headquarters office.)*

84.033
thru
84.038

Students should contact their educational institution. Public and private nonprofit organizations should contact grantee educational institutions. Educational institutions should contact the appropriate Regional Office, listed under **84.007**.

84.042
and
84.047

SECRETARY'S REGIONAL REPRESENTATIVES

REGION I—McCormack Post Office and Courthourse - Rm.540, Boston, MA 02109. Phone: (617)223-9317.

REGION II—75 Park Place - 12th fl., New York, NY 10007. Phone: (212)637-6283.

REGION III—100 Penn Square E. - Ste.505, Philadelphia, PA 19107. Phone: (215)656-6010.

REGION IV—61 Forsyth St. SW - Rm.19T40, Atlanta, GA 30303. Phone: (404)562-6225.

REGION V—111 N. Canal St. - Rm.1094, Chicago, IL 60606. Phone: (312)553-8192.

REGION VI—1999 Bryan St. - Ste.2700, Dallas, TX 75201-6817. Phone: (214)880-3011.

REGION VII—10220 N. Exccutive Hills Blvd. - Ste.720, Kansas City, MO 64153-1367. Phone: (816)880-4000.

REGION VIII—Federal Regional Office Bldg. - Rm.310, 1244 Speer Blvd., Denver, CO 80204-3582. Phone: (303)844-3544.

REGION IX—50 United Nations Plaza - Rm.205, San Francisco, CA 94102-4987. Phone: (415)437-7520.

REGION X—915 2nd Ave. - Rm.3362, Seattle, WA 98174-1099. Phone: (206)220-7800.

84.063 Federal Student Aid Information Center. Phone: (800)433-3243. *Or, contact the director of student financial aid at the institution the student wishes to attend, high school guidance counselors, directors of state agencies, or regional office listed under* **84.007.**

84.069 *List of state student scholarship or assistance agencies available in the Regional Offices listed under* **84.007.** *Program administered from headquarters.*

84.126 thru 84.132

REGIONAL COMMISSIONERS/REHABILITATIVE SERVICES

REGION I—McCormack Post Office and Courthouse - Rm.232, Boston, MA 02109-4557. Phone: (617)223-4085.

REGION II—75 Park Place - 12th fl., New York, NY 10007. Phone: (212)264-4016.

REGION III—100 Penn Square E. - Ste.512, Philadelphia, PA 19107. Phone: (215)656-8531.

REGION IV—61 Forsyth St. SW - Rm.18T91, Atlanta, GA 30303. Phone: (404)562-6330.

REGION V—10220 N. Executive Hills Blvd., Kansas City, MO 64153-1367. Phone: (816)880-4107.

REGION VI—1999 Bryan St. - Rm.2740, Dallas, TX 75202. Phone: (214)808-4927.

REGION VII—111 N. Canal St. - Ste.510, Chicago, IL 60606. Phone: (816)880-4107.

REGION VIII—Harwood Center, 1999 Bryan St., Dallas, TX 75201-6817. Phone: (214)880-4927.

REGION IX—Federal Office Bldg. - Rm.215, 50 United Nations Plaza, San Francisco, CA 94102. Phone: (415)437-7840.

REGION X—915 2nd Ave. - Rm.2848, Seattle, WA 98174-1099. Phone: (206)220-7840.

84.145

FEDERAL REAL PROPERTY ASSISTANCE PROGRAM

REGIONAL OFFICES

EASTERN ZONE (Regions I, II, III, IV, V)—Director, Office of Administrator/Management Services, McCormack Post Office and Courthouse - Rm.536, Boston, MA 02109-4557. Phone: (617)223-9321.

WESTERN ZONE (Regions VI, VII, XIII, IX, X)—Director, Office of Administrator/Management Services, 400 Maryland Ave. SW - Rm.2C107, Washington, DC 20202. Phone: (202)401-0506.

84.161 and 84.169 Listed under **84.126.**

84.173 *Contact the state educational agency.*

84.177 thru 84.250 Listed under **84.126.**

84.256	Contact Pacific Resources for Education and Learning, Honolulu, HI. Phone: (no number provided).
84.263 thru 84.265	Listed under **84.126**.
84.268	Listed under **84.007**.
84.275	Listed under **84.126**.
84.281	Each state has an SEA and SAHE coordinator; obtain addresses from headquarters office.
84.315	Listed under **84.126**.

SCHOLARSHIP AND FELLOWSHIP FOUNDATIONS

85.400	American College Testing (ACT), 2201 N. Dodge, P.O. Box 168, Iowa City, IA 52243. Phones: (319)337-1707; FAX (319)337-1204.
85.402	110 S. Church - Ste.3350, Tucson, AZ 85701. Phones: (520)670-5529; FAX (520)670-5530.

PENSION BENEFIT GUARANTY CORPORATION

86.001	*Contact the nearest Pension and Welfare Benefits Administration (Department of Labor) office listed under* **17.150**.

NATIONAL ARCHIVES AND RECORDS ADMINISTRATION

89.001   PRESIDENTIAL LIBRARIES

California—Ronald Reagan Library, 40 Presidential Dr., Simi Valley, CA 93065-0600. Phone: (800)410-8354.

Georgia—Jimmy Carter Library, 441 Freedom Pkwy., Atlanta, GA 30307-1498. Phone: (404)331-3942.

Kansas—Dwight D. Eisenhower Library, 200 SE 4th St., Abilene, KS 67410-2900. Phone: (785)263-4751.

Iowa—Herbert Hoover Library, 210 Parkside Dr., West Branch, IA 52358-0488. Phone: (319)643-5301.

Maryland—Nixon Presidential Materials Staff, National Archives at College Park, College Park, MD 20740-6001. Phone: (301)713-6950.

Massachusetts—John F. Kennedy Library, Columbia Point, Boston, MA 02125-3398. Phone: (617)929-4500.

Michigan—Gerald R. Ford Museum, 303 Pearl St. NW, Grand Rapids, MI 49504-5353. Phone (616)451-9263.

▪ Gerald R. Ford Library, 1000 Beal Ave., Ann Arbor, MI 48109-2114. Phone: (734) 741-2218.

Missouri—Harry S. Truman Library, 500 W. U.S. Hwy. 24, Independence, MO 64050-1798. Phone: (816)833-1400.

New York—Franklin D. Roosevelt Library, 511 Albany Post Rd., Hyde Park, NY 12538-1999. Phone: (914)229-8114.

Texas—Lyndon B. Johnson Library, 2313 Red River St., Austin, TX 78705-5702. Phone: (512)916-5137.

▪ George Bush Library, 1000 George Bush Dr. W., College Station, TX 77843. Phone: (409)260-9554.

OFFICE OF REGIONAL RECORDS SERVICES

Alaska - Pacific Alaska Region—654 W. 3rd Ave., Anchorage, AK 99501-2145. Phones: (907)271-2443; FAX (907)271-2442; e-mail, archives@alaska.nara.gov

California - Pacific Region—24000 Avila Rd. - 1st fl. (east entrance), Laguna Niguel, CA 92667-3497. *For mail:* Laguna Niguel, CA 92607-6719. Phones: (949)360-2618; FAX (949)360-2624; e-mail, archives@laguna.nara.gov

▪ 1000 Commodore Dr., San Bruno, CA 94066-2350. Phones: (650)876-9249; FAX (650)876-9233; e-mail, archives@sanbruno.nara.gov

Colorado - Rocky Mountain Region—Denver Federal Center - Bldg. 48, Denver, CO 80225-0307. Phones: (303)236-0801; FAX (303)236-9297; e-mail, center@denver. nara.gov

District of Columbia—Washington National Records Center, Reference Service Branch, Washington, DC 20409-0002. Phone: (301)457-7010.

▪ Archives I - Research Room Services Branch, 700 Pennsylvania Ave. NW, Washington, DC 20408. Phone: (202)501-5403.

Georgia - Southeast Region—1557 St. Joseph Ave., East Point, GA 30344-2593. Phones: (404)763-7438; FAX (404)763-7059; e-mail, center@atlanta.nara.gov

Illinois - Great Lakes Region—7358 S. Pulaski Rd., Chicago, IL 60629-5898. Phones: (773)581-9688; FAX (312)886-7883; e-mail, center@chicago.nara.gov

Maryland—Archives II - Research Room Support Branch, College Park, MD 20740-6001. Phone: (301)713-6800.

Massachusetts - Northeast Region—380 Trapelo Rd., Waltham, MA 02154-6399. Phones: (617)647-8108; FAX (617)647-8008; e-mail, archives@waltham.nara.gov

▪ 100 Conte Dr., Pittsfield, MA 01201-8230. Phones: (413)445-6885; FAX (413)445-7305.

Missouri - Central Plains Region—200 Space Center Dr., Lee's Summit, MO 64064-1182. Phones: (816)478-7089; FAX (816)478-7623.

▪ 2312 E. Bannister Rd., Kansas City, MO 64131-3011. Phones: (816)926-6920; FAX (816)926-6982; e-mail, archives@kansascity.nara.gov

▪ (Military Records) 9700 Page Ave., St. Louis, MO 63132-5100. Phones: (314)538-4247; FAX (314)538-4005; e-mail, center@stlouis.nara.gov

▪ (Civilian Records) 111 Winnebago St., St. Louis, MO 63118-4199. Phones: (314)425-5722; FAX (314)425-5719; e-mail, center@cpr.nara.gov

New York - Northeast Region—201 Varick St., New York, NY 10014-4811. Phones: (212)337-1300; FAX (212)337-1306; e-mail, archives@newyork.nara.gov

Ohio - Great Lakes Region—3150 Springboro Rd., Dayton, OH 45439-1883. Phones: (937)225-2852; FAX (937)225-7236; e-mail, center@dayton.nara.gov

89.001
(cont.)

Pennsylvania - Mid Atlantic Region—900 Market St., Philadelphia, PA 19107-4292. Phones: (215)597-3000, -9752; FAX (215)597-2303; e-mail, archives@philarch. nara.gov

▪ 14700 Townsend Rd., Philadelphia, PA 19154-1096. Phones: (215)671-8005; FAX (215)671-8001.

Texas - Southwest Region—Bldg. 1, 501 W. Felix St., Ft. Worth, TX 76115-3405. *For mail:*P.O. Box 6216, Ft. Worth, TX 76115-0216. Phones: (817)334-5736; FAX (817)334-5621; e-mail, archives@ftworth.nara.gov

Washington - Pacific Alaska Region—6125 Sand Point Way NE, Seattle, WA 98115-7999. Phones: (206)526-6501; FAX (206)526-6545; e-mail, archives@seattle.nara.gov

DEPARTMENT OF HEALTH AND HUMAN SERVICES

OFFICE OF THE SECRETARY

93.001   **HHS REGIONAL OFFICES**

Regional Managers, Office for Civil Rights:

REGION I—JFK Federal Bldg. - Rm.1875, Boston, MA 02203. Phones: (617)565-1340; TDD (617)565-1343.

REGION II—Javits Federal Bldg. - Ste.3312, 26 Federal Plaza, New York, NY 10278. Phones: (212)264-3313; TDD (212)264-8900.

REGION III—3535 Market St. - Rm.6300, Philadelphia, PA 19101. Phones: (215)596-1262; TDD (215)596-5195.

REGION IV—101 Marietta Tower Bldg. - Ste.1504, Atlanta, GA 30323. Phones: (404)562-7886; TDD (404)841-2867.

REGION V—105 W. Adams - 16th fl., Chicago, IL 60603. Phones: (312)886-2359; TDD (312)353-5693.

REGION VI—1301 Young St. - Ste.1169, Dallas, TX 75202. Phones: (214)562-7886; TDD (214)767-8940.

REGION VII—601 E. 12th St. - Rm.248, Kansas City, MO 64106. Phones: (816)426-7278; TDD (816)426-7065.

REGION VIII—1961 Stout St. - Rm.840, Denver, CO 80294. Phones: (303)844-2024; TDD (303)844-3439.

REGION IX—50 United Nations Plaza - Rm.322, San Francisco, CA 94103. Phones: (415)437-8310; TDD (415)437-8311.

REGION X—2201 6th Ave. - Ste.900, Seattle, WA 98121. Phones: (206)615-2287; TDD (206)615-2293.

ADMINISTRATION ON AGING

REGIONAL OFFICES

93.041
thru
93.051

Regional Administrator, Administration on Aging, DHHS:

REGION I *(Connecticut, Maine, Massachusetts, New Hampshire, Rhode Island, Vermont)*—JFK Federal Bldg. - Rm.2100, Government Center, Boston, MA 02203. Phone: (617)565-1500.

REGION II *(New York, New Jersey, Puerto Rico, Virgin Islands)*—26 Federal Plaza - Rm.3835, New York, NY 10278. Phone: (212)264-4600.

REGION III *(Delaware, District of Columbia, Maryland, Pennsylvania, Virginia, West Virginia)*—Gateway Bldg. - Rm.11480, 3535 Market St., Philadelphia, PA 19104. Phone: (215)596-6492.

REGION IV *(Alabama, Florida, Georgia, Kentucky, Mississippi, North Carolina, South Carolina, Tennessee)*—101 Marietta Tower Bldg. - Ste.1515, Atlanta, GA 30323. Phone: (404)331-2442.

REGION V *(Illinois, Indiana, Michigan, Minnesota, Ohio, Wisconsin)*—105 W. Adams - 23rd fl., Chicago, IL 60603. Phone: (312)353-5160.

REGION VI *(Arkansas, Louisiana, New Mexico, Oklahoma, Texas)*—1301 Young St. - Ste.1124, Dallas, TX 75202. Phone: (214)767-3301.

REGION VII *(Iowa, Kansas, Missouri, Nebraska)*—601 E. 12th St. - Rm.210, Kansas City, MO 64106. Phone: (816)426-2821.

REGION VIII *(Colorado, Montana, North Dakota, South Dakota, Utah, Wyoming)*— Federal Bldg. - Rm.325, 1961 Stout St., Denver, CO 80294-3538. Phone: (303)844-3372.

REGION IX *(American Samoa, Arizona, California, Guam, Hawaii, Nevada, Northern Mariana Islands, Trust Territories of the Pacific Islands)*—Federal Office Bldg. - Rm.431, 50 United Nations Plaza, San Francisco, CA 94102. Phone: (415)437-8500.

REGION X *(Alaska, Idaho, Oregon, Washington)*—2201 6th Ave. - Rm.1208, Seattle, WA 98121. Phone: (206)615-2010.

FOOD AND DRUG ADMINISTRATION

93.103   **DISTRICT OFFICES**

No field offices. Direct contact with HQ concerning grants. See main entry. However, for general information concerning Food and Drug Administration activities contact the nearest district office, following:

California—1431 Harbor Bay Pkwy., Alameda, CA 94502-7070. Phone: (510)337-6783.

  ▪ 19900 McArthur Blvd. - Ste.300, Irvine, CA 92715-2445. Phone: (714)798-7714.

Colorado—Denver Federal Center, 6th and Kipling St., Denver, CO 80225-0087. Phone: (303)236-3016.

Florida—7200 Lake Ellenor Dr. - Ste.120, Orlando, FL 32809. Phone: (407)648-6995.

Georgia—60 8th St. NE, Atlanta, GA 30309. Phone: (404)347-4344.

Illinois—300 S. Riverside Plaza - Ste.550 S., Chicago, IL 60606. Phone: (312)353-7379.

Kansas—11630 W. 80th St., Lenexa, KS 66285-5905. Phone: (913)752-2144.

Louisiana—4298 Elysian Fields Ave., New Orleans, LA 70122. Phone: (504)589-2401, ext.124.

Maryland—900 Madison Ave., Baltimore, MD 21201. Phone: (410)962-4012.

Massachusetts—One Montvale Ave. - 4th fl., Stoneham, MA 02180. Phone: (617)279-1675, ext.155.

Michigan—1560 E. Jefferson Ave., Detroit, MI 48207. Phone: (313)226-6260, ext.101.

Minnesota—240 Hennepin Ave., Minneapolis, MN 55401-1912. Phone: (612)334-4100, ext.121.

New Jersey—Waterview Corporate Center - 3rd fl., 10 Waterview Blvd., Parsippany, NJ 07054. Phone: (973)331-2901.

New York—850 3rd Ave., Brooklyn, NY 11232-1593. Phone: (718)340-7000, ext.5301.

  ▪ 599 Delaware Ave., Buffalo, NY 14202. Phone: (716)551-4461.

93.103
(cont.)

Ohio—1141 Central Pkwy., Cincinnati, OH 45202-1097. Phone: (513)684-3504.

Pennsylvania—U.S. Customhouse - Rm.900, 2nd & Chestnut St., Philadelphia, PA 19106. Phone: (215)597-4390, ext.4200.

Puerto Rico—466 Fernandez Juncos Ave., San Juan, PR 00901-3223. Phone: (787)729-6842.

Tennessee—297 Plus Park Blvd., Nashville, TN 37217. Phone: (615)781-5392, ext.128.

Texas—3310 Live Oak St., Dallas, TX 75204. Phone: (214)655-5315, ext.302.

Washington—Federal Office Bldg., 22201 23rd Dr. SE, Bothell, WA 98041-3012. Phone: (425)483-4950.

HEALTH RESOURCES AND SERVICES ADMINISTRATION

93.110
thru
93.151

Regional Health Administrator *or* Regional Grants Coordinator. *Use addresses listed under **93.041**.*

INDIAN HEALTH SERVICE

93.164   **AREA OFFICES**

Alaska Area *(Alaska)*—4141 Ambassador Dr., Anchorage, AK 99508-5928. Phone: (907)257-3686.

Arizona: Navajo Area *(Arizona, Colorado, New Mexico, Utah)*—Window Rock, AZ 86515-9020. Phone: (520)871-5811.

▪ **Phoenix Area** *(Arizona,Nevada,Utah)*—3738 N. 16th St. - Ste.A, Phoenix, AZ 85016-5981. Phone: (602)640-2052.

▪ **Tucson Area** *(Arizona)*—OHPRD, 7900 S. "J" Stock Rd., Tucson, AZ 85746-9352. Phone: (520)295-2406.

California Area *(California)*—1825 Bell St. - Ste.200, Sacramento, CA 95825-1097. Phone: (916)566-7101.

Maryland: Headquarters Office—5600 Fishers Ln. - Rm.6-05, Rockville, MD 20857. Phone: (301)443-1083.

Minnesota: Bemidji Area *(Michigan, Minnesota, Wisconsin)*—127 Federal Bldg., Bemidji, MN 56601. Phone: (218)759-3412.

Montana: Billings Area *(Montana, Wyoming)*—2900 4th Genuire N. - P.O. Box 2143, Billings, MT 59103. Phone: (406)247-7107.

New Mexico: Albuquerque Area *(Colorado, New Mexico)*—505 Marquette NW - Ste.1502, Albuquerque, NM 87102-2163. Phone: (505)248-4500.

▪ **Headquarters West Office**—5300 Homestead Rd. NE, Albuquerque, NM 87110. Phone: (505)248-4102.

Oklahoma: Oklahoma City Area *(Kansas, Oklahoma)*—5 Corporate Plaza, 3625 NW 56th St., Oklahoma City, OK 73112. Phone: (405)951-3768.

Oregon: Portland Area *(Idaho, Oregon, Washington)*—1220 SW 3rd Ave. - Rm.476, Portland, OR 97204-2892. Phone: (503)326-2020.

South Dakota: Aberdeen Area *(Iowa, Nebraska, North Dakota, South Dakota)*—Federal Bldg., 115 4th Ave. SE, Aberdeen, SD 57401. Phone: (605)226-7581.

Tennessee: Nashville Area *(Alabama, Arkansas, Connecticut, Delaware, Florida, Georgia, Illinois, Indiana, Kentucky, Louisiana, Maine, Maryland, Massachusetts, Mississippi, Missouri, New Hampshire, New Jersey, New York, North Carolina, Ohio,*

Pennsylvania, Rhode Island, South Carolina, Tennessee, Texas, Vermont, Virginia, West Virginia)—711 Stewarts Ferry Pike, Nashville, TN 37214-2634. Phone: (615) 736-2400.

93.215 National Ambulatory Hansen's Disease Program, G.W. Long Hansen's Disease Center, 5445 Point Clair Rd., Carville, LA 70721. Phone: (504)642-4769.

93.217 and 93.224 Same as **93.110**.

93.228 Listed under **93.164**.

93.246 and 93.260 Same as **93.110**.

ADMINISTRATION FOR CHILDREN AND FAMILIES

93.556 thru 93.674 Regional Administrator, ACF, HHS Regional Office. *Use addresses listed under* **93.041**.

HEALTH CARE FINANCING ADMINISTRATION

93.767 thru 93.777 Regional Administrator, HCFA, HHS Regional Office. *Use addresses listed under* **93.041**.

93.778 Associate Regional Administrator, Division of Medicaid, HCFA, HHS Regional Office. *Use addresses listed under* **93.041**.

93.779 and 93.900 Same as **93.767**

93.926 Listed under 93.041.

93.927 thru 93.932 Same as 93.110.

93.965 Listed under 93.041.

93.971 and 93.972 Same as **93.164**.

93.982 Regional Director, FEMA Regional Office. *See addresses listed under* **83.011**.

93.984 Same as **93.110**.

CORPORATION FOR NATIONAL AND COMMUNITY SERVICE

94.002 thru 94.016 **ATLANTIC CLUSTER OFFICES**

CLUSTER DIRECTOR—801 Arch St. - Ste.103, Philadelphia, PA 19107-2416. Phones: (215)597-9972; FAX (215)597-4933.

**94.002
thru
94.016
(cont.)**

Connecticut—One Commercial Plaza - 21st fl., Hartford, CT 06103-3510. Phones: (860)240-3237; FAX (860)240-3238.

Delaware—*see* **Maryland.**

Maine—*see*New Hampshire.

Maryland—One Market Center - Ste.702 and 703 (Box 5), 300 W. Lexington St., Baltimore, MD 21201-3418. Phones: (410)962-4443; FAX (410)962-3201.

Massachusetts—10 Causeway St. - Rm.473, Boston, MA 02222-1038. Phones: (617) 565-7000; FAX (617)565-7011.

New Hampshire—The Whitebridge, 91-93 N. State St., Concord, NH 03301-3939. Phones: (603)225-1450; FAX (603)225-1459.

New Jersey—44 S. Clinton Ave. - Ste.702, Trenton, NJ 08609-1507. Phones: (609)989-2243; FAX (609)989-2304.

New York—O'Brien Federal Bldg. -Rm.818, Clinton Ave. and Pearl St., Albany, NY 12207. Phones: (518)431-4150: FAX (518)431-4154.

- 6 World Trade Center - Rm.758, New York, NY 10048-0206. Phones: (212)466-4471; FAX (212)466-4195.

Pennsylvania—Gateway Bldg. - Rm.2460, 3535 Market St., Philadelphia, PA 19104-2996. Phones: (215)596-4077; FAX (215)596-4072.

Puerto Rico - Virgin Islands—Federal Bldg. - Ste.662, 150 Carlos Chardon Ave., Hato Rey, PR 00918-1737. Phones: (787)766-5314; FAX (787)766-5189.

Rhode Island—400 Westminster St. - Rm.203, Providence, RI 02903. Phones: (401) 528-5424; FAX (401)528-5220.

Vermont—*See* **New Hampshire.**

NORTH CENTRAL CLUSTER OFFICES

CLUSTER DIRECTOR—77 W. Jackson Blvd. - Ste.442, Chicago, IL 60604-3511. Phones: (312)353-7705; FAX (312)353-5343.

Illinois—77 W. Jackson Blvd. - Ste.442, Chicago, IL 60604-3511. Phones: (312)353-3622; FAX (312)353-5343.

Indiana—46 E. Ohio St. - Rm.457, Indianapolis, IN 46204-1922. Phones: (317)226-6724; FAX (317)226-5437.

Iowa—Federal Bldg. - Rm.917, 210 Walnut St., Des Moines, IA 50309-2195. Phones: (515)284-4816; FAX (515)284-6640.

Michigan—211 W. Fort St. - Ste.1408, Detroit, MI 48226-2799. Phones: (313)226-7848; FAX (313)226-2557.

Minnesota—431 S. 7th St. - Ste.2480, Minneapolis, MN 55415-1854. Phones: (612) 334-4083; FAX (612)334-4084.

Nebraska—Federal Bldg. - Rm.156, 100 Centennial Mall N., Lincoln, NE 68508-3896. Phones: (402)437-5493; FAX (402)437-5495.

North Dakota - South Dakota—Federal Bldg. - Rm.225, 225 S. Pierre St., Pierre, SD 57501-2452. Phones: (605)224-5996; FAX (605)224-9201.

Ohio—51 N. High St. - Ste.451, Columbus, OH 43215. Phones: (614)469-7441; FAX (614)469-2125.

Wisconsin—Reuss Federal Plaza - Rm.1240, 310 W. Wisconsin Ave., Milwaukee, WI 53203-2211. Phones: (414)297-1118; FAX (414)297-1863.

PACIFIC CLUSTER OFFICES

CLUSTER DIRECTOR—P.O. Box 29996, Presidio of San Francisco, CA 94129-0996. Phones: (415)561-5960; FAX (415)561-5970.

Alaska—*See* **Washington.** Phones: (206)220-7736; FAX (206)553-4415.

California—Federal Bldg. - Rm.11221, 11000 Wilshire Blvd., Los Angeles, CA 90024-3671. Phones: (310)235-7421; FAX (310)235-7422.

Hawaii, Guam, American Samoa—Federal Bldg. - Rm.6326, 300 Ala Moana Blvd., Honolulu, HI 96850-0001. Phones: (808)541-2832; FAX (808)541-3603.

Idaho—304 N. 8th St. - Rm.344, Boise, ID 83702-5835. Phones: (208)334-1707; FAX (208)334-1421.

Montana—Capitol One Center - Ste.206, 208 N. Montana Ave. Helena, MT 59601-3837. Phones: (406)449-5404; FAX (406)449-5412.

Nevada—4600 Kietzke Ln. - Ste.E-141, Reno, NV 89502-5033. Phones: (702)784-5314; FAX (702)784-5026.

Oregon—2010 Lloyd Center, Portland, OR 97232. Phones: (503)231-2103; FAX (503) 231-2106.

Utah—350 S. Main St. - Rm.504, Salt Lake City, UT 84101-2198. Phones: (801)524-5411; FAX (801)524-3599.

Washington—Jackson Federal Bldg. - Ste.3190, 915 2nd Ave., Seattle, WA 98174-1103. Phones: (206)220-7745; FAX (206)553-4415.

Wyoming—Federal Bldg. - Rm.1110, 2120 Capitol Ave., Cheyenne, WY 82001-3649. Phones: (307)772-2385; FAX (307)772-2389.

SOUTHERN CLUSTER OFFICES

CLUSTER DIRECTOR—101 Marietta St NW - Ste.1003, Atlanta, GA 30323-2301. Phones: (404)331-2860; FAX (404)331-2438.

Alabama—Medical Forum - Ste.428, 950 22nd St. N,, Birmingham, AL 35203. Phones: (205)731-0027; FAX(205)731-0031.

District of Columbia—*See* **Virginia.**

Florida—3165 McCrory St. - Ste.115, Orlando, FL 32803-3750. Phones: (407)648-6117; FAX (407)648-6116.

Georgia—75 Piedmont Ave. NE - Ste.462, Atlanta, GA 30303-2587. Phones: (404)331-4646; FAX (404)331-2898.

Kentucky—Federal Bldg. - Rm.372-D, 600 Martin Luther King Place, Louisville, KY 40202-2230. Phones: (502)582-6384; FAX (502)582-6386.

Mississippi—100 W. Capitol St. - Rm.1005A, Jackson, MS 39269-1092. Phones: (601)965-5664; FAX (601)965-4617.

North Carolina—300 Fayetteville St. Mall - Rm.131, Raleigh, NC 27601-1739. Phones: (919)856-4731; FAX (919)856-4738.

South Carolina—1835 Assembly St. - Ste.872, Columbia, SC 29201-2430. Phones: (803)765-5771; FAX (803)765-5777.

Tennessee—265 Cumberland Bend Dr., Nashville, TN 37228. Phones: (615)736-5561; FAX (615)736-7937.

Virginia—400 N. 8th St. - Rm.1119, P.O. Box 10066, Richmond, VA 23240-1832. Phones: (804)771-2197; FAX (804)771-2157.

West Virginia—10 Hale St. - Ste.203, Charleston, WV 25301-1409. Phones: (304)347-5246; FAX (304)347-5464.

SOUTHWEST CLUSTER OFFICES

CLUSTER DIRECTOR—1999 Bryan St. - Rm.2050, Dallas, TX 75201. Phones: (214)880-7050; FAX (214)880-7074.

Arizona—522 N. Central - Rm.205A, Phoenix, AZ 85004-2190. Phones: (602)379-4825; FAX (602)379-4030.

Arkansas—Federal Bldg. - Rm.2506, 700 W. Capitol St., Little Rock, AR 72201. Phones: (501)324-5234; FAX (501)324-6949.

94.002
thru
94.016
(cont.)

Colorado—One Sherman Place - Ste.120, 140 E. 19th Ave., Denver, CO 80203-1167. Phones: (303)866-1070; FAX (303)866-1081.

Kansas—444 SE Quincy - Rm.260, Topeka, KS 66683-3572. Phones: (785)295-2540; FAX (785)295-2596.

Louisiana—640 Main St. - Ste.102, Baton Rouge, LA 70801-1910. Phones: (504)389-0471; FAX (504)389-0510.

Missouri—801 Walnut St. - Ste.504, Kansas City, MO 64106-2009. Phones: (816)347-6300; FAX (816)347-6305.

New Mexico—120 S. Federal Place - Rm.315, Santa Fe, NM 87501-2026. Phones: (505)988-6577; FAX (505)988-6661.

Oklahoma—215 Dean A. McGee - Ste.324, Oklahoma City, OK 73102. Phones: (405)231-5201; FAX (405)231-4329.

Texas—903 San Jacinto St. - Ste.130, Austin, TX 78701-3747. Phones: (512)916-5671; FAX (512)916-5806.

SOCIAL SECURITY ADMINISTRATION

96.001
thru
96.006

There are some 1,296 district and branch SSA offices located in cities and towns throughout the U.S. Consult the local phone directory under "Social Security Administration" or "U.S. Government" or ask for address at local U.S. Post Office.

NOTE: Entries cover administrative units and sub-units, referring to program numbers used in Parts II, III, and IV. The program numbering system is explained on page 12.

APPALACHIAN REGIONAL COMMISSION, 23.001-23.011

ARCHITECTURAL AND TRANSPORTATION BARRIERS COMPLIANCE BOARD, 88.001

COMMISSION ON CIVIL RIGHTS, 29.001

COMMODITY FUTURES TRADING COMMISSION, 78.004

CORPORATION FOR NATIONAL AND COMMUNITY SERVICE, 94.002-94.016

DEPARTMENT OF AGRICULTURE, 10.001-10.963
Agricultural Marketing Service, 10.153-10.167
Agricultural Research Service, 10.001, 10.700
Alternative Agricultural Research and Commercialization Center, 10.240
Animal and Plant Health Inspection Service, 10.025-10.028
Cooperative State Research, Education and Extension Service, 10.200-10.226, 10.500, 10.501
Economic Research Service, 10.250
Farm Service Agency, 10.051-10.055, 10.069, 10.071, 10.404, 10.406, 10.407, 10.421, 10.435-10.437, 10.451-10.453
Food and Nutrition Service, 10.550-10.574
Food Safety and Inspection Service, 10.475-10.477
Foreign Agricultural Service, 10.600, 10.601, 10.960-10.962
Forest Service, 10.652-10.671
Grain Inspection, Packers and Stockyard Administration, 10.800
National Agricultural Statistics Service, 10.950
National Sheep Industry Improvement Center, 10.774
Natural Resources Conservation Service, 10.062, 10.064, 10.070, 10.072, 10.900-10.914
Office of Community Development, 10.772
Office of Outreach, 10.443
Risk Management Agency, 10.450, 10.454
Rural Business-Cooperative Service, 10.350, 10.767-10.769, 10.771, 10.773, 10.854

Rural Housing Service, 10.405, 10.410-10.420, 10.427, 10.433, 10.438, 10.441, 10.442, 10.444, 10.445, 10.766

Rural Utilities Service, 10.760-10.763, 10.770, 10.850-10.852, 10.855

DEPARTMENT OF COMMERCE, 11.001-11.900

Bureau of the Census, 11.001-11.006

Bureau of Export Administration, 11.150

Economic Development Administration, 11.300-11.313

Economics and Statistics Administration, 11.025-11.027

International Trade Administration, 11.106-11.115

Minority Business Development Agency, 11.800-11.802

National Institute of Standards and Technology, 11.601-11.614

National Oceanic and Atmospheric Administration, 11.400-11.480

National Technical Information Service, 11.650

National Telecommunications and Information Administration, 11.550-11.552

Office of the Secretary, 11.702

Patent and Trademark Office, 11.900

DEPARTMENT OF DEFENSE, 12.002-12.911

Defense Advanced Research Projects Agency, 12.910, 12.911

Defense Logistics Agency, 12.002

Department of the Air Force, Material Command, 12.800

Department of the Army, Aviation Applied Technology Directorate, 12.640

Department of the Army, Office of the Chief of Engineers, 12.100-12.114

Department of the Navy, Naval Surface Warfare Center, 12.301

Department of the Navy, Office of Naval Research, 12.300

National Guard Bureau, 12.400, 12.401

National Security Agency, 12.900-12.902

Office of Assistant Secretary/Strategy and Requirements, 12.550-12.552

Office of Economic Adjustment, 12.600-12.613

Office of the Secretary, 12.630

Secretaries of Military Departments, 12.700

U.S. Army Materiel Command, 12.431

U.S. Army Medical Command, 12.420

DEPARTMENT OF EDUCATION, 84.002-84.343
National Institute for Literacy, 84.257
Office of Administrator/Management Services, 84.145
Office of Bilingual Education and Minority Languages Affairs,
84.162, 84.194, 84.195, 84.288-84.293
Office of Educational Research and Improvement, 84.168, 84.203,
84.206, 84.215, 84.286, 84.287, 84.295, 84.302-84.309, 84.319
Office of Elementary and Secondary Education, 84.004, 84.010-
84.013, 84.040, 84.041, 84.060, 84.083, 84.141, 84.144,
84.149, 84.165, 84.184, 84.186, 84.196, 84.209-84.214,
84.216, 84.256, 84.258, 84.276-84.283, 84.296-84.298,
84.310, 84.314, 84.318, 84.320-84.322, 84.330, 84.332,
84.338, 84.340
Office of Postsecondary Education, 84.007, 84.015-84.022,
84.031, 84.042-84.047, 84.066, 84.103-84.120, 84.153,
84.170, 84.185, 84.200, 84.217, 84.220, 84.229, 84.252,
84.269-84.274, 84.316, 84.333-84.337, 84.339, 84.342
Office of Special Education and Rehabilitative Services, 84.027,
84.126-84.133, 84.160, 84.161, 84.169, 84.173-84.181,
84.187, 84.221-84.224, 84.234-84.240, 84.246-84.250,
84.263-84.265, 84.275, 84.315, 84.323-84.329
Office of Student Financial Assistance, 84.007, 84.032-84.038,
84.063, 84.069, 84.268, 84.343
Office of Vocational and Adult Education, 84.002, 84.048, 84.051,
84.101, 84.191, 84.243-84.245, 84.255, 84.259, 84.331,
84.341

DEPARTMENT OF ENERGY, 81.003-81.116
Energy Information Administration, 81.039
Office of Civil Rights and Diversity Management, 81.116
Office of Civilian Radioactive Waste Management, 81.065
Office of Defense Programs, 81.110-81.112
Office of Economic Impact and Diversity, 81.082
Office of Energy Efficiency and Renewable Energy, 81.036,
81.041, 81.042, 81.079, 81.081, 81.086, 81.087, 81.105,
81.117, 81.118
Office of Energy Research, 81.064
Office of Environment, Safety and Health, 81.108
Office of Environmental Management, 81.104, 81.106
Office of Fossil Energy, 81.057, 81.089

Office of General Counsel, 81.003
Office of Nonproliferation and National Security, 81.113
Office of Nuclear Energy, Science and Technology, 81.114
Office of Science, 81.022. 81.049,

DEPARTMENT OF HEALTH AND HUMAN SERVICES, 93.001-93.995

Administration for Children and Families, 93.550-93.674
Administration on Aging, 93.041-93.051
Agency for Health Care Policy and Research, 93.225, 93.226
Centers for Disease Control and Prevention, 93.116, 93.118, 93.135, 93.136, 93.161, 93.184, 93.185, 93.197-93.208, 93.227, 93.262-93.268, 93.283, 93.919, 93.938-93.947, 93.955-93.957, 93.977, 93.978, 93.988, 93.991
Food and Drug Administration, 93.103, 93.245, 93.948
Health Care Financing Administration, 93.767, 93.773, 93.774, 93.777-93.779
Health Resources and Services Administration, 93.107, 93.108, 93.110, 93.117, 93.124, 93.127, 93.129, 93.130, 93.134, 93.139, 93.145, 93.151, 93.153, 93.155-93.157, 93.162, 93.165, 93.178, 93.181, 93.186, 93.188-93.192, 93.211, 93.212, 93.215, 93.222-93.224, 93.234-93.236, 93.241, 93.246, 93.288, 93.298, 93.299, 93.342-93.359, 93.364, 93.379, 93.820, 93.822, 93.824, 93.884-93.887, 93.895-93.900, 93.906-93.908, 93.912-93.918, 93.923-93.928, 93.931, 93.932, 93.951, 93.962-93.969, 93.984, 93.994
Indian Health Service, 93.123, 93.164, 93.193, 93.210, 93.219, 93.228, 93.231, 93.237, 93.905, 93.933, 93.954, 93.970-93.972
National Institutes of Health, 93.106, 93.113-93.115, 93.121, 93.140-93.143, 93.154, 93.168, 93.172, 93.173, 93.187, 93.209, 93.213, 93.220, 93.232, 93.233, 93.242, 93.271-93.273, 93.277-93.282, 93.306, 93.333, 93.361, 93.371, 93.375, 93.389-93.399, 93.821, 93.837-93.880, 93.891, 93.894, 93.929, 93.934, 93.936, 93.960, 93.989
Office of Disease Prevention and Health Promotion, 93.990
Office of Minority Health, 93.004-93.006, 93.105, 93.137, 93.910
Office of Population Affairs, 93.111, 93.217, 93.260, 93.974, 93.995
Office of the Secretary, 93.001-93.003, 93.239, 93.775

National Institute of Corrections, 16.601-16.603
National Institute of Justice, 16.560-16.566
Office for State and Local Domestic Preparedness Support,
    16.006, 16.007
Office of Community Oriented Policing Services, 16.710-16.712
Office of Juvenile Justice and Delinquency Prevention, 16.523,
    16.540-16.549, 16.726-16.732
Office of Victims of Crime, 16.575, 16.576, 16.582, 16.583
Violence Against Women Office, 16.524, 16.525, 16.587-16.590

DEPARTMENT OF LABOR, 17.002-17.805
Bureau of Labor Statistics, 17.002-17.006
Employment and Training Administration, 17.201-17.257
Employment Standards Administration, 17.301-17.308
Mine Safety and Health Administration, 17.600-17.602
Occupational Safety and Health Administration, 17.502-17.504
Office of Assistant Secretary for Veterans' Employment and
    Training, 17.801-17.805
Office of Labor-Management Standards, 17.140, 17.309
Office of the Secretary, Women's Bureau, 17.700
Pension and Welfare Benefits Administration, 17.150

DEPARTMENT OF STATE, 19.200-19.300
Bureau of Intelligence and Research, 19.300
Bureau of Oceans and International Environmental and Scientific
    Affairs, 19.204
Bureau of Personnel, 19.202
Office of Legal Adviser, 19.200, 19.201

DEPARTMENT OF TRANSPORTATION, 20.001-20.907
Federal Aviation Administration, 20.100-20.109
Federal Highway Administration, 20.205-20.219
Federal Railroad Administration, 20.301-20.312
Federal Transit Administration, 20.500-20.515
Maritime Administration, 20.801-20.813
National Highway Traffic Safety Administration, 20.600, 20.601
Office of the Secretary, 20.900-20.907
Research and Special Programs Administration, 20.700-20.703
U.S. Coast Guard, 20.001-20.007

FEDERAL MARITIME COMMISSION, 33.001

FEDERAL MEDIATION AND CONCILIATION SERVICE, 34.001-34.002

FEDERAL TRADE COMMISSION, 36.001

GENERAL SERVICES ADMINISTRATION, 39.001-39.009

GOVERNMENT PRINTING OFFICE, 40.001-40.002

INTERNATIONAL TRADE COMMISSION, 61.001

LIBRARY OF CONGRESS, 42.001-42.008

NATIONAL AERONAUTICS AND SPACE ADMINISTRATION, 43.001-43.002

NATIONAL ARCHIVES AND RECORDS ADMINISTRATION, 89.001-89.003

NATIONAL COUNCIL ON DISABILITY, 92.001

NATIONAL CREDIT UNION ADMINISTRATION, 44.001-44.002

NATIONAL FOUNDATION ON THE ARTS AND THE HUMANITIES, 45.024-45.312
Federal Council on the Arts and the Humanities, 45.201
Institute of Museum and Library Services, 45.301-45.312
National Endowment for the Arts, 45.024-45.026
National Endowment for the Humanities, 45.129-45.164

NATIONAL GALLERY OF ART, 68.001

NATIONAL LABOR RELATIONS BOARD, 46.001

NATIONAL SCIENCE FOUNDATION, 47.041-47.078

NUCLEAR REGULATORY COMMISSION, 77.001-77.005

OFFICE OF PERSONNEL MANAGEMENT, 27.001-27.013

MASTER INDEX

NOTES

Index entries refer to program numbers used in Part II. The numbering system is explained on page 12.

- Italicized program *numbers* indicate programs that provide financial assistance. Example:

  ABANDONED MINE LAND RECLAMATION (AMLR) PROGRAM, *15.252*

  Assistance classifications are explained on page 4.

- Subject headings are in bold-face type. Example:

  Adult education

- Program titles are in capital letters. Bracketed agency identifiers are inserted when the title inadequately describes program focus. Examples:

  ACADEMIC RESEARCH ENHANCEMENT AWARD [HHS], *93.390*
  BUILDINGS AND FACILITIES PROGRAM [USDA], *10.218*
  GENERAL RESEARCH AND TECHNOLOGY ACTIVITY [HUD], *14.506*

- Also provided are (1) popular and abbreviated program titles, (2) government departments and independent agencies, (3) names of Acts, (4) section and title numbers of Acts, and (5) some general references to programs. Examples:

  (1) Age Search, 11.006
      AG*SAT ("Agricultural Satellite"), *10.501*

  (2) Appalachian Regional Commission, 23.001 through 23.011

  (3) AIDS Housing Opportunity Act, *14.241*

  (4) Section 22, Water Resources Development Act, 12.110
      Title I, ESEA, migrants, *84.011*

  (5) Acid precipitation research, NOAA, *11.432, 11.459*
      Aid to Families with Dependent Children (AFDC), *93.560, 93.563, 93.583, 93.658, 93.659*
      National Institute on Drug Abuse (NIDA), NIH, 93.277 through 93.279

Remarks on using the index are offered in Part I in the section on "Obtaining Federal Assistance," under "STEP ONE: USE THE MASTER INDEX," beginning on page 15.

homeless, mental health, social services, *93.150*
juveniles, prevention, *16.542*
minority community health coalitions, *93.137*
offenders, health, social services networks, *93.229*
pregnant, postpartum women, infants, *93.169*
prevention, community coalitions, *93.194*
prevention, rehabilitation, treatment research training, *93.271, 93.272*
research centers, *93.891*
Social Services Block Grant, *93.667*
Substance Abuse Pilot Treatment Block Grant monitoring, evaluation, *93.238*
Substance Abuse Prevention and Treatment Block Grant, *93.959*
substance abuse-related treatment, women, infants, children, *93.101, 93.102*
treatment systems, culturally distinct, remote, rural populations, *93.122*
Tribal Youth Program, OJJDP, *16.731*
urban Indian program, *93.193*
veterans, DVA transitional housing loans, *64.025*
veterans program, 64.019
Welfare-to-Work Grants, *17.253*
youth, prevention, *93.144*
see also Behavioral sciences, education, services; Drug abuse; Family therapy; Mental health; Social services; Volunteers
Aleuts, *see* Alaska natives; Indian *entries*
Aliens, refugees
citizenship education, training, 16.400
citizenship verification, 11.006
Cuban, Haitian entrants, *93.566*
Cuban, Haitian resettlement, *16.201*
discretionary grants, *93.576*
employment, civil rights education, enforcement, *16.110*
immigrant children, supplementary education, *84.162*
job services, *93.583*
labor certification, 17.202, 17.203
Office of Refugee Resettlement programs, *93.566, 93.567, 93.576, 93.579, 93.583, 93.584*
resettlement agencies, services, *93.567*
specialty occupations, employer attestation, 17.252
State Criminal Alien Assistance Program, DOJ, *16.606*
substance abuse treatment systems, *93.122*
targeted assistance, jobs, *93.584*
temporary work, 17.202, 17.203
U.S. Repatriation Program, *93.579*
Wilson/Fish programs, *93.583*
see also Bilingual education, services; English as a second language; Farm workers; Social services; Volunteers
ALL-VOLUNTEER FORCE EDUCATIONAL ASSISTANCE [DVA], *64.124*
ALLERGY, IMMUNOLOGY AND TRANSPLANTATION RESEARCH, *93.855*
Allied health professions, *see* Health professions
ALLIED HEALTH PROJECTS, *93.191*
Alternative Agricultural Research and Commercialization Center (AARC), USDA, *see* Agency Index
ALTERNATIVE AGRICULTURAL RESEARCH AND COMMERCIALIZATION PROGRAM, *10.240*

Alternative medicine, *93.213*
Alzheimer's disease, related disorders, *see* Aging and the aged
Amblyopia research, *93.867*
Ambulance service, *see* Rescue services
AMD (acid mine drainage), DOI, *15.253*
AMERICAN BATTLEFIELD PROTECTION, *15.926*
AMERICAN BUSINESS CENTER, *11.115*
AMERICAN COUNCIL OF YOUNG POLITICAL LEADERS [USIA], *82.006*
American Indian Environmental Office, EPA, *see* Agency Index
American Indians, *see* Indian *entries*
American natives, *see* Alaska natives; Hawaii, Hawaii natives; Indian *entries*; U.S. possessions, territories
AMERICAN OVERSEAS RESEARCH CENTERS, *84.274*
American Samoa, *see* U.S. possessions, territories
Americans with Disabilities Act (ADA), 14.414, *16.108, 20.106, 20.507, 30.002,* 30.005, 30.011, 53.001, 88.001, *92.001,* 93.001
AMERICANS WITH DISABILITIES ACT TECHNICAL ASSISTANCE PROGRAM, *16.108*
AmeriCorps
higher education, *94.005*
planning, development, *94.007*
projects, *94.006*
school, community programs, *94.004*
state commissions, *94.003*
training, technical assistance, *94.009*
VISTA program, 94.013
see also Volunteers
AMLR (Abandoned Mine Land Reclamation), *15.252*
AMS (Agricultural Marketing Service), USDA, *see* Agency Index
ANADROMOUS FISH CONSERVATION ACT PROGRAM, *11.405*
ANE (Alaska Native Education), DOED, *84.320, 84.321, 84.322*
Anesthesiology, *see* Pharmacology, pharmacy
Anesthetists, *93.124, 93.907, 93.916*
ANILCA (Alaska National Interest Lands Conservation Act), *15.055*
Animal and Plant Health Inspection Service, USDA, *see* Agency Index
Animal Damage Control, *10.028*
Animal disease control, health, welfare
Comparative Medicine, *93.306*
competitive research grants, *10.206*
endangered species conservation, *15.615*
FEMA, disaster home study, 83.529
international assistance, *10.960*
international, elephant conservation, *15.620, 15.621*
international research exchanges, *10.961*
international, rhinoceros, tiger conservation, *15.619*
interstate control, technical assistance, training, *10.025*
Lyme Disease, *93.942*
marine mammal data, *11.439*
pest management research, *10.200*

Animal disease control, health, welfare *(continued)*
  research, *10.207*
  research, SBIR, *10.212*
  rodent control, preventive health services block grant, *93.991*
  waterfowl, Water Bank Program, *10.062*
  wildlife-borne diseases, *10.028*
  see also Birds; Environmental management; Laboratory animals; Livestock industry; Poultry, egg products; Veterinary medicine; Wildlife
Animal drugs, *see* Animal disease control, health, welfare; Veterinary medicine
ANIMAL HEALTH AND DISEASE RESEARCH, *10.207*
Animal welfare, *see* Animal disease control, health, welfare
Anorexia research, *93.848*
Antarctic, Arctic research, *47.078*
Anthropology, *see* History; Humanities *entries*; Social sciences
Anti-discrimination, *see* Civil rights; Complaint investigation
Antidumping duties, *see* International commerce, investment; Trade adjustment assistance
Anti-terrorism, terrorism, *see* Civil defense
Anti-terrorism training, FEMA, *83.547*
AOA (Administration on Aging), HHS, *see* Agency Index
AORC (American Overseas Research Centers), *84.274*
APPALACHIAN AREA DEVELOPMENT, *23.002*
Appalachian Corridors, *23.003*
APPALACHIAN DEVELOPMENT HIGHWAY SYSTEM, *23.003*
APPALACHIAN LOCAL ACCESS ROADS, *23.008*
APPALACHIAN LOCAL DEVELOPMENT DISTRICT ASSISTANCE, *23.009*
Appalachian Program, *23.001*
Appalachian region
  Appalachian Corridors, *23.003*
  Appalachian Program, *23.001*
  economic, social development technical assistance, *23.011*
  flood warning systems, *11.450*
  highway system development, *23.003*
  Local Development Districts (LDD), planning assistance, *23.009*
  road construction, *23.008*
  State Research, *23.011*
  Supplemental and Direct Grants, *23.002*
Appalachian Regional Commission, 23.001 through 23.011
APPALACHIAN REGIONAL DEVELOPMENT, *23.001*
APPALACHIAN STATE RESEARCH, TECHNICAL ASSISTANCE, AND DEMONSTRATION PROJECTS, *23.011*
APPLIED TOXICOLOGICAL RESEARCH AND TESTING, *93.114*
Apprenticeship training
  coastal ecosystem management, NOAA, *11.473*
  community development work-study, *14.512, 14.513*
  Community Food Projects, USDA, *10.225*
  demonstration projects, *17.249*

disabled veterans, *17.801*
HUD Youthbuild Program, *14.243*
ironworkers, native Americans, *15.146*
native American language preservation, *93.587*
native Americans, JTPA, *17.251*
program development, registration, 17.201
Tech-Prep Education, *84.243*
Weed and Seed Program, *16.595*
work study programs, *84.033*
see also Disadvantaged, employment and training; Employment development, training; Fellowships, scholarships, traineeships; Technical training; Veterans education, training; Vocational education
Apprenticeship Training, 17.201
Aquaculture
  agricultural marketing improvement, *10.156*
  business financing, *11.415*
  disaster assistance, noninsured crops, *10.451*
  emergency loans, *10.404*
  farm operating loans, *10.406*
  fisheries development, utilization research, *11.427*
  hatcheries, anadromous, *11.405*
  Hawaii program, *11.444*
  international research exchanges, *10.961*
  loans, farm enterprises *10.407, 10.453*
  research, agricultural experiment stations, *10.203*
  research, SBIR, *10.212*
  research, Sea Grant Support, *11.417*
  special research, *10.200*
  sport fish research, development, *15.605*
  see also Farm, nonfarm enterprises; Fish; Fisheries industry
AQUACULTURE PROGRAM, *11.444*
Aquariums, *see* Museums, galleries
AQUATIC PLANT CONTROL, 12.100
Aquatic plants, *see* Marine sciences; Plants
Arboreta, *see* Museums, galleries
Archaeology
  American Battlefield Protection, NPS, *15.926*
  Cultural Resource Management, BLM, *15.224*
  historic preservation, *15.904, 15.923*
  Indian programs, *15.041*
  National Register of Historic Places, 15.914
  native American graves protection, repatriation, *15.922*
  watershed, river basin projects, 10.906
  see also History; Historic preservation; Humanities *entries*; Social sciences
ARCHITECTURAL AND TRANSPORTATION BARRIERS COMPLIANCE BOARD, 88.001
Architectural and Transportation Barriers Compliance Board (ATBCB), 88.001
Architectural Barriers Act, 88.001
ARCHITECTURAL BARRIERS ACT ENFORCEMENT, 14.407
Architecture
  ADA technical assistance, *16.108*
  Architectural Barriers Act Enforcement, HUD programs, 14.407
  disaster-resistant communities, standards, training, *83.551*
  earthquake hazards mitigation, *15.807*
  energy conservation, renewable energy outreach, training, *81.117*

handicapped, architectural barriers standards, 88.001
Hazard Mitigation Grant, FEMA, *83.548*
HBCU structures preservation, NPS, *15.924*
historic preservation, *15.904, 15.923*
historic properties preservation, technical services, 15.915
National Register of Historic Places, 15.914
see also Arts, arts education; Buildings; Construction; Historic preservation; Housing research; Interior design; Urban planning
Arctic, Antarctic research, *47.078*
AREA (Academic Research Enhancement Award), NIH, *93.390*
Area studies, *see* Foreign languages; International studies
Armed forces, *see* Military; Veterans *entries*
ARMS (Adjustable Rate Mortgages), *14.175*
Army Corps of Engineers, DOD, *see* Agency Index (DOD, Department of the Army, Office of the Chief of Engineers)
Army Materiel Command, DOD, *see* Agency Index
Army Medical Command, DOD, *see* Agency Index
ARS (Agricultural Research Service), USDA, *see* Agency Index
Arson, *see* Crime; Fire fighting, prevention, control
Art, *see* Arts, arts education
Art galleries, *see* Museums, galleries
ARTHRITIS, MUSCULOSKELETAL AND SKIN DISEASES RESEARCH, *93.846*
Arthritis research, *see* Health, medical research
Artifacts indemnity, *45.201*
ARTS AND ARTIFACTS INDEMNITY, *45.201*
Arts, arts education
art works, artifacts indemnity, *45.201*
employees, grant-assisted productions, wage standards, 17.303
graduate fellowships, *84.170*
historical collections, preservation, *89.003*
history, Woodrow Wilson Center fellowships, *85.300*
IMLS assistance, *45.301*
Indian arts, crafts, 15.850
international festivals, USIA, *82.030, 82.032*
International Visitors Program, USIA, *82.004*
Library of Congress Publications, 42.005
National Gallery exhibits, schools, libraries, 68.001
native arts, crafts development, 15.850
NEA grants, organizations, individuals, *45.024*
NEA Leadership Initiatives, *45.026*
NEA Partnership Agreements, *45.025*
USIA Creative Arts Grants, *82.015*
Woodrow Wilson Center fellowships, *85.300*
see also Audiovisual aids, film, video; Copyright services; Education *entries*; Foreign languages; Historic preservation; Humanities *entries*; Literature; Museums, galleries; Music; Teacher education, training
ASCS (Agricultural Stabilization and Conservation Service), *see* Agency Index (USDA, Farm Service Agency)
ASIAN ELEPHANT CONSERVATION, *15.621*
ASSISTANCE FOR INDIAN CHILDREN WITH SEVERE DISABILITIES, *15.045*

ASSISTANCE TO STATE WATER RESOURCES RESEARCH INSTITUTES, *15.805*
ASSISTANCE TO TRIBALLY CONTROLLED COMMUNITY COLLEGES AND UNIVERSITIES, *15.027*
Assisted housing, *see* Housing, subsidized
ASSISTIVE TECHNOLOGY, *84.224*
ASSISTIVE TECHNOLOGY—STATE GRANTS FOR PROTECTION AND ADVOCACY [DOED], *84.343*
Asthma research, *93.855*
Astronomy
basic research, *47.049*
environmental systems research, NOAA, *11.432*
see also Aeronautics, space; Physical sciences; Scientific research
ATBCB (Architectural and Transportation Barriers Compliance Board), 88.001
ATF (Bureau of Alcohol, Tobacco and Firearms), Department of the Treasury, *see* Agency Index
ATLANTIC COAST FISHERIES COOPERATIVE MANAGEMENT ACT, *11.474*
Atmospheric science, *see* Aeronautics, space; Astronomy; Climate; Geology; Physical sciences; Scientific research
Atomic energy, *see* Nuclear sciences, technology; Public safety; Radiation
Atomic Energy Act, *see* Nuclear sciences, technology
ATP (Advanced Technology Program), *11.612*
ATT (Anti-Terrorism Training), FEMA, *83.547*
ATTESTATIONS BY EMPLOYERS USING NON-IMMIGRANT ALIENS IN SPECIALTY OCCUPATIONS, 17.252
ATTORNEY FEES—INDIAN RIGHTS, *15.053*
Attorneys, *see* Legal services
Audiology, *see* Audiovisual aids, film, video; Deafness and the deaf; Speech pathology
Audiovisual aids, film, video
ADA technical assistance, *16.108*
aerospace, 43.001
AIDS prevention, school health projects, *93.938*
Aviation Education, 20.100
blind, handicapped persons, braille, cassette, talking books, instructional, library services, 42.001
chemical emergency planning, EPA, *66.810*
child abuse, closed-circuit TV, DOJ, *16.611*
civil rights, aliens, *16.110*
drug abuse prevention, 16.005
humanities collections preservation, *45.149*
mine safety, 17.602
National Audiovisual Center, NTIS, 11.650
National Gallery exhibits, schools, libraries, 68.001
Rural Business-Cooperative Service, 10.350
small business assistance, 59.005
taxpayer services, 21.003
telecommunications, instructional programming, Star Schools, *84.203*
USIA Creative Arts Grants, *82.015*
USIA Cultural Exchange, *82.032*
see also Arts, arts education; Educational resources; Libraries; Museums, galleries; Radio, television
Auditory defects, *see* Deafness and the deaf
Autistic children, *see* Handicapped children

Corps of Engineers, DOD, *see* Agency Index (DOD, Department of the Army, Office of the Chief of Engineers)

CORRECTIONAL GRANT PROGRAM FOR INDIAN TRIBES, *16.596*

Corrections
adult education, offenders, *84.002, 84.191*
Byrne Formula Grant Program, *16.579*
civil rights, inmates, 16.105
Delinquency Prevention Program, *16.548, 16.549*
Drug Court Program, *16.585*
education, institutionalized neglected, delinquent youth, *84.013*
ex-offenders, job training, *17.249, 17.250*
facilities, federal surplus property transfer, 16.578, 39.002
Indian detention facilities improvement, repair, *15.063*
Indian tribes, jail construction, *16.596*
inmate education, federal surplus real property transfer, 84.145
juvenile delinquency programs, facilities, *16.541*
juvenile facilities improvements, personnel training, *16.523*
juvenile gangs program, *16.544*
juvenile, personnel training, research, *16.542*
Literacy Program for Prisoners, *84.255*
personnel families support projects, research, *16.563*
personnel, student loan cancellations, *84.037*
Prison Grants, *16.586*
research, program evaluation, *16.602*
Residential Substance Abuse Treatment, DOJ, *16.593*
staff, ex-offenders development, training, *16.601*
State Criminal Alien Assistance Program, DOJ, *16.606*
substance abusers, health, social services networks, *93.229*
tribal detention facilities, *15.030*
upgrading facilities operation, clearinghouse, *16.603*
vocational education, offenders, *84.048*
youth, offenders, education, employment services, *84.331*
see also Crime; Criminal justice system; Education counseling; Juvenile delinquency; Law enforcement education, training; Police

CORRECTIONS AND LAW ENFORCEMENT FAMILY SUPPORT, *16.563*

CORRECTIONS—RESEARCH AND EVALUATION AND POLICY FORMULATION, *16.602*

CORRECTIONS—TECHNICAL ASSISTANCE/CLEARINGHOUSE, *16.603*

CORRECTIONS—TRAINING AND STAFF DEVELOPMENT, *16.601*

Cotton, *see* Agricultural commodities, stabilization

Counseling, *see* Behavioral sciences, education, services; Education counseling; Home management; Mental health; Social services

Counseling on Doing Business with the Federal Government, 39.001

Counter-Terrorism Training, FEMA, *83.547*

COUNTY AND MUNICIPAL AGENCY DOMESTIC PREPAREDNESS EQUIPMENT SUPPORT PROGRAM [DOJ], *16.006*

Court Appointed Special Advocates (CASA), child abuse, *16.547*

Courts, *see* Criminal justice system; Indian affairs; Legal services

Courtesy Marine Examinations, 20.001

CP (Conservation Project Support), IMLS, *45.303*

CPAR (Construction Productivity Advanced Research), Corps of Engineers, *12.114*

CPHF (Community Partners for Healthy Farming), *93.956*

Cranston-Gonzalez National Affordable Housing Act, *see* National housing acts (National Affordable Housing Act)

CRBSCP (Colorado River Basin Salinity Control Program), *10.070*

CREATIVE ARTS GRANTS [USIA], *82.015*

CREDIT UNION CHARTER, EXAMINATION, SUPERVISION AND INSURANCE, *44.001*

Credit unions
Community Development Credit Union, *44.002*
establishment, operation, *44.001*
financial counseling, *44.002*
guaranteed student loans, *84.032*
health education loans, *93.108*
housing counseling assistance, *14.169*
insurance, *44.001*
revolving loan fund, *44.002*
see also Banks, banking

Crew Leader, farm labor, 17.308

CRF (Construction Reserve Fund), ships, *20.812*

Crime
anti-drug grants, low-income housing areas, *14.868*
arrest records, criminal history, 16.304
ATF crime control training, 21.052
Bulletproof Vest Partnership Program, *16.607*
campus crime grants, *16.552*
Civil Rights Prosecution, 16.109
Combined DNA Index System, *16.307*
computer fraud detection, training, 16.302
Cops Grants, *16.710*
Counter-Terrorism Training, FEMA, *83.547*
criminal conspiracy information sharing, *16.610*
criminal history record systems, *16.554*
domestic violence arrest policy development, *16.590*
drug abuse prevention, low-income housing areas, HUD, *14.193*
drug control improvement, *16.579, 16.580*
Drug-Free Schools and Communities, national programs, *84.184*
Emergency Federal Law Enforcement Assistance, *16.577*
violence, children's exposure, prevention initiative, *16.730*
FBI fingerprint identification, 16.303
Food Stamp fraud, *10.561*
gang-related, reduction programs, *16.544*
Medicaid, Medicare fraud, *93.042, 93.775*
Motor Vehicle Theft Protection Act Program, *16.597*
National Crime Information Center, 16.304
Omnibus Crime Control and Safe Streets Act (OCCSSA), *16.564, 16.565, 16.566, 16.571, 16.579, 16.580, 16.585, 16.587, 16.588, 16.589, 16.590, 16.592, 16.593, 16.609, 16.610, 16.612, 16.710, 16.711*, 21.052

independent living centers, *84.132, 84.169*
Indians, vocational rehabilitation, *84.250*
longshore, harbor workers benefits, *17.302*
maintenance assistance, Guam, Puerto Rico, Virgin Islands, *93.560*
meals, nutrition services, *93.045*
Medicare, *93.773*
Medicare supplementary, *93.774*
National Council on Disability, research, studies, *92.001*
National Limb Loss Information Center, *93.184*
programs, research, studies, evaluation, *92.001*
Protection and Advocacy, *84.240*
public housing, supportive services, *14.864*
rehabilitation personnel training, *84.129, 84.246, 84.263, 84.264, 84.265, 84.275*
rehabilitation personnel training, minorities, *84.315*
rehabilitation research, fellowships, *84.133*
research, Center for Medical Rehabilitation, *93.929*
scientists, biomedical research training, alcoholism, *93.272*
scientists, NIH intramural research training, *93.140*
scientists, NSF research opportunities, *47.049, 47.050, 47.075, 47.078*
Senior Companion Program, *94.016*
Social Security disability insurance, *96.001*
Social Security, disabled dependents of retirees, *96.002*
Social Security survivors insurance, *96.004*
Social Services Block Grant, *93.667*
special vocational rehabilitation services, *84.235*
Supplemental Security Income, *96.006*
supported employment, severely handicapped, *84.187*
supportive housing, *14.181*
veterans, adaptive equipment, automobiles, *64.100*
veterans pension, *64.104*
vocational rehabilitation services, *84.126, 84.128*
see also Behavioral sciences, education, services; Blindness and the blind; Deafness and the deaf; Employee benefits; Handicapped *entries*; Mental retardation; Social services; Veterans, disabled; Victim assistance; Vocational rehabilitation; Volunteers
Disabled veterans, *see* Veterans, disabled
DISABLED VETERANS' OUTREACH PROGRAM (DVOP), *17.801*
Disadvantaged
community food, nutrition CSBG, *93.571*
Community Services Block Grant, *93.569, 93.570*
Family Life Centers, violence prevention, *93.910*
Low-Income Taxpayer Clinics, *21.008*
Medicaid, *93.778*
Social Services Block Grant, *93.667*
see also Depressed areas; Disadvantaged *entries*; Homeless persons; Indian *entries*; Minority *entries*; Public assistance; Social services; Volunteers; Women; Youth *entries*
Disadvantaged, business development
DOT contracts, Bonding Assistance Program, *20.904*
DOT contracts, Short Term Lending Program, *20.905*

equity capital, loans, *59.011*
farmer outreach, *10.443*
government contracts, 39.001, 59.006
HUD project contracts complaints, 14.412
management, technical assistance, *59.007*
Microloan Demonstration Program, *59.046*
New Assets for Independence Demonstration, *93.602*
public transportation, *20.511*
transportation, DOT contracts, *20.903, 20.906, 20.907*
see also Business development; Economic development; Government contracts; Indian economic, business development; Minority business enterprise; Small business; Small Business Innovation Research (SBIR); Women
DISADVANTAGED BUSINESS ENTERPRISES— SHORT TERM LENDING PROGRAM [DOT], *20.905*
Disadvantaged, education
adult education, basic skills, *84.002*
adults, Educational Opportunity Centers, *84.066*
advanced placement test fee payment, DOED, *84.330*
at-risk students research, *84.306*
Colorado diversity-related engineering, science training, DOE, *81.116*
community development work-study, HUD, *14.512, 14.513*
Community Learning Centers, *84.287*
Community Services Block Grant, *93.569*
compensatory, *84.010*
Comprehensive School Reform Demonstration, *84.332*
early childhood research, *84.307*
elementary, secondary, innovative strategies, *84.298*
Even Start, *84.213*
Even Start, family literacy, *84.314*
Extension Service, *10.500*
Foster Grandparent Program, *94.011*
graduate study, *84.217*
Head Start, *93.600*
health, allied health, *93.822*
health professions faculty loan repayments, *93.923*
health professions scholarships, *93.139, 93.925*
health professions student loans, *93.342*
institutionalized neglected, delinquent children, *84.013*
Leveraging Educational Assistance Partnership (LEAP), *84.069*
Low-Income Taxpayer Clinics, *21.008*
Magnet Schools Assistance, *84.165*
medical, research, *93.222*
minority health professions schools, Centers of Excellence, *93.157*
minority IHEs, institutional aid, *84.031*
New Assets for Independence Demonstration, *93.602*
NIH Clinical Research Loan Repayment Program, *93.220*
NIH Undergraduate Scholarship Program, *93.187*
nursing, *93.178*
parent assistance, Goals 2000, *84.310*
postsecondary academic preparation, *84.042, 84.047*

Disadvantaged, education *(continued)*
postsecondary low-income student-parents, child care, *84.335*
postsecondary, staff training, *84.103*
private schools, Title 1 capital expenses, *84.216*
secondary students, supportive services, scholarships, *84.334*
teacher quality enhancement, recruitment, partnership, *84.336*
telecommunications instructional programming, Star Schools, *84.203*
undergraduate, SEOG, *84.007*
Upward Bound, academic stipends, *84.047*
Urban Community Service, IHEs, *84.252*
VISTA volunteers, 94.013
vocational, *84.048*
youth, secondary, postsecondary, dropout prevention, Talent Search, *84.044*
see also Agricultural education; Education counseling; Indian education, training; Minority education; Student financial aid; Tutoring; Volunteers; Women; Youth *entries*
Disadvantaged, employment and training
community development work-study, HUD, *14.512, 14.513*
Community Services Block Grant, discretionary, *93.570*
elderly, community services, *17.235*
Empowerment Zones Program, *14.244*
federal employment, 27.001
HUD projects employment complaints, 14.412
HUD Youthbuild Program, *14.243*
Job Opportunities for Low-Income Individuals, TANF, *93.593*
Job Training Partnership Act, *17.250*
One-Stop Career Center Initiative, *17.257*
pilot projects, *17.249*
public transportation careers, *20.511*
U.S. Employment Service, *17.207*
Welfare-to-Work Grants, *17.253*
Workforce Investment Act, *17.255*
see also Employment *entries*; Indian employment; Women; Youth employment
DISADVANTAGED HEALTH PROFESSIONS FACULTY LOAN REPAYMENT AND FELLOWSHIP PROGRAM, *93.923*
Disaster assistance
atmospheric, climate research, *11.431*
climate monitoring, assessment, *11.428*
Community Disaster Loans, FEMA, *83.537*
Crisis Counseling, FEMA, *83.539*
Crop Insurance, *10.450*
crops, noninsured, *10.451*
Disaster Preparedness Improvement Grants, *83.505*
disaster-resistant communities, standards, training, *83.551*
dislocated workers, *17.246*
economic development assistance, *11.307*
Emergency Management Performance Grants, *83.552*
EMI training, *83.527*, 83.530
engineering, earthquake hazard mitigation research, *47.041*
farm emergency loans, *10.404*
farmlands, Emergency Conservation Program (ECP), USDA, *10.054*

FEMA Mitigation Assistance, planning, training, *83.535*
FEMA Public Assistance Grants, *83.544*
FEMA state, local formula grants, *83.534*
Fisheries Disaster Relief, *11.477*
fisheries restoration, *11.407*
flood fighting, rescue, 12.103
flood, hurricane damage, 12.102
flood insurance, *83.100*
Flood Mitigation Assistance, FEMA, *83.536*
flood threat assistance, 12.111
highway, public works protection, 12.105
highway repairs, *20.205*
housing, FEMA program, *83.545*
housing purchase, reconstruction, *14.119, 14.120*
Individual and Family Grants, FEMA, *83.543*
legal services, *83.540*
library, archival humanities collections, planning, *45.149*
livestock, Disaster Reserve Assistance, *10.452*
mental health counseling, training, *93.982*
National Guard operations, maintenance, *12.401*
property repair, replacement, businesses, homeowners, nonprofits, renters *59.008*
public health, social services, *93.003*
rental housing, *14.139*
rural housing, *10.444, 10.445*
search, rescue services, *83.526*
small business loans, *59.002*
taxes, special IRS procedures, 21.003
training, EMI home study courses, 83.529
unemployment assistance, *83.541*
Unemployment Insurance, *17.225*
victim assistance, Cora Brown Fund, *83.538*
victim identification, FBI, 16.303
see also Agricultural commodities, stabilization; Civil defense; Climate; Earthquakes; Emergency assistance; Fire fighting, prevention, control; Flood prevention, control; Health, medical services; Hurricanes; Missing persons; Rescue services; Small business; Victim assistance
DISASTER HOUSING PROGRAM, *83.545*
DISASTER LEGAL SERVICES, *83.540*
Disaster Preparedness Improvement Grants, *83.505*
DISASTER RESERVE ASSISTANCE [FSA], *10.452*
DISASTER UNEMPLOYMENT ASSISTANCE, *83.541*
Discretionary Drug and Criminal Justice Assistance Program, *16.580*
Discrimination, *see* Civil rights; Complaint investigation
Disease control
animal disease, pest control, *10.025*
CDCP assistance, *93.283*
cell biology, biophysics research, *93.821*
Clinical Research, *93.333*
diabetes, *93.988*
disease prevention research, *93.135*
Hemophilia Surveillance, *93.227*
Immunization Grants, *93.268*
immunization research, information, *93.185*
Indians, epidemiology centers, *93.231*
Infant Health Initiative, *93.946*
Lyme Disease, *93.942*

community development work-study, *14.512, 14.513*
CSBG, discretionary, *93.570*
defense program changes impact, *11.307, 12.611, 12.612, 12.613*
Economic Adjustment Program, EDA, *11.307*
Economic Recovery, forest-dependent communities, *10.670*
evaluation, research, HUD, *14.506*
foreign trade zones (U.S.), 11.111
Fund for Rural America, *10.224*
HBCU Program, HUD, *14.237*
higher education institutions outreach, HUD, *14.511*
Hispanic IHEs community assistance, HUD, *14.514*
Indians, Alaska natives, *14.862*
insular areas, *14.225*
military base impact, 12.600, *12.607*
native American programs, *93.612*
planning assistance, *11.305*
public facilities construction, EDA projects, *11.300*
public housing, Economic Development and Supportive Services, *14.864*
public housing residents opportunities, *14.870*
revolving loan funds, *11.307*
revolving loan funds, credit unions, *44.002*
rural business, industrial development, *10.769*
rural business, industry financing, *10.768*
Rural Business Opportunity Grants, *10.773*
Rural Housing and Economic Development, HUD, *14.250*
rural, Intermediary Relending Program, *10.767*
rural loans, grants, RBCS, *10.854*
rural public facilities loans, *10.766*
rural resource development, *10.901*
Section 108 Loan Guarantees, *14.248*
Small Business Investment Companies, *59.011*
Southeast Alaska Economic Disaster Fund, Forest Service, *10.671*
technical assistance, *11.303, 14.227*
Trade Adjustment Assistance, *11.313*
U.S. insular areas, *15.875*
see also Appalachian region; Business development; Community development; Depressed areas; Economics, research, statistics; Employment *entries*; Indian economic, business development; Job creation; Private sector; Rural areas; Small business; Trade adjustment assistance; Urban planning
Economic Development Administration (EDA), USDC, *see* Agency Index
ECONOMIC DEVELOPMENT AND SUPPORTIVE SERVICES PROGRAM, *14.864*
Economic Development Initiative (EDI), HUD, *14.246*
ECONOMIC DEVELOPMENT—STATE AND LOCAL ECONOMIC DEVELOPMENT PLANNING, *11.305*
ECONOMIC DEVELOPMENT—TECHNICAL ASSISTANCE, *11.303*
Economic injury, *see* Community development; Complaint investigation; Consumers, consumer services; Disaster assistance; Fisheries industry; Insurance; Legal services; Small business; Trade adjustment assistance

ECONOMIC INJURY DISASTER LOANS, *59.002*
Economic Recovery, Forest Service, *10.670*
Economic Research Service, USDA, *see* Agency Index
ECONOMIC, SOCIAL, AND POLITICAL DEVELOPMENT OF THE TERRITORIES AND THE FREELY ASSOCIATED STATES, *15.875*
Economics and Statistics Administration, USDC, *see* Agency Index
Economics, research, statistics
agricultural, rural, 10.250, 10.950
Census Bureau data, 11.001
Consumer Price Index, 17.003
Economic Bulletin Board, 11.027
economic data, analysis, national, 11.025
economic depression research, training, *11.312*
employment projections, 17.006
export, import price index, 17.003
foreign trade, industry studies, 11.110
International Education Exchange, *84.304*
labor force, *17.002*
Medicaid, Medicare research, *93.779*
National Trade Data Bank, 11.026
NOAA unallied projects, *11.452, 11.454*
NSF research, *47.075*
Producer Price Index, 17.003
productivity studies, 17.004
Social Security program research, *96.007*
Welfare Reform Research, *93.595*
Woodrow Wilson Center fellowships, *85.300*
see also Agricultural statistics; Census services; Economic development; Housing research; Information *entries*; Social sciences; Statistics
ECP (Emergency Conservation Program), USDA, *10.054*
EDA (Economic Development Administration), USDC, *see* Agency Index
EDI (Economic Development Initiative), HUD, *14.246*
EDMAP, Geological Survey, *15.810*
EDSS (Economic Development and Supportive Services), HUD, *14.864*
Education
Agricultural Telecommunications Program, *10.501*
boating safety, 20.001, *20.005*
Charter Schools, *84.282*
desegregation, legal services, 16.100
elementary, secondary, innovative strategies, *84.298*
elementary, secondary teaching, Eisenhower professional development, *84.281*
environmental education professionals training, *66.950*
environmental education projects, *66.951*
fair housing outreach, *14.409*
Gifted and Talented, *84.206*
highway transportation, 20.215
international exchange, *84.304*
international peace, conflict management, *91.001, 91.002*
leadership development, *84.308*
library-museum partnerships, *45.312*
Magnet Schools Assistance, *84.165*
model projects, *84.215*
museum partnerships, *45.306*

Energy *(continued)*
wood fuel, *10.664*
see also Energy *entries*; Mineral resources;
Nuclear sciences, technology; Public utilities;
Solar energy
Energy conservation
community development block grants, *14.218,*
14.219, 14.225, 14.228, 14.862
improvement, health facilities, multifamily
housing, *14.151*
industrial waste reduction, *81.105*
inventions development assistance, *81.036*
low-income, assistance, *81.042, 93.568*
outreach, training, *81.117*
public housing, Comprehensive Grant Program,
14.859
Residential Energy Assistance Challenge Program
(REACH), ACF, *93.568*
state plans, *81.041*
sustainable agriculture research, *10.215*
technology research, development, *81.086*
Urban Consortium, *81.081*
weatherization, *81.042*
see also Housing rehabilitation; Weatherization
ENERGY EFFICIENCY AND RENEWABLE
ENERGY INFORMATION,
DISSEMINATION, OUTREACH, TRAINING
AND TECHNICAL
ANALYSIS/ASSISTANCE, *81.117*
Energy Information Administration (EIA), DOE, *see*
Agency Index
Energy information center, 81.039
ENERGY-RELATED INVENTIONS, *81.036*
Energy research
aviation, *20.108*
basic research, science, technology, *81.049*
biomass technology, *81.079*
coal, *81.057*
conservation technology development, *81.086*
environmental pollution control, *66.500*
DOE nuclear, education, fellowships, *81.114*
DOE nuclear weapons nonproliferation, *81.113*
DOE workers, epidemiology, health studies,
81.108
fossil, *81.089*
gas pipeline safety, *20.700*
Hydrologic Research, *11.462*
industrial waste reduction, *81.105*
Inertial Confinement Fusion, stockpile
stewardship, *81.112*
inventions development assistance, *81.036*
municipal solid waste technology, *81.079*
renewable resources, research, development, *81.087*
TVA energy, environmental research, services,
62.001
Used Equipment Grants, 81.022
see also Engineering *entries*; Nuclear sciences,
technology; Scientific research; Solar energy
ENERGY TASK FORCE FOR THE URBAN
CONSORTIUM, *81.081*
ENFORCING UNDERAGE DRINKING LAWS
PROGRAM, *16.727*
ENG (Engineering Grants), NSF, *47.041*
Engineering
agricultural, graduate fellowships, *10.210*
Barry M. Goldwater Scholarship Program, *85.200*

calibration, testing, 11.601
Colorado diversity-related engineering, science
training, DOE, *81.116*
DOD science, technology projects, *12.910*
earthquakes hazards mitigation, *15.807*
energy information, 81.064
energy-related inventions development, *81.036*
EPA fellowships, *66.500*
Hazard Mitigation Grant, FEMA, *83.548*
hazardous waste site remediation technology
development, *66.807*
health-related, preprofessional scholarships,
Indians, *93.971*
historic properties preservation, *15.904*
historic register, 15.914
Hydrometeorological Development, NOAA,
11.467
manufacturing technology commercialization,
11.612
mass transit, *20.505*
minority institutions, program improvements,
84.120
National Standard Reference Data System, *11.603*
National Technical Information Service, 11.650
NOAA Colorado areas math, engineering, science
education, *11.449*
NSF education, *47.041, 47.076*
soil survey data, 10.903
Standard Reference Materials, 11.604
standards, *11.609*
standards and certification information center,
11.610
Tech-Prep Education, secondary, postsecondary,
84.243
Technology Reinvestment Project, DOD, *12.911*
transportation, *20.515*
vocational rehabilitation engineering scholarships,
84.129
watershed, river basin projects, 10.906
Weights and Measures Service, NIST, 11.606
see also Computer products, sciences, services;
Energy *entries*; Engineering research;
Highways, roads, bridges; Mass transportation;
Mathematics; Physical sciences; Public works;
Science education; Scientific research;
Technology transfer, utilization; Transportation
ENGINEERING GRANTS, *47.041*
Engineering research
Air Force Defense Research Sciences Program,
12.800
Army Research Office, *12.431*
biomedical, biotechnological, *93.371*
biomedical, hazardous materials, *93.143*
biophysics, *93.821*
Christopher Columbus Fellowship Program, *85.100*
Construction Productivity Advanced Research,
Corps of Engineers, *12.114*
deafness, communicative disorders, *93.173*
DOD Integrated Helicopter Design Tools, *12.640*
DOD science, technology projects, *12.910*
DOD sciences research, fellowships, *12.630*
DOE nuclear, education, fellowships, *81.114*
DOE nuclear weapons nonproliferation, *81.113*
energy-related, basic sciences, technology, *81.049*
energy-related, conservation technology
development, *81.086*

energy-related, used equipment, 81.022
environmental systems, NOAA, *11.432*
high-speed passenger rail systems, *20.312*
Hydrologic Research, *11.462*
injury prevention research, *93.136*
manufacturing technology, *11.611*
NASA Technology Transfer, 43.002
Navy, education support, *12.300*
Navy research, *12.301*
NSF computer engineering, *47.070*
NSF grants, *47.041*
standards, projects, *11.609*
water desalination development, *15.506*
see also Biological sciences; Computer products,
    sciences, services; Energy *entries*; Engineering;
    Mathematics; Nuclear sciences, technology;
    Physical sciences; Scientific research;
    Technology transfer, utilization
English as a second language
adult education research, technical assistance,
    84.191
at-risk students research, *84.306*
citizenship education, 16.400
English Language Programs, USIA, *82.034*
Low-Income Taxpayer Clinics, *21.008*
Ready-to-Learn TV, early childhood education,
    84.295
refugees, *93.566, 93.567, 93.584*
school civil rights compliance, *84.004*
see also Aliens, refugees; Bilingual education,
    services; Disadvantaged, education
English language, *see* Adult education; Bilingual
    education, services; Illiteracy; Literature
English Language Programs, USIA, *82.034, 82.035*
Enterprise Communities, *10.772, 14.244*
ENTREPRENEURIAL TRAINING AND
    TECHNICAL ASSISTANCE PROGRAM
    [DOT], *20.907*
Environmental education
coastal ecosystem management, NOAA, *11.473*
elementary, secondary, exemplary projects, *84.168*
Environmental Education and Training Program,
    66.950
Environmental Education Grants, *66.951*
environmental justice projects, *66.604, 66.711*
EPA fellowships, engineering, environmental
    sciences, *66.500*
EPA, training and fellowships, *66.607*
NOAA intern program, *11.480*
Udall doctoral fellowships, *85.401*
Udall undergraduate scholarships, *85.400*
Wildlife Conservation and Appreciation, *15.617*
Woodrow Wilson Center fellowships, *85.300*
see also Environmental *entries*; Science
    education; Teacher education, training
ENVIRONMENTAL EDUCATION AND
    TRAINING PROGRAM, *66.950*
ENVIRONMENTAL EDUCATION GRANTS,
    66.951
Environmental health, research, services
blood-lead surveillance, *93.957*
community, environmental health centers, *93.224*
disabilities prevention, *93.184*
energy-related, *81.049*
environmental justice projects, *66.604, 66.710*
environmental hazards, *93.113*

EPA Children's Health Protection, *66.609*
EPA research, *66.500*
Great Lakes fish consumption effects, *93.208*
hazardous substances, biomedical research,
    graduate education, *93.143*
hazardous substances emergencies, state
    surveillance systems, *93.204*
hazardous waste sites health studies, *93.206*
Indians, preprofessional scholarships, *93.971*
lead poisoning prevention, *66.605, 93.197*
migrant health centers, *93.246*
multi-disciplinary, training, *93.894*
Occupational Health and Surveillance, fatality
    assessment, *93.957*
Pesticide Environmental Stewardship, *66.714*
plutonium center, *81.110*
pollution, air, water, lead poisoning, biometry, risk
    estimation, *93.115*
public health, graduate traineeships, *93.964*
research, manpower development, *93.894*
surveys, studies, special grants, EPA, *66.606*
toxic substances compliance programs, *66.701*
toxicology, *93.114*
see also Air pollution; Behavioral sciences,
    education, services; Community health
    services; Environmental *entries*; Hazardous
    materials, waste; Health, medical research;
    Pesticides; Pollution abatement; Public health;
    Radiation; Toxic substances, toxicology; Waste
    treatment, disposal; Water *entries*
Environmental Health Sciences Centers (EHS
    Centers), *93.894*
Environmental justice, *see* Community development
ENVIRONMENTAL JUSTICE COMMUNITY/
    UNIVERSITY PARTNERSHIP GRANTS
    PROGRAM, *66.710*
ENVIRONMENTAL JUSTICE GRANTS TO
    SMALL COMMUNITY GROUPS, *66.604*
ENVIRONMENTAL JUSTICE THROUGH
    POLLUTION PREVENTION GRANTS,
    66.711
Environmental management
abandoned mine land reclamation, *15.252*
agricultural experiment stations, research, *10.203*
aviation research, *20.108*
BLM projects, Cultural Resource Management,
    15.224
brownfield sites redevelopment, training, EPA,
    66.811
Chesapeake Bay Program, *66.466*
coastal ecosystem, NOAA, *11.473*
Coastal Ocean Program, research, *11.478*
conservation law enforcement training, 15.602
Defense Environmental Restoration Program,
    12.113
defense program changes, *12.612*
DOE technology development, *81.104*
endangered species conservation, *15.615*
environmental justice projects, *66.604, 66.710,*
    66.711
Environmental Quality Incentives Program,
    NRCS, *10.912*
EPA projects, One Stop Reporting, *66.608*
EPA, training and fellowships, *66.607*
estuary protection, *66.456*
forestry, rangeland research, *10.202*

Government *(continued)*
international public policy, minority student
fellowships, *84.269*
International Visitors Program, USIA, *82.004*
National Archives Reference Services, 89.001
native Americans, Udall congressional
internships, *85.402*
officials misconduct, prosecution, 16.109
productivity data, 17.004
Professional Exchange, USIA, *82.033*
public service career scholarships, *85.001*
publications, depository libraries, 40.001
publications sales, 40.002
statistical area boundaries, census, 11.003
teaching, Madison fellowships, *85.500*
telecommunications infrastructure, *11.552*
tribal, assistance, *15.020*
tribal self-government, *15.022, 15.023*
U.S. insular areas, *15.875*
USDC postsecondary student internships, *11.702*
whistle-blower protection, 17.303
Woodrow Wilson Center fellowships, *85.300*
young political leaders, international exchange,
82.006
see also Aliens, refugees; Civil rights; Complaint
investigation; Federal employment;
Government contracts; History; Indian affairs;
Information *entries*; International studies;
Legislation; Publications; Social sciences
Government Bookstore, 40.002
Government contracts
advisory services, counseling, 39.001
defense procurement assistance, *12.002*
DOE technical assistance, minorities, women,
81.082
employment discrimination, legal services, 16.101
equal opportunity, 17.301
federal contract compliance, 17.301
Minority Business Development, *11.802*
minority, Indian enterprises, technical assistance,
11.800
minority, SBA procurement assistance, 59.006
Native American Program, technical assistance,
11.801
small business technical assistance, 59.009
wage, hour standards, 17.303
see also Business development; Civil rights;
Disadvantaged, business development; Indian
economic, business development; Minority
business enterprise; Small business; Small
Business Innovation Research (SBIR)
Government employment, *see* Federal employment
Government Printing Office (GPO), 40.001 through
40.002
GOVERNMENT PUBLICATIONS SALES AND
DISTRIBUTION, 40.002
Governmental statistics, *see* Agricultural statistics;
Census services; Computer products, sciences,
services; Economics, research, statistics;
Information *entries*; Publications; Statistics
GPO (Government Printing Office), 40.001 through
40.002
GR-LRP (General Research Loan Repayment
Program), NIH, *93.232*
GRADUATE ASSISTANCE IN AREAS OF
NATIONAL NEED, *84.200*

Graduate fellowships, *see* Fellowships, scholarships,
traineeships
Graduate Research Fellowship Program, DOJ,
16.562
Graduated Payment Mortgage Program, *14.159*
Grain, *see* Feed grains
Grain Inspection, Packers and Stockyard
Administration, USDA, *see* Agency Index
GRANTING OF PATENT LICENSES, 81.003
GRANTS FOR AGRICULTURAL RESEARCH—
COMPETITIVE RESEARCH GRANTS,
10.206
GRANTS FOR AGRICULTURAL RESEARCH,
SPECIAL RESEARCH GRANTS, *10.200*
GRANTS FOR DENTAL PUBLIC HEALTH,
93.236
GRANTS FOR FACULTY DEVELOPMENT IN
FAMILY MEDICINE, *93.895*
GRANTS FOR FACULTY DEVELOPMENT IN
GENERAL INTERNAL MEDICINE AND/OR
GENERAL PEDIATRICS, *93.900*
GRANTS FOR GERIATRIC EDUCATION
CENTERS, *93.969*
GRANTS FOR GRADUATE TRAINING IN
FAMILY MEDICINE, *93.379*
GRANTS FOR NURSE ANESTHETIST
FACULTY FELLOWSHIPS, *93.907*
GRANTS FOR PREDOCTORAL TRAINING IN
FAMILY MEDICINE, *93.896*
GRANTS FOR PREVENTIVE MEDICINE, *93.117*
GRANTS FOR PUBLIC WORKS AND
INFRASTRUCTURE DEVELOPMENT,
11.300
GRANTS FOR RESIDENCY TRAINING IN
GENERAL INTERNAL MEDICINE AND/OR
GENERAL PEDIATRICS, *93.884*
GRANTS FOR RESIDENTIAL TREATMENT
PROGRAMS FOR PREGNANT AND
POSTPARTUM WOMEN, *93.101*
GRANTS FOR STATE LOAN REPAYMENT
[HHS], *93.165*
GRANTS-IN-AID FOR RAILROAD SAFETY—
STATE PARTICIPATION, *20.303*
GRANTS TO COMBAT VIOLENT CRIMES
AGAINST WOMEN ON CAMPUSES, *16.552*
GRANTS TO ENCOURAGE ARREST POLICIES,
16.590
GRANTS TO INCREASE ORGAN DONATIONS,
93.134
GRANTS TO PROVIDE OUTPATIENT EARLY
INTERVENTION SERVICES WITH
RESPECT TO HIV DISEASE, *93.918*
GRANTS TO STATES FOR ACCESS AND
VISITATION PROGRAMS [ACF], *93.597*
GRANTS TO STATES FOR CONSTRUCTION OF
STATE HOME FACILITIES, *64.005*
GRANTS TO STATES FOR INCARCERATED
YOUTH OFFENDERS, *84.331*
GRANTS TO STATES FOR OPERATION OF
OFFICES OF RURAL HEALTH, *93.913*
Graphic arts, *see* Arts, arts education; Audiovisual
aids, film, video
Great Lakes
Clean Vessel Act, pumpout/dump stations,
15.616
coastal wetlands protection, *15.614*

coastal zone management, *11.419*
ecosystem restoration, *66.469*
estuary research reserves, *11.420*
fish consumption health effects research, *93.208*
fish resources management, *11.405*
research, Coastal Ocean Program, *11.478*
research, Sea Grant Support, *11.417*
shipping, ship construction, reconstruction financing, *20.802*
shipping, ship construction, reconstruction subsidies, *20.808*
see also Water navigation
GREAT LAKES HUMAN HEALTH EFFECTS RESEARCH, *93.208*
GREAT LAKES PROGRAM, *66.469*
GREAT PLAINS CONSERVATION, *10.900*
Group homes
AIDS-afflicted persons, *14.241*
board and care, assisted living facilities, *14.129*
disabled, supportive housing, *14.181*
emergency housing, homeless, *14.231*
food donations, commodities, *10.569, 10.570*
handicapped, independent living, *84.132, 84.169*
juveniles, half-way houses, *16.540*
meals services, elderly, handicapped, *93.045*
mentally ill, supported housing, *93.125*
rehabilitation personnel training, *84.263, 84.264*
rural facilities, *10.766*
SED, children, adolescents, mental health services, *93.104*
Senior Companion Program, *94.016*
transitional housing, homeless *14.235*
veterans, DVA transitional housing loans, *64.025*
veterans, homeless, DVA provider grants, *64.024*
vocational rehabilitation personnel training, *84.129, 84.275*
see also Handicapped, housing; Homeless persons; Housing, congregate; Maternal, child health, welfare
Group practice, *see* Health facilities *entries*
Group Projects Abroad, DOED, *84.021*
Growing Equity Mortgages (GEMs), *14.172*
GROWTH MANAGEMENT PLANNING ASSISTANCE [DOD], *12.613*
GSA (General Services Administration), 39.001 through 39.009
Guam, *see* U.S. possessions, territories
Guaranteed Student Loans, *84.032*
Guidance counseling, testing, *see* Education counseling; Employment services; Veterans education, training; Veterans employment; Vocational education
Gun control, *see* Crime

HABITAT CONSERVATION, *11.463*
Haitians, *see* Aliens, refugees
Halfway houses, *see* Group homes
Handicapped
ADA technical assistance, *16.108*
Architectural Barriers Act Enforcement, HUD, 14.407
architectural, transportation barriers, facilities accessibility standards enforcement, design, research, 88.001
assistive technology, *84.224*
assistive technology protection, advocacy, *84.343*

Client Assistance Program, benefits, services information, *84.161*
developmental disabilities, national projects, *93.631*
developmental disabilities, personnel training, *93.632*
developmentally disabled, advocacy, support, *93.630*
discrimination, housing, HUD programs, 14.404, 14.414
food, meals assistance, *10.558*
Food Stamps, *10.551*
independent living centers, *84.132*
independent living services, severely handicapped, *84.169*
instructional services, 42.001
library services, 42.001
meal services, *93.045*
mentally retarded, President's Committee, 93.613
programs, research, studies, evaluation, *92.001*
Protection and Advocacy, *84.240*
rehabilitation personnel training, *84.129, 84.246 84.263, 84.264, 84.265*
rehabilitation research, fellowships, *84.133*
rehabilitation services, *84.126, 84.128*
research, Center for Medical Rehabilitation, *93.929*
Senior Companion Program, *94.016*
special vocational rehabilitation services, *84.235*
small business loans, *59.012*
transportation services, specialized vehicle purchases, *20.513*
see also Behavioral sciences, education, services; Blindness and the blind; Deafness and the deaf; Disabled; Handicapped *entries*; Mental health; Mental retardation; Social services; Veterans, disabled; Vocational rehabilitation; Volunteers
Handicapped children
Adoption Assistance, *93.659*
developmental disabilities research, *93.865*
developmentally disabled, advocacy, support, *93.630*
early intervention, special education, *84.027, 84.181, 84.323, 84.324, 84.325, 84.326, 84.327, 84.328, 84.329*
food, meals assistance, *10.558*
Foster Grandparent Program, *94.011*
Hawaii, special education programs, *84.221*
Head Start Program, *93.600*
Indian, institutionalized handicapped, *15.045*
milk program, *10.556*
preschool special education, *84.173*
programs, research, studies, evaluation, *92.001*
School Breakfast Program, *10.553*
School Lunch Program, *10.555*
see also Disabled; Handicapped; Handicapped, education; Maternal, child health, welfare, Volunteers
Handicapped, education
Colorado diversity-related engineering, science training, DOE, *81.116*
early intervention, special education, *84.027, 84.181, 84.323, 84.324, 84.325, 84.326, 84.327, 84.328, 84.329*
Hawaii, special education programs, *84.221*
Head Start Program, *93.600*

Health facilities construction, rehabilitation
(conintued)
  vocational rehabilitation, *84.126*
  see also Community health services; Education
    facilities; Nursing homes
Health insurance
  Children's Insurance Program, HCFA, *93.767*
  elders benefits counseling, *93.049*
  health care systems research, *93.226, 93.239*
  HIV coverage, *93.917*
  Medicaid, *93.778*
  Medicaid fraud control, *93.775*
  Medicaid, Medicare research, *93.779*
  Medicare hospital insurance, *93.773*
  Medicare supplementary, *93.774*
  railroad workers, *57.001*
  Social Security, disability, *96.001*
  see also Employee benefits; Insurance; Social
    Security Act; Veterans health, medical services
Health, maternal and child, *see* Maternal, child
  health, welfare
Health, medical education, training
  Academic Research Enhancement Award, *93.390*
  agricultural health, safety, *93.956*
  AIDS, NIH research education loan repayments,
    93.936
  AIDS-related, *93.145, 93.938, 93.939*
  alcoholism research, *93.271, 93.272*
  allied professions, *93.191*
  anesthetists, nurse, *93.124, 93.916*
  Area Health Education Centers Model Programs,
    93.107
  bilingual, bicultural demonstrations, *93.105*
  biodiversity research, *93.168*
  cancer-related, *93.398, 93.919*
  Clinical Research, *93.333*
  communicable, chronic diseases control, *93.283*
  contraception, infertility research, education loan
    repayments, *93.209*
  developmentally disabled, personnel, *93.632*
  disabilities prevention, *93.184*
  disadvantaged, assistance, *93.139, 93.220,*
    93.342, 93.822, 93.925
  DOT emergency medical services, disasters,
    highway safety, *20.600*
  education loan repayments, states, *93.165*
  faculty education loan repayments, disadvantaged,
    93.923
  family medicine, *93.379, 93.895, 93.896, 93.984*
  family planning paramedical, paraprofessional
    personnel, *93.260*
  geriatrics-related, *93.156, 93.969*
  HEAL program, *93.108*
  health center technical assistance, *93.129*
  health education centers, *93.189, 93.824*
  health planning, policy, graduate traineeships,
    93.962
  health professions community scholarships, *93.931*
  health services research, NRSA, *93.225*
  highway accidents, training, DOT, *20.600*
  HIV projects, *93.928*
  hospital administration graduate, *93.962*
  IHS education loan repayment, *93.164*
  independent living center personnel, *84.132*
  Indians, *93.123, 93.970, 93.972*
  Indians, preprofessional, *93.971*

  injury prevention, control, *93.136*
  internal medicine, *93.884, 93.900*
  librarians, medical, *93.879*
  loans, *93.108*
  maternal, child health, *93.110*
  mental health-related, *93.150, 93.244, 93.982*
  minority faculty, students, *93.157*
  minority health status improvement, *93.004*
  minority research, *93.106*
  minority schools, biomedical research, *93.375*
  neurological disorders research, minority faculty,
    93.853
  NHSC education loan repayments, *93.162*
  NHSC education scholarships, *93.288*
  NIH General Research Loan Repayment Program,
    93.232
  NIH Undergraduate Scholarship Program, *93.187*
  nurse anesthetist faculty, *93.907*
  nursing-related, *93.298, 93.299, 93.359*
  occupational health, safety personnel, *93.263*
  osteopathy faculty development, *93.900*
  pediatrics, *93.884*
  pediatrics faculty development, *93.900*
  pharmacology, *93.948*
  physician assistants, *93.886*
  podiatry postgraduate programs, *93.181*
  preventive medicine residency, *93.117*
  public education, promotion, *93.990*
  public health, *93.188, 93.964*
  radiation control, NRC training, *77.001*
  rehabilitation medicine, *84.129*
  rehabilitation personnel, *84.246 84.263, 84.264,*
    84.265, 84.275
  research, *93.222*
  rural computer networks, RUS, *10.855*
  rural physician residency, *93.906*
  rural specialists, *93.192*
  scholarships, Exceptional Financial Need, *93.820*
  search, rescue, *83.526*
  sexually transmitted diseases, *93.977*
  student loans, *93.342*
  substance abuse, health faculty, *93.274*
  Tech-Prep Education, secondary, postsecondary,
    84.243
  tuberculosis prevention, control, *93.947*
  vocational rehabilitation personnel, *84.129*
  see also Behavioral sciences, education, services;
    Chiropractic; Dental education, training;
    Family medicine; Fellowships, scholarships,
    traineeships; Health, medical research; Health
    professions; Libraries; National Research
    Service Awards; Nursing; Optometry;
    Osteopathy; Pediatrics; Pharmacology,
    pharmacy; Podiatry; Social sciences; Speech
    pathology; Technical training; Veterinary
    medicine; Vocational rehabilitation
Health, medical research
  Academic Research Enhancement Award, *93.390*
  aging, behavioral, biomedical, social sciences,
    93.866
  aging, care, *93.048*
  agricultural health, safety, *93.956*
  AIDS/HIV epidemiologic studies, *93.943*
  AIDS, international, *93.154*
  AIDS, NIH research education loan repayments,
    93.936

national forests, USDA payments to states, *10.665*
national grasslands, USDA payments to counties,
  10.666
parking facilities, *20.205*
pedestrian walkways, *20.205*
planning, research, *20.205*
railroad grade crossings, *20.205*
relocation assistance, *20.205*
rest areas, *20.205*
road, street improvement, *20.205*
state, community highway safety, equipment,
  public education, training, *20.600*
U.S. insular areas, *15.875*
see also Community development; Interstate
  commerce; Mass transportation; Motor
  vehicles; Public safety; Public works;
  Transportation
HIP (Housing Improvement Program), Indian,
  15.141
HISPANIC INSTITUTIONS WORK-STUDY
  PROGRAM [HUD], *14.513*
HISPANIC-SERVING INSTITUTIONS
  ASSISTING COMMUNITIES [HUD], *14.514*
HISPANIC SERVING INSTITUTIONS
  EDUCATION GRANTS [USDA], *10.223*
HISPANIC SERVING INSTITUTIONS—
  ENTREPRENEURIAL TRAINING AND
  TECHNICAL ASSISTANCE [DOT], *20.906*
Historic monuments
advisory services, counseling, 15.915
DOD donations, loans, 12.700
federal surplus property, 15.918, 39.003
federal surplus real property, 39.002
see also Buildings; Historic preservation; History;
  Museums, galleries
Historic preservation
advisory services, counseling, 15.912, 15.914,
  15.915
American Battlefield Protection, *15.926*
BLM projects, Cultural Resource Management,
  15.224
community development grants, *14.218, 14.219,
  14.225, 14.228, 14.862*
federal surplus property, 15.918
grants-in-aid, *15.904*
HBCU structures, *15.924*
highways, *20.205*
historic landmarks registry, 15.912
humanities research materials preservation,
  45.149
Indian programs, *15.041*
maritime heritage grants, *15.925*
museum collections preservation, planning,
  training, *45.301*
National Center for Preservation Technology and
  Training, *15.923*
National Register of Historic Places, *15.904,
  15.914*
native American graves protection, repatriation,
  15.922
natural landmarks registry, 15.910
planning, repair, *15.904*, 15.914
rural resource development, *10.901*
tax incentives, *15.904*, 15.912, 15.914
technical information, 15.915
transportation facilities, *20.507*

see also Community development; Historic
  monuments; History; Museums, galleries;
  National Register of Historic Places
HISTORIC PRESERVATION FUND GRANTS-
  IN-AID, *15.904*
Historic Surplus Property Program, DOI, 15.918
HISTORICALLY BLACK COLLEGES AND
  UNIVERSITIES PRESERVATION
  INITIATIVE, *15.924*
HISTORICALLY BLACK COLLEGES AND
  UNIVERSITIES PROGRAM [HUD], *14.237*
History
collections preservation, arrangement, training,
  89.003
historical organizations, challenge grants, *45.130*
humanities, NEH Public Programs, *45.164*
Indian history, tribal heritage, elementary,
  secondary education, *84.060*
National Archives Reference Services, federal
  records, Presidential Libraries, 89.001
National Historical Publications and Records
  Commission, *89.003*
native American language preservation, *93.587*
research materials preservation, *45.149*
teaching, Madison fellowships, *85.500*
Woodrow Wilson Center fellowships, *85.300*
see also Government; Historic preservation;
  Humanities entries; International studies;
  Museums, galleries; Social sciences
HIV (human immunodeficiency virus), see AIDS
  (Acquired Immunodeficiency Syndrome)
HIV/AIDS Dental Reimbursements, *93.924*
HIV/AIDS MENTAL HEALTH SERVICES
  DEMONSTRATION PROGRAM, *93.216*
HIV CARE FORMULA GRANTS, *93.917*
HIV DEMONSTRATION PROGRAM FOR
  CHILDREN, ADOLESCENTS, AND
  WOMEN, *93.153*
HIV DEMONSTRATION, RESEARCH, PUBLIC
  AND PROFESSIONAL EDUCATION
  PROJECTS, *93.941*
HIV EMERGENCY RELIEF FORMULA
  GRANTS, *93.915*
HIV PREVENTION ACTIVITIES—HEALTH
  DEPARTMENT BASED, *93.940*
HIV PREVENTION ACTIVITIES—
  NON-GOVERNMENTAL ORGANIZATION
  BASED, *93.939*
HMEP (Hazardous Materials Emergency
  Preparedness) Training and Planning Grants,
  20.703
HMGP (Hazard Mitigation Grant Program), FEMA,
  83.548
Home economics
child welfare services, *93.645*
Community Food Projects, USDA, *10.225*
Extension Service, *10.500*
Minority Scholars Program, scholarships, *10.220*
New Assets for Independence Demonstration,
  93.602
vocational education program, *84.048*
see also Adult education; Consumers, consumer
  services; Food, nutrition; Home management;
  Volunteers
HOME EQUITY CONVERSION MORTGAGES,
  14.183

libraries, collections preservation training, *45.149*
local, state, regional projects, *45.129*
National Gallery of Art exhibits, 68.001
native American language preservation, *93.587*
NEH Public Programs, *45.164*
USIA Creative Arts Grants, *82.015*
young political leaders, international exchange, *82.006*
see also Arts, arts education; Historic preservation; History; Humanities education, research; International studies; Social sciences

Humanities education, research
Alaska natives, *84.320*
BLM projects, Cultural Resource Management, *15.224*
challenge grants, *45.130*
graduate fellowships, *84.170*
Indian history, tribal heritage, elementary, secondary education, *84.060*
international exchange, *82.026, 82.038*
international peace, conflict management, *91.001, 91.002*
NEH centers support, *45.161*
NEH development, demonstration, *45.162*
NEH fellowships, *45.160, 45.161*
NEH Public Programs, *45.164*
NEH Seminars and Institutes, *45.163*
NSF, cultural anthropology, *47.075*
teacher training seminars abroad, *84.018*
Woodrow Wilson Center fellowships, *85.300*
see also Arts, arts education; Foreign languages; History; Humanities; International studies; Libraries; Museums, galleries; Social sciences; Teacher education, training
Hunter safety programs, *15.611*
Hunting, *see* Public safety; Wildlife

Hurricanes
coastal zone management, *11.419*
coastal zone rehabilitation, 12.102
disaster-resistant communities, standards, training, *83.551*
emergency rescue, 12.103
farmland rehabilitation, *10.054*
FEMA Community Disaster Loans, *83.537*
FEMA Mitigation Assistance, planning, training, *83.535*
Hazard Mitigation Grant, FEMA, *83.548*
search, rescue services, *83.526*
see also Climate; Coastal zone; Disaster assistance; Emergency assistance; Flood prevention, control
HYDROLOGIC RESEARCH, *11.462*
Hydrometeorological Development, NOAA, *11.467*
Hydropower, *see* Energy *entries*; Public utilities
Hypertension, *see* Health, medical *entries*; Preventive health services

ICBG (International Cooperative Biodiversity Groups) Program, HHS, *93.168*
ICF (Inertial Confinement Fusion), DOE, *81.112*
IDEA (Individuals with Disabilities Education Act), *see* Handicapped education
IFG (Individual and Family Grants), FEMA, *83.543*
IFLOWS (Integrated Flood Observing and Warning System), *11.450*

IHE (institution of higher education), *see* Higher education institutions
IHI (Infant Health Initiatives), *93.946*
IHS (Indian Health Service), HHS, *see* Agency Index
IHS (Indian Health Service) Loan Repayment Program, *93.164*
IIPP (Institute for International Public Policy), *84.269*

Illiteracy
adult education programs, *84.002*
education technology consortia, *84.302*
Even Start, families, *84.314*
Even Start, Indians, *84.258*
Even Start, state, *84.213*
JTPA research, *17.248*
Literacy Program for Prisoners, *84.255*
National Institute for Literacy, fellowships, *84.257*
Ready-to-Learn TV, early childhood education, *84.295*
workplace literacy model, *17.249*
see also Adult education; Bilingual education, services; Education counseling; Libraries; Tutoring; Volunteers
IMLS (Institute of Museum and Library Services), National Foundation on the Arts and the Humanities, *see* Agency Index
IMMIGRANT EDUCATION, *84.162*
Immigration and Nationality Act, *16.110,* 16.400, *16.606,* 17.202, 17.203, 17.252
Immigration and Naturalization Service (INS), DOJ, *see* Agency Index
Immigration, citizenship, *see* Adult education; Aliens, refugees
IMMUNIZATION GRANTS, *93.268*

Immunization, immunology
cancer research, *93.393, 93.395, 93.396*
childhood immunization, state, local programs, *93.283*
Clinical Research, *93.333*
deafness, communicative disorders research, *93.173*
hazardous waste sites health studies, *93.206*
health services block grant activities, *93.991*
Immunization Grants, *93.268*
immunology, immunological diseases research, *93.855*
neurological disorders research, *93.853*
research, information, *93.185*
Urban Indian Health Services, *93.193*
see also Communicable diseases; Disease control; Epidemiology; Health, medical *entries*; Preventive health services
IMMUNIZATION RESEARCH, DEMONSTRATION, PUBLIC INFORMATION AND EDUCATION— TRAINING AND CLINICAL SKILLS IMPROVEMENT PROJECTS, *93.185*
IMPACT AID [DOED], *84.041*
IMPACT AID—FACILITIES MAINTENANCE [DOED], *84.040*
Import Price Index, 17.003
IMPORT RELIEF (INDUSTRY), 61.001
Imports, *see* International commerce, investment
IMPROVEMENT AND REPAIR OF INDIAN DETENTION FACILITIES, *15.063*

Head Start parent programs, *93.600*
health, allied professions recruitment, *93.970*
health professions scholarships, *93.123, 93.219,*
    93.971, 93.972
higher education grants, *15.114*
higher education strengthening, *84.031*
IHS education loan repayments, *93.164*
Indian School Equalization Program, *15.042*
Ironworker Training Program, *15.146*
language preservation, *93.587, 93.612*
Native American Library Services, *45.311*
school administrative costs, *15.046*
school operations costs, *15.047*
school repair, replacement, *15.062*
Special Higher Education Scholarships, *15.059*
student transportation, *15.044*
supplemental education programs, *15.130, 84.060*
Tech-Prep Education, *84.243*
tribally-controlled IHEs, *15.027, 15.028*
Udall congressional internships, *85.402*
Udall doctoral fellowships, *85.401*
Udall undergraduate scholarships, *85.400*
vocational, *84.101*
vocational, employment assistance, *15.108*
vocational rehabilitation, *84.250*
vocational, technical, tribally controlled, *84.245*
vocational, United Tribes Technical College,
    15.060
Welfare-to-Work Grants, *17.254*
see also Adult education; Alaska natives;
    Education *entries*; Hawaii, Hawaii natives;
    Technical training; Vocational education
Indian employment
community development block grants, *14.862*
employment rights, *30.009*
Ironworker Training Program, *15.146*
One-Stop Career Center Initiative, *17.257*
referrals, United Sioux Tribes Development
    Corporation, *15.061*
training, services, *17.251*
tribal self-government, *15.022*
Tribal Work Grants, *93.594*
vocational rehabilitation, *84.250*
vocational training, employment assistance,
    15.108
vocational, United Tribes Technical College,
    15.060
Welfare-to-Work Grants, *17.254*
Workforce Investment Act, *17.255*
see also Alaska natives; Employment *entries*;
    Hawaii, Hawaii natives; Vocational education
INDIAN EMPLOYMENT ASSISTANCE, *15.108*
INDIAN ENVIRONMENTAL GENERAL
    ASSISTANCE PROGRAM, *66.926*
INDIAN GRADUATE STUDENT
    SCHOLARSHIPS, *15.059*
Indian Health Service (IHS), HHS, *see* Agency Index
INDIAN HEALTH SERVICE EDUCATIONAL
    LOAN REPAYMENT, *93.164*
INDIAN HEALTH SERVICE—HEALTH
    MANAGEMENT DEVELOPMENT
    PROGRAM, *93.228*
INDIAN HEALTH SERVICE RESEARCH, *93.905*
Indian health, social services
bilingual, bicultural health demonstrations, *93.105*
block grants, community development, *14.862*

child welfare, day care, foster care, counseling,
    family assistance, *15.144*
children's justice act, *16.583*
community health coalitions, *93.137*
diabetes program, *93.237*
elderly, special programs, *93.047*
epidemiology centers, *93.231*
family violence prevention services, *93.671*
food assistance, 10.550, *10.565, 10.567*
food assistance, WIC, *10.557*
Great Lakes fish consumption effects, *93.208*
health care research, demonstration, *93.933*
health management development, *93.228*
health professionals recruitment, *93.954, 93.970*
health professions scholarships, *93.219, 93.971,*
    93.972
health programs, tribal self-governance, *93.210*
IHS education loan repayments, *93.164*
IHS research, development projects, *93.905*
Indian housing authorities, drug elimination
    program, *14.854*
injury prevention, *93.228*
nurses, education loan repayments, *93.908*
social, economic self-sufficiency development,
    93.612
Social Services program, *15.025*
substance abuse treatment systems, *93.122*
tribal self-government, *15.022*
Udall doctoral fellowships, *85.401*
Udall undergraduate scholarships, *85.400*
urban Indians, *93.193*
violence against women, victim services, *16.587*
vocational rehabilitation, *84.250*
welfare assistance, *15.113*
Welfare-to-Work Grants, *17.254*
see also Alaska natives; Community health
    services; Hawaii, Hawaii natives; Health,
    medical services; Social services; Volunteers
Indian housing
anti-drug grants, *14.868*
block grants, *14.867*
construction, rehabilitation, *14.862*
counseling program, *10.441*
drug elimination program, *14.854*
Economic Development and Supportive Services,
    14.864
farm laborers, *10.405*
federal housing guarantees, *14.869*
Housing Improvement Program (HIP), *15.141*
HUD, Rural Housing and Economic
    Development, *14.250*
loan guarantees, *14.865*
modernization, Comprehensive Grant Program,
    14.859
outreach, socially disadvantaged, *10.443*
rehabilitation, *10.433*
tribal self-government, *15.022*
veterans, *64.126*
see also Housing *entries*
INDIAN HOUSING ASSISTANCE, *15.141*
INDIAN HOUSING BLOCK GRANTS, *14.867*
Indian Housing Improvement Program (HIP),
    15.141
INDIAN JOB PLACEMENT—UNITED SIOUX
    TRIBES DEVELOPMENT CORPORATION,
    15.061

criminal justice research, graduate fellowships, *16.561*
Delinquency Prevention Program, *16.548, 16.549*
Drug Court Program, *16.585*
Drug-Free Schools and Communities, national programs, *84.184*
education of institutionalized children, *84.013*
Foster Grandparent Program, *94.011*
gangs, drug abuse, trafficking, *16.544*
halfway houses, group homes, *16.540*
Juvenile Justice and Delinquency Prevention Act (JJDPA), *16.540, 16.541, 16.543, 16.544, 16.548, 16.549, 16.601, 16.602, 16.603, 16.726*
juvenile justice system improvement, *16.523*
Juvenile Mentoring Program, *16.726*
local law enforcement block grants, *16.592*
personnel training, *16.542*
prevention, control demonstrations, *16.541*
prevention, control research, *16.542*
prevention programs, research, *16.540*
Prison Grants, *16.586*
research fellowships, *16.566*
Safe Schools/Healthy Students National Evaluation, DOJ, *16.732*
State Court Improvement Program, ACF, *93.586*
state plan development, *16.540*
substance abusers, health, social services networks, *93.229*
Tribal Youth Program, OJJDP, *16.731*
see also Alcoholism; Corrections; Criminal justice system; Drug abuse; Volunteers; Youth *entries*
Juvenile Justice and Delinquency Prevention Act (JJDPA), *see* Juvenile delinquency
JUVENILE JUSTICE AND DELINQUENCY PREVENTION—ALLOCATION TO STATES, *16.540*
JUVENILE JUSTICE AND DELINQUENCY PREVENTION—SPECIAL EMPHASIS, *16.541*
JUVENILE MENTORING PROGRAM, *16.726*

K Awards, alcoholism, *93.271*
K Awards, drug abuse, *93.277*
K Awards, mental health, *93.281*
KD&A (Knowledge Development and Application), SAMHSA, *93.230*
Kidney disease research, *see* Health, medical research
KIDNEY DISEASES, UROLOGY AND HEMATOLOGY RESEARCH, *93.849*
Kings Point, *20.807*
Knowledge Development and Application (KD&A), SAMHSA, *93.230*

LAAP (Learning Anytime Anywhere Partnerships), DOED, *84.339*
LABOR CERTIFICATION FOR ALIEN WORKERS, 17.203
LABOR FORCE STATISTICS, *17.002*
Labor Housing, USDA, *10.405*
LABOR-MANAGEMENT COOPERATION, *34.002*
Labor-management relations
BLS data, *17.005*
collective bargaining, conciliation, mediation, FMCS, 34.001
labor-management committees, FMCS, *34.002*

labor organization practices, reports, 17.140, 17.309
Landrum-Griffin Act, 17.140, 17.309
unfair labor practices, 46.001
union representation elections, 46.001
see also Labor *entries*
LABOR-MANAGEMENT RELATIONS, 46.001
LABOR MEDIATION AND CONCILIATION, 34.001
LABOR ORGANIZATION REPORTS, 17.140, 17.309
Labor standards
child labor standards, 17.303
Equal Pay Act, 30.010
farm labor contractor registration, 17.308
Federal Wage Garnishment Law, 17.306
federal wage hour law, 17.303
federally assisted construction, 17.301, 17.303
labor-management committees, FMCS, *34.002*
performing arts employees, 17.303
prevailing wage determinations, 17.303
railroad employees, 20.301
safety, health, *17.503, 17.504*
sex-based wage differentials, 30.010
union practices, 17.140, 17.309
wage-hour standards, 17.303
whistle-blowers, 17.303
working conditions data, *17.005*
see also Employee benefits; Farm workers; Labor *entries*; Occupational health, safety
Labor statistics, *see* Economics, research, statistics; Statistics
Labor unions
collective bargaining data, *17.005*
collective bargaining, mediation assistance, FMCS, 34.001
disabled, employment, Projects with Industry, *84.234*
disclosure, reporting, 17.140, 17.309
employment discrimination, 16.101
labor-management committees, FMCS, *34.002*
representation elections, 46.001
unfair practices, regulation, 46.001
union members rights, election standards, 17.140, 17.309
see also Labor *entries*
Laboratory animals
alternative medicine research, *93.213*
cancer research, *93.393, 93.394, 93.395, 93.396, 93.399*
cancer research facilities, *93.392*
comparative medicine, *93.306*
environmental risk research, *93.115*
mental health research, *93.242*
microbiology, infectious diseases research, *93.856*
Lyme Disease, *93.942*
Lung Diseases Research, *93.838*
primate research centers, *93.306*
Research Infrastructure, minority institutions, *93.389*
see also Animal disease control, health, welfare; Veterinary medicine
Lake Champlain fish resources management, *11.405*
Lakes, *see* Great Lakes; Recreation, water; Water resources, supply, management; Wetlands

Liaison and Outreach Services Program (LOSP), DOT, *20.903*

Libraries
agriculture, 10.700
bibliographic, reference services, LC, 42.006
bibliographic, reference services, science, technology, LC, 42.007
Books for the Blind, handicapped, 42.001
depository, government publications, 40.001
DOD property donations, loans, 12.700
education technology, *84.302, 84.303*
environmental education, *66.950*
EPA Air Information Center, 66.009
federal surplus personal property donations, 39.003
federal surplus real property transfer, 84.145
foreign information access, education technology, *84.337*
foreign language, international studies resources, *84.015, 84.016*
government publications, 40.001
Hispanic-serving institutions, agricultural, food sciences, *10.223*
historical collections, preservation, training, *89.003*
humanities, archival, collections preservation, *45.149*
humanities development, challenge grants, *45.130*
humanities, NEH Public Programs, *45.164*
IMLS National Leadership Grants, *45.312*
international peace, conflict management, *91.001, 91.002*
LC catalog cards, tapes, microforms, 42.003
library-museum partnerships, research, model programs, fellowships, traineeships, *45.312*
Library of Congress publications, 42.005
lifelong learning, research, OERI, *84.309*
medical information sciences NRSA, *93.225*
minority college, university strengthening, *84.031*
minority health professions schools, *93.157*
National Agricultural Library, 10.700
National Archives, 89.001
National Gallery of Art exhibits, 68.001
National Library of Medicine, *93.879*
Native American Library Services, *45.311*
NIH medical libraries resource development, librarians training, *93.879*
NIH medical library research training, *93.140*
NRC local public document rooms, *77.005*
nutrition education resources, schools, FCS, *10.574*
postsecondary education access projects, FIPSE, *84.116*
preservation practices, training, *45.149*
Presidential Libraries, 89.001
rural computer networks, RUS, *10.855*
Senior Community Service Employment Program, *17.235*
State Library Program, *45.310*
telecommunications infrastructure, *11.552*
see also Adult education; Arts, arts education; Computer products, sciences, services; Humanities; Information *entries*
Library of Congress (LC), 42.001 through 42.008
LIBRARY OF CONGRESS—LIBRARY SERVICES, 42.006

LIBRARY OF CONGRESS PUBLICATIONS, 42.005
Life insurance, *see* Insurance
LIFE INSURANCE FOR VETERANS, *64.103*
LIHEAP (Low-Income Home Energy Assistance Program), HHS, *93.568*
Literacy, *see* Illiteracy
LITERACY PROGRAM FOR PRISONERS, *84.255*
Literature
creative writing, NEA, *45.024*
Library of Congress Publications, 42.005
USIA Creative Arts Grants, *82.015*
Woodrow Wilson Center fellowships, *85.300*
see also Arts, arts education; Copyright services; Foreign languages; Humanities *entries*; Publications
LITIGATION SUPPORT FOR INDIAN RIGHTS, *15.052*
Livestock industry
animal health research, *10.207*
dairy products indemnification, *10.053*
Disaster Reserve Assistance, *10.452*
Environmental Quality Incentives Program, NRCS, *10.912*
export market development, *10.600*
farm enterprises, research, *10.205*
farm operating loans, *10.406*
forage research, *10.202*
Indian lands, *10.421, 15.034*
inspection, grading, 10.162, *10.475,* 10.477
international assistance, *10.960*
international research training, *10.962*
market supervision, 10.800
Navajo-Hopi Joint Use Area, *15.057*
production data, statistics, 10.950
research, *10.200*
sheep, goat industry improvement center, *10.774*
subsidized loans, *10.437*
sustainable agriculture research, *10.215*
Wetlands Reserve Program, *10.072*
wildlife disease control, *10.028*
see also Agricultural *entries*; Animal disease control, health, welfare; Dairy industry; Poultry, egg products; Veterinary medicine
LIVESTOCK, MEAT AND POULTRY MARKET SUPERVISION, 10.800
Loan Guarantees for Indian Housing, *14.865*
Loan Guaranty Program, BIA, *15.124*
LOAN REPAYMENT PROGRAM FOR GENERAL RESEARCH [NIH], *93.232*
Loans for Disadvantaged Students (LDS), HHS, *93.342*
Local Development Districts (LDD), Appalachian region, *23.009*
Local government, *see* Community development; Government; Indian affairs; Urban planning
LOCAL LAW ENFORCEMENT BLOCK GRANTS PROGRAM, *16.592*
LOCAL RAIL FREIGHT ASSISTANCE, *20.308*
LOCAL VETERANS' EMPLOYMENT REPRESENTATIVE PROGRAM, *17.804*
Logging, *see* Farm, nonfarm enterprises; Farm workers; Forestry; Timber industry; Woodlands
Long-Term Economic Deterioration (LTED), *11.307*
Long Term Resource Monitoring Program (LTRMP), DOI, *15.978*

infant mortality initiative, *93.926*
labor standards, 17.303
lead poisoning prevention, *93.197*
Medicaid, *93.778*
mentally disturbed, services, *93.125*
missing children programs, public education, research, *16.543*
nurse midwife education, *93.298*
parent access, visitation programs, *93.597*
personnel training, *93.648*
Population Research, reproductive processes, *93.864*
primary care coordination, *93.130*
public health graduate traineeships, *93.964*
public housing residents, health services, *93.927*
research, training, *93.110*
runaway children, *93.645*
rural domestic violence, *16.589*
rural health services, *93.912*
Safe Schools/Healthy Students National Evaluation, DOJ, *16.732*
SED, children, adolescents, mental health services, *93.104*
services, block grants, *93.994*
Social Security, children of disabled parents, *96.001, 96.002*
Social Security survivors, *96.004*
Social Services Block Grant, *93.667*
social services research, demonstration, *93.647*
spina bifida, veterans dependents, *64.127*
state assistance programs, *93.645*
State Court Improvement Program, ACF, *93.586*
substance abuse, model projects, pregnant, postpartum women, infants, *93.169*
Substance Abuse Prevention and Treatment Block Grant, *93.959*
substance abuse-related treatment, women, infants, children, *93.101, 93.102*
Traumatic Brain Injury, *93.234*
Welfare Reform Research, *93.595*
WIC Farmers' Market Nutrition Program (FMNP), *10.572*
youth, independent living education, training, *93.674*
see also Child care services; Community health services; Early childhood education; Family planning; Family therapy; Handicapped children; Head Start Program; Health, medical *entries*; Indian children; Indian health, social services; Juvenile delinquency; Parenting; Social Security Act; Social services; Volunteers; Youth *entries*
MATHEMATICAL AND PHYSICAL SCIENCES, *47.049*
MATHEMATICAL SCIENCES GRANTS PROGRAM, *12.901*
Mathematics
Air Force Defense Research Sciences Program, *12.800*
Alaska natives student enrichment, *84.322*
Army Research Office, *12.431*
Barry M. Goldwater Scholarship Program, *85.200*
centers, Upward Bound, *84.047*
Colorado diversity-related engineering, science training, DOE, *81.116*
DOD sciences research, fellowships, *12.630*

Eisenhower Professional Development, exemplary math, science projects, *84.168*
Eisenhower regional education consortia, *84.319*
energy sciences research, *81.049*
math telecommunications demonstrations, *84.286*
mathematical sciences research, *47.049*
mathematical sciences research, education, NSA, *12.901*
mental health research models, *93.242*
NASA education services, 43.001
Navy research, *12.301*
Navy research, education support, *12.300*
NOAA Colorado areas math, engineering, science education, *11.449*
NSF, education improvement, *47.076*
Star Schools Program, *84.203*
Tech-Prep Education, secondary, postsecondary, *84.243*
Women's Educational Equity Program, *84.083*
see also Adult education; Computer products, sciences, services; Education *entries*; Engineering *entries*; Physical sciences; Science education; Scientific research; Teacher education, training
Mathematics, Engineering, Science Achievement (MESA), Colorado, NOAA, *11.449*
MBDA (Minority Business Development Agency), USDC, *see* Agency Index
MBDC (Minority Business Development Centers), *11.800*
MBRS (Minority Biomedical Research Support), *93.375*
MCHEP (Maternal and Child Health Epidemiology Program), *93.946*
McIntire-Stennis Act, forestry, *10.202*
McKinney homeless assistance, *see* National housing acts
MCNAIR POST-BACCALAUREATE ACHIEVEMENT, *84.217*
MCSAP (Motor Carrier Safety Assistance Program), *20.218*
Measurement
business internships, Soviet, Eastern European, *11.114*
calibration, testing, 11.601
geodetic surveys, *11.400*
National Standard Reference Data System, *11.603*
research, *11.609*
Standard Reference Materials, 11.604
standards and certification information center, 11.610
weights, measures service, 11.606
see also Engineering *entries*; Maps, charts; Physical sciences; Scientific research
MEASUREMENT AND ENGINEERING RESEARCH AND STANDARDS, *11.609*
MEASURES AND ANALYSES OF THE U.S. ECONOMY, 11.025
Meat, *see* Food inspection, grading; Livestock industry; Poultry, egg products
Meat and Poultry Inspection State Programs, *10.475*
MEAT, POULTRY, AND EGG PRODUCTS INSPECTION, 10.477
MECEA (Mutual Educational and Cultural Exchange Act), *see* International studies

vocational rehabilitation personnel training, *84.129*

vocational rehabilitation service projects, *84.128*

see also Disabled; Education *entries*; Group homes; Handicapped *entries*; Mental health; Vocational rehabilitation; Volunteers

MENTAL RETARDATION—PRESIDENT'S COMMITTEE ON MENTAL RETARDATION, 93.613

Mentoring programs, *see* Education counseling; Tutoring

Merchant Marine, *see* Maritime industry; U.S. Merchant Marine

Merchant Marine Act (MMA), 20.801, *20.802, 20.803, 20.804,* 20.805, *20.808,* 20.810, *20.812, 20.813*

MESA (Mathematics, Engineering, Science Achievement), Colorado, NOAA, *11.449*

MESBIC (Minority Enterprise Small Business Investment Companies), *59.011*

Metabolism research, *93.847*

METEOROLOGIC AND HYDROLOGIC MODERNIZATION DEVELOPMENT, *11.467*

Metropolitan Planning, mass transit, *20.505*

MFB (Marine and Freshwater Biomedical) Centers, *93.894*

MGIB (Montgomery GI Bill), *64.124*

MICROBIOLOGY AND INFECTIOUS DISEASES RESEARCH, *93.856*

Microgram, DOJ, 16.003

MICROLOAN DEMONSTRATION PROGRAM, *59.046*

Micronesia, *see* U.S. possessions, territories

Midwife training, *see* Health professions; Nursing

MIGRANT AND SEASONAL FARMWORKERS, *17.247*

MIGRANT EDUCATION—BASIC STATE GRANT PROGRAM, *84.011*

MIGRANT EDUCATION—COLLEGE ASSISTANCE MIGRANT PROGRAM, *84.149*

MIGRANT EDUCATION—COORDINATION PROGRAM, *84.144*

MIGRANT EDUCATION—HIGH SCHOOL EQUIVALENCY PROGRAM, *84.141*

Migrant labor, *see* Farm workers

MIGRATORY BIRD BANDING AND DATA ANALYSIS, 15.976

Military

Air Force Defense Research Sciences Program, *12.800*

American Battlefield Protection, NPS, *15.926*

anti-terrorism training, *16.614*

Army Research Office, *12.431*

base reuse studies, *12.607*

biological/chemical/nuclear warfare, domestic preparedness, *16.006, 16.007*

biological-medical research, *12.420*

chemical stockpile emergency preparedness, FEMA, *83.549*

community economic impact, 12.600, *12.607*

community land use planning, *12.610*

defense cutbacks, unemployment, *17.246*

defense program changes impact, *11.307, 12.611, 12.612, 12.613*

DOD property donations, loans, 12.700

DOE nuclear weapons nonproliferation research, *81.113*

education assistance, dependents, survivors, *64.117*

education assistance, post-Vietnam personnel, *64.120*

employment counseling, 64.125

foreign language, area studies, NSEP, *12.551, 12.552*

home loans, improvement, repair, *64.114*

home mortgage insurance, *14.166*

impact assistance, schools, *84.040, 84.041*

impacted areas, home mortgage insurance, *14.165*

Indian lands environmental impact mitigation, *93.582*

Integrated Helicopter Design Tools, *12.640*

interment in national cemeteries, 64.201

Montgomery GI Bill education benefits, *64.124*

National Guard facilities, *12.400*

National Guard operations, maintenance, *12.401*

National Maritime Heritage Grants, NPS, *15.925*

National Security Education Program, DOD, *12.550*

NSA language grants, *12.900*

plutonium center, *81.110*

scientific research, Navy, *12.300*

student loan cancellations, *84.037*

Technology Reinvestment Project, DOD, *12.911*

Troops to Cops program, *16.711*

veterans employment, reemployment rights, 17.803

vocational rehabilitation, disabled, hospitalized service personnel, *64.116*

see also Civil defense; Government contracts; Maritime industry; Veterans *entries*

MILITARY CONSTRUCTION, NATIONAL GUARD, *12.400*

MILITARY MEDICAL RESEARCH AND DEVELOPMENT, *12.420*

Milk, *see* Dairy industry

Milk Orders, 10.155

MINE HEALTH AND SAFETY COUNSELING AND TECHNICAL ASSISTANCE, 17.601

MINE HEALTH AND SAFETY EDUCATION AND TRAINING, 17.602

MINE HEALTH AND SAFETY GRANTS, *17.600*

Mine safety, *see* Coal Mining; Mining, mining industries; Occupational health, safety

Mine Safety and Health Administration, DOL, *see* Agency Index

Mineral resources

Census Bureau data, 11.001

geologic research, *15.808*

Indian lands, assessments, *15.038*

minerals disposal, BLM lands, 15.214

see also Coal mining; Energy *entries*; Geology; Mining, mining industries; Natural resources; Nuclear sciences, technology; Physical sciences; Public lands; Statistics

MINERALS AND MINING ON INDIAN LANDS, *15.038*

Minimum wage, *see* Labor standards

Mining, mining industries

abandoned mine land reclamation, *15.252*

futures trading information, customer complaints, 78.004

Cuban, Haitian entrants, *16.201*
educational assistance, missing-in-action veterans dependents, *64.117*
fingerprint identification, FBI, 16.303
runaway youth, *93.623, 93.645*
see also Census services; Homeless persons; Veterans *entries*; Volunteers; Youth *entries*
MLI (Museum Leadership Initiatives), IMLS, *45.306*
MITIGATION ASSISTANCE [FEMA], *83.535*
Mitigation Directorate, FEMA, *see* Agency Index
MITIGATION OF ENVIRONMENTAL IMPACTS TO INDIAN LANDS DUE TO DEPARTMENT OF DEFENSE ACTIVITIES, *93.582*
MMA, *see* Merchant Marine Act
Mobile homes, *see* Homes, manufactured
Mobility, intergovernmental, *see* Federal employment; Government
MODEL STATE-SUPPORTED AREA HEALTH EDUCATION CENTERS, *93.107*
Moderate income, *see* Disadvantaged *entries*; Housing, low to moderate income; Housing, subsidized; Rural poor
Moderate Rehabilitation, Section 8, *14.856*
Mohair, *see* Agricultural commodities, stabilization; Livestock industry
Mold and Moisture Control Grants, HUD, *14.900*
Monopolistic practices, 36.001
Montgomery GI Bill Act Active Duty, *64.124*
MONTHLY ALLOWANCE FOR CHILDREN OF VIETNAM VETERANS BORN WITH SPINA BIFIDA, *64.127*
Monthly Labor Review, *17.002*
MORRIS K. UDALL FELLOWSHIP PROGRAM, *85.401*
MORRIS K. UDALL NATIVE AMERICAN CONGRESSIONAL INTERNSHIP PROGRAM, *85.402*
Morris K. Udall Scholarship and Excellence in National Environmental Policy Foundation, *see* Agency Index (Scholarship and Fellowship Foundations)
MORRIS K. UDALL SCHOLARSHIP PROGRAM, *85.400*
Mortgage and loan insurance, *see* Housing mortgage, loan insurance; Insurance
MORTGAGE INSURANCE—COMBINATION AND MANUFACTURED HOME LOT LOANS, *14.162*
MORTGAGE INSURANCE—COOPERATIVE PROJECTS, *14.126*
MORTGAGE INSURANCE FOR CONSTRUCTION OR SUBSTANTIAL REHABILITATION OF CONDOMINIUM PROJECTS, *14.112*
MORTGAGE INSURANCE FOR SINGLE ROOM OCCUPANCY (SRO) PROJECTS, *14.184*
MORTGAGE INSURANCE FOR THE PURCHASE OR REFINANCING OF EXISTING MULTIFAMILY HOUSING PROJECTS, *14.155*
MORTGAGE INSURANCE—GROUP PRACTICE FACILITIES, *14.116*
MORTGAGE INSURANCE—GROWING EQUITY MORTGAGES, *14.172*
MORTGAGE INSURANCE—HOMES, *14.117*

MORTGAGE INSURANCE—HOMES FOR DISASTER VICTIMS, *14.119*
MORTGAGE INSURANCE—HOMES FOR LOW AND MODERATE INCOME FAMILIES, *14.120*
MORTGAGE INSURANCE—HOMES FOR MEMBERS OF THE ARMED SERVICES, *14.166*
MORTGAGE INSURANCE—HOMES IN OUTLYING AREAS, *14.121*
MORTGAGE INSURANCE—HOMES IN URBAN RENEWAL AREAS, *14.122*
MORTGAGE INSURANCE—HOMES—MILITARY IMPACTED AREAS, *14.165*
MORTGAGE INSURANCE—HOSPITALS, *14.128*
MORTGAGE INSURANCE—HOUSING IN OLDER, DECLINING AREAS, *14.123*
MORTGAGE INSURANCE—MANUFACTURED HOME PARKS, *14.127*
MORTGAGE INSURANCE—NURSING HOMES, INTERMEDIATE CARE FACILITIES, BOARD AND CARE HOMES AND ASSISTED LIVING FACILITIES, *14.129*
MORTGAGE INSURANCE—PURCHASE BY HOMEOWNERS OF FEE SIMPLE TITLE FROM LESSORS, *14.130*
MORTGAGE INSURANCE—PURCHASE OF SALES-TYPE COOPERATIVE HOUSING UNITS, *14.132*
MORTGAGE INSURANCE—PURCHASE OF UNITS IN CONDOMINIUMS, *14.133*
MORTGAGE INSURANCE—RENTAL AND COOPERATIVE HOUSING FOR MODERATE INCOME FAMILIES AND ELDERLY, MARKET INTEREST RATE, *14.135*
MORTGAGE INSURANCE—RENTAL HOUSING, *14.134*
MORTGAGE INSURANCE—RENTAL HOUSING FOR THE ELDERLY, *14.138*
MORTGAGE INSURANCE—RENTAL HOUSING IN URBAN RENEWAL AREAS, *14.139*
MORTGAGE INSURANCE—SINGLE-FAMILY COOPERATIVE HOUSING, *14.163*
MORTGAGE INSURANCE—SPECIAL CREDIT RISKS, *14.140*
MORTGAGE INSURANCE—TWO YEAR OPERATING LOSS LOANS, SECTION 223(D), *14.167*
Mothers, *see* Child care services; Family planning; Maternal, child health, welfare; Parenting; Women
MOTOR CARRIER SAFETY, 20.217
MOTOR VEHICLE THEFT PROTECTION ACT PROGRAM, *16.597*
Motor vehicles
automobiles, disabled veterans, *64.100*
elderly, disabled, transportation services, *20.513*
energy conservation, renewable energy outreach, training, *81.117*
energy conservation technology development, *81.086*
hazardous materials transport, 20.217
hazardous materials transport regulation, *20.218*
mass transit park-and-ride lots, *20.500*

Pharmacology, pharmacy
AIDS, anti-viral drugs development, *93.821*
alternative agricultural product, process
  development, commercialization, *10.240*
biodiversity research, *93.168*
cancer treatment research, *93.395*
clinical training programs, *93.948*
deafness, communicative disorders research,
  93.173
DVA prescription service, 64.012
education assistance, disadvantaged, *93.342,*
  93.925
education loans, *93.108, 93.342*
faculty loan repayments, disadvantaged, *93.923*
Indians, health professions scholarships, *93.972*
Indians, scholarships, preprofessional, *93.971*
narcotics, dangerous drugs, personnel training,
  16.004
pharmacological sciences research, fellowships,
  93.859
rural specialists training, *93.192*
see also Biological sciences; Chemicals,
  chemistry; Drugs, drug research; Health,
  medical education, training; Health, medical
  research; Health professions
PHARMACOLOGY, PHYSIOLOGY, AND
  BIORELATED CHEMISTRY RESEARCH,
  93.859
PHASE (Practical Hands-on Application to Science
  Education, NOAS, *11.449*
PHDEP (Public Housing Drug Elimination
  Program), *14.854*
PHHS (Preventive Health and Health Services)
  Block Grants, *93.991*
Photography, *see* Arts, arts education; Audiovisual
  aids, film, video
PHS (Public Health Service), HHS, *see* Public health
PHYSICAL DISASTER LOANS, *59.008*
Physical disasters, *see* Disaster assistance;
  Earthquakes; Flood prevention, control;
  Hurricanes
Physical fitness, *see* Health, medical services;
  Occupational health, safety; Recreation
Physical Fitness and Sports, 93.289
Physical sciences
Air Force Defense Research Sciences Program,
  12.800
Army Research Office, *12.431*
atmospheric, marine sciences education, research
  facilities, NOAA, *11.469*
Barry M. Goldwater Scholarship Program, *85.200*
biodiversity research, *93.168*
biophysics, cell biology, *93.821*
calibration, testing, NIST, 11.601
climate, air quality research, services, *11.459*
climate monitoring, assessment, *11.428*
climate, short-term fluctuations, *11.443*
coal research, *81.057*
coastal ecosystem management, NOAA, *11.473*
DOD research, fellowships, *12.630*
DOD science, technology projects, *12.910*
DOE used equipment, 81.022
energy-related, renewable resources research,
  81.087
energy sciences research, *81.049*
forestry research, *10.652*

geosciences research, *47.050*
hazardous substances, multi-disciplinary research,
  education, *93.143*
National Standard Reference Data System, *11.603*
Navy research, *12.301*
Navy research, education support, *12.300*
NMFS marine education, science projects, *11.455*
NOAA special projects, *11.460*
NOAA unallied program, *11.472*
Polar Programs, *47.078*
research support, *47.049*
rural, research, education, *10.224*
see also Aeronautics, space; Astronomy;
  Agricultural research, sciences; Biological
  sciences; Chemicals, chemistry; Climate; Earth
  sciences; Energy *entries*; Engineering *entries*;
  Environmental sciences; Forensic science;
  Geology; Marine sciences; Mathematics;
  Minority education; Nuclear sciences,
  technology; Science education; Scientific
  research
Physical therapy, *see* Occupational health, safety;
  Vocational rehabilitation
Physically handicapped, *see* Disabled; Handicapped
  entries; Veterans, disabled
PHYSICIAN ASSISTANT TRAINING IN
  PRIMARY CARE, *93.886*
Physicians, *see* Family medicine; Health, medical
  education, training; Health professions;
  Osteopathy; Pediatrics
Physics, *see* Engineering *entries*; Nuclear sciences,
  technology; Physical sciences; Scientific
  research
Physiology research, *93.859*
PILOT CLINICAL PHARMACOLOGY
  TRAINING, *93.948*
PILT (Payments in Lieu of Taxes), BLM, *15.226*
PIPELINE SAFETY, *20.700*
Pittman-Robertson (P-R) Program, DOI, *15.611*
PL-566, NRCS, *10.904,* 10.906
Planetariums, *see* Museums, galleries
PLANNING AND PROGRAM DEVELOPMENT
  GRANTS [CNCS], *94.007*
PLANNING ASSISTANCE TO STATES [DOD],
  12.110
PLANNING, IMPLEMENTING, AND
  ENHANCING STRATEGIES IN
  COMMUNITY PROSECUTION, *16.609*
PLANT AND ANIMAL DISEASE, PEST
  CONTROL, AND ANIMAL CARE, *10.025*
PLANT MATERIALS FOR CONSERVATION,
  10.905
Plant Variety Protection Program, 10.163
Plants
agricultural, inspection 10.162
aquatic plant control, rivers, harbors, 12.100
biodiversity research, NIH, *93.168*
competitive research grants, *10.206*
conservation use, *10.069,* 10.905
Crop Insurance, *10.450*
disaster assistance, noninsured crops, *10.451*
disease, pest control, *10.025*
endangered species conservation, *10.914, 15.615*
endangered species, Indian lands, *15.051*
endangered species, pesticides enforcement,
  66.700

Public utilities
Census Bureau data, 11.001
compensation to states for federally-acquired lands, hydropower, *12.112*
disaster-resistant communities, standards, training, *83.551*
economic development loans, RBCS, *10.854*
energy conservation technology research, *81.086*
geodetic surveys, *11.400*
Hydrologic Research, *11.462*
industrial development, rural, *10.769*
insular area, *15.875*
NRC local public document rooms, *77.005*
rural telecommunications service, RUS loans, *10.852*
rural telephone service, RUS loans, *10.851*
rural facilities loans, *10.766*
RUS electrification loans, *10.850*
Urban Consortium, DOE, *81.081*
water supply forecasts, 10.907
see also Communications, telecommunications; Energy; Nuclear sciences, technology; Public works

Public works
Appalachian region, *23.002*
Aquatic Plant Control, Corps of Engineers, 12.100
Beach Erosion Control, Corps of Engineers, 12.101
Bridge Alteration, *20.007*
CDBG, *14.218*, *14.219*, *14.225*, *14.228*, *14.862*
Community Disaster Loans, *83.537*
Construction Productivity Advanced Research, Corps of Engineers, *12.114*
dam safety program, FEMA, *83.550*
defense program changes impact, *12.613*
disaster-resistant communities, standards, training, *83.551*
disasters, Public Assistance Grants, FEMA, *83.544*
economic assistance, *11.307*
flood-caused erosion protection, 12.105
flood control emergencies, 12.102, 12.103
flood control projects, Corps of Engineers, 12.106
flood control projects, snagging, clearing, Corps of Engineers, 12.108
highway personnel training, *20.215*
Indian lands, dam safety, *15.049*, *15.065*
navigation projects, Corps of Engineers, 12.107, 12.109
public facilities construction, EDA projects, *11.300*
U.S. insular areas, *15.875*
water reclamation, reuse, *15.504*
see also Coastal zone; Community development; Economic development; Flood prevention, control; Highways, roads, bridges; Public utilities; Sewage facilities, treatment; Transportation; Urban renewal; Waste treatment, disposal; Water *entries*
Public Works and Economic Development Act, *11.300* through *11.312*

Publications
ADA compliance, *16.108*
aerospace technology, 43.002
air pollution control, 66.009
bibliographies, catalogs, LC, 42.005

boating safety, 20.001
books for the blind, handicapped, 42.001
census studies, 11.001
citizenship, 16.400
civil aviation, 20.100
civil rights, 29.001
consumer information, 39.009
depository libraries, government publications, 40.001
drug abuse prevention, 16.005
energy-related, 81.039, 81.064
exporting, 11.108
Government Bookstore, 40.002
historical documents collection, preservation, *89.003*
international peace, conflict management, *91.001*, *91.002*
medical, health, National Library of Medicine, *93.879*
Microgram, DEA, 16.003
National Archives and Reference Administration, 89.001
National Center for Standards and Certification Information, 11.610
National Technical Information Service, 11.650
National Trade Data Bank, 11.026
newspaper cataloguing, preservation, *45.149*
small business programs, 59.005
Uniform Crime Reports, 16.305
see also Agricultural statistics; Arts, arts education; Audiovisual aids, film, video; Census services; Computer products, sciences, services; Consumers, consumer services; Copyright services; Economics, research, statistics; Education resources; Humanities *entries*; Information *entries*; International studies; Libraries; Literature; Statistics

Puerto Rico
aged, blind, disabled persons maintenance assistance, *93.560*
food assistance, *10.566*
home mortgage insurance, armed services members, *14.166*
see also U.S. possessions, territories
PWBA (Pension and Welfare Benefits Administration), 17.150
PWI (Projects with Industry), DOED, *84.234*

QUALIFIED PARTICIPATING ENTITIES (QPE) RISK SHARING PILOT PROGRAM [HUD], *14.189*
QUENTIN N. BURDICK PROGRAMS FOR RURAL INTERDISCIPLINARY TRAINING [HHS], *93.192*

Racial discrimination, *see* Civil rights; Community development

Radiation
biohazard contaminant, cancer research facilities, *93.392*
biological/chemical/nuclear warfare, domestic preparedness, *16.006*, *16.007*
cancer research, *93.395*, *93.399*
control, EMI home study courses, 83.529
control, NRC health, safety training, 77.001
dairy products contamination, *10.053*

computer sciences, NSF, *47.070*
DOD research, fellowships, *12.630*
DOD science, technology projects, *12.910*
DOE environmental restoration, waste
    management technology development, *81.104*
DOE nuclear, education, fellowships, *81.114*
DOE nuclear weapons nonproliferation, *81.113*
DOE used equipment, 81.022
energy information, OSTI, 81.064
energy sciences, *81.049*
fossil energy, development, *81.089*
Geosciences, NSF, *47.050*
hazardous substances multi-disciplinary research,
    93.143
hydrology, *15.805*
Hydrometeorological Development, NOAA,
    11.467
Inertial Confinement Fusion, stockpile
    stewardship, *81.112*
LC reference services, 42.007
marine sanctuaries, *11.429*
measurement, engineering projects, *11.609*
measurement, Standard Reference Materials,
    11.604
mental health research, *93.242*
minority biomedical, health research training,
    93.880
National Standard Reference Data System, *11.603*
Navy research, *12.301*
Navy, education support, *12.300*
NIH international, *93.934*
NIH intramural research training, *93.140*
NMFS marine education, science projects, *11.455*
NOAA, *11.432*
NOAA special projects, *11.460*
NOAA unallied projects, *11.452*
NSF, behavioral, economic, social sciences,
    47.075
NSF engineering education, research, *47.041*
NSF Mathematical and Physical Sciences,
    47.049
Polar Programs, *47.078*
register of research in progress, 11.650
remote sensing research, *11.440*
Sea Grant Support, *11.417*
Special Minority Initiatives, biomedical sciences,
    93.960
undersea, *11.430*
see also Aeronautics, space; Agricultural
    experiment stations; Agricultural research,
    sciences; Astronomy; Behavioral sciences,
    education, services; Biological sciences;
    Cancer control, prevention, research;
    Chemicals, chemistry; Climate; Computer
    products, sciences, services; Dental health,
    dental research; Earth sciences; Energy
    research; Engineering research; Environmental
    health, research, services; Environmental
    sciences; Food, nutrition research, science;
    Geology; Health, medical research;
    Immunization, immunology; Information,
    scientific and technical; Marine sciences;
    Mathematics; National Research Service
    Awards; Nuclear sciences, technology;
    Physical sciences; Social sciences; Technology
    transfer, utilization

SCORE (Service Corps of Retired Executives),
    59.005, *59.026*
SCP (Senior Companion Program), *94.016*
SCS (Soil Conservation Service), *see* Agency Index
    (USDA, Natural Resource Conservation Service)
SCSEP (Senior Community Service Employment
    Program), *17.235*
Sculptors, sculpture, *see* Arts, arts education;
    Fellowships, scholarships, traineeships;
    Museums, galleries
SDI (Services Delivery Improvement), family
    planning, *93.974*
SDS (Scholarships for Disadvantaged Students),
    HHS, *93.925*
SEA GRANT SUPPORT, *11.417*
SDWA (Safe Drinking Water Act), *see* Water
    pollution abatement, prevention
SEAMAP (Southeast Area Monitoring and
    Assessment Program), *11.435*
Seamen, *see* Fisheries industry; Maritime industry;
    U.S. Merchant Marine; Water navigation
Seasonal workers, *see* Aliens, refugees; Farm
    workers; Fisheries industry
SEC (Securities and Exchange Commission), 58.001
SECONDARY AGRICULTURE EDUCATION
    GRANTS, *10.226*
Secondary education, *see* Elementary and secondary
    education
SECONDARY MARKET FOR
    NON-CONFORMING LOANS TO
    LOW-WEALTH BORROWERS
    DEMONSTRATION PROGRAM [HUD],
    14.196
SECRET SERVICE—TRAINING ACTIVITIES,
    21.100
Secretaries of Military Departments, DOD, *see*
    Agency Index
Section 3 Emergency Dredging Projects, 12.109
Section 3, employment opportunities, HUD, 14.412
Section 7, Fishermen's Protective Act, *19.204*
Section 7(a) Loans, SBA, *59.012*
Section 7(b) Loans, SBA, *59.008*
Section 7(J) Development Assistance Program,
    SBA, *59.007*
Section 8 Housing Assistance Payments Program for
    Very Low Income Families—Moderate
    Rehabilitation, *14.856*
SECTION 8 HOUSING ASSISTANCE
    PAYMENTS PROGRAM—SPECIAL
    ALLOCATIONS, *14.195*
SECTION 8 MODERATE REHABILITATION
    SINGLE ROOM OCCUPANCY, *14.249*
SECTION 8 RENTAL CERTIFICATE PROGRAM,
    14.857
SECTION 8 RENTAL VOUCHER PROGRAM,
    14.855
Section 8(a) Business Development, SBA, 59.006
Section 22, Water Resources Development Act,
    12.110
Section 106 Grants, Clean Water Act, *66.419*
Section 106, 111, Clean Air Act, *66.033*
Section 108, CDBG Economic Development
    Initiative, *14.246*
Section 108 Loan Guarantees, HUD, *14.248*
Section 109, Title I, Housing and Community
    Development Act, nondiscrimination, 14.406

SELF-HELP HOMEOWNERSHIP
    OPPORTUNITY PROGRAM, *14.247*
Self-help housing, *10.420*
Self-help housing site loans, *10.411*
SEMICONDUCTOR CHIP PROTECTION
    SERVICE, 42.008
SEMFISH (Stock Enhancement of Marine Fish),
    11.445
Senior citizens, *see* Aging and the aged; Housing,
    elderly
SENIOR COMMUNITY SERVICE
    EMPLOYMENT PROGRAM, *17.235*
SENIOR COMPANION PROGRAM, *94.016*
SENIOR ENVIRONMENTAL EMPLOYMENT
    PROGRAM, *66.508*
SENIOR INTERNATIONAL FELLOWSHIPS
    [HHS], *93.989*
SEOG (Supplemental Educational Opportunity
    Grants), *84.007*
SEP (Student Expense Program), FEMA, *83.527*
Serious Emotional Disturbances (SED), HHS, *93.104*
SERVICE CORPS OF RETIRED EXECUTIVES,
    59.026
Servicemen's Readjustment Act, *17.804*
Services Delivery Improvement (SDI), family
    planning, *93.974*
SERVICES TO INDIAN CHILDREN, ELDERLY
    AND FAMILIES, *15.025*
Sewage facilities, treatment
    Appalachian region, *23.002*
    CDBG, *14.218, 14.219, 14.225, 14.228, 14.862*
    Clean Vessel Act, pumpout/dump stations, *15.616*
    EPA consolidated program support, *66.600*
    Performance Partnership Grants, EPA, *66.605*
    public works, EDA projects, *11.300*
    rural areas, *10.760*
    rural housing loans, *10.410*
    rural loans, *10.411*
    U.S. insular areas, *15.875*
    wastewater operator technical assistance, training,
        66.467
    wastewater, revolving fund, *66.458*
    see also Hazardous materials, waste; Pollution
        abatement; Public works; Waste treatment,
        disposal; Water systems, treatment
Sex discrimination, *see* Civil rights; Women
Sexual abuse
    campus crime grants, *16.552*
    child, investigation, prosecution, *93.643*
    children, services, research, *93.670*
    Combined DNA Index System, FBI, *16.307*
    homeless, runaway youth, Street Outreach
        Program, *93.557*
    Indian children, *16.583*
    investigations training, FBI Academy, 16.300
    offender registry, *16.554*
    victim assistance, *16.524, 16.575, 16.582*
    victim assistance, block grant, *93.991*
    see also Crime; Family therapy; Maternal, child
        health, welfare; Parenting; Social services;
        Victim assistance
Sexual relations, *see* Family planning; Parenting;
    Youth
Sexually transmitted diseases, *see* AIDS (Acquired
    Immune Deficiency Syndrome);
    Communicable diseases

Sharing Contracts (Exchange of Use or Mutual
    Use), DVA, 64.018
SHARING SPECIALIZED MEDICAL
    RESOURCES, 64.018
Sheep, *see* Agricultural marketing; Livestock
    industry
SHELTER PLUS CARE, *14.238*
Shelters, *see* Civil defense; Emergency assistance;
    Homeless persons; Victim assistance
SHEPSA (School Health Education to Prevent the
    Spread of AIDS), *93.938*
SHIP SALES, 20.805
Shipping, *see* Interstate commerce; Maritime
    industry; Railroads; Transportation
Shipping Act of 1984, 33.001
SHIPPING—INVESTIGATION OF
    COMPLAINTS, 33.001
Ships, *see* Fisheries industry; Maritime industry;
    Water navigation
SHORT TERM CLIMATE FLUCTUATIONS,
    11.443
Short Term Lending Program, DOT, *20.905*
Sign language, *see* Deafness and the deaf
Single room occupancy (SRO) housing, *14.135,
    14.184, 14.188, 14.238, 14.241, 14.249*
SIPI (Southwestern Indian Polytechnic Institute),
    15.058
SIRG (State Indoor Radon Grants), *66.032*
SIS (State Identification Systems), DOJ, *16.598*
Site Loans, Sections 523 and 524, *10.411*
Site Specific Cooperative Agreement Program,
    CDCP, *93.240*
SITE (Superfund Innovative Technology
    Evaluation), *66.807*
Skin diseases research, *93.846*
SLATT (State and Local Anti-Terrorism Training),
    DOJ, *16.614*
Sleep disorders, *93.233, 93.853*
Slides, *see* Audiovisual aids, film, video
SLS (Supplemental Loans for Students), *84.032*
Slum elimination, *14.218, 14.219, 14.225, 14.228,
    14.862*
Small Beach Erosion Control Projects, 12.101
Small business
    BIA Loan Guaranty Program, *15.124*
    bid, payment, performance bonds, *59.016*
    bond guarantees, surety companies, *59.016*
    CDBG, *14.218, 14.219, 14.225, 14.228, 14.862*
    Certified Development Company loans, *59.041*
    community development credit union loans,
        44.002
    Counseling on Doing Business with the Federal
        Government, 39.001
    credit union establishment, *44.001*
    defense procurement assistance, *12.002*
    disadvantaged, management, technical assistance,
        59.007
    disadvantaged, transportation, DOT contracts,
        20.903, 20.906, 20.907
    disaster loans, *59.002, 59.008*
    DOE contracts, technical assistance, 81.082
    DOE patent licensing, 81.003
    DOT contracts, Bonding Assistance Program,
        minority-, women-owned, *20.904*
    DOT contracts, Short Term Lending Program,
        minority-, women-owned, *20.905*

STATE PLANNING AND RESEARCH [DOT], *20.515*

STATE PUBLIC WATER SYSTEM SUPERVISION, *66.432*

State Revolving Fund, wastewater treatment, *66.458*

STATE RURAL HOSPITAL FLEXIBILITY PROGRAM, *93.241*

STATE SURVEY AND CERTIFICATION OF HEALTH CARE PROVIDERS AND SUPPLIERS, *93.777*

STATE UNDERGROUND STORAGE TANKS PROGRAM, *66.804*

STATE UNDERGROUND WATER SOURCE PROTECTION, *66.433*

STATEMAP, Geological Survey, *15.810*

States community development block grants, *14.228*

Statistical Analysis Centers (SACs), DOJ, *16.550*

Statistics
  agricultural, rural, 10.950
  biostatistics NRSA, *93.225*
  biostatistics, public health graduate traineeships, *93.964*
  business, 11.025
  census data, services, 11.001, 11.002, 11.005
  census geography, 11.003
  Census Intergovernmental Services, 11.004
  census use training, 11.002
  Consumer Price Index, 17.003
  crime, criminal justice, 16.304, 16.305, *16.550*
  disabled, *92.001*
  Economic Bulletin Board, 11.027
  economic data, analysis, national, 11.025
  employment, labor force projections, 17.006
  energy, 81.039
  environmental health, biometry, *93.115*
  export, import price index, 17.003
  fisheries, southeast area, *11.434*
  international industrial data, 11.110
  juvenile delinquency, *16.542*
  labor force, *17.002*
  labor-management relations, *17.005*
  mathematical sciences research, education, NSA, *12.901*
  National Trade Data Bank, 11.026
  occupational health, safety, *17.005*
  overseas trade markets, 11.108
  Pacific fisheries, *11.437*
  Producer Price Index, 17.003
  productivity, 17.004
  TIGER (Topologically Integrated Geographic Encoding and Referencing) system, 11.003
  wages, benefits, *17.005*
  Welfare Reform Research, *93.595*
  see also Agricultural statistics; Census services; Computer products, sciences, services; Economics, research, statistics; Epidemiology; Information *entries*; Publications

STEJ (State and Tribal Environmental Justice), *66.713*

STELA (System for Tracking Export License Applications), 11.150

STEWARDSHIP SCIENCE GRANT PROGRAM [DOE], *81.112*

Stewart B. McKinney Homeless Assistance Act, *see* National housing acts

STOCK ENHANCEMENT OF MARINE FISH IN THE STATE OF HAWAII, *11.445*

Storage, agricultural, *see* Agricultural storage

Strabismus research, *93.867*

Street Outreach Program, ACF, *93.557*

Streets, *see* Community development; Highways, roads, bridges; Public works

Stroke, nervous system trauma research, *93.853*

STRUCTURAL FIRE PROTECTION—BUREAU OF INDIAN AFFAIRS FACILITIES, *15.064*

Student financial aid
  advanced placement test fee payment, DOED, *84.330*
  AIDS, NIH research education loan repayments, *93.936*
  AmeriCorps, *94.006*
  child care, postsecondary low-income student-parents, *84.335*
  community development work-study, HUD, *14.512, 14.513*
  contraception, infertility research, education loan repayments, *93.209*
  disadvantaged, graduate opportunities, *84.217*
  disadvantaged, stipends, Upward Bound, *84.047*
  disadvantaged, talented youth, information, Talent Search, *84.044*
  elementary, secondary students, Social Security survivors benefits, *96.002, 96.004*
  emergency management personnel, FEMA stipends, *83.527*
  Federal Direct Student Loan, graduate, undergraduate, *84.268*
  guaranteed loans, *84.032*
  health, allied health information, disadvantaged, *93.822*
  health education loan repayments, states, *93.165*
  health education loans, *93.108, 93.342*
  health professions faculty loan repayments, disadvantaged, *93.923*
  IHS education loan repayments, *93.164*
  Indian Employment Assistance, *15.108*
  information for adults, *84.066*
  Leveraging Educational Assistance Partnership (LEAP), *84.069*
  low-income, postsecondary, New Assets for Independence Demonstration, *93.602*
  low-income secondary students, TRIO supportive services, scholarships, *84.334*
  marine schools, *20.806*
  merchant marine officers, *20.806, 20.807*
  migrants, *84.141, 84.149*
  NHSC education loan repayment, *93.162*
  NIH Clinical Research Loan Repayment Program, *93.220*
  NIH General Research Loan Repayment Program, *93.232*
  nursing education loan repayments, *93.908*
  nursing student loans, *93.364*
  Pell grants, *84.063*
  post-Vietnam era veterans, *64.120*
  public safety officers' dependents, *16.615*
  State Student Incentive Grants, *84.069*
  student loan cancellations, *84.037*
  Summer Jobs in Federal Agencies, 27.006
  undergraduate, graduate, Perkins loans, *84.038*
  undergraduate, SEOG, *84.007*

Technology Reinvestment Project (TRP), DOD, *12.911*

TECHNOLOGY TRANSFER [NASA], 43.002

Technology transfer, utilization
Advanced Technology Program, *11.612*
agricultural, alternative product, process development, commercialization, *10.240*
agriculture, international, *10.960, 10.961*
agriculture-related, SBIR, *10.212*
Air Force Defense Research Sciences Program, *12.800*
anti-terrorism technology development, DOJ, *16.565*
biomass energy, *81.079*
biomedical, research, *93.371*
coastal ecosystem management, NOAA, *11.473*
Community-Based Technology Centers, DOED, *84.341*
competitive technology (EPSCoT), *11.614*
computer sciences research, *47.070*
Corps of Engineers Construction Productivity Advanced Research, *12.114*
data, trends, 17.004
disabled, assistive technology, *84.224*
disabled, devices, services, research, studies, *92.001*
disabled, education technology, *84.327*
DOD Integrated Helicopter Design Tools, *12.640*
DOD science, technology projects, *12.910*
DOD Technology Reinvestment Project, *12.911*
DOE environmental restoration, waste management technology development, *81.104*
DOE patent licensing, 81.003
education technology, *84.302, 84.303*
energy conservation, research, *81.086*
energy, invention assistance, *81.036*
energy-related, renewable resources, research, development, *81.087*
energy sciences research, *81.049*
foreign information access, education, *84.337*
foreign language resource centers, *84.229*
forestry assistance, *10.664*
Fund for Rural America, *10.224*
geosciences, research, *47.050*
hazardous waste site remediation, *66.807*
measurement, engineering projects, *11.609*
medical rehabilitation research, *93.929*
NASA education services, 43.001
NASA Technology Transfer, 43.002
National Center for Preservation Technology and Training, *15.923*
National Technical Information Service, 11.650
NSF engineering, *47.041*
NSF research, *47.075*
NSF technology K-16 education reform, *47.076*
patent, trademark information, 11.900
pollution prevention, *66.708*
regional centers, *11.611*
LC science, technology references, 42.007
Teacher Training in Technology, *84.342*
Tech-Prep Education, *84.243*
transportation, *20.701*
Urban Community Service, IHEs, *84.252*
see also Business development; Computer products, sciences, services; Engineering *entries*; Information *entries*; Nuclear sciences,

technology; Patents, trademarks, inventions; Private sector; Scientific research; Small Business Innovation Research (SBIR)

Teenagers, *see* Juvenile delinquency; Maternal, child health, welfare; Youth *entries*

TEFAP (Temporary Emergency Food Assistance Program), 10.550, *10.557*

Telecommunication, *see* Communications, telecommunications; Computer products, sciences, services

TELECOMMUNICATIONS AND INFORMATION INFRASTRUCTURE ASSISTANCE PROGRAM, *11.552*

TELECOMMUNICATIONS DEMONSTRATION PROJECT FOR MATHEMATICS, *84.286*

Telephone service, *see* Communications, telecommunications; Hotlines; Public utilities

Television, *see* Radio, television

Television Demonstration Grants (TDG), rural, *10.769*

TEMPORARY ASSISTANCE FOR NEEDY FAMILIES, *93.558*

Temporary Emergency Food Assistance Program (TEFAP), 10.550, *10.557*

Tenant Opportunities Program (TOP), HUD, *14.853*

Tennessee Valley Authority, 62.001

Tennis courts, public, *15.916*

TERO (Tribal Employment Rights Office), *30.009*

Terrorism, anti-terrorism, *see* Civil defense

Theater, *see* Arts, arts education; Music

Thermal energy, *see* Energy *entries*

TIGER (Topologically Integrated Geographic Encoding and Referencing) system, 11.003

TIIAP (Telecommunications and Information Infrastructure Assistance Program), *11.552*

Timber industry
cooperative forestry assistance, *10.664*
Economic Recovery, forest-dependent communities, *10.670*
export market development, *10.600*
Fire Suppression Assistance, FEMA, *83.542*
foreign workers certification, 17.202
forest products utilization research, *10.202*
Forestry Incentives Program, nonindustrial lands, *10.064*
futures trading information, customer complaints, 78.004
Indian lands, *15.035*
loans, family farms, *10.406*
research, forestry, *10.652*
Southeast Alaska Economic Disaster Fund, Forest Service, *10.671*
Wetlands Reserve Program, *10.072*
see also Farm, nonfarm enterprises; Forestry; Woodlands

Title I, ADA, 30.011

Title I, ESEA, Capital Expenses, *84.216*

Title I, ESEA, compensatory, *84.010*

Title I, ESEA, Even Start, *84.213, 84.214, 84.258*

Title I, ESEA, migrants, *84.011*

Title I, ESEA, neglected, delinquent, *84.013*

TITLE I GRANTS TO LOCAL EDUCATIONAL AGENCIES, *84.010*

Title I, Section 2, NHA, manufactured homes, *14.110, 14.162*

technical assistance, training, rural, *10.761*
U.S. insular areas, *14.225, 15.875*
wastewater operator technical assistance, training, *66.467*
see also Irrigation; Public works; Sewage facilities, treatment; Waste treatment, disposal; Water *entries*
Waterfowl, *see* Birds; Wildlife
WATERSHED PROTECTION AND FLOOD PREVENTION, *10.904*
WATERSHED SURVEYS AND PLANNING, 10.906
Watersheds, *see* Natural resources; Water resources, supply, management; Wetlands
Weapons of Mass Destruction (WMD), domestic preparedness, *16.006, 16.007*
Weather, *see* Climate
Weatherization
CDBG projects, business, residential, *14.218, 14.219*
low-income, assistance, *81.042, 93.568*
rural low-income housing grants, loans, *10.433*
rural low-income housing loans, *10.410*
very low-income rural housing grants, loans, *10.417*
veterans housing loans, *64.114*
see also Energy conservation; Housing rehabilitation
WEATHERIZATION ASSISTANCE FOR LOW-INCOME PERSONS, *81.042*
Weed and Seed Program, *16.595*
WEIGHTS AND MEASURES SERVICE, 11.606
Weights, measures, *see* Measurement
Welfare payments, *see* Public assistance; Social Security Act; Subsidies
WELFARE REFORM RESEARCH, EVALUATIONS, AND NATIONAL STUDIES, *93.595*
Welfare services, *see* Homeless persons; Indian health, social services; Maternal, child health, welfare; Public assistance; Social Security Act; Social services
WELFARE-TO-WORK GRANTS TO FEDERALLY-RECOGNIZED TRIBES AND ALASKA NATIVES, *17.254*
WELFARE-TO-WORK GRANTS TO STATES AND LOCALITIES, *17.253*
Wetlands
acid mine drainage (AMD), *15.253*
coastal, protection, *11.419, 15.614*
conservation, contract commodity production, *10.055*
EPA Nonpoint Source Implementation Grants, *66.460*
farmland conservation, *10.069*
Federal-Aid Highway Program, mitigation, *20.205*
flood plain data, services, 12.104
flood plain management, *83.100*
North American Wetlands Conservation Fund, *15.623*
Performance Partnership Grants, EPA, *66.605*
protection, development grants, *66.461*
research, forestry, *10.202*
restoration program, *10.072*
Water Bank Program, *10.062*
watershed protection, *10.904*

watershed, river basin projects, 10.906
watersheds, forestry research, *10.652*
Wildlife Habitat Incentive Program, *10.914*
see also Coastal zone; Estuaries; Environmental management; Forestry; Water conservation; Water resources, supply, management
WETLANDS PROTECTION—DEVELOPMENT GRANTS, *66.461*
WETLANDS RESERVE PROGRAM, *10.072*
Wheat, *see* Agricultural commodities, stabilization; Agricultural marketing
WHIP (Wildlife Habitat Incentive Program), *10.914*
Whistle-blowers, *see* Complaint investigation
White collar crime, *see* Crime
WHOLESALE MARKET DEVELOPMENT [USDA], 10.164
WIA (Workforce Investment Act), *17.255*
WIC FARMERS' MARKET NUTRITION PROGRAM (FMNP), *10.572*
WIC (Women, Infants, and Children) Program, FNS, *10.557, 10.565, 10.572*
Wildlife
animal, pest damage, disease control, *10.028*
BLM Recreation Resource Management, *15.225*
coastal wetlands protection, *15.614*
conservation law enforcement training, 15.602
cooperative forestry assistance, *10.664*
disease research, *10.207*
endangered species, Indian lands, *15.051*
endangered species, pesticides enforcement, *66.700*
endangered, threatened species, *15.615*
federal surplus real property, 39.002
Great Plains Conservation, *10.900*
habitat improvement, agricultural conservation, *10.069*
habitat management research, *10.652*
hunter safety, *15.611*
Indian hunting rights, *15.050, 15.052*
Indian lands, *15.039*
Indian Rights Protection, *15.036*
international, elephant conservation, *15.620, 15.621*
international, rhinoceros, tiger conservation, *15.619*
Lyme Disease, *93.942*
migratory bird data repository, 15.976
natural landmarks registry, 15.910
North American Wetlands Conservation Fund, *15.623*
Pittman-Robertson (P-R) Program, *15.611*
plant materials for conservation, 10.905
research, DOI, *15.611*
research, forestry, *10.202*
resource management, 15.608
restoration, management, *15.611*
restoration programs, *15.618*
rural resource conservation, development, *10.901*
waterfowl, Water Bank Program, *10.062*
watershed projects, *10.904*
Wildlife Conservation and Appreciation, *15.617*
Wildlife Habitat Incentive Program, *10.914*
see also Animal disease control, health, welfare; Birds; Environmental management; Fish; Forestry; Natural resources; Recreation
Wildlife and Parks, BIA, *15.039*